KEEPING
★ SCORE

FILM AND TELEVISION
MUSIC, 1980 - 1988

(with additional coverage of 1921-1979)

JAMES L. LIMBACHER
and
H. STEPHEN WRIGHT

The Scarecrow Press, Inc.
Metuchen, N.J., & London
1991

This volume supplements and provides additional coverage for two previous works by James L. Limbacher--Film Music: From Violins to Video (Scarecrow, 1974) and Keeping Score: Film Music, 1972-1979 (Scarecrow, 1981).

British Library Cataloguing-in-Publication Data available

Library of Congress Cataloging-in-Publication Data

Limbacher, James L.
    Keeping score : film and television music, 1980-1988 : with additional coverage of 1921-1979 / by James L. Limbacher and H. Stephen Wright, Jr.
       p.   cm.
    Discography: p.
    Includes bibliographical references and index.
    ISBN 0-8108-2453-1 (alk. paper)
    1. Motion picture music--Bibliography. I. Wright, H. Stephen. II. Title.
ML128.M7L5   1991
016.7815'42--dc20   91-21180

CONTENTS

iii

INTRODUCTION

This third volume covers the 1980s and updates the earlier eras of film music. The best news we could have for our readers is that movies and television have somewhat turned back to romantic scores in that decade.

The most important event of the 1980s was the introduction of the compact disc (CD), which brought more film and television scores to the collector with better sound and also brought back scores from past productions. The CD made collections of long-playing records (LP) more valuable and at the same time out-dated. I personally donated my film and television music LP collection to the Popular Culture Library at Bowling Green State University in Ohio, where it has already proved valuable as a reference tool.

"Fan clubs" still exist for Miklos Rozsa, Max Steiner, Erich Wolfgang Korngold, John Barry, Elmer Bernstein, and others.

The introductory notes for the second volume in this series names the people who have been enthusiastic about these reference books and who have helped me in some way in compiling them. The only new name to be mentioned is H. Stephen Wright, Jr., who prepared the discography for this new edition.

In the alphabetical order of entries, I should repeat that in the title list initial articles (a, an, der, die, el, gli, la, le, the, etc.) are printed at the end of the individual title; they are not considered part of the alphabetization.

But enough technicalities. It's time to start reminiscing about the 1980s and look forward to the creative output of film and television music for the 1990s. Let's continue keeping score!

James Limbacher
Dearborn, MI

BIBLIOGRAPHY

Halliwell, Leslie. Halliwell's Film Guide. London: Granada, 1977.

Harris, Steve. Film, Television and Stage Music on Phonograph
  Records: A Discography. Jefferson, N.C.: McFarland, 1988.

International Motion Picture Almanac. New York: Quigley, annual.

International Television and Video Almanac. New York: Quigley,
  annual.

Limbacher, James L. Film Music: From Violins to Video.
  Metuchen, N.J.: Scarecrow, 1974.

_____. Keeping Score: Film Music 1972-1979. Metuchen, N.J.:
  Scarecrow, 1981.

Marill, Alvin H. Movies Made for Television: The Telefeature and
  the Mini-Series, 1964-1986. New York: New York Zoetrope,
  1987.

Nash, Jay Robert, and Stanley Ralph Ross. The Motion Picture
  Guide. Chicago: Cinebooks, 1985-1988.

Phonolog. Los Angeles: Trade Service Publications, weekly.

Reed, James W. 1984 Price Guide for Sound Track Records.
  Quarryville, Pa.: Sound Track Album Retailers, 1984.

Schwann. Boston: ABC Consumer Magazines, monthly (to 1986);
  quarterly (from 1987).

Schwann Compact Disc Catalog. Boston: ABC Consumer Magazines,
  monthly.

Screen World. Ed. John Willis. New York: Crown, annual.

Soundtrack! The Collector's Quarterly. Ed. Luc Van de Ven.
  Mechelen, Belgium.

KEY TO ABBREVIATIONS

AA	Allied Artists	CEY	Ceylon (Sri Lanka)
A&E	Arts & Entertainment	CHE	Chesterfield
ABC	American Broadcasting	CHI	Childhood
	Corp.	CHL	Chile
ACR	American Cinema	CHN	China
	Releasing	CIN	Cinerama
AFD	Associated Film	CIV	Cinema 5
	Distribution	COL	Columbia
AFG	Afghanistan	CRO	Crown International
AFI	American Film Institute	CUB	Cuba
AFR	Africa	CYP	Cyprus
AI or AIP	American International	CZE	Czechoslovakia
ALB	Albania	DCA	Distributors Corp. of
ALG	Algeria		America
ALL	Allied	DEG	DeLaurentiis Entertain-
ALM	Almi		ment Group
AMB	Ambassador	DEN	Denmark
ARC	Atlantic Releasing	DIS	Disney (Buena Vista)
ARG	Argentina	EBE	Encyclopaedia Britannica
ARM	Armenia	ECU	Ecuador
AST	Astor	EGY	Egypt
ATL	Atlantic	EL	Eagle-Lion
AUS	Austria	EMB	Avco Embassy
AUT	Australia	EMP	Empire
BAN	Bangladesh	EPC	Epoch
BAR	Barr	EST	Estonia
BEL	Belgium	FAM	Famous Players/Lasky
BIO	Biograph	FC	Film Classics
BKW	Blackwood	FIL	Filmmakers/Filmways
BLU	Bluebird	FIN	Finland
BRA	Brazil	FMC	Filmmakers Cooperative
BRI	Great Britain	FN	First National
BRY	Bryanston	FOR	Formosa
BUL	Bulgaria	FOX or TCF	Twentieth Century-
CAN	Canada		Fox
CBC	Canadian Broadcasting	FRA	France
	Corp.	FVI	Film Ventures Interna-
CBS	Columbia Broadcasting		tional
	System	GAM	Gamma
CC	Cinema Center	GER	Germany

GHA	Ghana	NAF	New American Films
GN	Grand National	NBC	National Broadcasting Co.
GOL	Goldwyn		
GRA	Graphic	NDF	New Day Films
GRE	Greece	NEP	Nepal
GRI	D. W. Griffith	NET	National Educational TV
HB	Hanna-Barbera	NGP	National General
HBO	Home Boxoffice	NGS	National Geographic Society
HK	Hong Kong		
HOL	Holland/Netherlands	NIC	Nicaragua
HOW	Howco	NIG	Nigeria
HUN	Hungary	NLC	New Line Cinema
ICE	Iceland	NOR	Norway
IN	India	NWP	New World
INC	Ince	NYF	New Yorker Films
IND	Independent release	NZ	New Zealand
INO	Indochina	OLI	Oliver Morosco
INV	Invincible	ORI	Orion
IRAN	Iran	PAK	Pakistan
IRE	Ireland	PAL	Palestine
ISL	Island	PAP	Papua New Guinea
ISR	Israel	PAR	Paramount
ITA	Italy	PBS	Public Broadcasting System
JAM	Jamaica		
JAP	Japan	PHI	Philippine Islands
JEN	Jensen-Farley	PIC	Pictorial Clubs/Ohio Film
KAL	Kalem		
KLE	Kleine/Edward F. Klein	POL	Poland
KOR	Korea	POR	Portugal
KUW	Kuwait	PR	Puerto Rico
LAS	Lasky	PRC	Producers Releasing Corp.
LAT	Latvia		
LEB	Lebanon	PRI	Principal
LIB	Liberty	PUR	Puritan
LIBYA	Libya	PYR	Pyramid
LIP	Lippert	RAN	Rankin/Bass
LIT	Lithuania	REA	Realart
LOR	Lorimar	REP	Republic
MAJ	Majestic	RKO	Radio Pictures/RKO Radio Pictures
MAL	Malaysia		
MAS	Mascot	RUM or ROU	Rumania
MAY	Mayfair	RUS	Russia
MET	Metro	SA	South America
MEX	Mexico	SEN	Senegal
MGM	Metro-Goldwyn-Mayer	SHO	Showtime
MHF	McGraw-Hill	SIG	Sigma 3
MOG	Mongolia	SPA	Spain
MON	Monogram	SRI	Sri Lanka
MOR	Morocco	SWE	Sweden
MOZ	Mozambique	SWI	Switzerland
MTP	Modern Talking Pictures	SYR	Syria

TAH	Tahiti	UA	United Artists
TAI	Taiwan/Taipei	UMC	Universal Marion
TCF	Fox/Twentieth Century-Fox (see also FOX)	UN	Universal
		URU	Uruguay
THAI	Thailand	VEN	Venezuela
TIF	Tiffany	VES	Vestron
TIM	Time/Life	VIE	Vietnam
TMC	Movie Channel	VIT	Vitagraph
TRI	Triangle	WB	Warner Brothers
TST	Tri-Star	WNP	World Northal
TUN	Tunisia	WOL	Wolper
TUR	Turkey	WOO	Woolner
TV	television production	YUG	Yugoslavia

FILMS AND THEIR COMPOSERS/ADAPTORS

1921

Destiny (Mude Tod, Der)	GER	Guiseppe Becce

1922

Beyond the River	GER	Gerdinand Hummel
Dr. Mabuse der Spieler	GER	Konrad Elfers
Nosferatu	GER	Hans Erdmann
Phantom	GER	Leo Speiss

1923

Inhumaine, L'	FRA	Darius Milhaud

1926

Charleston (short)	FRA	Clement Doucet
Metropolis (reissue)	GER	Konrad Elfers

1928

Adventures of Dr. Dolittle	GER	Philip Braham
Alraune (Daughter of Evil)	GER	Bronislaw Kaper
Last Warning, The	UN	Joseph Cherniavsky
October	RUS	Edmund Meisel

1929

Evangeline	UA	Hugo Riesenfeld
Queen Kelly	UA	Adolph Tandler

1930

End of the World, The	FRA	Michel Michelet
Ingagi	IND	Edward Gage
Liliom	FOX	Richard Fall/Samuel Kaylin
Procureau Hallers, Le	FRA	Frederick Hollander

1

1931

Frankenstein	UN	Bernhard Kaun
Galloping Ghost, The (serial)	MAS	Lee Zahler
Lightning Warrior, The (serial)	MAS	Lee Zahler
Surrender	FOX	Carli Elinor
Vanishing Legion, The (serial)	MAS	Lee Zahler

1932

Atlantide, L' (Lost Atlantis)	GER	Wolfgang Zeller
Doctor X	FN	Bernhard Kaun
Farewell to Arms, A	PAR	Bernhard Kaun
Freaks	MGM	Gavin Barns
I Am a Fugitive from a Chain Gang	WB	Bernhard Kaun
Intruder, The	IND	Val Burton
King Solomon's Mines	BRI	Mischa Spoliansky
Last of the Mohicans, The (serial)	MAS	Lee Zahler
Mummy, The	UN	James Dietrich
One Way Passage	WB	Bernhard Kaun
Phantom of Crestwood, The	MGM	Max Steiner
Testament of Dr. Mabuse (Crimes of Dr. Mabuse)	GER	Hans Erdmann

1933

Ciboulette	FRA	Renaldo Hahn
Fighting with Kit Carson (serial)	MAS	Lee Zahler
Ghoul, The	BRI	Louis Levy
His Double Life	PAR	James Hanley/Karl Stark
Little Schemer, The	GER	Oscar Straus
Mystery of the Wax Museum, The	FN	Bernhard Kaun
Mystery Squadron (serial)	MAS	Lee Zahler
Study in Scarlet, A	IND	Val Burton
Supernatural	PAR	Karl Hajos/Howard Jackson/Milan Roder
Three Musketeers, The (serial)	MAS	Lee Zahler
20,000 Years in Sing Sing	FN	Bernhard Kaun
Whispering Shadow, The (serial)	MAS	Lee Zahler
Wolf Dog, The (serial)	MAS	Lee Zahler

1934

Adieu, les Beaux Jours	FRA	E. E. Buder/Raoul Ploquin
Black Cat, The	UN	Heinz Roemheld
Broken Shoes	RUS	D. S. Block/V. J. Shelabin
Burn 'Em Up Barnes (serial)	MAS	Lee Zahler
Champion of Pontresina	GER	Willi Meisl
Dawn to Dawn	IND	Cameron Macpherson

Death Takes a Holiday	PAR	Bernhard Kaun/John Leipold/Milan Roder
Gold (Or, L')	FRA/GER	Hans Otto Borgmann
Hell on Earth	GER	Hanns Eisler
Hitlerjunge Quex	GER	Hans Otto Borgmann
House of Greed	RUS	A. F. Paschenko
Idea, The (short)	FRA	Arthur Honegger
Lac aux Dames	FRA	Georges Auric
Law of the Wild (serial)	MAS	Lee Zahler
Liliom	FRA	Jean Lenoir/Franz Waxman
Lily of Kilarney (Bride of the Lake)	IRE	William Trytell
Little Friend	BRI	Louis Levy
Lost Jungle, The (serial)	MAS	Lee Zahler
Love, Death and the Devil	GER	Theo Mackeben
Man of Aran	BRI	John Greenwood
Miserables, Les	FRA	Arthur Honegger
Mystery Mountain (serial)	MAS	Lee Zahler
No Funny Business	BRI	Noel Gay
Norah O'Neale	IRE	Herbert Hughes
On a Vole un Homme	FRA	Walter Jurmann/ Bronislau Kaper
Phantom of the Convent	MEX	Mac Urban
Return of the Terror, The	WB	Bernhard Kaun
Romance in Budapest	HUN	Nicholas Brodzsky
Romance of Ida	HUN	Szaboles Fenyes
Thunderstorm	RUS	Vladimir Tscherbatchov
Trapeze	GER	Arthur Guttmann/ Walter Jurmann
Viktor und Viktoria	GER	Franz Doelle
Wajan (Son of a Witch)	GER	Wolfgang Zeller
Water in the Ground	SPA	Francisco Alonso
Young Love	CZE	Josef Dobe

1935

Adventures of Rex and Rinty, The (serial)	MAS	Lee Zahler
After a Night of Love	ITA	Antonio Pedace
Amphytryon	FRA/GER	Franz Doelle
Bandera, La	FRA	Roland Manuel/Jean Weiner
Black Sheep	TCF	Samuel Kaylin
Bride of Frankenstein, The	UN	Franz Waxman
Charlie Chan in Shanghai	TCF	Samuel Kaylin
Charlie Chan's Secret	TCF	Samuel Kaylin
Cowboy Millionaire	TCF	Abe Meyer
Crisis Is Over, The	FRA	Jean Lenoir
Dance Music	AUS	Max Niederberger
Don Quintin, the Bitter	SPA	Jacinto Guerrero

Dream of the Rhine	GER	Willi Ostermann
Fahrmann Maria	GER	Herbert Windt
Fighting Marines, The (serial)	MAS	Lee Zahler
Ganga Avtaran	IN	Viswanathbuva Jadhav
Golden Riaga	RUS	S. N. Vasilenko
Golgotha	FRA	Jacques Ibert
Green Is the Heath	GER	Walter Ulfig
Gridiron Flash	RKO	Max Steiner
Hectic Days	RUS	V. Shelobinski
Itto	FRA	Albert Wolff
Kermesse Heroique, La	FRA	Louis Beydts
King of the Champs-Elysee	FRA	Joe Hajos
Land of Promise	IND	Boris Morros
Little Men	MAS	Hugo Riesenfeld
Little Mother	HUN	Nicholas Brodzsky
Look Up and Laugh	BRI	Harry Parr Davies
Lost City, The	PRI	Lee Zahler
Loves of a Dictator	BRI	Karol Rathaus
Mad Love	MGM	Dimitri Tiomkin
Maria Chapdeleine	FRA	Jean Weiner
Maternity	FRA	Jacques Ibert
Men on Wings	RUS	Nicolai Kryukov
Mimi	BRI	G. H. Glutsam
Miracle Rider, The (serial)	MAS	Lee Zahler
Moscow Laughs	RUS	Isaac O. Dunayevsky
My Marriage	TCF	Samuel Kaylin
My Song for You	BRI	Mischa Spoliansky
Mystery of the Pallid Face, The	MEX	Max Urban
Navy Wife	TCF	David Buttolph
New Gulliver, The	RUS	Lev Schwartz
On the Road to Cairo	SPA	Jacinto Guerrero
Paddy O'Day	TCF	Samuel Kaylin
Peasants	RUS	V. Poushkov
Pepo	RUS	Aram Khachaturian
Peter	HUN	Nicholas Brodszky
Phantom Empire, The (serial)	MAS	Lee Zahler
Plain Girl	TUN	Fred Markush
Prodigal Son, The	AUS	Guiseppe Becce
Rare Bird	FRA	H. Poussique
Raven, The	UN	Clifford Vaughan
Red Village, The	RUS	Isaac O. Dunayevsky
Remous	FRA	Al Sendrey
Rich Uncle, The	ITA	C. A. Bixio
She	RKO	Max Steiner
		(not Alfred Newman)
Shir Hashirim	IND	Joseph Rumshinsky
Story of Louis Pasteur, The	WB	Bernhard Kaun
Student of Prague, The	GER	Theo Mackeben
Sunny Youth	RUS	Jack Zelony
Sweet Stepmother	HUN	Sandor Szlatinay
This Woman Is Mine	BRI	Alexis Archangelski

Villa for Sale	HUN	Paul Gyongy
Wandering Jew, The	BRI	Hugo Riesenfeld
Werewolf of London	UN	Karl Hajos
What Am I Without You?	GER	Franz Stolzenwald
Winter Night's Dream, A	GER	Franz Grothe
Young Forest	POL	Roman Palester

1936

Abduction, The	GER	Franz Grothe
Abdul the Damned	BRI	Hanns Eisler
Accused	BRI	Percival Mackey
Alla en el Rancho Grande	MEX	Lorenzo Barcelata
Anna and Elizabeth	GER	Paul Desseau
Annette in Paradise	GER	Willi Meisl
Back to Nature	TCF	Samuel Kaylin
Ball at the Savoy, The	BRI	Paul Abraham
Battle, The	RUS	Hans Hauska
Be Good unto Death	HUN	Paul Gyongy
Boccaccio (Love Tales of Boccaccio)	GER	Franz Doelle
Boundary Fire	GER	Toni Thoms
Brave Seaman	GER	Haraldt Boehmelt
Budapest Candy Store	HUN	Imre Hajdu
Burg Theater	AUS	Peter Kreuder
Cafe Moscow	HUN	Sandor Laslo
Career Woman	TCF	Samuel Kaylin
Castle in Flanders	GER	Franz Grothe
Castle Vogeloed	GER	Friedrich Wilhelm Rust
Charlie Chan at the Circus	TCF	Samuel Kaylin
Charlie Chan at the Opera	TCF	Samuel Kaylin
Charlie Chan at the Race Track	TCF	Samuel Kaylin
Children of Fortune	GER	Peter Kreuder
Crack-Up	TCF	Samuel Kaylin
Crime of Dr. Forbes, The	TCF	Samuel Kaylin
Dancer and the Worker, The	SPA	Francisco Alonso
Deuxieme Bureau (Second Bureau)	FRA	Jean Lenoir
Dinner Is Served	GER	Leo Leux
Dissatisfied Woman	GER	Michael Jary
Educating Father	TCF	Samuel Kaylin
Emperor of California	GER	Guiseppe Becce
Everybody's Woman	ITA	Daniele Amfitheatrof
Everything for the Woman	GER	Alfred Abel
Feminine Regina	GER	E. E. Buder
First Baby, The	TCF	Samuel Kaylin
Flying Doctor, The	AUT	Alfred Lawrence/Willy Redstone
Flying Hostess	UN	Charles Previn
Friendly Expression, Please	HUN	Nicholas Brodzsky
Gentle Julia	TCF	Samuel Kaylin
German Destiny	GER	Walter Gronostay

Ghost Goes West, The	BRI	Mischa Spoliansky
Girls' Dormitory	GER	Ralph Benatzky
Golden Lake	RUS	V. Vasilenko
Golem, The	FRA	Joseph Kumok
Greater Promise, The	RUS	Isaac O. Dunayevsky
Guilty Melody	BRI	Nicholas Brodzsky
Gypsies	RUS	C. G. Lobachev
Higher Command	GER	Werner Eisbrenner
His Daughter Is Peter	AUS	Willy Schmidt-Gentner
His Official Wife	GER	Kurt Schroeder
Hoax	GER	Victor Corzilius
Hokum	GER	Peter Kreuder
Hot Blood	GER	Franz Doelle
Human Cargo	TCF	Samuel Kaylin
Hunter of Fall	GER	Albert Fischer
I Am Longing for You	GER	Willi Engleberger
I Love You Only	ITA	Salvatore Allegra
Inheritance in Pretoria	GER	Hans Carste
Intermezzo	GER	Theo Mackeben
Isn't My Husband Wonderful?	GER	Walter Kiesow/Theodor Knobel
Jana	GER	Karl Hasler
Jungle Princess, The	PAR	Gregory Stone
Kind Stepmother	HUN	Sandor Szlatinay
Knock-Out	GER	Leo Leux
Land That Dies, The	FRA	Jane Bos
Life of Don Bosco, The	ITA	G. Federico Ghendini
Light Cavalry	GER	Hans-Otto Borgmann
Little Miss Nobody	TCF	Samuel Kaylin
Little Nightingale, The	RUS	Yakov Stollar
Lost Valley	GER	Fritz Wennels
Love and Kisses--Veronica	HUN	Franz Waxman
Love and Sacrifice	IND	Abe Schwartz
Love at Court	GER	Max Niederberger
Love Maneuvers	POL	Henry Vars
Love's Awakening	GER	Alois Melichar
Madonna, Where Are You?	GER	Franz Grothe
Magic Mountain	SWI	Arthur Honegger
Man Who Could Work Miracles, The	BRI	Mischa Spoliansky
Maria the Servant	GER	Leo Leux
Marija Valewska	AUS	Guiseppe Becce
Milizia Territoriale	ITA	Guilio Bennard
Morality	GER	Leo Leux
Moutonnet	FRA	Paul Misraki
My Song Goes Around the World	GER	Hans May
New Squire, The	HUN	Tibor Polgar/Gyorgy Ranki
90 Minute Stop	GER	Ernst Leenen
Open Door to the Sea	FRA	Michael Levine
Our Boy	SWE	Erik Baumann/Evert Taube

Paloma, La	GER	Willi Meisl
Pappi	GER	Walter Ulfig
Private Life of Louis XIV, The	GER	Alois Melichar
Private Secretary Marie	GER	Willi Schmidt-Gentner
Queen of Love	GER	Hans-Otto Borgmann
Queen's Hussar, The	HUN	Imre Farkas
Raggen	SWE	Erik Baumann
Rakoszy March	HUN	Paul Abraham
Regular Fellow, A	GER	Hans Carste
Rembrandt	BRI	Geoffrey Toyo
Revolt of the Zombies	IND	Abe Meyer
Romance	AUS	August Popoeck
Royal Waltz, The	GER	Franz Doelle
Rubber	HOL	Walter Gronostay
Senorita de Travelez, La	SPA	Rodolfo Halffter
Shadows of the Past	GER	Anton Profes
Shanty Town	SWE	Sten Axelson/Erik Baumann
Sharpshooter Bruggler	GER	Herbert Windt
Southern Roses	BRI	Hans May
Story of a Trickster, The	FRA	Adolphe Borchard
Stowaway	TCF	Louis Silvers
Strange Guest, A	GER	Guiseppe Becce
Street Music	GER	Walter Gronostay
Stronger Than Paragraphs	GER	Rudolf Perak
Tender Enemy	FRA	Albert Wolff
This Girl Irene	GER	Alois Melichar
Those Three About Christine	GER	Toni Thoms
Three-Cornered Hat, The	ITA	E. Tagliaferri
Two Hundred a Month	HUN	Alexander Rozenval
Uncivilized	AUT	Lindley Evans
Under Western Eyes	FRA	Georges Auric
Unknown, The	GER	Hans Otto Borgmann
113, El	SPA	Jose Padilla
Wackere Schustermeister	GER	Ludwig Rueth
Walking Dead, The	WB	Bernhard Kaun
Waltz for You, A	GER	Willi Meisl
We Are from Kronstadt	RUS	Nicolai Kryukov
Wedding Dream, A	GER	Peter Kreuder
Woman of No Importance, A	GER	Clemens Schmalstich
Work (Avodah)	HUN	Paul Desseau
You Are My Joy	GER	Guiseppe Becce
Young Blood	GER	Carl Emil Fuchs
Young Count, The	GER	Leo Leux
Youth of Today	SWE	Sune Waldmir

1937

African Holiday	IND	Edward Kilenyi
Angel's Holiday	TCF	Samuel Kaylin

Arshin Mal Alan	ARM	Serge Houshnareff
Baby Doctor Engel	GER	Hans Sommer
Beethoven Concerto	RUS	Isaac O. Dunayevsky
Beloved Vagabond, The	BRI	Darius Milhaud
Big Business	TCF	Samuel Kaylin
Big Town Girl	TCF	Samuel Kaylin
Blessed Rose, The	MEX	Max Urban
Born Reckless	TCF	Samuel Kaylin
Borrowed Chateau	HUN	Jeno Sandor
Borrowing Trouble	TCF	Samuel Kaylin
Bride of Tarocke	HUN	Tibor Polgar
Carnet de Bal, Un	FRA	Maurice Jaubert
Charlie Chan at Monte Carlo	TCF	Samuel Kaylin
Charlie Chan at the Olympics	TCF	Samuel Kaylin
Charlie Chan on Broadway	TCF	Samuel Kaylin
Checkers	TCF	Samuel Kaylin
Cinderella	FRA	Vincent Scotto
Citadel of Silence	FRA	Arthur Honegger
City Girl	TCF	Samuel Kaylin
Confession	WB	Peter Kreuder
Court Concert	GER	Edmund Nick
Crossroads (Shi Zi Jie Tou)	CHN	Ho Lu-ding
Dangerously Yours	TCF	Samuel Kaylin
Date by the Danube	HUN	Imre Hajdu
Dead March, The	IND	Erno Rapee
Divine Jette, The	GER	Georg Hentschel
Dr. Knock	FRA	Jean Wiener
Duchess of Parma, The	ITA	Amedeo Escobar/Giovanni Fusco/E. Montagnini
Ecce Homo	FRA	Jacques Ibert
Episode	AUS	Willi Schmidt-Gentner
Eternal Mask, The	SWI	Anton Profes
Every Woman Has a Secret	GER	Willi Meisl
Evil Eye, The	BEL	Marcel Poot
Exception to the Rule	HUN	George Feyer
Fair and Warmer	GER	Hans Sommer
Family on Parade	GER	Fritz Domina/Willi Meisl
45 Fathers	TCF	Samuel Kaylin
Frozen Child, The	HUN	Victor Papir
Girl from the Chorus, A	GER	Paul Huehn/Walter Kollo/ Paul Linke
Gleisdreick	GER	Hans Otto Borgmann
Gobsek	RUS	V. Y. Shebalin
Great Hospital Mystery, The	TCF	Samuel Kaylin
Green Fields	IND	Vladimir Heifetz
Happy Days	POL	Henry Vars
Help! I'm an Heir!	HUN	Istvan Basthal
Holy Terror, The	TCF	Samuel Kaylin
Hot Water	TCF	Samuel Kaylin
Hotel Kikelet	HUN	Paul Abraham

I Will Give a Million	ITA	Gian Luca Tocchi
Ideal Husband, An	GER	Werner Bochman
In the Far East	RUS	Yuri Millutin
Incognito	GER	Friedrich Wilhelm Rust
Invisible Menace, The	WB	Bernhard Kaun
I've Lost My Husband	ITA	Amedeo Escobar
Jenny (Jadzia)	POL	Fred Scher
Jester, The	POL	Nicholas Brodzsky
Kimiko	JAP	Noburu Itoh
King August the Strong	GER	Hans Erdmann
Lady Escapes, The	TCF	Samuel Kaylin
Lady Killer	FRA	Arthur Honegger
Lady Seeks Room	HUN	Paul Szigmondy
Late Matthew Pascal, The	FRA/ITA	Jacques Ibert
Laughing at Trouble	TCF	Samuel Kaylin
Lessons in Love	GER	Theo Mackeben
Lie of Nina Petrovna, The	FRA	Joe Hajos/Michael Levine
Love or a Kingdom	POL	Jan Maklakiewicz
Love Under Fire	TCF	Arthur Lange
Lower Depths, The	FRA	Jean Wiener
Loyalty of Love	ITA	C. A. Bixio
Mademoiselle Docteur	FRA	Arthur Honegger
Mammy	HUN	Denes Buday/Jeno Sandor
Man Who Was Sherlock Holmes, The	BRI	Hans Sommer
Marthe Richard	FRA	Arthur Honegger
Maskerade	AUS	Willi Schmidt-Gentner
Messenger, The	FRA	Georges Auric
Midnight Taxi	TCF	Samuel Kaylin
Modern Girls	HUN	Paul Abraham
My Song of Love	ITA	Dan Caslar
Mysteries of Paris	FRA	Georges Auric
New Earth, The	JAP	Kosaku Yamada
Night with the Emperor, A	GER	Hans Otto Borgmann
Off to the Races	TCF	Samuel Kaylin
One Mile from Heaven	TCF	Samuel Kaylin
Pan Twardowski	POL	Jan Maklakiewicz
Paris Commune	RUS	Nicolai Kruykov
Pearls of the Crown	FRA	Jean Francaix
Pesti-Mese	HUN	Paul Abraham
Peter the First	RUS	Vladimir Tscherbatchov
Play on the Tenne, The	GER	Hans Carste
Police Mondaine	FRA	Jane Bos
Premiere	AUS	Szaboles Fenyes/Denes Buday
Prisoners	RUS	Y. Shaporin
Queen of Spades (Pique Dame)	FRA	Karol Rathaus
Ready for Action	SWE	Jules Sylvain
Renfrew of the Royal Mounted	GN	Arthur Kay
Riding on Air	RKO	Arthur Morton

Romance and Riches (Amazing Adventure, The)	BRI	Werner Bachman
Sarati the Terrible	FRA	Jacques Janin/Vincent Scotto
Scipio, the African	ITA	Ildebrando Pizzetti
Sensation	HUN	Tibor Polgar
She Had to Eat	TCF	Samuel Kaylin
Sister Maria	HUN	Szaboles Fenyes
Smiling Gentleman, The	ITA	C. A. Bixio
Son of the Pusta	HUN	Laszlo Angyal
South of the Highway	SWE	Erik Baumann/Edvin Lindberg
Step Lively, Jeeves!	TCF	Samuel Kaylin
Storm of the Plains	HUN	Tibor Polgar
Study of Suzanne, A	GER	Haraldt Boehmelt
Talking About Josephine	GER	Anton Profes
Tall Timbers	AUT	W. Hamilton Webber
Thank You, Mr. Moto	TCF	Samuel Kaylin
That I May Live	TCF	Samuel Kaylin
There's But One Love	GER	Eduard Kuennecke
These Children	ITA	Giovanni Fusco/Umberto Mancini
Think Fast, Mr. Moto	TCF	Samuel Kaylin
Thirty Seconds of Love	ITA	Guido Bonnard
This Is China	IND	Alfred Uhl
This Is My Affair	TCF	Arthur Lange
Three Sailors and a Blonde	GER	Eduard Kuennecke
Time Out for Romance	TCF	Samuel Kaylin
Tomb of the Angels	ITA	Enzo Massetti
Tommy	HUN	Victor Papir
Truxa	GER	Leo Leux
Under a False Flag	SWE	Jules Sylvain
Under the Red Robe	BRI	Sir Arthur Benjamin
Viki	HUN	Paul Abraham
Vivere	ITA	Domenico Savino
Voice of the Heart, The	GER	Guiseppe Becce
Wave, The (Redes)	MEX	Sylvestre Revueltas
Ways of Love are Strange	GER	Leo Leux
Wedding of Palo	IND	Emil Reesen
Wee Willie Winkie	TCF	Alfred Newman
Western Gold	TCF	Arthur Lange
Wife, Doctor and Nurse	TCF	Arthur Lange
Wild and Woolly	TCF	Samuel Kaylin
Woman Wise	TCF	Samuel Kaylin
Young Pushkin	RUS	Yuri Kochurov

1938

Abused Confidence	FRA	Georges van Parys
Affairs of Maupassant	AUS	Paul Abraham

Altitude 3,200	FRA	Maurice Jaubert
Andalusian Nights	GER	Jose Munoz-Molleda
Artist's Entrance	FRA	Georges Auric
Avocate d'Amour	FRA	Georges van Parys
Azure Express	HUN	Carlo de Fries
Bergslagsfolk	SWE	Hilding Rosenberg
Black Diamonds	HUN	Lajos Akom
Broken Melody	AUT	Alfred Hill
Cafe de Paris	FRA	Georges van Parys
Carrefour	FRA	Michel Emer
Cheri-Bibi	FRA	Paul Misraki
Childhood of Maxim Gorky, The	RUS	L. Shvarts
Children Must Laugh	POL	H. Kon
City of Youth	RUS	V. Pushkov
College Girl, The	CZE	Josef Dobe
Concert in Tyrol	AUS	Willy Schmidt-Gentner
Country Bride, The	RUS	Isaac O. Dunayevsky
Courier of Lyons	FRA	Louis Beydts
Covered Tracks	GER	Hans Otto Borgmann
Crime of Dr. Hallet, The	UN	Charles Previn
Cuckoo Clock, The	ITA	Vittorio Rieti
Damsel of Bard (Destino, Il)	ITA	Anchise Bruzzi/Teo Muccy
Dangerous Secrets	BRI	George Walter
Dark Eyes	FRA	Michel Levine
Devil's Party, The	UN	Charles Previn
Double Cross	IN	Badri Prasad
Dreiklang	GER	Kurt Schroeder
Equipage, L'	FRA	Arthur Honegger
Escadrille of Change	FRA	Georges van Parys
Eternal Street	HUN	Geza Koudela
Family Bonus	HUN	Paul Abraham
Foolish Virgin	FRA	Michel Michelet
For Freedom and Love	GER	Werner Bochmann
For You Only	ITA	Alois Melichar
Four Men and a Prayer	FOX	Louis Silvers
Gaiety Girls	BRI	Mischa Spoliansky
Gay Misery	HUN	Joseph Paksy
Generals Without Buttons	FRA	Wal-Berg
Girl Refugee, The	GRE	J. Yannides
Girl Thief, The	BRI	Clifford Grey/Mischa Spoliansky
Glory of Faith	FRA	Jane Bos
Great John Ericsson, The	SWE	Eric Bengtson
Hercule	FRA	Manuel Rosenthal
House of the Maltese	FRA	Jacques Ibert
I Married a Spy	GN	Walter Goehr
I Want to Live with Joy	ITA	Guiseppe Rosati
If War Comes Tomorrow	RUS	Brothers Pokrass
Indian Tomb, The	GER	Harald Rochmelt

International Settlement	FOX	Samuel Kaylin
Island in the Sky	FOX	Samuel Kaylin
I've Made a Love Match	HUN	Imre Hajdu
Katia	FRA	Wal-Berg
Katzensteg, Der	GER	Walter Gronostay
Kreutzer Sonata	FRA	Adolphe Borchard
Legions of Honor	FRA	Henri Tomasi
Lenin in October	RUS	A. Alexandrov
Let George Do It	AUT	Maurice Gilman/Hamilton Webber
Love on a Budget	FOX	Samuel Kaylin
Man of the Sea	RUS	Vladimir Scherbachev
Man With 100 Faces	BRI	Louis Levy
Merry Wives, The	CZE	Jaroslav Kricka
Midnight Happenings	GER	Werner Bochman
Missing from St.-Agil	FRA	Henri Verdun
Mistakes Will Happen	HUN	Denes Buday
Mother Love	FRA	Georges van Parys
Mother Song	GER/ITA	Alois Melichar
Mountain Calls, The	GER	Guiseppe Becce
My Daughter Is Different	HUN	Sandor Szlatinay
My Foster Sister	FRA	Georges van Parys
Naples of Former Days	ITA	Allessandro Cicognini
Naples Under the Kiss of Fire	FRA	Vincent Scotto
Number 111	HUN	Denes Budey
Odd Mr. Victor	FRA	Roland Manuel
One Wild Night	FOX	Samuel Kaylin
Orloff and Tarakanova	FRA	Ricardo Zandenat
Patriot, The	FRA	Jacques Ibert
Poet and Tsar	RUS	N. Streinikov
Princess Tarakanova	FRA/ITA	Antonio Veretti
Professor Mamlock	RUS	Yuri Kochurov/N. Timofeyev
Quadrille	FRA	Adolphe Bochard
Quai de Brumes	FRA	Maurice Jaubert
Remounting the Champs-Elysee	FRA	Adolphe Borchard
Return to the Dawn	FRA	Paul Misraki
Rothschild	FRA	Guido Curto
S.O.S. Sahara	GER	L. Brunner
Sacrifice of Honor	FRA	Jean Lenoir
Saga, En (Laili)	SWE	Bengt Rodhe
Savoy Lancers	ITA	Enzo Masetti
Sinners in Paradise	UN	Charles Previn
Ski Chase, The	FRA	Paul Dessau
Slipper Episode	FRA	Paul Segnitz/Jean Wiener
South Riding	BRI	Muir Mathieson
Southern Bar	FRA	Henri Verdun
Storm over Asia	FRA	Ralph Erwin
Storms in May	GER	Hans Elert

Stream, The	FRA	Tiarko Richepin
Sun over Sweden	SWE	Eric Baumann
13 Girls Smile at the Sky	HUN	Denes Buday
Three Argentines in Paris	ARG	Enrique Delfino
Tiger von Eschnapur	GER	Harald Rochmelt
Tokay Rhapsody	HUN	Imre Hajdu
Troopship	BRI	Richard Addinsell
Troubled Heart	FRA	Jane Bos
Two Prisoners	HUN	Lajos Akom
Two Sisters	IND	Joseph Rumshinsky
Ultimatum	FRA	Adolphe Borchard
Volga Boatman, The	FRA	Michel Levine
We Were Seven Sisters	ITA	C. A. Bixio/Umberto Mancini
Wide Open Faces	COL	Hugo Riesenfeld
Woman Thief, The	FRA	Henri Verdun
Women of Niskavuori	FIN	Harry Bergstrom
Women's Prison	FRA	Jean Lenoir
Yellow Flag, The	GER	Guiseppe Becce
Young Noszty and Mary Toth	HUN	Szabolcs Fenyes
You're Only Young Once	MGM	David Snell
Youth (Jugend)	GER	Hans-Otto Bergmann
Yvette	GER	Hanson-Milde Meissner
Zamboanga	GN	Edward Kilenyi

1939

Affair Lafont, The	FRA	Wal-Berg
Amangeldy	RUS	N. Gnessin/A. Zhubanov
Andersson Family, The	SWE	Kaj Gullmar
Behind the Facade	FRA	Z. Galihard
Betrayal (Taran Kova)	FRA	Ricardo Zandenat
Beware Spooks!	COL	Morris Stoloff
Black Pirate, The	ITA	Alessandro Cicognini
Captain Grant's Children	RUS	Isaac O. Dunayevsky
Charlie Chan at Treasure Island	FOX	Samuel Kaylin
Checker Player, The	FRA	Jean Lenoir
Circumstantial Evidence	FRA	Georges van Parys
Cocoanut	FRA	Georges van Parys
College Girls (Girls Who Study)	ARG	Francisco Lomuto
Concentration Camp	RUS	Lev Schwartz
Conquest of Peter the Great, The	RUS	Vladimir Tscherbatchov
Cossacks in Exile	RUS	Anthony Rudnicky
Crisis	IND	Haroslav Harvan/ H. W. Susskind
Deserter, The	FRA	Arthur Honegger/Henri Verdun
End of the Day	FRA	Maurice Jaubert
Exile Express	GN	George Parrish
Five-Forty	HUN	Szaboles Fenyes
400 Million, The	IND	Hanns Eisler

From the Hills to the Valley	ARG	Jose Cane
Gibralter	FRA	Paul Desseau/P. Simon
Governor, The	GER	Wolfgang Zeller
Great Citizen, The	RUS	Dmitri Shostakovich
Green Emperor, The	GER	Hans Ebert
Harvest	FRA	Arthur Honegger
Heartbeat	FRA	Vincent Scotto
Heroes of the Marne	FRA	Jacques Ibert
Hotel du Nord	FRA	Maurice Jaubert
Human Monster, The (Dark Eyes of London)	BRI	Guy Jones
I Accuse	FRA	Henri Verdun
I Was an Adventuress	FRA	Paul Misraki
Istvan Bors	HUN	Szaboles Fenyes
I've Never Stolen in My Life	HUN	Lajos Akom
Jeanne Dore	ITA	Guiseppe Mule
Jour se Leve, Le	FRA	Maurice Jaubert
Lenin in 1918	RUS	Nicolai Kryukov
Life on the Hegns Farm	DEN	Poul Bang
Little Flower of Jesus	FRA	F. L. Streapy
Mamele	POL	Abe Ellstein
Marguerite Drei	GER	Peter Ingelhoff
Midnight Phantom, The	MEX	Raul Lavista
Midnight Tradition	FRA	Jean Lenoir
Minister's Friend, The	HUN	Michael Eisemann
Mirele Efros	IND	Vladimir Heifetz
Mr. Chedworth Steps Out	AUT	Hamilton Webber
Naples That Never Dies	ITA	Alessandro Cicognini/ Valente E. Frustaci
Neighbors (Apartment Above)	POL	Henry Vars
New Horizons	RUS	Dmitri Shostakovich
Night of the Mayas	SPA	Cornello Cardenas
On His Own	RUS	Lev Schwartz
On the Night of the Fire	BRI	Miklos Rozsa
Oppenheim Family, The	RUS	Nicolai Kryukov
Pete Roleum and His Cousins (short)	IND	Hanns Eisler/Oscar Levant
Prisoner of Corbal	BRI	Allan Gray
Puszta Princess	HUN	Miklos Laurisin
Rappel Immediat	FRA	Michel Levine
Return of Dr. X, The	WB	Bernhard Kaun
Ripening Wheat	HUN	Sandor Szlatinay
Rules of the Game, The	FRA	Joseph Kosma
Skanor-Falsterbo	SWE	Erik Baumann/Lasse Dalquist
Song of the Butterfly	ITA	Luigi Ricci
Song of the Streets	FRA	Hanns Eisler
Stars of Variety	HUN	Georg Hentzschel
Sun Shines, The	HUN	Zoltan Kodaly
Tevya	IND	Sholem Secunda
There Were Nine Bachelors	FRA	Adolphe Borchard

This Man Is News	BRI	Percival Mackey
Unholy Wish, The	GER	Wolfgang Zeller
Union Pacific	PAR	George Anthiel

1940

Adventure of Salvator Rosa, An	ITA	Alessandro Cicognini
Ape, The	MON	Edward J. Kay
Battlement de Coeur (Heartbeat)	FRA	Paul Misraki
Boy	SPA	Martinez Azaora
Cavalcade of Love	FRA	Arthur Honegger
Contraband	BRI	Richard Addinsell
Deadly Spring	HUN	Tibor Polgar
Duration Family, The	FRA	Paul Misraki
Everything Is Rhythm	BRI	Cyril Ray
Fight for Life, The	IND	Louis Gruenberg
Florian	MGM	Franz Waxman/ Eugene Zador
Gallant Sons	MGM	Eugene Zador
Great Beginning, The	RUS	N. Timofeyev
House Across the Bay, The	UA	Werner Janssen
King of the Royal Mounted (serial)	REP	Cy Feuer
Kiss of Fire	FRA	Vincent Scotto
Leopard Men of Africa	IND	James Dietrich
Living Corpse, The	FRA	Jean Wiener
Mad Men of Europe	BRI	Louis Levy
Man from the Niger, The	FRA	Henri Tomasi
Man of the Hour	FRA	Michel Emer/Vincent Scotto/Jean Wiener
More About Nostradamus (short)	MGM	Eugene Zador
Mortal Storm, The	MGM	Edward Kane/Eugene Zador
Night Train	BRI	Louis Levy
Phantom Chariot, The	FRA	Jacques Ibert
Pomegranate Girl	IN	M. Mahomed
Power and the Land	RKO	Douglas Moore
Ramparts We Watch, The	RKO	Louis de Francesco
Semmelweis	HUN	Charles Froehlich
Tempest, The	FRA	Marcel Delannoy
They Wanted Peace	RUS	I. Gokieli
Two Mothers, The	ITA	Umberto Mancini

1941

Best Father in the World, The	ARG	Enrique Delfino
Black Dragons	MON	Johnny Lange/Lew Porter
Devil Bat	PRC	David Chudnow
Dick Tracy vs. Crime Incorporated (serial)	REP	Cy Feuer
Freedom Radio	BRI	Nicholas Brodszky

Greece on the March	GRE	Stephen Bartsens
Green Archer, The (serial)	COL	Lee Zahler
Hangman's Noose	FRA	Jean Lenoir
Hot Spot (I Wake Up Screaming)	TCF	Cyril Mockridge
Invisible Ghost, The	MON	Johnny Lange/Lew Porter
Iron Claw, The (serial)	COL	Lee Zahler
Jungle Cavalcade	RKO	Nathaniel Shilkret
Jungle Girl (serial)	REP	Cy Feuer
King of the White Elephants	THAI	Phra Chen Durtyang
King of the Zombies	MON	Edward J. Kay
Kukan	IND	Edward Craig
Musical Story, A	RUS	D. Astradantsev
New Teacher, The	RUS	V. Pushkov
Shark Woman, The	WOR	Abe Meyer
Siege of the Alcazar	ITA/SPA	Antonio Veretti
Smiling Ghost, The	WB	Bernhard Kaun/William Lava
This England	BRI	Richard Addinsell
Tower of Terror	BRI	Eddie Benson
University of Life	RUS	Lev Schwartz
Volga Volga	RUS	Isaac O. Dunayevsky
Wings of Victory	RUS	V. Pushkov

1942

Angel Down from Heaven, An	ARG	Mario Maurano
Aniki-Bobo	POR	Jaime Silva Filho
Ashes to the Wind	ARG	Julian Bautista
Baron Fantome, Le (Phantom Baron, The)	FRA	Louis Beydts
Bedeviled Gold	GER	Wolfgang Zeller
Corpse Vanishes, The	MON	Johnny Lange/Lew Porter
Devil's Envoys, The	FRA	Joseph Kosma/Maurice Thiriet
Devil's Hand, The	FRA	Roger Dumas
Gaucho War, The	ARG	Lucio Demare
Gold Rush, The (reissue)	UA	Charles Chaplin
Guerrilla Brigade	RUS	Sergei Pototsky
Her Melody	SWE	Erik Baumann/Nathan Goerling/Kaj Gullmar
King Midas Jr. (short)	COL	Paul Worth
Land, The	IND	Richard Arnell
Malambo	ARG	Alberto Ginastera
Moscow Strikes Back	RUS	Dimitri Tiomkin
My Merry Widow	MEX	Rafael de Paz
Sable Cicada	CHN	K. S. Yen
Secret Code, The (serial)	COL	Lee Zahler
Ships with Wings	BRI	Geoffrey Wright
Strange Holiday	PRC	Gordon Jenkins
Tanya	RUS	Isaac O. Dunayevsky

Undying Monster, The	FOX	Arthur Lange/Cyril Mockridge/David Raksin
Visiteurs du Soir, Les (Devil's Envoys, The)	FRA	Joseph Kosma/Maurice Thiriet
Wolves of the Malveneurs, The	FRA	Maurice Thiriet

1943

Adventures of Baron Munchaussen	GER	G. Haentzschel
Day of Wrath	DEN	Paul Schierbeck
Devil with Hitler, The	UA	Edward Ward
Eternal Return, The	FRA	Georges Auric
Imagination (short)	COL	Paul Worth
Jitterbugs	TCF	Charles Newman
Masked Marvel, The (serial)	REP	Mort Glickman
Mysterious Doctor, The	WB	Howard Jackson/William Lava
Rikisha Man, The	JAP	Goro Nishi
Secret Service in Darkest Africa, The (serial)	REP	Mort Glickman
Terror House	BRI	Charles Williams

1944

Mummy's Curse, The	UN	Oliver Drake/Frank Orth
Murder in the Blue Room	UN	Sam Freed, Jr.
When Spring Makes a Mistake	ARG	Julian Bautista

1945

Brighton Strangler, The	RKO	Leigh Harline/Franz Waxman
Castillo de las Bofetadas, El	SPA	Juan Hernandez
Day with the Devil, A	MEX	Rosalio Ramirez
Fog Island	PRC	Karl Hajos
He Who Died of Love	MEX	Manuel Esperon
Jade Mask, The	MON	Edward J. Kay
Jungle Captive	UN	William Lava/Charles Previn/Hans Salter
Kickapoo Juice (short)	COL	Eddie Kilfeather
Red Dragon, The	MON	Edward J. Kay
Satan's Five Warnings	MEX	Rosalio Ramirez
Walk in the Sun, A	TCF	Frederic Efrem Rich

1946

Battle of the Rails	FRA	Yves Baudrier

Decoy	MON	Edward J. Kay
Fabulous Joe	UA	Heinz Roemheld
Heritage of the Crying Women, The	MEX	Rosalio Ramirez
Kuruk Shetra	IN	Ganpat Rao
Lady and Death, The	CHL	Jorge Andreani
Leda and the Elephant (short)	RUS	Lev Schwartz
Night Editor	COL	Mischa Bakaleinkoff
Rebellion of the Ghosts	MEX	Leo Cardona
Scared to Death	SG	Carl Hoefle
Singin' in the Corn	COL	George Duning
Stone Flower, The	RUS	Lev Schwartz
Strange Mr. Gregory, The	MON	Edward J. Kay
Valley of the Zombies	REP	Richard Cherwin

1947

Adventure in the Night	MEX	Rosalio Ramirez
Chips Are Down, The	FRA	Georges Auric
Colonel Bogey	BRI	Norman Fulton
Down to Earth	COL	George Duning
Fantomas vs. Fantomas	FRA	Joe Hajos
Francis the First	FRA	Rene Sylviano
Ghost Goes Wild, The	REP	Joseph Dubin/Morton Scott
Ghosts of Berkeley Square, The	BRI	Hans May
Gokul (Shepherd)	IN	Sudhir Phadke
Howdy Doody (series)	NBC-TV	Edward Kean
If Youth Only Knew	FRA	Paul Misraki
Music of Govind (short)	IN	Gyan Dutt
Mysterious Uncle Silas	ARG	Juan Ehler
Petit Soldat, Le (short)	FRA	Joseph Kosma
Prelude to Madness (Kreutzer Sonata)	ITA	Nino Rota
Woman	ITA	Renzo Rosselini

1948

Angel's Coat, The (short)	CZE	Jan Rychlik
Behind Locked Doors	EL	Irving Friedman (not Albert Glasser)
Calling Paul Temple	BRI	Percival Mackey
Counterblast	BRI	Hans May
Devil's Wanton, The (Fangelse)	SWE	Erland von Koch
Drunken Angel	JAP	Fumio Hayasaka
Fatal Night, The	BRI	Stanley Black
He Walked by Night	EL	Leonid Raab (not Irving Friedman)
Hollow Triumph (Scar, The)	EL	Sol Kaplan (not Irving Friedman)
House of Darkness, The	BRI	George Melachrino

Kitty Foiled (short)	MGM	Scott Bradley
Kukla, Fran and Ollie (series)	NBC-TV	Jack Fascinato
Lullaby (short)	CZE	Zedenek Liska
Machine That Kills Bad People, The	ITA	Renzo Rossellini
Monkey's Paw, The	BRI	Stanley Black
Siren's Song, The (Canto de la Sirena, El/Song of the Siren)	MEX	Manuel Esperon
Super Scientist, The	MEX	Gonzalo Curiel
Things Happen at Night	BRI	George Melachrino

1949

Affairs of a Rogue, The	BRI	Lennox Berkeley
All Roads Lead to Rome	FRA	Paul Misraki
Amazing Mr. Beecham, The	BRI	Benjamin Frankel
Antonio di Padova	ITA	Carlo Innocenzi
Appointment with Life	FRA	Jean Weiner
Arsenic and Old Lace	CBS-TV	Cy Feuer
Bad Lord Byron	BRI	Cedric Thorpe Davie
Barkleys of Broadway, The	MGM	Lennie Hayton
Behind the Barriers	FRA/ITA	Roman Vlad
Beloved of the World	AUS	Nicholas Brodzsky/ Frank Fox
Berliner Ballade	GER	Werner Eisbrenner
Beyond the Forest	WB	Max Steiner
Black Shadows	FRA	Pierre Moulaert
Blondie Hits the Jackpot	COL	Mischa Bakaleinikoff
Bom, the Soldier	SWE	Kaj Gullmar
Carmela	ITA	Franco Sacavola
Chiltern Hundreds, The (see Amazing Mr. Beecham)		
Criss Cross	UN	Miklos Rozsa
Cry of the Earth	ITA	Bruno Cicognini
Cuckoo's Egg, The	AUS	Peter Wehle
Cure de Village, Le	FRA	Morris C. Davis
Dalton Gang, The	LIP	Walter Greene
Dear Mr. Prohack	BRI	Temple Abady
Dedee	FRA	Jacques Besse
Desterrado, O	POR	Jaime Mendez
Diamond City	BRI	Clifton Parker
Docteur Laennec	FRA	Jean-Jacques Gruenwald
Dolores	SPA	Luis Hernandez Breton
Don't Ever Leave Me	BRI	Lambert Williamson
Dynamite Brothers, The	ITA	Guiseppe Piazzi
Elizabeth of Ladymead	BRI	Robert Farnon
Eva	SWE	Erik Nordgren
Fairy of Happiness	AUS	Frans Thurner
First Front, The	RUS	Aram Khatchaturian
Flight into France	ITA	Nino Rota
For Them That Trespass	BRI	Philip Green

Forbidden Jungle	EL	David Chudnow
Girdhar Gopal Ki Mira	IN	Brijlal Varma
Girl from a Mountain Village	SWE	Sven Skjold
Girl from the Dress Circle, The	SWE	Sune Waldimir
Give Us This Day (Christ in Concrete)	BRI	Benjamin Frankel
Glass Mountain, The (see Legend of the Glass Mountain, The)		
Gros Bill, Le	CAN	Maurice Blackburn
Gun Crazy (Deadly Is the Female)	UA	Victor Young
Hans the Sailor	FRA	Joseph Kosma
Harvest Is Plentiful, The	SPA	Manuel Parada
Heaven over the Marshes	ITA	Antonio Veretti
Hellish Love	AUS	Hans Elin
Hey, Boy! (Guaglio)	ITA	Nino Rota
Holy Nun, The	ITA	Ezio Caraballa/Antonio Valli
I Remember Mama (series)	CBS-TV	Billy Nalle
Inspiration (short)	CZE	A. Liska
Jour de Fete	FRA	Jean Yatove
Just a Big, Simple Girl	FRA	P. Capedevielle
Katrina	SWE	Gunnar Johansson
King of the Rocket Men (Lost Planet Airmen) (serial)	REP	Stanley Wilson
Kingdom for a Horse, A	HOL	Harry Hilm/Erich Ziegler
Kiss of a Dead Woman	ITA	Enzo Massetti
Lambert Is Threatened	AUS	Hanns Elin
Last Days of Dolwyn, The	BRI	John Greenwood
Last Stop, The	POL	Roman Palester
Legend of the Glass Mountain, The (Glass Mountain, The)	BRI	Georges Anthiel
Leprechaun's Gold (short)	PAR	Winston Sharples
Life of Riley, The (series)	NBC-TV	Lou Kosloff
Lights Out (series)	NBC-TV	Fred Howard
Lone Ranger, The (series)	ABC-TV	Alias Alfriede/Ralph Cushman
Look After Amelia	FRA	Rene Cloerec
Lost in the Dark	ITA	Virginio Marchi
Love Locked Out	FRA	Joseph Kosma
Magic Sword, The	YUG	Kresimir Baranovich
Man on the Run	BRI	Philip Green
Man with the Grey Glove, The	ITA	Ezio Carabella
Massacre River	MON	Lucien Moraweck
Maya	FRA	Georges Auric
Maytime in Mayfair	BRI	Robert Farnon
Merchant of Slaves	ITA	Piero Giorgi
Mill on the Po, The	ITA	Ildebrando Pizzetti
Nail, The	SPA	Joaquin Quintero
Now Barabbas Was a Robber	BRI	George Melachrino

Omoo-Omoo, the Shark God	SG	Albert Glasser
Pact with the Devil	ITA	Achille Longo
Palace Scandal	GER	Wolfgang Zeller
Parents Terribles, Les	FRA	Georges Auric
Peddlin' in Society	ITA	E. Montagnini
Pretty Little Beach, A	FRA	Maurice Thiriet
Prison, The	SWE	Erland von Kock
Quiet One, The	IND	Ulysses Kay
Radar Patrol vs. Spy King (serial)	REP	Stanley Wilson
Rapture	ITA	Giuseppe Rosati
Ribatejo	POR	Jaime Mendez
Romantic Age, The	BRI	Charles Williams
Rose of Bagdad, The	ITA	Riccardo Pick Mangiagalli
Rugged O'Riordans, The	AUT	Henry Cripps
Ruggles, The (series)	ABC-TV	Fred Howard
Run for Your Money, A	BRI	Sir Ernest Irving
Saints and Sinners	BRI	Philip Green
Secrets of a Ballerina	FRA	Arthur Honegger
Shadows of the West	MON	Edward J. Kay
Shamrock Hill	EL	Herschel Burke Gilbert
Silence of the Sea	FRA	Edgar Bischoff
Slave Merchant (see Merchant of Slaves)		
Somewhere in Berlin	GER	Erich Einegg
Stallion Canyon	AST	Emil Velazco
Strange Bargain	RKO	Constantin Bakaleinikoff
Strangers in the House	FRA	Roland Manuel
Sun Comes Up, The	MGM	Andre Previn
Suspense (series)	CBS-TV	Henry Sylvern
Swiss Tour	SWI	Robert Blum
Symphony of Life	RUS	Nicolai Kryukov
Third Time Lucky	BRI	Stanley Black
Toa	FRA	Louiguy
Town Tale (Pueberlina)	MEX	Antonio Dias Conde
Train Goes East, The	RUS	Tikhon Khrennikov
Ulli und Marei	GER	Alois Melichar
Under the Sun of Rome	ITA	Nino Rota
Vagabonds	AUS	Anton Profes
Van Gogh (short)	FRA	Jacques Besse
Volume One (series)	ABC-TV	Albert Buhrmann
Wench, The	FRA	Joseph Kosma
Wild Weed	IND	Rudolph Friml, Jr.
Wiseguy (Avivato)	ARG	Rudolfo Sciammarella
Woman in White	SWE	Hakan von Eichwald
Woman of Evil	FRA	Yves Baudrier
Young Guard, The	RUS	Dmitri Shostakovich
Youth of Athens	GRE	M. Katinanos/Andreas Poggis

1950

Adam and Eve	ITA	Pippo Barzizza
Almafuerte	ARG	Alejandro Gutierrez del Barrio
Angel with the Trumpet, The	BRI	Willy Schmidt-Gentner
Angels of the Streets	FRA	Jean-Jacques Grunewald
Astounding She Monster	IND	Gene Kauer
Beautiful Galatea, The	GER	Franz Grothe
Between Midnight and Dawn	COL	George Duning
Big Town (series)	CBS-TV	Albert Glasser
Blue Lamp, The	BRI	Sir Ernest Irving
Boys from the Streets	NOR	Gunnar Sonstevold
Bullet for Stefano, A	ITA	Enzo Massetti
Cavaliero della Montagna	ITA	Massimo Dalamanno
Children of Chance	ITA	Nino Rota
Cisco Kid, The (series)	IND-TV	Albert Glasser
City of Torment	GER	Theo Mackeben
Cold Heart (Heart of Stone)	E.GER	Herbert Trantow
Congolaise	FC	Bernardo Segall
Danger (series)	CBS-TV	Tony Motolla
Dangerous Guests	GER	Michael Jary
Daybreak in Udi (short)	BRI	William Alwyn
Death in Love	MEX	Manuel Esperon
Death of a Dream	EL	Jack Shaindlin
Demon in Art, The (short)	ITA	Roman Vlad
Dishonored	ITA	Ezio Carabella
Dream No More	IND	Lan Adomian
Duchess of Benameji, The	SPA	Juan Quintero
Duel Without Honor	ITA	Ezio Carabella
Emperor of Capri, The	ITA	Felice Montagnini
Escape (series)	CBS-TV	Cy Feuer
Fame and the Devil	ITA	Carlo Franci/Mario Funaro
Farewell to Yesterday	TCF	Louis Applebaum/Robert McBride/Richard Mohaupt
Faust and the Devil	ITA	Alessandro Cicognini
50 Years Before Your Eyes	WB	Howard Jackson/William Lava
Fighting Stallion, The	EL	Edward Paul
Film Without a Name, The	GER	Bernhard Eichhorn
Flesh Will Surrender	ITA	Fernando Previtali
Gabrielle	GER	Michael Jary
Girl from Jungfrusund	SWE	Sune Waldimir
Girls Behind Bars	GER	Herbert Trantow
God, Man and Devil	IND	Sholem Secunda
Golden Salamander, The	BRI	William Alwyn
Guilt Is My Shadow	BRI	Hans May
Here Is the Beauty	FRA	Joseph Kosma
Histoires Extraordinaires	FRA	Georges van Parys

House by the River, The	REP	George Anthiel
I Cover Times Square (series)	ABC-TV	Ethel Stevens
Inn of Sin, The	FRA	Henri Verdun
Invisible Monster, The (serial)	REP	Stanley Wilson
Julie de Carnellhan	FRA	Henri Sauguet
Lady Paname	FRA	Georges van Parys
Last Days of Pompeii, The	FRA	Roman Vlad
Loves and Poisons	ITA	Salvatore Allegra
Lure of the Sila (Wolf of the Sila)	ITA	Enzo Massetti
Lux Video Theater (series)	CBS-TV	Vladimir Selinsky/ Milton Weinstein
Man Who Returns from Afar, The	FRA	Yves Beaudrier
Man Without a Face, The	MEX	Raul Lavista
Marshal of Gunfight Pass, The (series)	ABC-TV	Anthony Parker
Midsummer Holiday	ITA	Roman Vlad
Miss Pilgrim's Progress	BRI	Philip Martell
Monsignor	FRA	Henri Verdun
Mousetrap, The	FRA	Jean Marion
Mulatto, The	ITA	Annibal Bizzelli
My Friend Who Can't Say No	AUS	Robert Stolz
My Widow and I	ITA	Nino Rota
Nacha Regules	ARG	Juan Ehler
No More Vacation for the Good Lord	FRA	Jean Weiner
No Place for Jennifer	BRI	Allen Gray
On the Isle of Samoa	COL	Mischa Bakaleinkoff
Only a Mother	SWE	Dag Wiren
Our Daily Bread	GER	Hanns Eisler
Pancho Villa Returns	MEX	Elias Breeskin
Paper Gallows	BRI	John Wooldridge
Portrait of an Assassin	FRA	Maurice Thiriet
Portrait of Clare	BRI	Leighton Lucas
Pulitzer Prize Playhouse (series)	ABC-TV	Glenn Osser
Red Rain	MEX	Manuel Esperon
Rita	FRA	Francis Lopez
Roi, Le	FRA	Jean Marion
Scandal (Shuban)	JAP	Fumio Hayasaka
Scandals of Clochemerle	FRA	Henri Sauguet
Shadow of the Past	BRI	Stanley Black
Sicilian Uprising	ITA	Enzo Massetti
Singoalla	FRA	Hugo Alfven
Son of D'Artagnan	ITA	Carlo Jachino
Strange Appointment	ITA	Francesco Lavagnino
Summer Storm	FRA	Marcel Delannoy
Susana (Devil and Flesh)	MEX	Raul Lavista
Swedish Horseman	SWE	Bertil Bokstedt
Sylvie and the Phantom	FRA	Rene Cloerec
That Wonderful Guy (series)	ABC-TV	Bernard Green
This Is the Half Century	FRA	Georges Auric/Henri Sauguet

Thus Ends the Night	FRA	Joe Hoyos
Toto Wants a Home	ITA	Giacome Rustichesi
Treasure of Cantenac, The	FRA	Louiguy
Two Lost Worlds	EL	Alex Alexander/Michael Terr
Unconquered People	YUG	Fran Lotka
Volcano	ITA	Enzo Massetti
Walls of Malapaga	ITA	Roman Vlad
We Shall Go to Paris	FRA	Paul Misraki
Where the Sidewalk Ends	TCF	Cyril Mockridge (not Lionel Newman)
With These Hands	IND	Morris Mamorsky
Woman on the Run	UN	Arthur Lange/Emil Newman
You Can't Fool an Irishman	IRE	Eamonn O'Galehur

1951

Accusation	ITA	Carlo Rustichelli
Adventures of Captain Fabian, The	REP	Rene Cloerec
Adventuress, The	BRI	Cedric Thorpe Davie
Andalousie	FRA/SPA	Francis Lopez
Appointment with Venus	BRI	Benjamin Frankel
Axe of Wandsbek, The	E.GER	Ernst Roters
Bethsabee	FRA	Joseph Kosma
Blackmailed	BRI	John Wooldridge
Boston Blackie (series)	IND-TV	Joseph Hooven
Celanese Theater (series)	ABC-TV	Bernard Green
Circle of Danger	BRI	Robert Farnon
City Park	AUS	Frank Filip
Crime Photographer (series)	CBS-TV	Morton Gould
Crossroads of Passion	FRA	Joseph Kosma
Doctor Beware	ITA	Renzo Rossellini
Door with No Name, The (series)	NBC-TV	Charles Paul
Dragnet (series)	NBC-TV	Frank Comstock/Lyn Murray/Walter Schumann/Nathan Scott/ Stanley Wilson
Emperor's Nightingale, The	CZE	Vaclav Trojan
Eva Inherits Paradise	AUS	Hans Lang
Far from Moscow	RUS	Nicolai Kryukov
Feminine Wiles (Coasa de Mujer)	ARG	Peter Kreuder
Fire Test (Agni Pariksha)	IN	G. P. Narasimha
First Legion, The	UA	Hans Sommer
Flesh and Blood	BRI	Charles Williams
Forbidden Christ	ITA	Curzio Malaparte
Foreign Intrigue (series)	IND-TV	Erik Baumann/Ervin Drake/Charles Norman/Eland von Koch
Four in a Jeep	SWI	Robert Blum

Frightened Ghosts	ARG	Tito Ribero
Galloping Major, The	BRI	Georges Auric
Ghost Chasers	MON	Edward J. Kay
Grand Terrace, The	FRA	Joseph Kosma
Green Grow the Rushes	BRI	Lambert Williamson
Her Panelled Door	BRI	Allan Gray
Horseman, The	RUS	A. Spadavekpia
Hotel Sahara	BRI	Benjamin Frankel
Housemaid, Highly Presentable, Seeks Job	ITA	Alessandro Cicognini
Jungle of Chang	RKO	Gunnar Johansson/ Jules Sylvain
Krakatit	CZE	Kiri Srnka
Lady With a Lamp	BRI	Anthony Collins
Last Illusion, The	GER	Georg Haentzschel
Laughter in Paradise	BRI	Stanley Black
Lav Kush	IN	Shankar Rao Vyas
Lavender Hill Mob, The	BRI	Georges Auric
Love of Life (series)	CBS-TV	Carey Gold
Lovers of Verona	FRA	Joseph Kosma
M	COL	Michel Michelet (not Bert Shefter)
Meet Corliss Archer (series)	CBS-TV	Felix Mills
Midnight Episode	BRI	Mischa Spoliansky
Miracle in Milan	ITA	Alessandro Cicognini
Mr. District Attorney (series)	ABC-TV	Peter Van Steeden
Mr. Peek-a-Boo	FRA	Georges van Parys
Musolino the Bandit	ITA	Enzo Massetti
Native Son	ARG	Juan Ehler
Neapolitan Millionaire	ITA	Nino Rota
Night Without Stars	BRI	William Alwyn
Obsession	BRI	Allan Gray
One Wild Oat	BRI	Stanley Black
Pandora and the Flying Dutchman	MGM	Alan Rawsthorne
Pickup	COL	Harold Byrns
Prowler, The	UA	Lyn Murray (not Irving Friedman)
Radar Men of the Moon (serial)	REP	Stanley Wilson
Range Ridger, The (series)	IND-TV	Carl Cotner
Red Inn, The	FRA	Rene Cloerec
Road to Hope	ITA	Carlo Rustichelli
St. Benny the Dip	UA	Robert Stringer
Saturday's Hero	COL	Elmer Bernstein
Search for Tomorrow (series)	CBS-TV	Elliott Lawrence
Second Woman, The	UA	Nat W. Finston
Secret Brigade, The	RUS	A. Bogatyrov
Secret Flight	BRI	Alan Rawsthorne
Seven Journeys	GER	Bernhard Eichhorn
Sickle or the Cross, The	AST	Alberto Colombo
Signori in Carrozza	FRA/ITA	Renzo Rossellini
Sky King (series)	IND-TV	Alec Compinsky

Sommarlek (She Only Danced One Summer)	SWE	Erik Nordgren
Street Urchin	ITA	Nino Rota
Strictly Dishonorable (opera sequence)	MGM	Mario Castelnuovo Tedesco
Swamp Fox	ABC-TV	Buddy Baker
Tale of Five Cities	BRI	Hans May
Tales of Tomorrow (series)	ABC-TV	Robert Christian
There Is Another Sun	BRI	Wilfred Burns
Three Steps North	UA	Roman Vlad
Tony Draws a Horse	BRI	Bretton Byrd
Travellers Joy	BRI	Arthur Wilkinson
Treasured Earth	HUN	Sandor Veres
Try and Get Me (Sound of Fury, The)	UA	Hugo Friedhofer
Two Pennies Worth of Violets	FRA	Georges van Parys
Unwanted, The	ARG	Alejandro del Barrio
Without a Flag	ITA	Renzo Rossellini
Woman Without Love, A	MEX	Raul Lavista
Women and Bandits	ITA	Nino Rota
Wonder Child	AUS/BRI	Willy Schmidt-Gentner
Wonderful Times	GER	Werner Eisbrenner
Young Caruso, The (Enrico Caruso, Legend of a Voice)	ITA	Carlo Franci

1952

Aan (Pride)	IN	Naushad
Abbott and Costello Show, The (series)	IND-TV	Raoul Kraushaar
Absentee, The	MEX	Raul Lavista
Adventures in Vienna	GER	Richard Hageman
Adventures of Ozzie and Harriet, The (series)	ABC-TV	Basil Adlam
Affairs of a Model	SWE	E. Eckert-Lundin
Affairs of China Smith, The	IND-TV	Melvyn Lenard
Amazing Monsieur Fabre, The	FRA	Hubert d'Auriol
Angelo in the Crowd	ITA	Gino Filippini
Angels of the District	ITA	Nino Rota
Assignment--Paris	COL	George Duning
Babes in Bagdad	UA	J. Leoz
Bandit of Tacca del Lup	ITA	Carlo Rustichelli
Barbara Atomica	ARG	Tito Ribero
Battles of Chief Pontiac	REA	Elmer Bernstein
Beauty and the Thieves	JAP	Fumio Hayasaka
Behind Closed Shutters	ITA	Carlo Rustichelli
Bela Lugosi Meets a Brooklyn Gorilla	IND	Richard Hazard
Bountiful Summer	RUS	E. Zhubovsky
Bride for a Night	ITA	Alessandro Cicognini
Brief Rapture	ITA	Constantino Ferri

Castles in the Air	BRI	Francis Chagrin
Clash by Night	RKO	Roy Webb
		(not C. Bakaleinikoff)
Cloudburst	UA	Frank Spencer
Cops and Robbers	ITA	Alessandro Cicognini
Curious Adventures of Mr. Wonderbird, The	FRA	Joseph Kosma
Daughter of the Sands	FRA	Georges Auric
Dishonor	ARG	Julian Bautista
Doorway to Danger (series)	NBC-TV	Charles Paul
Dream of a Cossack	RUS	Tikhon Khrennikov
Europe '51	ITA	Renzo Rossellini
Firebrand, The (Eldfageln)	SWE	Stig Rybrant
Forever My Love	JAP	Hidemaro Konoe
French Way, The	FRA	Wal-Berg/Vincent Scotto
Gift Horse, The	BRI	Clifton Parker
Grand Melies, Le	FRA	Georges van Parys
Guiding Light, The (series)	CBS-TV	Charles Paul
Hell's Kitchen	MEX	Perez Prado
His Excellency	BRI	Sir Ernest Irving
His Hand Slipped	MEX	Jose de la Vega
Hunted	BRI	Hubert Clifford
Hunter, The (series)	CBS-TV	Frank Lewin
Husband and Wife	ITA	Nino Rota
I Was a Prisoner in Siberia	JAP	Akira Ifukube
Ideal Woman Sought	AUS	Johannes Fehring
In Olden Days	ITA	Alessandro Cicognini
Jungle, The	LIP	Dakshnimurti
Jupiter	FRA	Georges van Parys
Last Meeting, The	ITA	Enzo Massetti
Last Mission, The	GRE	Costa Yiannide
Life Begins Tomorrow	FRA	Darius Milhaud
Little Love of My Life	MEX	Manuel Esperon
Mad Woman, The	MEX	Manuel Esperon
Made in Heaven	BRI	Ronald Hammer
Maria Theresia	AUS	Alois Melichar
Mr. Denning Drives North	BRI	Benjamin Frankel
Mr. Peepers (series)	NBC-TV	Bernard Green
Mr. Walkie Talkie	LIP	Leon Klatzkin
Murder Will Out	BRI	Frank Cordell
My Friend Irma (series)	CBS-TV	Lud Gluskin
My Little Margie (series)	CBS-TV	Lud Gluskin
My Son, the Vampire	BRI	Linda Southworth
Old Mother Riley	BRI	George Melachrino
Once a Sinner	BRI	Ronald Binge
100 Little Mothers	ITA	Carlo Innocenzi
One Summer of Happiness	SWE	Sven Skjold
Our Miss Brooks (series)	CBS-TV	Lud Gluskin
Paris Is Always Paris	FRA	Joseph Kosma
Pleasure Garden, The (short)	BRI	Stanley Bate

Poison, Le	FRA	Louiguy
Port Sinister (Beast of Paradise Isle)	RKO	Albert Glasser
Red Curtain, The	FRA	Joseph Kosma
Red Shirts	FRA/ITA	Enzo Massetti
Rendezvous (series)	ABC-TV	Edward Vito
Right to Be Born, The	MEX	Raul Lavista
Simple Case of Money, A	FRA	Jean Marion
Sisters of Nishijin	JAP	Akira Ifukube
Sky Is Red, The	ITA	Valentino Bucchi
Sniper, The	COL	George Anthiel (not Morris Stoloff)
Something Money Can't Buy	BRI	Nino Rota
Song of Paris	BRI	Cyril Martell
Stormbound	ITA	Alessandro Cicognini
Strange Fascination	COL	Vaclav Divinia
Tembo	RKO	Claude Sweeten
Three Forbidden Stories	ITA	Antonio Veretti
Three Sinners	FRA	Raymond Legrand
Tragic Spell	ITA	Roman Vlad
Treasure of Bird Island, The (short)	CZE	Zdenek Liska
Trip to America, A	FRA	Francis Poulenc
Tromba, the Tiger Man	GER	Adolf Steimel
Vacation with a Gangster	ITA	Mario Nascimbene
Victory at Sea (series)	NBC-TV	Richard Rodgers
Was It He? Yes! Yes!	ITA	Pippo Barzizza
White Hell of Pitz-Palu, The	GER	Mark Lothar
White Slave Trade, The	ITA	Armando Trovajoli
Who Goes There?	BRI	Muir Mathieson
Wonder Boy	BRI	Willi Schmidt-Gentner
Zombies of the Stratosphere (serial)	REP	Stanley Wilson

1953

Alerte au Sud	FRA/ITA	Joseph Kosma
Alif Laila	IN	Shyam Sunder
April 1, 2000	AUS	Josef Fiedler/Alois Melichar
Article 519, Penal Code	FRA/ITA	Carlo Innocenzi
Assignation, The (short)	IND	Ernest Gold
Bad Blonde	LIP	Ivor Slaney
Beautiful Dreamer, The	MEX	Manuel Esperon
Ben and Me (short)	DIS	Oliver Wallace
Black Ermine	ARG	Julian Bautista
Bonjour Paris	FRA	Jean Yatove
Brutality (Flight into the Reeds)	AUS	Paul Kont
Cat Women of the Moon	AST	Elmer Bernstein
Children of Love, The	FRA	Joseph Kosma
China Venture	COL	Ross di Maggio

Christopher Crumpet (short)	COL	George Bruns
City That Never Sleeps, The	REP	Dale Butts
Confusion (Yessa Mossa)	JAP	Hiroyuki Nagaoka
Cosh Boy	BRI	Lambert Williamson
Counterfeiters, The	ITA	Carlo Rustichelli
Dementia	AI	Georges Anthiel
Desperate Moment	BRI	Ronald Binge
Devotion	ITA	Antonio Veretti
Donovan's Brain	UA	Eddie Dunstedter
Don't Be Offended, Beatrice	MEX	Luis Hernandez Breton
Eager to Love	ITA	Enzo Massetti
Easy Years, The	ITA	Nino Rota
Flash Gordon (series)	IND-TV	Kurt Heuser
Flight of the Tertia	GER	Herbert Windt
Four-Sided Triangle	BRI	Malcolm Arnold
Ganga Malya	IN	Shankar Rao Vyas
General Electric Theater, The (series)	CBS-TV	Elmer Bernstein/Wilbur Hatch/Melvyn Lenard/ Johnny Mandel
Genie, The	BRI	Allan Gray
Grandstand for the General Staff, A	AUS	Anton Profes
Hindu, The	IN	Dakshnimurti
His Last 12 Hours	ITA	Nino Rota
Horse's Mouth, The (Oracle, The)	BRI	Temple Abady
House of Life	GER	Bernhard Eichorn
I and My Wife	AUS	Bruno Uher
I Chose Love	ITA	Roman Vlad
I'll Get You	LIP	Hans May
I'm the Law (series)	IND-TV	Raoul Kraushaar
Intruder, The	BRI	Francis Chagrin
Invaders from Mars	FOX	Mort Glickman/Raoul Kraushaar
Irene in Need	AUS	Bojan Adamic
Is Your Honeymoon Really Necessary?	BRI	William Trytell
Isn't Life Wonderful?	BRI	Philip Green
It Came from Outer Space	UN	Irving Gertz/Henry Mancini/Herman Stein (not Joseph Gershenson)
Johnny Saves Nebrador	GER	Werner Eisbrenner
Keepers of the Night (Night Watch)	BRI	Mark Lothar
Letter to Loretta, A (series)	NBC-TV	Harry Lubin
Life of Riley, The (series)	NBC-TV	Jerry Fielding
Life with Father (series)	CBS-TV	David Raksin
Love in Pawn	BRI	Temple Abady
Lucrece Borgia	FRA	Maurice Thiriet
Mahatma Gandhi--20th Century Prophet	UA	Edward Paul

Mailman Mueller	GER	Friedrich Schroeder
Make Room for Daddy (series)	ABC-TV	Earle Hagen/Herbert Spencer
Man from Cairo, The	LIP	Renzo Rossellini
Man of Conflict	IND	Albert Glasser
Man of Music	RUS	Vladimir Scherbachev
Manon of the Spring	FRA	Raymond Legrand
Maze, The	AA	Marlin Skiles
Meet Mr. Lucifer	BRI	Eric Rogers
Merchant of Venice, The	FRA/ITA	Giovanni Fusco
Mr. Photographer	MEX	Raul Lavista
Muddy Waters	ARG	Tito Ribero
My Darling Clementine	MEX	Antonio Dias Conde
Neapolitans in Milan	ITA	Renzo Rossellini
Net, The	BRI	Benjamin Frankel
Net, The	MEX	Antonio Dias Conde
99 River Street	UA	Arthur Lange
Nothing to Lose (Time, Gentlemen, Please)	BRI	John Addison
On Both Sides of the Rollbahn	GER	Rudolf Perak
One Girl's Confession	COL	Vaclav Divina
Overdoing It	MEX	Jose de la Vega
Paolo and Francesca	ITA	Alessandro Cicognini
Pimpernel Svensson	SWE	Knut Edgardt
Pride of the Family (series)	ABC-TV	Stanley Wilson
Private Secretary (series)	CBS-TV	Mahlon Merrick
Project Moonbase	IND	Herschel Burke Gilbert
Return to Youth	MEX	Raul Lavista
Ring Around the Clock	ITA	Alessandro Cicognini/ I. Cini
Robot Monster	AST	Elmer Bernstein
Secretly, Quietly and Softly	GER	Michael Jary/Paul Lincke
Seven of the Big Bear	ITA	Nino Rota
Seven Ravens, The	GER	Walter Popper
Shadow Man (Street of Shadows)	BRI	Eric Spear
Sky Commando	COL	Ross di Maggio
So Little Time	BRI	Louis Levy
Spaceways	BRI	Ivor Slaney
Stolen Identity	IND	Richard Hageman
Strange Deception	ITA	Curzio Malaparte
Street Corner	BRI	Temple Abady
Tanga-Tika	IND	Les Baxter
Terror Street	BRI	Ivor Slaney
That Was Our Rommel	GER	Gustav Adolf Schlemm
Till Five Minutes Past Twelve	GER	Rudolf Perak
Time Bomb	BRI	John Addison
Topper (series)	CBS-TV	Charles Koff
Tormento	ITA	Gino Campase
Ugetsu	JAP	Fumio Hayasaka
Uncle from America	GER	Lotar Olias
Undercover Agent	LIP	Eric Spear

Voice of Silence	FRA/ITA	Enzo Massetti
What Price Innocence?	ITA	Gino Filippini
Will Any Gentleman?	BRI	Wally Stott
Woman Without Camelias, The	ITA	Giovanni Fusco
Women of Destiny	ITA	Roman Vlad
You Are There (series)	CBS-TV	Tom Scott

1954

Adventures of Rin-Tin-Tin, The (series)	ABC	Hal Hopper
Age of Love, The	FRA	Mario Nascimbene
Aladdin Takes Off (Dringue, Castrito and Aladdin's Lamp)	ARG	Eduardo Armani
Ali Baba and the 40 Thieves	FRA	Paul Misraki
Anathan (Devil's Pitchfork, The)	JAP	Akira Ifukube
Angel Who Pawned Her Harp, The	BRI	Anthony Hopkins
Angelika	GER	Mark Lothar
Annie Oakley (series)	IND-TV	Erma Levin
Anxiety	MEX	Manuel Esperon
Appointment for Murder	ITA	Gino Marinuzzi, Jr.
Bailiff, The (Sancho Dayu)	JAP	Fumio Hayasaka
Beautiful Stranger	BRI	Malcolm Arnold
Belle Otero, La	FRA	Georges van Parys
Black Widow	FOX	Leigh Harline
Bread, Love and Fantasy	ITA	Alessandro Cicognini
Bread of Love, The	SWE	Sven Skjold
Cadet-Rousselle	FRA	Jean Marion
Caliph Stork (short)	BRI	Freddie Phillips
Captain Midnight (series)	CBS-TV	Don Ferris
Carnival Story	RKO	Willi Schmidt-Gentner
Cave of Ali Baba, The	ARG	Fernando M. Lopez
Chevalier de la Nuit	FRA	Jean-Jacques Gruenwald
Circus (short)	POL	Zbigniew Turski
Confession at Dawn	CHILE	Acario Cotapos/Alfonso Letelier/Juan Orrego Solas
Confession Under Four Eyes	GER	Werner Eisbrenner
Conflict of Wings	BRI	Philip Green
Dames Get Along	FRA	Paul Misraki
Davy Crockett (series)	DIS-TV	George Bruns
Days of Love	ITA	Mario Nascimbene
December Bride (series)	CBS-TV	Eliot Daniel
Descent into Hell	ARG	Tito Ribero
Destiny in Trouble	BRA	Francisco Mignoni
Devil Girl from Mars, The	BRI	Edwin Astley
Devil on Horseback, The	BRI	Malcolm Arnold
Diamond Wizard, The	BRI	Matyas Seiber
Dringue Castrito and Aladdin's Lamp (see Aladdin Takes Off)		

Egyptian, The	FOX	Bernard Herrmann/ Alfred Newman
Eight O'Clock Walk	BRI	George Melachrino
End of the Road, The	BRI	John Addison
Face That Launched a Thousand Ships, The	ITA	Nino Rota
Fast and Furious, The	IND	Alexander Gerens
Father Brown	BRI	Georges Auric
Father Knows Best (series)	CBS-TV	Irving Friedman
Femmes de Paris	FRA	Paul Misraki
Fireworks	GER	Paul Burkhard
For Better for Worse	BRI	Wally Stott
Forbidden Cargo	BRI	Lambert Williamson
French Touch, The	FRA	Paul Misraki
Frog Prince, The (short)	BRI	Freddie Phillips
Front Page Story	BRI	Jackie Brown
Gallant Little Tailor, The (short)	BRI	Freddie Phillips
Gaucho	ARG	Lucio Demare
Girls Marked Danger	ITA	Armando Trovajoli
Golden Demon, The	JAP	Ichiro Saito
Golden Link, The	BRI	Eric Spear
Golden Mask, The	UA	Robert Gill
Good Die Young, The	BRI	Georges Auric
Grasshopper and the Ant, The (short)	BRI-TV	Freddie Phillips
Great Gildersleeve, The (series)	IND-TV	Jack Meakin
Great Hope, The	ITA	Nino Rota
Halls of Ivy, The (series)	CBS-TV	Les Baxter
Hansel and Gretel (short)	BRI-TV	Freddie Phillips
Happiness of Three Women, The	BRI	Edwin Astley
Helen Keller in Her Own Story (Unconquered, The)	IND	Morgan Lewis
High and Dry (Maggie, The)	BRI	John Addison
His Royal Highness	GER	Mark Lothar
Holly and the Ivy, The	BRI	Malcolm Arnold
Honestly, Celeste! (series)	CBS-TV	Jerry Fielding
I and You	GER	Lother Bruehne
If Versailles Were Told to Me (see Royal Affair in Versailles)		
Immediate Disaster	BRI	Eric Spear
Indra Leela	IN	Ajit Merchant
Inspector Calls, An	BRI	Francis Chagrin
It's a Great Life (series)	NBC-TV	David Rose
It's the Paris Life	FRA	Roger Roger
Jack and the Beanstalk (short)	BRI	Freddie Phillips
Janet Dean, Registered Nurse (series)	IND-TV	Albert Glasser
John Wesley	BRI	Henry Reed
Journey to Italy	ITA	Renzo Rossellini
Karamoja	IND	Ernest Gold
Lassie (series)	CBS-TV	Raoul Kraushaar/Nathan Scott/Sid Sidney

Last Stagecoach West	IND-TV	Gerald Roberts
Life Begins at 17	GER	Wolfgang Zeller
Line-Up, The (series)	CBS-TV	Mischa Bakaleinkoff/ Jerry Goldsmith
Little Kidnappers, The (Kidnappers, The)	BRI	Bruce Montgomery
Little Mook	E.GER	Ernst Roters
Little Town Will Go to Sleep, The	GER	Werner Bochmann
Lonely Night, The	IND	Mel Powell
Loretta Young Theater, The (series)	NBC-TV	Harry Lubin
Mad About Men	BRI	Benjamin Frankel
Mam'selle Nitouche	FRA	Georges van Parys
Man with a Million (Million Pound Note, The)	BRI	William Alwyn
Mayor of the Town (series)	IND-TV	Albert Glasser
Medic (series)	NBC-TV	Victor Young
Melody of Love	ITA	Gino Filippini
Men at Dangerous Age	GER	Hans-Martin Majewski
Monsieur Ripois	FRA	Roman Vlad
Monster from the Ocean Floor, The	LIP	Andre S. Brummer
Native Pony	ARG	Alberto Ginastera
Nenita Unit	PHI	Ariston Avelino
Paris Incident	FRA	Joseph Kosma
Phantom of the Red House, The	MEX	Jose de la Vega
Portia Faces Life (serial)	CBS-TV	Tony Mottola
Princess Sen, The	JAP	Fumio Hayasaka
Prisoner of Love	GER	Werner Eisbrenner
Public Enemy No. 1	FRA	Raymond Legrand/Nino Rota
Punktchen und Anton	AUS	Heino Gaze/Herbert Trantow
Puss in Boots	BRI	Freddie Phillips
Renegade Satellite, The	TV	Alexander Laszlo
Runaway Bus, The	BRI	Ronald Binge
Sacred Call, The	ARG	Tito Ribero
Salt of the Earth	IND	Sol Kaplan
Sauerbruch	GER	Mark Lothar
Schlagerparade (Hit Parade)	GER	Heino Gaze
School for Connubial Bliss	GER	Ulrich Sommerlatte
Sea Shall Not Have Them, The	BRI	Malcolm Arnold
Secret Document--Vienna	IND	Van Hoorebeke
Secret File, U.S.A. (series)	IND-TV	Ella Sacco
Secret of Pancho Villa	MEX	Sergio Guerrero
Secret Storm, The (series)	CBS-TV	Carey Gould
Sherlock Holmes (series)	BRI-TV	Claude Durant
Silent Raiders	IND	Elmer Bernstein
Sister Unafraid (Path to the Kingdom)	SPA	Juan Quintero/Joaquin Rodrego/Joaquin Turina
Sixth Continent, The	ITA	Roberto Nicolosi

Skanderbeg	RUS	Yuri Sviridov/Cesk Zadeja
Sleeping Tiger, The	BRI	Malcolm Arnold
Stranger, The (series)	IND-TV	Tony Mottola
Stratford Adventure	CAN	Louis Applebaum
Sun of St. Moritz, The	GER	Bert Grund
This Is Your Army	FOX	Jack Shaindlin
Tobor the Great	REP	Howard Jackson/William Lava
Unholy Four, The	LIP	Ivor Slaney
Villa Borghese	FRA	Mario Nascimbene
Vise, The (series)	ABC-TV	Albert Elms
Waterfront (series)	IND-TV	Alexander Laszlo
Whistler, The (series)	IND-TV	Rene Garriguenc/Wilbur Hatch
World Without End	IND	Elizabeth Lutyens
Young Wives' Tale	BRI	Philip Green

1955

Adventure in Warsaw	POL	Tadeusz Sygietynski
Adventures of Champion, The (series)	CBS-TV	Carl Cotner
Adventures of Robin Hood, The (series)	CBS-TV	Edwin Astley/Albert Elms
Air Strike	LIP	Andre S. Brummer
Alias John Preston	BRI	Edward Astley/Albert Elms
Art of Getting Along, The	ITA	Alessandro Cicognini
As Long as You Live	GER	Jose Munoz Molleda
Bandits of the Highway	GER	Michael Jary
Barretts of Wimpole Street, The	CBS-TV	Don Ray
Beast with a Million Eyes, The	AI	John Bickford
Big Chamorro Circus, The	CHILE	Jose Bohr
Big Family, A	RUS	V. Pushkov
Bread, Love and Jealousy	ITA	Alessandro Cicognini
Bride of the Monster	IND	Frank Worth
Broadway	CBS-TV	Alfredo Antonini
Bruja, La (Witch, The)	MEX	Raul Lavista
Buffalo Bill, Jr. (series)	IND-TV	Carl Cotner
Burlesque	CBS-TV	David Rose
Canaris	GER	Siegfried Franz
Captain and His Hero, The	GER	Martin Boetticher
Captain Gallant of the Foreign Legion (series)	NBC-TV	Guy Luypaertz
Captain Kangaroo (series)	CBS-TV	John Myer
Case of Poisons, The	FRA	Rene Cloerec
Cavalry Captain Wronski	GER	Norbert Schultze
Children, Mother and a General	GER	Werner Eisbrenner
Christopher Crumpet's Playmate (short)	COL	Dennis Farnon

Clerk and the Coat, The	IN	Amar Nath
Come In, Jupiter (short)	IND	Lloyd von Haden
Cow Girl of St. Catherine	AUS	Anton Karas/Carl Loube
Creeping Unknown, The (Quatermass Experiment, The)	BRI	James Bernard
Criminal Life of Archibaldo de la Cruz, The	MEX	Jesus Bracho/Jorge Perez Herrera
Crusader, The (series)	CBS-TV	Edmund Wilson/Stanley Wilson
Dark Star, The	GER	Bernhard Eichhorn
Dementia (Daughter of Horror)	IND	George Anthiel
Devotee to the God	IN	K. Dutta
Diabolique	FRA	Georges van Parys
Disbanded, The	ITA	Giovanni Fusco
Double Destiny	FRA/GER	Hans Martin Majewski
Drop the Curtain	MEX	Federico Ruiz
Fear (Angst)	GER/ITA	Renzo Rossellini
Friends for Life	ITA	Nino Rota
Frou-Frou	FRA	Louiguy
Fugitives, The	FRA	Joseph Kosma
Future Stars	FRA	Jean Wiener
Gamma People, The	BRI	George Melachrino
Gerald McBoing Boing on the Planet Moo (short)	COL	Ernest Gold
Girl and the Oak, The	YUG	Branimir Sakac
Girl Days of a Queen	AUS	Anton Profes
Girl Friends, The	ITA	Giovanni Fusco
Girls of San Francisco, The	ITA	Mario Zafred
Gold of Naples, The	ITA	Alessandro Cicognini
Golden Pestilence, The	GER	Hans-Martin Majewski
Grasshopper and the Ant, The (short)	FRA	Joseph Kosma
Green Shadow, The	MEX	Gustavo C. Carreon
Gunsmoke (series)	CBS-TV	Jerrold Immel/Rex Koury /John Parker/Richard Shores
Half Human	JAP	Masaru Sato
Heroes Are Tired, The	FRA	Louiguy
Hotel Adlon	GER	Georg Haentzschel
House of Bamboo	TCF	Leigh Harline (not Lionel Newman)
If I Had Seven Daughters	FRA/ITA	Fred Freed
Imposter, The	JAP	Seiichi Suzuki
Ingrid: Story of a Model	GER	Hans-Martin Majewski
Intermediate Landing in Paris	FRA	Paul Misraki
It's Always Jan (series)	CBS-TV	Earle Hagen/Herbert Spencer
Joe and Mabel (series)	CBS-TV	Wilbur Hatch
Joe Macbeth	COL	Richard Taylor
Josephine and Men	BRI	John Addison
Jungle Jim (series)	IND-TV	Alec Compinsky

King Dinosaur	LIP	Michael Terr
King's Row (series)	ABC-TV	David Buttolph
Last Act, The	GER	Erwin Halletz
Last Five Minutes, The	FRA/ITA	Alessandro Cicognini
Living Bread, The	FRA	Michel Magne
Lost Dogs Without Collars	FRA	Paul Misraki
Love That Bob (series)	NBC-TV	Gene LeGrande/Mahlon Merrick
Loving Couples	AUT	Lotar Olias
Magic Strings (short)	BRI	Tolbert Gordon
Man of the Moment	BRI	Philip Green
Marguerite of the Night	FRA/ITA	Rene Cloerec
Master over Life and Death	GER	Hans-Martin Majewski
Mickey Mouse Club, The (series)	DIS-TV	Buddy Baker/Joseph Dubin/William Lava/ Franklin Marks/ Joseph Mullendore
Mighty Mouse Playhouse, The (series)	CBS-TV	Philip Scheib
Millionaire, The (series)	CBS-TV	George Sharder/Stanley Wilson
Moonfleet	MGM	Vicente Gomez/Miklos Rozsa
Napoleon Bonaparte (reissue)	FRA	Henri Verdun
One Bullet Is Enough	FRA/SPA	Jean Marion
One Good Turn	BRI	John Addison
One Woman Is Not Enough	GER	Peter Igelhoff
Operation Sleeping Bag	GER	Bert Grund
Ordet (Word, The)	DEN	Paul Schierbeck
Parson of Kirchfeld, The	GER	Heinrich Riethmueller
People's Choice, The (series)	CBS-TV	Raven Kosakoff/Lou Kosloff
Phil Silver Show, The (series)	CBS-TV	John Strauss
Rats, The	GER	Werner Eisbrenner
School for Vagabonds	MEX	Manuel Esperon
Second Life, The	FRA/GER	Hans-Martin Majewski
Seducer, The	MEX	Antonio Dias Conde
Serie Noir	FRA	Sidney Bechet
Silver Star, The	LIP	Leon Klatzkin
So This Is Hollywood (series)	NBC-TV	Bernard Green
Strangers	ITA	Renzo Rossellini
Tender Hearts	IND	Ernest Gold
Three Men in the Snow	AUS	Alexander von Slatina
To the Four Winds	MEX	Francisco Ruiz
Tower of Nesle, The	FRA/ITA	Henri Verdun
Town Is Full of Secrets, The	GER	Michael Jary
Variety Stars	RUS	Isaac Dunayevsky/ A. Tsfasman
Watch Out for Love	MEX	Manuel Esperon
Witch, The	MEX	Raul Lavista
Woman for Joe, A	BRI	Malcolm Arnold

World's Most Beautiful Woman, The	ITA	Renzo Rossellini
Yokihi	JAP	Fumio Hayasaka
Yours Truly, Blake	FRA	Jeff Davis
Zemlya (Land, The)	RUS	V. Gomolyaka/B. Krizhanovsky

1956

Adventures of Long John Silver, The (series)	IND-TV	David Buttolph
All for Mary	BRI	Robert Farnon
Along the Sidewalks	FRA	Joseph Kosma
As the World Turns (series)	CBS-TV	Charles Paul
Astic	IN	Narayan
Attempt at a Crime	MEX	Jesus Bracho
Awara	IN	Shankar Jaikishan/ Ravi Shankar
Baby and the Battleship, The	BRI	Humphrey Searle/ James Stevens
Bachelor, The	ITA/SPA	Francesco Lavagnino
Bandits of Cold River, The	MEX	Gonzalo Curiel
Basket of Mexican Tales	MEX	Lan Adomian
Before Sundown	GER	Werner Eisbrenner
Bewitching Love of Madam Pai, The	JAP	Ikuma Dan
Blonde Bait	BRI	Leonard Salzedo
Boy Detectives, The	JAP	Hiroshi Kusakawa
Broken Arrow (series)	ABC-TV	Paul Sawtell/Stanley Wilson
Brothers, The (series)	CBS-TV	Irving Miller
Buccaneers, The (series)	CBS-TV	Edwin Astley
Charley Moon	BRI	Francis Chagrin
Charley's Aunt	GER	Friedrich Schroeder
Cheyenne (series)	ABC-TV	Stan Jones/William Lava/Paul Sawtell
Child in the House	BRI	Mario Nascimbene
Communications Primer, A (short)	IND	Elmer Bernstein
Confidential File	WB	Paul Misraki
Conflict (series)	ABC-TV	David Buttolph
Day the World Ended, The	AI	Ronald Stein
Devdas	IN	S. D. Burman
Devil in Silk, The	GER	Mark Lothar
Devil's Commandment, The	ITA	Franco Mannino/Roman Vlad
Doctor Christian (series)	IND-TV	Albert Glasser
Dracos	GRE	Manos Hadjidakis
Eames Lounge Chair (short)	IND	Elmer Bernstein
Edge of Night, The (series)	CBS-TV	Elliott Lawrence/Paul Taubman
18-Year-Olds	ITA	Armando Trovajoli
Extra Day, The	BRI	Philip Green

Eyewitness	BRI	Bruce Montgomery
Flying Carpet, The	RUS	M. Simonyan
Fruit Without Love	GER	Willi Mattes
Gadfly, The	RUS	Dmitri Shostakovich
Gerald McBoing Boing (series)	CBS-TV	Ernest Gold/Lyn Murray
Gervaise	FRA	Georges Auric
Girl in Black, The	GRE	Arghyris Kounadis
Godzilla, King of the Monsters	JAP	Akira Ifukube
Heels Go to Hell	FRA	Andre Gosselain
Hidden One, The	MEX	Raul Lavista
Hill in Korea, A	BRI	Malcolm Arnold
Horoscope of the Hesselbach Family	GER	Wolf Droysen
House of Secrets	BRI	Sir Hubert Clifford
I Spy (series)	IND-TV	Frank Lewin
It Conquered the World	AI	Ronald Stein
It's Great to Be Young	BRI	Ray Martin
Jedda, the Uncivilized	AUT	Isador Goodman
Jumping for Joy	BRI	Larry Adler
Ladron de Cadaveres (Grave Robbers)	MEX	Federico Ruiz
Last Man, The	GER	Werner Eisbrenner
Legend of the White Serpent, The (White Madam's Strange Love)	JAP	Ikuma Dan
Legends of Anika	YUG	Kresimir Baranovich
Like Once Lili Marlene	GER	Norbert Schultze
Long Arm, The	BRI	Gerard Schurmann
Lost	BRI	Benjamin Frankel
Lovers, The	MEX	Raul Lavista
Major and the Steers, The	GER	Bert Grund
Man of Africa	BRI	Malcolm Arnold
Manfish (Calypso)	UA	Francesco Lavagnino
Many Passed By	GER	Peter Sandloff
Meeting in Paris	FRA	Georges van Parys
Moment in Love, A (short)	IND	Norman Lloyd
Music School	MEX	Manuel Esperon
My Friend Flicka (series)	CBS-TV	Alec Compinsky
My Teenage Daughter	BRI	Stanley Black
Mystery of Picasso (Picasso)	FRA	Georges Auric
Narcissus	IND	Alan Hovhannes
Naughty Ball, The (short)	CZE	Zdenek Liska
Noah's Ark (series)	NBC-TV	David Buttolph
Not of This Earth	AA	Ronald Stein
Now and Forever	BRI	Stanley Black
08/15 at Home	GER	Rolf Alexander Wilhelm
Odongo	BRI	George Melachrino
Oklahoma Woman, The	AI	Ronald Stein
One Wish Too Many	BRI	Douglas Gamley
Passport to Treason	BRI	Stanley Black
People of No Importance	FRA	Joseph Kosma
Pepote	ITA/SPA	Roman Vlad

Phantom from 10,000 Leagues, The	IND	Ronald Stein
Pintore a Cidade, O	POR	Padre Luis Rodrigues
Playhouse 90 (theme)	CBS	Alex North
Postmark for Danger	BRI	John Veale
Railroad Man, The	ITA	Carlo Rustichelli
Red Light District	JAP	Toshiro Mayuzumi
Rice Field, The	ITA	Francesco Lavagnino
River Changes, The	GER	Roy Webb
Road of Life, The	MEX	Gustavo C. Carreon
Roman Tales	ITA	Mario Nascimbene
Sailor Beware	BRI	Peter Akister
Satellite in the Sky	BRI	Albert Elms
She Creature, The	AI	Ronald Stein
Short History, A (short)	RUM	Dimitru Capoianu
Short Vision, A (short)	BRI	Matyas Seiber
Stanley (series)	NBC-TV	Charles Sanford
Stories of the Century (series)	IND-TV	Gerald Roberts
Storm Fear	UA	Elmer Bernstein
Supersonic Saucer	BRI	Jack Beaver
Swamp Woman	WOO	Willis Holman
That Darned Kid	FRA	Henri Crolla
That Is the Dawn	FRA/ITA	Joseph Kosma
Together	BRI	Daniele Paris
Toro!	MEX	R. Staffler
Trapp Family, The	GER	Franz Grothe
Trip Across Paris, The	FRA	Rene Cloerec
Twin Maneuver	AUS	Hans Lang
Two-Gun Lady	IND	Leon Klatzkin
Uli the Tenant	SWI	Robert Blum
Unknown Soldier, The	FIN	Jean Sibelius/Ahti Sonninen
War in the Air (short)	BRI-TV	Sir Arthur Bliss
Wedding in Monaco, The	MGM	Daniel J. White
When the Child Appears	FRA	Henri Sauguet
White Vertigo	ITA	Francesco Lavagnino
Who Done It?	BRI	Philip Green
Windfall in Athens	GRE	Andre Ryder
Yield to the Night	BRI	Ray Martin
Zane Grey Theater, The (series)	CBS-TV	Herschel Burke Gilbert/ Joseph Mullendore

1957

Abominable Snowman, The	FOX	Humphrey Searle
Action	CBS-TV	Herschel Burke Gilbert
Adventures of Til Eulenspiegel	FRA/E.GER	Georges Auric
After the Ball	BRI	Muir Mathieson
Air Heroes	SPA	Emilio Lemberg
All at Sea	MGM	John Addison
Appeal on the Cross	JAP	Yushizo Kaji
Back from the Dead	FOX	Dave Kahn/Raoul Kraushaar

Bayou	UA	Edward I. Fessler
Be Dear to Me	DEN	Erik Fiehn
Bed of Grass	GRE	Manos Hadjidakis
Beginning or the End, The	REP	Albert Glasser
Behind the Show Window	RUS	A. Isfasman
Beloved Corrine	GER	Lothar Bruehne
Birthday Present, The	BRI	Clifton Parker
Black Scorpion, The	WB	Jack Cookerly/Paul Sawtell/Bert Shefter
Bliss on Earth	JAP	Chuji Kinoshita
Blondie (series)	NBC-TV	Leon Klatzkin
Bon Soir, Paris, Bonjour L'Amour	FRA	L. Glass
Brothers-in-Law	BRI	Benjamin Frankel
Carnival Night	RUS	Anatole Lepin
Casino de Paris	FRA/GER	Gilbert Becaud/Paul Durand
Castle of the Monsters	MEX	Gustavo Cesar Carreon
Child's Play	BRI	Anthony Hopkins
City at Night	ITA	Nino Rota
Colonel March of Scotland Yard (series)	IND-TV	Philip Green
Colt .45 (series)	ABC-TV	Paul Sawtell
Communist, The	RUS	Rodion Shchedrin
Cowboy Jim	YUG	Aleksander Bubanovic
Cursed Money	YUG	Bojan Adamic
Dangerous Exile	BRI	Georges Auric
Daughter of Dr. Jekyll, The	AA	Melvyn Leonard/Robert Wiley Miller
Day in Moscow, A	RUS	Anatole Lepin
Day of Fear	SPA	Leon Arnaud
Day of the Dead	IND	Elmer Bernstein
Dear Family	AUS	Johannes Fehring
Death by Witchcraft	JAP	Yutaka Makino
Death in Small Doses	AA	Lionel Newman
Decision Against Time	MGM	Gerhard Schurmann
Delicate Delinquent, The	PAR	Buddy Bregman
Dick and the Duchess (series)	BRI-TV	Edwin Astley
Don't Trifle With Women	ITA	Francesco Lavagnino
Door in the Wall (short)	BRI	James Bernard
Dreams in a Drawer	FRA/ITA	Roman Vlad
Eve Arden Show, The (series)	CBS-TV	Jerry Fielding
Eye for an Eye, An	FRA/ITA	Louiguy
Family Schimek	AUS	Heinz Sandauer
Felicidad	MEX	Raul Lavista
Flesh Is Weak, The	BRI	Tristram Cary
Flying Dutchman, The	HOL	Henk Badings
Footsteps	SPA	Salvador Ruiz de Luna
Forbidden Desert	WB	Howard Jackson
Fortune Is a Woman	COL	William Alwyn
Four Just Men (series)	BRI-TV	Edwin Astley/Albert Elms

Freedom	AFR	James W. Owens
Fukusuke (Top Heavy Frog, The)	JAP	Ryoichi Hattori
Garconne, La	FRA	Jean Wiener
Girl from Korfu, The	GRE	Menelos Theofanides
Girl from the Salt Fields, The	GER/ITA	Bert Grund
Girls in Tails	SWE	Hakan von Eichwald
Grandfather Automobile, The	CZE	J. F. Fischer
Great Day, The	ITA/SPA	Jesus Guridi
Guendalina	FRA/ITA	Piero Morgan
Gumby Special, The	TV	Les Baxter
Harbor Command (series)	IND-TV	Albert Glasser
Herr Puntila and His Chauffeur Matti	AUS	Hanns Eisler
Holy Heritage	AUS	Haraldt Boehmelt
Horse Boy, The	JAP	Shiro Fukai
Ikiru	JAP	Fumio Hayasaka
Immortal Garrison, The	RUS	V. Basner
In Soldier's Uniform	HUN	Tibor Polgar
Information Machine, The (short)	IND	Elmer Bernstein
Invasion of the Saucer Men	AI	Ronald Stein
It Happened on the 36 Candles	FRA	Francis Lopez
It Was Not in Vain	YUG	Milo Cipra
Ivanhoe (series)	BRI-TV	Edwin Astley/Albert Elms
Jamboree	WB	Neal Hefti
Je Reviendrai a Kandara	FRA	Joseph Kosma
Jonas	GER	Duke Ellington/Winifried Zillig
Juha	FIN	Tauno Pylkkanen
Junior Miss (series)	CBS-TV	Burton Lane
Just My Luck	BRI	Philip Green
Kabuliwala	IN	Ravi Shankar
Kanikosen	JAP	Akira Ifukube
Lapland Calendar	NOR	Christian Hartmann
Last Night of Love, The	ITA/SPA	Carlo Innocenzi
Leave It to Beaver (series)	CBS-TV	Pete Rugolo/Paul Smith
Little Black Sambo Hunts the Tiger (short)	JAP	Mitsuo Kato
Love Laughs at All	GER	Herbert Trantow
Love Slaves of the Amazon	UN	Herman Stein/Stanley Wilson
M Squad (series)	NBC-TV	Stanley Wilson
Magic of the Kite (short)	CHN/FRA	Louis Bessieres/Tuan-Se-Tchung
Man Called Demon, A	JAP	Masaru Sato
Man in the Raincoat, The	FRA	Georges van Parys
Man in the Sky	BRI	Gerbrand Schurmann
Man Who Wagged His Tail, The	ITA/SPA	Bruno Canfora
Man Without a Body, The	BRI	Albert Elms

Manuela	BRI	William Alwyn
Maverick (series)	ABC-TV	David Buttolph
Meet Mr. Kringle	CBS-TV	Kenny Ascher
Men and Wolves	ITA	Guido Nardone
Mexican, The	RUS	M. Chulaki
Michel Strogoff	FRA	Norbert Glanzberg
Miracle in Soho	BRI	Brian Easdale
Mr. Adams and Eve (series)	CBS-TV	Mahlon Merrick
Monolith Monsters, The	UN	Irving Gertz (not Joseph Gershenson)
Monster from Green Hell, The	DCA	Albert Glasser
Mysteries of Black Magic, The	MEX	Jose de la Vega
Naked Paradise	AI	Ronald Stein
Naked Truth, The	BRI	Stanley Black
New Invisible Man, The	MEX	Antonio Dias Conde
New Year's Sacrifice	CHN	Chen Yen-Si
1918--A Man and His Conscience	FIN	Heikki Asltoila
No Road Back	RKO	John Veale
No Time for Tears	BRI	Francis Chagrin
Not Wanted on the Voyage	BRI	Tony Lowry
Panic! (series)	NBC-TV	Mahlon Merrick
Paradise on Earth	FRA/ITA	Roman Vlad
Passionate Strangers, The	BRI	Humphrey Searle
Peaceful Valley, The	YUG	Marijan Kozina
Pepito and the Monster	MEX	Sergio Guerrero
Perri	DIS	Carl Brandt
Perry Mason (series)	CBS-TV	Richard Shores/Fred Steiner
Philosopher's Stone	IN	Ravi Shankar
Prolog	RUS	Nicolai Kryukov
Queen Louise	GER	Franz Grothe
Real McCoys, The (series)	ABC-TV	Jack Cookerly/William Loose/Ed Norton/ Harry Ruby
Rendez-vous in Melbourne	FRA	Christian Chevalier
Rendezvous with Forgotten Years	NOR	Bjoern Woll
Restless Gun, The (series)	NBC-TV	Stanley Wilson
Revenge of the Vampire	MAL	Sabir Said
Richard Diamond, Private Detective (series)	CBS-TV	Pete Rugolo/Richard Shores
Scamp, The	BRI	Francis Chagrin
Scotland Yard (series)	BRI-TV	Edwin Astley
Secret Scrolls, The	JAP	Akira Ifukube
Seven Lively Arts, The (series)	CBS-TV	Alfredo Antonini
Seven Thunders	BRI	Anthony Hopkins
Seven Waves Away	BRI	Sir Arthur Bliss
Seven Year's Bad Luck	AUS	Anton Profes
Seventh Seal, The	SWE	Erik Nordgren
Shiralee, The	BRI	John Addison
Star of Africa	GER	Hans-Martin Majewski
Stars Never Die	FRA	Jean Wiener

Sugarfoot (series)	ABC-TV	Paul Sawtell
Susanna and Me	SPA	Francis Lopez
Sword of Freedom, The (series)	BRI-TV	Edwin Astley/Albert Elms
Tales of Wells Fargo, The (series)	NBC-TV	Melvyn Lenard/Morton Stevens/Stanley Wilson
Talpa	MEX	Lan Adomian
Taxi Driver Baenz	GER/SWI	Robert Blum
10th of May, The	SWI	Robert Blum
That Woman Opposite	BRI	Stanley Black
These Dangerous Years	BRI	Bert Waller
Thin Man, The (series)	NBC-TV	Pete Rugolo
Third Sex, The	GER	Erwin Halletz
Time Lock	BRI	Stanley Black
Time of Desire	SWE	Harry Arnold
Timmy and Lassie (series)	CBS-TV	Nathan Scott/Sid Sidney
Tizoc	MEX	Raul Lavista
Tom Terrific (series)	CBS-TV	Philip Scheib
Trackdown (series)	CBS-TV	Herschel Burke Gilbert
Traitors	JAP	Shiro Fukai
True as a Turtle	BRI	Robert Farnon
Twentieth Century, The (series)	CBS-TV	Alfredo Antonini/Kenyon Hopkins/Leonard Rosenthal
27 Men (series)	IND-TV	Hal Hopper/Gordon Zahler
Two Men and a Wardrobe (short)	POL	Kryzystof Komeda
Undead, The	AI	Ronald Stein
Under Cover of Night	IN	Salil Chowdhury
Undercurrent	JAP	Nari Ikeno
Up in the World	BRI	Philip Green
Vampires, The	ITA	Roman Vlad
Voodoo Woman	AI	Darrell Calker
Wagon Train (series)	NBC-TV	Melvyn Lenard/Jerome Moross/Hans Salter/Richard Sendry
Wedding Day, The	KOR	Lim Won Shik
Witness for the Prosecution	UA	Matty Malneck
Women in Prison	JAP	Ichiro Saito
Women Times Three	ITA	Francesco Lavagnino
Yangtse Incident	BRI	Leighton Lucas
Youth at Play	DEN	Arne Lamberth
Zorro (series)	ABC-TV	George Bruns

1958

Adventures of Sun Wu Kung	JAP	Ikuma Dan
Aleksa Dundic	RUS/YUG	Nikita Bogoslowski
Antarctic Crossing	BRI	Humphrey Searle
Ash Wednesday	MEX	Antonio Diaz Conde

At Green Cockatoos by Night	GER	Michael Jary
Attack of the Puppet People, The (Six Inches Tall)	AI	Albert Glasser
Azimat	MAL	Dick Abel
Bachelor of Hearts	BRI	Hubert Clifford
Ballerina and God, The	ITA	Piero Morgan
Behind the Mask	BRI	Geoffrey Wright
Big Money, The	BRI	Van Phillips
Black Pearls	YUG	Bojan Adamic
Brain Eaters, The	AI	Tom Jonson
Brain from Planet Arous, The	IND	Walter Greene
Bronco (series)	ABC-TV	Paul Sawtell
Buckskin (series)	NBC-TV	Mort Green/Stanley Wilson
Candidates for Marriage	AUS	Hans Lang
Catcher, The	GER	Hans-Martin Majewski
Challenge, The	ITA/SPA	Roman Vlad
Charming Boys	FRA	Guy Bearts/Georges van Parys
Colossus of New York, The	PAR	Fred Steiner/Nathan van Cleave
Cosmic Monsters, The (Strange World of Planet X, The)	WB	Robert Sharples
Creation of the World	CZE	Jan Rychlik
Day the Sky Exploded, The	ITA	Carlo Rustichelli
Desert Lovers	ITA/SPA	Michel Michelet
Doc Holliday	CBS-TV	Herschel Burke Gilbert
Doctor and the Healer, The	FRA/ITA	Nino Rota
Dr. Crippen Lives!	GER	Siegfried Franz
Doctor of Stalingrad	GER	Siegfried Franz
Earth vs. the Spider (Spider, The)	AI	Albert Glasser
Ed Wynn Show, The (series)	NBC-TV	Jerry Fielding
Eighth Day of the Week, The	GER/POL	Kazimietz Serocki
Elevator to the Gallows	FRA	Miles Davis
Elfego Baca (series)	ABC-TV	William Lava
Embezzled Heaven	GER	Anton Profes
Escapement	BRI	Richard Taylor
Eve Wants to Sleep	POL	Henryk Boyz
Every Day Has Its Secret	FRA	Eddie Barclay
Fear of Power	SWI	Robert Blum
Fiend Without a Face, The	MGM	Buxton Orr
Fly, The	FOX	Paul Sawtell/Bert Shefter
Fox of Paris, The	GER	Hans-Martin Majewski
Frankenstein's Daughter	AST	Nicholas Carras
Further Up the Creek	COL	Stanley Black
General Electric Theater (series)	TV	Elmer Bernstein
Giant from the Unknown	AST	Albert Glasser
Girl from Valladolid	SPA	Cristobal Halffter
Girl on the Run	ABC-TV	Howard Jackson
Girls at Sea	BRI	Laurie Johnson

Golden Age of Comedy, The	DCA	George Steiner
Golden Mountains	DEN	Svend Erik Tarp
Golden Ox Inn	SWI	Hans Moeckel
Great Fear, The (short)	YUG	Tomislav Simovic
Guns, Girls and Gangsters	UA	Emil Newman
H 8	YUG	Dragutin Savin
Happy End (short)	YUG	Bojan Adamic
High Flight	BRI	Douglas Gamley/Kenneth V. Jones
Horror of Dracula	BRI	James Bernard
Hot Dog Gang	AI	Ronald Stein
How to Make a Monster	AI	Paul Dunlap
I Only Arsked	BRI	Benjamin Frankel
It Happens in Spain	IND-TV	Joe Bushkin
Italian Journey--Love Included	GER	Friedrich Schroeder
Jungle Saga, The	SWE	Ravi Shankar
Lawman (series)	ABC-TV	Frank Perkins/Paul Sawtell
Legend of Sleepy Hollow, The	NBC-TV	Vic Mizzy
Lighthouse, The	JAP	Chuji Kinoshita
Lights of the Night	SWE	Lars-Erik Larsson
Lineup, The	COL	Mischa Balaleinikoff
Love and Chatter	FRA/ITA/SPA	Mario Nascimbene
Lucky Galoshes	POL	Stefan Kisielewski
Machine Gun Kelly	AA	Gerald Fried
Magician, The	SWE	Erik Nordgren
Man of Straw	ITA	Carlo Rustichelli
Man with a Camera (series)	ABC-TV	Pete Rugolo
Man Without a Gun, The	IND-TV	Lionel Newman
Mine, The	ITA/SPA	Carlo Rustichelli
Missile to the Moon	AST	Nicholas Carras
Monster on the Campus	UN	William Lava
My World Dies Screaming	IND	Darrell Calker
Naked City (series)	ABC-TV	George Duning/Billy May/Nelson Riddle
Narcotics Story, The	IND	Alexander Laszlo
Night in Hell, A	IRAN	Del Kash
Night of the Blood Beast	AI	Alexander Laszlo
Night Prowl	IND-TV	Elmer Bernstein
No Time to Die	COL	Kenneth V. Jones
One Step Beyond (series)	ABC-TV	Harry Lubin
Osvetnik	YUG	Aleksander Bubanovic
Otar's Widow	RUS	S. Sinzadze
Panda and the Magic Serpent	JAP	Chuji Kinoshita
Passionate Summer	BRI	Francesco Lavagnino
Passport to Shame	BRI	Kenneth V. Jones
Peter Gunn (series)	NBC-TV	Henry Mancini
Pezzo, Capopezzo e Capitano	GER/ITA	Francesco Lavagnino
Precipice, The	JAP	Akira Ifukube
Quatermass and the Pit (series)	BRI-TV	Trevor Duncan
Que Linda Cha Cha Cha!	MEX	Manuel Esperon

Rainbow Dilemma, The	SWE	Eric Nordgren
Rescue 8 (series)	IND-TV	Douglas Heyes
Revenge of Frankenstein	BRI	Leonard Salzedo
Rifleman, The (series)	ABC-TV	Herschel Burke Gilbert
Rio Zone Norte	BRA	Urgel de Castro/Ze Keti
Road a Year Long, The	YUG	Vladimir Kraus
Rockets Galore	BRI	Cedric Thorpe Davie
Saddle the Wind	MGM	Jeff Alexander/Elmer Bernstein
Sally's Irish Rogue	BRI	Ivor Slaney
Screaming Skull, The	AI	Ernest Gold
Sea Fury	BRI	Philip Green
Sea of Sand	BRI	Clifton Parker
Secret of Magic Island	FRA	Richard Cornu
77 Sunset Strip (series)	ABC-TV	Warren Barker/Jerry Fielding/William Lava/ Frank Ortega/Frank Perkins/Paul Sawtell/ Nathan Van Cleve
Sharpshooter, The	CBS-TV	Herschel Burke Gilbert
She Demons	AST	Nicholas Carras
She Didn't Say "No"	BRI	Tristram Cary
She-Gods of Shark Reef	AI	Ronald Stein
Shirley Temple's Storybook (series)	NBC-TV	Mack David/Vic Mizzy/ Walter Scharf/Vic Schoen
Shots in the Sky	YUG	Bojan Adamic
Silent Enemy, The	BRI	William Alwyn
Soledad	ITA/SPA	Francesco Lavagnino
Square Peg, The	BRI	Philip Green
Steve Canyon (series)	NBC-TV	Walter Schumann/Nathan Scott
Stormy Crossing	BRI	Stanley Black
Story of a Pure Love, The	JAP	Masao Oki
Strange Gods, The	ARG	Waldo de los Rios
Strange World of Planet X, The	IND	Robert Sharples
Tabarin	FRA	Francis Lopez
Tank Battalion	AI	Richard La Salle
Teenage Casanova	AI	Albert Glasser
Teenage Caveman	AI	Albert Glasser
Teenage Monster	IND	Walter Greene
Temptress, The	JAP	Yukata Makino
Texas John Slaughter (series)	ABC-TV	Buddy Baker
Trapp Family in America, The	GER	Franz Grothe
Trollenberg Terror, The (Crawling Eye, The)	BRI	Stanley Black
Two Eyes, Twelve Hands	IN	Vasant Desai
Two Ghosts and a Girl	MEX	Sergio Guerrero
Under Age	AUS	Carl de Groof
Unexcused Hour, The	AUS	Heinz Sandauer
Unseen Heroes	BRI	Robert Sharples

Up the Creek	BRI	Tony Fones
Veil, The (series)	IND-TV	Edwin Astley/Leon Klatzkin
Vicious Breed, The	SWE	Les Baxter
Vienna, City of My Dreams	AUS	Hans Lang/Alfred Uhl
Viking Women and the Sea Serpent, The	AI	Albert Glasser
Virgin Island	BRI	Clifton Parker
Wanted: Dead or Alive (series)	CBS-TV	Herschel Burke Gilbert/ Harry King
War of the Colossal Beast, The	AI	Albert Glasser
War Starts in Cuba	SPA	Salvador Ruiz de Luna
Weapons of Destruction	CZE	Zdenek Liska
Weddings and Babies	IND	Eddy Manson
When the Devil Came at Night	GER	Siegfried Franz
White Onion, Red Onion	MAL	Sabir Said
Wichita Town (series)	NBC-TV	Hans Salter
Wild Strawberries	SWE	Erik Nordgren
Windsong (short)	IND	Harry Partsch
Woman and the Beast, The	MEX	Manuel Esperon
Woman in a Fur Coat, The	SWE	Harry Arnold
Wonderful Things	BRI	Harold Rome
Yancy Derringer (series)	CBS-TV	Leon Klatzkin
Young Husbands	FRA/ITA	Mario Zafred
Youth Comes Only Twice	AUS	Hans Lang

1959

Adolescence of Cain	VEN	Eduardo Serrano
Adventures in Paradise (series)	ABC-TV	Lionel Newman
Alaskans, The (series)	ABC-TV	Paul Sawtell
Alive and Kicking	BRI	Philip Green
And That on Monday Morning	GER	Hans-Martin Majewski
Angry Red Planet, The	IND	Paul Dunlap
Asa-Nisse in Military Uniform	SWE	Sven Runo
Astronauts, The (short)	FRA	Jan Markowsky
At the Photographer's (short)	YUG	Aleksander Bubanovic
Back to the Door	SPA	Ramon Vives
Ballad of Louie the Louse, The	CBS-TV	Gordon Jenkins
Beautiful Adventure	GER	Franz Grothe
Betty Hutton Show, The (series)	CBS-TV	Jerry Fielding
Black Saddle (series)	ABC-TV	Jerry Goldsmith/Arthur Morton
Bloody Brood, The	CAN	Harry Freedman
Bomb Mania	CZE	Jan Rychlik
Bonanza (series)	NBC-TV	Raoul Kraushaar/David Rose/Harry Sukman
Bourbon Street Beat (series)	ABC-TV	Paul Sawtell
Boy and the Bridge, The	COL	Malcolm Arnold
Cafe Odeon	SWI	Walter Baumgartner
Caltiki, the Immortal Monster	ITA	Roman Vlad

Calypso	FRA/ITA	Francesco Lavagnino
Caravan to Russia	RUS	Alexander Zorov
Carmen of Granada	SPA	Gregory Segura
Carrousel Boreal (short)	FRA	Daniel White
Carry On, Teacher	BRI	Bruce Montgomery
Castle Is Swinging, The	SWE	Bengt Hallberg
Challenge (series)	NBC-TV	Warren Barker
Christ in Bronze	JAP	Toshiro Mayuzumi
Cote d'Azur	ITA	Roberto Nicolosi
Crazy Heart, A (short)	YUG	Aleksandar Bubanovic
Cucuracha, La	MEX	Raul Lavista
D.A.'s Man, The (series)	NBC-TV	Frank Comstock
Danger Within	BRI	Francis Chagrin
Death of a Friend	ITA	Mario Nascimbene
Dennis the Menace (series)	CBS-TV	Irving Friedman
Departure for the Clouds	GER	Werner Eisbrenner
Deputy, The (series)	NBC-TV	Jack Marshall
Detectives, The (series)	ABC-TV	Herschel Burke Gilbert
Devil Incarnate, The (Super Giant #8)	JAP	Sadao Nagase
Devouring Rock, The	MAL	Osman Ahmad/R. Ramlee
Diego Corrientes	SPA	Xavier Mort Salvatge
Dobie Gillis (series)	CBS-TV	Lionel Newman
Don't Panic, Chaps!	BRI	Philip Green
Door Remains Open, The	YUG	Borut Lesjak
Dubrovsky	ITA/YUG	Carlo Rustichelli
Eighth Door, The	YUG	Dragutin Savin
Elisabeth McQueeney Story, The	NBC-TV	Jerome Moross
Enjo	JAP	Toshiro Mayuzumi
Europe by Night	FRA/ITA	Carlo Savina
Face of the Screaming Werewolf, The (House of Terror)	MEX	Luis Hernandez Breton
Factory B	YUG	Vojkan Simic
False Passport, The	YUG	Bojan Adamic
First Love	ITA	Francesco Lavagnino
First Spaceship on Venus, The	IND	Gordon Zahler
Five Fingers (series)	NBC-TV	David Raksin
Five Minutes of Paradise	YUG	Bojan Adamic
Flor de Mayo	MEX	Gustavo Cesar Carreon
Follies of Barbara, The	MEX	Casas Auge/Franceso Lavagnino
Follow a Star	BRI	Philip Green
For Better or Worse (serial)	CBS-TV	Kip Walton
48 Hours to Live	SWE	Harry Arnold
Four Desperate Men (Siege of Pinchgut, The)	BRI	Kenneth V. Jones
General Delle Rovere	FRA/ITA	Renzo Rossellini
Giant Gila Monster, The	IND	Jack Marshall
Gigantis, the Fire Monster	JAP	Masaru Sato
Good Old Piano, The	YUG	Marijan Lipovsek
Great Is My Country (Wide Is My Country)	RUS	V. Knushevitsky/ K. Moichanov

Green Mansions	MGM	Bronislau Kaper/Heitor Villa-Lobos
Green Mare, The	FRA	Rene Cloerec
Gringalet	ARG	Tito Ribero
Handwritten (short)	IND	Teiji Ito
Happiness	MEX	Raul Lavista
Hawaiian Eye (series)	ABC-TV	Frank Perkins/Paul Sawtell
Headless Ghost, The	AI	Gerard Schurmann
Heart of a Man, The	BRI	Wally Stott
Heaven Without Love	YUG	Bojan Adamic
Hell in the City	ITA	Roman Vlad
Hennesey	CBS-TV	Sonny Burke
Hercules and the Queen of Lydia	FRA/ITA	Enzo Massetti
Hero of Our Times, A	ITA	Giovanni Fusco
Heroes (Helden)	GER	Franz Grothe
Hidden Fortress, The	JAP	Masaru Sato
Hideous Sun Demon, The	IND	John Seely
Holy Island, The	IN	B. C. Corel
Homo Sapiens (short)	RUM	Dimitru Capoianu
Hoppla, Now Comes Eddie	GER	Michael Jary
Horrors of the Black Museum	AI	Gerard Schurmann
Hotel de Paree (series)	CBS-TV	Van Alexander
I Was Born in Buenos Aires	ARG	Sebastian Plana
Ideal Woman, The	GER	Georg Haentzschel
Idle on Parade	BRI	Bill Shepherd
I'll Carry You on My Hands	GER	Werner Eisbrenner
I'm All Right, Jack	BRI	Ken Hare
Indestructible, The	FRA	Loulou Gaste
Indian, The	ABC-TV	Herschel Burke Gilbert
Indian Tomb, The	GER	Gerhard Becker
Inferno	GER	Herbert Windt
Inhabitants of the Uninhabited House, The	SPA	Federico Contreras
Inspector Returns Home, The	YUG	Kurt Grieden
International Detective (series)	IND-TV	Edwin Astley/Harry Booth
Invaders of the Space Ship (Prince of Space)	JAP	Katsuhisa Hattori
Invitation to Monte Carlo	IND	(William) Hill Bowen
Isn't Mama Fabulous?	GER	Norbert Schultze
Jack the Ripper	BRI	Stanley Black
Jet Storm	BRI	Thomas Hajna
Johnny Ringo (series)	CBS-TV	Laurindo Almeida/Rudy Schrager
Johnny Staccato (series)	NBC-TV	Elmer Bernstein
Killer Shrews, The	IND	Harry Bluestone/Emil Cadkin
Kingdom of the Venomous Moth, The (Super Giant #9)	JAP	Sadao Nagase
Korkarlen	SWE	Dag Wiren
Krammer, The	GER	Karl von Feilitzsch

Labyrinth	GER/ITA	Hans-Martin Majewski
Laramie (series)	NBC-TV	Cyril Mockridge/Hans Salter/Richard Sendry
Law of the Plainsman, The (series)	NBC-TV	Leonard Rosenman
Lazarillo (Ragamuffin of Tormes)	SPA	Salvador Ruiz de Luna
Leap to Fame	SPA	Isidoro Maiztegui
Lend Me Your Wife	SWE	Jules Sylvain
Life Around Us	SPA	Rafael de Andres
Life in Emergency Ward 10	BRI	Philip Green
Life in Your Hands	RUS	O. Karavanich
Little One	BUL	Parashkev Hadjiev
Little Red Riding Hood and Her Friends	MEX	Sergio Guerrero
Living Head, The	MEX	Gustavo Cesar Carreon
Loner, The	CBS-TV	Herschel Burke Gilbert
Love and Marriage (series)	NBC-TV	Earle Hagen/Herbert Spencer
Magic Boy, The	JAP	Toru Funaura
Mamula Camp	YUG	Bojan Adamic
Man and the Monster, The	MEX	Gustavo Cesar Carreon
Man from Denver, The	CBS-TV	Herschel Burke Gilbert
Man in a Cocked Hat, The (Carlton-Browne of the F.O.)	BRI	John Addison
Man Who Sold Himself, The	GER	Georg Haentzschel
Manster, The	JAP	Niroaki Ogawa
Markham (series)	CBS-TV	Stanley Wilson
Men into Space (series)	CBS-TV	David Rose
Miss April	SWE	Harry Arnold
Miss Cuple	SPA	Augusto Alguero
Miss Stone	YUG	Ivan Pupnik
Mr. Lucky (series)	CBS-TV	Henry Mancini
Mistress, The	JAP	Ikama Dan
Molokai	SPA	Salvador Ruiz de Luna
Moralist, The	ITA	Carlo Savina
My Daughter Patricia	AUS	Heinz Neubrand
Mystery of Three Continents, The	FRA/GER/ITA	Roman Vlad
Naked Sun, The	JAP	Yasushi Akutagawa
Navy Lark, The	BRI	James Moody/Tommy Reilly
Night of the Ghouls	IND	Gordon Zahler
Night We Dropped a Clanger, The	BRI	Edwin Branden
Non-Scheduled Train, A	YUG	Vladimir Kraus-Rajteric
Not for Hire (series)	IND-TV	Joseph Hooven
Oh! Que Mambo	FRA	Guy Magenta
Operation Bullshine	BRI	Laurie Johnson
Operation Dames	AI	Richard Markowitz
Paradise and Fire Oven (Heaven and Hell)	GER	Bernhard Eichhorn
Peck's Bad Girl (series)	CBS-TV	Jerry Goldsmith

Pete Kelly's Blues (series)	NBC-TV	Frank Comstock
Piccolo (short)	YUG	Branimir Sakac
Picnic on the Grass	FRA	Joseph Kosma
Prisoner 1.040	ARG	Juan Ehler
Quick Draw McGraw Show, The (series)	IND-TV	Ted Nichols
Race for Space, The	TV	Elmer Bernstein
Rawhide (series)	CBS-TV	Dimitri Tiomkin
Riko Na Oyome-San	JAP	Hiraku Hayashi
Riverboat (series)	NBC-TV	Elmer Bernstein/ Richard Sendry/Leo Shuken
Robot vs. the Aztec Mummy, The	MEX	Antonio Dias Conde
Rocky and His Friends (series)	ABC-TV	Frank Comstock/Fred Steiner
Room at the Top	BRI	Mario Nascimbene
Rough and the Smooth, The	BRI	Douglas Gamley
S.O.S. Glacier Pilot	SWI	Hans Moeckel
St. Valentine's Day	SPA	Augusto Alguero
Sam (Alone)	YUG	Bojan Adamic
Santa Claus	MEX	Antonio Diaz Conde
Savage Eye, The	IND	Leonard Rosenman
Schinderhannes, Der	GER	Bernard Eichhorn
Search for Chorefto	YUG	Friedrich Meyer
Serenade	MGM	Georgie Stoll
Serious Charge	BRI	Leighton Lucas
77 Sunset Strip	ABC-TV	Alex North
Shadow of the Past	EGY	Andre Ryder
Sheriff of Fractured Jaw, The	FOX	Robert Farnon
Shotgun Slade (series)	IND-TV	Gerald Fried/Stanley Wilson
Skeleton of Mrs. Morales, The	MEX	Raul Lavista
Sleepless Years	HUN	Raul Lavista
Sonatas	MEX/SPA	Isidoro Maiztegui
Star Goes to the South, The	CZE/YUG	Jirzi Baur
Stomach In, Chest Out	FIN	Toivo Karki
Story of a Goldfish, The (short)	FRA	Henri Crolla/Andre Hodier
Strange Guests	ARG	Juan Carlo Paz
Strictly Confidential	BRI	Malcolm Lockyer
Tank Commandos	AI	Ronald Stein
Tarzan the Ape Man	ABC-TV	Shorty Rogers
10 Ready Rifles	ITA/SPA	Francisco Escudero/ Tomas Garbizu
Third Commandment, The	NBC-TV	Fred Katz
Three Quarters of a Sun	YUG	Bojan Adamic
Three Rascals in the Hidden Forest	JAP	Masaru Sato
Tiger Bay	BRI	Laurie Johnson
Tiger of Eschnapur, The	GER	Michel Michelet
Tightrope (series)	CBS-TV	George Duning

Too Many Crooks	BRI	Stanley Black
Treasure of San Teresa	BRI	Jeff Davis
Trip to the Moon, A	AUS	Oskar Wagner
Turn the Key Softly	NBC-TV	Frank DeVol/Stan Zabka
12 Girls and One Man	AUS	Franz Grothe
Twilight Zone, The (series)	CBS-TV	Jerry Goldsmith/Bernard Herrmann/William Lava/ Tommy Morgan/Leonard Rosenman/Nathan Scott/ Fred Steiner/Nathan Van Cleave
Two Men in Town	SPA/SWE	Cristobal Halffter
Ugly Duckling, The	BRI	Douglas Gamley
Untouchables, The (series)	CBS-TV	Wilbur Hatch/Nelson Riddle
Uomo Facile, Un	ITA	Carlo Rustichelli
Up and Down	MEX	Raul Lavista
Vargas Inn	SPA	Guillermo Cases
Very Edge of Night, The (short)	IND	Louis and Bebe Barron
Village on the River, The	HOL	Jurrihan Andriessen
Violent Fate	SPA	Miguel Asins Arbo
Whirlpool	BRI	Ron Goodwin
Wolves in the Abyss	ITA	Bruno Canfora
You're On Your Own	ITA	Carlo Rustichelli
Zamach (Partisan Prison)	POL	Adam Walacinski

1960

Adua and the Colleagues	ITA	Piero Piccioni
Amazing Transparent Man, The	AI	Darrell Calker
... And Saucy at That!	GER	Ernst Simon
Andy Griffith Show, The (series)	CBS-TV	Earle Hagen
Aquanauts, The (series)	CBS-TV	Andre Previn
Ardent Love	HOL	Herman van der Horst
As the Sea Rages	GER	Friedrich Meyer
Assignment Outer Space (Space Men)	AI	J. K. Broady
Astronauts, The	MEX	Gustavo Cesar Carreon
Atom Age Vampire (Seddok)	ITA	Armando Trovajoli
Atomic Submarine, The	AA	Neil Brunnenkant/ Alexander Laszlo
Bacchantes, The	ITA	Mario Nascimbene
Barbara Stanwyck Theater, The (series)	NBC-TV	Earle Hagen
Bernadette of Lourdes	FRA	Maurice Thiriet
Beyond the Time Barrier	AI	Darrell Calker
Blazing Sand	GER/ISR	Siegfried Wegener
Boomerang	GER	Hans-Martin Majewski
Bottoms Up	BRI	Stanley Black
Braggarts, The	MEX	Jesus Zarzosa
Brainiac, The (Baron of Terror)	MEX	Gustavo Cesar Carreon

Bringing Up Buddy (series)	CBS-TV	Michael Johnson
Bulldog Breed, The	BRI	Philip Green
Cape Canaveral Monster, The	IND	Gene Kauer
Captain Leshi	YUG	Redzo Mulle
Carry On, Constable	BRI	Bruce Montgomery
Challenge, The	BRI	Bill McGuffie
Checkmate (series)	CBS-TV	Pete Rugolo/Morton Stevens/John Williams
Children's Dream (short)	AUS	Oskar Wagner
Chip on the Shoulder	MEX	Manuel Esperon
Comrade President Center-Forward	YUG	Bojan Adamic
Conquest of the Moon	MEX	Raul Lavista
Crack in the Mirror	FOX	Maurice Jarre
Crime of Silence	BRI	Gerald Schurmann
Criminal, The	BRI	John Dankworth
Cruel Story of Youth	JAP	Riichiro Manabe
Dan Raven (series)	NBC-TV	Billy May
Dante (series)	NBC-TV	Leith Stevens
Darkness Fell on Gotenhafen	GER	Hans-Martin Majewski
Dauphins, The	ITA	Giovanni Fusco
Day of Reckoning (short)	CZE	Zdenek Liska
Dear Augustin, The	GER	Bernd Kampka
Dentist in the Chair	BRI	Kenneth V. Jones
Desert Mice	BRI	Philip Green
Desire in the Dust	FOX	Paul Dunlap
Devil May Well Laugh, The	SWI	Walter Baumgartner
Diary of Sueko, The	JAP	Toshiro Mayazumi
Division Brandenburg	GER	Hans-Martin Majewski
Dreams Come by Coach	YUG	Berivoje Simic
Empty Star, The	MEX	Gustavo Cesar Carreon
Enchanting Shadow	HK	Chi Hsiang-tang
End of Innocence	ARG	Juan Carlos Paz
Esther and the King	FOX	Francesco Lavagnino/ Roberto Nicolosi
Faces in the Dark	BRI	Edwin Astley
Fair, The	GER	Werner Pohl
Faith, Hope and Witchcraft	DEN	Svend Erik Tarp
Fanatics, The	FRA	Sasha Distel
Faust	GER	Mark Lothar
Flesh and the Fiends	BRI	Stanley Black
Flight	IND	Laurindo Almeida
Follow That Horse	BRI	Stanley Black
Forbidden Sands	JAP	Chuji Kinoshita
Foxhole in Cairo	BRI	Douglas Gamley/Kenneth V. Jones/Wolfram Roehrig
Frantic (Double Deception)	FRA	Georges van Parys
Get Outta Town	IND	Bill Holman
Ghosts in Rome	ITA	Nino Rota
Goliath Against the Giants	ITA	Carlo Innocenzi

Gorgo	BRI	Francesco Lavagnino
Grand Jury	TV	Ray Ellis
Guapo del 1900, Un	ARG	Hector Stamponi
Guestward Ho! (series)	ABC-TV	Jerry Fielding
Hands of Orlac	FRA	Claude Bolling
Harrigan and Son (series)	ABC-TV	Jerry Fielding/Earle Hagen/Pete Rugolo
Hercules' Pills	ITA	Armando Trovajoli
Heritage of Bjoerndal	AUS	Rolf Alexander Wilhelm
Hong Kong (series)	ABC-TV	Lionel Newman
How to Furnish a Flat (short)	CZE	William Bukovy
Hypnotic Eye, The	AA	Marlin Skiles
I, a Sinner	MEX	Raul Lavista
I Passed for White	AA	Jerry Irving
Immoral Mr. Teas, The	IND	Edward Lasko
Impatient Heart, The	MEX	Raul Lavista
In Love, But Doubly	FIN	Toivo Karki
In the Nick	BRI	Ron Goodwin
Ingeborg	GER	Peter Thomas
Introduction to Feedback (short)	IND	Elmer Bernstein
Invasion of the Animal People	SWE	Harry Arnold/Allan Johannson
Invisible Creature, The	BRI	John Veale
Islanders, The (series)	ABC-TV	Sonny Burke
Israel (short)	IND	Elmer Bernstein
It Goes Better with Raspberry Juice	AUS	Johannes Febring
Johnny Midnight (series)	IND-TV	Joe Bushkin
Josephine Little: The Miraculous Journey of Tadpole Chan	NBC-TV	Earle Hagen
Judge for the Young, The	GER	Raimund Rosenberger
Killers of Kilimanjaro	COL	William Alwyn
Klondike (series)	NBC-TV	Vic Mizzy
Knights of the Teutonic Order	POL	Kazimierz Serocki
Last Woman on Earth	IND	Ronald Stein
Law and Mr. Jones, The (series)	ABC-TV	Herschel Burke Gilbert/ Hans Salter
League of Gentlemen	BRI	Philip Green
Leningrad Skies	RUS	Lev Schwartz
Let's Get Married	BRI	Edwin Astley
Life Is a Circus	BRI	Philip Green
Light Up the Sky	BRI	Douglas Gamley
Little Red Riding Hood and the Monster	MEX	Raul Lavista
Lost Pencil, The	YUG	Miroslav Belamaric
Low Midnight	YUG	Aleksander Bubanovic
Macario	MEX	Raul Lavista
Macbeth	NBC-TV	Richard Addinsell
Magnificent Seven, The	UA	Elmer Bernstein
Malpas Mystery, The	BRI	Elisabeth Lutyens

Man from Interpol, The (series)	NBC-TV	Tony Crombie
Man Is a Social Being (short)	CZE	J. F. Fiser
Man Who Couldn't Walk, The	BRI	Wilfred Burns
Mania (Fiendish Girls, The)	BRI	Stanley Black
Master of Horror	ARG	Victor Schlichter
Matter of Dignity, A	GRE	Manos Hadjidakis
Michael Shayne, Private Detective (series)	NBC-TV	Leith Stevens
Mighty Hercules, The (series)	IND-TV	Winston Sharples
Mill of the Stone Women	ITA	Carlo Innocenzi
Millionairess, The	FOX	Georges van Parys
Mischief Makers, The (series)	IND-TV	Jack Saunders
Mr. Ed (series)	IND-TV	Dave Kahn/Raoul Kraushaar
Mr. Garlund (series)	CBS-TV	Jerry Fielding/Pete Rugolo
Mrs. Warren's Profession	GER	Siegfried Franz
Motherland	PAK	Inayat Hussain
My Friend Death	JAP	Hachiro Matsui
My Niece Doesn't Do That	AUS	Charly Niessen
My Second Brother	JAP	Toshiro Mayazumi
My Sister Eileen (series)	CBS-TV	Warren Barker
My Three Sons (series)	ABC-TV	Jeff Alexander/Frank deVol/Gerald Fried/ Nathan Scott
Mysterious Case of Rygseck Murders	FIN	Osmo Lindeman
National Velvet (series)	NBC-TV	Alexander Courage
Never Take Candy from a Stranger	BRI	Elisabeth Lutyens
Night in Rome, A	ITA	Renzo Rossellini
Night They Killed Rasputin, The	FRA/ITA	Francesco Lavagnino
Of Love and Lust	SWE	Herbert Sandburg
Operation	YUG	Alojz Srebotnjak
Our Last Spring	GRE	Arghyris Kounadis
Our Man in Havana	COL	Hernand Deniz
Outlaws, The	NBC-TV	Hugo Friedhofer
Overland Trail (series)	IND-TV	Stanley Wilson
Partisan Stories	YUG	Bojan Adamic
Peeping Tom (Face of Fear)	BRI	Brian Easdale
Penalty Battalion 999	GER	Willy Mattes
Pete and Gladys (series)	CBS-TV	Wilbur Hatch
Peter Loves Mary (series)	NBC-TV	Jerry Fielding/Herschel Burke Gilbert
Peter Voss, Hero of the Day	GER	Erwin Halletz
Phantom of the Operetta, The	MEX	Manuel Esperon
Piccadilly Third Stop	BRI	Philip Green
Pioneers, The	BRA/FRA	Henri Crolla
Playgirls and the Vampire, The	ITA	Aldo Piga
Pleasures of Saturday Night	ITA	Armando Trovajoli

Point 905	YUG	Danilo Danev
Pony Express (series)	IND-TV	Marlin Skiles
Prime Time, The	IND	Buddy Frye/Martin Rubenstein
Pure Hell at St. Trinian's	BRI	Malcolm Arnold
Red Lips	FRA/ITA	Piero Umiliani
Right Man, The	CBS-TV	George Kleinsinger
Roaring Twenties, The (series)	ABC-TV	Alexander Courage
Robert Herridge Theater, The (series)	IND-TV	Tom Scott
Roses for the Prosecutor	GER	Raimund Rosenberger
Route 66 (series)	CBS-TV	Nelson Riddle
Sands of the Desert	BRI	Stanley Black
Saturday Night and Sunday Morning	BRI	John Dankworth
School for Scoundrels	BRI	John Addison
September Storm	FOX	Edward L. Alperson Jr./Raoul Kraushaar
Serge	RUS	Boris Chaikovsky
Siege of Sidney St., The	BRI	Stanley Black
Simon Lash	IND-TV	Richard LaSalle
Ski Troop Attack	IND	Fred Katz
Son of Samson	ITA	Carlo Innocenzi
Song to Remember, A	MEX	Jesus Zarzosa
South Wind	ITA	Gino Marinuzzi, Jr.
Spook Castle in Spessart, The	GER	Frederick Hollander
Stagecoach West (series)	ABC-TV	Jerry Fielding/Herschel Burke Gilbert
Story of David, A	BRI-TV	Kenneth V. Jones
Studs Lonigan	UA	Jerry Goldsmith
Summer of the 17th Doll, The	UA	Benjamin Frankel
Super He-Man, The (Supermacho, El)	MEX	Sergio Guerrero
Surfside 6 (series)	ABC-TV	Frank Ortega/Frank Perkins/Paul Sawtell
Tab Hunter Show, The (series)	NBC-TV	Pete Rugolo
Tall Man, The (series)	NBC-TV	Juan Esquivel
Thief in the Bedroom, The	SWE	Harry Arnold
Three Came to Kill	UA	Paul Sawtell
Three Girls Named Anna	YUG	Bojan Adamic
Three Moves to Freedom	GER	Hans-Martin Majewski
Three Treasures, The	JAP	Akira Ifukube
Thriller (series)	NBC-TV	Jerry Goldsmith/Pete Rugolo
To Each His Life	MEX	Raul Lavista
Tommy the Toreador	BRI	Stanley Black
Too Hot to Handle	BRI	Eric Spear
Too Young to Love	BRI	Bruce Montgomery
Trials of Oscar Wilde, The	BRI	Ron Goodwin

Two Faces West (series)	IND-TV	Irving Friedman/ Joseph Weiss
Unheeded Crisis	KOR	Sang Ki Han
Until Money Departs You	GER	Herbert Trantow
Utamaro, Painter of Women	JAP	Hiroyoshi Ogawa
Valiant Years, The (series)	ABC-TV	Richard Rodgers
Venner	NOR	Maj Sonstevold
Via Margutta	ITA	Piero Piccioni
Violent Summer	FRA/ITA	Mario Nascimbene
War (Rat)	YUG	Vladimir Kraus-Rajteric
Wasp Woman, The	IND	Fred Katz
We Cellar Children	GER	Peter Sandloff
Westerner, The (series)	NBC-TV	Joseph Mullendore/ Rudy Schrager
When the Bells Sound Clearly	AUS	Willy Mattes
Where the Devil Cannot Go	CZE	Zdenek Liska
Where the Hot Wind Blows	MGM	Roman Vlad
White Dove, The	CZE	Zdenek Liska
Word of a Cat, The (short)	CZE	Miles Vacek
World, the Flesh and the Devil, The	MEX	Antonio Dias Conde
Years of Youth	RUS	Platon Maiboroda
Young Sinner, The	GER	Ernest Simon
Your Money or Your Wife	BRI	Philip Green

1961

A for Andromeda	BRI-TV	Trevor Duncan
Acapulco (series)	NBC-TV	Billy May
Adventure at the Door	YUG	Aleksander Bubanovic
Along the Barbary Coast	NBC-TV	Earle Hagen
Antinea (Atlantide, L')	FRA/ITA	Carlo Rustichelli
At the Terminus	CZE	Zdenek Liska
Ballad About a Trumpet and a Cloud, A	YUG	Alojz Srebotnjak
Balloon Man	MEX	Antonio Diaz Conde
Bandits of Orgosolo	ITA	Valentino Bucchi
Baron Munchausen	CZE	Zdenek Liska
Battle at Bloody Beach	FOX	Henry Vars/Sonny Burke
Beachcomber, The (series)	IND-TV	Elmer Bernstein/Joseph Hooven/Raoul Kraushaar/Marlin Skiles
Beast of Yucca Flats, The	IND	Irwin Nafshun/Al Remington
Beautiful and Beloved Mexico	MEX	Jesus Zarzosa
Ben Casey (series)	ABC-TV	George Bassman/Gerald Fried/Jerry Goldsmith/ Richard Markowitz/ David Raksin/Walter Scharf/Richard Sendry/ Morton Stevens

Big Show, The	FOX	Paul Sawtell/Bert Shefter
Burning Court, The	FRA/GER/ITA	Georges Auric
Bus Stop (series)	ABC-TV	Frank De Vol
Cain's Hundred (series)	NBC-TV	Jerry Goldsmith/Lyn Murray/Pete Rugolo/ Morton Stevens
Call Me Genius (Rebel, The)	BRI	Frank Cordell
Canadians, The	FOX	Muir Mathieson (not Ken Darby)
Capture That Capsule!	IND	Arthur Hopkins
Car 54, Where Are You? (series)	NBC-TV	John Strauss
Carry On Regardless	BRI	Bruce Montgomery
Cat, The	MEX	Raul Lavista
Corsican Brothers, The	ITA	Francesco Lavagnino
Courageous Cat (series)	IND-TV	Johnny Holiday
Curse of the Aztec Mummy, The	MEX	Antonio Diaz Conde
Curse of the Crying Woman, The	MEX	Gustavo Cesar Carreon
Curse of the Doll People, The	MEX	Antonio Diaz Conde
Dancing in the Rain	YUG	Bojan Adamic
Danger Man (series)	CBS-TV	Edwin Astley
Deceived Women	MEX	Sergio Guerrero
Defenders, The (series)	CBS-TV	Leonard Rosenman
Devil Played the Balalaika, The	GER	Z. Barodow
Dick Tracy Show, The (series)	IND-TV	Carl Brandt
Dick Van Dyke Show, The (series)	CBS-TV	Earle Hagen
Doctor Kildare (series)	NBC-TV	Jerry Goldsmith/Pete Rugolo/Harry Sukman
Doll, A (Lutkica) (short)	YUG	Tomislav Simovic
Don't Meddle with Fortune	YUG	Dusan Radic
Dreamer, The (Sanjar)	YUG	Branimir Sakac
Dreamland of Desire	GER	Manos Hadjidakis
87th Precinct (series)	NBC-TV	Morton Stevens
Escape to Berlin	GER	Peter Thomas
Everything Happens to Me	CBS-TV	Earle Hagen
Father of the Bride (series)	CBS-TV	Jerry Fielding
Five Days--Five Nights	E.GER/RUS	Dmitri Shostakovich
Flame in the Streets	BRI	Philip Green
Follow the Sun (series)	ABC-TV	Sonny Burke
Fountain of Life	GER	Gerhard Becker
14 Days, The	YUG	Vladimir Kraus-Rajteric
Frontier Circus (series)	CBS-TV	Jeff Alexander
Full Treatment, The	BRI	Stanley Black
Gang Leader	MEX	Gustavo Cesar Carreon
Gioia Vivere, Che	FRA/ITA	Francesco Lavagnino
Girl in the Window	FRA/ITA	Roman Vlad
Grand Olympiade, The	ITA	Francesco Lavagnino/ Armando Trovajoli
Grass Eater, The	IND	Jaime Mendoza-Nava

Hathaways, The (series)	ABC-TV	Jeff Alexander/Jerry Fielding/Pete Rugolo
Haunted Castle, The	GER	Frederick Hollander
Hazel (series)	NBC-TV	Charles Albertine/Van Alexander/Howard Blake/Ed Forsyth
Heaven Can Wait	NBC-TV	Robert Cobert
Heiress, The	CBS-TV	Robert Cobert
Hercules Against the Haunted World	ITA	Armando Trovajoli
Hercules and the Captive Women	ITA	Gino Marinuzzi
High Princip	CZE	Zdenek Liska
His and Hers	BRI	John Addison
Hollywood and the Stars (series)	TV	Elmer Bernstein
Hollywood: The Golden Years	WOL	Elmer Bernstein
Horse With the Flying Tail, The	DIS	William Lava
House of Fright	AI	John Hollingsworth
I Like Mike (Surprise Party)	ISR	Arie Levanon
I Love, You Love	FRA/ITA	Carlo Savina
Ichabod and Me (series)	CBS-TV	Frank Morris/Pete Rugolo
Invasion of the Zombies	MEX	Raul Lavista
Invisible Dr. Mabuse, The	GER	Peter Sandloff
Jakobli and Meyeii	ISR	Robert Blum
Josephine Little: Adventures in Happiness	NBC-TV	Earle Hagen
Josephine Little: Dragon by the Tail	NBC-TV	Earle Hagen
Journey to the Seventh Planet	AI	Ib Glindenmann/Ronald Stein
Juana Gallo	MEX	Manuel Esperon
King of Diamonds (series)	IND-TV	Frank Ortega
King of the Roaring Twenties	AA	Franz Waxman
King's New Clothes, The	YUG	Andelko Klobucar
Kitchen, The	BRI	David Lee
Knife, The	HOL	Pim Jacobs
Konga	AI	Gerard Schurmann
Last War, The	JAP	Ikuma Dan
Last Witness, The	GER	Werner Eisbrenner
Like Father, Like Son	IND	Shelley Manne
Lion Tamer, The (short)	YUG	Miljenko Prohaska
Little Shop of Horrors, The	IND	Fred Katz
Long and the Short and the Tall, The	BRI	Stanley Black
Long Live Jalisco, Land of My Birth	MEX	Manuel Esperon
Looking for Death	MEX	Sergio Guerrero
Lost Atlantis	ITA	Carlo Rustichelli
Love at Every Fair, A	MEX	Gustavo Cesar Carreon
Love Hangs on the Gibbet	GER	Ernst Roters
Love of Anuradka	IN	Ravi Shankar

Magic Fountain, The	IND	Jacques Belasco
Malibu Run (series)	CBS-TV	Andre Previn
Man Wants to Live!	FRA	Joseph Kosma
Margie (series)	ABC-TV	Cyril Mockridge/Lionel Newman
Mark of Death, The	MEX	Gustavo Cesar Carreon
Marriage of Mr. Mississippi, The	SWI	Hans-Martin Majewski
Martin in the Clouds	YUG	Aleksander Bubanovic
Mathematical Peep Show (short)	IND	Elmer Bernstein
Miracle of Malachias	GER	Hans-Martin Majewski
Mr. Topaze	FOX	Georges van Parys
Mole Men vs. the Son of Hercules	ITA	Armando Trovajoli
Mother Courage and Her Children	E.GER	Paul Desseau
Mrs. G Goes to College (series)	CBS-TV	Herschel Burke Gilbert
My Son the Hero	ITA	Carlo Rustichelli
Neutron Against the Death Robots	MEX	Enrico Cabiati
Neutron and the Black Mask	MEX	Enrico Cabiati
New Adventures of Pinocchio, The (series)	IND-TV	Jules Bass
New Breed, The (series)	ABC-TV	Dominic Frontiere
Night We Got the Bird, The	BRI	Tommy Watts
Ninth Circle, The	YUG	Bianimir Sakak
Not Tonight, Henry	IND	Hal Borne
Of Stars and Men	IND	Walter Trampler
Offbeat	BRI	Kenneth V. Jones
One Happy Family (series)	NBC-TV	Jerry Fielding/Pete Rugolo
1,000 Eyes of Dr. Mabuse, The	GER	Bert Grund
Orlak, the Hell of Frankenstein	MEX	Ruben Fuentes
Phantom Planet, The	IND	Hayes Pagel
Piece of Blue Sky, A	YUG	Bojan Adamic
Pigs and Battleships	JAP	Toshiro Mayuzumi
Pine Lake Lodge	IND-TV	Raoul Kraushaar
Planets Against Us	ITA	Armando Trovajoli
Power and the Glory, The	CBS-TV	Laurence Rosenthal
Project: Man in Space	TV	Elmer Bernstein
Purple Hills, The	FOX	Richard LaSalle
Quiet Summer, A	YUG	Dragutin Savin
Red Blossoms	MEX	Antonio Dias Conde
Red Dove, The	FIN	Osmo Lindeman
Return of Dr. Mabuse, The	GER	Peter Sandloff
Ripcord (series)	IND-TV	Stanley Wilson
Sacred Waters	GER/SWI	Hans-Martin Majewski
Salonka Terrorists, The	YUG	Dusan Radic
Sam Hill	NBC-TV	David Rose
Sampson	POL	Tadeusz Baird
Sea Gypsies, The	PHI	F. Buencamino
Shadows Are Getting Longer, The	GER/SWI	Robert Blum
Shannon (series)	IND-TV	Joe Bushkin
Signal Over the City	YUG	Bojan Adamic

Spare the Rod	BRI	Laurie Johnson
Spiritism (Espiritismo)	MEX	Antonio Diaz Conde
Swindler and the Lord, The	GER	Norbert Schultze
Sword of Sherwood Forest	COL	Stanley Black/Alun Hoddinott
Target: The Corrupters (series)	ABC-TV	Jerry Fielding/Pete Rugolo/Hans Salter/ Rudy Schrager
Teddy Boys (Potota, La)	ARG	Lucio Milena
Three Romeos and a Juliet	MEX	Antonio Dias Conde
Throne of Blood	JAP	Masaru Sato
Tonight for Sure	IND	Carmine Coppola
Ulysses Against the Sons of Hercules	ITA	Francesco Lavagnino
Ursus in the Valley of the Lions	ITA	Riz Ortolani
Vacations in Acapulco	MEX	Navarro Brothers/ Antonio Prieto
Very Important Person, A	BRI	Reg Owen
Viaccia, La	ITA	Piero Piccioni
Violence at the Square	YUG	Dusan Radic
Voyage to the Bottom of the Sea	FOX	Paul Sawtell/Bert Shefter
Werewolf in a Girl's Dormitory	ITA	F. Berman
Whispering Smith (series)	NBC-TV	Richard Shores/Leo Shuken
Who Killed Julie Greer?	NBC-TV	Herschel Burke Gilbert
Wilhelm Tell	SWI	Hans Haug
Window on Main Street	CBS-TV	Irving Friedman
Witch's Mirror, The	MEX	Gustavo Cesar Carreon
Yes Yes Nanette (series)	NBC-TV	Axel Stordahl/Stanley Wilson
Young Ones, The	IND	Leon Bibb

1962

Affair at Akitsu	JAP	Hikaru Hayashi
Allegro Non Troppo (short)	PYR	Francois de Roubaix
Amphibian Man	RUS	Tirentev
Apple, The (short)	BRI	Ernst Naser
Attack of the Robots (Cards on the Table)	AI	Paul Misraki
Beverly Hillbillies, The (series)	CBS-TV	Perry Botkin/Curt Massey
Biography (series)	IND-TV	Jack Tillar
Bomb Was Stolen, A	RUM	Dimitru Capoianu
Boston Terrier, The	NBC-TV	Herschel Burke Gilbert
Brain, The (Vengeance)	BRI	Kenneth V. Jones
Carnival of Souls	BRI	Gene Moore
Charlie Angelo	CBS-TV	Sonny Burke
Cobra Girl	IN	S. N. Tripathi
Colossus and the Headhunters	AI	Guido Robuschi/Gian Stellari

Combat (series)	ABC-TV	George Bassman/Leonard Rosenman
Curse of the Blood Ghouls, The	ITA	Aldo Piga
Cybernetic Grandmother (short)	CZE	Jan Novak
D-Day	TV	Elmer Bernstein
Death of the Ape Man	CZE	Evgen Illin
Devil and the Ten Commandments, The	FRA	Michel Magne
Devil's Messenger	BRI	Alfred Gwynn
Don't Call Me Charlie (series)	NBC-TV	Jerry Fielding
Eleventh Hour, The (series)	NBC-TV	Harry Sukman
Empire (series)	NBC-TV	John Green
Ensign O'Toole (series)	NBC-TV	Frank Comstock
F.B.I. Code 98	IND-TV	Max Steiner
Face of Terror	SPA	Jose Buenagu
Fair Exchange (series)	CBS-TV	Cyril Mockridge
First Hundred Years, The	CBS-TV	John Williams
Floyd Gibbons, Reporter	ABC-TV	Nelson Riddle
Frankenstein, the Vampire and Co.	MEX	Gustavo Cesar Carreon
Game, The (short)	YUG	Tomislav Simovic
Giant of Metropolis, The	ITA	Armando Trovajoli
Going My Way (series)	ABC-TV	Leo Shuken
Golden Rabbit, The	BRI	Bill McGuffie
Horrible Dr. Hitchcock, The	ITA	Roman Vlad
House of Science (short)	IND	Elmer Bernstein
House on Bare Mountain, The	IND	Pierre Martel
Hypnosis	GER/ITA/SPA	Roman Vlad
I'm Dickens ... He's Fenster (series)	ABC-TV	Frank DeVol/Irving Szathmary
Immortelle, L'	FRA	Georges Delerue
Invasion of the Star Creatures	AI	Jack Cookerly/Elliott Fisher
It's a Man's World (series)	NBC-TV	Jack Marshall
Jetsons, The (series)	CBS-TV	Hoyt Curtin
King of Terror	IND	James Cairncross
Knight's Gambit	NBC-TV	John Williams
Labyrinth (short)	POL	Wlodzimierz Kotonski
Lecture on Man, A (short)	BRI	Tristram Cary
Lloyd Bridges Show, The (series)	CBS-TV	Leith Stevens
Loretta Young Show, The (series)	CBS-TV	Harry Lubin
Lucy Show, The (series)	CBS-TV	Wilbur Hatch
McHale's Navy (series)	ABC-TV	Jerry Fielding/Axel Stordahl
McKeever and the Colonel (series)	NBC-TV	Jerry Fielding/Herschel Burke Gilbert
Man from Independence, The	TV	Elmer Bernstein
Man of the World (series)	BRI-TV	Edwin Astley
Medusa vs. the Son of Hercules	ITA	Carlo Franci/Manuel Parada
Mermaids of Tiburon, The	IND	Richard La Salle

Our Man Higgins (series)	ABC-TV	Frank DeVol
Plunderers of the Moon	CZE	Adam Walacinski
Rocket to Nowhere	CZE	Evgen Illin
Rogopag	ITA	Carlo Rustichelli
Room for One More (series)	ABC-TV	Frank Perkins/Paul Sawtell
Safari	NBC-TV	Herschel Burke Gilbert
Saints and Sinners (series)	NBC-TV	Elmer Bernstein
Sam Benedict (series)	NBC-TV	Jeff Alexander/Nelson Riddle
Saturday's Children	CBS-TV	Alfredo Antonini
Savage Sunday	NBC-TV	Herschel Burke Gilbert
Stoney Burke (series)	ABC-TV	Dominic Frontiere
Story of --, The (series)	IND-TV	Ruby Raksin
Supercar (series)	IND-TV	Barry Gray
Swingin' Along	FOX	Arthur Morton
Tack Reynolds	ABC-TV	Dominic Frontiere
Terrible Snow Giant, The	MEX	Sergio Guerrero
Terrified	BRI	Michael Anderson
Testament of Dr. Mabuse, The	GER	Raimund Rosenberger
330 Independence S.W.	NBC-TV	Herschel Burke Gilbert
Vampires and the Ballerina, The	ITA	Aldo Piga
Varan, the Unbelievable	JAP	Akira Ifukube
Venus Against the Son of Hercules	ITA	Gino Marinuzzi
Virginian, The (series)	NBC-TV	Percy Faith/Leonard Rosenman/Hans J. Salter/Leo Shuken
Vulcan, Son of Jupiter	ITA	Marcello Giombini
Wally Gator (series)	IND-TV	Ted Nichols
Young Guns of Texas	FOX	Paul Sawtell/Bert Shefter

1963

Adam Mackenzie Story, The	NBC-TV	Jerome Moross
Attack of the Mayan Mummy	MEX	Luis de Leon
Blancheville Monster, The	ITA/SPA	Carlo Franci
Blood Feast	IND	Hershell Gordon Lewis
Border Town	ABC-TV	Dominic Frontiere
Breaking Point (series)	ABC-TV	David Raksin
Burke's Law (series)	ABC-TV	Herschel Burke Gilbert/ Joseph Mullendore
Captain Sinbad	MGM	Michel Michelet
Case Against Paul Ryker, The	NBC-TV	John Williams
Channing (series)	ABC-TV	Jack Marshall
Charlie Wooster--Outlaw	NBC-TV	Jerome Moross
Colossus	NBC-TV	Herschel Burke Gilbert
Conquest of Mycene	ITA	Carlo Rustichelli
Dakotas, The (series)	ABC-TV	Warren Barker/Frank Perkins

Death on the Fourposter	FRA/ITA	Marcello de Martino
Devil on Vacation, The	SPA	Modesto Rebollo
Diagnosis: Danger	CBS-TV	Lyn Murray
Dionysus (short)	FMC	Teiji Ito
Do You Keep a Lion at Home?	CZE	William Buckovy
Doctors, The (series)	NBC-TV	John Geller/Charles Gross
East Side/West Side (series)	CBS-TV	Kenyon Hopkins
Eyes Without a Face (Horror Chamber of Dr. Faustus/ Shadowman)	FRA	Georges Franju
Farmer's Daughter, The (series)	ABC-TV	George Duning/Dave Grusin
Fugitive, The (series)	ABC-TV	Pete Rugolo
General Hospital (series)	ABC-TV	Charles Paul
Ghost, The	ITA	Franco Mannino/Roman Vlad
Glynis (series)	CBS-TV	George Duning
Golden Hairpin, The	HK	Pan Chao
Great Adventure, The (series)	CBS-TV	Richard Rodgers
Greatest Show on Earth, The (series)	ABC-TV	Jeff Alexander
Grindl (series)	NBC-TV	Frank DeVol
Hand of a Dead Man	SPA	Daniel J. White
Harbor Lights	FOX	Paul Sawtell/Bert Shefter
Harry's Girls (series)	NBC-TV	Van Alexander/Jerry Fielding
Horror Castle (Virgin of Nuremberg)	ITA	Riz Ortolani
Horror Hotel	BRI	Douglas Gamley
Horror of Party Beach	FOX	Bill Holmes
House on the Moon, The	BRI	Ron Grainer
Incredibly Strange Creatures Who Stopped Living and Became Mixed-Up Zombies, The	IND	Henry Price
Indian Scarf, The	GER	Peter Thomas
Invisible Terror, The	GER	Jean Thome
It Takes a Thief (series)	ABC-TV	Ralph Ferraro/Benny Golson/Dave Grusin
Jetee, La (short)	FRA	Trevor Duncan
Kincaid	ABC-TV	Dominic Frontiere
Kulicka	CZE	Evgen Illin
Last of the Private Eyes, The	NBC-TV	Herschel Burke Gilbert
Little Ball, The (short)	CZE	Evgen Illin
Little Prince and the Eight-Headed Dragon, The	JAP	Akira Ifukube
Losers, The	NBC-TV	Richard Shores
Loves of Salammbo, The	FOX	Alexander Derevitzky
Luxury Liner	NBC-TV	Herschel Burke Gilbert

Mad Executioners, The	GER	Raimund Rosenberger
Making of the President, The	TV	Elmer Bernstein
Man from Galveston, The	IND-TV	David Buttolph
Matango (Attack of the Mushroom People)	JAP	Betsumia Sadao
Mr. Magoo (series)	IND-TV	Shorty Rogers
Monk of Monza, The	ITA	Armando Trovajoli
Museum of Horror, The	MEX	Sergio Guerrero
My Favorite Husband (series)	CBS-TV	Lud Gluskin
My Favorite Martian (series)	CBS-TV	George Greeley
Omicron	ITA	Piero Umiliani
Outer Limits, The (series)	ABC-TV	Dominic Frontiere
Pasi Spre Luna	RUM	Dimitru Capoianu
Patriarchs of the Bible	ITA	Gino Marinuzzi/Teo Usuelli
Patty Duke Show, The (series)	ABC-TV	Harry Geller/Sid Ramin
Petticoat Junction (series)	CBS-TV	Curt Massey
Redigo (series)	NBC-TV	Nelson Riddle
Richard Boone Show, The (series)	NBC-TV	Vic Mizzy
Samson vs. the Giant King	ITA	Carlo Rustichelli
Samson vs. the Pirates	ITA	Francesco Lavagnino
Secret of the Telegian, The	JAP	Sei Ikeno
Sergeant Ryker	TV	John Williams
Shock Corridor	AA	Gordon Zahler
Slime People, The	IND	Lou Foman
Son of Hercules in the Land of Fire	ITA	Carlo Savina
Strangler of Blackmoor Castle, The	GER	Oskar Sala
Superloco, El	MEX	D. Castaneda
Tarzan's Three Challenges	BRI	Joseph Horowitz
Temple Houston (series)	NBC-TV	Frank Comstock
Terror in the Crypt	ITA	Carlo Savina
Think! (View from the People Wall, The) (short)	IND	Elmer Bernstein
Tifusari (short)	YUG	Branimir Sakac
Unearthly Stranger, The	BRI	Edward Williams
Weapons Man	ABC-TV	Dominic Frontiere
Weapons of Vengeance	ITA	Francesco de Masi
What?	ITA	Carlo Rustichelli
Which Way'd They Go?	ABC-TV	Herschel Burke Gilbert
Wild Kingdom (series)	NBC-TV	James Bourgeois

1964

Addams Family, The (series)	ABC	Vic Mizzy
Adventures of Jonny Quest, The (series)	ABC-TV	Hoyt Curtin
Alf, Bill and Fred (short)	BRI	Arthur Dulay
Alone with Ghosts	JAP	Hiroaki Watanabe
Another World (series)	NBC-TV	Chet Kingsbury
Appearances	BEL/FRA	Georges Delerue

Baileys of Balboa, The (series)	CBS-TV	Harry Geller
Bewitched (pilot)	ABC-TV	Jerry Fielding
Bewitched (series)	ABC-TV	Warren Barker/Jimmie Haskell
Black Torment, The	BRI	Bobby Richards
Boat Without a Fisherman, The	SPA	Eduardo Sainz de la Maza
Brass Bottle, The	UN	Bernard Green
Broadside (series)	ABC-TV	Jerry Fielding/Axel Stordahl
Bullwinkle Show, The (series)	ABC-TV	Dennis Farnon/Fred Steiner
Canon (short)	CAN	Eldon Rathburn
Cara Williams Show, The (series)	CBS-TV	Frank Comstock/Kenyon Hopkins
Carol for Another Christmas, A	ABC-TV	Henry Mancini
Carpetbaggers, The	PAR	Elmer Bernstein
Castle of Terror (Danse Macabre)	ITA	Riz Ortolani
Castle of the Living Dead, The	ITA	Francesco Lavagnino
Daniel Boone (series)	NBC-TV	Alexander Courage/ Irving Gertz/Leigh Harline/Joseph Mullendore/Lyn Murray/ Lionel Newman/Herman Stein/Fred Steiner/ Leith Stevens/Harry Sukman
Demon in the Blood	ARG	Rudolfo Arizaga
Diabolical Axe, The	MEX	Jorge Perez Herrera
Doctor of Doom, The	MEX	Antonio Diaz Conde
Dr. Terror's House of Horrors [Double-O Two] (see 00-2 Secret Agents)	BRI	Elisabeth Lutyens
Every Sparrow Must Fall	IND	J. A. Kroculick
Famous Adventures of Mr. Magoo, The (series)	NBC-TV	Carl Brandt
Fantomas	FRA	Michel Magne
Far Away I Saw Mist and Mud	YUG	Tomislav Simovic
Fifi la Plume	FRA	Jean-Michel Defaye
Flesh Eaters, The	IND	Julian Stein
Flipper (series)	NBC-TV	Al Mack/Samuel Motlovsky/Henry Vars
Four Days in November	TV	Elmer Bernstein
Games of Angels	FRA	Bernard Parmeggiani
Ghost Jesters, The	MEX	Ruben Fuentes
Gilligan's Island (series)	CBS-TV	Gerald Fried/Herschel Burke Gilbert/Sherwood Schwartz/Morton Stevens/John Williams
Girl Who Danced into Life, The	HUN	Tihamer Vujicsies
Gomer Pyle, U.S.M.C. (series)	CBS-TV	Earle Hagen

Gorath	JAP	Kan Ishii
Hanged Man, The	UN	Stanley Wilson
Hangman (short)	IND	Serge Hovey
Harris Against the World (series)	NBC-TV	Lalo Schifrin
Help, My Snowman Is Burning Down (short)	IND	Jerry Mulligan
Hercules Against Rome	ITA	Francesco Lavagnino
Hercules Against the Moon Men	ITA	Carlo Franci
Hercules Against the Sun	ITA	Lallo Gori
Hercules and the Tyrants of Babylon	ITA	Francesco Lavagnino
Hercules of the Desert	ITA	Carlo Rustichelli
Human Jungle, The (series)	BRI-TV	Edwin Astley/Albert Elms
Human Vapor, The	JAP	Kunio Miyauchi
Hunger Canal	JAP	Isao Tomita
Hyena of London, The	ITA	Francesco de Masi
Impossible on Saturday	ISR	Alexander (Sacha) Argov
Invasion	ITA	Luis de Pablo
Invincible Maciste Brothers, The	ITA	Felice di Stefano
Invincible Three, The	ITA	Francesco Lavagnino
Invisible Assassin, The	MEX	Sergio Guerrero
Jester's Tale, A	CZE	Jan Novak
Karen (series)	NBC-TV	Jack Marshall
Kentucky Jones (series)	NBC-TV	Vic Mizzy
Kiss from Beyond the Grave, The	MEX	Sergio Guerrero
Lady in a Cage	PAR	Paul Glass
Lassie (series)	CBS-TV	Nathan Scott
Littlest Hobo, The (series)	CAN-TV	Douglas Lackey
Long Hair of Death, The	ITA	Carlo Rustichelli
Lost World of Sinbad, The	JAP	Masaru Sato
Maciste and the Queen of Samar	ITA	Carlo Franci
Maciste, Gladiator of Sparta	ITA	Carlo Franci
Magic World of Topo Gigio, The	ITA	Aldo Rossi
Magilla Gorilla Show, The (series)	IND-TV	Ted Nichols
Man from UNCLE, The (series)	NBC-TV	Gerald Fried/Jerry Goldsmith/Lalo Schiffrin/Leith Stevens/Morton Stevens
Man in the Middle	FOX	John Barry/Lionel Bart
Many Happy Returns (series)	CBS-TV	Kenyon Hopkins
Martians Have Arrived, The	ITA	Ennio Morricone
Mickey (series)	ABC-TV	Bobby Hammack
Mr. Broadway (series)	CBS-TV	Dave Brubeck
Monstrosity	IND	Gene Kauer
Munsters, The (series)	CBS-TV	Jack Marshall
My Living Doll (series)	CBS-TV	George Greeley
Nightmare in Chicago	TV	John Williams
No Time for Sergeants (series)	ABC-TV	George Duning
Nut House, The	CBS-TV	Jerry Fielding

00-2 Secret Agents	ITA	Piero Umiliani
One Hundred Cries of Terror	MEX	Rafael Carrion
Peter Potamus Show, The (series)	IND-TV	Ted Nichols
Peyton Place (serial)	ABC-TV	Lee Holdridge/Cyril Mockridge/Arthur Morton/Lionel Newman
Ready for the People	IND-TV	Frank Perkins
Red Army's Bridge, The	CHN	Chang Tung
Reporter, The (series)	CBS-TV	Kenyon Hopkins
Rhythm 'n' Greens (short)	BRI	Norrie Paramour
Rogues, The (series)	NBC-TV	Nelson Riddle
Samson and the Mighty Challenge	ITA	Piero Umiliani
Samson in King Solomon's Mines	ITA	Francesco de Masi
Santa Claus Conquers the Martians	EMB	Milton Delugg
Santo Attacks the Witches	MEX	George Perez
Second Look	NBC-TV	Lalo Schifrin
Secret of Dr. Mabuse, The	GER	Carlos Dierhammer
See How They Run	UN	Lalo Schifrin
Seven Little Foys, The	NBC-TV	Johnny Mandel
Shadow of Evil	FRA	Michel Magne
Sky Above Heaven	FRA/ITA	Jacques Loussier
Slattery's People (series)	CBS-TV	Elmer Bernstein/Nathan Scott
Sophia Loren in Rome	ABC-TV	John Barry
Sound of Horror, The	SPA	Luis de Pablo
Surf Party	FOX	Jimmie Haskell
Survival (series)	IND-TV	Nelson Riddle
Tarzan and the Leopard Man	ITA	Aldo Piga
Temple of the White Elephants, The	FRA	Georges Garvarentz
Tiger Walks, A	DIS	Buddy Baker
Tom, Dick and Mary (series)	NBC-TV	Pete Rugolo
Tomb of Lygeia, The	AI	Kenneth V. Jones
Twelve O'Clock High (series)	ABC-TV	Dominic Frontiere
2,000 Maniacs	IND	Larry Wellington
Tycoon, The (series)	ABC-TV	Earle Hagen
Unknown, The	ABC-TV	Dominic Frontiere
Unknown Hour, The	SPA	Adolfo Waitzman
Valentine's Day (series)	ABC-TV	Lionel Newman
Voyage to the Bottom of the Sea (series)	ABC-TV	Alexander Courage/Harry Geller/Jerry Goldsmith/Lionel Newman/Nelson Riddle/Paul Sawtell/John Williams
We Shall See	BRI	Bernard Ebbinghouse
Wendy and Me (series)	ABC-TV	George Duning
Witchcraft	BRI	Carlo Martelli
Woman of the Dunes	JAP	Toru Takemitsu
World War I (series)	CBS-TV	Morton Gould
[Zero Zero Two] (see 00-2 Secret Agents)		

1965

A-008 Operation Exterminate	ITA	Francesco Lavagnino
Adventure at the Center of the Earth, The	MEX	Sergio Guerrero
Adventures of Takla Makan	JAP	Akira Ifukube
Agent 505	FRA/GER/ITA	Ennio Morricone
All Men Are Apes	BRI	Irv Dweir
Amos Burke, Secret Agent (series)	ABC-TV	Herschel Burke Gilbert/ Leith Stevens
Baby the Rain Must Fall	COL	Elmer Bernstein
Bad Joke, A	RUS	Nikolai Karetnikov
Banner, The (short)	POL	Kryzystof Komeda
Big Valley, The (series)	ABC-TV	Elmer Bernstein/Joseph Mullendore
Blood Beast from Outer Space (Night Caller)	BRI	Johnny Gregory
Bloody Pit of Horror	ITA	Gino Peguri
Branded (series)	NBC-TV	Dominic Frontiere
Burning of a Thousand Suns, The	FRA	Bernard Parmeggiani
Camp Runamuck (series)	NBC-TV	Frank De Vol/Ed Forsyth
Cave of the Living Dead	GER/YUG	Herbert Jarczyk
Cavern, The	FOX	Carlo Rustichelli/Gene de Novi
Ceremony, The (short)	YUG	Tomislav Simovic
Christmas That Almost Wasn't, The	CHI	Bruno Nicolai
Chromophobia (short)	BEL	Ralph Darbo
Convoy (series)	NBC-TV	Bernard Herrmann
Crazy Leg (Luda Noga) (short)	YUG	Bosco Petrovic
Creature of the Walking Dead, The	MEX	Gustavo Cesar Carreon
Days of Our Lives (series)	NBC-TV	Charles Albertine/ Tommy Boyce/Bobby Hart/Barry Mann
Diabolical Dr. Z, The	SPA	Daniel J. White
Disintegrating Ray, or the Adventures of Quique and Arthur the Robot, The	SPA	Carmelo Barnaola
Double-Barrelled Detective Story	IND	Meyer Kupferman
Elge, Queen of Snakes	RUS	E. Balsia
Embalmer, The	ITA	Marcello Gigante
End of August at the Hotel Ozone, The	CZE	Jan Klusak
Espionage in Tangiers	ITA/SPA	Benedetto Ghiglia
Exterminators, The	FRA	Michel Magne
F.B.I., The (series)	ABC-TV	Sidney Cutner/John Elizalde/Dominic Frontiere/Bronislau Kaper/Richard Markowitz/Duane Tatro

F Troop (series)	ABC-TV	Frank Comstock/Richard LaSalle/William Lava
Fiend with the Electronic Brain, The (Psycho a Go-Go)	TV	Don McGinnis
Fliers, The	NBC-TV	Cyril Mockridge
For the People (series)	CBS-TV	George Kleinsinger
French Without Dressing	CAN	Jean Dore
Get Smart (series)	NBC-TV	Irving Szathmary
Gidget (series)	ABC-TV	Charles Albertine/Dave Grusin/Stu Phillips
Gift of Oscar, The (short)	BEL	Alain Goraguer
Gonks Go Beat	BRI	Robert Richards
Green Acres (series)	CBS-TV	Vic Mizzy
Gulliver's Travels Beyond the Moon	JAP	Milton Delugg
Hank (series)	NBC-TV	Frank Perkins
Hawks and the Sparrows, The	ITA	Ennio Morricone
Hen With the Wrong Chick, The (short)	GER	Gunter Klein
Hogan's Heroes (series)	CBS-TV	Jerry Fielding/Fred Steiner
Honey West (series)	ABC-TV	Joseph Mullendore/ Alfred Perry
I Dream of Jeannie (series)	NBC-TV	Buddy Kaye/Hugo Montenegro/Richard Wess
I Spy (series)	NBC-TV	Carl Brandt
Joachim's Dictionary	FRA	Bernard Parmeggiani
John Forsythe Show, The (series)	NBC-TV	Jeff Alexander/Jerry Fielding
Killers Are Challenged	ITA	Carlo Savina
Kind-Hearted Ant, The (short)	YUG	Miljenko Prohaska
Kiss Kiss, Kill Kill	GER/ITA/YUG	Mladen Gutesha
Kreimhild's Revenge (re-issue)	GER	Rolf Wilhelm
Laredo (series)	NBC-TV	Russell Garcia/Stanley Wilson
Legend of Jesse James, The (series)	ABC-TV	Joseph Hooven
Loner, The (series)	CBS-TV	Jerry Goldsmith/Nelson Riddle/Lalo Schifrin
Lost in Space (series)	CBS-TV	Alexander Courage/ Robert Drasnin/Gerald Fried/Lionel Newman/ Herman Stein/John Williams
Meeting at the Fashion Show	YUG	Tomislav Simovic
Milton the Monster Cartoon, The (series)	ABC-TV	Winston Sharples
Mr. Roberts (series)	NBC-TV	Frank Perkins
Mona McCluskey (series)	NBC-TV	Sonny Burke
My Mother the Car (series)	NBC-TV	Ralph Carmichael

O.K. Crackerby (series)	ABC-TV	Ralph Carmichael
O.S.S. Mission for a Killer	FRA/ITA	Michel Magne
Operation Atlantis	ITA	Teo Usuelli
Operation Poker	ITA	Piero Umiliani
Patrick Stone	CBS-TV	Earle Hagen
Peanuts (series)	CBS-TV	Vince Guaraldi
Please Don't Eat the Daisies (series)	NBC-TV	Jeff Alexander
Psychopaths, The	BRI	Elisabeth Lutyens
Rapture at Two-Forty	NBC-TV	Pete Rugolo
Run for Your Life (series)	NBC-TV	Pete Rugolo
Sandokan the Great	ITA	Giovanni Fusco
Seaway (series)	BRI-TV	Edwin Astley
Secret Agent (series)	CBS-TV	Edwin Astley
Secret Agent Fireball	ITA	Carlo Savina
She Wolf, The (Horrors of the Black Forest)	MEX	Raul Lavista
Siegfried (re-issue)	GER	Rolf Wilhelm
Simon of the Desert	MEX	Raul Lavista
Snails, The	FRA	Alain Gorageur
Space Monster	AI	Marlin Skiles
Stingray (series)	IND-TV	Barry Gray
Sweet Sound of Death, The	SPA	Gregory Segura
Sword of Ali Baba, The	UN	William Lava
Tammy (series)	ABC-TV	Jack Marshall
Tarzan and King Kong	IN	A. Banerjee
Tarzan and the Valley of Gold	AI	Van Alexander
Thrill Killers, The	IND	Henry Price
Trials of O'Brien, The (series)	CBS-TV	Sid Ramin
Two Cosmonauts Against Their Will	ITA/SPA	Lallo Gori
Ultraman	JAP-TV	Kunio Miyauchi
Valentine for Marie, A (short)	IND	Teijo Ito
Wackiest Ship in the Army, The (series)	NBC-TV	Jeff Alexander/Nelson Riddle
Wall, The (short)	YUG	Tomislav Simovic
War Between the Planets, The	ITA	Francesco Lavagnino
War Gods of the Deep	AI	Stanley Black
Who Has Seen the Wind?	ABC-TV	John Green
Who Killed the Jackpot?	ABC-TV	Herschel Burke Gilbert
Wild Wild West, The (series)	CBS-TV	Richard Markowitz/ Richard Shores/ Morton Stevens

1966

A-077--Challenge to the Killers	FRA/ITA	Carlo Savina
Adultery, Italian Style	ITA	Ennio Morricone
Adventurer, The	ITA	Ennio Morricone
Affair in Port Said	ITA	Francesco de Masi
Agent 353, Massacre in the Sun	FRA/ITA/SPA	Piero Umiliani
Agent Z-55: Desperate Mission	ITA	Francesco de Masi
Alice in Wonderland	BRI-TV	Ravi Shankar

Almost Perfect Crime, The	FRA/ITA	Carlo Rustichelli
Ambush at Devil's Gap (serial)	BRI	Albert Elms
America, God's Country	ITA	Francesco Lavagnino/ Armando Trovajoli
Angel (short)	CAN	Leonard Cohen
Angel for Satan, An	ITA	Francesco de Masi
Apocalypse in Berlin	ITA	Bruno Nicolai
Arizona Colt	ITA	Francesco de Masi
Assassin 77, Life or Death	ITA	Giorgio Zinzi
Avengers, The (series)	BRI-TV	Howard Blake/John Dankworth/Laurie Johnson
Ballad for a Thousand Million	ITA	Luis Enrique Bacalov
Baron, The (series)	ABC-TV	Edwin Astley
Batman (series)	ABC-TV	Billy May/Nelson Riddle
Battle of the Mods, The	ITA	Robby Poitevin
Beast of Morocco	BRI	John and Joan Shakespeare
Beckett Affair, The	FRA/ITA	Nora Orlandi
Bible ... in the Beginning, The	FOX	Toshiro Mayuzumi
Birdman (series)	NBC-TV	Ted Nichols
Bitter Bread	ITA	Francesco Lavagnino
Black Box Affair, The	ITA	Gianni Ferrio
Black One, The	ITA	Piero Umiliani
Blade in the Body, The	FRA/ITA	Francesco de Masi
Blue Light, The (series)	ABC-TV	Joseph Mullendore/Lalo Schifrin
Blues for Lovers	FOX	Stanley Black
Bounty Killer, The	ITA	Stelvio Cipriani
Brides of Fu Manchu	BRI	Johnny Douglas
Brilliant Benjamin Boggs	NBC-TV	John Williams
Bubble, The	IND	Bert Shefter/Paul Sawtell
Christmas Memory, A	ABC-TV	Meyer Kupferman
Ciascuno il Suo, A	ITA	Luis Enrique Bacalov
Cisco, El	ITA	Bruno Nicolai
Cliff Dwellers, The	ABC-TV	Lalo Schifrin
Comando de Asesinos	GER/POR/SPA	Jose Luis Alonso
Coup of a Thousand Milliards, A	ITA	Piero Umiliani
Creatures, Les	FRA	Pierre Barbaud
Criminal	ITA	Raymond Full
Cruel Ones, The	ITA	Leo Nichols
Cyborg 2087	IND	Paul Dunlap
Daktari! (series)	CBS-TV	Warren Barker/Harold Gelman/Shelly Manne/ Ruby Raksin
Dangerous Days of Kiowa Jones, The	ABC-TV	Samuel Matlovsky
Danny the Dragon	BRI	Harry Robinson
Dark Shadows (series)	ABC-TV	Robert Cobert
Death Curse of Tartu, The	IND	A. Green/Al Jacobs
Death March (Morte Cammina con Loro, La)	ITA	Lallo Gori

Deguejo	ITA	Alexander Derevitzky
Devil in Love, The	ITA	Armando Trovajoli
Devil's Mistress, The	IND	Billy Allen/Doug Warren
Dick Smart 2/007	ITA	Mario Nascimbene
Dimension 5	IND	Paul Dunlap
Django	ITA	Luis Enrique Bacalov
Django Spara per Primo	ITA	Bruno Nicolai
Dr. Satan	MEX	Luis Hernandez Breton
Dollar a Head, A	ITA	Ennio Morricone
Dollar Between the Teeth, A	ITA	Benedetto Ghiglia
Domani non Siamo piu Qui	ITA	Enzo Fusco
Doomsday Flight	UN	Lalo Schifrin
Double Life of Henry Phyfe, The (series)	ABC-TV	Vic Mizzy
Duel Over the World	ITA	Piero Umiliani
Dynamite in the Pentagon	ITA	Armando Trovajoli
Dyurado	ITA	Gianni Ferrio
Fame Is The Name of the Game	NBC-TV	Benny Carter
Family Affair (series)	CBS-TV	Jeff Alexander/Frank DeVol/Gerald Fried/ Nathan Scott
Fantasia ... 3	SPA	Fernando Garcia Morillo
Fate, The	ITA	Armando Trovajoli
Felony Squad, The (series)	ABC-TV	Pete Rugolo
Fischio al Naso, Il	ITA	Teo Usuelli
Five Men with a Vendetta	ITA	Franco Salina
For a Few Dollars Less	ITA	Marcello Giombini
For a Few Dollars More	ITA	Gianni Ferrio/Ennio Morricone
For a Thousand Dollars a Day	ITA/SPA	Gino Peguri
For Love ... For Magic ...	ITA	Luis Enrique Bacalov
For the Taste of Killing	ITA/SPA	Nico Fidenco
Frankenstein Conquers the World	JAP	Akira Ifukube
Fury at Marrakeck	FRA/ITA	Carlo Savina
Gangster from Brooklyn, The	ITA	Walter Romano
Ghost Goes Gear, The	BRI	John and Joan Shake- speare
Gigantor (short)	IND	Lou Singer
Girl from Bersagliere, The	ITA	Riz Ortolani
Girl from U.N.C.L.E., The (series)	NBC-TV	Jerry Goldsmith/Dave Grusin/Jack Marshall/ Richard Shores
Give a Dog a Bone	IND	George Fraser
Gold and Lead	FRA	Michel Legrand
Goldsnake "Killer's Company"	ITA	Carlo Savina
Golem, Le	FRA	Jean Wiener
Goodbye, Texas	ITA	Anton Garcia Abril
Great Coup of the 7 Golden Men, The	ITA	Armando Trovajoli
Green Hornet, The (series)	ABC-TV	Billy May/Lionel Newman
Guilty or Not Guilty	NBC-TV	Johnny Mandel

Hawk (series)	ABC-TV	Kenyon Hopkins/Nelson Riddle
Heart Trump in Tokyo for O.S.S. 117	FRA/ITA	Michel Magne
Hero, The (series)	NBC-TV	Jack Marshall
Hey, Landlord (series)	NBC-TV	Quincy Jones
Holidays in the Snow	ITA	Mario D'Amici
Holloway's Daughters	NBC-TV	John Williams
How the Grinch Stole Christmas (short)	TV	Albert Hague/Eugene Poddany
How to Steal the Crown of England (Argoman Superdiabolico)	ITA	Piero Umiliani
I Don't Love War, I Love Love	ITA	Riz Ortolani
If All the Women in the World (Operation Paradise)	ITA	Mario Nascimbene
Illusion of Blood	JAP	Toru Takemitsu
Ironside (series)	NBC-TV	Oliver Nelson/Marty Paich
It Happened Here	BRI	Jack Beaver
It's a Long and Difficult Summer, But ... What a Night, My Dears	ITA	Piero Umiliani
It's About Time (series)	CBS-TV	Gerald Fried
James Tont, Operation D.U.E.	FRA/ITA	Bruno Canfora
Jericho (series)	CBS-TV	Jerry Goldsmith
Jerry Land, Spy Hunter	ITA	Piero Umiliani
Joe Dynamite	ITA	Carlo Savina
Kill Johnny Ringo	ITA	Pippo Caruso
Kill or Be Killed	ITA	Carlo Rustichelli
King Kong Show, The (series)	ABC-TV	Maury Laws
Kiss Kiss ... Bang Bang	ITA	Bruno Nicolai
Long Days of Vengeance, The	ITA	Ennio Morricone
Long Night of Veronique, The	ITA	Giorgio Gaslini
Love on a Rooftop (series)	ABC-TV	Warren Barker/Mundell Lowe
Loves of Angelica, The	ITA/SPA	Marcello Gigante
Magic Serpent, The	JAP	Toshiaki Tsushima
Magician of Dreams	SPA	Jose Sola
Maigret in Pigalle	ITA	Armando Trovajoli
Majin, the Hideous Idol	JAP	Akira Ifukube
Man Who Never Was, The (series)	ABC-TV	Frank Cordell
Marine Boy (series)	IND-TV	Norman Gould
Matchless	ITA	Gino Marinuzzi, Jr./ Piero Piccioni
Million Dollars for Seven Assassins, A	ITA	Francesco Lavagnino
Mission: Impossible (series)	CBS-TV	Robert Drasnin/Jerry Fielding/Gerald Fried/ Harry Geller/Benny Golson/Richard Haig/ Kenyon Hopkins/ Richard Markowitz/

		Robert Prince/Lalo Schifrin/Leith Stevens
Monkees, The (series)	NBC-TV	Stu Phillips
Monroes, The	ABC-TV	David Rose
Monroes, The (series)	ABC-TV	Robert Drasnin/Harry Sukman
Monster of Highgate Ponds, The	BRI	Francis Chagrin
Murder, Czech Style	CZE	Zdenek Liska
Naked Evil	BRI	Bernard Ebbinghouse
Navy vs. the Night Monsters, The	IND	Gordon Zahler
New Adventures of Superman, The (animated series)	CBS-TV	Yvette Blais/George Michael
New Three Stooges, The (series)	IND-TV	Paul Horn/Gordon Zahler
Nobody Can Judge Me	ITA	Gianfranco Monaldi
Occasional Wife (series)	NBC-TV	Warren Barker
087 "Mission Apocalypse"	ITA	Francesco de Masi
$100,000 for Lassiter	ITA	Marcello Giombini
Only a Coffin	SPA	Ramon Femeria
Operation Goldman	ITA	Riz Ortolani
Operation Goldseven	ITA	Piero Umiliani
Operation Lady Chaplin	FRA/ITA/SPA	Bruno Nicolai
Operation San Gennaro	ITA	Armando Trovajoli
Operation "Three Yellow Cats"	ITA	Gino Marinuzzi, Jr.
Original TV Adventures of King Kong, The	TV	Maury Laws
Our Husbands	ITA	Armando Trovajoli
Pardon	ITA	Gianfranco Monaldi
Pardon Me, But Are You For or Against?	ITA	Piero Piccioni
Password: Kill Agent Gordon	ITA	Piero Umiliani
Peaceful Nights	ITA	Gino Marinuzzi, Jr.
Picture Mommy Dead	EMB	Robert Drasnin
Pistol for Ringo, A	ITA	Ennio Morricone
Pistols 'n' Petticoats (series)	CBS-TV	Jack Elliott/George Tibbles/Stanley Wilson
Pitiless Colt of the Gringo, The	ITA/SPA	Francesco de Masi
Please Don't Shoot the Cannon	ITA	Angel Oliver Pina
Poppy Is Also a Flower, The	ABC-TV	Georges Auric
Private Matter, A	ITA	Ettore Ballotta
Pruitts of Southampton, The (series)	ABC-TV	Vic Mizzy
Quien Sabe?	ITA	Luis Enrique Bacalov/Ennio Morricone
Ramon, the Mexican	ITA	Felice di Stefano
Rat Patrol, The (series)	ABC-TV	Dominic Frontiere
Red Roses for Angelique	ITA	Francesco Lavagnino
Reluctant Astronaut, The	UN	Vic Mizzy
Reptile, The	FOX	Don Banks
Requiem for a Secret Agent	ITA	Antonio Perez Olea
Rete Piena di Sabbia, Una	ITA	Teo Usuelli

Ringo and Gringo Against All	ITA	Gianni Ferrio
Ringo: The Face of Revenge	ITA	Francesco de Masi
Rita la Zanzara	ITA	Bruno Canfora
River of Dollars, A	ITA	Ennio Morricone
Road West, The (series)	NBC-TV	Leonard Rosenman
Rojo, El	ITA	Benedetto Ghiglia
Rounders, The (series)	ABC-TV	Jeff Alexander
Run, Buddy, Run (series)	CBS-TV	Jerry Fielding
Scalplock	ABC-TV	Richard Markowitz
Scandal, The	ITA	Ralph Ferraro
Seasons of Our Love, The	ITA	Carlo Rustichelli
Secret	ITA	Piero Umiliani
Seven Golden Women Against Two 07s	ITA	Felice di Stefano
Seven Wives for the McGregors	ITA/SPA	Ennio Morricone
Seventh Floor, The	ITA	Teo Usuelli
Shane (series)	ABC-TV	Jerry Fielding
She Freak	IND	Billy Allen
Sheriff All in Gold, A	ITA	Nora Orlandi
Shiver of Skin, A	ITA	Stefano Torossi
Singapore Zero Hour	ITA	Carlo Savina
Snow Queen, The	RUS	M. Simonyan
Space Ghost (series)	CBS-TV	Ted Nichols
Space Kidettes (series)	NBC-TV	Ted Nichols
Special Code	ITA	Riz Ortolani
Spies Kill Silently	ITA/SPA	Francesco di Masi
Spies Love Flowers	ITA	Francesco Lavagnino/ Armando Trovajoli
Spy Spying	ITA	Federigo Martinez Tudo
Spy Who Came from the Sea, The	ITA	Franco Pisano
Star Trek (series)	NBC-TV	Alexander Courage/ George Duning/Gerald Fried/Wilbur Hatch/ Sol Kaplan/Fred Steiner
Starblack	ITA	Benedetto Ghiglia
Sting of Death, The	IND	Al Jacobs/Lon Norman
Story of a Night, The	ITA	Armando Trovajoli
Stroke of a Thousand Million	ITA	Piero Umiliani
Sugar Colt	ITA	Luis Enrique Bacalov
Summer	ITA	Gianni Boncompagni
Superargo vs. Diabolicus	ITA	Franco Pisano
T.H.E. Cat (series)	NBC-TV	Lalo Schifrin
Tamer of Wild Horses (short)	YUG	Tomislav Simovic
Tammy Grimes Show, The (series)	ABC-TV	Warren Barker
Target for Killing, A	ITA	Marcello Giombini
Tarzan (pilot)	NBC-TV	Jerry Fielding
Tarzan (series)	NBC-TV	Walter Greene/Nelson Riddle
Technique for a Massacre	ITA	Piero Umiliani

Technique of a Murder	ITA	Robby Poitevin
Terrornauts, The	BRI	Elizabeth Lutyens
Testadirapa	ITA	Piero Umiliani
That Girl (series)	ABC-TV	Warren Barker/Harry Geller/Earle Hagen/ Walter Scharf
Three Golden Men	ITA	Marcello Giombini
Three Violent Nights	ITA	Franco Pisano
Time of Massacre	ITA	Lallo Gori
Time Tunnel, The (series)	ABC-TV	Robert Drasnin/George Duning/Joseph Mullen- dore/Lyn Murray/ Lionel Newman/John Williams
Tom and Jerry Show, The (series)	CBS-TV	Scott Bradley/Carl Brandt/Eugene Poddany
Tom of T.H.U.M.B.	TV	Maury Laws
Top Crack	ITA	Riz Ortolani
Two Men of the Mafia Against Al Capone	ITA/SPA	Piero Umiliani
2 + 5: Mission Hydra	ITA	Nico Fidenco
Two Sanculotti, The	ITA	Piero Umiliani
Two Sons of Ringo, The	ITA	Piero Umiliani
Vagabond Hero	ITA/SPA	Francesco de Masi
Vaya con Dios Gringo	ITA	Felice di Stefano
Velvet Hand	ITA	Franco Salina
Voyage of the Brigantine Yankee	TV	Elmer Bernstein
Wake Up and Kill	ITA	Ennio Morricone
War of the Giants	ITA/SPA	Marcello Gigante
War of the Monsters	JAP	Chuji Kinoshita
Weekend at Dunkirk	FOX	Maurice Jarre
When the Skin Burns	ITA	Bruno Chiavegato/ Harumi Ibe/Oscar Pacelli/Michiaki Watanabe
Where's Everett?	CBS-TV	Frank DeVol
Witch in Love, A	ITA	Luis Enrique Bacalov
Witch Without a Broom, A	SPA	Gregory Segura
Woman and the General, The	ITA	Ennio Morricone
You'll See Me Come Back	ITA	Ennio Morricone
Your Son and Brother	RUS	Pavel Bachmetiv
Zorro the Rebel	ITA	Francesco Lavagnino

1967

Accidental Family (series)	NBC-TV	Earle Hagen
Alaska	NGS	Walter Scharf
Alberto Giacometti (short)	IND	Arnold Gamson
Amazing Three, The (series)	IND-TV	Nobuyoshi Koshibe
Ambushers, The	COL	Hugo Montenegro
American Vision, The (short)	EBE	Frank Ledlie Moore

Arizona and Its Natural Resources   IND   Gene Kauer/Douglas
  (short)   Lackey
Art Scene USA (short)   IND   Harold Fargerman
Atomic Power Today (short)   IND   Don Elliot
Autumn Flight (short)   IND   Stuart Scharf
Bang! (short)   BRI   Johnny Hawksworth
Behind the Spaceman (short)   IND   Walter Raim
Berserk!   COL   Patrick John Scott
Between the Nets   FRA/ITA/SPA Jacques Lacome

Bit of Immortality, A   HUN   Gyorgy Ranki
Blood Demon, The   GER   Peter Thomas
Bogart   NBC-TV   Nelson Riddle
Borgia Stick, The   UN   Kenyon Hopkins
Brief Encounters   RUS   Oleg Karavaichuk/
                                                  Valdimir Visotski
Brookhaven Spectrum (short)   IND   Frank Lewin
Caldron of Blood   SPA   Jose Luis Navarro
Captain Nice (series)   NBC-TV   Vic Mizzy
Captain Scarlet and the   IND-TV   Barry Gray
  Mysterons (series)
Carol   CBS-TV   Vic Mizzy
Champions, The   BRI-TV   Edwin Astley/Albert
                                                  Elms
Charles Burchfield--Fifty Years   IND   Robert Muszynski/
  of His Art (short)   Wallace Rushkin
China: The Roots of Madness   EBE   Harry Freedman
Christ Is Born   IND   Rayburn Wright
Cimarron Strip (series)   CBS-TV   Maurice Jarre/Morton
                                                  Stevens
Code Name: Heraclitus   NBC-TV   Johnny Mandel/John
                                                  Williams
Commissar   RUS   Alfred Schnitke
Computer Glossary, A (short)   IND   Elmer Bernstein
Coronet Blue (series)   CBS-TV   Laurence Rosenthal
Cowboy (short)   IND   Laurindo Almeida
Cowboys in Africa (series)   BRI-TV   Malcolm Arnold/George
                                                  Bruns
Cyborg 009--Underground Duel   JAP   Taichiro Kasugi
Disembodied, The   AA   Marlin Skiles
Dr. Leakey and the Dawn of Man   NGS   Leonard Rosenman
Dorellik   ITA   Franco Pisano
End of the Trail   MHF   Robert Russell Bennett
Equinox   IND   John Caper
Face of Genius, The   IND   Teo Macero
Fantabulous Inc.   ITA   Sandro Brugnolini
Fantastic Four, The (series)   ABC-TV   Hoyt Curtin/Dean Elliott
Further Perils of Laurel & Hardy,   FOX   John Parker
  The
Garrison's Gorillas (series)   ABC-TV   Leonard Rosenman
Gentle Ben (series)   CBS-TV   Samuel Matlowsky/Harry
                                                  Sukman

George of the Jungle (series)	ABC-TV	Sheldon Allman/Stan Worth
Glorious Times in the Spessart	GER	Franz Grothe
Goldface, the Fantastic Superman	ITA	Piero Umiliani
Good Morning World (series)	CBS-TV	Dave Grusin
Grand Duel in Magic	JAP	Toshiaki Tsushima
Gungala, the Virgin of the Jungle	ITA	Francesco Lavagnino
Guns of Will Sonnett, The (series)	ABC-TV	Earle Hagen/Fred Steiner
Happeners, The	IND-TV	Bob Bower
Happiness Is a Three-Legged Dog (short)	AUT	Ian Clarkson
He and She (series)	CBS-TV	Jerry Fielding
Herculoids, The (animated series)	CBS-TV	Ted Nichols
Hidden World, The	EBE	Ruby Raksin/Lalo Schifrin
High Chaparral, The (series)	NBC-TV	David Rose/Harry Sukman
Hole, The (Dupkata)	BUL	Simeon Pironkov
Hondo (series)	ABC-TV	Richard Markowitz
How I Spent My Summer Vacation (Deadly Roulette)	UN	Lalo Schifrin
How to Make a Doll	IND	Larry Wellington
How We Stole the Atomic Bomb	ITA	Lallo Gori
Invaders, The (series)	ABC-TV	Dominic Frontiere/Duane Tatro
Ironside	NBC-TV	Quincy Jones
Ironside (series)	NBC-TV	Oliver Nelson/Marty Paich
Island Called Ellis, The	MHF	Robert Russell Bennett
Island of the Burning Doomed	BRI	Malcolm Lockyer
It's a Dog's World	WOL	Gary Geld/Peter Udell
Jack and the Witch	JAP	Seiichiro Uno
Jet Pink	UA	Walter Greene
Journey to the Beginning of Time	CZE	E. F. Burian
Journey to the Center of the Earth (animated series)	ABC-TV	Gordon Zahler
Judd, for the Defense (series)	ABC-TV	Alexander Courage/George Duning/Harry Geller/Lionel Newman/Leith Stevens
Legend of Custer, The (series)	ABC-TV	Elmer Bernstein/Richard Markowitz/Joseph Mullendore/Leith Stevens
Legend of the Skylark, The (short)	RUM	Dimitru Capoianu
Life in the Balance (short)	MTP	David Diamond
Longest Hundred Miles, The	UN	Franz Waxman
Love Is a Many-Splendored Thing (series)	CBS-TV	Eddie Layton
Mad Monster Party, The	EMB	Maury Laws
Madcap Island (Hyokkori Hyotan Jima)	JAP	Seiichiro Uno

Magnificence in Trust	IND	Albert Glasser
Majin Strikes Again	JAP	Akira Ifukube
Make Room for Daddy	NBC-TV	Earle Hagen
Mannix (series)	CBS-TV	Kenyon Hopkins/Lalo Schifrin
Maya (series)	NBC-TV	Hans Salter
Miraculous Virgin (Panna Zazranica)	CZE	Ilja Zeljenka
Mr. Terrific (series)	CBS-TV	Gerald Fried
Monster from a Prehistoric Planet (Gappa)	JAP	Seitaro Omori
Mothers-in-Law, The (series)	NBC-TV	Wilbur Hatch
N.Y.P.D. (series)	ABC-TV	Charles Gross
Omegans, The	BRI-TV	Albert Elms
Outsider, The	NBC-TV	Pete Rugolo
Pancho (short)	MTP	Sol Kaplan
Pearl Harbor	NBC	Joe Belasco
Pink Blueprint, The (short)	UA	William Lava
Post No Bills! (short)	IND	Charles Gross
Prehistoric Women	FOX	Carlo Martelli
Privilege	UN	Mike Leander
Rango (series)	ABC-TV	Carl Brandt/Earle Hagen
Reason Nobody Hardly Ever Seen a Fat Outlaw in the Old West Is as Follows:, The	NBC-TV	Johnny Mandel
Reflections (short)	ABC	William Loose
Return of the Giant Majin, The	JAP	Akira Ifukube
Return of the Giant Monsters, The (Gammera vs. Gaos)	JAP	Tadashi Yamaguchi
Return of the Gunfighter	MGM	Hans J. Salter
Rififi in Amsterdam	ITA/SPA	Piero Umiliani
Rocket Robin Hood (series)	IND-TV	Winston Sharples
Saint, The (series)	BRI-TV	Edwin Astley
Scorpio Letters, The	MGM	Dave Grusin
Second Hundred Years, The (series)	ABC-TV	George Duning
Secret of the Ninja	JAP	Harumi Ibe
Seventh Continent, The	YUG	Tomislav Simovic
Shazzam! (series)	CBS-TV	Ted Nichols
Sighet (short)	IND	Jimmy Guiffre
Sky of Our Childhood, The	RUS	T. Yermatov
Soldier in Love	NBC-TV	Bernard Green
Speed Racer (series)	JAP-TV	Tatsuo Koshibe
Spirits of the Dead (sequence)	AI	Diego Masson/Jean Prodromides/Nino Rota
Strange Case of Dr. Jekyll and Mr. Hyde, The	TV	Robert Cobert
Stranger on the Run	UN	Leonard Rosenman
Summer Children, The	IND	Richard Markowitz

Symmetry (short)	IND	Gene Forrell
Terror in the Jungle	CRO	Les Baxter/Stan Hoffman
Theatre of Mr. and Mrs. Kabal, The	FRA	Avenir de Monfried
Thing of Beauty, A	IND	Ulysses Kay
Those Fantastic Flying Fools (Rocket to the Moon/Blast-Off)	AI	Patrick John Scott
Time of the West (short)	IND	Robert Wykes
To Be a Man	IND	Paul Butterfield
Transportation USA (short)	IND	Don Elliot
Ultraman	JAP-TV	Rohru Fuyuki
Vampire Women, The	FRA	Yvon Geraud/Francois Tusques
Vergette Making a Pot (short)	IND	Teiji Ito
Winchester '73	UN	Sol Kaplan
Wings of Fire	UN	Samuel Matlovsky
Wishing Machine, The	CZE	William Buckovy
X from Outer Space	JAP	Taku Izumi
Yankee Sails Across Europe	TV	Elmer Bernstein
Year Toward Tomorrow, A	IND	Frank Lewin
Z-7 Operation Rembrandt	ITA	Aldo Piga

1968

Adam-12 (series)	NBC-TV	Frank Comstock
Adios Gringo	FRA/ITA/SPA	Benedetto Ghiglia
Agent Sigma 3--Mission Goldwather	ITA/SPA	Manuel Carra
America and Americans	NBC	Norman Dello Joio
American Image, The	NBC	Glen Paxton
Americans on Everest	NGS	Franco Ferrara
Aroused	IND	Edmund Mitchell
Assignment Earth (series)	NBC-TV	Alexander Courage
Asterix and Cleopatra	BEL/FRA	Gerard Calvi
Banana Splits Adventure Hour, The (series)	NBC-TV	Hoyt Curtin/Jack Eskew
Baptism	HUN	Andras Szollosy
Bed Sitting Room, The	BRI	Ken Thorne
Between the Glass and the Lip	YUG	Tomislav Simovic
Big People--Little People (short)	IND	Peter Schickele
Blondie (series)	CBS-TV	Bernard Green
Bloodthirsty Fairy, The (short)	BEL	Paul Lambert
Bondage (Kotolek)	HUN	Imre Vincze
Boston Strangler, The	FOX	Lionel Newman
Bride from Hades, The	JAP	Sei Ikeno
Case of the Two Beauties, The	SPA	Fernando Garcia Morillo
Castle of Fu Manchu, The (Assignment Istanbul)	BRI/GER/ITA/SPA	Carlo Camilleri/Malcolm Shelby
Castle of Lust	GER	Jerry van Rooyen

Chamber of Fear	MEX	Alice Uretta
Champions, The (series)	BRI-TV	Edwin Astley/Albert Elms/Robert Farnon
Chinese and Mini-Skirts, The	GER/ITA/SPA	Piero Umiliani
City: Time of Decision, The (short)	IND	Bernardo Segall
Clowns on the Wall	HUN	Zdenko Tamassy
Companions in Nightmare	UN	Bernard Herrmann
Competition	CZE	Jiri Slitr
Day of the Owl	FRA/ITA	Giovanni Fusco
Death by Hanging	JAP	Hikaru Hayashi
Detective, The	FOX	Jerry Goldsmith
Diabolic Pact, The	MEX	Gustavo Cesar Carreon
Dirty Story of the West, A	ITA	Francesco de Masi
Doris Day Show, The (series)	CBS-TV	Jimmie Haskell/William Loose
Draw Me a Telephone (short)	IND	Michael Small
Emperor Lee	HK	Yu Lun
Escape to Mindanao	UN	Lyn Murray
Eve, the Savage Venus	ITA	Roberto Pregadio
Fables from Hans Christian Andersen	JAP	Seiichiro Uno
Face of Eve, The	BRI	Malcolm Lockyer
Family Planning (short)	DIS	Buddy Baker
Fando and Lys (Tar Babies)	MEX	Pepe Avila
Fantastic Ballad (short)	YUG	Bojan Adamic
Fantastic Voyage, The (series)	ABC-TV	Gordon Zahler
Flat, The (Byt)	CZE	Zdenek Liska
48 Hours to Acapulco	GER	Roland Kovac
Fusion (short)	IND	Alwin Nikolais
Ghost and Mrs. Muir, The (series)	NBC-TV	Warren Barker/George Greeley/David Grusin
Godzilla vs. the Sea Monster (Ebirah)	JAP	Masaru Sato
Good Guys, The (series)	CBS-TV	Jerry Fielding
Grand Ceremonial, The	FRA	Jacques Arel
Grand Jete (short)	IND	Dave Brubeck
Grizzly!	WOL	Jerome Moross
Guardian of the Atom (short)	IND	Pim Jacobs
Hall of Kings	ABC	Clinton Elliot
Harem	FRA/GER/ITA	Ennio Morricone
Hawaii Five-O (series)	CBS-TV	Bruce Broughton/ Richard Clements/ James di Pasquale/ Don B. Ray/Pete Rugolo/Morton Stevens/ Duane Tatro
He Walked Through the Fields	ISR	Alexander (Sacha) Argov
Heidi	TV	John Williams
Here Come the Brides (series)	ABC-TV	Warren Barker/Hugo Montenegro/Shorty Rogers/Paul Sawtell

Here's Lucy (series)	CBS-TV	Marl Young
Home Country, USA	NBC	Charlie Byrd
Hour of the Wolf	SWE	Lars Johan Werle
House of Evil	MEX	Alice Uretta
How to Steal an Airplane (Only One Day Left Before Tomorrow)	UN	Pete Rugolo
Istanbul Express	UN	Oliver Nelson
Journey to the Unknown	ABC-TV	David Lindup/Harry Robinson
Julia (series)	NBC-TV	Van Alexander/Elmer Bernstein
Kaidan Botan Doro	JAP	Shigeru Ikeno
King of Kong Island	ITA-TV	Roberto Pregadio
Kiss and Kill	SPA	Daniel J. White/Barney Wilen
Kiss Me, Monster	SPA	Fernando Garcia Morillo
Lancer (series)	CBS-TV	Hugo Friedhofer/Joseph Mullendore
Land of the Giants (series)	ABC-TV	Lionel Newman/John Williams
Laura	ABC-TV	David Raksin
Legend of the Boy and the Eagle, The	DIS	Franklyn Marks
Living Skeleton, The	JAP	Noburu Nishiyama
Long Shadow, The (short)	IND	Gene Kauer/Douglas Lackey
Lost Continent, The	FOX	Gerard Schurmann
Love Mates	SWE	Torbjorn Lundquist
Luana, Daughter of the Virgin Forest	ITA	Stelvio Cipriani
Magic Guitar, The	PHI	Danny Holmsen
Magic Ring, The (short)	IND	Michael Small
Malenka	ITA	Carlo Savina
Man in a Suitcase (series)	ABC-TV	Albert Elms
Manhunter, The	UN	Benny Carter
Mantis in Lace	IND	Frank Coe
Mayberry R.F.D. (series)	CBS-TV	Earle Hagen
Mod Squad (series)	ABC-TV	Earle Hagen/Billy May/ Shorty Rogers
Monument to the Dream	IND	Robert Wykes
Morianna--I the Body	SWE	Georg Riedel
Name of the Game, The (series)	NBC-TV	Dominic Frontiere/Dave Grusin/Stanley Wilson
National Gallery of Art, The	MHF	George Kleinsinger
Negresco	GER	Klaus Doldinger
New Adventures of Huckleberry Finn, The (series)	NBC-TV	Hoyt Curtin/Ted Nichols
Night of the Bloody Apes, The (Horror and Sex)	MEX	Antonio Dias Conde
Night of the Living Dead	IND	William Loose

Nitakayama Nobore	JAP	Kingo Someya/Sadai Wakemiya
Now You See It, Now You Don't	UN	Lyn Murray
100 Monsters	JAP	Ghumei Watanabe
Opera Cordis (short)	YUG	Tomislav Simovic
Opus Op (short)	IND	Teo Macero
Outcasts, The (series)	ABC-TV	Hugo Montenegro
Outsider, The (series)	NBC-TV	Pete Rugolo/Stanley Wilson
Petzi (short)	BEL	Paul Uyttebroeck
Prescription: Murder	NBC-TV	Dave Grusin
Primordium (short)	PYR	Ravi Shankar
Prisoner, The (series)	CBS-TV	Albert Elms
Prisoner, The	BRI-TV	Ron Grainer
Quality and Promise (short)	IND	Robert Wykes
Quiet Revolution (short)	IND	Jaime Mendoza Nava
Robert Scott and the Race for the South Pole	ABC	Ulpio Minucci
Santo vs. the Blue Demon in Atlantis	MEX	Gustavo Cesar Carreon
Satanik	SPA	Manuel Parada
Secret Diary of a Minor	ITA	Giovanni Marchetti
Seventh Satellite, The	RUS	I. Shvarc
Shadow on the Land	COL	Sol Kaplan
Shadow Over Elveron	UN	Leonard Rosenman
She-Devils on Wheels	IND	Hershell Gordon Lewis/ Robert Lewis
Slave of Paradise, The	ITA	Nico Fidenco
Smugglers, The	UN	Lyn Murray
Snake People, The (Isle of the Dead)	MEX	Enrico Cabiati/Alice Uretta
Snow Ghost, The	JAP	Akira Ifukube
So Goes the Day	HUN	Lehel Szorenyi
Solitary Man Attacks, The	FRA	Bernard Gerard
Something for a Lonely Man	UN	Jack Marshall
Sophia!	ABC-TV	Jack Tillar
Sound of Anger, The	NBC-TV	Pete Rugolo
Split Second to an Epitaph	UN	Quincy Jones
Spook Warfare	JAP	Shigeru Ikeno
Stain on His Conscience, A (short)	YUG	Tomislav Simovic
Succubus	GER	Friedrich Gulda/Jerry van Rooyen
Sunshine Patriot, The	UN	Stanley Wilson
Super VIP's, The	ITA	Franco Godi
Tarzan and the Jungle Boy	PAR	William Loose
Thanksgiving Visitor, The	ABC-TV	Meyer Kupferman
Thunderbirds (series)	IND-TV	Barry Gray
Travels with Charley	NBC-TV	Rod McKuen

Tunnel Under the World, The	ITA	Claudio Calzolari
Twiddle Twaddle (short)	GER/YUG	Tomislav Simovic
Ugliest Girl in Town, The (series)	ABC-TV	George Romanis
Valley of Bees, The	CZE	Zdenek Liska
Voice in the City, A (short)	IND	Charlie Byrd
Wacky Races, The (series)	CBS-TV	Hoyt Curtin
Walls (Falak)	HUN	Mikis Theodorakis
War of the Insects (Genocide)	JAP	Shunsuke Kikuchi
Weapons of Gordon Parks, The (short)	MHF	Gordon Parks
Wild 90	IND	Charlie Brown
Winged World, The	NGS	Gerald Fried
Winter Geyser (short)	PYR	Buddy Colette
Women Who Care (short)	IND	Charles Fox
World of Horror (sequence)	POL	A. Karzynska/Andrezaj Lapicki/Jarzy Maksymiuck
Wyeth Phenomenon, The (short)	CBS	Glenn Paxton
Yellow Submarine, The	UA	George Martin
Young, the Evil and the Savage, The	ITA	Carlo Savina

1969

Adam 2	GER	Joseph Anton Riedl
Admiral Yamamoto	JAP	Masaru Sato
Aladdin and the Wonderful Lamp	FRA	Fred Freed
Any Second Now	UN	Leonard Rosenman
Arena	HUN	Ivan Patrachich
Astro-Zombies, The	IND	Nicholas Carras
Attack of the Monsters	JAP	Shunsuke Kikuchi
Ballad of Andy Crocker, The	IND	Billy May
Bill Cosby Show, The (series)	NBC-TV	Quincy Jones
Black Lizard	JAP	Isao Tomita
Boys of Paul Street, The	FOX	Emil Petrovics
Bracken's World (series)	NBC-TV	Warren Barker/Robert Drasnin/Jack Elliott/ Harry Geller/Lionel Newman/David Rose
Brady Bunch, The (series)	ABC-TV	Frank De Vol/David Rose
Brain, The	PAR	Georges Delerue
Brownout	PHI	Tito Arevalo
Caldi Amori di una Minorenne, I	ITA/SPA	Gianni Ferrio
Captain Nemo and the Underwater City	MGM	Wally Stott
Cattanooga Cats, The (series)	ABC-TV	Hoyt Curtin
Celestina, La	SPA	Angel Arteaga
Computer Free-for-All	JAP	Naozumi Yamamoto
Courtship of Eddie's Father, The (series)	ABC-TV	George Aliceson Tipton

Curious Female, The	IND	Stu Phillips
Curse of the Blood	JAP	Hajime Kaburage
D.A.: Murder One, The	NBC-TV	Frank Comstock
Dastardly and Muttley and Their Flying Machines (series)	CBS-TV	Hoyt Curtin
Daughter of the Mind	FOX	Robert Drasnin
Deadlock	NBC-TV	Stanley Wilson
Debbie Reynolds Show, The (series)	NBC-TV	Jack Marshall/Tony Romero
Desperate Mission (Joaquin Murieta)	FOX	Jerry Goldsmith
Destiny of a Spy	BRI	Ron Grainer
Destroy All Monsters	JAP	Akira Ifukube
Doc (series)	NBC-TV	Vic Mizzy
Doctors, The (series)	NBC-TV	Richard Clements
Don't Push, I'll Charge When I'm Ready	UN	Lyn Murray
Dragnet	UN	Lyn Murray
Drifting Avenger	JAP	Masao Yagi
Dudley Do-Right Show, The (series)	ABC-TV	Sheldon Allman/Stan Worth
Emperor and a General, The	JAP	Masaru Sato
Escarlotta	PHI	Danny Holmsen
Fables from Hans Christian Andersen	JAP	Seiichiro Koyama
Father, Dear Father (series)	BRI-TV	Gordon Franks
Fear No Evil	UN	Billy Goldenberg
Final Winner?, The	JAP	Soji Yokouchi
Forsyte Saga, The (series)	BRI-TV	Marcus Dods
Fountain of Love	AUS	Claudius Alzner
Fox With Nine Tails, The	JAP	Shigeru Ikeno
Gamera vs. Viras	JAP	Kenjiro Hirose
Gangster VIP	JAP	Naozumi Yamamoto
Genii (Devils)	CZE	Ilja Zeljenka
Gidget Grows Up	ABC-TV	Shorty Rogers
Girl Who Couldn't Say No, The	FOX	Riz Ortolani
Goke, Body Snatcher from Hell	JAP	Shunsuke Kikuchi
Golden Mob, The	JAP	Harumi Ibe
Governor and J.J., The (series)	CBS-TV	Jerry Fielding
Guru, The	FOX	Ustad Vilaya Khan
Hardy Boys, The (series)	ABC-TV	Gordon Zahler
Haunted Castle, The	JAP	Chumei Watanabe
Honeymoon with a Stranger	FOX	Marc Bucci
Hot Wheels (series)	ABC-TV	Jack Fascinato
House of the Sleeping Virgins, The	JAP	Shigeru Ikeno
Immortal, The	ABC-TV	Dominic Frontiere
In Name Only	COL	Sunset Editorial
In the Dead of Night	ABC-TV	Robert Cobert
Industrial Spy	JAP	Masao Yagi
Invasion of the Body Stealers, The	BRI	Reg Tilsley

Invincible Invisible Man, The	ITA	Carlo Savina
Invocation of My Demon Brother (short)	BRI	Mick Jagger
Kill!	JAP	Masaru Sato
King Kong Escapes	JAP	Akira Ifukube
Kuroneko	JAP	Hikaru Hayashi
Little Norse Prince	JAP	Yoshio Mamiya
Lonely Profession, The	UN	Pete Rugolo
Love, American Style (series)	ABC-TV	Charles Fox
Mad Doctor of Blood Island	PHI	Tito Arevalo
Magic Samurai, The	PHI	Paquito Toledo
Marcus Welby, M.D. (series)	ABC-TV	Leonard Rosenman
Masque of the Red Death, The (short)	YUG	Branimir Sakac
Mayhem (Scream, Baby, Scream)	IND	"The Charles Austin Group"
Medical Center (series)	CBS-TV	John Parker/George Romanis/Lalo Schifrin/ Philip Springer
Men of Action Meet Women of Dracula	PHI	"Britz"
Mind of Mr. Soames, The	COL	Michael Dress
Mr. Deeds Goes to Town (series)	ABC-TV	Warren Barker/Shorty Rogers
Moju (Blind Beast, The)	JAP	Hiraku Hayashi
Monk, The	ABC-TV	Earle Hagen
Movement, Movement	BRI/FRA	Tony Meehan
My Friend Tony (series)	NBC-TV	Earle Hagen
My World ... and Welcome to It (series)	NBC-TV	Danny Arnold/Warren Barker
New People, The (series)	ABC-TV	Earle Hagen
New Phil Silvers Show, The (series)	CBS-TV	Harry Geller
Night Gallery	UN	Billy Goldenberg
Night Guy	JAP	Masao Yagi
Operation Negligee	JAP	Hikaru Hayashi
Our Lady of Compassion	BRA	Sergio Bicardo
Over-the-Hill Gang, The	TV	Hugo Friedhofer
Pauk (short)	YUG	Andelko Klobucar
Perils of Penelope Pitstop, The (series)	CBS-TV	Hoyt Curtin/Ted Nichols
Pigeon, The	ABC-TV	Billy May
Pink Panther, The (series)	NBC-TV	Doug Goodwin/Walter Greene/William Lava
Pioneer Spirit	NBC-TV	Vic Mizzy
Psycho Lover, The	IND	Gary Lee Mell
Queen and I, The (series)	CBS-TV	Jerry Fielding
Recess (short)	IND	Luther Henderson
Return of the Filthy Seven, The	JAP	Koichi Sakata/Naozumi Yamamoto
Revenge of the Vampire Women, The	MEX	Gustavo Cesar Carreon

Room 222 (series)	ABC-TV	Jerry Goldsmith/Benny Golson/Richard La Salle/Lionel Newman
Run a Crooked Mile	UN	Mike Leander
Scabies (short)	YUG	Tomislav Simovic
Scooby-Doo, Where Are You? (series)	CBS-TV	Hoyt Curtin/Paul DeKorte/Ted Nichols
Scoundrels, The (Cannales, Los)	MEX	Gustavo Cesar Carreon
Secret World, The	FOX	Antoine Duhamel
Sesame Street (series)	PBS-TV	Joe Raposo
Set This Town on Fire (Profane Comedy, The)	UN	Pete Rugolo
Seven in Darkness	PAR	Mark Bucci
Sex Check, The	JAP	Tadashi Yamauchi
Silent Gun, The	PAR	Leith Stevens
Silent Night, Lonely Night	UN	Billy Goldenberg
Singapore, Singapore	SPA	Antoine Duhamel
Skyhawks, The (series)	ABC-TV	Jack Fascinato
Smokey the Bear Show, The (series)	ABC-TV	Maury Laws
Son of Godzilla	JAP	Masaru Sato
Space Giants (series)	JAP-TV	Naozumi Yamamoto
Spider Elephant, The (short)	FRA	Bernard Parmeggiani
Spider-Man (series)	ABC-TV	Ray Ellis
Spy Killer, The	BRI	Philip Martel
Strange Case of Dr. Faustus, The	SPA	S. Pueyo
Then Came Bronson	NBC-TV	George Duning
Then Came Bronson (series)	NBC-TV	George Duning/Richard Shores
They Call It Murder	FOX	Robert Drasnin
Three Seconds to Zero Hour	JAP	Seitaro Omori
Three's a Crowd	COL	Boyce and Hart
Tiger! Tiger!	NBC-TV	Harry Sukman
To Rome With Love (series)	CBS-TV	Frank DeVol
Trial Run	UN	Stanley Wilson
U.M.C. (Operation Heartbeat)	CBS-TV	George Romanis/Lalo Schifrin
Under the Yum Yum Tree	NBC-TV	Johnny Mandel
Wake Me When the War Is Over	TV	Fred Steiner
Wasted Sunday, A	CZE	Jiri Sust
We Are All Demons!	DEN	Finn Savery
Where the Heart Is (series)	CBS-TV	Eddie Layton
Whole World Is Watching, The	NBC-TV	Pete Rugolo
Witchcraft '70	ITA	Piero Umiliani
Witchcraft Through the Ages (reissue)	IND	Daniel Humair/Jean-Luc Ponty
Wolf Men, The	TV	Elmer Bernstein
Young Lawyers, The	ABC-TV	Lalo Schifrin
Yukionna	JAP	Akira Ifukube
Zatoichi Challenged	JAP	Akira Ifukube

1970

All My Children (series)	ABC-TV	Sid Ramin/James Reichert /Teri Smith
Alliance (Wedding Ring, The)	FRA	Gilbert Amy
Along Came a Spider	FOX	David Rose
Angel Levine, The	UA	William Eaton
Anti-Climax	MEX	Jimmie Nichol/G. Gas
Aoom	SPA	Alfonso Sainz
Aquarians, The	UN	Lalo Schifrin
Aquasex	IND	Richard LaSalle
Archie Comedy Hour, The (series)	CBS-TV	George Blais/Jeff Michael
Arnie (series)	CBS-TV	Harry Geller
Barefoot in the Park (series)	ABC-TV	Charles Fox/J.J. Johnson
Berlin Affair	UN	Francis Lai
Beyond Love and Evil	FRA	Jean-Claude Pelletier
Black Water Gold	TV	Mike Curb/Jerry Steiner
Blind Woman's Curse, The	JAP	Hajimi Kubarasi
Blood of the Vampires (Dugo No Vampires)	PHI	Tito Arevalo
Brazil Year 2000	BRA	Caetano Valeso Capinan/ Rogerio Duprat/ Gilberto Gil
Breakout	UN	Shorty Rogers
Brotherhood of the Bell, The	TV	Jerry Goldsmith
Bugaloos, The (series)	NBC-TV	Charles Fox
But I Don't Want to Get Married!	TV	George Duning
Carter's Army	TV	Fred Steiner
Castle for a Young Hangman, A	CZE	Zdenek Liska
Challenge, The	FOX	Harry Geller
Cherry Blossoms in the Air--The Suicide Raiders--Oh, Buddies!	JAP	Masayoshi Ikeda
City of Beasts	JAP	Masaru Sato
Clear and Present Danger, A	UN	Billy Goldenberg
Comeback Trail, The	IND	Igo Cantor
Cover Me, Babe	FOX	Fred Karlin
Creature Called Man, The	JAP	Mitsuhiko Satoh
Crimson Bat-Oichi: Wanted, Dead or Alive	JAP	Takeo Watanabe
Crowhaven Farm	TV	Robert Drasnin
Curious Dr. Humpp, The	ARG	V. Buchino
Curse of the Vampires	PHI	Tiro Arevalo
Cutter's Trail	CBS	John Parker
Dan August (series)	ABC-TV	Dave Grusin/Don Vincent
David Copperfield	BRI	Malcolm Arnold
Dawn of Judo	JAP	Yukata Makino
Deadly Odor, The	CZE	Lubos Fiser
Devil Woman	PHI	d'Amarillo
Dial Hotline	ABC-TV	Oliver Nelson

Disciple of Satan	PHI	Manuel Franco
Doctor Dolittle (series)	NBC-TV	Doug Goodwin/Arthur Leonardi/Eric Rogers
Dr. Frankenstein on Campus	CAN	Paul Hoffert/Skip Prokop
Doctors Wear Scarlet	BRI	Bobby Richards
Egghead's Robot	BRI	Gordon Langford
Evening with Edgar Allan Poe, An	TV	Les Baxter
Females, The	GER	Peter Thomas
Fools	CIN	Shorty Rogers
Foreign Exchange	BRI	Philip Martell
Frisson des Vampires (Sex and the Vampire)	FRA	George Acanthus
God Bless the Children	NBC-TV	Roger Kellaway
Hamlet	NBC-TV	John Addison
Hansel and Gretel Get Lost in the Woods	GER	Attila Zoller
Happiness Is a Warm Clue	UN	Robert Prince
Happy Days (series)	CBS-TV	Jack Elliott/Allyn Ferguson
Harlem Globetrotters, The (animated series)	CBS-TV	Hoyt Curtin
Harmony of Nature and Man (short)	IND	Elmer Bernstein
Hauser's Memory	UN	Billy Byers
Headmaster (series)	CBS-TV	Patrick Williams
Helene and Fernanda	FRA	Georges Garvarentz
Horror of the Blood Monsters (Creatures of the Prehistoric Planet)	IND	Mike Velarde
House of 'Dark Shadows, The	MGM	Robert Cobert
House on Greenapple Road, The	ABC-TV	Duane Tatro
House That Screamed, The	AI	Waldo de los Rios
House That Wouldn't Die, The	TV	George Duning/Laurence Rosenthal
How Awful About Allan	TV	Laurence Rosenthal
Hunters Are for Killing	TV	Jerry Fielding
Hurrah for Adventure	SPA	Gregory Segura
Immortal, The (series)	ABC-TV	Dominic Frontiere/Leith Stevens
Interns, The (series)	CBS-TV	Shorty Rogers
Intruders, The	UN	Dave Grusin
Josie and the Pussycats (series)	CBS-TV	Hoyt Curtin
Joshua in a Box (short)	IND	Mat Andes
Kamikaze Cop, A	JAP	Masao Yagi
Kifaru	TV	Elmer Bernstein
Kowboys, The (pilot)	NBC-TV	Jeff Barry/Don Kirshner
Lady Called Andres, A	SPA	Augusto Alguero

Lame Devil, The	SPA	Angel Arteaga
Latitude Zero	JAP	Akira Ifukube
Lokis	POL	Wojiech Kilar
Love War, The	TV	Dominic Frontiere
McCloud: Who Killed Miss U.S.A.?	NBC-TV	David Shire
McCloud (series)	NBC-TV	Richard Clements/Billy Goldenberg/Stu Phillips/ David Shire
Magic Typewriter, The (short)	PHI	Dominic Valdez
Make Room for Granddaddy (series)	ABC-TV	Earle Hagen
Man from Shiloh, The	UN-TV	Ennio Morricone
Man Who Died Twice, The	TV	John Parker
Man Who Had to Sing, The (short)	YUG	Tomislav Simovic
Man Who Haunted Himself, The	BRI	Michael J. Lewis
Man Who Wanted to Live Forever, The (Only Way Out Is Dead, The)	TV	Dolores Claman
Mark of the Witch	IND	Whitey Thomas
Mary Tyler Moore Show, The (series)	CBS-TV	Patrick Williams
Mask of Sheba, The	MGM	Lalo Schifrin
Matt Lincoln (series)	ABC-TV	Oliver Nelson
Men from Shiloh, The (series)	NBC-TV	Leonard Rosenman
Mga Hagibis	PHI	Manuel Franco
Mighty Gorga, The	IND	Charles Walden
Mini-Skirt Gambler, A	JAP	Chuji Kinoshita
Mister Jericho	BRI	Laurie Johnson
Mr. Rogers' Neighborhood (series)	PBS-TV	John Costa
Monster Zero	JAP	Akira Ifukube
Most Deadly Game, The (Zig Zag) (series)	ABC-TV	George Duning
Motor Mouse (series)	ABC-TV	Hoyt Curtin
Movie Murderer, The	UN	Stanley Wilson
My Sweet Charlie	UN	Gil Melle
Name for Evil, A	CIN	Dominic Frontiere
Nancy (series)	NBC-TV	Sid Ramin
Nanny and the Professor (series)	ABC-TV	Charles Fox/George Greeley
Necropolis	ITA	Gavin Bryars
Night Chase	TV	Laurence Rosenthal
Night of the Witches	IND	Sean Bonniwell
Night Slaves	TV	Bernado Segall
Nine Lives of a Cat, The	SPA	Anton Garcia Abril
Nobody's Boy	JAP	Chuji Kinoshita
Odd Couple, The (series)	ABC-TV	Neil Hefti/Kenyon Hopkins
Ogre, The	SPA	Les Baxter
Old Man Who Cried Wolf, The	TV	Robert Drasnin
On the Comet	CZE	Lubos Fiser
Orloff and the Invisible Man	FRA	Camille Sauvage
Other Man, The	UN	Michel Colombier
Over-the-Hill Gang Rides Again, The	ABC-TV	David Raksin

Paris 7000 (series)	ABC-TV	Stanley Wilson
Partridge Family, The (series)	ABC-TV	George Duning/Benny Golson/Hugo Montenegro/Shorty Rogers
Play It Cool	JAP	Hikaru Hayashi
Portraits (short)	YUG	Tomislav Simovic
Psychiatrist: God Bless the Children, The	UN	Roger Kellaway
Quarantined	PAR	George Duning
Ritual of Evil	UN	Billy Goldenberg
Run, Simon, Run	TV	"The Orphanage"
San Francisco International Airport (series)	NBC-TV	Patrick Williams
Scandalous Adventures of Buraikan, The	JAP	Masaru Sato
Scream of the Demon Lover, The	ITA	Luigi Malatesta
Serpent God, The	ITA	Augusto Martelli
Sex and the Vampire (Vampire Thrills/Frisson des Vampires, Les)	FRA	George Acanthus
Shadow Within, The	JAP	Yasushi Akutagawa
Shameful Secrets of Hastings Corners, The (pilot)	NBC-TV	George Duning
Sicilian Clan, The	FOX	Ennio Morricone
Silent Force, The (series)	ABC-TV	George Duning
Sole Survivor	TV	Paul Glass
Somerset (series)	NBC-TV	Chet Kingsbury/Charles Paul
Something Is Creeping in the Dark	ITA	Francesco Lavagnino
Storefront Lawyers, The (series)	CBS-TV	Harper McKay/Morton Stevens
Thomas and ... the Bewitched	ITA	Amedeo Tommasi
Three Coins in the Fountain (series)	NBC-TV	Jeff Alexander
Three for Tahiti (pilot)	ABC-TV	Jack Elliott/Allyn Ferguson
Tim Conway Show, The (series)	CBS-TV	Harry Geller
Tora! Tora! Tora!	FOX	Jerry Goldsmith
Transplant	SPA	Gregory Segura
Tribes (Soldier Who Declared Peace, The)	FOX	Al Capps/Marty Cooper
Vampire Doll, The	JAP	Riichiro Manabe
Virgin Witch, The	BRI	Burnell Whibley
War of the Gargantuas	JAP	Akira Ifukube
Way Out, Way In	JAP	Harumi Ibe
Weekend of Terror	PAR	Richard Markowitz
Where's Huddles? (series)	CBS-TV	Hoyt Curtin
Wild Women	TV	Fred Steiner
Wildcat Rock	JAP	Kunihiko Suzuki

Will the Real Jerry Lewis Please Sit Down? (series)	ABC-TV	Yvette Blais/George Michael
Young Country, The	UN	Pete Rugolo
Young Lawyers, The (series)	ABC-TV	Lalo Schifrin/Leith Stevens
Young Man's Stronghold, A	JAP	Jiro Inagaki/Hiroki Tamaki
Young Rebels, The (series)	ABC-TV	Dominic Frontiere

1971

Abominable Dr. Phibes, The	BRI	Basil Kirchen
Alaska	TV	Elmer Bernstein
Ali-Baba and the Forty Thieves	JAP	Seiichiro Uno
Alias Smith and Jones (series)	ABC-TV	Billy Goldenberg/Robert Prince
All in the Family (series)	CBS-TV	Roger Kellaway
All-Out Game, The	JAP	Harumi Ibe
Amants del Diablo, Les	SPA	Mariano Girolami/Carlo Savina
Aphrousa	BRI	Carl Crossman/George Potamianos
Archie's TV Funnies (series)	CBS-TV	George Blais/Jeff Michael
Arnold's Closet Review (pilot)	NBC-TV	Ian Bernard
Arthur & the Britons (series)	BRI	Elmer Bernstein
Assault on the Wayne	PAR	Leith Stevens
Ballad of Death	JAP	Takeo Yamashita
Banyon	WB	Leonard Rosenman
Battle of Okinawa	JAP	Masaru Sato
Bearcats! (series)	CBS-TV	Dave Kahn
Beast in the Cellar, The	BRI	Tony Macauley
Beat '71	JAP	Hiroki Tamaki
Birdmen, The	UN	David Rose
Black Noon	COL	George Duning
Blinker's Spy Spotter	BRI-TV	Harry Robinson
Blood Bath (Gore-Gore Girls, The)	IND	Hershell Gordon Lewis
Blood Rose	FRA	J. P. Dorsay
Blood Vendetta	JAP	Taichiro Kosugi
Boss with the Samurai Spirit, A	JAP	Takeo Yamashita
Brian's Song	COL	Michel Legrand
Buford and the Ghost (series)	NBC-TV	Hoyt Curtin
Burke and Hare	BRI	Roger Webb
Cable Car Murder, The	WB	Jerry Goldsmith
Cade's County (series)	CBS-TV	Henry Mancini
Cannon (series)	CBS-TV	John Cannon/Robert Drasnin/John Parker/ George Romanis/Duane Tatro
Carnage (Antefatto)	ITA	Stelvio Cipriani
Chicago Teddy Bears, The (series)	CBS-TV	Jerry Fielding

Christ of the Ocean	ITA	Bruno Nicolai
City, The	ABC-TV	Billy Goldenberg
City Beneath the Sea, The	CBS-TV	Richard LaSalle
Colossal	ITA	Nico Fidenco
Columbo (series)	NBC-TV	Jeff Alexander/Dick de Benedictis/Billy Goldenberg/Henry Mancini/Oliver Nelson/Robert Prince/Bernardo Segall
Congratulations, It's a Boy!	TV	Richard Baskin/Basil Poledouris
Crucible of Horror (Velvet House)	BRI	John Hotchkiss
Crucible of Terror	BRI	Paris Rutherford
Curiosity Shop (series)	ABC-TV	Dick Elliott/Henry Mancini
D.A., The (series)	NBC-TV	Frank Comstock
D.A.: Conspiracy to Kill, The	NBC-TV	Frank Comstock
Dead Men Tell No Tales	FOX	Robert Drasnin
Deadly Dream, The	UN	Dave Grusin
Deadly Hunt, The	TV	Vic Mizzy
Death by Invitation	IND	Sonny Kohl
Death of Innocence, A	TV	Morton Stevens
Death of Me Yet, The	TV	Pete Rugolo
Death Takes a Holiday	UN	Laurindo Almeida
Deathmaster, The	AI	Bill Marx
Department S (series)	BRI-TV	Edwin Astley
Devil and Miss Sarah, The	UN	David Rose
Devil's Nightmare, The	ITA	Alessandro Alessandroni
Do Not Fold, Spindle or Mutilate	TV	Jerry Goldsmith
Do You Take This Stranger?	UN	Pete Rugolo
Dr. Cook's Garden	PAR	Robert Drasnin
Dr. Mabuse	GER/SPA	Daniel J. White
Doctor's Wives	COL	Elmer Bernstein
Dodes ka-Den	JAP	Toru Takemitsu
Duel	UN	Billy Goldenberg
Duel at the Cape Shiretoko	JAP	Masao Yagi
Earth II	MGM	Lalo Schifrin
Ellery Queen: Don't Look Behind You	NBC-TV	Jerry Fielding
Enter the Devil	TV	Sam Douglas
Escape (pilot)	ABC-TV	Lalo Schifrin
Expo '70	JAP	Yoshio Mamiya
Eye of the Labyrinth, The (Blood)	ITA	Roberto Nicolosi
Face of Fear, The	TV	Morton Stevens
Failing of Raymond, The	UN	Pat Williams
Fear Has a Thousand Eyes	SWE	Mats Olsson
Feminist and the Fuzz, The	COL	Jack Elliott/Allyn Ferguson
Five Desperate Women	TV	Paul Glass
Forbidden Affair	JAP	Sei Ikeno
Forbidden Fruit, The	JAP	Harumi Ibe

Forgotten Man, The	TV	David Shire
Frankenstein's Bloody Terror	SPA	Angel Arteaga
From a Bird's Eye View (series)	BRI-TV	Frank Barber
Funky Phantom, The (series)	ABC-TV	John Sangster
Funny Face (Sandy Duncan Show, The) (series)	CBS-TV	Patrick Williams
G.I. Executioner, The (Wit's End/ Dragon Lady)	IND	Elliot Chiprut/Jason Garfield
Gamblers in Okinawa	JAP	Takeo Yamashita
Gamera vs. Zigra	JAP	Shunsuke Kikuchi
Getting Together (series)	ABC-TV	George Duning/Hugo Montenegro/David Shire
Gift of the Fox, The	JAP	Hajime Kaburagi
Go-Between, The	COL	Michel Legrand
Godzilla vs. Hedorah	JAP	Riichiro Manabe
Godzilla's Revenge	JAP	Kunio Miyauchi
Golem's Daughter, The (Erotic Witchcraft)	FRA	Guy Boulanger
Good Life, The (series)	NBC-TV	Sacha Distel/Jack Elliott/Allyn Ferguson
Goodbye Raggedy Ann	TV	Wladimir Selinsky
Groovie Goolies, The (series)	CBS-TV	George Mahana
Hand of Power	GER	Peter Thomas
Hands of the Ripper	BRI	Christopher Gunning
Harness, The	UN	Billy Goldenberg
Harpy	TV	David Shire
Help! It's the Hair Bear Bunch (series)	CBS-TV	Hoyt Curtin
High School Outcasts	JAP	Tomohiro Koyama
Home in My Heart	JAP	Hajime Kaburagi
Homecoming, The	TV	Jerry Goldsmith
Horror on Snape Island	BRI	Kenneth V. Jones
Hot Little Girl, The	JAP	Tadashi Yamauchi
Howling in the Woods, A	UN	Dave Grusin
Human Target	JAP	Taku Izumi
Hunter	CBS	Lalo Schifrin
Hypnos	ITA/SPA	Carlo Savina
I Drink Your Blood	IND	Clay Pitts
I Hear the Whistle	JAP	Masaaki Hayakawa
If Tomorrow Comes	TV	Gil Melle
Impatient Heart, The	UN	David Shire
In Broad Daylight	TV	Leonard Rosenman
In Search of America	TV	Fred Myrow
Incident in San Francisco	TV	Pat Williams
Incredible Invasion, The	MEX	Enrico Cabiati/Alice Uretta
Inn of Evil	JAP	Toru Takemitsu
Inside O.U.T.	CBS-TV	Jerry Fielding
Is There a Doctor in the House?	CBS-TV	David Shire
Jackson Five, The (series)	ABC-TV	Maury Laws

Jane Eyre	TV	John Williams
Jekyll and Hyde Portfolio, The	BRI	Randy Scott
Jimmy Stewart Show, The (series)	NBC-TV	Van Alexander
Johnstown Monster, The	BRI	Harry Robinson
Kamikaze Cop, Marihuana Syndicate	JAP	Masao Yagi
Kamikaze Cop, No Epitaph to Us	JAP	Masao Yagi
Kamikaze Cop, The Poison Gas Affair	JAP	Masao Yagi
Killer, The	JAP	Koichi Sakata
Knight in Shining Armour, A	ABC-TV	George Duning
Lady Frankenstein	ITA	Alessandro Alessandroni
Lake of Dracula	JAP	Riichiro Manabe
Last Child, The	TV	Laurence Rosenthal
Law of the Outlaw	JAP	Harumi Ibe
Legacy of Blood	IND	Jaime Mendoza-Nava
Legend of Hillbilly John, The	IND	Roger Kellaway
Li'l Abner (pilot)	ABC-TV	Earl Brown/Jimmy Dale
Lineup of Kanto Outlaws	JAP	Hiroki Tamaki
Little Game, A	UN	Robert Prince
Little Women (series)	BRI-TV	Patrick Harvey
Live and Learn	JAP	Sei Ikeno
Live My Share, Mother	JAP	Takeo Watanabe
Live Today; Die Tomorrow!	JAP	Hikaru Hayashi
Lock, Stock and Barrel (pilot)	NBC-TV	Patrick Williams
Long Goodbye, The	RUS	O. Karabanchiuk
Long, Swift Sword of Siegfried, The	GER	Daniele Patucchi
Longstreet	ABC-TV	Robert Drasnin
Longstreet (series)	ABC-TV	Robert Drasnin/Billy Goldenberg/Oliver Nelson
Lost Treasure	CBS-TV	Mimis Plessas
Love and Death	JAP	Katsuhisha Hattori
Love for Eternity	JAP	Harumi Ibe
Love, Hate, Love	TV	Lyn Murray
Macbeth	BRI	Paul Buckmaster
McMillan and Wife (series)	NBC-TV	Jerry Fielding
Maidstone	IND	Isaac Hayes
Mako, the Bad Girl	JAP	So Tsumiki
Man and the City, The (series)	ABC-TV	Alex North
Man on a False Flight	JAP	Shigeru Ikeno
Man with the Synthetic Brain, The (Blood of Ghastly Horror)	TV	Don McGinnis/Jimmy Roosa
Marriage Year One	UN	David Shire
Maybe I'll Come Home in the Spring	TV	Earl Robinson
Med Kaerlig Hilsen (Love Me, Darling)	DEN	Bent Fabricius-Bjerre
Men at Law (series)	CBS-TV	Harper McKay

Metamorphosis	SPA	Carlos Maleras
Million Dollar Duck, The	DIS	Buddy Baker
Mr. and Mrs. Bo Jo Jones	FOX	Fred Karlin
Mr. Horatio Knibbles	BRI	Muir Mathieson
Mongo's Back in Town	TV	Michael Melvoin
Monty Nash (series)	IND-TV	The Good Stuff
Murder Once Removed	TV	Robert Drasnin
Necrophagus	SPA	Alfonso Santisteben
Neon Ceiling, The	UN	Billy Goldenberg
New Dick Van Dyke Show, The (series)	CBS-TV	Jack Elliott/Allyn Ferguson
Nichols (series)	NBC-TV	Bernardo Segall
Night Butterflies	JAP	Najime Kaburagi
Night Gallery (series)	NBC-TV	Billy Goldenberg/Gil Melle/Eddie Sauter
Night God Screamed, The	IND	Don Vincent
Night Hair Child	BRI	Stelvio Cipriani
Night of the Damned, The	ITA	Carlo Savina
Oh, My Comrade!	JAP	Seitaro Omori
O'Hara, United States Treasury (series)	CBS-TV	Ray Heindorf
O'Hara, United States Treasury: Operation Cobra	UN	Ray Heindorf/William Lava
Once Upon a Dead Man	NBC-TV	Jerry Fielding
Our Street (series)	PBS-TV	Don Schwartz
Owen Marshall: Counselor at Law (series)	ABC-TV	Elmer Bernstein/ Richard Clements
Paper Man	FOX	Duane Tatro
Partners, The (series)	NBC-TV	Lalo Schifrin
Pebbles and Bamm Bamm (series)	CBS-TV	Hoyt Curtin/Ted Nichols
Persuaders, The (series)	ABC-TV	John Barry/Ken Thorne
Pilgrimage to Japanese Baths	JAP	Ichiro Araki
Powderkeg	CBS-TV	John Andrew Tartaglia
Priest Killer, The	UN	David Shire
Primus (series)	IND-TV	Leonard Rosenman
Psychiatrist, The (series)	NBC-TV	Gil Melle
Queens of Evil, The	ITA	Francesco Lavagnino
Ransom for a Dead Man	NBC-TV	Billy Goldenberg
Reluctant Heroes, The	TV	Frank DeVol
Requiem for a Vampire	FRA	Piere Raph
Revenge	TV	Dominic Frontiere
River of Gold	TV	Fred Steiner
River of Mystery	UN	Luis Bonfa
Road Runner Show, The (series)	ABC-TV	Milt Franklin/William Lava/John Seely/ Carl Stalling
Sabrina, the Teenage Witch (series)	CBS-TV	George Blais/Jeff Michael
Sam Hill: Who Killed the Mysterious Mr. Foster? (pilot)	NBC	Pete Rugolo

Sarge: The Badge or the Cross	UN	Dave Grusin
Sarge (series)	NBC-TV	David Shire
Secret Rites	BRI	Bryn Walton
Secret Zone of Tokyo	JAP	Yutaka Makino
See the Man Run	UN	David Shire
Sex Comedy, Quick on the Trigger	JAP	Toshiaki Tsushima
Shadow of Deception	JAP	Katsuhisa Hattori
Sheriff, The	COL	Dominic Frontiere
Shirley's World (series)	ABC-TV	John Barry/Laurie Johnson
Sign of the Jack	JAP	Hajime Kaburagi
Six Wives of Henry VIII, The (series)	BRI-TV	David Munrow
Smith Family, The (series)	ABC-TV	Frank DeVol
Snow Country Elegy	JAP	Shunsuke Kikuchi
Someone Behind the Door	FRA	Georges Garvarentz
Soul to Devils, A (Chimimorya)	JAP	Toshiro Mayazumi
Step on the Gas!	JAP	Hiroki Tamaki
Step Out of Line, A	TV	Jerry Goldsmith
Strange Report, The (series)	NBC-TV	Edwin Astley/Roger Webb
Suddenly Single	TV	Billy Goldenberg
Suicide Mission	MEX	Gustavo Cesar Carreon
Superman on Gale	JAP	Hajime Kaburagi
Sweet, Sweet Rachel	ABC	Laurence Rosenthal
Swords of Death	JAP	Taichiro Kosugi
Taste of Evil, A	TV	Robert Drasnin
Tattered Web, A	TV	Robert Drasnin
Terror in the Sky	PAR	Patrick Williams
They Call It Murder (pilot)	NBC-TV	Robert Drasnin
Thief	TV	Ron Grainer
13th Day: The Story of Esther, The (pilot)	ABC-TV	Morton Stevens
Three Supermen in the Jungle	ITA	Sante Maria Romitelli
Thursday's Game	ABC	Billy Goldenberg
To Love Again	JAP	Shun-ichi Magaino
Tokyo Bad Girls	JAP	Toshiaki Tsushima
Tora-san, The Good Samaritan	JAP	Naozumi Yamamoto
Trackers, The	TV	Johnny Mandel
Travis Logan, D.A.	CBS-TV	Patrick Williams
Treasure Island	JAP	Naozumi Yamamoto
Troublesome Double, The	BRI-TV	Gordon Langford
Twilight People	PHI	Tito Arevalo/Ariston Avelino
Two on a Bench	UN	Pete Carpenter/Mike Post
Up Pompeii	BRI	Alan Blaikey/Carl Davis/Ken Howard
Up the Chastity Belt	BRI	Carl Davis
Vanished	UN	Leonard Rosenman

Velvet Vampire, The	IND	Roger Dollarhide/ Clancy B. Grass
Water Spider, The	FRA	Serge Kaufmann
Waterfront Blues	JAP	Seitaro Omori
What's a Nice Girl Like You...?	UN	Robert Prince
When Women Played Ding Dong	ITA	Giancarlo Chiarmello
Where Spring Comes Late	JAP	Masaru Sato
Where's Huddles? (series)	CBS-TV	Hoyt Curtin
Whistling Cobblestone, The	HUN	Lajos Illes
Who Killed the Mysterious Mr. Foster?	NBC-TV	Pete Rugolo
Will to Conquer	JAP	Akira Ifukube
Wizard of Gore, The	IND	Larry Wellington
Wolf Man, The	BRA	Gabriel Migliori
Women Smell of Night	JAP	Taichiro Kosugi
Yog, Monster from Space	JAP	Akira Ifukube
You Are There (series)	CBS-TV	Glenn Paxton
Yuma (pilot)	ABC-TV	George Duning

1972

ABC After School Special, The (series)	ABC	John Morris
Adventurer, The (series)	IND-TV	John Barry/Jerry Goldsmith
Adventures of Nick Carter, The (series)	ABC-TV	John Andrew Tartaglia
All My Darling Daughters	UN	Billy Goldenberg
Amanda Fallon (pilot)	NBC-TV	Richard Clements
Amazing Chan and the Chan Clan, The (series)	CBS-TV	Hoyt Curtin
Amazing Mr. Blunden, The	BRI	Elmer Bernstein
America (series)	NBC-TV	Charles Chilton/William Davies
American Lifestyle (series)	IND-TV	Michael Shapiro
Anna and the King (series)	CBS-TV	Richard Shores
Around the World in 80 Days (series)	NBC-TV	John Sangster
Assignment: Munich (pilot)	ABC-TV	George Romanis
Assignment: Vienna (series)	ABC-TV	Dave Grusin/John Parker
Astronaut, The	UN	Gil Melle
Asylum	BRI	Douglas Gamley
Banacek	NBC-TV	Jack Elliott/Allyn Ferguson/Billy Goldenberg
Banyon (series)	NBC-TV	Leonard Rosenman
Barkleys, The (animated series)	NBC-TV	Doug Goodwin/Eric Rogers
Beware the Brethren	IND	Richard Kerr/Tony Osborne

Big Game, The	ITA	Francesco de Masi
Bigfoot	IND	Richard A. Podolar
Blood Waters of Dr. Z, The	IND	Jami DeFrates/Barry Hodgin
Bob Newhart Show, The (series)	CBS-TV	Patrick Williams
Bobby Jo and the Big Apple Goodtime Band (pilot)	CBS-TV	Jerry Fuller/Michael Murphy
Bounty Man, The	ABC	"The Orphanage"
Brady Kids, The (series)	CBS-TV	Yvette Blais/Jeff Michael
Bravos, The	UN	Leonard Rosenman
Bridget Loves Bernie (series)	CBS-TV	Jerry Fielding/George Romanis
Call Holme	NBC-TV	Johnny Mandel
Castle Orgies	JAP	Taichi Tsukimisato
Catcher, The (pilot)	CBS-TV	Bill Walker
Century Turns, The	NBC-TV	Fred Steiner
Champions of Justice Return, The	MEX	Gustavo Cesar Carreon
Chase That Man	JAP	Hajime Kaburagi
Children Shouldn't Play With Dead Things	IND	Carl Zitterer
Chimimoryo	JAP	Toshiro Mayazumi
Climb an Angry Mountain	WB	George Duning
Clones, The	IND	Allen D. Allen
Cool Million (Mask of Marcella)	NBC-TV	Robert Prince
Cool Million (series)	NBC-TV	Billy Goldenberg
Corner Bar, The (series)	ABC-TV	Norman Paris
Coronation Street (series)	BRI-TV	Eric Spear
Corpse Grinders, The	IND	Ted V. Mikels
Couple Takes a Wife, The	UN	Dick DeBenedictis
Crawlspace	TV	Jerry Goldsmith
Cremators, The	CZE	Albert Glasser
Crime Does Not Pay	IN	S. Jagmohan
Crooked Hearts, The	TV	Billy Goldenberg
Daughters of Joshua Cabe, The	TV	Jeff Alexander
Deadhead Miles	IND	Tom T. Hall
Deadly Harvest	CBS	Morton Stevens
Dear Dead Delilah	IND	Bill Justis
Death of the Flea Circus Operator, or Ottocardo Weiss Reforms His Firm	SWI	Ernest Kolz
Deer-Golden Antlers	RUS	Anatoli Filippenko
Dell of the Virginis	MEX	Joaquin Gutierrez Heras
Delphi Bureau, The (series)	ABC-TV	Frank DeVol/Harper McKay
Detour to Nowhere	NBC-TV	Billy Goldenberg
Devil in the Brain	ITA	Ennio Morricone
Dig (short)	TV	Quincy Jones
Dr. X	IN	Sonik-Omi
Don Rickles Show, The (series)	CBS-TV	Earle Hagen
Doomwatch	BRI	John Scott

Dougal and the Blue Cat (Pollux and the Blue Cat)	FRA	Joss Basselli
Emergency! (series)	NBC-TV	Gerald Fried/Billy May/ Nelson Riddle
Every Man Needs One	ABC	Jack Elliott/Allyn Ferguson
Evil Roy Slade (pilot)	NBC-TV	Murray McLeod/Stuart Margolin/Jerry Riopelle
Excite Me	ITA	Bruno Nicolai
Family Flight	UN	Fred Steiner
Family Rico, The	CBS	Dave Grusin
Father on Trial (pilot)	NBC-TV	Walter Marks
Fear in the Night	BRI	John McCabe
Female Instinct	NBC-TV	Jerry Fielding
Fighting Cuban Against the Demons, The	CUB	Leo Brouwer
Fireball Forward	FOX	Lionel Newman
Flintstones Comedy Hour, The (series)	CBS-TV	Hoyt Curtin
Footsteps	TV	Dennis Gold
Fright	BRI	Harry Robinson
From Three to Sex	JAP	Hajime Okusawa
Garden of the Dead (Tomb of the Undead)	IND	Jaime Mendoza-Nava
Gargoyles	TV	Robert Prince
Ghost Story (series)	NBC-TV	Billy Goldenberg
Gidget Gets Married	ABC-TV	Pete Carpenter/Mike Post
Go for a Take	BRI	Glen Mason
Godzilla vs. Gigan	JAP	Akira Ifukube
Godzilla vs. the Smog Monster	JAP	Riichiro Manabe
Goodnight My Love	ABC	Harry Betts
Great American Tragedy, A	TV	George Duning
Groundstar Conspiracy, The	UN	Paul Hoffert
Hands of Cormac Joyce, The	AUT	Bob Young
Hardcase	HB	Patrick Williams
Hari Darshan	IN	K. Anadji
Haunts of the Very Rich	ABC	Dominic Frontiere
Hec Ramsey (series)	NBC-TV	Lee Holdridge/Fred Steiner
Heist, The	PAR	Robert Drasnin
Highway Circuit (Hairpin Circus)	JAP	Masaaki Kikuchi
Home for the Holidays	ABC	George Aliceson Tipton
Honeymoon Suite (pilot)	ABC-TV	Jack Elliott/Allyn Ferguson
Houndcats, The (series)	NBC-TV	Doug Goodwin
Hungry Wives	IND	Steve Gorn
I Dismember Mama (Poor Albert and Little Annie)	IND	Herschel Burke Gilbert
I, Monster	BRI	Carl Davis

Insatiable, The	JAP	Hajime Kaburagi
Jangal Mein Mangal	IN	Shankar Jaikishan
Jigsaw (series)	ABC-TV	Robert Drasnin/Harper McKay
Joshua and the Blob (short)	IND	Maxine Sellers/Larry Wolff
Josie and the Pussycats in Outer Space (series)	CBS-TV	Hoyt Curtin
Judge and Jake Wyler, The (pilot)	NBC-TV	Gil Melle
Kadoyng	BRI	Edwin Astley
Kid Power (series)	ABC-TV	Perry Botkin, Jr.
Killer by Night (pilot)	CBS-TV	Quincy Jones
Kung Fu (series)	ABC-TV	Jim Helms
Lady James Bond	IN	Sathyam
Last House on the Left, The	IND	David Alex Hess
Lieutenant Schuster's Wife	UN	Gil Melle
Lill, My Darling Witch	JAP	Kenjiro Hirose
Lisa and the Devil	ITA	Carlo Savina
Little People, The (series)	NBC-TV	Artie Butler/Jerry Fielding
Lloyd Bridges Water World	IND-TV	Marty Gould
Lone Assassin, A	JAP	Toshiaki Tsushima
Longest Night, The	UN	Hal Mooney
Love and the Happy Days	ABC-TV	Charles Fox
M*A*S*H (series)	CBS-TV	Earle Hagen/Johnny Mandel/Lionel Newman/Duane Tatro
Macunaima	BRA	M. de Andrade
Madame Sin (pilot)	ABC-TV	Michael Gibbs
Madigan (series)	NBC-TV	Jerry Fielding
Magic Carpet	UN	Lyn Murray
Man and the Snake, The	BRI	Marc Wilkinson
Man in the Middle (pilot)	CBS-TV	Jerry Fielding
Man on the Move	ABC-TV	Robert Drasnin
Mask of Marcella, The	NBC-TV	Robert Prince
Me and the Chimp (series)	CBS-TV	Artie Butler/Jerry Fielding
Mind Snatchers, The	CIN	Phil Ramone
Miss Leslie's Dolls	IND	Imer Leaf
Moon of the Wolf	ABC-TV	Bernardo Segall
Moonchild	TV	Billy Byers/Patrick Williams
Mouse Factory, The (series)	IND-TV	George Bruns
Movin' On (pilot)	NBC-TV	Dominic Frontiere
My Darling Witch--A Kiss Before Death	JAP	Kenjiro Hirose
My Voiceless Friends	JAP	Hitoshi Ohmuro
New Andy Griffith Show, The (series)	CBS-TV	Earle Hagen
New Healers, The	ABC-TV	Kenyon Hopkins
Night of Terror	PAR	Robert Drasnin

Night of the Blood Monster (Throne of Fire)	ITA	Bruno Nicolai
Night Stalker, The (pilot)	ABC-TV	Robert Cobert
No Place to Run	ABC	George Aliceson Tipton
Nun at Casino	JAP	Toshiaki Tsushima
Orgy of the Dead (Dracula--The Terror of the Living Dead)	ITA	Francesco de Masi
Osmonds, The (animated series)	ABC-TV	Maury Laws
Ozzie's Girls (series)	NBC-TV	Frank McKelvey
Paul Bernard--Psychiatrist (series)	IND-TV	Milani Kymlicka
Paul Lynde Show, The (series)	ABC-TV	Shorty Rogers
People, The	TV	Carmine Coppola
Phoenix, The	TV	Arthur B. Rubinstein, Jr.
Pigs, The (Daddy's Deadly Darling)	IND	Charles Bernstein
Playmates	ABC	Jack Elliott/Allyn Ferguson
Police Surgeon (series)	CAN-TV	Lewis Helkman
Poor Albert and Little Annie	IND	Herschel Burke Gilbert
Probe	NBC-TV	Dominic Frontiere
Protectors, The (series)	BRI-TV	John Cameron
Pursuit	ABC	Jerry Goldsmith
Queen Bee Strikes Again	JAP	Hajime Kaburagi
Rajdhani Express	IN	Utpalendu Chakraborti
Raw Meat	AI	Wil Malone/Jeremy Rose
Rendezvous, The	JAP	Yashushi Miyagawa
Rentadick	BRI	Carl Davis
Rex Harrison Presents Short Stories of Love	NBC-TV	David Shire
Rolling Man	ABC	Murray McLeod/Stuart Margolin
Roman Holidays, The (series)	NBC-TV	Hoyt Curtin
Rookies, The (series)	ABC-TV	Elmer Bernstein/Jack Elliott/Allyn Ferguson/ Laurence Rosenthal/ Pete Rugolo
Sand Castles	TV	Paul Glass
Sandy Duncan Show, The (series)	CBS-TV	Patrick Williams
Sanford and Son (series)	NBC-TV	Quincy Jones
Santo and the Daughter of Frankenstein	MEX	Gustavo Cesar Carreon
Santo vs. the Black Magic	MEX	Gustavo Desar Carreon
Satan of All Horrors	MEX	Ernesto Cortazar
Say Goodbye, Maggie Cole	TV	Hugo Montenegro
Screaming Woman, The	UN	John Williams
Sealab 2020 (series)	NBC-TV	Hoyt Curtin
Search (series)	NBC-TV	Dominic Frontiere
Search for the Nile, The (series)	NBC-TV	Joseph Horowitz
Seeds of Evil	IND	Marc Fredericks
She Beasts' Warm Bodies	JAP	Noboru Yoda

Blacksnake (Slaves/Sweet Suzy)	IND	William Loose
Blood Orgy of the She Devils	IND	Carl Zitterer
Blood Sport	TV	Randy Edelman
Blue Knight, The	NBC-TV	Nelson Riddle
Bob & Carol & Ted & Alice (series)	ABC-TV	Artie Butler
Borrowers, The	NBC-TV	Billy Byers/Rod McKuen
Brand New Life, A	TV	Billy Goldenberg
Brock's Last Case (pilot)	NBC-TV	Charles Gross
Butch Cassidy and the Sundance Kids (series)	NBC-TV	Hoyt Curtin
Call to Danger (pilot)	CBS-TV	Laurence Rosenthal
Calucci's Department (series)	CBS-TV	Marvin Hamlisch
Carnation Killer, The	BRI-TV	Laurie Johnson
Cat Creature, The	COL	Leonard Rosenman
Catholics	TV	Carl Davis
Chase (series)	NBC-TV	Oliver Nelson
Circle of Fear (series)	NBC-TV	Billy Goldenberg/Robert Prince
Class of '63	TV	Tom Scott
Coffee Tea or Me?	CBS	Morton Stevens
Cold Night's Death, A	ABC	Gil Melle
Connection	TV	John Murtaugh
Crime Club, The (pilot)	CBS-TV	George Romanis
Crypt of the Living Dead	SPA	Philip Lambro
Daddy's Girl (pilot)	CBS-TV	Vic Mizzy
Dear Summer Sister	JAP	Toru Takemitsu
Death in Small Doses	BRI-TV	Laurie Johnson
Death Race	UN	Milton Rosen
Del Terror Ciego	SPA	Anton Garcia Abril
Deliver Us from Evil	TV	Andrew Belling
Demons of the Mind	BRI	Harry Robinson
Devil's Daughter, The	PAR	Laurence Rosenthal
Devil's Triangle, The	TV	"King Crimson"
Diana (series)	NBC-TV	Jerry Fielding
Divorce His/Divorce Hers	TV	Stanley Myers
Doc Elliot (series)	ABC-TV	Earle Hagen/Marvin Hamlisch
Dr. Jekyll and Mrs. Hyde	BRI-TV	Lionel Bart
Dr. Who (series)	BRI-TV	Geoffrey Burgon/Ron Grainer/Malcolm Lockyer/Bill McGuffie
Don't Be Afraid of the Dark	TV	Billy Goldenberg
Don't Look in the Basement	IND	Robert Farrar
Double Indemnity	UN	Billy Goldenberg
Dream for Christmas, A (pilot)	ABC-TV	David Rose
Drive Hard, Drive Fast	UN	Pete Rugolo

Dusty's Trail (series)	IND-TV	Frank DeVol/Jack Plees
Dying Room Only	TV	Charles Fox
Echo of Theresa, An	BRI-TV	Laurie Johnson
Egan	ABC-TV	Lalo Schifrin
Escape (series)	NBC-TV	Frank Comstock
Eternal Cause	JAP	Masaru Sato
Everything's Archie (series)	CBS-TV	George Blais/Jeff Michael
Evil Touch, The (series)	IND-TV	Laurie Lewis
Faraday and Company (series)	NBC-TV	Jerry Fielding
Female Artillery	UN	Frank DeVol
File It Under Fear	BRI-TV	Laurie Johnson
Firehouse (pilot)	ABC-TV	Tom Scott
500-Pound Jerk, The	WOL	Neal Hefti
Frankenstein	ABC-TV	Robert Cobert
Frankenstein: The True Story	UN	Gil Melle
Friends of Eddie Coyle, The	PAR	Dave Grusin
Fuzz Brothers, The (pilot)	ABC-TV	J. J. Johnson
'Gator Bait	IND	William A. Castleman/ William Loose
Gemini Affair--A Diary, The	IND	Herschel Burke Gilbert
Genesis II (pilot)	ABC-TV	Harry Sukman
Ghost in the Noonday Sun	BRI	Denis King
Ghost Story	BRI	Ron Geeson
Gidget Makes the Wrong Connection	ABC-TV	Hoyt Curtin
Girl Most Likely to ..., The	ABC	Bernardo Segall
Girl with Something Extra, The (series)	NBC-TV	Dave Grusin
Girls of Huntington House, The	TV	Tom Scott
Glass Menagerie, The	TV	John Barry
Go Ask Alice	TV	Michael O'Martin/Bill Schnee/Joel Sill
Godzilla vs. Megalon	JAP	Riichiro Manabe
Going Places (pilot)	NBC-TV	Charles Fox
Goober and the Ghost Chasers (series)	ABC-TV	Hoyt Curtin
Great American Beauty Contest, The	ABC	Ken Wannberg
Great Man's Whiskers, The	UN	Earl Robinson
Griff (series)	ABC-TV	Pete Carpenter/Elliot Kaplan/Mike Post
Guess Who's Sleeping in My Bed?	ABC	Morton Stevens
Harry O	CBS-TV	Richard Hazard
Hawkins (series)	CBS-TV	Jerry Goldsmith/George Romanis
Hawkins on Murder	CBS-TV	Jerry Goldsmith
Here Comes the Bride (Bride, The/House That Cried Murder, The)	IND	Peter Bernstein
Here We Go Again (series)	ABC-TV	Al DeLory

Hijack!	TV	Jack Elliott/Allyn Ferguson
Hitched (pilot)	NBC-TV	Patrick Williams
Home from the Sea	JAP	Masaru Sato
Honor Thy Father	TV	George Duning
Horror at 37,000 Feet, The	CBS	Morton Stevens
House in Nightmare Park	BRI	Harry Robinson
Hunter (pilot)	CBS-TV	Lalo Schifrin
I Heard the Owl Call My Name	TV	Peter Matz
I Love a Mystery	NBC-TV	Oliver Nelson
Inch High, Private Eye (series)	NBC-TV	Hoyt Curtin
Incident on a Dark Street	FOX	Elmer Bernstein
Invasion of the Bee Girls, The	IND	Charles Bernstein
Isn't It Shocking?	ABC	David Shire
Jarrett	NBC-TV	Jack Elliott/Allyn Ferguson/Jeff McDuff
Jeannie (series)	CBS-TV	Hoyt Curtin/Paul DeKorte
Journey into Solitude	JAP	Takuro Yoshida
Key West (pilot)	NBC-TV	Frank DeVol
Kojak (series)	CBS-TV	John Cacavas/Billy Goldenberg/Jerry Fielding/Kim Richmond
Lady Killer	BRI-TV	Laurie Johnson
Lady Luck (pilot)	NBC-TV	Hal Mooney
Lassie's Rescue Rangers (series)	ABC-TV	Yvette Blais/Jeff Michael
Letters, The	ABC	Pete Rugolo
Letters from Three Lovers (pilot)	ABC-TV	Pete Rugolo
Linda	UN	John Cacavas
Lisa, Bright and Dark	NBC-TV	Rod McKuen
Long Darkness, The	JAP	Teizo Matsumura
Long Goodbye, The	UA	John Williams
Lost in Space (animated series)	ABC-TV	Hoyt Curtin
Lotsa Luck (series)	NBC-TV	Jack Elliott/Allyn Ferguson
Love Story (series)	NBC-TV	Peter Matz/David Shire
Love Thy Neighbor (series)	ABC-TV	Pete Rugolo
Magician, The (series)	NBC-TV	Patrick Williams
Man Who Could Talk to Kids, The	TV	Fred Karlin
Man Without a Country, The	TV	Jack Elliott/Allyn Ferguson
Maneater	UN	George Romanis
Marcus-Nelson Murders, The	UN	Billy Goldenberg
Message to My Daughter	TV	Fred Myrow
Miracle on 34th Street	FOX	Sid Ramin
Mission Magic (series)	ABC-TV	Yvette Blais/Jeff Michael
Mr. Inside/Mr. Outside	TV	Charles Gross

Money to Burn	UN	Oliver Nelson
Monster of the Island, The	ITA	Carlo Innocenzi
Moonbase 3	BRI-TV	Dudley Simpson
Mousey	BRI-TV	Ron Grainer
Murdock's Gang	CBS-TV	Frank DeVol
My Darling Daughters' Anniversary	UN	Hal Mooney
My Favorite Martian (series)	CBS-TV	George Mahana
My Partner the Ghost (series)	BRI-TV	Edwin Astley
Mystery of Life, The	IN	A. Banerjee
Needles and Pins	NBC-TV	Pete Carpenter/Marvin Hamlisch/Mike Post
New Adventures of Perry Mason, The (series)	CBS-TV	Earle Hagen
New Temperatures Rising Show, The (series)	ABC-TV	Vic Mizzy
New Voice, The (series)	PBS-TV	Chico O'Farrell
Night in the Cemetery, A	FRA	Piere Raph
Night Strangler, The (pilot)	ABC-TV	Robert Cobert
Nightmare Hotel	SPA	Antonio Perez Olea
Norliss Tapes, The (pilot)	NBC-TV	Robert Cobert/John Mick
One Deadly Owner	BRI-TV	Laurie Johnson
Ordeal	FOX	Patrick Williams
Orson Welles' Great Mysteries (series)	BRI-TV	John Barry
Outrage!	ABC	Jimmie Haskell
Ozzie's Girls (series)	IND-TV	Frank McKelvey
Partners in Crime (pilot)	NBC-TV	Gil Melle
Picture of Dorian Gray, The	ABC-TV	Robert Cobert
Pioneer Woman	FIL	Al DeLory
Police Story (series)	NBC-TV	Jack Elliott/Allyn Ferguson/Jerry Goldsmith/Richard Markowitz/John Parker
Poor Devil (pilot)	NBC-TV	Morton Stevens
Possession	BRI-TV	Laurie Johnson
President's Plane Is Missing, The	ABC	Gil Melle
Red Pony, The	UN	Jerry Goldsmith
Reincarnation of Isabel (Ghastly Orgies of Count Dracula)	ITA	Remolo Forlai/Gianfranco Reverberi
Return, The	BRI	Marc Wilkinson
Reunion	CBS	George Romanis
Roll Out! (series)	CBS-TV	Benny Golson/Dave Grusin
Romantic Agony, The (Vaarwel)	ITA	Ennio Morricone
Rose of Iron, The	FRA	Piere Raph
Run, Stranger, Run	IND	Don Vincent
Runaway!	UN	Hal Mooney
Sanka	JAP	Hikaru Hayashi
Satan's School for Girls	TV	Laurence Rosenthal
Savage (pilot)	NBC-TV	Gil Melle

Scream, Pretty Peggy	UN	Robert Prince
Severed Arm, The	IND	Phillan Bishop
Shaft (series)	CBS-TV	Johnny Pate
She Cried "Murder!"	UN	John Cacavas
Shirts/Skins	MGM	Jerry Fielding
Sigmund and the Sea Monsters (series)	NBC-TV	Wes Farrell/Jimmie Haskell/Michael Lloyd
Six Million Dollar Man, The (series)	ABC-TV	Richard Clements/J. J. Johnson/Gil Melle/ Oliver Nelson/Stu Phillips
Slaughter in San Francisco	HK	Joe Curtis
Snatched	ABC	Randy Edelman
Someone at the Top of the Stairs	BRI-TV	Laurie Johnson
Speed Buggy (series)	CBS-TV	Hoyt Curtin/Paul DeKorte
Spell of Evil	ABC-TV	Laurie Johnson
Star Trek (series)	NBC-TV	Yvette Blais/Jeff Michael
Strange Places (Other People, Other Places)	BRI-TV	Gerherd Trede
Stranger, The (pilot)	NBC-TV	Richard Markowitz
Suicide Club, The	TV	Michael Lang
Summer Without Boys, A	TV	Andrew Belling
Sunshine	UN	John Denver
Super Friends (series)	ABC-TV	Hoyt Curtin/Paul DeKorte
Taste of Hell, A	PHI	Nestor Robles
Teacher's Pet	ABC-TV	Yvette Blais/Jeff Michael
Tenafly (series)	NBC-TV	Gil Melle
Terror Circus	IND	Tommy Vig
Terror on the Beach	FOX	Billy Goldenberg
There's Always Room	CBS-TV	Bill Conti
Thicker Than Water (series)	ABC-TV	Michael Melvoin
Third Girl from the Left	TV	Dory Previn
Thrill Seekers (series)	IND-TV	David Davis
Thriller (series)	BRI-TV	Laurie Johnson
Time for Love, A (pilot)	NBC	Patrick Williams
Time Within Memory	JAP	Toru Takemitsu
Tom Sawyer	UN	Hal Mooney
Toma (series)	ABC-TV	Pete Carpenter/Mike Post/Pete Rugolo
Tombs of the Blind Dead	SPA	Anton Garcia Abril
Topper Returns (pilot)	NBC-TV	Patrick Williams
Toru-san's Dream Come True	JAP	Naozumi Yamamoto
Touch of Grace, A (series)	ABC-TV	Pete Rugolo
Trapped	UN	Gil Melle
Trouble Comes to Town	ABC	Tom Scott
Twilight Years	JAP	Masaru Sato
Voices	BRI	Richard Rodney Bennett

Voyage of the Yes, The	NBC-TV	Richard Markowitz
Werewolf of Washington, The (White House Horrors, The)	IND	Arnold Freed
What Are Best Friends For?	ABC	Jack Elliott/Allyn Ferguson
Wheeler and Murdoch (pilot)	ABC-TV	Robert Drasnin
Wild Wild World of Animals, The (series)	IND-TV	Gerherd Trede/Beatrice Witkin
Wonder Girl	IND-TV	Steve St. Claire
Wonder Woman	TV	Carson Whitsett
World at War, The (series)	IND-TV	Carl Davis
Yogi's Gang (series)	ABC-TV	Hoyt Curtin
You'll Never See Me Again	UN	Richard Clements
Young and the Restless, The (series)	CBS-TV	David McGinnis/B. Todd/J. Wood
Zoo Robbers, The	BRI	De Wolfe

1974

Aces Up (pilot)	CBS-TV	Earle Hagen
Adam and Yves	IND	David Ernest
All the Kind Strangers	TV	Ron Frangipane
Aloha Means Goodbye	UN	Charles Fox
Anatomy of Terror	BRI-TV	Laurie Johnson
Ann in Blue (pilot)	ABC-TV	Jack Elliott/Allyn Ferguson
Apple's Way (series)	CBS-TV	Alexander Courage/ Morton Stevens
Asylum of Satan	IND	William Girdler
Autobiography of Miss Jane Pittman, The	TV	Fred Karlin
Bad Ronald	TV	Fred Karlin
Bat People, The (It Lives by Night)	AI	Artie Kane
Beast Must Die, The	BRI	Douglas Gamley
Bedtime with Rosie	BRI	Roger Webb
Betrayal	TV	Ernest Gold
Beyond the Darkness (Magdelena --Possessed by the Devil)	GER	Hans-Martin Majewski
Big Rose (pilot)	CBS-TV	Robert Prince
Blood	JAP	Hiroshi Takada
Blood-Spattered Bride, The	SPA	Antonio Perez Olea
Bobby Parker and Company	CBS-TV	Jack Elliott/Allyn Ferguson
Born Free (series)	NBC-TV	Dick de Benedictis/ Richard Shores
Born Innocent	TV	Fred Karlin
Boy With Two Heads, The	BRI	Harry Robinson
Brief Encounter	NBC-TV	Cyril Ornadel
California Kid, The	UN	Luchi de Jesus
Can Ellen Be Saved?	ABC	The Orphanage

Canterville Ghost, The	TV	Carl Davis
Case of Rape, A	UN	Hal Mooney
Chadana	IN	Ramesh Naidu
Chadwick Family, The (pilot)	ABC-TV	Hal Mooney
Change at 125th Street	CBS-TV	Nick Ashford/Valerie Simpson
Chico and the Man (series)	NBC-TV	Jose Feliciano
Chopper One	ABC-TV	Dominic Frontiere
Claretta and Ben	FRA/ITA	Carlo Rustichelli
Clinic on 18th Street (pilot)	NBC-TV	Frank Comstock
Closed Mondays (short)	IND	Billy Scream
Color Him Dead	BRI-TV	Laurie Johnson
Come Out, Come Out, Wherever You Are	BRI-TV	Laurie Johnson
Cosmos (series)	PBS-TV	Gordon Skene
Cowboys, The (series)	ABC-TV	Harry Sukman/John Williams
Craze	WB	Patrick John Scott
Creeping Terror, The (Dangerous Charter)	TV	Frederick Kopp
Cry in the Wilderness, A	UN	Robert Prince
Cry Panic	TV	Jack Elliott/Allyn Ferguson
Cyborg 009	TV	Kiochi Sugiyama
Dark Star	BRY	John Carpenter
Day the Earth Moved, The	ABC	Bobby Sherman
Death Cruise	TV	Pete Rugolo
Death Dream (Night Andy Came Home, The)	IND	Carl Zitterer
Death Sentence	TV	Laurence Rosenthal
Death Squad, The	TV	Dave Grusin
Deborah	ITA	Albert Verrechia
Demoniaques, Les	FRA	Piere Raph
Devil's Web, The	BRI-TV	Laurie Johnson
Devlin (series)	ABC-TV	Hoyt Curtin
Dion Brothers, The	IND-TV	Fred Karlin
Dirty Sally (series)	CBS-TV	John Parker
Disappearance of Flight 412, The	TV	Morton Stevens
Doctor Dan	CBS-TV	David Shire
Dr. Jekyll and the Wolfman	SPA	Anton Garcia Abril
Doctor Max (pilot)	NBC-TV	Billy Goldenberg
Dominic's Dream	CBS-TV	Buz Cohan
Dracula	UN	Robert Cobert
Drive!	IND	David Ernest
Elevator, The	UN	John Cacavas
Eunice	CBS-TV	Peter Matz
Evel Knievel (pilot)	CBS-TV	Gil Melle
Execution of Private Slovik, The	UN	Hal Mooney
Exorcism	SPA	Alberto Argudo
Exorcism's Daughter	SPA	Jaime Perez
Eyes Have It, The	BRI-TV	Laurie Johnson

F.B.I. Story: The F.B.I. Versus Alvin Karpis, Public Enemy Number One	TV	Duane Tatro
F. Scott Fitzgerald and "The Last of the Belles"	TV	Don Sebesky
Family Kovack, The (pilot)	NBC-TV	Harry Sukman
Fer-de-Lance	TV	Dominic Frontiere
Fess Parker Show, The	CBS-TV	Frank De Vol
Firehouse (series)	ABC-TV	Billy Goldenberg
Flesh and Blood Show, The	BRI	Cyril Ornadel
Fools, Females and Fun	NBC-TV	Jerry Fielding/Lee Holdridge
Friends and Lovers (series)	CBS-TV	Patrick Williams
Get Christie Love! (series)	ABC-TV	Luchi de Jesus/Jack Elliott/Allyn Ferguson
Girl on the Late, Late Show, The	COL	Richard Markowitz
Girl Who Came Gift-Wrapped, The	TV	Jack Elliott/Allyn Ferguson
Godchild, The	MGM	David Shire
Good Times (series)	CBS-TV	Dave Grusin
Great Expectations	TV	Maurice Jarre
Great Ice Rip-Off, The	ABC	Robert Cobert
Great Niagara, The	TV	Peter Link
Greatest Gift, The	UN	Dick DeBenedictis
Gun and the Pulpit, The (pilot)	ABC-TV	George Aliceson Tipton
Hanged Man, The	TV	Richard Markowitz
Happy Anniversary and Goodbye	CBS-TV	Nelson Riddle
Happy Days (series)	ABC-TV	Frank Comstock/Hack Hays/Pete King
Harry O (series)	ABC-TV	Billy Goldenberg/Kim Richmond
Hatchet for a Honeymoon, A	ITA	Sante Maria Romitelli
Healers, The (pilot)	NBC-TV	David Shire
Heatwave!	UN	Fred Steiner
High Riders	IND	Rusty Haller
Hit Lady	TV	George Aliceson Tipton
Hitchhike!	UN	Gil Melle
Hong Kong Phooey (series)	ABC-TV	Hoyt Curtin
Honky Tonk	MGM	Jerry Fielding
Hot Dreams (Free Love)	ITA	Fabio Frizzi
House of Whipcord	BRI	Stanley Myers
House That Vanished, The	BRI	Terry Warr
Houston, We've Got a Problem	UN	Richard Clements
Hurricane	TV	Vic Mizzy
I Eat Your Skin	IND	Lon Norman
I Love You, Goodbye	TV	Billy Goldenberg
If I Love You, Am I Trapped Forever? (pilot)	CBS-TV	Benny Golson
I'm the Girl He Wants to Kill	BRI-TV	Laurie Johnson
Imposter, The	WB	Gil Melle
In Tandem	TV	Don Ellis

In the Devil's Garden	BRI	Eric Rogers
Indict and Convict	UN	Jerry Goldsmith
It Couldn't Happen to a Nicer Guy	TV	Fred Karlin
It's Good to Be Alive	TV	Michel Legrand
Jack the Ripper (series)	BRI-TV	Bill Southgate
Jerry	CBS-TV	Marvin Hamlisch
Jongara	JAP	Genpachiro Shirakawa
Jo's Cousins	NBC-TV	Al Burton/Gloria Loring/ Alan Thicke
Judge Dee and the Monastery Murders (pilot)	ABC-TV	Leonard Rosenman
Kelly's Kids	ABC-TV	Frank DeVol
Killdozer	UN	Gil Melle
Killer Bees	TV	David Shire
Killer in Every Corner, A	BRI-TV	Laurie Johnson
Killer With Two Faces, The	BRI-TV	Laurie Johnson
Kiss Kiss, Kill Kill	BRI-TV	Laurie Johnson
Kodiak (series)	ABC-TV	Morton Stevens
Korg: 70,000 B.C. (series)	ABC-TV	Hoyt Curtin
Land of the Lost (series)	NBC-TV	Jimmie Haskell/Linda Laurie/Michael Lloyd
Larry	TV	Peter Matz
Last Angry Man, The (pilot)	ABC-TV	Gil Melle
Last of the Wild (series)	IND-TV	William Loose/Jack Tillar
Legend of the Spider Forest, The	BRI	J. S. Harrison
Little House on the Prairie, The (series)	NBC-TV	David Rose
Live Again, Die Again	UN	George Romanis
Locusts	PAR	Pete Carpenter/Mike Post
Long Journey into Love	JAP	Masaru Sato
Love Betrayed	JAP	Hikaru Hayashi
Love Stopped the Runaway Train	JAP	Chuji Kinoshita
Lucas Tanner (series)	NBC-TV	Richard Clements/David Shire
Ma and Pa	CBS-TV	Marvin Hamlisch
Maid for Pleasure	FRA	Bernard Gerard/Allen Toussaint
Manhunter, The (series)	CBS-TV	Duane Tatro
Mark of Zorro, The	FOX-TV	Dominic Frontiere/ Alfred Newman
Melvin Purvis--G-Man (pilot)	ABC-TV	Robert Cobert
Men and War	JAP	Masaru Sato
Men of the Dragon (pilot)	ABC-TV	Elmer Bernstein
Michelle Lee Show, The (pilot)	CBS-TV	Stephen Lawrence
Migrants, The	CBS	Billy Goldenberg
Mr. and Mrs. Cop	CBS-TV	Peter Matz
Mrs. Sundance	FOX	Patrick Williams
Monty Python's Flying Circus (series)	BRI-TV	John Gould

Morning After, The	WOL	Pete Carpenter/Mike Post
Movin' On (Series)	NBC-TV	Earle Hagen/George Romanis
Murder Is a One-Act Play	BRI-TV	Laurie Johnson
Murder or Mercy	TV	Patrick Williams
Naked Magic (Shocking Cannibals)	ITA	Francesco Lavagnino
Nakia (series)	ABC-TV	Leonard Rosenman
New Adventures of Gilligan, The (series)	ABC-TV	Yvette Blais/Jeff Michael
New Land, The (series)	ABC-TV	"The Orphanage"
Nickel Ride, The	TCF	Dave Grusin
Nicky's World	TV	Charles Gross
Night Games	PAR	Lalo Schifrin
Night of a Thousand Cats	MEX	Raul Lavista
Night Stalker, The (series)	ABC-TV	Jerry Fielding/Gerig McRitchie/Gil Melle
Nightmare	CBS	Peter Link
Nine Lives of Fritz the Cat	IND	Tom Scott
Not Guilty	BRI-TV	Laurie Johnson
Once the Killing Starts	BRI-TV	Laurie Johnson
Only a Scream Away	BRI-TV	Laurie Johnson
Only with Married Men	TV	Jack Elliott/Allyn Ferguson
Panic on the 5:22	TV	Richard Markowitz
Paradise	CBS-TV	Fotu Leao
Partridge Family: 2200 A.D., The (series)	CBS-TV	Hoyt Curtin
Perfume of the Woman in Black, The	ITA	Nicola Piovani
Pete 'n' Tillie	CBS-TV	Michael Melvoin
Petrocelli (series)	NBC-TV	Lalo Schifrin
Phantom of Hollywood, The	MGM	Leonard Rosenman
Place to Die, A	BRI-TV	Laurie Johnson
Planet Earth (pilot)	ABC-TV	Harry Sukman
Planet of the Apes (series)	CBS-TV	Lionel Newman/Lalo Schifrin
Police Woman (series)	NBC-TV	Jeff Alexander/Bruce Broughton/Gerald Fried/Jerry Goldsmith/Richard Markowitz/George Romanis/Pete Rugolo/Morton Stevens
Pray for the Wildcats	ABC	Fred Myrow
Professor Popper's Problems	BRI	Kenneth V. Jones
Psycho from Texas	IND	Jaime Mendoza-Nava
Psychopath	IND	Al Ross
Punch and Jody	TV	Fred Karlin

QB VII	COL	Jerry Goldsmith
Questor Tapes, The (pilot)	NBC-TV	Gil Melle
Rangers, The	UN	Lee Holdridge
Ready or Not	CBS-TV	Don Costa
Red Badge of Courage, The	FOX	Jack Elliott
Reflections of Murder	ABC	Billy Goldenberg
Remember When	TV	George Aliceson Tipton
Rhoda (series)	CBS-TV	Billy Goldenberg/Les Hooper/Richard Warren Lewis
Riddle at 24,000 (pilot)	NBC-TV	Quincy Jones/Marty Paich
Rise, Fair Sun	JAP	Teizo Matsumura
Robinson Crusoe	BRI	Wilfred Josephs
Rockford Files, The (series)	NBC-TV	Pete Carpenter/Artie Kane/Mike Post
Roll, Freddy, Roll!	ABC	Jack Elliott/Allyn Ferguson
Run, Joe, Run (series)	NBC-TV	Richard LaSalle
Salty (series)	IND-TV	Samuel Matlovsky
Savage Curse, The	BRI-TV	Laurie Johnson
Savages	TV	Murray MacLeod
Scream of the Wolf	TV	Robert Cobert
Screamer	BRI-TV	Laurie Johnson
Senior Year	UN	James DiPasquale
Seven Women for Satan (Count Zaroff)	FRA	Guy Bonnett
Sex Symbol, The	COL	Jeff Williams
Sexorcists, The	IND	Lex de Azevedo
Shazam! (series)	CBS-TV	Yvette Blais/Jeff Michael
Shootout in a One-Dog Town	HB	Hoyt Curtin
Sidekicks (pilot)	CBS-TV	David Shire
Sierra (series)	NBC-TV	Lee Holdridge
Sign It Death	BRI-TV	Laurie Johnson
Silk Tree Ballad, The	JAP	Mariko Miyagi
6 Rms Riv Vu	CBS-TV	Pater Matz
Skyway to Death	UN	Lee Holdridge
Smile, Jenny, You're Dead	WB	Billy Goldenberg
Snoop Sisters, The (series)	NBC-TV	Jerry Fielding
Sons and Daughters (series)	CBS-TV	James di Pasquale
Spasm	ITA	Ennio Morricone
Story of Jacob and Joseph, The	COL	Mikis Theodorakis
Story of Pretty Boy Floyd, The	UN	Pete Rugolo
Strange and Deadly Occurrence, The	TV	Robert Prince
Strange Homecoming	TV	John Parker
Stranger Who Looks Like Me, The	FIL	George Aliceson Tipton
Stranger Within, The	TV	Charles Fox
Sugar Hill (Voodoo Girl)	IND	Dino Fekaris/Nick Zesses

Tales of 1001 Nights	CZE	Frantisek Bulein
Tell Me Where It Hurts	TV	David Shire
Tempter, The (Antichrist, The)	ITA	Bruno Nicolai
Terror from Within	BRI-TV	Laurie Johnson
Terror on the 40th Floor	TV	Vic Mizzy
Texas Chainsaw Massacre, The	IND	Wayne Bell/Tobe Hooper
Texas Wheelers, The	ABC-TV	Pete Carpenter/Mike Post/John Andrew Tartaglia
That's My Mama (series)	ABC-TV	Lamont Dozier/Jack Eskew
These Are the Days (series)	ABC-TV	Hoyt Curtin
Things in Their Season	TV	Ken Lauber
This Was the West That Was	UN	Dick DeBenedictis
Tora-san Loves an Artist	JAP	Hirozumi Yamamoto
Torso	ITA	Guido and Maurizio de Angelis
Trapped Beneath the Sea	ABC	Joel Hirschhorn/Al Kasha
Tree Grows in Brooklyn, A	FOX	Jerry Goldsmith
Tribe, The	UN-TV	Hal Mooney/David Shire
Turn of the Screw	TV	Robert Cobert
Twice in a Lifetime	NBC-TV	Al Capps
Twisted Brain, The (Horror High)	CRO	Don Hulette
UFO Target Earth	TV	Aminidav Aloni
U.S. of Archie, The (series)	CBS-TV	George Blais/Jeff Michael
Under the Flag of the Rising Sun	JAP	Hikaru Hayashi
Underground Man, The	PAR	Richard Hazard
Underground Man, The (pilot)	NBC-TV	Marvin Hamlisch
Unwed Father	WOL	Jerry Fielding
Upstairs, Downstairs (series)	BRI-TV	Alexander Faris
Valley of the Dinosaurs (series)	CBS-TV	Hoyt Curtin
Virginia Hill Story, The	TV	David Shire
Wanderers, The	JAP	Yukio Asami/Kuri Shitei
Warlock Moon	IND	Charles Blaker
Welcome to Arrow Beach (Tender Flesh)	WB	Tony Camillo
Wheelie and the Chopper Bunch (series)	NBC-TV	Hoyt Curtin
Where Have All the People Gone?	TV	Robert Prince
Whispers of Fear	BRI	Harry Bromley Davenport
Who?	BRI/GER	John Cameron
Wicker Man, The	BRI	Paul Giovani
Winter Kill	MGM	Jerry Goldsmith
Wonder Woman	WB	Artie Butler

1975

| Abduction of Saint Anne, The | TV | George Duning |

Adams of Eagle Lake (series)	ABC-TV	Jerry Goldsmith/Harry Lojewski
Adventures of Pinocchio, The	ITA	Fiorenzo Carpi
Adventures of the Queen	FOX	Richard LaSalle
Aililia	HK	Wong Tse Yan
All Creatures Great and Small	BRI	Wilfred Josephs
All Together Now	TV	John Rubenstein
Angels of 2000, The	ITA	Mario Molino
Appointment with a Killer	ABC-TV	Laurie Johnson
Art of Crime, The (pilot)	NBC-TV	Gil Melle
Asaki Yememishi	JAP	Ryohei Hirose
Assassination of Ryoma, The	JAP	Teizo Matsumura
Assassin's Quarry	JAP	Hajime Kaburagi
Attack on Terror: The F.B.I. vs. the Ku Klux Klan	TV	Mundell Lowe
Bangalore Bhoota	IN	Guna Singh
Barbary Coast, The (series)	ABC-TV	John Andrew Tartaglia/ George Aliceson Tipton
Bare-Breasted Countess, The	SPA	Daniel J. White
Barney Miller (series)	ABC-TV	Jack Elliott/Allyn Ferguson
Beacon Hill (series)	CBS-TV	Marvin Hamlisch
Benilde, ou a Virgem Mae	POR	Joao Paes
Beyond the Bermuda Triangle	TV	Harry Sukman
Big Eddie (series)	CBS-TV	Jack Elliott/Allyn Ferguson/Earle Hagen
Big Ripoff, The	UN	Dick DeBenedictis
Bigfoot--Man or Beast?	TV	Jeff Gilman
Blue Knight, The (series)	CBS-TV	Henry Mancini/Robert Prince/Pete Rugolo
Bob Crane Show, The (series)	NBC-TV	Pete Carpenter/Mike Post
Bronk	CBS-TV	Robert Drasnin/George Romanis/Lalo Schifrin
Bullet Train Blast	JAP	Hachiro Aoyama
Cage Without a Key	COL	Jerry Fielding
Caribe (series)	ABC-TV	John Elizalde/Nelson Riddle
Castle of Sand, The	JAP	Mitsuaki Kanno
Celina's Cry	ARG	Victor Proncet
Charlotte	IND	Mike Oldfield
Children of the Snow Country	JAP	Taku Izumi
Classroom No. 205	JAP	Taku Izumi
Cobra	JAP	Seitaro Ohmori
Conspiracy of Terror (pilot)	NBC-TV	Neal Hefti
Cop and the Kid, The (series)	NBC-TV	Jerry Fielding/Joe Reisman
Copacabana, Mon Amour	BRA	Gilberto Gil
Count of Monte Cristo, The	TV	Allyn Ferguson
Crime Club, The (pilot)	CBS-TV	Gil Melle
Crossfire	TV	Patrick Williams

Cry for Help, A	UN	Gil Melle
Cry Terror!	BRI-TV	Laurie Johnson
Dark August	IND	William S. Fisher
Daughters of Joshua McCabe Return, The	TV	Jeff Alexander
Day After Tomorrow, The	TV	Derek Wadsworth
Dead Don't Die, The	TV	Robert Prince
Dead Man on the Run (pilot)	ABC-TV	Harry Geller
Dead Tower, The	MGM	Don Ellis
Death Among Friends (pilot)	NBC-TV	Jim Helms
Death Be Not Proud	TV	Fred Karlin
Death in Deep Water	BRI-TV	Laurie Johnson
Death Scream	TV	Gil Melle
Death Stalk	WOL	Pete Rugolo
Deep Red	ITA	"Goblin"
Delancey Street: The Crisis Within (pilot)	NBC-TV	Lalo Schifrin
Desperate Miles, The	UN	Robert Prince
Devilish Dolls, The	BRA	D. D. Sanches
Devil's Web, The	BRI-TV	Laurie Johnson
Dial a Deadly Number	BRI-TV	Laurie Johnson
Doc (series)	CBS-TV	Dick De Benedictis/ Patrick Williams
Doctors Hospital (series)	NBC-TV	Don Ellis
Double Kill	BRI-TV	Laurie Johnson
Dracula in the Provinces	ITA	C. A. Bixio/Fabio Frizzi/Franco Nebbia/ Vincenzo Tempera
Dream Makers, The	MGM	Fred Karlin
Easter Promise, The	CBS-TV	Arthur B. Rubinstein
Ellery Queen (series)	NBC-TV	Elmer Bernstein/Dana Kaproff/Hal Mooney
Ellery Queen (Too Many Suspects)	UN	Elmer Bernstein
Eric	NBC-TV	Dave Grusin
Erotomania Daimyo, The	JAP	Ichiro Araki
Espy	JAP	Masaaki Hirao
Evil Eye, The (Maldiccio)	ITA	Stelvio Cipriani
Evil of Dracula	JAP	Riichiro Manabe
Exorcist--Italian Style, The	ITA	Franco Godi
Family Holvak, The (series)	NBC-TV	Dick de Benedictis/ Lee Holdridge
Family Nobody Wanted, The	UN	George Romanis
Far-Out Space Nuts (series)	CBS-TV	Michael Lloyd/Reg Powell
Fear Is Spreading, The	BRI-TV	Laurie Johnson
Fireball on the Highway	JAP	Tadashi Kinoshita
First 36 Hours of Dr. Durant, The (pilot)	ABC-TV	Leonard Rosenman
Flavia, Priestess of Violence	ITA	Nicola Piovani

Flying Sorcerer, The	BRI	Harry Robinson
Forbidden Zone, The	RUS	Ivar Vigner
Force Five (pilot)	CBS-TV	James di Pasquale
Forced Entry (Last Victim, The)	IND	Tommy Vig
Forever Emmanuelle (Laure)	FRA/ITA	Franco Micalizzi
Foster and Laurie	TV	Lalo Schifrin
Friendly Persuasion	TV	John Cacavas
Frightmare	BRI	Stanley Myers
Ghost Busters, The (series)	CBS-TV	Yvette Blais/Jeff Michael
Ghost Hunter, The	BRA	Stefan Wohl
Girl Named Sooner, A	FOX	Jerry Goldsmith
Go--U.S.A. (series)	NBC-TV	Robert Maxwell
Godzilla vs. Mechagodzilla	JAP	Masaru Sato
Gold, Code and the Sea	JAP	Hachiro Aoyama
Grady (series)	NBC-TV	John Addison
Grandpa Max	CBS-TV	Peter Matz
Grave of the Vampire	IND	Jaime Mendoza-Nava
Guilty or Innocent: The Sam Sheppard Murder Case	UN	Lalo Schifrin
Hatfields and the McCoys, The	TV	Ken Lauber
Hereafter	NBC-TV	Jeff Barry
Hex	FOX	Patrick Williams
Hey, I'm Alive!	TV	Frank DeVol
Himiko	JAP	Toru Takemitsu
Home of Our Own, A	TV	Laurence Rosenthal
Horror Hospital	BRI	De Wolfe
Hot L Baltimore (series)	ABC-TV	Marvin Hamlisch
Huckleberry Finn	ABC	Earl Robinson
Hustle	PAR	Frank de Vol
Hustling	FIL	Jerry Fielding
I Will Fight No More Forever	WOL	Gerald Fried
If It's a Man, Hang Up	BRI-TV	Laurie Johnson
In This House of Brede	TV	Peter Matz
Inner Space (series)	IND-TV	Sven Liback
International Animation Festival, The (series)	PBS-TV	Gerig McRitchie
Invisible Man, The (series)	NBC-TV	Richard Clements/Henry Mancini/Pete Rugolo
Isis (series)	CBS-TV	Yvette Blais/Jeff Michael
Jeffersons, The (series)	CBS-TV	Jeff Barry/Ja'net Dubois /Don Great
Jennie: Lady Randolph Churchill (series)	PBS-TV	Tom McCall
Joe and Sons (series)	CBS-TV	David Shire
Joe Forrester (series)	NBC-TV	Robert Drasnin/Richard Markowitz
Journey from Darkness	TV	Ken Lauber
Kansas City Massacre, The	ABC	Robert Cobert
Karate Lady in Danger	JAP	Toshisuke Kikuchi
Karen (series)	ABC-TV	Benny Golson

Kate McShane (series)	CBS-TV	Charles Bernstein/John Cacavas
Keep On Truckin' (series)	ABC-TV	Marvin Laird
Khan! (series)	CBS-TV	Bruce Broughton/Morton Stevens
Killing Blows	JAP	Toshiaki Tsushima
Killing Game, The	BRI-TV	Laurie Johnson
Kiss Me, Monster	GER	Jerry van Rooyen
Kun Pi	THAI	Sahat Tuchinda
Last Day, The	PAR	Carmine Coppola
Last Hours Before Morning (pilot)	NBC-TV	Pete Rugolo
Last Survivors, The	TV	Michael Melvoin
Legend of Bigfoot, The	IND	Don Peake
Legend of Lizzie Borden, The	PAR	Billy Goldenberg
Legend of the Werewolf, The	BRI	Harry Robinson
Legend of Valentino, The	TV	Charles Fox
Lemora, the Lady Dracula (Child's Tale of the Supernatural, A)	IND	Dan Neufeld
Let's Switch	UN	Harry Geller
Lives of Jenny Dolan, The (pilot)	NBC-TV	Patrick Williams
Living Together	JAP	Hachiro Aoyama
Log of the Black Pearl, The	UN	Laurence Rosenthal
Look Back in Darkness	BRI-TV	Laurie Johnson
Lost Saucer, The (series)	IND-TV	Marvin Laird/Michael Lloyd
Love Among the Ruins	ABC	John Barry
Love Butcher, The	IND	Richard Hieronymous
Lowell Thomas Remembers (series)	PBS-TV	Jack Shaindlin
McCoy (series)	NBC-TV	Dick de Benedictis/Billy Goldenberg
Man on the Outside	UN	Elliot Kaplan
Mansion of the Doomed (Terror of Dr. Cheney, The)	IND	Robert O. Ragland
Matt Helm	COL	Jerry Fielding/Oliver Nelson
Matt Helm (series)	ABC-TV	Jerrold Immel/John Parker/Morton Stevens
Matter of Wife and Death, A (pilot)	NBC-TV	Richard Shores
Medical One	COL	Arthur Morton
Medical Story (series)	NBC-TV	Jerry Goldsmith/Arthur Morton/Richard Shores
Melody of Hate	BRI-TV	Laurie Johnson
Miles to Go Before I Sleep	TV	Wladimir Selinsky
Mirror of Deception, The	BRI-TV	Laurie Johnson
Missing Are Deadly, The	TV	Gil Melle
Mobile One (series)	ABC-TV	Nelson Riddle
Mobile Two (series)	ABC-TV	Nelson Riddle
Moll Flanders (series)	BRI-TV	Martin Caithy
Montefuscos, The	NBC-TV	Jack Elliott/Allyn Ferguson

Monty Python and the Holy Grail	BRI	Neil Innes/De Wolfe
Murder Motel	BRI-TV	Laurie Johnson
Murder on Flight 502	TV	Laurence Rosenthal
Murder on the Midnight Express	BRI-TV	Laurie Johnson
My Father's House	FIL	Charles Fox
My Way	JAP	Hikaru Hayashi
Mysteries from Beyond Earth	TV	Jaime Mendoza-Nava
Naked Exorcism	ITA	M. Sorghini
Nevada Smith (pilot)	NBC-TV	Lamont Dozier
New, Original Wonder Woman, The	WB	Charles Fox
Next Victim, The	BRI-TV	Laurie Johnson
Night That Panicked America, The	PAR	Frank Comstock
No, Honestly (series)	BRI-TV	Lynsey DePaul
Nothing But the Night	BRI	Malcolm Williamson
Oddball Couple, The (series)	ABC-TV	Doug Goodwin
On the Rocks (series)	ABC-TV	Jerry Fielding
One of Our Own	UN	Hal Mooney
Operation Summit	JAP	Toshiaki Tsushima
Oregon Trail, The	UN	David Shire
Outer Space Connection, The	IND	Roger Wagner
Phyllis (series)	CBS-TV	Dick de Benedictis
Pop!	CBS-TV	Sid Ramin
Princess Mermaid	JAP	Tsuokuni Hirayoshi
Professional Killers--Assassin's Quarry (see "Assassin's Quarry")		
Promise Him Anything ...	ABC	Nelson Riddle
Prophecies of Nostradamus	JAP	Isao Tomita
Queen of the Stardust Ballroom	TV	Billy Goldenberg
Return of Joe Forrester, The	COL	Richard Markowitz
Return to the Planet of the Apes (series)	NBC-TV	Dean Elliott/Eric Rogers
Returning Home	ABC-TV	Ken Lauber
Rivalry, The	NBC-TV	Mauro Bruno
Rivals of Sherlock Holmes, The (series)	PBS-TV	Robert Sharples
Rosenthal and Jones (pilot)	CBS-TV	Joel Hirschhorn/Al Kasha
Runaway Barge, The	TV	Nelson Riddle
Runaways, The	TV	Earle Hagen
S.W.A.T. (series)	ABC-TV	Barry de Vorzon/John Parker
Saint, The (series)	NBC-TV	Edwin Astley
Sandakan No. 8	JAP	Akira Ifukube
Sarah T.--Portrait of a Teenage Alcoholic	UN	James DiPasquale
Satan's Triangle	TV	Johnny Pate
Search for the Gods	WB	Billy Goldenberg
Secret Lives of Waldo Kitty, The (series)	NBC-TV	Yvette Blais/Jeff Michael
Secret Night Caller, The	TV	John Parker

Seduzidas Pelo Demonio	BRA	E. Coelho
Sex Express	BRI	De Wolfe
Shadow in the Streets, A	TV	Charles Bernstein
Shell Game	TV	Lenny Stack
Shock Waves (Death Corps)	IND	Richard Einhorn
Silence, The	TV	Maurice Jarre
Sin in the Vestry	BRA	Remo Usai
Sky Heist	WB	Leonard Rosenman
Sleepwalker	BRI-TV	Laurie Johnson
So This Is Love	JAP	Takamichi Ryuzaki
Someone I Touched	TV	Joel Hirschhorn/Al Kasha
Song of the Sun	JAP	Takeshi Shibuya
Space: 1999 (series)	BRI-TV	Vic Elms/Barry Gray/ Derek Wadsworth
Specialists, The (pilot)	NBC-TV	Billy May
Spiral Staircase, The	TV	David Lindup
Starsky and Hutch (series)	ABC-TV	Jack Elliott/Allyn Ferguson/Andrew Kulberg/Shorty Rogers /Lalo Schifrin/Tom Scott/Mark Snow
Stowaway to the Moon	FOX	Patrick Williams
Strange New World	WB	Richard Clements/Elliott Kaplan
Strike Force	TV	John Murtaugh
Sunshine (series)	NBC-TV	Hal Mooney
Supercops (pilot)	CBS-TV	Jacques Urbont
Swamy Aiyyappan	IN	Devarajan
Sweet Hostage	TV	Luchi de Jesus
Swiss Family Robinson	FOX	Richard LaSalle
Swiss Family Robinson (series)	ABC-TV	Richard LaSalle/Arthur Morton/Lionel Newman
Switch (series)	CBS-TV	James di Pasquale/Glen A. Larson/Dick Halli- gan/Stu Phillips/Eddie Sauter/Don Vincent
Target Risk (pilot)	NBC-TV	Eumir Deodato
Tattered Banner, The	JAP	Kazuo Okada
Tender Dracula (Confessions of a Blood Drinker)	GER	Karl-Heinz Shafer
Terror of Sheba, The (Persecution)	BRI	Paul Ferris
They Only Come Out at Night	MGM	"The Orphanage"
Three for the Road (series)	CBS-TV	James di Pasquale/David Shire
Three Old Women	JAP	Naozumi Yamamoto
Thundercrack!	IND	Mark Ellinger
Trial of Chaplain Jensen, The	FOX	Dave Grusin
Trilogy of Terror	ABC	Robert Cobert

Turning Point of Jim Malloy, The	COL	Johnny Mandel
Two Faces, The	IN	Ramzan Hammu
Vampyres	BRI	James Clark
Wave of Lust	ITA	Marcello Giombini
Welcome Back, Kotter (series)	ABC-TV	John Sebastian
We'll Get By (series)	CBS-TV	Sheldon Harnick/Joe Raposo
Westwind, The (series)	NBC-TV	Richard LaSalle
Wet Sand in August	JAP	Hiroshi Mutsu
When Things Were Rotten (series)	ABC-TV	Artie Butler
Who Is the Black Dahlia?	TV	Dominic Frontiere
Wildcat Rock-Beat '71	JAP	Hiroki Tamaki
Winner Take All	TV	David Shire
Wives (pilot)	CBS-TV	Buzz Kohen
You Lie So Deep, My Love	UN	Elliot Kaplan
Zoo Gang, The (series)	NBC-TV	Ken Thorne

1976

Ace (pilot)	NBC-TV	Patrick Williams
Adams Chronicles, The (series)	PBS	John Morris
Addie and the King of Hearts	CBS-TV	Arthur B. Rubinstein
African Bird, The	JAP	Kazuo Sugita
Alice (series)	CBS-TV	David Shire
Alien Factor, The	IND	Kenneth Walker
All the Colors of Darkness (They're Coming to Get You)	ITA	Bruno Nicolai
All's Fair (series)	CBS-TV	Jeff Barry
Amelia Earhart	UN	David Shire
Archie (pilot)	ABC-TV	Larry Farrow/Stu Gardner
Ark II (series)	CBS-TV	Yvette Blais/Jeff Michael
Assault on Precinct 13	IND	John Carpenter
Ball Four	CBS-TV	Harry Chapin
Banjo Hackett (pilot)	NBC-TV	Morton Stevens
Beauty and the Beast	NBC-TV	Ron Goodwin
Bert D'Angelo/Superstar (series)	ABC-TV	John Elizalde/Duane Tatro/Patrick Williams
Big John, Little John (series)	NBC-TV	Richard La Salle
Bionic Woman, The (series)	ABC-TV	Charles Albertine/ Bobby Bryant/Jerry Fielding/Joe Harnell/ J. J. Johnson
Bloodsucking Freaks (Incredible Torture Show, The)	IND	Michael Sahl
Blue Bird, The	RUS	Irwin Kostal/Lionel Newman/Andrei Petrov
Boy in the Plastic Bubble, The	TV	Mark Snow/Paul Williams
Brenda Starr (pilot)	ABC-TV	Lalo Schifrin
Bridger (pilot)	ABC-TV	Elliot Kaplan

Brink's: The Great Robbery	TV	Richard Markowitz
Bubble, The	IND	Paul Miraki
Bureau, The	NBC-TV	Peter Matz
C.P.O. Sharkey (series)	ABC-TV	Peter Matz
Call of the Wild, The	TV	Peter Matz
Captains and the Kings	UN	Elmer Bernstein
Cat on a Hot Tin Roof	TV	Derek Hilton
Charlie's Angels (series)	ABC-TV	Jack Elliott/Allyn Ferguson
Cheerleaders, The (pilot)	NBC-TV	Earle Hagen
City of Angels (series)	NBC-TV	Hal Mooney/Nelson Riddle
Clue Club, The (series)	CBS-TV	Hoyt Curtin
Code Name: Hercules	TV	Johnny Mandel
Coral Jungle, The (series)	IND-TV	Tom Anthony
Creature from Black Lake	IND	Jaime Mendoza-Nava
Crimes of Passion (series)	IND-TV	Derek Scott
Crimes of the Black Cat	ITA	Manuel de Sica
Dark Side of Innocence, The	WB	Peter Matz
Dark Victory	UN	Billy Goldenberg
Dawn: Portrait of a Teenage Runaway	TV	Fred Karlin
Death at Love House	TV	Laurence Rosenthal
Delvecchio (series)	CBS-TV	Richard Clements/Billy Goldenberg
Demain des Momes	FRA	Eric Demarsan
Devil's Mountain, The	IND	Gene Kauer/Douglas Lackey
Devude Gelichad	IN	Ramesh Naidu
Disappearance of Aimee, The	NBC-TV	Steve Byrne
Doctor Maniac (House of the Living Dead)	IND	Peter J. Elliott
Doctor Shrinker (series)	ABC-TV	Jimmie Haskell
Dr. Tarr's Torture Dungeon	IND	Nacho Mendez
Dogs	IND	Alan Oldfield
Don't Call Us (pilot)	CBS-TV	Patrick Williams
Dumplings, The (series)	NBC-TV	Billy Goldenberg
Dynasty	TV	Gil Melle
Eaten Alive (Death Trap)	IND	Wayne Bell
Eleanor and Franklin	TV	John Barry
Electra Woman and Dyna Girl (series)	ABC-TV	Jimmie Haskell
Entertainer, The	TV	Marvin Hamlisch
Everybody Rides the Carousel	CBS-TV	William Russo
Executive Suite (series)	CBS-TV	Bill Conti/Gerald Fried/Billy Goldenberg/Gil Melle/John Parker/Nelson Riddle
F. Scott Fitzgerald in Hollywood	TV	Morton Stevens
Face of Darkness, The	BRI	Martin Jacklin
Family (series)	ABC-TV	John Rubenstein/Pete Rugolo/Mark Snow

Farewell to Manzanar	UN	Paul Chihara
Fay (series)	NBC-TV	George Aliceson Tipton
Flatbush/Avenue J (pilot)	ABC-TV	Paul Jabara
Flood	FOX	Richard LaSalle
Forbidden Letters	IND	Jeff Olsom
Francis Gary Powers: The True Story of the U-2 Spy Incident	TV	Gerald Fried
Full House (pilot)	NBC-TV	Harper McKay
Future Cop	PAR	Billy Goldenberg
Gemini Man	UN	Billy Goldenberg
Gemini Man, The (series)	NBC-TV	Lee Holdridge/Mark Snow
Gibbsville (series)	NBC-TV	Jack Elliott/Allyn Ferguson/Leonard Rosenman
God Told Me To (Demon)	NWP	Frank Cordell
Good Heavens (series)	ABC-TV	Patrick Williams
Goodies, The (series)	BRI-TV	Michael Gibbs/Bill Oddie
Green Eyes	TV	Fred Karlin
Griffin and Phoenix	ABC	George Aliceson Tipton
Haunts (Veil, The)	IND	Pino Donaggio
Having Babies	TV	Earle Hagen
Hazard's People (pilot)	CBS-TV	John Cacavas
Heart of Glass	GER	"Popol Vuh"
Heck's Angels (pilot)	CBS-TV	Jack Elliott/Allyn Ferguson
Helter Skelter	TV	Billy Goldenberg
High Risk (pilot)	ABC-TV	Billy Goldenberg
Holmes and Yoyo (series)	ABC-TV	Dick Halligan/Leonard Rosenman
Horror of the Zombies	SPA	Anton Garcia Abril
House of Terror	JAP	Ugi Oni
How to Break Up a Happy Divorce	TV	Nelson Riddle
I Want to Keep My Baby	CBS	George Aliceson Tipton
I'll Never Forget What's Her Name	ABC-TV	Jerry Fielding
In Search of ... (series)	IND-TV	Michael J. Lewis/Laurin Rinder
Invasion of Johnson County, The	UN	Pete Carpenter/Mike Post
Invisible Strangler (Astral Factor, The)	IND	Richard Hieronymous/Alan Oldfield
Ivan the Terrible (series)	CBS-TV	Joe Raposo
Jabberjaw (series)	ABC-TV	Hoyt Curtin/Paul DeKorte
James Dean	TV	Billy Goldenberg
Jeremiah of Jacob's Neck (pilot)	CBS-TV	Harry Sukman
Jigsaw John (series)	NBC-TV	Harry Lojewski/Pete Rugolo
Just an Old Sweet Song	IND	Peter Matz
Kaseki	JAP	Toru Takemitsu
Keegans, The (pilot)	CBS-TV	Paul Chihara
Kids from C.A.P.E.R., The (series)	NBC-TV	Wally Gold/Jay Siegel

Killer Who Wouldn't Die, The	ABC-TV	George Garvarentz
Kingston: The Power Play	NBC-TV	Leonard Rosenman
Kiss Me, Kill Me (pilot)	ABC-TV	Richard Markowitz
Land of Hope (pilot)	CBS-TV	Morton Gould
Lanigan's Rabbi	UN	Leonard Rosenman
Laverne and Shirley (series)	ABC-TV	John Beal/Richard Clements/Charles Fox
Law and Order	PAR	Richard Hazard
Law of the Land (pilot)	NBC-TV	John Parker
Legend of Bigfoot, The	IND	Al Capps
Legend of the Wolf Woman (Werewolf Woman)	ITA	Lallo Gori
Lindbergh Kidnapping Case, The	COL	Billy Goldenberg
Loneliest Runner, The	NBC	David Rose
Look What's Happened to Rosemary's Baby	PAR	Charles Bernstein
Louis Armstrong--Chicago Style	TV	Benny Carter
Love Boat, The	TV	Charles Fox
Macahans, The	MGM	Jerrold Immel
McDuff, The Talking Dog (series)	NBC-TV	Richard LaSalle
McLean Stevenson Show, The (series)	NBC-TV	Paul Williams
McMillan (series)	NBC-TV	Jerry Fielding
McNaughton's Daughter (series)	NBC-TV	George Romanis/David Shire
Magic Man, The	ITA-TV	Ennio Morricone
Mallory: Circumstantial Evidence (pilot)	NBC-TV	James di Pasquale
Man from Nowhere, The	BRI	John Cameron
Man Who Fell to Earth, The	BRI	John Phillips/Stomu Yamashita
Mary Hartman, Mary Hartman (series)	IND-TV	Earle Hagen
Maureen (pilot)	CBS-TV	Arthur B. Rubinstein, Jr.
Maya Manushya	IN	Vijaya Bhaskar
Mayday at 40,000 Feet	WB	Richard Markowitz
Million Dollar Rip-Off, The	TV	Vic Mizzy
Milpitas Monster, The	IND	Robert R. Berry, Jr.
Mr. T and Tina (series)	ABC-TV	George Aliceson Tipton
Moneychangers, The	PAR	Henry Mancini
Monster Squad, The (series)	NBC-TV	Richard La Salle
Moses--The Lawgiver	ITA	Ennio Morricone
Most Wanted (series)	ABC-TV	Richard Markowitz/Lalo Schifrin/Patrick Williams
My Friends Need Killing	IND	Mark Bucci
Mysteries of the Gods	GER	Peter Thomas
Naag Champag	IN	S. N. Tripathi
Nagin	IN	Laxmikant Pyarelal

New Daughters of Joshua Cabe, The (pilot)	ABC-TV	Jeff Alexander
Newman's Drug Store (pilot)	NBC-TV	Charles Fox
Nightmare in Badham County	ABC	Charles Bernstein
Oath: The Sad and Lonely Sundays, The	ABC-TV	Dave Grusin
Once an Eagle (series)	NBC-TV	Dana Kaproff
One of My Wives Is Missing (pilot)	ABC-TV	Billy Goldenberg
Onedin Line, The (series)	BRI-TV	Anthony Isaac
Over and Out (pilot)	NBC-TV	Peter Matz
Panache (pilot)	ABC-TV	Frank DeVol
Passing Strangers	IND	Jeff Olsom
Perennial Weed, The	JAP	Mitsuaki Kanno
Perilous Voyage	UN	Gil Melle
Popi (series)	CBS-TV	George Del Barrio
Possessed, The (Witch Yoba, The)	JAP	Riichiro Manabe
Practice, The (series)	NBC-TV	James DiPasquale/David Shire
Preparations for the Festival	JAP	Teizo Matsumura
Quest, The (series)	NBC-TV	Richard Shores
Quincy (series)	NBC-TV	Bob Alcivar/Bruce Broughton/Vic Mizzy/ Stu Phillips
Red	BRI	Anthony Bowles
Return of the World's Greatest Detective, The	UN	Dick DeBenedictis
Return to Earth	TV	Billy Goldenberg
Revenge for a Rape	TV	Jerrold Immel
Rich Man, Poor Man, Book I	ABC-TV	Alex North
Rich Man, Poor Man, Book II	ABC-TV	Michael Isaacson/Alex North
Richie Brockelman: Missing 24 Hours	UN	Pete Carpenter/Mike Post
Royce (pilot)	CBS-TV	Jerrold Immel
Sara (series)	CBS-TV	Lee Holdridge
Satan's Slave	IND	Patrick John Scott
Savage Bees, The	TV	Walter Murphy
Schizo	BRI	Stanley Myers
Scooby-Doo/Dynomutt Hour, The	ABC-TV	Ted Nichols
Scott Free (pilot)	NBC-TV	Pete Carpenter/Mike Post
Secret Life of John Chapman, The	TV	Fred Myrow
Serpico (series)	NBC-TV	Elmer Bernstein/Robert Drasnin
Serpico: The Deadly Game	PAR	Elmer Bernstein
Sex Machine, The	ITA	Fred Bongusto
Shark Kill	TV	George Romanis
Sherlock Holmes in New York	FOX	Richard Rodney Bennett
Sirota's Court (series)	NBC-TV	David Shire
Smash-Up on Interstate 5	FIL	Bill Conti
Someday, Somewhere	JAP	Hachiro Aoyama

Song of the Demon	JAP	Hikaru Hayashi
Special Branch (series)	BRI-TV	Robert Earley
Spencer's Pilots (series)	CBS-TV	Bruce Broughton/ Jerrold Immel/Morton Stevens
Spermula	FRA	Jose Bartel
Stalk the Wild Child	TV	John Rubenstein
State Fair	CBS-TV	Laurence Rosenthal
Stranded (pilot)	CBS-TV	Gordon Jenkins
Street Killing (pilot)	ABC-TV	J. J. Johnson
Sweeney, The (series)	BRI-TV	Harry South
Sybil	TV	Leonard Rosenman
Sylvester and Tweety (series)	CBS-TV	Milt Franklin/William Lava/John Seely/Carl Stalling
Symptons	IND	Patrick John Scott
Tarzan: Lord of the Jungle (series)	CBS-TV	Yvette Blais/Jeff Michael
That Was the Year That Was	NBC-TV	Joe Raposo
They Came from Within (Shivers/ Parasite Murders, The)	CAN	Ivan Reitman
This Better Be It (pilot)	CBS	David Shire
Three Times Daley (pilot)	CBS	Don Costa
Time Travelers (pilot)	ABC	Morton Stevens
To the Devil, a Daughter	BRI	Paul Glass
Tongue	IND	Roger Hamilton Spotts
Tony Randall Show, The (series)	ABC-TV	Patrick Williams
Tora-san's Rise and Fall	JAP	Naozumi Yamamoto
21 Hours at Munich	FIL	Laurence Rosenthal
Twin Detectives (pilot)	ABC-TV	Tom Scott
UFO's: It Has Begun	TV	Robert Emenegger
Under the Blossoming Cherry Trees	JAP	Toru Takemitsu
Valley Forge	NBC-TV	Wladimir Selinsky
Vandedevatha	IN	Devarajan
Victory at Entebbe	WOL	Charles Fox
Village, The	JAP	Kyoko Okada
Visions (series)	PBS-TV	Joe Raposo/Mark Snow
Viva Valdez (series)	ABC-TV	Shorty Rogers
Wanted: The Sundance Woman	FOX	Fred Karlin
What's Happening? (series)	ABC-TV	Henry Mancini
Whispers in the Dark	IND	Pino Donaggio
Who Can Kill a Child? (Island of the Damned)	SPA	Waldo de los Rios
Widow	TV	Billy Goldenberg
Witch Who Came from the Sea, The	IND	Herschel Burke Gilbert
Woman of the Year	MGM	Fred Karlin
Wonder Woman (series)	ABC-TV	Charles Fox/Artie Kane
Wonderbug (series)	ABC-TV	Jimmie Haskell
Young Pioneers	ABC	Laurence Rosenthal

| Young Pioneers' Christmas | ABC-TV | Laurence Rosenthal |
| You're Just Like Your Father (pilot) | CBS-TV | Harry Geller |

1977

African Queen, The (pilot)	CBS-TV	John Murtaugh
Alaska Story, The	JAP	Masaru Sato
Alexander: The Other Side of Dawn	TV	Fred Karlin
All That Glitters (series)	IND-TV	Ray Brown/Shelly Manne
Amazing Howard Hughes, The	BRI	Laurence Rosenthal
Amazing Spiderman, The	TV	Johnnie Spence
Amy Prentiss (series)	NBC-TV	John Cacavas/Don Costa
Andros Targets, The (series)	CBS-TV	Bill Conti/Jerry Fielding/ Morton Stevens/Patrick Williams
Aspen	UN	Mike Melvoin/Tom Scott
Baggy Pants and the Nitwits (series)	NBC-TV	Steve DePatie/Doug Goodwin
Bang-Shang Lalapalooza Show, The (series)	NBC-TV	Yvette Blais/Jeff Michael
Battle of the Planets	TV	Koichi Sugiyama
Beach Girls, The (pilot)	IND-TV	Dick Smedley
Benny and Barney, Las Vegas Undercover (pilot)	NBC-TV	Stu Phillips
Betty White Show, The (series)	CBS-TV	Dick de Benedictis
Beyond Reason (Mati)	IND	Robert Randles
Big Hawaii (series)	NBC-TV	Jack Elliott/Allyn Ferguson
Billy: Portrait of a Street Kid	TV	Fred Karlin
Black Magic II	HK	Chan Yang Yu
Black Market Baby	TV	Richard Bellis/George Wilkins
Black Sheep Squadron, The (series)	NBC-TV	Pete Carpenter/Mike Post
Blansky's Beauties (series)	ABC-TV	Charles Fox
Bless This House (series)	BRI-TV	Geoff Love
Blood Relations	HOL	J. M. de Scarano
Blue Sunshine	IND	Charles Gross
Bumpers (pilot)	NBC-TV	The Brecker Brothers
Bunco	NBC-TV	John Parker
Busting Loose (series)	CBS-TV	Jack Elliott/Allyn Ferguson
C.B. Bears, The (series)	NBC-TV	Hoyt Curtin/Paul DeKorte
Cabot Connection, The (pilot)	CBS-TV	George Romanis
Calmos (Femmes Fatales)	FRA	Georges Delerue
Captains Courageous	TV	Allyn Ferguson
Carter Country (series)	ABC-TV	Pete Rugolo
Charlie Cobb: Nice Night for a Hanging (pilot)	NBC-TV	Pete Carpenter/Mike Post

Child, The (Kill and Go Hide)	NAF	Rob Wallace
Chopped Liver Brothers, The	ABC-TV	Patrick Williams
Christmas Miracle in Caufield, U.S.A.	FOX	Fred Karlin
Cinderella 2000	IND	Sparky Sugarman
Circle of Children, A	FOX	Nelson Riddle
City, The (pilot)	NBC-TV	John Elizalde
Claws	IND	Gene Kauer/Douglas Lackey
Cliffwood Avenue Kids, The (series)	IND-TV	Larry Taylor
Code Name: Diamond Head (pilot)	NBC-TV	Morton Stevens
Code R (series)	CBS-TV	Lee Holdridge
Come Back, Little Sheba	TV	John McCabe
Comeback, The (Day the Screaming Stopped, The)	BRI	Stanley Myers
Confessional, The	BRI	Stanley Myers
Contract on Cherry Street	COL	Jerry Goldsmith
Corey: For the People (pilot)	NBC-TV	Ed Kalehoff
Counterfeit Commandos (see Unglorious Bastards)		
Cover Girls (pilot)	NBC-TV	Richard Shores
Crash! (Akaza, God of Vengeance)	IND	Andrew Belling
Curse of the Black Widow	ABC	Robert Cobert
Curse of the Mayan Temple, The	IND	Gene Kauer/Douglas Lackey
Danger in Paradise	FIL	Jack Elliott/Allyn Ferguson
Darinda	IN	K. Anandji
Dead of Night	TV	Robert Cobert
Deadliest Season, The	TV	Dick Hyman
Deadly Game, The	MGM	Mundell Lowe
Deadly Triangle, The (pilot)	NBC-TV	Dick de Benedictis
Death of Richie, The	TV	Fred Karlin
Delta County, U.S.A. (pilot)	ABC-TV	Jack Elliott/Jack Ferguson
Devil's Ecstasy, The	IND	Bill Phyx
Diabolica	ITA	Franco Micalizzi
Dickens of London	BRI-TV	Monty Norman
Dog and Cat (series)	ABC-TV	Barry de Vorzon
Dominique (Dominique Is Dead)	BRI	David Whittaker
Eddie and Herbert (pilot)	CBS-TV	Ray Charles
Eight Is Enough (series)	ABC-TV	Earle Hagen/Fred Wagner
Eleanor and Franklin: The White House Years	TV	John Barry
Elixir of the Devil, The	GER	Hans-Martin Majewski
Emmanuelle and the Last Cannibals (Trap Them and Kill Them)	ITA	Nico Fidenco
End of the World	IND	Andrew Belling
Enigma	CBS-TV	Harry Sukman

Escape from Brogen County	PAR	Charles Bernstein
Exo-Man (pilot)	NBC-TV	Dana Kaproff
Fantastic Journey, The (series)	NBC-TV	Dick de Benedictis/ Robert Prince
Fantasy Island	TV	Laurence Rosenthal
Father, Dear Father (series)	IND-TV	Gordon Frankes
Father Knows Best: Home for Christmas	NBC-TV	George Duning
Father Knows Best Reunion	NBC-TV	George Duning
Fawlty Towers (series)	BRI-TV	Dennis Wilson
Feather and Father Gang, The (series)	ABC-TV	Bert Gold/George Romanis
Fire!	TV	Richard LaSalle
Fish (series)	ABC-TV	Jack Elliott/Allyn Ferguson
Fitzpatricks, The (series)	CBS-TV	John Rubenstein/Fred Werner
Flag, Class A, Grade 4, The	JAP	Takahiko Ishikawa
Flight to Holocaust	TV	Paul Williams
Flying Without Wings	HOL	Tonny Eyk
Foes	IND	Jeff Bruner
Forever Fernwood (series)	IND-TV	Bobby Knight
Four of Us, The (pilot)	ABC-TV	Morton Gould
Future Cop (series)	ABC-TV	J. J. Johnson
Gasp!	YUG	Walter Scharf
Gathering, The	HB	John Barry
Giant Iron Man 1-7--The Ariel Battleship	JAP	Chumei Watanabe
Girl Called Hatter Fox, The	TV	Fred Karlin
Girl in the Empty Grave, The	MGM	Mundell Lowe
Glitterball, The	BRI	Harry Robinson
Goldenrod	CAN	Franklin Boyd
Good Against Evil (pilot)	ABC-TV	Lalo Schifrin
Great Day	ABC-TV	Peter Matz
Great Grape Ape Show, The (series)	ABC-TV	Hoyt Curtin/Paul DeKorte
Greatest Thing That Almost Happened, The	TV	David Shire
Green, Green Grass of Home, The	RUM	Radu Serban
Hardy Boys Mysteries, The (series)	ABC-TV	Stu Phillips
Haunting	JAP	Shunsuke Kikuchi
Having Babies II	TV	Fred Karlin
Hell Island	JAP	Shinichi Tanabe
Hostage Heart, The	MGM	Fred Karlin
House by the Lake, The	CAN	Ivan Reitman
How the West Was Won (series)	ABC-TV	Bruce Broughton/Jerrold Immel/John Parker

Hunted Lady, The	TV	Laurence Rosenthal
Hunter (series)	CBS-TV	Richard Shores
I Am the Greatest: The Adventures of Muhammad Ali (series)	NBC-TV	Charles Blaker
In the Glitter Palace	TV	John Parker
In the Matter of Karen Ann Quinlan	TV	Bill Conti
Incredible Rocky Mountain Race, The	SUN	Robert Summers
Intimate Strangers	TV	Fred Karlin
Inugamis, The	JAP	Yuji Ohno
It Happened at Lake Wood Manor	TV	Kim Richmond
It Happened One Christmas	UN	Stephen Lawrence
Jadu Tona	IN	H. Bhoshe
James at 15	FOX	Richard Baskin
James at 15 (series)	NBC-TV	Miles Goodman/Jimmie Haskell/J. A. C. Redford
Jesus of Nazareth	BRI	Maurice Jarre
Johnny, We Hardly Knew Ye	TV	Garry Sherman
Journey into the Beyond	IND	Don Great
Just a Little Inconvenience	UN	Jimmie Haskell
Kallikaks, The (series)	NBC-TV	Tom Wells
Keeper of the Wild (pilot)	IND-TV	Bill Marx
Kill Me If You Can	COL	Bill Conti
Killer on Board	TV	Earle Hagen
Killing Affair, A	COL	Richard Shores
King of Kensington (series)	CAN-TV	Bob McMillin
Kingston: Confidential (series)	NBC-TV	Henry Mancini/Pete Rugolo/Richard Shores
Land of the Minotaur	BRI	Brian Eno
Lanigan's Rabbi (series)	NBC-TV	Don Costa
Last Dinosaur, The	TV	Maury Laws
Last Hurrah, The	NBC-TV	Peter Matz
Last of the Mohicans, The	SUN	Bob Summers
Legend of Dinosaurs and Monster Birds	JAP	Masao Yagi
Life and Assassination of the Kingfish, The	TV	Fred Karlin
Life and Times of Grizzly Adams, The (series)	NBC-TV	Bob Summers
Little Girl Who Lives Down the Lane, The	AI	Christian Gaubert
Little Ladies of the Night	TV	Jerry Fielding
Logan's Run (series)	CBS-TV	Jerrold Immel/Laurence Rosenthal
Lou Grant (series)	CBS-TV	Michael Melvoin/Patrick Williams
Love Boat, The (series)	ABC-TV	Charles Fox/Artie Kane/John Parker/Duane

		Tatro/George Aliceson Tipton
Love Boat II, The	TV	Charles Fox
Loves Me, Loves Me Not (series)	CBS-TV	George Aliceson Tipton
Lucan	MGM	Fred Karlin
Lucan (series)	ABC-TV	J. J. Johnson
Lullaby of the Good Earth	JAP	Jiro Takemura
McLaren's Riders (pilot)	CBS-TV	Fred Karlin
Mad Bull	TV	Al DeLory
Magic Mongo (series)	ABC-TV	Michael Melvoin
Magnificent Magnet of Santa Mesa, The	COL	Jack Elliott/Allyn Ferguson
Man from Atlantis, The (series)	NBC-TV	Fred Karlin
Man in the Iron Mask, The	TV	Allyn Ferguson
Man With the Power, The (pilot)	NBC-TV	Patrick Williams
Mariko-Mother	JAP	Mariko Miyagi
Marlo and the Magic Movie Machine (series)	CBS-TV	Pete Dino
Mary Jane Harper Cried Last Night	PAR	Billy Goldenberg
Mary White	TV	Leonard Rosenman
Messalina, Messalina	ITA	Maurizio and Guido de Angelis
Minstrel Man	TV	Fred Karlin
Miss Jones and Son (series)	BRI-TV	Roger Webb
Mulligan's Stew (series)	NBC-TV	Morton Stevens/George Aliceson Tipton
Murder at the World Series	ABC	John Cacavas
Murder in Peyton Place	FOX	Laurence Rosenthal
Mysteries from Beyond the Triangle	TV	Jeff Gilman
Nana (series)	BRI-TV	Mark Lubrock
Nancy Drew Mysteries, The (series)	ABC-TV	Glen A. Larson/Stu Phillips
Nashville 99 (series)	CBS-TV	Earle Hagen
Natural Look, The (pilot)	NBC-TV	Charles Fox
New Adventures of Batman, The (series)	CBS-TV	Yvette Blais/Jeff Michael
New Adventures of Wonder Woman, The (series)	CBS-TV	Johnny Harris/Artie Kane/Richard La Salle/Angela Morley/ Stu Phillips/ Robert Prince
New Archie/Sabrina Hour, The (series)	NBC-TV	Yvette Blais/Jeff Michael
New Super Friends Hour, The (series)	ABC-TV	Hoyt Curtin/Paul DeKorte
Night of the Seagulls	SPA	Anton Garcia Abril
Night Terror	TV	Fred Steiner
Night They Took Miss Beautiful, The	TV	Walter Murphy
Nowhere to Hide (pilot)	NBC-TV	Ray Ellis

Nowhere to Hide	TV	Ray Ellis
Off the Wall (pilot)	NBC-TV	Pete Carpenter/Mike Post
Operation Petticoat (series)	ABC-TV	Artie Butler/Hal Mooney
Oregon Trail, The (series)	NBC-TV	Dick de Benedictis
Outside Man, The (pilot)	CBS-TV	Tom Scott
Pallisers, The (series)	BRI-TV	Herbert Chappel/Wilfred Josephs
Panic in Echo Park	TV	Johnnie Spence
Peter Lundy and the Medicine Hat Stallion (pilot)	NBC-TV	Morton Stevens
Pine Canyon Is Burning (pilot)	NBC-TV	Lee Holdridge
Possessed, The (pilot)	NBC-TV	Leonard Rosenman
Prey	BRI	Ivor Slaney
Primary English Class, The (pilot)	ABC-TV	Joe Hamilton/Peter Matz
Prince of Central Park, The	TV	Arthur B. Rubenstein
Quinns, The (pilot)	NBC-TV	John Scott
Rabid	CAN	Ivan Reitman
Rafferty (series)	CBS-TV	Richard Clements/ Leonard Rosenman
Raid on Entebbe	FOX	David Shire
Raja Nartakiya Rahasya	IN	E. Vasantha
Ransom for Alice (pilot)	NBC-TV	David Rose
Red Alert	PAR	George Aliceson Tipton
Relentless (pilot)	CBS-TV	John Cacavas
Rhinemann Exchange, The	NBC-TV	Michel Colombier
Robin's Nest (series)	BRI-TV	Brian Bennett
Roger and Harry: The Mitera Target (pilot)	ABC-TV	Jack Elliott/Allyn Ferguson
Roots	WOL	Gerald Fried/Quincy Jones
Rosetti and Ryan (series)	NBC-TV	Gordon Jenkins/Peter Matz
SST--Death Flight	ABC	John Cacavas
San Pedro Beach Bums, The (series)	ABC-TV	Pete Rugolo/Mark Snow
Sanford Arms (series)	NBC-TV	Henry Mancini
Satan's Cheerleaders	IND	Gerald Lee
Scream from Nowhere, A (Hidden Beast, The)	JAP	Hajimi Kubarasi
Search and Rescue: The Alpha Team (series)	NBC-TV	Lew Lehman
Secrets	TV	George Aliceson Tipton
Sensitive, Passionate Man, A	TV	Bill Conti
Seventh Avenue (series)	NBC-TV	Nelson Riddle
79 Park Avenue (series)	NBC-TV	Nelson Riddle
Sex and the Married Woman	UN	Gerald Fried
Shadow of Chikara, The	IND	Jaime Mendoza-Nava
Sharon: Portrait of a Mistress	PAR	Roger Kellaway
Skatebirds, The (series)	CBS-TV	Hoyt Curtin

Snowbeast	TV	Robert Prince
Soap (series)	ABC-TV	George Aliceson Tipton
Something for Joey	TV	David Shire
Space Academy (series)	CBS-TV	Yvette Blais/Jeff Michael
Spectre	FOX	John Cameron
Spell, The	TV	Gerald Fried
Spider-Man	CBS-TV	Johnnie Spence
Stonestreet: Who Killed the Centerfold Model?	NBC-TV	Patrick Williams
Storyteller, The	UN	David Shire/Hal Mooney
Strange Possession of Mrs. Oliver, The	TV	Morton Stevens
Sunshine Christmas	UN	Tony Berg
Super Witch (series)	NBC-TV	Yvette Blais/Jeff Michael
Szysznyk (series)	CBS-TV	Doug Gilmore
Tabitha (series)	ABC-TV	Dick de Benedictis/ Shorty Rogers
Tail Gunner Joe	UN	Billy May
Tales of the Unexpected (series)	NBC-TV	Richard Markowitz/ David Shire
Tarantulas: The Deadly Cargo	TV	Mundell Lowe
Telethon	ABC	Peter Matz
Tell Me My Name	TV	Mickey Erbe/Hagood Hardy
Temple of the Golden Pavilion, The	JAP	Toru Kurashima
Terraces (pilot)	NBC-TV	Peter Matz
Terror of Godzilla (Revenge of Mecha-Godzilla)	JAP	Akira Ifukube
Testimony of Two Men	UN	Michel Colombier/ Gerald Fried
That's Cat	IND-TV	John Sebastian
That's Hollywood (series)	IND-TV	Ruby Raksin/Jack Smalley
3,000 Mile Chase, The	UN	Elmer Bernstein
Three's Company (series)	ABC-TV	Joe Raposo
Thunder (series)	NBC-TV	Ray Ellis
Tintorera	IND	Basil Poledouris
Tora-san's Sunrise and Sunset	JAP	Naozumi Yamamoto
Towards the Year 2000 (series)	IND-TV	George Greeley
Trial of Lee Harvey Oswald, The	TV	Fred Karlin
Troupe, The (Halahaka)	ISR	Yair Rosenblum
Two Iida	JAP	Chuji Kinoshita
Uncanny, The	BRI	Wilfred Josephs
Unglorious Bastards (Counterfeit Commandos)	ITA	Francesco de Masi
Unicorn Tales (series)	IND-TV	Jack Feldman
Voyage of the Canoe "Che-Che-Meni," The	JAP	Saburo Iwakawa
War Between the Tates, The	TV	John Barry
War in Space	ITA	Marcello Giombini
Washington Affair, The	IND	Geordie Hormel

Washington: Behind Closed Doors (series)	ABC-TV	Dominic Frontiere/ Richard Markowitz
Westside Medical (series)	ABC-TV	Billy Goldenberg
We've Got Each Other (series)	CBS-TV	Nino Candido
What Really Happened to the Class of '65? (series)	NBC-TV	Don Costa/James de Pasquale/Jimmie Haskell/Stu Phillips
Whatever Happened to Dobie Gillis?	CBS-TV	Randy Newman
Wilma	TV	Irwin Bazelon
Winner Take All (pilot)	CBS-TV	John Elizalde
Wodehouse Playhouse (series)	BRI-TV	Raymond Jones
Wombling Free	BRI	Mike Batt
World of Darkness, The (pilot)	CBS-TV	Fred Karlin
Worm Eaters, The	IND	Theodore Stern
Yesterday's Child	PAR	Dominic Frontiere
Young Dan'l Boone (series)	CBS-TV	Earle Hagen
Young Joe, the Forgotten Kennedy	ABC	John Barry
Young Sentinels, The (series)	NBC-TV	Yvette Blais/Jeff Michael
You're Gonna Love It Here (pilot)	CBS-TV	Peter Matz

1978

A.E.S. Hudson Street (series)	ABC	Jack Elliott/Allyn Ferguson
Alice, Sweet Alice (Communion)	IND	Stephen Lawrence
All-New Popeye Hour, The (series)	CBS-TV	Hoyt Curtin
Almost Heaven (pilot)	ABC-TV	Paul Chihara
American Girls, The (series)	CBS-TV	Jerrold Immel
And I Alone Survived	TV	Laurence Rosenthal
Anna and the King (series)	CBS-TV	Paul Williams
Annie Flynn (pilot)	CBS-TV	Gene Page
Another Day (series)	CBS-TV	Paul Williams
Are You in the House Alone?	TV	Charles Bernstein
Arrevederci Yamato	JAP	Hiroshi Miyagawa
Awakening Land, The	WB	Fred Karlin
B. J. and the Bear	UN	Glen A. Larson
Baby, I'm Back (series)	CBS-TV	Jeff Barry
Baretta (series)	ABC-TV	Dave Grusin/Tom Scott
Barracuda	GER	Klaus Schulze
Bastard/Kent Family Chronicles, The	IND-TV	John Addison
Battered	TV	Don Peake
Battle of the Planets (series)	IND-TV	Hoyt Curtin
Battlestar Galactica	ABC-TV	Stu Phillips
Beasts Are on the Streets, The	HB	Gerald Fried
Bell, Book and Candle	ABC-TV	Ian Fraser
Bermuda Depths, The	ABC-TV	Maury Laws

Bermuda Triangle, The	BRI	John Cameron
Bermuda Triangle, The	ITA	Stelvio Cipriani
Betrayal	TV	Paul Chihara
Between the Wars (series)	IND-TV	William Loose/Jack Tillar
Big Bob Johnson and His Fantastic Speed Circus (pilot)	NBC-TV	Mark Snow
Black Beauty	NBC-TV	John Addison
Bog	IND	Bill Walker
Brain Leeches, The	IND	Paul Jones
Breaking Up	IND	Walt Levinsky
Bud and Lou	TV	Fred Karlin
Bushido Blade, The	JAP	Maury Laws
Busters, The	CBS-TV	Jerrold Immel
Cat from Outer Space, The	DIS	Lalo Schifrin
Centennial	UN	John Addison
Charmurti	IN	Ajoy Das
Child of Glass	DIS-TV	George Duning
Chinese Web, The	TV	Johnnie Spence
Christmas to Remember, A	TV	Jimmie Haskell
Cindy	TV	Howard Roberts
Clone Master, The	PAR	Glen Paxton
Cocktales	IND	Jacques Moreli
Colorado C.I. (pilot)	CBS-TV	Dave Grusin
Comedy Company, The	MGM	Tom Scott
Comedy Shop, The (series)	IND-TV	Jack Elliott/Allyn Ferguson
Cops and Robin	PAR	Charles Bernstein
Cotton Candy	TV	Joe Renzetti
Count Dracula	BRI-TV	Kenyon Emrys-Roberts
Courage and the Passion, The	COL	Richard Shores
Crash	TV	Eddie Manson
Crisis in Sun Valley (pilot)	NBC-TV	Dick de Benedictis
Critical List, The	TV	James DePasquale
Cruise into Terror	TV	Gerald Fried
Daddy, I Don't Like It Like This	CBS	David Shire
Dain Curse, The (series)	CBS	Charles Gross
Dallas (series)	CBS-TV	Bruce Broughton/Jerrold Immel/John Parker/Michael Warren/Richard Lewis Warren
Danny and the Mermaid	CBS-TV	Allen D. Allen
Dark Secret of Harvest Home, The	UN	Paul Chihara
Darwaza	IN	S. Jagmohan
Daughters of Fire	BRA	Rogerio Duprat
David Cassidy--Man Undercover (series)	NBC-TV	Harold Betts
Deadman's Curve	TV	Fred Karlin
Death in Canaan, A	WB	John Addison
Death Moon	TV	Paul Chihara

Deerslayer, The	SUN	Andrew Belling/Bob Summers
Defection of Simas Kudirka, The	PAR	David Shire
Desperate Women	TV	Dick DeBenedictis
Devil Dog: The Hound of Hell	TV	Artie Kane
Die, Sister, Die!	IND	Hugo Friedhofer
Diff'rent Strokes (series)	NBC-TV	Al Burton/Gloria Loring/ Alan Thicke
Dr. Jekyll's Dungeon of Death	IND	Marty Allen
Doctor Scorpion (pilot)	ABC-TV	Pete Carpenter/Mike Post
Doctor Strange (pilot)	CBS-TV	Paul Chihara
Doctors' Private Lives	ABC-TV	John Cacavas/Richard Markowitz
Dominique	BRI	David Whittaker
Donner Pass: The Road to Survival	SUN	Bob Summers
Eddie Capra Mysteries, The (series)	NBC-TV	John Addison/John Cacavas
Empire of Passion	JAP	Toru Takemitsu
Escapade (pilot)	CBS-TV	Patrick Williams
Escape from Women's Prison	ITA	Pippo Caruso
Evening in Byzantium (series)	IND-TV	Stu Phillips
Eyeball	ITA	Bruno Nicolai
Eyes Behind the Stars	ITA	Marcello Giombini
Fabulous Funnies, The (series)	NBC-TV	Yvette Blais/David Jeffrey/Mark Jeffrey/ Jeff Michael
Fall and Rise of Reginald Perrin, The (series)	BRI-TV	Ronnie Hazelhurst
Family Upside, Down, A	PAR	Henry Mancini
Fang Face (series)	ABC-TV	Dean Elliott
Fantasy Island (series)	ABC-TV	Charles Albertine/Ken Harrison/Elliot Kaplan/ Shorty Rogers/Laurence Rosenthal/Lance Rubin
Fertility God, The	IN	B. V. Karanth
Fighting Nightingales, The (pilot)	CBS-TV	Steve Kagan
Fire in the Sky, A	TV	Paul Chihara
First You Cry	TV	Peter Matz
Flashpoint Africa	AFR/GER	Eric Smith
Flying High	CBS-TV	David Shire/Jonathan Tunick
Flying High (series)	CBS-TV	Robert Prince/Arthur B. Rubinstein Jr.
Force on Thunder Mountain, The	TV	Christopher Cain
Forever	CBS-TV	Fred Karlin
Four Feathers, The	BRI	Allyn Ferguson
Free Country (series)	ABC-TV	Jack Elliott/Allyn Ferguson
Friends	CBS-TV	Gene Page

Funny Note	JAP	Masao Yagi
Funny World of Fred and Bunni, The (pilot)	CBS-TV	Jack Elliott/Allyn Ferguson
Galaxy Goofups, The (series)	NBC-TV	Hoyt Curtin
Gate of Youth--Part II, The	JAP	Riichiro Manabe
Getting Married	PAR	Craig Safan
Ghost of Flight 401, The	PAR	David Raksin
Ghosts That Still Walk	IND	Ronald Stein/Hod David Schudson
Gift of Love, The	TV	Fred Karlin
Girl from Starship Venus, The (Diary of a Space Virgin)	BRI	John Shakespeare
Glove, The	IND	Robert O. Ragland
Go West, Young Girl	ABC-TV	Jerrold Immel
Godzilla Power Hour, The (series)	NBC-TV	Hoyt Curtin
Grand Prix Hawk	JAP-TV	Hiroshi Miyagawa
Grandpa Goes to Washington (series)	NBC-TV	Artie Butler
Grass Is Always Greener Over the Septic Tank, The	TV	Peter Matz
Great Wallendas, The	NBC-TV	Bill Soden/Joe Weber
Greatest Heroes of the Bible (series)	NBC-TV	Bob Summers
Guide for the Married Woman, A	FOX	Jack Elliott/Allyn Ferguson
Happily Ever After	TV	Peter Matz
Harold Robbins' The Pirate	WB	Bill Conti
Harvey Korman Show, The (series)	ABC-TV	Peter Matz
Having Babies III	PAR	Lee Holdridge
Hitch in Time, A	BRI	Harry Robinson
Holocaust	TV	Morton Gould
Home to Stay	TIM	Hagood Hardy
How to Pick Up Girls!	TV	Don Debesky
Human Feelings (pilot)	NBC-TV	John Cacavas
Hunchback of Notre Dame, The	BRI	Wilfred Josephs
Hunters of the Reef	PAR	Richard Markowitz
Husbands, Wives and Lovers (series)	CBS-TV	Jack Elliott/Allyn Ferguson
Immigrants, The	IND-TV	Gerald Fried
In the Beginning (series)	CBS-TV	Barry DeVorzon
Incredible Hulk, The (series)	CBS-TV	Charles R. Casey/Joe Harnell
Initiation of Sarah, The	TV	Johnny Harris
Ishi: The Last of His Tribe	TV	Maurice Jarre
Islander, The	CBS-TV	Stu Phillips
Islander, The (pilot)	CBS-TV	John Andrew Tartaglia
Jack	IND	"The Beautiful People"
Jagan Mohini	IN	V. Krishnamurthy
Joe and Valerie (series)	NBC-TV	Jack Elliott/Allyn Ferguson/Joe Raposo
Jordan Chance, The (pilot)	CBS-TV	Pete Rugolo

Jubilee	BRI	Brian Eno
Julie Farr, M.D. (series)	ABC-TV	Lee Holdridge/George Aliceson Tipton
Just Me and You	TV	Fred Karlin
Kasturi	IN	Utam Singh
Kate Bliss and the Ticker Tape Kid (pilot)	ABC-TV	Jeff Alexander
Katie: Portrait of a Centerfold	WB	Charles Bernstein
Kaz (series)	CBS-TV	Fred Karlin
Keefer	COL	Duane Tatro
Killer's Moon	BRI	John Shakespeare/ Derek Warne
Killing Stone	UN	David Rose
King	FIL	Billy Goldenberg
King of the Road (pilot)	CBS-TV	Larry Cansler/Don Piestrup
Kiss Meets the Phantom of the Park	HB	Hoyt Curtin/Fred Karlin
Lacy and the Mississippi Queen (pilot)	NBC-TV	Barry De Vorzon
Lady of the House	TV	Fred Karlin
Laserblast	IND	Richard Band/Joel Goldsmith
Lassie: The New Beginning (pilot)	ABC-TV	Jerrold Immel
Last of the Good Guys	COL	Dana Kaproff
Last Tenant, The	TV	Dick Hyman
Late Great Planet Earth, The	IND	Dana Kaproff
Leave Yesterday Behind	ABC	Fred Karlin
Legs	ABC-TV	Charles Bernstein
Life of Chikuzan, Tsugaru Shamisen Player, The	JAP	Hikaru Hayashi
Like Mom, Like Me	CBS	Lee Holdridge
Little Lulu (series)	ABC-TV	Tommy Leonetti
Little Mo	TV	Carl Brandt/Billy May
Little Vic (series)	IND-TV	Tom Scott
Little Women	UN	Elmer Bernstein
Liza	IN	K. J. Joy
Long Journey Back	TV	Fred Karlin
Loose Change (series)	NBC-TV	Don Costa
Lost City of Atlantis	TV	Aminidav Aloni
Love Affair: The Eleanor and Lou Gehrig Story, A	TV	Eddie Manson
Love Is Not Enough	UN	Coleridge-Taylor Perkinson
Love's Dark Ride	TV	John D'Andrea/Michael Lloyd/Tom Sullivan
Lovey: A Circle of Children, Part II	TIM	Jerry Fielding
Lucifer Complex, The	TV	William Loose
Lupin III	JAP	Ugi Oni

Lusty Transparent Man, The	JAP	Shin Takada
Madhouse Brigade, The (series)	IND-TV	Tony Monte
Man from S.E.X., The	BRI	Simon Bell
Maneaters Are Loose!	TV	Gerald Fried
Many Loves of Arthur, The (pilot)	NBC-TV	Patrick Williams
Medusa Touch, The	BRI	Michael J. Lewis
Melody in Gray	JAP	Toru Takemitsu
Microwave Massacre	IND	Leif Horvath
Millionaire, The (pilot)	CBS-TV	Frank DeVol
Miserables, Les	TV	Allyn Ferguson
More Than Friends	COL	Fred Karlin
Mork and Mindy (series)	ABC-TV	Perry Botkin Jr.
Mt. Hakkoda	JAP	Yasushi Akutagawa
Murder at the Mardi Gras	PAR	Peter Matz
My Husband Is Missing	TV	Joseph Wells
Mysterious Big Tactics	JAP	Hiroki Tamaki/Naozumi Yamamoto
Naa Ninna Bidenu	IN	G. K. Venkatesh
Nativity, The	FOX	Lalo Schifrin
New Avengers, The (series)	CBS-TV	Laurie Johnson
New Maverick, The	WB	David Buttolph/John Rubenstein
New Operation Petticoat, The (series)	ABC-TV	Peter Matz
Next Step Beyond, The (series)	IND-TV	Ron Ramin/Mark Snow
Night Cries	TV	Paul Chihara
Nocturna	IND	Norman Bergen/Reid Whitelaw
Nowhere to Run	TV	Jerrold Immel
Obsessed, The (Eerie Midnight Horror Show, The)	ITA	Marcello Giombini
On Our Own	CBS-TV	Bob Israel
On Trial (pilot)	IND-TV	John Parker
One in a Million: The Ron LaFlore Story	TV	Peter Matz
Operation: Runaway	NBC-TV	Richard Markowitz
Other Side of Hell, The	TV	Leonard Rosenman
Outside Chance	TV	Michael Dunne/Lou Levy
Overboard	TV	Carol Connors Shaw
Paper Chase, The (series)	CBS-TV	Charles Fox/Stephen Sevetan/Richard Shores
Pearl	ABC-TV	John Addison
Perfect Gentlemen	PAR	Dominic Frontiere
Phoenix	JAP	Jun Fukumachi
Planetary Robot Vanguard: Ace Naval Battle in Space	JAP	Shunsuke Kikuchi
Please Stand By (series)	IND-TV	Phil Cody
President's Mistress, The	TV	Lalo Schifrin
Prisoner of the Cannibal God	ITA	Guido and Maurizio de Angelis

Project U.F.O. (series)	NBC-TV	Nelson Riddle
Quark (series)	NBC-TV	Perry Botkin, Jr.
Question of Guilt, A	TV	Artie Kane
Question of Love, A	TV	Billy Goldenberg
Rainbow	TV	Charles Fox
Raisins de la Mort, Les	FRA	Philippe Sissman
Real American Hero, A	TV	Walter Scharf
Redeemer ... Son of Satan, The	IND	Phil Gallo/Clem Vicari
Rescue from Gilligan's Island	NBC-TV	Gerald Fried
Return Engagement	NBC-TV	Arthur B. Rubenstein
Return of Captain Nemo, The (series)	CBS-TV	Richard LaSalle
Return to Boggy Creek	IND	Darrell Deck
Return to Fantasy Island	ABC	Leonard Rosenthal
Rhyme of Vengeance, A	JAP	Kunihiko Murai
Ring of Passion	FOX	Bill Conti
Richie Brockelman, Private Eye (series)	NBC-TV	Pete Carpenter/Mike Post
Rita Moreno Show, The (pilot)	CBS-TV	Peter Matz
Rock Rainbow, The	ABC-TV	Tony Berg
Roll of Thunder, Hear My Cry	ABC-TV	Fred Karlin
Rollergirls, The (series)	NBC-TV	Tony Asher/John Bahler /Kevin Clark
Sam (series)	CBS-TV	Billy May
Sammy's Super T-Shirt	BRI	Harry Robinson
Secrets of the Bermuda Triangle	IND	W. Michael Lewis/Laurin Rinder
Secrets of Three Hungry Wives	TV	John Parker
See How She Runs	TV	Jimmie Haskell
Sergeant Matlovich vs. the U.S. Air Force	TV	Teo Macero
She-Wolf of the Devil's Moon, The (Devil's Bed, The)	AUS	Gerhard Heinz
Shipshape (pilot)	CBS-TV	Michael Lloyd
Shout, The	BRI	A. Bank/Michael Rutherford
Siege	TV	Charles Gross
Sister Terri (pilot)	ABC-TV	Don Peake
Ski Lift to Death	PAR	Barry DeVorzon
Skies of Haruo, The	JAP	Taku Izumi
Someone Is Watching Me!	WB	Harry Sukman
Space Fantasy Emeraldus	JAP	Seiji Yokoyama
Space Pirate Captain Harlock	JAP-TV	Masaki Hirao/Seiji Yokoyama
Sparrow (pilot)	CBS-TV	Paul Williams
Special Olympics (Special Kind of Love, A)	TV	Peter Matz
Speedtrap	IND	Anthony Harris
Spiderman (series)	TV	Don Ellis
Spiderman Strikes Back	TV	Stu Phillips
Standing Tall	TV	Richard Markowitz

Star Wolf	JAP	Norio Maeda
Steel Cowboy	TV	Charles Bernstein
Sticking Together	TV	John Rubenstein
Stranger in Our House	TV	John D'Andrea/Michael Lloyd
Stubby Pringle's Christmas	NBC-TV	Garry Sherman
Suddenly, Love	TV	David Rose
Summer of My German Soldier, The	TV	Stanley Myers
Superdome	ABC	John Cacavas
Sword of Justice (series)	NBC-TV	John Andrew Tartaglia
Take-Off	IND	"Elephant's Memory"
Tame re Champo ne Ame Kel	IN	Mahesh Naresh
Tarao Bannai	JAP	Shunsuke Kikuchi
Tarzan and the Super Seven (series)	CBS-TV	Yvette Blais/Jeff Michael
Taxi (series)	ABC-TV	Bob James
Ted Knight Show, The (series)	CBS-TV	Michael Leonard
Terror Out of the Sky	TV	William Goldstein
Thaddeus Rose and Eddie	CBS	Charles Bernstein
That Thing on ABC	ABC-TV	Peter Matz
Thou Shalt Not Commit Adultery	TV	Paul Chihara
Three on a Date	ABC	George Aliceson Tipton
Three Robonic Stooges, The (series)	CBS-TV	Hoyt Curtin/Paul DeKorte
Time Machine, The	SUN	John Cacavas
To Kill a Cop	COL	Lee Holdridge
Tom and Joann (pilot)	CBS-TV	Hagood Hardy
Top Secret (pilot)	NBC-TV	Stu Gardner/Teo Macero
Tora-san Meets His Lordship	JAP	Naozumi Yamamoto
True Grit	PAR	Earle Hagen
Two-Five, The (pilot)	ABC-TV	Peter Matz
Two Ronnies, The (series)	BRI-TV	Ronnie Hazelhurst
2069: A Sex Odyssey	GER	Hans Hammerschmid
Users, The	TV	Maurice Jarre
Vampire Hookers, The	IND	Jaime Mendoza-Nava
Vayanadan Thampan	IN	Devarajan
Vega$ (series)	ABC-TV	John Beal/Frank deVol/ Dominic Frontiere/ Artie Kane/Shorty Rogers/Mark Snow
Veil of Blood (Devil's Plaything, The)	SWE	Rolf-Sans Mueller
Venetian Black (Damned in Venice)	IND	Pino Donaggio
W.E.B. (series)	NBC-TV	Jerry Fielding/David Rose/Morton Stevens
WKRP in Cincinnati (series)	CBS-TV	Tom Wells
War in Space, The	JAP	Toshiaki Tsushima
War of the Wizards (Phoenix, The)	IND	Lawrence Borden
Water Babies, The	BRI	Phil Coulter
Waverly Wonders, The (series)	NBC-TV	Fred Karlin
What's New, Mr. Magoo? (series)	CBS-TV	Dean Elliott/Doug Goodwin/Eric Rogers

What's Up, Doc? (pilot)	ABC-TV	Ian Freebairn-Smith
Wheels	UN	Morton Stevens
When Every Day Was the Fourth of July	TV	Walter Scharf
When Havoc Struck (series)	IND-TV	Harry Robinson
White House on the Beach, The	JAP	Hiroshi Kamayatsu/Herb Ohta
White Shadow, The (series)	CBS-TV	Pete Carpenter/Mike Post
Who'll Save Our Children?	TIM	Fred Karlin
Who's Watching the Kids? (series)	NBC-TV	Charles Bernstein
Wild and Wooly (pilot)	ABC-TV	Charles Bernstein
Wild Swans, The	JAP	Akihiro Komori
Wilds of Ten Thousand Islands, The (pilot)	CBS-TV	Dominic Frontiere
Wind	BRI-TV	Bob Summers
Winds of Change (Metamorphosis)	FRA	Alec R. Costandinos
Winds of Kitty Hawk, The	TV	Charles Bernstein
Witches' Brew (Which Witch Is Which?)	IND	John Parker
With This Ring	PAR	George Aliceson Tipton
Wolf Lake	IND	Ken Thorne
Wolfman--A Lycanthrope	IND	David Floyd/Arthur Smith
Woman Called Moses, A	TV	Coleridge-Taylor Perkinson
Word, The	TV	Alex North
World Beyond, The (pilot)	CBS-TV	Fred Karlin
World's Greatest Superheroes, The (series)	ABC-TV	Hoyt Curtin
Yellow Handkerchief, The	JAP	Masaru Sato
Yogi's Space Race (series)	NBC-TV	Hoyt Curtin
Young Pioneers, The (series)	ABC-TV	Dominic Frontiere/ Laurence Rosenthal
Ziegfeld: The Man and His Women	COL	Dick DeBenedictis
Zuma Beach	TV	Dick Halligan

1979

Act of Violence	CBS-TV	Paul Chihara
Against the Wind (series)	AUT	Jon English/Mario Millo
Alien Encounters, The	TV	William Loose
All Quiet on the Western Front	CBS-TV	Allyn Ferguson
Amateur Night at the Dixie Bar and Grill	UN	Bradford Craig
America 2100 (pilot)	ABC-TV	Jonathan Tunick
American Christmas Carol, An	ABC-TV	Hagood Hardy
Americathon	UA	Earl Brown, Jr./Tom Scott
Anatomy of a Seduction	FIL	Hagood Hardy
And Baby Makes Six	NBC-TV	Fred Karlin

And Your Name Is Jonah	TV	Fred Karlin
Angie (series)	ABC-TV	Dan Foliart/Howard Pearl
Arabian Adventure	BRI	Ken Thorne
Archie Bunker's Place (series)	CBS-TV	Ray Conniff
At Your Own Request	POL	unlisted
Attack of the Killer Tomatoes, The	IND	Gordon Goodwin/Paul Sundfor
B. J. and the Bear	NBC-TV	William Broughton/John Cacavas/Dave Fisher/ Dick Halligan/Peter Ives/Stu Phillips
Backstairs at the White House (series)	NBC-TV	Morton Stevens
Bad News Bears, The (series)	CBS-TV	David Frank
Baxters, The (series)	IND-TV	Marvin Laird
Beach Patrol (pilot)	ABC-TV	Barry de Vorzon
Beane's of Boston (pilot)	CBS-TV	Don Peake
Bees, The	IND	Richard Gillis
Beggarman, Thief	NBC-TV	Eddie Sauter
Bender (pilot)	CBS-TV	Ralph Ferraro
Benson (series)	ABC-TV	George Aliceson Tipton
Best Place to Be, The	TV	Henry Mancini
Better Late Than Never	NBC-TV	Charles Fox
Beyond Death's Door	TV	Bob Summers
Beyond the Door II (Shock/ Suspense)	IND	"Libra"
Big Shamus, Little Shamus (series)	CBS-TV	Pete Carpenter/James Di Pasquale/Mike Post
Billion Dollar Threat, The (pilot)	ABC-TV	Morton Stevens
Billy (series)	CBS-TV	Earle Hagen
Bizarre (pilot)	ABC-TV	D'Vaughn Pershing
Blind Ambition	TIM	Fred Karlin/Walter Scharf
Breaking Up Is Hard to Do	ABC-TV	Gerald Fried
Brenda Starr, Reporter (pilot)	IND-TV	Richard LaSalle
Brood, The	NWP	Howard Shore
Brothers and Sisters (series)	NBC-TV	Mark Snow
Buck Rogers in the 25th Century (series)	NBC-TV	Les Baxter/John Cacavas/Johnny Harris/J. J. Johnson/ Robert Prince/Stu Phillips
Buffalo Soldiers, The (pilot)	NBC-TV	Jerrold Immel
Buford and the Ghost (series)	NBC-TV	Hoyt Curtin
But Mother! (pilot)	NBC-TV	Jeff Alexander/Larry Orenstein
California Fever (series)	CBS-TV	Harry Betts/Artie Butler/Dick Halligan/ Don Peake
Can You Hear the Laughter?: The Story of Freddie Prinze	CBS-TV	Peter Matz

Cannibal Holocaust	ITA	Riz Ortolani
Captain America (pilot)	CBS-TV	Pete Carpenter/Mike Post
Captain America II	CBS-TV	Pete Carpenter/Mike Post
Car Wash (pilot)	NBC-TV	Dave Fisher
Casper and the Angels (series)	NBC-TV	Hoyt Curtin
Castaways on Gilligan's Island, The	NBC-TV	Gerald Fried
Cemetery Girls	IND	Carmelo Belona
Champions: A Love Story	WB	John Rubenstein
Charleston	TV	Elmer Bernstein
Child Stealer, The	COL	Jimmie Haskell
Chisholms, The (series)	CBS-TV	Elmer Bernstein/Aaron Copland
Christmas for Boomer, A (pilot)	NBC-TV	David Frank
Christmas Lilies of the Field	NBC-TV	George Aliceson Tipton
Christmas Without Snow, A	CBS-TV	Ed Bogas
Churchill and the Generals	BRI-TV	Wilfred Josephs
Circle of Iron	AUT	Bruce Smeaton
Cliffhangers (series)	TV	Charles R. Casey/Joe Harnell
Co-Ed Fever (pilot)	CBS-TV	Henry Mancini
Concrete Cowboys	CBS-TV	Earle Hagen
Corn Is Green, The	WB	John Barry
Cracker Factory, The	TV	Billy Goldenberg
Crisis in Mid-Air	CBS	Robert Drasnin
Crunch (Kinky Coaches and the Pom-Pom Pussycats, The)	CAN	unlisted
Curse of Dracula, The (series)	NBC-TV	Les Baxter/Charles R. Casey/Joe Harnell
Dallas Cowboys Cheerleaders, The (pilot)	ABC-TV	Jimmie Haskell
Danny	IND	Harry Manfredini
Darker Side of Terror, The	TV	Paul Chihara
Day It Came to Earth, The	IND	Joe Southerland
Day the Dreaming Stopped, The (Comeback, The)	BRI	Stanley Myers
Deadline (Anatomy of a Horror)	CAN	Dwayne Ford/Carole Pope/"Rough Trade"
Deadly Games	IND	Hod David Schudson/ Richard S. Thompson
Dear Detective (series)	CBS-TV	Dick and Dean de Benedictis
Death Car on the Freeway	TV	Richard Markowitz
Death of Ocean View Park, The	ABC-TV	Fred Werner
Delta House (series)	ABC-TV	Elmer Bernstein/Dick De Benedictis/Vic Mizzy/David Spear
Demonoid (Macabra)	IND	Richard Gillis
Detective School (series)	ABC-TV	Peter Matz

Devil Times Five, The (Horrible House on the Hill, The)	TV	William Loose
Diary of a Hitchhiker, The	ABC-TV	Joe Renzetti
Dooley Brothers, The (pilot)	CBS-TV	Murray McLeod/Herb Martin/ J. A. C. Redford
Doomsday Chronicles, The	IND	Joel Goldsmith
Dorothy (series)	CBS-TV	Billy Goldenberg
Dracula and Son	FRA	Vladimir Cosma
Dracula Blows His Cool	GER	Gerhard Heinz
Duke, The (series)	NBC-TV	Pete Carpenter/Mike Post
Dukes of Hazzard, The (series)	CBS-TV	Waylon Jennings
Dummy	WB	Gil Askey
Earthquake Islands	JAP	Toshiaki Tsushima
Ebony, Ivory and Jade (pilot)	CBS-TV	Earle Hagen
Eischied (series)	NBC-TV	John Cacavas
Electric Eskimo, The	BRI	Harry Robinson
11th Victim, The	CBS-TV	Michel Colombier
Elvis	TV	Joe Renzetti
Emergency! (series)	NBC-TV	Gerald Fried
Facts of Life, The (series)	NBC-TV	Al Burton/Gloria Loring /Alan Thicke
Fairy Tales	IND	Andrew Belling
Family Man, The	CBS-TV	Billy Goldenberg
Fast Friends	COL	Donald Pearce
Featherstone's Nest (pilot)	CBS-TV	Earle Hagen
Flame Is Love, The	NBC-TV	Morton Stevens
Flash Gordon (series)	NBC-TV	Yvette Blais/George Mahana/Jeff Michael
Flatbed Annie and Sweetiepie: Lady Truckers (pilot)	CBS-TV	Don Peake
Flatbush (series)	CBS-TV	Mark Snow
Flesh and Blood	CBS-TV	Billy Goldenberg
416th, The (pilot)	CBS-TV	Pete Carpenter/Mike Post
Fred and Barney Meet the Thing (series)	NBC-TV	Hoyt Curtin
Freedom Road	NBC-TV	Terrence James/Cole-ridge-Taylor Perkinson
French Atlantic Affair, The (series)	ABC-TV	John Addison
Friday the 13th ... The Orphan (Don't Open the Door)	IND	Teo Macero
Friendly Fire	TV	Leonard Rosenman
Friends (series)	ABC-TV	Fred Karlin
Friendships, Secrets and Lies	NBC-TV	Angela Morley
From Here to Eternity	COL	Walter Scharf
Gathering, Part II, The	NBC-TV	Robert Prince
Ghost Festival at Saint's Village	JAP-TV	Toshiaki Yokota
Gift, The	CBS-TV	George Aliceson Tipton

Girls in the Office, The	ABC	John Parker
Gold of the Amazon Women	TV	Gil Melle
Golden Gate Murders, The	CBS-TV	Sol Kaplan
Good Ol' Boys (pilot)	NBC-TV	Jack Elliott/Allyn Ferguson
Gossip (pilot)	NBC-TV	Art Twain
Hanging by a Thread	WB	Richard LaSalle
Hanging In (series)	CBS-TV	Billy Byers
Harris and Company (series)	NBC-TV	J. J. Johnson
Hart to Hart (series)	ABC-TV	Mark Snow
Heaven on Earth (pilot)	NBC-TV	Stephen Cohn
Hello, Larry (series)	NBC-TV	John La Salle/Tom Smith
High Ice	NBC-TV	Robert O. Ragland
High Midnight	CBS-TV	Jerry Fielding
Highcliffe Manor (series)	NBC-TV	Robert Alberti/Frank DeVol
Highpoint	NWP	John Addison
Hizzoner (series)	NBC-TV	Robert Alberti
Hollow Image	TV	Don Debesky
Homework (Growing Pains)	IND	Tony Jones
Hot Rod	ABC	Michael Simpson
House Calls (series)	CBS-TV	Jack Elliott/Allyn Ferguson/Michael Lang
House on Garibaldi Street, The	TV	Charles Bernstein
Hunter's Moon (pilot)	CBS-TV	Harry Sukman
I, Claudius (series)	BRI-TV	Wilfred Josephs
I Know Why the Caged Bird Sings	TV	Peter Matz
Ike	ABC-TV	Fred Karlin
Incredible Journey of Dr. Meg Laurel	COL	Gerald Fried
Inferno, The	JAP	Riichiro Manabe
Institute for Revenge (pilot)	NBC-TV	Lalo Schifrin
It Can't Happen to Me	IND-TV	Christopher Stone
Jason of Star Command (series)	CBS-TV	Yvette Blais/Jeff Michael
Jaws of Satan (King Cobra)	UA	Roger Kellaway
Jennifer: A Woman's Story	TV	William Goldstein
Jericho Mile, The	ABC	Jimmie Haskell
Joe's World (series)	NBC-TV	Alan Thicke
Just Friends (series)	CBS-TV	Doug Gilmore
Kate Loves a Mystery (series)	NBC-TV	John Cacavas/Charles R. Casey
Kid from Left Field, The	NBC-TV	David Frank
King and the Mockingbird, The	POL	Wojiech Kilar
Kinky Coaches and the Pom-Pom Pussycats, The (see Crunch)		
Knot's Landing (series)	CBS-TV	Ron Grant/Jerrold Immel/Lance Rubin
Last Convertible, The (series)	NBC-TV	Pete Rugolo
Last Cry for Help, A	TV	Miles Goodman
Last Giraffe, The	TV	Fred Karlin

Last Resort, The (series)	CBS-TV	Patrick Williams
Last Ride of the Dalton Gang, The	NBC-TV	Robert Cobert
Laurel & Hardy Laughtoons (series)	IND-TV	George Korngold
Lazarus Syndrome, The (series)	ABC-TV	Billy Goldenberg/John Rubenstein
Legend of Sleepy Hollow, The	TV	Bob Summers
Legend of the Golden Gun (pilot)	NBC-TV	Jerrold Immel
Legend of the 7 Golden Vampires, The (7 Brothers Meet Dracula, The)	BRI	James Bernard
Letters from Frank	CBS-TV	Ernest Gold
Licensed to Love and Kill	BRI	Simon Bell
Like Normal People	FOX	John Addison
Lion, the Witch and the Wardrobe, The	TV	Michael J. Lewis
Love and Learn (pilot)	NBC-TV	Dick de Benedictis/Paul Wayne
Love for Lydia (series)	BRI-TV	Barry Rabinowitz
Love for Rent	ABC-TV	Peter Matz
Lovebirds, The (pilot)	CBS-TV	Peter Matz
Love's Savage Fury	TV	John Addison
M-3: The Gemini Strain (Plague)	IND	Eric Robertson
MacKenzies of Paradise Cove, The (series)	ABC-TV	John Rubenstein/Fred Werner
Makin' It (series)	ABC-TV	Don Peake
Man Called Intrepid, A (series)	BRI-TV	Robert Farnon
Man Called Sloane, A (series)	NBC-TV	Don Bagley/Billy Byers/ Les Hooper/Tom Scott/ Patrick Williams
Man in the Santa Claus Suit, The	NBC-TV	Peter Matz
Mandrake (pilot)	NBC-TV	Morton Stevens
Marciano	ABC-TV	Ernest Gold
Marie (pilot)	ABC-TV	Denny Crocket
Marie Curie (series)	BRI-TV	Carl Davis
Married: The First Year (series)	CBS-TV	Jerrold Immel
Mary and Joseph: A Story of Faith	NBC-TV	Robert Farnon
Mayflower: The Pilgrim's Adventure	CBS-TV	Brad Fiedel
Me and Ducky (pilot)	NBC-TV	Larry Weiss
Meat	GER	Eugen Thomass
Mind Over Murder	TV	Paul Chihara
Miracle Worker, The	NBC-TV	Billy Goldenberg
Mirror, Mirror	NBC-TV	Jimmie Haskell
Misadventures of Sheriff Lobo, The (series)	NBC-TV	William Broughton/ Jimmie Haskell/John Andrew Tartaglia
Miss Winslow and Son (series)	CBS-TV	Pete Rugolo
Mr. Horn	TV	Jerry Fielding

Mr. Slotter's Jubilee	HOL	Jurre Haanstra
Mrs. Columbo (series)	NBC-TV	John Cacavas
Mrs. R's Daughter	NBC-TV	Robert Cobert
Mistress of the Apes	IND	"The Missing Link"
Monique (Flashing Lights/New York After Dark)	IND	Jacques Morali
Mother and Me, M.D. (pilot)	NBC-TV	Patrick Williams
Muppet Movie, The	BRI	Kenny Ascher/Patrick Williams
Murder by Decree	EMB	Paul J. Zaza/Carl Zitterer
Murder by Natural Causes	TV	Dick De Benedictis
Murder in Music City (pilot)	NBC-TV	Earle Hagen
My Buddy (pilot)	NBC-TV	Gerald Wilson
My Old Man	CBS-TV	Dominic Frontiere
Mysterious Island of Beautiful Women, The	CBS-TV	William Loose/Jack Tillar
Nero Wolfe	ABC-TV	Leonard Rosenman
Never Say Never (pilot)	CBS-TV	Danny Wells
New Fred and Barney Show, The (series)	NBC-TV	Hoyt Curtin
New Kind of Family, A (series)	ABC-TV	Dan Foliart/Howard Pearl
New Schmoo, The (series)	NBC-TV	Hoyt Curtin
Night of the Zombies (Gamma 693)	IND	Matt Kaplowitz/Maggie Nolin
Night Rider, The (pilot)	ABC-TV	Pete Carpenter/Mike Post
Nightingales, The (pilot)	NBC-TV	Barry DeVorzon
No Other Love	TV	Charles Gross
Nocturna	IND	Reid Whitelaw
Not Until Today	NBC-TV	Johnny Mandel
Notes for an African Orestes	ITA	Leandro "Gato" Barbieri
Ohms	CBS-TV	Elizabeth Swados
Operating Room (pilot)	NBC-TV	Pete Carpenter/Mike Post
Ordeal of Patty Hearst, The	TV	John Rubenstein
Orphan Train	CBS-TV	Laurence Rosenthal
Out of the Blue (series)	ABC-TV	Ben Lanzarone
Outer Touch (Spaced Out)	BRI	Alan Brawer/Anna Pepper
Paradise Connection, The	CBS-TV	Bruce Broughton
Paris (series)	CBS-TV	Fred Karlin
Percy's Progress (It's Not the Size That Counts)	BRI	Tony Macauley
Piper's Pets (pilot)	NBC-TV	Jack Elliott/Allyn Ferguson
Plasticman Comedy/Adventure Show, The (series)	ABC-TV	Dean Elliott
Pleasure Cove (pilot)	NBC-TV	Perry Botkin, Jr.
Power Within, The (pilot)	ABC-TV	John Addison

Prime of Miss Jean Brodie, The (series)	BRI-TV	Marvin Hamlisch
Prisoner: Cell Block H (series)	AUT-TV	William Motzing
Queen of the Cannibals	ITA	Nico Fidenco
Ravagers	TV	Fred Karlin
Rebels, The	UN	Gerald Fried
Remington Steele (series)	NBC-TV	Richard Lewis Warren
Rendezvous Hotel (pilot)	CBS-TV	Jonathan Tunick
Return of Charlie Chan, The	ABC-TV	Robert Prince
Return of the Mod Squad, The	ABC-TV	Shorty Rogers/Mark Snow
Return of the Saint, The (series)	CBS-TV	John Scott
Roots: The Next Generations	WOL	Gerald Fried
Ropers, The (series)	ABC-TV	Joe Raposo
Runaways, The (series)	NBC-TV	Bruce Broughton/ Robert Drasnin/John Elizalde/Ralph Kessler/ Richard Markowitz/ Nelson Riddle/Duane Tatro
S.O.S. Titanic	ABC-TV	Howard Blake
Sacketts, The	TV	Jerrold Immel
Salem's Lot	TV	Harry Sukman
Salvage I (series)	ABC-TV	Richard Clements/Ken Harrison/Walter Scharf
Samurai (pilot)	ABC-TV	Fred Karlin
Sanctuary of Fear	TV	Jack Elliott/Allyn Ferguson
Scarlet Letter, The	PBS-TV	John Morris
Scooby-Doo and Scrappy-Doo (series)	ABC-TV	Hoyt Curtin
Second Time Around, The (pilot)	ABC-TV	Don Costa
Secret, The	HK	Violet Lam
Secret Empire, The (series)	NBC-TV	Les Baxter/Charles R. Casey/Joe Harnell
Seeding of Sarah Burns, The	TV	Jimmie Haskell
Seekers, The	IND-TV	Gerald Fried
Sgt. T. K. Yu (pilot)	NBC-TV	Al Kasha
Sex and the Single Parent	CBS-TV	Fred Karlin
Sheriff and the Satellite Kid, The	ITA	Guido and Maurizio de Angelis
She's Dressed to Kill	NBC-TV	George Romanis
Shining Season, A	CBS-TV	Richard Bellis
Shirley (series)	NBC-TV	Richard Clements/Ben Lanzarone/Arthur B. Rubinstein, Jr.
Silent Victory: The Kitty O'Neil Story	TV	Jimmie Haskell
Sinthia, The Devil's Doll	IND	Henry Price
Solitary Man, The	CBS-TV	Jack Elliott
Some Kind of Miracle	TV	Jimmie Haskell/Robie Porter

Son Rise: A Miracle of Love	FIL	Gerald Fried
Sooner or Later	NBC	Stephen Lawrence
Space Cruiser Yamato--The New Voyage	JAP-TV	Hiroshi Miyagawa
Spaced Out (see Outer Touch)		
Spider-Men: The Dragon's Challenge	TV	Dana Kaproff
Spider-Woman (series)	ABC-TV	Eric Rogers
Starstruck (pilot)	CBS-TV	Alan Alper
Starting Fresh (pilot)	NBC-TV	Norman Sacs
Stone	ABC-TV	Pete Carpenter/Mike Post
Stop Susan Williams (series)	NBC-TV	Les Baxter/Charles R. Casey/Joe Harnell
Strangers: The Story of a Mother and Daughter	TV	Fred Karlin
Streets of L.A., The	CBS-TV	Jimmie Haskell
Struck by Lightning (series)	CBS-TV	Thomas Talbert
Studs Lonigan	NBC-TV	Ken Lauber
Stung Seven (pilot)	CBS-TV	Bill Conti/Jack Eskew
Suicide's Wife, The	CBS-TV	David Raksin
Super Globetrotters, The (series)	NBC-TV	Hoyt Curtin
Supertrain (series)	NBC-TV	Robert Cobert
Survival of Dana	TV	Craig Safan
Sweepstakes (series)	NBC-TV	George Aliceson Tipton/ Fred Werner
TV Show, The (pilot)	ABC-TV	Steve Kagan
Tales of the Unexpected (series)	BRI-TV	Ron Grainer/Elizabeth Swados
Taro of the Dragons	JAP	Riichiro Manabe
Tenth Month, The	CBS-TV	Peter Matz
Thief of Bagdad, The	BRI-TV	John Cameron
13 Queens Boulevard (series)	ABC-TV	Barry de Vorzon
This Man Stands Alone	TV	Fred Karlin
Three Wives of David Wheeler, The (pilot)	NBC-TV	Jack Elliott/Allyn Ferguson
Tigers in Lipstick	ITA	Riz Ortolani
Time Express (series)	CBS-TV	Richard Hazard
Too Far to Go	TV	Elizabeth Swados
Topper (pilot)	ABC-TV	Fred Karlin
Torn Between Two Lovers	TV	Ian Fraser
Transplant	TIM	Fred Karlin
Trapper John, M.D. (series)	CBS-TV	John Parker
Triangle Factory Fire Scandal, The	TV	Walter Scharf
Triton of the Seas	JAP	Kosetsu Minami
Turnabout (series)	NBC-TV	Jack Elliott/Allyn Ferguson

240-Robert (series)	ABC-TV	Pete Carpenter/Murray MacLeod/Mike Post
Two Worlds of Jennie Logan, The	CBS-TV	Glen Paxton
U.F.O. Blue Christmas	JAP	Masaru Sato
Ultimate Imposter, The (pilot)	CBS-TV	Dana Kaproff
Undercover with the KKK	NBC-TV	Morton Stevens
Unidentified Flying Oddball	DIS	Ron Goodwin
Up from the Depths	NWP	James Horner
Uptown Saturday Night (pilot)	NBC-TV	Gary Lemel
Vacation in Hell, A	TV	Gil Melle
Vampire	ABC-TV	Fred Karlin
Vampire Dracula Comes to Kobe: Evil Makes Women Beautiful	JAP	Katsumi Nakamura
Virgin and the Monster, The	CZE	Petr Hapka
Voltus V	JAP	Hiroshi Tsutsui
Walking Through the Fire	TIM	Fred Karlin
When Hell Was in Session	NBC-TV	Jimmie Haskell
When She Was Bad ...	ABC-TV	Perry Botkin, Jr.
Where's Poppa? (pilot)	ABC-TV	Alan Douglas/Ken Lauber
Whitney and the Robot (series)	IND-TV	Corky Greene
Who's on Call? (pilot)	ABC-TV	Glen Page
Wild Wild West Revisited, The	CBS	Jeff Alexander/Richard Markowitz
Willa	TV	John Barry
Wise Blood	IRE	Alex North
Women at West Point	TV	Charles Bernstein
Women in White (series)	NBC-TV	Morton Stevens
Working Stiffs (series)	CBS-TV	John Cacavas/Jack Carone
Worlds Apart (see "Don't Ask Me If I Love")		
You Can't Go Home Again	CBS	Charles Gross
Young Guy Christian (pilot)	ABC-TV	Murray MacLeod
Young Love, First Love	CBS-TV	Artie Kane
Young Maverick (series)	CBS-TV	Lex deAzevedo/Lee Holdridge

1980

Act of Violence	BRA	Egberto Gismonti
Action	ITA	Riccardo Giovannini
Adventures of Nellie Bly	NBC-TV	Bob Summers
Aeroport: Charter 2020	FRA-TV	Guy Boulanger
Aftermath, The	IND	John Morgan
Age of the Earth, The	BRA	Rogerio Duarte
Agee	IND	Kenton Coe
Agency	CAN	Lewis Furey
Airplane	PAR	Elmer Bernstein
Alcatraz: The Whole Shocking Story	NBC-TV	Jerrold Immel

Alex and the Doberman Gang (pilot)	NBC-TV	Earle Hagen
Alexander the Great (O Megalexandros)	GRE/ITA	Christidulos Halaris
Alien, The (De Plaats van de Vreemdeling)	HOL	Louis Andriessen
Alien Contamination	ITA	"Goblin"
Alien Dead, The	IND	Franklin Sledge
Aliens Are Coming, The (pilot)	NBC-TV	William Goldstein
All-American Pie (pilot)	ABC-TV	Billy Goldenberg
All God's Children	ABC-TV	Billy Goldenberg
All Is Love	BUL	Vesselin Nikolov
All-Stars (Tous Vedettes)	FRA	Mort Schuman
Alley Cat	IND	Quito Colayco
Almost a Love Story	BUL	Mitko Sterev
Almost Human (Milano Odia)	ITA	Ennio Morricone
Almost Transparent Blue	JAP	Masaru Hoshii
Alone at Last (pilot)	NBC-TV	Joe Harnell
Altered States	WB	John Corigliano
Amber Waves	ABC-TV	John Rubenstein
American Gigolo	PAR	Giorgio Moroder
Anastasia Passed By	RUM	Lucian Metianu
... And the Third Year, He Resuscitated	SPA	Gregorio Garcia Segura
Angel City	CBS-TV	Mark Snow
Angel on My Shoulder	ABC-TV	Artie Butler
Anti-Clock	BRI	Mihai Dragutescu
Any Body ... Any Way	IND	H. R. Kugley
Apple, The	IND	Coby Recht
April Has 30 Days	E.GER	Udo Zimmermann
Aria for an Athlete	POL	Zdzislaw Szostak
Asphalt Cowboy, The (pilot)	NBC-TV	Ken Harrison
Asphalt Night	GER	Lothar Meid
Assassination (Attentat)	DEN	Ole Hoeyer
Atlantic City, U.S.A.	CAN/FRA	Michel Legrand
Attica	ABC-TV	Gil Melle
Augh! Augh!	ITA	Pino Donaggio
Aunt Alexandra	MEX	Luis Hernandez Breton
Aunt Mary	CBS-TV	Arthur B. Rubinstein, Jr.
Auschwitz Street	GER	Christobal Halffter
Authorized Instructor	ITA	Egisto Macchi
Awakening, The	WB	Claude Bolling
Aziza	ALG/TUN	Ahmed Malek
B.A.D. Cats (series)	ABC-TV	Barry DeVorzon/Andrew Kulberg/Mundell Lowe
B. B. Beegle Show, The	IND-TV	Bob Buckley
Baby Come Home	CBS-TV	Fred Karlin
Babylon	BRI	Denis Bovell
Back to the Planet of the Apes	TV	Richard LaSalle/Lalo Schifrin
Bad Son, A	FRA	Philippe Sarde
Bad Sorts (Warui Yatsura)	JAP	Satoshi Akutagawa

Bad Timing	BRI	Richard Hartley
Balint Fabian Meets God	HUN	Gyorgy Vukan
Baltimore Bullet, The	EMB	Johnny Mandel
Battle Beyond the Stars	NWP	James Horner
Battles: The Murder That Wouldn't Die (pilot)	NBC	Joe Harnell/Glen A. Larson/Stu Phillips
Be Forever Yamato	JAP	Hiroshi Miyagawa
Beach House, The (Casotto, Il)	ITA	Gianni Mazza
Beads of One Rosary, The	POL	Wojiech Kilar
Bear Island	COL	Robert Farnon
Being, The (Easter Sunday)	IND	Don Preston
Belle Starr	CBS-TV	Dana Kaproff
Bells (Murder by Phone)	CAN	John Barry
Bells of Autumn (Autumn Chimes)	RUS	A. Kogan
Below the Belt	ARC	Jerry Fielding
Beneficiary, The	BRI	Trevor Jones
Berlin Alexanderplatz	GER/ITA	Peer Raben
Between the Lines (pilot)	ABC-TV	Kenny Loggins/Richard Stekol
Beulah Land (series)	NBC-TV	Allyn Ferguson
Beyond Evil	IND	Pino Donaggio
Beyond Reasonable Doubt	NZ	Dave Fraser
Beyond Westworld (series)	CBS-TV	George Romanis
Big Brawl, The	WB	Lalo Schifrin
Big City Comedy (series)	IND-TV	Ian Bernard
Big Red One, The	UA	Dana Kaproff
Birthday, The	POL	Jerzy Maksymiuck
Black Hand, The	SPA	Jose Nieto
Black Marble, The	EMB	Maurice Jarre
Blake's Seven (series)	IND-TV	Dudley Simpson
Blinded by the Light	CBS-TV	Jonathan Tunick
Blood Tide (Red Tide, The)	BRI/GRE	Jerry Moseley
Bloodeaters	IND	Ted Shapiro
Blue Jeans (pilot)	ABC-TV	Don Foliart/Howard Pearl
Blue Lagoon	COL	Basil Poledouris
Bogie	CBS-TV	Charles Bernstein
Bon Voyage, Charlie Brown (And Don't Come Back)	PAR	Ed Bogas/Judy Munsen
Boogeyman	IND	Tim Krog
Borderline	IND	Gil Melle
Bosom Buddies (series)	ABC-TV	Dan Foliart/Howard Pearl
Boxer from the Temple, The	HK	Eddie Wang
Boy Who Drank Too Much, The	CBS-TV	Michael Small
Brave New World	TV	Paul Chihara
Break Away (Frzed Odlotem)	POL	Elzbieta Sikora
Breaker Morant	AUT	Phil Cunneen
Breaking Away (series)	ABC-TV	Lance Rubin
Broken Promise	CBS-TV	Fred Karlin
Bronco Billy	WB	Snuff Garrett

Brothers (pilot)	CBS-TV	Hod-David Schudson
Brothers and Sisters	BRI	Trevor Jones
Brubaker	TCF	Lalo Schifrin
Build a House, Plant a Tree	CZE	Petr Hapka
Buried Alive	ITA	"Goblin"
Byé Bye Brazil	BRA/FRA	Chico Buarque/ Roberto Menescal
Cabaret Mineiro	BRA	Tavinho Moura
Caddyshack	WB	Johnny Mandel
Cafe Express	ITA	Giovanna Marini
Cage aux Folles II, La	FRA/ITA	Ennio Morricone
Camp Grizzly (pilot)	ABC-TV	Ken Lauber
Camp Wilderness (series)	IND-TV	William Loose/Don Peake/ Michael Tschedin
Can-Cannes	ITA	Detto Mariano
Cannibals in the Streets	ITA/SPA	Alex Blonksteiner
Captain Caveman and the Teen Angels (series)	ABC-TV	Hoyt Curtin/Paul DeKorte
Carlton, Your Doorman (pilot)	CBS-TV	Stephen Cohn
Carny	UA	Alex North
Carry On Laughing (series)	BRI-TV	Max Harris/John Marshall/Richard Tattersall
Casino (pilot)	ABC-TV	Mark Snow
Catalan Cuckold (Salut I Forca al Canut)	SPA	Joseph Maria Duran
Cathy's Curse	FRA	Didier Vasseur
Caught on a Train	BRI-TV	Mike Westbrook
Caution to the Wind	SPA	Juan C. Senante
Celtic Ghosts	TV	Don Great
Cerromaior	POR	Constanca Capdeville
C'est La Vie! (That's Life)	FRA	Roland Vincent
Chain Reaction	AUT	Andrew Thomas Wilson
Chance (Szansa)	POL	Jan Kanty Pawluslziewicz
Chance Meeting on the Ocean	POL	Piotr Figiel
Change of Seasons, A	TCF	Henry Mancini
Changeling, The	CAN	Rick Wilkins
Characters (pilot)	NBC-TV	Hod David Schudson
Charlie Bravo	FRA	Alain Goraguer
Charter Trip, The	SWE	Bengt Palmers
Cheap Detective, The (pilot)	NBC-TV	Don Costa
Cheaper to Keep Her	IND	Dick Halligan
Cheech and Chong's Next Movie	UN	Mark Davis
Child of Divorce	NBC-TV	Minette Alltan/Raoul Kraushaar
Child Woman, The	FRA	Vladimir Cosma
Children, The	NWP	Harry Manfredini
Children from Blue Lake Mountain, The	SWE	Bernt Rosengren
Children from No. 67, The	GER	Andi Brauer
Children of An Lac, The	CBS-TV	Paul Chihara

Children of Babylon	JAM	Harold Butler
Children of Divorce	NBC-TV	Minette Alton/Raoul Kraushaar
Children of the Wind	ALG	Djiali Detto Carlos
Chisholms, The (second series)	CBS-TV	Gerald Fried/William Kraft
Circle of Two	CAN	Paul Hoffert
City in Fear	ABC-TV	Leonard Rosenman
City of the Walking Dead (Nightmare City)	ITA/SPA	Stelvio Cipriani
City of Women	FRA/ITA	Luis Enrique Bacalov
Clan of the White Lotus	HK	Eddie Wang
Clarence and Angel	IND	Philip Wilson
Cloud Dancer	IND	Fred Karlin
Club, The	AUT	Mike Brady
Coach of the Year	NBC-TV	Pete Carpenter/Mike Post
Coal Miner's Daughter	UN	Owen Bradley
Coast to Coast	PAR	Charles Bernstein
Cocktail Molotov	FRA	Yves Simon
Coffin Affair, The	CAN/FRA	Anne Laubert
Comeback Kid, The	ABC-TV	Barry De Vorzon
Concert at the End of Summer	CZE	Jaromil Burghauser
Condominium	IND-TV	Gerald Fried
Con-fusion	ITA	Arturo Annecchion
Conquest of the Earth	TV	Stu Phillips
Contender, The (series)	CBS-TV	James Di Pasquale
Contract (Kontrakt)	POL	Wojiech Kilar
Convict Killer, The	HK	Eddie Wang
Cordelia	CAN	Maurice Blackburn
Coup d'Etat (Zamach Stanu)	POL	Piotr Marczewski
Courage of Kavik, the Wolf Dog, The	NBC-TV	Harry Freedman
Crime at Porta Romana	ITA	Franco Micalizzi
Cruise, The (Rejs)	POL	Wojiech Kilar
Cruising	UA	Jack Nitzsche
Cry for Love, A	NBC-TV	Jimmie Haskell
Cry of the Innocent	NBC-TV	Allyn Ferguson
Cuenca Crime, The	SPA	Anton Garcia Abril
Curse of King Tut's Tomb, The	TV	Gil Melle
Damien: The Leper Priest	NBC-TV	Peter Matz
Dark Sun (Temne Slunce)	CZE	Martin Kratochvili
Day Christ Died, The	CBS-TV	Laurence Rosenthal
Day of Judgment, A	IND	Arthur Smith/Clay Smith
Day of the Vistula, The	POL	Waldemar Kazanecki
Day the Earth Got Stoned, The	IND	Richard Theiss
Day Time Ended, The	IND	Richard Band

Days of Dreams	YUG	Ksenija Zecevic
Dead End, A (Peruvaziambalan)	IN	M. G. Radhikishman
Dead or Alive (Elve Vagy Halva)	HUN	Geza Berki
Dear Boys (Lieve Jongens)	HOL	Laurens van Rooyen
Dear Friends	ARG	Victor Proncet
Death Ship	BRI	Ivor Slaney
Deathwatch	FRA/GER	Antoine Duhamel
Defiance	AI	Basil Poledouris/Gerard McMahon
Defiant Delta	YUG	Vangelis Papathanassiou
Demise of Herman Durer, The	HOL	Angelo Branduardi
Demon Pond (Yashaga Ike)	JAP	Isao Tomita
Demons of the South (Demons du Midi)	BEL/FRA/SPA	Michel Bernholc
Denmark Closed Down	DEN	Benny Andersen
Desideria, La Vita Interiore (Desire, the Interior Life)	GER/ITA	Pino Donaggio
Desperate Moves	IND	Steve Power
Desperate Voyage	CBS-TV	Bruce Broughton
Detour to Terror	NBC-TV	Morton Stevens
Diary of Anne Frank, The	NBC-TV	Billy Goldenberg
Did You Hear About Josh and Kelly? (pilot)	CBS-TV	Hal Cooper/Rod Parker
Die Laughing	WB	Robby Benson/Jerry Segal
Diaster on the Coastliner	ABC-TV	Gerald Fried
Disco of Love, The	ARG	Emilio Kauderer
Distant Cry from Spring, A	JAP	Masaru Sato
Divine Emma	CZE	Zdenek Liska
Dr. Butcher M.D. (Queen of the Cannibals)	ITA	Walter Sear
Dr. Franken	NBC-TV	John Morris
Dr. Heckyl & Mr. Hype	IND	Richard Band
Dogs of War, The	UA	Geoffrey Burgon
Don't Answer the Phone	CRO	Byron Allred
Don't Go in the House	IND	Richard Einhorn
Don't Go into the Woods	IND	Gunther Klein/H. Kingsley Thurber
Double, The (Kagemusha)	JAP	Shinjiro Ikebe
Double Negative	CAN	Paul Hoffert
Dracula Sucks	IND	Lionel Thomas
Drak Pack, The (series)	CBS-TV	Hoyt Curtin/Paul De Korte
Dream Merchants, The	IND-TV	George Duning
Dreams, Life, the Death of Filip Filipovic	YUG	Kornelije Kovac
Dressed to Kill	FIL	Pino Donaggio
Dribble (pilot)	NBC-TV	Joey Levine
Echoes	IND	Gerard Bernard Cohen/ Stephen Schwartz
Eclipse (Grhana)	IN	Vijaya Bhaskar

Edward and Mrs. Simpson (series)	BRI-TV	Ron Grainer
Edward the King	TV	Cyril Ornadel
Eight Kilos of Happiness	YUG	Vojkan Simic
Eleftherios Venizelos 1910-1927	GRE	Loukianos Kelaedonis
Elephant Man, The	PAR	John Morris
Elephant Story	JAP	Makato Kawaguchi
Empire Strikes Back, The	FOX	John Williams
Encore	HK	Danny Chan
Enemy, The (Dusman)	TUR	Yavuz Top
Enola Gay	NBC-TV	Maurice Jarre
Enos (series)	CBS-TV	Dennis McCarthy
Escapade	E.GER	Peter Rabenalt
Escape	CBS-TV	James di Pasquale
Escape from Iran: The Canadian Caper	CBS-TV	Peter Jermyn
Esthappan	IN	Aravindam/Kanardham/ Isaac Thomas Kottukapally
Ethel Is an Elephant (pilot)	ABC-TV	Ken Harrison
Eugenio	FRA/ITA	Romano Checcacci
Everyone for Himself in Life	FRA/SWI	Gabriel Yared
Evil Dead, The (Book of the Dead)	NLC	Joe LoDuca
Exit ... But No Panic	AUS	Otto M. Zykan
Exterior Night	FRA	Karl-Heinz Schafer
Exterminator, The	EMB	Joe Renzetti
Eyes of Texas, The (pilot)	NBC-TV	Stu Phillips
FDR--The Last Year	NBC-TV	Laurence Rosenthal
Fabian	GER	Charles Kalman
Face to the Sun	FRA	Sergio Godinho
Fade to Black	IND	Craig Safan
Falling in Love Again	IND	Michel Legrand
Fame	MGM	Michael Gore
Family, Fine, Thanks, The	SPA	Juan Carlos Calderon
Fantastica	CAN	Lewis Furey
Fantozzi Against the World	ITA	Fred Bongusto
Faraway Tomorrow (Toi Ashita)	JAP	Kawachi Kuni
Fascist Jew, The	ITA	Aldo Salvi
Fat Angels	IND	Bob Dorough
Father Figure	CBS-TV	Billy Goldenberg
Fatso	TCF	Joe Renzetti
Fatty Finn	AUT	Graham Bond/Rory O'Donohue
Fault, The (A Culpa)	POR	Antonio Victorino d'Almeida
Fear (Murder Syndrome/ Unconscious)	FRA/ITA	Franco Mannino
Fears (Miedos, Los)	ARG	Luis Maria Serra
Fernand	FRA	Michel Coeuriot
ffolkes	UN	Michael J. Lewis
Fiancee, The (Verlobte, Die)	E.GER	Karl-Ernst Sasse
Fiendish Plot of Dr. Fu Manchu, The	WB	Marc Wilkinson

Final Assignment	CAN	Peter Germyn
Final Countdown, The	UN	John Scott
Final Cut	AUT	Howard Davidson
First Deadly Sin, The	FIL	Gordon Jenkins
First Family	WB	Ralph Burns
First Time, The (Goldmine)	NLC	Lanny Meyers
First Time, Second Time (pilot)	CBS-TV	Michael Cannon/Cort Casady
First Voyage	FRA	Georges Delerue
Fist of Fear, Touch of Death	IND	Keith Mansfield
$5.20 an Hour Dream, The	CBS-TV	Jimmie Haskell
Five Forks (Cinco Tenedores)	SPA	Anton Garcia Abril
5% Risk	BEL/FRA	Eric Demarsan
Flambards, The (series)	PBS-TV	David Fanshawe
Flamingo Road	NBC-TV	Gerald Fried
Flash Gordon	UN	"Queen"
Flight Level 450	SWE	Ralph Lundsten
Flipside of Dominick Hyde, The	BRI-TV	Rick Jones/David Pierce
Flo (series)	CBS-TV	Fred Werner
Flourishing Times	SWE	Bjoern Isfaelt
Fog, The	EMB	John Carpenter
Fontamara	ITA	Roberto DeSimone
Fonz and the Happy Days Gang (series)	ABC-TV	Hoyt Curtin
Foolin' Around	COL	Charles Bernstein
For the Love of It	ABC-TV	Jimmie Haskell
Formula, The	MGM	Bill Conti
Foxes	UA	Giorgio Moroder
Friday the 13th	PAR	Harry Manfredini
From Here to Eternity (series)	NBC-TV	Richard Clements/ Walter Scharf
From the Abyss (Desde el Abismo)	ARG	Oscar Cardozo Ocampo
From the Life of the Marionettes	GER	Rolf Wilhelm
Frozen Heart, The	AUS/GER/SWI	Hardy Hepp
Fugitive Family	CBS-TV	Morton Stevens
Full Moon (Pelnia)	POL	Wlodzimierz Nahorny
Fun and Games	ABC-TV	Peter Matz
Fun Is Beautiful (Sacco Bello, Un)	ITA	Ennio Morricone
Further Adventures of Wally Brown, The (pilot)	NBC-TV	Don Peake
G.I.'s (pilot)	CBS-TV	Jack Elliott
Galactica 1980 (series)	ABC-tV	Glen A. Larson/Stu Phillips
Gambler, The	CBS-TV	Larry Cansler
Gates of Hell, The	ITA	Fabio Frizzi
Gauguin the Savage	CBS-TV	Gerald Fried
Georgia Peaches, The (pilot)	CBS-TV	R. Donovan Fox
German Spring	AUS/GER/SWI	Peer Raben
Germany, Bitter Land	TUR	Rahmi Saltuk
Germany, Pale Mother	GER	Juergen Knieper
Getting There (pilot)	CBS-TV	Jeff Barry

Ghost of a Chance (pilot)	ABC-TV	Earle Hagen
Ghosts of Buxley Hall, The	TV	Frank de Vol
Ghosts of Cape Horn	IND	Ed Kalehoff
Girl from Millelire Street, The	ITA	Luis Enrique Bacalov
Girl, the Gold Watch, and Everything, The	IND-TV	Hod David Schudson
Girl with the Golden Panties, The	SPA/VEN	Manuel Camp
Give Me Five (Qua la Mano)	ITA	Detto Mariano
Gloria	COL	Bill Conti
Godsend, The	IND	Roger Webb
Gold Bug, The	TV	Charles Gross
Golden Moment--An Olympic Love Story, The	NBC-TV	Perry Botkin Jr.
Goldie and the Boxer	NBC-TV	Jimmie Haskell
Golge	GER	Jo Liebau
Gong Show Movie, The	UN	Milton de Lugg
Good Neighbors (series)	PBS-TV	Burt Rhodes
Good Thief, The (Ladrone, Il)	FRA/ITA	Ennio Morricone
Good Time Harry (series)	NBC-TV	Peter Matz
Goodtime Girls (series)	ABC-TV	John Beal/Charles Fox/ Ben Lanzarone
Gossip Columnist, The	IND-TV	Allyn Ferguson
Great American Traffic Jam, The	NBC-TV	Arthur B. Rubinstein, Jr.
Great Cash Giveaway Getaway, The	NBC-TV	John Parker
Gridlock	NBC-TV	Arthur B. Rubinstein, Jr.
Grimaces	HUN	Andras Szollosy
Growing Pains (Acne '80)	ISR	Gary Eckstein
Guardians, The (Formynderne)	NOR	Synne Skouen
Guignolo, Le	FRA	Philippe Sarde
Gundam	JAP	Wakiko Fukuda/Tetsuo Takei
Guyana: Cult of the Damned	UN	Nelson Riddle/Bob Sum- mers/George S. Price
Guyana Tragedy: The Story of Jim Jones	CBS-TV	Elmer Bernstein
Hagen (series)	CBS-TV	George Romanis
Hangar 18	IND	John Cacavas
Happy Birthday, Gemini	UA	Rich Look/Cathy Chamberlain
Hardhat and Legs	CBS-TV	Brad Fiedel
Harlem Globetrotters on Gilligan's Island, The	NBC-TV	Gerald Fried
Harlequin	AUT	Brian May
Hate (Haine)	FRA	Alain Jomy
Hawk the Slayer	BRI	Harry Robinson
Haywire	CBS-TV	Billy Goldenberg

Hazal	TUR	Arif Sag
He Is Heading to the Glory Again	GRE	Mimis Plessas
He Knows You're Alone	MGM	Alexander Peskanov/ Mark Peskanov
Headless Ghost, The	THAI	S. Klongvesa
Heads or Tails (Pile ou Face)	FRA	Lino Leonardi
Hearse, The	CRO	Webster Lewis
Heartland	IND	Charles Gross
Heathcliff and Dingbat Show, The (series)	ABC-TV	Dean Elliott
Heaven's Gate	UA	David Mansfield
Heinrich Heine Revue	GER	Peter Jassens
Hellinger's Law	CBS-TV	John Cacavas
Henderson Monster, The	TV	Dick Hyman
Herbie Goes Bananas	DIS	Frank de Vol
Here's Boomer (series)	NBC-TV	David Frank
Hero at Large	MGM	Patrick Williams
Heroin	ITA	The Pretenders
Hidden in the Sunlight	POL	Zbigniew Namyslawski
Hide in Plain Sight	MGM	Leonard Rosenman
Hide 'n' Seek (Miskhak Makhbuim)	ISR	Ammon Wolman
Hiding Place, The (Versteck, Das)	E.GER	Guenther Fischer
Hill Street Blues	NBC-TV	Mike Post
Hinotori	JAP	Michel Legrand/Jun Fukamachi
His Master's Eye (Oeil du Maitre, L')	FRA	Pierre Jansen
Hollywood (series)	IND-TV	Carl Davis
Home Front, The (pilot)	CBS-TV	Pete Rugolo
Homeland Fever (Shigaon Shel Moledeth)	ISR	Yoav Kutner/Nir Hakhlili
Homeward Bound	CBS-TV	Fred Karlin
Homme a tout Faire, L'	CAN	Francois Lanctot
Hopscotch	EMB	Ian Fraser
Hordubal	CZE	Karol Mares
Horse of Pride	FRA	Pierre Jansen
Hospital Massacre	IND	Arlon Ober
Hostage Tower, The	CBS-TV	John Scott
Hot Potato (Patata Bollente, La)	ITA	Tato Savio
Hounds ... of Notre Dame, The	CAN	Maurice Marshall
House by the Sea, The	DEN	Hans Dal
House Where Death Lives, The (Delusion)	IND	Don Peake
Housewarming, The (Grihapravesh)	IN	Kanu Roy
Human Experiments	IND	Marc Bucci
Humanoids of the Deep	NWP	James Horner
Hunger Years	GER	Johannes Schmoelling
Hunter, The	PAR	Michel Legrand

Hussy	BRI	George Fenton
Hustler of Muscle Beach, The (pilot)	ABC-TV	Earle Hagen
I Am Maria	SWE	Bengt Edquist
I As in Icarus	FRA	Ennio Morricone
I Sent a Letter to My Love (Chere Inconnue)	FRA	Philippe Sarde
If Things Were Different	CBS-TV	Lee Holdridge
If Your Heart Can Feel	POL	Piotr Marczewski
I'll Love You Tomorrow	THAI	Okawee Sathakovit
Illusion	BUL	Georgi Genkov
I'm a Big Girl Now (series)	ABC-TV	George Aliceson Tipton
I'm Photogenic	FRA/ITA	Manuel de Sica
Images of Indians (series)	PBS-TV	Mark Hoover
Immacolata and Concetta: The Other Jealousy	ITA	Remo Ugolinelli
Imprint of Giants, The	FRA/GER	Karl Heinz Schafer
In God We Trust	UN	John Morris
In My Life (Honningmane)	DEN	"Fuzzy"
In Search of Historic Jesus	SUN	Bob Summers
In the Heart of the Hurricane	GER	Irmin Schmidt
In the Lost City of Sarzana	ITA	Gianni Nocenzi
Inferno	ITA	Keith Emerson
Inside Moves	AFD	John Barry
Inside Woman (Kvindesind)	DEN	Anne Linnet/Ralph Lundsten
Inspection of the Scene of a Crime 1901	POL	Zdzislaw Szostak
Inspector Blunder	FRA	Vladimir Cosma
Inventor, The (Erfinder, Der)	SWI	Jonas C. Haefeli
Io Sono Anna Magnani	GEL	Willyl de Maesschalk
Irreconcilable Memories	GER	Andi Brauer
Island, The	UN	Ennio Morricone
It All Depends on Girls	FRA	Michel Bernholc
I'ts a Living (series)	ABC-TV	George Aliceson Tipton
It's a World Full of Children	DEN	Henning Christiansen
It's My Turn	COL	Patrick Williams
It's Not Me, It's Him	FRA	Vladimir Cosma
Ivory Ape, The	ABC-TV	Bernard Hoffer/Maury Laws
JFK Years--A Political Trajectory, The	BRA	Caique Botkay
Jaguar	PHI	Max Jocson
Jake's Way (pilot)	CBS-TV	Frank Lewin
Jane Austen in Manhattan	IND	Richard Robbins
Jayne Mansfield Story, The	CBS-TV	Jimmie Haskell
Jazz Singer, The	AFD	Leonard Rosenman
Jigsaw	CAN/FRA	Claude Bolling
Jimmy B. & Andre	CBS-TV	Bruce Langhorne
Joe Dancer: The Big Black Pill	NBC-TV	George Romanis
Joni	IND	Ralph Carmichael

Joshua's World (pilot)	CBS-TV	Leonard Rosenman
Jula Treekul River	THAI	Prachin Songpao
Just Tell Me What You Want	WB	Charles Strouse
Kent State	NBC-TV	Ken Lauber
Kidnapping of the President, The	CRO	Paul J. Zaza
Killers, The (Kilas, O Mau da Fita)	POR	Sergio Godinho
Killin' Cousin, The	CBS-TV	Walter Scharf
Killing of Randy Webster, The	CBS-TV	Peter Matz
King Crab	ABC-TV	Dick Hyman
King of the Joropo	VEN	Leo Brouwer
Klondike Fever	IND	Hagood Hardy
Knight, The (Rycerz)	POL	Zdzislaw Szostak
Kosuke Kindaichi's Adventure	JAP	Katsumi Kobayashi
Kung-Fu	POL	Jacek Bednarek
Ladies in Blue (pilot)	ABC-TV	John Beal
Ladies' Man (series)	CBS-TV	Jack Elliott
Lady Grey	IND	Arthur Smith/Clay Smith
Land and Sons	ICE	Gunnar Raynir Svensson
Land of Love, The (Pendin Heng Kuam Rak)	THAI	Chalie Intravijit/Smarn Kanjanaparint/Bang Laeh
Landon, Landon and Landon (pilot)	CBS-TV	Perry Botkin, Jr.
Last Flight of Noah's Ark, The	DIS	Maurice Jarre
Last Outlaw, The	AUT-TV	Brian May
Last Rites (Dracula's Last Rites)	IND	Paul Jost/George Small
Last Song, The	CBS-TV	Johnny Harris
Last Subway, The (Dernier Metro, Le)	FRA	Georges Delerue
Laura: Shadows of Summer	FRA	Patrick Juyet
Lead Brigade, The	YUG	Ilja Pejovski
Leap from the Bridge, The	SWI	Markus Fischer
Leap into the Void (Salto nel Vuoto)	FRA/ITA	Nicola Piovani
Leave Me Not Alone	SWE	Lennart Sjoeholm
Legend of Julian Makabayan, The	PHI	Lutgardo Labad
Legend of the Fox	HK	Eddie Wang
Lena Rais	GER	Eberhard Schoener
Loe and Loree	UA	Lance Rubin
Lesson of a Dead Language	POL	Andrzej Kurylewicz
Liar's Dice	IND	Coleman Burke/Gary Yamani
Life and Times of Eddie Roberts, The (L.A.T.E.R.) (series)	IND-TV	Harry Betts
Life Guard, The	RUS	Isaak Svarc
Life on the Mississippi	IND-TV	William Perry
Lightning Over Water (Nick's Movie)	GER/SWE	Ronee Blakley
Little Darlings	PAR	Charles Fox

Little Dragons, The	IND	Ken Lauber
Little Lord Fauntleroy	CBS-TV	Allyn Ferguson
Little Miss Marker	UN	Henry Mancini
Little Siren, The	FRA	Alain Jomy
Little Virgil and Frogeater Orla	DEN	Peter Bastian
Littlest Hobo, The (series)	IND-TV	Jacques Urbont
Lobo (series)	NBC-TV	John Andrew Tartaglia
Long Days of Summer, The	ABC-TV	Walter Scharf
Long Good Friday, The	BRI	Francis Monkman
Long Riders, The	UA	Ry Cooder
Lost Souls	HK	Eddie Wang
Lost Way, The (Chemin Perdu, Le)	BEL/FRA/SWI	Patrick Moraz
Love (Kaerleken)	SWE	Monica Dominique
Love at First Sight (pilot)	CBS-TV	Jose Feliciano
Love Between the Raindrops	CZE	Lubos Fiser
Love in a Taxi	IND	Susan Minsky
Love, Natalie (pilot)	NBC-TV	John Foster
Love, Natalie (series)	NBC-TV	Billy Byers/John Foster
Love of Perdition	POR	Joao Paes
Love Tapes, The	ABC-TV	Billy Goldenberg
Loving Couples	TCF	Fred Karlin
Lucky Star, The	CAN	Art Phillips
Lucy Moves to NBC	NBC-TV	Morton Stevens
M Station: Hawaii (pilot)	CBS-TV	Morton Stevens
Ma Cherie	BEL/FRA	Jean-Pierre Mas
McVicar	BRI	Jeff Wayne
Mad Dog (Wsciekly)	POL	Jerzy Matula
Madhouse (Scared to Death/I Will Scare You to Death/There Was Once a Child)	ITA	Riz Ortolani
Magnum, P.I. (series)	CBS-TV	Ian Freebairn-Smith
Make Me an Offer	ABC-TV	Ralph Burns
Maluala	CUB	Sergio Vitier
Mama Dracula	BEL	Roy Budd
Man of Fashion	SPA	Luis Eduardo Aute
Man on the Run, A	FRA/SWI	Pierre Jansen
Man Who Stole the Sun, The	JAP	Takayuki Inoue
Man with Bogart's Face, The	TCF	George Duning
Man with the Red Carnation, The	GRE	Mikis Theodorakis
Manos	ITA/MEX/SPA	Fabio Frizzi
Mandy's Grandmother	IND-TV	Linda Schreyer
Manaos	GER/VEN	Victor Cuica
Marathon	CBS-TV	Joe Renzetti
Mark, I Love You	CBS-TV	Jimmie Haskell
Marmalade Revolution, The	SWE	Antoine Forqueray
Marriage Is Alive and Well (pilot)	NBC-TV	Fred Karlin
Married for the First Time	RUS	Oleg Karavalchuk
Martian Chronicles, The (series)	NBC-TV	Stanley Myers
Masoch	ITA	Gianfranco di Fonzo/ Tonio Paoletti
Me and Maxx (series)	NBC-TV	Michael Lloyd

Medal, The	CZE	Zdenek Liska
Melvin and Howard	UN	Bruce Langhorne
Men or Not Men	ITA	Ennio Morricone
Marilyn: The Untold Story	ABC-TV	William Goldstein
Mating Season, The	CBS-TV	John Morris
Middle Age Crazy	TCF	Matthew McCauley
Midnight	IND	Eastman Color
Midnight Lace	NBC-TV	Stu Phillips
Midnight Madness	DIS	Julius Wechter
Migration of Sparrows	RUS	Teimuraz Babluani
Mike Test	RUM	Maja Stepanenco
Milionario and Ze Rico in the Highway of Life	BRA	Dooby Ghizzy
Mirror Crack'd, The	AFD	John Cameron
Miser, The (L'Avare)	FRA	Jean Bizet
Miss Keow (Keow)	THAI	Saravuth Pachaiyo
Miss Right	ITA	Michael Small
Missing Link, The	FRA	Roy Budd
Mr. & Mrs. & Mr. (pilot)	CBS-TV	Billy Byers
Mr. and Mrs. Dracula	TV	Jack Elliott/Ken Lauber
Mr. Patman	CAN	Paul Hoffert
Molotov Cocktail (see Cocktail Molotov)		
Mom, the Wolfman and Me	IND-TV	Fred Karlin
Moment, The	DEN	Lars Henning-Jensen
Moon Over the Alley	BRI	Galt MacDermot
More Wild, Wild West	CBS-TV	Jeff Alexander
Mosch	GER	Peer Raben
Motel Hell	UTA	Lance Rubin
Moth, The (Cma)	POL	Jan Kanty Pawluskiewicz
Mother and Daughter: The Loving War	ABC-TV	Lee Holdridge
Mother, Dearly Beloved	SPA	Vangelis Papathanassiou
Mother's Day	IND	Phil Gallo/Clem Vicari
Mountain Men, The	COL	Michel Legrand
Moving (see On the Move)		
Moviola: The Scarlett O'Hara War	NBC-TV	Walter Scharf
Moviola: The Silent Lovers	NBC-TV	Gerald Fried
Moviola: This Year's Blonde	NBC-TV	Elmer Bernstein
Murder Can Hurt You (pilot)	ABC-TV	Artie Kane
Music Mart, The	NBC-TV	Morton Stevens
My American Uncle	FRA	Arie Dzierlatka
My Bodyguard	TCF	Dave Grusin
My Days with Veronica	ARG	Luis Maria Serra
My Fabulous Girlfriends	ITA	Gioele and Elvio Boeri
My Heart Is Upside Down	FRA/SPA	Jean Musy
My Son, My Son (series)	BRI-TV	Kenyon Roberts
Nedtur (If Music Be the Food of Love)	NOR	Christian Reim

Nest Break	SWI	Cornelius Wernle
Nest in the Wind	RUS	Lepo Sumera
Next Stop Paradise	DEN	Gunnar Moeller Pedersen
Nick and the Dobermans (pilot)	NBC-TV	Jerrold Immel
Night Games	EMB	John Barry
Night of the Juggler	COL	Artie Kane
Night of the Zombies (Hell of the Living Dead/Apocalipsis Canibal)	ITA/SPA	"Goblin"
Night Warning (Thrilled to Death/ Momma's Boy/Butcher, Baker, Nightmare Maker)	IND	Bruce Langhorne
Nightside (pilot)	ABC-TV	John Andrew Tartaglia
Nine to Five	TCF	Charles Fox
Ninth Heart, The	CZE	Petr Hapka
No Holds Barred (series)	CBS-TV	Tony Romero
No More Easy Going	JAP	Michi Tanaka
Nobody's Perfect (series)	ABC-TV	Jack Elliott/Allyn Ferguson/Hal Mooney
Nomugi Pass	JAP	Masaru Sato
Nude Bomb, The	UN	Lalo Schifrin
Nuit des Traquees, La	FRA	Philippe Brejean
Number 96 (series)	NBC-TV	Gerald Fried
Nurse	CBS-TV	Charles Gross
Octagon, The	IND	Dick Halligan
Off Season (Fuori Stagione)	ITA	Amedeo Tommasi
Oficio de Tinieblas	MEX	Manuel Enriquez
Oh, God! Book II	WB	Charles Fox
Oh, Heavenly Dog	TCF	Ewel Box
Olympics 40	POL	Andrzej Korzynski
Omniscient, The (Sarvasakshi)	IN	Bhaskar Chandawarkar
On the Far Side of Adventure	ARG	Luis Maria Serra
On the Move (Utkozben)	HUN	Zygmunt Konieczny
On the Nickel	IND	Fred Myrow
Once Upon a Family	CBS-TV	Fred Karlin
Once Upon a Spy (pilot)	ABC-TV	John Cacavas
One-Armed Executioner, The	PHI	Gene Kavel
One in a Million (series)	ABC-TV	Harry Betts
One Man's Loss ...	SWE	Christer Boustedt
One Trick Pony	WB	Paul Simon
Opera Prima (First Effort)	FRA/SPA	Fernando Ember
Operation Leopard (La Legion Saute sur Kolwezi)	FRA	Serge Franklin
Ordeal of Dr. Mudd, The	CBS-TV	Gerald Fried
Order	GER	Rolf Bauer
Ordinary People	PAR	Marvin Hamlisch
Ortlieb Women, The	GER	Peer Raben
Other One's Mug, The (Gueule de l'autre, La)	FRA	Claude Bolling
Our Johnny	AUS	Dieter Kaufmann/Bel Koreni/"Clockwork"

Out of the Blue	IND	Tom Lavin
Pacific High	DIS	Robert F. Brunner
Paco the Infallible	FRA/SPA	Serge Perathoner
Palmerstown, U.S.A. (series)	CBS-TV	Al Schackman
Panagoulis Lives	ITA	Dimitri Nicolau
Paraguelia	GRE	Kyriacos Sfetsas
Parallels	CAN	Don Archbold
Partners of Adventure	BRA	Paulo Moura
Per, Jom and Phen	THAI	Buan Savatcho
Perfect Match, A	CBS-TV	Billy Goldenberg
Persian Lamb Coat, The	ITA	Bruno Nicolai
Perverse Tales	FRA/ITA	Martial Carceles
Petrija's Wreath	YUG	Zoran Simjanovic
Phil and Mikhy (series)	CBS-TV	Hal Cooper/Rod Parker
Phobia	CAN	Andre Gagnon
Pioneers, The	CHN/TAI	Ching-Shi, Oun
Pit, The	CAN	Victor Davies
Plan of His 19 Years, The (Jukyu-Sai no Chizu)	JAP	Fumio Itabashi
Planet of Dinosaurs	IND	Kelly Lammers/John O'Verlin
Playing for Time	CBS-TV	Brad Fiedel
Pleasure Palace	CBS-TV	Allyn Ferguson
Plumber, The	AUT	Gerry Tolland
Plutonium Incident, The	CBS-TV	Fred Karlin
Popeye	PAR	Harry Nilsson
Portrait of a Female Drunkard	GER	Peer Raben
Portrait of a Rebel: Margaret Sanger	CBS-TV	Arthur B. Rubinstein, Jr.
Portrait of an Escort	CBS-TV	Hagood Hardy
Pottsville (pilot)	CBS-TV	Larry Cansler
Power	NBC-TV	Jerrold Immel
Power of Men Is the Patience of Women, The	GER	Flying Lesbians
Precarious Bank Teller, The	ITA	Piero Piccioni
Prey, The	NWP	Don Peake
Price of Survival, The	GER	Joe Haider
Priceless Day, A (Ajandek .ez a Nap)	HUN	Gyorgy Selmeczi
Prickly Pears (Fico d'India)	ITA	Giancarlo Chiaromello
Pride and Prejudice	BRI-TV	Wilfred Josephs
Primal Fear	CAN	Maurice Blackburn
Princess	IND-TV	Richard Rand/Charles Stone
Private Battle, A	CBS-TV	Charles Gross
Private Benjamin	WB	Bill Conti
Private Eyes, The	NWP	Peter Matz
Prom Night	EMB	Carl Zittrer/Paul J. Zaza
Promise of Love, A	CBS-TV	Paul Chihara
Proper Way, The	JAP	Shinjiro Ikebe

Provincial Actors	POL	Andrzej Zarycki
Provinciale, La	FRA/SWI	Arie Dzierlatka
Psychotronic Man, The	IND	Rommy Irons
Purity of Heart	GER	Peer Raben
Put on Ice (Kaltgestellt)	GER	Charly Mariano/Jasper Van T'Hoft/Mike Thatcher
Quatermass Conclusion	BRI	Marc Wilkinson/Nick Rowley
Queen's Father, The	POL	Maciej Malecki
Rabbit Case, The	CZE	Vadim Petrov
Rage	NBC-TV	Laurence Rosenthal
Raise the Titanic!	AFD	John Barry
Rape and Marriage: The Rideout Case	CBS-TV	Gil Melle
Rapture (Arrebato)	SPA	Ivan Zulueta
Rascals (Turlupins, Les)	FRA	Roland Romanelli
Rat Race, The (Je Vais Craquer!)	FRA	Jean-Pierre Sabar
Real Game, The	ISR	Alona Tur-El
Rebel Intruders, The	HK	Eddie Wang
Red Mansion, The	THAI	Prachin Songpao
Red Stocking, The	GER	Eberhard Weber/Rainer Brueninghaus
Resurrection	UN	Maurice Jarre
Return, The	IND	Dan Wyman
Return in Bond	FRA	William Sheller
Return of Frank Cannon, The	CBS-TV	Bruce Broughton
Return of the Banished, The	RUM	Anatol Vieru
Return of the Secaucus Seven	IND	K. Mason Daring
Return tó Marseilles	FRA	Lucien Bertolina
Reunion	CBS-TV	George Romanis
Revenge of the Stepford Wives, The	TV	Laurence Rosenthal
Reward	ABC-TV	Barry De Vorzon
Richard's Things	BRI	Georges Delerue
Riding for the Pony Express (pilot)	CBS-TV	Ralph Ferraro
Right Out óf History--The Making of Judy Chicago's Dinner Party	IND	Catherine MacDonald
Rising Damp	BRI	David Lindup
Risk of Living, The	FRA	Georges Prost
Roadie	UA	Craig Hundley
Rodeo Girl	CBS-TV	Al DeLory
Rough Cut	TCF	Nelson Riddle/Duke Ellington
Roughnecks (series)	IND-TV	Jerrold Immel
Royal Vacation	FRA	Francois Tusques
Rumor of War, A	CBS-TV	Charles Gross
S*H*E (pilot)	CBS-TV	Michael Kamen

Sabine Wulff	E.GER	Karl-Heinz Sasse
Salad Days (Sielone Lata)	POL	Andrezej Korzynski
Salamander, The	BRI/ITA	Jerry Goldsmith
Sanford (series)	NBC-TV	Quincy Jones
Santa Esperanza	RUS	Gabriel Castro/Adrian Chamorro/Ramiro Soriano
Satan's Mistress	IND	Roger Kellaway
Saturn 3	AFD	Elmer Bernstein
Savage Breed (Razza Selvaggia)	ITA	Tullio de Piscopo
Saviour, The	HK	Teddy Robin
Scalpels (pilot)	NBC-TV	John LaSandra
Scared Straight: Another Story	CBS-TV	Dana Kaproff
Scared to Death	IND	Tom Chase/Ardell Hake
Schilten	SWI	Cornelius Wernle
Schizoid	IND	Craig Hundley
Scout's Honor	NBC-TV	Mike Post
Scruples	CBS-TV	Charles Bernstein
Sea of Roses	BRA	Paolo Herculano
Sea Wolves, The	BRI	Roy Budd
Second-Hand Hearts	IND	Willis Alan Ramsey
Second Shift, The	NOR	Arne Garvang
Secret of Nikola Tesla, The	YUG	Andelko Klobucar
Secret War of Jackie's Girls, The (pilot)	NBC-TV	Fred Karlin
Seduction of Miss Leona, The	CBS-TV	Robert Prince
See You in the Next War	YUG	Bojan Adamic
Seems Like Old Times	COL	Marvin Hamlisch
Seizure: The Story of Kathy Morris	CBS-TV	George Aliceson Tipton
Self-Portrait in Brains	IND	James D. Lumsden
Semi-Tough (series)	ABC-TV	Doug Gilmore/Tom Wells
Semmelweis	ITA/SWI	Gino Negri
September Wheat	GER	Rolf Riehm
Serial	PAR	Lalo Schifrin
Seven Brothers	FIN	Pekka Jalkannen
Shadow Box, The	ABC-TV	Henry Mancini
Shadow Line	ITA	Manuel De Sica
Shillingbury Blowers, The	BRI	Ed Welch
Shogun	NBC	Maurice Jarre
Shogun Assassin	JAP	W. Michael Lewis/Mark Lindsay
Sidney Shorr	NBC-TV	Bill Newkirk
Silent Lovers, The	NBC-TV	Gerald Fried
Silent Scream	ACR	Roger Kellaway
Simon	WB	Stanley Silverman
Sinful Life of Franciszek Buła, The	POL	Zygmunt Zgraja
Single Life, The (pilot)	NBC-TV	David Frank
Sir Henry at Rawlinson End	BRI	Vivian Stanshall
Six O'Clock Follies, The (series)	NBC-TV	Harry Betts/Artie Butler

Skag (series)	NBC-TV	Bruce Broughton/Billy Goldenberg/Morton Stevens
Skyward	NBC-TV	Lee Holdridge
Small Circle of Friends, A	UA	Jim Steinman
Smokey and the Bandit II	UN	Snuff Garrett
Sniper, The	IRAQ	Talib El-Qaraghooli
So Feared a Hell	ARG	Astor Piazzolla
Solo Sunny	E.GER	Guenther Fischer
Somebody's Stolen the Thigh of Jupiter	FRA	Georges Hatzinassios
Something Out of Nothing	BUL	Boris Karadimchev
Somewhere in Time	UN	John Barry
Son-in-Law, The (pilot)	NBC-TV	Pete Rugolo
Sophia Loren: Her Own Story	NBC-TV	Fred Karlin
Sorry to Have Imposed	DEN	Fuzzy
Sous-Doues, Les (Les Gifted, The)	FRA	Bob Brault
Space Movie, The	BRI	Mike Oldfield
Spetters	HOL	Ton Scherpenzeel
Spooky Bunch, The	HK	Tang Boom-Kei
Squeeze, The	ITA	Paolo Vasile
Star Inspector	RUS	Boris Rychkov
Steel	WNP	Michel Colombier
Stir	AUT	Cameron Allan
Stockard Channing Show, The (series)	CBS-TV	Doug Gilmore
Storm, The (Jhor)	IN	P. Bhattacharya
Story of a Good Guy, The	MOG	T. Namsraizhav
Story of an Unknown Man	RUS	A. Firtic
Strangers--The Road to Liberty	BRA	John Neschling
Stronger Than the Sun	BRI	Howard Blake
Stuckey's Last Stand	IND	Carson Whitsett
Stung Man, The	IND	Dominic Frontiere
Stunts Unlimited	ABC-TV	Barry de Vorzon
Sunday Lovers	FRA/ITA	Manuel de Sica
Sunday Parents (Vasarnapi Szulok)	HUN	Levente Szorenyi
Super Monster Gamera	JAP	Shunsuke Kikuchi
Survival Run	IND	Gary William Friedman
Suzanne	CAN	Francois Cousineau
Svetozar Markovic	YUG	Zoran Hristic
Swan Song	ABC-TV	Jonathan Tunick
Sweden for the Swedes	SWE	Carl-Axel Dominique
Swindle, The (Entourloupe, L')	FRA	Django Reinhardt
Tale of Two Cities, A	CBS-TV	Allyn Ferguson
Target ... Earth	TV	Joey Levine
Target: Harry	ABC	Les Baxter

Tarzan and Lone Ranger Adventure Hour, The (series)	CBS-TV	Yvette Blais/Jeff Michael
Tattoo Connection, The	WNP	Anders Nelsson/Perry Martin
Tears on the Lion's Mane	JAP	Toru Takemitsu
Telephone Bar, The	FRA	Vladimir Cosma
Tell Me a Riddle	FIL	Sheldon Shkolnik
Tenspeed and Brownshoe (series)	ABC-TV	Pete Carpenter/Mike Post
Terrace, The (Terrazza, La)	ITA	Armando Trovajoli
Terror on Tour	IND	The Names
Terror Train	TCF	John Mills-Cockell
Texas (series)	NBC-TV	Elliot Lawrence
That House in the Outskirts	SPA	Carmelo Bernaola
That's My Line (series)	CBS-TV	Robert Cobert
Their Golden Years	SPA	"Suburbano"
Theo Against the Rest of the World	GER	Lothar Meid
There Goes the Bride	BRI	Harry Robinson
They Call Him Hurricane (Jao Payu)	THAI	Orn-iem, Montri
This Age Without Pity	FRA	Alain Jomy
Those Amazing Animals (series)	ABC-TV	Roy Prendergast
Those Lips Those Eyes	UA	Michael Small
Three Men to Destroy	FRA	Claude Bolling
Thundarr the Barbarian (series)	ABC-TV	Dean Elliott
Thunderbirds to the Rescue	BRI	Barry Gray
Time for Miracles, A	ABC-TV	Fred Karlin
Tinker, Tailor, Soldier, Spy	BRI-TV	Geoffrey Burgon
To Find My Son	CBS-TV	Ralph Grierson
To Live a Long Life	RUS	Martyn Vertazaryan
To Love the Damned	ITA	Tullio Giordana
To Race the Wind	CBS-TV	John Rubinstein
To the Last Drop	BRA	Paul de Castro
Today Is for the Championship	IND	Buddy Collette
Todo Modo	ITA	Ennio Morricone
Tom Horn	WB	Ernest Gold
Tomb of Dracula	JAP	Seiji Yokoyama
Toni's Boys (pilot)	ABC-TV	Jack Elliott/Allyn Ferguson
Too Close for Comfort (series)	ABC-TV	Johnny Mandel
Top of the Hill	IND-TV	George Duning
Touched by Love	COL	John Barry
Tourist	IND-TV	Jack Smalley
Toward the Terror	JAP	Masaru Sato
Transit	ISR	Shlomo Gronich
Treachery and Greed on the Planet of the Apes	TV	Earle Hagen/Lalo Schifrin
Trouble in High Timber Country	ABC-TV	George Aliceson Tipton
Truth on the Savolta Affair, The	FRA/ITA/SPA	Egisto Macchi

Turnover Smith	ABC-TV	Bernardo Segall
Tusk	FRA	Jean-Claude Petit/Guy Skornik
22nd June, 1897	IN	Anand Modak
Twinkle, Twinkle, Killer Kane (Ninth Configuration, The)	WB	Barry de Vorzon
Two Champions of Shaolin	HK	Eddie Wang
Two Lions in the Sun	FRA	Albert Marcoeur
Uforia	UN	Richard Baskin
Ugily Family, The (pilot)	ABC-TV	Michael Leonard
Umbrella Coup, The	FRA	Vladimir Cosma
Under Lock and Key	GER	Edgar Froese
Union City	IND	Chris Stein
United States (series)	NBC-TV	Jack Elliott
Unpredictable Guy (Tiro Al Aire)	ARG	Victor Proncet
Until Death Do Us Part	E.GER	Peter Gotthardt
Up the Academy	WB	Jody Taylor Worth
Urban Cowboy	PAR	Ralph Burns
Used Cars	COL	Patrick Williams
Vacations in Val Trebbia	ITA	Nicola Piovani
Valentine Magic on Love Island (pilot)	NBC-TV	Peter Matz
Velvet Hands	ITA	Nando de Luca
Vengeance Is Mine	JAP	Shinjiro Ikebe
Vicious Circle (Cardena Perpetua)	MEX	Miguel Pons
Virus	JAP	Teo Macero
Visitor, The	IND	Franco Micalizzi
Voices of the Sylphides, The	GER-TV	Hubert Stuppner
Waikiki (pilot)	ABC-TV	Stu Phillips
Waiting for Daddy	SPA	Rafael Ferro/Julio Iglesias
Wandering Soul (Ashwathama)	IN	A. Padmanabhan
Watcher in the Woods, The	DIS	Stanley Myers
We Were One Man	FRA	Jean Jacques Ruhlmann
Week's Vacation, A (Une Semaine de Vacances)	FRA	Pierre Papadiamandis
Whale for the Killing, A	ABC-TV	Basil Poledouris
What Did I Ever Do to the Good Lord to Deserve a Wife Who Drinks in Cafes with Men?	FRA	Georges and Pierre-Marie Baux
Whatever You Can Spare (Daj Sto Das)	YUG	Ozren Depolo
When, Jenny, When?	IND-TV	Richard La Salle
When the Screaming Stops (Lorelei's Grasp, The)	SPA	Anton Garcia Abril
When the Whistle Blows (series)	ABC-TV	Mark Snow
When Time Ran Out	WB	Lalo Schifrin
Where the Buffalo Roam	UN	Neil Young
White Mama	CBS-TV	Peter Matz

Whitey (De Witte Van Sichem)	BEL	Juergen Knieper
Wholly Moses!	COL	Patrick Williams
Who's That Singing Over There?	YUG	Vojislav Kostic
Why Would I Lie?	MGM	Charles Fox
Widow Montiel, The	CUB/MEX/SA	Leo Brouwer
Wife, The (Savithri)	IN	Gunasingh
Wild and the Free, The	CBS-TV	Gerald Fried
Wild Times	IND-TV	Jerrold Immel
Willie and Phil	TCF	Claude Bolling
Willow B: Women in Prison (pilot)	ABC-TV	James di Pasquale
Windows	UA	Ennio Morricone
Windwalker	IND	Merrill Jensen
Without a Promised Land	HK	Polygram
Without Love	POL	Seweryn Krajewski
Without Warning	AI	Dan Wyman
Wolf-Cubs of Niquoluna, The (Prune des Bois)	BEL	Pierre Perret
Woman and a Woman, A	POL	Wojciech Trzcinski
Woman Banker, The	FRA	Ennio Morricone
Woman Cop, The	FRA	Philippe Sarde
Woman Like Eve, A	HOL	Laurens van Rooyen
Women's Room, The	ABC-TV	Billy Goldenberg
Wonderful Years, The	GER	Rolf Wilhelm
Xanadu	UN	Barry de Vorzon
Yamato 3	JAP-TV	Hiroshi Miyagawa
Yeagers, The (series)	ABC-TV	George Aliceson Tipton
Young Master, The	HK	Frankie Chan
You've Been Had ... You Turkey! (Achalta Ota)	ISR	Ilan Mochiach
Zombie	ITA	Fabio Frizzi/Giorgio Tucci

1981

Absence of Malice	COL	Dave Grusin
Absolution	BRI	Stanley Myers
Ace	ITA	Detto Mariano
Acorn People, The	NBC-TV	Craig Hundley
Act of Love	NBC-TV	Billy Goldenberg
Acting: Lee Strasberg and the Actors Studio	IND	Werner Janssen
Adventures of Enrique and Ana, The	SPA	L. Gomez Escolar/ Honorio Herrero
Adventures of Huckleberry Finn	NBC-TV	Bob Summers
Advice to the Lovelorn	NBC-TV	James Di Pasquale
Al di La	ITA	Fabio Frizzi
Al Qadisiyya	IRAQ	Walid Ghulmiyya
All Night Long	UN	Richard Hazard/Ira Newborn

Casanova (series)	IND-TV	John Burrows
Cassette Love	SWI	Jonas C. Haefeli
Castle Rock	TV	Kerry Crawford/Jonathan Goldsmith
Catherine and I	FRA/ITA	Piero Piccioni
Cattle Annie and Little Britches	UN	Sanh Berti
Caveman	UA	Lalo Schifrin
Chakra	IN	Hridayanath Mangeshkar
Champagne for Breakfast	IND	Jack Stern
Chance, History, Art ...	BRI	Simon Brint
Chanel Solitaire	FRA	Paul Jabara
Charge (Szarza)	POL	Czeslaw Hieman
Chariots of Fire	BRI	Vangelis
Charlie and the Great Balloon Race	NBC-TV	Glen Paxton
Charlie Chan and the Curse of the Dragon Queen	IND	Patrick Williams
Charlotte	GER/HOL	Egisto Macchi
Checking In (series)	CBS-TV	David Talisman/Horace Tapscott
Cheech & Chong's Nice Dreams	COL	Herry Betts
Cherokee Trail, The	CBS-TV	Jerrold Immel
Chicago Story	NBC-TV	Lalo Schifrin
Child Bride of Short Creek	NBC-TV	John Cacavas
Children Nobody Wanted, The	CBS-TV	Barry De Vorzon
Children's Island	SWE	Jean-Michel Jarre
Choice of Weapons	FRA	Philippe Sarde
Chosen, The	IND	Elmer Bernstein
Chu Chu and the Philly Flash	TCF	Pete Rugolo
Circus Casablanca	DEN	Leif Sylvester Petersen
Circus Maximus	HUN	Szaboles Fenyes
City Birds	ITA/SPA	Fabio Frizzi
Clara and the Swell Guys	FRA	Michel Jonasz
Clash of the Titans	MGM	Laurence Rosenthal
Code Red (series)	ABC-TV	Richard La Salle/Gerig McRitchie/Morton Stevens
Coldest Winter in Peking, The	TAI	Lo Ming-Tao
Come Back Swallow	CHN	Ji Ming/Ou We
Come to My Place, I'm Living at My Girlfriend's	FRA	Renaud
Comedy of Horrors	CBS-TV	Jonathan Tunick
Commanding Sea, The	BRI-TV	Carl Davis
Condorman	DIS	Henry Mancini
Continental Divide	UN	Michael Small
Conversations with Willard Van Dyke	IND	Amy Rubin
Coup de Torchon (Pop. 1280)	FRA	Philippe Sarde
Covergirl (Dreamworld)	CAN	Christopher Stone
Coward of the County	CBS-TV	Larry Cansler

Falling Stars (Zvezdopad)	RUS	Alfred Schnitke
Family Album	BRA	John Neschling
Family Reunion	NBC-TV	Wladimir Selinsky
Fan, The	PAR	Pino Donaggio
Father and Sun	HK	Violet Lam/Yu Lun
Father Murphy (series)	NBC-TV	David Rose
Father Will Beat Me Anyway	HUN	Ali Brezovsky
Fear No Evil	EMB	Frank LaLoggia/David Spear
Fear Not, Jacob!	GER	Kalus Obermeyer
Fever (Goraczka)	POL	Jan Kanty Pawluskiewicz
Few Days in Weasel Creek, A	CBS-TV	James Horner
Few Days More, A	CAN	Pierre Leduc
Fiend	IND	Paul Woznicki
5th Movement, The	JAP	Hikaru Hayashi
Filthy Business, A	FRA	Daniel Humair/Francois Jeanneau/Henri Texier
Final Conflict,--Damien III, The	TCF	Jerry Goldsmith
Final Exam	HUN	Edda
Final Exam	IND	Gary Scott
Final Terror, The	IND	Susan Justin
Find a Way, Comrade	YUG	Alfi Kabiljo
Fisherman's Wharf	NBC-TV	Earle Hagen
Fit to Be Untied (Matti da Slegare)	ITA	Nicola Piovani
Fitz and Bones (series)	NBC-TV	Stu Phillips
Five of Me, The	CBS-TV	Fred Karlin
Flame Top (Tulipaa)	FIN	Heikki Valpola
Fly Away Home	ABC-TV	Lee Holdridge
Flying Machine, The (Letaloto)	BUL	Yuri Stupel
Folk Tale, A	IN	Gaurang Vyas
Follies of Elodie, The	FRA	Claude Pimpere
For Ladies Only	NBC-TV	Lee Holdridge
For Your Eyes Only	UA	Bill Conti
Force: Five	IND	William Goldstein
Forest, The	IND	Richard Hieronymus/ Alan Oldfield
Fort Apache, the Bronx	TCF	Jonathan Tunick
Foul Play (series)	ABC-TV	David Frank
Four Friends	FIL	Elizabeth Swados
Four Seasons of Natsuko, The	JAP	Michi Tanaka
Fox and the Hound, The	DIS	Buddy Baker
Francisca	POR	Joao Paes
Freebie and the Bean (series)	CBS-TV	Dominic Frontiere
Friday Is Not the Weekend	CZE	Petr Hapka
Friday the 13th Part 2	PAR	Harry Manfredini
Fridays of Eternity, The	ARG	Lalo Schifrin
Frightmare (Horror Star, The)	IND	Jerry Moseley
From a Far Country--Pope John Paul II	BRI/ITA	Wojiech Kilar
From Mysterious Buenos Aires	ARG	Luis Maria Serra

Front Line	AUT	Lindsay Lee/Midnight Oil/Denise Wykes
Fruits of Passion, The	FRA/JAP	J. A. Seazer
Fugitive from the Empire	NBC-TV	Ian Underwood
Funeral Racket, The	JAP	Hajime Kaburagi
Funhouse	IND	John Beal
Gabe and Walker	ABC-TV	Ian Freebairn-Smith
Galaxina	IND	Arlon Ober
Galaxy of Terror	NWP	Barry Schrader
Gangster Chronicles, The	NBC-TV	John Cacavas/Billy Goldenberg
Gary Cooper, Who Are in Heaven	SPA	Anton Garcia Abril
Gas	PAR	Paul J. Zaza
Gazija	YUG	Zoran Simjanovic
Gentleman Bandit, The	CBS-TV	Stanley Myers
German Sisters, The	GER	Nicolas Economou
Getting Even	IND	Richard Greene
Getting Over	IND	Johnny Rodgers
Ghost of Love	FRA/GER/ITA	Riz Ortolani
Ghost Story	UN	Philippe Sarde
Gimmie a Break (series)	NBC-TV	Bob Christianson/Jay Graydon
Girl, the Gold Watch & Dynamite, The	IND-TV	Bruce Broughton
Girl with a Sea Shell	CZE	Petr Hapka
Girl with the Red Hair, The	HOL	Nicola Piovani
Girl's Tear, A	RUM	Anca Dumitrescu
Glowing Autumn	JAP	Toru Takemitsu
Going Ape!	PAR	Elmer Bernstein
Golden Age of Television, The (series)	PBS-TV	Fred Steiner/Ralph Norman Wilkinson
Golden Gate	ABC-TV	Ralph Burns
Goldie and the Boxer Go to Hollywood	NBC-TV	Jimmie Haskell
Goliath Awaits	IND-TV	George Duning
Goodbye Galaxy Express	JAP	Osamu Shoji
Goodbye Pork Pie	NZ	John Charles
Goslings (Housata)	CZE	Zdenek John
Graduation Day	IND	Arthur Kempel
Grady Nutt Show, The	NBC-TV	Charlie McCoy
Grambling's White Tiger	NBC-TV	John D'Andrea/Michael Lloyd
Grass Is Singing, The	BRI/SWE	Lasse Dahlberg/Bjoern Isfaelt
Grass Recruits	SPA/VEN	Joseph Maria Duran
Great Alligator, The	ITA	Stelvio Cipriani
Great Guy at Heart, A	YUG	Vojislav Kostic
Great Mysteries of Hollywood, The	IND-TV	Arthur B. Rubinstein
Greatest American Hero, The	ABC-TV	Pete Carpenter/Mike Post
Green Ice	BRI	Bill Wyman

Grendel Grendel Grendel	AUT	Bruce Smeaton
Grilling, The (Garde a Vue)	FRA	Georges Delerue
Guepiot, Le	FRA	Gerard Gustin
Gun in the House, A	CBS-TV	Jimmie Haskell
Halloween II	UN	John Carpenter
Ham Actors (Ripacsok)	HUN	Gabor Presser
Hand, The	WB	James Horner
Hands Up! (Rece Do Gory)	POL	Kryzystof Komeda/ Kryzystof Penderecki/ Jozef Skrzek
Happy Birthday, Marilyn!	HUN	Zdenko Tamassy
Happy Birthday to Me	CAN	Bo Harwood/Lance Rubin
Hard Country	AFD	Jimmie Haskell/Michael Martin Murphey
Hard Knocks	ABC-TV	Ken Harrison
Hardcase	NBC-TV	Craig Safan
Hardly Working	TCF	Morton Stevens
Harper Valley (series)	NBC-TV	Tom T. Hall
Harper Valley P.T.A. (series)	NBC-TV	Nelson Riddle
Harry's War	IND	Merrill Jensen
Haunting of M, The	IND	Leos Janacek
Have You Seen Alice?	DEN	Leif Sylvester Petersen
Heading South (Plein Sud)	FRA/SPA	Eric Demarsan
Head-Stand	AUS	Karl Ratzer
Heartaches	CAN	Simon Michael Martin
Heartbeeps	UN	John Williams
Heatwave	AUT	Cameron Allan
Heaven on Earth	NBC-TV	Dick de Benedictis
Heavy Metal	COL	Elmer Bernstein
Hell Night	IND	Dan Wyman
Help Me Dream	ITA	Riz Ortolani
High Voltage	YUG	Miljenko Prohaska
History of the World--Part 1	TCF	John Morris
Hollywood High Part II	IND	Doug Goodwin
Home for Gentle Souls, A	BUL	Bojidar Perkov
Home Room	ABC-TV	David Shire
Honky Tonk Freeway	UN	Elmer Bernstein/George Martin
Hot and Deadly (Retrievers, The)	IND	Ted Ashford/Paul Fontana
Hot W.A.C.S.	ABC-TV	David Frank
House of Death (Pee-Mak)	S.KOR	Hee-Kap Kim
House Outside the Cemetery, The	ITA	Walter Rizzati
Howling, The	CAN	Pino Donaggio
Hoyt Axton Show, The	NBC-TV	Dennis McCarthy
I Confess	PHI	Ernani Cuenco
I Hate Blondes	ITA	Piero Umiliani

Film	Country	Composer
I Love You (Eu te Amo)	BRA	Cesar Camargo Mariano
I Love You (Je Vous Aime)	FRA	Serge Gainsbourg
I Made a Splash	ITA	Detto Mariani
I'm Blushing	SWE	Bengt Ernryd
I'm Getting a Yacht	ITA	Gianni Ferrio
Improper Channels	CAN	Mickey Erbe/Maribeth Solomon
In Broad Daylight	POL	Stanislaw Radwan
In Search of Famine	IN	Silil Chowdhury
In the Pope's Eye	ITA	Renzo Arbore
In Trouble	ABC-TV	George Aliceson Tipton
Inchon	IND	Jerry Goldsmith
Incident at Crestridge	CBS-TV	Arthur B. Rubinstein, Jr.
Incredible Shrinking Woman, The	UN	Suzanne Ciani
Index	POL	Jacek Bednarek
Inmates: A Love Story	ABC-TV	Dana Kaproff
Ins and the Outs, The	FRA	Francis Lai
Inseminoid	IND	Patrick John Scott
Interrail	SWE	Ulf Dageby
Intruder Within, The	ABC-TV	Gil Melle
Is This Really Reasonable?	FRA	Philippe Sarde
Isabel's Choice	CBS-TV	Glen Paxton
Island of the Evil Spirit	JAP	Johji Yuassa
Island on the Lake, The	E.GER	Wolfgang Voigt
It Can't Be Winter, We Haven't Had Summer Yet	CAN	Marc O'Farrell
It Is Cold in Brandenburg--Kill Hitler	SWI	Frank Wolff
It's Handy When People Don't Die	IRE	Michael O'Sulleabhein
Jacqueline Bouvier Kennedy	ABC-TV	Billy Goldenberg
Jacqueline Susann's Valley of the Dolls 1981	CBS-TV	Fred Karlin
Jaws of the Wolf, The	FRA	Benoit Charvet/Jean Schwartz
Jealousy Tango	ITA	Gianni Mazza
Jeanne the Frenchwoman	BRA/FRA	Chico Buarque
Jeppe of the Hill	DEN	Erling D. Bjerno
Jessica Novak (series)	CBS-TV	Fred Karlin
Jet Lag (Vertigo in Manhattan)	SPA	Carlos Santos
Jewel of Shiva, The	IN	K. V. Mahadevan
Job Hunter	HK	Dominic Chung
Journey, The	BUL	Bozhidar Petkov
Judgment Day	NBC-TV	Morton Stevens
Julia Julia	NOR	Svein Gundersen
Jupiter Menace, The	IND	"Synergy"
Just Before Dawn	IND	Brad Fiedel
Just Whistle a Little	CZE	Zdenek John
Kaleidoscope (Challchitra)	IN	Aloknath Dey
Kargus	SPA	Pedro Luis Domingo
Karla's Marriages	CZE	Vitezslav Hadl

Kelly	CAN	Mickey Erbe/Maribeth Solomon
Key Tortuga	CBS-TV	Tim Simon
Khan Asparukh	BUL	Simeon Pironkov
Kill and Kill Again	IND	Igo Kantor
Kill the Shogun	HK	Hee Kap Kim
Kill to Love	HK	Tam Kar Ming/Joyce Cahn
Killing at Hell's Gate	CBS-TV	David Bell
Killing Hour, The (Clairvoyant, The)	FOX	Alexander Peskanov
Killing of Angel Street, The	AUT	Brian May
King and His Fool, The	GER	Guenther Fischer
King of Jerks, The	FRA	Laurent Petitgerard/ Nicolas Samuel
King of the Mountain	UN	Michael Melvoin
Kiss, The	BRA	Guta Graca Melo
Knife in the Heart, The	DEN	Johnny Bjoern/Helle Ryslinge
Knightriders	IND	Donald Rubinstein
Ladies Choice	BUL	Georgi Genkov
Lady Chatterley's Lover	BRI/FRA	Stanley Myers
Lamentations (Dung-Aw)	PHI	Lutgardo Labad
Land of Fire All Night Long	SWI	"Asphalt Blues Company"
Land of No Return, The	IND	Ralph Geddes
Last Chase, The	TV	Gil Melle
Last of the Knucklemen, The	AUT	Bruce Smeaton
Last Stop Freedom	GER	Irmin Schmidt
Lathe of Heaven	IND-TV	Michael Small
Laverne and Shirley in the Army (series)	ABC-TV	Hoyt Curtin
Leave 'Em Laughing	CBS-TV	Jimmie Haskell
Leaves Are Wide, The	YUG	Zoran Hristic
Legend of the Lone Ranger, The	UN	John Barry
Legends of the West: Truth and Tall Tales	ABC-TV	Dennis McCarthy
Lena	ISR	Itzhak Klepter
Lenin in Paris	RUS	Ludmila Kusskova
Leprechaun's Christmas Gold, The	ABC-TV	Maury Laws
Levin's Mill	E.GER	Horst Seemann
Lewis and Clark (series)	NBC-TV	Nathan Sassover
Life Goes On	FRA	Georges Delerue
Life of the Summer People, The	RUS	Isal Chivari
Light Years, The (Annees Lumiere, Les)	FRA/SWI	Arie Dzierlatka
Like a Stranger	GER	Carla Bley
Lili Marleen	GER	Peer Raben
Lion of the Desert	BRI/LIB	Maurice Jarre
Little Ida	NOR/SWE	Eyvind Solaas
Living in Paradise	NBC-TV	George Wyle
Lola	GER	Peer Raben

Lon, the Curse of Land	RUM	Gheorghe Zamfir
Lonely Woman, A	POL	Jan Kanty Pawluskiewicz
Loners (Seuls)	SWI	Michael Galasso
Long Way Home, A	ABC-TV	William Goldstein
Looker	WB	Barry DeVorzan
Loophole	BRI	Lalo Schifrin
Looping	GER	Brian Ferry
Loose Shoes	IND	Murphy Dunne
Lot of Bills to Pay, A	GER	Bernd Adamkewitz
Love Forgives	POL	Waldemar Kazanecki
Love, Love, But Don't Lose Your Head	YUG	Kornelije Nikolic
Love of a Princess, The	JAP	Ichiro Saito
Love, Sidney (series)	NBC-TV	Billy Goldenberg
Lovers' Exile, The	CAN/JAP	Carl Zittrer
Lucifer Rising	IND	Bobby Beausoleil
Lucio Flavio	BRA	John Neschling
Lunch Wagon	IND	Richard Band
Lynx (Rys)	POL	Lucjan Kaszycki
Mad Max 2	AUT	Brian May
Madame Claude 2 (Intimate Moments)	FRA	Francis Lai
Madame X	NBC-TV	Angela Morley
Maggie (series)	ABC-TV	Patrick Williams
Making a Living (series)	ABC-TV	George Aliceson Tipton
Malevil	FRA/GER	Gabriel Yared
Malou	GER	Peer Raben
Man of Iron	POL	Andrezej Korzynski
Man Unnecessary	POL	Jerzy Stanowski
Man Who Saw Tomorrow, The	WB	William Loose
Man Who Went Up in Smoke, The	GER/HUN/SWE	Jacques Loussier
Maniac	IND	Jay Chattaway
Manions of America, The	ABC-TV	Morton Stevens
Man's Affair, A	FRA	Vladimir Cosma
Man's Tragedy, A	ITA	Ennio Morricone
Maravillas	SPA	Nina Hagens
Mark of the Beast	HOL	Ruud Bos
Marva Collins Story, The	CBS-TV	Fred Karlin
Masada	ABC-TV	Jerry Goldsmith/Morton Stevens
Mass Miracle	BUL	Georgi Genkov
Master of Byana, The	BUL	Vassil Kazandjiev
Mausoleum	IND	Frank Primata
Maxwell Street Blues	IND	Jim Brewer/Arvella Gray
McClain's Law (series)	NBC-TV	James di Pasquale/ Angela Morley
Measure for Measure	BUL	Bozhidar Petkov
Melody Haunts My Reverie, The	YUG	Branislav Zivkovic
Member for Chelsea, The	BRI-TV	Joseph Horowitz
Memoirs of a Survivor	BRI	Mike Thorn
Memories of Fear	BRA	Armenio Graca

Men Prefer Fat Girls	FRA	Catherine Lara
Michiko	JAP	Yuji Takahashi
Mickey Spillane's Margin for Murder	CBS-TV	Nelson Riddle
Midnight Offerings	ABC-TV	Walter Scharf
Milka	FIN	Kari Rydman
Million Dollar Face, The	NBC-TV	Morton Stevens
Minestrone	ITA	Nicola Piovani
Minister's Wife, The	MEX/SPA	L. Santiesteban
Miracle of Kathy Miller, The	CBS-TV	Patrick Williams
Miracle on Ice	ABC-TV	Fred Karlin
Mr. Merlin (series)	TV	Ken Harrison
Mistress of Paradise	ABC-TV	John Addison
Mitchell and Woods	NBC-TV	Alan Silvestri
Modern Problems	TCF	Dominic Frontiere
Modern Romance	COL	Lance Rubin
Moments	ARG	Luis Maria Serra
Momma the Detective (pilot)	NBC-TV	Joey Levine/Chris Palermo
Mommie Dearest	PAR	Henry Mancini
Monkey Mission, The	NBC-TV	George Romanis
Monster Club, The	BRI	Douglas Gamley
Monster Island	IND	Alfonso Agullo
Montenegro (Pigs and Pearls)	BRI/SWE	Kornell Kovach
Moon's Only a Naked Ball, The	GER	Peer Raben
Mortuary	IND	John Cacavas
Ms. 45	IND	Joseph Delia
Munster's Revenge, The	NBC-TV	Vic Mizzy
Murder in Texas	NBC-TV	Leonard Rosenman
My Bloody Valentine	PAR	Paul J. Zaza
My Champion	JAP	David Campbell/Jun Sato
My Dinner with Andre	NYF	Allen Shawn
My Father's Secret	GER	Floh de Cologne
My Kidnapper, My Love	NBC-TV	Fred Karlin
My Mother, My Daughter	IND	Harvey Fisher
My Road	JAP	Lee Oskar
My Young Auntie	HK	Eddie Wang
Mysterious Castle in the Carpathians	CZE	Lubos Fiser
Mystique	IND	Richard Markowitz
Naked Love	FRA	Richard de Bordeaux
Nameless Band, A	BUL	Boris Karadimchev
Napoleon (re-issue)	IND	Carmine Coppola
Narcissus and Psyche	HUN	Laszlo Vidovszky
Nashville Grab	NBC-TV	Bob Summers
National Lampoon's Two Reelers	NBC-TV	Jeffrey Tipton
Neighbors	COL	Bill Conti
Neighbors (Vecinos)	SPA	Fernando Ember
Nero Wolfe (series)	NBC-TV	John Addison
Nesting, The	IND	Jack Malken/Kim Sholes
New Year's Evil	IND	W. Michael Lewis/ Laurin Rinder

Next One, The	GRE	Stanley Myers
Next Year If All Goes Well	FRA	Vladimir Cosma
Nichols and Dymes	NBC-TV	Cort Casady/Michael Connor
Night River	JAP	Sei Ikeno
Night School (Terror Eyes)	PAR	Brad Fiedel
Night the Lights Went Out in Georgia, The	EMB	David Shire
Nighthawks	UN	Keith Emerson
Nightmare	IND	Jack Eric Williams
Nights at O'Rear's	AFI	George Aliceson Tipton
Ninja, The	IN	W. Michael Lewis/ Laurin Rinder
No Place to Hide	CBS-TV	John Cacavas
No Terrace-House for Robin Hood	GER	Charles Kalman
Nobody's Perfekt	COL	David McHugh
Norma Rae	NBC-TV	David Shire
North Bridge (Pont du Nord, Le)	FRA	Astor Piazzola
Nuts and Bolts	ABC-TV	Perry Botkin
O.K. ... Laliberte	CAN	Francois Dompierre
Obscene	AUS	Ambroos Seelos
Occupied Palestine	PAL	Adli Fakhri/Marcel Kahlifa/Mustapha Kurd
Of Mice and Men	NBC-TV	George Romanis
Off the Air	ISR	Yoni Rechter
Oklahoma City Dolls, The	ABC-TV	Jerrold Immel
Older Master Cute	HK	Tang Siu Lam
Olsen Gang Jumps the Fence, The	DEN	Bent Fabricius-Bjerre
Olsen Gang Over the Hill, The	DEN	Bent Fabricius-Bjerre
Omega Factor, The (series)	BRI-TV	Anthony Isaac
On Golden Pond	UN	Dave Grusin
On the Right Track	TCF	Arthur B. Rubinstein
On the Time of Hellenes	GRE	George Papadakis
On the Track (Strange Voyage)	FRA	Maurice Le Roux
100 Days	POL	Przemyslaw Gintrowski
One Way Ticket	ALG	Ahmed Malek
Only When I Laugh	COL	David Shire
Open All Night (series)	ABC-TV	Tom Wells
Open Eyes	EGY	Ibrahim Hagag
Ordeal of Bill Carney, The	CBS-TV	Billy Goldenberg
Other Victim, The	CBS-TV	Richard Bellis
Our Bodies Are Still Alive	GER	Hans Wittstadt
Our Family Business	ABC-TV	Tom Scott
Our Short Life	E.GER	Gerhard Rosenfels
Outland	WB	Jerry Goldsmith
Paddington Bear	BRI-TV	Herbert Chappel
Park Place (series)	CBS-TV	Jack Elliott
Parkers, The	NBC-TV	Al Burton/Gloria Loring/ Alan Thicke
Party, The	FRA	Vladimir Cosma

Passing Killer, A	FRA	Jean-Pierre Mas
Passion of Love	FRA/ITA	Armando Trovajoli
Paternity	PAR	David Shire
Patricia Neal Story, The	CBS-TV	Laurence Rosenthal
Pearl of the Caribbean, The	GER	Andi Brauer
Peddler (Matlosa)	SWI	Enzo Jannacci
People vs. Jean Harris	NBC-TV	Brad Fiedel
Peter and Paul	CBS-TV	Allyn Ferguson
Petrol, Petrol	FRA	Eric Demarsan
Phalanstery, The	RUM	H. Maiorovici
Phoenix, The	ABC-TV	Arthur B. Rubinstein, Jr.
Pick-Up Summer	CAN	Jay Voivin/Germain Gauthier
Picnic Among the Poplars	YUG	Branca Vranjesevic
Pictures	NZ	Jan Preston
Pieces	ITA/SPA	"Cam"
Pierino Against the World	ITA	Berto Pisano
Pinchcliffe Grand Prix	DEN	Bent Fabricius-Bjerre
Piranha II (Spawning, The)	ITA	Steve Powder
Pixtoe, Survival of the Weakest	BRA	John Neschling
Please Look After Amelia	ITA/SPA	Detto Mariano
Plum Juice	YUG	Zoran Simjanovic
Polonia Restituta	POL	Czeslaw Nieman
Polyester	NLC	Michael Kamen/Chris Stein
Porky's	CAN	Paul J. Zaza/Carl Zittrer
Portrait of a Woman, Nude (Nudo di Donna)	FRA/ITA	Roberto Gatto/ Maurizio Giammarco
Possession	FRA/GER	Andrzej Korzynski
Postman Always Rings Twice, The	PAR	Michael Small
Post-Mortem (Moyna Tadanta)	IN	Utpalendu Chakraborti
Potteries	HUN	Andras Szollosy
Pretenders, The	HOL	"Hekket"
Pride of Jesse Hallam, The	CBS-TV	Johnny Cash
Priest of Love	FIL	Joseph James
Prince of the City	WB	Paul Chihara
Princess and the Cabbie, The	CBS-TV	Patrick Williams
Private Benjamin (series)	CBS-TV	Barry de Vorzon/Dennis McCarthy/George Aliceson Tipton
Professional, The	FRA	Ennio Morricone
Prohibited Area	HK/TAI	Chow Kun Cheung
Prowler, The	CAN	Richard Einhorn
Psy	FRA	Mort Schuman
Pursuit of D. B. Cooper, The	UN	James Horner
Quartet	BRI/FRA	Richard Robbins
Quest for Fire	CAN/FRA	Philippe Sarde
Quick and Quiet	CBS-TV	Jack Elliott
Race to the Yankee Zephyr	AUS/NZ	Brian May

Raggedy Man	UN	Jerry Goldsmith
Ragtime	PAR	Randy Newman
Raiders of the Lost Ark	PAR	John Williams
Raindrops	GER	Louis Bloom
Rare Breed, A	NWP	Bob Summers
Reborn	SPA	Scott Harper
Red Flag: The Ultimate Game	CBS-TV	Allyn Ferguson
Red Horse, The	YUG	Ljupco-Konstantinov
Red Shadow, The	FRA	Michel Portal
Reds	PAR	Dave Grusin/Stephen Sondheim
Refuge	IND	"Rich Look"
Return of the Beverly Hillbillies, The	CBS-TV	Billy May
Return of the Champ	JAP	Kosaku Dan/Kenichiro Morioka
Return of the Rebels	CBS-TV	Michael Melvoin
Revenge	RUM	Ileana Popovici
Revenge in Hong Kong	HK	Chow Fuk Leung
Revenge of the Gray Gang, The	NBC-TV	Pete Rugolo
Revenge of the Mysterians from Mars	BRI	Barry Gray
Rhythm of Crime	YUG	Hrvoje Hegedusic
Rich and Famous	MGM	Georges Delerue
Riker (series)	CBS-TV	John Cacavas
Rise and Shine	CBS-TV	Jack Elliott
Rising from the Surface	IN	Zia Fareeduddin
Rivkin: Bounty Hunter	CBS-TV	Arthur B. Rubinstein
Road, The (Droga)	POL	Andrezej Kurylewicz
Road Games	AUT	Brian May
Roads of Love Are Night Roads, The	GRE	George Papadakis
Roar	AUT	Dominic Frontiere
Rock and a Hard Place, A	NBC-TV	Keith Allison
Rollover	WB	Michael Small
Romaneto	CZE	Zdenek Bartak, Jr.
Rooster, The (Tuppen)	SWE	Georg Riedel/Gunnar Raynir Svensson
Rosi and the Big City	GER	Wolfgang Danner/Rainer Gansera
Royal Romp	SPA	Antonio Perez Olea
Rubber Tarzan	DEN	Kenneth Knudsen
Running Blind (series)	BRI-TV	Christopher Guinnes
Rush	IND	Johnny Loeffler
S.O.B.	PAR	Henry Mancini
St. Helens	IND	Buckboard/Goblin
Saint Peter	NBC-TV	Jeff Barry
Sally and Freedom	SWE	Stefan Nilsson
Saturday the 14th	NWP	Parmer Fuller
Savage Harvest	TCF	Robert Folk
Savage Land, The (Yuan Ye)	HK	Du Mingxin

Scanners	EMB	Howard Shore
Schoolmaster, The	FRA	Claude Engel
Scream (Outing, The)	IND	Joseph Conlan
Seal, The	NBC-TV	Joe Harnell
Sealed With a Kiss	HK	Chow Kam Cheung
Search, The (Shodh)	IN	Shantanu Mahpatra
Search for Alexander the Great, The	IND-TV	Robert Sharples
Season of Peace in Paris	FRA/YUG	Kornelije Kovac
Secrets of Midland Heights (series)	CBS-TV	Jerrold Immel
Security, The	HK	Philip Chan
Security Unlimited	HK	Sam Hui
Segovia Escape, The	SPA	Xabier Lasa/Amaia Zubiria
Senior Trip!	CBS-TV	Joe Harnell
Sense of Freedom, A	BRI-TV	Frankie Miller
Sentimental	ARG	Julian Plaza
Seven Dials Mystery, The	BRI-TV	Joseph Horowitz
Shannon (series)	CBS-TV	John Cacavas
She Dances Alone	AUS	Gustavo Santolalla
Sherlock Holmes	HBO-C	Arthur B. Rubinstein, Jr.
She's in the Army Now	ABC-TV	Artie Butler
Shilly-Shally (Wahadelko)	POL	Zdzislaw Szostak
Shock Treatment	TCF	Richard Hartley
Short Circuits	FRA	Dominique Dalmasso
Short Cut (Postriziny)	CZE	Jiri Sust
Shut Up When You Speak!	FRA/ITA	Armando Trovajoli
Side Show	NBC-TV	Ralph Burns
Sidney Shorr: A Girl's Best Friend	NBC-TV	Billy Goldenberg
Silence of the North	CAN	Allan Macmillan
Sixth Gear (Sesta Brzina)	YUG	Dusko Karuovic
Sixty Years of Seduction	ABC-TV	Peter Matz
Sizzle	ABC-TV	Artie Butler
Skin, The	FRA/ITA	Lalo Schifrin
Slap in the Face, A	RUS	Tigran Mansuyan
Slayer, The	IND	Robert Folk
Small Killing, A	CBS-TV	Fred Werner
Smaller Sky	POL	Zygmunt Krause
Smash Hit, A (Trhak)	CZE	Vitezslav Hadl
Smash Palace	NZ	Sharon O'Neill
Smokey Bites the Dust	NWP	Bent Myggen
Smurfs, The (series)	NBC-TV	Hoyt Curtin
Snapshot Around the Family Table	RUM	Jean Lazaroiu
Snow (Miege)	FRA	Francois Breant/Bernard Lavilliers
So Fine	WB	Ennio Morricone
So What? (Eijanaika)	JAP	Shinjiro Ikebe
Sophisticated Gents, The	NBC-TV	Benny Golson

Two Lives of Carl Letner, The	CBS-TV	Roger Kellaway
Two of Us, The (series)	CBS-TV	Patrick Williams
Two Stage Sisters	HK	Huang Zhun
Two the Hard Way	CBS-TV	Lee Holdridge
Unattended Party, The	ITA	Gregorio Cosentino
Uncle Scam	NWP	Michael Levanios, Jr.
Under the Rainbow	WB	Joe Renzetti
Underground Man, The	ARG	Maria Gondell
Undisciplined Sailors, The (Ken Galasi)	THAI	Maitree Janjarasskul
Unit 4	CBS-TV	Tom Scott
Unseen, The	NWP	Michael J. Lewis
Valley of the Dolls 1981 (see Jacqueline Susann's Valley of the Dolls 1981)		
Vicar of Olot, The	SPA	Josep M. Mainat
Victory	PAR	Bill Conti
Village in the Jungle	SRI	Nimal Mandis
Violation of Sarah McDavid, The	CBS-TV	Robert Prince
Visitors from the Galaxy	YUG	Tomislav Simovic
Vulture, The	ISR	Doron Salomon
Walking Tall (series)	NBC-TV	Ed Kalehoff
War of the Worlds--Next Century, The	POL	Jozef Skrzek
Way Back Home	BEL	Pol Kessels
We Are the Guinea Pigs	IND	"Fourth Wall Repertory Company"
We Won't Commit Hara-Kiri	ITA	Fiorenzo Carpi
Weak Man, The	FRA	Jean-Marie Senia
Wendy Hooper--U.S. Army	NBC-TV	Earle Hagen
We're Fighting Back	CBS-TV	Fred Karlin
Whacked Out	NBC-TV	Terri Falconi
When It Rains, It Pours (Alles Im Eimer)	GER	Juergen Knieper
When the Circus Came to Town	CBS-TV	Charles Gross
White and Reno	NBC-TV	Keith Allison
White Raven, The	RUS	Isaak Shwarz
White, Red and Verdone Green	ITA	Ennio Morricone
Whodunnit? (Island of Blood)	IND	Joel Goldsmith
Whose Life Is It Anyway?	MGM	Arthur B. Rubinstein
Why Albert Pinto Is Angry	IN	Bhaskar Chanadawarkar
Why Didn't They Ask Evans?	IND-TV	Joseph Horowitz
Why Us?	NBC-TV	Tom Scott
Willmar 8, The	IND	Peter Yarrow
Window, The (Prozoretsut)	BUL	Simeon Pironkov
Wings of the Dove	FRA/ITA	Philippe Sarde
Winter City	SWI	Benedict Jeger
Winter of Our Dreams, The	AUT	Sharon Calcraft
Witch Hunt, The (Forfoelgelsen)	NOR/SWE	Arne Nordheim

Witness, A	HUN	Szaboles Fenyes
Wobbly Waltz, The (Slingrevalsen)	DEN	Bent Fabricius-Bjerre
Wolfen	WB	James Horner
Woman Inside, The	TCF	Eddie Manson
Woman Next Door, The	FRA	Georges Delerue
Women of Russia	IND-TV	John Mortarott
Women's Love	FRA/SWI	Patrick Juvet
Wonderful World of Philip Malley, The	CBS-TV	Perry Botkin
Wood of Love	ITA	Carlo Rustichelli
Word of Honor	CBS-TV	Bruce Langhorne
Would You Believe It	YUG	Zoran Simjanovic
X-Ray	IND	Arlon Ober
Years of Crisis	YUG	Ljupco-Konstantinov
Yo-Ho-Ho	BUL	Kiril Dontchev
Young Lives (series)	IND-TV	Douglas Dutton
Your Neighbor's Son	DEN/SWE	Arghyris Kounadis
Zechmeister	AUS	Christian Geerdes/Fritz Mikesch/Ursula Weck
Zigeunerweisen	JAP	Kaname Kawachi
Zoot Suit	UN	Daniel Valdez
Zorro, the Gay Blade	TCF	Ian Fraser

1982

Abandoned	JAP	Gen-ichi Kawakami
About Judges and Other Sympathizers	GER	"Tangerine Dream"
Ace of Aces	FRA/GER	Vladimir Cosma
Aces Go Places	HK	Sam Hui
Adventures of Pollyanna, The (pilot)	CBS-TV	Jerrold Immel
After Midnight	GER	Charles Kalman
Agatha Christie's "Murder Is Easy"	CBS-TV	Gerald Fried
Airplane II: The Sequel	PAR	Elmer Bernstein
Alien 2	ITA	Guido and Maurizio de Angelis
All Fired Up (Tout Feu, Tout Flamme)	FRA	Michel Berger
Alone in the Dark	NLC	Renato Serio
Amateur, The	TCF	Ken Wannberg
Ambush Murders, The	CBS-TV	Paul Chihara
American Nightmare	CAN	Paul J. Zaza
Amityville II: The Possession	WB	Lalo Schifrin
And Next Year at Balaton	E.GER	Guenther Fischer
Android	NWP	Don Preston
Angel	IRE	Paddy Meegan
Angel (Anguelos)	GRE	Stamatis Spandoudakis
Angel, The	FRA	Michele Bokanowski
Angelic Pubis	ARG	Charly Garcia

Antonieta	FRA/MEX/SPA	Jose Antonio Zavala
Aphrodite	FRA	Jean-Pierre Stora
Appalling Days (Schoene Tage)	AUS/GER/SWI	Bert Breit
Apprenticeship of Snail the Inventor, The	YUG	Deco Zgur
Arpa-Colla	GRE	Nicos Mamagakis
Artichoke	AUS	"Chaos de Luxe"

Assistant, The (Pomocnik)	CZE	Svetozar Stur
Asya	E.GER/RUS	Oleg Karavalchuk
At This Late Date, the Charleston	JAP	Masaru Sato
August Requiem, An	IN	Louis Banks
Author! Author!	FOX	Dave Grusin

Axe of Wandsbek, The	GER	Annette Humpe

Bad Blood	BRI/NZ	Richard Hartley
Bad Luck Bullet (Kyodan)	JAP	Kentaro Hada
Baker's Dozen (series)	CBS-TV	Elliot Lawrence
Ballad of Mamlouk, The	CZE/TUN	Armando Trovajoli
Banana Joe	GER/ITA	Guido and Maurizio de Angelis
Barbarosa	UN	Bruce Smeaton
Bare Essence	CBS-TV	Billy Goldenberg
Barricade, The	GER	Peter Schirmann
Basket Case	IND	Gus Russo
Batch '81	PHI	Lorrie Ilustre
Battle at Poziralnik, The	YUG	Bojan Adamic
Battle for the Republic of China, The	HK	Lo Ming-tao
Battletruck	NWP	Kevin Peek
Beach Girls, The	CRO	Michael Lloyd
Beach House (Down the Shore)	NLC	C. P. Roth
Beast, The	BEL	Egisto Macchi
Beast Within, The	IND	Les Baxter
Beastmaster, The	MGM	Lee Holdridge
Bee-Hive, The (Colmena, La)	SPA	Anton Garcia Abril
Before the Dawn (A Rutana Pera)	SRI	W. B. Makuloluwa
Benny's Place	ABC-TV	Harold Wheeler
Best Friends	WB	Michel Legrand
Best Little Whorehouse in Texas, The	UN	Patrick Williams
Between Brothers	CBS-TV	Richard Hazard
Beyond the Door	ITA	Pino Donaggio

Bicycle, The	E.GER	Peter Rabenalt
Big Brother, The	FRA	Pierre Jansen
Big Easy, The	NBC-TV	J. J. Johnson
Big Meat Eater	CAN	J. Douglas Dodd
Big Pardon, The (Grand Pardon, Le)	FRA	Serge Franklin
Bit of Living, A (Croque la Vie)	FRA	Gerard Anfosso
Black Hen, The	RUS	Oleg Karavalchuk
Blade Master, The (Ator the Invincible)	NLC	Carlo Rustichelli
Blade Runner	WB	Vangelis
Blood and Honor: Young Under Hitler	IND-TV	Ernst Bradner
Blood of the Statues, The	GRE	George Kouroupos
Blue and the Gray, The	CBS-TV	Bruce Broughton
Blue Jeans Memory	JAP	Kyohei Tsutsumi
Blue Paradise (Adam and Eve)	ITA/SPA	Guido and Maurizio de Angelis
Boat People	HK	Lo Wing-fai
Bolivar, Tropical Symphony	VEN	Alejandro Blanco Uribe
Bonjour Monsieur Lewis	FRA	Gerard Calvi
Boogens, The	IND	Bob Summers
Border, The	UN	Ry Cooder
Born Beautiful	NBC-TV	Brad Fiedel
Born for Diesel	GER	Irmin Schmidt/ Raimundo Sodre
Bourgeois Gentilhomme, Le (Would-Be Gentleman, The)	FRA	Jean Bouchety
Boxoffice	IND	Ornette Coleman
Boy from Rio, The	BRA	Guto Graca Mello
Brain Burning (Hirnbrennen)	AUS	Bruno Spoerri
Brain Waves	IND	Robert O. Ragland
Brand Marks	GER	Edgar Froese
Breakfast in Paris	AUT	Brian May
Breathless (Ademloos)	HOL	Lodewijk de Boer
Brimstone and Treacle	BRI	"Sting"
Bring 'em Back Alive (series)	CBS-TV	Arthur B. Rubinstein
Britannia Hospital	BRI	Alan Price
Broken Sky	SWE	Bjoern Isfaelt
Brothers	AUT	Bob Young
Bugs Bunny's Third Movie: 1001 Rabbit Tales	WB	Milt Franklin/William Lava/Carl Stalling/ Bob Walsh
Burning an Illusion	BRI	Seyoum Nefta
Bus Driver, The	EGY	Kamel Bakir
Bush Doctor	IND-TV	Rod Levitt
Butterflies (series)	PBS-TV	Ronnie Hazelhurst
Cain and Abel	PHI	Max Jocson
Callahan	ABC-TV	Peggy Black/Nick Driver
Cannery Row	MGM	Jack Nitzsche
Capitol	CBS-TV	Bob Israel
Captain's Honor, A	FRA	Philippe Sarde

Capture of Grizzly Adams, The	NBC-TV	Bob Summers
Carl Gustav, the Gang and the Parking Lot Bandits	NOR	Peter Knutsen
Carry Me Back	NZ	Tom Bridgewater
Cass Malloy	CBS-TV	Tom Wells
Cassie and Company (series)	NBC-TV	Lex de Avezedo/J. J. Johnson/Mundell Lowe/ Mischa Segal
Cat People	RKO/UN	Giorgio Moroder
Catalina C-Lab	NBC-TV	Fred Karlin
Catherine's Wedding	ITA	Manuel de Sica
Cecilia	CUB	Leo Brouwer
Challenge, The	IND	Jerry Goldsmith
Chan Is Missing	IND	Robert Kikuchi-Yngojo
Charles & Diana: A Royal Love Story	ABC-TV	John Addison
Cheers	NBC-TV	Steve Nelson/Craig Safan
Chicago Story (series)	NBC-TV	Dick Halligan/Stu Phillips
Christmas Carol, A	A&E-C	Hiram Titus
Christmas Eve	POL	Krzyztof Konieczny
Chronopolis	FRA	Luc Ferrari
Ciao Nemico (Bridge Between, The)	ITA	Franco Micalizzi
Claire and Darkness	SWI	Nicos Kypourgos
Class Murmurs	SWI	Benedict Jeger
Class of 1984	CAN	Lalo Schifrin
Class Whispers (see "Class Murmurs")		
Coast of Love, The	FRA	Jean-Pierre Mas
Cold River	IND	Michael Gibson
Come Along to Monte Carlo	GER	Matthias Raue
Come Back (Volver)	ARG	Astor Piazzolla
Comeback	GER	Eric Burdon
Coming Out of the Ice	CBS-TV	Maurice Jarre
Computerside	NBC-TV	Jack Elliott/Allyn Ferguson
Conan the Barbarian	UN	Basil Poledouris
Conceived Desires	CHILE	Tomas Lefever
Concrete Jungle, The	IND	Joseph Conlan
Consul, The (Daimler-Benz Limuzvna)	GER/POL	Zdzislaw Szostak
Cool Lakes of Death, The	HOL	Peter Faber/Erik van't Wout
Counterattack: Crime in America	ABC-TV	Craig Safan
Country Gold	CBS-TV	Billy Goldenberg
Countryman	JAM	Wally Badarou
Crab (Cangrejo)	VEN	Miguel Angel Foster
Creepshow	IND	John Harrison
Cries in the Night	CAN	Jerry Fielding
Crossing Over (Traversees)	BEL/TUN	Francesco Accolai

Crosstalk	AUT	Chris Neal
Cry for the Strangers	CBS-TV	John Cacavas
Cyclops	YUG	Miljenko Prohaska
Dangerous Company	CBS-TV	Creed Bratton
Dan's Motel	IND	Rick Burnley
Danton	FRA/POL	Jean Prodromides
Dark Circle	IND	Bernard Krause/Gary Remal
Dark Crystal, The	UN	Trevor Jones
Dark Room, The	AUT	Cameron Allan
Day Before Yesterday, The (Tegnapelott)	HUN	Gyorgy Vukan
Day for Thanks on Waltons Mountain, A	NBC-TV	Alexander Courage
Day in a Taxi, A	CAN	Pierre Brault/Michel Robidoux
Day of the Idiots	GER	Peer Raben
Day of the Triffids, The (series)	BRI-TV	Christopher Gunning
Day the Bubble Burst, The	NBC-TV	Jack Elliott
Dead Easy	AUT	William Motzing
Dead End Street	ISR	Itzhak Klepter
Dead Men Don't Wear Plaid	UN	Miklos Rozsa
Dead Ringer	IND	Jim Steinman
Deadly Game (Jaeger, Die)	GER	Roland Baumgartner
Dear Mr. Wonderful	GER	Klaus Bantzer
Death in the Vatican	ITA/MEX/SPA	Pino Donaggio
Death Valley	UN	Dana Kaproff
Death Wish II	COL/WB	Jimmy Page
Deathtrap	WB	Johnny Mandell
Deliverance (Sadgati)	IN	Satyajit Ray
Demons in the Garden	SPA	Javier Iturralde
Depart to Arrive	GER	"FemSession Berlin"
Desperate Lives	CBS-TV	Bruce Broughton
Detective Story	JAP	Yo Misaka
Devil at Your Heels, The	CAN	Arthur Phillips
Devlin Connection, The (series)	NBC-TV	John Addison/Nan Schwartz/Patrick Williams
Devonshire Terror, The	IND	Ed Hill
Diamond Square	SPA	Ramon Muntaner
Dignity (Jom)	SEN	Lamine Konte
Direct-Line Heir, The	RUS	Isaak Shwarz
Displaced Person	YUG	Jerko Novak
Distant Sky, The	YUG	Ksenija Zecevic
Divorce Wars	ABC-TV	Paul Chihara
Dr. Slump	JAP-TV	Shunsuke Kikuchi
Doktor Faustus	GER	Rolf Alexander Wilhelm
Domino	GER	Christian Kunert
Don Juan, Karl-Liebknecht-Str. 78	E.GER	Karl-Ernst Sasse
Don't Go to Sleep	ABC-TV	Dominic Frontiere

Dot and Santa Claus	AUT	Bob Young
Double Trouble	GER	Juergen Knieper
Dragon Force	HK	Chris Babida
Dragon Lord	HK	Jackie Chan
Draughtsman's Contract, The	BRI	Michael Nyman
Dream Is Not Over, The	BRA	Paul de Castro
Dreams Don't Die	ABC-TV	Brad Fiedel
Drop-Out Father	CBS-TV	Peter Matz
Duet for Four	AUT	Peter Sullivan
E. T. & Friends--Magical Movie Visitors	CBS-TV	William Loose
E. T., the Extra-Terrestrial	UN	John Williams
Easy Money (Plata Dulce)	ARG	Emilio Kauderer
Eating Raoul	IND	Arlon Ober
Edo Porn	JAP	Hikaru Hayashi
Egyptian Story, An	EGY	Gamal Salama
Eijanaika	JAP	Shinjiro Ikebe
Eleanor, First Lady of the World	CBS-TV	John Addison
Electric Grandmother, The (short)	TV	John Morris
Enchanted Grove, The	RUM	Cornelia Tautu
Enchanted Sail, The	ITA	Nicola Piovani
Endangered Species	MGM	Gary Wright
Endeavor	YUG	Josip Magdic
Enter the Ninja	IND	W. Michael Lewis/ Laurin Rinder
Entity, The	TCF	Charles Bernstein
Escape Artist, The	WB	Georges Delerue
Eva's Dreams	IND	Hale Smith
Everybody Is Good	SPA	Carlos Vizziello
Executioner's Song, The	NBC-TV	John Cacavas
Eyes, the Mouth, The	FRA/ITA	Nicola Piovani
Factory, The	GRE	Domna Samiou
Facts of Life Goes to Paris, The	NBC-TV	Misha Segal
Faerie Tale Theater	SHO-C	Stephen Barber
Fake-Out	IND	Arthur B. Rubinstein, Jr.
Falcon's Gold	SHO-C	Lalo Schifrin
Fall of the House of Usher, The	NBC-TV	Bob Summers
False Eyelashes	SPA	Jose Miguel Lopez Saez
Family Affair, A (series)	BRI-TV	Francis Shaw
Family in Blue	CBS-TV	Patrick Williams
Family Rock	FRA	Guy Boulanger
Family Ties (series)	NBC-TV	Tom Scott/Tim Simon
Fanny and Alexander	FRA/GER/SWE	Daniel Bell
Fanny by Gaslight	BRI-TV	Alexander Paris
Fantasies	ABC-TV	James di Pasquale
Far East	AUT	Sharon Calcraft
Farewell, Beloved Land	JAP	Toshiaki Yokota
Farrell for the People	NBC-TV	Bill Conti
Fast Times at Ridgemont High	UN	Joe Walsh

Fast-Walking	IND	Lalo Schifrin
Father by Accident	SA	German Arrieta
Fear in the City of the Living Dead	ITA	Fabio Frizzi
Felix	DEN	Leif Sylvester Petersen
Fellows (Muzhyki)	RUS	Vladimir Komarov
Ferdinanda, La	GER	Ingfried Hoffmann
Fifth of July, The	SHO-C	John Adams
Fighting Back	PAR	Piero Piccioni
Fighting Back	AUT	Colin Stead
Fighting for Two	HOL	Tonny Eyk
Filthy Rich (series)	CBS-TV	Bucky Jones
Firefox	WB	Maurice Jarre
First Blood	ORI	Jerry Goldsmith
First Love (Ahava Rishona)	ISR	Francis Lewin
First Time, The	ABC-TV	Fred Karlin
Fistful of Chopsticks, A	IND	Tommy Vig
Fit for a King	NBC-TV	John Addison
Fitzcarraldo	GER	Popol Vuh
Five and the Skin	FRA	Benoit Charvet
Five Days One Summer	WB	Elmer Bernstein
Five-Legged Hare, The	YUG	Bashim Shehu
Flame Trees of Thika, The (series)	PBS-TV	Alan Blaikley/Ken Howard
Flatfoots	NBC-TV	David Frank
Flight of the Eagle, The	GER/NOR/SWE	Hans-Erik Philip
Flight of Whimbrels, A	HOL	Laurens Van Rooyen
Flight Year, The (Flugjahr, Das)	SWI	Heinz Reutlinger
Fluteman	AUT	John Sangster
Fond Memories (Beaux Souvenirs, Les)	CAN	Jean Cousineau
For Lovers Only	ABC-TV	Pete Rugolo
For 200 Grand, You Get Nothing Now	FRA	Murray Head
Forbidden Love	CBS-TV	Hagood Hardy
Forbidden World	NWP	Susan Justin
Forced Vengeance	MGM	William Goldstein
Forties, The	CAN	Joel Bienvenue
Forty Deuce	IND	Manu Dibango
48 Hrs.	PAR	James Horner
Foundation Stone, The	IN	Ranjit Kapoor
Fracchia, the Human Beast	ITA	Fred Bongusto
Frances	UN	John Barry
Freedom	AUT	Don Walker
Friday the 13th--Part 3	PAR	Harry Manfredini
Friend or Foe	BRI	Robert Farnon
Funeral Home	IND	Jerry Fielding
Future War 198X	JAP	Seiji Yokoyama
Galaxy Express 999	JAP	Nozumi Aoki
Games Mother Never Taught You	CBS-TV	Mark Snow
Gandhi	COL	Ravi Shankar/George Fenton

Gapi	CAN	Edith Butler/Neil Chotem
Gardener, The	FRA	Pierre Alrand
Gate of Youth, The	JAP	Hako Yamazaki
Gavilan (series)	NBC-TV	Steve Dorff
Genocide	IND	Elmer Bernstein
German Revolution, A	GER	Ernst Bechert/Theo Janssen
Gift, The (Cadean, Le)	FRA/ITA	Michel Legrand
Gift of Life, The	CBS-TV	Billy Goldenberg
Gilligan's Planet (series)	CBS-TV	Yvette Blais
Ginger Meggs	AUT	"Front"
Girl from India	IND	Ved Pal/Amal Deu
Girl with the Horse, The	E.GER	Gunther Erdmann
Giro City	BRI	Martin Evans
Gloria (series)	CBS-TV	Tony Greco
Gloria Comes Home	CBS-TV	Ray Conniff
Goat, The (Chevre, La)	FRA	Vladimir Cosma
God's Gift		
(see Wend Kuuni)		
Goin' All the Way	IND	Richard Hieronymus
Good Luck Love	JAP	Kazuo Otani
Goodbye Paradise	AUT	Peter Best
Gordon Pinsent and the Life and Times of Edwin Alonzo Boyd	CAN	Zina Louie/Alex Pauk
Grand Hotel Excelsior	ITA	Armando Trovajoli
Grass Widowers	SWE	Bjoern Jason Lindh
Great Expectation (series)	BRI-TV	Paul Reade
Great White	TV	Morton Stevens
Green, Green Grass of Home	TAI	Zuo Hongyuan
Gregory's Girl	BRI	Colin Tully
Grey Fox, The	CAN	Michael Conway Baker
Grog	ITA	Paolo Conte
Guaguasi	CUB	Chico O'Farrill
Guy de Maupassant	FRA	Georges Delerue
Halloween III: Season of the Witch	UN	John Carpenter/Alan Howarth
Hammett	WB	John Barry
Hamsin	ISR	Raviv Gazit
Hanky Panky	COL	Tom Scott
Happy Birthday (Creeps/Bloody Birthday)	IND	Arlon Ober
Happy Birthday, Mama	JAP	Maohiko Terashima
Hard Feelings	CAN	Mickey Erbe/Maribeth Solomon
Hatter's Ghosts, The	FRA	Mathieu Chabrol
Having It All	ABC-TV	Miles Goodman
Head Hunter, The	HK	Tang Siu-Lam
Hear No Evil	CBS-TV	Lance Rubin
Hearts and Guts	BRA	Paolo Herculano
Hecate	FRA/SWI	Carlos d'Alessio
Heidi's Song	PAR	Hoyt Curtin

Hello, Cane Stick	THAI	Prachin Songpao/ Chalie Intravijit
Help Wanted: Male	CBS-TV	Nelson Riddle
Henry's Back Room	NOR	Lars Martin Myhre
Herbie, The Love Bug (series)	CBS-TV	Frank De Vol/Tom Worrall
Hero	BRI	Paul Stern
High Five	NBC-TV	Fred Hamm/Art Wilson
Hit and Run	IND	Brad Fiedel
Hole in the Wall, The	ARG	Lito Vitale
Honeyboy	NBC-TV	J. A. C. Redford
Honkytonk Man	WB	Steve Dorff
Hooray Brazil	BRA	Egberto Gismonti
Horror Planet (Inseminoid)	BRI	John Scott
Horse, The	TUR	Okay Temiz
Horseman Riding By, A (series)	BRI-TV	Max Harris
Hot Touch	CAN	Andre Gagnon
Hotel of the Americas	FRA	Philippe Sarde
Hotel Polan and Its Guests	E.GER	Horst Seemann
Hotline	CBS-TV	Johnny Harris
House Arrest	SEN	Francis Bebey
House of Glass	CZE	Jiri Stivin
House Where Evil Dwells, The	MGM	Ken Thorne
Houseboat No. 70	EGY	Gehad Daoud
How Do I Kill a Thief--Let Me Count the Ways	ABC-TV	Stu Phillips
Human Lanterns	HK	So Chun-hou/Stephen Shing
Humongous	CAN	John Mills Cockell
Hunchback of Notre Dame, The	CBS-TV	Ken Thorne
Hunting Ground	GER	Robert Lovas
I, Desire	ABC-TV	Don Peake
I Know That You Know That I Know	ITA	Piero Piccioni
I Ought to Be in Pictures	TCF	Marvin Hamlisch
I, the Jury	FOX	Bill Conti
I Want to Live	YUG	Alfi Kabiljo
I Was a Mail Order Bride	CBS-TV	John Addison
I'd Rather Be Calm	CBS-TV	Mark Snow
If You Could See What I Hear	CAN	Eric Robertson
I'm Dancing as Fast as I Can	PAR	Stanley Silverman
I'm in a Crisis!	SPA	Jose Nieto
Imperative	GER	Wojiech Kilar
Imperial Japanese Empire, The	JAP	Naozumi Yamamoto
Imperial Navy (Great Fleet, The)	JAP	Katsuhisa Hattori/Shinji Tanimura
Imprudent Lover, The	DEN	Holger Laumann
In Just the Wink of an Eye	PHI	Lorrie Ilustre
In Love With an Older Woman	CBS-TV	Lee Holdridge
In Security	CBS-TV	Patrick Williams
In September	SPA	Jesus Aranguren

In the Custody of Strangers	ABC-TV	Matthew McCauley
In the King of Prussia	IND	Jackson Browne/Graham Nash
In the Land of My Parents	GER	Jakob Lichtmann
Incubus, The	CAN	Stanley Myers
India, Daughter of the Sun	BRA	Perinho Albuquerque/ Caetano Veloso
Indiscretion, The	FRA	Eric Demarsan
Innocent Love, An	CBS-TV	David Frank
Inside the Third Reich	ABC-TV	Fred Karlin
Interrupted Traces, The	SWI	Roland Moser
Inti Anti, the Road to the Sun	ARG	Horacio Corral
Intimate Friends: An Historic Legend	CHN	Wang Ming
Invitation, The	ARG	Marcelo Etchemendi/ Panchi Quesada
Invitation to a Trip	FRA	Gabriel Yared
Ironmaster	FRA/ITA	Guido and Maurizio de Angelis
Is There a Frenchman in the House?	FRA	Roger Loubet
It Takes Two (series)	ABC-TV	George Aliceson Tipton
It's Nice to Meet You (Muito Prazer)	BRA	Carlos Moletta
Ivanhoe	CBS-TV	Allyn Ferguson
James Boys, The	NBC-TV	Patrick Williams
Jekyll and Hyde ... Together Again	PAR	Barry DeVorzon
Jimmy the Kid	NWP	John Cameron
Jinxed!	MGM	Miles Goodman/Bruce Roberts
Joanie Loves Chachi (series)	ABC-TV	Dan Foliart/Howard Pearl
Jocondes, Les	FRA	Jacques Dutronc/John Lennon
Johnny Belinda	CBS-TV	John Rubinstein
Josepha	FRA	Georges Delerue
Juggler of Notre Dame, The	IND-TV	Christopher Stone
Julie Darling	CAN/GER	Joachim van Ludwig
Kaliyugaya	SRI	Premasiri Khemadasa
Kamikaze	GER	Edgar Froese/Tangerine Dream
Kamikaze, the Adventurer	JAP	Masakatsu Suzuki
Kangaroos in the Kitchen	NBC-TV	Earle Hagen
Kellers Hof--Portrait of a German Farmer	GER	Heiner Goebbels
Kid from Nowhere, The	NBC-TV	Garry Sherman
Kid With the Broken Halo, The	NBC-TV	Tommy Vig
Kidnapping, The	DEN	"Fuzzy"
Kidnapping Blues	JAP	Yosuke Yamashita
Kill Squad	IND	Joseph Conlan

Killing of America, The	JAP	Mark Lindsay/W. Michael Lewis
King's Crossing (series)	ABC-TV	Miles Goodwin/Jerrold Immel/J. A. C. Redford
Kisapmata	PHI	Lorrie Ilustre
Kiss Me Goodbye	FOX	Ralph Burns
Kitty and the Bagman	AUT	Brian May
Knight Rider	NBC-TV	Don Peake/Dave Phillips/ Stu Phillips/Morton Stevens
Krabat (Sorcerer's Apprentice, The)	CZE	Juroslav Moucka
Ladies' Turn (American Quarter Hour, The)	FRA	Jean Morlier
Lady, Stay Dead	IND	Bob Young
Lame Ducks	FRA	Daniel Huck/Marc Pindar
Land of Look Behind	IND	K. Leimer
Last of the Summer Wine, The (series)	BRI-TV	Ronnie Hazelhurst
Last Unicorn, The	IND	Jimmy Webb
Latitude 55°	CAN	Victor Davies
Laverne and Shirley with the Fonz (series)	ABC-TV	Hoyt Curtin
Lawful Violence	FRA	Jean-Marie Senia
Leadfoot	IND-TV	Christopher Stone
Left Without Leaving an Address	FRA/SWI	Carlos d'Alessio
Legend of the Drum, The	MEX/SPA	Santi Arisa
Legend of Walks Far Woman, The	NBC-TV	Paul Chihara
Let's Go On	YUG	Dusan Karuovic
Letter, The	ABC-TV	Laurence Rosenthal
Life Is Wonderful	ITA/RUS	Armando Trovajoli
Life of the Party: The Story of Beatrice	CBS-TV	Ian Fraser
Liquid Sky	IND	Brenda Hutchinson/ Clive Smith/Slava Tsukerman
Listen to the Sound of the Wind	JAP	Shuichi Hoshino
Litan	FRA	Nino Ferrer
Little Gloria ... Happy at Last	NBC-TV	Berthold Carriere
Little Joseph	FRA	Gerard Clavel
Little People	IND	Randy Arneson
Little Rascals, The (series)	ABC-TV	Hoyt Curtin
Little Sex, A	UN	Georges Delerue
Little Wars	LEB	Gabriel Yared
Live Broadcast	YUG	Zoran Radetic
Living Like the Rest of Us	YUG	Kornelije Kovac
Lois Gibbs and the Love Canal	CBS-TV	John D. Berkman
Lonely Hearts	AUT	Norman Kaye
Lonely Hearts (Kofuku)	JAP	Takahiro Ishikawa/ Toru Okada

Long Summer of George Adams, The	NBC-TV	Murray McLeod/Stuart Margolin/J. A. C. Redford
Lookin' to Get Out	PAR	Johnny Mandell/Miles Goodman
Looking for Jesus	FRA/ITA	Fiorenzo Carpi
Louis L'Amour's "The Shadow Riders"	CBS-TV	Jerrold Immel
Love	CAN	Tim McCauley
Love and Lies	RUS	Alexej Rybnikov
Love & Money	PAR	Aaron Copland
Love Can Make a Rainbow	JAP	Mitshiko Satoh
Love Child	WB	Charles Fox
Love in a Cold Climate	PBS-TV	Julian Slade
Love of My Heart (Core Mio)	ITA	Patrizio Trampetti
Love Suicides at Sonezaki, The	JAP	Matsunosuke Nozawa
Luc ou la Part des Choses	CAN	Christian Parent
Luz del Fuego	BRA	Carlos Moletta
Mackenzie (series)	BRI-TV	Anthony Isaac
Madly in Love (Innamorato Pazzo)	ITA	Bruno Zandrini
Madman	IND	Stephen Horelick/Gary Sales
Madonna, Che Silenzio c'e Stasera (Wow, How Quiet It Is Tonight)	ITA	"I Barluna"
Mae West	ABC-TV	Brad Fiedel
Magic Mountain, The	FRA/GER/ITA	Juergen Knieper
Maid in America	CBS-TV	David Frank
Making It (Ningyo Girai)	JAP	Motoaki Masuo
Making Love	TCF	Leonard Rosenman
Making the Grade (series)	CBS-TV	Tom Scott
Malamore	ITA	Aldo Salvi
Mamma	SWE	Gunnar Edander
Man from Snowy River, The	AUT	Bruce Rowland
Man on the Wall, The	GER	Irmin Schmidt
Manhattan Baby	ITA	Fabio Frizzi
Manon	JAP	Ichiro Araki
Marathon Runners, The	YUG	Zoran Simjanovic
Marco Polo	NBC-TV	Ennio Morricone
Marian Rose White	CBS-TV	Billy Goldenberg
Mark, The (Stigma, To)	GRE	Kyriacos Sfetsas
Marquis of Grillo, The	FRA/ITA	Nicola Piovani
Mascot (Kabala)	HUN	Levente Szorenyi
Massarati and the Brain	ABC-TV	Billy Goldenberg
Matagi (Old Bear Hunter, The)	JAP	Kentaro Haneda
Matt Houston (series)	ABC-TV	Dominic Frontiere/ Nelson Riddle
Megaforce	FOX	Jerrold Immel
Melanie	EMB	Paul J. Zaza
Memories Never Die	CBS-TV	Morton Stevens
Metin	GER	Graziano Mandozzi

Mexico in Flames	ITA/MEX/RUS	Jorges Eras
Midnight	IND	"Quintessence"
Million Dollar Infield	CBS-TV	Artie Kane
Minuet	BEL	Egisto Macchi
Miss All-American Beauty	CBS-TV	Paul Chihara
Missing	UN	Vangelis
Mission Hill	IND	Don Wilkins
Missionary, The	COL	Mike Moran
Mr. Leon	ISR	Dov Seltzer
Modesty Blaise	ABC-TV	Kevin Knelman/Paul J. Zaza
Money on the Side	ABC-TV	Richard Bellis
Monkey Grip	AUT	Bruce Smeaton
Monsignor	FOX	John Williams
Moonlight	CBS-TV	Patrick Williams
Mork and Mindy (animated series)	ABC-TV	Hoyt Curtin
Mother Lode	IND	Ken Wannberg
Mother's Day on Waltons Mountain	NBC-TV	Alexander Courage
Muggable Mary: Street Cop	CBS-TV	Earle Hagen
Murder in the Central Committee	SPA	Manuel Camp
Mute Love	ISR	Kobi Oshrath
My Body, My Child	ABC-TV	Charles Gross
My Favorite Year	MGM	Ralph Burns
My Therapist (Love Ya, Florence Nightingale)	IND	Rob Walsh
My Trip with Dad	ITA	Piero Piccioni
Mysterious Two, The	NBC-TV	Joe Renzetti
National Lampoon's Class Reunion	TCF	Peter Bernstein/Mark Goldenberg
Neighborhood, The	NBC-TV	Richard Markowitz
Nestor Burma, Detective of Shock	FRA	Alain Bashung
New Odd Couple, The (series)	ABC-TV	Dan Foliart/Howard Pearl
New York Ripper	ITA	Francesco de Masi
Newhart (series)	CBS-TV	Henry Mancini/Nelson Riddle
Next of Kin	AUT	Klaus Schulze
Night of Destiny	GER	Andreas Markus Klug
Night of the Falling Stars (Night of San Lorenzo)	ITA	Nicola Piovani
Night of the Wolves	GER	Joerg Evers
Night of Varennes, The	FRA/ITA	Armando Trovajoli
Night Shift	WB	Burt Bacharach
Nightfall (Head Shot)	GER	"The 39 Clocks"
Nine to Five (series)	ABC-TV	Jack Elliott/Dan Foliart/ Jimmie Haskell/Howard Pearl
Nine Ways to Approach Helsinki	FIN	Matti Bergstrom
No Soap, Radio (series)	ABC-TV	Barry Goldberg/Danny Goldberg
No Thanks, Coffee Makes Me Nervous	ITA	James Senese

Noa at 17	ISR	Itzhak Steiner
Nobody's Wife (Senora de Naide)	ARG	Luis Maria Serra
Norman Loves Rose	AUT	Mike Perjanik
North Star, The	FRA	Philippe Sarde
Not in Front of the Children	IND-TV	Fred Karlin
Not Just Another Affair	CBS-TV	Arthur B. Rubinstein, Jr.
Nutcracker	BRI	Simon Park
O Is for Oblomov	SWI	Benedict Jeger
Occupation, The (Dakhal)	IN	Goutam Ghose
Octavia	IND	Gerald Michenaud
Odds and Evens	SPA	Jose Nieto
Of Worms and Roses	PHI	George Canseco
Officer and a Gentleman, An	PAR	Jack Nitzsche
O'Hara's Wife	IND	Artie Butler
Old Bear Hunter, The	JAP	Kentaro Haneda
Oliver Twist	CBS-TV	Nick Bicat
On Probation (Buergschaft Fuer Ein Jahr)	E.GER	Guenther Fischer
On the Road	JAP	Taiho Nagato
On the Run	AUT	Laurie Lewis
One Among Many	MEX	Jose Elorza
One Down Two to Go	ALM	Herb Hetzer/Joe Trunzo
One from the Heart	COL	Tom Waits
One More Try	CBS-TV	Dan Foliart/Howard Pearl
One Shoe Makes It Murder	CBS-TV	Bruce Broughton
Open All Hours	BRI-TV	Max Harris
Open Day and Night	ARG	Oscar Cardozo Ocampo
Open Grave ... an Empty Coffin, An	ITA	Piero Piccioni
Oppenheimer (series)	PBS-TV	Carl Davis
Orderly, The (Paramedico, Il)	ITA	Armando Trovajoli
Orozco Family, The	PERU	Jorge Reyes
Outlaw: The Saga of Gisli (Utlaginn)	ICE	Askell Masson
P. X.	PHI	Ed Gatchalian
Pablo Picasso	FRA/SPA	Vangelis
Painter, The (Maalaren)	SWE	Ulf Dageby
Palms Precinct	NBC-TV	Pete Carpenter/Mike Post
Pandemonium (Thursday the 12th)	MGM	Dana Kaproff
Pandemonium (series)	CBS-TV	Johnny Douglas
Paper Dolls	ABC-TV	Mark Snow
Paper Heart	SPA	Carmelo Bernaola
Paradise	EMB	Paul Hoffert
Paradise for All	FRA	Rene Koening
Parallel Corpse, The	DEN	Hans-Erik Philip
Parasite	EMB	Richard Band
Parole	CBS-TV	George Fenton

Partners	PAR	Georges Delerue
Party II, The	FRA	Vladimir Cosma
Passengers of the Garden, The	ARG	Alejandro Lerner
Passerby of the San Souci Cafe, The	FRA/GER	Georges Delerue
Paths of Life (Lebenslaeufe)	E.GER	Gerhard Rosenfels
Penitentiary II	MGM	Jack W. Wheaton
Penmarric (series)	BRI-TV	Richard Hartley
Perfect Marriage, A (Beau Mariage, Le)	FRA	Ronan Girre/Simon des Innocents
Permanent Vacation	IND	Jim Jarmusch/John Lurie
Personal Best	WB	Jack Nitzsche/Jill Fraser
Personals, The	NWP	Will Sumner
Pest, The (Tete a Claques)	FRA	Yves Guillaine
Peter No-Tail	SWE	Bernd Egerblahd
Piano for Mrs. Cimino, A	CBS-TV	James Horner
Piranha 2	ITA	Stelvio Cipriani
Plague Dogs, The	BRI	Patrick Gleeson/Alan Price
Plains of Heaven, The	AUT	Andrew Duffield
Plainsong	IND	Brian Eno/Meredith Monk/Bill Peck
Poachers (Krypskyttere)	NOR	Jo Tore Baeverfjord/Hans Rotmo
Polar	FRA	Karl-Heinz Schafer
Police Squad! (series)	ABC-TV	Ira Newborn
Poltergeist	MGM	Jerry Goldsmith
Pool Without Water, A	JAP	Katsuo Ono
Portrait of a Showgirl	CBS-TV	Jimmie Haskell
Powerhouse (series)	PBS-TV	Frank Karns
Powers of Matthew Starr, The (series)	NBC-TV	Charles Albertine/Pete Carpenter/Johnny Harris/Denny Jaeger/Mike Post/Michel Rubini
Pranks	IND	Chris Young
Pray TV	ABC-TV	Dennis McCarthy
Praying Mantis	BRI	Carl Davis
Prime Suspect	CBS-TV	Charles Gross
Prince and the Fawn, The	IRAN	Ismail Vasseghi
Privates on Parade	BRI	Denis King
Privileged	BRI	Rachel Portman
Pure and the Evil, The	HK	So Chun-Hou/Stephen Shing
Pure Blood (Pura Sangre)	SA	Bernardo and Gabriel Ossa
Q	IND	Robert O. Ragland
Q.E.D. (series)	CBS-TV	Ken Howard
Quarter to Two Before Jesus Christ, A	FRA	Raymond Alessandrini/Jean Yanne

Querelle	FRA/GER	Peer Raben
Quest, The (series)	ABC-TV	Pete Carpenter/Mike Post
Question of Honor, A	CBS-TV	Billy Goldenberg
Rainbow Girl, The	NBC-TV	Dennis McCarthy
Rascals and Robbers--The Secret Adventures of Tom Sawyer and Huck Finn	CBS-TV	James Horner
Rasmus Hits the Road	SWE	Goesta Linderholm
Rat Trap, The	IN	M. B. Srinivasan
Raw Force	IND	Walter Murphy
Really ... Incredible	ITA	Detto Mariano
Red Dust (Polvo Rojo)	CUB	Jose Maria Vitier
Rehearsal for Murder	CBS-TV	Billy Goldenberg
Remembrance of Love	NBC-TV	William Goldstein
Renegades, The	ABC-TV	Joseph Conlan/Barry De Vorzon
Repeat Dive	ISR	Zohar Levi
Return of Martin Guerre, The	FRA	Michel Portal
Return of the Soldier, The	BRI	Richard Rodney Bennett
Return to Haifa	PAL	Ziad Rahbany
Revenge of the Dead (Zeder)	ITA	Riz Ortolani
Revolt of the Birds, The	SPA	Manuel Cobedo
Reward, The (Beloenningen)	NOR	"Fuzzy"
Richard Pryor Live on the Sunset Strip	COL	Harry Betts
Rise Up, Spy	FRA	Ennio Morricone
Road, The (Yol)	SWI/TUR	Sebastian Argol/Kendal
Roaring Forties, The	FRA/GER	Henri Lanoe
Robbers of the Sacred Mountain (Falcon's Gold)	CAN	Lalo Schifrin
Rock Disconcert	ITA	Gianna Nannini
Rocky III	UA	Bill Conti
Roger Doesn't Live Here Anymore (series)	BRI-TV	Ronnie Hazelhurst
Romance Theater	IND-TV	Bob Summers
Romance with Amelie	E.GER	Guenther Fischer
Rona Jaffe's "Mazes and Monsters"	CBS-TV	Hagood Hardy
Roof, A Family, A	ALG	Ahmed Malek
Room in Town, A	FRA	Michel Colombier
Room 666	IND	Juergen Knieper
Roommates	IND	Jonathan Hannah
Rooster	ABC-TV	Stu Phillips
Rosa	GRE	Heleni Karaendrou
Rosie: The Rosemary Clooney Story	CBS-TV	Frank Ortega
Royal Romance of Charles and Diana, The	CBS-TV	David Palmer
Rules of Marriage, The	CBS-TV	Paul Chihara
Run, Rebecca, Run!	AUT	Simon Walker

Sabine	HOL	Ruud Bos
Safari 3000 (Rally)	MGM	Ernest Gold
St. Elsewhere (series)	NBC-TV	Dave Grusin/J. A. C. Redford
Samurai Reincarnation	JAP	Hozan Yamamoto
Santa Claus Is a Louse	FRA	Vladimir Cosma
Sarah (The Seventh Match)	AUT	Glora Freidman
Savamala	YUG	Zoran Hristic
Savannah Smiles	IND	Ken Sutherland
Save the Lady	AUT	Peter McKinley
Scamps	NBC-TV	George Wyle
Scarecrow, The	NZ	Andrew Hagen/Morton Wilson
Scared Silly	ABC-TV	Joe Harnell
Scarlet Pimpernel, The	CBS-TV	Nick Bicat
Scent of Quince, The	YUG	Esad Arnautalic
Scoop	ITA	Marcello Giombini
Screamers	NWP	Luciano Michelini/Sandy Berman
Scrubbers	BRI	Michael Hurd
Sea Devils	SPA	Alfonso Qgullo
Sea Prince and the Fire Child, The	JAP	Koichi Sugiyama
Secret of NIMH, The	MGM	Jerry Goldsmith
Seduction, The	EMB	Lalo Schifrin
Sender, The	PAR	Trevor Jones
Serpent's Poison (Hadi Jed)	CZE	Lubos Fiser
Servants from a Small Town	YUG	Zdenko Runjic
Seven Magnificent Gladiators, The	IND	Dov Seltzer
She	ITA	Rick Wakeman
Shock, The (Choc, Le)	FRA	Philippe Sarde
Shocking Asia	GER/HK	Erwin Halletz
Shocktraume	IND-TV	Eric Robertson
Shot Pattern (Tir Groupe)	FRA	Hubert Rostaing
Showdown (Anametrissi)	GRE	H. S. Vrontos
Side by Side: The True Story of the Osmond Family	NBC-TV	George Aliceson Tipton
Signs and Wonders	GER	"Patchwork"/Michael Rueggeberg
Silence Around Christina M., The	HOL	Lodewijk de Boer
Silent Rage	COL	Peter Bernstein
Silver Spoons (series)	NBC-TV	Rik Howard/Robert Wirth
Simon and Simon (series)	CBS-TV	Joseph Conlan/Barry de Vorzon/Michael Towers
Sing, Cowboy, Sing	E.GER	Karel Svoboda
Singles (Ma Femme s'appelle Reviens)	FRA	William Sheller
Sister, Sister	NBC-TV	Alex North
Six of Us, The	NBC-TV	Mark Snow

Six Pack	FOX	Charles Fox
Six Weeks	UN	Dudley Moore
Skeezer	NBC-TV	Arthur B. Rubinstein, Jr.
Skin of the Fool (Narrohut)	AUS	Ludwig Eschman/Hans Koller/Wolfgang Puschnig
Slapstick	IND	Michel Legrand
Slumber Party Massacre, The	IND	Ralph Jones
Smiley's People	IND-TV	Patrick Gowers
Smithereens	IND	"The Feelies"
Snow Fairy, The (Yuki)	JAP	Kawachi Chito
Society Limited (Fine Gesellschaft, Beschraenkte Haftung)	GER	Hans Martin Majewski
Soldier, The	EMB	"Tangerine Dream"
Some Kind of Hero	PAR	Patrick Williams
Something Becomes Evident	GER	Markus Spies
Something Like That (No Yonamono)	JAP	Sai Shomura
Something So Right	CBS-TV	Charles Gross
Sophie's Choice	UN	Marvin Hamlisch
Soup for One	WB	Bernard Edwards/ Johnny Mandel/Nile Rodgers
Southern Cross, The	AUT/JAP	Masaru Sato
Southern Trail, The	YUG	Ljupco Konstantinov
Space Cruiser Yamato	JAP-TV	Kentaro Haneda
Space Cruiser Yamato--Final	JAP-TV	Kentaro Haneda/ Hiroshi Miyagawa
Space Firebird 2772 (Hi No Tori-2772)	JAP	Yauo Higuchi
Space Runway Ideon: A Contact	JAP	Koichi Sugiyama
Space Runway Ideon: Be Invoked	JAP	Koichi Sugiyama
Spaghetti House	ITA	Gianfranco Plenixio
Split Image	ORI	Bill Conti
Sport Billy (series)	NBC-TV	George Mahana
Spring in Autumn	TAI	Tso Hong Yuan
Square Pegs (series)	CBS-TV	Tom Scott
Squizzy Taylor	AUT	Bruce Smeaton
Stacy's Knights (Double Down)	CRO	Norton Buffalo
Star of the Family (series)	ABC-TV	Steve Nelson
Star Trek: The Wrath of Khan	PAR	James Horner
State of Things, The	GER/POR	Juergen Knieper
Station (Eki)	JAP	Ryudo Uzaki
Stigma (Oth Kayin)	ISR	Yoni Rechter
Still of the Night	MGM	John Kander
Straits (Kaikyo)	JAP	Kosetsu Minami
Strange Affair, A	FRA	Philippe Sarde
Stranger Is Watching, A	MGM	Lalo Schifrin
Street Corner Kids (Fichissimi, I)	ITA	Detto Mariano

Strike at the Heart	ITA	Franco Piersani
Summer Lovers	FIL	Basil Poledouris
Sunday Lunch	YUG	Vojislav Kostic
Sunset	YUG	Gabor Lendjel
Superelectromagnetic Robot "Combatler V"	JAP	Hiroshi Tsutsui
Swamp Thing	EMB	Harry Manfredini
Sweet Inquest on Violence	FRA	Albert Marcoeur
Sweet Lies and Loving Oaths (Doux Aveau)	CAN	Rejean Marois
Sword and the Sorcerer, The	IND	David Whittaker
Syncopated Time	SPA	Arie Dzierlatka
T A G (The Assassination Game)	NWP	Craig Safan
T. J. Hooker (series)	ABC-TV	John Davis/Mark Snow
Talcum Powder (Borotalco)	ITA	Lucio Dalla
Tale of Love and Friendship	ITA	Mario Nascimbene
Tales of the Apple Dumpling Gang	CBS-TV	Frank de Vol/Tom Worrall
Tales of the Gold Monkey	ABC-TV	Pete Carpenter/Frank Denison/Mike Post
Talk to Me	IND	Coleridge-Taylor Perkinson
Talking Walls	IND	Richard Glasser
Target Eagle (Playing with Death)	MEX/SPA	Pino Donaggio/Daniele Patucchi/Renato Serio
Taste of Water, The	HOL	Jan Musch
Tattoo	JAP	Ryudo Uzaki
Teachers Only (series)	NBC-TV	Earle Hagen
Technopolice 21-C	JAP	Hisaishi, Jo
Tempest	COL	Stomu Yamashita
Tender Mercies	UN	George Dreyfus
Terminal Choice (Trauma/Death List/Critical List)	CAN	Brian Bennett
Terror at Alcatraz	NBC-TV	Stu Phillips
Test of Strength (Kraftprobe)	GER	Rudolf Schenker
Tex	DIS	Pino Donaggio
That Championship Season	IND	Bill Conti
That's TV	NBC-TV	Edward Gordon
Theater of Shimmering Heat	JAP	Nori Kawauchi
There Was a War When I Was a Child	JAP	Masaru Sato
They Call That an Accident	FRA	Wally Badarou/Steve Winwood
They Were Nobody	CHL	Angel Parra/Pablo Bravo
Thing, The	UN	Ennio Morricone
Things That Teachers Do	JAP	Kazuo Okada
36 Chowringhee Lane	IN	Vanraj Bhatia
This Is Kate Bennett ...	ABC-TV	Lee Holdridge
This Is Noriko	JAP	Kenichiro Morioka
Thorvald and Linda	DEN	"Jairo"

Thou Shalt Not Kill	NBC-TV	Lee Holdridge
Thousand Billion Dollars, A	FRA	Philippe Sarde
Three Eyes	NBC-TV	Barry de Vorzon
Thyagayya	IN	K. V. Mahadevan
Time Masters, The	FRA/GER/SWI	Francoise Bourgoin/Pierre Tardy/Christian Zanesi
Time to Be Happy	BEL	Lydia Chagoll
Time Walker	NWP	Richard Band
To Hell with the Devil	HK	Tang Siu Lam
To Kill a Stranger	IND	Mort Garson
To the Manor Born (series)	BRI-TV	Ronnie Hazelhurst
Tomorrow We Dance	ITA	Eugenio Bennato
Tomorrow's Child	ABC-TV	Patrick Williams
Too Scared to Scream (Doorman, The)	IND	Georges Garvarentz
Tootsie	COL	Dave Grusin
Top Speed (Toute Allure, A)	FRA	Barre Philips
Toward Magic Island	JAP	Nozumi Aoki
Tower of the Lilies	JAP	Soichiro Watanabe
Toy, The	COL	Patrick Williams
Tradition in the World of Spirit, A	JAP-TV	Maruyama/Naozumi Yamamoto
Tradition of Terror: Frankenstein, A	JAP-TV	Kentaro Haneda
Trail of the Pink Panther	UA	Henry Mancini
Train to Kraljevo, The	YUG	Vojislav Kostic
Trance	GER	"Rheingold"
Tron	DIS	Wendy Carlos
Trout, The	FRA	Richard Hartley
Tucker's Witch (series)	CBS-TV	Brad Fiedel/Shirley Walker
25th Man, The	NBC-TV	Frank Comstock
Twins, The	ICE	Egill Olafsson
Two Guys from Muck	NBC-TV	Al Kasha
Two of a Kind	CBS-TV	James di Pasquale
2020 Texas Gladiators	ITA	Francis Taylor
Unapproachable, The	AUS/GER	Wojiech Kilar
Uncensored Cartoons	UA	Carl Stalling
Undernose	ISR	Shlomo Gronich
Uneasiness After School	JAP	Ginji Ito
Unfinished Game of Go, The	CHN/JAP	Jiang Dingxian/Lin Guang
Untamable Shrews, The	ARG	Oscar Cardozo Ocampo
Valentina	SPA	Riz Ortolani
Variola Vera	YUG	Zoran Simjanovic
Vasily and Vasilisa	RUS	Alexei Muravlov
Venom	PAR	Michael Kamen
Verdict, The	FOX	Johnny Mandel
Veronika Voss	GER	Peer Raben

Vice Squad	EMB	Keith Rubenstein
Victims	NBC-TV	Lalo Schifrin
Victor/Victoria	MGM	Henry Mancini
Visiting Hours	CAN	Jonathan Goldsmith
Voice (Golos)	RUS	N. Karithnikov
Voice, The	ITA/YUG	Stelvio Cipriani
Voyagers (series)	NBC-TV	Jerrold Immel/Elliot Kaplan/Peter Myers/ Joel Rosenbaum
Wait Until Dark	HBO-C	Lalo Schifrin
Wall, The	CBS-TV	Leonard Rosenman
Wanted: Good Looking Receptionist and Messenger with His Own Motorcycle	VEN	Juan Carlos Nunnes
War Story, A	CAN	Maurice Marshall
Washington Mistress	CBS-TV	Billy Goldenberg
Wasted Lives	HUN	Gyorgy Selmeczi
Wasteland	YUG	Bojan Adamic
Water Water (Thaneer Thaneer)	IN	M. S. Visvanathan
Waves (Golven)	HOL	Louis Andreissen
We of the Never Never	AUT	Peter Best
Wedding, The (Boda, La)	VEN	Juan Carlo Nunez
Wedding on Waltons Mountain, A	NBC-TV	Alexander Courage
Wend Kuuni	AFR	Rene Guirma
What Makes David Run?	FRA	Michel Legrand
What Now, Little Man?	GER	Hans A. Wittstadt
White Dog	PAR	Ennio Morricone
White Rose, The	GER	Konstantin Wecker
Who Dares Win?	BRI	Roy Budd/Jerry and Marc Donohue
Who Pulled the Plug? (Goeta Kanal)	SWE	Bjoern Isfaelt
Wild Beasts	ITA	Daniele Patucchi
Wild Daisy, The	JAP	Shunsuke Nikuchi
Wild Flowers	CAN	Raoul Dugnay
Wild Women of Chastity Gulch, The	ABC-TV	Frank De Vol/Tom Worrall
Will, G. Gordon Liddy	NBC-TV	Pete Carpenter/Mike Post
Will the High Salaried Workers Please Raise Their Hands!!!	FRA	Philippe Sarde
Willful Murder	JAP	Masaru Sato
Winged Serpent, The	IND	Robert O. Ragland
Witness for the Prosecution	CBS-TV	John Cameron
Wizard of Babylon, The	GER	Peer Raben
Woman Called Golda, A	IND-TV	Michel Legrand
Woman in Love with Mechanic Gavrilov, The	RUS	Alexi Mashukov
World According to Garp, The	WB	David Shire
World War III	TV	Gil Melle
Wrong Is Right	COL	Artie Kane
Year of Living Dangerously, The	AUT	Maurice Jarre

Yes, Minister (series)	BRI-TV	Ronnie Hazelhurst
Young Doctors in Love	FOX	Maurice Jarre
Young Teacher, The (Miao Miao)	CHN	Zhueng Liu
Your Money or Your Life	DEN	Jimmy Guiffre
(Pengene Eller Livet)		
Zapped!	EMB	Charles Fox

1983

A-Team, The (series)	NBC-TV	Pete Carpenter/Mike Post
Abuse	IND	Shawn Phillips/Jeffrey Olmsted
Acceptable Levels	BRI	Nick Garvey
Ace Crawford, Private Eye (series)	CBS-TV	Peter Matz
Adam	NBC-TV	Mike Post
Adam's House	CBS-TV	Stuart Katz
Addressee Unknown	GER	Wolfgang Heinze
Adios Miami	VEN	Chuchito Sanoja
Aerodrome, The	BRI-TV	Carl Davis
African, The	FRA	Georges Delerue
After Love	BEL	Jean Blaute
Agatha Christie's "A Caribbean Mystery"	CBS-TV	Lee Holdridge
Agatha Christie's "Sparkling Cyanide"	CBS-TV	James di Pasquale
Ah Ying	HK	Violet Lam
Airship, The	E.GER	Friedrich Goldmann
Alexander the Little	E.GER/RUS	Eduard Artemyev
Alexandre	SWI	Gaspard Glaus
All My Friends 2	ITA	Carlo Rustichelli
All Right, My Friend	JAP	Kazuhiko Katoh
All the Right Moves	FOX	David Campbell
All the Wrong Spies	HK	Chris Babida
Allegement, L'	SWI	Michel Hostettler
Allies	AUT	Greg Maclain/John Stuart
Alsino and the Condor	CUB/MEX/NIC	Leo Brouwer
Amada	CUBA	Leo Brouwer
Amagi Pass	JAP	Mitsuaki Kanno
Amanda's (series)	ABC-TV	Peter Matz
Amityville 3-D	ORI	Howard Blake
Amok	MOR	Miriam Makeba
An Bloem	HOL	Bob Zimmerman
And the Ship Sails On	FRA/ITA	Gianfranco Plenixio
Angelo, My Love	IND	Michael Kamen
Another Time, Another Place	BRI	John McLeod
Another Woman's Child	CBS-TV	Billy Goldenberg
Antique Dealer's Wife, The	JAP	Toshiyuki Komori
Ark of the Sun God, The	ITA/TUR	Aldo Tamborrelli

Art of Love, The	FRA/ITA	Luis Enrique Bacalov
Ascendancy	BRI	Ronnie Leahy
At the Cinema Palace--Liam O'Leary	IRE	Bill Whelan
Assassination Run, The	IND-C	John Scott
At Ease (series)	ABC-TV	Jack Elliott
At the Top of the Stairs	FRA	Roland Vincent
Ator	IND	Carlo Maria Cordio
Attention, One Woman May Be Hiding Another (Double Husbands)	FRA	Philippe Sarde
Austeria	POL	Leopold Kozlowski
Automan (series)	ABC-TV	Stu Phillips/Morton Stevens
Autumn Born	CAN	Don Bouchai
Awakening of Candra, The	CBS-TV	Billy Goldenberg
Awry in the Wings	DEN	Helle Ryslinge/ "Paravion"
Axe (Lisa, Lisa)	IND	George Newman Shaw/ John Wilhelm
BMX Bandits	AUT	Colin Stead/Frank Stangio
Baby Makes Five (series)	ABC-TV	Mischa Segal
Baby Sister	ABC-TV	Fred Karlin
Bad Boys	UN	Bill Conti
Bad Hats (Amour Fugitif, L')	BRI/FRA	Jeff Cohen
Balance (Ravnovessie)	BUL	Boris Karadimchev
Ball, The	ALG/FRA/ITA	Vladimir Cosma
Ballad of Gregorio Cortez, The	IND	W. Michael Lewis
Ballad of Narayama, The	JAP	Shinjiro Ikebe
Banks and Robbers	GER	Peter Schmitt
Banzai	FRA	Vladimir Cosma
Bar Esperanca: Last to Close	BRA	Thomas Improta
Basic Training (Up the Pentagon)	IND	Michael Cruz
Bastard, The	FRA	Norbert Aboudarham
Bay City Blues (series)	NBC-TV	Mike Post
Be Tough, Victor!	HUN	Zdenko Tamassy
Bearn	SPA	Francisco Guerrero
Beauty and the Beast, The	DEN	Gunnar Moeller Pedersen
Bed, The (Lit, Le)	BEL	Serge Kochyne
Before the Battle	BEL	Fabien Audooren
Bell for Nirvana, A	KOR	Chung Minsup
Bella Donna	GER	Astor Piazzolla
Benvenuta	BEL/FRA	Frederic Devreese
Best of Times, The	CBS-TV	Craig Safan
Betrayal	FOX	Dominic Muldowney
Better Late Than Never	BRI	Henry Mancini
Between Friends	HBO-C	James Horner
Beyond the Limit	PAR	Stanley Myers
Beyond Witch Mountain	TV	George Duning
Biddy	BRI	Michael Sanvoisin

Big Bang in Bender, The	SWE	Stefan Nilsson
Big Blonde (Iso Valee)	FIN	Heikki Valpola
Big Carnival, The	FRA	Serge Franklin
Big John	NBC-TV	Pete Carpenter/Mike Post
Big Score, The	IND	Jay Chattaway
Bill on His Own	CBS-TV	Lee Curreri
Bingo Bongo	ITA	Pinuccio Pirazzoli
Biohazard	IND	Drew Neumann/Eric Rasmussen
Biquefarre	FRA	Yves Gilbert
Bird Watch, The	FRA	Jean Musy
Biskitts, The (series)	CBS-TV	Hoyt Curtin
Black Crows	NOR/SWE	Anne-Grete Preus
Black Goddess	BRA/NIG	Reni Kababa
Black Rider	HOL	Clous van Mechelen
Black Spider, The	SWI	Veronique Muller/ "Yello"
Black Stallion Returns, The	MGM/UA	Georges Delerue
Black Tiger, The	EGY	Gamal Salama
Black Venus	IND	Gregory Segura
Blade in the Dark, A	ITA	Guido and Maurizio de Angelis
Blastfighter	ITA	Andrew Barrymore
Blood Brothers	HUN	Gyula Babos
Blood Feud	IND-TV	Fred Steiner
Blue Skies Again	WB	John Kander
Blue Thunder	COL	Arthur B. Rubinstein, Jr.
Body Is Willing, The	HK	Michael Lai
Bolero	GER	Joerg Evers
Boogeyman II	IND	Craig Hundley/Tim Krog
Boone (series)	NBC-TV	Alexander Courage/ William Goldstein/ Arthur Kempel
Boy Like Many Others, A	ITA	Enrico Pieranunzi
Brainstorm	MGM/UA	James Horner
Branagan and Mapes	CBS-TV	Artie Butler
Break-In (Effraction)	FRA	Maurice Vander
Breath of Air, A (DIH)	YUG	Jani Golob
Breathless	ORI	Jack Nitzsche
Broken-Hearted Love Story, A	TUR	Cahit Berkay
Brussels by Night	BEL	Raymond van het Groenewoud
Buddies	AUT	Chris Neal
Buffalo Bill (series)	NBC-TV	Tom Wells
Bullshot	BRI	John Du Prez
Burning Love	HOL	Laurens van Rooyen
Burning of the Imperial Palace, The	CHN	Li Hang Chiang

Bush Christmas	AUT	Mike Perjanik
Cabaret Tears (Send in the Clowns)	HK	Lo Ta Yu
Cabbie, The	ITA	Piero Piccioni
Cache, The (Battant, Le)	FRA	Christian Dorisse
Camminacammina	ITA	Bruno Nicolai
Can She Bake a Cherry Pie	IND	Karen Black
Cap Canaille	BEL/FRA	Elisabeth Wiener
Careful, He Might Hear You	AUT	Ray Cook
Carmen	SPA	Paco de Lucia
Carpool	CBS-TV	Jimmie Haskell
Casablanca	NBC-TV	Peter Matz
Case Is Closed, The (Kharij)	IN	B. V. Karanth
Catch Your Dreams ...	GER	"Kitaro"
Caution: Danger	GRE	Christodoulos Halaris
Cave-In!	NBC-TV	Richard LaSalle
Chained Heat	JEN	Joseph Conlan
Chained Justice	HUN	Adrian Enescu
Charlie Brown and Snoopy Show, The (series)	CBS-TV	Ed Bogas/Desarae Goyette
Chiefs	CBS-TV	Michael Small
Children of God's Earth	NOR	Peter Knutsen
China Rose	CBS-TV	Charles Gross
Choices of the Heart	NBC-TV	John Rubinstein
Christine	COL	John Carpenter
Christmas Story, A	MGM/UA	Paul Zaza/Carl Zittrer
Circle of Passions	FRA/SPA	Egisto Macchi
Citadel, The (series)	PBS-TV	Michael Stuckey
Citizen: The Political Life of Allard K. Lowenstein	IND	Stephen Thompson
Class	ORI	Elmer Bernstein
Close Ties	A&E-C	Jerry Frankel
Cocaine and Blue Eyes	NBC-TV	Morton Stevens
Cocaine: One Man's Seduction	NBC-TV	Brad Fiedel
Co-Fathers, The	FRA	Vladimir Cosma
Cold Feet	IND	Todd Rundgren
Come Dire	ITA	Gaetano Liguori
Comeback	FOX	Klaus Doldinger
Concrete Pastures	CZE	Svetozar Stur
Condo (series)	ABC-TV	George Aliceson Tipton
Confessions of a Married Man	ABC-TV	Billy Goldenberg
Conquest of Albania, The	SPA	Alberto Iglesias
Cook & Peary: The Race to the Pole	CBS-TV	Charles Gross
Count Tacchia	ITA	Armando Trovajoli
Coup de Foudre	FRA	Luis Enrique Bacalov
Coverup (Crime, La)	FRA	Reinhardt Wagner
Cowboy	CBS-TV	Bruce Broughton
Crack II, El	SPA	Jesus Gluck
Cradle Will Fall, The	CBS-TV	Elliot Lawrence
Cross Country	NWP	Chris Rea

Cross Creek	UN	Leonard Rosenman
Cujo	WB	Charles Bernstein
Curse of the Pink Panther	MGM/UA	Henry Mancini
Curtains	CAN	Paul J. Zaza
Cutter to Houston (series)	CBS-TV	Ray Cooper/Dennis McCarthy
D.C. Cab	UN	Giorgio Moroder
Daniel Takes a Train	HUN	Gyorgy Selmeczi
Danni	GER	Lothar Meid
Dawn, The	INO	Embie C. Noer
Day After, The	ABC-TV	David Raksin
Dead Wrong	CAN	Karl Kobylansky
Dead Zone, The	PAR	Michael Kamen
Deadly Circuit	FRA	Carla Bley
Deadly Force	EMB	Gary Scott
Deadly Impact	ITA	Frank Pentarey
Deadly Lessons	ABC-TV	Ian Freebairn-Smith
Deal, The	ARG	Jorge Valcarcel
Deal of the Century	WB	Arthur B. Rubinstein
Death of Mario Ricci, The	FRA/SWI	Arie Dzierlatka
Deathmask (Unknown)	IND	Robert Rugieri
Deception of Benjamin Steiner, The	IND	Todd Gould/Rick Hamouris
Def-Con 4 (Dark Eyes/Ground Zero)	CAN	Chris Young
Demon Murder Case, The	TV	George Aliceson Tipton
Demon of the Isle, The	FRA	Christian Gaubert
Dempsey	CBS-TV	Billy Goldenberg
Deserters	CAN	Michael Conway Baker
Desire	PHI	Ryan Cayabyab
Desperate Intruder	IND-TV	Tim Simon
Devil and the Lady, The	FRA/MEX	Augustin Lara/Beto Mendez
... Difficult to Become Engaged	E.GER	Reinhard Lakonny
Digital Dreams	BRI	Mike Batt/Bill Wyman
Diner	CBS-TV	Harry Lojewski
Dirty Hero (Yogoreta Eiyu)	JAP	Yuichiro Oda
Disappearance of Harry, The	BRI	Nick Bicat
Distinguishing Marks: Handsome	ITA	Gino Santercole
Dixie: Changing Habits	CBS-TV	Jimmie Haskell
Doctor Detroit	UN	Lalo Schifrin
Doctor Who--The Five Doctors	BRI-TV	Ron Grainer
Dog in a Game of Nine-Pins, A	FRA	Patrice Caratini
Dog's Night Song, The	HUN	"Bizottsag Group"
Doll, The	GER	Hainer Dutjer
Don't Panic, Please!	HUN	Karoly Frenreisz
Dot and the Bunny	AUT	Bob Young
Dream Flights	RUS	Vadim Khrapachev
Dream House (series)	NBC-TV	Michael Malone
Dreamland	FRF	Henry Butler
Dresser, The	COL	James Horner

Drifting (Nagua)	ISR	Arik Rudich
Dropout, The	JAP	Katsuo Ono
Drummer, The	HK	Joseph Koo
Due to an Act of God	GER	Jens-Peter Ostendorf
Dukes, The (series)	CBS-TV	Hoyt Curtin
Dungeons and Dragons	CBS-TV	Johnny Douglas/Rob Walsh
Dust of Empire	FRA	Nguyen Thien Dao
Dusty	NBC-TV	Jerry Goldsmith
Dusty	AUT	Frank Strangio
Easy Money	ORI	Laurence Rosenthal
Eddie and the Cruisers	EMB	John Cafferty
Eddie Macon's Run	UN	Norton Buffalo
Edith and Marcel	FRA	Francis Lai
Edith's Diary	GER	Juergen Knieper
Educating Rita	COL	David Hentschel
1893-1915 (series)	BRI-TV	Bruce Smeaton
Emerald Point (series)	CBS-TV	Bill Conti/Lance Rubin
Emergency Room	IND-TV	Richard Shores
Enemies, The	ARG	Luis Maria Serra
Englishman Abroad, An	BRI	George Fenton
Epitaph for Barbara Radziwill, An	POL	Bohdan Mazurek/ Zdzislaw Szostak
Equator	FRA	Serge Gainsbourg
Erendira	FRA/GER/MEX	Maurice Lecoeur
Eureka	UA	Stanley Myers
Exposed	MGM/UA	Georges Delerue
Eyes of the Birds	BRI/FRA	Carlos Andreau/ Francois Tusques
Face of Rage, The	ABC-TV	Miles Goodman
Falasha: Exile of the Black Jews	CAN	Sara Jacobovici
Falcon, The	FRA	Del Rabenja
Family Business	ABC-TV	Johnny Mandel
Family Relations (Rodnia)	RUS	Eduard Artemyev
Family Tree, The	NBC-TV	Mark Snow
Far from Where	ITA	Lucio Dalla
Farmers Arms	BRI	Ilona Sekacz
Fat Guy Goes Nutzoid	IND	Leo Kottke
Fat Tilla	E.GER	Kiril Cibulka
Father and Child	JAP	Shinji Tanimura
Favorite, The (Rock and Torah)	FRA	Jean-Philippe Goude/ Ramon Pipin
Favorites and Winners	ITA	Alfredo E. Muschietti
Feel the Heat	ABC-TV	Bennett Salvay
Femmes	FRA	Yves Dessca/Marc Hillman
Ferat Vampire	CZE	Petr Kapka
Fiancee Who Came in From the Cold, The	FRA	Robert Charlebois
Field of Honor, The	HOL	"Au Pairs"/"Tuxide- moon"

Fighter, The	CBS-TV	Patrick Williams
Final Executioner, The	ITA	Carlo De Nonno
Finals	ISR	Naftali Alter
Fire and Ice	FOX	William Kraft
Firm, The	NBC-TV	John Morris
First Affair	CBS-TV	Lee Holdridge
First Desires	FRA/GER	Philippe Sarde
Fist Full of Talons, A	HK	So Chun Hou/Stephen Shing
Flash Gordon--The Greatest Adventure of All	NBC-TV	Yvette Blais
Flashdance	PAR	Giorgio Moroder
Flax Field, The	BEL/HOL	Rogier van Otterloo
Flirt	ITA	Francesco De Gregori
Flower in the Raining Night, A	TAI	Chang Hun I
Foolish Years of the Twist, The	ALG	Richard Anthony
Foot in the Door (series)	CBS-TV	Joe Raposo
For Love and Honor (series)	NBC-TV	Ian Freebairn-Smith
For Those I Loved	CAN/FRA	Maurice Jarre
Fords on Water	BRI	Keith Donald
Forgive Me for Betraying Me	BRA	Chico Buarque
Found Money	NBC-TV	Jack Elliott
Fourth Man, The	HOL	Loek Dikker
Francois Reichenbach's Japan	FRA	Jean-Claude Eloi
Friend of Vincent, A	FRA	Philippe Sarde
Full House	CBS-TV	Fred Karlin
Fun (Boarding House)	ISR	Ronny Brown/Yorik Ben David
Funny Farm, The	CAN	Pierre Brousseau
Funny Money	BRI	James Kenelm Clarke
Gabriela	BRA	Antonio Carlos Jobim
Garcon!	FRA	Philippe Sarde
Get Crazy	EMB	Michael Boddicker
Getting It On	IND	Ricky Keller
Ghost Dance	BRI/GER	David Cunningham/ Michael Giles/James Muir
Ghost Dancing	ABC-TV	John Morris
Gift of Love: A Christmas Story, The	CBS-TV	Fred Karlin
Girl's Life, A	NBC-TV	Patrick Williams
Girls of the White Orchid	NBC-TV	Brad Fiedel
Going Berserk	UN	Tom Scott
Gold Diggers, The	BRI	Lindsay Cooper
Gold, Silver, Bad Luck	PHI	Jose Gentica
Golden Girl	BRA	Guilherme Arantes
Golden 80's, The	BEL	Marc Herouet
Golden Seal, The	IND	John Barry
G'Ole	BRI	Rick Wakeman
Goodnight, Beantown (series)	CBS-TV	Dennis McCarthy
Gorky Park	ORI	James Horner

Grace Kelly	ABC-TV	John Andrew Tartaglia
Gramps Is in the Resistance	FRA	Jean Musy
Great Day	CBS-TV	Jack Elliott
Guerrilla from the North	MEX	Rafael Carrion
Gulliver's Travels	SPA	Antonio Areta
Gun Shy	CBS-TV	Dennis McCarthy
Gunman (Meu-Peun)	THAI	Pisate Sangsuwan
Haiti Express	DEN	"D. P. Express/Fuzzy"
Hamptons, The (series)	ABC-TV	Marvin Laird
Hannah K.	FRA	Gabriel Yared
Hans, Life Before Death	HOL	Misha Mengalberg
Happy	CBS-TV	Billy Goldenberg
Happy Endings	NBC-TV	J. A. C. Redford
Happy Endings	CBS-TV	William Goldstein
Hardcastle and McCormick (series)	ABC-TV	Pete Carpenter/Mike Post
Haunting Passion, The	NBC-TV	Paul Chihara
Heads or Tails	ITA	Carlo Rustichelli/Paolo Rustichelli
Heads or Tails	YUG	Bojan Adamic
Heart Like a Wheel	FOX	Laurence Rosenthal
Heart of Steel	ABC-TV	Brad Fiedel
Heartbreakers, The	GER	Lothar Meid
Heat and Dust	IN	Richard Robbins
Heavenly Hosts	HUN	Gyorgy Selmczi
Heinrich Penthesilea von Kleist	GER	Heiner Goebbels
Held for Questioning	E.GER	Guenther Fischer
Hell Riders	IND	"Electra Nova"
Hell Squad	IND	Charles P. Barnett
Hello, Taxi	YUG	Kornelije Kovac
Hell's Kitchen (Kiez)	GER	Gunther Erfurt
Hercules	MGM/UA	Pino Donaggio
Hercules II	IND	Pino Donaggio
Here Are Ladies	IRE	David Fanshawe
Herndon and Me	ABC-TV	John D'Andrea/David Wheatley
Hidden Dances	SWI	Oberwalliser Spillit
High Road to China	WB	John Barry
High School U.S.A.	NBC-TV	Tony Berg/Miles Goodman
Highway Honeys	NBC-TV	Ken Harrison
Hill on the Dark Side of the Moon, A	SWE	Lars-Erik Brossner
Hills Have Eyes II, The	IND	Harry Manfredini
Hitchhiker, The (series)	HBO-C	Paul Hoffert/Michel Rubini
Hobson's Choice	CBS-TV	Robert Drasnin
Hockey Fever	NOR	Bent Aswerud/Geir Boehren
Home at Hong Kong	HK	Ng Tai Kong
Home Free All	IND	Jay Chattaway

Homecoming Song	GRE	Demetris Papademetriou
Honeymoon	YUG	Alfi Kabiljo
Hong Kong, Hong Kong	HK	Lam Man-Yee
Hong Kong Playboys	HK	Stephen Ching/So Chun Hou
Horatio I.P.I.	BRI/HK	Anders Nelson
Hostage--The Christine Maresch Story	AUT	Davood Tabrizi
Hot Summer in Kabul, A	RUS	Eduard Artemyev
Hotel	ABC-TV	Artie Kane
Hotel Central	BUL	Bozhidar Petkov
House, The	ICE	Thorir Bladursson
House in the Park	GER	Wilhelm Dieter Siebert
House of the Long Shadows	BRI	Richard Harvey
House of the Yellow Carpet	ITA	Stelvio Cipriani
House on Sorority Row, The	IND	Richard Band
Hunger, The	MGM/UA	Denny Jaeger/Michel Rubini
I Am the Cheese	IND	Jonathan Tunick
I Do	HK	Lam Man Eiee
I Married a Dead Man	FRA	Philippe Sarde
I Married Wyatt Earp	NBC-TV	Morton Stevens
I Take These Men	CBS-TV	Earle Hagen
I Want to Live!	ABC-TV	Lee Holdridge
Ice Birds (Isfugle)	DEN	Kenneth Knudsen
If I Were for Real	TAI	Ch'en Hsin-yi
If You Know What I Mean	HOL	Herman Schoonderwalt
Igman March, The	YUG	Kornelije Kovac
Illusionist, The	HOL	William Beruker
Illusions	CBS-TV	Robert Drasnin
I'm Going to Be Famous	IND	Jay Asher
I'm Not Living With You Anymore	ITA	Fernando Falcao
In the White City	POR/SWI	Jean-Luc Barbier
In the Year of the Ape	FIN	Pekka Rechardt
Incident of the Half-Meter, The	SYR	Marcel Kalipheh
Incomplete Eclipse	CZE	Zdenek Pololanik
Independence Day	WB	Charles Bernstein
Informer, The (Indic, L')	FRA	Michel Magne
Initiation, The	NWP	Gabriel Black/Lance Ong
Inspector Gadget (series)	IND-TV	Shuki Levy/Haim Saban
Inspector Perez	NBC-TV	Fred Karlin
Instructor, The	IND	Marti Lunn
Insult, The	HUN	Szaboles Fenyes
Intimate Agony	ABC-TV	Billy Goldenberg
Invisible Woman, The	NBC-TV	David Frank
Invitation to the Wedding	BRI	Joseph Brooks
Irezumi--Spirit of Tattoo	JAP	Masaru Sato
Issa's Valley	POL	Zygmunt Konieczny
It's Not Easy (series)	ABC-TV	Charles Fox

Jacobo Timerman: Prisoner Without a Name, Cell Without a Number	NBC-TV	Brad Fiedel
Jane Doe	CBS-TV	Paul Chihara
Jaws 3-D	UN	Alan Parker
Jazz Man, The	RUS	Anatoli Kroll
Jeans and a T-Shirt	ITA	Franco Chiaravalle/Nino D'Angelo
Jennifer Slept Here (series)	NBC-TV	Perry Botkin
John Steinbeck's "The Winter of Our Discontent"	CBS-TV	Mark Snow
Joke of Destiny Lying in Wait Around the Corner Like a Robber, A	ITA	Paolo Conte
Jon--A Story About the End of the World	FIN	Antti Hytti
Joseph's Daughter	GER/SPA	Roland Baumgartner
Josie	IND-TV	Richard Lyman
Joy	CAN	Francois Valery/Alain Wisniak
Joy Ride (Schwarzfahrer)	GER	Kevin Coyne
Joysticks (Video Madness)	JEN	John Caper, Jr.
Juliette's Fate	FRA	Bernard Lubat
Jungle Warriors	GER/MEX	Roland Baumgartner
Just a Game	CAN	Yves Lafferriere
Just Once More	YUG	Mladen Vranesevic/ Predrag Vranesevic
Keep, The	PAR	"Tangerine Dream"
Kennedy	NBC-TV	Richard Hartley
Kenny Rogers as the Gambler-- The Adventure Continues	CBS-TV	Larry Cansler
Kentucky Woman	CBS-TV	George Romanis
Key, The (Chiave, La)	ITA	Ennio Morricone
Kid Who Couldn't Miss, The	CAN	Ben Low
Kid with the 200 I.Q., The	NBC-TV	Dennis McCarthy
Killer, The	GRE	Michalis Christodoulidis
Killer in the Family, A	ABC-TV	Gerald Fried
King Blank	IND	Anton Fig
King of Comedy	FOX	Robbie Robertson
Klakier (Applause-Getter, The)	POL	Krzysztof Mayer
Knocking Down Building Blocks	JAP	Kentaro Haneda
Konopielka	POL	Wojciech Karolak
Koyaanisqatsi	IND	Philip Glass/Michael Hoenig/Murt Munkacsi
Krull	COL	James Horner
Kudzu	CBS-TV	Tim Simon
Kukurantumi--The Road to Accra	GHA	Amartey Hedzoleh
Kuni Lemel in Cairo	ISR	Kobi Oshrath
Kurt and Valde	DEN	Jesper Klein/Svend Skipper

Land of Cops and Robbers	GER	"Nightwork"
Landscape with Figures	ITA	Matteo di Guida
Larose, Pierrot el la Luce	CAN	June Wallack
Last Combat, The	FRA	Eric Serra
Last Diva: Francesca Bertini, The	ITA	Egisto Macchi
Last Flight, The	IND	Jay Chattaway
Last Ninja, The	ABC-TV	Robert Cobert
Last Winter, The	ISR	Nahum Heyman
Last Wishes	BUL	Kiril Dontchev
Legend of Plumeria--Heaven's Kiss, The	JAP	Ryo Fukui
Legend of Tianyun Mountain	CHN	Ge Yan
Legs	ABC-TV	Lee Holdridge
Let It Be Sunday	FRA	Georges Delerue
Lianna	UA	K. Mason Daring
Liberty Belle	FRA	Georges Delerue
Lies	IND	Marc Donahue
Life and Blood of the Polish	BRA	Henrique de Curitiba
Life Is a Novel	FRA	Philippe Gerard
Like Grandfather, Like Grandson	YUG	Dimitrije-Mikan Obradovic
Limpan	SWE	Bjoern Isfaelt
Listen to Your Heart	CBS-TV	James di Pasquale
Little Brother, The	GER	Juergen Knieper
Little Bunch, The	FRA	Edgar Cosma
Little Devil from the Quarter	ARG	Mike Rivas
Little Girl Who Conquered Time, The	JAP	Masataka Matsutoya
Little House: Look Back to Yesterday	NBC-TV	David Rose
Little Shots	NBC-TV	John Beal
Littles, The	ABC-TV	Shuki Levy/Haim Saban
Local Hero	WB	Mark Knopfler
Lone Wolf McQuade	ORI	Francesco de Masi
Lonely Lady, The	UN	Charles Calello
Loose Connections	BRI	Dominic Muldowney/ Andy Roberts
Lords of Discipline, The	PAR	Howard Blake
Losin' It	EMB	Ken Wannberg
Lost Empire, The	IND	Alan Howarth
Lost Illusions	HUN	Istvan Martha
Lost Republic, The	ARG	Luis Maria Serra
Lost Tribe, The	NZ	David Fraser
Lottery (series)	ABC-TV	Mark Snow
Love by Request	RUS	Igor Tsvetkuv
Love in Germany, A	FRA/GER	Michel Legrand
Love Is Forever	NBC-TV	Klaus Doldinger
Love, Sex and Marriage	ABC-TV	Danny Goldberg
Loved One, The	BRA	Tavinho Moura
Lovely But Deadly	IND	Robert O. Ragland
Lovers and Other Strangers	ABC-TV	Fred Karlin
Lovesick	WB	Philippe Sarde

Loving (series)	ABC-TV	Michael Karp
Lucie Sur Seine	FRA	Gabriel Yared
Luggage of the Gods	IND	Cengiz Valtkaya
M.A.D.D.: Mothers Against Drunk Drivers	NBC-TV	Bruce Broughton
Macross--Super Time Fortress	JAP-TV	Kentaro Haneda
Making of a Model, The	ABC-TV	Artie Butler
Malibu	ABC-TV	Mark Snow
Mama's Family (series)	NBC-TV	Peter Matz
Man in the Top Hat, The	FRA	Theirry Durbet
Man of My Measure, A	FRA/GER	Pierre Bachelet
Man Who Loved Women, The	COL	Henry Mancini
Man Who Wasn't There, The	PAR	Miles Goodman
Man With Two Brains, The	WB	Joel Goldsmith
Man, Woman and Child	PAR	Georges Delerue
Manchurian Avenger	IND	Paul Conly
Mandi (Market Place)	IN	Vanraj Bhatia
Manimal (series)	NBC-TV	Paul Chihara/Alan Silvestri
Maria Chapdelaine	CAN/FRA	Lewis Furey
Marriage, A	IND	Jack Waldman
Maruja in Hell	PERU	Arturo Kike Pinto
Marvin and Tige	IND	Patrick Williams
Masquerade	YUG	Bojan Adamic
Masquerade (series)	ABC-TV	Stu Phillips
Matushka (Viadukt)	GER/HUN	Zdenko Tamassy
Max	NBC-TV	Bob Christianson
Max Dugan Returns	FOX	David Shire
Me, Light and Darkness	ITA	"I Barluna"
Meantime	BRI	Andrew Dickson
Mediterranean, The	IND	Martin Bresnick
Megilah '83	ISR	Dov Seltzer
Melzer	GER/SWI	Jan Garbarek
Memorial Day	CBS-TV	Billy Goldenberg
Men from the Gutter	HK	So Chun Hou/Stephen Shing
Merry Christmas, Mr. Lawrence	UN	Ryuichi Sakamoto
Metalstorm: The Destruction of Jared-Syn	UN	Richard Band
Metropolis (reissue)	GER	Giorgio Moroder
Metropolis	ITA	Luciano Berio
Mickey Spillane's Mike Hammer: More Than Murder	CBS-TV	Earle Hagen
Mickey Spillane's Mike Hammer: Murder Me, Murder You	CBS-TV	Earle Hagen
Midnight Rehearsal	HUN	Zsolt Dome
Midnight Spares	AUT	Cameron Allan
Midsummer Night's Dream, A	ITA	Mauro Pagani
Millennial Bee, The	CZE/GER/ITA	Petr Hapka
Milo Barus--The Strongest Man in the World	GER	Jiri Sust

Miss Lonelyhearts	IND	Leonard Rosenman
Mission Thunderbolt	HK	Johnny Tsang
Mississippi, The	CBS-TV	Lee Holdridge/Dennis McCarthy
Mr. Mom	FOX	Lee Holdridge
Mr. Smith (series)	NBC-TV	Patrick Williams
Modern Day Houdini	IND	Jeffrey Boze
Moment of Adventure, The	ITA	Manuel de Sica
Monchhichis (series)	CBS-TV	Hoyt Curtin
Moon in the Gutter, The	FRA/ITA	Gabriel Yared
Moonshine Bowling	CAN	Joel Bienvenue
Moral	PHI	George Canseco
Mosquito on the Tenth Floor	JAP	Katsuo Ono
Moss-Covered Asphalt	YUG	Arsen Dedic
Mother Maria	RUS	Alexej Rybnikov
Move Along, There's Nothing to See	FRA	Jean-Philippe Goude/Ramon Pipin
Murder in Coweta County	CBS-TV	Brad Fiedel
Murder Ink	CBS-TV	Duane Tatro
Murder 1, Dancer 0	NBC-TV	George Romanis
My Aunt Nora	ECU	Claudio Jacome
My Country, My Hat	AFR	Barry Bekker/Colin Shapiro
My Love Letters	NWP	Ralph Jones
My Temporary Father	YUG	Vojislav Kostic
My Tutor	CRO	Webster Lewis
Mystere	ITA	Armando Trovajoli
Mystery	MEX	Leonardo Velazquez
Mystery Mansion	IND	William Loose/Jack Tillar/Marty Wereski
National Lampoon's Vacation	WB	Ralph Burns
National Snoop, The	NBC-TV	Perry Botkin, Jr.
Nelly's Version	BRI	Michael Nyman
Never Cry Wolf	DIS	Mark Isham
Never Say Never Again	WB	Michel Legrand
News Is the News, The (series)	NBC-TV	Bob Mounsey
Night After Death	YUG	Alfi Kabiljo
Night Beast (Bete Noir, La)	FRA	Jean-Claude Vannier
Night in Heaven, A	FOX	Jan Hammer
Night Partners	CBS-TV	Fred Karlin
Night the Bridge Fell Down, The	NBC-TV	Richard LaSalle
Nightmares	UN	Craig Safan/Black Flag
1990: The Bronx Warriors	ITA	Walter Rizzati
1919	SPA	Riz Ortolani
No Clues	HUN	Laszlo Des/"Dimenzio Group"
Nostalgia	ITA/RUS	Gino Peguri
Nothing Left to Lose	GER	Peer Raben
Now and Forever	AUT	Bruce Rowland
Nut in Action, A	ARG	Horacio Malvicino
Octopussy	MGM/UA	John Barry

Odd Balls	IND	Dave Harrison/Ron Harrison
Odyssey of the Pacific	CAN	Edith Butler
Of Unknown Origin	CAN	Ken Wannberg
Off the Wall	JEN	Dennis McCarthy
Oh Madeline (series)	ABC-TV	Dan Foliart/Howard Pearl
Okay, Okay	ITA	Gaetano Liguori
Okinawan Boys	JAP	Shinichiro Ikebe
O'Malley	NBC-TV	Pete Rugolo
On the Wrong Track	HK	Li Hsiao Tien
On Your Feet, Crabs, the Tide Is Up	FRA	Eric Demarsan
One Cooks, the Other Doesn't	CBS-TV	Fred Karlin
One Could Laugh in Former Days	HOL	Jurre Haanstra
One Dark Night	IND	Bob Summers
One Deadly Summer	FRA	Georges Delerue
One Night Band	CBS-TV	Michael Cannon/Cort Casady
One Night Only (New Year's Eve)	CAN	Lawrence Shragge
Onimasa	JAP	Mitsukai Karno
Open Ends (Grenzenlos)	GER	Peer Raben
Order of Death	ITA	Ennio Morricone
Orientation Course (Concurs)	RUM	Adrian Enescu
Osterman Weekend, The	FOX	Lalo Schifrin
Other Woman, The	CBS-TV	Artie Butler
Otto Is a Rhino	DEN	Jacob Groth
Our Aunt Tao	CHN	Liu Yan-xi
Outer Signs of Wealth	FRA	Pierre Billon/Eric Bouad/Johnny Hallyday
Outside the Day	ITA	Maurizio Giammarco
Outsider, The (Marginal, Le)	FRA	Ennio Morricone
Outsider in Amsterdam	HOL	Rogier van Otterloo
Outsiders, The	WB	Carmine Coppola
P. K. and the Kid	IND	James Horner
Pac-Man	ABC-TV	Hoyt Curtin
Packin' It In	CBS-TV	Mark Snow
Paper Chase: The Second Year, The	SHO-C	Stephen Sevetan
Parahyba Woman	BRA	Paulo Moura
Parallel Divergences	ITA	Renato Meneghetti
Paso Doble	GER	Albert Kittler/"Brutto Netto"
Passionate People	AUS/GER/SWI	Ernst Koelz
Pastorale Heroica	POL/RUS	Jerzy Maksymiuck
Pauline at the Seaside	FRA	Jean-Louis Valero
Peppermint Peace	GER	Konstantin Wecker
Perfect Strangers (Blind Alley)	NLC	Dwight Dixon
Perfect Wife, The	HK	Teddy Robin

Phantom of the Opera	CBS-TV	Ralph Burns
Phar Lap	AUT	Bruce Rowland
Phatik and the Juggler	IN	Satyajit Ray
Philip Marlowe, Private Eye (series)	HBO-C	John Cameron
Pico, El (Needle, The)	SPA	Luis Iriondo
Pink Motel (Motel)	IND	Larry K. Smith
Pirates, The	NOR	Odd A. Eilersten
Planet "Tailor," The	POL	Marek Wilczynski
Play Catch	HK	Teddy Robin/Tang Shiulam
Ploughman's Lunch, The	BRI	Dominic Muldowney
Policewoman Centerfold	NBC-TV	Fred Karlin
Porky's II: The Next Day	FOX	Carl Zittrer
Prime Times	NBC-TV	William Loose
Prince of Homburg, The	ITA	Giorgio Carnini
Princes, The	FRA	Tony Gatlif
Princess Daisy	NBC-TV	Lalo Schifrin
Prisoners of the Lost Universe	HBO-C	Harry Robinson
Private Life, A	GER	Evelyne Crochet
Prize of Peril, The	FRA	Vladimir Cosma
Prototype	CBS-TV	Billy Goldenberg
Psycho II	UN	Jerry Goldsmith
Puen and Paeng	THAI	Kadee Atkakorn/Samra Karnchanapalin
Quarantine	RUS	Alexej Rybnikov
Quarterback Princess	CBS-TV	James di Pasquale
Quite Far Away	GER	Bernhard Schmitz
Radical Cut	CZE	Zdenek Mart
Rage of Angels	NBC-TV	Billy Goldenberg
Raskenstam	SWE	Lasse Samuelsson
Reaching Out	IND	Elizabeth Mazel
Rebetico	GRE	Stavros Xarhacos
Red Bells: I've Seen the Birth of the New World	ITA/MEX/RUS	Georgy Sviridov
Red Boogie	YUG	Janez Gregorc
Refugees from Dead Man's Cave, The	CUBA	Leo Brouwer/Silvio Rodriguez
Research in Mark Brandenberg	E.GER	Guenther Fischer
Return Engagement	IND	Adrien Belew
Return from Hell	RUM	Cornel Taranu
Return of Captain Invincible, The	AUT	William Motzing
Return of the Jedi	FOX	John Williams
Return of the Man from U.N.C.L.E., The	CBS-TV	Gerald Fried
Return to Eden	BRI	Ton Pa/David Scholastique/Patrick Victor
Returning, The	IND	Harry Manfredini
Reuben, Reuben	FOX	Billy Goldenberg
Revenge, The	ARG	Baby Lopez Furst
Revenge	GRE	Demetris Papademetriou

Revenge of the Ninja	MGM/UA	W. Michael Lewis/Rob Walsh
Revolt of Job	GER/HUN	Zoltan Jeny
Rickshaw Boy	CHN	Qu Xixian
Right of Way	HBO-C	Brad Fiedel
Right Stuff, The	WB	Bill Conti
Right Way, The	SWI	Stephan Wittwer
Riptide	NBC-TV	Pete Carpenter/Mike Post
Risky Business	WB	"Tangerine Dream"
Rita Hayworth: The Love Goddess	CBS-TV	Lalo Schifrin
Roarin' Fifties, The	GER	Klaus Doldinger
Rock & Rule	MGM/UA	Patricia Cullen
Rocking Silver	DEN	Leif Sylvester Petersen
Rogues (Truhanes)	SPA	Jose Nieto
Romantic Comedy	MGM/UA	Marvin Hamlisch
Romantic Story	CZE	Oldrich Flosman
Rose of the Winds, The	CUB/SPA/VEN	Leo Brouwer
Rousters, The (series)	NBC-TV	Pete Carpenter/Mike Post
Ruffian, The	CAN/FRA	Ennio Morricone
Rumble Fish	UN	Stewart Copeland
Rumor, A (Bruit qui Court, Un)	FRA	Pierre Alrand
Runners	BRI	George Fenton
Running Brave	CAN	Mike Post
Running Out	CBS-TV	Lee Holdridge
Ryan's Four (series)	ABC-TV	Randy Edelman
S.A.S.--Terminate with Extreme Prejudice	FRA/GER	Michel Magne
SL-1	IND	Brian Eno/"Popol Vuh"
Sabine Kleist, 7 Years Old	E.GER	Christian Steyer
Sadat	IND-TV	Charles Bernstein
Saddled With a Girl	SWE	Ragnar Grippe
Sahara	MGM/UA	Ennio Morricone
Saigon--Year of the Cat	BRI	George Fenton
Same As It Ever Was	AUT	Brian Eno/"Talking Heads"
Sarah	FRA	Gabriel Yared
Sasame Yuki	JAP	Shinnosuke Okawa
Savage: In the Orient	CBS-TV	Morton Stevens
Savage Weekend	IND	Dov Seltzer
Sawyer and Finn	NBC-TV	Arthur B. Rubinstein
Scalps	IND	Drew Neumann/Eric Rassmussen
Scarecrow and Mrs. King (series)	CBS-TV	Mark Hoder/Arthur B. Rubinstein
Scarface	UN	Giorgio Moroder
Scarlet and the Black, The	CBS-TV	Ennio Morricone
School Outing, A	ITA	Riz Ortolani
Scream, The (Krzyk)	POL	Wojciech Trzcinski
Screwballs	NWP	Tim McCauley

Season in Hakkari, A	GER/TUR	Timur Selcuk
Second Dance	SWE	Jan Bandell
Second Generation, The	YUG	Disciplina Kicme i Azra
Second Thoughts	UN	Henry Mancini
Secret Child, The	FRA	Faton Cahen
Seeing Things (series)	CAN-TV	Philip Schreibman
Separate Tables	HBO-C	Phil Smith
September Gun	CBS-TV	Larry Cansler
Sessions	ABC-TV	Charles Gross
Seventh Man, The	IN	Vaithilaxman
Shadow Dance	FRA	Gabriel Yared
Shadow of Sam Penny, The	CBS-TV	Barry de Vorzon
Shadow of the Earth	FRA/TUN	unlisted
Shane, The (El-aar)	EGY	Hassan Abu el Soud
Shaolin Drunkard	HK	Tang Siu Lam
Shirt Tales, The (series)	NBC-TV	Hoyt Curtin
Shooting Stars	ABC-TV	Dominic Frontiere
Sideroads	FRA	Jean Musy
Siege	CAN	Peter Jermyn/Drew King
Silent Madness (Omega Factor/ Night Killer)	ALM	Barry Salmon
Silent Ocean, The	AUS/GER	Bert Breit
Silkwood	FOX	Georges Delerue
Sins of Dorian Gray, The	ABC-TV	Bernard Hoffer
Sitcom	HBO-C	Tom Wells
Six Pack	NBC-TV	Lance Rubin
Skinny Chico	POR	Rui Veloso
Sky on Location, The	GER	Ann Hankinson
Sleepaway Camp	IND	Edward Bilous
Sleight of Hand (Jogo de Mao)	POR	Luis Cilia
Small and Frye (series)	CBS-TV	Dennis McCarthy
Smokey and the Bandit--Part 3	UN	Larry Cansler
Smorgasbord	WB	Morton Stevens
Smurfs and the Magic Flute, The	IND	Michel Legrand
So Long, Stooge (Tchao Pantin)	FRA	Charelie Couture
Soap and Water	ITA	Fabio Liberatori
Something in Between	YUG	Zoran Simjanovic
Something Wicked This Way Comes	DIS	James Horner
Sonata for a Redhead	CZE	Petr Ulrych
Sorry I'm Late	ITA	Antonio Singara
South Bronx Heroes (Runaways/ Revenge of the Innocents)	IND	Al Zima
Space Cobra	JAP-TV	Kentaro Haneda/Yuji Ohno
Space Raiders	NWP	James Horner
Spacehunter: Adventures in the Forbidden Zone	COL	Elmer Bernstein
Spring Fever	CAN	Fred Mollin
Star Chamber, The	FOX	Michael Small
Star 80	WB	Ralph Burns
Starflight: The Plane That Couldn't Land	ABC-TV	Lalo Schifrin

Station for Two	RUS	Andrei Petrov
Stella	FRA	Philippe Sarde
Still Smokin'	PAR	George S. Clinton
Still the Beaver	CBS-TV	John Cacavas
Sting Is Over, The	ARG/PERU	Luis Maria Serra
Sting II, The	UN	Lalo Schifrin
Stone in the Mouth, A	FRA	Egisto Macchi
Stone River, The	GER	Guenther Fischer
Story of an Encounter	ALG	Safy Bontella
Story of Piera	ITA	Renato Angiulini
Strange Brew	MGM/UA	Charles Fox
Strange Friends	CHN	Zhang Piji
Strange Fruits (Eisenhans)	GER	Bert Grund
Strange Invaders	ORI	John Addison
Strangers in Paradise	IND	"Moonlight Drive"
Stranger's Kiss	ORI	Leandro "Gato" Barbieri
Strata	NZ	Mike Nock
Stray Bullets	FRA	Michel Portal
Street of Mirrors	ITA	Pino Donaggio
Street of the Black Shacks	FRA	Groupe Malavoi
Stroke of Luck (Baraka, La)	FRA	Jacques Arel
Stroker Ace	UN	Al Capps
Stryker	PHI	Ed Gatchalian
Sudden Impact	WB	Lalo Schifrin
Summer Girl	CBS-TV	Angela Morley
Summerspell	IND	Toni Marcus
Sunset Limousine	CBS-TV	Frank Denson
Superman III	WB	Ken Thorne/John Williams
Surprise Party	FRA	Michel Magne/Sergio Renucci
Survivors, The	COL	Paul Chihara
Sutter's Bay	CBS-TV	Artie Butler
Sweet Bunch	GRE	George Hatzinassios
Sweet Sixteen	IND	Ray Ellis
Swing, The	GER	Peer Raben
Sword of the Barbarians, The	ITA	Franco Campanino
Syndicate Sadists (Rambo Takes on the City)	ITA	Franco Micalizzi
Table for Five	WB	Miles Goodman/John Morris
Taste of Sea, A	ITA	Mariano Parrella/ Edouardo Vianello
Taste of Sin, A	IND	Joel Goldsmith
Teacher, The (Sensei)	JAP	Masaru Sato
Tears Are Flowing	RUS	Guy Kancheli
Teddy Baer	SWI	Bruno Spoerri
Teenaged Girl	THAI	Virat Yuthaworn
10 to Midnight	IND	Robert O. Ragland
Terms of Endearment	PAR	Michael Gore
Territory, The	POR	Jorge Arriagada
Terror in the Swamp	IND	Jaime Mendoza-Nava

"Terrorists" in Retirement	FRA	Benoit Charvet/Jean Schwarz
Terry Fox Story, The	CAN	Bill Conti
Testament	PAR	James Horner
There Goes the Neighborhood	NBC-TV	Tom Wells
There Will Be No More Sorrows Nor Oblivion	ARG	Oscar Cardozo Ocampo
These Children Survive Me	JAP	Tadashi Kinoshita
Third Key, The	YUG	Aleksandar Bubanovic
13 Thirteenth Avenue	CBS-TV	Denny Jaeger/Michel Rubini
This Girl for Hire	CBS-TV	Bruce Broughton
Thorn Birds, The	ABC-TV	Henry Mancini
Three Crowns of the Sailor, The	FRA	Jorge Arriagada
Through Naked Eyes	ABC-TV	Gil Melle
Thursday's Child	CBS-TV	Lee Holdridge
Tiger Town	DIS	Eddie Manson
Tight Spot, A (Tesna Koza)	YUG	Vojislav Kostic
Time to Die, A	IND	Ennio Morricone/Robert O. Ragland
Timerider	IND	Michael Nesmith
Tin Man	IND	Bishop Holiday
To Be or Not to Be	FOX	John Morris
To the Rhythm of My Heart	CAN	Jean-Pierre Lefebvre
Tom Swift and Linda Craig Mystery Hour, The	ABC-TV	Jerrold Immel
Too Good to Be True	ABC-TV	Tony Berg
Tornado	ITA	Aldo Tamborrelli
Touched	IND	Shirley Walker
Tough Enough	FOX	Michael Lloyd/Steve Wax
Toxic Love	ITA	Detto Mariano
Trace, The	FRA/SWI	Marc Perrone/Nicola Piovani
Track Two	CAN	Carol Pope/Kevin Staples
Trackdown: Finding the Goodbar Killer	CBS-TV	Stephen Lawrence
Trading Places	PAR	Elmer Bernstein
Trail, The	HK	Bobby Chan
Traitors, The	DEN	Ib Glindemann
Trauma Center (series)	ABC-TV	James di Pasquale
Travis McGee	ABC-TV	Jerrold Immel
Treasure of the Four Crowns	ITA/SPA	Ennio Morricone
Trenchcoat	DIS	Charles Fox
Trespasses	NZ	Bernie Hill
Turkey Shoot	AUT	Brian May
20th Century Chocolate Cake, A	CAN	Andre Vincelli
Twilight Time	MGM/UA	Walter Scharf
Twilight Zone--The Movie	WB	Jerry Goldsmith
Two Guys and a Gal	SWE	Anders Berglund
Two Kinds of Love	CBS-TV	Mark Snow

Two Marriages (series)	ABC-TV	Bruce Broughton/Bodie Chandler
Two of a Kind	FOX	Patrick Williams
Two Worlds of Angelita, The	FRF	Dom Salvador
Uliisees	GER	Anthony Moore/Helge Schneider
Uncommon Love, An	CBS-TV	Miles Goodman
Uncommon Valor	CBS-TV	Bob Summers
Uncommon Valor	PAR	James Horner
Under Fire	ORI	Jerry Goldsmith
Under the Mosquito Net	INDONESIA	Eros Djarot
Underground Passage	GRE	Michalis Grigoriou
Ups & Downs	CAN	Bo Harwood
Utilities	CAN	John Erbe/Mickey Solomon
Utopia	GER	Rolf Bauer
Utu	NZ	John Charles
V	NBC-TV	Joe Harnell
Variety	IND	John Lurie
Vassa	RUS	Vadim Bibergan
Venice Medical	ABC-TV	Jack Elliott
Videodrome	UN	Howard Shore
Vienna Story--Gemini Y and S	JAP	Kazuo Oya
Vigilante	FVI	Jay Chattaway
Violent Breed, The	ITA	Paolo Rustichelli
Virgin People	PHI	Rey Rames
Vive la Sociale!	FRA	Jean-Claude Petit
Vulture, The	HUN	Gyorgy Kovacs
Wacko	IND	Arthur Kempel
Wagner	AUS/BRI/HUN	Ivan Fischer
Wait for Me a Long Time	ARG	Baby Lopez Furst
Wait Till Your Mother Gets Home!	NBC-TV	Ken Harrison
Wall, The (Mur, La)	FRA	Ozan Garip Sahin
Waltz Across Texas	ATL	Steve Dorff
War Games	MGM/UA	Arthur B. Rubinstein, Jr.
Warrior and the Sorceress, The (Kain of Dark Planet)	IND	Louis Saunders
Warrior of the Lost World	ITA	Daniele Patucchi
Warriors of the Wasteland	ITA	Claudio Simonetti
Wars, The	CAN	Glenn Gould
Wavelength	NWP	Tangerine Dream
We Got It Made (series)	NBC-TV	Tom Wells
Weather in the Streets, The	BRI	Carl Davis
Webster (series)	ABC-TV	Steve Nelson
What Price Victory?	AUS	Hans Kann
When Your Lover Leaves	NBC-TV	Randy Edelman
White Lions, The	IND	William Goldstein
White Magic	BUL	Georgi Genkov
White Water Rebels	CBS-TV	Ken Thorne
Whiz Kids (series)	CBS-TV	Paul Chihara

Who Will Love My Children?	ABC-TV	Laurence Rosenthal
Whole of Life, The	SWI	Benedict Jeger
Wicked Lady, The	MGM/UA	Tony Banks
Wife for My Son, A	ALG	Philippe Arthuys
Wild Bunch	GER	"Extrabreit"/Marianne Rosenberg
Wild Duck, The	AUT	Simon Walker
Wild Horses	NZ	Dave Fraser
Wild Side, The (Suburbia)	NWP	Alex Gibson
Wild Style	IND	Fred Brathwaite/Chris Stein
Will There Really Be a Morning?	CBS-TV	Billy Goldenberg
Winds of Jarrah, The	AUT	Bruce Smeaton
Winds of War, The	ABC-TV	Robert Cobert
Windy Places: Torn Apart	SWI	"West Block"
Winter Journey	BEL	Marc Herouet
Winter, 1960	BEL	Marc Herouet
Wishman	ABC-TV	Fred Karlin
With Burning Patience	GER/POR	Roberto Lecaros
Without a Trace	FOX	Jack Nitzsche
Without Witnesses	RUS	Eduard Artemyev
Wizards and Warriors (series)	TV	Lee Holdridge
Woman Across the Way, The	GRE	Stavrous Logaridis
Woman Flambee, A	GER	Peer Raben
Women of San Quentin	NBC-TV	John Cacavas
Words to Say It	FRA	Jean-Marie Senia
Xtro	NLC	Harry Bromley Davenport/Sheldon Leigh Palmer
Yellow Rose, The (series)	NBC-TV	Jerrold Immel
Yellowbeard	ORI	John Morris
Yentl	MGM/UA	Michel Legrand
Yor, the Hunter from the Future	COL	John Scott/Maurizio and Guido de Angelis
You Disturb Me	ITA	Paolo Conte
Young Bridegroom, The	FRA	Luis Enrique Bacalov
Young Ladies' War, The	FRA	Georges and Pierre-Maria Baux
Young Lovers	ISR	Nurit Hirsch
Young Olympians, The	IND	Michael Shadow
Your Place or Mine	CBS-TV	Gerald Alters
Youth of a Genius, The	RUS	Eduard Artemyev
Zaman	BEL	Franois Glorieux
Zappa	DEN	Bo Holten
Zelig	WB	Dick Hyman
Zig Zag Story	FRA	Patrick Schulmann
Zombie Island Massacre	IND	Harry Manfredini
Zorro and Son (series)	CBS-TV	George Duning
Zu (Warriors from the Magic Mountain)	HK	Tang Siu-Lam

1984

Abel Gance and His Napoleon	FRA	Hubert Rostaing/Betty Willemetz
Aces Go Places III	HK	Noel Quinlan
Act, The	FVI	Phil Goldston/John Sebastian
Adventures of Buckaroo Banzai: Across the 8th Dimension, The	FOX	Bones Howe
Afternoon Affair, An	HUN	Gabor Presser
Against All Odds	COL	Larry Carlton/Michel Colombier
Agitated Winds	GRE	Costas Haralambides/ Pieris Pieretis/George Spanos
Air of Crime, The	SWI	Peer Raben
Airwolf	CBS-TV	Sylvester Levay
Ake and His World	SWE	Thomas Lindahl
Akropolis Now	SWI	Benedict Jeger
Aldo and Junior	FRA	Patrick Schulmann
Alexyz	IND	John Aschenbrenner
All of Me	UN	Patrick Williams
All That Rhythm	ITA	Ettore Fioravanti/ Marcello Modugno
All the Rivers Run	HBO-C	Bruce Rowland
Almeria Case, The	SPA	Ricardo Miralles
Almonds and Raisins	BRI	John Altman
Almost You	FOX	Jonathan Elias
Alphabet City	IND	Nile Rodgers
Amazons	ABC-TV	Basil Poledouris
Ambassador, The	IND	Dov Seltzer
Ambassador, The	YUG	Alfi Kabiljo
American Dreamer	WB	Lewis Furey
American Taboo	IND	Dan Brandt/Dana Libonati
Among the Cinders	GER/NZ	Jan Preston
Anatomy of an Illness	CBS-TV	Brad Fiedel
... And Pigs Might Fly	BRI	Trevor Jones
Angel	NWP	Craig Safan
Angela	CAN	Henry Mancini
Angela's War	FIN	Esa Helasvuo
Anna's Mother	GER	Kristian Schultze
Anne Devlin	IRE	Robert Boyle
Annie's Coming Out	AUT	Simon Walker
Annunciation	HUN	Istvan Martha
Another Country	BRI	Michael Storey
Another Man's Shoes	CBS-TV	Jeff Barry/Nancy Barry
Antarctica	JAP	Vangelis
Arctic Sea Calls, The	E.GER	Uwe Hilprecht
At Your Service	NBC-TV	David Wheatley

Athalia	ISR	Nahum Heiman
Atomic Station	ICE	Karl Sighvatsson
Aussie Assault	AUT	Mario Millo
Autograph, The	FRA/GER	Juan Jose Mosalini
Autumn Almanac	HUN	Mihaly Uigh
Ave Maria	FRA	Jorge Arriagada
Baby	GER	"SPLIFF"
Bachelor Party	FOX	Robert Folk
Back Together	CBS-TV	David Franko
Balkan Spy, The	YUG	Vojislav Kostic
Bao and His Son	CHN	Wang Ming
Bastille	HOL	Boudewijn Tarenskeen
Bay Boy	CAN	Claude Bolling
Bear, The	EMB	Martin Bandier/Bill Conti/Martin Koppelman
Beasts, The	FRA	Philippe Servain
Bedroom Eyes	CAN	Paul Hoffert/John Tucker
Bedrooms	HBO-C	Ray Ellis
Before Stonewall	IND	Roy Ramsing/Lori Seligman
Bertoldo, Bertoldino and Cacasenno	ITA	Nicola Piovani
Best Defense	PAR	Patrick Williams
Best Kept Secrets	ABC-TV	Gil Melle
Best Legs in the Eighth Grade, The	HBO-C	Lee Holdridge
Beverly Hills Cop	PAR	Harold Faltermeyer
Beyond Sorrow, Beyond Pain	SWE	Gunnar Edander
Beyond the Walls	ISR	Ilan Wirtzberg
Bianca	ITA	Franco Piersanti
Bicycles Are for the Summer	SPA	Francisco Guerrero
Bill, The (Addition, L')	FRA	Jean-Claude Petit
Birdy	TST	Peter Gabriel
Black Cat, The	ITA	Pino Donaggio
Black List	FRA	Alain Wisniak
Black Room, The	IND	James Achley/Art Podell
Blame It on Rio	FOX	Oscar Castro Neves/Ken Wannberg
Blame It on the Night	TST	Ted Whitfield
Blind Date	NLC	Stanley Myers
Bliss	ABC-TV	J. A. C. Redford
Blood Is Always Hot	CHN	Zhang Piji
Blood of Others, The	CAN/FRA	Mathieu Chabrol/Francois Dompierre
Blood Simple	IND	Carter Burwell
Blue Thunder (series)	ABC-TV	Frank Denison
Bluebeard	GER/SWI	Wojiech Kilar
Boatman, The	PHI	Jaime Fabregas
Body Double	COL	Pino Donaggio

Bolero	IND	Elmer Bernstein/Peter Bernstein
Bon Plaisir, Le	FRA	Georges Delerue
Born Again	RUS	Edisson Denissov
Bostonians, The	BRI	Richard Robbins
Bounder, The	CBS-TV	Dana Kaproff
Bounty, The	ORI	Vangelis
Boy and a Girl, A	ITA	Manuel de Sica
Boy from Ebalus, The	ITA	Marcello Pasquali
Boy Who Disappeared, The	DEN	Kenneth Knudsen
Boys in Blue, The	CBS-TV	Lee Holdridge
Brady's Escape	IND	Charles Gross
Breakin'	MGM	Michael Boyd/Gary Remal
Breakin' 2: Electric Boogaloo	TST	Mike Linn
Breaking the Silence: The Generation After the Holocaust	IND	Rosalie Gerut
Breakout	BRI	Harry Robertson
Breed Apart, A	ORI	Maurice Gibb
Broadway Boys	IND	David Mann
Broadway Danny Rose	ORI	Dick Hyman
Broken Mirrors	HOL	Lodewijk de Boer
Brother from Another Planet, The	IND	K. Mason Daring
Brothers (series)	SHO-C	Dan Foliart/Howard Pearl
Buddy System, The	FOX	Patrick Williams
Bulldogs and Cherries	CZE	Petr Hapka
Bums, The (Strawanzer)	AUS/GER	Peter Zwetkoff
Burning Angel	FIN	"Hector"
Burning Land	ISR	Gerard Pullicino
Buster's World	DEN	Bo Holten
C.H.U.D.	NWP	Cooper Hughes
Caged Fury	PHI	Ernani Cuenco
Caged Women	FRA/ITA	Luigi Ceccarelli
Cal	IRE	Mark Knopfler
Calamity Jane	CBS-TV	Fred Karlin
Calendar Girl Murders, The	ABC-TV	Brad Fiedel
Call to Glory (Air Force) (series)	ABC-TV	Charles Gross
Camel Boy, The	AUT	Bob Young
Camila	ARG/SPA	Luis Maria Serra
Camille	CBS-TV	Allyn Ferguson
Campo Europa	SWI	Jacques Robellaz
Cannonball Run II	WB	Al Capps
Carpet Change (Knock on the Wrong Door)	GER	Joerg Evers
Case of Irresponsibility, A	ITA	Luis Enrique Bacalov
Cat on a Hot Tin Roof	SHO	Tom Scott
Celebrity	NBC-TV	Leonard Rosenman
Census Taker, The	IND	Kay Seagrave
Champions	BRI	Carl Davis
Chaos	ITA	Nicola Piovani

Chapiteau	SWI	Rich Schwab
Charmer, The (Joli Coeur, Le)	FRA	Yves Gilbert
Cheaters, The (Tricheurs, Les)	FRA/GER	Peer Raben
Cheech & Chong's The Corsican Brothers	ORI	"Geo"
Chewingum	ITA	Giancarlo Bigazzi
Chieftain, The	NOR	Bent Aserud/Geir Boehren
Childhood Garden, A	RUS	Gleb May
Children in the Crossfire	NBC-TV	Brad Fiedel
Children of Pride	IND	Tim Cappello
Children of the Corn	NWP	Jonathan Elias
Children of the Steps	ISR	Alex Kagan
Chile, I Do Not Call Your Name in Vain	FRA/CHILE	Isabel Parra
Chinese Boxes	BRI/GER	Guenther Fischer
Choose Me	IND	Teddy Pendergrass
Christina	SPA	Ted Scotto
Christmas Carol, A	CBS-TV	Nick Bicat
Christmas Vacation	ITA	Giorgio Calabrese
Cinderella '80	FRA/ITA	Guido and Maurizio de Angelis
Ciske the Rat	HOL	Erik van der Wurff
City Girl, The	CAN	Scott Wilk
City Heat	WB	Lennie Niehaus
City Never Sleeps, The	GRE	Yannis Kostidakis
Claretta	ITA	Gerard Schurmann
Cloak and Dagger	UN	Brian May
Close Behind the Door	AUS	Heinz Leonhardsberger
Cold Room, The	BRI	Michael Nyman
Comfort and Joy	BRI	Mark Knopfler
Committed	IND	Phillip Johnston
Company of Wolves, The	BRI	George Fenton
Conan the Destroyer	UN	Basil Poledouris
Concrete Beat	ABC-TV	Artie Kane
Conquest	ITA/MEX/SPA	Claudio Simonetti
Constance	NZ	John Charles
Contract for Life: The S.A.D.D. Story	CBS-TV	Misha Segal
Coolangatta Gold, The	AUT	Bill Conti
Cotton Club, The	ORI	John Barry
Country	DIS	Charles Gross
Courageous Blacksmith, The	CZE	Petr Ulrych
Cover Up	CBS-TV	Richard Lewis Warren
Cracker Brothers, The	NBC-TV	Artie Butler
Crackers	UN	Paul Chihara
Crazy Like a Fox	CBS-TV	Mark Snow
Crime, A	ITA	Guido and Maurizio de Angelis
Crime at the Blue Gay	ITA	Fabio Frizzi
Crimes of Passion	NWP	Rick Wakeman

Crossing, The (Paar)	IN	Goutam Ghose
Daddy Dearest	IND	"New York City Jazz Quadrille"
Dance Music	ITA	Paolo Casa
Danube Waltzes	AUS	Bert Breit
Dark Enemy	BRI	David Hewson
Dark Mirror	ABC-TV	Dominic Frontiere
Darlings!	HOL	Van Hamert
Day at the Beach, A	HOL	Rheiner Henzel/Willem van Echeren
Day Longer Than the Night, The	RUS	Guy Kancheli
Day Pedro Infante Died, The	MEX	Nicolas Echevarria
Dead Teach the Living, The	CZE	Svetozar Stur
Deadly Intruder	IND	John McCauley
Dear Karl (Lieber Karl)	AUS/GER	Maran Gosov
Death Warmed Up	NZ	Mark Nicholas
Deathstalker	NWP	Oscar Cardoso Ocampo
Descent of the Nine, The	GRE	Michalis Christodoulidis
Desire (Desiderio)	ITA	Nicola Piovani
Desiree	HOL	Ronald Snijders
Diary (Naplo)	HUN	Zsolt Dome
Didi and His Double	GER	Harold Faltermeyer
Discotheque, The	ITA	Franco Chiaravalle/ Nino D'Angelo
Doctor's Story, A	NBC-TV	Randy Edelman
Dog, The (Chien, Le)	FRA	"The Scorpions"
Dog Day (Canicule)	FRA	Francis Lai
Dollmaker, The	ABC-TV	John Rubinstein
Domestic Life (series)	CBS-TV	David Frank
Don Quixote	ITA	Eugenio Bennato
Don't Kill God	BRI	Ennio Morricone
Don't Open Till Christmas	BRI	Des Dolan
Doom of the Berhof Lonely Farm, The	CZE/POL	Jozef Revallo
Doomed Love	IND	Evan Lurie
Dorado--One Way	GER	Gernot Voltz
Double Deal	AUT	Bruce Smeaton
Double Decker	HK	Chris Babida
Double Feature (Sesion Continua)	SPA	Jesus Gluck
Double Trouble	NBC-TV	Ray Colcord/Mark Snow
Down Home	CBS-TV	Patrick Williams
Dragon's Lair	ABC-TV	John Debney
Draw!	HBO-C	Ken Wannberg
Dreams (series)	CBS-TV	Trevor Veitch
Dreamscape	FOX	Maurice Jarre
Duck and Drake Adventure, A	HUN	Istvan Martha
Duck Factory, The (series)	NBC-TV	Tom Wells
Dune	UN	"Toto"
E/R (series)	CBS-TV	Jimmy Webb
Early Snowfall in Munich	YUG	Ozren Depolo
Earthlings, The	ABC-TV	Jack Elliott

Easy Times Are Over, The	GER	"Hurricane"
Electric Dreams	MGM	Giorgio Moroder
Element of Crime, The	DEN	Bo Holten
Ellie	FVI	Bob Pickering
Ellis Island	CBS-TV	John Addison
Emmanuelle 4	FRA	Michel Magne
Empire (series)	CBS-TV	Patrick Williams
End of the Miracle, The	HUN	"Veszi"
Enrico IV (Henry IV)	ITA	Astor Piazzolla
Epilog	SPA	Juan Jose Garcia Caffi
Ernie Kovacs: Between the Laughter	ABC-TV	Ralph Burns
Errant Lives	MEX	Antonio Avitia
Escape from Grumble Gulch	FRA/HB	Claude Bolling/Shuki Levy/Haim Saban
Eskimo Woman Feels Cold	HUN	Gabor Lukin/Mihaly Vigh
Eternal Feelings, The	AUS/GER	Herbert Groenemeyer
Every Picture Tells a Story	BRI	Michael Storey
Evil That Men Do, The	TST	Ken Thorne
Evita--Who Wants to Hear May Hear	ARG	Lito Nebbia
Exterminator 2	IND	David Spear
Exterminators of the Year 3000, The	ITA/SPA	Detto Mariano
Eyes of Fire	IND	Brad Fiedel
Fair Game (Freiwild)	GER/POL	Andrzej Korzynski
Fairy Tale of Wanderings, A	CZE/RUM/RUS	Alfred Schnitke
Falling in Love	PAR	Dave Grusin
False Confidences, The	FRA	Jean Musy
Family Affair, A	HK	Mahmood Rumjahn
Family Light Affair	HK	So Chun Hou/Stephen Shing
Family Secrets	NBC-TV	Charles Fox
Fantasize	IND	Garth Evans
Fantastic World of D. C. Collins, The	NBC-TV	A. S. Dimond/Dennis Dreith/Mitch Margo
Fantasy Man	AUT	Adrian Payne
Fantozzi Takes It on the Chin Again	ITA	Gambrini
Far from Poland	IND	Michael Sahl
Far Pavilions, The	HBO-C	Carl Davis
Fast Talking	AUT	Sharon Calcraft
Fatal Games	IND	Shuki Levy
Fatally Wounded for Love of Life	RUM	Adrian Enescu
Fear (Angst)	AUS	Klaus Schulze
Fear City	IND	Dick Halligan
Fear of Falling	GER	Eberhard Schoener
Fellow Travellers	ISR	Rafi Kadishsohn
Femme de l'Hotel, La	CAN	Yves Lafferriere
Ferocious	SPA	"Coro Infantil Villa de Madrid"

Festival (Utsav)	IN	Laxmikant Pyarelal
Final Call	GER	Nicolas Economou
Finder of Lost Loves	ABC-TV	Artie Kane
Finders Keepers	GER	Peter Lentz/Horst Zinsmeister
Finders Keepers	WB	Ken Thorne
Fire on East Train 34	RUS	Marc Minkov
Fire on Sight (Tir a Vue)	FRA	Gabriel Yared
Firestarter	UN	"Tangerine Dream"
Firm Forever, A	GER	Claus Deubel/Paul Esslinger
First & Ten (series)	HBO-C	Dave Fisher/Bruce Kernohan
First Contact	IND	Ron Carpenter
First Olympics--Athens, The	NBC-TV	Bruce Broughton
Firstborn	PAR	Michael Small
Five-O-One	IND	Rick Rodwell
Flash of Green, A	IND	Charles Engstrom
Flashpoint	TST	"Tangerine Dream"
Flesh of Your Flesh	SA	Mario Gomez Vignes
Fleshburn	CRO	Don Felder
Flight #90: Disaster on the Potomac	NBC-TV	Gil Melle
Flight of the Raven	ICE/SWE	Hans-Erik Phillip
Flight of the Sphinx, The	FRA	Michel Goguelat
Flight to Berlin	BRI/GER	Irmin Schmidt
Foggy Landscapes	YUG	Aleksandar Habic
Footloose	PAR	Miles Goodman/Becky Shargo
For a Young Lady and Her Male Companions	BUL	Kiril Dontchev
For All People, For All Time	IND	Sheldon Leigh Palmer
Forced Witness	ISR	Dov Seltzer
Fort Saganne	FRA	Philippe Sarde
Four Days in July	BRI	Rachel Portman
Four Eyes	NBC-TV	Pete Carpenter/Mike Post
Four Seasons, The (series)	CBS-TV	John Cacavas
"Frank" and I (Liberated Lady)	FRA	Marc Hillman
Frankenstein 90	FRA	Armando Trovajoli
French Lieutenant's Boys, The	IND	Costello Presley
Friday the 13th--The Final Chapter	PAR	Harry Manfredini
From Somalia with Love	FRA	Jean Wiener
Front Romance, A	RUS	Igor Kantjukov/Petr Todorovskij
Frontier (De Grens)	HOL	Boudewijn Tarenskeen
Future Interior, The	CAN	Ginette Bellavance/Alain Corneau
Future Is Woman, The	FRA/GER/ITA	Carlo Savina
Future of Emily, The	FRA/GER	Juergen Knieper
Future Schlock	AUT	John McCubbery

Ganga Maya	FRA	Dominique Bertrand
Garbo Talks	MGM	Cy Coleman
Gasping (Atemnot)	AUS	Dead Nittels/Konstantin Wecker
Generation Apart, A	IND	Peter Arnow
George and Mildred (series)	BRI-TV	Roger Webb
George Stevens: A Filmmaker's Journey	IND	Carl Davis
George Washington	CBS-TV	Laurence Rosenthal
Get Along Gang, The (series)	CBS-TV	Shuki Levy/Haim Saban
Getting Physical	CBS-TV	William Goldstein
Ghost from Bahia, The	BRA	Denoy de Oliveira/Luiz Carlos Gomes/Julinho Vicente
Ghostbusters	COL	Elmer Bernstein
Giarres (City of Wolves)	GER	Peer Raben
Gimmie an "F"	FOX	Jan Hammer
Giuseppe Fava: Sicilian Like Me	ITA	Riz Ortolani
Give My Regards to Broad Street	FOX	George Martin
Glassful of Snow, A	ITA	Carlo Rustichelli/Paolo Rustichelli
Glitter	ABC-TV	Peter Eric Meyers/ Lalo Schifrin
Go Tell It on the Mountain	IND	Webster Lewis
Going Bananas (series)	NBC-TV	Shuki Levy/Haim Saban
Golden River	BUL	Mitko Shterev
Gone to Seed	ARG	Pocho Lapouble
Good Bourgeois, The	BRA	Paulo Moura
Good Fight, The	FRF	Wendy Blackstone/ Bernardo Palombo
Good King Dagobert	FRA/ITA	Guido and Maurizio de Angelis
Good Sport, A	CBS-TV	Mark Snow
Grandview, U.S.A.	WB	Thomas Newman
Green Years	BRA	Nelson Coelho de Castro/ Augusto Licks/Nei Lisboa
Gremlins	WB	Jerry Goldsmith
Greystoke: The Legend of Tarzan, Lord of the Apes	WB	John Scott
Growing Pains	NWP	"Sparks"
Guelibik	GER/TUR	Zulfi Livaneli
Gwendoline	FRA	Pierre Bachelet
Habris (Ybris)	ITA	Pietro Sassu
Hadley's Rebellion	IND	Mike Post
Hairdresser, The	ISR	Ilan Mokhiakh
Half-Truth (Ardh Satya)	IN	Ajit Verman
Hambone and Hillie	NWP	Georges Garvarentz
Happy Alcoholic, The	BRI	Ifor Ab Gwilym
Happy Easter	FRA	Philippe Sarde
Hard Choices	IND	Jay Chattaway

Hard Knox	NBC-TV	Pete Carpenter/Mike Post
Hard to Hold	UN	Tom Scott
Harry & Son	ORI	Henry Mancini
Hawaiian Heat	ABC-TV	J. A. C. Redford/Tom Scott
Heart of the Stag	NZ	Leonard Rosenman
Heart Side, Garden Side	FRA	Serge Franklin
Heartbreakers	ORI	"Tangerine Dream"
Heaven Earth Man	BRI	David Hewson
Hector	SPA	Ovidi Montilor/Toti Soler
Helen Keller--The Miracle Continues	IND-TV	J. A. C. Redford
Hell Train	FRA	Michel Legrand
Helter-Skelter	HUN	"KFT Group"
Her Life as a Man	NBC-TV	John Cacavas
Heroes and Sidekicks--Indiana Jones and the Temple of Doom	CBS-TV	William Loose/Jack Tillar/ John Williams
Hey Babe!	CAN	Roger Pilon/"Mature Adults"/Gino Soccio
Highway to Heaven (series)	NBC-TV	David Rose
Hinterland Nights	BRA	Tavinho Moura
His and Hers	CBS-TV	Dan Foliart/Howard Pearl
Hit, The	BRI	Paco de Lucia
Hollywood Hot Tubs	IND	Joel Goldsmith
Holy Innocents, The	SPA	Anton Garcia Abril
Home and the World, The (Ghare Baire)	IN	Satyajit Ray
Homecoming	CHN/HK	"Kitaro"
Homeland	GER	Nikos Mamangakis
Hookers on Davie Street	CAN	"The Crusaders"
Horizon, The	JAP	Hikaru Hiyayashi
Horror Vacui	GER	Maran Gosov
Horsemen of the Storm, The	FRA/YUG	Michel Portal
Hot Dog--The Movie	MGM/UA	Peter Bernstein
Hot Men Observed	IND	Shawn Foreman
Hot Moves	IND	Louis Forestieri
Hot Pursuit (series)	NBC-TV	Joe Harnell
Hotel New York	IND	Lee Erwin
House of Water, The	VEN	Juan Carlo Nunez
Housewarming, The	HUN	Gyorgy Ukan
How Chileans Love	CHILE	Jose Luis Correa
Howling II ... Your Sister Is a Werewolf, The	BRI	Steve Parsons
Hundra	SPA	Ennio Morricone
Hunter of the Heart	GER	Andreas Darau
Hunters of the Golden Cobra	ITA	Carlo Savina
Hustlers	IND	"The Riddlemedics"
Husty	JAP	Kentaro Haneda

I Don't Want to Be Grown-Up	RUS	Gennadi Gladkov/Igor Kantyukov
I Gave at the Office	NBC-TV	Tony Greco
I Shall Always Stand Guard	POL	Wojiech Kilar
I Told You So	YUG	Ljupco Konstantinov
Ice Pirates, The	MGM/UA	Bruce Broughton
Iceman	UN	Bruce Smeaton
Illusive Summer of '68, The	YUG	Zoran Hristic
Image of Dorian Gray in the Yellow Press, The	GER	Peer Raben
Imposter, The	ABC-TV	Craig Safan
Impulse	FOX	Paul Chihara
In the Middle of the Night	DEN	Kim Larsen
Incinerator, The	ITA	Richard Benson
Indiana Jones and the Temple of Doom	PAR	John Williams
Innocent Prey	AUT	Brian May
Inside Man, The	BRI/SWE	Stefan Nilsson
Investigators, The	HBO-C	Bruce Kernohan
Invitation to Hell	ABC-TV	Sylvester Levay
Irreconcilable Differences	IND	Paul de Senneville
Isaac Littlefeathers	CAN	Paul J. Zaza
It Came Upon a Midnight Clear	IND-TV	Arthur B. Rubinstein, Jr.
Jack of Spades	GER	Hubert Bartholomae
Jacques Mesrine	FRA	Gil Slavin
Jagger & Spaghetti--The Supper Bluffers	GER	Bodo Staiger
Jan Amos' Peregrination	CZE	Otmar Macha
Jaws of Life, The	YUG	Brana Zivkovic
Jealousy	ABC-TV	Jimmie Haskell/Gil Melle
Jean-Louis Barrault--A Man of the Theater	FRA	Pierre Boulez/Jean-Pierre Stora
Jerk, Two, The	NBC-TV	Frank Denison/Phil Galdston/John Sebastian
Jesse Owens Story, The	IND-TV	Michel Legrand
Jessie (series)	ABC-TV	John Cacavas
Jewel in the Crown, The	PBS-TV	George Fenton
Jigsaw Man, The	BRI	John Cameron
Joe Louis--For All Time	IND	Bill Zampino
Johnny Dangerously	FOX	John Morris
Joint Custody: A New Kind of Family	NDF	Peter Fish
Journey Into a Secret Life	GER	Heiner Goebbels
Journey to the Capital	GRE	Thanos Mikroutsikos
Joy of Sex	PAR	Bishop Holiday/Scott Lipsker/Harold Payne
Judge, The	FRA	Luis Enrique Bacalov
Just the Way You Are	MGM	Vladimir Cosma
K. u. K.	AUS	Gabi Kepplinger
Kaddish	IND	Andy Statman

Karate Kid, The	COL	Bill Conti
Karkalou	GRE	Charlotte Van Gelder
Karnal	PHI	Ryan Cayabyab
Kate and Allie (series)	CBS-TV	John Leffler/Ralph Schuckett
Keeping Up with the Joneses	CBS-TV	Jack Elliott/Allyn Ferguson
Kemira: Diary of a Strike	AUT	Elizabeth Drake
Khandar	IN	Bhaskar Chandawarkar
Kidd Video	NBC	Shuki Levy/Haim Saban
Kidnapping, The (Rapt, Le)	FRA/SWI	Serge Franklin
Kill the Referee	FRA	Alain Chamfort
Killers, The	IND	Bill Boydstun/Doug Lynner
Killing Fields, The	WB	Mike Oldfield
Killpoint	CRO	Herman Jeffreys/Daryl Stevenett
Kim	CBS-TV	Marc Wilkinson
King of China, The	FRA	Michel Portal
Kipperbang	BRI	David Earl
Kitchen Table Talk with Women Rebels	AUS	Carla Bley
Knights of the City (Cry of the City)	NWP	Misha Segal
Knockout (Nacaut)	MEX	Gerardo Suarez
Kovacs	GER	Roman Schwaller
Kusameikyu	FRA/JAP	J. A. Seazer
Lace	ABC-TV	Nick Bicat
Ladies and Gentlemen	ITA	Mauro Pagani
Lady Doctors (Arztinnen)	GER/SWE/SWI	Horst Seemann
Laisse-Beton	ALG/FRA	Jean-Pierre Mas
Land of Doom	IND	Mark Governor
Land of Miracles	HUN	Zsolt Dome
Lassiter	WB	Ken Thorne
Last Bastion, The	AUT-TV	Colin Stead
Last Broomete, The	CHILE	Carlos Fernandez
Last Days of Pompeii, The	ABC-TV	Trevor Jones
Last Evenings with Theresa	SPA	J. M. Bardagi
Last Horror Film, The	IND	Jesse Frederick/Jeff Koz
Last Hunter, The	ITA	Franco Micalizzi
Last Leaf, The	IND-TV	Larry Bastian
Last Night of Madam Chin, The	HK/TAI	Chen Chi Yuan
Last of the Great Survivors, The	CBS-TV	Artie Butler
Last Starfighter, The	UN	Craig Safan
Last Summer, The	FIN/SWE	Ragnar Grippe
Laughterhouse	BRI	Dominic Muldowney
Lawyer, The	EGY	Haney Shenouda
Lead Soldiers	SPA	Josef Mas
Led by the Nose	FRA	Vladimir Cosma
Legend of the Mermaid	JAP	Toshiyuki Honda

Lekha's Death--A Flashback	IN	M. B. Srinivasan
Leopard, The	FRA	Claude Bolling
Liberty at Night	FRA	Faton Cahen
License to Kill	CBS-TV	Laurence Rosenthal
Light Physical Injuries	HUN	Tamas Somlo
Lion of Flanders, The	BEL	Ruud Bos
Listen to the City	CAN	Gordon Deppe
Little Drummer Girl, The	WB	Dave Grusin
Little House: Bless All the Dear Children	NBC-TV	David Rose
Little House: The Last Farewell	NBC-TV	David Rose
Little Jerk (P'tit Con)	FRA	Vladimir Cosma
Little Klas in the Trunk	DEN/SWE	Monica Dominique
Little Train Robbery, The	YUG	Neven Franges
Lives (Vidas/Survivors)	POR	To Neto
Loafing and Camouflage	GRE	Nicos Mamangakis
London and Davis in New York	CBS-TV	Arthur Kempel
Lonely Guy, The	UN	Jerry Goldsmith
Long Live Life!	FRA	Didier Barbelivien
Long Live Women!	FRA	Nicolas Errera
Lost Honor of Kathryn Beck, The	CBS-TV	Laurence Rosenthal
Louisiana	CAN/FRA/ITA	Claude Bolling
Love in a Fallen City	HK	Lam Man-Yee
Love Is Not an Argument	GER	Gunther Fischer
Love Is Where the Trouble Begins	GER	Heiner Goebbels
Love Streams	MGM/UA	Bo Harwood
Love Thy Neighbor	ABC-TV	Georges Delerue
Love Unto Death	FRA	Hans Werner Henze
Lovers of the Lord of the Night, The	MEX	Pedro Pacencia/Pancho Saenz
Low Visibility	CAN	Martin Gotfrit
Lunar Rainbow	RUS	Eduard Artemyev
Lust in the Dust	IND	Peter Matz
Luther Is Dead	GER	Reiner Bohm/Reinhard Hoffmann/Dagmar Jaenicke/Bernhard Wageringel
Magic Moments	ITA	Matia Bazar
Main Theme	JAP	Osamu Shiomura
Majdhar	BRI	Ustad Imrat Khan
Making the Grade	MGM	Basil Poledouris
Malambo	AUS	Flora St. Loup
Mama Happy ...?	AUS	Roli Krauss
Man from Mallorca, The	SWE	Bjoern Jason Lindh
Man Labeled to Die, A	BRA	Rogerio Rossini
Man With a Valise, The	FRA	Jerome Levy (noise score)
Man Without Memory	SWI	Jonas C. Haefeli
Manhunt, The	GOL	Francesco de Masi
Maria de mi Corazon	MEX	Joaquin Gutierrez Heras
Maria's Lovers	MGM	Gary Remal

Mario	CAN	Francois Dompierre
Married Man, A	IND-TV	Wilfred Josephs
Masculine Mystique, The	CAN	Richard Gresko
Mass Appeal	UN	Bill Conti
Massive Retaliation	IND	Paul Potyen/Harn Soper
Master, The (series)	NBC-TV	Les Hooper/Gene Kraft
Master of Ballantrae, The	CBS-TV	Bruce Broughton
Master of the Game	CBS-TV	Allyn Ferguson
Matter of Sex, A	NBC-TV	Matthew McCauley
Maybe It's Love	HK	Noel Quinlan
Meatballs II	TST	Ken Harrison
Melvin, Son of Alvin	AUT	Colin Stead
Memed My Hawk	BRI/YUG	Manos Hadjidakis
Merry Marriage, The	YUG	Jani Golob
Mesrine	FRA	Jean-Pierre Rusconi
Miami Vice (series)	NBC-TV	Jan Hammer
Micki & Maude	COL	Lee Holdridge
Midsummer Night's Dream, A	BRI/SPA	Carlos Miranda
Mighty Orbots, The (series)	ABC-TV	Yuji Ohno
Mike's Murder	WB	John Barry/Joe Jackson
Milan '83	ITA	Mike Oldfield
Mint Tea	FRA	Lahlou Tighrent
Miracle of Joe Petrel, The	JAP	Ryudo Uzaki
Mirage, The (Maya Miriga)	IN	Bhaskar Chandawarkar
Mirror, The	GER	Brynmor Jones
Mirrors (Marianne)	IND	Stephen Lawrence
Mischief (Frevel)	GER	Brian Eno
Missing in Action	IND	Jay Chattaway
Mission of No Return	N.KOR	Kim Chi-hon
Mr. Mom	ABC-TV	Dave Fisher
Mr. Success	NBC-TV	David Frank
Mrs. Latter's Pension	POL	Zdzislaw Szostak
Mrs. Soffel	MGM	Mark Isham
Mistral's Daughter	CBS-TV	Vladimir Cosma
Misunderstanding	GRE	Michalis Grigoriou
Misunderstood	MGM/UA	Michael Hoppe
Mixed Blood	IND	Andy Hernandez
Mob War	IND	Bobby Davis
Model Behavior	IND	Phil Galdston/Andy Goldmark
Modern American Composers I	BRI	John Cage/Meredith Monk
Moritz Inside the Advertising Pillar	E.GER	Karl-Ernst Sasse
Morning in Alabama (German Lawyer, A)	GER	Markus Urchs
Morning Mist	AUS	Georg Herrnstadt
Moscow on the Hudson	COL	David McHugh
Motel	MEX	Eduardo Diazmunoz
Mother's Meat and Freud's Flesh	CAN	"Trio"

Muppets Take Manhattan, The	TST	Ralph Burns
Murder at the Nation's Senate	ARG	Baby Lopez Furst
Murder in Ecstasy	HOL	Arthur Cune
Murder, She Wrote (series)	CBS-TV	John Addison/David Bell
Mutilator, The (Fall Break)	IND	Michael Minard
My Granny's House	DEN	Bent Fabricius-Bjerre
My Kind of Town	CAN	Charles Wilkinson
My Mother's Secret Life	ABC-TV	Brad Fiedel
My Soul's Adventure	GER	Ariel Kalma
Mystery of the Morca, The	ITA	Giovanna Marini
Mystic Warrior, The	ABC-TV	Gerald Fried
Nadia	IND-TV	Christopher L. Stone
Naked Face, The	MGM	Michael J. Lewis
Nancy Astor (series)	PBS-TV	Stanley Myers
Natural, The	TST	Randy Newman
Nature's Revenge	SWE	Ulf Dageby
Naughty Boys	HOL	Mark Naes
Nemo (Dream Cne)	BRI/FRA	Gabriel Yared
Never Again	ABC-TV	Ira Newborn
Neverending Story, The	GER	Klaus Doldinger/Giorgio Moroder
New York Nights	IND	Linda Schreyer
Next Victim, The	BRA	Marcus Vinicius
Night and Its Price, The	GER	Piet Klocke
Night Court (series)	NBC-TV	Jack Elliott
Night Patrol (Ronde de Nuit)	FRA	Ivan Julien/Hubert Rostaing
Night Shadows (Mutant)	FVI	Richard Band
Night Soldier	ISR	Alex Kagan
Night They Arrested Fatima, The	EGY	Omar Khairat
Night They Saved Christmas, The	ABC-TV	Charles Gross
Nightmare on Elm Street, A	NLC	Charles Bernstein
Nights Without Moons or Suns	ARG	Roberto Lar
Nightsongs	IND	R. I. P. Hayman
1984	BRI	Dominic Muldowney
1919	BRI	Brian Gascoigne
Ninja Mission, The	BRI	Danny Young
No Man's Land	NBC-TV	Pete Carpenter/Mike Post
No One Twice	POR	Hans Werner Henze
No Small Affair	COL	Rupert Holmes
Noah's Ark Principle, The	GER	Hubert Bartholomae
Nobody's Women	FRA	Georges Delerue
Not in Front of the Kids	ABC-TV	David Garfield
Nothing But Words of Praise for the Deceased	YUG	Vojislav Kostic
Nucleus Zero	ITA	Stelvio Cipriani
Number One	BRI	David Mackay
Oasis, The	IND	Chris Young
Off Sides	NBC-TV	Mark Snow

Off the Rack	ABC-TV	Fred Karlin
Oh, Bloody Life! ...	HUN	Gyorgy Vukan
Oh, God! You Devil	WB	David Shire
Old Enough	ORI	Julian Marshall
Old Friends	ABC-TV	Artie Butler
On a First-Name Basis	ITA	La Bionda Brothers, The
On a River Without Navigation Marks	CHN	Xu Youfu
On the Line (Rio Abajo)	MEX	Armando Manzanero/ George Michalski/ Manuel Munoz/Pam Savage
On the Threshold	NOR	Freddy Lindquist
Once Upon a Time in America	WB	Ennio Morricone
100 Centre Street	ABC-TV	Artie Butler
100 Days in Palermo	ITA	Vittorio Gelmetti
One Night Stand	AUT	William Motzing
One Rainy Night	ITA	Gianfranco Plenixio
Open Balcony, The	SPA	Emilio de Diego
Oracle, The	IND	Walter E. Sear
Ordeal by Innocence	MGM	Pino Donaggio
Orinoko--Nuevo Mundo	VEN	Alejandro Bianco Uribe
Ostria (South Wind)	GRE	Thanassis Bikos/"O.K. Charlie"
Other Halves	NZ	Don McGlashan
Other Side of a Gentleman, The	HK	Alan Tam
Out of Order (Abwarts/Going Down)	GER	Jacques Zwart
Outlaws, The	ABC-TV	Jerrold Immel
Over the Brooklyn Bridge	MGM/UA	Pino Donaggio
Oxford Blues	MGM	John DuPrez
P & B	SWE	Gunnar Raynir Svensson
P. O. P.	NBC-TV	Dave Grusin
Pale Passion	HK	Stephen Shing/Lin Min Yi
Pallet on the Floor	NZ	Bruno Lawrence
Pankow '95	GER	Tom Dukoupil
Papa, Can You Hear Me Sing?	HK	C. Y. Chen/S. C. Lee
Paper Bird	NOR	Jan Garbarek
Parade, The	CBS-TV	Arthur B. Rubinstein, Jr.
Paris Seen by ... 20 Years After (sequence)	FRA	Jorge Arriagada/Michel Bernholc/Jean-Claude Deblais/Faton Cahen/Jean-Marie Hausser/Roger Pouly/ Silvano Santorio
Paris, Texas	FRA/GER	Ry Cooder
Parodontosis Now	AUS	Karl Ellinger
Partners in Crime (series)	NBC-TV	Nathan Sassover

Passage to India, A	COL	Maurice Jarre
Passengers of a Nightmare	ARG	Oscar Cardozo Ocampo
Passing Fancy	HUN	Gyorgy Selmeczi
Patience (Ayoub)	EGY	Moustapha Nagi
Pavlova	BRI/RUS	Eugene Dogas
Peaceful Days	GER	Loek Dikker
Pedro and the Captain	MEX	Gerardo Batiz
Pessi and Illusia	FIN	Kari Rydman
Phantom, The (Widziadlo)	POL	Krzysztof Knittel
Photographing Patricia	ITA	Fred Bongusto
Pianoforte	ITA	Guido and Maurizio de Angelis
Picone Sent Me	ITA	Tullio de Piscopo
Pigeon Jill	E.GER	Christian Steyer
Pigs	IRE	Roger Doyle
Pinot, Just a Cop	FRA	Louis Chedid
Pirate, The	FRA	Philippe Sarde
Places in the Heart	TST	John Kander
Police Academy	WB	Robert Folk
Ponirah Terpidana	IN	Eros Djarot
Poor Richard	CBS-TV	Craig Safan
Pope John Paul II	CBS-TV	Wilfred Josephs
Pope of Greenwich Village, The	MGM	Dave Grusin
Power, The	IND	Chris Young
Preppies	IND	Ian Shaw
Price of Love, The	GRE	Heleni Karaendrou
Prince Charming	HK	So Chun Hou
Prince Jack	FVI	Elmer Bernstein
Private Function, A	BRI	John duPrez
Proper Scandal, A	ITA	Riz Ortolani
Protocol	WB	Basil Poledouris
Pryor's Place (series)	CBS-TV	Gene Page
Public Woman, The	FRA	Alain Wisniak
Pulsebeat	SPA	Walter Murphy
Punky Brewster (series)	NBC-TV	Rik Howard
Purple Hearts	WB	Robert Folk
Purple Rain	WB	Michel Colombier
Put 'Em All in Jail (Tutti Dentro)	ITA	Piero Piccioni
Quilombo	BRA	Gilberto Gil
R.S.V.P.	IND	Ian Shaw
Races (Uindii)	GER/JAP	Akira Inoue
Racing With the Moon	PAR	Dave Grusin
Raffl	AUS	Bert Breit
Rage and Glory	ISR	Rami Kleinstein
Rainfox	DEN	Ole Koch-Hansen
Ratings Game, The	TMC-C	David Spear
Razorback	AUT	Iva Davies
Razor's Edge, The	COL	Jack Nitzsche
Real Life	BRI	David Mindel
Rearview Mirror	NBC-TV	William Goldstein

Reason Asleep	GER	Helmut Timpelan
Rebelote	FRA	Pierre Jansen
Reckless	MGM/UA	Thomas Newman
Red Dawn	MGM	Basil Poledouris
Red-Light Sting, The	CBS-TV	James di Pasquale
Reflections	BRI	Rachel Portman
Reilly, Ace of Spies (series)	PBS-TV	Barry Rabinowitz
Remedy	TUR	Yeni Turku Gurubu
Return of Luther Gillis, The	CBS-TV	Pete Carpenter/Mike Post
Return of Marcus Welby, M.D., The	ABC-TV	Leonard Rosenman
Revenge of the Nerds	FOX	Thomas Newman
Right Bank, Left Bank	FRA	Michel Berger
Ripoux, Les	FRA	Francis Lai
Ritual (series)	IND-TV	Tom Wolfe
River, The	UN	John Williams
River Rat, The	PAR	Mike Post
River Trip with Hen	GER	Martin Cyrus/Matthias Raue
Roadhouse 66	ATL	Gary Scott
Robin Hood and the Sorcerer	SHO-C	"Clannard"
Rocktober Blood	IND	Nigel Benjamin/Richard Onori/Patrick Regan
Romancing the Stone	FOX	Alan Silvestri
Ronya--The Robber's Daughter	SWE	Bjoern Isfaelt
Roommates	IND	Alan Bacus
Roro Mendut	IN	Franki Raden
Rue Barbare	FRA	Bernard Lavilliers
Runaway	TST	Jerry Goldsmith
Running Hot (Lucky 13)	NLC	Al Capps
Rush	ITA	Francesco de Masi
"S" Day, The	CAN	Barbara Easto/Jean-Pierre Lefebvre
Scared Hearts	BRI	Dirk Higgins
Sakharov	HBO-C	Carl Davis
Sam's Son	IND	David Rose
Samson and Delilah	ABC-TV	Maurice Jarre
Santa Barbara (series)	NBC-TV	Joe Harnell
Savage Streets	IND	John D'Andrea/Michael Lloyd
Savage Women	MEX	Juan Jose Calayud
Scandalous	ORI	Dave Grusin
Scarlet Fever	FRA	Gabriel Yared
Scene of the Crime, The	NBC-TV	James di Pasquale
Scorpion, The	HOL	Nicola Piovani
Scream for Help	IND	John Paul Jones
Sea Serpent, The	SPA	Robin Davis
Second Edition	CBS-TV	Chick Corea
Second Sight: A Love Story	CBS-TV	Dana Kaproff
Second Time Lucky	AUT/NA	Garry McDonald/Laurie Stone

Secret Agent, The	IND	Country Joe McDonald
Secret Diary of Sigmund Freud, The	IND	V. Boris
Secret Honor	IND	George Burt
Secret Places	BRI	Michel Legrand
Secrets	BRI	Guy Woolfenden
Seduction of Gina, The	CBS-TV	Thomas Newman
Sentimental Reasons	CAN	Paul J. Zaza
Seraphim Polubes and Other Humans	RUS	Alexej Rybinkov
Sex Mission (Seksmisja)	POL	Henryk Kuzniak
Shaping Up (series)	ABC-TV	Fletcher Adams
Shattered Vows	NBC-TV	Lee Holdridge
Sheena	COL	Richard Hartley
Sheriff and the Astronaut, The	CBS-TV	Basil Poledouris
Shoe Called Melichar, A	CZE	Karel Wagner
Shooting Party, The	BRI	John Scott
Side by Side	ABC-TV	Peter Matz
Signal 7	IND	Andy Narrell
Signals Through the Flames	IND	Carlo Altomare
Silent Night, Deadly Night	TST	Perry Botkin
Silent Ocean, The	BEL/HOL	Peter Vermeersch
Silent One, The	NZ	Jenny McLeod
Silver City	AUT	William Motzing
Sins of the Past	ABC-TV	Arthur B. Rubinstein, Jr.
681 A.D. The Glory of Khan	BUL	Gene Kauer/Douglas Lackey/Simeon Pironkov
Sixteen Candles	UN	Ira Newborn
Sky's No Limit, The	CBS-TV	Maurice Jarre
Slapstick of Another Kind	IND	Morton Stevens
Slayground	BRI	Colin Towns
Sleeps Six	BRI	Richard Holmes
Sloane	IND	Phil Marshall
Smoke Should Not Fly, The	EGY	Gamal Salama
Sno-Line (Texas Sno-Line)	IND	Richard Bellis
Snorks (series)	NBC-TV	Hoyt Curtin
Snow, the Movie	AUT	George Woronstschak
Snowdrop Celebrations	CZE	Jiri Sust
Soldier's Story, A	COL	Herbie Hancock
Something About Amelia	ABC-TV	Mark Snow
Songwriter	TST	Larry Cansler
Souvenirs, Souvenirs	FRA	Cyril Assous/Jean-Paul Dreau
Spencer (series)	NBC-TV	Barry Goldberg
Spiaccichicciacaticelo	ITA	Leone Creti
Splash	DIS	Lee Holdridge
Splatter University	IND	Chris Burke
Splitz	FVI	George Small

Spraggue	ABC-TV	Lalo Schifrin
Sprinter, The	GER	Paul Vincent
Stanley	AUT	William Motzing
Star Trek III: The Search for Spock	PAR	James Horner
Starman	COL	Jack Nitzsche
State of Wonder	BRI	Alan Gill/Michael Parker
Steambath (series)	SHO-C	Artie Butler
Stigma	GRE	Kyriacos Sfetsas
Stilts, The	SPA	"Madrid Judeo-Spanish Musical Group"
Stone Boy, The	FOX	James Horner
Story of the Good Scoundrels, The	POR	Rui Veloso
Strange Love	E.GER	Juergen Ecke
Strange Passion, A	FRA/ITA	Luis Enrique Bacalov
Stranger Than Paradise	IND	John Lurie
Strangler vs. Strangler	YUG	Vuk Kelenovic
Street Hero	AUT	Bruce Smeaton
Streetcar Named Desire, A	ABC-TV	Marvin Hamlisch
Streets of Fire	UN	Ry Cooder
Strikebound	AUT	Declan Affley
Success Is the Best Revenge	BRI	Stanley Myers/Hans Zimmer
Sudden Love	GRE	Stamatis Spandoudakis
Sugar Water	YUG	Goran Paljatic
Summer	CBS-TV	Setven Wolfson
Summer Fantasy	NBC-TV	Peter Bernstein
Summer in Hell, A	FRA/SPA	Francois Valery
Summons for Mohan Joshi	IN	Vanraj Bhatia
Sun Also Rises, The	NBC-TV	Billy Goldenberg
Supergirl	TST	Jerry Goldsmith
Surrogate, The	CAN	Daniel Lanois
Suzanne and Leonard	DEN	Elisabeth G. Nielsen/ Finn Verwohlt
Suzanne Pleshette Is Maggie Briggs (series)	CBS-TV	Patrick Williams
Swallow and the Titmouse, The (reissue)	FRA	Raymond Alessandrini/ Maurice Jaubert
Swann in Love	ORI	Hans-Werner Henze
Sweet Revenge	CBS-TV	Gil Melle
Swing Shift	WB	Patrick Williams
Swingin' Betty (Bete Balanco)	BRA	"Cazuza"/Roberto Frejat
Swordkill	IND	Richard Band
Syringe, The	FRA	Jacques Revaux
Tail of the Tiger	AUT	Steve Arnold/Graham Tardif
Tales of Beatrix Potter, The (series)	PBS-TV	Carl Davis

Tango Is History	MEX	Astor Piazzola/Osvaldo Pugliese/Susana Rinaldo
Tank	UN	Lalo Schifrin
Tasio	SPA	Angel Illarramendi
10 Days in Calcutta	GER	Bhaskar Chandawarkar/Salil Chowdhury/Vijay Raphava/Roa
Ten Violent Women	IND	Nicholas Carras
Teppanyaki	HK	Chris Babida
Terminator, The	ORI	Brad Fiedel
Terrible Joe Moran	CBS-TV	Charles Gross
Terror in the Aisles	UN	Richard Johnston/Doug Timm
There Was No Sun	POL	Janusz Hajdun
They're Playing With Fire	NWP	John Cacavas
Thief of Hearts	PAR	Harold Faltermeyer
Thieves (Voleurs)	FRA	Nicolas Zourabichvill
Thieves After Dark	FRA	Ennio Morricone
Things Are Looking Up	CBS-TV	Miles Goodman/Bruce Roberts
This and That	ITA	Gacio Chiocchio/Luciano Rossi
Thousand Eyes	GER	Hubert Bartholomae
Three Sorts of Slovene Madness	YUG	Zoran Simjanovic
Three Wishes of Billy Grier	ABC-TV	Brad Fiedel
Thrillkill	CAN	Tim McCauley
Thus Spake Bellavista	ITA	Claudio Mattone
Tightrope	WB	Lennie Niehaus
Time Bomb	NBC-TV	Sylvester Levay
Times of Harvey Milk, The	TEL	Mark Isham
Tiznao	VEN	Miguel Angel Fuster
To Catch a Cop	FRA	Vladimir Cosma
To Catch a King	HBO-C	Nick Bicat
Tomorrow I'm Getting Married	ITA	Detto Mariano
Top Secret	PAR	Maurice Jarre
Torchlight	FVI	Michael Cannon
Torn Allegiance	IND	Johnny Boshoff
Toughest Man in the World, The	CBS-TV	William Goldstein
Town Mayor, The	SWI	Benedict Jeger
Toxic Time Bomb	HBO-C	Robert Boress
Toy Soldiers	NWP	Leland Bond
Trapped Women (Atrapadas)	ARG	Luis Maria Serra
Trauma	GER	Paul Vincent Gunia
Trial Run	NZ	Jan Preston
Tribe, The (Smala, La)	FRA	Michel Goguelat
Triumphs of a Man Called Horse, The	JEN	Georges Garvarentz
Tuff Turf	NWP	Jonathan Elias
Tug of Love (Etincelle, L')	FRA	Vladimir Cosma
Twins, The	FRA	Vladimir Cosma

Twist & Shout (Faith, Hope and Charity)	DEN	Bo Holten
2010	MGM	David Shire
Ultimate Solution of Grace Quigley, The	MGM	John Addison
Ultimatum	POL	Henryk Kuzniak
Under the Volcano	UN	Alex North
Undercover	AUT	Dorothy Dodds/William Motzing/Bruce Smeaton
Unfair Exchanges	BRI	Bruce Cole
Unfaithfully Yours	FOX	Bill Conti
Unfinished Business	CAN	Patricia Cullen
Unseen Wonder	YUG	Boro Tamindzic
Until September	MGM	John Barry
Up the Creek	ORI	William Goldstein
Up to a Certain Point	CUB	Leo Brouwer
Uphill All the Way	NWP	Dennis M. Pratt
Used Cars	CBS-TV	Charles Fox/Norman Gimbel
V (series)	NBC-TV	Dennis McCarthy
V--The Final Battle	NBC-TV	Joseph Conlan/Barry De Vorzon/Dennis McCarthy
Vacation in America	ITA	Manuel de Sica
Vagrants (Fariaho)	E.GER	Guenther Fischer
Vamping	ATL	Ken Kaufman
Velvet	ABC-TV	Dominic Frontiere
Vengeance of the Plumed Serpent, The	FRA	Michel Polnareff
Venus	FRA	Jean Louis d'Oraro
Very Late Afternoon of a Faun, The	CZE	Miroslav Korinek
Victims for Victims: The Theresa Saldana Story	NBC-TV	Paul Chihara
Victory (Victoria)	SPA	Manuel Valls Gorina
Vigil	NZ	Jack Body
Village in the Mist	S.KOR	Kim Chong-kil
Violent Stories	MEX	Joaquin Gutierrez Heras
Voyage, The	FRA	Michel Portal
Voyage to Cythera	GRE	Heleni Karaendrou
Voyager	GER	Konstantin Wecker
Vultures, The	FRA	Georges Delerue
Walls	CAN	J. Douglas Dodd/Michael Oczko
Walter	CBS-TV	Patrick Williams
Warming Up	AUT	Mike Perjanik
Waterwalker	CAN	Bruce Cockburn/Hugh Marsh
We Have Never Been So Happy	BRA	Sergio G. Saraceni
We Three (Noi Tre)	ITA	Riz Ortolani
Weekend Pass	CRO	John Baer

Welcome to Paradise	CBS-TV	Pete Carpenter/Mike Post
Wet Gold	ABC-TV	John Scott
What Have I Done to Deserve This?	SPA	Bernardo Bonezzi
What My Eyes Are Going to See	GRE	Nicos Tatsis
What Waits Below (Secrets of the Phantom Caverns)	IND	Denny Jaeger/Michel Rubini
What Will We Do on Sunday?	FRA/TUN	Mohammed Abdel Waheb
What You Take for Granted	IND	Karen Pritikin
What's Up, Nina?	YUG	Zoran Simjanovic
Wheel, The	S.KOR	Chong Yun-chu
When She Says No	ABC-TV	Brad Fiedel
When the Mountains Tremble	IND	Ruben Blades
Where Is Parsifal?	BRI	Ivan Julien/Hubert Rostaing
Where the Boys Are '84	IND	Sylvester Levay
White Delusion, The	HOL	Clous van Mechelen
White Slave (Amazonia)	ITA	Franco Campanino
Who'll Help Me?	ITA	Carlo Siliotto
Why Me?	ABC-TV	Billy Goldenberg
Wild Life, The	UN	Donn Landee/Edward Van Halen
Wildrose	IND	Bernard Krause/Gary Remal
Windy City	WB	Jack Nitzsche
Winter Flight	BRI	Richard Harvey
Wishing Time	RUS	Alexander Belyaiev
Witches' Sabbath	HUN	Zdenko Tamassy
Witches' Sabbath	SPA	Carmelo Bernaola
Withdrawal (En Retirada)	ARG	Baby Lopez Furst
Wodzeck	GER	Andrew Hofner
Wolf Rock TV (series)	ABC-TV	Shuki Levy/Haim Saban
Woman and Her Four Men, A	RUS	Yuozas Sirvinskas
Woman in Red, The	ORI	John Morris
Woman in the Mirror, A	ITA	Gino Paoli
Woman of Substance, A	BRI-TV	Nigel Hess
Words and Music	CAN/FRA	Michel Legrand
World Safari II	AUT	Mario Marlo/Glenn Shorrock
Wrong Timing	GRE	Giorgos Tsangaris
Year of the Medusa	FRA	Alain Wisniak
Year of the Quiet Sun, The	GER/POL	Wojiech Kilar
Yellow Hair and the Pecos Kid	IND	Franco Piersanti
You Alone (Tu Solo)	SPA	Vainica Doble/Antonio Solera
You Are the Jury	NBC-TV	Peter Matz
Young Hearts	NBC-TV	Bennett Salvay
Young Visiters, The	BRI	John Cameron
Zany Adventures of Robin Hood, The	CBS-TV	Stanley Myers

1985

Film	Country	Composer
A. D.	NBC-TV	Anthony Burgess/Lalo Schifrin
A. K.	FRA	Toru Takemitsu
Ablakon	AFR	"Les Mystics"
Abortion: Stories from North and South	CAN	Micky Erbe/Maribeth Solomon
Accomplished Fact, An	CHILE	Patricio Solovera
Adela	RUM	Adrian Enescu
Adieu, Bonaparte	EGY/FRA	Gabriel Yared
Adolescent Sugar of Love, The (Gazi El Banat)	CAN/FRA/LEB	Siegfried Kessler
Adventures of Sherlock Holmes, The	PBS-TV	Patrick Gowers
Affair, The (Relasyon)	PHI	Winston Ravel
After Darkness	BRI/SWI	Giacomo Peier/Susanne Pisieur
After Hours	WB	Howard Shore
After the Fall of New York	FRA/ITA	Oliver Onions
Again Forever (Dime Novel)	ISR	Shem-Tov Levi
Agatha	KOR	I Pil-weon
Agnes of God	COL	Georges Delerue
Agony	VEN	Gilberto Harquez
AIDS--A Danger for Love	FRA/GER	Francis Lai/Roman Romanelli
Alamo Bay	TST	Ry Cooder
Alcove, The	ITA	Manuel de Sica
Alice in Wonderland	CBS-TV	Morton Stevens
All Mixed Up	FRA	Michel Goguelat
Alley Cat, The (Matou, Le)	CAN/FRA	Francois Dompierre
Alone Among His Own	POL	Zbigniew Gorny
Alpine Fire	SWI	Mario Beretta
Amazing Stories (series)	NBC-TV	John Williams
American Caesar	IND-TV	Art Phillips
American Drive-In	IND	Paul Sabu
American Flyers	WB	Lee Ritenour
American Ninja	IND	Michael Linn
Amigos	IND	Sergio Garcia-Marruz
And Never the Twain Shall Meet	HOL	Zeth Mustamu
... And When They Shall Ask	CAN	Victor Davies
Angel of Fire	POL	Romuald Twardowski
Angelic Conversations	BRI	"Coil"
Angels in Love	DEN	Anne Dorte Michelsen
Annie Oakley	SHO-C	Ry Cooder
Antonio Gaudi	JAP/SPA	Shinji Hori/Hurodo Mori/Toru Takemitsu
Anzacs	AUT-TV	Bruce Rowland
Apple of Our Eye, The (Eszterlanc)	HUN	Zoltan Jeney
Appointment with Fear	IND	Andrea Saparoff
April Fool's Day	IND	Harry Manfredini

Arch of Triumph	CBS-TV	Georges Delerue
Architecture of Frank Lloyd Wright, The	ABC	Frank Spedding
Arhats in Fury	CHN/HK	Wu Dai Jang
Arthur the King	CBS-TV	Charles Gross
Assam Garden, The	BRI	Richard Harvey
Assisi Underground, The	IND	Dov Seltzer
Asterix vs. Caesar	FRA	Vladimir Cosma
Atlanta Child Murders, The	CBS-TV	Billy Goldenberg
Attention	ITA	Pino Donaggio
Avenging Angel	NWP	Chris Young
Baby	DIS	Jerry Goldsmith
Back-Jet Family, The	JAP	"1984"
Back to the Future	UN	Alan Silvestri
Bad Girls Dormitory	IND	Man Parrish
Bad Medicine	FOX	Lalo Schifrin
Badge of the Assassin	CBS-TV	Tom Scott
Ballad of the Irish Horse	PBS-TV	Paddy Moloney
Barbarian Queen	IND	James Horner/Chris Young
Baritone, The	POL	Jerzy Satanowski
Baton Rouge	FRA	John Faure
Battlefield	POL	Andrzej Zarycki
Bayo	CAN	Loreena McKennit
Be Unfaithful and Don't Be Concerned With Whom	SPA	Angel Munoz
Beaver Track, The	E.GER	Guenther Fischer
Becoming Aware	ARG	Silvio Rodriguez
Beer	ORI	Bill Conti
Before & After	IND	Steve Bernstein
Before the Future	ITA	Riccardo Senigallia
Beni Walks By Himself	ALB	Limos Dizdari
Berlin Affair, The	GER/ITA	Pino Donaggio
Berlin Love Story, A	GER	Juergen Knieper
Berrenger's (series)	NBC-TV	Jerrold Immel
Best Times, The	NBC-TV	Miles Goodman/Bruce Roberts
Bet, The (short)	IND-TV	Chris Stone
Better Off Dead	WB	Rupert Hine
Between the Times	GER	Ludvik Mann/Astor Piazzolla
Bhombal Sardar	IN	Anupam Mookerji
Big Shots	ISR	Shlomo Gronich
Billy Ze Kick	FRA	Jean-Claude Petit
Bimini Code	IND	Marc Ellis
Birds Will Fly	CUB	Juan Formell
Bite, The	GER	Gerd Pasemann
Bitter Harvest	GER	Jorg Strassburger
Black Caldron, The	DIS	Elmer Bernstein
Black Hills	GER	Buddy Red Bow/John Surman

Black Orchestra, The	BEL	Jean-Francois Maljean
Blackout	HBO-C	Laurence Rosenthal
Blazing Sun, The (Deng-Byod)	KOR	Young Dong Kim
Bleak House	BRI-TV	Geoffrey Burgon
Blind Alley (Mienai)	JAP	Gulliver Otsuka
Bliss	AUT	Peter Best
Blue Heaven	IND	Fonda Feingold
Blue Money	BRI	Richard Hartley
Blue Mountains, The	RUS	Guia Kancheli
Boggy Creek II	IND	Frank McKelvey
Bombs Away	IND	Skeets McCraw
Bonded Until Death (Damul)	IN	Raghunath Sheth
Boodle, The (Pactole, Le)	FRA	Roger Loubet
Bordello	GRE	Nikos Mamangakis
Boy Who Had Everything, The	AUT	Ralph Schneider
Brazil	BRI	Michael Kamen
Breakfast Club, The	UN	Keith Forsey
Breakfast with Les & Bess	IND-TV	James Dale
Breaking (Shovrim)	ISR	Izhar Ashdoth
Breaking All the Rules	CAN	Paul Zaza
Breaking Silence	IND	Paul de Benedictis
Brewster's Millions	UN	Ry Cooder
Bride, The	COL	Maurice Jarre
Bridge Across Time	NBC-TV	Lalo Schifrin
Broken Hearts and Noses (see Crimewave)		
Broken Rainbow	IND	Laura Nyro
Brotherly Love	CBS-TV	Jonathan Tunick
Brothers (Fratelli)	ITA	Egisto Macchi
Buddies	NLC	Jeffrey Olmsted
Burke & Wills	AUT	Peter Sculthorpe
Burmese Harp, The	JAP	Naozumi Yamamoto
Burning Flowers	NOR	Bent Aserud/Geir Bohren
Business Is Booming	SWE	Bengt Palmers
Caffe Italia	CAN	Pierre Flynn/Andrea Piazza
Cage, The	ITA/SPA	Ennio Morricone
Cage Aux Folles III, La	FRA/ITA	Ennio Morricone
Calamari Union	FIN	"Casablanca Vox"
California Summer	IND	Costello Presley
Came a Hot Friday	NZ	Stephen McCurdy
Canary Cage, The	RUS	Igor Kantyukov
Captive of the Dragon	NOR/RUS	Egil Monn-Iversen
Care Bears Movie, The	CAN	John Sebastian
Carne: The Man Behind the Camera	FRA	Georges Delerue
Carnival	SPA	"The Comediants"
Carnival (Fasnacht)	GER/SWI	Norbert Juergen Schneider
Cats, The	ARG	Jorge Candia

Cat's Eye	MGM	Alan Silvestri
Caught in the Throat	YUG	Zoran Simjanovic
Cave Girl	CRO	Jon St. James
Cease Fire	IND	Gary Fry
Cemetery of Terror	MEX	Chucho Sarsoza
Certain Fury	NWP	Russell Kunkel/George Massenburg/Bill Payne
Chain, The	BRI	Stanley Myers
Chain Letters	IND	Robert Previte
Challenge of a Lifetime	ABC-TV	Mark Snow
Chase	CBS-TV	Robert Drasnin
Chekhov in My Life	GER	Nicolas Economou
Chick for Cairo, A	GER	Matthias Raue
Chicks, The (Nanas, Les)	FRA	Francois Valery
Children, The	FRA	Carlos d'Alessio
Children of Chronos	GRE	Manolis Logiadis
Children of the Night	CBS-TV	Miles Goodman
Children of the War, The	ARG	Luis Maria Serra
Chiller	CBS-TV	Dana Kaproff
Chilly Nights (Han Ye)	CHN	Lu Quiming
Chipmunk Reunion, A	NBC-TV	Dean Elliott
Choice of a People, The	CAN	Pierre Langevin/Marc O'Farrell
Christmas Present	BRI	Nick Bicat
Christopher Columbus	ITA-TV	Riz Ortolani
Chronic Innocence	DEN	Anne Linnet
City and the Dogs, The	PERU	Enrique Iturriaga
City Hero	HK	Danny Chung
City Limits	IND	John Lurie
City of Pirates	FRA/POR	Jorge Arriagada
Clan: Tale of the Frogs, The	FIN	Anssi Tikanmaki
Clean Loving Never Stays That Way for Long	FRA	Jean-Claude Vannier
Closed Case	SPA	Bernardo Feverrigel/ Luis Mendo
Clowns, The	RUM	Tomistocle Popa
Clue	PAR	John Morris
Cobalt Blue	ITA	Daniele Bacalov
Coca-Cola Kid, The	AUT	William Motzing
Cocoon	FOX	James Horner
Code Name: Emerald	MGM	John Addison
Code Name: Foxfire	NBC-TV	Joe Sample
Code of Silence	ORI	David Frank
Code of Vengeance	NBC-TV	Don Peake
Cold in Colombia	GER	Michael McLernon/ Peter Maloney
Color Purple, The	WB	Quincy Jones
Commando	FOX	James Horner
Compromising Positions	PAR	Brad Fiedel
Contract with Death	MEX	Raul Alcantara
Contrary Warriors	IND	Todd Boekelheide

Cop and the Girl, The	AUS/GER	"Alphaville"/Brynmor Jones/George Kranz
Cop's Honor	FRA	Pino Marchese
Corsican Brothers, The	CBS-TV	Allyn Ferguson
Count to Ten	ARG	Luis Maria Serra
Cowboy, Le	FRA	Philippe Sarde
Cowra Breakout, The	AUT-TV	William Motzing
Crack in the Facade, The (Sprung, Der)	GER	Thorsten Nater
Crazy Like a Fox (series)	CBS-TV	Mark Snow
Creator	UN	Sylvester Levay
Creature	IND	Thomas Chase
Crimewave (Broken Hearts and Noses/XYZ Murders, The)	EMB	Arlon Ober
Criminal, The	MEX	Ernesto Cortazar
D.A.R.Y.L.	PAR	Marvin Hamlisch
Da Capo	FIN	Atso Alima
Dance With a Stranger	BRI	Richard Hartley
Dances Sacred and Profane	IND	Larry Gelb
Dangerous Moves	SWI	Gabriel Yared
Dark Lullabies	CAN	Michael Beinhorn/Lauri Conger
Day of the Dead	IND	John Harrison
Days in June	ARG	Luis Maria Serra
Days of Torment	AFR	Sotigui Kouyate
Deadly Intentions	ABC-TV	Georges Delerue
Deadly Passion	AFR	Jay Ferguson
Death in California, A	ABC-TV	John Cacavas
Death of a Patriot	MAL	A. Abu Hassan
Death of an Angel	FOX	Peter Myers
Death of the White Steed, The	GER	Erhard Grosskopf
Death Wish 3	IND	Jimmy Page
Deceptions	NBC-TV	Nigel Hess
Deceptions (Inganni)	ITA	Luis Enrique Bacalov
Deep Blue Night	KOR	Chung Seong-Jo
Defense of the Realm	BRI	Richard Hartley
Deja Vu	BRI	Pino Donaggio
Delos Adventure, The	IND	Richard DeLabio/Kenny Kotwitz
Delta Pi (Mugsy's Girls)	IND	Nelson Kole
Demons	ITA	Claudio Simonetti
Departure, Return	FRA	Michel Legrand
Descendant of the Snow Leopard, The	RUS	M. Begalijev
Desert Bloom	COL	Brad Fiedel
Desert Warrior	IND	Chris Young
Desperately Seeking Susan	ORI	Thomas Newman
Detective in the House	CBS-TV	Craig Safan
Devil in the Flesh	AUT	Philippe Sarde
Devil on the Hill, The	ITA	Guido and Maurizio de Angelis

Didi and the Revenge of the Disinherited	GER	Guenther Fischer
Dim Sum: A Little Bit of Heart	ORI	Todd Boekelheide
Dinosaur!	CBS-TV	John Holbrook/Peter Sherer
Dirty Dozen: Next Mission, The	NBC-TV	Richard Harvey
Dirty Story	FIN/SWE	Pedro Hietanen
Disciples, The	HUN	Ferenc Darvas
Displaced Persons	AUT-TV	Martin Armiger
Do You Remember Love?	CBS-TV	David Shire
Doctor and the Devils, The	FOX	John Morris
Dr. Fischer of Geneva	BRI	Trevor Jones
Dogface	FRA	Didier Vasseur
Doin' Time	WB	Charles Fox
Domina--The Burden of Lust	GER	"Fono Dor"
Don Mouse and Don Thief	MEX	Nacho Mendez
Donkey Skin	RUS	Moissej Weinberg
Don't Touch	ABC-TV	Garry Sherman
Dormire	GER	Andreas Hofner
Dot and the Koala	AUT	John Sangster/Bob Young
Double Dare	CBS-TV	Sylvester Levay
Double Start to Act, The	RUS	Vadim Bibergan
Doubletake	CBS-TV	Arthur B. Rubinstein, Jr.
Down and Out in Beverly Hills	DIS	Andy Summers
Down with the Germans	GER	Wolfgang Hamm
Dream, The	HOL	Cees Bijlstra
Dreamchild	BRI	Max Harris/Stanley Myers
Dreams and Needs	ITA-TV	Francesco de Masi
Dreams Come True	IND	"Spooner"
Dunera Boys, The	AUT-TV	Greg Sneddon
Dungeonmaster, The	IND	Richard Band/Shirley Walker
Dust	BEL/FRA	Martin St. Pierre
Dynasty II: The Colbys	ABC-TV	Peter Myers
Early Frost, An	NBC-TV	John Kander
Eating Your Heart Out	AUT	Mark McSherry
Echo Park	AUS	David Rickets
Edge of Darkness	BRI-TV	Eric Clapton/Michael Kamen
Eleni	WB	Bruce Smeaton
Elsa! Elsa!	FRA	Eric Lalann
Emergency	FRA	Jean-Hector Drand
Emoh Ruo	AUT	Cameron Allan
Empire	IND-TV	Neil Chotem
Employees (Impiegati)	ITA	Riz Ortolani
Empty Beach, The	AUT	Martin Armiger/Red Symons
Enchantress, The	GRE	Demetris Papademetriou

End of the War, The (Kraj Rata)	YUG	Mladen and Predrag Vranjesevic
End of the World Man, The	IRE	John Anderson
Enemy Mine	FOX	Maurice Jarre
Enraged Toy, The	ARG	Luis Maria Serra
Er Woo Dong (Entertainer, The)	KOR	Lee Chong-ku
Escape, The (Firar)	TUR	Yeni Turku Gurubu
Escape from the Bronx	NLC	Francesco de Masi
Ete and Ali	E.GER	Rainer Boehm
Eternal Fire	SPA	Roberto Iglesias
Event, An	IN	Bhubaneswar Misra
Evils of the Night	IND	Robert O. Ragland
Ewoks: The Battle for Endor	ABC-TV	Peter Bernstein
Execution of Raymond Graham, The	ABC-TV	James E. Dale
Explorers	PAR	Jerry Goldsmith
Explosion Happens at Five O'Clock, The	CZE	Zdenek John
Extramurals	SPA	Jose Nieto
Eye to Eye	ABC-TV	Jimmie Haskell
Falcon and the Snowman, The	ORI	Lyle Mays/Pat Metheny
Fall Guy, The	JAP	Masato Kai
False as Water	SWE	Stefan Nilsson
Fandango	WB	Alan Silvestri
Farewell to the Ark	JAP	J. A. Seazer
Fast Forward	COL	Jack Hayes/Tom Scott
Fate of a Family	JAP	Toru Takemitsu
Fathers and Sons	NBC-TV	Patrick Williams
Festival of Fire (Holi)	IN	Rajat Dholakia
Fetish and Dreams	SWI	William Stephen
Fever Pitch	MGM	Thomas Dolby
Final Jeopardy	NBC-TV	Fred Karlin
Final Justice	IND	David Bell
Fire Festival (Himatsuri)	JAP	Toru Takemitsu
First Son	KOR	I Jeol-hyeok
First Steps	CBS-TV	Leonard Rosenman
Flesh & Blood	ORI	Basil Poledouris
Fletch	UN	Harold Faltermeyer
Florence Nightingale	NBC-TV	Stanley Myers
Flowers of Reverie	HUN	Gyorgy Selmeczi
Flying Devils, The	DEN	Kaspar Winding
Foley Square (series)	CBS-TV	Gordon Lustig
Fool for Love	IND	George Burt
For Kayako	JAP	Durodo Mohri
For Your Heart Only	HK	Danny Chung
Forbidden	HBO-C	"Tangerine Dream"
Forester's Sons, The	AUS/GER	Ennio Morricone
Forgive Me, Alyosha	RUS	Vladimir Komarov
Fortress	HBO-C	Danny Beckerman
45/85	ABC-TV	Bill Conti
44 or Tales of the Night	MOR	Benjamin Yarmolinsky

Four Americans in China	PBS-TV	William Loose/Tsun-Yuen Lui/Jack Tillar
Four Seasons, The	POL	Andrzej Kondratiuk
Fourth Power, The	FRA	Alain Bashung
Fourth Wise Man, The	ABC-TV	Bruce Langhorne
Fran	AUT	Greg Schultz
Frankenstein's Great Aunt Tillie	MEX	Ronald Stein
Fraternity Vacation	NWP	Brad Fiedel
French Quarter Undercover	IND	Bill Ginn/Larry Seyer
Friday the 13th V: A New Beginning	PAR	Harry Manfredini
Fright Night	COL	Brad Fiedel
Frog Dreaming	AUT	Brian May
From Normandie to Berlin: A War Remembered	IND-TV	Peter Howell
Funeral, The	JAP	Johji Yuassa
Funeral Ceremony	BRI/POL	Henri Seroka
Future Cop	IND	Phil Davies/Mark Ryder
Future-Kill	IND	Robert Renfrow
Gag Kings, The	FRA	Vladimir Cosma
Game of Survival (Tenement)	IND	Walter F. Sear
Gathering of Spirits, A	GER	Irmin Schmidt
Gaza Ghetto: Portrait of a Palestinian Family, 1948-84	SWE	George Totari
Generation	ABC-TV	Charles Bernstein
George Burns Comedy Week	CBS-TV	Charles Fox
Ghost in the Garden, A	RUS	Juris Karlsons
Ghoulies	IND	Richard Band/Shirley Walker
Gidget's Summer Reunion	COL-TV	George Aliceson Tipton
Gift of Life, The	CBS-TV	Brian Howard/Igor Saulsky
Ginger and Fred	FRA/GER/ITA	Nicola Piovani
Girlfriend for David, A	CUB	Pablo Milanes
Girls (Banoth)	ISR	Jaroslav Jocobowicz
Girls Just Want to Have Fun	NWP	Thomas Newman
Glass Babies	AUT-TV	Frank Strangio
Glissandro	RUM	Vasile Sirli
Go and See	RUS	Oleg Yanchenko
Godzilla	JAP	Rejiro Koroku
Going for the Gold: The Bill Johnson Story	CBS-TV	J. A. C. Redford
Golden Pennies	AUT-TV	Maurie Sheldon
Golden Sands	ICE	Darryl Runswick
Goldie and the Bears	ABC-TV	Dick de Benedictis
Goodbye Charlie (pilot)	ABC-TV	Charles Fox
Goodbye New York	ISR	Michael Abene
Goodbye, Robert	ARG	Pocho Lapouble/Pablo Ziegler
Goodbye, Solidarity	NOR	Svein Gundersen
Goonies, The	WB	Dave Grusin

Gotcha	UN	Bill Conti
Goya	SPA-TV	Javier Montsalvage
Graduation Party	ITA	Riz Ortolani
Greenhouse	GRE	Michalis Christodoulides
Gregorio	PERU	Arturo Ruiz del Pozo
Gringo	IND	Chuck Kentis
Gruenstein's Clever Move	GER	Guenther Fischer
Grunt! The Wrestling Movie	NWP	Susan Justin
Guard, The (Bekci)	TUR	Sarper Ozhan
Guilty Conscience	CBS-TV	Billy Goldenberg
Gulag	HBO-C	Elmer Bernstein
Gulf of Biscay	SPA	Angel Munoz
Gus Brown and Midnight Brewster	NBC-TV	Harry Middlebrooks
Gwen, or the Book of Sand	FRA	Pierre Alrand
Gymkata	MGM	Alfi Kabiljo
Half of Life, A	E.GER	Georg Katzer
Half of Love	BEL	Ramon de Herrera
Happy Ghost II, The	HK	Mahood Rumjahn
Happy New Year	HK	Mahood Rumjahn
Hard Traveling	IND	Ernie Sheldon
Harem	FRA	Philippe Sarde
Hearst-Davies Affair, The	ABC-TV	Laurence Rosenthal
Heart (Cuore)	ITA	Manuel de Sica
Heart Beats (Herzklopfen)	AUS	Roland Baumgartner
Heart of a Champion	CBS-TV	Mike Post
Heart of the Garden	IND	J. Aaron Diamond
Heart on the Land, The	CUB	Jose Maria Vitier
Heated Vengeance	IND	Jim Price
Heaven Help Us	TST	James Horner
Heavenly Kid, The	ORI	Kennard Ramsey
Hell Town	NBC-TV	George Romanis
Hellhole	IND	Jeff Sturges
Here Come the Littles	ATL	Shuki Levy/Haim Saban
Here Comes Santa Claus	FRA	Francis Lai
Heroic Times	GER/HUN	Janos Decsenyi
Hit and Run	FRA	Kristian Tabuchi
Hodja from Pjort	DEN	Sebastian
Holcroft Covenant, The	BRI	"Stanislas"
Hold-Up	CAN/FRA	Serge Franklin
Hollywood Harry	IND	Michael Lang
Hollywood Wives	ABC-TV	Lalo Schifrin
Holy Robe of the Shaolin Temple, The	CHN	Joseph Koo Kai Fai
Hometown	CBS-TV	Nicholas Kirgo/Mark Snow
Honest, Decent and True	BRI	Simon Brint
Honeymoon	CAN	Boris Bergman/Robert Charlebois
Hong Kong Graffiti	HK	Alvin Kwok
Honor, Profit and Pleasure	BRI	Nicholas Kraemer
Hopscotch (Pisingana)	SA	Paul Dominguez

Hostage Flight	NBC-TV	Fred Karlin
Hot Resort	IND	Ken Brown/Dave Powell
Hot Target	NZ	Gil Melle
Hot Water	CAN	Allen Gerber/Ken Roberts
House for Swap	CUB	Juan Marquez
House on the Edge of the Park, The	ITA	Riz Ortolani
Howard's Way	BRI-TV	Simon May/Leslie Osborne
Huey Long	IND	John Colby/Randy Newman
Hussy, The (Effrontee, L')	FRA	Alain Jomy
I Am Not Afraid Anymore	CZE	Vadim Petrov
I Dream of Jeannie: 15 Years Later	NBC-TV	Mark Snow
I Had Three Wives	CBS-TV	Bill Conti
I Like Her	ITA	Vincent Tempera
I Live, But ...	JAP	Kojun Saito
Idol	POL	Jan Kanty
Igor and the Lunatics	IND	Sonia Rutstein
In Heaven All Hell Is Breaking Loose	GER	Andreas Markus Klug
In Her Own Time	IND	James Horner
Indebted to Death	POL	Wlodzimierz Nahorny
Indecent Exposure (Tosha 1/250 Byo)	JAP	Takayuki Inoue
Indecent Obsession, An	AUT	Dave Skinner
Infatuation	HK	Lowell Lo
Innocent, The	BRI	Francis Monkman
Inside the Whale	GER	Klaus Bantzer
Insignificance	BRI	Stanley Myers
Insomniac on the Bridge, The	GRA	Gerard Maimone
Insurance Man, The	BRI	Dominic Muldowney
International Airport	ABC-TV	Mark Snow
Into the Night	UN	Ira Newborn
Into Thin Air	CBS-TV	Brad Fiedel
Invasion U.S.A.	IND	Jay Chattaway
Irith, Irith	ISR	Naftali Alter
Is That It?	BRI	Schaun Tozer
It Only Happens to Me	FRA	Philippe Sarde
Italians, The	AUT-TV	Ann Carr-Boyd
J. O. E. and the Colonel	ABC-TV	Joseph Conlan
Jacques and November	CAN	Michel Rivard
Jacques Costeau: The First 75 Years	IND-TV	John Scott
Jade Love	TAI	Zhang Jongyi
Jagged Edge	COL	John Barry
Jailmates	IND	Andrew James
Jenny Kissed Me	AUT	Trevor Incas/Ian Mason
Jenny's War	IND-TV	John Cacavas

Jewel of the Nile, The	FOX	Jack Nitzsche
Job, The (Fucha)	POL	Zygmunt Konieczny
Joey	GER	Hubert Bartholomae
Joey	IND	Jim Roberge
Johanna	ABC-TV	Dan Foliart/Howard Pearl
John Huston's Dublin	PBS-TV	John Mills-Cockell
John's Secret	DEN	Anders Koppel
Jonny Roova	SWE	Hans Sandin
Joshua Then and Now	CAN	Philippe Sarde
Journey of Natty Gann, The	DIS	James Horner
Journey to Paimpol	FRA	Serge Franklin
Just Married (series)	ABC-TV	George Aliceson Tipton
Just One of the Guys	COL	Tom Scott
Kaiser and One Night	SWI	Markus Fischer
Kaminsky	GER	Robert C. Detree
Kane and Abel	CBS-TV	Billy Goldenberg
Key Exchange	FOX	Mason Daring
Key to Rebecca, The	IND-TV	J. A. C. Redford
Kids from the South Side, The	ITA	Alessandro Sbordoni
Kill Zone	IND	Robert A. Higgins
Killing Auntie	POL	Janusz Hajdun
Killing 'em Softly	CAN	Art Phillips
King David	PAR	Carl Davis
King for a Day	BUL	Ivan Staikov
King Kong's Fist	GER	Gerhard Staebler
King of the Streets	IND	"Contraband"
King Solomon's Mines	IND	Jerry Goldsmith
Kingpin	NZ	"Schtung"
Kiss of the Spider Woman	IND	John Neschling
Kissyfur	NBC-TV	Shuki Levy/Haim Saban
Kojak: The Belarus File	CBS-TV	Joseph Conlan/Barry de Vorzon
Koko at 19	ISR	Shlomo Mizrahi
Kolp	GER	Roland Suso Richter/ Frank Roth
Lace II	ABC-TV	Nick Bicat
Lady Blue	ABC-TV	John Cacavas
Lady from Yesterday, The	CBS-TV	Mark Snow
Ladyhawke	WB	Andrew Powell
Lamb	BRI	Van Morrison
Land in Two	GER/HOL	Rosanna and Oliviero Barbanera
Land of the Tiger	CBS-TV	Terry Oldfield
Land of William Tell, The	SWI	Daniel Brunetti
Last Dragon, The	TST	Mischa Segal
Last Glacier, The	CAN	Jean Derome/Rene Lussier
Last Hunt, The	IND	"Gray Castle"
Latino	IND	Diane Louie
Leave All Fair	NZ	Stephen McCurdy

Legend	UN	Jerry Goldsmith
Legend of Billie Jean, The	TST	Craig Safan
Legend of Suram Fortress, The	RUS	Dzhansug Kakhidze
Let Ye Inherit	GER/HUN	Gyorgy Pesko
Let's Make Laugh II	HK	Stephen Shing
Letter to Brezhnev	BRI	Alan Gill
Letter to Three Wives, A	NBC-TV	Johnny Mandel
Letters to an Unknown Lover	BRI/FRA	Raymond Alessandrini
Letting Go	ABC-TV	Lee Holdridge
Liberty, Equality, Sauerkraut	FRA/ITA	Jean Yanne
Lie of the Land, The	NZ	Dale Gold
Life and Adventures of Santa Claus, The	CBS-TV	Bernard Hoffer
Life in Wittstock	E.GER	Rainer Boehm
Life Is Beautiful	YUG	Vojislav Voki Kostic
Life, Love, Tears	RUS	Igor Nazarouk
Lifeforce	TST	Henry Mancini/Michael Kamen
Light Blast	ITA	Guido and Maurizio de Angelis
Lightship, The	WB	Stanley Myers
Like Life Itself	CUB	Silvio Rodriguez
Lily in Love	HUN	Szabolcs Fenyes
Lime Street	ABC-TV	Lee Holdridge
Link, The	ITA	Ennio Morricone
Little Bit of You ... A Little Bit of Me, A	HUN	Gyorgy Selmeczi
Little Bull, The	SPA	Miguel Asins Arbo
Little Fires	ITA	Riccardo Zampa
Little Sister, The	IND	Pat Metheny
Living Off Love	SWI	Teresa Gatta
Living Planet, The	BRI-TV	Elizabeth Parker
Long Hot Summer, The	NBC-TV	Charles Bernstein
Look, The	IND	Sylvester Levay
Looming Shadow, A	POL	Zbigniew Rudzinski
Loose Screws	CAN	Fred Mollin
Lorca and the Outlaws	BRI	Tony Banks
Lost in America	WB	Arthur B. Rubinstein
Lost in London	CBS-TV	Ken Thorne
Lost Paradises, The	SPA	Carmelo Bernaola
Lots of Luck	DIS-C	William Goldstein
Louise the Rebel	FRA	Jean-Marie Senia
Love and Death	GER	Guy Boulanger/Jean Yves Rigaud
Love Atop the Pyramids	EGY	Hani Mehama
Love Circles	BRI	Bunny Anton
Love Is Never Silent	NBC-TV	Billy Goldenberg
Love Lives On	ABC-TV	James di Pasquale
Love Movie, The	FIN	Anssi Tikanmaki
Love on the Run	NBC-TV	Billy Goldenberg
Love Strange Love	BRA	Rogerio Duprat

Love's Labor's Lost	PBS-TV	Stephen Oliver
Lucy Arnaz Show, The	CBS-TV	Jack Elliott
Lute of the Blind Monks of Satsuma, The	JAP	Takeo Yamashita
Macaroni	ITA	Armando Trovajoli
MacArthur's Children	JAP	Shinichiro Ikebe
MacGyver (series)	ABC-TV	Randy Edelman
McGruder & Loud	ABC-TV	Paul Chihara
McGuffin, The	BRI	Richard Hartley
Mad Love (Amour Braque, L')	FRA	Stanislas Syrewicz
Mad Max Beyond Thunderdome	AUT	Maurice Jarre
Madman at War	FRA/ITA	Guido and Maurizio de Angelis
Magic Is Alive, My Friends	AFR	Terry Dempsey
Magician and the Police Commissioner, The	BRA	Nelson Jacobina
Make-Up (Kesho)	JAP	Sei Akeno
Malady of Death, The	AUS	Sambuca Nigra
Male and Female	VEN	Alejandro Blanco Uribe
Malibu Express	IND	Henry Strzelecki
Malice in Wonderland	CBS-TV	Charles Bernstein
Mamma Ebe	ITA	Franco Piersanti
Man from Moscow, The	PBS-TV	Jim Parker
Man With One Red Shoe, The	FOX	Thomas Newman
Man with the Mandolin, The	MEX	Leonardo Valazquez
Man with the Silver Eyes, The	FRA	Philippe Sarde
Mania	GRE	Nicos Zidakis
Manuel's Destinies	FRA/POR	Jorge Arriagada
Marie	MGM	Francis Lai
Marie Ward	GER	Elmer Bernstein
Mark Twain	IND	Billy Scream
Marriage of the Century, The	FRA	Jean Morlier
Martha Dubronski	SWI	Konstantin Wecker
Martin Niemoeller	GER	Frank Wolff
Martin's Day	MGM	Wilfred Josephs
Mary (series)	CBS-TV	Dan Foliart/Howard Pearl
Mass Is Over, The	ITA	Nicola Piovani
Mata Hari	IND	Wilfred Josephs
Maxie	ORI	Georges Delerue
Maximum Security	HBO-C	Jay Asher/David Frank
Me and Mom	ABC-TV	Miles Goodman
Me Want You	FRA	Eric Demarsan
Mean Season, The	ORI	Lalo Schifrin
Medium (Deja Vu)	POL	Krzesimir Debski
Melek Leaves	GER	Jakob Lichtmann
Memoirs	CAN	Julia Gilmore/Edward Straviak/Philip Vezina
Men (Manner)	GER	Klaus Bantzer
Meteor and Shadow	GRE	Marinos Athanassopoulous
Metropolitan Avenue	IND	Glen Daum

Midas Valley	ABC-TV	Jerrold Immel
Midnight Hour, The	ABC-TV	Brad Fiedel
Miranda	ITA	Riz Ortolani
Mischief	FOX	Barry De Vorzon
Mishima	WB	Philip Glass
Missing--Have You Seen This Person?	NBC-TV	Gary Remal
Missing in Action 2--The Beginning	IND	Brian May
Mission Kill	IND	Jesse Frederick/Jeff Koz
Mr. Clock (What Time Is It, Mr. Clock?)	HUN	Gyorgy Vukan
Mr. Love	BRI	Willy Russell
Mr. Wrong	NZ	Jonathan Crayford
Mode in France	FRA	Serge Gainsbourg
Monday, a Parody	GER	Thomas Lachnit
Monkey Mia	AUT	"The Bahloo Music Show"
Monsieur de Pourceaugnac	FRA	Pierre Jansen
Moonlighting	ABC-TV	Lee Holdridge
More Things Change, The	AUT	Peter Best
Morons from Outer Space	BRI	Peter Brewis
Mother Teresa	IND	Suzanne Ciani
Movers & Shakers	MGM	Ken and Mitzi Welch
Moving Targets (Zielscheiben)	GER	Edward Aniol
Moving Violations	FOX	Ralph Burns
Murphy's Romance	COL	Carole King
Mussolini: The Decline and Fall of Il Duce	HBO-C	Egisto Macchi
Mussolini: The Untold Story	NBC-TV	Laurence Rosenthal
My Beautiful Laundrette	BRI	Stanley Myers
My Darling, My Beloved	RUS	Victor Kisine
My Dearest Son	ITA	Guido and Maurizio de Angelis
My Father, My Rival	HBO-C	Fred Mollin
My Life as a Dog	SWE	Bjoern Isfaelt
My Science Project	DIS	Peter Bernstein
My Son Che: A Family Portrait by Don Ernesto Guevara	CUB/ITA/SPA	Tata Cedron
Naked Country, The	AUT	Bruce Smeaton
Nana	MEX	Rafael Elizondo
Narrow Bridge, The	INDONESIA	Franki Raden
National Lampoon's European Vacation	WB	Charles Fox
Neglected Miracle, The	NZ	Jenny McLeod
Neighbours	AUT-TV	Tony Hatch
Neither Chana Nor Juana	MEX	J. Antonio Zavala
New Kids, The	COL	Lalo Schifrin
New Year's Eve at Bob's House	FRA	Michel Magne
Next Summer	FRA	Philippe Sarde

Nickel Mountain	IND	Lincoln Mayorga
Niel Lynne	AUT	Chris Neal
Niemann's Time--A German "Heimatfilm"	GER	Jolyon Brettingham-Smith
Night	BRA	Sergio G. Saraceni
Night Caller	HK	Romeo Diaz
Night Heat	CBS-TV	Domenic Troiano
Night Magic	CAN/FRA	Lewis Furey
Night of the Emerald Moon, The	CZE	Jiri Svoboda
Night Stalker, The	ALM	David Kitay
Nightmare	MOR	Haj Younous
Nightmare on Elm Street, Part 2: Freddy's Revenge, A	NLC	Chris Young
9 Deaths of the Ninja	CRO	Cecile Colayco
Ninety Days	CAN	Richard Gresco
Ninja Thunderbolt	HK	Stephen Tsang
Niskavouri Saga, The	FIN	Rauno Lehtinen
No End	POL	Zbigniew Preisner
No Harvest But a Thorn	MAY	Ooi Eow Jin
No Man's Land	FRA/SWI	Terry Riley
No Place Like Home	CBS-TV	Joe Raposo
No Sad Songs	CAN	Allen Booth/David Woodhead
No Surrender	BRI	Darryl Runswick
Noblewoman, The	S.KOR	Han Sang-Key
Noise Kill, The (Schalltot)	GER	Fred van der Kooij
Nomads	IND	Bill Conti
North Beach and Rawhide	CBS-TV	Earle Hagen
Northern Lights (Havlandet)	NOR	Klaus Schultze
Not My Kid	CBS-TV	Mark Snow
Not Nothing Without You	GER	Horst Muhlbradt
Not Quite Jerusalem	BRI	Gianfranco Reverberi
Not With You, Not Without You	FRA	Kolinka
Nothing Left to Do But Cry	ITA	Pino Donaggio
Nothing Underneath	ITA	Pino Donaggio
Notorious Nobodies	FRA	Benito Merlino
November Moon	FRA/GER	Egisto Macchi
Nuclear Gypsies, The	JAP	Ryudo Uzaki
O-Bi, O-Ba--The End of Civilization	POL	Jerzy Satanowski
Objection	POL	"Siekiera"
Odd Birds	IND	Dick Hamilton
Official History, The	ARG	Atilio Stampone
Ohan	JAP	Shinnosuke Ohkawa
Old Forest, The	IND	Mark Blumberg
Old Henry	E.GER	Peter Rabenalt
On a Narrow Bridge	ISR	Poldi Shatzman
On Course (En Plo)	GRE	Heleni Karaendrou
On Our Way	CBS-TV	Dennis McCarthy
On the Edge	IND	Herb Pilhofer

On the Loose	AUT	Todd Hunter
Once Bitten	GOL	John du Prez
One Magic Christmas	DIS	Michael Conway Baker
One Woman or Two	FRA	Kevin Mulligan/Toots Thielmans/Evert Verhees
Operation Judas (Iron Hands)	FRA	Michel Portal
Ophelia Hits Town	DEN	Henrik Langkilde/Hans-Erik Philip
Order of the Black Eagle, The	IND	Dee Barton
Oriana	FRA/VEN	Eduardo Marturet
Orion's Belt	NOR	Bent Aserud/Geir Bohren
Osa	IND	Mason Daring
Other, The	MEX	Chucho Zarzoza
Other Cuba, The	ITA	Paquito D'Rivera
Otherworld	CBS-TV	Sylvester Levay
Otto--The Film	GER	Herb Geller
Our Marriage	FRA	Jorge Arriagada
Out of Africa	UN	John Barry
Out of the Darkness	CBS-TV	Billy Goldenberg
Out of the Darkness	BRI	Ed Welch
Outlaws	FRA	Philippe Sarde
Over the Summer	IND	Steven Heller
P. P. Rider	JAP	Masaru Hoshi
P.R.O.F.S.	FRA	Patrick Schulmann
Package Tour II--Snowroller, The	SWE	Bengt Palmers
Palace	FRA/GER	Michel Legrand
Palace of Dreams	AUT-TV	Chris Neal
Pale Face	CAN	Jerome Langlois
Pale Rider	WB	Lennie Niehaus
Parade of the Planets	RUS	Vyacheslav Ganelin
Paradise Motel	IND	Mark Governor/Rick White
Paradise View	JAP	Haruomi Hosono
Parfait Amour	HOL	Johanna d'Armagnac
Parking	FRA	Michel Legrand
Passing, The	IND	William-John Tudor
Past Caring	BRI	George Fenton
Patakin	CUB	Rembert Egues Gomez
Paul Chevrolet and the Ultimate Hallucination	HOL	Lodewijk de Boer
Paul's Awakening	ITA	Marco Canepa/Kalib Khallab
Peanut Butter Solution, The	CAN	Lewis Furey
Peephole and the Key, The	HUN	Zoltan Papp
Pee-Wee's Big Adventure	WB	Danny Elfman
Perfect	COL	Ralph Burns
Perfectionist, The	AUT-TV	John Charles
Permeke	BEL	David Darling/John Surman

Perry Mason Returns	NBC-TV	Dick de Benedictis
Peter No-Tail in America	SWE	Bernd Egerbladh
Peyton Place: The Next Generation	NBC-TV	Jerrold Immel
Pharaoh's Court	SPA	Luis Cobos
Philadelphia Attraction, The (Uramisten)	HUN	Janos Novak
Picking Up the Pieces	CBS-TV	Paul Chihara
Pink Nights	IND	Jim Tullio/Jeffrey Vanston
Pizza Connection, The	ITA	Carlo Savina
Playing with Fire	NBC-TV	Dennis McCarthy
Police	FRA	Henryk Mikolaj Gorecki
Police Academy 2: Their First Assignment	WB	Robert Folk
Porky's Revenge	FOX	Dave Edmonds
Possession	AUT-TV	Mick Harvey
Postcard from a Journey	POL	Zygmunt Konieczny
Poulet au Vinaigre	FRA	Matthieu Chabrol
Power of Evil, The	FRA/ITA	Wojciech Kilar
Practice of Love, The	AUS/GER	Stephen Ferguson
Prague	CZE/ITA	Michael Kocab
Pray for Death	IND	Thomas Chase/Steve Rucker
Prey, The	HOL	Henny Vrienten
Prime Risk	ALM	Phil Marshall
Private Conversations	IND	Alex North
Private Passions (Clair)	AUS/FRA	"The Performer's Band"
Private Practices: The Story of a Sex Surrogate	IND	Tom Recchion
Private Sessions	NBC-TV	Lalo Schifrin
Private Show	PHI	Jaime Fabregas
Prizzi's Honor	FOX	Alex North
Promises to Keep	CBS-TV	Michel Legrand
Protector, The	WB	Ken Thorne
Pumping Iron II: The Women	IND	David McHugh/Michael Montes
Purple Rose of Cairo, The	ORI	Dick Hyman
Pushkin Trilogy, A	RUS	Alfred Schnitke
Queen of Mate, The	SPA	Jose Nieto
Question Time	BUL	Victor Chuchkov
Quiet Earth, The	NZ	John Charles
Rabid Ones, The	FRA	Vincent Gemignani
Rainbow Brite and the Star Stealer	WB	Shuki Levy/Haim Saban
Rainbow Serpent, The	AUT-TV	Peter Miller
Rainy Day Friends	IND	Jimmie Haskell
Rambo: First Blood Part II	TST	Jerry Goldsmith
Ran (King Lear)	FRA/JAP	Toru Takemitsu
Rape of Aphrodite, The	GRE	Michalis Christodoulidis

Rape of Richard Beck, The	ABC-TV	Peter Bernstein
Rappin'	IND	Michael Linn
Rate It X	IND	Elizabeth Swados
Real Genius	TST	Thomas Newman
Re-Animator	IND	Richard Band
Rebel	AUT	Chris Neal
Record, The	GER	"The Chance"
Red Caviar	FRA/SWI	Jean-Claude Petti/ Claude Michel Schonberg/Gheorghe Zamfir
Red Countess, The	HUN	Laszlo Vidovszky
Red Guards in Hong Kong	HK	Mahmood Rumjahn
Red Heat	GER	"Tangerine Dream"
Red Kiss	FRA/GER	Jean-Marie Senia
Red Sonja	MGM	Ennio Morricone
Reference	BUL	Victor Chuchkov
Relatives	AUT	Norman Kaye
Remo Williams: The Adventure Begins	ORI	Craig Safan
Rendezvous	FRA	Philippe Sarde
Rendezvous Leipzig	GER	Franz Bartzsch/Peter Schirmann
Repenter, The	ITA	Ennio Morricone
Report from an Abandoned Planet	GER	Rolf Riehm
Requiem for a Spanish Peasant	SPA	Anton Garcia Abril
Restless Natives	BRI	Stuart Adamson
Return	IND	Ragnar Grippe/Michael Shrieve
Return of the Living Dead, The	ORI	Matt Clifford
Return to Eden	AUT-TV	Brian May
Return to Oz	DIS	David Shire
Reunion at Fairborough	HBO-C	Nigel Hess
Revenge for Justice	PHI	Jaime Fabregas
Revenge of the Teenage Vixens from Outer Space, The	IND	Louis X. Erlanger/Lane James/Gary Schmidt
Revolution	WB	John Corigliano
Rigged	IND	Brian Banks/Anthony Marinelli
Right Man for a Delicate Job, The	HUN	Matyas Varkonyi
Right to Kill?	ABC-TV	Paul Chihara
Robbery Under Arms	AUT	Garry McDonald/Laurie Stone
Robert Kennedy and His Times	CBS-TV	Fred Karlin
Rockhopper (pilot)	CBS-TV	Mark Snow
Rocky IV	MGM	Bill Conti/Vince Di Cola
Romance of Betty Boop, The (short)	CBS-TV	Goyette & John Bogus
Rosso	FIN	Marco Cucinatta
Rumble, The	FRA	Ivan Jullien/Hubert Rostaing

Runaway Train	IND	Trevor Jones
Rustlers' Rhapsody	PAR	Steve Dorff
Ruthless Romance	RUS	Andrei Petrov
Sadness and Beauty	FRA	Jean-Claude Petit
Sadness of Knowing, The	ITA	Fiorenzo Rizzone
Sahara (Lost in the Sahara)	SPA	Carlos Vizziello
St. Elmo's Fire	COL	David Foster
Salt on the Skin	BEL/CAN/FRA	Christian Lete
Samuel Lount	CAN	"Kitaro"
Sanford Meisner--The Theater's Best Kept Secret	COL	Skip Kennon
Santa Claus--the Movie	TST	Henry Mancini
Sara	NBC-TV	Tom Scott
Satin Spider, The	FRA	Bruno Gillet
Savage Island	IND	Phil Davies/Mark Ryder
Scalpel, Please	CZE	Jozef Revallo
Scandalous Gilda	ITA	Giorgio Carnini
Scenario	GRE	George Hadzinassios
School Spirit	IND	Tom Bruner
Scout Forever, A	FRA	Gabriel Yared
Screamplay	IND	Basil J. Bova/George Cordeiro
Screen Test	IND	Don Harrow
Seburi Story, The	JAP	Takayuki Inoue
Secret Admirer	ORI	Jan Hammer
Secret Garden, The	SPA	Alberto Bourbon
Secret Passage	FRA	Jean-Claude Nachon
Secret Weapons	NBC-TV	Charles Bernstein
Secrets Secrets	ITA	Nicola Piovani
Seduced	CBS-TV	Patrick Williams
Sequa, La	MEX	Orlando Garcia/Benjamin Gutierrez
Sesame Street Presents: Follow That Bird	WB	Lennie Niehaus/Van Dyke Parks
Seven in the Viewfinder	MEX	Nacho Mendez
Seventh Target, The	FRA	Vladimir Cosma
Shadey	BRI	Colin Towns
Shadow Chasers, The	ABC-TV	Joe Harnell
Shadows of the Future	GER	Wolfgang Hamm
Shaker Run	NZ	Stephen McCurdy
She'll Be Wearing Pink Pajamas	BRI	John du Prez
Shipwreck of Liguria, The	MEX	Juan Jose Calatayud
Shoud I Be Good?	NZ	Geoff Castle
Signed Charlotte	FRA	Philippe Sarde
Signed Renart	FRA/SWI	Tom Novembre
Silas Marner	BRI	Carl Davis
Silent Twins, The	BRI	Nicholas Carr
Silent Witness	NBC-TV	Michael Hoenig
Silip	PHI	Lutgardo Labad
Silk	PHI	Willie Cruz
Silver Bullet	PAR	Jay Chattaway
Silverado	COL	Bruce Broughton

Sins of the Father	NBC-TV	Sylvester Levay
Six Days in June	YUG	Vladimir Divijan
Skyhigh	IND	Denis Haines
Slammer Girls (Big Slammer, The)	IND	Marc Ubell (Chuck Vincent)
Slices of Life	FRA	Jean-Claude Petit
Slugger's Wife, The	COL	Patrick Williams
Smooth Talk	IND	Russell Kunkel/George Masenburg/Bill Payne
Smuggler King, The	SWE	Stefan Nilsson
Sniffing Around	GER	Wilhelm Dieter Siebert
Snowman, The	GER	Paul Vincent Gunia
Softly ... Softly	ITA	Paolo Conte
Song-Filled Tomorrows	FRA	Jean-Marie Senia
Song for Europe, The	BRI	Carl Davis
Soul Is Greater Than the World, The	SWE	Ulf Dageby
Space	CBS-TV	Tony Berg/Miles Goodman
Special Effects	NLC	Michael Minard
Specialists, The	FRA	Eric Demarsan
Spies Like Us	WB	Elmer Bernstein
Staff of "Life," The	ABC-TV	Michael Lloyd
Staircase C	FRA	Raymond Alessandrini
Star Games	IND-TV	Kevin Kinen
Starchaser: The Legend of Orin	ATL	Dale Gold
Starcrossed	ABC-TV	Gil Melle
Stark	CBS-TV	Bill Conti/Peter Myers
Station to Station	IND	Wyatt Helin
Steaming	BRI	Richard Harvey
Stick	UN	Joseph Conlan/Barry de Vorzon
Stingray	NBC-TV	Pete Carpenter/Mike Post
Stitches	IND	Bob Floke
Stone Pillow	CBS-TV	Georges Delerue
Stone Years	GRE	Stamatis Spandoudakis
Stoogemania	ATL	Hummue Mann/Gary Tigerman
Storm	CAN	Amin Bhatia
Stormin' Home	CBS-TV	Bruce Broughton
Stranger at Home	HOL	Boudewijn Tarenskeen
Stranger Than Fiction	BRI	Benedict Mason
Stravinsky--A Life	SWE-TV	Hans-Erik Philip
Strawberry Fields	GER	Eberhard Weber
Street Comedy	CAN-TV	Cliff Jones
Street Hawk (series)	ABC-TV	"Tangerine Dream"
Street to Die, A	AUT	Michael Atkinson
Streetwalkin'	IND	Matthew Ender/Doug Timm

Streetwise	IND	Tom Waits
Strictly Personal	FRA	Serge Perathoner
Stripper	FOX	Jack Nitzsche/Buffy Sainte-Marie
Subway	FRA	Eric Serra
Such a Long Absence	GRE	Stamatis Spandoudakis
Sudden Death	IND	Arthur Baker
Summer at Grandpa's, A	TAI	Edward Yang
Summer Rental	PAR	Alan Silvestri
Summer to Remember, A	CBS-TV	Charles Fox
Supergrass, The	BRI	Keith Tippet
Superslob	FRA	Yasuaki Shimizu
Superstition	ALM	David Gibney
Sure Thing, The	EMB	Tom Scott
Surviving	ABC-TV	James Horner
Sweet Dreams	TST	Charles Gross
Sweet 17	NOR	Anne Grete Preus
Sword of Heaven	IND	Christopher L. Stone
Sylvester	COL	Lee Holdridge
Sylvia	NZ	Leonard Rosenman
TV and the Hotel, The	ARG	Mike Ribas
Tainted	IND	Hayden Wayne
Taipei Story, The	TAI	Edward Yang
Taiwan Canasta	YUG	Zoran Simjanovic
Tango in the Belly	GER	Andreas Koebner
Tango of Our Childhood	RUS	Tigran Mansuryan
Tangos--Gardel's Exile	ARG/FRA	Astor Piazzola
Target	WB	Michael Small
Taulant Wants a Sister	ALB	Hajg Zaharian
Tea in the Harem of Archimedes	FRA	Karim Kacel
Tears in Florence	GER	Charles Kalmann
Teen Wolf	ATL	Miles Goodman
Telephone Always Rings Twice, The	FRA	Gabriel Yared
Temptation of Isabelle, The	FRA/SWI	Philippe Sarde
Terrible Lovers, The	FRA	Jorge Arriagada
Terry on the Fence	BRI	Harry Robertson
Tex and the Lord of the Deep	ITA	Gianni Ferrio
That Couple	BRA	Augusto Licks
That Damned Meat	BRA	Rogerio Duprat
That's Dancing!	MGM	Henry Mancini
That's My Baby	CAN	Eric N. Robertson
There Are Some Guys Downstairs	ARG	Jorge Lopez Ruiz
There Were Times, Dear	IND	Jay Gruska
13 at Dinner	CBS-TV	John Addison
Three Feet Above the Ground	POL	Zbigniew Raj
Three Sovereigns for Sarah	PBS-TV	Charles Gross
Thunder Alley	IND	Ken Topolsky
Time After Time	BRI-TV	Jim Parker
Time Destroyed: Letters from a War, 1939-40	FRA	Maurice Jaubert

Time of Leopards, The	MOZ/YUG	Kornelije Kovac
Time of the Star, The	BRA	Marcus Vinicius
Time to Die, A	CUB	Leo Brower/Nafer Duran
Time to Live, A	NBC-TV	Georges Delerue
Timing	CAN	James Dale
To Live and Die in L.A.	MGM	Wang Chung
To See the Light (Eszmejes)	HUN	Gyorgy Jurtag, Jr./ Peter Peterdi
Tokyo-Ga	GER	Meche Mamecier/Chico Rojo Ortega/Loorie Petitgand
Tomb, The	IND	Drew Neumann
Tomboy	CRO	Michael Lloyd
Tooth for a Tooth, A (On the Tracks of the Killers)	GER	"Klaus Lage Band"
Topos	GRE	Giorgos Apergis
Torpedo Planes	RUS	Alexander Knaifel
Toughlove	ABC-TV	Paul Chihara
Toxic Avenger, The	IND	Marc Katz
Tracks in the Snow (Pervola)	HOL	Maarten Koopman
Transylvania 6-5000	NWP	Lee Holdridge
Treasure of the Amazon, The	MEX	Daniel Lopez
Tree Under the Sea, The	FRA	Luc Le Masne
Trip to Bountiful, A	IND	J. A. C. Redford
Trouble in Mind	IND	Mark Isham
Tub Studs	IND	Andrew James
Tupac Amaru	CUB/PERU	Juan Marquez
Turk 182	FOX	Paul Zaza
Turn of the Screw, The	SPA	Luis Iriondo
Turncoat, The	FRA/GER	Luis Enrique Bacalov
Turn-On (Declic, Le)	FRA	Jacques Lecoeur
Turtle Diary	BRI	Geoffrey Burgon
Twice in a Lifetime	IND	Pat Metheny
Twisted Passion	HK	So Chun Hou/Stephen Shing
Two Cops, The	ITA	Fabio Liberatori
Two Lives of Mattia Pascal, The	ITA	Nicola Piovani
Two Valentinos	GER	Otto Beatus
Una	YUG	Kornelije Kodec
Undergrads, The	DIS-C	Matthew McCauley
Unit, The (Otryad)	RUS	Valdimir Kamolikov
Va Banque II	POL	Henryk Kuzniak
Vagabond	FRA	Joanna Druzdowicz
Vibrations (Tarang)	IN	Vanraj Bhatia
View to a Kill, A	MGM	John Barry
Vision Quest	WB	"Tangerine Dream"
Volley for a Black Buffalo	FRA/HUN	Elek Petrovics
Volunteers	TST	James Horner
Walking the Edge	IND	Jay Chattaway
Wallenberg: A Hero's Story	NBC-TV	Ernest Gold

Film	Country	Composer
Walter and Carlo: Up at Dad's Hat	DEN	Jan Glasel
Warning Sign	FOX	Craig Safan
Water	BRI	Mike Moran
Water and Man (short)	IND	Gabriel Yared
Way It Is or Eurydice in the Avenues, The	IND	Vincent Gallo
Weird Science	UN	Ira Newborn
Weirdo (Chuchela)	RUS	Sofia Cabaidulina
Wetherby	MGM	Nick Bicat
What Number?	CAN	Jean Sauvageau
When Dreams Come True	ABC-TV	Gil Melle
When Nature Calls	IND	Arthur Custer
When Night Falls	ISR	Itzhak Klepter
Where Others Keep Silent	E.GER	Peter Gotthardt
White Nights	COL	Michel Colombier
White Water Summer (Rites of Summer)	COL	Michael Boddicker
Who Is That Man?	POL	Jerzy Maksymiuk
Wild and Beautiful	FRA	Vangelis
Wild Geese II	BRI	Roy Budd
Wild Horses	CBS-TV	Stanley Myers/Hans Zimmer
Wildschut	BEL/HOL	Alain Pierre
Wildside	ABC-TV	Jack Elliott
Wind in the Willows, The	ABC-TV	Maury Laws
Witchfire	IND	Dave Puchan
Witching Hour, The	SPA	Alejandro Masso
Witness	PAR	Maurice Jarre
Wolf's Bride, The	GER	Pete Wyoming-Bender
Woman and the Stranger, The	E.GER	Rainer Bredemeyer
Woman from the Provinces, The	POL	Henryk Kuzniak
Woman in a Hat	POL	Jerzy Satanowski
Woman of Wonders	ITA	Carlo and Paolo Rustichelli
Women	HK	Law Wing-fai
Women's Prison Massacre	FRA/ITA	Luigi Ceccarelli
Working Class	HK	Teddy Robin
Wrestler, The (Pehlivan)	TUR	Tarik Ocal
Write and Fight (Pismak)	POL	Jerzy Maksymiuk
Wrong World	AUT	Eric Gradman
Wurlitzer	GER	Budi Seibert/Wolfgang Stryi
Yamaha Fish Stall	CHN	Chen Qixiong
Yasha	JAP	Mitshuhiko Saito
Year of the Dragon	MGM	David Mansfield
Yearbook: Class of '67	CBS-TV	Mike Melvoin
Yellow Earth	CHN	Zhao Jiping
Yerma	CAN/GER/HUN	Zoltan Pesko
You Haven't Got a Chance-- Take It!	NOR-TV	Svart Framtid

You Only Die Twice	FRA	Claude Bolling
You Really Got Me	MEX	"Grupo Manchuria"
Young Lady Chatterley II	IND	Mischa Segal
Young Sherlock Holmes	PAR	Bruce Broughton
Zed and Two Noughts, A	BRI/HOL	Michael Nyman
Zina	BRI	David Cunningham/ Barry Guard/Simon Heyworth

1986

Abandon (Afzien)	HOL	Berend Hunnekink
Abducted	CAN	Michel Rubini
Abel	HOL	Vincent van Warmerdam
About Last Night	TST	Miles Goodman
Absentee, The	HUN	Laszlo Sary
Acceptable Risks	ABC-TV	Mark Snow
Act of Violence	HBO-C	Frankie Miller
Adam: His Song Continues	NBC-TV	Mike Post
Adams Apple	CBS-TV	Lee Holdridge
Adventures of Chatran, The	JAP	Ryuichi Sakamoto
Adventures of Faustus Bidgood, The	CAN	Robert Joy/Patricia Morgan/Paul Seffer
Affliction (Dahan)	AFR	Amanul Haque
After Pilkington	BRI	Stephen Oliver
Agent on Ice (And Then You Die/Silent Partners)	IND	Ian Carpenter
Alchemist, The	IND	Richard Band
Alex: The Life of a Child	ABC-TV	J. A. C. Redford
Alice to Nowhere	AUT-TV	Peter Best
Aliens	FOX	James Horner
All Because of a Wedding Dress	MEX	Luis Arcaraz
Almacita de Desolata	HOL	"Grupo Issoco"
Alter Ego (Letters from a Doctor in Africa)	HOL	Daniel Smith
Amerasia	GER	Terry Allen/Surachai Jantimatorn
America 3000	IND	Tony Berg
American Anthem	COL	Alan Silvestri
American Commandos (Hitman)	IND	Ole Hoeyer
American Geisha	CBS-TV	Miles Goodman
American Tail, An	UN	James Horner
American Way, The	BRI	Brian Bennett
Among the Shadows	SPA	Fernando Civil/Mariano Diaz
Anastasia: The Mystery of Anna	NBC-TV	Laurence Rosenthal
And Then (Sorekara)	JAP	Shigaru Umnhoyoshi
Anemia	ITA	Lorenzo Ferrero
Angel River	IND	"Garcia Campos, El"
Angel Skin	FRA	Philippe Servain

Anne Trister	CAN	Rene Dupere
Another Love (Ina Laska)	CZE	Marian Varga
Apology	HBO-C	Maurice Jarre
April Fool's Day	PAR	Charles Bernstein
Are We Winning, Mommy? America and the Cold War	IND	Wendy Blackstone
Armed and Dangerous	COL	Bill Meyers
Armed Response (Jade Jungle)	IND	Tom Chase/Steve Rucker
Armour of God, The	HK	Michael Rai
Around the World in Eighty Ways	AUT	Chris Neal
Arriving Tuesday	NZ	Scott Calhoun
As Is	SHO-C	Peter Matz
Ask Max	DIS-TV	Robert Folk
Assassin	CBS-TV	Anthony Guefen
Assault, The	HOL	Jurrihan Andriessen
Assignment Africa	PBS-TV	Toure Kunda
Asterix in Britain	DEN/FRA	Vladimir Cosma
At Close Range	ORI	Patrick Leonard
Aurora Encounter, The	NWP	Ron F. Dilulio
Avanti Popolo	ISR	Uri Ofir
Avenging Force	IND	George S. Clinton
Awesome Lotus	IND	Paul Conly
B.R.A.T. Patrol, The	DIS-TV	Jonathan Tunick
Babies Having Babies	CBS-TV	Ken Lauber
Back to School	ORI	Danny Elfman
Backlash	AUT	Michael Atkinson/ Michael Spicer
Bad Guys	IND	William Goldstein
Bad Night (Mala Noche)	IND	Creighton Lindsay
Balboa	IND	Richard Hieronymus
Ballad of Eve, The	ITA	Tony Esposito
Ballet Black	BRI	Schaun Tozer
Band of the Hand	TST	Michel Rubini
Bar 51	ISR	Erich Rudich
Barnum	CBS-TV	Charles Gross
Bastard Brother of God, The	SPA	Juan Pablo Munoz Zielinski
Beast, The	ICE	Oddson W. A. Mozart/ Hrodmar Sigurdbjorns- son
Beauty of Vice, The	YUG	Zoran Simjanovic
Bedroom Window, The	DEG	Patrick Gleeson/ Michael Shrieve
Bee Keeper, The	FRA/GRE/ITA	Heleni Karaendrou
Beginner's Luck	NWP	Richard Lavsky
Behind Enemy Lines	NBC-TV	Jack Chipman/Steve Lindsey
Believe It or Not (Impossible Things)	RUS	I. Matzievsky
Belzaire the Cajun	IND	Michael Doucet

Best Man, The	BRI	Eamon Friel
Best of Times, The	UN	Arthur B. Rubinstein
Betrayed by Innocence	CBS-TV	Charles Fox
Better Days (series)	CBS-TV	Jesse Frederick/Bennett Salvay
Better Tomorrow, A	HK	Joseph Koo
Betty Blue	FRA	Gabriel Yared
Between Two Women	ABC-TV	Charles Gross
Beverly Hills Madam	NBC-TV	Lalo Schifrin
Beyond Passion	SPA	Leo Marino
Bi and the Ba, The	ITA	Detto Mariano
Big Deal on Madonna Street-- 20 Years Later	ITA	Bruno Moretti/Nino Rota
Big Easy, The	IND	Brad Fiedel
Big Hurt, The	AUT	Allan Zavod
Big Joys, Small Sorrows	JAP	Chuji Kinoshita
Big Trouble	COL	Bill Conti
Big Trouble in Little China	FOX	John Carpenter
Birds of Prey	CAN	Paul Zaza
Bitter Coffee	IND	Eros Djarot
Bitter Truth, The	HUN	Ferenc Farkas
Black and Without Sugar	GER	Adrian Vonwiller
Black Flag	SPA	Carmelo Bernaola
Black Hanky Panky	FRA	Ray Lema
Black Moon Rising	NWP	Lalo Schifrin
Black Tanner	AUS/GER/SWI	Hardy Hepp
Blacke's Magic	NBC-TV	David Bell
Blackout	NOR	Oistein Boassen
Blame It on Paradise	ITA	Giovanni Nuti
Blind Endeavor	HUN	Ferenc Balazs
Blind Justice	CBS-TV	Miles Goodman
Blood (Kan)	TUR	Zuifu Livaneli
Blood and Orchids	CBS-TV	Mark Snow
Blood of Brothers (Aghaat)	IN	Ajit Varman
Blood Sport	CBS	John Davis
Blood Ties	ITA	Celso Valli
Blood Tracks	SWE	Dag Unenge
Bloody Birthday	IND	Arlon Ober
Blue City	PAR	Ry Cooder
Blue DeVille	NBC-TV	Don Felder
Blue Like Hell	FRA	Pierre Porte
Blue Mammy, The	FIN	Pekka Jalkannen
Blue Velvet	DEG	Angelo Badalamenti
Bokuchan's Battlefield	JAP	Masao Hario
Boris Godunov	RUS	Vyacheslav Ovchinnikov
Born American	IND	Richard Mitchell
Boss' Wife, The	TST	Bill Conti
Boy in Blue, The	FOX	Roger Webb
Boy Soldier	BRI	Graham Williams
Boy Who Could Fly, The	FOX	Bruce Broughton
Breeders	EMP	Don Great/Tom Milano

Bricklayers Day, Part II	MEX	Ernesto Cortazar
Bridge to Nowhere	NZ	Stephen McCurdy
Bridges to Cross	CBS-TV	Mark Snow
Brighton Beach Memoirs	UN	Michael Small
Broken Arrow 29	BRI	"Los Iberos"
Broken Images	EGY	Mohamed Hilal
Bronco, El	MEX	Ernesto Cortazar
Bullies	CAN	Paul Zaza
Burst of Lead	MEX	Ricardo Carrion
Busted Up	CAN	Charles Barnett
Butterflies and Flowers	THAI	"Butterfly"
C.A.T. Squad	NBC-TV	Ennio Morricone
Calacan	MEX	Luis Guzman
Camarena Taken Hostage	MEX	Marco Flores
Camorra	ITA	Tony Esposito
Can You Feel Me Dancing?	NBC-TV	Johnny Harris
Canterville Ghost, The	IND-TV	Howard Blake
Capablanca	CUB/RUS	Sergio Vitier
Captive	BRI/FRA	Michael Berkeley/ "The Edge"
Caravaggio	BRI	Simon Fisher Turner
Caravan Palace	GRE	Giorgos Tsanguaris
Care Bears Movie II: A New Generation	COL	Patricia Cullen
Carefree Giovanni	ITA	Lamberto Macchi
Case of the Shooting Star, The	NBC-TV	Dick de Benedictis/ Fred Steiner
Castaway	BRI	Stanley Myers
Castle, The (Linna)	FIN	Otto Donner
Catch, The	JAP	Shigeaki Saegusa
Cat's Whiskers and Green Peas	SWE	Stefan Nilsson
Cavanaughs, The (series)	CBS-TV	William Moloney/Paul Pilger/Dennis Polen
Certain Desire, A	FRA	Gabriel Yared
Challenge, The	AUT-TV	Martin Armiger
Champions Part 3--The Final Battle, The	CAN	Eldon Rathburn
Charley Hannah	ABC-TV	Jan Hammer
Check Is in the Mail, The	IND	David Frank
Chicano Connection, The	MEX	Rafael Elizondo
Chicherin	RUS	Irakli Gabeli
Chidambaram	IN	Devarajan
Child God, The	IN	Utpalendu Chakraborti
Children of a Lesser God	PAR	Michael Convertino
Children of Bullerby Village, The	SWE	Georg Riedel
Children of the Cold War	CHILE/FRA	Jorge Arriagada
Children of Times Square	ABC-TV	Michael Shrieve
Child's Cry	CBS-TV	Garry Sherman
Choices	ABC-TV	Charles Gross
Choke Canyon	IND	Sylvester Levay
Chopper	IN	Nikhil Chattopadhyay

Chopping Mall (Kilbots)	IND	Chuck Cirino
Christmas Present	ITA	Riz Ortolani
Christmas Snow	NBC-TV	Michael Convertino
Christmas Star, The	DIS-TV	Ralph Burns
Circle of Violence: A Family Drama	CBS-TV	"Blue Daisies"/Gil Melle
City, The	ABC-TV	J. A. C. Redford
Clan of the Cave Bear, The	WB	Alan Silvestri
Class of Nuke 'Em High	IND	Michael Lattanzi
Classified Love	CBS-TV	Artie Butler
Clockwise	BRI	George Fenton
Close to Home	CAN	Ken Ilemmerick
Clowns of God, The	FRA	Teddy Lasry/Mikis Theodorakis
Club Med	ABC-TV	Peter Bernstein
Club Paradise	WB	David Mansfield/Van Dyke Parks
Clue: Movies, Murder and Mystery	CBS-TV	Kevin Kinen
Cobra	WB	Sylvester Levay
Codename: Wildgeese	GER/ITA	Jan Nemec
Color of Money, The	DIS	Robbie Robertson
Combat High	NBC-TV	Robert Folk
Combat Shock	IND	Ricky Giovinazzo
Comic Magazine	JAP	Katsuo Ono
Coming Up Roses	BRI	Michael Storey
Comrades	BRI	David Graham/Hans-Werner Henze
Condor	ABC-TV	Ken Heller
Condor	IND-TV	Tom Salisbury
Confidential	CAN	Bruce Ley
Congo Express	BEL	"Kreuners Group"
Contraband Aces	MEX	Diego Herrera
Cool Change	AUT	Bruce Rowland
Cormorant	YUG	Zoran Predin
Corner Forsaken by Love, The	CHN	Wang Ming
Countdown	HUN	Jozsef Czencz
Courage	CBS-TV	Craig Safan
Cowboys	HUN	Janos Novak
Crawlspace	IND	Pino Donaggio
Crazy Dan	NBC-TV	Peter Myers
Crime Story	NBC-TV	Todd Rundgren
Crimes of the Heart	DEG	Georges Delerue
Critters	NLC	David Newman
Crocodile Dundee	AUT	Peter Best
Crossings	ABC-TV	Michel Legrand
Crossroads	COL	Ry Cooder
Cry from the Mountain	IND	J. A. C. Redford
Cut and Run	ITA	Claudio Simonetti
Cyclone Tracy	AUT-TV	Martin Armiger
D.C. Cop	CBS-TV	Tony Berg

Dads (series)	ABC-TV	Alf Clausen
Dallas: The Early Years	CBS-TV	Jerrold Immel
Dalton: Code of Vengeance II	NBC-TV	Don Peake
Dancing Daze	AUT-TV	Martin Armiger
Dancing on Water	YUG	Zoran Simjanovic
Dangerous Orphans	NZ	Jonathan Crayford
Dangerously Close	IND	Michael McCarty
Dark Mansions	ABC-TV	Ken Harrison
Dark Night	HK/TAI	Peter Chang
Dawn, The	FRA/ISR	Zoltan Simon
Day of Wrath	RUS	Gija Kantscheli
Days of Hell	ITA	Francesco de Masi
Dead-End Drive-In	AUT	Frank Strangio
Dead End Kids	IND	David Byrne/Philip Glass
Dead Man's Folly	CBS-TV	John Addison
Deadly Business, A	CBS-TV	Paul Chihara
Deadly Friend	WB	Charles Bernstein
Death Game, The	MEX	Susan (Suzy) Rodriguez
Death of a Soldier	AUT	Allan Zavod
Death of the Heart, The	BRI	Geoffrey Burgon
Death on a Rainy Sunday	FRA/SWI	Vladimir Cosma
Deaths in Tokimeki	JAP	Osamu Shiomura
Debutante, The	FRA	Yves Gilbert
Deep Lakes	SWI	Daniele Mainardi
Deliberate Stranger, The	NBC-TV	Gil Melle
Delta Force, The	IND	Alan Silvestri
Demons 2--The Nightmare Is Back	ITA	Simon Boswell
Department Store	ITA	Detto Mariano
Departure	AUT	Bruce Smeaton
Descent into Hell	FRA	Georges Delerue
Desiring Giulia	ITA	Antonio Sechi
Desperate Road, The	TUR	Ugur Dikmen
Detached Mission, The	RUS	Victor Babushkin
Detachment, The (Burys)	RUS	Vladimir Kamolikov
Devastator, The (Kings Ransom)	IND	Matthew Ender/Mark Governor
Devil in the Flesh	FRA/ITA	Carlo Crivelli
Diapason	ARG	Lito Vitale
Diary of a Perfect Murder, The	NBC-TV	Dick de Benedictis
Diggers	IND	Ken McIntyre
Dirt Bike Kid, The	IND	Bill Bowersock
Dirt Cheap	AUT	"The Early Kookas"
Disconnected	IND	Steve Asetta
Disorder	FRA	Gabriel Yared
Dr. Otto and the Riddle of the Gloom Beam	IND	Shane Keister
Dogs of the Night	ARG	Leion Gieco/Tarrago Ros
Doing Life	NBC-TV	Arthur B. Rubinstein
Dot and the Whale	AUT	Guy Gross

Double Switch	DIS-TV	Michel Colombier
Double Talk	ABC-TV	Bob Cobert
Down by Law	IND	John Lurie
Downtown	CBS-TV	Johnny Harris
Dragon Rapide	SPA	Javier Montsalvatje
Dream Castle, The	NOR	Svein Gundersen
Dream Lover	MGM	Michael Small
Dream Lovers	HK	Law Wing Fai
Dream West	CBS-TV	Fred Karlin
Dreams of Gold	CBS-TV	Ernest Gold
Dress Gray	NBC-TV	Billy Goldenberg
Drug Knot, The	CBS-TV	Robert De La Garza
Drunken Night	FRA	Jacques Delaporte
Dublin Suite, The	IRE-TV	Robert Lamb
Dumb Dicks	ITA	Guido and Maurizio de Angelis
Dunki-Schott (Don Quixote)	GER/SWI	Ruedi Haeusermann
Dying to Sing	ITA-TV	Luis Enrique Bacalov
Easy Prey	ABC-TV	J. A. C. Redford
Easy Street	NBC-TV	Palmer Fuller
Eat and Run	NWP	Donald Pippin
Eat the Peach	IRE	Donal Lunny
8 Million Ways to Die	TST	James Newton Howard
Elephant Got Lost, An	RUS	Sandor Kallosh
Eliminators	IND	Bob Summers
Embryo	HUN	Zdenko Tamassy
Emperor Caligula: The Untold Story, The	ITA	Carlo Maria Cordio
Enchanted Dollars, The	HUN	Karoly Frenreisz
Endgame	ITA	Carlo Maria Cordio
Endless Dream	BRA	Antonio Adolfo
Equinox	CAN	Jean Sauvageau
Evening Bells	YUG	Vladimir Kraus-Rajteric
Evening Dress	FRA	Serge Gainsbourg
Every Time We Say Goodbye	TST	Philippe Sarde
Extremities	ATL	J. A. C. Redford
F/X	ORI	Bill Conti
Face to Face	IN	M. B. Srinivasan
Faculty, The (pilot)	ABC-TV	Patrick Williams
Failure, The	HOL	Lelijke Mannen
Fair Game	AUT	Ashley Irwin
False One, The	AUS/GER/SWI	Muzzi Loffredo
Family, The	HK	Lam Mun Yee
Family Council	FRA	Georges Delerue
Fantasist, The	IRE	Stanislas Syrewicz
Fast Times (series)	CBS-TV	Danny Elfman/Barry Goldberg
Fatherland	BRI/GER	Christian Kunert/Gerulf Pannach
Father's Day	ABC-TV	Barry Goldberg

Faubourg Saint-Martin	FRA	Serge Tomassi
Ferris Bueller's Day Off	PAR	Ira Newborn
Ferrywoman, The	ITA	Franco Piersanti
Fetters	EGY	Intisar Abdul-Fatah
15 Pounds in 7 Days	ITA	Pino Donaggio
Fifth Missile, The	NBC-TV	Pino Donaggio
52 Pick-Up	IND	Gary Chang
50 Years of Action!	IND	Bill Conti
Fighting Choice	ABC-TV	Brad Fiedel
Final Mission	IND	Georges Garvarentz
Final Take: The Golden Days of the Movies	JAP	Naozumi Yamamoto
Fine Mess, A	COL	Henry Mancini
Fine Weather, but Storms Due Towards Evening	FRA	Roland Vincent
Fire in the Night	IND	Toti Fuentes
Fire with Fire	PAR	Howard Shore
Firefighter	CBS-TV	John Addison
Firewalker	IND	Gary Chang
Flames in the Ashes	ISR	Yossi Mar-Haim
Flaming Hearts	DEN	Peer Raben
Flies in the Light	SWI	Stephan Wittwer
Flight of the Navigator	DIS	Alan Silvestri
Flight of the Spruce Goose	IND	Henri Seroka
Flight 222	RUS	Sergei Banevitch
Flodder	HOL	Dick Maas
Florida Straits	HBO-C	Michel Colombier
Fly, The	FOX	Howard Shore
Flying	CAN	Ollie E. Brown
Follow My Gaze	FRA	Tom Novembre
Fools on the Hill, The	PBS-TV	Denis King
Footrot Flats	NZ	Dave Dobbyn
Forbidden of the World, The	FRA	"Big Bucks"
Foreign Body	ORI	Ken Howard
Forget That Case	BUL	Kiril Dontchev
Formula for Murder	ITA	Francesco de Masi
Fortune Dane	ABC-TV	Douglas Fraser/David Kurtz
45th Parallel	ITA	Manuel de Sica
40 Square Meters of Germany	GER	Klaus Bantzer
Fouette	RUS	Anatoly Balchev/Oleg Karavalchuk
Fox, The	SWE	Bo Anders Persson
Foxtrap	IND	Patrizio Fariselli
Fracchia vs. Dracula	ITA	Bruno Zambrini
Frankenstein '88 (Vindicator, The)	CAN	Paul Zaza
Franza	AUS	Bert Breit
Fresno	CBS-TV	John Morris
Friday the 13th, Part VI: Jason Lives	PAR	Harry Manfredini
Fringe Dwellers, The	AUT	George Dreyfus

Frogs, The	TUR	Atilla Ozdemiroglu
From Beyond	IND	Richard Band
Frontier	CAN-TV	Hagood Hardy
Frozen Leopard, The	SWE	Leifur Thorarensson
Fugitives, The	FRA	Vladimir Cosma
Fulaninha	BRA	Sergio G. Saraceni
Full Moon High	ORI	Gary William Friedman
Funny Farm	ISR	Naftali Alter
Garbagemen	CAN	Yves Godin/"Lady Luck"
General Document on Chile	CUB	Angel Parra
Genesis	BEL/FRA/IN/SWI	Ravi Shankar
Gentle France	FRA/GER	Nicolas Skorsky
Gentleman, The	EGY	Mohamed Hellal
George McKenna Story, The	CBS-TV	Herbie Hancock
George Washington: The Forging of a Nation	CBS-TV	Bruce Broughton
German Dreams	GER	Juergen Buchner
Geronima	ARG	Arnaldo di Pace/Aime Paine
Getting Even (Hostage: Dallas)	IND	Chris Young
Gift of Amazing Grace, The	ABC-TV	Harold Wheeler
Gilsodom	KOR	Kim Jong-Kil
Girl from Mani, The	BRI/GRE	Theodore Antoniou
Girl in Red, The	CHN	Wang Ming
Girl of Good Family, A	CHN	Shi Wanchum
Girl Who Spelled Freedom, The	DIS-TV	Mark Snow
Girls School Screamers	IND	John Hodian
Gladiator, The	ABC-TV	David Frank
Global Assembly Line, The	IND	Steven Gray
Gloves	ISR	Shalom Hanoch
Godson, The	POL	Waldemar Kazanecki
Going Sane	AUT	Cameron Allan
Golden Child, The	PAR	Michel Colombier
Gonza the Spearman	JAP	Toru Takemitsu
Good Hope, The	HOL	Rogier van Otterloo
Good Wife, The	AUT	Cameron Allan
Gosta Berling's Saga	SWE-TV	Arnold Ostman/Leif Stinnrbom
Gothic	BRI	Thomas Dolby
Grand Illusion, The	FIN	Kaija Saariaho
Granny General	RUS	Mikhail Makmudov
Great Bookie Robbery, The (series)	AUT-TV	Dave Skinner
Great Mouse Detective, The	DIS	Henry Mancini
Great Wall Is a Great Wall, The	ORI	David Liang
Gritta of the Rat Castle	E.GER	Stefan Carow
Grown Up Today	E.GER	Juergen Balitzki
Gung Ho	PAR	Thomas Newman
Gypsy, The	FRA	Claude Bolling
Half Moon Street	FOX	Richard Harvey

Half of the Sky	SPA	"Milladoiro"
Hamburger--The Motion Picture	IND	Peter Bernstein
Hame'ahev	ISR	Dov Seltzer
Handful of Paradise, A	TUR	Tarik Ocal
Hands of Steel (After the Fall of New York)	ITA	Claudio Simonetti
Happiness Strikes Again	FRA	Jean-Claude Deblais
Happy Din Don	HK	Michael Lai
Happy Homecoming, Comrade	GRE	Heleni Karaendrou
Happy New Year--1949	YUG	Ljupco Konstantinov
Happy Valley, The	BRI	Geoffrey Burgon
Hard Asphalt	NOR	Marius Mueller
Hard Game	BRA	Mauro Giorgetti
Hardbodies 2	IND	Ed Arkin/Jay Levy
Hardesty House	ABC-TV	Fred Karlin
Harem	ABC-TV	John Scott
Haunted Honeymoon	ORI	John Morris
He Looks Dead ... But He Just Fainted	ITA	Lamberto Macchi
Head of the Class (series)	ABC-TV	Ed Alton
Head Office	TST	James Newtom Howard
Heart of the City	ABC-TV	Patrick Williams
Heartbreak Ridge	WB	Lennie Niehaus
Heartburn	PAR	Carly Simon
Heavenly Pursuits	BRI	B. A. Robertson
Hellfire	IND	Mark Knox
Help Wanted: Kids	ABC-TV	Craig Safan
Henri	CAN	Denis Larochelle
Her Name Is Vasfiye	TUR	Atilla Ozdemiroglu
Hero in the Family	NBC-TV	William Goldstein
He's the Mayor (series)	ABC-TV	Glen Ballard
He's Too Much (Troppo Forte)	ITA	Antonello Venditti
High Speed	FRA	Olivier Hutman
Highlander	FOX	Michael Kamen
History	ITA	Fiorenzo Carpi
Hitcher, The	TST	Mark Isham
Hold the Dream	BRI-TV	Barrie Guard
Hollywood Vice Squad	IND	Michael Convertino/ Keith Levine
Hoosiers	ORI	Jerry Goldsmith
Hot Shots	CBS-TV	Domenic Troiano
House	NWP	Harry Manfredini
House Committee Rivalry	ISR	Erich Rudich
House of Gloom	YUG-TV	Vojkan Borisavljevic
House on the River, The	E.GER	Guenther Fischer
House Poised on the Edge, A	ITA	Franco Piersanti
Houston: The Legend of Texas	CBS-TV	Dennis McCarthy
How Young We Were Then	RUS	Yuri Vinnik
Howard the Duck	UN	John Barry/Sylvester Levay
Hunger	EGY	George Kaza Zayani

Hyper Sapien: People from Another Star	TST	Arthur B. Rubinstein
I Go to Tokyo	JAP	Hiroshi Wada
I Hate Actors	FRA	Roland Vincent
I Love Dollars	FRA/HOL/SWI	Willem Breuker
I-Man	DIS-TV	Craig Safan
I Married a Vampire	IND	Steve Monahan
I Need a Moustache	SPA	Carlos Vizziello
I Own the Racecourse	AUT	Martin Armiger/Red Symons
I Was Caught in the Night	CZE	Michael Kocab
Ideal Landscape	EST	Jaanus Nogisto
Idiots May Apply	HUN	Janos Masik
If Tomorrow Comes	CBS-TV	Nick Bicat
Imagemaker, The	IND	Fred Karns
Images of an Everyday War	CAN/CHILE	Rodrigo Villaseka
Impure Thoughts	IND	James Oliviero
In a Glass Cage	SPA	Javier Navaretor
In 'n' Out (Gringo Mojado)	MEX	T-Bone Burnett
In Search of the Trojan War	PBS-TV	Terry Oldfield/David Pash
In the Name of the Law	SWE	Ulf Dageby
In the Shadow of Kilimanjaro	IND	Arlon Ober
In the Shadow of Victory	HOL	Henny Vrienten
Informer, The	SWI	Benedikt Jeger
Innocence	ITA	Graziano Mandozzi
Inside Out	IND	Peer Raben
Insomniacs, The	ARG	Luis Maria Serra
Inspector Lavardin	FRA	Mathieu Chabrol
Intimate Encounters	NBC-TV	Sylvester Levay
Intimate Strangers	CBS-TV	Barry de Vorzon
Invaders from Mars	IND	Christopher Young
Invitation to Dance	GER	Ingfried Hoffmann
Iron Eagle	TST	Basil Poledouris
Isaac in America	IND	Ross Levinson
Island, An	ITA-TV	Armando Trovajoli
Islands	IND	Scott Cossu
Isle of Fantasy	HK	Mahmood Rumjahn
Italian Fast Food	ITA	Detto Mariano
It's Gary Shandling's Show (series)	SHO-C	Joey Carbonne
It's My Life (Noa Noa 2, El)	MEX	Gabriel and Eduardo Malallemo
Jack and Mike (series)	ABC-TV	Johnny Mandel
Jackals	IND	Paul Chihara
Jake Speed	NWP	Mark Snow
Jo Jo Dancer, Your Life Is Calling	COL	Herbie Hancock
Joe Bash (series)	ABC-TV	Jack Elliott
John Lennon: A Journey in the Life	PBS-TV	John Altman
Johnnie Mae Gibson: FBI	CBS-TV	Billy Goldenberg

Joint Brothers, The	FRA	Jacques Delaporte
Journey, The (Reise, Die)	GER/SWI	Franco Ambrosetti
Jubiaba	BRA/FRA	Gilberto Gil
Judgment in Stone, A	CAN	Patrick Coleman/ Robert Murphy
Jumpin' Jack Flash	FOX	Thomas Newman
Jumping (Springen)	BEL	Dirk Brosse
Jungle Raiders	ITA	Cal Taormina
Just Between Friends	ORI	Patrick Williams
Kaj Munk	DEN-TV	Ole Schmidt
Kamikaze	FRA	Eric Serra
Kamikaze Hearts	IND	Walt Fowler/Paul M. Young
Kangaroo	AUT	Nathan Waks
Kangaroo Complex, The	FRA	Serge Perathoner
Karate Kid Part II, The	COL	Bill Conti
Karsh: The Searching Eye	CAN	Louis Applebaum
Keep Smiling, Baby!	EST	Lepo Sumera
Kid, The (Mome, Le)	FRA	Otis Redding
Killer in the Mirror	NBC-TV	Gil Melle
Killer Party	MGM	John Beal
Killing Cars	GER	Michael Landau
Killing Machine, The	MEX/SPA	Guido and Maurizio de Angelis
Kind of English, A	BRI	"Fire House"
King and His Movie, A	ARG	Carlos Franzetti
King Kong Lives	DEG	John Scott
Kingdom Chums: Little David's Adventure, The	ABC-TV	Joe Raposo
Kiss Me, Witch	ITA-TV	Stelvio Cipriani
Knight of the Dragon, The	SPA	Jose Nieto
Knock Out	GRE	Georges Hatzinassios
Komba, God of the Pygmies	AFR/FRA	Hector Zazou
Kuei-Mei, A Woman	TAI	Chang Hung-Yi
Kung Fu: The Movie	CBS-TV	Lalo Schifrin
L.A. Law	NBC-TV	Mike Post
Labyrinth	TST	Trevor Jones
Ladies Club, The	NLC	Lalo Schifrin
Lady Jane	BRI	Stephen Oliver
Lake of Constance, The	POL	Jerzy Satanowski
Laputa	GER	Matthis Meyer
Las Vegas Weekend	IND	Scarlet Rivera/Alan St. Jons
Last Days of Frank and Jesse James, The	NBC-TV	Paul Chihara
Last Days of Patton, The	CBS-TV	Allyn Ferguson
Last Electric Knight, The	DIS-TV	David Kurtz/James Roberts
Last Faust, The (Filme Demencia)	BRA	Luiz Chagas/Manuel Paiva
Last Frontier, The	CBS-TV	Brian May

Last Mazurka, The	ITA	Gino Negri
Last of Philip Banter, The	SPA/SWI	Phil Marshall
Last Precinct, The	NBC-TV	Pete Carpenter/Mike Post
Last Resort	IND	Steve Nelson
Last Song	FRA/SWI	Stephane Vilar
Last Tango, The	ALG/FRA	Philippe Arthuys/ Jean Paul Cara
Legal Eagles	UN	Elmer Bernstein
Legend of Sleepy Hollow, The	SHO-C	Robert Folk
Leo and Liz in Beverly Hills	CBS-TV	David Frank
Leonora	AUT	Derek Strahan
Let Them Kill Me Once and For All	MEX	Joaquin Lopez Chapman
Lethal (KGB--The Secret War)	IND	Misha Segal
Let's Hope It's a Girl	FRA/ITA	Nicola Piovani
Letters from a Dead Man	RUS	Alexander Zhurbin
Life and Loves of a She-Devil, The	BRI-TV	Peter Filleul
Like Poison (Jako Jed)	CZE	Jiri Stivin
Lily	CBS-TV	Robert Folk
Link	BRI	Jerry Goldsmith
Lisi and the General	SWI	Renato Anselmi
Lit Lantern, The	RUS	Tigran Mansuyan
Little Shop of Horrors, The	WB	Miles Goodman
Little Sister, The	IND-TV	Pat Metheny
Little Spies	ABC-TV	Peter Bernstein
Lock 17	GER	Paul Hornyak
Lola	SPA	Jose Manuel Pagan
Long Coats, The	ARG/FRA	Jean-Francois Leon
Long Time Gone	ABC-TV	Artie Kane
Longshot, The	ORI	Charles Fox
Lord Mountbatten: The Last Viceroy	PBS-TV	John Scott
Lost!	CAN	Mickey Erbe/Maribeth Solomon
Lost Empires	BRI-TV	Derek Hilton/Joseph Ward
Lost in the Wilderness	JAP	William Ackerman
Lost Republic II, The	ARG	Luis Maria Serra
Love Around the Corner	MEX	Jose Elorza
Love in Bagdad	IRAQ	Abdul Amir Alcarraf
Love Letter (Koibumi)	JAP	Takayuki Inoue
Love Scenes	IND	Ted Scotto
Love Story (Storia d'Amore)	ITA	Giovanna Marini
Love Till First Blood	HUN	Laszlo Des
Love With a Perfect Stranger	SHO-C	John Du Prez
Love with the Perfect Stranger	HK	So Chun-hou/Stephen Shing
Lover, The (Asheke, Al)	IRAQ	Helmi Al Wadi
Loving Walter	BRI	George Fenton

Low Blow	CRO	Steve Amundsen
Lucas	FOX	Dave Grusin
Lulu by Night	SPA	Angel Munoz
Madness My Love	ITA	Francesco De Masi
Madres: The Mothers of Plaza de Payo, Las	FRF	"Inti-Illimani"/Astor Piazzola
Mafia Princess	NBC-TV	Lee Holdridge
Maggie	CBS-TV	Charles Fox
Magic Toyshop, The	BRI	Bill Connor
Maine-Ocean Express	FRA	Chico Buarque/Hubert Dege/Anne Frederic
Make a Note of This Face	AUS	Pas Paravant
Malady of Love, The	FRA/ITA	Egisto Macchi
Malayunta	ARG	Lito Nebbia
Mama Is Mad!	HOL	Ruud van Hemert
Membru Went to War	SPA	Carmelo Bernaola
Mammame	FRA	Serge Houppin/Henry Torque
Man About Town	ABC-TV	David Shire
Man and a Woman: 20 Years Later, A	FRA	Francis Lai
Man in the Moon, The	DEN	Robert Broberg
Man Looking Southeast	ARG	Pedro Aznar
Man of Ashes	TUN	Salah Mahdi
Man With the Black Coat, The	BRA	David Tygel
Manhattan Project, The	FOX	Philippe Sarde
Manhunter, The	DEG	Michel Rubini
Manly Education, A	RUS	Nury Chalmamedov
Manon	VEN	Federico Ruiz
Manon des Sources	FRA	Jean-Claude Lepit
Many Happy Returns	CBS-TV	Matthew McCauley
Maria	HOL	Tonny Eyk
Market of the Humble	MEX	H. Baltazar
Marriage of Convenience	RUS	Isaak Schwarz
Massey Sahib	IN	Vanraj Bhatia
Master, The	RUS	Tigran Mansuyan
Matador	SPA	Bernardo Bonezzi
Matlock	NBC-TV	Dick de Benedictis
Matter of Heart	IND	John Adams
Max My Love	FRA	Michel Portal
Maximum Overdrive	IND	"AC/DC"
May We Borrow Your Husband?	BRI-TV	Joe Campbell/Paul Hart
Me and Mrs. C	NBC-TV	Harry Middlebrooks
Melo	FRA	Philippe Gerard
Mementos	INDONESIA	Idris Sardi
Memoirs of a Sinner, The	POL	Jerzy Maksymiuck
Men's Club, The	ATL	Lee Holdridge
Mesmerized	AUT/BRI/NZ	Georges Delerue
Mexican, You Can Do It	MEX	Pedro Plascencia
Miles to Go	CBS-TV	Ken Wannberg

Mind of Clay, The	IN	T. R. Mahalingam
Miracle of the Heart: The Boys Town Story	IND-TV	Lee Holdridge
Mirza Nowrouz's Shoes	IRAN	Freydoun Nasseri
Miss Mary	ARG	Luis Maria Serra
Mission, The	BRI	Ennio Morricone
Mr. and Mrs. Ryan	ABC-TV	John Davis
Mr. Boogedy	ABC-TV	John Addison
Mr. Fabre's Mill	ALG	Noutil Fadel
Mr. Sunshine (series)	ABC-TV	Randy Edelman
Mr. Vampire	HK	Anders Nelson
Mrs. Delafield Wants to Marry	CBS-TV	Peter Matz
Mix-Up (Meli-Melo)	FRA	Nicolas Frize
Modern Girls	ATL	Ed Arkin/Jay Levy
Moments of Play	DEN	Antonio Carlos Jobim
Mona Lisa	BRI	Michael Kamen
Money Pit, The	UN	Michel Colombier
Monster Dog	IND	"Grupo Dichotomy"
Monster in the Closet	IND	Barrie Guard
Monster of Florence, The	ITA	Paolo Rustichelli
Monster Shark (Red Ocean)	FRA/ITA	Antony Barrymore
Moods (Etats d'Ame)	FRA	Jean-Marie Senia
Morning After, The	FOX	Paul Chihara
Moro Affair, The	ITA	Pino Donaggio
Moscow Bureau	ABC-TV	George Aliceson Tipton
Mosquito Coast, The	WB	Maurice Jarre
Mountaintop Motel Massacre	NWP	Ron F. Dilulio
Mueller's Bureau	AUS	Ernie Seuberth
Mulberry Tree, The (Pong)	KOR	Choi Chang-kwon
Murder in the Dark	DEN	Michael Falck/Pete Repete
Murders in the Rue Morgue	CBS-TV	Charles Gross
Murphy's Law	IND	Marc Donahue
Murrow	HBO-C	Carl Davis
My Brother-in-Law Has Killed My Sister	FRA	Philippe Sarde
My Brother Tom	AUT-TV	Garry McDonald/Laurie Stone
My Case	FRA/POR	Joao Pais
My Chauffeur	CRO	Paul Hertzog
My Darling, My Darling	BUL	Mitko Schtorev
My Friend Ivan Lapshin	RUS	Arkadi Gagulachvili
My Little Pony	IND	Rob Walsh
My Man Adam	TST	Sylvester Levay
My Sister Sam (series)	CBS-TV	Steve Dorff
My Sweet Little Village	CZE	Jiri Sust
My Town	DIS	Craig Safan
My Two Loves	ABC-TV	Gary William Friedman
Mystery of Bellavista, The	ITA	Renzo Arbore
Nadia	ISR	Yoni Rechter
Naked Cage, The	IND	Christopher Stone

Naked Vengeance	IND	Ron Jones
Name of the Rose, The	FOX	James Horner
Nanou	BRI/FRA	John Kean
Narc--Red Duel, The	MEX	Hector Sanchez
Native Son	IND	James Mtume
Nazi Hunter: The Beate Klarsfeld Story	ABC-TV	Richard Hartley
Neighborhood--Oh, Those Hot Mexicans, The	MEX	Ernesto Cortazar
Nemesio	CHILE	Payo Grondona
Neon Maniacs	IND	Kendall Schmidt
New Delhi Times	IN	Louis Banks
New Mike Hammer, The	CBS-TV	Ron Ramin
New Morning of Billy the Kid, The	JAP	Shuichi Chino
New World	BRI	Stanley Myers
News at Eleven	CBS-TV	Mark Snow
Next of Kin	FRA	Bruno Coulais
'night, Mother	UN	David Shire
Night of the Creeps	TST	Barry de Vorzon
Night of the Pencils, The	ARG	Jose Luis Castineira de Dios
Night on the Town, A	MEX	Nacho Mendez
Night with Silena, The	GRE	Kyriacos Sfetsas
Nightmare Weekend	BRI	Martin Kershaw
Nine-and-a-Half Weeks	MGM	Michael Hoenig/Jack Nitzsche
Ninja Turf (L.A. Streetfighters)	IND	Charles Pavlosky
No Mercy	TST	Alan Silvestri
No Retreat No Surrender	NWP	Paul Gilbreath
No Time to Die	GER/INDONESIA	Hans Hammer-schmid
Noah and the Cowboy	SWI	Andreas Litmanowitsch
Nobody's Child	CBS-TV	Michael Small
Nobody's Fool	IND	James Newton Howard
Nocturnal Voyage, The	AUS	Polio Brezina
North & South, Book II	ABC-TV	Bill Conti
Not Everything Is Ture	BRA	Joao Gilberto
Nothing in Common	TST	Patrick Leonard
November Cats	GER	Gunter Ress
Now or Never	GER	Chris Rea
Number 14	TUR	"Kurtalan Ekspres"/ Baris Manco
Ocean Drive Weekend	IND	Alan Kaufman
Oceans of Fire	CBS-TV	Patrick Williams
Octopus--Pt. 2, The	ITA-TV	Ennio Morricone
Of Pure Blood	CBS-TV	Brad Fiedel
Off Beat	DIS	James Horner
On the Next Morning the Minister Didn't Return to His Post	GER	Frieder Butzmann
On the Razzle	PBS-TV	Derek Bourgeois

On Valentine's Day	IND	Jonathan Shefter
On Wings of Eagles	NBC-TV	Laurence Rosenthal
One and Only, The (Unique, L')	FRA	Guy Boulanger
One Big Family	IND-TV	George Aliceson Tipton
One Crazy Summer	WB	Cory Lerios
One Look--and Love Begins	GER	Brynmor Jones
One More Saturday Night	COL	David McHugh
One Police Plaza	CBS-TV	Mark Snow
One Terrific Guy	CBS-TV	Mark Snow
Operation Violin Case	E.GER	Bernd Menzel
Opinion, The (Rai)	ALG	Farid Balkhirrat
Ordinary Heroes	ABC-TV	Perry Botkin
Other People's Passions	LAT	Uldis Stabulneiks
Out of Bounds	COL	Stewart Copeland
Outlaws	CBS-TV	Joseph Conlan
Outrage	CBS-TV	Morton Stevens
Ovation (Applause, Applause)	RUS	Alexander Morozov
Overnight	CAN	Michael Conway Baker/ Glenn Morley
P.O.W. The Escape	IND	David Storrs
Pack of Women, The	AUT-TV	Andrew Bell
Panther Squad	BEL/FRA	Douglas Cooper Getschal/ Jeffrey G. Gusman
Paradise	GER	Klaus Bantzer/"Combo Cocktail"
Paradise Camp	AUT-TV	Adam Hoptman
Paris Midnight	FRA	Christopher Donnet
Paso Doble for Three	CZE	Angelo Michajilov
Passage, The	FRA	Jean-Felix Lalanne
Passiflora	CAN	Jean Derome/Andre Duchesne/Rene Lussier
Passion	HK	Lowell Lo
Passion Flower	CBS-TV	Miles Goodman
Passion of Remembrance, The	BRI	Tony Remy
Past, Present, Future (Trikal)	IN	Vanraj Bhatia
Patriot, The	CRO	Jay Ferguson
Paul Cadmus: Enfant Terrible at 80	PBS-TV	Edward Korwin
Paulette	FRA	Nicolas Errera
Peggy Sue Got Married	TST	John Barry
Peking Central	FRA	Michel Hardy
Peking Opera Blues	HK	James Wong
Perry Mason: The Case of the Notorious Nun	NBC	Dick de Benedictis
Peter the Great	NBC-TV	Laurence Rosenthal
Photograph, The	GRE	Christidulos Halaris
Picture Hunters, The	HUN	Zsolt Dome
Piece of the Royal Pie, A	FRA	Vladimir Cosma
Pied Piper of Hamelin, The (Krysar)	CZE	Michael Kocab
Ping Pong	BRI	Richard Harvey

Pink Chiquitas, The	CAN	Paul Zaza
Pinky's Gang	DEN	Elizabeth Nielsen
Pirates	IND	Philippe Sarde
Placido	CUB	Sergio Vitier
Platoon	ORI	Georges Delerue
Play Dead	IND	Robert Farrar
Playing Away	BRI	Simon Webb
Playing Beatie Bow	AUT	Garry McDonald/Laurie Stone
Pleasures	ABC-TV	Lee Holdridge
Pointsman, The	HOL	Michel Mulders
Poison for Fairies	MEX	Carlos Jimenez Mabarak
Poker Face	AUT-TV	Joe Chindamo/Mark Domoney
Police Academy 3: Back in Training	WB	Robert Folk
Police Story	HK	Michael Lai
Polish War Worker, The	GER	Thomas Timmler
Poltergeist II	MGM	Jerry Goldsmith
Pony Express Boy, The	ITA	Umberto Smaila
Popeye Doyle	NBC-TV	Brad Fiedel
Population: One	IND	Daniel Schwartz
Pouvoir Intime	CAN	Richard Gregoire
Power	FOX	Cy Coleman
PPPerformer, The	HOL	Willem Breuker
Pretty in Pink	PAR	Michael Gore
Prince of Bel Air	ABC-TV	Robert Folk
Princess of Babylonia, The	SWE-TV	Thomas Lindahl
Private Classes	FRA	Philippe Sarde
Prodigal Son, The	LIT	Yuozas Sirvinskas
Professor, The	ITA	Nicola Piovani
Proka	YUG	Krist Lekaj
Prom Queen	ISR	Alex Kagan
Promise	CBS-TV	David Shire
Promise, The	JAP	Haruomi Hosono
Promised Land, The	MEX	Rafael Carrion
Promised Land, The	YUG	Alfi Kabiljo
Protect Me, My Talisman	RUS	Vadim Khrasatchev
Prude, The (Puritaine, La)	BEL/FRA	Philippe Sarde
Prunelle Blues	FRA	Ivan Julian/Hubert Rostaing
Psycho III	UN	Carter Burwell
Quicksilver	COL	Tony Banks
Quiet Cool	NLC	Jay Ferguson
RAD	TST	James di Pasquale
Radioactive Dreams	DEG	Pete Robinson
Rage	ITA/SPA	Stelvio Cipriani
Rage of Angels: The Story Continues	NBC-TV	Billy Goldenberg
Rao Saheb	IN	Bhaskar Chandawarkar
Ratboy	WB	Lennie Niehaus

Realm of Fortune, The	MEX	Lucia Alvarez
Rebel Love	IND	Bobby Horton
Recruits	IND	Steve Parsons
Red Desert Penitentiary	HOL	James Michael Taylor
Red Zone	FRA	Gabriel Yared
Redd Foxx Show, The (series)	ABC-TV	Sonny Burke
Reform School Girls	NWP	Tedra Gabriel
Reporter X	POR	Antonio Emiliano
Resting Place	CBS-TV	Paul Chihara
Retouche	GER	Konrad Haas
Return of a Citizen	EGY	Kamal Bakir
Return of Josey Wales, The	IND	Rusty Thornhill
Return of Mickey Spillane's Mike Hammer, The	CBS-TV	Earle Hagen
Return of the Jonsson League, The	SWE	Ragnar Grippe
Return to the Right Path	VIE	Hong Dang
Revenge	IND	Rod Slane
Richest Cat in the World, The	DIS-TV	Peter Bernstein
Ricochets	ISR	Benny Nagari
Right at the Bottom	GER	Heinrich Huber/Nehmet Ipek
Rise and Rise of Daniel Rocket, The	PBS-TV	Jonathan Shefter
Riverbed, The	IND	Josh Colow
River's Edge	IND	Juergen Knieper
Roanoak	PBS-TV	Paul Chihara
Robinsoniad: Or, My English Grandfather	RUS	Enri Lolaschwili
Rocinante	BRI	Juergen Knieper
Rockabye	CBS-TV	Charles Bernstein
Rockin' Road Trip (Summertime Blues)	IND	Ricky Keller
Roller Blade	NWP	Robert Garrett
Romance	ITA	Andrea Centazzo
Romantic Story	BUL	Aleksander Burzitsov
Room With a View, A	IND	Richard Robbins
Rosa Luxemburg	GER	Nicolas Economou
Rosa-the-Rose, Public Woman	FRA	Roland Vincent
'Round Midnight	FRA	Herbie Hancock
Round My Head in 40 Days	CZE	Peter & Pavel Orm
Ruder, P.I.	IND	Kevin Kelly
Run for Your Life, Lola	CAN	Lewis Furey
Running Scared	MGM	Rod Temperton
Ruthless People	DIS	Michel Colombier
Sacrifice, The (Offret)	FRA/SWE	Watazumido Shuso
Sacrifice of Youth	CHN	Liu Suola/Qu Xiasong
Salome	FRA/ITA	Egisto Macchi
Salty Sweets	CZE	Andrej Seban
Salvador	IND	Georges Delerue
Samaritan: The Mitch Snyder Story	CBS-TV	Craig Safan

San Antonito	SA	Juan Lanz
Sand	HK	"Jam Machine"
Sarraounia	AFR	Pierre Akendengue
Satan's Empire (Beginning, The)	EGY	Ammar El Cherii/Sayed Hegab
Saxon Splendor and Prussian Glory	E.GER-TV	Karl-Ernst Sasse
Scene of the Crime, The	FRA	Philippe Sarde
School for Vandals	BRI	David Hewson
Schumtz	AUT	"Yollo"
Scorpion (Summons, The)	CRO	Sean Murray
Second Night, The	ITA	Luigi Cinque
Second Serve	CBS-TV	Brad Fiedel
Second Victory, The	BRI	Stanley Myers
Secret Wife, The	FRA	Bruno Coulais
See You After School	SA	Alejandro Blanco Uribe
Seize the Day	IND	Elizabeth Swados
Sensi (Evil Senses)	ITA	Fabio Frizzi
Seven Female Vampires, The	BRA	Julio Medaglia
Sex Appeal	IND	Kai Joffee/Ian Shaw
Shadow Play	NWP	Jon Newton
Shaka Zulu (Part 1)	IND-TV	Dave Pollecutt
Shanghai Surprise	MGM	George Harrison/ Michael Kamen
Shark's Paradise	AUT-TV	Nigel Plunker
Sharma and Beyond	BRI	Rachel Portman
Shattered Spirits	ABC-TV	Michael Hoenig
Sheriff's Strange Son, The	MEX	Rafael Carrion
She's Gotta Have It	IND	Bill Lee
Shoot for the Sun	BRI	Michael Kamen
Short Changed	AUT	Chris Neal
Short Circuit	TST	David Shire
Shot from the Heart, A	DEN	Lars Hug
Shroud for a Nightingale	PBS-TV	Richard Harvey
Sidekicks (series)	ABC-TV	"Rareview"
Silence of the Poets, The	GER	Klaus Bantzer
Sin of Innocence	CBS-TV	Georges Delerue
Sins	CBS-TV	Francis Lai
16 Days of Glory	PAR	Lee Holdridge
Sixth Day, The	EGY	Omar Khairat
Sixth Sense, The	GER	Albert Kittler
Skin (Hud)	NOR	Arne Nordheim
Sky Bandits	BRI	Alfi Kabiljo
Sky Pirates	AUT	Brian May
Slaughter in Matamoros	MEX	Susan (Suzy) Rodriquez
Sledge Hammer (series)	ABC-TV	Arthur B. Rubinstein
Sleepwalk	IND	Phil Kline
Smart Alec	IND	Morgan Cavett/Stephen Hunter/Jan King/ Bruce Langhorne
Smile of the Lamb, The	ISR	Ilan Virtzberg
Smoky Mountain Christmas, A	ABC-TV	Dana Kaproff

Solarbabies	MGM	Maurice Jarre
Soldier's Revenge	IND	Don Great/Gary Rist
Something Entirely Different	NOR	Nissa Nyberget
Something in Common	CBS-TV	John Addison
Something Wild	ORI	John Cale/Laurie Anderson
Soul Man	NWP	Tom Scott
Space Camp	FOX	John Williams
Spell II, The	MEX	Guillermo Mendez
Spiker	IND	Jeff Barry
Spookies	IND	James Calabrese/Kenneth Higgins
Stammheim	GER	Marcel Wengler
Stand Alone	NWP	David Campbell
Stand by Me	COL	Jack Nitzsche
Star Crystal	NWP	Doug Katsaros
Star Trek VI: The Voyage Home	PAR	Leonard Rosenman
Stark: Mirror Image	CBS-TV	Bill Conti/Peter Myers
Starman (series)	ABC-TV	Dana Kaproff
State of Emergency, A	IND	Georges Garvarentz
State of Grace	FRA	Philippe Sarde
Stepfather, The	IND	Patrick Moraz
Still Point, The	AUT	Pierre Pierre
Stranded	NBC-TV	Alf Clausen
Street of Departures	FRA	Charles Benarroch
Street of My Childhood	DEN	Anne Linnet
Streets of Gold	FOX	Jack Nitzsche
Strong Medicine	IND-TV	Stanley Myers
Subarnarekha	IN	Ustad Khan
Successful Man, A	CUB	Luigi Nono
Summer (Rayon Vert, Le)	FRA	Jean-Louis Valero
Summer of the Samurai	GER	K. Bartholome
Sun on a Hazy Day, The	SYR	Soulhi el Wadi
Sun Searchers, The	E.GER	Joachim Werzlau
Sunday Drive	DIS-TV	Brad Fiedel
Sunrise (Rezhou)	CHN	Xu Jingxin
Sunset Strip	IND	David Storrs
Super Citizen	CHN	Li Show Chaun
SuperFanta Genio	ITA	Fabio Frizzi
Superfantozzi	ITA	Fred Bongusto
Supernaturals, The	REP	Robert O. Ragland
Swallow Storm, The	TUR	Engin Noyan
Swan Song	CHN	Zhao Xiaoyuan
Swedish Mess	SWE-TV	Anders Ekhadi
Sweet Absence	ITA	Mauro Pahani
Sweet Liberty	UN	Bruce Broughton
Swimmer, The (Plovec)	RUS	Temo Bakuzadze
Tai-Pan	DEG	Maurice Jarre
Take It Easy	DEN	Leo Mathisen
Taking It Home	NBC-TV	Tom Scott
Tandem	HUN	Janos Masik/Jiri Stivin

Tarot	GER	Christoph Oliver
Taste of Corn, The	ITA	Franco Piersanti
Taxi Boy	FRA	Charelie Couture
Ted Kennedy Jr. Story, The	NBC-TV	Teo Macero
Teo the Redhead	SPA	Jan Garbarek/Rosita Perrer
Terror and Black Lace	MEX	Pedro Plascencia
TerrorVision	IND	Richard Band
Texas Chainsaw Massacre Part 2, The	IND	Tobe Hooper/Jerry Lambert
Thanatos	MEX	Edgar Sosa Corona
Thanksgiving Promise, The	ABC-TV	Bruce Broughton
That Mad Mad Hospital	MEX	Carlos Torres
That Secret Sunday	CBS-TV	Bob Alcivar
That's Life!	COL	Henry Mancini
There Must Be a Pony	ABC-TV	Billy Goldenberg
Thief Academy	ITA	Bruno Zambrini
Third Dragon, The	CZE	Petr Hapka
'38	AUS/GER	Bert Grund
Thomas and Senior on the Track of Barend the Brute	HOL	Tonny Eyk
Thompson's Last Run	CBS-TV	Miles Goodman
Thousand and One Daisies, A	FRA	Philippe Eidel
Thrashin'	IND	Barry Goldberg
Three Amigos	ORI	Elmer Bernstein
Three Fifteen	IND	Gary Chang
Three's Happiness	YUG	Bogdan Arsovski/ Vlatko Stefanovski
Throb	IND-TV	Tena Clark
Throne of Fire, The	ITA	Carlo Rustichelli
Thumbscrew, The	DEN-TV	Anders Koppel
Thunder Run	IND	Jay Levy/Matthew McCauley
Thunder Warrior	ITA	Francesco de Masi
Time (Ido Van)	HUN	Gyorgy Selmeczi
Time Flyer	ABC-TV	David Shire
Time Stops	EGY	Georges Kazazian
Time That Remains, The	E.GER	Guenther Fischer
Time to Live and a Time to Die, A	TAI	Wu Ch'uch'u
Time to Triumph, A	CBS-TV	John Cacavas
To Church and Work You Go	HOL	Pieter de Bruin
To Live and Die in Westallgau	GER	Klaus Roggers
To Marry the Captain	RUS	Isaak Schwarz
Too Much Kissing (Qui Trop Embrasse)	FRA	Bruno Coulais
To Sleep So As to Dream	JAP	Hidehiko Urayama
Toby McTeague	CAN	Claude Demers
Together We Stand	CBS-TV	David Kurtz
Tommaso Blu	GER/ITA	Peer Raben
Tomorrow	FIN	Edward Vesala

Top Gun	PAR	Harold Faltermeyer
Torment	NWP	Christopher Young
Touch and Go	TST	Sylvester Levay
Touching	POL-TV	Zbigniew Preisner
Tough Cookies (series)	CBS-TV	George Aliceson Tipton
Tough Guys	DIS	James Newton Howard
Tragedy of the Afghan, The	SWI	Mark M. Rissi/Malek Salam
Train, The (Kettar, Al)	EGY	Tarak Sarara
Train of the Pioneers, The	SA	Mauricio Mejia
Tramp at the Door	CAN	Randolph Peters
Transformers, The	DEG	Vince DeCola
Transit Dreams	GER	Bernhard Voss
Trees We Were Hurting, The	GRE	Demetris Papademetriou
Trial on the Road	RUS	Isaak Schwarz
Trick or Treat	DEG	Christopher Young
Triple Cross	ABC-TV	Lalo Schifrin
Troll	IND	Richard Band
Trumpet Solo	RUS	R. Ledenew
Twelfth Night	AUT	Allen John/Nathan Waks
Twist Again in Moscow	FRA	Michel Goguelat
2-1/2 Dads	DIS-TV	Robert Folk
Two Faces of January	GER	Eberhard Schoener
Under Siege	NBC-TV	Brad Fiedel
Under the Influence	CBS-TV	Nan Schwartz
Unmasking the Idol	IND	Dee Barton
Unsewing Machine, The	FRA	Jacky Giordano
Va Banque	GER	Achim Reichel
Valerie (series)	NBC-TV	Charles Fox
Valhalla	DEN	Ron Goodwin
Vamp	NWP	Jonathan Elias
Vanishing Act	CBS-TV	Ken Wannberg
Vasectomy: A Delicate Matter	IND	Fred Karlin
Vendetta	IND	David Newman
Venetian Woman, The	ITA	Ennio Morricone
Vengeance: The Story of Tony Cimo	CBS-TV	Charles Gross
Very Close Quarters (Communal Flat, The)	IND	Jay Chattaway
Victim, The	EGY	Gamal Salama
Video Dead, The	IND	Kevin McMahon/Leonard Marcel/Stuart Rabinowitsch
Violated	IND	Lee Shapiro
Violent Man, A	MEX	Ernesto Cortazar
Violets Are Blue	COL	Patrick Williams
Virus Knows No Morals, A	GER	"Bermudas, The"/Maran Gosov
Visa U.S.A.	CUB	Leo Brower
Vital Signs	CBS-TV	Glen Paxton
Vladimir Horowitz: The Last Romantic	IND	Jack Pfeiffer

Volunteers	YUG	Kornelije Kovac
Voyage to Nowhere	SPA	Pedro Iturralde
Waiting for Darkness	FIN	Raoul Bjorkenheim
Wall Driller, The (Falfuro)	HUN	Janos Karacsony
Wasp, The	CAN	Osvaldo Montes
Weekend Warriors	IND	Perry Botkin
Welcome Home, Bobby	CBS-TV	David McHugh
Welcome to 18	IND	Tony Berg
Welcome to the Parade	CAN	Robb Wright
Westler	GER	Englebert Rehm
What Comes Around	IND	Al Delory
What Happened Next Year	SYR	Ziad Rahbany
What Really Happened Between the Images?	GER	Anthony Moore
Whatever It Takes	IND	Garry Sherman
When the Bough Breaks	NBC-TV	Paul Chihara
Where Are the Children?	COL	Sylvester Levay
Where Are You Going?	BUL	Kiril Dontchev
Where the River Runs Black	MGM	James Horner
Whistle Blower, The	BRI	John Scott
White Dwarf, The	FIN	Johnny Lee Michaels
Who Is Julia?	CBS-TV	Robert Drasnin
Whoopee Boys, The	PAR	Jack Nitzsche
Whoops Apocalypse	BRI	Patrick Gowers
Wild Clown, The	GER	Eberhard Schoener
Wild Dove, The	RUS	Isaak Schwarz
Wild Mountains	CHN	Xu Youfu
Wild Wind, The	RUS/YUG	Eugene Dogas
Wildcats	WB	Hawk Wolinski
Willy/Milly	IND	David McHugh
Windrider	AUT	Kevin Peak
Windshade	HOL	Berend Hunnekink
Winter Night in Gagra, A	RUS	Anatoly Kroll
Wired to Kill	IND	Russell Ferrante
Wisdom	FOX	Danny Elfman
Wise Guys	MGM	Ira Newborn
With All Hands (Corps et Biens)	FRA	Eric Lelann
Wizard, The	CBS-TV	Arthur B. Rubinstein
Wolf at the Door, The	DEN/FRA	Ole Schmidt
Wolves Among Themselves, The	FRA	Pino Marchese
Woman of My Life, The	FRA	Romano Musumarra
Women from South Lebanon	LEB	Jawed Berri/Ali Jihad Rassi
Women of Valor	CBS-TV	Georges Delerue
Working Girls	IND	David Van Tieghem
Wraith, The	IND	Michael Hoenig/J. Peter Robinson
X	NOR	Andrej Nebb/Holy Toy
Yako--Hunter of the Damned	MEX	Pedro Galarra
Year of Awakening, The	SPA	Francisco Guerrero
Yes, It's Your Father!	DEN	Jan Glasel
Yiddish Connection	FRA	Georges Garvarentz

Young Again	ABC-TV	James di Pasquale
Young Girl and Hell, The	FRA/SPA	Michel Stelio
Youngblood	MGM	William Orbit
Yuppies 2	ITA	Manuel de Sica
Yuppies, Youngsters Who Succeed	ITA	Detto Mariano
Yuri Mosenko KGB	HBO-C	Peter Howell
Yu'suf from Kuyucak	TUR	Timur Selcuk
Zone Troopers	IND	Richard Band
Zoning	GER	"Tangerine Dream"

1987

Aah, Belinda!	TUR	Omno Tunc
Abduction of Kari Swenson, The	NBC-TV	Sylvester Levay
About Love	SWE	Wlodek Gulgowski/Ulf Wahlberg
Absences	GRE	Stamatis Spandoudakis
Actress (Eiga Joyu)	JAP	Kensaku Tanigawa
Adventure of the Action Hunters, The	IND	John Pallumbo
Adventures in Babysitting	DIS	Michael Kamen
After Rubicon	NOR	Bent Aserud/Geir Bohren
After the Promise	CBS-TV	Ralph Burns
Alamo: 13 Days to Glory, The	NBC-TV	Peter Bernstein
Alfred Laliberte, Sculptor	CAN	Dominique Tremblay
All Life Long	MEX	Carlos Torres Marin
Allan Quatermain and the Lost City of Gold	IND	Michael Linn
Allnighter, The	UN	Charles Bernstein
Almost Partners	IND-TV	Paul Chihara
Amazing Grace and Chuck	TST	Elmer Bernstein
Amazons	IND	Oscar Camp
American Harvest	CBS-TV	Christopher Young
American Ninja 2: The Confrontation	IND	George S. Clinton
Amerika	ABC-TV	Basil Poledouris
And Then You Die	CAN	Marty Simons
And Two Eggs from Turkey	GRE	Nicos Portocaloglou
Andersen's Run	NOR	Bent Aserud/Geir Bohren
Angel Dust	FRA	Vincent-Marie Bouvot/ Leon Senza
Angel Heart	TST	Trevor Jones
Angel of Vengeance	IND	Chuck Dodson
Angelus Novus	ITA	Vittorio Gelmetti
Anguish	SPA	Jose Manuel Pagan
Anita--Dances of Vice	GER	Konrad Elfers/Ed Lieber/ Alan Marks/Rainer Rubert
Anne of Avonlea	DIS-TV	Hagood Hardy
Anzacs: The War Down Under	IND-TV	Bruce Rowland

April Is a Deadly Month	FRA	Philippe Sarde
Army Wives	AUT-TV	Chris Neal
As Long as There Are Women	FRA	Jean-Claude Petit
As Time Goes By	AUT	Peter Sullivan
Assassination	IND	Valentine McCallum/
		Robert O. Ragland
Assault & Matrimony	NBC-TV	Johnny Mandel
Association of Wrongdoers	FRA	Francis Lai
At Mother's Request	CBS-TV	Charles Gross
Attention, Bandits	FRA	Francis Lai
Aurelia	ITA	Paolo Conte
Australian Dream	AUT	Colin Timms
Autumn's Tale, An	HK	Lowell Lo
Axiliad	POL	Jerzy Satanowski
Babette's Feast	DEN	Per Norgaard
Baby Boom	MGM	Bill Conti
Baby Girl Scott	CBS-TV	Paul Chihara
Bach and Broccoli	CAN	Pierick Houdy
Bachelor Girl	AUT	Burkhart von Dallwitz
Back to the Beach	PAR	Steve Dorff
Backfire	IND	David Shire
Ballad of Dogs' Beach, The	POR/SPA	Alberto Iglesias
Bamba, La	COL	Miles Goodman/Carlos
		Santana
Banana Skin Waltz	HUN	Gyorgy Vukan
Bang! You're Dead!	GER	Piet Klocke
Banzai Runner	IND	Joel Goldsmith
Barbarians, The	IND	Pino Donaggio
Barbarous Wedding, The	BEL/FRA	Frederic Devrees
Barrington	CBS-TV	Patrick Williams
Bates Motel, The	NBC-TV	Peter Robinson
Batteries Not Included	UN	James Horner
Bay Coven	NBC-TV	Shuki Levy
Beaks (Birds of Prey)	IND	Stelvio Cipriani
Bear-Skinned Man	E.GER	Gunter Fischer
Beat, The	IND	Carter Burwell
Beat Generation--An American Dream, The	IND	David Amram
Beauf, Le	FRA	Alain Bashung
Beauty and the Beast	CBS-TV	Lee Holdridge
Beggars, The	FRA/SWI	Jorge Arriagada
Beirut: The Last Home Movie	IND	Lanny Meyers
Believers, The	ORI	Peter Robinson
Bell Diamond	IND	Jon English
Bellman and True	BRI	Colin Towns
Belly of an Architect, The	BRI	Glenn Branca/Wim
		Mertens
Below the Chinese Restaurant	ITA	Ugo Rossi
Beneath the World	ARG/CZE	Jose Luis Castineira de Dios
Benji the Hunted	DIS	Euel Box
Bennett Brothers, The (series)	NBC-TV	David Fishberg

Berserker	IND	Chuck Francour/Gary Griffin
Best Seller	ORI	Jay Ferguson
Better Than Bread	MEX	Gustavo Pimentel
Better Tomorrow II, A	HK	Joseph Koo
Betty Ford Story, The	ABC-TV	Arthur B. Rubinstein
Beverly Hills Buntz	NBC-TV	Ry Cooder
Beverly Hills Cop II	PAR	Harold Faltermeyer
Bewitched (Stregati)	ITA	Giovanni Nuti
Beyond Silence	VEN	Vincio Ludovic
Beyond Therapy	NWP	Gabriel Yared
Big Bad Mama II	IND	Chuck Cirino
Big Bang, The	BEL/FRA	Roy Budd
Big Parade, The	CHN	Zhao Quiping/Qu Xiasong
Big Race, The	POL	Jerzy Matula
Big Road, The	FRA	Georges Granier
Big Shots	FOX	Bruce Broughton
Big Town, The	COL	Michael Melvoin
Bigfoot	DIS-TV	Bruce Rowland
Billboard (series)	AUT-TV	Peter Crosbie
Billionaire Boys Club	NBC-TV	Jorge Calandrelli
Bird in the Hand Is Worth ..., A	MEX	Gustavo Cesar Carreon
Birthday Town	GRE	Thomas Sliomis
Bit Part, The	AUT	Paul Grabowsky
Black Eye, A	FRA	Francois Bernheim
Black Sheep, The	VEN	Federico Ruiz
Black Side of Blackie, The	MEX	Carlos Torres Marin
Black Swans	BUL	Bozhidar Petkov
Black Widow	FOX	Michael Small
Blind Chance (Przypadek)	POL	Wojciech Kilar
Blind Date	TST	Henry Mancini
Blindside	CAN	Paul Zaza
Blonde at the Bar, The	SPA	Gato Perez
Blood Diner	VES	Don Preston
Blood Hook	IND	Thomas A. Naunas
Blood Sisters (Slash)	IND	Walter E. Sear
Bloody New Year	BRI	Nick Magnus
Bloody Weed	MEX	Ernesto Cortazar
Blue Monkey	IND	Patrick Coleman/Paul Novotny
Blue Window	PBS-TV	Craig Carnelia
Bluffing It	ABC-TV	Brad Fiedel
Body Slam	DEG	John D'Andrea/Michael Lloyd
Boran--Time to Aim	BEL/GER	Okko Berger/Jan Kruger/Lonzo Westphal
Border	BRI	Jiri Stanislav
Born Again: Life in a Funda- mentalist Baptist Church	IND	Paul Moravec
Born in East L.A.	UN	Lee Holdridge

Born of Fire	BRI	Kudsi Erguner/Colin Towns
Bouba	ISR	Dov Seltzer
Boy With the Big Black Dog, The	E.GER	Gerhard Schone
Brand New Day	BRI/FRA	"The Eurythmics"
Brave Little Toaster, The	IND	David Newman
Bride of Boogedy	ABC-TV	John Addison
Bride Was Radiant, The	HUN/ITA	Nicola Piovani
Brightness (Yeelen)	MALI	Michel Portal
Broadcast News	FOX	Bill Conti
Broken April	FRA	Steve Beresford
Broken Vows	CBS-TV	Charles Gross
Bronx Zoo, The	NBC-TV	Gary Scott
Brute, The	FRA	Jean-Marie Senia
Buddha's Lock	CHN/HK	Zhao Ji Ping
Bullseye	AUT	Chris Neal
Burglar	RUS	Victor Kisine
Burglar	WB	Sylvester Levay
Burnin' Love	DEG	Charles Fox
Burning Bush	FRA	Jorge Arriagada
Bus	JAP	Kiyoshi Takeo
Bushfire Moon	AUT	Bruce Rowland
Business as Usual	BRI	Andrew Scott/Paul Weller
Buster Keaton: A Hard Act to Follow	PBS-TV	Carl Davis
Cain	SPA	Santi Arisa
Call Me Mister	AUT-TV	George Fenton
Caller, The	EMP	Richard Band
Calm Night (Nuit Docile)	FRA	Vincent Marie
Campus Man	PAR	James Newton Howard
Can't Buy Me Love	DIS	Robert Folk
Capriccio (Letters from Capri)	ITA	Riz Ortolani
Captain James Cook	AUT-TV	Jose Nieto
Captive Hearts	MGM	Osamu Kitajima
Carly's Web	NBC-TV	Richard Lewis Warren
Caro's Escape--Kill the Fugitive	MEX	Ernesto Cortazar
Carrasco's Escape	MEX	Chilo Moran
Casanova	ABC-TV	Michel Legrand
Case of the Murdered Madam, The	NBC-TV	Dick De Benedictis
Case of the Scandalous Scoundrel, The	NBC-TV	Dick De Benedictis
Caspar David Friedrich	GER	Hans Posegga
Cassandra	AUT	Trevor Lucas/Ian Mason
Cat City (Macskafogo)	CAN/GER/HUN	Tamas Deak
Cathy	CBS-TV	Jimmie Haskell/James Lee Stanley
Caught	IND	Ted Neeley
Caught in a Web: L'Impasse	BRI	Mike Westbrook
Cayenne-Palace	FRA	Jean-Francois Leon
Celebration Family	ABC-TV	Fred Karlin

Cemil	GER	"Fancy"/Frank Flebig
Certain Josette Bauer, A	SWI	Ramon Kuss
Challenge to Life	MEX	Armando Manzanero
Changing Patterns (short)	CBS-TV	John Debney
Charlie Dingo	FRA	Christian Chevalier
Charmings, The (series)	ABC-TV	Jonathan Wolff
Chechechela--A Girl of the Barrio	ARG	Jose Luis Castineira de Dios
Children of the Swallow, The	GRE	Giorgos Tsanguaris
Childstealers	MEX	Leonardo Valazquez
China Girl	IND	Joe Delia
China Run	IND	Brian Mendelsohn
Chinese Are Coming, The	GER	Rio Reiser
Chinese Ghost Story, A	HK	Romeo Diaz/James Wong
Choice, The (Yam Daabo)	AFR	Francis Bebey
Christmas Comes to Willow Creek	CBS-TV	Charles Fox
Christmas Visitor, The	DIS-C	Bruce Rowland
Chronicle of a Death Foretold	FRA/ITA	Piero Piccioni
Circus	ABC-TV	Henry Mancini
City on Fire	HK	Teddy Robin
City Rats	MEX	Marco Flores
Climb, The	CAN	Peter Jermyn
Closing Ranks	BRI	Tony Britten
Cloud Dancing	SHO-C	Richie Clode
Coach!	IND-TV	Jeff Cain
Cocked Gun	MEX	Carlos Torres Marin
Coda	AUT	Frank Strangio
Code Name: Zebra	IND	Louis Febre/Peter Rotter
Cold Steel	IND	David A. Jackson
Collapse	MEX	Alberto Nunez Palacio
Collar and the Bracelet, The	EGY	Intisar Abdul-Fatah
Color of Destiny, The	BRA	David Tygel
Comedy!	FRA	Philippe Sarde
Concerto for the Right Hand	GER	Fernando Lafferriere/ Lothar Mankewitz
Conspiracy of Love	CBS-TV	John Rubinstein
Contract Mother (Sibaji)	KOR	Shin Byung-ha
Control	HBO-C	Ennio Morricone
Convicted: A Mother's Story	NBC-TV	David Shire
Corruption	MEX	Ernesto Cortazar
Count Your Blessings	HOL	Cees Bijlstra
Cracked Up	ABC-TV	Mark Snow
Crazy Boys	GER	Franz Plasa
Crazy Love	BEL	Raymond Van Het Groenewoud
Creampuffs and Lollipops	DEN	Sanne Bruel
Creepozoids	IND	Guy Moon
Creepshow 2	NWP	Les Reed/Rick Wakeman
Critical Condition	PAR	Alan Silvestri
Crooks	ARG	Leo Sujatovich
Cross	FRA	Michel Goguelat

Cross My Heart	UN	Bruce Broughton
Crossed Hearts	FRA	Vladimir Cosma
Cry Freedom	UN	George Fenton/Jonas Gwangwa
Cry of the Owl, The	FRA/ITA	Mathieu Chabrol
Cry Wilderness	IND	Fritz Heede
Crystal Heart	NWP	Joel Goldsmith
Custody	AUT	Peter Best
Cyclone	IND	David A. Jackson/ James Saad
Daddy	ABC-TV	Simon Rogers
Dance of the Dolls	BRA	Nivaldo Ornelas
Dancers	CRC	Pino Donaggio
Danger Zone, The	IND	Robert Etoll
Dangerous Characters	BRI	Jonathan Kahn
Daniel & the Towers	PBS-TV	Dennis Dreith
D'Annunzio	ITA	Sergio Sandrelli
Dark Eyes (Oci Ciornie)	ITA	Francis Lai
Darkside, The	CAN	Greg Diakun
Date With an Angel	DEG	Randy Kerber
Day My Kid Went Punk, The	ABC-TV	John Debney/Larry & Tom Weill
Day They Came to Arrest the Book, The	CBS-TV	Udi Harpaz
Day to Day	CBS-TV	Marvin Hamlisch
Days and Nights of Molly Dodd, The (series)	NBC-TV	Patrick Williams
Days to Remember	GER/YUG	Juergen Knieper
Dead, The	VES	Alex North
Dead Ball, The	FRA/HUN	Gyorgy Vukan
Dead of Winter	MGM	Richard Einhorn
Deadline	GER	Hans Jansen/Jacques Zwart
Deadly Care	CBS-TV	"Tangerine Dream"
Deadly Illusion (Love You to Death)	IND	Patrick Gleeson
Deadly Prey	IND	Tim Heintz/Tim James/ Steve McClintock
Deaf in the City, The	CAN	Ginette Bellavance
Dear America	IND	Todd Boekelheide
Dear Cardholder	AUT	Michael Atkinson
Death Before Dishonor	IND	Brian May
Death in the Family, A	NZ-TV	Wayne Laird
Death of a Beautiful Dream	CZE	Lubos Fiser
Death of Palomo, The	MEX	Ricardo Carrion
Death Stone	GER	Luigi Ceccarelli
Death Wish 4: The Crackdown	CRC	John Bisharat/Paul McCallum/Valentine McCallum
Deathrow Gameshow	CRO	Gregg Gross
Deathstalker II	IND	Chuck Cirino

Debauched Life of Gerard Floque, The	FRA	"Daily News"
Deep Dark Secrets	NBC-TV	Charles Fox
Deep Illusion	BRA	Antonio Carlos Jobim
Deja Vu (Veo Videno)	YUG	Zoran Simjanovic
Delinquent	MEX	Jonathan Zarzosa
Deranged	IND	Bill Heller
Deserters, The	HUN/POL	Gyorgy Selmeczi
Desperado	NBC-TV	Michel Colombier
Destination America	ABC-TV	Mike Post
Detail in Cyprus, A	CYP	Michael Christodoulidis
Devil Lurks Among Bar-Girls, The	MEX	Gustavo Cesar Carreon
Devil, the Saint and the Fool, The	MEX	Heriberto Aceves
Devil's Paradise	GER	Juergen Knieper
Diary for My Lovers	HUN	Zsolt Dome
Diary of a Mad Old Man	BEL/FRA/HOL	Egisto Macchi
Diary of a Madman, The	FRA	Jean Musy
Different Affair, A	CBS-TV	Jim Gross
Dirty Dancing	IND	John Morris
Dirty Laundry	IND	Elliot Solomon
Distant Lights	ITA	Angelo Branduardi
Distortions	IND	David Morgan
Doctors Wilde	CBS-TV	Dana Kaproff
Dolly In (Travelling Avant)	FRA	Raymond Alessandrini
Don't Give a Damn	ISR	Benny Nagari
Don't Press the Button	SPA-TV	Jorge Chartoriski
Double Agent	ABC-TV	Alf Clausen
Down and Out with Donald Duck	NBC-TV	Christopher Stone
Down the Long Hills	ABC-TV	Mark Snow
Doxobus	GRE	Costas Vomvolos
Dragnet	UN	Ira Newborn
Dragon Food	GER/SWI	Klaus Bantzer
Dreams Lost, Dreams Found	SHO-C	Alan Hawkshaw
Duet	FOX-TV	John Beasley/Buddy Budson
Dumb Waiter, The	ABC-TV	Judith Gruber-Stitzer
Dutch Treat	IND	Steve Bates
Dylan Thomas' A Child's Christmas in Wales	PBS-TV	Louis Natale
Ears Between the Teeth	FRA	Patrick Schulmann
Eat the Rich	BRI	"Motorhead"
Ebony Tower, The	BRI-TV	Richard Rodney Bennett
Echoes in the Darkness	CBS-TV	David Shire
Edge of Hell, The (Rock 'n' Roll Nightmare)	CAN	"The Tritonz"
Eight Is Enough: A Family Reunion	NBC-TV	Lee Holdridge
84 Charing Cross Road	COL	George Fenton
El Lute--Forge On or Die	SPA	Jose Nieto

Emanon	IND	Lennie Niehaus
Emilio Varela's Band	MEX	Rafael Carrion
Emmanuelle 5	FRA	Pierre Bachelet
Empire of the Sun	WB	John Williams
Enchanted Forest, The	SPA	Jose Nieto
Enemy Among Us, An	CBS-TV	Mischa Segal
Enemy Territory	EMP	Richard Koz Kosinaki/ Sam Winans
Entire Life, The	ARG	Rodolfo Mederos
Equalizer 2000	IND	Edward Achacoso
Ernest Goes to Camp	DIS	Shane Keister
Escape from Sobibor	CBS-TV	Georges Delerue
Essence, The (Susman)	IN	Vanraj Bhatia/Sharang Dev
Eulalia	IND	Alvaro Esquivel
Eunuchs	KOR	Chong Yon-joo
Eva: Guerrillera	CAN	Barry Goold
Everything's Relative (series)	CBS-TV	David Horowitz
Evil Spawn (Alive by Night/ Deadly Sting)	IND	Paul Natzke
Evil Town	IND	Michael Linn
Exploits of a Young Don Juan, The	FRA/ITA	Nicola Piovani
Extreme Prejudice	TST	Jerry Goldsmith
Eye on the Sparrow	NBC-TV	Eddie Manson
F...ing Fernand	FRA/GER	Jean-Claude Petit
Facts of Life Down Under, The	NBC-TV	Fred Karlin
Fair at Dharmatalia, The	IN	Dilip Balakrishnan
Faithful River, The	POL	Jerzy Matuszkiewicz
Fake Five	CBS-TV	David Frank
Fall, The	HUN	Gyorgy Selmeczi
Falsch	BEL/FRA	Jean-Marie Billy/ Jan Franssen
False Word, The	GER	George Boulanger
Family, The	FRA/ITA	Armando Trovajoli
Family Sins	CBS-TV	Elizabeth Swados
Family Viewing	CAN	Michael Danna
Far Country, The	AUT-TV	Garry McDonald/Laurie Stone
Farewell Green Summer	RUS	Eduard Artemyev
Fatal Attraction	PAR	Maurice Jarre
Fatal Beauty	MGM	Harold Faltermeyer
Fatal Confession: A Father Dowling Mystery	NBC-TV	Dick De Benedictis/ Artie Kane
Fatal Telephone, The	YUG	Otroci Socializma
Father Clements Story, The	NBC-TV	Mark Snow
Fearnot	NBC-TV	Rachel Portman
Federico Fellini's Interview	ITA	Nicola Piovani/Nino Rota
Feelings: Mirta from Liniers to Istanbul	ARG	Leo Sujatovich
Feldmann Case, The	NOR	Nissa Nyberget

Female Cabbie, The	MEX	Gustavo Pimentel
Field Agent, The	FRA	Vladimir Cosma
Field of Honor	FRA	Michel Portal
Fields of Fire	AUT-TV	Wayne Goodwin/Mark Moffat
Fig Tree, The	PBS-TV	John Morris
Fight for the Red Cow, The	DEN	Jan Glasel/Friis Mikkelsen
Fire and Ice	BRI-TV	Carl Davis
Fire from the Mountain	IND	Charlie Haden
Firehouse	IND	Michael Montes
First Among Equals	AUT-TV	Richard Harvey
First Killing Frost, The	IND	Michael Rendish/Don Wilkens
Fists in the Dark	CZE	Zdenek Bartak, Jr.
Five Corners	BRI	James Newton Howard
Five Nerds Take Las Vegas	MEX	Luis Alcaraz
Flicks (Hollyweird/Loose Joints)	IND	John Morgan
Flowers in the Attic	NWP	Christopher Young
Flyer, The	GER	Andreas Kobner
Flying Doctors, The	AUT-TV	Gary McDonald/Laurie Stone
Fond Farewell to the Prince, A	HUN	Istvan Martha
For Keeps	TST	Bill Conti
Forest of Little Bear (Itszu)	JAP	Masaru Sato
Forever Friends	DEN	Kim Sagild/Christian Skeel/Mort Vizki
Forgive Me (Prosti)	RUS	Vadim Bibergan
Forty Days of Musa Dagh	IND	Jaime Mendoza Nava
Forward, God's Army	JAP	Shigeru Yamakawa
Four Adventures of Reinette and Mirabelle	FRA	Ronan Cirre/Jean-Louis Valero
Four Hands (Quatre Mains)	GER/HOL	Paul Prenen
Fourth Protocol, The	BRI	Lalo Schifrin
Foxfire	CBS-TV	Johnny Mandel
Francesca	GER	Fulvio de Stefano/ Leopoldo Sanfelice
Frank's Place (series)	CBS-TV	Michael Stokes
Frenchman's Farm	AUT	Tommy Tycho
Friend of a Jolly Devil, The	POL	Marek Bilinski
Friends and Enemies	AUT	Paul Charlier
Friendship's Death	BRI	Barrington Pheloung
From a Whisper to a Scream	IND	Jim Manzie
From Neither Here Nor There	MEX	Chucho Zarzosa
From Pole to Equator	GER/ITA	Charles Anderson/ Keith Ulrich
From the Hip	DEG	Paul Zaza
Frosty Roads	IRAN	Kambiz Roshan Ravan
Full Metal Jacket	WB	Abigail Mead

Fuegos	FRA	Jean-Marie Senia
Funland	IND	James Oliviero
Gaby--A True Story	TST	Maurice Jarre
Gambler III, The Legend Continues, The	CBS-TV	Larry Cansler
Games for School Children	RUS	Lepo Sumera
Games of Artifice	FRA	Andre Demay
Garbage Pail Kids, The	ATL	Michael Lloyd
Gardens of Stone	TST	Carmine Coppola
Garfield Goes Hollywood (short)	CBS-TV	Ed Bogas/Desiree Goyette
Gate, The	CAN	Michael Hoenig/J. Peter Robinson
Gathering of Old Men, A	CBS-TV	Ron Carter/Papa John Creach
Gavea Girls	BRA	Sergio G. Saraceni
Geek	IND	Skeet Bushor
Ghost Fever	IND	James Hart
Ghost of a Chance	CBS-TV	Charles Bernstein
Ghost Valley, The	FRA/SWI	Arie Dzierlatka
Gigio	SPA-TV	Beco Rotta
Girl, The	BRI	Alfi Kabiljo
Glass Menagerie, The	IND	Henry Mancini
Gold Rimmed Glasses, The	FRA/ITA/YUG	Ennio Morricone
Gondola	JAP	Satoru Yoshida
Good Morning, Babylon	FRA/ITA	Nicola Piovani
Good Morning, Miss Bliss	NBC-TV	Charles Fox
Good Morning, Vietnam	DIS	Alex North
Goodbye, Little Girl	SPA	Alberto Iglesias
Goodbye, Mr. Chips	PBS-TV	Dudley Simpson
Goodbye, Mr. President	FIN	Neikki Sarmanto
Goofballs	IND	Robert Rettberg
Great Land of Small, The	CAN	Normand Dube/Guy Trepanier
Gran Fiesta, La	PR	Angel (Cucco) Pena
Graveyard Shift	IND	Nicholas Pike
Grizzlies, The	PBS-TV	Scott Harper
Grouch, The	ITA	Detto Mariano
Ground Zero	AUT	Chris Neal
Guardian Angel	YUG	Zoran Simjanovic
Guilty of Innocence: The Lennel Geter Story	CBS-TV	Ira Newborn
Gunfighters, The	IND-TV	Domenic Troiano
Gunpowder	BRI	Jeffrey Wood
Ha-Ha	SPA-TV	Jesus Blanco
Hamburger Hill	PAR	Philip Glass
Hammerhead Jones	IND	Larry Demer/Joe Galdo
Hangmen	IND	Michael Montes
Hanoi Hilton, The	IND	Jimmy Webb
Happy Hour	IND	Neal Fox/Rick Patterson
Happy New Year	COL	Bill Conti

Hard Ticket to Hawaii	IND	Gary Stockdale
Harp in the South	AUT-TV	Peter Best
Harry (series)	ABC-TV	Alf Clausen
Harry and the Hendersons	UN	Bruce Broughton
Harry's Hong Kong	ABC-TV	Dominic Frontiere
Haunted by Her Past	NBC-TV	Paul Chihara
Haunting of Barney Palmer, The	PBS-TV	Jenny McLeod
Havinck	HOL	Egisto Macchi
Hazard of Hearts, A	CBS-TV	Laurie Johnson
He, the Dolphin	BRA	Wagner Tiso
Heart	NWP	Geoff Levin/Chris Many
Heartbeat 100	HK	David Wu
Heartbreak Yakuza, The	JAP	Toshihiro Nakanishi
Hearts of Fire	LOR	John Barry
Heat	IND	Michael Gibbs
Heat and Sunlight	IND	David Byrne/Brian Eno
Heaven	ISL	Howard Shore
Hello Again	DIS	William Goldstein
Hello Mary Lou: Prom Night II	CAN	Paul Zaza
Hellraiser	BRI	Christopher Young
Her Name Is Lisa	IND	Richard Sohl
Her Secret Life	ABC-TV	Georges Delerue
Hero of the Year	POL	Jan Kanty Pawuluskiewicz
Hidden, The	NLC	Michael Convertino
Hidden City	BRI	Michael Storey
Hiding Out	DEG	Anne Dudley
Hi-Fi	YUG	Ljupco Konstantinov
High Mountain Rangers	CBS-TV	Robert Folk
High Season	BRI	Jason Osborn
High Stakes	CAN	Paul Zaza
High Tide	AUT	Ricky Fataar/Mark Moffat
Higher Education	CAN	Paul Zaza
Himmo, King of Jerusalem	ISR	Ilan Virtzberg
Hobo's Christmas, A	CBS-TV	Mark Snow
Holiday Australia	AUT-TV	Ken Davis
Hollywood Shuffle	IND	Udi Harpaz/Patrice Rushen
Home	ABC-TV	Nan Schwartz
Home Is Where the Hart Is	ATL	Eric N. Robertson
Home Remedy (Xero)	IND	Steve Katz
Hooperman (series)	ABC-TV	Mike Post
Hoover vs. the Kennedys: The Second Civil War	IND-TV	Paul Hoffert
Hope and Glory	BRI	Peter Martin
Hot Child in the City	IND	W. Michael Lewis
Hot Pursuit	PAR	"Rareview"
Hotel Colonial	COL	Pino Donaggio
Hotel du Paradis	BRI/FRA	Rodolfo Mederos
Hotshot	IND	William Orbit
Hour of the Assassin (License to Kill)	IND	Richard Emmett

Hours of Wedlock, The	JAP	Saeko Suzuki
House of Games	ORI	Alric Jans
House on Fire	JAP	Takayuki Inoue
House II: The Second Story	NWP	Harry Manfredini
Housekeeping	COL	Michael Gibbs
Houston Knights	CBS-TV	Dennis McCarthy
Hoxsey: The Quack Who Cured Cancer	IND	Jeff Nelson/Peter Rowan
Hunk	CRO	David Kurtz
Hunter's Blood	IND	John D'Andrea
I Do 'em In	MEX	Gustavo Cesar Carreon
I Dreamed of My Elk	E.GER	Hans Jurgen Wenzel
I Love N.Y.	IND	Bill Conti
I Love You	DEN	Claus & Svend Agmussen
I Married Dora (series)	ABC-TV	Glenn Jordan
I, the Executioner	MEX	Kiki Campos
I Was a Teenage Zombie	IND	Jonathan Roberts/Craig Seaman
If Looks Could Kill	IND	Jonathan Hannah/Susan Jopson
If the Sun Never Returned	FRA/SWI	Antoine Auberson
I'll Take Manhattan	CBS-TV	Lee Holdridge
Imaginary Friends	BRI-TV	Ilona Sekacz
Impossible Spy, The	HBO-C	Richard Hartley
In an Old Manor House	POL	Zbigniew Raj
In Between	AUT-TV	Marc McSherry
In Love and War	NBC-TV	Charles Gross
In Retirement	ARG	Baby Lopez Furst
In Self Defense	ABC-TV	Patrick Gleeson
In the Last Resort	CAN	Francois Dompierre
In the Lion's Den (pilot)	CBS-TV	Dan Foliart/Howard Pearl
In the Mood (Woo Woo Kid, The)	IND	Ralph Burns
In the Name of God	CHILE/SPA	Jose Antonio Quintano
In the Name of the People	YUG	Vuk Kulenovic
In the Name of the Son	ARG	Pepe Motta
In the Shadow of the Wind	CAN/FRA	Richard Gregoire
In the Shadow of Vesuvius	PBS-TV	William Loose/Jack Tillar
Incredible Ida Early, The	NBC-TV	Fred Mollin
Independence	NBC-TV	J. A. C. Redford
Indian Summer	BRI	Barry Guard/Ilaya Raja
Infidelity	ABC-TV	Steve Dorff
Infiltrator	CBS-TV	Barry Goldberg
Innerspace	WB	Jerry Goldsmith
Instant Justice (Marine Issue)	WB	David Kurtz
Interrogation of the Witness	E.GER	Friedbert Wissmann
Intimate Contact	BRI-TV	Ilona Sekacz
Intimate Enemies	FRA	Philippe Sarde
Into the Homeland	HBO-C	David Mansfield
Intoxicated (Als in Een Roes)	HOL	Lodewijk de Boer

Investigation, The	ITA	Riz Ortolani
Invisible Man, The	GER	Boris Jojic
Iris	HOL	Loek Dikker
Iron Earth, Copper Sky	GER/TUR	Zulfi Livaneli
Iron Warrior (Echoes of Wizardry)	ITA	Charles Scott
Ironweed	TST	John Morris
Is It Easy to Be Young?	RUS	Martin Brauns
Island Sons	ABC-TV	Basil Poledouris
Italian Night	ITA	Fiorenzo Carpi
Italian Postcards	ITA	Stefano Mainotti
It's Alive III: Island of the Alive	WB	Laurie Johnson
I've Heard the Mermaids Singing	CAN	Mark Korven
J. Edgar Hoover	SHO-C	Peter Robinson
Jake and the Fatman (series)	CBS-TV	Dick De Benedictis
Jake's M.O.	NBC-TV	Lalo Schifrin
Jaws IV--The Revenge	UN	Michael Small
Jeantsch	FRA/SWI	Pino Donaggio
Jester, The (Bobo, O)	POR	Carlos Azevedo/Pedro Caldeira Cabral/ Carlos Zingaro
Jilted	AUT	Michael Atkinson
Jim & the Pirates	SWE	Stefan Nilsson
Jocks	CRO	David McHugh
John and the Missus	CAN	Michael Conway Baker
John Huston and the Dubliners	IND	Alex North
Johnny Flash	GER	Helge Schneider
Johnny Monroe	FRA	Jean Musy
Joyous Photographs	ITA	Simon Boswell
Juana the Saloon Keeper	MEX	Javier del Rio
Julia & Julia	ITA	Maurice Jarre
Juvi	CBS-TV	Jimmy Haskell
Kapax: The Man from the Amazon	SA	Miguel Angel Rincon
Keep Up Your Right	FRA/SWI	Rita Mitsouko
Keeping Track	CAN	Ben Low
Kid Brother, The	CAN/JAP	Francois Dompierre
Kid Who Wouldn't Quit/The Brad Silverman Story, The	ABC-TV	Roger Bellon
Kidnapped	IND	Ron Jones
Kids Like These	CBS-TV	Mark Snow
Kill or Die	MEX	Carlos Torres
Killer Workout (Aerobicide)	IND	Todd Hayen
Killing Time, The	NWP	Paul Chihara
Kindred, The	IND	David Newman
King of Endings	YUG	Vuk Kulenovic
King of Love, The	ABC-TV	Paul Chihara
Kiss Me a Lot	BRA	Wagner Tiso
Kitchen Toto, The	BRI	John Kean
Kojak: The Price of Justice	NBC-TV	John Cacavas
Kreutzer Sonata, The	RUS	Sofia Gubaidulina
Kung Fu: The Next Generation	CBS-TV	Stanley Clarke

LBJ: The Early Years	NBC-TV	Johnny Mandel
Ladies of the Lotus	CAN	Greg Ray
Lady Beware	IND	Craig Safan
Lady Coyote II, The	MEX	Susy Rodriguez
Land of the Brave	MEX	Rafael Carrion
Landslides	AUT	Cameron Allan
Laputa	JAP	Jo Hisaishi
Last Assault, The	RUM	Adrian Enescu
Last Day of Winter, The	CHN	Wang Xilin
Last Emperor, The	COL	David Byrne/Ryuichi Sakamoto/Cong Su
Last Fling, The	ABC-TV	Charles Bernstein
Last Innocent Man, The	HBO-C	Brad Fiedel
Last Man of Urfa, The	TUR	Haluk Ozkan
Last Manuscript, The	HUN	Laszlo Vidovsky
Last Moment	ITA	Riz Ortolani
Last Straw, The	CAN	Robert Lauzon/Fernand Martel
Last Summer in Tangiers	FRA	Philippe Sarde
Late Summer Blues	ISR	Rafi Kadishohn
Laura	HUN	Gyorgy Selmeczi
Laura (From Heaven to Hell)	SPA	Jordi Cervello
Law and Harry McGraw, The (series)	CBS-TV	Richard Markowitz
Leading Edge, The	NZ	Mike Farrell
Left-Hander (Levsha)	RUS	Igor Matsievski
Leg Work	CBS-TV	Michael O'Martin
Legacy of the Brave	MEX	Diego Herrera
Legend of Wolf Lodge, The	CAN	Andy Thompson
Leif	SWE	Claes Eriksson/Charles Falk
Leila Diniz	BRA	David Tygel
Lemon Sky	IND	Pat Metheny
Lena: My 100 Children	NBC-TV	Misha Segal
Leonard Part 6	COL	Elmer Bernstein
Les Patterson Saves the World	AUT	Tim Finn
Less Than Zero	FOX	Thomas Newman
Lethal Weapon	WB	Eric Clapton/Michael Kamen
Let's Get Harry	TST	Brad Fiedel
Levy and Goliath	FRA	Vladimir Cosma
Liberators, The	ABC-TV	Joe Harnell
Life Classes	CAN	Alexandra Tilley
Life Is a Dream	FRA	Jorge Arriagada
Life Is Rosy	AFR/BEL/FRA	Papa Wemba
Light of Day	TST	Thomas Newman
Light Years (Gandahar)	IND	Gabriel Yared
Lighthorsemen, The	AUT	Mario Millo
Like Father, Like Daughter	CUB	Aneiro Tano/Tony Tano
Like Father, Like Son	TST	Miles Goodman

Line, The (pilot)	NBC-TV	Scott Gale
Lion of Africa, The	HBO-C	George S. Clinton
Lionheart	ORI	Jerry Goldsmith
Little Match Girl, The	NBC-TV	John Morris
Little Prosecutor, The	GER	Toots Thielmans
Living Dangerously	GRE	Nicos Mamangakis
Living Daylights, The	UA	John Barry
Lock and Seal	GER	Peter Schmitt
Lonely Hearts Club	FRA	Michel Legrand
Lonely Passion of Judith Hearne, The	BRI	Georges Delerue
Lonely Woman Seeks Life Companion	RUS	Vadim Khrasatchev
Long Journey Home, The	CBS-TV	J. A. C. Redford
Long Strider	SPA	Emilio de Diego
Looking for Eileen	HOL	Pim Kops/Boudewijn Tarenskeen
Lost Boys, The	WB	Thomas Newman
Love Among Thieves	ABC-TV	Arthur B. Rubinstein
Love in a Minefield	CUB	Chico Buarque
Love is a Fat Woman	ARG	Paul Michael van Brugge
Love Letter	JAP	Michi Tanaka
Love, Mother	HUN	Janos Brody
Love Odyssey	HOL	Eddy Bennett/Adriaan van Noord
Love Unto Waste	HK	Violet Lam
Lovelock	FRA	Luc Le Masne
Lucky Ravi	FRA	Laurent Grangier
Luminous Woman	JAP	Shigeaki Saegusa
Lust for Freedom	IND	John Messari
Mabel and Max (pilot)	CBS-TV	Steve Dorff
Mace	IND	James Oliviero
Macho That Barks Doesn't Bite II	MEX	Marcos Lifshitz
Macu, the Policeman's Wife	VEN	Victor Cuica
Made in Argentina	ARG	Emilio Kauderer
Made in Heaven	IND	Mark Isham
Made in U.S.A.	DEG	"Sonic Youth"
Madhvacharya	IN	Balamurali Krishna
Madrid	SPA	Carmelo Bernaola
Magdalena Viraga	IND	"Grupo Travieso"
Magic Snowman, The	YUG	John Berenzy
Magic Sticks	AUS/GER	George Kranz
Magnate, The	POL	Jerzy Satanowski
Magnificent Warriors	HK	Chan Wing Leong
Magpie's Strategy, The	YUG	Vranjesevic Brothers
Maid to Order	IND	Georges Delerue
Maiden of the Woods	RUM	Cornel Taranu
Making Mr. Right	ORI	Chaz Jankel
Malady of Love	FRA	Romano Musumarra
Malone	ORI	David Newman
Man in Love, A	FRA	Georges Delerue

Man of the Foreign Debt, The	ARG	Daniel Beradi/Carlos Fradkin
Man on Fire	FRA/ITA	John Scott
Man Outside	IND	John McEuen
Man Who Assassinated Ryoma, The	JAP	Shuichi Chino
Man Who Broke 1,000 Chains, The	HBO-C	Charles Bernstein
Man Who Fell to Earth, The	ABC-TV	Doug Timm
Man With Three Coffins, The	S.KOR	Jong-gu Lee
Mandela	HBO-C	Richard Hartley
Mankillers (Twelve Wild Women)	IND	Tim James/Steve McClintock/Mark Mancina
Mannequin	FOX	Sylvester Levay
Marauders	AUT	Mark Horpinitch/John Merakovsky
Mariah	ABC-TV	Bill Conti
Mariana, Mariana	MEX	Carlos Warman
Marsupials: The Howling III, The	AUT	Allan Zavod
Mascara	BEL/FRA/HOL	Egisto Macchi
Maschenka	BRI/GER	Nick Glowna
Masks	FRA	Matthieu Chabrol
Masterblaster	IND	Alain Salvati
Masters of the Universe	IND	Bill Conti
Matewan	IND	Mason Daring
Matter of Life and Death, A	SWE	Ilja Cmiral
Max Headroom	ABC-TV	Corey Lerious
Me, Myself and I (Eu)	BRA	Julio Madaglia
Means and Ends	IND	Gerald Michenaud
Meatballs II	IND	Paul Zaza
Mercy or Murder?	NBC-TV	Peter Matz
Messenger, The	IND	William Stuckey
Messenger Boy (Kurier)	RUS	Eduard Artemyev
Method, The	IND	Ray Obiedo
Mexican Double-Entendre	MEX	Pedro Placenicia
Mickey & Nora (short)	CBS-TV	John Beasley/Cheryl Wheeler
Migrating Birds	AFG	Mohamed Shah Hakparast
Miklos Akli	HUN	Istvan Marta/Levente Szorenyi
Mill, The	TUR	Arif Erkin
Million Dollar Mystery	DEG	Al Gorgoni
Mind Killer	IND	Jeffrey Wood
Miracle, The	FRA	Jorge Arriagada
Miracles	ORI	Peter Bernstein
Mirage	CHN/HK	Joseph Koo
Miss Mona	FRA	Bernard Lubat
Miss ... or Myth?	IND	Liz Story
Mr. Nice Guy	CAN	Paul Hoffert
Mr. President (series)	FOX-TV	Patrick Williams
Mistress	CBS-TV	Michael Convertino

Moa	SWE	Gunnar Edander
Mofles' Escapades	MEX	Gustavo Pimentel
Momo	GER/ITA	Angelo Branduardi
Monsignor Quixote	PBS-TV	Anton Garcia Abril
Monster Squad, The	TST	Bruce Broughton
Monte Napoleone	ITA	Beppe Cantarelli
Montecarlo, Montecarlo	ITA	Carmelo and Michelangelo La Bionda
Month in the Country, A	BRI	Howard Blake
Month Later, A	HOL	Rob van Donselaar
Moon and Sun	INDONESIA	Franki Raden
Moonstruck	MGM	Dick Hyman
More About the Children of Bullerby Village	SWE	Georg Riedel
Morgan Stewart's Coming Home	IND	Peter Bernstein
Morning Man, The	IND	Diane Juster
Morning Patrol	GRE	Georges Hatzinassios
Moscow Farewell	ITA	Ennio Morricone
Mother (Ibunda)	INDONESIA	Idris Sardi
Mother of Kings, The	POL	Przemyslaw Gintrowski
Motherland Hotel	TUR	Atilla Ozdemiroglu
Mountains of the Moon	FRA/POR	Philippe Hersant
Moving Day	PBS-TV	Robert Kraft
Muckrakers, The	AUS	Ernie Seuberth
Muffler and the Mechanics	MEX	Gustavo Pimentel
Muppet Family Christmas, A	ABC-TV	Larry Grossman
Murder Lust	IND	James Lane
Murder Ordained	CBS-TV	Mark Snow
My Dark Lady	IND	Ken Kaufman
My Demon Lover	NLC	David Newman
My Dissident Mom	CBS-TV	Robert Drasnin
My First 40 Years	ITA	Umberto Smaila
My General	SPA	Vainica Doble
My Girl Friend's Boy Friend	FRA	Jean-Louis Valero
My Name Is Gatillo	MEX	Manuel Esperon
Nadine	TST	Howard Shore
Nail Gun Massacre	IND	Whitey Thomas
Naked Man, The	MEX	Javier Castro/Francisco Rodriguez
Napoleon and Josephine: A Love Story	ABC-TV	Bill Conti
Narcotics Police	MEX	Gustavo Pimentel
Narcotics Terror	MEX	Jesus Zarzosa
Near Dark	DEG	"Tangerine Dream"
Necropolis	EMP	Don Great/Tom Milano
Neighbor, The	GER/SWI	"Pi-Rats"
Neighborhood	ITA	Ennio Morricone
Nice Girls Don't Explode	NWP	Brian Banks/Anthony Marinelli
Night Angels	BRA	Servulo Augusto
Night of Courage	ABC-TV	Gary William Friedman

Night Voyage	NOR	Bent Aserud/Geir Bohren
Night Zoo	CAN	Jean Corriveau
Nightflyers	IND	Doug Timm
Nightforce	VES	Nigel Harrison/Bob Rose
Nightmare at Shadow Woods	IND	Richard Einhorn
Nightmare on Elm Street 3: Dream Warriors, A	NLC	Angelo Badalamenti/Don Dokken/Ken Harrison
Nights in White Satin	HBO-C	Paul Farerro
Nightstick	IND	Robert O. Ragland
Nitwits	HOL	Vladimir Cosma
No Dead Heroes	IND	Marita M. Wellman
No Drowning Allowed	FRA/ITA	Philippe Sarde
No Man's Land	ORI	Basil Poledouris
No Way Out	ORI	Maurice Jarre
Noistottus	ITA	Mauro di Rienzi
Noose, The	GRE	Arghyris Kounadis
Norman Rockwell's "Breaking Home Ties"	ABC-TV	Jerrold Immel
North Shore	UN	Richard Stone
Not Quite Human	ABC-TV	Tom Scott
Nothing in Common (series)	NBC-TV	James P. Dunne
Nowhere to Hide	CAN	Brad Fiedel
Nuclear Split	GER	Ulrich Bassenge/ Wolfgang Neumann
Number One With a Bullet	IND	Alf Clausen
Nursemaid Mine	SPA	Jacobo Duran-Loriga
Nuts	WB	Barbra Streisand
Odd Jobs	TST	Robert Folk
Off the Mark (Crazy Legs)	IND	David Frank
Oktoberfest	YUG	Vranesevic Brothers
Old Well, The	CHN	Xu Youfu
Oldest Rookie, The (series)	CBS-TV	Steve Dorff
Omega Syndrome, The	NWP	Nicholas Carras/Jack Cookerly
On Fire	ABC-TV	William Goldstein
On the Edge	NBC-TV	Dave Grusin
On the Green Path	VEN	Ruben Blades
On the Road to Katanga	YUG	Baronijan Vartkes
Once Again (Retake)	MEX	Amparo Rubin
Once We Were Dreamers	ISR	Misha Segal
100% Brazilian Film, A	BRA	Luiz Eca
One More Saturday	MEX	Jorge Zarzosa
One Straight and Two with Salt	MEX	Carlos Torres Marin
One Way Out	IND	Vincent Smith
Open House	IND	Jim Studer
Operation Marijuana	MEX	Susy Rodriguez
Opposing Force (Clay Pigeons/ Hell Camp)	ORI	Marc Donohue
Orion Nebula	HOL	Arjen Hogendorp/ Jurrien Rood
Orphans	LOR	Michael Small

Otto--The New Film	GER	Thomas Kukuck/Christoph Leis Hendorff
Out of Rosenheim	GER	Bob Telson
Out on a Limb	ABC-TV	Lalo Schifrin
Outing, The	IND	Bruce Miller/Joel Rosenbaum
Outlaws in the Viewfinder	MEX	Gustavo Cesar Carreon
Outrageous Fortune	DIS	Alan Silvestri
Outtakes	IND	Rich Daniels/Chris Lay/ Jack M. Sell
Over the Top	WB	Giorgio Moroder
Overboard	MGM	Alan Silvestri
Owners of Silence, The	ARG/SWE	Luis de Matteo
Owners of the Sun, The	ARG	Mario Ferre
P.O.W.--American in Enemy Hands	IND-TV	James McVay
Pack of Lies	CBS-TV	Stanley Myers
Pals	CBS-TV	Mark Snow
Paper Bridge, The	AUS	Arvo Part
Parent Trap II, The	DIS-TV	Charles Fox
Partner of God, The	CUB/PERU	Juan Marquez
Party Camp	IND	Dennis Dreith
Passing the Course	SPA	Jesus Gluck
Passion of Beatrice, The	FRA/ITA	Lili Boulanger/Ron Carter
Pathfinder	NOR	Kjetil Bjerkestrand/ Marius Mueller/ Nils-Aslak Valkeapaa
Patti Rocks	IND	Doug Maynard
Pelle the Conqueror	DEN/SWE	Stefan Nilsson
Penitentiary III	CRC	Garry Schyman
Perfect Match, The	IND	Tim Torrance
Perry Mason: The Case of the Lost Love	NBC-TV	Dick De Benedictis
Perry Mason: The Case of the Sinister Spirit	NBC-TV	Dick de Benedictis/ Fred Steiner
Personal Foul	IND	Greg Brown
Peter von Scholten	DEN	Bent Fabricius-Bjerre
Petrov Affair, The	AUT-TV	Paul Grabowsky
Picaros, The	ITA/SPA	Lucio Della/Claudio Malavasi
Pick-Up Artist, The	FOX	Georges Delerue
Pierre and Djemila	FRA	Olivier Kowalski/Gabor Kristof
Pimp, The (Zegen)	JAP	Shinjiro Ikebe
Pinocchio and the Emperor of the Night	NWP	Brian Banks/Anthony Marinelli
Pirates of the Lake	SWE	Thomas Lindahl
Place at the Coast, The	AUT	Chris Neal
Place to Call Home, A	CBS-TV	Fred Karlin
Planes, Trains & Automobiles	PAR	Ira Newborn
Play ... Boy	POR	Antonio Emiliano

Pleasure of Vengeance, The	MEX	Carlos Torres Marin
Plumber, The	ISR	Micky Gavrielov
Plumbum, or a Dangerous Game	RUS	Vladimir Dashkevich
Poisons	FRA/SWI	Jacques Robellaz
Poker Alice	CBS-TV	Billy Goldenberg
Poking Fun at the Border Patrol	MEX	Marcos Lifshitz
Police Academy 4: Citizens on Patrol	WB	Robert Folk
Police Story: The Freeway Killings	NBC-TV	John Cacavas
Poor Little Rich Girl, The Barbara Hutton Story	NBC-TV	Richard Rodney Bennett
Poor Man's Orange	AUT-TV	Peter Best
Popcorn Kid	CBS-TV	Judy Hart Angelo/ Gary Portnoy
Potlatch	GRE	Demitris Papademetriou
Prayer for the Dying, A	GOL	Bill Conti
Predator	FOX	Alan Silvestri
Pretty Smart	NWP	Eddie Arkin/Jay Levy
Prettykill	IND	Robert O. Ragland
Prick Up Your Ears	BRI	Stanley Myers
Prince of Darkness	UN	John Carpenter
Princess Academy, The	EMP	Roger Bellon
Princess Bride, The	FOX	Mark Knopfler
Principal, The	TST	Jay Gruska
Prison on Fire	HK	Lowell Lo
Prison Ship (Star Slammer)	IND	Anthony Harris
Private Eye	NBC-TV	Joe Jackson
Private Investigation	POL	Zbigniew Gorny
Private Investigations	MGM	Murray Munro
Prodigious Hickey	PBS-TV	Hagood Hardy
Programmed to Kill	IND	Craig Huxley/Jerrold Immel
Project X	FOX	James Horner
Proud Men	ABC-TV	Laurence Rosenthal
Psycho Girls	CAN	Joel Rosenbaum
Psychos in Love	IND	Carmine Capobianco
Puppetman (short)	CBS-TV	Nick Glennie-Smith/ Phil Ramone
Quartermain's Terms	PBS-TV	Jeremy Nicholas
Queen City Rocker	NZ	Dave McCartney
Queenie	ABC-TV	Georges Delerue
Quest Beyond Time	PBS-TV	Chris Neal
Quick and the Dead, The	HBO-C	Steve Dorff
Race Never Loses--It Smells Like Gas, The	MEX	Marcos Lifshitz
Rachel River	IND	Arvo Part
Radio Bikini	ITA-TV	Robert Fitzsimmons
Radio Speed	SPA	Joan Enric Garde
Radium City	IND	Tim Cappello
Rage of Honor	IND	Stelvio Cipriani

Rags to Riches	NBC-TV	Peter Robinson
Raising Arizona	FOX	Carter Burwell
Rampage	DEG	Ennio Morricone
Rattlerat, The	HOL	Ruud Bos
Red Ants (Passkey to Paradise)	GRE	Michalis Gregoriou
Red Riding Hood	IND	Stephen Lawrence
Red Shirt, The	FRA	Joanna Bruzdowicz
Redondela	SPA	Jesus Gluck
Regina	ITA	Helmut Laberer
Relative Merits	AUT-TV	Martin Armiger
Reno and Yolanda	CBS-TV	Patrick Williams
Retribution	IND	Alan Howarth
Return of Sherlock Holmes, The	CBS-TV	Ken Thorne
Return of the Shaggy Dog, The	ABC-TV	David Bell
Return of the Six Million Dollar Man and the Bionic Woman	NBC-TV	Marvin Hamlisch
Return to Earth	BUL	Raicho Lyubenov
Return to Horror High	NWP	Stacy Widelitz
Return to Oegstgeest	HOL	Rainer Hensel
Return to Salem's Lot, A	WB	Michael Minard
Reunion (Yi Lou Yi)	HK	Roland Morales/Herman Yau
Revenge of the Nerds II: Nerds in Paradise	FOX	Gerald V. Casale/Mark Mothersbaugh
Right Hand Man, The	AUT	Allan Zavod
Right to Die, The	NBC-TV	Brad Fiedel
Rising Stock	NOR	Egil Monn-Iverson
Rita, Sue and Bob Too	BRI	Michael Kamen
River of Fireflies	JAP	Masatsugu Shinozaki
Robocop	ORI	Basil Poledouris
Rolling Vengeance	IND	Phil Marshall
Romance in Paris, A	FRA	Jean-Marie Senia
Rome, 2072 A.D.--The New Gladiators	ITA	Riz Ortolani
Roofs at Dawn	HUN	Zdenko Tamassy
Room, The	ABC-TV	Judith Gruber-Stitzer
Room to Move	PBS-TV	William Motzing
Room Upstairs, The	CBS-TV	Robert Folk
Rosary Murders, The	NLC	Bobby Laurel/Don Sebesky
Rose of the Border	MEX	Ricardo Carrion
Rose of the Names, The	ITA	Claudio Scannavini
Roses Are for the Rich	CBS-TV	Arthur B. Rubinstein
Rotten Fate! (Sale Destin!)	FRA	Pascal Arroyo
Roxanne	COL	Bruce Smeaton
Roxie (series)	CBS-TV	Perry Botkin
Rumba, The	FRA	Claude Bolling
Rumpelstiltskin	IND	Max Robert
Running from the Guns	AUT	Bruce Rowland
Running Man, The	TST	Harold Faltermeyer
Russkies	IND	James Newton Howard

Sable	ABC-TV	Michael Shrieve
Sadie and Son	CBS-TV	Billy Goldenberg
Saint, The	CBS-TV	Mark Snow
Sakura Killers	IND	William Scott
Sammy and Rosie Get Laid	BRI	Stanley Myers
Saturday Night at the Palace	AFR	Johnny Cleff
Savage Creatures in Heat	MEX	Ernesto Cortazar
Sawdust (short)	CBS-TV	Ralph Burns
Scared Stiff	IND	The Barber Brothers
Scent of Death	MEX	Ernesto Cortazar
Screwball Academy	CAN	Charles Barnett/Brian Bell
Sea and Poison, The	JAP	Teizo Matsumura
Search, The	ARG	Baby Lopez Furst
Season of Dreams	EMB	Patrick Gleeson
Season of Monsters	HUN	Zoltan Simon
Secret Garden, The	CBS-TV	John Cameron
Secret Life of Sergei Eisenstein, The	ITA-TV	Graziano Mandozzi
Secret of My Success, The	UN	David Foster
Serpent's Way Up to the Naked Rock, The	SWE	Stefan Nilsson
Set in Berlin	GER	Andi Brauer
Seven Years Itch	HK	Anders Nelsson
Shadows of the Peacock	AUT	William Motzing
Shameless ... But Honorable	MEX	Carlos Torres
Shattered Dreams--Picking Up the Pieces	BRI	Shlomo Bar/Shalom Hanoch/Arik Rudich
Shaved Heads	GRE	N. Mavroudis
She Must Be Seeing Things	IND	John Zorn
Shell Game	CBS-TV	Michel Colombier/ Richard Lewis Warren
Shelley	CAN	Michael Conway Baker
Shy People	IND	"Tangerine Dream"
Sicilian, The	FOX	David Mansfield
Siegfried	POL	Jerzy Satanowski
Siesta	LOR	Marcus Miller
Silent Night, Deadly Night, Part II	IND	Michael Armstrong
Sirens	CBS-TV	Mike Post
Sister, Sister	NWP	Richard Einhorn
Six Against the Rock	NBC-TV	William Goldstein
'68	IND	Shony Alex Braun/ John Cipollina
Skin Deep	ITA	Roberto Cacciapaglia
Skipper, The (Abba Ganuv)	ISR	Shlomo Gronich
Sky Over Berlin, The (Wings of Desire)	FRA/GER	Juergen Knieper
Slam Dance	ISL	Mitchell Froom
Slate, Wyn & Me	AUT	Peter Sullivan

Slave Girls from Beyond Infinity	IND	Carl Dante
Sleep Well, My Love	BRI/SWE	Alfi Kabiljo
Slumber Party Massacre II	IND	Richard Cox
Snow Queen, The	FIN	Jukka Linkola
Snowballing	IND	Larry Whitley
So Many Dreams	E.GER	Stefan Carow
So What?	GER	Nicki Reiser
Soldiers--365 Till Dawn	ITA	Manuel de Sica
Some Kind of Wonderful	PAR	John Musser/Stephen Rague
Someone to Watch Over Me	COL	Michael Kamen
Sophia	ARG	Luis Maria Serra
Sorceress	FRA	Michel Portal
Sorority House Massacre	IND	Michael Wetherwax
Soul	HK	Danny Chung
South of Reno	IND	Nigel Holton/Clive Wright
Space Rage	VES	Billy Ferrick/Zander Schloss
Spaceballs	MGM	John Morris
Special Friendship, A	CBS-TV	Teo Macero
Specters	ITA	Lele Marchitelli/Daniele Rea
Spies	CBS-TV	Craig Safan
Spinach Face	SPA	Ricardo Miralles
Spiral	FRA	Michel Legrand
Spirit, The	ABC-TV	Billy Goldenberg
Square Dance	IND	Bruce Broughton
Squeeze, The	TST	Miles Goodman
Stadtrand	GER	Bernhard Voss
Stakeout	DIS	Arthur B. Rubinstein
Stand-In, The (Cuo Wei)	CHN	Han Yong
Star Trek--The Next Generation	IND-TV	Dennis McCarthy
Steel Dawn	VES	Brian May
Stella on Vacation	ICE	Valgeir Gudjonsson
Stewardess School	COL	Robert Folk
Still Crazy Like a Fox	CBS-TV	Mark Snow
Still Watch	CBS-TV	Gil Melle
Stone Fox	NBC-TV	Allyn Ferguson/Peter Matz
Stony Lion	IRAN	Fareidoun Shabazian
Story of a Marriage, Part I: Courtship, The	PBS-TV	Jonathan Shefter
Storyteller, The	NBC-TV	Rachel Portman
Straight to Hell	ISL	"The Pogues"
Stranded	NLC	Stacy Widelitz
Strange Case of Dr. Jekyll and Mr. Hyde, The	RUS	Edouard Artemyev
Strange Voices	NBC-TV	John Addison
Stranger, The	COL	Craig Safan
Stranger, The	POL	Anna Izykowska-Mironowicz

Stranger Waits, A	CBS-TV	James di Pasquale
Street Smart	IND	Robert Irving III
Street Trash	IND	Rick Ulfik
Strike Commando	ITA	Luigi Ceccarelli
Stripped to Kill	IND	John O'Kennedy
Student Confidential	IND	Richard Horian
Student Exchange	ABC-TV	Phil Marshall
Suburban Angels	BRA	Luiz Chagas/Manuel Paiva
Subway to Paradise	DEN	"Fuzzy"
Suffer Mammon	SPA	David Summers
Suicide Club, The	IND	Joel Diamond
Summer Camp Nightmare (Butterfly Revolution, The)	IND	Gary Chase/Ted Neeley
Summer Heat	ATL	Richard Stone
Summer Nights	SWE	Goran Klintberg/ "Thirteen Moons"
Summer on a Soft Slope	FRA	Roland Vincent
Summer School	PAR	Danny Elfman
Sunday Pranks	POL	Lech Branski
Superman IV: The Quest for Peace	WB	Alexander Courage/ John Williams
Sure Death 4	JAP	Masaaki Hirao
Surf Nazis Must Die	IND	Jon McCallum
Surfer, The	AUT	Davood Tabrizi
Surrender	WB	Michel Colombier
Survival Game	IND	Michael Linn/Tom Simonec
Suspect	TST	Michael Kamen
Suspended	POL	Jerzy Satanowski
Suzi's Story	AUT-TV	David Hirschfelder
Sweet Country	IND	Stavros Xarhacos
Sweet Lorraine	IND	Richard Robbins
Sweet Revenge	IND	Ernest Troost
Swimming to Cambodia	IND	Laurie Anderson
Sword to Silence	ABC-TV	Dennis McCarthy
Sworn Brothers	HK	Chris Babida
Taggart	BRI-TV	Mike Moran
Taking Care	CAN	Jane Fair
Tale of Ruby Rose, The	AUT	Paul Schitze
Tales from the Hollywood Hills (series)	PBS-TV	Dick Hyman
Tales from the Magino Village	JAP	Masahiko Togashi
Talmae and Pomdari	N.KOR	Chon Chang II
Tandem	FRA	Francois Bernheim
Taxi to Cairo	GER	Peter Breiner
Taxing Woman, A	JAP	Toshiyuki Honda
Teen Wolf Too	ATL	Mark Goldenberg
Tel Aviv-Berlin	ISR	Shalom Weinstein
Tequiman	ECU	Julio Bueno
Teresa	ITA	Claudio Maioli
Terminus	FRA/GER	David Cunningham

Test, The	SWE	Eva Dahlgren/Andres Glenmark
Testament of a Murdered Jewish Poet, The	FRA	Gabriel Yared
Texas Comedy Massacre, The	IND	Van Bavel
Then Nothing Was the Same Anymore	GER	Lutz Koehler
Theofilos	GRE	George Papadakis
There Was a Village	IN	Aravindam
They Died in the Middle of the River	MEX	Joel Goldsmith
They Still Call Me Bruce	IND	Morton Stevens
Thirteenth Bride of the Prince, The	BUL	Georgi Genkov
Thirty Million Rush, The	HK	Alvin Kwok
This Is Not Our Destination	IN	Rajat Dholakla
Those Dear Departed	AUT	Phil Scott
Thou Shalt Not Kill ... Except	IND	Joseph Lo Duca
Threat, The	SWE	Ulf Dageby
Three for the Road	IND	Barry Goldberg
Three Kinds of Heat	IND	Michael Bishop/Scott Page
Three Kings, The	ABC-TV	William Goldstein
Three Men and a Baby	DIS	Marvin Hamlisch
Three O'Clock High	UN	"Tangerine Dream"
Throw Momma from the Train	ORI	David Newman
Thunder Warrior 2	ITA	Walter Ritz
Tiger's Tale, A	ATL	Lee Holdridge
Time Guardian, The	AUT	Allan Zavod
Timestalkers	CBS-TV	Craig Safan
Tin Men	DIS	Andy Cox/"Fine Young Cannibals"/David Steele
To a Safer Place	CAN	Loreena McKennit
To Hurt and to Heal	CAN	Patrick Godfrey
Together (Juntos)	MEX	Marco Flores
Tokyo Blackout	JAP	Maurice Jarre
Tokyo Bordello	JAP	Masaru Sato
Tolerance	HUN	Ferenc Balazs
Tonight Pancho Dines Out (Bachelor Party)	MEX	Marcos Lifshitz
Tonight's the Night	ABC-TV	"Tangerine Dream"/ "Billy and the Beaters"
Too Much	CRC	George S. Clinton
Too Outrageous!	CAN	Russ Little
Top Flight	CBS-TV	James McVay
Top Kid	PBS-TV	Chris Neal/Phillip Scott
Touch of Spice, A	IN	Rajat Choudhury
Tough Guys Don't Dance	IND	Angelo Badalamenti
Tour of Duty (series)	CBS-TV	Joseph Conlan

Tragic Earthquake in Mexico	MEX	Jep Epstein
Train for Hollywood	POL	Jerzy Matula
Train for the Stars, A	BRA	Gilberto Gil
Train of Dreams	CAN	Malcolm MacKenzi, Jr.
Train to Holland	HOL	Gyorgy Vukan
Travelling Man	CBS-TV	Brad Fiedel
Treasure of the Moon Goddess	IND	Victor Hall/Stephen Metz
Treichville Story	FRA	Francois Breant
Trespasses	IND	Wayne Bell/Chuck Pennell
Trip to Paradise	MEX	Leonardo Velazquez
Triumph of the Just	GER	Rudolf Gregor Knabl
Trouble Agent	FRA	Gabriel Yared
Trouble with Dick, The	IND	Roger Bourland
Trouble with Spies, The	DEG	Ken Thorne
True and Accurate Report, A	POR	Jose Alberto Gil
True Colors	HK	Danny Chung
Tuesday Wednesday	CAN	Mark Carmody
21 Jump Street	FOX-TV	Peter Bernstein
Two Crocodiles	FRA	Philippe Sarde
Two Mrs. Grenvilles, The	NBC-TV	Marvin Hamlisch
Ulama, The Game of Life and Death	MEX	Antonio Zepeda
Ultimate Stuntman: A Tribute to Dar Robinson, The	ABC-TV	Joel Hirschhorn/Al Kasha/Michael Lloyd
Umbruch	SWI	Bruno Spoerri
Uncle Tom's Cabin	SHO-C	Kennard Ramsay
Under Cover	IND	Todd Rundgren
Under the Sun of Satan	FRA	Henri Dutilleux
Unfinished Business ...	AFI	Patricia Lee Stotter
Unknown Country	AUS/FRA	Heinz Leonhardsberger
Unsane (Tenebrae)	ITA	Massimo Morante/Fabio Pignatelli/Claudio Simonetti
Untouchables, The	PAR	Ennio Morricone
Up Line	BRI-TV	Kenny Craddock/Colin Gibson
Urge to Kill, The	MEX	Diego Herrera
Ursula	FIN	Antti Hytti/Raine Salo
Us Real Men	ITA	Beppe Cantarelli
Valet Girls	EMP	Robert Parr
Veiled Man, The	FRA/LEB	Gabriel Yared
Vera	BRA	Arrigo Barnabe
Verne Miller	IND	Tom Chase/Steve Rucker
Vietnam	AUT-TV	William Motzing
Violins Came with the Americans, The	IND	Fred Weinberg
Vision, The	BRI	Bill Connor
Visit, The	PBS-TV	James Newton Howard
Visitors	BRI-TV	Marc Wilkinson

Voice, The (SES)	TUR	Tarik Ocal
Waiting for the Pallbearers	ARG	Feliciano Brunelli
Walk Like a Man	MGM	Lee Holdridge
Walk on the Moon, A	IND	Paul Chihara
Walker	UN	Joe Strummer
Wall Street	FOX	Stewart Copeland
Wanted: Dead or Alive	NWP	Joseph Renzetti
Warm Hearts, Cold Feet	CBS-TV	Mark Snow
Warm Nights on a Slow Moving Train	AUT	Peter Sullivan
Warrior Queen	IND	Kai Joffee/Ian Shaw
Warriors of the Apocalypse	PHI	Ole Hoeyer
Water Also Burns	TUR	Sarper Ozhan
Way of the Lotus, The	SRI	Sarath Fernando
Way Upstream	BRI	Alan Brown
Ways of the Lord Are Finite, The	ITA	Pino Daniele
We Are the Children	ABC-TV	Paul Chihara
We Must Undo the House	SPA	Miguel Morales
Weave of Time, A	IND	Jim Pepper
Wedding in Galilee, A	BEL/FRA	Jean-Marie Senia
Weeds	DEG	Angelo Badalamenti
Welcome, Maria	MEX	Miguel Angel Alonso
Werewolf	FOX-TV	Sylvester Levay
Whales of August, The	IND	Alan Price
What If I'm Gay?	CBS-TV	Howard Goodall
What Is Caesar's	MEX	Amparo Rubin
What's Past Is Dead	HOL	Simon Burger
Wheels of Terror	IND	Ole Hoeyer
When the Time Comes	ABC-TV	Marvin Hamlisch
While There Is Light	SPA	Bernardo Bonezzi
White Mischief	BRI	George Fenton
White of the Eye	BRI	Rick Fenn/Nick Mason
White Phantom	IND	Robert J. Resetar
Whoever Is Here, Is Here	ITA	Lamberto Macchi
Whooping Cough	HUN	Janos Novak
Wide Net, The	PBS-TV	Glenn Roven
Wife of an Important Man	EGY	Georges Kazazian
Wild Pair, The	IND	John Debney
Wild Pony, The	IND-TV	Hagood Hardy
Wild Thing	ATL	George S. Clinton
Willing and Abel (series)	BRI-TV	Ashley Irwin
Wimps	IND	Kai Joffee/Ian Shaw
Wind, The	IND	Stanley Myers/Hans Zimmer
Winners Take All	IND	Doug Timm
Winter Tan, A	CAN	Ahmend Hassan/John Lang
Winter Wayfarers, The	S.KOR	Kim Nam-yoon
Wiseguy (series)	CBS-TV	Mike Post
Wish You Were Here	BRI	Stanley Myers

Witch Hunt	AUT	Thomas Mexis
Witchboard	IND	Dennis Michael Tenney
Witches of Eastwick, The	WB	John Williams
With Time to Kill	AUT	Stephen Cummings/ Chris Knowles/Ollie Olsen
Withnail and I	BRI	David Dundas
Witness to a Killing	SRI	Sarath Fernando
Wolf's Lair	CZE	Michael Kocab
Woman to Woman	SA	Alejandro Blanco Uribe
Woman's Day	YUG	Zoran Simjanovic
Women in Prison (series)	FOX-TV	Ray Colcord
Women of the Frontier	CUB/NIC	Cedrick d'lla Torre
Women's Club, The	IND	Paul E. Antonelli/ David Wheatley
Worker's Life, A	YUG	Zoran Simjanovic
Year of the Rabbit, The	ARG	Leo Sujatovich
You Ruined My Life	ABC-TV	Jonathan Tunick
You Talking to Me?	MGM	Joel McNeely
Young Magician, The	CAN/POL	Krzesmir Debski
Zabou	GER	Klaus Lage
Zacharias	GER	Alan Marks
Zero Boys, The	IND	Stanley Myers/Hans Zimmer
Zjoek	HOL	Henk Hofstede
Zombie High	IND	Daniel May
Zombie Nightmare	IND	Jon-Miki Thor

1988

Aaron's Way	NBC-TV	Mark Snow
Above the Law	WB	David Frank
Abracadabra	JAP	Haruna Miyake
Absent-Minded Professor, The	DIS-TV	Tom Scott
Abyss, The	BEL/FRA	Frederic Devreese
Accidental Tourist, The	WB	John Williams
Accomplices	GER	Franz Hummel
According to Pontius Pilate	ITA	Angelo Branduari
Accordionist's Wedding, The	SA	Adolfo Pacheco/Luis Pulido
Accused, The	PAR	Brad Fiedel
Action Jackson	LOR	Herbie Hancock/ Michael Kamen
Actress, The	E.GER	Stefan Carow
Addicted to His Love	ABC-TV	Richard Bellis
Aetherrausch	GER	Kristian Schultze
Afflicted, The	POL	Przemyslaw Gintrowski
Afraid to Dance	AUT	Chris Neal
African Odyssey	PBS-TV	William Loose/Jack Tillar
Age of the Wolf	SWE	Stefan Nilsson

Alias Will James	CAN	Robert M. Lepage
Alien Years, The	AUT-TV	Bruce Smeaton
All the Way	AUT-TV	Peter Chambers/Ashley Irwin
Almost Grown	CBS-TV	Craig Safan
Aloa--The Whore's Feast	YUG	Igor Savin
Aloha Summer	IND	Jesse Frederick/Bennett Salvay
Alone in the Neon Jungle	CBS-TV	Mark Snow
Always Afternoon	AUT-TV	Mario Millo
Ambassador from India, The	SA	Jorge Villamil
America, Unknown Land	VEN	Alejandro Blanco Uribe
American Roulette	BRI	Michael Gibbs
American Scream, The	IND	Richard Cox
Amsterdamned	HOL	Dick Maas
... And God Created Woman	VES	Thomas Chase/Steve Rucker
Ann Jillian Story, The	NBC-TV	Morton Stevens
Annie McGuire (series)	CBS-TV	J. A. C. Redford
Another Chance	IND	Ron Bloom
Antarctica Project, The	GER	Marcel Mengler
Apartment Zero	BRI	Elja Cmiral
Appointment in Liverpool	ITA	Carlo Crivelli
Appointment with Death	CRC	Pino Donaggio
Apprentice to Murder	NWP	Charles Gross
April Morning	CBS-TV	Allyn Ferguson
Arder and Yul	SPA	Pascal Gaigne/Amaia Zubiria
Arizona Heat	IND	Gary Stockdale
Arthur 2 on the Rocks	WB	Burt Bacharach
Asa Branca--A Brazilian Dream	BRA	Mario Valerio Zaccaro
Asik Kerib	RUS	Shavanshir Kuliev
Assa	RUS	Boris Grebenschikov
Assault of the Killer Bimbos	EMP	Marc Ellis/Fred Lapides
Astonished	IND	Michael Urbaniak
Attic: The Hiding of Anne Frank, The	CBS-TV	Richard Rodney Bennett
August	FRA/POR	Jose Mario Branco
Australian Daze	AUT	Davood Tabrizi
Australia's Twilight of the Dreamtime	PBS-TV	Terry Oldfield
Avia's Summer	ISR	Shem-Tov Levi
Azra	YUG	Esad Arnautalic
Azul	IND	Russell Curie
Baby Doll	DEN	Gunnar Moeller Pedersen
Baby M	ABC-TV	Charles Fox
Baby on Board	CBS-TV	Stephen Lawrence
Backstage	AUT	Bruce Rowland
Bad Dreams	FOX	Jay Ferguson
Bad Taste	NZ	Michelle Scullion
Badlands 2005	ABC-TV	Bruce Roland

Baja Oklahoma	HBO-TV	Stanley Myers
Bat 21	TST	Christopher Young
Baton Rouge	SPA	Bernardo Bonezzi
Beach Balls	IND	Mark Governor
Beaches	DIS	Georges Delerue
Bears, The	FRA	Philippe Sarde
Beast, The	COL	Mark Isham
Because of That War	ISR	Yehuda Poliker
Beetlejuice	WB	Danny Elfman
Beginning of a Story, The	NOR	Christian Eggen
Bengali Night, The	FRA	Brij Narayan/Michel Portal/Steve Potts
Berlin Blues	SPA	Lalo Schifrin
Bernadette	FRA	Francis Lai
Beryl Markham: A Shadow on the Sun	CBS-TV	John Addison
Best Wishes	BRA	Guto Graca Melo
Betrayal, The (Petos)	FIN	Upi Sorvali
Betrayed	UA	Bill Conti
Beyond the Rising Moon	IND	David Bartley
Big	FOX	Howard Shore
Big Blue, The	FRA	Eric Serra
Big Blue, The	IND	Jill Jaffe
Big Business	DIS	Lee Holdridge
Big Money	CZE	Ondrei Soukup
Big Top Pee-wee	PAR	Danny Elfman
Biloxi Blues	UN	Georges Delerue
Bingo, Bridesmaids and Braces	AUT	Mark Moffat
Bird	WB	Lennie Niehaus
Black Monk, The	RUS	Teimuraz Bakuradze
Blackbird	YUG	Kornelije Kovac
Blackout	IND	Don Davis
Blob, The	TST	Michael Hoenig
Bloodspell	IND	Randy Miller
Bloodsport	CRC	Paul Hertzog
Blue City Slammers	CAN	Tim McCauley
Blue Iguana, The	PAR	Ethan James
Blue Movies	IND	Patrick Gleeson/Michael Shrieve
Blue Pyramids, The (Paradise Calling)	FRA/MEX	Francis Lai
Blue Scar	BRI	Grace Williams
Blue Skies	CBS-TV	Miles Goodman
Blueberry Hill	IND	Ira Ingber
Bluecher	NOR	Lillebjorn Nilsen
Bluegrass	CBS-TV	Don Davis/Mark Snow
Bodily Restraint	FRA	Oliver Meston
Body Beat (Dance Academy)	ITA	Guido and Maurizio de Angelis
Body Count	IND	Bob Summers
Body of Evidence	CBS-TV	John Cacavas

Bodywatching	CBS-TV	Teo Macero
Bonanza: The Next Generation	IND-TV	Robert Cobert
Book of Days	IND	Meredith Monk
Boost, The	IND	Stanley Myers
Borderline	AUS	Guido Mancusi
Born to Race	MGM	Ross Vannelli
Boulevard of Broken Dreams	AUT	John Capek
Boundaries of the Heart	AUT	Sharon Calcraft
Bourne Identity, The	ABC-TV	Laurence Rosenthal
Box of Sun, The	CAN	Jean-Pierre Lefebvre
Braddock: Missing in Action III	CRC	Jay Chattaway
Brain, The	CAN	Paul Zaza
Brain Damage	IND	Clutch Reiser/Gus Russo
Bravestarr	IND	Frank W. Becker
Break of Dawn	IND	Mark Adler
Breaking Loose	AUT	Jan Michalak
Bright Lights, Big City	MGM	Donald Fagen
Bring Me the Head of Dobie Gillis	CBS-TV	Jimmie Haskell
Broken Angel	ABC-TV	James di Pasquale
Broken Victory	IND	Tom Howard
Buckeye and Blue	IND	Bruno Nicolai
Bull Durham	ORI	Michael Convertino
Bulletproof	IND	Tom Chase/Steve Rucker
Bum Rap	IND	Robert Kessler/Ethan Neuburg
Burning Beds	GER	Horst Muhlbradt
Burning Secret	VES	Hans Zimmer
Buster	TST	Anne Dudley
Bu-Su	JAP	Bun Ikatura
Buy and Cell	EMP	Mark Shreeve
Buying Time	CAN	David Krystal
By the Sword Divided	PBS-TV	Alan Blaikley/Ken Howard
C.A.T. Squad: Python Wolf	NBC-TV	Ennio Morricone
Caddyshack II	WB	Ira Newborn
Caftan of Love	FRA/MOR	Jorge Arriagada
Call Me	VES	David Frank
Calling the Shots	CAN	Lauri Conger
Camels, The	ITA	Nicola Piovani
Camille Claudel	FRA	Gabriel Yared
Camomille	FRA	Tony Coe
Camp Thiaroye	AFR	Ismaila Lo
Campaign	BRI-TV	Nigel Beaham-Powell/ Bella Russel
Cannot Run Away	HOL	Patricio Wang
Captain Khorshid	IRAN	F. Naseri
Captive Rage	IND	Mick Hope Bailie/Mark Mitchell
Caribe	CAN	Michael Danna

Carpenter, The	CAN	Pierre Bundock
Cary Grant: A Celebration	ABC-TV	Arthur Kempel
Casual Sex?	UN	Van Dyke Parks
Cat, The	GER	Andreas Koebner
Catacombs	EMP	Pino Donaggio
Catastrophe, The	IN	Satya Barua
Catwalk, The	FRA	Herve Lavandier
Cause Celebre	PBS-TV	Richard Harvey
Cellar Dweller	EMP	Carl Dante
Chair, The	IND	Eddie Reyes
Channel 99 (pilot)	NBC-TV	Alf Clausen
Chasing Rainbows	CAN-TV	Neil Chotem
Cheap Shots	IND	Jeff Beal
Cheerleader Camp	ATL	Joel Hamilton/Murielle Hodler-Hamilton
Cherry 2000	ORI	Basil Poledouris
Chess King	CHN	Guo Wenjing
Chief Zabu	IND	Andrew Asch
Child Saver, The	NBC-TV	Lennie Niehaus
Childhood of Art	FRA	Romano Musumura
Child's Play	UA	Joe Renzetti
China Beach	ABC-TV	John Rubinstein
China Ranch	ISR	Erich Rudich
Chinese White	FRA	Raoul Coutard
Chocolate	FRA	Abdullah Ibrahim
Chouans!	FRA	Georges Delerue
Christmas Wife, The	HBO-C	Max Harris
Citadel, The	ALG	Jawad Fasla
Clandestine Destinies	MEX	Carlos Esege
Clara's Heart	WB	Dave Grusin
Clean and Sober	WB	Gabriel Yared
Clean Machine, The	AUT-TV	Cameron Allan
Clinton and Nadine (Blood Money)	HBO-C	Jan Hammer
Closing Time	DEN	Elit (Nulle) Nykjar
Cloth Doll	TUR	Melih Kibar/Gulsen Tuncer
Cocktail	DIS	J. Peter Robinson
Cocoon: The Return	FOX	James Horner
Code Name: The Russian	SPA	Anton Garcia Abril
Codename: Kyril	SHO-C	Alan Lisk
Cohen and Tate	TST	Bill Conti
Cold March	RUS	Anatoli Dergachev
Color of the Wind, The	FRA	Philippe Sarde
Colors	ORI	Herbie Hancock
Coming of Age (series)	CBS-TV	Tim Truman
Coming to America	PAR	Nile Rodgers
Compromise, The	VEN	Waldemar de Lima
Consuming Passions	GOL	Richard Hartley
Contagion	AUT	Frank Strangio
Cop	ATL	Michel Colombier
Couch Trip, The	ORI	Michel Colombier

Coverup: Behind the Iran Contra Affair	IND	Richard Elliott
Cowboys Don't Cry	CAN	Louis Natale
Crack in the Mirror	IND	Nile Rodgers/Philippe Saisse
Crash Course	NBC-TV	Mark Davis
Crazy Lola	IND	Daniel Indart
Crime Zone	IND	Rick Conrad
Criminal Law	TST	Jerry Goldsmith
Critters 2: The Main Course	NLC	Nicholas Pike
Crocodile Dundee II	PAR	Peter Best
Cross My Heart	FRA	Vladimir Cosma
Crossfire	BRI-TV	Richard Harvey
Crossing Delancey	WB	Paul Chihara
Crossing the Mob	NBC-TV	Michel Rubini
Crusoe	ISL	Michael Kamen
Cry and Cry Again	HUN	Gyorgy Selmeczi
Cry in the Dark, A	WB	Bruce Smeaton
Crystalstone	IND	Fernando Uribe
Cubagua	CUB/VEN	Gilberto Marquez
Da	IND	Elmer Bernstein
Dadah Is Death	CBS-TV	Fred Karlin
Daddy's Boys	IND	Sasha Matson
Dakota	IND	Chris Christian
Damn Real	HUN	Janos Masik
Damnation	HUN	Mihaly Vigh
Dandin	FRA	Jean-Pierre Fouquey
Danger Down Under	NBC-TV	Bruce Rowland
Dangerous Game	AUT	Steve Ball/Les Gock
Dangerous Liaisons	WB	George Fenton
Dangerous Life, A	HBO-C	Brian May
Daniya, Garden of the Harem	SPA	Enric Murillo
Dark Before Dawn	IND	Ken Sutherland
Dark Side of Midnight, The	IND	Doug Holroyd
Darkness (Tamas)	IN-TV	Vanraj Bhatia
Date Rape	ABC-TV	Steven Margoshes
David	ABC-TV	Marvin Hamlisch
Davy Crockett: Rainbow in the Thunder	NBC-TV	Joel McNeely
Dawning, The	BRI	Simon May
Day by Day (series)	NBC-TV	Robert Kraft
Day of the Panther	AUT	Brian Beamish/Gary Hardman
Dead Heat	NWP	Ernest Troost
Dead Man Walking	IND	Claude (Coffee) Cave
Dead or Alive	GER	Wolfgang Dauner
Dead Pool, The	WB	Lalo Schifrin
Dead Ringers	CAN	Howard Shore
Dead Solid Perfect	HBO-C	"Tangerine Dream"
Deadline	BRI-TV	Jim Parker
Deadly Addiction	IND	John Cascella

Deadly Dreams	IND	Todd Boekelheide
Deadly Intent	IND	Ethan James
Deadly Stranger	IND	Chuck Cirino/Mayf Nutter
Dear Gorbachev	ITA	Luis Enrique Bacalov
Debt, The	ARG/BRI	Jaime Torres
Deceivers, The	BRI/IN	John Scott
Dede Mamata	BRA	Caetano Veloso
Deep (Profundo)	SA	Miguel Angel Fuster
Deep Space	IND	Alan Oldfield/Robert O. Ragland
Defense Play	IND	Arthur B. Rubinstein
Demonwarp	IND	Dan Slider
Deserter	GRE	Eleni Karaendrou
Desperado: Avalanche at Devil's Ridge	NBC-TV	Michel Colombier
Despite Everything	TUR	Cahit Berkay
Destined to Live	NBC-TV	James McVay
Destroyer (Shadow of Death)	IND	Patrick O'Hearn
Determinations	CAN	Dennis Burke
Diamond Trap, The	CBS-TV	Ron Ramin
Die Hard	FOX	Michael Kamen
Difficult Days	MEX	Arturo Martinez
Dirtwater Dynasty, The	AUT-TV	Brian Beamish/Garry Hardman
Dirty Dealings Between Friends	MEX	Ernesto Cortazar
Dirty Dozen, The (series)	FOX-TV	Doug Timm
Dirty Dozen: The Fatal Mission, The	NBC-TV	John Cacavas
Dirty Rotten Scoundrels	ORI	Miles Goodman
Disaster at Silo 7	ABC-TV	Mark Snow
Distant Thunder	PAR	Maurice Jarre
Divided We Stand	ABC-TV	Artie Kane
Dixie Lanes	IND	Pat Coleman/Paul Novotny
Doc's Kingdom	FRA	Barre Phillips
Doin' Time on Planet Earth	CRC	Dana Kaproff
Dominick and Eugene	ORI	Trevor Jones
Donna Donna!	HOL	Bert Hermelink
Doom Asylum	IND	Jonathan Stuart
Door	JAP	Moritsune Tsuno
Door on Heaven, A	FRA/MOR	Anouar Braham
Door on the Left as You Leave the Elevator, The	FRA	Murray Head
Double Standard	NBC-TV	Patrick Williams
Dream Demon	BRI	Bill Nelson
Dreaming, The	AUT	Frank Strangio
Dreams of Hind and Camelia	EGY	Ammar Shevai
Dressmaker, The	BRI	George Fenton
Drifter, The	IND	Rick Conrad
Drop-Out Mother	CBS-TV	Gerald Fried

Drowning by Numbers	BRI	Michael Nyman
Dueling Techniques	CUB/SA	Juan Marquez
Dun-Huang	JAP	Masaru Sato
Earth Girls Are Easy	VES	Nile Rodgers
Earth Star Voyager	DIS	Lalo Schifrin
Echoes of a Distant Drum	AUT-TV	Sean O'Riada
Eden Miseria	FRA	A. Z. Dyne
Egg (Ei)	HOL	Michel Mulders
Eight Men Out	ORI	Mason Daring
18 Again	NWP	Billy Goldenberg
Eisenhower & Lutz	CBS-TV	Amanda McBroom/ Patrick Williams
Electric Blue	ITA	Stelvio Cipriani
Elvira, Mistress of the Dark	NWP	James Campbell
Elvis & Me	ABC-TV	Richard Stone
Elvis Hansen--A Pillar of Society	DEN	Michael Hardinger/ Joergen Thorup
Emmanuelle 6	FRA	Oliver Day
Emma's Shadow	DEN	Thomas Lindahl
Empty Nest (series)	NBC-TV	George Aliceson Tipton
Encore (Once More)	FRA	Roland Vincent
End of the Line	ORI	Andy Summers
Ernest Saves Christmas	DIS	Mark Snow
Eternal Evil	CAN	Marvin Dolgay
Eva Peron Mystery, The	ARG	Oscar Cardozo Ocampo
Everlasting Secret Family, The	AUT	Tony Bremner
Everybody's All-American	WB	James Newton Howard
Evil Laugh	IND	David Shapiro
Exquisite Corpses	IND	Gary Knox
FM--Frequency Murder	FRA	Philippe Gall
Fable of the Beautiful Pigeon Fancier, The	SPA	Egberto Gismonti
Faceless (Night Predators)	FRA	Romano Musumurra
Fairytale Country, The	SWE	Tom Wolgers
Family Again, A	ABC-TV	Randy Edelman
Family Man (series)	ABC-TV	Roger Steinman
Far North	IND	"The Red Clay Ramblers"
Farewell to You	HUN	Zdenko Tamassy
Fatal Judgment	CBS-TV	Lee Holdridge
Father's Homecoming, A	NBC-TV	Tom Scott
Father's Revenge, A	ABC-TV	Klaus Doldinger
Fear	IND	Alfi Kabiljo
Fear, The	BRI-TV	Colin Towns
Feds	WB	Randy Edelman
Fever	AUT	Frank Strangio
Few Days with Me, A	FRA	Philippe Sarde
Fictive Marriage	ISR	Itzhak Klepter
Final Arrangement, The	FIN	Leo Friman
Final Season	IND	Jim Jacobsen

Finding Mary March	CAN	Pam Morgan/Paul Steffler
Fire and Passion	BRA	Servulo Augusto/Gil Reyes
Fish Called Wanda, A	MGM	John Du Prez
Flag (Flagrante Delicto)	CAN	Jean-Pierre Mas
Folks and Robbers of Cardamom City	NOR/SWE	Torbjorn Egner
For Queen and Country	BRI	Michael Kamen
For the Sake of Peace	FRA	Philippe Sarde
Forgotten Ones, The	YUG	Vlatko Stefanovski
Forgotten Tune for the Flute, A	RUS	Andrei Petrov
Fort Figueroa	CBS-TV	Miles Goodman
Fortunate Pilgrim, The	NBC-TV	Lucio Dalla/Mauro Malavasi
Four-Minute Mile, The	AUT-TV	Richard Hartley
14 Going on 30	ABC-TV	Lee Holdridge
Foxhunting	RUS	Eduard Artemyev
Foxtrot	ICE	Erik Gunvaldsen/Stein B. Svendsen
Frankenstein General Hospital	IND	John Ross
Frantic	WB	Ennio Morricone
Freedom Fighter	NBC-TV	Laurence Rosenthal
Freedom Fighters (Mercenary Fighters)	CRC	Howard Morgan
Freeway	NWP	Joe Delia
Fresh Horses	COL	David Foster/Patrick Williams
Friday the 13th Part VII--The New Blood	PAR	Harry Manfredini/Fred Mollin
Friday the 13th: The Series	IND-TV	Fred Mollin
Friends	SWE	Anders Hillborg
Fright Night Part 2	IND	Brad Fiedel
From Hollywood to Deadwood	IND	Alex Gibson/Gregory Kuehn
Frosty Paradise	SWI	Gerald Karfiol
Fruit Machine, The	BRI	Hans Zimmer
Full Moon	TUR	Server Acim
Full Moon in Blue Water	IND	Phil Marshall
Funny Farm	WB	Elmer Bernstein
Further and Particular	BRI	Schaun Tozer
Galactic Gigolo	IND	Michael Bernard/Bob Esty
Gambler	CBS-TV	Brad Fiedel
Gardener, The (Sadovnik)	RUS	Algirdas Paulavicus
Gaspard and Son	CAN	Denis Larochelle
Gates of Flesh, The	JAP	Mochifumi Izumimori
Geierwally	GER	Horst Hornung
Gentlemen	EGY	Mohamed Helal
Georgia	AUT	Paul Grabowsky
Ghost Town	IND	Harvey R. Cohen

Ghosts of the Civil Dead	AUT	Nick Cave
Ghoulies II	EMP	Fuzzbee Morse
Girl Cops--Counterattack of the Three Sisters	JAP	Ichiro Natti
Girl in a Swing, The	BRI	Carl Davis
Girlfriend, The	ARG/GER	Jose Luis Castineira de Dios
Gladiator School	ABC-TV	Sylvester Levay
Glass Heart, The	DEN	Pernille Urzon Ravn
Glass Heaven, The	GER	Flora St. Loup
Glembays, The	YUG	Arsen Dedïc
Glitz	NBC-TV	Dana Kaproff
Glory Days	CBS-TV	Robert Folk
Go Toward the Light	CBS-TV	James Newton Howard
God Bless the Child	ABC-TV	David Shire
Goddess of Love, The	NBC-TV	A. S. Diamond/Dennis Dreith/Mitch Margo
Going to the Chapel	NBC-TV	Charles Fox
Going Undercover	BRI	Alan Hawkshaw
Gombrowicz	ARG	Adrian Russovich
Good Mother, The	DIS	Elmer Bernstein
Gore Vidal's Lincoln	NBC-TV	Ernest Gold
Gorillas in the Mist	UN	Maurice Jarre
Great Escape II: The Untold Story, The	NBC-TV	Johnny Mandel
Great Outdoors, The	UN	Thomas Newman
Grievous Bodily Harm	AUT	Chris Neal
Grotesque	IND	Jack Cookerly/William Loose
Growing Up (De Grande)	ITA	Pino Massara
Guardians of the Fog	YUG	Gjon Gjevelekaj
Haitian Corner	FRA/GER	Mino Cinelu
Half Brothers	YUG	Dusan Karuovic
Half 'n' Half	CBS-TV	James de Pasquale
Halloween 4: The Return of Michael Myers	IND	Alan Howarth
Handful of Dust, A	BRI	George Fenton
Hanna's War	CRC	Dov Seltzer
Hanussen	GER/HUN	Gyorgy Vukan
Happy End	SWI	Leon Francioli
Happy Old Year	BRA	Luiz Henrique Xavier
Hard Times	POR	Antonio Pinho Vargas
Harms Case, The	YUG	Aleksandar Habic
Haunted Summer	CRC	Christopher Young
Hawks	IND	Barry Gibb
Heart of Midnight	GOL	"Yanni"
Heartbeat	ABC-TV	Ken Harrison
Heartbreak Hotel	DIS	Georges Delerue
Heat Line, The	CAN	Richard Gregoire
Heaven and Hell	DEN	Ole Arnfred
Heaven on Earth	PBS-TV	Loreena McKennitt

Hector	BEL	Jan de Wilde
Hell Comes to Frogtown	NWP	David Shapiro
Hellbound: Hellraiser II	NWP	Christopher Young
Helsinki Napoli All Night Long	FIN/SWI	Jacques Zwart
Hemingway	IND-TV	James Calebrese/Kenneth Higgins
Hero and the Terror	CRC	David Frank
Hey, Maestro!	RUS	Nodar Mamissachvili
Hibiscus Town	CHN	Ge Yan
High Frequency (Aquarium)	ITA	Pino Donaggio
High Hopes	BRI	Andrew Dixon
High Spirits	TST	George Fenton
Higher Ground	CBS-TV	John Denver/Lee Holdridge
Highwayman, The (series)	NBC-TV	Rocky Davis/Dave Fisher
Hint of a Crime, The	SPA	Francisco Aguarod/Luis Fatas
Hiroshima Maiden	PBS-TV	Richard Stone
History of Wind, A	FRA	Michel Portal
Holes in the Soup	DEN	Frans Bak
Hollywood Chainsaw Hookers	IND	Michael Perilstein
Hollywood Cop	IND	Elton Farokh Ahi
Home and Away	AUT-TV	Mike Perjanik
Home Free	NBC-TV	Kennard Ramsey
Home Sweet Homeless	CBS-TV	Misha Segal
Homeboy	IND	Eric Clapton/Michael Kamen
Honeybunch	HOL	Ruud Van Hemert/ Peter Schon
Horses in Winter	CAN	Fred Torak
Hostage	CBS-TV	Brad Fiedel
Hot Paint	CBS-TV	Brad Fiedel
Hot to Trot	WB	Danny Elfman
Hotel St. Pauli	NOR	Svein Gundersen
House by the Railway Tracks, The	YUG	Vojkan Borisavljevic
House for Two, A	CZE	Pavel Drazan/Jan Paukert
House of Jade	FRA	Philippe Sarde
House on Carroll Street, The	ORI	Georges Delerue
Howling IV ... The Original Nightmare	IND	David George
Hunting Time	TUR	Sarper Oszan
Hurray, He's Coming!	CZE	Dusan Rapos/Jozef Slovak
Husbands, Wives, Lovers	FRA	Marine Rosier
I Saw What You Did	CBS-TV	Dana Kaproff
Ice Palace, The	NOR	Bent Aserud/Geir Bohren

Icebreaker	FRA/SWE	Jorge Arriagada/ David Jisse
Iguana	SWI	Franco Campanino
I'll Be Home for Christmas	NBC-TV	Joseph Callendrelli
Illegally Yours	UA	Phil Marshall
Illustrious Energy	NZ	Jan Preston
I'm Gonna Git You Sucka	UA	David Michael Frank
In a Shallow Grave	LOR	Jonathan Shefter
In Blood and Sand	FRA	Nina Corti/Anne-Marie Fijal
In Crowd, The	ORI	Mark Snow
In Dangerous Company	IND	Berington Van Campen
In the Heat of the Night	NBC-TV	Dick De Benedictis
In the Line of Duty: The F.B.I. Murders	NBC-TV	Laurence Rosenthal
In the Shadow of Fear	GRE	Demetris Papademetriou
In the Shadow of the Raven	ICE/SWE	Hans-Erik Philip
Incident at Raven's Gate	AUT	Roman Kornen/Graham Tardif
Incredible Hulk Returns, The	NBC-TV	Lance Rubin
Indiscreet	CBS-TV	Arthur B. Rubinstein
Inherit the Wind	NBC-TV	Arthur B. Rubinstein
Innocents, The	FRA	Philippe Sarde
Inside Story	ABC-TV	Richard Harvey
Inside the Sexes	CBS-TV	Teo Macero
Internal Affairs	CBS-TV	Arthur B. Rubinstein
Intrigue	CBS-TV	Basil Poledouris
Inuksuk	FIN	Hans Sandin/Mikael Segerstrom
Invasion Earth: The Aliens Are Here	NWP	Anthony R. Jones
Invisible Kid, The	IND	Steve Hunter/Jan King
Invisibles, The	ITA	Renato Serio
Iron Eagle II	TST	Amin Bhatia
Island Wind, The	SPA	Alexandro Marcello
Issue de Secours	BEL	Marc Herouet
It Takes Two	MGM	Carter Burwell
Itinerary of a Spoiled Child	FRA/GER	Francis Lai
It'll Happen Tomorrow	ITA	Nicola Piovani
It's the Girl in the Red Truck, Charlie Brown	CBS-TV	Paul Rodriguez
Jack Simpson	AUT-TV	William Motzing
Jack the Ripper	CBS-TV	John Cameron
Jack's Back	IND	Danny Di Paolo
Jacob Behind the Blue Door	GER	David Knopfler
Jarrapellejos	SPA	Carmelo A. Bernaola
Jeanne's House	FRA	Raymond Alessandrini
Jenny's Song	IND-TV	Mason Daring
Jesse	CBS-TV	David Shire
Jester and the Queen, The	CZE	Jiri Bulis
John Huston	IND	Steven Goldstein

Johnny Be Good	ORI	Jay Ferguson
Johnsons Are Home, The	CBS-TV	David Burke
Joshua, Joshua	ISR	Adi Rennert
Journey to Spirit Island	IND	Fred Myrow
Juarez	ABC-TV	Udi Harpaz
Judgment in Berlin	NLC	Peter Goldfoot
Juicy Romance, A	CZE	Miky Jelinek
July in September	FRA	Eric Demarsan
Just Ask for Diamond	BRI	Trevor Jones
Just Forget It	GER	Thomas Bauer
Just in Time (series)	ABC-TV	Lee Holdridge
Justin Case	DIS-TV	Henry Mancini
Kadaicha	AUT	Peter Westheimer
Kalamazoo	CAN	Joel Bienvenue
Kamilla and the Thief	BRI/NOR	Ragnar Bjerkreim/ Benny Borg
Kandyland	NWP	George Michalski
Kansas	IND	Pino Donaggio/Natale Massara
Karma	KOR	Choi Chang-Kwon
Katinka	DEN/SWE	Georg Riedel
Killer Instinct	NBC-TV	Paul Chihara
Killer Klowns from Outer Space	IND	John Massari
Killing Affair, A	IND	John Barry
King James Version	IND	Wendy Blackstone
King of the Children	CHN	Qu Xiasong
King Size	POL	Krzesimir Debski
Kiss, The	TST	J. Peter Robinson
Kiss of Judas, The	ITA	Stefano Bambini
Kiss the Night	AUT	Graeme Isaac
Knightwatch	ABC-TV	Stanley Clarke
Krik? Krak! Tales of a Nightmare	IND	Juan Marquez/Jean- Claude Martineau
Kung Fu Master!	FRA	Joanna Bruzdowicz
Lady from the Shanghai Cinema, The	BRA	Hermelino Nader
Lady in White	IND	Frank LaLoggia
Lady Mobster	ABC-TV	Fred Karlin
Ladykillers	ABC-TV	Mark Snow
Lair of the White Worm, The	VES	Stanislas Syrewicz
Lame Go Christmas, The	GER	Andreas Koebner
Land Before Time, The	UN	James Horner
Land for Rose	BRA	Paula Andre/Marcelo Pascoal/Ricardo Pavao
Land of Fathers, Land of Sons	GER	Peter Zwetkoff
Land of Little Rain	PBS-TV	Bruce Odland
Landscape in the Mist	FRA/GRE/ITA	Eleni Karaendrou
Landscape with Furniture	CZE	Emil Viklicky
Lark, The (Alouette)	FRA	Jean-Philippe Rameau
Laser Man, The	IND	Mason Daring
Last Man Standing	CAN	Charles Barnett

Last Rites	MGM	Bruce Broughton
Last Story of Koningswald Castle, The	GER	Ralph Siegel
Last Temptation of Christ, The	UN	Peter Gabriel
Last Voyage, The	HOL	Matthijs Vermeulen
Latent Image	CHILE	Jaime de Aguirre
Laura Lansing Slept Here	NBC-TV	Peter Matz
Leap of Faith	CBS-TV	Charles Gross
Leave to Remain	BRI	Simon Brint/Rowland Rivron
Let Down Your Hair	SPA	Angel Munoz/David Summers
Lethal Pursuit	IND	Richard Hieronymous
Letters from the Park	CUB	Gonzalo Rubalcaba
Liberace	ABC-TV	Gary William Friedman
Liberace: Behind the Music	CBS-TV	Hagood Hardy
License to Drive	FOX	Jay Ferguson
Life Is a Long Quiet River	FRA	Gerard Kawczynski
Life Is Strange	ITA	Nicola Piovani
Life with Alkis	GRE	Michalis Grigoriou
Lightning Over Braddock: A Rustbowl Fantasy	IND	Stephen Pellegrino
Lights and Shadows	SPA	Javier Montsalvage
Line One	GER	Birger Heymann
Lion's Den, The	PERU/SPA	Bernardo Bonezzi
Little Devil	ITA	Evan Lurie
Little Girl Lost	ABC-TV	Billy Goldenberg
Little Nikita	COL	Marvin Hamlisch
Little Sweetheart	BRI	Lalo Schifrin
Living Dreams	IND	Paul Murciano/Andrew Rosen/John Salton
Living Legends (Amagleba)	RUS	Nodar Gabunia
Lodz Ghetto	IND	Wendy Blackstone
Lone Runner, The	ITA	Carlo Maria Cordio
Longarm	ABC-TV	Richard Stone
Lords of the Streets, The (Aduefue)	FRA	Serge Franklin
Lou, Pat and Joe D.	IND	Daryll Dobson
Lounge Chair, The	FRA/SWI	Antoine Auberson/ Gaspard Glaus
Love Is Strange	SPA	Emili Baleriola
Love Till Second Blood	HUN	Laszlo Des
Luck Child, The (short)	NBC-TV	Rachel Portman
Lurkers	CRO	Walter Sear
Mac and Me	ORI	Alan Silvestri
Mad About You	IND	John England
Madame Sousatzka	UN	Gerald Gouriet
Madonna Man, The	GER	Manfred Schoof
Maiden Voyage	SWE	Bjoern Isfaelt
Mamba (Fair Game)	ITA	Giorgio Moroder
Man Eaters	IND	Aldo Frank

Man for All Seasons, A	TNT-C	Julia Downes
Man from Boulevard des Capucines, The	RUS	Gennadi Gladkov
Man Spricht Deutsch	GER	Hanns Christian Mueller
Man Who Mistook His Wife for a Hat, The	BRI	Michael Nyman
Maneuvers	GER	Jurgen Knieper
Maniac Cop	IND	Jay Chattaway
Manifesto	CRC	Nicola Piovani
Marcus Welby, M.D.--A Holiday Affair	NBC-TV	Georges Garvarentz
Marie in the City	CAN	Michel Rivard
Married to the Mob	ORI	David Byrne
Martha, Ruth and Edie	CAN	Alexina Louie/Alex Pauk
Mask, The	ITA	Luis Enrique Bacalov
Masquerade	MGM	John Barry
Mauri	NZ	Hirini Melbourne
Maybe Baby	NBC-TV	Patrick Williams
Me and My Sister	ITA	Fabio Liberatori
Meantime, It's Already Noon	AUS/GER	Christian Brandauer
Meet the Munceys	ABC-TV	Stephen Lawrence
Melba	AUT-TV	William Motzing
Memories of Me	MGM	Georges Delerue
Memories of You (Love Story)	JAP	Akiyuki Asakawa
Messenger of Death	CRC	Robert O. Ragland
Microscope, The	GER	Gabriela di Rosa/ Hanno Rinne
Midas Touch, The (Eldorado)	HUN	Ferenc Darvas
Midnight Caller	NBC-TV	Brad Fiedel
Midnight Crossing	VES	Steve Tyrell
Midnight Movie Massacre	IND	Bill Crain
Midnight Run	UN	Danny Elfman
Mignon Has Gone	FRA/ITA	Roberto Gatto/ Battista Lena
Milagro Beanfield War, The	UN	Dave Grusin
Miles from Home	IND	Robert Folk
Milk and Honey	BRI/CAN	Mickey Erbe/Maribeth Solomon
Milk Train	ITA	Ludovico Einaudi
Mills of Power (Part 1)	CAN	Martin Fournier
Miracle Mile	TST	"Tangerine Dream"
Mirages of Love	RUS/SYR	Rumil Vildanov
Miser, The	PBS-TV	Jim Parker
Miss Arizona	HUN/ITA	Armando Trovajoli
Miss Million	RUS	Vladislav Panchenko
Mission: Impossible (series)	ABC-TV	Lalo Schifrin
Mississippi Burning	ORI	Trevor Jones
Mr. Muhsin	TUR	Attila Ozdemiroglu
Mr. North	GOL	David McHugh
Moderns, The	IND	Mark Isham

Moloka'i Solo	IND	Kapono Beamer
Mondo New York	ISL	Luis Perico Ortiz/ Johnny Pecheco
Monkey Shines	ORI	David Shire
Monolog	IN	M. B. Srinivasan
Monster Manor	ABC-TV	John Lurie
Montecarlo Gran Casino	ITA	Manuel de Sica
Moon in Scorpio	IND	Robert O. Ragland
Moon Over Parador	UN	Maurice Jarre
Moonwalker	WB	Bruce Broughton
More Light!	RUS	L. Ovtshinskaia
More Than Broken Glass: Memories of Kristallnacht	PBS-TV	Brooke Halpin
Mortu Nega	AFR	Djanun Dabo/Sidonio Pais Quaresma
Mortuary Academy	IND	David Spear
Most Amusing Game, The	SPA	Angel Munoz
Most Dangerous Man in the World, The	BRI-TV	Stanley Myers
Moving	WB	Howard Shore
Mullaway	AUT	Michael Atkinson/ Trevor Lucas
Murder in Paradise	NOR	Pete Repete
Murder of Mary Phagan, The	NBC-TV	Maurice Jarre
Murder One	CAN	Michael Danna
Murdered House, The	FRA	Philippe Sarde
Murphy Brown (series)	CBS-TV	Steve Dorff
Murphy's Law (series)	ABC-TV	Mike Post
My Africa	CBS-TV	Lee Holdridge
My Best Friend Is a Vampire	IND	Steve Dorff
My Dad, The Socialist Kulak	YUG	Joze Privsek
My Dream, My Love and You	TUR	Esin Engin
My Father, My Son	CBS-TV	Laurence Rosenthal
My First Love	ABC-TV	Alf Clausen
My Friend the Traitor	FRA	Jean-Marie Senia
My Stepmother Is an Alien	COL	Alan Silvestri
My Uncle's Legacy	YUG	Branislav Zivkovic
Mystic Pizza	GOL	David McHugh
Naked Gun, The	PAR	Ira Newborn
Nature of the Beast, The	BRI	Stanley Myers/Hans Zimmer
Navigator, The	NZ	Davood A. Tabrizi
Necessary Parties	PBS-TV	Richard Einhorn
Nest, The	IND	Rick Conrad
Never Say Die	NZ	Billy Kristian/Sam Negri
New Adventures of Pippi Longstocking, The	COL	Misha Segal
New Life, A	PAR	Joseph Turrin
New Paradise Cinema	FRA/ITA	Ennio Morricone
Night at the National Assembly, A	FRA	Gabriel Yared
Night Friend	CAN	Heather Conkie/Rory Cummings

Night in the Life of Jimmy Valentine, A	FOX	Bill Conti
Night Journey	TUR	Atilla Ozdemiroglu
Night of the Demon	IND	Dennis Michael Tenney
Night of the Marten, The	GER	Ranier Fabich
Night Train to Kathmandu, The	DIS-C	Paul Baillargeon
Night Wars	IND	Tim James/Steve McClintock/Mark Mancina
Night with Hortense, The	CAN	Richard Desjardins
Nightfall	IND	Frank Serafine
Nightingales	NBC-TV	William Olvis
Nightmare at Bitter Creek	CBS-TV	Arthur B. Rubinstein
Nightmare on Elm Street 4: The Dream Master, A	NLC	Craig Safan
Nightmare on Elm Street-- Freddy's Nightmare: The Series, A	IND-TV	Nicholas Pike
1969	ATL	Michael Small
No Harm Intended	FRA	Michel Portal
Noble House	DEG	Paul Chihara
Nosferatu in Venice	ITA	Luigi Ceccarelli
Not Since Casanova	IND	John Debney
Now I Know	IRE	Stan Beard
Obsessed	CAN	Jean-Alain Roussel
Odipussi	GER	Rolf Wilhelm
Off Limits	FOX	James Newton Howard
Off Season	AUS/GER	Bert Breit
Office Party	CAN	Billy Bryans
Old Money	CBS-TV	John Debney
Oliver & Company	DIS	J. A. C. Redford
On the Black Hill	BRI	Robert Lockhart
Onassis: The Richest Man in the World	ABC-TV	Billy Goldenberg
Once in a Lifetime	PBS-TV	Carl Davis
Once Upon a Texas Train	CBS-TV	Arthur B. Rubinstein
One and the Others	TUR	Suheyl Denizci
One Way Ticket	SWE	Ola Hakonson/Tim Norell
One-Way Ticket, A	IND	Rafael Solano
Onimaru	JAP	Toru Takemitsu
Open Admissions	CBS-TV	Charles Gross
Other Night, The	FRA	Eric Tabuchi
Otto Spalt ... for Instance	GER	Klaus Doldinger
Out of the Body	AUT	Peter Westheimer
Out of Time	NBC-TV	Andy Summers
Outback Bound	CBS-TV	Miles Goodman
Outlaw Force	IND	Donald Hulette
Pagu Forever	BRA	Roberto Gnatalli/ Turibio Santos
Painted Faces	HK	Lowell Lo
Palais Royale	CAN	Jonathan Goldsmith

Palanquin of Tears, The	CAN	Maurice Jarre
Pancho Barnes	CBS-TV	Allyn Ferguson
Pandemonium	AUT	Cameron Allan
Paper Gramophone, The	RUS	Gennadi Banshchikov
Paperhouse	VES	Stanley Myers/Hans Zimmer
Paradise (series)	CBS-TV	Jerrold Immel
Paramedics	VES	Murray McLeod
Party Line	IND	Sam Winans
Pascali's Island	BRI	Loek Dikker
Pass the Ammo	IND	Carter Burwell
Pathetic Fallacy (Ajantrik)	IN	Ali Akbar Khan
Patty Hearst	ATL	Scott Johnson
Penitent, The	IND	Alex North
People of the Forest	IND	Jennie Muskett
People's Hero	HK	Lowell Lo
Perfect Murder, The	BRI/IN	Richard Robbins
Perfect People	ABC-TV	Patrick Gleeson
Perfect Spy, The	AUT-TV	Michael Storey
Perfect Victims	IND	Shuki Levy
Permanent Record	PAR	Joe Strummer
Perry Mason: The Case of the Avenging Ace	NBC-TV	Dick De Benedictis/ Fred Steiner
Perry Mason: The Case of the Lady in the Lake	NBC-TV	Dick de Benedictis/ Fred Steiner
Pestonjee	IN	Vanraj Bhatia
Peter in Wonderland	GER/HUN	Ferenc Darvas/ "Neurotic Group"
Phantasm II	UN	Fred Myrow/Christopher Stone
Phobia	AUT	Ross Edwards
Picasso Trigger	IND	Gary Stockdale
Pickles Make Me Cry	HK	Tan Dun
Pictures from the Unconscious	BRA	Edu Lobo
Pictures of the Old World	CZE	Vaclav Halek/Josef Malovec
Pigeon Feathers	PBS-TV	David Amram
Pin	NWP	Peter Manning Robinson
Place at the Table, A	NBC-TV	Nan Schwartz
Place by the Sea, A	ISR	Dov Seltzer
Place in the Sun, The	KOR	Kim Soo Chul
Plagues	IND-TV	Michael Bacon
Plain Clothes	PAR	Scott Wilk
Plainlands	FIN	Antti Hytti
Platoon Leader	CRC	George S. Clinton
Pleasure of Killing, The	SPA	Carlos Miranda
Police Academy 5: Assignment Miami Beach	WB	Robert Folk
Polk File on the Air	GRE	Costas Mylonas
Poltergeist III	MGM	Joe Renzetti
Portrait of a Life	IN	Raja Mitra

Portrait of the Soviet Union	IND-TV	Nigel Hess
Possessed, The	FRA	Zygmunt Konieczny
Powaqqatsi	CRC	Philip Glass
Powwow Highway	IND	Barry Goldberg
Presidio, The	PAR	Bruce Broughton
Prime Evil	CRO	Walter Sear
Prison	EMP	Richard Band
Prisoner of Rio	SWI	Luis Bonfa/Hans Zimmer
Probe	ABC-TV	Sylvester Levay
Promised a Miracle	CBS-TV	Leonard Rosenman
Promised Land	VES	James Newton Howard
Pulse	COL	Jay Ferguson
Pumpkinhead	UA	Richard Stone
Punchline	COL	Charles Gross
Purgatory	AUS	Karl-Heinz Miklin
Quebec, une Ville	CAN	Francois Guy
Quest for Love	AFR	Tony Rudner
Quiet Victory: The Charlie Wedemeyer Story	CBS-TV	Don Davis
Quite by Chance	ITA	Celso Valli
Raggedy Rawney, The	BRI	Michael Kamen
Rain Man	UA	Hans Zimmer
Raising Miranda (series)	CBS-TV	Martin Silvestri
Rambo III	TST	Jerry Goldsmith
Rat Winter	SWE	Nils Landgren/Bengt Anre Wallin
Red Dock	MEX	Rafael Carrion
Red Heat	TST	James Horner
Red Nights	IND	"Tangerine Dream"
Red River	CBS-TV	Ken Wannberg
Red Sorghum	CHN	Zhao Jiping
Red Spider, The	CBS-TV	Artie Kane
Redtops Meet Tyrannos, The	DEN	Anders Koppel
Reefer and the Model	IRA	Andy Roberts
Rejuvenator, The	IND	Larry Juris
Remembering Marilyn	ABC-TV	Kevin Kinen
Remembrance	JAP	Tashinoori Kondo
Remote Control	IND	Peter Bernstein
Rent-a-Cop	IND	Jerry Goldsmith
Report on Pollution at the Women's Kingdom	CHN	Gu De
Rescue, The	DIS	Bruce Broughton
Return, The (Phera)	IN	Jyotishka Dasgupta
Return, The	BRI-TV	Donal Junny
Return of Ben Casey, The	IND-TV	Mark Snow
Return of Desperado, The	NBC-TV	Michel Colombier
Return of Hickey, The	PBS-TV	Hagood Hardy
Return of Robin Hood, The	IN	Tapan Sinha
Return of the Killer Tomatoes	NWP	Neal Fox/Rick Patterson
Return of the Living Dead Part II	LOR	J. Peter Robinson

Return to Snowy River (Part II)	AUT	Bruce Rowland
Revolving Doors	CAN/FRA	Francois Dompierre
Richmond Hill	AUT-TV	Ashley Irwin
Rikky and Pete	AUT	Phil Judd/Eddie Raynor
Ring, The	DEN-TV	Bo Holten
Road Home, The	BRI/POL	Zygmunt Konieczny
Road South, The	ARG/YUG	Zoran Simjanovic
Robert Frost	PBS-TV	Michael Bacon
Rock 'n' Roll Mom	ABC-TV	Lee Ritenour
Rocket Gibralter	COL	Andrew Powell
Roger Rabbit & the Secrets of Toontown	CBS-TV	Alan Silvestri
Rogue of the North	TAI	Peter Chang
Roots: The Gift	ABC-TV	Gerald Fried
Rorret	ITA	Ferruccio Busoni/ Florian Schneider
Rowing With the Wind	SPA	Alejandro Masso
Run Till You Fall	CBS-TV	Tom Scott
Running on Empty	WB	Tony Mottola
Russians Are Coming!, The	E.GER	Peter Gotthardt
Saigon Commandos	IND	Samuel Asuncion/Noli Aurillo
Salaam Bombay	IN	L. Subramaniam
Salt (Uppu)	IN	Sarath Chandra Maratte
Sandwich Years, The	FRA	Roland Romanelli
Satisfaction	FOX	Michel Colombier
Savannah (Ballade, La)	FRA	Jean-Claude Petit
Scavengers	IND	Nick Picard
School Daze	COL	Bill Lee
Scrooged	PAR	Danny Elfman
Seasons of Pleasure, The	FRA	Gabriel Yared
Sebastian and the Sparrow	AUT	Allan Zavod
Secret Access	ITA	Giovanna Marini Salviucci
Secret Life of Kathy McCormick, The	NBC-TV	Mark Snow
Secret Witness	CBS-TV	Robert Drasnin
Send a Gorilla	NZ	Peter Blake
Senior Week	IND	Russ Landau/Ken Mazur
Sensations	IND	Joey Mennonna
Seppan	SWE	Mikael Renliden
Serpent and the Rainbow, The	UN	Brad Fiedel
Seven Hours to Judgment	IND	John Debney
Seventh Sign, The	TST	Jack Nitzsche
Severance	IND	Daniel May
Sexpot	IND	Joey Mennonna
Shadow Dancing	CAN	Jay Gruska
Shadows in the Storm	IND	Sasha Matson
Shakedown	UN	Jonathan Elias
Shakedown on the Sunset Strip	CBS-TV	Lalo Schifrin
Shallow Grave	IND	Mason Daring

Sharing Richard	CBS-TV	Michael Melvoin
Shattered Innocence	CBS-TV	Richard Bellis
She Was Marked for Murder	NBC-TV	Nan Schwartz
She's Having a Baby	PAR	Stewart Copeland
Shiralee, The	AUT-TV	Chris Neal
Shoot to Kill	DIS	John Scott
Shooter	NBC-TV	Paul Chihara
Short Circuit 2	TST	Charles Fox
Short Film About Killing, A	POL	Zbigniew Preisner
Short Film About Love, A	POL	Zbigniew Preisner
Showers of Gold	DEN	Jacob Groth
Side by Side	CBS-TV	Charles Gross
Silence at Bethany, The	IND	Lalo Schifrin
Silent Assassins	IND	Paul Gillman
Silent Night	GER	Cliff Eidelman
Silent Whisper	CBS-TV	Bill Conti
Silver Globe, The	POL	Andrzej Korzynski
Sins of the Fathers	SHO-C	Peer Raben
Slaughterhouse	IND	Joseph Garrison
Slaughterhouse Rock	IND	Gerald V. Casale/Mark Mothersbaugh
Slave Coast (Cobra Verde)	GER	"Popol Vuh"
Sleepaway Camp 2: Unhappy Campers	IND	James Oliviero
Slime City	IND	Robert Tomaro
Snakes: Eden's Deadly Charmers	CBS-TV	Guy Michelmore
Snuff Bottle	HK	Wang Zian
Soldier's Tale, A	NZ	John Charles
Solo Sailor, The	E.GER	Guenther Fischer
Something About Love	CAN	Lou Forestieri
Something Is Out There	NBC-TV	Sylvester Levay
Sonny Spoon	NBC-TV	Mike Post
Soursweet	BRI	Richard Hartley
South (Sur)	ARG/FRA	Astor Piazzolla
Souvenir	SHO-C	Tony Linsey
Special Affections	ITA	Lamberto Macchi
Spellbinder	MGM	Basil Poledouris
Spies, Lies & Naked Thighs	CBS-TV	Jack Elliott
Spike of Bensonhurst	IND	Coati Mundi
Splash, Too	ABC-TV	Joel McNeely
Split Decisions	IND	Basil Poledouris
Stallion Didn't Like Him, The	YUG	Zoran Mulic
Stand and Deliver	WB	Craig Safan
Star Wormwood, The	POL	Andrzej Trzaskowski
Stars and Bars	COL	Stanley Myers
Stealing Heaven	BRI/YUG	Nick Bicat
Stealing Home	WB	David Foster
Stick, The	AFR	Dana Kaproff
Sticky Fingers	IND	Gary Chang
Still Looking for a Good Title	YUG	Zoran Simjanovic

Stoning in Fulham County, A	NBC-TV	Don Davis
Stormquest	ARG	Oscar Cardozo Ocampo
Stormy Monday	BRI	Mike Figgis
Story of Fausta, The	BRA	Ruben Blades
Story of Hollywood--Part 1, The	TNT-TV	Richard Rodney Bennett
Straight from the Heart	CAN/SWI	Osvaldo Montes
Stranger on My Land	ABC-TV	Ron Ramin
Strangers in a Strange Land: The Adventures of a Canadian Film Crew in China	CAN	Terence McKeown
Street of Dreams	CBS-TV	Laurence Rosenthal
Street Story	IND	Edward W. Burrows
Striker With the No. 9	GRE	Stamatis Spandoudakis
Student, The	FRA/ITA	Vladimir Cosma
Suitors, The	IND	Nicholas Kean/Fareidoun Shabazian/A. Veseghi
Summer Story, A	ATL	Georges Delerue
Summer Thefts	EGY	Omar Khayrat
Sunset	TST	Henry Mancini
Superboy (series)	IND-TV	Kevin Kinen
Supercarrier	ABC-TV	Bill Conti/Jack Eskew
Suspicion	PBS-TV	Larry Crossman
Swan's Song	POL	Henryk Kuzniak
Sweetwater	NOR	Stefan Nilsson
Swiss Named Notzli, A	GER/SWI	Walter Baumgartner
Switching Channels	TST	Michel Legrand
Tabataba	FRA	Eddy Louis
Taboo	POL	Zygmunt Konieczny
Tadpole and the Whale	CAN	Normand Dube/Guy Trepanier
Taffin	MGM	Stanley Myers/Hans Zimmer
Take Two	IND	Donald Hulette
Talk Radio	UN	Stewart Copeland
Tango Bar	ARG	Atilio Stampone
Tango: Our Dance	ARG	Daniel Binelli
Tapeheads	DEG	"Fishbone"
Tattinger's (series)	NBC-TV	Jonathan Tunick
Taxing Woman II, A	JAP	Toshiyuki Honda
Tears in the Rain	SHO-C	Barrie Guard
Telephone, The	NWP	Christopher Young
Temptation, The	AUS	Mathias Rugg
Tender Hooks	AUT	Graham Bidstrup
Tenth Man, The	CBS-TV	Lee Holdridge
Tequila Sunrise	WB	Dave Grusin
Terminal Entry	IND	Gene Hobson
Terror Squad	IND	Chuck Cirino
Terrorist on Trial: The United States vs. Salim Ajami	CBS-TV	Jimmie Haskell
Testament	BRI	T. Mathison
They Live	UN	John Carpenter

Thin Blue Line, The	IND	Philip Glass
Things Change	COL	Alric Jans
Things Forgotten and Not	ARG	Rodolfo Mederos
Thinkin' Big	IND	John Boy Cooke
Thirst (Dorst)	HOL	Boudewijn Tarenskeen
32nd of December, The	ITA	Tullio De Piscopo
This Is America, Charlie Brown	CBS-TV	Ed Bogas
This Love of Mine	TAI	Chang Hung-Yi
Thorn Under the Fingernail, A	HUN	Peter Eotvoss
Three Minus Me	FRA/POR	Jose Mario Branco
Three Seats for the 26th	FRA	Michel Legrand
Three Sisters (Fear and Love)	FRA/GER/ITA	Franco Piersanti
Three to Get Ready	IND	"Duran Duran"
Tickets Please (pilot)	CBS-TV	David Benoit
Tiger Warsaw	IND	Ernest Troost
Time of Destiny, A	COL	Ennio Morricone
Time of Violence	BUL	Georgi Genkov
Time Out	DEN	Anne Linnet
Tin Star Void	IND	"Sound X"
To Heal a Nation	NBC-TV	Laurence Rosenthal
To Kill a Priest	FRA	Georges Delerue
To Our Late Unlamented Husband	FRA	Alain Goraguer
Tokyo Pop	IND	Alan Brewer
Tomorrow I'll Be Free (Lute II, El)	SPA	Jose Nieto
Tomorrow It Is Over	DEN	Yorgen Vestergaard
Too Good to Be True	NBC-TV	Michael Rubini
Too Young the Hero	CBS-TV	Steve Dorff
Tottering Lives (House on a Limb, A)	ITA	Franco Piersanti
Touch of Blue, A	FRA	Robert Cohen-Solal
Town Bully, The	ABC-TV	Jorge Calandrelli
Track 29	BRI	Stanley Myers
Tracker, The	HBO-C	Sylvester Levay
Trading Hearts	IND	Stanley Myers
Train of Lenin, The	ITA-TV	Nicola Piovani
Transvestite, The	FRA	Philippe Sarde
Traxx	DEG	Jay Gruska
Treasure	PR	Gilberto Marquez
Tribulations of Balthazar Kobera	FRA/POL	Zdislaw Szostak
Tricks of the Trade	CBS-TV	Walter Murphy
Trip to the Sea, A	RUS	Oleg Karavalchuk
Tucker: The Man and His Dream	PAR	Carmine Coppola/Joe Jackson
Tudawali	AUT-TV	Raphael Apuatimi
Tunnel, The	SPA	Augusto Alguero
Twice Dead	IND	David Bergeaud
Twins	UN	Georges Delerue/Randy Edelman
Two Moon Junction	LOR	Jonathan Elias
Two More Minutes of Sunlight	FRA	Michel Portal
Two-Step (Pasodoble)	SPA	Carmelo Bernaola

Two Virtuous Women	CHN	Shi Wanchum
Under the Boardwalk	NWP	David Kitay
Underachievers, The	IND	Don Preston
Unholy, The	VES	Roger Bellon
Uninvited	IND	Dan Slider
Unnamable, The	IND	David Bergeaud
Upstairs, Downstairs	POL	Jerzy Satanowski
Urinal	CAN	Glenn Schellenberg
Vampire at Midnight	IND	Robert Etoll
Vampires (Abadon)	IND	Chris Burke
Vampire's Kiss	IND	Colin Towns
Van Dyke Show, The (series)	CBS-TV	Stewart Levin
Vanishing, The	HOL	Henny Vrienten
Venus Trap, The	GER	Peer Raben
Very Brady Christmas, A	CBS-TV	Laurence Juber
Very Old Man with Enormous Wings, A	CUB/ITA/SPA	Pablo Mianes/ Gianni Nocenzi/Jose Maria Vitier
Vibes	COL	James Horner
Vice Versa	COL	David Shire
Vicious	AUT	Robert Scott/John Sleith
Vietnam War Story	HBO-C	Jonathan Sheffer/Mark Snow
Viper	IND	Scott Roewe
Visitor, The	SWE	Peter Wallin
Volpone (Big Fox, The)	ITA	Fabio Liberatori
Voyage Beyond	IN	Goutam Ghose
Voyage of the Rock Aliens	IND	Jack White
Vroom	BRI	Adam Kidron/Michael McEvoy
Wait for Me in Heaven	SPA	Carmelo Bernaola
Walking After Midnight	CAN	Mychael Dana
Wanted: Loving Father and Mother	HOL	Ig Henneman
War	IND	Christopher De Marco
War & Remembrance	ABC-TV	Robert Cobert
Warning: Medicine May Be Hazardous to Your Health	HBO-C	Robert Lieberman
Wash, The	IND	John Morris
Wasps' Nest, The	RUM	Paul Urmuzescu
Watchers	UN	Joel Goldsmith
Waxwork	VES	Roger Bellon
We the Living	ITA	Renzo Rossellini
We Think the World of You	BRI	Julian Jacobson
Weekend War	ABC-TV	Brad Fiedel
Welcome to Germany	GER	Guenther Fischer
Well, the (Jin)	CHN	Tang Qingshi
Werewolf of W., The	GER	Volker Rogall
West Is West	IND	Sheila Chandra/Jai Uttal
What If Gargiulo Finds Out?	ITA	Pino Daniele
What Is to Come	ARG	Charly Garcia

What Price Victory	ABC-TV	Fred Karlin
When, If Not Now?	GER	Klaus Bantzer
Where Do We Go From Here?	BUL	Kiril Dontchev
Where the Hell's That Gold?	CBS-TV	Arthur B. Rubinstein
Where to Go? (Wohin?)	GER	Tom Waits
Wherever You Are	BRI/GER/POL	Wojiech Kilar
Whisper Kills, A	ABC-TV	Charles Bernstein
White Ghost	IND	Palmer Fuller
Who Framed Roger Rabbit	DIS	Alan Silvestri
Why (Proc)	CZE	Michael Pavlicek
Why on Earth?	ABC-TV	Craig Huxley/Jerrold Immel
Wild Things	BRI	Richard Hartley
Wildfire	IND	Maurice Jarre
Willow	MGM	James Horner
Windmills of the Gods	CBS-TV	Perry Botkin
Witches' Sabbath, The	FRA/ITA	Carlo Crivelli
With Feathers	SPA	Jose Manuel Pagan
Without a Clue	ORI	Henry Mancini
Without Fear or Blame	FRA	Yves de Bujadoux
Wizard of Loneliness, The	IND	Michel Colombier
Wizard of Speed and Time, The	IND	John Massari
Wolves' Moon	SPA	Bernardo Fuster/Luis Mendo
Woman Destroyed, A	ITA	Egisto Macchi
Woman He Loved, The	CBS-TV	Allyn Ferguson
Woman in the Moon	ITA	Franco Piersanti
Women in Prison	FRA	Michel Portal
Women on the Verge of a Nervous Breakdown	SPA	Bernardo Bonezzi
Women's Affair, A	FRA	Mathieu Chabrol
Wonder Years, The	ABC-TV	Stewart Levin/W. G. Snuffy Walden
Working Girl	FOX	Carly Simon
World Apart, A	BRI	Hans Zimmer
World Gone Wild	LOR	Laurence Juber
Wrong Guys, The	NWP	Joseph Conlan
Xaver	GER	Hans Juergen Buchner Baindling
Yasemin	GER	Jens-Peter Ostendorf
Yen Family	JAP	Katsuo Ohne
You Can't Hurry Love	IND	Bob Esty
Young Einstein	WB	Martin Armiger/William Motzing/Tommy Tycho
Young Guns	FOX	Brian Banks/Anthony Marinelli
Zan Boko	AFR	Georges Ouedraogo
Zelly and Me	COL	Pino Donaggio
ZEN--Zone of Expansion North	ITA	Laura Fisher
Zina, Dear Zina	RUS	Marc Minkov
Zombie Brigade	AUT	John Charles/Todd Hunter
Zucchini Flowers	ITA	Piero Montanari

COMPOSERS AND THEIR FILMS

AC/DC
Maximum Overdrive (1986)

ABADY, TEMPLE
Dear Mr. Prohack (1949)
Horse's Mouth, The (Oracle,
The) (1953)
Love in Pawn (1953)
Street Corner (1953)

ABDUL-FATAH, INTISAR
Fetters (1986)
Collar and the Bracelet,
The (1987)

ABEL, ALFRED
Everything for the Woman
(1936)

ABEL, DICK
Azimat (1958)

ABENE, MICHAEL
Goodbye New York (1985)

ABOUDARHAM, NORBERT
Bastard, The (1983)

ABRAHAM, PAUL
Ball at the Savoy, The (1936)
Rakoszy March (1936)
Hotel Kikelet (1937)
Modern Girls (1937)
Pesti-Mese (1937)
Viki (1937)

ABRIL, ANTON GARCIA
Goodbye, Texas (1966)
Nine Lives of a Cat, The
(1970)

Werewolf vs. the Vampire
Woman, The (1972)
Del Terror Ciego (1973)
Tombs of the Blind Dead
(1973)
Dr. Jekyll and the Wolfman
(1974)
Horror of the Zombies (1976)
Night of the Seagulls (1977)
When the Screaming Stops
(1980)
Cuenca Crime, The (1980)
Five Forks (1980)
Gary Cooper, Who Art in
Heaven (1981)
Bee-Hive, The (1982)
Holy Innocents, The (1984)
Requiem for a Spanish
Peasant (1985)
Monsignor Quixote (1987)
Code Name: The Russian
(1988)

ACANTHUS, GEORGE
Sex and the Vampire (Vampire
Thrills) (1970)

ACCOLAI, FRANCESCO
Crossing Over (1982)

ACEVES, HERIBERTO
Devil, the Saint and the Fool,
The (1987)

ACHACOSO, EDWARD
Equalizer 2000 (1987)

ACHLEY, JAMES
Black Room, The (1981)

ACIM, SERVER
  Full Moon (1988)

ACKERMAN, WILLIAM
  Lost in the Wilderness (1986)

ADAMIC, BOJAN
  Irene in Need (1953)
  Cursed Money (1957)
  Black Pearls (1958)
  Happy End (1958)
  Shots in the Sky (1958)
  False Passport, The (1959)
  Five Minutes of Paradise (1959)
  Heaven Without Love (1959)
  Mamula Camp (1959)
  Sam (Alone) (1959)
  Three Quarters of a Sun (1959)
  Comrade President Center-
    Forward (1960)
  Partisan Stories (1960)
  Three Girls Named Anna (1960)
  Dancing in the Rain (1961)
  Piece of Blue Sky, A (1961)
  Signal Over the City (1961)
  Fantastic Ballad (1968)
  See You in the Next Year
    (1980)
  Wasteland (1982)
  Battle at Poziralnik, The (1982)
  Masquerade (1983)
  Heads or Tails (1983)

ADAMKEWITZ, BERND
  Lot of Bills to Pay, A (1981)

ADAMS, FLETCHER
  Shaping Up (1984)

ADAMS, JOHN
  Fifth of July (1982)
  Matter of Heart (1986)

ADAMSON, STUART
  Restless Natives (1985)

ADDINSELL, RICHARD
  Contraband (1940)
  This England (1941)
  Time Bomb (1953)

ADDISON, JOHN
  Nothing to Lose (Time,
    Gentlemen, Please) (1953)
  End of the Road, The (1954)
  One Good Turn (1955)
  Josephine and Men (1955)
  Shiralee, The (1957)
  All at Sea (1957)
  Man in a Cocked Hat (1959)
  School for Scoundrels (1960)
  His and Hers (1961)
  Hamlet (1970)
  Grady (1975)
  Centennial (1978)
  Black Beauty (1978)
  Bastard/Kent Family Chroni-
    cles, The (1978)
  Death in Canaan, A (1978)
  Pearl (1978)
  Eddie Capra Mysteries, The
    (1978)
  French Atlantic Affair, The
    (1979)
  Like Normal People (1979)
  Love's Savage Fury (1979)
  Power Within, The (1979)
  Highpoint (1979)
  Mistress of Paradise (1981)
  Nero Wolfe (1981)
  Charles and Diana: A Royal
    Love Story (1982)
  Eleanor, First Lady of the
    World (1982)
  I Was a Mail Order Bride
    (1982)
  Devlin Connection, The (1982)
  Fit for a King (1982)
  Strange Invaders (1983)
  Murder, She Wrote (1984)
  Ultimate Solution of Grace
    Quigley, The (1984)
  Ellis Island (1984)
  Code Name: Emerald (1985)
  13 at Dinner (1985)
  Dead Man's Folly (1986)
  Firefighter (1986)
  Mr. Boogedy (1986)
  Something in Common (1986)
  Bride of Boogedy (1987)
  Strange Voices (1987)

Beryl Markham: A Shadow
on the Sun (1988)

ADLER, LARRY
Jumping for Joy (1956)

ADLER, MARK
Break of Dawn (1988)

ADOLFO, ANTONIO
Endless Dream (1986)

ADOMIAN, LAN
Dream No More (1950)
Basket of Mexican Tales
(1956)
Talpa (1957)

AFFLEY, DECLAN
Strikebound (1984)

AGMUSSEN, CLAUS & SVEND
I Love You (1987)

AGUAROD, FRANCISCO
Hint of a Crime, A (1988)

AGULLO, ALFONSO
Monster Island (1981)

AHI, ELTON FAROKH
Hollywood Cop (1988)

AHMAD, OSMAN
Devouring Rock, The (1959)

AKENDENGUE, PIERRE
Sarraounia (1986)

AKENO, SEI
Make-Up (1985)

AKISTER, PETER
Sailor Beware (1956)

AKOM, LAJOS
Black Diamonds (1938)
I've Never Stolen in My
Life (1939)

AKUTAGAWA, SATOSHI
Bad Sorts (1980)

AKUTAGAWA, YASUSHI
Naked Sun, The (1959)
Mt. Hakkoda (1978)
Shadow Within, The (1970)
Bonchi (1981)

AL WADI, HELMI
Lover, The (1986)

ALBENIZ, ISAAC
Pictura (1952)

ALBERTI, ROBERT
Highcliffe Manor (1979)
Hizzoner (1979)

ALBERTINE, CHARLES
Days of Our Lives (1965)
Bionic Woman, The (1976)
Fantasy Island (1978)
Powers of Matthew Starr,
The (1982)

ALBUQUERQUE, PERINHO
India, Daughter of the Sun
(1982)

ALCANTARA, RAUL
Contract with Death (1985)

ALCARAZ, LUIS
Five Nerds Take Las Vegas
(1987)

ALCARRAF, ABDUL AMIR
Love in Bagdad (1986)

ALCIVAR, BOB
Quincy (1976)
That Secret Sunday (1986)

ALESSANDRINI, RAYMOND
Quarter to Two Before Jesus
Christ, A (1982)
Swallow and the Titmouse,
The (1984)
Staircase C (1985)
Letters to an Unknown Lover
(1985)
Dolly In (1987)
Jeanne's House (1988)

ALESSANDRONI, ALESSANDRO
Devil's Nightmare, The
(1971)
Lady Frankenstein (1971)

ALEXANDER, ALEX
Two Lost Worlds (1950)

ALEXANDER, JEFF
My Three Sons (1960)
Family Affair, A (1966)
Julia (1968)
Columbo (1971)
Daughters of Joshua Cabe,
The (1972)
Barnaby Jones (1973)
Barney and Me (1973)
Police Woman (1974)
Daughters of Joshua Cabe
Return, The (1975)
New Daughters of Joshua
Cabe, The (1976)
Kate Bliss and the Ticker
Tape Kid (1978)
But Mother! (1979)
Wild Wild West Revisited,
The (1979)
More Wild, Wild West (1980)

ALEXANDER, VAN
Tarzan and the Valley of
Gold (1965)
Jimmy Stewart Show, The
(1971)

ALFVEN, HUGO
Singoalla (1950)

ALGUERO, AUGUSTO
Miss Cuple (1959)
St. Valentine's Day (1959)
Lady Called Andres, A (1970)
Tunnel, The (1988)

ALIMA, ATSO
Da Capo (1985)

ALLAM, DJAMEL
Take 10,000 Francs and
Settle Down (1981)

ALLAN, CAMERON
Stir (1980)
Heatwave (1981)
Dark Room, The (1982)
Midnight Spares (1983)
Emoh Ruo (1985)
Going Sane (1986)
Good Wife, The (1986)
Landslides (1987)
Clean Machine, The (1988)
Pandemonium (1988)

ALLEGRA, SALVATORE
I Love You Only (1936)
Loves and Poisons (1950)

ALLEN, ALLEN D.
Clones, The (1972)
Danny and the Mermaid (1978)

ALLEN, BILLY
She Freak (1966)

ALLEN, MARTY
Dr. Jekyll's Dungeon of
Death (1978)

ALLEN, TERRY
Amerasia (1986)

ALLISON, KEITH
Rock and a Hard Place, A
(1981)
White and Reno (1981)

ALLMAN, SHELDON
George of the Jungle (1967)
Dudley Do-Right Show, The
(1969)

ALLRED, BYRON
Don't Answer the Phone
(1980)

ALLTAN, MINETTE
Children of Divorce (1980)

ALMEIDA, LAURINDO
Flight (1960)
Cowboy (1967)
Death Takes a Holiday (1971)

ALONI, AMINIDAV
  UFO Target Earth (1974)
  Lost City of Atlantis (1978)

ALONSO, FRANCISCO
  Water in the Ground (1934)
  Dancer and the Worker, The
    (1936)

ALONSO, MIGUEL ANGEL
  Welcome, Maria (1987)

ALPER, ALAN
  Starstruck (1979)

ALPERSON, EDWARD L., JR.
  September Storm (1960)

"ALPHAVILLE"
  Cop and the Girl, The (1985)

ALRAND, PIERRE
  Gardener, The (1982)
  Rumor, A (1983)
  Gwen, or the Book of Sand
    (1985)

ALTER, NAFTALI
  Finals (1983)
  Irith, Irith (1985)
  Funny Farm (1986)

ALTERS, GERALD
  Your Place or Mine (1983)

ALTMAN, JOHN
  Almonds and Raisins (1984)
  John Lennon: A Journey
    in the Life (1986)

ALTON, ED
  Head of the Class (1986)

ALTON, MINETTE
  Children of Divorce (1980)

ALTOMARE, CARLO
  Signals Through the Flames
    (1984)

ALVAREZ, LUCIA
  Realm of Fortune, The (1986)

ALWYN, WILLIAM
  Daybreak in Udi (1950)
  Golden Salamander, The
    (1950)
  Night Without Stars (1951)
  Man With a Million (1954)
  Fortune Is a Woman (1957)
  Manuela (1957)
  Silent Enemy, The (1958)
  Killers of Kilimanjaro (1960)

ALZNER, CLAUDIUS
  Fountain of Love (1969)

AMBROSETTI, FRANCO
  Journey, The (1986)

AMFITHEATROF, DANIELE
  Everybody's Woman (1936)

AMRAM, DAVID
  Beat Generation--An American
    Dream, The (1987)
  Pigeon Feathers (1988)

AMUNDSEN, STEVE
  Low Blow (1986)

AMY, GILBERT
  Alliance (1970)

ANANDJI, K.
  Hari Darshan (1972)
  Darinda (1977)

ANDERSEN, BENNY
  Denmark Closed Down (1980)

ANDERSON, CHARLES
  From Pole to Equator (1987)

ANDERSON, JOHN
  End of the World Man, The
    (1985)

ANDERSON, LAURIE
  Something Wild (1986)
  Swimming to Cambodia (1987)

ANDERSON, MICHAEL
  Terrified (1962)

ANDES, MAT
  Joshua in a Box (1970)

ANDOMIAN, LAN
  Pictura (1952)

ANDRE, PAULA
  Land for Rose (1988)

ANDREANI, JORGE
  Lady and Death, The (1946)

ANDREAU, CARLOS
  Eyes of the Birds (1983)

ANDRIESSEN, JURRIHAN
  Village on the River, The
    (1959)
  Assault, The (1986)

ANDRIESSEN, LOUIS
  Alien, The (1980)
  Waves (1982)

ANFOSSO, GERARD
  Bit of Living, A (1982)

ANGELO, JUDY HART
  Popcorn Kid (1987)

ANGIULINI, RENATO
  Story of Piera (1983)

ANGYLA, LASZLO
  Son of the Pusta (1937)

ANIOL, EDWARD
  Moving Targets (1985)

ANNECCHION, ARTURO
  Con-fusion (1980)

ANSELMI, RENATO
  Lisi and the General (1986)

ANTHIEL, GEORGES
  Union Pacific (1939)
  Legend of the Glass Moun-
    tain, The (1949)
  House by the River, The
    (1950)

Sniper, The (1952)
Dementia (1953)

ANTHONY, RICHARD
  Foolish Years of the Twist,
    The (1983)

ANTHONY, TOM
  Coral Jungle, The (1976)

ANTON, BUNNY
  Love Circles (1985)

ANTONELLI, PAUL E.
  Women's Club, The (1987)

ANTONIOU, THEODORE
  Girl from Mani, The (1986)

AOKI, NOZUMI
  Toward Magic Island (1982)
  Galaxy Express 999 (1982)

AOYAMA, HACHIRO
  Bullet Train Blast (1975)
  Gold, Code and the Sea
    (1975)
  Living Together (1975)
  Someday, Somewhere (1976)

APERGIS, GIORGOS
  Topos (1985)

APPLEBAUM, LOUIS
  Farewell to Yesterday (1950)
  Stratford Adventure (1954)
  Karsh: The Searching Eye
    (1986)

APUATIMI, RAPHAEL
  Tudawali (1988)

ARAKI, ICHIRO
  Pilgrimage to Japanese Baths
    (1971)
  Twisted Sex (1972)
  Erotomania Daimyo, The
    (1975)
  Manon (1982)

ARANGUREN, JESUS
  In September (1982)

ARANTES, GUILHERME
    Golden Girl (1983)

ARAVINDAM
    Esthappan (1980)
    There Was a Village (1987)

ARBO, MIGUEL ASINS
    Violent Fate (1959)
    Little Bull, The (1985)

ARBORE, RENZO
    In the Pope's Eye (1981)
    Mystery of Bellavista, The
        (1986)

ARCARAZ, LUIS
    All Because of a Wedding
        Dress (1986)

ARCHANGELSKI, ALEXIS
    This Woman Is Mine (1935)

ARCHBOLD, DON
    Parallels (1980)

AREL, JACQUES
    Grand Ceremonial, The
        (1968)
    Stroke of Luck (1983)

ARETA, ANTONIO
    Gulliver's Travels (1983)

AREVALO, TITO
    Mad Doctor of Blood Island
        (1969)
    Beast of Blood (1970)
    Curse of the Vampires
        (1970)
    Blood of the Vampires
        (1970)
    Twilight People (1971)

ARGOL, SEBASTIAN
    Road, The (1982)

ARGOV, ALEXANDER (SACHA)
    Impossible on Saturday
        (1964)
    He Walked Through the
        Fields (1968)

ARGUDO, ALBERTO
    Exorcism (1974)

ARISA, SANTI
    Legend of the Drum, The
        (1982)
    Cain (1987)

ARIZAGA, RUDOLFO
    Demon in the Blood (1964)

ARKIN, ED (EDDIE)
    Hardbodies 2 (1986)
    Modern Girls (1986)
    Pretty Smart (1987)

ARMANI, EDUARDO
    Aladdin Takes Off (Dringue
        Castrito and Aladdin's
        Lamp) (1954)

ARMIGER, MARTIN
    Empty Beach, The (1985)
    Displaced Persons (1985)
    Challenge, The (1986)
    Cyclone Tracy (1986)
    Dancing Daze (1986)
    I Own the Racecourse (1986)
    Relative Merits (1987)
    Young Einstein (1988)

ARMSTRONG, MICHAEL
    Silent Night, Deadly Night,
        Part II (1987)

ARNAUD, LEON
    Day of Fear (1957)

ARNAUTALIC, ESAD
    Scent of Quince, The (1982)
    Azra (1988)

ARNELL, RICHARD
    Land, The (1942)

ARNESON, RANDY
    Little People (1982)

ARNFRED, OLE
    Heaven and Hell
        (1988)

ARNOLD, DANNY
My World ... and Welcome
to It (1969)

ARNOLD, HARRY
Time of Desire (1957)
Woman in a Fur Coat, The
(1958)
Miss April (1959)
48 Hours to Live (1959)
Invasion of the Animal People
(1960)
Thief in the Bedroom, The
(1960)

ARNOLD, MALCOLM
Four-Sided Triangle (1953)
Holly and the Ivy, The
(1954)
Devil on Horseback, The
(1954)
Beautiful Stranger (1954)
Sea Shall Not Have Them,
The (1954)
Sleeping Tiger, The (1954)
Woman for Joe, A (1955)
Hill in Korea, A (1956)
Man of Africa (1956)
Boy and the Bridge, The
(1959)
Pure Hell at St. Trinian's
(1960)
David Copperfield (1970)

ARNOLD, STEVE
Tail of the Tiger (1984)

ARNOW, PETER
Generation Apart, A (1984)

ARRIAGADA, JORGE
Territory, The (1983)
Three Crowns of the Sailor,
The (1983)
Paris Seen By ... 20 Years
After (1984)
Ave Maria (1984)
Our Marriage (1985)
Terrible Lovers, The (1985)
Manuel's Destinies (1985)
City of Pirates (1985)

Children of the Cold War
(1986)
Beggars, The (1987)
Burning Bush (1987)
Life Is a Dream (1987)
Miracle, The (1987)
Caftan of Love (1988)
Icebreaker (1988)

ARRIETA, GERMAN
Father by Accident (1982)

ARROYO, PASCAL
Rotten Fate! (1987)

ARSOVSKI, BOGDAN
Three's Happiness (1986)

ARTEAGA, ANGEL
Celestina, La (1969)
Lame Devil, The (1970)
Frankenstein's Bloody Terror
(1971)

ARTEMYEV, EDUARD
Alexander the Little (1983)
Family Relations (1983)
Without Witnesses (1983)
Hot Summer in Kabul, A
(1983)
Youth of a Genius, The
(1983)
Lunar Rainbow (1984)
Farewell Green Summer (1987)
Messenger Boy (1987)
Strange Case of Dr. Jekyll
and Mr. Hyde, The (1987)
Foxhunting (1988)

ARTHUYS, PHILIPPE
Wife for My Son, A (1983)
Last Tango, The (1986)

ASAKAWA, AKIYUKI
Memories of You (1988)

ASAMI, YUKIO
Wanderers, The (1974)

ASCH, ANDREW
Chief Zabu (1988)

ASCHENBRENNER, JOHN
  Alexyz (1984)

ASCHER, KENNY
  Meet Mr. Kringle (1957)
  Muppet Movie, The (1979)

ASERUD, BENT
  Hockey Fever (1983)
  Chieftain, The (1984)
  Orion's Belt (1985)
  Burning Flowers (1985)
  After Rubicon (1987)
  Andersen's Run (1987)
  Night Voyage (1987)
  Ice Palace, The (1988)

ASETTA, STEVE
  Disconnected (1986)

ASHDOTH, ISHAR
  Breaking (1985)

ASHER, JAY
  I'm Going to Be Famous
    (1983)
  Maximum Security (1985)

ASHER, TONY
  Rollergirls, The (1978)

ASHFORD, NICK
  Change at 125th Street
    (1974)

ASHFORD, TED
  Hot and Deadly (1981)

ASKEY, GIL
  Dummy (1979)

ASLTOILA, HEIKKI
  1918--A Man and His
    Conscience (1957)

"ASPHALT BLUES COMPANY"
  Land of Fire All Night
    Long (1981)

ASSOUS, CYRIL
  Souvenirs, Souvenirs (1984)

ASTLEY, EDWIN
  Devil Girl from Mars, The
    (1954)
  Happiness of Three Women,
    The (1954)
  Alias John Preston (1955)
  Veil, The (1958)
  Faces in the Dark (1960)
  Let's Get Married (1960)
  Saint, The (1967)
  Champions, The (1967)
  Department S (1971)
  Strange Report, The (1971)
  Kadoyng (1972)
  My Partner the Ghost (1973)
  Saint, The (1975)

ASTRADANTSEV, D.
  Musical Story, A (1941)

ASUNCION, SAMUEL
  Saigon Commandos (1988)

ATHANASSOPOULOUS, MARINOS
  Meteor and Shadow (1985)

ATKAKORN, KADEE
  Puen and Paeng (1983)

ATKINSON, MICHAEL
  Street to Die, A (1985)
  Backlash (1986)
  Dear Cardholder (1987)
  Jilted (1987)
  Mullaway (1988)

"AU PAIRS"
  Field of Honor, The (1983)

AUBERSON, ANTOINE
  If the Sun Never Returned
    (1987)
  Lounge Chair, The (1988)

AUBIN, TONY
  Greenland (1952)

AUDOOREN, FABIEN
  Before the Battle (1983)

AUGE, CASAS
  Follies of Barbara, The
    (1959)

AUGUSTO, SERVULO
  Night Angels (1987)
  Fire and Passion (1988)

AURIC, GEORGES
  Lac aux Dames (1934)
  Under Western Eyes (1936)
  Messenger, The (1937)
  Mysteries of Paris (1937)
  Artist's Entrance (1938)
  Eternal Return, The (1943)
  Chips Are Down, The (1947)
  Parents Terribles, Les
    (1949)
  Maya (1949)
  This Is the Half Century
    (1950)
  Galloping Major, The (1951)
  Lavender Hill Mob, The
    (1951)
  Daughter of the Sands
    (1952)
  Father Brown (1954)
  Good Die Young, The (1954)
  Mystery of Picasso (Picasso)
    (1956)
  Gervaise (1956)
  Adventures of Til Eulenspiegel
    (1957)
  Dangerous Exile (1957)
  Burning Court, The (1961)
  Innocents, The (1961)

AURILLO, NOLI
  Saigon Commandos (1988)

AUTE, LUIS EDUARDO
  Man of Fashion (1980)
  Evening Performance (1981)

AVELINO, ARISTON
  Nenita Unit (1954)
  Twilight People (1971)

AVILA, PEPE
  Fando and Lys (Tar Babies)
    (1968)

AVITIA, ANTONIO
  Errant Lives (1984)

AVRAMOVSKI, RISTO
  Time and Tide (1981)
  Australia, Australia (1981)

AXELSON, STEN
  Shanty Town (1936)

AZAORA, MARTINEZ
  Boy (1940)

AZEVEDO, CARLOS
  Jester, The (1987)

AZNAR, PEDRO
  Man Looking Southeast (1986)

BABIDA, CHRIS
  Dragon Force (1982)
  All the Wrong Spies (1983)
  Teppanyaki (1984)
  Double Decker (1984)
  Sworn Brothers (1987)

BABOS, GYULA
  Blood Brothers (1983)

BABUSHKIN, VICTOR
  Detached Mission, The (1986)

BACALOV, DANIELE
  Cobalt Blue (1985)

BACALOV, LUIS ENRIQUE
  Ballad for a Thousand Million
    (1966)
  Django (1966)
  Ciascuno il Suo, A (1966)
  For Love ... For Magic ...
    (1966)
  Quien Sabe? (1966)
  Sugar Colt (1966)
  Witch in Love, A (1966)
  City of Women (1980)
  Girl from Millelire Street,
    The (1980)
  Coup de Foudre (1983)
  Young Bridegroom, The
    (1983)

Art of Love, The (1983)
Judge, The (1984)
Strange Passion, A (1984)
Case of Irresponsibility, A
    (1984)
Deceptions (1985)
Turncoat, The (1985)
Dying to Sing (1986)
Dear Gorbachev (1988)
Mask, The (1988)

BACHARACH, BURT
Arthur (1981)
Night Shift (1982)
Arthur 2 on the Rocks
    (1988)

BACHELET, PIERRE
Man of My Measure, A
    (1983)
Gwendoline (1984)
Emmanuelle 5 (1987)

BACHMAN, WERNER
Romance and Riches (1937)

BACHMETIV, PAVEL
Your Son and Brother
    (1966)

BACON, MICHAEL
Plagues (1988)
Robert Frost (1988)

BACUS, ALAN
Roommates (1984)

BADALAMENTI, ANGELO
Blue Velvet (1986)
Nightmare on Elm Street 3:
    Dream Warriors, A (1987)
Tough Guys Don't Dance
    (1987)
Weeds (1987)

BADAROU, WALLY
Countryman (1982)
They Call That an Accident
    (1982)

BADLINGS, HENK
Flying Dutchman, The (1957)

BAER, JOHN
Weekend Pass (1984)

BAEVERFJORD, JO TORE
Poachers (1982)

BAGLEY, DON
Man Called Sloane, A (1979)

BAHLER, JOHN
Rollergirls, The (1978)

"BAHLOO MUSIC SHOW, THE"
Monkey Mia (1985)

BAILIE, MICK HOPE
Captive Rage (1988)

BAILLARGEON, PAUL
Night Train to Kathmandu,
    The (1988)

BAINDLING, HANS JUERGEN
BUCHNER
Xaver (1988)

BAIRD, TADEUSZ
Sampson (1961)

BAK, FRANS
Holes in the Soup (1988)

BAKALEINIKOFF, CONSTANTIN
Strange Bargain (1949)

BAKALEINIKOFF, MISCHA
Night Editor (1946)
Blondie Hits the Jackpot
    (1949)
On the Isle of Samoa (1950)
Lineup, The (1958)

BAKER, Arthur
Sudden Death (1985)

BAKER, BUDDY
Tiger Walks, A (1964)
Family Planning (1968)
Million Dollar Duck, The
    (1971)
Devil and Max Devlin, The
    (1981)

Fox and the Hound, The
(1981)

BAKER, MICHAEL CONWAY
Grey Fox, The (1982)
Deserters (1983)
One Magic Christmas (1985)
Overnight (1986)
John and the Missus (1987)
Shelley (1987)

BAKIR, KAMAL
Bus Driver, The (1982)
Return of a Citizen (1986)

BAKUZADZE, TEMO (TEIMURAZ)
Swimmer, The (1986)
Black Monk, The (1988)

BALAKRISHNA, DILIP
Fair at Dharamtalia, The
(1987)

BALAZS, FERENC
Blind Endeavor (1986)
Tolerance (1987)

BALCHEV, ANATOLY
Fouette (1986)

BALERIOLA, EMILI
Love Is Strange (1988)

BALITZKI, JUERGEN
Grown Up Today (1986)

BALKHIRRAT, FARID
Opinion, The (1986)

BALL, STEVE
Dangerous Game (1988)

BALLARD, GLEN
He's the Mayor (1986)

BALLOTTA, ETTORE
Private Matter, A (1966)

BALSIA, E.
Elge, Queen of Snakes
(1965)

BALTAZAR, H.
Market of the Humble (1986)

BAMBINI, STEFANO
Kiss of Judas, The (1988)

BAND, RICHARD
Laserblast (1978)
Dr. Heckyl & Mr. Hype (1980)
Day Time Ended, The (1980)
Lunch Wagon (1981)
Parasite (1982)
Time Walker (1982)
House on Sorority Row, The
(1983)
Metalstorm: The Destruction
of Jared-Syn (1983)
Night Shadows (Mutant)
(1984)
Swordkill (1984)
Ghoulies (1985)
Dungeonmaster, The (1985)
Re-Animator (1985)
Alchemist, The (1986)
From Beyond (1986)
TerrorVision (1986)
Troll (1986)
Zone Troopers (1986)
Caller, The (1987)
Prison (1988)

BANDELL, JAN
Second Dance (1983)

BANDIER, MARTIN
Bear, The (1984)

BANERJEE, A.
Tarzan and King Kong (1965)
Mystery of Life, The (1973)

BANEVITCH, SERGEI
Flight 222 (1986)

BANG, POUL
Life on the Hegns Farm
(1939)

BANKS, BRIAN
Rigged (1985)
Nice Girls Don't Explode (1987)

Pinocchio and the Emperor
  of the Night (1987)
Young Guns (1988)

BANKS, DON
  Reptile, The (1966)

BANKS, LOUIS
  August Requiem, An (1982)
  New Delhi Times (1986)

BANKS, TONY
  Wicked Lady, The (1983)
  Lorca and the Outlaws (1985)
  Quicksilver (1986)

BANSHCHIKOV, GENNADI
  Paper Gramophone, The
    (1988)

BANTZER, KLAUS
  Dear Mr. Wonderful (1982)
  Inside the Whale (1985)
  Men (1985)
  40 Square Meters of Germany
    (1986)
  Paradise (1986)
  Silence of the Poets, The
    (1986)
  Dragon Food (1987)
  When, If Not Now? (1988)

BAR, SHLOMO
  Shattered Dreams--Picking
    Up the Pieces (1987)

BARANOVICH, KRESIMIR
  Magic Sword, The (1949)
  Legends of Anika (1956)

BARBANERA, ROSANNA AND
    OLIVIERO
  Land in Two (1985)

BARBAUD, PIERRE
  Creatures, Les (1966)

BARBELIVIEN, DIDIER
  Long Live Life! (1984)

BARBER, FRANK
  From a Bird's Eye View
    (1971)

BARBER, STEPHEN
  Faerie Tale Theater (1982)

BARBER BROTHERS, THE
  Scared Stiff (1987)

BARBIER, JEAN-LUC
  In the White City (1983)

BARBIERI, LEANDRO "GATO"
  Notes for an African Orestes
    (1979)
  Stranger's Kiss (1983)

BARCELATA, LORENZO
  Alla en el Rancho Grande
    (1936)

BARCLAY, EDDIE
  Every Day Has Its Secret
    (1958)

BARDAGI, J. M.
  Last Evenings with Theresa
    (1984)

BARKER, WARREN
  Bewitched (1964)
  Love on a Rooftop (1966)
  That Girl (1966)
  Ghost and Mrs. Muir, The
    (1968)
  Here Come the Brides (1968)
  Bracken's World (1969)
  My World ... and Welcome
    to It (1969)

"I BARLUNA"
  Madonna, Che Silenzio c'e
    Stasera (1982)
  Me, Light and Darkness (1983)

BARNABE, ARRIGO
  Vera (1987)

BARNETT, CHARLES P.
  Hell Squad (1983)

Busted Up (1986)
Screwball Academy (1987)
Last Man Standing (1988)

BARNS, GAVIN
Freaks (1932)

BARODOW, Z.
Devil Played the Balalaika,
The (1961)

BARRIO, ALEJANDRO see
GUTIERREZ DEL BARRIO,
ALEJANDRO

BARRON, LOUIS AND BEBE
Very Edge of Night, The
(1959)
Spaceboy (1972)

BARRY, JEFF
Kowboys, The (1970)
Jeffersons, The (1975)
All's Fair (1976)
Baby I'm Back (1978)
Getting There (1980)
Saint Peter (1981)
Another Man's Shoes (1984)
Hereafter (1985)
Spiker (1986)

BARRY, JOHN
Persuaders, The (1971)
Shirley's World (1971)
Adventurer, The (1972)
Orson Welles' Great
Mysteries (1973)
Glass Menagerie, The (1973)
Love Among the Ruins (1975)
Eleanor and Franklin (1976)
Eleanor and Franklin: The
White House Years (1977)
Gathering, The (1977)
War Between the Tates, The
(1977)
Young Joe, the Forgotten
Kennedy (1977)
Corn is Green, The (1979)
Willa (1979)
Night Games (1980)
Touched by Love (1980)
Raise the Titanic! (1980)

Somewhere in Time (1980)
Inside Moves (1980)
Legend of the Lone Ranger,
The (1981)
Body Heat (1981)
Hammett (1982)
Frances (1982)
High Road to China (1982)
Octopussy (1983)
Golden Seal, The (1983)
Mike's Murder (1984)
Until September (1984)
Cotton Club, The (1984)
View to a Kill, A (1985)
Jagged Edge (1985)
Out of Africa (1985)
Howard the Duck (1986)
Peggy Sue Got Married (1986)
Hearts of Fire (1987)
Living Daylights, The (1987)
Killing Affair, A (1988)
Masquerade (1988)

BARRY, NANCY
Another Man's Shoes (1984)

BARRYMORE, ANDREW (ANTONY)
Blastfighter (1983)
Monster Shark (1986)

BART, LIONEL
Man in the Middle (1964)
Dr. Jekyll and Mrs. Hyde
(1973)

BARTAK, ZDENEK, JR.
Romaneto (1981)
Fists in the Dark (1987)

BARTEL, JOSE
Spermula (1976)

BARTHOLOMAE, HUBERT
Noah's Ark Principle, The
(1984)
Thousand Eyes (1984)
Jack of Spades (1984)
Joey (1985)

BARTHOLOME, K.
Summer of the Samurai (1986)

BARTLEY, DAVID
    Beyond the Rising Moon
        (1988)

BARTON, DEE
    Unmasking the Idol (1986)

BARTSENS, STEPHEN
    Greece on the March (1941)

BARTZSCH, FRANZ
    Rendezvous Leipzig (1985)

BARUA, SATYA
    Catastrophe, The (1988)

BARZIZZA, PIPPO
    Adam and Eve (1950)
    Was It He? Yes! Yes!
        (1952)

BASHUNG, ALAIN
    Nestor Burma, Detective of
        Shock (1982)
    Fourth Power, The (1985)
    Beauf, The (1987)

BASKIN, RICHARD
    Congratulations, It's a Boy!
        (1971)
    James at 15 (1977)
    Uforia (1980)

BASNER, V.
    Immortal Garrison, The
        (1957)

BASS, JULES
    New Adventures of Pinocchio

BASSELLI, JOSS
    Dougal and the Blue Cat
        (1972)

BASSENGE, ULRICH
    Nuclear Split (1987)

BASTHAL, ISTVAN
    Help! I'm an Heir! (1937)

BASTIAN, LARRY
    Last Leaf, The (1984)

BASTIAN, PETER
    Little Virgil and Frogeater
    Orla (1980)

BATE, STANLEY
    Pleasure Garden, The (1952)

BATES, STEVE
    Dutch Treat (1987)

BATIZ, GERARDO
    Pedro and the Captain (1984)

BATT, MIKE
    Wombling Free (1977)
    Digital Dreams (1983)

BAUDRIER, YVES
    Women of Evil (1949)

BAUER, ROLF
    Order (1980)
    Utopia (1983)

BAUER, THOMAS
    Just Forget It (1988)

BAUMANN, ERIK
    Raggen (1936)
    Shanty Town (1936)
    Our Boy (1936)
    South of the Highway (1937)
    Skanor-Falsterbo (1939)
    Her Melody (1942)

BAUMGARTNER, ROLAND
    Deadly Game (1982)
    Joseph's Daughter (1983)
    Jungle Warriors (1983)
    Heart Beats (1985)

BAUMGARTNER, WALTER
    Palace Hotel (1952)
    Cafe Odeon (1959)
    Devil May Well Laugh, The
        (1960)
    Swiss Named Notzli, A (1988)

BAUR, JIRZI
    Star Goes to the South,
        The (1959)

BAUTISTA, JULIAN
  Ashes to the Wind (1942)
  When Spring Makes a Mistake
    (1944)
  Dishonor (1952)
  Black Ermine (1953)

BAUX, GEORGES
  What Did I Ever Do to the
    Good Lord to Deserve a
    Wife Who Drinks in Cafes
    with Men? (1980)
  Young Ladies' War, The
    (1983)

BAUX, PIERRE-MARIE
  What Did I Ever Do to the
    Good Lord to Deserve a
    Wife Who Drinks in Cafes
    with Men? (1980)
  Young Ladies' War, The
    (1983)

BAVEL, VAN
  Texas Comedy Massacre,
    The (1987)

BAXTER, LES
  Tanga-Tika (1953)
  Gumby Special, The (1957)
  Vicious Breed, The (1958)
  Terror in the Jungle (1967)
  Evening with Edgar Allan
    Poe, An (1970)
  Ogre, The (1970)
  Buck Rogers in the 25th
    Century (1979)
  Curse of Dracula, The (1979)
  Secret Empire, The (1979)
  Stop Susan Williams (1979)
  Target: Harry (1980)
  Beast Within, The (1982)

BAZAR, MATIA
  Magic Moments (1984)

BAZELON, IRWIN
  Wilma (1977)

BEACHAM-POWELL, NIGEL
  Campaign (1988)

BEAL, JEFF
  Cheap Shots (1988)

BEAL, JOHN
  Laverne and Shirley (1976)
  Vega$ (1978)
  Goodtime Girls (1980)
  Ladies in Blue (1980)
  Funhouse (1981)
  Little Shots (1983)
  Killer Party (1986)

BEAMER, KAPONO
  Moloka'i Solo (1988)

BEAMISH, BRIAN
  Day of the Panther (1988)
  Dirtwater Dynasty, The (1988)

BEARD, STAN
  Now I Know (1988)

BEARTS, GUY
  Charming Boys (1958)

BEASLEY, JOHN
  Duet (1987)
  Mickey & Nora (1987)

BEATUS, OTTO
  Two Valentinos (1985)

BEAUDRIER, YVES
  Man Who Returns from Afar,
    The (1950)

BEAUSOLEIL, BOBBY
  Lucifer Rising (1981)

BEAVER, JACK
  Supersonic Saucer (1956)
  It Happened Here (1966)

BEBEY, FRANCIS
  House Arrest (1982)
  Choice, The (1987)

BECAUD, GILBERT
  Casino de Paris (1957)

BECCE, GUISEPPE
  Destiny (Mude Tod, Der)
    (1921)
  Prodigal Son, The (1935)
  Strange Guest, A (1936)
  Emperor of California (1936)
  Marija Valewska (1936)
  You Are My Joy (1936)
  Voice of the Heart, The
    (1937)

BECHERT, ERNST
  German Revolution, A (1982)

BECHET, SIDNEY
  Serie Noir (1955)

BECKER, FRANK W.
  Bravestar (1988)

BECKER, GERHARD
  Indian Tomb, The (1959)
  Fountain of Life (1961)

BECKERMAN, DANNY
  Fortress (1985)

BEDNAREK, JACEK
  Kung-Fu (1980)
  Index (1981)

BEGALIJEV, M.
  Descendant of the Snow
    Leopard, The (1985)

BEINHORN, MICHAEL
  Dark Lullabies (1985)

BEKKER, BARRY
  My Country, My Hat (1983)

BELAMARIC, MIROSLAV
  Lost Pencil, The

BELASCO, JACQUES
  Magic Fountain, The (1961)

BELASCO, JOE
  Pearl Harbor (1967)

BELEW, ADRIEN
  Return Engagement (1983)

BELL, ANDREW
  Pack of Women, A (1986)

BELL, BRIAN
  Screwball Academy (1987)

BELL, DANIEL
  Fanny and Alexander (1982)

BELL, DAVID
  Killing at Hell's Gate (1981)
  Murder, She Wrote (1984)
  Final Justice (1985)
  Blacke's Magic (1986)
  Return of the Shaggy Dog,
    The (1987)

BELL, SIMON
  Man from S.E.X., The (1978)
  Licensed to Love and Kill
    (1979)

BELL, WAYNE
  Texas Chainsaw Massacre,
    The (1974)
  Eaten Alive (Death Trap)
    (1976)
  Trespasses (1987)

BELLAVANCE, GINETTE
  Future Interior, The (1984)
  Deaf in the City (1987)

BELLING, ANDREW
  Deliver Us from Evil (1973)
  Summer Without Boys, A
    (1973)
  Crash! (1977)
  End of the World (1977)
  Deerslayer, The (1978)
  Fairy Tales (1979)

BELLIS, RICHARD
  Black Market Baby (1977)
  Shining Season, A (1979)
  Fallen Angel (1981)
  Dear Teacher (1981)
  Other Victim, The (1981)
  Money on the Side (1982)
  Addicted to His Love (1988)
  Shattered Innocence (1988)

BELLON, ROGER
Kid Who Wouldn't Quit/The
Brad Silverman Story,
The (1987)
Princess Academy, The
(1987)
Unholy, The (1988)
Waxwork (1988)

BELONA, CARMELO
Cemetery Girls (1979)

BELVAL, ROGER
Angel Life (1981)

BELYAIEV, ALEXANDER
Wishing Time (1984)

BEN MICHAEL, EDUARD
Faithful City (1952)

BENARROCH, CHARLES
Street of Departures (1986)

BENATZKY, RALPH
Girls' Dormitory (1936)

BENEDETTO, MARCELLO
Black Mirror (1981)

BENGTSON, ERIC
Great John Ericsson, The
(1938)

BENJAMIN, SIR ARTHUR
Under the Red Robe (1937)

BENNARD, GUILIO
Milizia Territoriale (1936)

BENNATO, EUGENIO
Tomorrow We Dance (1982)
Don Quixote (1984)

BENNETT, BRIAN
Robin's Nest (1977)
Terminal Choice (Trauma/
Death List/Critical List)
(1982)
American Way, The (1986)

BENNETT, EDDY
Love Odyssey (1987)

BENNETT, RICHARD RODNEY
Devil's Own, The (Witches,
The) (1967)
Voices (1973)
Sherlock Holmes in New York
(1976)
Return of the Soldier, The
(1982)
Ebony Tower, The (1987)
Poor Little Rich Girl: The
Barbara Hutton Story
(1987)
Attic: The Hiding of Anne
Frank, The (1988)
Story of Hollywood--Part 1,
The (1988)

BENNETT, ROBERT RUSSELL
End of the Trail (1967)
Island Called Ellis, The (1967)

BENOIT, DAVID
Tickets Please (1988)

BENSON, EDDIE
Tower of Terror (1941)

BENSON, RICHARD
Incinerator, The (1984)

BENSON, ROBBY
Die Laughing (1980)

BERADI, DANIEL
Man of the Foreign Debt,
The (1987)

BERENZY, JOHN
Magic Snowman, The (1987)

BERESFORD, STEVE
Broken April (1987)

BERETTA, MARIO
Alpine Fire (1985)

BERG, TONY
Sunshine Christmas (1977)

Rock Rainbow, The (1978)
High School U.S.A. (1983)
Too Good to Be True (1983)
Space (1985)
America 3000 (1986)
D.C. Cop (1986)
Welcome to 18 (1986)

BERGEAUD, DAVID
Twice Dead (1988)
Unnamable, The (1988)

BERGER, MICHEL
All Fired Up (1982)
Right Bank, Left Bank (1984)

BERGER, OKKO
Boran--Time to Aim (1987)

BERGLUND, ANDERS
Two Guys and a Gal (1983)

BERGMAN, ALAN AND MARILYN
All That Glitters (1977)

BERGMAN, BORIS
Honeymoon (1985)

BERGMANN, HANS-OTTO
Youth (Jugend) (1938)

BERGSTROM, HARRY
Women of Niskavuori (1938)

BERGSTROM, MATTI
Nine Ways to Approach
Helsinki (1982)

BERIO, LUCIANO
Metropolis (1983)

BERKAY, CAHIT
Broken-Hearted Love Story,
A (1983)
Despite Everything (1988)

BERKELEY, LENNO
Affairs of a Rogue, The
(1949)

BERKELEY, MICHAEL
Captive (1986)

BERKI, GEZA
Dead or Alive (1980)

BERKMAN, JOHN D.
Lois Gibbs and the Love Canal
(1982)

BERMAN, F.
Werewolf in a Girl's Dormitory
(1961)

BERMAN, SANDY
Screamers (1982)

"BERMUDAS, THE"
Virus Knows No Morals, A
(1986)

BERNAOLA, CARMELO
Disintegrating Ray, or the
Adventures of Quique and
Arthur the Robot, The
(1965)
That House in the Outskirts
(1980)
Paper Heart (1982)
Witches' Sabbath (1984)
Lost Paradises, The (1985)
Black Flag (1986)
Mambru Went to War (1986)
Madrid (1987)
Jarrapellejos (1988)
Two-Step (1988)
Wait for Me in Heaven (1988)

BERNARD, GUY
Pictura (1952)

BERNARD, IAN
Arnold's Closet Review (1971)
Big City Comedy (1980)

BERNARD, JAMES
Door in the Wall
(1957)

BERNARD, MICHAEL
Galactic Gigolo (1988)

BERNHEIM, FRANCIS (FRANCOIS)
Black Eye, A (1987)
Tandem (1987)

Legend of the 7 Golden
Vampires, The (1979)

BERNHOLC, MICHEL
Demons of the South (1980)
It All Depends on Girls
(1980)
Paris Seen By ... 20 Years
After (1984)

BERNSTEIN, CHARLES
Pigs, The (1972)
Invasion of the Bee Girls,
The (1973)
Kate McShane (1975)
Shadow in the Streets, A
(1975)
Look What's Happened to
Rosemary's Baby (1976)
Nightmare in Badham County
(1976)
Escape from Brogen County
(1977)
Cops and Robin (1978)
Katie: Portrait of a
Centerfold (1978)
Are You in the House Alone?
(1978)
Who's Watching the Kids?
(1978)
Wild and Wooly (1978)
Legs (1978)
Steel Cowboy (1978)
Thaddeus Rose and Eddie
(1978)
Winds of Kitty Hawk, The
(1978)
House on Garibaldi Street,
The (1979)
Women at West Point (1979)
Coast to Coast (1980)
Foolin' Around (1980)
Scruples (1980)
Bogie (1980)
Entity, The (1982)
Independence Day (1983)
Sadat (1983)
Cujo (1983)
Nightmare on Elm Street,
A (1984)
Secret Weapons (1985)

Malice in Wonderland (1985)
Generation (1985)
Long Hot Summer, The (1985)
April Fool's Day (1986)
Deadly Friend (1986)
Rockabye (1986)
Allnighter, The (1987)
Ghost of a Chance (1987)
Last Fling, The (1987)
Man Who Broke 1,000 Chains,
The (1987)
Whisper Kills, A (1988)

BERNSTEIN, ELMER
Saturday's Hero (1951)
Battles of Chief Pontiac
(1952)
Cat Women of the Moon (1953)
Robot Monster (1953)
Silent Raiders (1954)
Storm Fear (1956)
Communications Primer, A
(1956)
Eames Lounge Chair (1956)
Day of the Dead (1957)
Information Machine, The
(1957)
General Electric Theater
(1958)
Saddle the Wind (1958)
Race for Space, The (1959)
Introduction to Feedback
(1960)
Israel (1960)
Magnificent Seven, The (1960)
Beachcomber, The (1961)
Hollywood and the Stars
(1961)
Mathematical Peep Show (1961)
Project: Man in Space (1961)
Hollywood: The Golden
Years (1961)
D-Day (1962)
House of Science (1962)
Man from Independence, The
(1962)
Saints and Sinners (1962)
Making of the President,
The (1963)
Think! (1963)

Carpetbaggers, The (1964)
Four Days in November (1964)
Slattery's People (1964)
Baby the Rain Must Fall
  (1965)
Voyage of the Brigantine
  Yankee (1966)
Big Valley, The (1965)
Computer Glossary, A (1967)
Yankee Sails Across Europe
  (1967)
Julia (1968)
Wolf Men, The (1969)
Harmony of Nature and Man
  (1970)
Kifaru (1970)
Alaska (1971)
Arthur & the Britons (1971)
Doctor's Wives (1971)
Amazing Mr. Blunden, The
  (1972)
Owen Marshall, Counselor-
  at-Law (1971)
Rookies, The (1972)
Incident on a Dark Street
  (1973)
Men of the Dragon (1974)
Ellery Queen (Too Many
  Suspects) (1975)
Captains and the Kings
  (1976)
Serpico: The Deadly Game
  (1976)
3,000 Mile Chase, The (1977)
Little Women (1978)
Delta House (1979)
Charleston (1979)
Chisholms, The (1979)
Little Women (1979)
Airplane! (1980)
Saturn 3 (1980)
Guyana Tragedy: The Story
  of Jim Jones (1980)
Going Ape! (1981)
Moviola: This Year's
  Blonde (1980)
Stripes (1981)
Heavy Metal (1981)
American Werewolf in
  London, An (1981)
Honky Tonk Freeway (1981)

Chosen, The (1981)
Genocide (1982)
Five Days One Summer (1982)
Airplane II:= The Sequel
  (1982)
Spacehunter: Adventures in
  the Forbidden Zone (1983)
Trading Places (1983)
Class (1983)
Prince Jack (1984)
Ghostbusters (1984)
Bolero (1984)
Gulag (1985)
Marie Ward (1985)
Black Caldron, The (1985)
Spies Like Us (1985)
Legal Eagles (1986)
Three Amigos (1986)
Amazing Grace and Chuck
  (1987)
Leonard Part 6 (1987)
Da (1988)
Funny Farm (1988)
Good Mother, The (1988)

BERNSTEIN, PETER
  Here Comes the Bride (1973)
  Silent Rage (1982)
  National Lampoon's Class
    Reunion (1982)
  Hot Dog--The Movie (1984)
  Bolero (1984)
  Summer Fantasy (1984)
  Rape of Richard Beck, The
    (1985)
  My Science Project (1985)
  Ewoks: The Battle for
    Endor (1985)
  Club Med (1986)
  Hamburger--The Motion Pic-
    ture (1986)
  Little Spies (1986)
  Richest Cat in the World,
    The (1986)
  Alamo: 13 Days of Glory,
    The (1987)
  Miracles (1987)
  Morgan Stewart's Coming
    Home (1987)
  21 Jump Street (1987)
  Remote Control (1988)

BERNSTEIN, STEVE
  Before & After (1985)

BERRI, JAWED
  Women from South Lebanon
    (1986)

BERRY, ROBERT R., JR.
  Milpitas Monster, The (1976)

BERTEL, J. H.
  Trokadero (1981)

BERTI, SANH
  Cattle Annie and Little
    Britches (1981)

BERTOLINA, LUCIEN
  Return to Marseilles (1980)

BERTRAND, DOMINIQUE
  Ganga Maya (1984)

BERUKER, William
  Illusionist, The (1983)

BESSE, JACQUES
  Dedee (1949)
  Van Gogh (1949)

BESSIERES, LOUIS
  Magic of the Kite (1957)

BEST, PETER
  We of the Never Never (1982)
  Goodbye Paradise (1982)
  More Things Change, The
    (1985)
  Bliss (1985)
  Alice to Nowhere (1986)
  Crocodile Dundee (1986)
  Custody (1987)
  Harp in the South (1987)
  Poor Man's Orange (1987)
  Crocodile Dundee II (1988)

BETTS, HARRY
  Goodnight My Love (1972)
  David Cassidy--Man

Undercover (1978)
California Fever (1979)
Life and Times of Eddie
  Roberts, The (1980)
One in a Million (1980)
Six O'Clock Follies, The
  (1980)
Cheech & Chong's Nice
  Dreams (1981)
Richard Pryor Live on the
  Sunset Strip (1982)

BEYDTS, LOUIS
  Kermesse Heroique, La (1935)
  Courier of Lyons (1938)
  Baron Fantome, Le (1942)

BHASKAR, VIJAYA
  Maya Manushya (1976)
  Eclipse (1980)

BHATIA, AMIN
  Storm (1985)
  Iron Eagle II (1988)

BHATIA, VANRAJ
  36 Showringhee Lane (1982)
  Mandi (Market Place) (1983)
  Summons for Mohan Joshi
    (1984)
  Vibrations (1985)
  Massey Sahib (1986)
  Past, Present, Future (1986)
  Essence, The (1987)
  Darkness (1988)
  Pestonjee (1988)

BHATTACHARYA, P.
  Storm, The (1980)

BHOSHE, H.
  Jadu Tona (1977)

BIBB, LEON
  Young Ones, The (1961)

BIBERGAN, VADIM
  Vassa (1983)
  Double Start to Act, The
    (1985)
  Forgive Me (1987)

BICAT, NICK
   Oliver Twist (1982)
   Scarlet Pimpernel, The
      (1982)
   Disappearance of Harry, The
      (1983)
   Lace (1984)
   To Catch a King (1984)
   Christmas Carol, A (1984)
   Wetherby (1985)
   Lace II (1985)
   Christmas Present (1985)
   If Tomorrow Comes (1986)
   Stealing Heaven (1988)

BICKFORD, JOHN
   Beast With a Million Eyes,
      The (1955)

BIDSTRUP, GRAHAM
   Tender Hooks (1988)

BIENVENUE, JOEL
   Forties, The (1982)
   Moonshine Bowling (1983)
   Kalamazoo (1988)

"BIG BUCKS"
   Forbidden of the World,
      The (1986)

BIGAZZI, GIANCARLO
   Chewingum (1984)

BIJLSTRA, CEES
   Dream, The (1985)
   Count Your Blessings
      (1987)

BIKOS, THANASSIS
   Ostria (1984)

BILINSKI, MAREK
   Friend of a Jolly Devil,
      The (1987)

BILLON, PIERRE
   Outer Signs of Wealth
      (1983)

BILLY, JEAN-MARIE
   Falsch (1987)

"BILLY AND THE BEATERS"
   Tonight's the Night (1987)

BILOUS, EDWARD
   Sleepaway Camp (1983)

BINELLI, DANIEL
   Tango: Our Dance (1988)

BINGE, RONALD
   Once a Sinner (1952)
   Desperate Moment (1953)
   Runaway Bus, The (1954)

BIONDA BROTHERS see
   LA BIONDA BROTHERS

BISCHOFF, EDGAR
   Silence of the Sea (1949)

BISHARAT, JOHN
   Death Wish 4: The Crack-
      down (1987)

BISHOP, MICHAEL
   Three Kinds of Heat (1987)

BISHOP, PHILLAN
   Severed Arm, The (1973)

BIXIO, C. A.
   Rich Uncle, The (1935)
   Loyalty of Love (1937)
   Smiling Gentleman, The
      (1937)

BIXIO, FRANCO
   Dracula in the Provinces
      (1975)

BIZET, JEAN
   Last Rites (1980)

"BIZOTTSAG GROUP"
   Dog's Night Song, The
      (1983)

BIZZELLI, ANNIBAL
   Mulatto, The (1950)

BJERKESTRAND, KJETIL
   Pathfinder (1987)

BJERKREIM, RAGNAR
Kamilla and the Thief (1988)

BJERNO, ERLING D.
Jeppe of the Hill (1981)

BJERRE, BENT FABRICIUS
see FABRICIUS-BJERRE,
BENT

BJOERN, JOHNNY
Knife in the Heart, The
(1981)

BJORKENHEIM, RAOUL
Waiting for Darkness (1986)

BLACK, GABRIEL
Initiation, The (1983)

BLACK, KAREN
Can She Bake a Cherry
Pie? (1983)

BLACK, PEGGY
Callahan (1982)

BLACK, STANLEY
Monkey's Paw, The (1948)
Fatal Night, The (1948)
Third Time Lucky (1949)
Shadow of the Past (1950)
Laughter in Paradise (1951)
One Wild Oat (1951)
My Teenaged Daughter (1956)
Now and Forever (1956)
Passport to Treason (1956)
City After Midnight (That
Woman Opposite) (1957)
Naked Truth, The (1957)
Time Lock (1957)
Further Up the Creek (1958)
Stormy Crossing (1958)
Trollenberg Terror, The
(1958)
Jack the Ripper (1959)
Too Many Crooks (1959)
Mania (1960)
Bottoms Up (1960)
Flesh and the Fiends (1960)
Follow That Horse (1960)
Sands of the Desert (1960)

Siege of Sidney St., The
(1960)
Tommy the Toreador (1960)
Full Treatment, The (1961)
Long and the Short and the
Tall, The (1961)
War Gods of the Deep (1965)
Blues for Lovers (1966)

"BLACK FLAG"
Nightmares (1983)

BLACKBURN, MAURICE
Gros Bill, Le (1949)
Cordelia (1980)
Primal Fear (1980)

BLACKSTONE, WENDY
El Salvador: Another Vietnam
(1981)
Good Fight, The (1984)
Are We Winning, Mommy?
America and the Cold War
(1986)
King James Version (1988)
Lodz Ghetto (1988)

BLADES, RUBEN
When the Mountains Tremble
(1984)
On the Green Path (1987)
Story of Fausta, The (1988)

BLADURSSON, THORIR
House, The (1983)

BLAIKLEY, ALAN
Flame Trees of Thika, The
(1982)
By the Sword Divided (1988)

BLAIS, GEORGE
Archie Comedy House, The
(1970)
Archie's TV Funnies (1971)
Sabrina, the Teenage Witch
(1971)
Everything's Archie (1973)
U.S. of Archie, The (1974)

BLAIS, YVETTE
Brady Kids, The (1972)

Lassie's Rescue Rangers
(1973)
Mission Magic (1973)
Star Trek (1973)
New Adventures of Gilligan,
The (1974)
Shazam! (1974)
Ghost Busters, The (1975)
Secret Lives of Waldo Kitty,
The (1975)
Isis (1975)
Ark II (1976)
Tarzan: Lord of the Jungle
(1976)
Bang-Shang Lalalapooza
Show, The (1977)
New Adventures of Batman,
The (1977)
New Archie/Sabrina Hour,
The (1977)
Space Academy (1977)
Super Witch (1977)
Young Sentinels, The (1977)
Fabulous Funnies, The (1978)
Tarzan and the Super Seven
(1978)
Flash Gordon (1979)
Jason of Star Command
(1979)
Tarzan and Lone Ranger
Adventure Hour, The
(1980)
Blackstar (1981)
Gilligan's Planet (1982)
Flash Gordon--The Greatest
Adventure of All (1983)

BLAKE, HOWARD
Avengers, The (1966)
S.O.S. Titanic (1979)
Stronger Than the Sun
(1980)
Lords of Discipline, The
(1983)
Amityville 3-D (1983)
Canterville Ghost, The
(1986)
Month in the Country, A
(1987)

BLAKE, PETER
Send a Gorilla (1988)

BLAKER, CHARLES
Warlock Moon (1974)
I Am the Greatest; The
Adventures of Muhammad
Ali (1977)

BLAKLEY, RONEE
Lightning Over Water (Nick's
Movie) (1980)

BLANCO, JESUS
Ha-Ha (1987)

BLANCO URIBE, ALEJANDRO
Bolivar, Tropical Symphony
(1982)
Orinoko--Nuevo Mundo (1984)
Male and Female (1985)
See You After School (1986)
Woman to Woman (1987)
America, Unknown Land
(1988)

BLAUTE, JEAN
After Love (1983)

BLEY, CARLA
Like a Stranger (1981)
Deadly Circuit (1983)
Kitchen Table Talk with
Women Rebels (1984)

BLISS, SIR ARTHUR
Seven Waves Away (1957)

BLOCK, D. S.
Broken Shoes (1934)

BLONKSTEINER, ALEX
Cannibals in the Streets
(1980)

BLOOM, LOUIS
Raindrops (1981)

BLOOM, RON
Another Chance (1988)

"BLUE DAISIES"
Circle of Violence: A Family
Drama (1986)

BLUESTONE, HARRY
  Killer Shrews, The (1959)

BLUM, ROBERT
  Swiss Tour (1949)
  Four in a Jeep (1951)
  Uli the Tenant (1956)
  Taxi Driver Baenz (1957)
  10th of May, The (1957)
  Fear of Power (1958)
  Jakobli and Meyeii (1961)
  Shadows Are Getting Longer,
    The (1961)

BLUMBERG, MARK
  Old Forest, The (1985)

BOASSEN, OISTEIN
  Blackout (1986)

BOCHMANN, WERNER
  Ideal Husband, An (1937)
  Midnight Happenings (1938)
  Little Town Will Go to
    Sleep, The (1954)

BODDICKER, MICHAEL
  Get Crazy (1983)

BODY, JACK
  Vigil (1984)

BOEHM, RAINER
  Life in Wittstock (1985)
  Ete and Ali (1985)

BOEHMELT, HARALDT
  Brave Seaman (1936)
  Study of Suzanne, A (1937)
  Holy Heritage (1957)

BOEHREN, GEIR
  Hockey Fever (1983)
  Chieftain, The (1984)

BOEKELHEIDE, TODD
  Dim Sum: A Little Bit of
    Heart (1985)
  Contrary Warriors (1985)
  Dear America (1987)
  Deadly Dreams (1988)

BOERI, GIOELE AND ELVIO
  My Fabulous Girlfriends
    (1980)

BOETTCHER, MARTIN
  Captain and His Hero, The
    (1955)

BOGAS, ED
  Christmas Without Snow, A
    (1979)
  Bon Voyage, Charlie Brown
    (And Don't Come Back)
    (1980)
  Street Music (1981)
  Charlie Brown and Snoopy
    Show, The (1983)
  Garfield Goes Hollywood
    (1987)
  This Is America, Charlie
    Brown (1988)

BOGATYROV, A.
  Secret Brigade, The (1951)

BOGOSLOWSKI, NIKITA
  Aleksa Dundic (1958)

BOGUS, GOYETTE AND JOHN
  Romance of Betty Boop, The
    (1985)

BOHM, REINER
  Luther Is Dead (1984)

BOHR, JOSE
  Big Chamorro Circus, The
    (1955)

BOHREN, GEIR
  Orion's Belt (1985)
  Burning Flowers (1985)
  After Rubicon (1987)
  Andersen's Run (1987)
  Night Voyage (1987)
  Ice Palace, The (1988)

BOIVIN, JAY
  Pick-Up Summer (1981)

BOKANOWSKI, MICHELE
  Angel, The (1982)

BOKSTEDT, BERTIL
  Swedish Horseman (1950)

BOLLING, CLAUDE
  Hands of Orlac (1960)
  Other One's Mug, The (1980)
  Willie and Phil (1980)
  Awakening, The (1980)
  Three Men to Destroy (1980)
  Jigsaw (1980)
  Escape from Grumble Gulch
    (1984)
  Louisiana (1984)
  Leopard, The (1984)
  Bay Boy (1984)
  You Only Die Twice (1985)
  Gypsy, The (1986)
  Rumba, The (1987)

BONCOMPAGNI, GIANNI
  Summer (1966)

BOND, GRAHAM
  Fatty Finn (1980)

BOND, LELAND
  Toy Soldiers (1984)

BONEZZI, BERNARDO
  What Have I Done to Deserve
    This? (1984)
  Matador (1986)
  While There Is Light (1987)
  Baton Rouge (1988)
  Lion's Den, The (1988)
  Women on the Verge of a
    Nervous Breakdown (1988)

BONFA, LUIS
  River of Mystery (1971)
  Prisoner of Rio (1988)

BONGUSTO, FRED
  Sex Machine, The (1976)
  Fantozzi Against the World
    (1980)
  Fracchia, the Human Beast
    (1982)
  Photographing Patricia (1984)
  Superfantozzi (1986)

BONNARD, GUIDO
  Thirty Seconds of Love
    (1937)

BONNETT, GUY
  Seven Women for Satan
    (1974)

BONNIWELL, SEAN
  Night of the Witches (1970)

BONTELLA, SAFY
  Story of an Encounter (1983)

BOOM-KEI, TANG
  Spooky Bunch, The (1980)

BOOTH, ALLEN
  No Sad Songs (1985)

BORCHARD, ADOLPHE
  Story of a Trickster, The
    (1936)
  Kreutzer Sonata (1938)
  Remounting the Champs-
    Elysee (1938)
  Ultimatum (1938)
  There Were Nine Bachelors
    (1939)

BORDEN, LAWRENCE
  War of the Wizards (Phoenix,
    The) (1978)

BORESS, ROBERT
  Toxic Time Bomb (1984)

BORG, BENNY
  Kamilla and the Thief (1988)

BORGMANN, HANS OTTO
  Gold (Or, L') (1934)
  Hitlerjunge Quex (1934)
  Light Cavalry (1936)
  Queen of Love (1936)
  Unknown, The (1936)
  Gleisdreick (1937)
  Night with the Emperor, A
    (1937)
  Covered Tracks (1938)

BORIS, V.
  Secret Diary of Sigmund
    Freud, The (1984)

BORISAVLJEVIC, VOJKAN
  House of Gloom (1986)
  House by the Railroad
    Tracks, The (1988)

BORNE, HAL
  Not Tonight, Henry (1961)

BOROCOMAN, TIBERIU
  Between Parallel Mirrors
    (1981)

BOS, JANE
  Land That Dies, The (1936)
  Police Mondaine (1937)
  Troubled Heart (1938)
  Glory of Faith (1938)

BOS, RUUD
  Mark of the Beast (1981)
  Sabine (1982)
  Lion of Flanders, The (1984)
  Rattlerat, The (1987)

BOSHOFF, JOHNNY
  Torn Allegiance (1984)

BOSWELL, SIMON
  Demons 2--The Nightmare Is
    Back (1986)
  Joyous Photographs (1987)

BOTKAY, CAIQUE
  JFK Years--A Political
    Trajectory, The (1980)

BOTKIN, PERRY
  Beverly Hillbillies, The (1962)
  Tarzan, the Ape Man (1981)
  Nuts and Bolts (1981)
  Wonderful World of Philip
    Malley, The (1981)
  Jennifer Slept Here (1983)
  Silent Night, Deadly Night
    (1984)
  Ordinary Heroes (1986)

Weekend Warriors (1986)
Roxie (1987)
Windmills of the Gods (1988)

BOTKIN, PERRY, JR.
  Adam's Rib (1973)
  Mork and Mindy (1978)
  Quark (1978)
  Pleasure Cove (1979)
  When She Was Bad ... (1979)
  Landon, Landon and Landon
    (1980)
  Golden Moment--An Olympic
    Love Story, The (1980)
  National Snoop, The (1983)

BOUAD, ERIC
  Outer Signs of Wealth (1983)

BOUCHAI, DON
  Autumn Born (1983)

BOUCHETY, JEAN
  Bourgeois Gentilhomme, Le
    (Would-Be Gentleman,
    The) (1982)

BOULANGER, GEORGE
  False Word, The (1987)

BOULANGER, GUY
  Golem's Daughter, The (1971)
  Aeroport: Charter 2000
    (1980)
  Family Rock (1982)
  Love and Death (1985)
  One and Only, The (1986)

BOULANGER, LILI
  Passion of Beatrice, The
    (1987)

BOULEZ, PIERRE
  Jean-Louis Barrault--A Man
    of the Theater (1984)

BOURBON, ALBERTO
  Secret Garden, The (1985)

BOURGEOIS, DEREK
  On the Razzle (1986)

BOURGEOIS, JAMES
Wild Kingdom (1963)

BOURGOIN, FRANCOISE
Time Masters, The (1982)

BOURLAND, ROGER
Trouble with Dick, The
(1987)

BOUSTEDT, CHRISTER
One Man's Loss ... (1980)

BOUVOT, VINCENT-MARIE
Angel Dust (1987)

BOVA, BASIL J.
Screamplay (1985)

BOVELL, DENIS
Babylon (1980)

BOW, BUDDY RED
Black Hills (1985)

BOWDEN, RICHARD
Wait Till Your Father Gets
Home (1972)

BOWEN, (WILLIAM) HILL
Invitation to Monte Carlo
(1959)

BOWERSOCK, BILL
Dirt Bike Kid, The (1986)

BOWLES, ANTHONY
Red (1976)

BOX, EWEL
Oh, Heavenly Dog (1980)
Benji the Hunted (1987)

BOYCE AND HART
Three's a Crowd (1969)

BOYCE, TOMMY
Days of Our Lives (1965)

BOYD, FRANKLIN
Goldenrod (1977)

BOYD, MICHAEL
Breakin' (1984)

BOYDSTUN, BILL
Killers, The (1984)

BOYLE, ROBERT
Anne Devlin (1984)

BOYZ, HENRYK
Eve Wants to Sleep (1958)

BOZE, JEFFREY
Modern Day Houdini (1983)

BRACHO, JESUS
Criminal Life of Archibaldo
de la Cruz, The (1955)
Attempt at a Crime (1956)

BRADLEY, OWEN
Coal Miner's Daughter (1980)

BRADLEY, SCOTT
Kitty Foiled (1948)
Tom and Jerry Show, The
(1966)

BRADNER, ERNST
Blood and Honor: Young
Under Hitler (1982)

BRADY, MIKE
Club, The (1980)

BRAHAM, ANOUAR
Door on Heaven, A (1988)

BRANCA, GLENN
Belly of an Architect, The
(1987)

BRANCO, JOSE MARIO
August (1988)
Three Minus Me (1988)

BRANDAO, PAULO
Dina and Django (1981)

BRANDAUER, CHRISTIAN
Meantime, It's Already Noon
(1988)

BRANDEN, EDWIN
Night We Dropped a
Clanger, The (1959)

BRANDT, CARL
Perri (1957)
Tom and Jerry Show, The
(1966)
Little Mo (1978)

BRANDT, DAN
American Taboo (1984)

BRANDUARDI, ANGELO
Demise of Herman Durer,
The (1980)
Distant Lights (1987)
Momo (1987)
According to Pontius Pilate
(1988)

BRANSKI, LECH
Sunday Pranks (1987)

BRATHWAITE, FRED
Wild Style (1983)

BRATTON, CREED
Dangerous Company (1982)

BRAUER, ANDI
Children from No. 67, The
(1980)
Irreconcilable Memories
(1980)
Pearl of the Caribbean,
The (1981)
Set in Berlin (1987)

BRAULT, BOB
Sous-Doues, Les (1980)

BRAULT, PIERRE
Day in a Taxi, A (1982)

BRAUN, SHONY ALEX
'68 (1987)

BRAUNS, MARTIN
Is it Easy to Be Young?
(1987)

BRAVO, PABLO
They Were Nobody (1982)

BRAWER, ALAN
Outer Touch (Spaced Out)
(1979)

BREANT, FRANCOIS
Snow (1981)
Treichville Story (1987)

BRECKER BROTHERS, THE
Bumpers (1977)

BREDEMEYER, RAINER
Woman and the Stranger,
The (1985)

BREESKIN, ELIAS
Pancho Villa Returns (1950)

BREGMAN, BUDDY
Delicate Delinquent, The
(1957)

BREINER, PETER
Taxi to Cairo (1987)

BREIT, BERT
Appalling Days (1982)
Silent Ocean, The (1983)
Raffl (1984)
Danube Waltzes (1984)
Franza (1986)
Off Season (1988)

BREJEAM, PHILIPPE
Nuit des Traquees, La (1980)

BREMNER, TONY
Everlasting Secret Family,
The (1988)

BRESNICK, MARTIN
Mediterranean, The (1983)

BRETON, LUIS HERNANDEZ
Dolores (1949)
Don't Be Offended, Beatrice
(1953)
Face of the Screaming

Werewolf, The (House of
Terror) (1959)
Dr. Satan (1966)
Aunt Alexandra (1980)

BRETTINGHAM-SMITH, JOLYON
Deimann's Time--A German
"Heimatfilm" (1985)

BREUKER, WILLEM
I Love Dollars (1986)
PPPerformer, The (1986)

BREWER, ALAN
Tokyo Pop (1988)

BREWER, JIM
Maxwell Street Blues (1981)

BREWIS, PETER
Morons from Outer Space
(1985)

BREZINA, POLIO
Nocturnal Voyage, The
(1986)

BREZOVSKY, ALI
Father Will Beat Me Anyway
(1981)

BRICENO, ARNULFO
Canaguaro (1981)

BRIDGEWATER, TOM
Carry Me Back (1982)

BRINT, SIMON
Chance, History, Art ...
(1981)
Honest, Decent and True
(1985)
Leave to Remain (1988)

BRITTEN, SIR BENJAMIN
Doktor Faustus (1982)

BRITTEN, TONY
Closing Ranks (1987)

"BRITZ"
Men of Action Meet Women
of Dracula (1969)

BROADY, J. K.
Assignment Outer Space
(1960)

BROBERG, ROBERT
Man in the Moon, The (1986)

BRODY, JANOS
Love, Mother (1987)

BRODZSKY, NICHOLAS
Romance in Budapest (1934)
Peter (1935)
Little Mother (1935)
Friendly Expression, Please
(1936)
Guilty Melody (1936)
Jester, The (1937)
Freedom Radio (1941)
Beloved of the World (1949)

BRONSKI, LECH
Tender Spots (1981)

BROOKS, JOSEPH
Invitation to the Wedding
(1983)

BROOKS, PATTI
Joe and Valerie (1979)

BROSSE, DIRK
Jumping (1986)

BROSSNER, LARS-ERIK
Hill on the Dark Side of the
Moon, A (1983)

BROUGHTON, BRUCE
Hawaii Five-O (1968)
Barnaby Jones (1973)
Police Woman (1974)
Khan! (1975)
Quincy (1976)
Spencer's Pilots (1976)
How the West Was Won (1977)

Dallas (1978)
Paradise Connection, The
   (1979)
Runaways, The (1979)
Skag (1980)
Desperate Voyage (1980)
Return of Frank Cannon,
   The (1980)
Girl, the Gold Watch &
   Dynamite, The (1981)
Blue and the Gray, The
   (1982)
Desperate Lives (1982)
One Shoe Makes It Murder
   (1982)
Cowboy (1983)
M.A.D.D.: Mothers Against
   Drunk Drivers (1983)
This Girl for Hire (1983)
Two Marriages (1983)
Ice Pirates, The (1984)
First Olympics--Athens, The
   (1984)
Master of Ballantrae, The
   (1984)
Stormin' Home (1985)
Silverado (1985)
Young Sherlock Holmes (1985)
Boy Who Could Fly, The
   (1986)
George Washington: The
   Forging of a Nation (1986)
Sweet Liberty (1986)
Thanksgiving Promise, The
   (1986)
Big Shots (1987)
Cross My Heart (1987)
Harry and the Hendersons
   (1987)
Monster Squad, The (1987)
Square Dance (1987)
Last Rites (1988)
Moonwalker (1988)
Presidio, The (1988)
Rescue, The (1988)

BROUGHTON, WILLIAM
   B.J. and the Bear (1979)
   Misadventures of Sheriff
      Lobo, The (1979)

BROUSSEAU, PIERRE
   Funny Farm, The (1983)

BROUWER, LEO
   Fighting Cuban Against the
      Demons, The (1972)
   Widow Montiel, The (1980)
   King of the Joropo (1980)
   Cecilia (1982)
   Alsino and the Condor (1983)
   Rose of the Winds (1983)
   Amada (1983)
   Refugees from Dead Man's
      Cove, The (1983)
   Up to a Certain Point (1984)

BROWER, LEO
   Time to Die, A (1985)
   Visa U.S.A. (1986)

BROWN, ALAN
   Way Upstream (1987)

BROWN, CHARLIE
   Wild 90 (1968)

BROWN, EARL, JR.
   Li'l Abner (1971)
   Americathon (1979)

BROWN, GREG
   Personal Foul (1987)

BROWN, JACKIE
   Front Page Story (1954)

BROWN, KEN
   Hot Resort (1985)

BROWN, OLLIE E.
   Flying (1986)

BROWN, RAY
   All That Glitters (1977)

BROWN, RONNY
   Fun (Boarding House) (1983)

BROWNE, JACKSON
   In the King of Prussia (1982)

BRUBECK, DAVE
Grand Jete (1968)

BRUEHNE, LOTHER
I and You (1954)
Beloved Corrine (1957)

BRUEL, SANNE
Creampuffs and Lollipops
(1987)

BRUENINGHAUS, RAINER
Red Stocking, The (1980)

BRUGNOLINI, SANDRO
Fantabulous Inc. (1967)

BRUMMER, ANDRE S.
Monster from the Ocean Floor,
The (1954)
Air Strike (1955)

BRUNELLI, FELICIANO
Waiting for the Pallbearers
(1987)

BRUNER, JEFF
Foes (1977)

BRUNER, TOM
School Spirit (1985)

BRUNETTI, DANIEL
Land of William Tell, The
(1985)

BRUNNENKANT, NEIL
Atomic Submarine, The
(1960)

BRUNNER, L.
S.O.S. Sahara (1938)

BRUNNER, ROBERT F.
Pacific High (1980)
Amy (1981)

BRUZDOWICZ, JOANNA
Red Shirt, The (1987)
Kung Fu Master! (1988)

BRUZITSOV, ALEXANDER
Crime in Yellow (1981)

BRYANS, BILLY
Office Party (1988)

BRYANT, BOBBY
Bionic Woman, The (1976)

BRYARS, GAVIN
Necropolis (1970)

BUARQUE, CHICO (CHICO
BUARQUE DE HOLLANDA)
Bye Bye Brazil (1980)
Jeanne the Frenchwoman
(1981)
Forgive Me for Betraying Me
(1983)
Maine-Ocean Express (1986)
Love in a Minefield (1987)

BUBANOVIC, ALEKSANDER
Cowboy Jim (1957)
Osvetnik (1958)
At the Photographer's (1959)
Crazy Heart, A (1959)
Low Midnight (1960)
Martin in the Clouds (1961)
Adventure at the Door (1961)
Third Key, The (1983)

BUCCHI, VALENTINO
Sky Is Red, The (1952)
Bandits of Orgosolo (1961)

BUCCI, MARC
Honeymoon with a Stranger
(1969)
Seven in Darkness (1969)
My Friends Need Killing
(1976)
Human Experiments (1980)

BUCCIONE, MARIO
Girls of Piazza di Spagna,
The (1952)

BUCHINO, V.
Curious Dr. Humpp, The
(1970)

BUCHNER, JUERGEN
  German Dreams (1986)

"BUCKBOARD"
  St. Helens (1981)

BUCKLEY, BOB
  B. B. Beegle Show, The
    (1980)

BUCKMASTER, PAUL
  Macbeth (1971)

BUCKOVY, WILLIAM
  How to Furnish a Flat (1960)
  Do You Keep a Lion at Home?
    (1963)
  Wishing Machine, The (1967)

BUDAY, DENES
  Mammy (1937)
  Premiere (1937)
  13 Girls Smile at the Sky
    (1938)

BUDD, ROY
  Mama Dracula (1980)
  Missing Link, The (1980)
  Sea Wolves, The (1980)
  Who Dares Win? (1982)
  Wild Geese II (1985)
  Big Bang, The (1987)

BUDER, E. E.
  Adieu, les Beaux Jours
    (1934)
  Feminine Regina (1936)

BUDSON, BUDDY
  Duet (1987)

BUENAGU, JOSE
  Face of Terror (1962)

BUENCAMINO, F.
  Sea Gypsies, The (1961)

BUENO, JULIO
  Tequiman (1987)

BUFFALO, NORTON
  Stacy's Knights (1982)
  Eddie Macon's Run (1983)

BULEIN, FRANTISEK
  Tales of 1001 Nights (1974)

BULIA, JIRI
  Jester and the Queen, The
    (1988)

BUNDOCK, PIERRE
  Carpenter, The (1988)

BURDON, ERIC
  Comeback (1982)

BURGER, SIMON
  What's Past Is Dead (1987)

BURGESS, ANTHONY
  A.D. (1985)

BURGHAUSER, JAROMIL
  Concert at the End of Summer
    (1980)

BURGON, GEOFFREY
  Dr. Who (1973)
  Dogs of War, The (1980)
  Tinker, Tailor, Soldier, Spy
    (1980)
  Brideshead Revisited (1981)
  Bleak House (1985)
  Turtle Diary (1985)
  Death of the Heart, The
    (1986)
  Happy Valley, The (1986)

BURIAN, E. F.
  Journey to the Beginning of
    Time (1967)

BURKE, CHRIS
  Splatter University (1984)
  Vampires (1988)

BURKE, COLEMAN
  Liar's Dice (1980)

BURKE, DAVID
    Johnsons Are Home, The
    (1988)

BURKE, DENNIS
    Determinations (1988)

BURKE, SONNY
    Hennesey (1959)
    Battle at Bloody Beach (1961)
    Redd Foxx Show, The (1986)

BURKHARD, PAUL
    Fireworks (1954)

BURNETT, T-BONE
    In 'n' Out (1986)

BURNLEY, RICK
    Dan's Motel (1982)

BURNS, RALPH
    Make Me an Offer (1980)
    Urban Cowboy (1980)
    First Family (1980)
    Golden Gate (1981)
    Side Show (1981)
    My Favorite Year (1982)
    Kiss Me Goodbye (1982)
    National Lampoon's Vacation
        (1983)
    Star 80 (1983)
    Phantom of the Opera (1983)
    Muppets Take Manhattan, The
        (1984)
    Ernie Kovacs: Between the
        Laughter (1984)
    Moving Violations (1985)
    Perfect (1985)
    Christmas Star, The (1986)
    After the Promise (1987)
    In the Mood (Woo Woo Kid,
        The) (1987)
    Sawdust (1987)

BURNS, WILFRED
    There Is Another Sun (1951)
    Man Who Couldn't Talk, The
        (1960)

BURROWS, EDWARD W.
    Street Story (1988)

BURROWS, JOHN
    Casanova (1981)

BURT, GEORGE
    Secret Honor (1984)
    Fool for Love (1985)

BURTON, AL
    Jo's Cousins (1984)
    Diff'rent Strokes (1978)
    Facts of Life, The (1979)
    Parkers, The (1981)

BURTON, VAL
    Intruder, The (1932)
    Study in Scarlet, A (1933)

BURWELL, CARTER
    Blood Simple (1984)
    Psycho III (1986)
    Beat, The (1987)
    Raising Arizona (1987)
    It Takes Two (1988)
    Pass the Ammo (1988)

BURZITSOV, ALEKSANDER
    Romantic Story (1986)

BUSHOR, SKEET
    Geek (1987)

BUSONI, FERRUCCIO
    Rorret (1988)

BUTLER, ARTIE
    Me and the Chimp (1972)
    Bob & Carol & Ted & Alice
        (1973)
    Little People, The (1972)
    Wonder Woman (1974)
    When Things Were Rotten
        (1975)
    Operation Petticoat (1977)
    Grandpa Goes to Washington
        (1978)
    California Fever (1979)
    Six O'Clock Follies, The
        (1980)
    Angel on My Shoulder (1980)
    Sizzle (1981)
    American Dream (1981)
    She's in the Army Now (1981)

O'Hara's Wife (1982)
Sutter's Bay (1983)
Branagan and Mapes (1983)
Making of a Model, The (1983)
Other Woman, The (1983)
Last of the Great Survivors,
   The (1984)
Cracker Brothers, The (1984)
Old Friends (1984)
100 Centre Street (1984)
Steambath (1984)
Classified Love (1986)

BUTLER, EDITH
Gapi (1982)
Odyssey of the Pacific (1983)

BUTLER, HAROLD
Children of Babylon (1980)

BUTLER, HENRY
Dreamland (1983)

BUTTERFIELD, PAUL
To Be a Man (1967)

"BUTTERFLY"
Butterflies and Flowers (1986)

BUTTOLPH, DAVID
Navy Wife (1935)
Maverick (1957)
New Maverick, The (1978)

BUTTS, DALE
City That Never Sleeps,
   The (1953)

BUTZMANN, FRIEDER
On the Next Morning the
   Minister Didn't Return to
   His Post (1986)

BYERS, BILLY
Hauser's Memory (1970)
Moonchild (1972)
Borrowers, The (1973)
Hanging In (1979)
Man Called Sloane, A (1979)
Mr. & Mrs. & Mr. (1980)
Love, Natalie (1980)

And They All Lived Happily
   Ever After (1981)

BYRD, BRETTON
Tony Draws a Horse (1951)

BYRD, CHARLIE
Home Country, USA (1968)
Voice in the City, A (1968)

BYRNE, DAVID
Dead End Kids (1986)
Heat and Sunlight (1987)
Last Emperor, The (1987)
Married to the Mob (1988)

BYRNE, STEVE
Disappearance of Aimee,
   The (1976)

BYRNS, HAROLD
Pickup (1951)

BYUNG-HA, SHIN
Contract Mother (1987)

CABAIDULINA, SOFIA
Weirdo (1985)

CABIATI, ENRICO
Neutron Against the Death
   Robots (1961)
Neutron and the Black Mask
   (1961)
Snake People, The (1968)
Invincible Invasion, The
   (1971)

CABRAL, CALDEIRA
Jester, The (1987)

CACAVAS, JOHN
Kojak (1973)
Linda (1973)
She Cried "Murder!" (1973)
Elevator, The (1974)
Friendly Persuasion (1975)
Kate McShane (1975)
Hazard's People (1976)
Amy Prentiss (1977)
Murder at the World Series
   (1977)

Relentless (1977)
SST--Death Flight (1977)
Human Feelings (1978)
Superdome (1978)
Time Machine, The (1978)
B.J. and the Bear (1979)
Buck Rogers in the 25th
    Century (1979)
Doctors' Private Lives (1979)
Eischied (1979)
Kate Loves a Mystery (1979)
Mrs. Columbo (1979)
Working Stiffs (1979)
Once Upon a Spy (1980)
Hangar 18 (1980)
Hellinger's Law (1980)
Mortuary (1981)
Border Pals (1981)
Gangster Chronicles (1981)
California Gold Rush (1981)
Child Bride of Short Creek
    (1981)
Riker (1981)
No Place to Hide (1981)
Shannon (1981)
Today's F.B.I. (1981)
Cry for the Strangers (1982)
Executioner's Song, The
    (1982)
Still the Beaver (1983)
Women of San Quentin (1983)
They're Playing With Fire
    (1984)
Her Life as a Man (1984)
Four Seasons, The (1984)
Jessie (1984)
Lady Blue (1985)
Death in California, A (1985)
Jenny's War (1985)
Time to Triumph, A (1986)
Kojak: The Price of Justice
    (1987)
Police Story: The Freeway
    Killings (1987)
Body of Evidence (1988)
Dirty Dozen: The Fatal Mis-
    sion, The (1988)

CACCIAPAGLIA, ROBERTO
Skin Deep (1987)

CADKIN, EMIL
    Killer Shrews, The (1959)

CAFFERTY, JOHN
    Eddie and the Cruisers (1983)

CAFFI, JUAN JOSE see GARCIA
CAFFI, JUAN JOSE

CAGE, JOHN
    Modern American Composers I
        (1984)

CAHEN, FATON
    Secret Child, The (1983)
    Liberty at Night (1984)
    Paris Seen By ... 20 Years
        After (1984)

CAHN, JOYCE
    Kill to Love (1981)

CAIN, CHRISTOPHER
    Force on Thunder Mountain,
        The (1978)

CAIN, JEFF
    Coach! (1987)

CAIRNCROSS, JAMES
    King of Terror (1962)

CAITHY, MARTIN
    Moll Flanders (1975)

CALABRESE, GIORGIO
    Christmas Vacation (1984)

CALABRESE, JAMES
    Spookies (1986)
    Hemingway (1988)

CALANDRELLI, JORGE
    Billionaire Boys Club (1987)
    Town Bully, The (1988)

CALATAYUD, JUAN JOSE
    Shipwreck of Liguria, The
        (1985)

CALCRAFT, SHARON
   Winter of Our Dreams, The
      (1981)
   Far East (1982)
   Fast Talking (1984)
   Boundaries of the Heart
      (1988)

CALDERON, JUAN CARLOS
   Family, Fine, Thanks, The
      (1980)

CALE, JOHN
   Something Wild (1986)

CALELLO, CHARLES
   Lonely Lady, The (1983)

CALHOUN, SCOTT
   Arriving Tuesday (1986)

CALKER, DARRELL
   Voodoo Woman (1957)
   My World Dies Screaming
      (1958)
   Amazing Transparent Man,
      The (1960)
   Beyond the Time Barrier
      (1960)

CALLENDRELLI, JOSEPH
   I'll Be Home for Christmas
      (1988)

CALVI, GERARD
   Bonjour Monsieur Lewis
      (1982)

CALZOLATI, CLAUDIO
   Tunnel Under the World,
      The (1968)

"CAM"
   Pieces (1981)

CAMERON, JOHN
   Strange Vengeance of Rosalie,
      The (1972)
   Protectors, The (1972)
   Who? (1974)
   Man from Nowhere, The (1976)

Spectre (1977)
Bermuda Triangle, The (1978)
Thief of Bagdad, The (1979)
Mirror Crack'd, The (1980)
Jimmy the Kid (1982)
Witness for the Prosecution
   (1982)
Philip Marlowe, Private Eye
   (1983)
Jigsaw Man, The (1984)
Young Visiters, The (1984)
Secret Garden, The (1987)
Jack the Ripper (1988)

CAMILLERI, CARLO
   Castle of Fu Manchu, The
      (1968)

CAMILLO, TONY
   Welcome to Arrow Beach
      (1974)

CAMP, MANUEL
   Girl with the Golden Panties,
      The (1980)
   Murder in the Central Com-
      mittee (1982)

CAMP, OSCAR
   Amazons (1987)

CAMPANINO, FRANCO
   Sword of the Barbarians,
      The (1983)
   Iguana (1988)

CAMPASE, GINO
   Tormento (1953)

CAMPBELL, DAVID
   My Champion (1981)
   All the Right Moves (1983)
   Stand Alone (1986)

CAMPBELL, JAMES
   Elvira, Mistress of the Dark
      (1988)

CAMPBELL, JOE
   May We Borrow Your Hus-
      band? (1986)

CAMPOS, KIKI
  I, the Executioner (1987)

CANDIA, JORGE
  Cats, The (1985)

CANDIDO, NINO
  We've Got Each Other (1977)

CANE, JOSE
  From the Hills to the Valley
    (1939)

CANEPA, MARCO
  Paul's Awakening (1985)

CANFORA, BRUNO
  Man Who Wagged His Tail,
    The (1957)
  Wolves in the Abyss (1959)
  James Tont, Operation
    D.U.E. (1966)
  Rita la Zanzara (1966)

CANNON, JOHN
  Cannon (1971)

CANNON, MICHAEL
  First Time, Second Time
    (1980)
  One Night Band (1983)
  Torchlight (1984)

CANSECO, GEORGE
  Of Worms and Roses (1982)
  Moral (1983)

CANSLER, LARRY
  King of the Road (1978)
  Pittsville (1980)
  Gambler, The (1980)
  Coward of the County (1981)
  Smokey and the Bandit--
    Part 3 (1983)
  Kenny Rogers as the
    Gambler--The Adventure
    Continues (1983)
  September Gun (1983)
  Songwriter (1984)
  Gambler III, The Legend
    Continues, The (1987)

CANTARELLI, BEPPE
  Monte Napoleone (1987)
  Us Real Men (1987)

CANTOR, IGO
  Comeback Trail, The (1970)

CAPDEVILLE, CONSTANCA
  Cerromaior (1980)

CAPEDEVEILLE, P.
  Just a Big, Simple Girl
    (1949)

CAPEK, JOHN
  Boulevard of Broken Dreams
    (1988)

CAPER, JOHN, JR.
  Equinox (1967)
  Joysticks (1983)

CAPINAN, CAETANO VALESO
  Brazil Year 2000 (1970)

CAPOBIANCO, CARMINE
  Psychos in Love (1987)

CAPOIANU, DIMITRU
  Short History, A (1956)
  Homo Sapiens (1959)
  Bomb Was Stolen, A (1962)
  Pasi Spre Luna (1963)
  Legend of the Skylark, The
    (1967)

CAPPELLO, TIM
  Children of Pride (1984)
  Radium City (1987)

CAPPS, AL
  Tribes (1970)
  Twice in a Lifetime (1974)
  Legend of Bigfoot, The (1976)
  Stroker Ace (1983)
  Running Hot (1984)
  Cannonball Run II (1984)

CARA, JEAN PAUL
  Last Tango, The (1986)

CARABALLA, EZIO
Holy Nun, The (1949)
Man With the Grey Glove,
The (1949)
Duel Without Honor (1950)
Dishonored (1950)
Island of Procida (1952)

CARATINI, PATRICE
Dog in a Game of Nine-Pins,
A (1983)

CARBONNE, JOEY
It's Gary Shandling's Show
(1986)

CARCELES, MARTIAL
Perverse Tales (1980)

CARDENAS, CORNELLO
Night of the Mayas (1939)

CARDONA, LEO
Rebellion of the Ghosts (1946)

CARLOS, DJIALI DETTO
Children of the Wind (1980)

CARLOS, WENDY
Clockwork Orange, A (1971)
Shining, The (1980)
Tron (1982)

CARLTON, LARRY
Against All Odds (1984)

CARMICHAEL, RALPH
Joni (1980)

CARMODY, MARK
Tuesday Wednesday (1987)

CARNELIA, CRAIG
Blue Window (1987)

CARNINI, GIORGIO
Prince of Homburg, The
(1981)
Scandalous Gilda (1985)

CARONE, JACK
Working Stiffs (1979)

CAROW, STEFAN
Gritta of the Rat Castle
(1986)
So Many Dreams (1987)
Actress, The (1988)

CARPENTER, IAN
Agent on Ice (1986)

CARPENTER, JOHN
Dark Star (1974)
Assault on Precinct 13 (1976)
Fog, The (1980)
Escape from New York (1981)
Halloween II (1981)
Halloween III: Season of the
Witch (1982)
Christine (1983)
Big Trouble in Little China
(1986)
Prince of Darkness (1987)
They Live (1988)

CARPENTER, PETE
Two on a Bench (1971)
Gidget Gets Married (1972)
Griff (1973)
Needles and Pins (1973)
Toma (1973)
Locusts (1974)
Morning After, The (1974)
Rockford Files, The (1974)
Texas Wheelers, The (1974)
Bob Crane Show, The (1975)
Invasion of Johnson County,
The (1976)
Richie Brockelman: Missing
24 Hours (1976)
Scott Free (1976)
Black Sheep Squadron, The
(1977)
Charlie Cobb: Nice Night for
a Hanging (1977)
Off the Wall (1977)
Doctor Scorpion (1978)
Richie Brockelman, Private
Eye (1978)
White Shadow, The (1978)
Big Shamus, Little Shamus
(1979)
Captain America (1979)
Captain America II (1979)

Duke, The (1979)
416th, The (1979)
Night Rider, The (1979)
Operating Room (1979)
240-Robert (1979)
Stone (1979)
Tenspeed and Brownshoe
    (1980)
Coach of the Year (1980)
Magnum P.I. (1980)
Greatest American Hero,
    The (1981)
Palms Precinct (1982)
Powers of Matthew Starr,
    The (1982)
Quest, the (1982)
Tales of the Gold Monkey
    (1982)
Will, G. Gordon Liddy (1982)
A-Team, The (1983)
Big John (1983)
Hardcastle and McCormick
    (1983)
Riptide (1983)
Rousters, The (1983)
Four Eyes (1984)
Hard Knox (1984)
No Man's Land (1984)
Return of Luther Gillis,
    The (1984)
Welcome to Paradise (1984)
Stingray (1985)
Last Precinct, The (1986)

CARPENTER, RON
    First Contact (1984)

CARPI, FIORENZO
    Adventures of Pinocchio,
        The (1975)
    Greatest American Hero, The
        (1981)
    We Won't Commit Hara-Kiri
        (1981)
    Sweet Pea (1981)
    Looking for Jesus (1982)
    History (1986)
    Italian Night (1987)

CARR, NICHOLAS
    Silent Twins, The (1985)

CARR-BOYD, ANN
    Italians, The (1985)

CARRADINE, DAVID
    Americana (1981)

CARRAS, NICHOLAS
    Missile to the Moon (1958)
    She Demons (1958)
    Frankenstein's Daughter (1958)
    Astro-Zombies, The (1969)
    Ten Violent Women (1984)
    Omega Syndrome, The (1987)

CARREON, GUSTAVO CESAR
    Green Shadow, The (1955)
    Castle of the Monsters, The
        (1957)
    Living Head, The (1959)
    Flor de Mayo (1959)
    Man and the Monster, The
        (1959)
    'Astronauts, The (1960)
    Brainiac, The (1960)
    Empty Star, The (1960)
    Curse of the Crying Women,
        The (1961)
    Witch's Mirror, The (1961)
    Mark of Death, The (1961)
    Gang Leader (1961)
    Love at Every Fair, A (1961)
    Frankenstein, the Vampire
        and Co. (1962)
    Creature of the Walking Dead,
        The (1965)
    Diabolic Pact, The (1968)
    Santo vs. the Blue Demon in
        Atlantis (1968)
    Revenge of the Vampire
        Women, The (1969)
    Scoundrels, The (1969)
    Suicide Mission (1971)
    Champions of Justice Return,
        The (1972)
    Santo and the Daughter of
        Frankenstein (1972)
    Santo vs. the Black Magic
        (1972)
    Superman and the Space Boy
        (1972)
    Bird in the Hand Is Worth
        ..., A (1987)

Devil Lurks Among Bar-Girls,
The (1987)
I Do 'em In (1987)
Outlaws in the Viewfinder
(1987)

CARRIERE, BERTHOLD
Little Gloria ... Happy at
Last (1982)

CARRION, RAFAEL
One Hundred Cries of Terror
(1964)
Theft of the Mummies of
Gunjuato (1972)
Guerrilla from the North
(1983)
Promised Land, The (1986)
Sheriff's Strange Son, The
(1986)
Emilio Varela's Band (1987)
Land of the Brave (1987)
Red Dock (1988)

CARRION, RICARDO
Burst of Lead (1986)
Death of Palomo, The (1987)
Rose of the Border (1987)

CARSTE, HANS
Inheritance in Pretoria (1936)
Regular Fellow, A (1936)
Play on the Tenne, The
(1937)

CARTER, BENNY
Fame Is the Name of the
Game (1966)
Manhunter, The (1968)
Louis Armstrong--Chicago
Style (1976)

CARTER, RON
Gathering of Old Men, A
(1987)
Passion of Beatrice, The
(1987)

CARUSO, PIPPO
Kill Johnny Ringo (1966)
Escape from Women's Prison
(1978)

CARWITHIN, DARWEEN (MRS.
WILLIAM ALWYN)
Harvest from the Wilderness
(1948)
Boys in Brown (1950)
Man in Hiding (1953)
Break in the Circle (1957)

CARY, TRISTRAM
Flesh Is Weak, The (1957)
She Didn't Say "No" (1958)
Lecture on Man, A (1962)

CASA, PAOLO
Dance Music (1984)

"CASABLANCA VOX"
Calamari Union (1985)

CASADY, CORT
First Time, Second Time (1980)
Nichols and Dymes (1981)
One Night Band (1983)

CASALE, GERALD V.
Revenge of the Nerds II:
Nerds in Paradise (1987)
Slaughterhouse Rock (1988)

CASCELLA, JOHN
Deadly Addiction (1988)

CASES, GUILLERMO
Vargas Inn (1959)

CASEY, CHARLES R.
Incredible Hulk, The (1978)
Curse of Dracula, The (1979)
Kate Loves a Mystery (1979)
Secret Empire, The (1979)
Stop Susan Williams (1979)
Cliffhangers (1979)
Today's F.B.I. (1981)

CASH, JOHNNY
Pride of Jesse Hallam, The
(1981)

CASLAR, DAN
My Song of Love (1937)

CASTANEDA, D.
    Superloco, El (1963)

CASTINEIRA DE DIOS, JOSE
    LUIS
    Night of the Pencils, The
        (1986)
    Beneath the World (1987)
    Chechechela--A Girl of the
        Barrio (1987)
    Girlfriend, The (1988)

CASTLE, GEOFF
    Should I Be Good? (1985)

CASTLEMAN, WILLIAM A.
    'Gator Bait (1973)

CASTRO, GABRIEL
    Santa Esperanza (1980)

CASTRO, JAVIER
    Naked Man, The (1987)

CASTRO, PAUL DE see
    DE CASTRO, PAUL

CASWELL, ALLAN
    Prisoner: Cell Block H
        (1980)

CAVE, CLAUDE (COFFEE)
    Dead Man Walking (1988)

CAVE, NICK
    Ghosts of the Civil Dead
        (1988)

CAVETT, MORGAN
    Smart Alec (1986)

CAYABYAB, RYAN
    Desire (1983)
    Karnal (1984)

"CAZUZA"
    Swingin' Betty (1984)

CECCARELLI, LUIGI (LOU)
    Caged Women (1984)

Death Stone (1987)
Strike Commando (1987)
Nosferatu in Venice (1988)

CEDRON, TATA
    My Son Che: A Family Por-
        trait by Don Ernesto
        Guevara (1985)

CENTAZZO, ANDREA
    Romance (1986)

CERVELLO, JORDI
    Laura (1987)

CHABROL, MATHIEU
    Hatter's Ghosts, The (1982)
    Blood of Others, The (1984)
    Poulet au Vinaigre (1985)
    Inspector Lavardin (1986)
    Cry of the Owl, The (1987)
    Masks (1987)
    Women's Affair, A (1988)

CHAGAS, LUIZ
    Last Faust, The (1986)
    Suburban Angels (1987)

CHAGOLL, LYDIA
    Time to Be Happy (1982)

CHAGRIN, FRANCIS
    Castle in the Air (1952)
    Intruder, The (1953)
    Inspector Calls, An (1954)
    Charley Moon (1956)
    No Time for Tears (1957)
    Scamp, The (1957)
    Danger Within (1959)
    Monster of Highgate Ponds,
        The (1966)

CHAIKOVSKY, BORIS
    Serge (1960)

CHAKRABORTI, UTPALENDU
    Rajdhani Express (1972)
    Post-Mortem (1981)
    Child God, The (1986)

CHALMAMEDOV, NURY
    Manly Education, A (1986)

CHAMBERLAIN, CATHY
 Happy Birthday, Gemini
  (1980)

CHAMBERS, PETER
 All the Way (1988)

CHAMFORT, ALAIN
 Kill the Referee (1984)

CHAMORRO, ADRIAN
 Santa Esperanza (1980)

CHAN, BOBBY
 Trail, The (1983)

CHAN, DANNY
 Encore (1980)

CHAN, FRANKIE
 Young Master, The (1980)

CHAN, JACKIE
 Dragon Lord (1982)

CHAN, PHILIP
 Security, The (1981)

"CHANCE, THE"
 Record, The (1985)

CHANDAWARKAR, BHASKAR
 Omniscient, The (1980)
 Why Albert Pinto Is Angry
  (1981)
 Khandar (1984)
 Mirage, The (1984)
 10 Days in Calcutta (1984)
 Rao Saheb (1986)

CHANDLER, BODIE
 Two Marriages (1983)

CHANDRA, SHEILA
 West Is West (1988)

CHANG II, CHON
 Talmae and Pomdari (1987)

CHANG, GARY
 52 Pick-Up (1986)
 Firewalker (1986)

Three Fifteen (1986)
Sticky Fingers (1988)

CHANG, PETER
 Dark Night (1986)
 Rogue of the North (1988)

CHANG-KWON, CHOI
 Mulberry Tree, The (1986)
 Karma (1988)

CHAO, PAN
 Golden Hairpin, The (1963)

"CHAOS DE LUXE"
 Artichoke (1982)

CHAPIN, HARRY
 Ball Four (1976)

CHAPLIN, CHARLES
 Gold Rush, The (reissue)
  (1942)

CHAPMAN, JOAQUIN LOPEZ
 Let Them Kill Me Once and
  For All (1986)

CHAPPEL, HERBERT
 Pallisers, The (1977)
 Paddington Bear (1981)

CHARLEBOIS, ROBERT
 Fiancee Who Came in From
  the Cold, The (1983)
 Honeymoon (1985)

"CHARLES AUSTIN GROUP, THE"
 Mayhem (1969)

CHARLES, JOHN
 Goodbye Pork Pie (1981)
 Utu (1983)
 Constance (1984)
 Quiet Earth, The (1985)
 Perfectionist, The (1985)
 Soldier's Tale, A (1988)
 Zombie Brigade (1988)

CHARLES, RAY
 Eddie and Herbert (1977)

CHARLIER, PAUL
   Friends and Enemies (1987)

CHARTORISKI, JORGE
   Don't Press the Button (1987)

CHARVET, BENOIT
   Jaws of the Wolf, The (1981)
   Five and the Skin (1982)
   "Terrorists" in Retirement
      (1983)

CHASE, GARY
   Summer Camp Nightmare
      (1987)

CHASE, THOMAS (TOM)
   Scared to Death (1980)
   Creature (1985)
   Pray for Death (1985)
   Armed Response (1986)
   Verne Miller (1987)
   ... And God Created Woman
      (1988)
   Bulletproof (1988)

CHATTAWAY, JAY
   Maniac (1981)
   Vigilante (1983)
   Home Free All (1983)
   Last Flight, The (1983)
   Big Score, The (1983)
   Hard Choices (1984)
   Missing in Action (1984)
   Invasion U.S.A. (1985)
   Silver Bullet (1985)
   Very Close Quarters (1986)
   Braddock: Missing in
      Action (1988)
   Maniac Cop (1988)

CHATTOPADHYAY, NIKHIL
   Chopper (1986)

CHAUN, LI SHOW
   Super Citizen (1986)

CHECCACCI, ROMANO
   Eugenio (1980)

CHEDID, LOUIS
   Pinot, Just a Cop (1984)

CHEKALOV, PAVEL
   Stones and Benches (1972)

CHEN, C. Y.
   Papa, Can You Hear Me Sing?
      (1984)

CHERNIAVSKY, JOSEPH
   Last Warning, The (1928)

CHERWIN, RICHARD
   Valley of the Zombies (1946)

CHEUNG, CHOW KAM
   Sealed With a Kiss (1981)

CHEUNG, CHOW KUN
   Prohibited Area (1981)

CHEVALIER, CHRISTIAN
   Rendez-vous in Melbourne
      (1957)
   Charlie Dingo (1987)

CHIANG, LI HANG
   Burning of the Imperial
      Palace, The (1983)

CHIARAVALLE, FRANCO
   Jeans and a T-Shirt (1983)
   Discotheque, The (1984)

CHIAROMELLO, GIANCARLO
   When Women Played Ding Dong
      (1971)
   Prickly Pears (1980)

CHIAVEGATO, BRUNO
   When the Skin Burns (1966)

CHIHARA, PAUL
   Farewell to Manzanar (1976)
   Keegans, The (1976)
   Almost Heaven (1978)
   Betrayal (1978)
   Dark Secret of Harvest Home,
      The (1978)
   Death Moon (1978)
   Dr. Strange (1978)
   Fire in the Sky, A (1978)
   Night Cries (1978)
   Thou Shalt Not Commit

Adultery (1978)
Darker Side of Terror, The
  (1979)
Act of Violence (1979)
Mind Over Murder (1979)
Brave New World (1980)
Children of An Lac, The
  (1980)
Promise of Love, A (1980)
Prince of the City (1981)
Ambush Murders, The
  (1982)
Divorce Wars (1982)
Legend of Walks Far Woman,
  The (1982)
Miss All-American Beauty
  (1982)
Rules of Marriage, The (1982)
Haunting Passion, The (1983)
Jane Doe (1983)
Manimal (1983)
Survivors, The (1983)
Whiz Kids (1983)
Crackers (1984)
Impulse (1984)
Victims for Victims: The
  Theresa Saldana Story
  (1984)
McGruder & Loud (1985)
Right to Kill? (1985)
Toughlove (1985)
Picking Up the Pieces (1985)
Deadly Business, A (1986)
Jackals (1986)
Last Days of Frank and Jesse
  James, The (1986)
Morning After, The (1986)
Resting Place (1986)
Roanoak (1986)
When the Bough Breaks
  (1986)
Almost Partners (1987)
Baby Girl Scott (1987)
Haunted By Her Past (1987)
Killing Time, The (1987)
King of Love, The (1987)
Walk on the Moon, A (1987)
We Are the Children (1987)
Crossing Delancey (1988)
Killer Instinct (1988)
Noble House (1988)
Shooter (1988)

CHI-HON, KIM
  Mission of No Return (1984)

CHILTON, CHARLES
  America (1972)

CHINDAMO, JOE
  Poker Face (1986)

CHING, STEPHEN
  Hong Kong Playboys (1983)

CHING-SHI, OUN
  Pioneers, The (1980)

CHINO, SHUICHI
  Disciples of Hippocrates (1981)
  New Morning of Billy the Kid,
    The (1986)
  Man Who Assassinated Ryoma,
    The (1987)

CINQUE, LUIGI
  Second Night, The (1986)

CHIOCCHIO, GACIO
  This and That (1984)

CHIPMAN, JACK
  Behind Enemy Lines (1986)

CHIPRUT, ELLIOT
  G.I. Executioner, The (1971)

CHITO, KAWACHI
  Snow Fairy, The (Yuki)
    (1982)

CHIVARI, ISAL
  Life of the Summer People,
    The (1981)

CHONG-KIL, KIM
  Village in the Mist (1984)

CHOTEM, NEIL
  Gapi (1982)
  Empire (1985)
  Chasing Rainbows (1988)

CHOUDHURY, RAJAT
  Touch of Spice, A (1987)

CHOWDHURY, SALIL
    Under the Cover of Night
        (1957)
    In Search of Famine (1981)
    10 Days in Calcutta (1984)

CHRISTIAN, CHRIS
    Dakota (1988)

CHRISTIANSEN, HENNING
    It's a World Full of Children
        (1980)

CHRISTIANSON, BOB
    Gimmie a Break (1981)
    Max (1983)

CHRISTODOULIDIS, MICHALIS
    Killer, The (1983)
    Descent of the Nine, The
        (1984)
    Rape of Aprodite, The (1985)
    Greenhouse (1985)
    Detail in Cyprus, A (1987)

CHUCHKOV, VICTOR
    Question Time (1985)
    Reference (1985)

CH'UCH'U, WU
    Time to Live and a Time to
        Die, A (1986)

CHUDNOW, DAVID
    Devil Bat (1941)
    Forbidden Jungle (1949)

CHUL, KIM SOO
    Place in the Sun, The (1988)

CHULAKI, M.
    Mexican, The (1957)

CHUN-HOU, SO
    Human Lanterns (1982)
    Pure and the Evil, The
        (1982)
    Love With the Perfect
        Stranger (1986)

CHUNG, DANNY
    For Your Heart Only (1985)
    City Hero (1985)
    Soul (1987)
    True Colors (1987)

CHUNG, DOMINIC
    Job Hunter (1981)

CHUNG, WANG
    To Live and Die in L.A.
        (1985)

CIANI, SUZANNE
    Incredible Shrinking Woman,
        The (1981)
    Mother Teresa (1985)

CIBULKA, KIRIL
    Fat Tilla (1983)

CICOGNINI, ALESSANDRO
    Black Pirate, The (1939)
    Naples That Never Dies (1939)
    Adventure of Salvator Rosa,
        An (1940)
    Faust and the Devil (1950)
    Miracle in Milan (1951)
    Housemaid, Highly Presentable,
        Seeks Job (1951)
    Bride for a Night (1952)
    Cops and Robbers (1952)
    In Olden Days (1952)
    Life of Donizetti, The (1952)
    Little World of Don Camillo,
        The (1952)
    Stormbound (1952)
    Two Cents Worth of Hope
        (1952)
    Paolo and Francesca (1953)
    Ring Around the Clock (1953)
    Bread, Love and Fantasy (1954)
    Art of Getting Along, The
        (1955)
    Bread, Love and Jealousy
        (1955)
    Gold of Naples, The (1955)
    Last Five Minutes, The (1955)

CICOGNINI, BRUNO
    Cry of the Earth (1949)

CILIA, LUIS
Sleight of Hand (1983)

CINELU, MINO
Haitian Corner (1988)

CINI, I.
Ring Around the Clock (1953)

CIPOLLINA, JOHN
'68 (1987)

CIPRA, MILO
It Was Not in Vain (1957)

CIPRIANI, STELVIO
Bounty Killer, The (1966)
Luana, Daughter of the
Virgin Forest (1968)
Night Hair Child (1971)
What the Peeper Saw (1972)
Evil Eye, The (1975)
Bermuda Triangle, The (1978)
City of the Walking Dead
(1980)
Great Alligator, The (1981)
Piranha 2 (1982)
Voice, The (1982)
House of the Yellow Carpet
(1983)
Nucleus Zero (1984)
Kiss Me, Witch (1986)
Rage (1986)
Beaks (1987)
Rage of Honor (1987)
Electric Blue (1988)

CIRINO, CHUCK
Chopping Mall (1986)
Big Bad Mama II (1987)
Deathstalker II (1987)
Deadly Stranger (1988)
Terror Squad (1988)

CIVIL, FERNANDO
Among the Shadows (1986)

CLAMAN, DOLORES
Man Who Wanted to Live
Forever, The (Only

Way Out Is Dead, The)
(1970)

"CLANNARD"
Robin Hood and the Sorcerer
(1984)

CLAPTON, ERIC
Edge of Darkness (1985)
Lethal Weapon (1987)
Homeboy (1988)

CLARK, JAMES
Vampyres (1975)

CLARK, KEVIN
Rollergirls, The (1978)

CLARK, TENA
Throb (1986)

CLARKE, JAMES KENELM
Funny Money (1983)

CLARKE, STANLEY
Kung Fu: The Next Gener-
ation (1987)
Knightwatch (1988)

CLARKSON, IAN
Happiness Is a Three-Legged
Dog (1967)

CLAUSEN, ALF
Dads (1986)
Stranded (1986)
Double Agent (1987)
Harry (1987)
Number One With a Bullet
(1987)
Channel 99 (1988)
My First Love (1988)

CLAVEL, GERARD
Little Joseph (1982)

CLEFF, JOHNNY
Saturday Night at the Palace
(1987)

CLEMENTS, RICHARD
Hawaii Five-O (1968)

McCloud (1970)
Owen Marshall: Counselor
    at Law (1971)
Amanda Fallon (1972)
Six Million Dollar Man, The
    (1973)
You'll Never See Me Again
    (1973)
Houston, We've Got a Problem
    (1974)
Lucas Tanner (1974)
Invisible Man, The (1975)
Strange New World (1975)
Delvecchio (1976)
Laverne and Shirley (1976)
Rafferty (1977)
Salvage I (1979)
Shirley (1979)
From Here to Eternity (1980)

CLIFFORD, SIR HUBERT
Hunted (1952)
House of Secrets (1956)
Bachelor of Hearts (1958)

CLIFFORD, MATT
Return of the Living Dead,
    The (1985)

CLINTON, GEORGE S.
Still Smokin' (1983)
Avenging Force (1986)
American Ninja 2: The
    Confrontation (1987)
Lion of Africa, The (1987)
Too Much (1987)
Wild Thing (1987)
Platoon Leader (1988)

"CLOCKWORK"
Our Johnny (1980)

CLODE, RICHIE
Cloud Dancing (1987)

CLOEREC, RENE
Oh, Amelia (Look After
    Amelia) (1949)
Sylvie and the Phantom
    (1950)
Adventures of Captain
    Fabian, The (1951)

Red Inn, The (1951)
Case of Poisons, The (1955)
Marguerite of the Night (1955)
Trip Across Paris, The (1956)
Green Mare, The (1959)

CLUTSAM, G. H.
Mimi (1935)

CMIRAL, ILJA
Matter of Life and Death, A
    (1987)
Apartment Zero (1988)

COBEDO, MANUEL
Revolt of the Birds, The
    (1982)

COBERT, ROBERT
Heaven Can Wait (1962)
Dark Shadows (1966)
Strange Case of Dr. Jekyll
    and Mr. Hyde, The (1967)
House of Dark Shadows, The
    (1970)
Night Stalker, The (1972)
Frankenstein (1973)
Night Strangler, The (1973)
Norliss Tapes, The (1973)
Picture of Dorian Gray, The
    (1973)
Dracula (1974)
Great Ice Rip-Off, The (1974)
Melvin Purvis--G-Man (1974)
Scream of the Wolf (1974)
Turn of the Screw (1974)
Kansas City Massacre, The
    (1975)
Trilogy of Terror (1975)
Curse of the Black Widow
    (1977)
Dead of Night (1977)
Supertrain (1979)
Last of the Dalton Gang, The
    (1979)
Mrs. R's Daughter (1979)
That's My Line (1980)
Last Ninja, The (1983)
Winds of War, The (1983)
Double Talk (1986)
Bonanza: The Next
    Generation (1988)

War & Remembrance
    (1988)

COBOS, LUIS
    Pharaoh's Court (1985)

COCKBURN, BRUCE
    Waterwalker (1984)

COCKELL, JOHN MILLS
    Humongous (1982)

CODY, PHIL
    Please Stand By (1978)

COE, FRANK
    Mantis in Lace (1968)

COE, KENTON
    Agee (1980)

COE, TONY
    Camomille (1988)

COELHO, E.
    Seduzidas Pelo Demonio
        (1975)

COEURIOT, MICHEL
    Fernand (1980)

COHAN, BUZ
    Dominic's Dream (1974)

COHEN, GERARD BERNHARD
    Echoes (1980)

COHEN, HARVEY R.
    Ghost Town (1988)

COHEN, JEFF
    Bad Hats (Amour Fugitif, L')
        (1983)

COHEN-SOLAL, ROBERT
    Touch of Blue, A (1988)

COHN, STEPHEN
    Heaven on Earth (1979)
    Carlton, Your Doorman
        (1980)

"COIL"
    Angelic Conversations (1985)

COLAYCO, CECILE
    9 Deaths of the Ninja (1985)

COLAYCO, QUITO
    Alley Cat (1980)

COLBY, JOHN
    Huey Long (1985)

COLCORD, RAY
    Double Trouble (1984)
    Women in Prison (1987)

COLEMAN, CY
    Garbo Talks (1984)
    Power (1986)

COLEMAN, ORNETTE
    Boxoffice (1982)

COLEMAN, PATRICK
    Judgment in Stone, A (1986)
    Blue Monkey (1987)
    Dixie Lanes (1988)

COLLETTE, BUDDY
    Winter Geyser (1968)
    Today Is for the Champion-
        ship (1980)

COLLINS, ANTHONY
    Lady With a Lamp (1951)

COLOMBIER, MICHEL
    Other Man, The (1970)
    Rhinemann Exchange, The
        (1977)
    Testimony of Two Men (1977)
    11th Victim, The (1979)
    Steel (1980)
    Room in Town, A (1982)
    Against All Odds (1984)
    Purple Rain (1984)
    White Nights (1985)
    Double Switch (1986)
    Florida Straits (1986)
    Golden Child, The (1986)
    Money Pit, The (1986)

Ruthless People (1986)
Desperado (1987)
Shell Game (1987)
Surrender (1987)
Cop (1988)
Couch Trip, The (1988)
Desperado: Avalanche at
    Devil's Ridge (1988)
Return of Desperado, The
    (1988)
Satisfaction (1988)
Wizard of Loneliness, The
    (1988)

COLOW, JOSH
Riverbed, The (1986)

"COMBO COCKTAIL"
Paradise (1986)

"COMEDIANTS, THE"
Carnival (1985)

COMSTOCK, FRANK
Dragnet (1951)
Adam-12 (1968)
D.A.: Murder One, The
    (1969)
D.A., The (1971)
D.A.: Conspiracy to Kill,
    The (1971)
Barnaby Jones (1973)
Escape (1973)
Clinic on 18th Street (1974)
Happy Days (1974)
Night That Panicked
    America, The (1975)
25th Man, The (1982)

CONGER, LAURI
Dark Lullabies (1985)
Calling the Shots (1988)

CONKIE, HEATHER
Night Friend (1988)

CONLAN, JOSEPH
Scream (Outing, The) (1981)
Renegades, The (1982)
Kill Squad (1982)
Concrete Jungle, The (1982)

Simon and Simon (1982)
Chained Heat (1983)
High Performance (1983)
Just Our Luck (1983)
Lone Star (1983)
V--The Final Battle (1984)
Kojak: The Belarus File
    (1985)
Stick (1985)
J.O.E. and the Colonel (1985)
Outlaws (1986)
Tour of Duty (1987)
Wrong Guys, The (1988)

CONLY, PAUL
Manchurian Avenger (1983)
Awesome Lotus (1986)

CONNIFF, RAY
Archie Bunker's Place (1979)
Gloria Comes Home (1982)

CONNOR, BILL
Magic Toyshop, The (1986)
Vision, The (1987)

CONNOR, MICHAEL
Nichols and Dymes (1981)

CONRAD, RICK
Crime Zone (1988)
Drifter, The (1988)
Nest, The (1988)

CONTE, PAOLO
Grog (1982)
You Disturb Me (1983)
Joke of Destiny Lying in
    Wait Around the Corner
    Like a Robber, A (1983)
Softly ... Softly (1985)
Aurelia (1987)

CONTI, BILL
There's Always Room (1973)
Executive Suite (1976)
Smash-Up on Interstate 5
    (1976)
Andros Targets, The (1977)
In the Matter of Karen Ann
    Quinlan (1977)

Kill Me If You Can (1977)
Sensitive, Passionate Man,
 A (1977)
Harold Robbins' The Pirate
 (1978)
Ring of Passion (1978)
Stunt Seven (1979)
Gloria (1980)
Private Benjamin (1980)
Formula, The (1980)
Falcon Crest (1981)
For Your Eyes Only (1981)
Victory (1981)
Carbon Copy (1981)
Neighbors (1981)
Rocky III (1982)
I, the Jury (1982)
Farrell for the People (1982)
Split Image (1982)
That Championship Season
 (1982)
Bad Boys (1983)
Emerald Point (1983)
Terry Fox Story, The (1983)
Right Stuff, The (1983)
Unfaithfully Yours (1984)
Karate Kid, The (1984)
Bear, The (1984)
Coolangatta Gold, The (1984)
Mass Appeal (1984)
Stark (1985)
Rocky IV (1985)
Gotcha (1985)
Nomads (1985)
I Had Three Wives (1985)
Beer (1985)
45/85 (1985)
Big Trouble (1986)
Boss' Wife, The (1986)
50 Years of Action! (1986)
F/X (1986)
Karate Kid Part II, The
 (1986)
North & South, Book II
 (1986)
Stark: Mirror Image (1986)
Baby Boom (1987)
Broadcast News (1987)
For Keeps (1987)
Happy New Year (1987)
I Love N.Y. (1987)
Mariah (1987)

Masters of the Universe
 (1987)
Napoleon and Josephine: A
 Love Story (1987)
Prayer for the Dying, A
 (1987)
Betrayed (1988)
Cohen and Tate (1988)
Night in the Life of Jimmy
 Valentine, A (1988)
Silent Whisper (1988)
Supercarrier (1988)

"CONTRABAND"
 King of the Streets (1985)

CONTRERAS, FEDERICO
 Inhabitants of the Uninhabited
  House, The (1959)

CONVERTINO, MICHAEL
 Children of a Lesser God
  (1986)
 Christmas Snow (1986)
 Hollywood Vice Squad (1986)
 Hidden, The (1987)
 Mistress (1987)
 Bull Durham (1988)

COODER, RY
 Long Riders, The (1980)
 Southern Comfort (1981)
 Border, The (1982)
 Paris, Texas (1984)
 Streets of Fire (1984)
 Alamo Bay (1985)
 Brewster's Millions (1985)
 Annie Oakley (1985)
 Blue City (1986)
 Crossroads (1986)
 Beverly Hills Buntz (1987)

COOK, RAY
 Careful, He Might Hear You
  (1983)

COOKE, JOHN BOY
 Thinkin' Big (1988)

COOKERLY, JACK
 Black Scorpion, The (1957)

Invasion of the Star Creatures
(1962)
Omega Syndrome, The (1987)
Grotesque (1988)

COOPER, HAL
Did You Hear About Josh
and Kelly? (1980)
Phil and Mikhy (1980)

COOPER, LINDSAY
Gold Diggers, The (1983)

COOPER, MARTY
Tribes (1970)

COPELAND, STEWART
Rumble Fish (1983)
Out of Bounds (1986)
Wall Street (1987)
She's Having a Baby (1988)
Talk Radio (1988)

COPLAND, AARON
Chisholms, The (1979)
Love & Money (1982)

COPPOLA, CARMINE
Tonight for Sure (1961)
People, The (1972)
Last Day, The (1975)
Napoleon (1981)
Outsiders, The (1983)
Gardens of Stone (1987)
Tucker: The Man and His
Dream (1988)

CORDEIRO, GEORGE
Screamplay (1985)

CORDELL, FRANK
Murder Will Out (1952)
Call Me Genius (1961)

CORDIO, CARLO MARIA
Ator (1983)
Emperor Caligula: The
Untold Story, The (1986)
Endgame (1986)
Lone Ranger, The (1988)

COREA, CHICK
Second Edition (1984)

COREL, B. C.
Holy Island, The (1959)

CORIGLIANO, JOHN
Altered States (1980)
Revolution (1985)

CORNEAU, ALAIN
Future Interior, The (1984)

CORNU, RICHARD
Secret of Magic Island (1958)

"CORO INFANTIL VILLA DE
MADRID"
Ferocious (1984)

CORONA, EDGAR SOSA
Thanatos (1986)

CORRAL, HORACIO
Inti Anti, the Road to the
Sun (1982)

CORREA, JOSE LUIS
How Chileans Love (1984)

CORRIVEAU, JEAN
Night Zoo (1987)

CORTAZAR, ERNESTO
Satan of All Horrors (1972)
Criminal, The (1985)
Bricklayers Day, Part II
(1986)
Broncho, El (1986)
Neighborhood--Oh, Those
Hot Mexicans, The (1986)
Violent Man, A (1986)
Bloody Weed (1987)
Caro's Escape--Kill the
Fugitive (1987)
Corruption (1987)
Savage Creatures in Heat
(1987)
Scent of Death (1987)
Dirty Dealings Between Friends
(1988)

CORTES, DIEGO
Crypt, The (1981)

CORTI, NINA
In Blood and Sand (1988)

CORZILIUS, VICTOR
Hoax (1936)

COSBY, WILLIAM H., JR.
To All My Friends on Shore
(1972)

COSENTINO, GREGORIO
Unattended Party, The (1981)

COSMA, EDGAR
Little Bunch, The (1983)

COSMA, VLADIMIR
Dracula and Son (1979)
It's Not Me, It's Him (1980)
Child Woman, The (1980)
Telephone Bar, The (1980)
Umbrella Coup, The (1980)
Inspector Blunder (1980)
Party, The (1981)
Diva (1981)
Next Year If All Goes Well
(1981)
Man's Affair, A (1981)
Goat, The (1982)
Santa Claus is a Louse (1982)
Ace of Aces (1982)
Party II, The (1982)
Prize of Peril, The (1983)
Banzai (1983)
Co-Fathers, The (1983)
Ball, The (1983)
To Catch a Cop (1984)
Little Jerk (1984)
Tug of Love (1984)
Twins, The (1984)
Just the Way You Are (1984)
Led by the Nose (1984)
Mistral's Daughter (1984)
Seventh Target, The (1985)
Gag Kings, The (1985)
Asterix vs. Caesar (1985)
Asterix in Britain (1986)
Death on a Rainy Sunday
(1986)

Fugitives, The (1986)
Piece of the Royal Pie, A
(1986)
Crossed Hearts (1987)
Field Agent, The (1987)
Levy and Goliath (1987)
Nitwits (1987)
Cross My Heart (1988)
Student, The (1988)

COSSU, SCOTT
Islands (1986)

COSTA, DON
Ready or Not (1974)
Three Times Daley (1976)
Amy Prentiss (1977)
Lanigan's Rabbi (1977)
What Really Happened to the
Class of '65? (1977)
Loose Change (1978)
Second Time Around, The
(1979)
Cheap Detective, The (1980)

COSTANDINOS, ALEC R.
Winds of Change (1978)

COTAPOS, ACARIO
Confession at Dawn (1954)

COULAIS, BRUNO
Next of Kin (1986)
Secret Wife, The (1986)
Too Much Kissing (1986)

COULTER, PHIL
Water Babies, The (1978)

COURAGE, ALEXANDER
Voyage to the Bottom of the
Sea (1964)
Daniel Boone (1964)
Lost in Space (1965)
Star Trek (1966)
Waltons, The (1972)
Apple's Way (1974)
Day for Thanks on Waltons
Mountain, A (1982)
Mother's Day on Waltons
Mountain (1982)
Wedding on Waltons Mountain,

New Super Friends Hour,
   The (1977)
Skatebirds, The (1977)
All-New Popeye Hour, The
   (1978)
Battle of the Planets (1978)
Galaxy Goofups, The (1978)
Godzilla Power Hour, The
   (1978)
Kiss Meets the Phantom of
   the Park (1978)
Three Robonic Stooges, The
   (1978)
World's Greatest Superheroes,
   The (1978)
Yogi's Space Race (1978)
Buford and the Ghost (1979)
Casper and the Angels (1979)
Fred and Barney Meet the
   Thing (1979)
New Fred and Barney Show,
   The (1979)
New Schmoo, The (1979)
Scooby-Doo and Scrappy-Doo
   (1979)
Super Globetrotters, The
   (1979)
Captain Caveman and the
   Teen Angels (1980)
Drak Pack, The (1980)
Fonz and the Happy Days
   Gang (1980)
Laverne and Shirley in the
   Army (1981)
Smurfs, The (1981)
Space Stars (1981)
Trollkins (1981)
Heidi's Song (1982)
Laverne and Shirley with
   the Fonz (1982)
Little Rascals, The (1982)
Mork and Mindy (1982)
Biskitts, The (1983)
Dukes, The (1983)
Monchhichis (1983)
Pac-Man (1983)
Shirt Tales, The (1983)
Snorks (1984)

CURTIS, JOE
   Slaughter in San Francisco
      (1973)

CURTO, GUIDO
   Rothschild (1938)

CUSTER, ARTHUR
   When Nature Calls (1985)

CYRUS, MARTIN
   River Trip with Hen (1984)

CZENCZ, JOZSEF
   Countdown (1986)

"D. P. EXPRESS"
   Haiti Express (1983)

DABO, DJANUN
   Mortu Nega (1988)

DAGEBY, ULF
   Interrail (1981)
   Painter, The (1982)
   Nature's Revenge (1984)
   Soul Is Greater Than the
      World, The (1985)
   In the Name of the Law
      (1986)
   Threat, The (1987)

DAGLISH, MALCOLM
   Tuck Everlasting (1981)

DAHLBERG, LASSE
   Grass Is Singing, The (1981)

DAHLGREN, EVA
   Test, The (1987)

"DAILY NEWS"
   Debauched Life of Gerard
      Floque, The (1987)

DAKSHNIMURTI
   (DAHSKINAMOORTHY)
   Jungle, The (1952)
   Hindu, The (1953)

DAL, HANS
   House by the Sea, The (1980)

DALAMANNO, MASSIMO
   Cavaliero della Montagna
      (1950)

DALE, JAMES
Execution of Raymond Graham,
The (1985)
Breakfast with Les & Bess
(1985)
Timing (1985)

DALE, JIMMY
Li'l Abner (1971)

D'ALESSIO, CARLOS
Left Without Leaving an
Address (1982)
Hecate (1982)
Children, The (1985)

DALLA, LUCIO
Talcum Powder (1982)
Ear From Where (1983)
Fortunate Pilgrim, The (1988)

DALMASSO, DOMINIQUE
Short Circuits (1981)

D'ALMEIDA, ANTONIO VICTORINO
Fault, The (1980)

DALQUIST, LASSE
Skanor-Falsterbo (1939)

D'AMARILLO
Devil Woman (1970)

D'AMICI, MARIO
Holidays in the Snow (1966)

DAN, IKUMA
Legend of the White Serpent,
The (1956)
Adventures of Sun Wu Kung
(1958)
Mistress, The (1959)
Last War, The (1961)

DAN, KOSAKU
Return of the Champ (1981)

DANA, MYCHAEL
Walking After Midnight
(1988)

D'ANDREA, JOHN
Love's Dark Ride (1978)
Stranger in Our House (1978)
Grambling's White Tiger
(1981)
Savage Streets (1984)
Herndon and Me (1983)
Body Slam (1987)
Hunter's Blood (1987)

DANEV, DANILO
Point 905 (1960)

DANG, HONG
Return to the Right Path
(1986)

D'ANGELO, NINO
Jeans and a T-Shirt (1983)
Discotheque, The (1984)

DANIELE, PINO
Starting Over from Three
(1981)
Ways of the Lord Are Finite,
The (1987)
What If Gargiulo Finds Out?
(1988)

DANIELS, RICH
Outtakes (1987)

DANKWORTH, JOHN
Criminal, The (1960)
Saturday Night and Sunday
Morning (1960)
Avengers, The (1966)

DANNA, MICHAEL
Family Viewing (1987)
Caribe (1988)
Murder One (1988)

DANNER, WOLFGANG
Rosi and the Big City (1981)

DANTE, CARL
Slave Girls from Beyond
Infinity (1987)
Cellar Dweller (1988)

DAO, DGUYEN THIEN
  Dust of Empire (1983)

DAOUD, GEHAD
  Houseboat No. 70 (1982)

DARAU, ANDREAS
  Hunter of the Heart (1984)

DARBO, RALPH
  Chromophobia (1965)

DARING, K. MASON
  Return of the Secaucus Seven
    (1980)
  Lianna (1983)
  Brother from Another Planet,
    The (1984)
  Key Exchange (1985)
  Osa (1985)
  Matewan (1987)
  Eight Men Out (1988)
  Jenny's Song (1988)
  Laser Man, The (1988)
  Shallow Grave (1988)

DARLING, DAVID
  Permeke (1985)

D'ARMAGNAC, JOHANNA
  Parfait Amour (1985)

DARVAS, FERENC
  Disciples, The (1985)
  Midas Touch, The (1988)
  Peter in Wonderland (1988)

DAS, AJOY
  Charmurti (1978)

DASGUPTA, JYOTISHKA
  Return, The (1988)

DASHKEVICH, VLADIMIR
  Plumbum, or a Dangerous
    Game (1987)

DASSAULT, OLIVIER
  Black Gown for a Killer,
    A (1981)

DAUM, GLEN
  Metropolitan Avenue (1985)

DAUNER, WOLFGANG
  Dead or Alive (1988)

D'AURIOL, HUBERT
  Amazing Monsieur Fabre, The
    (1952)

DAVENPORT, HARRY BROMLEY
  Whispers of Fear (1974)
  Xtro (1983)

DAVID, YORIK BEN
  Fun (Boarding House) (1983)

DAVIDSON, HOWARD
  Final Cut (1980)

DAVIE, CEDRIC THORPE
  Bad Lord Byron (1949)
  Adventuress, The (1951)
  Rockets Galore (1958)

DAVIES, HARRY PARR
  Look Up and Laugh (1935)

DAVIES, IVA
  Razorback (1984)

DAVIES, PHIL
  Future Cop (1985)
  Savage Island (1985)

DAVIES, VICTOR
  Pit, The (1980)
  Latitude 55° (1982)
  ... And When They Shall
    Ask (1985)

DAVIES, WILLIAM
  America (1972)

DAVIS, BOBBY
  Mob War (1984)

DAVIS, CARL
  Up the Chastity Belt (1971)
  Up Pompeii (1971)
  I, Monster (1972)

Rentadick (1972)
What Became of Jack and
  Jill? (1972)
Catholics (1973)
World at War, The (1973)
Canterville Ghost, The (1974)
Marie Curie (1979)
Hollywood (1980)
Commanding Sea, The (1981)
Oppenheimer (1982)
Praying Mantis, The (1982)
Aerodrome, The (1983)
Weather in the Streets, The
  (1983)
Champions (1984)
George Stevens: A Film-
  maker's Journey (1984)
Far Pavillions, The (1984)
Sakharov (1984)
Tales of Beatrix Potter, The
  (1984)
King David (1985)
Song for Europe, The (1985)
Silas Marner (1985)
Murrow (1986)
Buster Keaton: A Hard Act
  to Follow (1987)
Fire and Ice (1987)
Silas Marner (1987)
Girl in a Swing, The (1988)
Once in a Lifetime (1988)

DAVIS, DON
  Blackout (1988)
  Bluegrass (1988)
  Quiet Victory: The Charlie
    Wedemeyer Story (1988)
  Stoning in Fulham County, A
    (1988)

DAVIS, JEFF
  Yours Truly, Blake (1955)
  Treasure of San Teresa
    (1959)

DAVIS, JOHN
  Strike Force (1981)
  T. J. Hooker (1982)
  Blood Sport (1986)
  Mr. and Mrs. Ryan (1986)

DAVIS, KEN
  Holiday Australia (1987)

DAVIS, MARK
  Cheech and Chong's Next
    Movie (1980)
  Bustin' Loose (1981)
  Crash Course (1988)

DAVIS, MILES
  Elevator to the Gallows (1958)

DAVIS, MORRIS C.
  Cure de Village, Le (1949)

DAVIS, ROCKY
  Highwayman, The (1988)

DAY, OLIVER
  Emmanuelle 6 (1988)

DE, GU
  Report on Pollution at the
    Women's Kingdom (1988)

DE AGUIRRE, JAIME
  Latent Image (1988)

DEAK, TAMAS
  Cat City (1987)

DE ANDRADE, M.
  Macunaima (1972)

DE ANDRES, RAFAEL
  Life Around Us (1959)

DE ANGELIS, GUIDO AND
  MAURIZIO
  Torso (1974)
  Prisoner of the Cannibal
    God (1978)
  Sheriff and the Satellite Kid,
    The (1979)
  Alien 2 (1982)
  Ironmaster (1982)
  Banana Joe (1982)
  Yor, the Hunter from the
    Future (1983)
  Cinderella '80 (1984)
  Crime, A (1984)

Pianoforte (1984)
Good King Dagobert (1984)
Devil on the Hill, The (1985)
Light Blast (1985)
Madman at War (1985)
My Dearest Son (1985)
Dumb Dicks (1986)
Killing Machine, The (1986)
Body Beat (1988)

DE AZEVEDO, LEX
Sexorcists, The (1974)
Young Maverick (1979)
Cassie and Company (1982)

DE BENEDICTIS, DEAN
Tabitha (1977)
Love and Learn (1979)
Earthling (1981)

DE BENEDICTIS, DICK
Columbo (1971)
Couple Takes a Wife, The
(1972)
Born Free (1974)
Greatest Gift, The (1974)
This Was the West That Was
(1974)
Big Ripoff, The (1975)
Doc (1975)
Family Hovak, The (1975)
McCoy (1975)
Phyllis (1975)
Return of the World's
Greatest Detective, The
(1976)
Betty White Show, The (1977)
Deadly Triangle, The (1977)
Fantastic Journey, The (1977)
Oregon Trail, The (1977)
Tabitha (1977)
Crisis in Sun Valley (1978)
Desperate Women (1978)
Ziegfeld: The Man and His
Women (1978)
Dear Detective (1979)
Delta House (1979)
Love and Learn (1979)
Murder by Natural Causes
(1979)
Heaven on Earth (1981)

Goldie and the Bears (1985)
Perry Mason Returns (1985)
Case of the Shooting Star,
The (1986)
Diary of a Perfect Murder,
The (1986)
Matlock (1986)
Perry Mason: The Clue of
the Notorious Nun (1986)
Case of the Murdered Madam,
The (1987)
Case of the Scandalous
Scoundrel, The (1987)
Fatal Confession: A Father
Dowling Mystery (1987)
Jake and the Fatman (1987)
Perry Mason: The Case of
the Lost Love (1987)
Perry Mason: The Case of
the Sinister Spirit (1987)
In the Heat of the Night
(1988)
Perry Mason: The Case of
the Avenging Ace (1988)
Perry Mason: The Case of
the Lady in the Lake
(1988)

DE BENEDICTIS, PAUL
Breaking Silence (1985)

DEBLAIS, JEAN-CLAUDE
Paris Seen By ... 20 Years
After (1984)
Happiness Strikes Again
(1986)

DEBNEY, JOHN
Dragon's Lair (1984)
Changing Patterns (1987)
Day My Kid Went Punk, The
(1987)
Wild Pair, The (1987)
Not Since Casanova (1988)
Old Money (1988)
Seven Hours to Judgment
(1988)

DE BOER, LODEWIJK
Silence Around Christina M.,
The (1982)

Breathless (1982)
Broken Mirrors (1984)
Paul Chevrolet and the
    Ultimate Hallucination
    (1985)
Intoxicated (1987)

DE BORDEAUX, RICHARD
Naked Love (1981)

DE BRUIN, PIETER
To Church and Work You Go
    (1986)

DEBSKI, KRZESIMIR
Medium (1985)
Young Magician, The (1987)
King Size (1988)

DE BUJADOUX, YVES
Without Fear or Blame (1988)

DE CASTRO, NELSON COELHO
Green Years (1984)

DE CASTRO, PAUL
To the Last Drop (1980)
Dream Is Not Over, The
    (1982)

DE CASTRO, URGEL
Rio Zone Norte (1958)

DECK, DARRELL
Return to Boggy Creek
    (1978)

DE COLA, VINCE
Transformers, The

DE COLOGNE, FLOH
My Father's Secret (1981)

DECSENYI, JANOS
Heroic Times (1985)

DE CURITIBA, HENRIQUE
Life and Blood of the
    Polish (1983)

DEDIC, ARSEN
Moss-Covered Asphalt (1983)
Glembays, The (1988)

DE DIEGO, EMILIO
Blood Wedding (1981)
Open Balcony, The (1984)
Long Strider (1987)

DE DIOS, JOSE LUIS see
CASTINEIRA DE DIOS,
JOSE LUIS

DEFAYE, JEAN-MICHEL
Fifi la Plume (1964)

DE FRANCESCO, LOUIS
Ramparts We Watch, The
    (1940)

DEFRATES, JAMI
Zaat (1972)
Blood Waters of Dr. Z, The
    (1972)

DE FRIES, CARLO
Azure Express (1938)

DEGE, HUBERT
Maine-Ocean Express (1986)

DE GREGORI, FRANCESCO
Flirt (1983)

DE GROOF, CARL
Under Age (1958)

DE HERRERA, RAMON
Half of Love (1985)

DE JESUS, LUCHI
California Kid, The (1974)
Get Christie Love! (1974)
Sweet Hostage (1975)

DE KORTE, PAUL
Scooby-Doo, Where Are You?
    (1969)
Jeannie (1973)
Speed Buggy (1973)
Super Friends (1973)

Jabberjaw (1976)
C. B. Bears, The (1977)
Great Grape Ape Show, The
    (1977)
New Super Friends Hour,
    The (1977)
Three Robonic Stooges, The
    (1978)
Captain Caveman and the
    Teen Angels (1980)
Drak Pack, The (1980)

DE LA GARZA, ROBERT
    Drug Knot, The (1986)

DE LA MAZA, EDUARDO see
SAINZ DE LA MAZA, EDUARDO

DELANNOY, MARCEL
    Tempest, The (1940)
    Summer Storm (1950)

DELAPORTE, JACQUES
    Drunken Night (1986)
    Joint Brothers, The (1986)

DE LA VEGA, JOSE
    His Hand Slipped (1952)
    Overdoing It (1953)
    Phantom of the Red House,
        The (1954)
    Mysteries of Black Magic,
        The (1957)

DEL BARRIO, ALEJANDRO
    Unwanted, The (1951)
    Tunnel, The (1952)

DEL BARRIO, GEORGE
    Popi (1976)

DE LEON, LUIS
    Attack of the Mayan Mummy
        (1963)

DELERUE, GEORGES
    Immortelle, L' (1962)
    Appearances (1964)
    Brain, The (1969)
    Calmos (Femmes Fatales)
        (1977)

First Voyage (1980)
Richard's Things (1980)
Last Subway, The (1980)
Woman Next Door, The (1981)
Grilling, The (1981)
Life Goes On (1981)
Documenteur: An Emotion
    Picture (1981)
Broken English (1981)
Rich and Famous (1981)
True Confessions (1981)
Josepha (1982)
Little Sex, A (1982)
Partners (1982)
Escape Artist, The (1982)
Guy de Maupassant (1982)
Passerby of the San Souci
    Cafe, The (1982)
Exposed (1983)
African, The (1983)
Black Stallion Returns, The
    (1983)
Man, Woman and Child (1983)
Let It Be Sunday (1983)
One Deadly Summer (1983)
Liberty Belle (1983)
Silkwood (1983)
Bon Plaisir, Le (1984)
Nobody's Women (1984)
Vultures, The (1984)
Love Thy Neighbor (1984)
Deadly Intentions (1985)
Arch of Triumph (1985)
Agnes of God (1985)
Maxie (1985)
Time to Live, A (1985)
Stone Pillow (1985)
Carne: The Man Behind
    the Camera (1985)
Crimes of the Heart (1986)
Descent into Hell (1986)
Family Council (1986)
Mesmerized (1986)
Platoon (1986)
Salvador (1986)
Sin of Innocence (1986)
Women of Valor (1986)
Escape from Sobibor (1987)
Her Secret Life (1987)
Lonely Passion of Judith
    Hearne, The (1987)

Maid to Order (1987)
Man in Love, A (1987)
Pick-Up Artist, The (1987)
Queenie (1987)
Beaches (1988)
Biloxi Blues (1988)
Chouans! (1988)
Heartbreak Hotel (1988)
House on Carroll Street,
   The (1988)
Memories of Me (1988)
Summer Story, A (1988)
To Kill a Priest (1988)
Twins (1988)

DELFINO, ENRIQUE
Best Father in the World,
   The (1941)

DELIA, JOSEPH (JOE)
Ms. .45 (1981)
China Girl (1987)
Freeway (1988)

DE LIMA, WALDEMAR
Compromise, The (1988)

DELLA, LUCIO
Picaros, The (1987)

DELLO JOIO, NORMAN
America and Americans (1968)

DE LORY, AL
Here We Go Again (1973)
Pioneer Woman (1973)
Mad Bull (1977)
Rodeo Girl (1980)
What Comes Around (1986)

DE LOS RIOS, WALDO
Strange Gods, The (1958)
House That Screamed, The
   (1970)

DEL RIO, JAVIER
Juana the Saloon Keeper
   (1987)

DE LUCA, NANDO
Velvet Hands (1980)

DE LUCIA, PACO
Carmen (1983)
Hit, The (1984)

DELUGG, MILTON
Santa Claus Conquers the
   Martians (1964)
Gulliver's Travels Beyond the
   Moon (1965)
Gong Show Movie, The (1980)

DE LUNA, SALVADOR see
RUIZ DE LUNA, SALVADOR

DEL POZO, ARTURO see RUIZ
DEL POZO, ARTURO

DE MAESSCHALK, WILLYL
Io Sono Anna Magnani (1980)

DE MARCO, CHRISTOPHER
War (1988)

DEMARE, LUCIO
Gaucho War, The (1942)
Gaucho (1954)

DEMARSAN, ERIC
Demain des Momes (1976)
5% Risk (1980)
Petrol, Petrol (1981)
Heading South (1981)
Indiscretion, The (1982)
On Your Feet, Crabs, the
   Tide is Up (1983)
Specialists, The (1985)
Me Want You (1985)
July in September (1988)

DE MARTINO, MARCELLO
Death on the Fourposter
   (1963)

DE MASI, FRANCESCO
Weapons of Vengeance (1963)
Hyena of London, The (1964)
Samson in King Solomon's
   Mines (1964)
Affair in Port Said (1966)
Agent Z-55: Desperate
   Mission (1966)

Angel for Satan, An (1966)
Arizona Colt (1966)
Blade in the Body (1966)
087 "Mission Apocalypse"
    (1966)
Pitiless Colt of the Gringo,
    The (1966)
Ringo: The Face of Revenge
    (1966)
Spies Kill Silently (1966)
Vagabond Hero (1966)
Dirty Story of the West, A
    (1968)
Big Game, The (1972)
Orgy of the Dead (1972)
Unglorious Bastards (Counter-
    feit Commandos) (1977)
New York Ripper (1982)
Lone Wolf McQuade (1983)
Manhunt (1984)
Rush (1984)
Escape from the Bronx (1985)
Dreams and Needs (1985)
Days of Hell (1986)
Formula for Murder (1986)
Madness My Love (1986)
Thunder Warrior (1986)

DE MATTEO, LUIS
    Owners of Silence, The
        (1987)

DEMAY, ANDRE
    Games of Artifice (1987)

DEMER, LARRY
    Hammerhead Jones (1987)

DEMERS, CLAUDE
    Toby McTeague (1986)

DE MONFRIED, AVENIR
    Theatre of Mr. and Mrs.
        Kabal, The (1967)

DEMPSEY, TERRY
    Magic Is Alive, My Friends
        (1985)

DENISON, FRANK
    Blue Thunder (1984)
    Jerk, Two, The (1984)

DENISSOV, EDISSON
    Born Again (1984)

DENIZ, HERNAND
    Our Man in Havana (1960)

DENIZCI, SUHEYL
    One and the Others (1988)

DE NONNO, CARLO
    Final Executioner, The (1983)

DE NOVI, GENE
    Cavern, The (1965)

DENSON, FRANK
    Sunset Limousine (1983)

DENVER, JOHN
    Sunshine (1973)
    Higher Ground (1988)

DEODATO, EUMIR
    Target Risk (1975)

DE OLIVEIRA, DENOY
    Ghost from Bahia, The (1984)

DE PABLO, LUIS
    Invasion (1964)
    Sound of Horror, The (1964)

DE PASQUALE, JAMES
    Half 'n' Half (1988)

DePATIE, STEVE
    Baggy Pants and the Nitwits
        (1977)

DE PAUL, LYNSEY
    No, Honestly (1975)

DE PAZ, RAFAEL
    My Merry Widow (1942)

DE PISCOPO, TULLIO
    Savage Breed (1980)
    Picone Sent Me (1984)
    32nd of December, The (1988)

DEPOLO, OZREN
  Whatever You Can Spare
    (1980)
  Early Snowfall in Munich
    (1984)

DEPPE, GORDON
  Listen to the City (1984)

DEREVITZKY, ALEXANDER
  Loves of Salammbo, The
    (1963)
  Deguejo (1966)

DERFEL, JERZY
  Teddy Bear (1981)

DERGACHEV, ANATOLI
  Cold March (1988)

DEROME, JEAN
  Last Glacier, The (1985)
  Passiflora (1986)

DES, LASZLO
  No Clues (1983)
  Love Till First Blood (1986)
  Love Till Second Blood
    (1988)

DESAI, VASANT
  Two Eyes, Twelve Hands
    (1958)

DE SCARANO, J. M.
  Blood Relations (1977)

DE SENNEVILLE, PAUL
  Irreconcilable Differences
    (1984)

DE SICA, MANUEL
  Crimes of the Black Cat
    (1976)
  I'm Photogenic (1980)
  Shadow Line (1980)
  Sunday Lovers (1980)
  Catherine's Wedding (1982)
  Moment of Adventure, The
    (1983)

Boy and a Girl, A (1984)
Vacation in America (1984)
Heart (Cuore) (1985)
Alcove, The (1985)
45th Parallel (1986)
Yuppies 2 (1986)
Soldiers--365 Till Dawn (1987)
Montecarlo Gran Casino (1988)

DE SIMONE, ROBERTO
  Fontamara (1980)

DESJARDINS, RICHARD
  Night With Hortense, The
    (1988)

DESSCA, YVES
  Femmes (1983)

DESSEAU, PAUL
  Anna and Elizabeth (1936)
  Work (Avodah) (1936)
  Gibralter (1939)
  Mother Courage and Her
    Children (1961)

DE STEFANO, FULVIO
  Francesca (1987)

DETREE, ROBERT C.
  Kaminsky (1985)

DEU, AMAL
  Girl from India (1982)

DEUBEL, CLAUS
  Firm Forever, A (1984)

DEV, SHARANG
  Essence, The (1987)

DEVARAJAN
  Swamy Aiyyappan (1975)
  Vandedevatha (1976)
  Vayanadan Thampan (1978)
  Chidambaram (1986)

DE VOL, FRANK
  Turn the Key Softly (1959)

My Three Sons (1960)
Family Affair (1966)
Brady Bunch, The (1969)
To Rome with Love (1969)
Reluctant Heroes, The (1971)
Smith Family, The (1971)
Delphi Bureau, The (1972)
Dusty's Trail (1973)
Key West (1973)
Murdock's Gang (1973)
Female Artillery (1973)
Key West (1973)
Murdock's Gang (1973)
Fess Parker Show, The
   (1974)
Hey, I'm Alive! (1975)
Hustle (1975)
Panache (1976)
Vega$ (1978)
Millionaire, The (1978)
Highcliffe Manor (1979)
Herbie Goes Bananas (1980)
Ghosts of Buxley Hall, The
   (1980)
... All the Marbles (1981)
Brady Brides, The (1981)
Brady Girls Get Married,
   The (1981)
Wild Women of Chastity Gulch,
   The (1982)
Herbie, the Love Bug (1982)
Tales of the Apple Dumpling
   Gang (1982)

DE VORZON, BARRY
   S.W.A.T. (1975)
   Dog and Cat (1977)
   In the Beginning (1978)
   Lacy and the Mississippi
      Queen (1978)
   Ski Lift to Death (1978)
   Beach Patrol (1979)
   Nightingales, The (1979)
   13 Queens Boulevard (1979)
   Stunts Unlimited (1980)
   Twinkle, Twinkle, Killer
      Kane (Ninth Configura-
      tion, The) (1980)
   Comeback Kid, The (1980)
   Stunts Unlimited (1980)
   Reward (1980)

B.A.D. Cats (1980)
Xanadu (1980)
Children Nobody Wanted,
   The (1981)
Tattoo (1981)
Looker (1981)
Private Benjamin (1981)
Jekyll and Hyde ... Together
   Again (1982)
Renegades, The (1982)
Simon and Simon (1982)
Three Eyes (1982)
Shadow of Sam Penny, The
   (1983)
High Performance (1983)
Just Our Luck (1983)
Lone Star (1983)
V--The Final Battle (1984)
Mischief (1985)
Kojak: The Belarus File
   (1985)
Stick (1985)
Intimate Strangers (1986)
Night of the Creeps (1986)

DEVREESE, FREDERIC
   Benvenuta (1983)
   Barbarous Wedding, The
      (1987)
   Abyss, The (1988)

DE WILDE, JAN
   Hector (1988)

DE WOLFE
   Fall of the House of Usher,
      The (1952)
   Zoo Robbers, The (1973)
   Horror Hospital (1975)
   Sex Express (1975)

DEY, ALOKNATH
   Kaleidoscope (1981)

DHOLAKIA, RAJAT
   Festival of Fire (1985)
   This is Not Our Destination
      (1987)

DIAKUN, GREG
   Darkside, The (1987)

DIAMOND, A. S.
Goddess of Love, The (1988)

DIAMOND, DAVID
Life in the Balance (1967)

DIAMOND, J. AARON
Heart of the Garden (1985)

DIAMOND, JOEL
Suicide Club, The (1987)

DIAZ, MARIANO
Among the Shadows (1986)

DIAZ, ROMEO
Night Caller (1985)
Chinese Ghost Story, A
(1987)

DIAZ CONDE, ANTONIO
Town Tale (Pueblerina)
(1949)
My Darling Clementine (1953)
Net, The (1953)
Seducer, The (1955)
New Invisible Man, The
(1957)
Ash Wednesday (1958)
Robot vs. the Aztec Mummy,
The (1959)
World, the Flesh and the
Devil, The (1960)
Santa Claus (1959)
Spiritism (Espiritismo) (1961)
Balloon Man (1961)
Curse of the Aztec Mummy,
The (1961)
Curse of the Doll People,
The (1961)
Red Blossoms (1961)
Three Romeos and a Juliet
(1961)
Doctor of Doom, The (1964)
Night of the Bloody Apes,
The (Horror and Sex)
(1968)

DIAZMUNOZ, EDUARDO
Motel (1984)

DIBANGO, MANU
Forty Deuce (1982)

DICKSON, ANDREW
Meantime (1983)

DI COLA, VINCE
Rocky IV (1985)

DIERHAMMER, CARLOS
Secret of Dr. Mabuse, The
(1964)

DIETRICH, JAMES
Mummy, The (1932)
Leopard Men of Africa (1940)

DI FONZO, GIANFRANCO
Masoch (1980)

DI GUIDA, MATTEO
Landscape with Figures
(1983)

DIKKER, LOEK
Fourth Man, The (1983)
Peaceful Days (1984)
Iris (1987)
Pascali's Island (1988)

DIKMEN, UGUR
Desperate Road, The (1986)

DILULIO, RON F.
Aurora Encounter, The
(1986)
Mountaintop Motel Massacre
(1986)

DI MAGGIO, ROSS
China Venture (1953)
Sky Commando (1953)

"DIMENZIO GROUP"
No Clues (1983)

DIMOND, A. S.
Fantastic World of D. C.
Collins, The (1984)

DINGXIAN, JIANG
  Unfinished Game of Go, The
    (1982)

DINO, PETE
  Marlo and the Magic Movie
    Machine (1977)

DI PACE, ARNALDO
  Geronima (1986)

DI PAOLO, DANNY
  Jack's Back (1988)

DI PASQUALE, JAMES
  Hawaii Five-O (1968)
  Senior Year (1974)
  Sons and Daughters (1974)
  Force Five (1975)
  Switch (1975)
  Sarah T.--Portrait of a
    Teenage Alcoholic (1975)
  Three for the Road (1975)
  Mallory: Circumstantial
    Evidence (1976)
  Practice, The (1976)
  What Really Happened to the
    Class of '65? (1977)
  Critical List, The (1978)
  Big Shamus, Little Shamus
    (1979)
  Contender, The (1980)
  Willow B: Women in Prison
    (1980)
  Escape (1980)
  Advice to the Lovelorn (1981)
  McClain's Law (1981)
  Fantasies (1982)
  Two of a Kind (1982)
  After George (1983)
  Agatha Christie's "Sparkling
    Cyanide" (1983)
  Trauma Center (1983)
  Listen to Your Heart (1983)
  Quarterback Princess (1983)
  Red-Light Sting, The (1984)
  Scene of the Crime (1984)
  Love Lives On (1985)
  RAD (1986)
  Young Again (1986)
  Stranger Waits, A (1987)
  Broken Angel (1988)

DI RIENZI, MAURO
  Noistottus (1987)

DI ROSA, GABRIELA
  Microscope, The (1988)

"DISCIPLINA KIOME I AZRA"
  Second Generation, The
    (1983)

DI STEFANO, FELICE
  Invincible Maciste Brothers,
    The (1964)
  Ramon, the Mexican (1966)
  Seven Golden Women Against
    Two 07s (1966)
  Vaya con Dios Gringo (1966)

DISTEL, SASHA
  Fanatics, The (1960)
  Good Life, The (1971)

DIVIJAN, VLADIMIR
  Six Days in June (1985)

DIVINA, VACLAV
  Strange Fascination (1952)
  One Girl's Confession (1953)

DIXON, ANDREW
  High Hopes (1988)

DIXON, DWIGHT
  Perfect Strangers (1983)

DIZDARI, LIMOS
  Beni Walks by Himself (1985)

DJAROT, EROS
  Under the Mosquito Net (1983)
  Ponirah Terpidana (1984)
  Bitter Coffee (1986)

D'LLA TORRE, CEDRICK
  Women of the Frontier (1987)

DOBBYN, DAVE
  Footrot Flats (1986)

DOBE, JOSEF
  Young Love (1934)

College Girl, The (1938)

DOBLE, VAINICA
You Alone (1984)
My General (1987)

DOBSON, DARYLL
Lou, Pat and Joe D. (1988)

DODD, J. DOUGLAS
Big Meat Eater (1982)
Walls (1984)

DODDS, DOROTHY
Undercover (1984)

DODSON, CHUCK
Angel of Vengeance (1987)

DOELLE, FRANZ
Viktor und Viktoria (1934)
Amphytrion (1935)
Royal Waltz, The (1936)
Hot Blood (1936)
Boccaccio (1936)

DOGAS, EUGENE
Pavlova (1984)
Wild Wind, The (1986)

DOKKEN, DON
Nightmare on Elm Street 3:
    Dream Warriors, A (1987)

DOKOUPIL, TOM
Pankow '95 (1984)

DOLAN, DES
Don't Open Till Christmas
    (1984)

DOLBY, THOMAS
Fever Pitch (1985)
Gothic (1986)

DOLDINGER, KLAUS
Negresco (1968)
Boat, The (1981)
Comeback (1983)
Love Is Forever (1983)
Roarin' Fifties, The (1983)

Neverending Story, The
    (1984)
Father's Revenge, A (1988)
Otto Spalt ... for Instance
    (1988)

DOLGAY, MARVIN
Eternal Evil (1988)

DOME, ZSOLT
Anna (1981)
Midnight Rehearsal (1983)
Diary (1984)
Land of Miracles (1984)
Picture Hunters, The (1986)
Diary for My Lovers (1987)

DOMINA, FRITZ
Family on Parade (1937)

DOMINGO, PEDRO LUIS
Kargus (1981)

DOMINGUEZ, PAUL
Hopscotch (1985)

DOMINIQUE, CARL-AXEL
Sweden for the Swedes (1980)

DOMINIQUE, MONICA
Love (1980)
Little Klas in the Trunk
    (1984)

DOMONEY, MARK
Poker Face (1986)

DOMPIERRE, FRANCOIS
O.K. ... Laliberte (1981)
Blood of Others, The (1984)
Mario (1984)
Alley Cat (1985)
In the Last Resort (1987)
Kid Brother, The (1987)
Revolving Doors (1988)

DONAGGIO, PINO
Haunts (Veil, The) (1976)
Whispers in the Dark (1976)
Venetian Black (1978)
Beyond Evil (1980)
Dressed to Kill (1980)

Augh! Augh! (1980)
Desideria, La Vita Interiore
    (1980)
Howling, The (1981)
Fan, The (1981)
Blow Out (1981)
Tex (1982)
Beyond the Door (1982)
Death in the Vatican (1982)
Target Eagle (1982)
Street of Mirrors (1983)
Hercules (1983)
Hercules II (1983)
Over the Brooklyn Bridge
    (1984)
Black Cat, The (1984)
Ordeal by Innocence (1984)
Body Double (1984)
Nothing Left to Do But Cry
    (1985)
Attention (1985)
Deja Vu (1985)
Berlin Affair, The (1985)
Nothing Underneath (1985)
Crawlspace (1986)
15 Pounds in 7 Days (1986)
Fifth Missile, The (1986)
Moro Affair, The (1986)
Barbarians, The (1987)
Dancers (1987)
Hotel Colonial (1987)
Jenatsch (1987)
Appointment with Death
    (1988)
Catacombs (1988)
High Frequency (1988)
Kansas (1988)
Zelly and Me (1988)

DONAHUE, MARC
    Murphy's Law (1986)

DONALD, KEITH
    Fords on Water (1983)

DONNER, OTTO
    Castle, The (1986)

DONNET, CHRISTOPHER
    Paris Midnight (1986)

DONOHUE, JERRY AND MARC
    Who Dares Win? (1982)

DONOHUE, MARC
    Opposing Force (1987)

DONTCHEV, KIRIL
    Yo-Ho-Ho (1981)
    Last Wishes (1983)
    For a Young Lady and Her
        Male Companions (1984)
    Forget That Case (1986)
    Where Are You Going? (1986)
    Where Do We Go From Here?
        (1988)

D'ORARO, JEAN LOUIS
    Venus (1984)

DORE, JEAN
    French Without Dressing
        (1965)

DORFF, STEVE
    Gavilan (1982)
    Honkytonk Man (1982)
    Waltz Across Texas (1983)
    Rustler's Rhapsody (1985)
    My Sister Sam (1986)
    Back to the Beach (1987)
    Infidelity (1987)
    Mabel and Max (1987)
    Oldest Rookie, The (1987)
    Quick and the Dead, The
        (1987)
    Murphy Brown (1988)
    My Best Friend is a Vampire
        (1988)
    Too Young the Hero (1988)

DORISSE, CHRISTIAN
    Cache, The (1983)

DOROUGH, BOB
    Fat Angels (1980)

DORSAY, J. P.
    Blood Rose (1971)

DOUCET, MICHAEL
    Belzaire the Cajun (1986)

DOUGLAS, ALAN
Where's Poppa? (1979)

DOUGLAS, JOHNNY
Brides of Fu Manchu (1966)
Pandemonium (1982)
Dungeons and Dragons (1983)

DOUGLAS, SAM
Enter the Devil (1971)

DOWNES, JULIA
Man for All Seasons, A (1988)

DOYLE, ROGER
Pigs (1984)

DOZIER, LAMONT
That's My Mama (1974)
Nevada Smith (1975)

DRAGUTESCU, MIHAI
Anti-Clock (1980)

DRAKE, ELIZABETH
Kemira: Diary of a Strike
(1984)

DRAKE, OLIVER
Mummy's Curse, The (1944)

DRAND, JEAN-HECTOR
Emergency (1985)

DRASNIN, ROBERT
Lost in Space (1965)
Time Tunnel, The (1966)
Picture Mommy Dead (1966)
Mission: Impossible (1966)
Bracken's World (1969)
Daughter of the Mind (1969)
They Call It Murder (1969)
Crowhaven Farm (1970)
Old Man Who Cried Wolf,
The (1970)
Cannon (1971)
Dead Men Tell No Tales
(1971)
Dr. Cook's Garden (1971)
Longstreet (1971)
Murder Once Removed (1971)

Taste of Evil, A (1971)
Tattered Web, A (1971)
They Call It Murder (1971)
Jigsaw (1972)
Heist, The (1972)
Night of Terror (1972)
Wheeler and Murdoch (1973)
Bronk (1975)
Joe Forrester (1975)
Serpico (1976)
Crisis in Mid-Air (1979)
Runaways, The (1979)
Hobson's Choice (1983)
Illusions (1983)
Chase (1985)
Who Is Julia? (1986)
My Dissident Mom (1987)
Secret Witness (1988)

DRAZAN, PAVEL
House for Two, A (1988)

DREAU, JEAN-PAUL
Souvenirs, Souvenirs (1984)

DREITH, DENNIS
Fantasic World of D. C.
Collins, The (1984)
Daniel & the Towers (1987)
Party Camp (1987)
Goddess of Love, The (1988)

DRESS, MICHAEL
Mind of Mr. Soames, The
(1969)

DREYFUS, GEORGE
Tender Mercies (1982)
Fringe Dwellers, The (1986)

DRIVER, NICK
Callahan (1982)

D'RIVERA, PAQUITO
Other Cuba, The (1985)

DROYSEN, WOLF
Horoscope of the Hesselbach
Family (1956)

DRUZDOWICZ, JOANNA
Vagabond (1985)

DUARTE, ROGERIO
    Age of the Earth, The
        (1980)

DUBE, NORMAND
    Great Land of Small, The
        (1987)
    Tadpole and the Whale (1988)

DUBIN, JOSEPH
    Ghost Goes Wild, The (1947)

DUBOIS, JA'NET
    Jeffersons, The (1975)

DUCHESNE, ANDRE
    Passiflora (1986)

DUDLEY, ANNE
    Hiding Out (1987)
    Buster (1988)

DUFFIELD, ANDREW
    Plains of Heaven, The
        (1982)

DUGNAY, RAOUL
    Wild Flowers (1982)

DUHAMEL, ANTOINE
    Secret World, The (1969)
    Singapore, Singapore (1969)
    Deathwatch (1980)

DUISSON, BERNARD
    Day by Day (1981)

DUMAS, ROGER
    Devil's Hand, The (1946)

DUMITRESCU, ANCA
    Girl's Tear, A (1981)

DUN, TAN
    Pickles Make Me Cry (1988)

DUNAYEVSKY, ISAAC O.
    Moscow Laughs (1935)
    Red Village, The (1935)
    Greater Promise, The (1936)
    Beethoven Concerto (1937)

Country Bride, The (1938)
Captain Grant's Children
    (1939)
Volga Volga (1941)
Tanya (1942)
Variety Stars (1955)

DUNCAN, TREVOR
    Quatermass and the Pit (1958)
    A for Andromeda (1961)
    Jetee, La (1963)

DUNDAS, DAVID
    Withnail and I (1987)

DUNING, GEORGE
    Singin' in the Corn (1946)
    Down to Earth (1947)
    Between Midnight and Dawn
        (1950)
    Assignment--Paris (1952)
    Star Trek (1966)
    Time Tunnel (1966)
    Then Came Bronson (1969)
    But I Don't Want to Get
        Married! (1970)
    Most Deadly Game, The (1970)
    Partridge Family, The (1970)
    Quarantined (1970)
    House That Wouldn't Die,
        The (1970)
    Shameful Secrets of Hastings
        Corners, The (1970)
    Silent Force, The (1970)
    Black Noon (1971)
    Getting Together (1971)
    Yuma (1971)
    Climb an Angry Mountain
        (1972)
    Great American Tragedy, A
        (1972)
    Woman Hater, The (1972)
    Honor Thy Father (1973)
    Abduction of Saint Anne,
        The (1975)
    Father Knows Best: Home
        for Christmas (1977)
    Father Knows Best Reunion
        (1977)
    Child of Glass (1978)
    Dream Merchants, The (1980)

Man with Bogart's Face, The
(1980)
Top of the Hill (1980)
Goliath Awaits (1981)
Zorro and Son (1983)
Beyond Witch Mountain
(1983)

DUNLAP, PAUL
How to Make a Monster (1958)
Angry Red Planet, The (1959)
Desire in the Dust (1960)
Dimension 5 (1966)
Cyborg 2087 (1966)

DUNNE, JAMES P.
Nothing in Common (1987)

DUNNE, MICHAEL
Outside Chance (1978)

DUNNE, MURPHY
Loose Shoes (1981)

DUNSTEDTER, EDDIE
Donovan's Brain (1953)

DUPERE, RENE
Anne Trister (1986)

DUPRAT, ROGERIO
Brazil Year 2000 (1970)
Daughters of Fire (1978)
That Damned Meat (1985)
Love Strange Love (1985)

DU PREZ, JOHN
Bullshot (1983)
Oxford Blues (1984)
Private Function, A (1984)
She'll Be Wearing Pink
Pajamas (1985)
Once Bitten (1985)
Love With the Perfect
Stranger (1986)
Fish Called Wanda, A (1988)

DURAN, JOSEPH MARIA
Catalan Cuckold (1980)
Grass Recruits (1981)

DURAN, NAFER
Time to Die, A (1985)

"DURAN DURAN"
Three to Get Ready (1988)

DURAN-LORIGA, JACOBO
Nursemaid Mine (1987)

DURAND, PAUL
Casino de Paris (1957)

DURBET, THEIRRY
Man in the Top Hat, The
(1983)

DURTYANG, PHRA CHEN
King of the White Elephants
(1941)

DUTILLEUX, HENRI
Under the Sun of Satan
(1987)

DUTJER, HAINER
Doll, The (1983)

DUTRONC, JACQUES
Jocondes, Les (1982)

DUTT, GYAN
Music of Govind (1947)

DUTTA, K.
Devotee to the God (1955)

DUTTON, DOUGLAS
Young Lives (1981)

DYER, BILL
Dorothy (1979)

DYNE, A. Z.
Eden Miseria (1988)

DZIERLATKA, ARIE
My American Uncle (1980)
Provinciale, La (1980)
Light Years, The (1981)
Syncopated Time (1982)
Death of Mario Ricci,

The (1983)
Ghost Valley, The (1987)

EARL, DAVID
Kipperbang (1984)

EARLEY, ROBERT
Special Branch (1976)

"EARLY KOOKAS, THE"
Dirt Cheap (1986)

EASDALE, BRIAN
Miracle in Soho (1957)
Peeping Tom (1960)

EASTO, BARBARA
"S" Day, The (1984)

EATON, WILLIAM
Angel Levine, The (1970)

EBBINGHOUSE, BERNARD
We Shall See (1964)
Naked Evil (1966)

EBERT, HANS
Green Emperor, The (1939)

ECA, LUIZ
100% Brazilian Film, A (1987)

ECHEVARRIA, NICOLAS
Day Pedro Infante Died,
The (1984)

ECKE, JUERGEN
Strange Love (1984)

ECKERT-LUNDIN, E.
Affairs of a Model (1952)

ECKSTEIN, GARY
Growing Pains (1980)

ECONOMOU, NICOLAS
German Sisters, The (1981)
Final Call (1984)
Chekhov in My Life (1985)
Rosa Luxemburg (1986)

EDANDER, GUNNAR
Mamma (1982)
Beyond Sorrow, Beyond Pain
(1984)
Moa (1987)

EDDA
Final Exam (1981)

EDELMAN, RANDY
Blood Sport (1973)
Snatched (1973)
Ryan's Four (1983)
When Your Lover Leaves
(1983)
Doctor's Story, A (1984)
MacGyver (1985)
Mr. Sunshine (1986)
Family Again, A (1988)
Feds (1988)
Twins (1988)

EDGARDT, KNUT
Pimpernel Svensson (1953)

"EDGE, THE"
Captive (1986)

EDMONDS, DAVE
Porky's Revenge (1985)

EDQUIST, BENGT
I Am Maria (1980)

EDWARDS, BERNARD
Soup for One (1982)

EDWARDS, ROSS
Phobia (1988)

EGERBLAHD, BERND
Peter No-Tail (1982)
Peter No-Tail in America
(1985)

EGGEN, CHRISTIAN
Beginning of a Story, The
(1988)

EGNER, TORBJORN
Folks and Robbers of Carda-
mon City (1988)

EHLER, JUAN
Mysterious Uncle Silas (1947)
Nacha Regules (1950)
Native Son (1951)
Black Vampire, The (1953)
Prisoner 1.040 (1959)
Black Vampire, The (1981)

EICHHORN, BERNHARD
Film Without a Name, The
(1950)
Seven Journeys (1951)
House of Life (1953)
Dark Star, The (1955)
Schinderhannes, Der (1959)
Paradise and Fire Oven (1959)

EIDEL, PHILIPPE
Thousand and One Daisies,
A (1986)

EIDELMAN, CLIFF
Silent Night (1988)

EIEE, LAM MAN
I Do (1983)

EILERSTEN, ODD A.
Pirates, The (1983)

EINAUDI, LUDOVICO
Milk Train (1988)

EINEGG, ERICH
Somewhere in Berlin (1949)

EINHORN, RICHARD
Shock Waves (Death Corps)
(1975)
Don't Go in the House (1980)
Eyes of a Stranger (1981)
Prowler, The (1981)
Dead of Winter (1987)
Nightmare at Shadow Woods
(1987)
Sister, Sister (1987)
Necessary Parties (1988)

EISBRENNER, WERNER
Higher Command (1936)
Berliner Ballade (1949)
Wonderful Times (1951)

Johnny Saves Nebrador (1953)
Confession Under Four Eyes
(1954)
Prisoner of Love (1954)
Children, Mother and a
General (1955)
Rate, The (1955)
Last Man, The (1956)
Before Sundown (1956)
Departure for the Clouds
(1959)
I'll Carry You on My Hands
(1959)
Last Witness, The (1961)

EISEMANN, MICHAEL
Minister's Friend, The (1939)

EISLER, HANNS
Hell on Earth (1934)
Abdul the Damned (1936)
Song of the Streets (1939)
Pete Roleum and His Cousins
(1939)
400 Million, The (1939)
Our Daily Bread (1950)
Herr Puntila and His
Chauffeur Matti (1957)

EKHADI, ANDERS
Swedish Mess (1986)

EL CHERII, AMMAR
Stan's Empire (1986)

EL-QARAGHOOLI, TALIB
Sniper, The (1980)

EL RIWANE, NASS see
RIWANE, NASS EL

EL SOUD, HASSAN ABU see
SOUD, HASSAN ABU EL

EL WADI, SOULHI
Sun on a Hazy Day, The
(1986)

"ELECTRA NOVA"
Hell Raiders (1983)

"ELEPHANT'S MEMORY"
  Take-Off (1978)

ELFERS, KONRAD
  Dr. Mabuse der Spieler
    (1922)
  Metropolis (1926)
  Anita--Dances of Vice (1987)

ELFMAN, DANNY
  Pee-Wee's Big Adventure (1985)
  Back to School (1986)
  Fast Times (1986)
  Wisdom (1986)
  Summer School (1987)
  Beetlejuice (1988)
  Big Top Pee-wee (1988)
  Hot to Trot (1988)
  Midnight Run (1988)
  Scrooged (1988)

ELIAS, JONATHAN
  Children of the Corn (1984)
  Almost You (1984)
  Tuff Turf (1984)
  Vamp (1986)
  Shakedown (1988)
  Two Moon Junction (1988)

ELIN, HANNS
  Lambert Is Threatened (1949)
  Hellish Love (1949)

ELINOR, CARLI
  Surrender (1931)

ELIZALDE, JOHN
  Streets of San Francisco,
    The (1972)
  Barnaby Jones (1973)
  Caribe (1975)
  Bert D'Angelo/Superstar
    (1976)
  City, The (1977)
  Winner Take All (1977)
  Runaways, The (1979)
  Death Ray 2000 (1981)

ELIZONDO, RAFAEL
  Nana (1985)
  Chicano Connection, The
    (1986)

ELLINGER, KARL
  Parodontosis Now (1984)

ELLINGER, MARK
  Thundercrack! (1975)

ELLINGTON, DUKE
  Jonas (1957)
  Rough Cut (1980)

ELLIOT, CLINTON
  Hall of Kings (1968)

ELLIOT, DON
  Atomic Power Today (1967)
  Transportation USA (1967)
ELLIOTT, DEAN
  Fantastic Four, The (1967)
  Return to the Planet of the
    Apes (1975)
  Fang Face (1978)
  What's New, Mr. Magoo?
    (1978)
  Plasticman Comedy/Adventure
    Show, The (1979)
  Heathcliff and Dingbat Show,
    The (1980)
  Thundarr the Barbarian (1980)
  Beauty and the Beast (1983)
  Mr. T (1983)
  Rubik, the Amazing Cube
    (1983)
  Chipmunk Reunion, A (1985)

ELLIOTT, DICK
  Curiosity Shop, The (1971)

ELLIOTT, JACK
  Bracken's World (1969)
  Three for Tahiti (1970)
  Feminist and the Fuzz, The
    (1971)
  Good Life, The (1971)
  New Dick Van Dyke Show,
    The (1971)
  Banacek (1972)
  Honeymoon Suite (1972)
  Playmates (1972)
  Rookies, The (1972)
  Bait, The (1973)
  Birds of Prey (1973)

Hijack! (1973)
Jarrett (1973)
Lotsa Luck (1973)
Man Without a Country, The
    (1973)
Police Story (1973)
What Are Best Friends For?
    (1973)
Ann in Blue (1974)
Cry Panic (1974)
Get Christie Love! (1974)
Girl Who Came Gift-Wrapped,
    The (1974)
Only With Married Men (1974)
Red Badge of Courage, The
    (1974)
Roll, Freddy, Roll! (1974)
Bobby Parker and Company
    (1974)
Barney Miller (1975)
Big Eddie (1975)
Montefuscos, The (1975)
Starsky and Hutch (1975)
Charlie's Angels (1976)
Gibbsville (1976)
Heck's Angels (1976)
Big Hawaii (1977)
Busting Loose (1977)
Danger in Paradise (1977)
Delta County, U.S.A. (1977)
Husbands and Wives (1977)
Fish (1977)
Magnificent Magnet of Santa
    Mesa, The (1977)
Roger and Harry: The
    Mitera Target (1977)
Comedy Shop, The (1978)
A.E.S. Hudson Street (1978)
Free Country (1978)
Funny World of Fred and
    Bunni, The (1978)
Guide for the Married Woman,
    A (1978)
Husbands, Wives and Lovers
    (1978)
Joe and Valerie (1978)
Good Ol' Boys (1979)
House Calls (1979)
Piper's Pets (1979)
Solitary Man, The (1979)
Sanctuary of Fear (1979)
Three Wives of David Wheeler,

The (1979)
Turnabout (1979)
G.I.'s (1980)
Ladies' Man (1980)
Nobody's Perfect (1980)
Toni's Boys (1980)
United States (1980)
Mr. and Mrs. Dracula (1980)
Don't Look Back (1981)
Park Place (1981)
Quick and Quiet (1981)
Ride and Shine (1981)
Computerside (1982)
Nine to Five (1982)
Day the Bubble Burst, The
    (1982)
At Ease (1983)
Found Money (1983)
Great Day (1983)
Venice Medical (1983)
Earthlings, The (1984)
Keeping Up with the Joneses
    (1984)
Night Court (1984)
Wildside (1985)
Lucy Arnaz Show, The (1985)
Joe Bash (1986)
Spies, Lies & Naked Thighs
    (1988)

ELLIOTT, PETER J.
    Doctor Maniac (1976)

ELLIOTT, RICHARD
    Coverup: Behind the Iran
        Contra Affair (1988)

ELLIS, DON
    In Tandem (1974)
    Deadly Tower, The (1975)
    Doctors Hospital (1975)
    Spiderman (1978)

ELLIS, MARC
    Bimini Code (1985)
    Assault of the Killer Bimbos
        (1988)

ELLIS, RAY
    Grand Jury (1960)

Nowhere to Hide (1977)
Thunder (1977)
Sweet Sixteen (1983)
Bedrooms (1984)

ELLSTEIN, ABE
Mamele (1939)

ELMS, ALBERT
Satellite in the Sky (1956)
Man Without a Body, The (1957)
Ambush at Devil's Cap (1966)
Champions, The (1967)
Omegans, The (1967)

ELMS, VIC
Space: 1999 (1975)

ELOI, JEAN-CLAUDE
Francois Reichenbach's Japan (1983)

ELORZA, JOSE
One Among Many (1982)
Love Around the Corner (1986)

EMBER, FERNANDO
Opera Prima (1980)
Neighbors (1981)

EMENEGGER, ROBERT
UFO's: It Has Begun (1976)

EMER, MICHEL
Carrefour (1938)
Man of the Hour (1940)

EMERSON, KEITH
Inferno (1980)
Nighthawks (1981)

EMILIANO, ANTONIO
Reporter X (1986)
Play ... Boy (1987)

EMMETT, RICHARD
Hour of the Assassin (1987)

EMRYS-ROBERTS, KENYON
Count Dracula (1978)

ENDER, MATTHEW
Streetwalkin' (1985)
Devastator, The (1986)

ENESCU, ADRIAN
Chained Justice (1983)
Orientation Course (Concurs) (1983)
Fatally Wounded for Love of Life (1984)
Adela (1985)
Last Assault, The (1987)

ENGEL, CLAUDE
Schoolmaster, The (1981)

ENGELBERGER, WILLI
I Am Longing for You (1936)

ENGIN, ESIN
My Dream, My Love and You (1988)

ENGLAND, JOHN
Mad About You (1988)

ENGLISH, JON
Against the Wind (1979)
Bell Diamond (1987)

ENGSTROM, CHARLES
Flash of Green, A (1984)

ENO, BRIAN
Land of the Minotaur (1977)
Jubilee (1978)
Egon Schiele--Excess and Punishment (1981)
Plainsong (1982)
Same As It Ever Was (1983)
SL-1 (1983)
Mischief (1984)
Heat and Sunlight (1987)

ENRIQUEZ, MANUEL
Oficio de Tinieblas (1980)

EOTVOSS, PETER
Thorn Under the Fingernail, A (1988)

EPSTEIN, JEP
  Tragic Earthquake in
    Mexico (1987)

ERAS, JORGES
  Mexico in Flames (1982)

ERBE, JOHN
  Utilities (1983)

ERBE, MICKEY
  Tell Me My Name (1977)
  Kelly (1981)
  Improper Channels (1981)
  Ticket to Heaven (1981)
  Threshold (1981)
  Hard Feelings (1982)
  Abortion: Stories from
    North and South (1985)
  Lost! (1986)
  Milk and Honey (1988)

ERDMANN, GUNTHER
  Girl with the Horse, The
    (1982)

ERDMANN, HANS
  Nosferatu (1922)
  Testament of Dr. Mabuse,
    The (1932)
  King August the Strong
    (1937)

ERFURT, GUNTHER
  Hell's Kitchen (1983)

ERGUNER, KUDAI
  Born of Fire (1987)

ERIKSSON, CLAES
  Leif (1987)

ERKIN, ARIF
  Elegie (1981)
  Mill, The (1987)

ERNRYD, BENGT
  I'm Blushing (1981)

ERRERA, NICOLAS
  Paulette (1986)

ERWIN, LEE
  Hotel New York (1984)

ERWIN, RALPH
  Storm Over Asia (1938)

ESCHMAN, LUDWIG
  Skin of the Fool (1982)

ESCOBAR, AMEDEO
  Duchess of Parma, The (1937)
  I've Lost My Husband (1937)

ESCOLAR, L. GOMEZ
  Adventures of Enrique and
    Ana, The (1981)

ESCUDERO, FRANCISCO
  10 Ready Rifles (1959)

ESEGE, CARLOS
  Clandestine Destinies (1988)

ESKEW, JACK
  Banana Splits Adventure
    Hour, The (1968)
  That's My Mama (1974)
  Stunt Seven (1979)
  Supercarrier (1988)

ESPERON, MANUEL
  He Who Died of Love (1945)
  Siren's Song (1948)
  Death in Love (1950)
  Red Rain (1950)
  Little Love of My Life (1952)
  Mad Woman, The (1952)
  Beautiful Dreamer, The
    (1953)
  Anxiety (1954)
  School for Vagabonds (1955)
  Watch Out for Love (1955)
  Music School (1956)
  Woman and the Beast, The
    (1958)
  Que Linda Cha Cha Cha!
    (1958)
  Phantom of the Operetta, The
    (1960)
  Chip on the Shoulder (1960)
  Juana Gallo (1961)

Long Live Jalisco, Land of
  My Birth (1961)
My Name Is Gatillo (1987)

ESPOSITO, TONY
  Ballad of Eve, The (1986)
  Camorra (1986)

ESQUIVEL, ALVARO
  Eulalia (1987)

ESSLINGER, PAUL
  ... And If We Don't Want
    To (1981)
  Firm Forever, A (1984)

ESTY, BOB
  Galactic Gigolo (1988)
  You Can't Hurry Love (1988)

ETCHEMENDI, MARCELO
  Invitation, The (1982)

ETOLL, ROBERT
  Danger Zone, The (1987)
  Vampire at Midnight (1988)

"EURYTHMICS, THE"
  Brand New Day (1987)

EVANS, LINDLEY
  Uncivilized (1936)

EVANS, MARTIN
  Giro City (1982)

EVERS, JOERG
  Night of the Wolves (1982)
  Bolero (1983)
  Carpet Change (1984)

"EXTRABREIT"
  Wild Bunch (1983)

EYK, TONNY
  Flying Without Wings (1977)
  Fighting for Two (1982)
  Maria (1986)
  Thomas and Senior on the
    Track of Barend the
    Brute (1986)

FABER, PETER
  Cool Lakes of Death, The
    (1982)

FABICH, RANIER
  Night of the Marten, The
    (1988)

FABREGAS, JAIME
  Boatman, The (1984)
  Private Show (1985)
  Revenge for Justice (1985)

FABRICIUS-BJERRE, BENT
  Med Kaerlig Hilsen (1971)
  Wobbly Waltz, The (1981)
  Olsen Gang Jumps the Fence,
    The (1981)
  Olsen Gang Over the Hill,
    The (1981)
  Pinchcliffe Grand Prix (1981)
  My Granny's House (1984)
  Peter von Scholten (1987)

FADEL, NOUTIL
  Mr. Fabre's Mill (1986)

FAGEN, DONALD
  Bright Lights, Big City (1988)

FAI, JOSEPH KOO KAI
  Holy Robe of the Shaolin
    Temple, The (1985)

FAI, LAW WING
  Dream Lovers (1986)

FAIR, JANE
  Taking Care (1987)

FAITH, PERCY
  Virginian, The (1962)

FAKHRI, ADLI
  Occupied Palestine (1981)

FALCAO, FERNANDO
  I'm Not Living With You
    Anymore (1983)

FALCK, MICHAEL
  Murder in the Dark (1986)

FALCONI, TERRI
  Whacked Out (1981)

FALK, CHARLES
  Leif (1987)

FALL, RICHARD
  Liliom (1930)

FALTERMEYER, HAROLD
  Didi and His Double (1984)
  Thief of Hearts (1984)
  Beverly Hills Cop (1984)
  Fletch (1985)
  Top Gun (1986)
  Beverly Hills Cop II (1987)
  Fatal Beauty (1987)
  Running Man, The (1987)

"FANCY"
  Cemil (1987)

FANSHAWE, DAVID
  Flambards, The (1980)
  Here Are Ladies (1983)

FARBERMAN, HAROLD
  Art Scene USA (1967)

FAREEDUDDIN, ZIA
  Rising from the Surface
    (1981)

FARERRO, PAUL
  Nights in White Satin (1987)

FARIS, ALEXANDER
  Upstairs, Downstairs (1974)

FARISELLI, PATRIZIO
  Foxtrap (1986)

FARKAS, FERENC
  Bitter Truth, The (1986)

FARKAS, IMRE
  Queen's Hussar, The (1936)

FARNON, ROBERT
  Elizabeth of Ladymead (1949)
  Maytime in Mayfair (1949)
  Circle of Danger (1951)
  All for Mary (1956)
  True as a Turtle (1957)
  Sheriff of Fractured Jaw,
    The (1959)
  Mary and Joseph: A Story
    of Faith (1979)
  Man Called Intrepid, A (1979)
  Bear Island (1980)
  Friend or Foe (1982)

FARRAR, ROBERT (BOB)
  Don't Look in the Basement
    (1973)
  Play Dead (1986)

FARRELL, MIKE
  Leading Edge, The (1987)

FARRELL, WES
  Sigmund and the Sea
    Monsters (1973)

FARROW, LARRY
  Archie (1976)

FASCINATO, JACK
  Kukla, Fran and Ollie (1948)
  Skyhawks, The (1969)

FASLA, JAWAD
  Citadel, The (1988)

FATAAR, RICKY
  High Tide (1987)

FATAS, LUIS
  Swallow It, Dog (1981)
  Hint of a Crime, The (1988)

FAURE, JOHN
  Baton Rouge (1985)

FEBRE, LOUIS
  Code Name: Zebra (1987)

FEBRING, JOHANNES
  It Goes Better with Rasp-
    berry Juice (1960)

"THE FEELIES"
  Smithereens (1982)

FEHRING, JOHANNES
  Ideal Woman Sought (1952)
  Dear Family (1957)

FEINGOLD, FONDA
  Blue Heaven (1985)

FEKARIS, DINO
  Sugar Hill (Voodoo Girl)
    (1974)

FELDER, DON
  Fleshburn (1984)
  Blue DeVille (1986)

FELDMAN, JACK
  Unicorn Tales (1977)

FELDMAN, NICK see CHUNG,
  WANG

FELICIANO, JOSE
  Chico and the Man (1974)
  Love at First Sight (1980)

FEMERIA, RAMON
  Only a Coffin (1966)

"FEMSESSION BERLIN"
  Depart to Arrive (1982)

FENN, RICK
  White of the Eye (1987)

FENTON, GEORGE
  Hussy (1980)
  Gandhi (1982)
  Parole (1982)
  Runners (1983)
  Englishman Abroad, An
    (1983)
  Saigon--Year of the Cat
    (1983)
  Company of Wolves, The
    (1984)
  Jewel in the Crown, The
    (1984)
  Past Caring (1985)

Clockwise (1986)
Loving Walter (1986)
Call Me Mister (1987)
Cry Freedom (1987)
84 Charing Cross Road
  (1987)
White Mischief (1987)
Dangerous Liaisons (1988)
Dressmaker, The (1988)
Handful of Dust, A (1988)
High Spirits (1988)

FENYES, SZABOLES
  Romance of Ida (1934)
  Premiere (1937)
  Sister Maria (1937)
  Five-Forty (1939)
  Istvan Bors (1939)
  Circus Maximus (1981)
  Witness, A (1981)
  Insult, The (1983)
  Lily in Love (1985)

FERGUSON, ALLYN
  Three for Tahiti (1970)
  Good Life, The (1971)
  Feminist and the Fuzz, The
    (1971)
  New Dick Van Dyke Show,
    The (1971)
  Banacek (1972)
  Every Man Needs One (1972)
  Honeymoon Suite (1972)
  Playmates (1972)
  Rookies, The (1972)
  Bait, The (1973)
  Birds of Prey (1973)
  Hijack! (1973)
  Jarrett (1973)
  Lotsa Luck (1973)
  Man Without a Country, The
    (1973)
  Police Story (1973)
  What Are Best Friends For?
    (1973)
  Ann in Blue (1974)
  Cry Panic (1974)
  Get Christie Love! (1974)
  Girl Who Came Gift-Wrapped,
    The (1974)
  Only With Married Men (1974)

Bobby Parker and Company
(1974)
Roll, Freddie, Roll! (1974)
Big Eddie (1975)
Count of Monte Cristo, The
(1975)
Barney Miller (1975)
Montefuscos, The (1975)
Starsky and Hutch (1975)
Charlie's Angels (1976)
Gibbsville (1976)
Heck's Angels (1976)
Big Hawaii (1977)
Busting Loose (1977)
Captains Courageous (1977)
Danger in Paradise (1977)
Delta County U.S.A. (1977)
Fish (1977)
Husbands and Wives (1977)
Magnificent Magnet of Santa
Mesa, The (1977)
Roger and Harry: The
Mitera Target (1977)
Man in the Iron Mask, The
(1977)
Comedy Shop, The (1978)
Four Feathers, The (1978)
Free Country (1978)
Funny World of Fred and
Bunni, The (1978)
A.E.S. Hudson Street (1978)
Guide for the Married Woman,
A (1978)
Husbands, Wives and Lovers
(1978)
Joe and Valerie (1978)
Miserables, Les (1978)
All Quiet on the Western
Front (1979)
Good Ol' Boys (1979)
House Calls (1979)
Piper's Pets (1979)
Sanctuary of Fear (1979)
Three Wives of David
Wheeler, The (1979)
Turnabout (1979)
Beulah Land (1980)
Gossip Columnist, The
(1980)
Cry of the Innocent (1980)
Nobody's Perfect (1980)
Pleasure Palace (1980)

Tale of Two Cities, A (1980)
Toni's Boys (1980)
Little Lord Fauntleroy (1980)
Big Bend Country (1981)
Elvis and the Beauty Queen
(1981)
Peter and Paul (1981)
Red Flag: The Ultimate Game
(1981)
Terror Among Us (1981)
Strike Force (1981)
Computerside (1982)
Ivanhoe (1982)
Master of the Game (1984)
Camille (1984)
Keeping Up with the Joneses
(1984)
Corsican Brothers, The
(1985)
Last Days of Patton, The
(1986)
Stone Fox (1987)
April Morning (1988)
Woman He Loved, The (1988)

FERGUSON, JAY
Deadly Passion (1985)
Patriot, The (1986)
Quiet Cool (1986)
Best Seller (1987)
Bad Dreams (1988)
Johnny Be Good (1988)
License to Drive (1988)
Pancho Barnes (1988)
Pulse (1988)

FERGUSON, STEPHEN
Practice of Love, The (1985)

FERNANDEZ, CARLOS
Last Broomete, The (1984)

FERNANDO, SARATH
Way of the Lotus, The
(1987)
Witness to a Killing (1987)

FERRANTE, RUSSELL
Wired to Kill (1986)

FERRARA, FRANCO
Americans on Everest (1968)

FERRARI, LUC
  Chronopolis (1982)

FERRARO, RALPH
  Scandal, The (1966)
  Bender (1979)
  Riding for the Pony Express
    (1980)

FERRE, MARIO
  Owners of the Sun, The
    (1987)

FERRER, NINO
  Litan (1982)

FERRERO, LORENZO
  Anemia (1986)

FERRI, CONSTANTINO
  Brief Rapture (1952)

FERRICK, BILLY
  Space Rage (1987)

FERRIO, GIANNI
  Black Box Affair, The (1966)
  Guyrado (1966)
  For a Few Dollars More (1966)
  Ringo and Gringo Against
    All (1966)
  I'm Getting a Yacht (1981)
  Tex and the Lord of the
    Deep (1985)

FERRIS, PAUL
  Terror of Sheba, The (1975)

FERRO, RAFAEL
  Waiting for Daddy (1980)

FERRY, BRIAN
  Looping (1981)

FESSLER, EDWARD I.
  Bayou (1957)

FEUER, CY
  King of the Royal Mounted
    (1940)

Jungle Girl (1941)
Dick Tracy vs. Crime
  Incorporated (1941)

FEVERRIGEL, BERNARDO
  Closed Case (1985)

FEYER, GEORGE
  Exception to the Rule (1937)

FIDENCO, NICO
  For the Taste of Killing (1966)
  2 + 5: Mission Hydra (1966)
  Slave of Paradise, The (1968)
  Colossal (1971)
  Ypotron--The Final Count-
    down (1972)
  Emmanuelle and the Last
    Cannibals (1977)
  Queen of the Cannibals (1979)

FIEDEL, BRAD
  Mayflower: The Pilgrim's
    Adventure (1979)
  Playing for Time (1980)
  Hardhat and Legs (1980)
  Day the Women Got Even,
    The (1981)
  Just Before Dawn (1981)
  Night School (1981)
  Bunker, The (1981)
  Dream House (1981)
  People vs. Jean Harris (1981)
  Born Beautiful (1982)
  Dreams Don't Die (1982)
  Mae West (1982)
  Tucker's Witch (1982)
  Hit and Run (1982)
  Cocaine: One Man's Seduc-
    tion (1983)
  Girls of the White Orchid
    (1983)
  Heart of Steel (1983)
  Jacobo Timerman: Prisoner
    Without a Name, Cell
    Without a Number (1983)
  Murder in Coweta County
    (1983)
  Right of Way (1983)
  Anatomy of an Illness (1984)

Calendar Girl Murders, The
   (1984)
My Mother's Secret Life (1984)
When She Says No (1984)
Children in the Crossfire
   (1984)
High School U.S.A. (1984)
Eyes of Fire (1984)
Terminator, The (1984)
Three Wishes of Billy Grier
   (1984)
Fraternity Vacation (1985)
Fright Night (1985)
Compromising Positions (1985)
Into Thin Air (1985)
Midnight Hour, The (1985)
Desert Bloom (1985)
Big Easy, The (1986)
Fighting Choice (1986)
Of Pure Blood (1986)
Popeye Doyle (1986)
Second Serve (1986)
Sunday Drive (1986)
Under Siege (1986)
Bluffing It (1987)
Last Innocent Man, The
   (1987)
Let's Get Harry (1987)
Nowhere to Hide (1987)
Right to Die, The (1987)
Travelling Man (1987)
Accused, The (1988)
Fright Night Part 2 (1988)
Gambler (1988)
Hostage (1988)
Hot Paint (1988)
Midnight Caller (1988)
Serpent and the Rainbow,
   The (1988)
Weekend War (1988)

FIEDLER, JOSEF
   April 1, 2000 (1953)

FIEHN, ERIK
   Be Dear to Me (1957)

FIELDING, JERRY
   Life of Riley, The (1953)
   Bewitched (1964)
   Hogan's Heroes (1965)

Mission: Impossible (1966)
Tarzan (1966)
He and She (1967)
Good Guys, The (1968)
Governor and J.J., The
   (1969)
Hunters Are for Killing
   (1970)
Chicago Teddy Bears, The
   (1971)
Ellery Queen: Don't Look
   Behind You (1971)
McMillan and Wife (1971)
Inside O.U.T. (1971)
Once Upon a Dead Man (1971)
Bridget Loves Bernie (1972)
Wednesday Night Out (1972)
Madigan (1972)
Man in the Middle (1972)
Me and the Chimp (1972)
Snoop Sisters, The (1972)
War of Children, A (1972)
Diana (1973)
Faraday and Company (1973)
Kojak (1973)
Barnaby Jones (1973)
Shirts/Skins (1973)
Fools, Females and Fun
   (1974)
Honky Tonk (1974)
Night Stalker, The (1974)
Snoop Sisters, The (1974)
Unwed Father (1974)
Cage Without a Key (1975)
Cop and the Kid, The (1975)
Hustling (1975)
Matt Helm (1975)
On the Rocks (1975)
Bionic Woman, The (1976)
McMillan (1976)
I'll Never Forget What's Her
   Name (1976)
Andros Targets, The (1977)
Little Ladies of the Night
   (1977)
Lovey: A Circle of Children,
   Part II (1978)
W.E.B. (1978)
High Midnight (1979)
Mr. Horn (1979)

Below the Belt (1980)
Cries in the Night (1982)
Funeral Home (1982)

FIG, ANTON
King Blank (1983)

FIGGIS, MIKE
Stormy Monday (1988)

FIGIEL, PIOTR
Chance Meeting on the
Ocean (1980)

FIJAL, ANNE-MARIE
In Blood and Sand (1988)

FILHO, JAIME SILVA
Aniki-Bobo (1942)

FILIP, FRANK
City Park (1951)

FILIPPENKO, ANATOLI
Deer-Golden Antlers (1972)

FILIPPINI, GINO
Angelo in the Crowd (1952)
What Price Innocence? (1953)
Melody of Love (1954)

FILLEUL, PETER
Life and Loves of a She-
Devil, The (1986)

"FINE YOUNG CANNIBALS"
Tin Men (1987)

FINN, TIM
Les Patterson Saves the
World (1987)

FINSTON, NAT W.
Second Woman, The (1951)

FIORAVANTI, ETTORE
All That Rhythm (1984)

"FIRE HOUSE"
Kind of English, A (1986)

FIRTIC, A.
Story of an Unknown Man
(1980)

FISCHER, ALBERT
Hunter of Fall (1936)

FISCHER, GUENTHER
Hiding Place, The (1980)
Solo Sunny (1980)
King and His Fool, The (1981)
On Probation (1982)
Romance with Amelie (1982)
And Next Year at Balaton
(1982)
Held for Questioning (1983)
Research in Mark Branden-
burg (1983)
Stone River, The (1983)
Love Is Not an Argument
(1984)
Vagrants (Fariaho) (1984)
Chinese Boxes (1984)
Didi and the Revenge of the
Disinherited (1985)
Gruenstein's Clever Move
(1985)
Beaver Track, The (1985)
House on the River, The
(1986)
Time That Remains, The
(1986)
Bear-Skinned Man (1987)
Solo Sailor, The (1988)
Welcome to Germany (1988)

FISCHER, IVAN
Wagner (1983)

FISCHER, J. F.
Grandfather Automobile, The
(1957)

FISCHER, MARKUS
Leap from the Bridge, A
(1980)
Kaiser and One Night (1985)

FISER, LUBOS
On the Comet (1970)

Deadly Odor, The (1970)
Love Between the Raindrops
(1980)
Mysterious Castle in the
Carpathians (1981)
Serpent's Poison (1982)
Death of a Beautiful Dream
(1987)

FISH, PETER
Joint Custody: A New Kind
of Family (1984)

FISHBERG, DAVID
Bennett Brothers, The (1987)

"FISHBONE"
Tapeheads (1988)

FISHER, DAVE
B.J. and the Bear (1979)
Car Wash (1979)
First and Ten (1984)
Mr. Mom (1984)
Highwayman, The (1988)

FISHER, ELLIOTT
Invasion of the Star
Creatures (1962)

FISHER, HARVEY
My Mother, My Daughter
(1981)

FISHER, LAURA
ZEN--Zone of Expansion
North (1988)

FISHER, WILLIAM S.
Dark August (1975)

FITZSIMMONS, ROBERT
Radio Bikini (1987)

FLEBIG, FRANK
Cemil (1987)

FLOKE, BOB
Stitches (1985)

FLORES, MARCO
Camarena Taken Hostage
(1986)
City Rats (1987)
Together (1987)

FLOSMAN, OLDRICH
Romantic Story (1983)

FLOYD, DAVID
Wolfman--A Lycanthrope (1978)

"FLYING LESBIANS"
Power of Men Is the Patience
of Women, The (1980)

FLYNN, PIERRE
Caffe Italia (1985)

FOLIART, DAN
Angie (1979)
New Kind of Family, A (1979)
Blue Jeans (1980)
Bosom Buddies (1980)
Joanie Loves Chachi (1982)
New Odd Couple, The (1982)
One More Try (1982)
Oh, Madeline (1983)
Brothers (1984)
His and Hers (1984)
Johanna (1985)
Mary (1985)
In the Lion's Den (1987)

FOLK, ROBERT
Savage Harvest (1981)
Slayer, The (1982)
Police Academy (1984)
Purple Hearts (1984)
Bachelor Party (1984)
Police Academy 2: Their
First Assignment (1985)
Ask Max (1986)
Combat High (1986)
Legend of Sleepy Hollow,
The (1986)
Lily (1986)
Police Academy 3: Back in
Training (1986)
Prince of Bel Air (1986)

2-1/2 Dads (1986)
Can't Buy Me Love
  (1987)
High Mountain Rangers
  (1987)
Odd Jobs (1987)
Police Academy 4: Citizens
  on Patrol (1987)
Room Upstairs, The (1987)
Stewardess School (1987)
Glory Days (1988)
Miles from Home (1988)
Police Academy 5: Assign-
  ment Miami Beach (1988)

FOMAN, LOU
  Slime People, The (1963)

FONES, TONY
  Up the Creek (1958)

"FONO DOR"
  Domina--The Burden of
  Lust (1985)

FONTANA, PAUL
  Hot and Deadly (1981)

FORD, DWAYNE
  Deadline (1979)

FORESTIERI, LOUIS (LOU)
  Hot Moves (1984)
  Something About Love (1988)

FORLAI, ROMOLO
  Reincarnation of Isabel,
  The (1973)

FORMELL, JUAN
  Birds Will Fly (1985)

FORQUERAY, ANTOINE
  Marmalade Revolution, The
  (1980)

FORRELL, GENE
  Symmetry (1967)

FORSEY, KEITH
  Breakfast Club, The (1985)

FOSTER, DAVID
  St. Elmo's Fire (1985)
  Secret of My Success, The
  (1987)
  Fresh Horses (1988)
  Stealing Home (1988)

FOSTER, JOHN
  Love, Natalie (1980)

FOSTER, MIGUEL ANGEL
  Crab (1982)

FOUQUEY, JEAN-PIERRE
  Dandin (1988)

FOURNIER, MARTIN
  Mills of Power (Part I)
  (1988)

"FOURTH WALL REPERTORY
  COMPANY"
  We Are the Guinea Pigs
  (1981)

FOWLER, WALT
  Kamikaze Hearts (1986)

FOX, CHARLES
  Women Who Care (1968)
  Love, American Style (1969)
  Barefoot in the Park (1970)
  Bugaloos, The (1970)
  Nanny and the Professor
  (1970)
  Weekend Nun, The (1972)
  Women in Chains (1972)
  Dying Room Only (1973)
  Going Places (1973)
  Alpha Means Goodbye (1974)
  Stranger Within, The (1974)
  Legend of Valentino, The
  (1975)
  My Father's House (1975)
  New, Original Wonder Woman,
  The (1975)
  Laverne and Shirley (1976)
  Love Boat, The (1976)
  Newman's Drug Store (1976)
  Victory at Entebbe (1976)
  Wonder Woman (1976)

Blansky's Beauties (1977)
Love Boat, The (1977)
Love Boat II, The (1977)
Natural Look, The (1977)
Paper Chase, The (1978)
Rainbow (1978)
Better Late Than Never
    (1979)
Goodtime Girls (1980)
Little Darlings (1980)
Why Would I Lie? (1980)
Oh, God! Book II (1980)
Nine to Five (1980)
Six Pack (1982)
Zapped! (1982)
Love Child (1982)
Trenchcoat (1983)
It's Not Easy (1983)
Strange Brew (1983)
Family Secrets (1984)
Used Cars (1984)
Summer to Remember, A
    (1985)
Goodbye Charlie (1985)
National Lampoon's
    European Vacation (1985)
George Burns Comedy Week
    (1985)
Doin' Time (1985)
Betrayed by Innocence
    (1986)
Longshot, The (1986)
Maggie (1986)
Valerie (1986)
Burnin' Love (1987)
Christmas Comes to Willow
    Creek (1987)
Deep Dark Secrets (1987)
Good Morning, Miss Bliss
    (1987)
Parent Trap II, The (1987)
Baby M (1988)
Going to the Chapel (1988)
Short Circuit 2 (1988)

FOX, FRANK
    Beloved of the World (1949)

FOX, NEAL
    Happy Hour (1987)
    Return of the Killer Tomatoes
        (1988)

FOX, R. DONOVAN
    Georgia Peaches, The (1980)

FRADKIN, CARLOS
    Man of the Foreign Debt,
        The (1987)

FRAMTID, SVART
    You Haven't Got a Chance--
        Take It! (1985)

FRANCAIX, JEAN
    Pearls of the Crown (1937)

FRANCI, CARLO
    Fame and the Devil (1950)
    Young Caruso, The (Enrico
        Caruso, Legend of a
        Voice) (1951)
    Medusa vs. the Son of
        Hercules (1962)
    Hercules Against the Moon
        Men (1964)
    Maciste and the Queen of
        Samar (1964)
    Maciste, Gladiator of Sparta
        (1964)

FRANCIOLI, LEON
    Happy End (1988)

FRANCO, MANUEL
    Mga Hagibis (1970)
    Disciple of Satan (1970)

FRANCOUR, CHUCK
    Berserker (1987)

FRANGES, NEVEN
    Little Train Robbery, The
        (1984)

FRANGIPANE, RON
    All the Kind Strangers
        (1974)

FRANJU, GEORGES
    Eyes Without a Face (1963)

FRANK, ALDO
    Man Eaters (1988)

FRANK, DAVID
  Bad News Bears, The (1979)
  Kid from Left Field, The
    (1979)
  Christmas for Boomer, A
    (1979)
  Here's Boomer (1980)
  Single Life, The (1980)
  Foul Play (1981)
  Hot W.A.C.S. (1981)
  Innocent Love, An (1982)
  Maid in America (1982)
  Flatfoots (1982)
  Invisible Woman, The (1983)
  Domestic Life (1984)
  Mr. Success (1984)
  Maximum Security (1985)
  Code of Silence (1985)
  Check Is in the Mail, The
    (1986)
  Gladiator, The (1986)
  Leo and Liz in Beverly Hills
    (1986)
  Fake Five (1987)
  Off the Mark (1987)
  Above the Law (1988)
  Call Me (1988)
  Hero and the Terror (1988)

FRANK, DAVID MICHAEL
  I'm Gonna Git You Sucka
    (1988)

FRANKEL, BENJAMIN
  Give Us This Day (1949)
  Hotel Sahara (1951)
  Appointment with Venus (1951)
  Mr. Denning Drives North
    (1952)
  Net, The (1953)
  Mad About Men (1954)
  Lost (Tears for Simon)
    (1956)
  Brothers-in-Law (1957)
  I Only Arsked (1958)
  Summer of the 17th Doll,
    The (1960)

FRANKEL, JERRY
  Close Ties (1983)

FRANKES, GORDON
  Father, Dear Father (1977)

FRANKLIN, MILT
  Road Runner Show, The
    (1971)
  Sylvester and Tweety (1976)
  Bugs Bunny's Third Movie:
    1001 Rabbit Tales (1982)

FRANKLIN, SERGE
  Operation Leopard (1980)
  Big Pardon, The (1982)
  Big Carnival, The (1983)
  Kidnapping, The (1984)
  Heart Side, Garden Side
    (1984)
  Journey to Paimpol (1985)
  Hold-Up (1985)
  Lords of the Streets, The
    (1988)

FRANKO, DAVID
  Back Together (1984)

FRANKS, GORDON
  Father, Dear Father (1969)

FRANSSEN, JAN
  Falsch (1987)

FRANZ, SIEGFRIED
  Canaris (1955)
  When the Devil Came at
    Night (1958)
  Doctor of Stalingrad (1958)
  Dr. Crippen Lives! (1958)
  Mrs. Warren's Profession
    (1960)

FRANZETTI, CARLOS
  King and His Movie, A
    (1986)

FRASER, DAVE (DAVID)
  Beyond Reasonable Doubt
    (1980)
  Wild Horses (1983)
  Lost Tribe, The (1983)

FRASER, DOUGLAS
    Fortune Dane (1986)

FRASER, GEORGE
    Give a Dog a Bone (1966)

FRASER, IAN
    Bell, Book and Candle (1978)
    Torn Between Two Lovers
        (1979)
    Hopscotch (1980)
    Zorro, the Gay Blade (1981)
    Life of the Party: The
        Story of Beatrice (1982)

FRASER, JILL
    Personal Best (1982)

FREDERIC, ANNE
    Maine-Ocean Express (1986)

FREDERICK, JESSE
    Last Horror Film, The
        (1984)
    Mission Kill (1985)
    Better Days (1986)
    Aloha Summer (1988)

FREDERICKS, MARC
    Seeds of Evil (1972)

FREEBAIRN-SMITH, IAN
    What's Up, Doc? (1978)
    Magnum, P.I. (1980)
    Gabe and Walker (1981)
    Deadly Lessons (1983)
    For Love and Honor (1983)

FREED, ARNOLD
    Werewolf of Washington,
        The (1973)

FREED, FRED
    If I Had Seven Daughters
        (1955)
    Aladdin and the Wonderful
        Lamp (1969)

FREED, SAM, JR.
    Murder in the Blue Room
        (1944)

FREEDMAN, HARRY
    Bloody Brood, The (1959)
    China: The Roots of Madness
        (1967)
    Courage of Kavik, The Wolf
        Dog, The (1980)

FREIDMAN, GLORA
    Sarah (The Seventh Match)
        (1982)

FREJAT, ROBERTO
    Swingin' Betty (1984)

FRENREISZ, KAROLY
    Don't Panic, Please! (1983)
    Enchanted Dollars, The (1986)

FRIED, GERALD
    Lost Missile, The (1958)
    Machine Gun Kelly (1958)
    Shotgun Slade (1959)
    My Three Sons (1960)
    Gilligan's Island (1964)
    Family Affair (1966)
    Mission: Impossible (1966)
    Star Trek (1966)
    Winged World, The (1968)
    Emergency! (1972)
    Police Woman (1974)
    I Will Fight No More Forever
        (1975)
    Executive Suite (1976)
    Francis Gary Powers: The
        True Story of the U-2
        Spy Incident (1976)
    Testimony of Two Men (1977)
    Roots (1977)
    Sex and the Married Woman
        (1977)
    Spell, The (1977)
    Beasts Are in the Streets,
        The (1978)
    Cruise into Terror (1978)
    Immigrants, The (1978)
    Maneaters Are Loose! (1978)
    Rescue from Gilligan's Island
        (1978)
    Castaways on Gilligan's Island,
        The (1979)
    Emergency! (1979)

Incredible Journey of Dr.
  Meg Laurel (1979)
Rebels, The (1979)
Roots: The Next Generation
  (1979)
Seekers, The (1979)
Breaking Up Is Hard to Do
  (1979)
Son Rise: A Miracle of Love
  (1979)
Chisholms, The (1980)
Condominium (1980)
Disaster on the Coast Liner
  (1980)
Flamingo Road (1980)
Number 96 (1980)
Moviola: The Silent Lovers
  (1980)
Harlem Globetrotters on
  Gilligan's Island, The
  (1980)
Ordeal of Dr. Mudd, The
  (1980)
Gauguin the Savage (1980)
Wild and the Free, The
  (1980)
Agatha Christie's "Murder Is
  Easy" (1982)
Killer in the Family, A (1983)
Return of the Man from
  U.N.C.L.E., The (1983)
Mystic Warrior, The (1984)
Drop-Out Mother (1988)
Roots: The Gift (1988)

FRIEDHOFER, HUGO
  Try and Get Me (1951)
  Lancer (1968)
  Over-the-Hill Gang, The
    (1969)
  Die, Sister, Die! (1978)

FRIEDMAN, GARY WILLIAM
  Survival Run (1980)
  Full Moon High (1986)
  My Two Loves (1986)
  Night of Courage (1987)
  Liberace (1988)

FRIEDMAN, IRVING
  Behind Locked Doors
    (1948)

Father Knows Best
  (1954)

FRIEL, EAMON
  Best Man, The (1986)

FRIMAN, LEO
  Final Arrangement, The
    (1988)

FRIML, RUDOLPH, JR.
  Wild Weed (1949)

FRIZE, NICOLAS
  Mix-Up (1986)

FRIZZI, FABIO
  Hot Dreams (Free Love)(1974)
  Dracula in the Provinces
    (1975)
  Gates of Hell, The (1980)
  Zombie (1980)
  Manaos (1980)
  Al di La (1981)
  And You'll Live in Terror!
    The Beyond (1981)
  City Birds (1981)
  Fear in the City of the
    Living Dead (1982)
  Manhattan Baby (1982)
  Crime at the Blue Gay (1984)
  Sensi (1986)
  SuperFantaGenio (1986)

FROEHLICH, CHARLES
  Semmelweis (1940)

FROESE, EDGAR
  Under Lock and Key (1980)
  Brand Marks (1982)
  Kamikaze (1982)

"FRONT"
  Ginger Meggs (1982)

FRONTIERE, DOMINIC
  Outer Limits, The (1963)
  Invaders, The (1967)
  Name of the Game, The
    (1968)
  Immortal, The (1969)

Immortal, The (1970)
Love War, The (1970)
Name for Evil, A (1970)
Young Rebels, The (1970)
Revenge (1971)
Sheriff, The (1971)
Haunts of the Very Rich
  (1972)
Movin' On (1972)
Probe (1972)
Search (1972)
Chopper One (1974)
Fer-de-Lance (1974)
Mark of Zorro, The (1974)
Who Is the Black Dahlia?
  (1975)
Young Pioneers, The (1976)
Washington: Behind Closed
  Doors (1977)
Yesterday's Child (1977)
Perfect Gentlemen (1978)
Vega$ (1978)
Wilds of Ten Thousand
  Islands, The (1978)
Young Pioneers, The (1978)
My Old Man (1979)
Stung Man, The (1980)
Freebie and the Bean (1981)
Roar (1981)
Modern Problems (1982)
Don't Go to Sleep (1982)
Matt Houston (1982)
Shooting Stars (1983)
Dark Mirror (1984)
Velvet (1984)
Harry's Hong Kong (1987)

FROOM, MITCHELL
  Slam Dance (1987)

FRUSTACI, VALENTE E.
  Naples That Never Dies (1939)

FRY, GARY
  Cease Fire (1985)

FRYE, BUDDY
  Prime Time, The (1960)

FUCHS, CARL EMIL
  Young Blood (1936)

FUENTES, RUBEN
  Orlak, the Hell of Franken-
    stein (1961)
  Ghost Jesters, The (1964)

FUENTES, TOTI
  Fire in the Night (1986)

FUKAI, SHIRO
  Traitors (1957)

FUKAMACHI, JUN
  Phoenix (1978)
  Hinotori (1980)

FUKAI, SHIRO
  Horse Boy, The (1957)

FUKUDA, WAKIKO
  Gundam (1980)

FUKUI, RYO
  Legend of Plumeria--Heaven's
    Kiss, The (1983)

FULL, RAYMOND
  Criminal (1966)

FULLER, JERRY
  Bobby Jo and the Big Apple
    Goodtime Band (1972)

FULLER, PALMER
  Saturday the 14th (1981)
  Easy Street (1986)
  White Ghost (1988)

FUNARO, MARIO
  Fame and the Devil (1950)

FUNAURA, TORU
  Magic Boy, The (1959)

FUN-KAY, CHAN
  Encounter of the Spooky
    Kind (1981)

FUREY, LEWIS
  Fantastica (1980)
  Agency (1980)
  Maria Chapdelaine (1983)

American Dreamer (1984)
Night Magic (1985)
Peanut Butter Solution, The
    (1985)
Run for Your Life, Lola
    (1986)

FURST, BABY LOPEZ
Revenge, The (1983)
Wait for Me a Long Time
    (1983)
Withdrawal (1984)
Murder at the Nation's Senate
    (1984)
In Retirement (1987)
Search, The (1987)

FUSCO, ENZO
Domani non Siamo piu Qui
    (1966)

FUSCO, GIOVANNI
Duchess of Parma (1937)
These Children (1937)
Merchant of Venice, The
    (1953)
Woman Without Camelias, The
    (1953)
Disbanded, The (1955)
Girl Friends, The (1955)
Hero of Our Times, A (1959)
Dauphins, The (1960)
Sandokan the Great (1965)
Day of the Owl, The (1968)

FUSTER, BERNARDO
Wolves' Moon (1988)

FUSTER, MIGUEL ANGEL
Tiznao (1984)
Deep (1988)

FUYUKI, TOHRU
Ultraman (1967)

"FUZZY"
In My Life (1980)
Sorry to Have Imposed (1980)

Reward, The (1982)
Kidnapping, The (1982)
Haiti Express (1983)
Subway to Paradise (1987)

GABELI, IRAKLI
26 Days in the Life of
    Dostoyevsky (1981)
Chicherin (1986)

GABRIEL, PETER
Birdy (1984)
Last Temptation of Christ,
    The (1988)

GABRIEL, TEDRA
Reform School Girls (1986)

GABUNIA, NODER
Living Legends (1988)

GAGE, EDWARD
Ingagi (1930)

GAGNON, ANDRE
Phobia (1980)
Hot Touch (1982)

GAGULACHVILI, ARKADI
My Friend Ivan Lapshin
    (1986)

GAIGNE, PASCAL
Arder and Yul (1988)

GAINSBOURG, SERGE
I Love You (1981)
Equator (1983)
Mode in France (1985)
Evening Dress (1986)

GALARRA, PEDRO
Yako--Hunter of the Damned
    (1986)

GALASSO, MICHAEL
Loners (1981)

GALDO, JOE
Hammerhead Jones (1987)

GALDSTON, PHIL
    Jerk, Two, The (1984)
    Model Behavior (1984)

GALE, SCOTT
    Line, The (1987)

GALIHARD, A.
    Behind the Facade (1939)

GALL, PHILIPPE
    FM--Frequency Murder (1988)

GALLO, PHILO
    Redeemer ... Son of Satan,
        The (1978)
    Mother's Day (1980)

GALLO, VINCENT
    Way It Is or Eurydice in the
        Avenues, The (1985)

GAMBRINI
    Fantozzi Takes It on the
        Chin Again (1984)

GAMLEY, DOUGLAS
    One Wish Too Many (1956)
    High Flight (1958)
    Rough and the Smooth, The
        (1959)
    Ugly Ducking, The (1959)
    Foxhole in Cairo (1960)
    Light Up the Sky (1960)
    Horror Hotel (1963)
    Tales from the Crypt (1972)
    Vault of Horror, The (1972)
    Asylum (1972)
    And Now the Screaming
        Starts (1973)
    Beast Must Die, The (1974)
    Monster Club, The (1981)

GAMSON, ARNOLD
    Alberto Giacometti (1967)

GANELIN, VYACHESLAV
    Parade of the Planets (1985)

GANSERA, RAINER
    Rosi and the Big City (1981)

GARBAREK, JAN
    Melzer (1983)
    Paper Bird (1984)
    Teo the Redhead (1986)

GARBIZU, TOMAS
    10 Ready Rifles (1959)

GARCIA, CHARLY
    Angelic Pubis (1982)
    What Is to Come (1988)

GARCIA, ORLANDO
    Sequa, La (1985)

GARCIA CAFFI, JUAN JOSE
    Epilog (1984)

"GARCIA CAMPOS, EL"
    Angel River (1986)

GARCIA-MARRUZ, SERGIO
    Amigos (1985)

GARDE, JOAN ENRIC
    Radio Speed (1987)

GARDNER, STU
    Archie (1976)
    Top Secret (1978)

GARFIELD, DAVID
    Not in Front of the Kids
        (1984)

GARFIELD, JASON
    G.I. Executioner, The
        (1971)

GARRETT, ROBERT
    Roller Blade (1986)

GARRETT, SNUFF
    Bronco Billy (1980)
    Smokey and the Bandit II
        (1980)

GARRISON, JOSEPH
    Slaughterhouse (1988)

454 Composers and Their Films

GARSON, MORT
To Kill a Stranger (1982)

GARVANG, ARNE
Second Shift, The (1980)

GARVARENTZ, GEORGES
Temple of the White Elephants,
The (1964)
Helene and Fernanda (1970)
Someone Behind the Door
(1971)
Killer Who Wouldn't Die, The
(1976)
Too Scared to Scream (Door-
man, The) (1982)
Triumphs of a Man Called
Horse, The (1984)
Hambone and Hillie (1984)
Final Mission (1986)
State of Emergency (1986)
Yiddish Connection (1986)
Marcus Welby, M.D.--A
Holiday Affair (1988)

GARVEY, NICK
Acceptable Levels (1983)

GAS, G.
Anti-Climax (1970)

GASCOIGNE, BRIAN
1919 (1984)

GASLINI, GIORGIO
Long Night of Veronique,
The (1966)

GASTE, LOULOU
Indestructible, The (1959)

GATCHALIAN, ED
P.X. (1982)
Stryker (1983)

GATLIF, TONY
Princes, The (1983)

GATTA, TERESA
Living Off Love (1985)

GATTO, ROBERTO
Portrait of a Woman, Nude
(1981)
Mignon Has Gone (1988)

GAUBERT, CHRISTIAN
Little Girl Who Lives Down
the Lane, The (1977)
Cute Chick and the Private
Eye, The (1981)
Demon of the Isle, The
(1983)

GAUTHIER, GERMAIN
Pick-Up Summer (1981)

GAVRIELOV, MICKY
Plumber, The (1987)

GAY, NOEL
No Funny Business (1934)

GAZE, HEINO
Punktchen und Anton (1954)
Schlagerparade (Hit Parade)
(1954)

GAZIT, RAVIV
Hamsin (1982)

GEDDES, RALPH
Land of No Return, The
(1981)

GEERDES, CHRISTIAN
Zechmeister (1981)

GEESON, RON
Ghost Story (1973)

GELB, LARRY
Dances Sacred and Profane
(1985)

GELD, GARY
It's a Dog's World (1967)

GELLER, HARRY (HAROLD)
Mission: Impossible (1966)
That Girl (1966)

Bracken's World (1969)
Arnie (1970)
Challenge, The (1970)
Tim Conway Show, The
    (1970)
Dead Man on the Run (1975)
Let's Switch (1975)
You're Just Like Your
    Father (1976)

GELLER, HERB
Otto--The Film (1985)

GELLER, JOHN
Doctors, The (1963)
Voyage to the Bottom of
    the Sea (1964)

GELMETTI, VITTORIO
100 Days in Palermo (1984)
Angelus Novus (1987)

GEMIGNANI, VINCENT
Rabid Ones, The (1985)

GENKOV, GEORGI
Illusion (1980)
Ladies Choice (1981)
Mass Miracle (1981)
White Magic (1983)
Thirteenth Bride of the
    Prince, The (1987)
Time of Violence (1988)

GENTICA, JOSE
Gold, Silver, Bad Luck
    (1983)

"GEO"
Cheech & Chong's The
    Corsican Brothers (1984)

GEORGE, DAVID
Howling IV ... The Original
    Nightmare (1988)

GERARD, BERNARD
Solitary Man Attacks, The
    (1968)
Maid for Pleasure (1974)

GERARD, PHILIPPE
Life Is a Novel (1983)
Melo (1986)

GERBER, ALLEN
Hot Water (1985)

GERE, DON
Sweet Sugar (1972)

GERENS, ALEXANDER
Fast and the Furious, The
    (1954)

GERMYN, PETER
Final Assignment (1980)

GERTZ, IRVING
It Came from Outer Space
    (1953)
Monolith Monster, The (1957)
Daniel Boone (1964)

GERUT, ROSALIE
Breaking the Silence: The
    Generation After the
    Holocaust (1984)

GETSCHAL, DOUGLAS COOPER
Panther Squad (1986)

GHENDINI, G. FEDERICO
Life of Don Bosco, The
    (1936)

GHIGLIA, BENEDETTO
Espionage in Tangiers (1965)
Dollar Between the Teeth, A
    (1966)
Rojo, El (1966)
Starblack (1966)
Adios Gringo (1968)

GHIZZY, DOOBY
Milionario and Ze Rico in the
    Highway of Life (1980)

GHOSE, GOUTAM
Occupation, The (1982)
Crossing, The (Paar) (1984)
Voyage Beyond (1988)

GHULMIYYA, WALID
    Al Qadisiyya (1981)

GIAMMARCO, MAURIZIO
    Portrait of a Woman, Nude
        (1981)
    Outside the Day (1983)

GIBB, BARRY
    Hawks (1988)

GIBB, MAURICE
    Breed Apart, A (1984)

GIBBS, MICHAEL
    Madame Sin (1972)
    Goodies, The (1976)
    Heat (1987)
    Housekeeping (1987)
    American Roulette (1988)

GIBNEY, DAVID
    Superstition (1985)

GIBSON, ALEX
    Wild Side, The (1983)
    From Hollywood to Deadwood
        (1988)

GIBSON, COLIN
    Up Line (1987)

GIBSON, MICHAEL
    Cold River (1982)

GIECO, LEION
    Dogs of the Night (1986)

GIGANTE, MARCELLO
    Embalmer, The (1965)
    Loves of Angelica, The
        (1966)
    War of the Giants (1966)

GIL, GILBERTO
    Brazil Year 2000 (1970)
    Copacabana, Mon Amour
        (1975)
    Quilombo (1984)
    Jubiaba (1986)
    Train for the Stars, A (1987)

GIL, JOSE ALBERTO
    True and Accurate Report,
        A (1987)

GILBERT, HERSCHEL BURKE
    Shamrock Hill (1949)
    Project Moonbase (1953)
    Gilligan's Island (1964)
    I Dismember Mama (1972)
    Poor Albert and Little Annie
        (1972)
    Gemini Affair--A Diary, The
        (1973)
    Witch Who Came from the
        Sea, The (1976)
    Man from Denver (1959)

GILBERT, YVES
    Biquefarre (1983)
    Charmer, The (1984)
    Debutante, The (1986)

GILBERTO, JOAO
    Not Everything Is True
        (1986)

GILBREATH, PAUL
    No Retreat No Surrender
        (1986)

GILES, MICHAEL
    Ghost Dance (1983)

GILL, ALAN
    State of Wonder (1984)
    Letter to Brezhnev (1985)

GILL, ROBERT
    So Little Time (1952)
    Golden Mask, The (1954)

GILLET, BRUNO
    Satin Spider, The (1985)

GILLIS, RICHARD
    Demonoid (Macabra) (1979)
    Bees, The (1979)

GILLMAN, PAUL
    Silent Assassins (1988)

GILLON, MARION
    Dark End of the Street,
        The (1981)

GILMAN, JEFF
    Bigfoot--Man or Beast? (1975)
    Mysteries from Beyond the
        Triangle (1977)

GILMAN, MAURICE
    Let George Do It (1938)

GILMORE, DOUG
    Szysznyk (1977)
    Just Friends (1979)
    Semi-Tough (1980)
    Stockard Channing Show,
        The (1980)

GILMORE, JULIA
    Memoirs (1985)

GIMBEL, NORMAN
    Used Cars (1984)

GINASTERA, ALBERTO
    Malambo (1942)
    Native Pony (1954)

GINN, BILL
    French Quarter Undercover
        (1985)

GINTROWSKI, PRZEMYSLAW
    100 Days (1981)
    Mother of Kings, The (1987)
    Afflicted, The (1988)

GIOMBINI, MARCELLO
    Vulcan, Son of Jupiter (1962)
    Target for Killing, A (1966)
    For a Few Dollars Less (1966)
    $100,000 for Lassiter (1966)
    Three Golden Men (1966)
    Wave of Lust (1975)
    War in Space (1977)
    Eyes Behind the Stars (1978)
    Obsessed, The (1978)
    Scoop (1982)

GIORDANA, TULLIO
    To Love the Damned (1980)

GIORDANO, JACKY
    Unsewing Machine, The (1986)

GIORGETTI, MAURO
    Hard Game (1986)

GIORGI, PIERO
    Merchant of Slaves (1949)

GIOVANI, PAUL
    Wicker Man, The (1974)

GIOVANNINI, RICCARDO
    Action (1980)

GIOVINAZZO, RICKY
    Combat Shock (1986)

GIRDLER, WILLIAM
    Asylum of Satan (1974)

GIROLAMI, MARIANO
    Amants del Diablo, Les
        (1971)

GIRRE, RONAN
    Perfect Marriage, A (1982)
    Four Adventures of Reinette
        and Mirabelle (1987)

GISMONTI, EGBERTO
    Act of Violence (1980)
    Hooray Brazil (1982)
    Fable of the Beautiful Pigeon
        Fancier, The (1988)

GIUA, GASPARE
    Thorn in the Flesh (1981)

GIUFFRE, JIMMY. See
    GUIFFRE, Jimmy

GJEVELEKAJ, GJON
    Guardians of the Fog (1988)

GLADKOV, GENNADI
    I Don't Want to Be Grown-
        Up (1984)
    Man from Boulevard des
        Capucines, The
        (1988)

GLANZBERG, NORBERT
  Michel Strogoff (1957)

GLASEL, JAN
  Walter and Carlo: Up at
    Dad's Hat (1985)
  Yes, It's Your Father! (1986)
  Fight for the Red Cow, The
    (1987)

GLASS, L.
  Bon Soir, Paris, Bonjour
    L'Amour (1957)

GLASS, PAUL
  Lady in a Cage (1964)
  Sole Survivor (1970)
  Five Desperate Women (1971)
  Sand Castles (1972)
  To the Devil, a Daughter
    (1976)

GLASS, PHILIP
  Koyaanisqatsi (1983)
  Mishima (1985)
  Dead End Kids (1986)
  Hamburger Hill (1987)
  Powaqqatsi (1988)
  Thin Blue Line, The (1988)

GLASSER, ALBERT
  Omoo-Omoo, the Shark God
    (1949)
  Port Sinister (1952)
  Man of Conflict (1953)
  Beginning or the End, The
    (1957)
  Monster from Green Hell,
    The (1957)
  Attack of the Puppet People,
    The (1958)
  Earth vs. the Spider (1958)
  Teenage Casanova (1958)
  Teenage Caveman (1958)
  Giant from the Unknown
    (1958)
  War of the Colossal Beast,
    The (1958)
  Viking Women and the Sea
    Serpent, The (1958)
  Magnificence in Trust (1967)
  Cremators, The (1972)

GLAUS, GASPARD
  Alexandre (1983)
  Lounge Chair, The (1988)

GLEESON, PATRICK
  Plague Dogs, The (1982)
  Bedroom Window, The (1986)
  Deadly Illusion (1987)
  In Self Defense (1987)
  Season of Dreams (1987)
  Blue Movies (1988)
  Perfect People (1988)

GLENMARK, ANDRES
  Test, The (1987)

GLENNIE-SMITH, NICK
  Puppetman (1987)

GLICKMAN, MORT
  Masked Marvel, The (1943)
  Secret Service in Darkest
    Africa, The (1943)
  Invaders from Mars (1953)

GLINDENMANN, IB
  Journey to the Seventh
    Planet (1961)
  Traitors, The (1983)

GLORIEUX, FRANCOIS
  Zaman (1983)

GLOWNA, NICK
  Maschenka (1987)

GLUCK, JESUS
  Crack, El (1981)
  Crack II, El (1983)
  Double Feature (1984)
  Passing the Course (1987)
  Redondela (1987)

GNATALLI, RADAMES
  They Don't Wear Black Ties
    (1981)

GNATALLI, ROBERTO
  Pagu Forever (1988)

GNESSIN, N.
  Amangeldy (1939)

"GOBLIN"
Deep Red (1975)
Alien Contamination (1980)
Buried Alive (1980)
St. Helens (1981)

GOCK, LES
Dangerous Game (1988)

GODFREY, PATRICK
To Hurt and to Heal (1987)

GODI, FRANCO
Super VIP's, The (1968)
Exorcist--Italian Style, The
(1975)

GODIN, YVES
Garbagemen (1986)

GODINHO, SERGIO
Face to the Sun (1980)
Killers, The (1980)

GOEBBELS, HEINER
Subjective Factor, The
(1981)
Kellers Hof--Portrait of a
German Farmer (1982)
Heinrich Penthesilea von
Kleist (1983)
Journey Into a Secret Life
(1984)
Love Is Where the Trouble
Begins (1984)

GOEHR, WALTER
I Married a Spy (1938)

GOERLING, NATHAN
Her Melody (1942)

GOGUELAT, MICHEL
Flight of the Sphinx, The
(1984)
Tribe, The (1984)
All Mixed Up (1985)
Twist Again in Moscow
(1986)
Cross (1987)

GOKIELI, I.
They Wanted Peace (1940)

GOLD, BERT
Feather and Father Gang,
The (1977)

GOLD, CAREY
Love of Life (1951)

GOLD, DALE
Lie of the Land, The (1985)
Starchaser: The Legend of
Orin (1985)

GOLD, DENNIS
Footsteps (1972)

GOLD, ERNEST
Assignation, The (1953)
Karamoja (1954)
Tender Hearts (1955)
Gerald McBoing Boing on the
Planet Moo (1955)
Screaming Skull, The (1958)
Betrayal (1974)
Letters from Frank (1979)
Marciano (1979)
Tom Horn (1980)
Safari 3000 (1982)
Wallenberg: A Hero's Story
(1985)
Dream of Gold (1986)
Gore Vidal's Lincoln (1988)

GOLD, WALLY
Kids from C.A.P.E.R., The
(1976)

GOLDBERG, BARRY
No Soap, Radio (1982)
Spencer (1984)
Fast Times (1986)
Father's Day (1986)
Thrashin' (1986)
Infiltrator (1987)
Three for the Road (1987)
Powwow Highway (1988)

GOLDBERG, DANNY
No Soap, Radio (1982)

Love, Sex and Marriage
  (1983)

GOLDENBERG, BILLY
  Fear No Evil (1969)
  Night Gallery (1969)
  Silent Night, Lonely Night
    (1969)
  Clear and Present Danger, A
    (1970)
  McCloud (1970)
  Ritual of Evil (1970)
  Alias Smith and Jones (1971)
  City, The (1971)
  Columbo (1971)
  Duel (1971)
  Harness, The (1971)
  Longstreet (1971)
  Neon Ceiling, The (1971)
  Ransom for a Dead Man
    (1971)
  Suddenly Single (1971)
  Thursday's Game (1971)
  All My Darling Daughters
    (1972)
  Banacek (1972)
  Banacek: Detour to Nowhere
    (1972)
  Cool Million (1972)
  Ghost Story (1972)
  Sixth Sense, The (1972)
  Truman Capote's The Glass
    House (1972)
  Brand New Life, A (1973)
  Circle of Fear (1973)
  Don't Be Afraid of the Dark
    (1973)
  Double Indemnity (1973)
  Kojak (1973)
  Marcus-Nelson Murders, The
    (1973)
  Terror on the Beach (1973)
  Dr. Max (1974)
  Firehouse (1974)
  Harry O (1974)
  I Love You, Goodbye (1974)
  Migrants, The (1974)
  Reflections of Murder (1974)
  Rhoda (1974)
  Smile, Jenny, You're Dead
    (1974)

Legend of Lizzie Borden,
  The (1975)
McCoy (1975)
Queen of the Stardust Ball-
  room, The (1975)
Search for the Gods (1975)
Dark Victory (1976)
Delvecchio (1976)
Dumplings, The (1976)
Executive Suite (1976)
Future Cop (1976)
Gemini Man (1976)
Helter Skelter (1976)
High Risk (1976)
James Dean (1976)
Lindbergh Kidnapping Case,
  The (1976)
One of My Wives is Missing
  (1976)
Return to Earth (1976)
Widow (1976)
Mary Jane Harper Cried Last
  Night (1977)
Westside Medical (1977)
King (1978)
Question of Love, A (1978)
Cracker Factory, The (1979)
Dorothy (1979)
Family Man, The (1979)
Flesh and Blood (1979)
Lazarus Syndrome, The
  (1979)
Miracle Worker, The (1979)
All-American Pie (1980)
Skag (1980)
Diary of Anne Frank, The
  (1980)
Women's Room, The (1980)
Father Figure (1980)
All God's Children (1980)
Haywire (1980)
Love Tapes, The (1980)
Perfect Match, A (1980)
Act of Love (1981)
Best Little Girl in the World,
  The (1981)
Callie & Son (1981)
Crisis at Central High (1981)
Dial M for Murder (1981)
Jacqueline Bouvier Kennedy

(1981)
Ordeal of Bill Carney, The
    (1981)
Gangster Chronicles, The
    (1981)
Love, Sidney (1981)
Sidney Shorr: A Girl's Best
    Friend (1981)
This House Possessed (1981)
Bare Essence (1982)
Country Gold (1982)
Gift of Life, The (1982)
Marian Rose White (1982)
Massarati and the Brain
    (1982)
Question of Honor, A (1982)
Rehearsal for Murder (1982)
Washington Mistress (1982)
Reuben, Reuben (1983)
Another Woman's Child (1983)
Awakening of Candra, The
    (1983)
Confessions of a Married
    Man (1983)
Dempsey (1983)
Happy (1983)
Intimate Agony (1983)
Memorial Day (1983)
Prototype (1983)
Rage of Angels (1983)
Will There Really Be a
    Morning? (1983)
Why Me? (1984)
Sun Also Rises, The (1984)
Atlanta Child Murders, The
    (1985)
Guilty Conscience (1985)
Out of the Darkness (1985)
Love on the Run (1985)
Kane and Abel (1985)
Love Is Never Silent (1985)
Dress Gray (1986)
Johnnie Mae Gibson: FBI
    (1986)
Rage of Angels: The Story
    Continues (1986)
There Must Be a Pony (1986)
Poker Alice (1987)
Sadie and Son (1987)
Spirit, The (1987)

18 Again (1988)
Little Girl Lost (1988)
Onassis: The Richest Man
    in the World (1988)

GOLDENBERG, MARK
    National Lampoon's Class
        Reunion (1982)
    Teen Wolf Too (1987)

GOLDFOOT, PETER
    Judgment in Berlin (1988)

GOLDMANN, FRIEDRICH
    Airship, The (1983)

GOLDMARK, ANDY
    Model Behavior (1984)

GOLDSMITH, JERRY (JERRALD)
    Studs Lonigan (1960)
    Doctor Kildare (1961)
    Detective, The (1968)
    Desperate Mission (1969)
    Room 222 (1969)
    Brotherhood of the Bell
        (1970)
    Tora! Tora! Tora! (1970)
    Cable Car Murder, The (1971)
    Do Not Fold, Spindle or
        Mutilate (1971)
    Homecoming, The (1971)
    Step Out of Line, A (1971)
    Crawlspace (1972)
    Pursuit (1972)
    Waltons, The (1972)
    Adventurer, The (1972)
    Hawkins (1973)
    Hawkins on Murder (1973)
    Barnaby Jones (1973)
    Police Story, The (1973)
    Red Pony, The (1973)
    Indict and Convict (1974)
    Police Woman (1974)
    QB VII (1974)
    Tree Grows in Brooklyn, A
        (1974)
    Winter Kill (1974)
    Girl Named Sooner, A (1975)
    Medical Story (1975)
    Adams of Eagle Lake (1975)

Contract on Cherry Street
  (1977)
Salamander, The (1980)
Caboblanco (1981)
Final Conflict: Damien III,
  The (1981)
Inchon (1981)
Masada (1981)
Outland (1981)
Raggedy Man (1981)
Challenge, The (1982)
Poltergeist (1982)
Secret of NIMH, The (1982)
First Blood (1982)
Dusty (1983)
Psycho II (1983)
Twilight Zone--The Movie
  (1983)
Under Fire (1983)
Lonely Guy, The (1984)
Gremlins (1984)
Supergirl (1984)
Runaway (1984)
Baby (1985)
Rambo: First Blood Part II
  (1985)
Explorers (1985)
Legend (1985)
King Solomon's Mines (1985)
Hoosiers (1986)
Link (1986)
Poltergeist II (1986)
Extreme Prejudice (1987)
Innerspace (1987)
Lionheart (1987)
Criminal Law (1988)
Rambo III (1988)
Rent-a-Cop (1988)

GOLDSMITH, JOEL
  Laserblast (1978)
  Doomsday Chronicles, The
    (1979)
  Taste of Sin, A (1983)
  Man With Two Brains, The
    (1983)
  Hollywood Hot Tubs (1984)
  Banzai Runner (1987)
  Crystal Heart (1987)
  They Died in the Middle of
    the River (1987)
  Watchers (1988)

GOLDSMITH, JONATHAN
  Castle Rock (1981)
  Visiting Hours (1982)
  Palais Royale (1988)

GOLDSTEIN, GIL
  Reckless Disregard (1984)

GOLDSTEIN, MICHAEL
  Bad Guys (1986)

GOLDSTEIN, STEVEN
  John Huston (1988)

GOLDSTEIN, WILLIAM
  Terror Out of the Sky (1978)
  Jennifer: A Woman's Story
    (1979)
  Aliens Are Coming, The
    (1980)
  Marilyn: The Untold Story
    (1980)
  Force: Five (1981)
  Eye for an Eye, An (1981)
  Long Way Home, A (1981)
  Forced Vengeance (1982)
  Remembrance of Love (1982)
  White Lions, The (1983)
  Happy Endings (1983)
  Boone (1983)
  Up the Creek (1984)
  Toughest Man in the World,
    The (1984)
  Rearview Mirror (1984)
  Getting Physical (1984)
  Lots of Luck (1985)
  Hero in the Family (1986)
  Hello Again (1987)
  On Fire (1987)
  Six Against the Rock (1987)
  Three Kings, The (1987)

GOLDSTON, PHIL
  Act, The (1984)

GOLOB, JANI
  Breath of Air, A (DIH)
    (1983)
  Merry Marriage, The (1984)

GOLSON, BENNY
  Mission: Impossible (1966)

Room 222 (1969)
Partridge Family, The (1970)
Roll Out! (1973)
If I Love You, Am I Trapped
   Forever? (1974)
Karen (1975)
Sophisticated Gents, The
   (1981)

GOMES, LUIZ CARLOS
Ghost from Bahia, The (1984)

GOMEZ, REMBERT EGUES
Patakin (1985)

GOMEZ, VICENTE
Moonfleet (1955)

GOMOLYAKA, V.
Zemlya (Land, The) (1955)

GONDELL, MARIA
Underground Man, The
   (1981)

"GOOD STUFF, THE"
Monty Nash (1971)

GOODALL, HOWARD
What If I'm Gay? (1987)

GOODMAN, ISADOR
Jedda, the Uncivilized (1956)

GOODMAN, MILES
James at 15 (1977)
Last Cry for Help, A (1979)
Having It All (1982)
Lookin' to Get Out (1982)
Jinxed! (1982)
King's Crossing (1982)
Table for Five (1983)
Man Who Wasn't There, The
   (1983)
Face of Rage, The (1983)
High School U.S.A. (1983)
Uncommon Love, An (1983)
Footloose (1984)
Things Are Looking Up
   (1984)
Me and Mom (1985)

Space (1985)
Best Times, The (1985)
Teen Wolf (1985)
Children of the Night (1985)
About Last Night (1986)
American Geisha (1986)
Blind Justice (1986)
Little Shop of Horrors, The
   (1986)
Passion Flower (1986)
Thompson's Last Run (1986)
Bamba, La (1987)
Like Father, Like Son (1987)
Squeeze, The (1987)
Blue Skies (1988)
Dirty Rotten Scoundrels
   (1988)
Fort Figueroa (1988)
Outback Bound (1988)

GOODWIN, DOUG
Pink Panther, The (1969)
Doctor Dolittle (1970)
Barkleys, The (1972)
Houndcats, The (1972)
Bailey's Comets (1973)
Oddball Couple, The (1975)
Baggy Pants and the Nitwits
   (1977)
What's New, Mr. Magoo?
   (1978)
Hollywood High Part II (1981)

GOODWIN, GORDON
Attack of the Killer Tomatoes,
   The (1979)

GOODWIN, RON
Whirlpool (1959)
In the Nick (1960)
Trials of Oscar Wilde, The
   (1960)
Beauty and the Beast (1976)
Unidentified Flying Oddball
   (1979)
Valhalla (1986)

GOODWIN, WAYNE
Fields of Fire (1987)

GOOLD, BARRY
    Eva: Guerrillera (1988)

GORAGUER, ALAIN
    Snails, The (1965)
    Gift of Oscar, The (1965)
    Charlie Bravo (1980)
    To Our Late Unlamented
        Husband (1988)

GORDON, EDWARD
    That's TV (1982)

GORDON, ROBERT
    Breakdown (1981)

GORDON, TOLBERT
    Magic Strings (1955)

GORE, MICHAEL
    Fame (1980)
    Terms of Endearment (1983)
    Pretty in Pink (1986)

GORECKI, HENRYK MIKOLAJ
    Police (1985)

GORGONI, AL
    Million Dollar Mystery (1987)

GORI, LALLO
    Hercules Against the Sun
        (1964)
    Two Cosmonauts Against Their
        Will (1965)
    Death March (Morte Cammina
        con Loro, La) (1966)
    Time of Massacre (1966)
    How We Stole the Atomic
        Bomb (1967)
    Legend of the Wolf Woman
        (1976)

GORINA, MANUEL VALLS
    Victory (1984)

GORN, STEVE
    Hungry Wives (1972)

GORNY, ZBIGNIEW
    Alone Among His Own (1985)

Private Investigations
    (1987)

GOSOV, MARAN
    Horror Vacui (1984)
    Dear Karl (1984)
    Virus Knows No Morals, A
        (1986)

GOSSELAIN, ANDRE
    Heels Go to Hell (1956)

GOTFRIT, MARTIN
    Low Visibility (1984)

GOTTHARDT, PETER
    Until Death Do Us Part
        (1980)
    Where Others Keep Silent
        (1985)
    Russians Are Coming, The
        (1988)

GOUDE, JEAN-PHILIPPE
    Move Along, There's Nothing
        to See (1983)
    Favorite, The (Rock and
        Torah) (1983)

GOULD, CAREY
    Secret Storm, The (1954)

GOULD, GLENN
    Wars, The (1983)

GOULD, JOHN
    Monty Python's Flying Circus
        (1974)

GOULD, MORTON
    Land of Hope (1976)
    Four of Us, The (1977)
    Holocaust (1978)

GOULD, TODD
    Deception of Benjamin Steiner,
        The (1983)

GOURIET, GERALD
    Madame Sousatzka (1988)

GOVERNOR, MARK
Paradise Motel (1985)
Devastator, The (1986)
Beach Balls (1988)

GOWERS, PATRICK
Therese Raquin (1981)
Smiley's People (1982)
Adventures of Sherlock Holmes,
The (1985)
Whoops Apocalypse (1986)

GOYETTE, DESARAE (DESIREE)
Charlie Brown and Snoopy
Show, The (1983)
Garfield Goes Hollywood
(1987)

GRABOWSKY, PAUL
Bit Part, The (1987)
Petrov Affair, The (1987)
Georgia (1988)

GRACA, ARMENIO
Memories of Fear (1981)

GRADMAN, ERIC
Wrong World (1985)

GRAHAM, DAVID
Comrades (1986)

GRAINER, RON
Mouse on the Moon, The
(1963)
Prisoner, The (1968)
Destiny of a Spy (1969)
Thief (1971)
And No One Could Save
Her (1973)
Mousey (1973)
Dr. Who (1973)
Tales of the Unexpected
(1979)
Edward and Mrs. Simpson
(1980)
Dr. Who--The Five Doctors
(1983)

GRANGIER, LAURENT
Lucky Ravi (1987)

GRANIER, GEORGES
Big Road, The (1987)

GRANT, RON
Knots Landing (1979)

GRASS, CLANCY B.
Velvet Vampire, The (1971)

GRAY, ALLAN
Prisoner of Corbal (1939)
No Place for Jennifer (1950)
Her Panelled Door (1951)
Obsession (1951)
Genie, The (1953)

GRAY, ARVELLA
Maxwell Street Blues (1981)

GRAY, BARRY
U.F.O. (1972)
Space: 1999 (1975)
Thunderbirds to the Rescue
(1980)
Revenge of the Mysterians from
Mars (1981)

GRAY, STEVE (STEVEN)
Erotica (1981)
Global Assembly Line, The
(1986)

"GRAY CASTLE"
Last Hunt, The (1985)

GRAYDON, JAY
Gimmie a Break (1981)

GREAT, DON
Jeffersons, The (1975)
Journey into the Beyond
(1977)
Celtic Ghosts (1980)
Breeders (1986)
Soldier's Revenge (1986)
Necropolis (1987)

GREBENSCHIKOV, BORIS
Assa (1988)

GRECO, TONY
  Gloria (1982)
  I Gave at the Office (1984)

GREELEY, GEORGE
  My Favorite Martian (1963)
  Ghost and Mrs. Muir, The
    (1968)
  Nanny and the Professor
    (1970)
  Towards the Year 2000 (1977)

GREEN, BERNARD
  Brass Bottle, The (1964)

GREEN, PHILIP
  For Them That Trespass
    (1949)
  Man on the Run (1949)
  Saint and Sinners (1949)
  Isn't Life Wonderful? (1953)
  Conflict of Wings (1954)
  Young Wives' Tale (1954)
  Man of the Moment (1955)
  Extra Day, The (1956)
  Who Done It? (1956)
  Up in the World (1957)
  Just My Luck (1957)
  Sea Fury (1958)
  Square Peg, The (1958)
  Life in Emergency Ward 10
    (1959)
  Alive and Kicking (1959)
  Don't Panic, Chaps! (1959)
  Follow a Star (1959)
  Bulldog Breed, The (1960)
  Desert Mice (1960)
  League of Gentlemen (1960)
  Life Is a Circus (1960)
  Piccadilly Third Stop (1960)
  Your Money or Your Wife
    (1960)
  Flame in the Streets (1961)

GREENE, AL
  Death Curse of Tartu (1966)

GREENE, CORKY
  Whitney and the Robot (1979)

GREENE, RICHARD
  Getting Even (1981)

GREENE, WALTER
  Dalton Gang, The (1949)
  Black Lash (1952)
  Brain from Planet Arous, The
    (1958)
  Teenage Monster (1958)
  Jet Pink (1967)
  Pink Panther, The (1969)

GREENSLADE, DAVID
  Dr. Jekyll and Mr. Hyde
    (1981)

GREENWOOD, JOHN
  Man of Aran (1934)
  Last Days of Dolwyn, The
    (1949)

GREGOIRE, RICHARD
  Pouvoir Intime (1986)
  In the Shadow of the Wind
    (1987)
  Heat Line, The (1988)

GREGORC, JANEZ
  Red Boogie (1983)

GREGORY, JOHNNY
  Blood Beast from Outer Space
    (1965)

GRESKO, RICHARD
  Masculine Mystique, The
    (1984)
  Ninety Days (1985)

GRIEDEN, KURT
  Inspector Returns Home, The
    (1959)

GRIERSON, RALPH
  To Find My Son (1980)

GRIFFIN, GARY
  Berserker (1987)

GRIGORIOU, MICHALIS
  Underground Passage (1983)
  Misunderstanding (1984)
  Red Ants (1987)
  Life with Alkis (1988)

GRIPPE, RAGNAR
  Saddles With a Girl (1983)
  Last Summer, The (1984)
  Return (1985)
  Return of the Jonsson
    League, The (1986)

GROENEMEYER, HERBERT
  Eternal Feelings, The (1984)

GRONDONA, PAYO
  Nemesio (1986)

GRONICH, SHLOMO
  Transit (1980)
  Thousand Little Kisses, A
    (1981)
  Undernose (1982)
  Big Shots (1985)
  Skipper, The (1987)

GRONOSTAY, WALTER
  Rubber (1936)
  German Destiny (1936)
  Street Music (1936)

GROSS, CHARLES
  Doctors, The (1963)
  Post No Bills! (1967)
  Brock's Last Case (1973)
  Mr. Inside/Mr. Outside (1973)
  Nicky's World (1974)
  Blue Sunshine (1977)
  Dain Curse, The (1978)
  Siege (1978)
  No Other Love (1979)
  You Can't Go Home Again
    (1979)
  Rumor of War, A (1980)
  Nurse (1980)
  Heartland (1980)
  Private Battle, A (1980)
  Gold Bug, The (1980)
  When the Circus Came to
    Town (1981)
  My Body, My Child (1982)
  Prime Suspect (1982)
  Something So Right (1982)
  China Rose (1983)
  Cook & Peary: The Race
    to the Pole (1983)
  Sessions (1983)

Brady's Escape (1984)
Country (1984)
Terrible Joe Morgan (1984)
Night They Saved Christmas,
  The (1984)
Call to Glory (1984)
Arthur the King (1985)
Three Sovereigns for Sarah
  (1985)
Sweet Dreams (1985)
Barnum (1986)
Between Two Women (1986)
Choices (1986)
Murders in the Rue Morgue
  (1986)
Vengeance: The Story of
  Tony Cimo (1986)
At Mother's Request (1987)
Broken Vows (1987)
In Love and War (1987)
Apprentice to Murder (1988)
Leap of Faith (1988)
Open Admissions (1988)
Punchline (1988)
Side by Side (1988)

GROSS, GREGG
  Deathrow Gameshow (1987)

GROSS, GUY
  Dot and the Whale (1986)

GROSS, JIM
  Different Affair, A (1987)

GROSSKOPF, ERHARD
  Death of the White Steed,
    The (1985)

GROSSMAN, LARRY
  Super, The (1972)
  Muppet Family Christmas, A
    (1987)
  Suspicion (1988)

GROTH, JACOB
  Otto Is a Rhino (1983)
  Showers of Gold (1988)

GROTHE, FRANZ
  Winter Night's Dream, A
    (1935)

Abduction, The (1936)
Castle in Flanders (1936)
Madonna, Where Are You?
  (1936)
Beautiful Galatea, The (1950)
Queen Louise (1957)
Trapp Family in America, The
  (1958)
Beautiful Adventure (1959)
Heroes (1959)
12 Girls and One Man (1959)
Glorious Times in the
  Spessart (1967)

GRUBER-STITZER, JUDITH
Dumb Waiter, The (1987)
Room, The (1987)

GRUENBERG, LOUIS
Fight for Life, The (1940)

GRUENWALD, JEAN-JACQUES
Docteur Laennec (1949)
Angels of the Streets (1950)
Chevalier de la Nuit (1954)

GRUND, BERT
Sun of St. Moritz, The (1954)
Operation Sleeping Bag (1955)
Major and the Steers, The
  (1956)
Girl from the Salt Fields, The
  (1957)
1,000 Eyes of Dr. Mabuse,
  The (1961)
Strange Fruits (1983)
'38 (1986)

"GRUPO DICHOTOMY"
Monster Dog (1986)

"GRUPO ISSOCO"
Almacita de Desolata (1986)

"GRUPO MANCHURIA"
You Really Got Me (1985)

"GRUPO TRAVIESO"
Magdalena Viraga (1987)

"GRUPPE KARAT"
Border, The (1981)

GRUSIN, DAVE
Scorpio Letters, The (1967)
Ghost and Mrs. Muir, The
  (1968)
Name of the Game, The
  (1968)
Prescription: Murder (1968)
Dan August (1970)
Intruders, The (1970)
Deadly Dream, The (1971)
Howling in the Woods, A
  (1971)
Sarge: The Badge or the
  Cross (1971)
Family Rico, The (1972)
Friends of Eddie Coyle, The
  (1973)
Girl With Something Extra,
  The (1973)
Roll Out! (1973)
Death Squad, The (1974)
Good Times (1974)
Nickel Ride, The (1974)
Eric (1975)
Trial of Chaplain Jensen,
  The (1975)
Oath: The Sad and Lonely
  Sundays (1976)
Baretta (1978)
Colorado C.I. (1978)
Assignment: Vienna (1979)
My Bodyguard (1980)
On Golden Pond (1981)
Absence of Malice (1981)
Reds (1981)
St. Elsewhere (1982)
Author! Author! (1982)
Tootsie (1982)
Scandalous (1984)
Pope of Greenwich Village,
  The (1984)
Little Drummer Girl, The
  (1984)
P.O.P. (1984)
Falling in Love (1984)
Goonies, The (1985)
Lucas (1986)
On the Edge (1987)
Clara's Heart (1988)
Milagro Beanfield War, The
  (1988)
Tequila Sunrise (1988)

GRUSKA, JAY
  There Were Times, Dear
    (1985)
  Principal, The (1987)
  Shadow Dancing (1988)
  Traxx (1988)

GUANG, LIN
  Unfinished Game of Go, The
    (1982)

GUARALDI, VINCE
  Peanuts (1965)

GUARD, BARRY
  Zina (1985)
  Hold the Dream (1986)
  Monster in the Closet (1986)
  Indian Summer (1987)
  Tears in the Rain (1988)

GUBAIDULINA, SOFIA
  Kreutzer Sonata, The (1987)

GUDJONSSON, VALGEIR
  Stella on Vacation (1987)

GUEFEN, ANTHONY
  Assassin (1986)

GUERRERO, FRANCISCO
  Bearn (1983)
  Bicycles Are for the Summer
    (1984)
  Year of Awakening, The
    (1986)

GUERRERO, JACINTO
  Don Quintin, the Bitter
    (1935)
  On the Road to Cairo (1935)

GUERRERO, SERGIO
  Secret of Pancho Villa (1954)
  Pepita and the Monster
    (1957)
  Two Ghosts and a Girl
    (1958)
  Little Red Riding Hood and
    Her Friends (1959)
  Super He-Man, The (1960)
  Deceived Women (1961)

Looking for Death (1961)
  Terrible Snow Giant, The
    (1962)
  Museum of Horror, The (1963)
  Kiss from Beyond the Grave,
    The (1964)
  Invisible Assassin (1964)
  Adventure at the Center of
    the Earth, The (1965)

GUIFFRE, JIMMY
  Sighet (1967)
  Your Money or Your Life
    (1982)

GUILLAINE, YVES
  Pest, The (1982)

GUINNES, CHRISTOPHER
  Running Blind (1981)

GUIRMA, RENE
  Wend Kuuni (1982)

GULGOWSKI, WLODEK
  About Love (1986)

GULLMAR, KAJ
  Andersson Family, The (1939)
  Her Melody (1942)
  Bom, the Soldier (1949)

GUNASINGH
  Wife, The (1980)

GUNDERSEN, SVEIN
  Julia Julia (1981)
  Goodbye, Solidarity (1985)
  Dream Castle, The (1986)
  Hotel St. Pauli (1988)

GUNIA, PAUL VINCENT
  Trauma (1984)
  Snowman, The (1985)

GUNNING, CHRISTOPHER
  Hands of the Ripper (1971)
  Day of the Triffids, The
    (1982)

GUNVALDSEN, ERIK
  Foxtrot (1988)

GURIDI, JESUS
Great Day, The (1957)

GURUBU, YENI TURKU
Remedy (1984)
Escape, The (1985)

GUSMAN, JEFFREY G.
Panther Squad (1986)

GUSTIN, GERARD
Guepiot, Le (1981)

GUTESHA, MLADEN
Kiss Kiss, Kill Kill (1965)

GUTIERREZ, BENJAMIN
Sequa, La (1985)

GUTIERREZ DEL BARRIO,
ALEJANDRO
Almafuerte (1950)

GUTIERREZ HERAS, JOAQUIN
Dell of the Virgins (1972)
Maria de mi Corazon (1984)
Violent Stories (1984)

GUTTMANN, ARTHUR
Trapeze (1934)

GUY, FRANCOIS
Quebec, Une Wille (1988)

GUZMAN, LUIS
Calacan (1986)

GWANGWA, JONAS
Cry Freedom (1987)

GWILYM, IFOR AB
Happy Alcoholic, The (1984)

GWYNN, ALFRED
Devil's Messenger, The
(1962)

GYONGY, PAUL
Villa for Sale (1935)
Be Good Unto Death (1936)

HAANSTRA, JURRE
Mr. Slotter's Jubilee (1979)
One Could Laugh in Former
Days (1983)

HAAS, KONRAD
Retouche (1986)

HABIC, ALEKSANDAR
Foggy Landscapes (1984)
Harms Case, The (1988)

HADA, KENTARO
Bad Luck Bullet (1982)

HADEN, CHARLIE
Fire from the Mountain (1987)

HADJIDAKIS, MANOS
Dracos (1956)
Matter of Dignity, A (1960)
Dreamland of Desire (1961)
Memed My Hawk (1984)

HADJIEV, PARASHKEV
Little One (1959)

HADL, VITEZSLAV
Karla's Marriages (1981)
Smash Hit, A (1981)

HADZINASSIOS, GEORGE
Scenario (1985)

HAEFELI, JONAS C.
Inventor, The (1980)
Cassette Love (1981)
Man Without Memory (1984)

HAENTZSCHEL, GEORG
Last Illusion, The (1951)
Hotel Adlon (1955)
Ideal Woman, The (1959)
Man Who Sold Himself, The
(1959)

HAEUSERMANN, RUEDI
Dunki-Schott (Don Quixote)
(1986)

HAGAG, IBRAHIM
Open Eyes (1981)

HAGEMAN, RICHARD
  Adventures in Vienna (1952)
  Stolen Identity (1953)

HAGEN, ANDREW
  Scarecrow, The (1982)

HAGEN, EARLE
  Make Room for Daddy (1953)
  Andy Griffith Show, The
    (1960)
  Dick Van Dyke Show, The
    (1961)
  Gomer Pyle, U.S.M.C. (1964)
  That Girl (1966)
  Mayberry, R.F.D. (1968)
  Mod Squad (1968)
  Monk, The (1969)
  New People, The (1969)
  Make Room for Granddaddy
    (1970)
  Don Rickles Show, The (1972)
  M*A*S*H (1972)
  New Andy Griffith Show,
    The (1972)
  Doc Elliot (1973)
  New Adventures of Perry
    Mason, The (1973)
  Aces Up (1974)
  Movin' On (1974)
  Big Eddie (1975)
  Runaways, The (1975)
  Cheerleaders, The (1976)
  Having Babies (1976)
  Mary Hartman, Mary Hartman
    (1976)
  Nashville 99 (1977)
  Eight Is Enough (1977)
  Killer on Board (1977)
  Young Dan'l Boone (1977)
  True Grit (1978)
  Billy (1979)
  Concrete Cowboys (1979)
  Ebony, Ivory and Jade (1979)
  Featherstone's Nest (1979)
  Murder in Music City (1979)
  Alex and the Doberman Gang
    (1980)
  Ghost of a Chance (1980)
  Hustler of Muscle Beach, The
    (1980)

Fisherman's Wharf (1981)
Wendy Hooper--U.S. Army
  (1981)
Stand By Your Man (1981)
Muggable Mary: Street Cop
  (1982)
Kangaroos in the Kitchen
  (1982)
Teachers Only (1982)
I Take These Men (1983)
Mickey Spillane's Mike Hammer:
  Murder Me, Murder You
  (1983)
Mickey Spillane's Mike Hammer:
  More Than Murder (1983)
North Beach and Rawhide
  (1985)
Return of Mickey Spillane's
  Mike Hammer, The (1986)

HAGENS, NINA
  Maravillas (1981)

HAGUE, ALBERT
  How the Grinch Stole Christ-
    mas (1966)

HAIDER, JOE
  Price of Survival, The (1980)

HAIG, RICHARD
  Mission: Impossible (1966)

HAINES, DENIS
  Skyhigh (1985)

HAJDU, IMRE
  Budapest Candy Store (1936)
  Date by the Danube (1937)

HAJDUN, JANUSZ
  There Was No Sun (1984)
  Killing Auntie (1985)

HAJNA, THOMAS
  Jet Storm (1959)

HAJOS, JOE
  King of the Champs-Elysee
    (1935)

Lie of Nina Petrovna, The
  (1937)
Danger Is a Woman (1952)

HAJOS, KARL
  Supernatural (1933)
  Werewolf of London (1935)
  Fog Island (1945)

HAKE, ARDELL
  Scared to Death (1980)

HAKHLILI, NIR
  Homeland Fever (1980)

HAKONSON, OLA
  One Way Ticket (1988)

HAKPARAST, MOHAMED SHAH
  Migrating Birds (1987)

HALARIS, CHRISTIDULOS
  Alexander the Great (1980)
  Caution: Danger (1983)
  Photograph, The (1986)

HALEK, VACLAV
  Pictures of the Old World
    (1988)

HALFFTER, CHRISTOBAL
  Girl from Valladolid (1958)
  Two Men in Town (1959)
  Auschwitz Street (1980)

HALFFTER, RODOLFO
  Senorita de Travelez, La
    (1936)

HALL, TOM T.
  Deadhead Miles (1972)
  Harper Valley (1981)

HALL, VICTOR
  Treasure of the Moon Goddess
    (1987)

HALLBERG, BENGT
  Castle Is Swinging, The
    (1959)

HALLETZ, ERWIN
  Last Act, The (1955)
  Third Sex, The (1957)
  Peter Voss, Hero of the Day
    (1960)
  Shocking Asia (1982)

HALLIGAN, DICK
  Switch (1975)
  Holmes and Yoyo (1976)
  Zuma Beach (1978)
  B.J. and the Bear (1979)
  California Fever (1979)
  Octagon, The (1980)
  Cheaper to Keep Her (1980)
  Chicago Story (1982)
  Fear City (1984)

HALLYDAY, JOHNNY
  Outer Signs of Wealth (1983)

HALPIN, BROOKE
  More Than Broken Glass:
    Memories of Kristallnacht
    (1988)

HAMBERGER, DAVID S.
  Stockers, The (1981)

HAMERT, VAN
  Darlings! (1984)

HAMILTON, CHICO
  By Design (1981)

HAMILTON, DICK
  Odd Birds (1985)

HAMILTON, JOE
  Primary English Class, The
    (1977)

HAMILTON, JOEL
  Cheerleader Camp (1988)

HAMLISCH, MARVIN
  Doc Elliot (1973)
  Needles and Pins (1973)
  Calucci's Department (1973)
  Underground Man, The (1974)

Jerry (1974)
Ma and Pa (1974)
Beacon Hill (1975)
Hot L. Baltimore (1975)
Entertainer, The (1976)
Prime of Miss Jean Brodie,
    The (1979)
Ordinary People (1980)
Seems Like Old Times (1980)
I Ought to Be in Pictures
    (1982)
Sophie's Choice (1982)
Romantic Comedy (1983)
Streetcar Named Desire, A
    (1984)
D.A.R.Y.L. (1985)
Day to Day (1987)
Return of the Six Million
    Dollar Man and the Bionic
    Woman (1987)
Three Men and a Baby (1987)
Two Mrs. Grenvilles, The
    (1987)
When the Time Comes (1987)
David (1988)
Little Nikita (1988)

HAMM, FRED
High Five (1982)

HAMM, WOLFGANG
Down with the Germans
    (1985)
Shadows of the Future (1985)

HAMMER, JAN
Night in Heaven, A (1983)
Gimmie an "F" (1984)
Miami Vice (1984)
Secret Admirer (1985)
Charley Hannah (1986)
Clinton and Nadine (1988)

HAMMER, RONALD
Made in Heaven (1952)

HAMMERSCHMID, HANS
2069: A Sex Odyssey (1978)
No Time to Die (1986)

HAMMU, RAMZAN
Two Faces, The (1975)

HAMOURIS, RICK
Deception of Benjamin Steiner,
    The (1983)

HAN, SANG KI
Unheeded Crisis (1960)

HANCOCK, HERBIE
Soldier's Story, A (1984)
George McKenna Story, The
    (1986)
Jo Jo Dancer, Your Life Is
    Calling (1986)
'Round Midnight (1986)
Action Jackson (1988)
Colors (1988)

HANEDA, KENTARO
Time Slip (1981)
Matagi (1982)
Old Bear Hunter, The (1982)
Tradition of Terror: Franken-
    stein, A (1982)
Space Cruiser Yamato (1982)
Macross--Super Time Fortress
    (1983)
Space Cobra (1983)
Knocking Down Building
    Blocks (1983)
Husty (1984)

HANKINSON, ANN
Sky on Location, The (1983)

HANLEY, JAMES
His Double Life (1933)

HANNAH, JONATHAN
C.O.D. (Snap) (1981)
Roommates (1982)
If Looks Could Kill (1987)

HANOCH, SHALOM
Gloves (1986)
Shattered Dreams--Picking
    Up the Pieces (1987)

HANZEL, RHEINER
Day at the Beach, A (1984)

HAPKA, PETR
Virgin and the Monster, The
(1979)
Build a House, Plant a Tree
(1980)
Ninth Heart, The (1980)
Friday Is Not the Weekend
(1981)
Girl With a Sea Shell (1981)
Ferat Vampire (1983)
Millennial Bee, The (1983)
Bulldogs and Cherries (1984)
Third Dragon, The (1986)

HAQUE, AMANUL
Affliction (1986)

HARALAMBIDES, COSTAS
Agitated Winds (1984)

HARDINGER, MICHAEL
Elvis Hansen--A Pillar of
Society (1988)

HARDMAN, GARY
Day of the Panther (1988)
Dirtwater Dynasty, The
(1988)

HARDY, HAGOOD
Tell Me My Name (1977)
Home to Stay (1978)
Tom and Joann (1978)
American Christmas Carol,
An (1979)
Anatomy of a Seduction (1979)
Klondike Fever (1980)
Portrait of an Escort (1980)
Dirty Tricks (1981)
Forbidden Love (1982)
Rona Jaffe's "Mazes and
Monsters" (1982)
Frontier (1986)
Anne of Avonlea (1987)
Prodigious Hickey (1987)
Wild Pony, The (1987)
Liberace: Behind the
Music (1988)

Return of Hickey, The
(1988)

HARDY, MICHEL
Peking Central (1986)

HARE, KEN
I'm All Right, Jack (1959)

HAREL, PIERRE
Angel Life (1981)

HARLINE, LEIGH
Black Widow (1954)
House of Bamboo (1955)
Daniel Boone (1964)

HARNELL, JOE
Bionic Woman, The (1976)
Incredible Hulk, The (1978)
Cliffhangers (1979)
Curse of Dracula, The (1979)
Secret Empire, The (1979)
Stop Susan Williams (1979)
Alone at Last (1980)
Battles: The Murder That
Wouldn't Die (1980)
Senior Trip! (1981)
Seal, The (1981)
Scared Silly (1982)
V (1983)
Hot Pursuit (1984)
Santa Barbara (1984)
Shadow Chasers, The (1985)
Liberators, The (1987)

HARNICK, SHELDON
We'll Get By (1975)

HARPAZ, UDI
Day They Came to Arrest the
Book, The (1987)
Hollywood Shuffle (1987)
Juarez (1988)

HARPER, SCOTT
Reborn (1981)
Grizzlies, The (1987)

HARQUEZ, GILBERTO
Agony (1985)

HARRIS, ANTHONY
Speedtrap (1978)
Prison Ship (1987)

HARRIS, JOHNNY
New Adventures of Wonder
Woman, The (1977)
Initiation of Sarah, The
(1978)
Buck Rogers in the 25th
Century (1979)
Last Song, The (1980)
Born to Be Sold (1981)
Hotline (1982)
Powers of Matthew Starr,
The (1982)
Can You Feel Me Dancing?
(1986)
Downtown (1986)

HARRIS, MAX
Carry On Laughing (1980)
Horseman Riding By, A
(1982)
Open All Hours (1982)
Dreamchild (1985)
Christmas Wife, The (1988)

HARRISON, GEORGE
Shanghai Surprise (1986)

HARRISON, JOHN
Creepshow (1982)
Day of the Dead (1985)

HARRISON, J. S.
Legend of the Spider Forest,
The (1974)

HARRISON, KEN
Fantasy Island (1978)
Salvage I (1979)
Asphalt Cowboy, The (1980)
Ethel is an Elephant (1980)
Mr. Merlin (1981)
Hard Knocks (1981)
Wait Till Your Mother Gets
Home! (1983)
Highway Honeys (1983)
Meatballs II (1984)
Dark Mansions (1986)

Nightmare on Elm Street 3:
Dream Warriors, A (1987)
Heartbeat (1988)

HARRISON, NIGEL
Nightforce (1987)

HARROW, DON
Screen Test (1985)

HART, BOBBY
Days of Our Lives (1965)

HART, JAMES
Ghost Fever (1987)

HART, PAUL
May We Borrow Your Husband?
(1986)

HARTLEY, RICHARD
Bad Timing (1980)
Shock Treatment (1981)
Penmarric (1982)
Bad Blood (1982)
Trout, The (1982)
Kennedy (1983)
Sheena (1984)
Dance With a Stranger (1985)
Blue Money (1985)
Defense of the Realm (1985)
McGuffin, The (1985)
Nazi Hunter: The Beate
Klarsfeld Story (1986)
Impossible Spy, The (1987)
Mandela (1987)
Consuming Passions (1988)
Four-Minute Mile, The (1988)
Soursweet (1988)
Wild Things (1988)

HARTMANN, CHRISTIAN
Lapland Calendar (1957)

HARVAN, HAROSLAV
Crisis (1939)

HARVEY, MICK
Possession (1985)

HARVEY, PATRICK
Little Women (1971)

HAZELHURST, RONNIE
Fall and Rise of Reginald
Perrin, The (1978)
Two Ronnies, The (1978)
Butterflies (1982)
Last of the Summer Wine,
The (1982)
Roger Doesn't Live Here
Anymore (1982)
To the Manor Born (1982)
Yes, Minister (1982)

HEAD, MURRAY
For 200 Grand, You Get
Nothing Now (1982)
Door on the Left as You
Leave the Elevator, The
(1988)

"HECTOR"
Burning Angel (1984)

HEDZOLEH, AMARTEY
Kukurantumi--The Road to
Accra (1983)

HEEDE, FRITZ
Cry Wilderness (1987)

HEFTI, NEAL
Jamboree (1957)
Odd Couple, The (1970)
500-Pound Jerk, The (1973)
Conspiracy of Terror (1975)

HEGAB, SAYED
Satan's Empire (1986)

HEGEDUSCI, HRVOJE
Rhythm of Crime (1981)

HEIFETZ, VLADIMIR
Green Fields (1937)
Mirele Efros (1939)

HEIMAN, NAHUM
Athalia (1984)

HEINDORF, RAY
O'Hara, United States
Treasury: Operation
Cobra (1971)

O'Hara, United States
Treasury (1971)

HEINTZ, TIM
Deadly Prey (1987)

HEINZ, GERHARD
She-Wolf of the Devil's Moon,
The (1978)
Dracula Blows His Cool (1979)

HEINZE, WOLFGANG
Addressee Unknown (1983)

"HEKKET"
Pretenders, The (1981)

HELAL, MOHAMED
Gentlemen (1988)

HELASVUO, ESA
Angel'a War (1984)

HELIN, WYATT
Station to Station (1985)

HELKMAN, LEWIS
Police Surgeon (1972)

HELLAL, MOHAMED
Gentleman, The (1986)

HELLER, BILL
Deranged (1987)

HELLER, KEN
Condor (1986)

HELLER, STEVEN
Over the Summer (1985)

HELMS, JIM
Kung Fu (1972)
Death Among Friends (1975)

HENDERSON, LUTHER
Recess (1969)

HENDORFF, CHRISTOPH LEIS
Otto--The New Film
(1987)

HENNEMAN, IG
  Wanted: Loving Father and
    Mother (1988)

HENNING-JENSEN, LARS
  Moment, The (1980)

HENSEL, RAINER
  Return to Oegstgeest (1987)

HENTSCHEL, DAVID
  Educating Rita (1983)

HENTZSCHEL, GEORG
  Divine Jette, The (1937)
  Stars of Variety (1939)

HENZE, HANS-WERNER
  Swann in Love (1984)
  Love Unto Death (1984)
  No One Twice (1984)
  Comrades (1986)

HEPP, HARDY
  Frozen Heart, The (1980)
  Black Tanner (1986)

HERAS, JOAQUIN see
  GUTIERREZ HERAS, JOAQUIN

HERBOLZHEIMER, PETER
  Dream House, The (1981)

HERCULANO, PAOLO
  Sea of Roses (1980)
  Hearts and Guts (1982)

HERMELINK, BERT
  Donna Donna! (1988)

HERNANDEZ, ANDY
  Mixed Blood (1984)

HERNANDEZ, JUAN
  Castillo de las Bofetadas,
    El (1945)

HEROUET, MARC
  Winter, 1960 (1983)
  Golden 80's, The (1983)
  Winter Journey (1983)

Issue de Secours (1988)

HERRERA, DIEGO
  Contraband Aces (1986)
  Legacy of the Brave (1987)
  Urge to Kill, The (1987)

HERRERA, JORGE see PEREZ
  HERRERA, JORGE

HERRERO, HONORIO
  Adventures of Enrique and
    Ana, The (1981)

HERRMANN, BERNARD
  Portrait of Jennie (1948)
  Egyptian, The (1954)
  Companions in Nightmare
    (1968)

HERRNSTADT, GEORG
  Morning Mist (1984)

HERSANT, PHILIPPE
  Mountains of the Moon (1987)

HERTZOG, PAUL
  My Chauffeur (1986)
  Bloodsport (1988)

HESS, DAVID ALEX
  Last House on the Left, The
    (1972)

HESS, NIGEL
  Woman of Substance, A
    (1984)
  Deceptions (1985)
  Reunion at Fairborough
    (1985)
  Portrait of the Soviet Union
    (1988)

HETZER, HERB
  One Down Two to Go (1982)

HEWSON, DAVID
  Dark Enemy (1984)
  Heaven Earth Man (1984)
  School for Vandals (1986)

HEYMAN, NAHUM
Last Winter, The (1983)

HEYMANN, BIRGER
Line One (1988)

HEYWORTH, SIMON
Zina (1985)

HIERONYMOUS, RICHARD
Love Butcher, The (1975)
Invisible Strangler (1976)
Forest, The (1981)
Goin' All the Way (1982)
Balboa (1986)
Lethal Pursuit (1988)

HIETANEN, PEDRO
Dirty Story (1985)

HIGGINS, DIRK
Sacred Hearts (1984)

HIGGINS, KENNETH
Spookies (1986)
Hemingway (1988)

HIGGINS, ROBERT A.
Kill Zone (1985)

HIGUCHI, YASUO
Space Firebird 2772 (1982)

HILAL, MOHAMED
Broken Images (1986)

HILL, ALFRED
Broken Melody (1938)

HILL, BERNIE
Trespasses (1983)

HILL, ED
Devonsville Terror, The (1982)

HILL, RICHARD
Baffled! (1973)

HILLBORG, ANDERS
Friends (1988)

HILLMAN, MARC
Femmes (1983)
"Frank" and I (1984)

HILM, HARRY
Kingdom for a Horse, A
(1949)

HILPRECHT, UWE
Arctic Sea Calls, The (1984)

HILTON, DEREK
Cat on a Hot Tin Roof (1976)
Lost Empires (1986)

HINCE, DONALD
Angel Life (1981)

HINE, RUPERT
Better Off Dead (1985)

HIRAO, MASAAKI
Espy (1975)
Space Pirate Captain Herlock
(1978)
Sure Death 4 (1987)

HIRAYOSHI, TSUOKUNI
Princess Mermaid (1975)

HIROSE, KENJIRO
Gamera vs. Viras (1969)
Lill, My Darling Witch (1972)
My Darling Witch--A Kiss
Before Death (1972)

HIROSE, RYOHEI
Asaki Yumemishi (1975)

HIRSCH, LUDWIG
Trokadero (1981)

HIRSCH, NURIT
Young Lovers (1983)

HIRSCHFELDER, DAVID
Suzi's Story (1987)

HIRSCHHORN, JOEL
Trapped Beneath the Sea
(1974)

Someone I Touched (1975)
Rosenthal and Jones (1975)
Ultimate Stuntman: A Tribute
  to Dar Robinson, The (1987)

HISAISHI, JO
Technopolice 21-C (1982)
Laputa (1987)

HIYAYASHI, HIKARU
Horizon, The (1984)

HOBSON, GENE
Student Bodies (1981)
Terminal Entry (1988)

HODDINOTT, ALUN
Sword of Sherwood Forest
  (1961)

HODER, MARK
Scarecrow and Mrs. King
  (1983)

HODGE, JONATHAN
Trouble with 2-B, The (1972)
Z.P.G. (1972)

HODGIN, BARRY
Blood Waters of Dr. Z, The
  (1972)
Zaat (1972)

HODIAN, JOHN
Girls School Screamers (1986)

HODIER, ANDRE
Story of a Goldfish, The
  (1959)

HODLER-HAMILTON, MURIELLE
Cheerleader Camp (1988)

HOEFLE, CARL (JAMES K.
  MAYFIELD)
Scared to Death (1956)

HOENIG, MICHAEL
Koyaanisqatsi (1982)
Silent Witness (1985)
Nine-and-a-Half Weeks (1986)

Shattered Spirits (1986)
Wraith, The (1986)
Gate, The (1987)
Blob, The (1988)

HOEYER, OLE
Assassination (1980)
American Commandos (1986)
Warriors of the Apocalypse
  (1987)
Wheels of Terror (1987)

HOFFER, BERNARD
Ivory Ape, The (1980)
Sins of Dorian Gray, The
  (1983)
Life and Adventures of Santa
  Claus, The (1985)

HOFFERT, PAUL
Dr. Frankenstein on Campus
  (1970)
Groundstar Conspiracy, The
  (1972)
Double Negative (1980)
Mr. Patman (1980)
Circle of Two (1980)
Paradise (1982)
Hitchhiker, The (1983)
Bedroom Eyes (1984)
Hoover vs. the Kennedys:
  The Second Civil War
  (1987)
Mr. Nice Guy (1987)

HOFFMAN, STAN
Terror in the Jungle (1967)

HOFFMANN, INGFRIED
Ferdinanda, La (1982)
Invitation to Dance (1986)

HOFFMANN, REINHARD
Luther Is Dead (1984)

HOFNER, ANDRES (ANDREAS)
Wodzeck (1984)
Dormire (1985)

HOFSTEDE, HENK
Zjoek (1987)

HOGENDORP, ARJEN
Orion Nebula (1987)

HOJDUN, JANUSZ
Supreme Value of a Free
Conscience, The (1981)

HOLBROOK, JOHN
Dinosaur! (1985)

HOLDRIDGE, LEE
Peyton Place (1964)
Hec Ramsey (1972)
Rangers (1974)
Fools, Females and Fun
(1974)
Sierra (1974)
Skyway to Death (1974)
Family Holvak, The (1975)
Gemini Man, The (1976)
Sara (1976)
Code R (1977)
Pine Canyon is Burning
(1977)
Having Babies III (1978)
Julie Farr, M.D. (1978)
Like Mom, Like Me (1978)
To Kill a Cop (1978)
Young Maverick (1979)
If Things Were Different
(1980)
Mother and Daughter: The
Loving War (1980)
Skyward (1980)
American Pop (1981)
East of Eden (1981)
Two the Hard Way (1981)
Fly Away Home (1981)
For Ladies Only (1981)
Three Hundred Miles for
Stephanie (1981)
In Love with an Older
Woman (1982)
This Is Kate Bennett ...
(1982)
Thou Shalt Not Kill (1982)
Beastmaster, The (1982)
Mr. Mom (1983)
Mississippi, The (1983)
Agatha Christie's "A
Caribbean Mystery" (1983)

First Affair (1983)
I Want to Live! (1983)
Legs (1983)
Running Out (1983)
Thursday's Child (1983)
Wizards and Warriors (1983)
Best Legs in the Eighth
Grade, The (1984)
Boys in Blue, The (1984)
Splash (1984)
Shattered Vows (1984)
Micki & Maude (1984)
Moonlighting (1985)
Sylvester (1985)
Letting Go (1985)
Lime Street (1985)
Transylvania 6-5000 (1985)
Adams Apple (1986)
Mafia Princess (1986)
Men's Club, The (1986)
Miracle of the Heart: The
Boys Town Story (1986)
Pleasures (1986)
16 Days of Glory (1986)
Beauty and the Beast (1987)
Born in East L.A. (1987)
Eight Is Enough: A Family
Reunion (1987)
I'll Take Manhattan (1987)
Tiger's Tale, A (1987)
Walk Like a Man (1987)
Big Business (1988)
Fatal Judgment (1988)
14 Going on 30 (1988)
Higher Ground (1988)
Just in Time (1988)
My Africa (1988)
Tenth Man, The (1988)

HOLIDAY, BISHOP
Tin Man (1983)
Joy of Sex (1984)

HOLLANDER, FREDERICK
Procureau Hallers, Le (1930)
Spook Castles in Spessart,
The (1960)
Haunted Castle, The (1961)

HOLLINGSWORTH, JOHN
House of Fright (1961)

HOLMAN, BILL
  Get Outta Town (1960)

HOLMES, BILL
  Horror of Party Beach (1963)

HOLMES, RICHARD
  Sleeps Six (1984)

HOLMES, RUPERT
  No Small Affair (1984)

HOLMSEN, DANNY
  Magic Guitar, The (1968)
  Escarlotta (1969)

HOLROYD, DOUG
  Dark Side of Midnight, The
    (1988)

HOLTEN, BO
  Zappa (1983)
  Element of Crime, The (1984)
  Buster's World (1984)
  Twist & Shout (1984)
  Ring, The (1988)

HOLTON, NIGEL
  South of Reno (1987)

HOMNA, WILLIS
  Swamp Woman (1956)

HONDA, TOSHIYUKI
  Legend of the Mermaid
    (1984)
  Taxing Woman, A (1987)
  Taxing Woman II, A (1988)

HONEGGER, ARTHUR
  Miserables, Les (1934)
  Idea, The (1934)
  Magic Mountain (1936)
  Citadel of Silence (1937)
  Lady Killer (1937)
  Mademoiselle Docteur (1937)
  Marthe Richard (1937)
  Equipage, L' (1938)
  Deserter, The (1939)
  Harvest (1939)
  Cavalcade of Love (1940)
  Secrets of a Ballerina (1949)

HONGYUAN, ZUO
  Green, Green Grass of Home
    (1982)

HOOPER, LES
  Rhoda (1974)
  Man Called Sloane, A (1979)
  Master, The (1984)

HOOPER, TOBE
  Texas Chainsaw Massacre,
    The (1974)
  Texas Chainsaw Massacre
    Part 2, The (1986)

HOOREBEKE, VAN
  Secret Document--Vienna
    (1954)

HOOVEN, JOSEPH
  Beachcomber, The (1961)

HOOVER, MARK
  Images of Indians (1980)

HOPKINS, ANTHONY
  Angel Who Pawned Her Harp,
    The (1954)
  Seven Thunders (1957)
  Child's Play (1957)
  Capture That Capsule! (1961)

HOPKINS, KENYON
  Hawk (1966)
  Mission: Impossible (1966)
  Borgia Stick, The (1967)
  Mannix (1967)
  Odd Couple, The (1970)
  New Healers, The (1972)

HOPPE, MICHAEL
  Misunderstood (1984)

HOPPER, HAL
  Adventures of Rin-Tin-Tin,
    The (1954)

HOPTMAN, ADAM
  Paradise Camp (1986)

HORELICK, STEPHEN
  Madman (1982)

HORI, SHINJI
  Antonio Gaudi (1985)

HORIAN, RICHARD
  Student Confidential (1987)

HORMEL, GEORDIE
  Washington Affair, The (1977)

HORNER, JAMES
  Up from the Depths (1979)
  Humanoids of the Deep (1980)
  Battle Beyond the Stars (1980)
  Angel Dusted (1981)
  Hand, The (1981)
  Wolfen (1981)
  Deadly Blessing (1981)
  Pursuit of D. B. Cooper,
    The (1981)
  Few Days in Weasel Creek,
    A (1981)
  Star Trek: The Wrath of
    Khan (1982)
  48 Hrs. (1982)
  Piano for Mrs. Cimino, A
    (1982)
  Rascals and Robbers--The
    Secret Adventures of Tom
    Sawyer and Huck Finn
    (1982)
  Something Wicked This Way
    Comes (1983)
  Krull (1983)
  Space Raiders (1983)
  Brainstorm (1983)
  Dresser, The (1983)
  Testament (1983)
  Gorky Park (1983)
  Uncommon Valor (1983)
  Between Friends (1983)
  Stone Boy, The (1984)
  Star Trek III: The Search
    for Spock (1984)
  Heaven Help Us (1985)
  Surviving (1985)
  Cocoon (1985)
  Volunteers (1985)
  Journey of Natty Gann, The
    (1985)
  Commando (1985)
  In Her Own Time (1985)

Barbarian Queen (1985)
  Aliens (1986)
  American Tail, An (1986)
  Name of the Rose, The
    (1986)
  Off Beat (1986)
  Where the River Runs Black
    (1986)
  Batteries Not Included (1987)
  Project X (1987)
  Cocoon: The Return (1988)
  Land Before Time, The (1988)
  Red Heat (1988)
  Vibes (1988)
  Willow (1988)

HORNUNG, HORST
  Geierwally (1988)

HORNYAK, PAUL
  Lock 17 (1986)

HOROWITZ, DAVID
  Everything's Relative (1987)

HOROWITZ, JOSEPH
  Tarzan's Three Challenges
    (1963)
  Search for the Nile (1972)
  Member for Chelsea, The
    (1981)
  Seven Dials Mystery, The
    (1981)
  Why Didn't They Ask Evans?
    (1981)

HORPINITCH, MARK
  Marauders (1987)

HORTON, BOBBY
  Rebel Love (1986)

HOSHII, MASARU
  Almost Transparent Blue
    (1980)
  P. P. Rider (1985)

HOSHINO, SHUICHI
  Listen to the Sound of the
    Wind (1982)

HOSONO, HARUOMI
Paradise View (1985)
Promise, The (1986)

HOSTETTLER, MICHEL
Allegement, L' (1983)

HOTCHKISS, JOHN
Crucible of Horror (1971)

HOU, SO CHUN
Fist Full of Talons, A (1983)
Hong Kong Playboys (1983)
Men from the Gutter (1983)
Family Light Affair (1984)
Prince Charming (1984)
Twisted Passion (1985)

HOUDY, PIERICK
Bach and Broccoli (1987)

HOUPPIN, SERGE
Mammame (1986)

HOUSHNAREFF, SERGE
Arshin Mal Alan (1937)

HOVEY, SERGE
Hangman (1964)

HOVHANNES, ALAN
Narcissus (1956)

HOWARD, BRIAN
Gift of Life, The (1985)

HOWARD, JAMES NEWTON
8 Million Ways to Die (1986)
Head Office (1986)
Nobody's Fool (1986)
Tough Guys (1986)
Campus Man (1987)
Five Corners (1987)
Russkies (1987)
Visit, The (1987)
Everybody's All-American
(1988)
Go Toward the Light (1988)
Off Limits (1988)
Promised Land (1988)

HOWARD, KEN
Flame Trees of Thika, The
(1982)
Q.E.D. (1982)
Foreign Body (1986)
By the Sword Divided (1988)

HOWARD, RIK
Silver Spoons (1982)
Punky Brewster (1984)

HOWARD, TOM
Broken Victory (1988)

HOWARTH, ALAN
Escape from New York (1981)
Halloween III: Season of the
Witch (1982)
Lost Empire, The (1983)
Retribution (1987)
Halloween 4: The Return of
Michael Myers (1988)

HOWE, BONES
Adventures of Buckaroo Banzai: Across the 8th Di-
mension, The (1984)

HOWELL, PETER
From Normandie to Berlin:
A War Remembered (1985)
Yuri Nosenko KGB (1986)

HOYOS, JOE
Thus Ends the Night (1950)

HRISTIC, ZORAN
Svetozar Markovic (1980)
Leaves Are Wide, The (1981)
Savamala (1982)
Illusive Summer of '68, The
(1984)

HSIANG-TANG, CHI
Enchanting Shadow (1960)

HSIN-YI, CH'EN
If I Were for Real (1983)

HUBER, HEINRICH
Right at the Bottom (1986)

HUCK, DANIEL
   Lame Ducks (1982)

HUEHN, PAUL
   Girl from the Chorus, A
      (1937)

HUES, JACK see CHUNG,
   WANG

HUG, LARS
   Shot from the Heart, A (1986)

HUGHES, COOPER
   C.H.U.D. (1984)

HUGHES, HERBERT
   Norah O'Neale (1934)

HUI, SAM
   Aces Go Places (1982)

HULETTE, DON (DONALD)
   Twisted Brain, The (Horror
      High) (1974)
   Outlaw Force (1988)
   Take Two (1988)

HUMAIR, DANIEL
   Filthy Business, A (1981)

HUMMEL, FERDINAND
   Beyond the River (1922)

HUMMEL, FRANZ
   Accomplices (1988)

HUMPE, ANNETTE
   Axe of Wandsbek, The
      (1982)

HUNDLEY, CRAIG
   Roadie (1980)
   Schizoid (1980)
   Acorn People, The (1981)
   Americana (1981)
   Boogeyman II (1983)

HUNG-YI, CHANG
   Kuei-Mei, A Woman (1986)
   This Love of Mine (1988)

HUNNEKINK, BEREND
   Abandon (1986)
   Windshade (1986)

HUNTER, STEPHEN (STEVE)
   Smart Alec (1986)
   Invisible Kid, The (1988)

HUNTER, TODD
   On the Loose (1985)
   Zombie Brigade (1988)

HURD, MICHAEL
   Scrubbers (1982)

"HURRICANE"
   Easy Times Are Over, The
      (1984)

HUSSAIN, INAYAT
   Motherland (1960)

HUTCHINSON, BRENDA
   Liquid Sky (1982)

HUTMAN, OLIVIER
   High Speed (1986)

HUXLEY, CRAIG
   Programmed to Kill (1987)
   Why on Earth? (1988)

HYMAN, DICK
   Deadliest Season, The (1977)
   Last Tenant, The (1978)
   King Crab (1980)
   Henderson Monster, The
      (1980)
   Zelig (1983)
   Broadway Danny Rose (1984)
   Purple Rose of Cairo, The
      (1985)
   Moonstruck (1987)
   Tales from the Hollywood
      Hills (1987)

HYTTI, ANTTI
   Jon--A Story About the End
      of the World (1983)
   Ursula (1987)
   Plainlands (1988)

I, CHANG HUN
   Flower in the Raining Night,
      A (1983)

I JEOL-HYEOK
   First Son (1985)

I PIL-WEON
   Agatha (1985)

IBE, HARUMI
   When the Skin Burns (1966)
   Secret of the Ninja (1967)
   Golden Mob, The (1969)
   Way Out, Way In (1970)
   All-Out Game, The (1971)
   Forbidden Fruit, The (1971)
   Law of the Outlaw (1971)
   Love for Eternity (1971)

"IBEROS, LOS"
   Broken Arrow 29 (1986)

IBERT, JACQUES
   Golgotha (1935)
   Maternity (1935)
   Ecce Homo (1937)
   Late Matthew Pascal, The
      (1937)
   Patriot, The (1938)
   House of the Maltese (1938)
   Heroes of the Marne (1939)
   Phantom Chariot, The (1940)

IBRAHIM, ABDULLAH
   Chocolate (1988)

IFUKUBE, AKIRA
   I Was a Prisoner in Siberia
      (1952)
   Sisters of Nishijin (1952)
   Anatahan (1954)
   Godzilla, King of the Monsters
      (1956)
   Kanikosen (1957)
   Secret Scrolls, The (1957)
   Precipice, The (1958)
   Three Treasures, The (1960)
   Varan, the Unbelievable
      (1962)
   Little Prince and the Eight-

Headed Dragon, The (1963)
Adventures of Takla Makan
   (1965)
Majin, the Hideous Idol (1966)
Return of the Giant Majin,
   The (1967)
Majin Strikes Again (1967)
Frankenstein Conquers the
   World (1966)
Snow Ghost, The (1968)
Destroy All Monsters (1969)
King Kong Escapes (1969)
Yukionna (1969)
Zatoichi Challenged (1969)
War of the Gargantuas (1970)
Latitude Zero (1970)
Monster Zero (1970)
Will to Conquer (1971)
Yog, Monster from Space
   (1971)
Godzilla vs. Gigan (1972)
Sandakan No. 8 (1975)
Terror of Godzilla (1977)

IGELHOFF, PETER
   One Woman Is Not Enough
      (1955)

IGLESIAS, ALBERTO
   Conquest of Albania, The
      (1983)
   Ballad of Dogs' Beach, The
      (1987)
   Goodbye, Little Girl (1987)

IGLESIAS, JULIO
   Waiting for Daddy (1980)

IGLESIAS, ROBERTO
   Eternal Fire (1985)

IKATURA, BUN
   Bu-Su (1988)

IKEBE, SHINJIRO (SHIN-ICHIRO)
   Proper Way, The (1980)
   Vengeance Is Mine (1980)
   Double, The (1980)
   So What? (1981)
   Eijanaika (1982)

Ballad of Narayama, The
 (1983)
Okinawan Boys (1983)
MacArthur's Children (1985)
Pimp, The (1987)

IKEDA, MASAYOSHI
Cherry Blossoms in the Air--
 The Suicide Raiders--
 Oh, Buddies! (1970)

IKENO, NARI
Undercurrent (1957)

IKENO, SEI
Secret of the Telegian, The
 (1963)
Bride from Hades, The (1968)
Forbidden Affair (1971)
Live and Learn (1971)
Night River (1981)

IKENO, SHIGERU
Kaidan Botan Doro (1968)
Spook Warfare (1968)
Fox With Nine Tails, The
 (1969)
House of the Sleeping Virgins,
 The (1969)
Man on a False Flight (1971)
Deluxe Animal (1981)

ILEMMERICK, KEN
Close to Home (1986)

ILLARRAMENDI, ANGEL
Tasio (1984)

ILLES, LAJOS
Whistling Cobblestone, The
 (1971)

ILLIN, EVGEN
Death of the Ape Man (1962)
Rocket to Nowhere (1962)
Little Ball, The (1963)
Kulicka (1963)

ILUSTRE, LORRIE
In Just the Wink of an Eye
 (1982)

Batch '81 (1982)
Kisapmata (1982)

IMMEL, JERROLD
Gunsmoke (1955)
Matt Helm (1975)
Macahans, The (1976)
Revenge for a Rape (1976)
Royce (1976)
Spencer's Pilots (1976)
How the West Was Won (1977)
Logan's Run (1977)
American Girls, The (1978)
Dallas (1978)
Go West, Young Girl (1978)
Busters, The (1978)
Lassie: The New Beginning
 (1978)
Nowhere to Run (1978)
Buffalo Soldiers, The (1979)
Knots Landing (1979)
Legend of the Golden Gun
 (1979)
Married: The First Year
 (1979)
Sacketts, The (1979)
Power (1980)
Alcatraz: The Whole Shocking
 Story (1980)
Nick and the Dobermans
 (1980)
Palmerstown, U.S.A. (1980)
Roughnecks (1980)
Wild Times (1980)
Death Hunt (1981)
Secrets of Midland Heights
 (1981)
Behind the Screen (1981)
Cherokee Trail, The (1981)
Oklahoma City Dolls, The
 (1981)
Texas Rangers, The (1981)
Adventures of Pollyanna, The
 (1982)
King's Crossing (1982)
Louis L'Amour's "The Shadow
 Riders" (1982)
Megaforce (1982)
Voyagers (1982)
Tom Swift and Linda Craig
 Mystery Hour, The (1983)

Travis McGee (1983)
Yellow Rose, The (1983)
Outlaws (1984)
Berrenger's (1985)
Peyton Place: The Next
  Generation (1985)
Midas Valley (1985)
Dallas: The Early Years
  (1986)
Norman Rockwell's "Breaking
  Home Ties" (1987)
Programmed to Kill (1987)
Paradise (1988)
Why on Earth? (1988)

IMPROTA, THOMAS
Bar Esperanca: Last to
  Close (1983)

INAGAKI, JIRO
Young Man's Stronghold, A
  (1970)

INCAS, TREVOR
Jenny Kissed Me (1985)

INDART, DANIEL
Crazy Lola (1988)

INGBER, IRA
Blueberry Hill (1988)

INGELHOFF, PETER
Marguerite Drei (1939)

INNES, NEIL
Monty Python and the Holy
  Grail (1975)

INNOCENTS, SIMON DES
Perfect Marriage, A (1982)

INNOCENZI, CARLO
Antonio di Padova (1949)
100 Little Mothers (1952)
Article 519, Penal Code
  (1953)
Last Night of Love, The
  (1957)
Goliath Against the Giants
  (1960)

Mill of the Stone Women (1960)
Son of Samson (1960)
Monster of the Island, The
  (1973)

INOUE, AKIRA
Races (1984)

INOUE, TAKAYUKI
Man Who Stole the Sun, The
  (1980)
Distant Thunder (1981)
Seburi Story, The (1985)
Indecent Exposure (1985)
Love Letter (1986)
House on Fire (1987)

"INTI-ILLIMANI"
Madres: The Mothers of Plaza
  de Payo, Las (1986)

INTRAVIJIT, GHALIE
Land of Love, The (1980)
Hello, Cane Stick (1982)

IPEK, NEHMET
Right at the Bottom (1986)

IRIONDO, LUIS
Pico, El (1983)
Turn of the Screw, The
  (1985)

IRONS, TOMMY
Psychotronic Man, The (1980)

IRVING, SIR ERNEST
Run for Your Money, A (1949)
Blue Lamp, The (1950)
His Excellency (1952)

IRVING, JERRY
I Passed for White (1960)

IRVING, ROBERT, III
Street Smart (1987)

IRWIN, ASHLEY
Fair Game (1986)
Willing and Abel (1987)
All the Way (1988)
Richmond Hill (1988)

ISAAC, ANTHONY
  Onedin Line, The (1976)
  Omega Factor, The (1981)
  Mackenzie (1982)

ISAAC, GRAEME
  Kiss the Night (1988)

ISAACSON, MICHAEL
  Rich Man, Poor Man,
    Book II (1976)

ISFAELT, BJOERN
  Flourishing Times (1980)
  Grass Is Singing, The
    (1981)
  Broken Sky (1982)
  Who Pulled the Plug? (1982)
  Limpan (1983)
  Ronya--The Robber's
    Daughter (1984)
  My Life as a Dog (1985)
  Maiden Voyage (1988)

ISFASMAN, A.
  Behind the Show Window
    (1957)

ISHAM, MARK
  Never Cry Wolf (1983)
  Times of Harvey Milk, The
    (1984)
  Mrs. Soffel (1984)
  Trouble in Mind (1985)
  Hitcher, The (1986)
  Made in Heaven (1987)
  Beast, The (1988)
  Moderns, The (1988)

ISHII, KAN
  Gorath (1964)

ISHIKAWA, TAKAHIRO
  Flag, Class A, Grade 4,
    The (1977)
  Lonely Hearts (1982)

ISAREL, BOB
  On Our Own (1978)
  Capitol (1982)

ITABASHI, FUMIO
  Plan of His 19 Years, The
    (1980)

ITO, GINJI
  Uneasiness After School
    (1982)

ITO, TEIJI
  Handwritten (1959)
  Valentine for Marie, A (1965)
  Vergette Making a Pot (1967)

ITOH, NOBURU
  Kimiko (1937)

ITURRALDE, JAVIER
  Demons in the Garden (1982)

ITURRALDE, PEDRO
  Voyage to Nowhere (1986)

ITURRIAGA, ENRIQUE
  City and the Dogs, The
    (1985)

IVES, PETER
  B.J. and the Bear (1979)

IWAKAWA, SABURO
  Voyage of the Canoe "Che-
    Che-Meni," The (1977)

IZUMI, TAKU
  X from Outer Space (1967)
  Human Target (1971)
  Children of the Snow Country
    (1975)
  Classroom No. 205 (1975)
  Skies of Haruo, The (1978)

IZUMIMORI, MOCHIFUMI
  Gates of Flesh, The (1988)

IZYKOWSKA-MIRONOWICZ, ANNA
  Stranger, The (1987)

JABARA, PAUL
  Flatbush/Avenue J (1976)
  Chanel Solitaire (1981)

JACHINO, CARLO
Son of D'Artagnan (1950)

JACKLIN, MARTIN
Face of Darkness, The (1976)

JACKOWSKI, MAREK
Big Picnic, The (1981)

JACKSON, DAVID A.
Cold Steel (1987)
Cyclone (1987)

JACKSON, HOWARD
Supernatural (1933)
Mysterious Doctor, The
(1943)
50 Years Before Your Eyes
(1950)
Forbidden Desert (1957)

JACKSON, JOE
Mike's Murder (1984)
Private Eye (1987)
Tucker: The Man and His
Dream (1988)

JACOBINA, NELSON
Magician and the Police
Commissioner, The (1985)

JACOBOVICI, SARA
Falasha: Exile of the Black
Jews (1983)

JACOBS, AL
Death Curse of Tartu (1966)
Sting of Death (1966)

JACOBS, PIM
Knife, The (1961)
Guardian of the Atom (1968)

JACOBSEN, JIM
Final Season (1988)

JACOBSON, JULIAN
We Think the World of You
(1988)

JACOME, CLAUDIO
My Aunt Nora (1983)

JADHAV, VISWANATHBUVA
Ganga Avtaran (1935)

JAEGER, DENNY
Hunger, The (1983)
13 Thirteenth Avenue (1983)

JAENICKE, DAGMAR
Luther Is Dead (1984)

JAFFE, JILL
Big Blue, The (1988)

JAGGER, MICK
Invocation of My Demon
Brother (1969)

JAGMOHAN, S.
Crime Does Not Pay (1972)
Darwaza (1978)

JAIKISHAN, SHANKAR
Awara (1956)
Jangal Mein Mangal (1972)

"JAIRO"
Thorvald and Linda (1982)

JALKANNEN, PEKKA
Seven Brothers (1980)
Blue Mammy, The (1986)

"JAM MACHINE"
Sand (1986)

JAMES, BOB
Taxi (1978)

JAMES, ETHAN
Blue Iguana, The (1988)
Deadly Intent (1988)

JAMES, JOSEPH
Priest of Love (1981)

JAMES, TERRENCE
Freedom Road (1979)

JAMES, TIM
  Deadly Prey (1987)
  Mankillers (1987)
  Night Wars (1988)

JANACEK, LEOS
  Haunting of M, The (1981)

JANG, WU DAI
  Arhats in Fury (1985)

JANIN, JACQUES
  Sarati the Terrible (1937)

JANJARASSKUL, MAITREE
  Undisciplined Sailors, The
    (1981)

JANKEL, CHAZ
  Making Mr. Right (1987)

JANNACCI, ENZO
  Peddler (1981)

JANS, ALRIC
  House of Games (1987)
  Things Change (1988)

JANSEN, HANS
  Deadline (1987)

JANSEN, PIERRE
  His Master's Eye (1980)
  Man on the Run, A (1980)
  Horse of Pride (1980)
  Big Brother, The (1982)
  Rebelote (1984)
  Monsieur de Pourceaugnac
    (1985)

JANSSEN, THEO
  German Revolution, A (1982)

JANSSEN, WERNER
  House Across the Bay, The
    (1940)
  Acting: Lee Strasberg and
    the Actors Studio (1981)

JANTIMATORN, SURACHAI
  Amerasia (1986)

JARCZYK, HERBERT
  Cave of the Living Dead,
    The (1965)

JARMUSCH, JIM
  Permanent Vacation (1982)

JARRE, JEAN-MICHEL
  Children's Island (1981)

JARRE, MAURICE
  Crack in the Mirror (1960)
  Weekend at Dunkirk (1966)
  Cimarron Strip (1967)
  Great Expectations (1974)
  Silence, The (1975)
  Jesus of Nazareth (1977)
  Ishi: The Last of His Tribe
    (1978)
  Users, The (1978)
  Black Marble, The (1980)
  Last Flight of Noah's Ark,
    The (1980)
  Resurrection (1980)
  Enola Gay (1980)
  Shogun (1980)
  Lion of the Desert (1981)
  Taps (1981)
  Firefox (1982)
  Young Doctors in Love (1982)
  Coming Out of the Ice (1982)
  Year of Living Dangerously,
    The (1982)
  For Those I Loved (1983)
  Dreamscape (1984)
  Top Secret (1984)
  Passage to India, A (1984)
  Samson and Delilah (1984)
  Sky's No Limit, The (1984)
  Witness (1985)
  Mad Max Beyond Thunder-
    dome (1985)
  Bride, The (1985)
  Enemy Mine (1985)
  Apology (1986)
  Mosquito Coast, The (1986)
  Solarbabies (1986)
  Tai-Pan (1986)
  Fatal Attraction (1987)
  Gaby--A True Story (1987)
  Julia & Julia (1987)

No Way Out (1987)
Tokyo Blackout (1987)
Distant Thunder (1988)
Gorillas in the Mist (1988)
Moon Over Parador (1988)
Murder of Mary Phagen, The (1988)
Palanquin of Tears, The (1988)
Wildfire (1988)

JARRETT, KEITH
Stepping Out (1981)

JARY, MICHAEL
Dissatisfied Woman (1936)
Dangerous Guests (1950)
Gabrielle (1950)
Secretly, Quietly and Softly (1953)
Town Is Full of Secrets, The (1955)
Bandits of the Highway (1955)
At Green Cockatoos by Night (1958)
Hoppla, Now Comes Eddie (1959)

JASSENS, PETER
Heinrich Heine Revue (1980)

JAUBERT, MAURICE
Carnet de Bal, Un (1937)
Altitude 3,200 (1938)
Quai de Brumes (1938)
Hotel du Nord (1939)
End of the Day (1939)
Jour se Leve, Le (1939)
Swallow and the Titmouse, The (1984)
Time Destroyed: Letters from a War, 1939-40 (1985)

JEANNEAU, FRANCOIS
Filthy Business, A (1981)

JEFFREY, DAVID
Fabulous Funnies, The (1978)

JEFFREY, MARK
Fabulous Funnies, The (1978)

JEFFREYS, HERMAN
Killpoint (1984)

JEGER, BENEDICT
Winter City (1981)
Class Whispering (1982)
O Is for Oblomov (1982)
Class Murmurs (1982)
Whole of Life, The (1983)
Town Mayor, The (1984)
Akropolis Now (1984)
Informer, The (1986)

JELINEK, MIKY
Juicy Romance, A (1988)

JENEY, ZOLTAN
Apple of Our Eye, The (1985)

JENKINS, GORDON
Strange Holiday (1942)
Stranded (1976)
Rosetti and Ryan (1977)
First Deadly Sin, The (1980)

JENNINGS, WAYLON
Dukes of Hazzard, The (1979)

JENSEN, MERRILL
Windwalker (1980)
Harry's War (1981)

JENY, ZOLTAN
Revolt of Job (1983)

JERMYN, PETER
Escape from Iran: The Canadian Caper (1980)
Siege (1983)
Climb, The (1987)

JIN, OOI EOW
No Harvest But a Thorn (1985)

JINGXIN, XU
Sunrise (1986)

JIPING, ZHAO
Yellow Earth (1985)
Red Sorghum (1988)

JISSE, DAVID
    Icebreaker (1988)

JOBIM, ANTONIO CARLOS
    Gabriela (1983)
    Moments of Play (1986)
    Deep Illusion (1987)

JOCOBOWICZ, JAROSLAV
    Girls (1985)

JOCSON, MAX
    Jaguar (1980)
    Bona (1981)
    Cain and Abel (1982)

JOFFEE, KAI
    Sex Appeal (1986)
    Warrior Queen (1987)
    Wimps (1987)

JOHANSSON, ALLAN
    Invasion of the Animal
        People (1960)

JOHANSSON, GUNNAR
    Katrina (1949)
    Jungle of Chang (1951)

JOHN, ALLEN
    Twelfth Night (1986)

JOHN, ZDENEK
    Goslings (1981)
    Just Whistle a Little (1981)
    Explosion Happens at Five
        O'Clock, The (1985)

JOHNSON, C. TYRONE
    Dark End of the Street,
        The (1981)

JOHNSON, J. J.
    Barefoot in the Park (1970)
    Fuzz Brothers, The (1973)
    Six Million Dollar Man, The
        (1973)
    Bionic Woman, The (1976)
    Street Killing (1976)
    Future Cop (1977)
    Lucan (1977)

Buck Rogers in the 25th
    Century (1979)
Harris and Company (1979)
Big Easy, The (1982)
Cassie and Company (1982)
Mickey Spillane's Mike Hammer
    (1984)

JOHNSON, LAURIE
    Girls at Sea (1958)
    Tiger Bay (1959)
    Operation Bullshine (1959)
    Spare the Rod (1961)
    Avengers, The (1966)
    Mister Jericho (1970)
    Shirley's World (1971)
    Someone at the Top of the
        Stairs (1973)
    Killer With Two Faces, The
        (1974)
    Anatomy of Terror (1974)
    Devil's Web, The (1974)
    One Deadly Owner (1973)
    Place to Die, A (1974)
    Terror from Within (1974)
    Savage Curse, The (1974)
    Spell of Evil (1973)
    New Avengers, The (1978)
    Color Him Dead (1974)
    Hazard of Hearts, A (1987)
    It's Alive III: Island of the
        Alive (1987)

JOHNSON, SCOTT
    Patty Hearst (1988)

JOHNSTON, PHILLIP
    Committed (1984)

JOHNSTON, RICHARD
    Terror in the Aisles (1984)

JOJIC, BORIS
    Invisible Man, The (1987)

JOMY, ALAIN
    Hate (1980)
    This Age Without Pity (1980)
    Little Siren, The (1980)
    Hussy, The (1985)

JONASZ, MICHEL
  Clara and the Swell Guys
    (1981)

JONES, ANTHONY R.
  Invasion Earth: The Aliens
    Are Here (1988)

JONES, BRYNMOR
  Mirror, The (1984)
  Cop and the Girl, The (1985)
  One Look--And Love Begins
    (1986)

JONES, BUCKY
  Filthy Rich (1982)

JONES, CLIFF
  Street Comedy (1985)

JONES, GUY
  Human Monster, The (Dark
    Eyes of London) (1939)

JONES, JOHN PAUL
  Scream for Help (1984)

JONES, KENNETH V.
  No Time to Die (1958)
  Passport to Shame (1958)
  Four Desperate Men (1959)
  Dentist in the Chair (1960)
  Foxhole in Cairo (1960)
  Story of David, A (1960)
  Offbeat (1961)
  Brain, The (Vengeance) (1962)
  Tomb of Lygeia, The (1964)
  Horror on Snape Island (1971)
  Professor Popper's Problems
    (1974)

JONES, PAUL
  Brain Leeches, The (1978)

JONES, QUINCY
  Ironside (1967)
  Split Second to an Epitaph
    (1968)
  Bill Cosby Show, The (1969)
  Killer by Night (1972)
  Sanford and Son (1972)

Riddle at 24,000 (1974)
Roots (1977)
Sanford (1980)
Color Purple, The (1985)

JONES, RALPH
  Slumber Party Massacre,
    The (1982)
  My Love Letters (1983)

JONES, RAYMOND
  Wodehouse Playhouse (1977)

JONES, RICK
  Flipside of Dominick Hyde,
    The (1980)

JONES, RON
  Naked Vengeance (1986)
  Kidnapped (1987)

JONES, TONY
  Homework (Growing Pains)
    (1979)

JONES, TREVOR
  Beneficiary, The (1980)
  Brothers and Sisters (1980)
  Black Angel (1981)
  Excalibur (1981)
  Sender, The (1982)
  Dark Crystal, The (1982)
  ... And Pigs Might Fly
    (1984)
  Last Days of Pompeii, The
    (1984)
  Dr. Fischer of Geneva (1985)
  Runaway Train (1985)
  Labyrinth (1986)
  Angel Heart (1987)
  Dominick and Eugene (1988)
  Just Ask for Diamond (1988)
  Mississippi Burning (1988)

JONG-KIL, KIM
  Gilsodom (1986)

JONGYI, ZHANG
  Jade Love (1985)

Raggedy Rawney, The
(1988)

KAMOLIKOV, VLADIMIR
Unit, The (1985)
Detachment, The (1986)

KAMPKA, BERND
Dear Augustin, The (1960)

KANARDHAM
Esthappan (1980)

KANCHELI, GUY (GUIA
KANTCHELI; see also
KANTSCHELI, GIJA)
Tears Are Flowing (1983)
Day Longer Than the Night,
The (1984)
Blue Mountains, The (1985)

KANDER, JOHN
Still of the Night (1982)
Blue Skies Again (1983)
Places in the Heart (1984)
Early Frost, An (1985)

KANDIA, KOUYATE SORI
Bloodline--A Modern Tale
(1981)

KANE, ARTIE
Bat People, The (It Lives by
Night) (1974)
Rockford Files, The (1974)
Blue Knight, The (1975)
Wonder Woman (1976)
New Adventures of Wonder
Woman, The (1977)
Devil Dog: The Hound of
Hell (1978)
Question of Guilt, A (1978)
Vega$ (1978)
Young Love, First Love (1979)
Murder Can Hurt You (1980)
Night of the Juggler (1980)
Wrong Is Right (1982)
Million Dollar Infield (1982)
Hotel (1983)
Concrete Beat (1984)
Finder of Lost Loves (1984)
Long Time Gone (1986)

Fatal Confession: A Father
Dowling Mystery (1987)
Divided We Stand (1988)
Red Spider, The (1988)

KANJANAPARINT, SMARN
Land of Love, The (1980)

KANN, HANS
What Price Victory? (1983)

KANNO, MITSUAKI
Castle of Sand, The (1975)
Perennial Weed, The (1976)
Amagi Pass (1983)

KANTCHELI, GUIA see
KANCHELI, GUY

KANTJUKOV, IGOR
Front Romance, A (1984)

KANTOR, IGO
Kill and Kill Again (1981)

KANTY, JAN
Idol (1985)

KANTSCHELI, GIJA (see also
KANCHELI, GUY)
Day of Wrath (1986)

KANTYUKOV, IGOR
I Don't Want to Be Grown-
Up (1984)
Canary Cage, The (1985)

KAPER, BRONISLAU
Alraune (Daughter of Evil)
(1928)
On a Vole un Homme (1934)
Green Mansions (1959)

KAPLAN, ELLIOT
Griff (1973)
Strange New World (1975)
Man on the Outside (1975)
You Lie So Deep, My Love
(1975)
Bridger (1976)
Fantasy Island (1978)

KAPLAN, SOL
  Hollow Triumph (Scar, The)
    (1948)
  Salt of the Earth (1954)
  Star Trek (1966)
  Pancho (1967)
  Winchester '73 (1967)
  Shadow on the Land (1968)
  Golden Gate Murders, The
    (1979)

KAPLOWITZ, MATT
  Night of the Zombies
    (Gamma 693) (1979)

KAPOOR, RANJIT
  Foundation Stone, The (1982)

KAPROFF, DANA
  Ellery Queen (1975)
  Once an Eagle (1976)
  Exo-Man (1977)
  Amazing Spider-Man, The
    (1977)
  Last of the Good Guys, The
    (1978)
  Late Great Planet Earth,
    The (1978)
  Spider-Men: The Dragon's
    Challenge (1979)
  Ultimate Imposter, The (1979)
  Big Red One, The (1980)
  Belle Starr (1980)
  Scared Straight: Another
    Story (1980)
  Every Stray Dog and Kid
    (1981)
  Berlin Tunnel (1981)
  Death Valley (1982)
  Second Sight: A Love Story
    (1984)
  Bounder, The (1984)
  Chiller (1985)
  Smoky Mountain Christmas,
    A (1986)
  Starman (1986)
  Doctors Wilde (1987)
  Doin' Time on Planet Earth
    (1988)
  Glitz (1988)
  I Saw What You Did (1988)
  Stick, The (1988)

KARACSONY, JANOS
  Wall Driller, The (1986)

KARADIMCHEV, BORIS
  Something Out of Nothing
    (1980)
  Nameless Band, A (1981)
  Balance (1983)

KARAENDROU, HELENI (ELENI)
  Rosa (1982)
  Price of Love, The (1984)
  Voyage to Cythera (1984)
  On Course (1985)
  Bee Keeper, The (1986)
  Happy Homecoming, Comrade
    (1986)
  Deserter (1988)
  Landscape in the Mist (1988)

KARAM, EDDIE
  Tulips (1981)

KARANTH, B. V.
  Fertility God, The (1978)
  Case Is Closed, The (Kharij)
    (1983)

KARAS, ANTON
  Cow Girl of St. Catherine
    (1955)

KARAVALCHUK, OLEG
  Married for the First Time
    (1980)
  Black Hen, The (1982)
  Asya (1982)
  Fouette (1986)
  Trip to the Sea, A (1988)

KARAVANISH, O.
  Life in Your Hands (1959)

KARFIOL, GERALD
  Frosty Paradise (1988)

KARITNIKOV, N.
  Voice (1982)

KARKI, TOIVO
  Stomach In, Chest Out
    (1959)

In Love, But Doubly
(1960)

KARLIN, FRED
Cover Me, Babe (1970)
Mr. and Mrs. Bo Jo Jones
(1971)
Man Who Could Talk to Kids,
The (1973)
Autobiography of Miss Jane
Pittman, The (1974)
Dion Brothers, The (1974)
Bad Ronald (1974)
Born Innocent (1974)
It Couldn't Happen to a Nicer
Guy (1974)
Punch and Jody (1974)
Death Be Not Proud (1975)
Dream Makers, The (1975)
Dawn: Portrait of a Teenage
Runaway (1976)
Green Eyes (1976)
Wanted: The Sundance
Woman (1976)
Woman of the Year (1976)
Alexander: The Other Side
of Dawn (1977)
Billy: Portrait of a Street
Kid (1977)
Christmas Miracle in Caufield,
U.S.A. (1977)
Death of Richie, The (1977)
Girl Called Hatter Fox, The
(1977)
Having Babies II (1977)
Hostage Heart, The (1977)
Intimate Strangers (1977)
Life and Assassination of the
Kingfish, The (1977)
Lucan (1977)
McLaren's Riders (1977)
Man from Atlantis, The
(1977)
Minstrel Man (1977)
Trial of Lee Harvey Oswald,
The (1977)
World of Darkness, The (1977)
Awakening Land, The (1978)
Bud and Lou (1978)
Deadman's Curve (1978)
Forever (1978)

Gift of Love, The (1978)
Just Me and You (1978)
Kaz (1978)
Kiss Meets the Phantom of
the Park (1978)
Lady of the House (1978)
Leave Yesterday Behind
(1978)
Long Journey Back (1978)
More Than Friends (1978)
Roll of Thunder, Hear My
Cry (1978)
Waverly Wonders, The (1978)
Who'll Save Our Children
(1978)
World Beyond, The (1978)
And Baby Makes Six (1979)
And Your Name Is Jonah
(1979)
Blind Ambition (1979)
Friends (1979)
Ike (1979)
Last Giraffe, The (1979)
Paris (1979)
Sex and the Single Parent
(1979)
Samurai (1979)
Strangers: The Story of a
Mother and Daughter (1979)
Ravagers (1979)
Vampire (1979)
This Man Stands Alone (1979)
Topper (1979)
Transplant (1979)
Walking Through the Fire
(1979)
Cloud Dancer (1980)
Loving Couples (1980)
Marriage Is Alive and Well
(1980)
Secret War of Jackie's Girls,
The (1980)
Baby Come Home (1980)
Broken Promise (1980)
Homeward Bound (1980)
Miracle on Ice (1980)
Mom, The Wolfman and Me
(1980)
Once Upon a Family (1980)
Plutonium Incident, The
(1980)

Sophia Loren: Her Own Story
   (1980)
Time for Miracles, A (1980)
Bitter Harvest (1981)
Five of Me, The (1981)
Jacqueline Susann's Valley
   of the Dolls 1981 (1981)
Jessica Novak (1981)
Marva Collins Story, The
   (1981)
My Kidnapper, My Love
   (1981)
Thornwell (1981)
We're Fighting Back (1981)
Catalina C-Lab (1982)
First Time, The (1982)
Inside the Third Reich
   (1982)
Not in Front of the Children
   (1982)
Full House (1983)
Inspector Perez (1983)
Lovers and Other Strangers
   (1983)
Wishman (1983)
Baby Sitter (1983)
Gift of Love: A Christmas
   Story, The (1983)
Night Partners (1983)
One Cooks, the Other
   Doesn't (1983)
Policewoman Centerfold (1983)
Calamity Jane (1984)
Off the Rack (1984)
Final Jeopardy (1985)
Hostage Flight (1985)
Robert Kennedy and His
   Times (1985)
Dream West (1986)
Hardesty House (1986)
Vasectomy: A Delicate
   Matter (1986)
Celebration Family (1987)
Facts of Life Down Under,
   The (1987)
Place to Call Home, A (1987)
Dadah is Death (1988)
Lady Mobster (1988)
What Price Victory (1988)

KARLSONS, JURIS
   Ghost in the Garden, A
      (1985)

KARNCHANAPALIN, SAMRA
   Puen and Paeng (1983)

KARNO, MITSUKAI
   Onimasa (1983)

KARNS, FRANK
   Powerhouse (1982)

KARNS, FRED
   Imagemaker, The (1986)

KAROLAK, WOJCIECH
   Konopielka (1983)

KARP, MICHAEL
   Loving (1983)

KARUOVIC, DUSKO (DUSAN)
   Sixth Gear (1981)
   Let's Go On (1982)
   Half Brothers (1988)

KARZYNSKA, A.
   World of Horror (1968)

KASH, DEL
   Night in Hell, A (1958)

KASHA, AL
   Trapped Beneath the Sea
      (1974)
   Someone I Touched (1975)
   Rosenthal and Jones (1975)
   Sgt. T. K. Yu (1979)
   Two Guys from Muck (1982)
   Ultimate Stuntman: A Tribute
      to Dar Robinson, The
      (1987)

KASUGI, TAICHIRO
   Cyborg 009--Underground
      Duel (1967)

KASZYCKI, LUCJAN
   Lynx (1981)

KATINANOS, M.
  Youth of Athens (1949)

KATOH, KAZUHIKO
  All Right, My Friend (1983)

KATSAROS, DOUG
  Star Crystal (1986)

KATZ, FRED
  Ski Troop Attack (1960)
  Wasp Woman, The (1960)
  Little Shop of Horrors, The
    (1961)

KATZ, MARC
  Toxic Avenger, The (1985)

KATZ, STEVE
  Home Remedy (1987)

KATZ, STUART
  Adam's House (1983)

KATZER, GEORG
  Half of Life, A (1985)

KAUDERER, EMILIO
  Disco of Love, The (1980)
  Easy Money (1982)
  Made in Argentina (1987)

KAUDERER, ENRIQUE
  Time for Revenge (1981)

KAUER, GENE (GUENTHER)
  Astounding She Monster
    (1950)
  Cape Canaveral Monster, The
    (1960)
  Monstrosity (1964)
  Arizona and Its Natural
    Resources (1967)
  Long Shadow, The (1968)
  Devil's Mountain, The (1976)
  Claws (1977)
  Curse of the Mayan Temple,
    The (1977)
  681 A.D. The Glory of Khan
    (1984)

KAUFMAN, ALAN
  Ocean Drive Weekend (1986)

KAUFMAN, KEN
  Vamping (1984)
  My Dark Lady (1987)

KAUFMANN, DIETER
  Our Johnny (1980)

KAUFMANN, SERGE
  Water Spider, The (1971)

KAUN, BERNHARD
  Frankenstein (1931)
  Doctor X (1932)
  Farewell to Arms, A (1932)
  I Am a Fugitive from a Chain
    Gang (1932)
  One Way Passage (1932)
  Mystery of the Wax Museum,
    The (1933)
  20,000 Years in Sing Sing
    (1933)
  Death Takes a Holiday (1934)
  Return of the Terror, The
    (1934)
  Story of Louis Pasteur, The
    (1935)
  Walking Dead, The (1936)
  Invisible Menace, The (1937)
  Return of Dr. X, The (1939)
  Smiling Ghost, The (1941)

KAVEL, GENE
  One-Armed Executioner, The
    (1980)

KAWACHI, KANAME
  Zigeunerweisen (1981)

KAWAGUCHI, MAKATO
  Elephant Story (1980)

KAWAKAMI, GEN-ICHI (YAMAHA)
  Abandoned (1982)

KAWAUCHI, NORI
  Theater of Shimmering Heat
    (1982)

KAWCZYNSKI, GERARD
Life is a Long Quiet River
(1988)

KAY, ARTHUR
Renfrew of the Royal Mounted
(1937)

KAY, EDWARD J.
Ape, The (1940)
King of the Zombies (1941)
Jade Mask, The (1945)
Red Dragon, The (1945)
Strange Mr. Gregory, The
(1946)
Decoy (1946)
Shadows of the West (1949)
Ghost Chasers (1951)

KAY, ULYSSES
Quiet One, The (1949)
Thing of Beauty, A (1967)

KAYE, BUDDY
I Dream of Jeannie (1965)

KAYE, NORMAN
Lonely Hearts (1982)
Relatives (1985)

KAYLIN, SAMUEL
Liliom (1930)
Black Sheep (1935)
Charlie Chan's Secret (1935)
Charlie Chan in Shanghai
(1935)
Paddy O'Day (1935)
My Marriage (1935)
Back to Nature (1936)
Career Woman (1936)
Charlie Chan at the Circus
(1936)
Charlie Chan at the Opera
(1936)
Charlie Chan at the Race
Track (1936)
Crack-Up (1936)
Crime of Dr. Forbes, The
(1936)
Educating Father (1936)

First Baby, The (1936)
Gentle Julia (1936)
Human Cargo (1936)
Little Miss Nobody (1936)
Angel's Holiday (1937)
Big Business (1937)
Big Town Girl (1937)
Born Reckless (1937)
Borrowing Trouble (1937)
Charlie Chan at Monte Carlo
(1937)
Charlie Chan at the Olympics
(1937)
Charlie Chan on Broadway
(1937)
Checkers (1937)
City Girl (1937)
Dangerously Yours (1937)
45 Fathers (1937)
Great Hospital Mystery, The
(1937)
Holy Terror, The (1937)
Hot Water (1937)
Lady Escapes, The (1937)
Laughing at Trouble (1937)
Midnight Taxi (1937)
Off to the Races (1937)
One Mile from Heaven (1937)
She Had to Eat (1937)
Step Lively, Jeeves! (1937)
Thank You, Mr. Moto (1937)
That I May Live (1937)
Think Fast, Mr. Moto (1937)
Time Out for Romance (1937)
Wild and Woolly (1937)
Woman Wise (1937)
One Wild Night (1938)
Charlie Chan at Treasure
Island (1939)

KAZANDJIEV, VASSIL
Master of Boyana, The (1981)

KAZANECKI, WALDEMAR
Day of the Vistula, The
(1980)
Love Forgives (1981)
Godson, The (1986)

KAZAZIAN, GEORGES
Time Stops (1986)

Wife of an Important Man
(1987)

KEAN, EDWARD
Howdy Doody (1947)

KEAN, JOHN
Nanou (1986)
Kitchen Toto, The (1987)

KEAN, NICHOLAS
Suitors, The (1988)

KEISTER, SHANE
Dr. Otto and the Riddle of
the Gloom Beam (1986)
Ernest Goes to Camp (1987)

KELAEDONIS, LOUKIANOS
Elefthoerios Venizelos
1910-1927 (1980)

KELAKOFF, ED
Corey: For the People (1977)

KELENOVIC, VUK
Strangler vs. Strangler
(1984)

KELLAWAY, ROGER
Psychiatrist: God Bless the
Children, The (1970)
All in the Family (1971)
Legend of Hillbilly John,
The (1971)
Sharon: Portrait of a
Mistress (1977)
Jaws of Satan (King Cobra)
(1979)
Satan's Mistress (1980)
Silent Scream (1980)
Evil Speak (1981)
Two Lives of Carol Letner,
The (1981)

KELLER, RICKY
Getting It On (1983)
Rockin' Road Trip (1986)

KELLY, KEVIN
Ruder, P.I. (1986)

KEMPEL, ARTHUR
Graduation Day (1981)
Wacko (1983)
Boone (1983)
London and Davis in New
York (1984)
Cary Grant: A Celebration
(1988)

KENDAL
Road, The (1982)

KENNER, AVNER
End of Milton Levi, The
(1981)

KENNON, SKIP
Sanford Meisner--The
Theater's Best Kept
Secret (1985)

KENTIS, CHUCK
Gringo (1985)

KEPPLINGER, GABI
K. u. K. (1984)

KERBER, RANDY
Date With an Angel (1987)

KERNOHAN, BRUCE
First & Ten (1984)
Investigators, The (1984)

KERSHAW, MARTIN
Nightmare Weekend (1986)

KESSELS, POL
Way Back Home (1981)

KESSLER, RALPH
Runaways, The (1979)

KESSLER, ROBERT
Bum Rap (1988)

KESSLER, SIEGFRIED
Adolescent Sugar of Love,
The (1985)

KETI, ZE
Rio Zone Norte (1958)

KHAIRAT, OMAR
Night They Arrested Fatima,
The (1984)
Sixth Day, The (1986)

KHALLAB, KALIB
Paul's Awakening (1985)

KHAN, ALI AKBAR
Pathetic Fallacy (1988)

KHAN, DAVE
Bearcats! (1971)

KHAN, USTAD IMRAT
Guru, The (1969)
Majdhar (1984)
Subarnarekha (1986)

KHATCHATURIAN, ARAM
Pepo (1935)
First Front, The (1949)

KHAYRAT, OMAR
Summer Thefts (1988)

KHEMADASA, PREMASIRI
Kaliyugaya (1982)

KHRASATCHEV, VADIM
Dream Flights (1983)
Protest Me, My Talisman
(1986)
Lonely Woman Seeks Life
Companion (1987)

KHRENNIKOV, TIKHON
Train Goes East, The (1949)
Dream of a Cossack (1952)

KIBAR, MELIH
Cloth Doll (1988)

KIDRON, ADAM
Vroom (1988)

KIESOW, WALTER
Isn't My Husband Wonder-
ful? (1936)

KIKUCHI, MASAAKI
Highway Circuit (Hairpin
Circus) (1972)

KIKUCHI, SHUNSUKE
War of the Insects (Genocide)
(1968)
Attack of the Monsters (1969)
Goke, Body Snatcher from
Hell (1969)
Gamera vs. Jiger (1970)
Gamera vs. Zigra (1971)
Snow Country Elegy (1971)
Haunting (1977)
Planetary Robot Vanguard:
Ace Naval Battle in Space
(1978)
Tarao Bannai (1978)
Super Monster Gamera (1980)
Dr. Slump (1982)
Wild Daisy, The (1982)

KIKUCHI, TOSHISUKE
Karate Lady in Danger (1975)

KIKUCHI-YNGOJO, ROBERT
Chan Is Missing (1982)

KILAR, WOJIECH
Lokis (1970)
King and the Mockingbird,
The (1979)
Beads of One Rosary, The
(1980)
Contract (1980)
Cruise, The (1980)
From a Far Country--Pope
John Paul II (1981)
Imperative (1982)
Unapproachable, The (1982)
Bluebeard (1984)
I Shall Always Stand Guard
(1984)
Year of the Quiet Sun, The
(1984)
Power of Evil, The (1985)
Blind Chance (1987)
Wherever You Are (1988)

KILENYI, EDWARD
African Holiday (1937)

KILFEATHER, EDDIE
  Kickapoo Juice (1945)

KIM, HEE-KAP
  Kill the Shogun (1981)
  House of Death (1981)

KIM, YOUNG DONG
  Blazing Sun, The (1985)

KINEN, KEVIN
  Star Games (1985)
  Clue: Movies, Murder and
    Mystery (1986)
  Remembering Marilyn (1988)
  Superboy (1988)

KING, CAROLE
  Murphy's Romance (1985)

KING, DENIS
  Ghost in the Noonday Sun
    (1973)
  Privates on Parade (1982)
  Fools on the Hill, The (1986)

KING, DREW
  Siege (1983)

KING, JAN
  Smart Alec (1986)
  Invisible Kid, The (1988)

KING, PETE
  Happy Days (1974)

"KING CRIMSON"
  Devil's Triangle, The (1973)

KINGSBURY, CHET
  Another World (1964)
  Somerset (1970)

KINGSLEY, GERSHON
  Silent Night, Bloody Night
    (1972)
  Deathhouse (1981)

KINOSHITA, CHUJI
  Bliss on Earth (1957)
  Lighthouse, The (1958)

Panda and the Magic Serpent
    (1958)
  Forbidden Sands (1960)
  War of the Monsters (1966)
  Nobody's Boy (1970)
  Mini-Skirt Gambler, A (1970)
  Love Stopped the Runaway
    Train (1974)
  Two Iida (1977)

KINOSHITA, TADASHI
  Fireball on the Highway
    (1975)
  These Children Survive Me
    (1983)
  Big Joys, Small Sorrows
    (1986)

KIRGO, NICHOLAS
  Hometown (1985)

KIRSCHNER, DON
  Kowboys, The (1970)

KISIELEWSKI, STEFAN
  Lucky Golashes (1958)

KISINE, VICTOR
  My Darling, My Beloved
    (1985)
  Burglar (1987)

KITAJIMA, OSAMU
  Captive Hearts (1987)

"KITARO"
  Catch Your Dreams ... (1983)
  Homecoming (1984)
  Samuel Lount (1985)

KITAY, DAVID
  Under the Boardwalk (1988)

KITTLER, ALBERT
  Paso Doble (1983)
  Sixth Sense, The (1986)

KLATZKIN, LEON
  Mr. Walkie Talkie (1952)
  Silver Star, The (1955)
  Two-Gun Lady (1956)
  Veil, The (1958)

"KLAUS LAGE BAND"
Tooth for a Tooth, A (1985)

KLEIN, GUNTER
Hen With the Wrong Chick,
The (1965)
Don't Go Into the Woods
(1980)

KLEIN, JESPER
Kurt and Valde (1983)

KLEINSINGER, GEORGE
National Gallery of Art, The
(1968)

KLEINSTEIN, RAMI
Rage and Glory (1984)

KLEPTER, ITZHAK
Lena (1981)
Dead End Street (1982)
When Night Falls (1985)
Fictive Marriage (1988)

KLINE, PHIL
Sleepwalk (1986)

KLINTBERG, GORAN
Summer Nights (1987)

KLOBUCAR, ANDELKO
King's New Clothes, The
(1961)
Pauk (1969)
Secret of Nikola Tesla, The
(1980)

KLOCKE, PIET
Night and Its Price, The
(1984)
Bang! You're Dead! (1987)

KLONGVESA, S.
Headless Ghost, The (1980)

KLUG, ANDREAS MARKUS
Night of Destiny (1982)
In Heaven All Hell Is Break-
ing Loose (1985)

KLUSAK, JAN
End of August at the Hotel
Ozone, The (1965)
That's Why (1981)

KNABL, RUDOLF GREGOR
Triumph of the Just (1987)

KNAIFEL, ALEXANDER
Torpedo Planes (1985)

KNELMAN, KEVIN
Modesty Blaise (1982)

KNIEPER, JUERGEN
Germany, Pale Mother (1980)
Whitey (1980)
Magic Mountain, The (1982)
Double Trouble (1982)
State of Things, The (1982)
Little Brother, The (1983)
Edith's Diary (1983)
Room 666 (1983)
Future of Emily, The (1984)
Berlin Love Story, A (1985)
River's Edge (1986)
Rocinante (1986)
Days to Remember (1987)
Devil's Paradise (1987)
Sky Over Berlin, The (1987)
Maneuvers (1988)

KNIGHT, BOBBY
Forever Fernwood (1977)

KNITTEL, KRZYSZTOF
Phantom, The (1984)

KNOBEL, THEODOR
Isn't My Husband Wonderful?
(1936)

KNOPFLER, DAVID
Jacob Behind the Blue Door
(1988)

KNOPFLER, MARK
Local Hero (1983)
Cal (1984)
Comfort and Joy (1984)
Princess Bride, The (1987)

KNOWLES, CHRIS
  With Time to Kill (1987)

KNOX, GARY
  Exquisite Corpses (1988)

KNOX, MARK
  Hellfire (1986)

KNUDSEN, KENNETH
  Rubber Tarzan (1981)
  Ice Birds (Isfugle) (1983)
  Boy Who Disappeared, The
    (1984)

KNUSHEVITSKY, V.
  Great Is My Country (1959)

KNUTSEN, PETER
  Carl Gustav, the Gang and
    the Parking Lot Bandits
    (1982)
  Children of God's Earth (1983)

KOBAYASHI, KATSUMI
  Kosuke Kinaichi's Adventure
    (1980)

KOBNER, ANDREAS
  Flyer, The (1987)

KOBYLANSKY, KARL
  Dead Wrong (1983)

KOCAB, MICHAEL
  Prague (1985)
  I Was Caught in the Night
    (1986)
  Pied Piper of Hamelin, The
    (1986)
  Wolf's Lair (1987)

KOCH-HANSEN, OLE
  Rainfox (1984)

KOCHUROV, YURI
  Young Pushkin (1937)
  Professor Mamlock (1938)

KOCHYNE, SERGE
  Bed, The (Lit, Le) (1983)

KOCK, ERLAND VON
  Prison, The (1949)

KODALY, ZOLTAN
  Sun Shines, The (1939)

KODEC, KORNELIJE
  Una (1985)

KOEBNER, ANDREAS
  Tango in the Belly (1985)
  Cat, The (1988)
  Lame Go Christmas, The
    (1988)

KOEHLER, LUTZ
  Then Nothing Was the Same
    Anymore (1987)

KOELZ, ERNST
  Passionate People (1983)

KOENING, RENE
  Paradise for All (1982)

KOGAN, A.
  Bells of Autumn (1980)

KOHEN, BUZZ
  Wives (1975)

KOHL, SONNY
  Death by Invitation (1971)

KOLE, NELSON
  Delta Pi (1985)

KOLINKA
  Not With You, Not Without
    You (1985)

KOLLER, HANS
  Skin of the Fool (1982)

KOLLO, WALTER
  Girl from the Chorus, A
    (1937)

KOLZ, ERNEST
  Death of the Flea Circus
    Operator, or Ottocardo

Weiss Reforms His Firm
(1972)

KOMAROV, VLADIMIR
Fellows (1982)
Forgive Me, Alyosha (1985)

KOMEDA, KRYZYSTOF
Two Men and a Wardrobe
(1957)
Banner, The (1965)
Hands Up! (1981)

KOMORI, AKIHIRO
Wild Swans, The (1978)

KOMORI, TOSHIYUKI
Antique Dealer's Wife, The
(1983)

KONDO, TASHINOORI
Remembrance (1988)

KONDRATIUK, ANDREZEJ
Four Seasons, The (1985)

KONG, NG TAI
Home at Hong Kong (1983)

KONIECZNY, KRZYZTOF
Christmas Eve (1982)

KONIECZNY, ZYGMUNT
On the Move (Moving) (1980)
Issa's Valley (1983)
Postcard from a Journey
(1985)
Job, The (1985)
Possessed, The (1988)
Road Home, The (1988)
Taboo (1988)

KONOE, HIDEMARO
Forever My Love (1952)

KONSTANTIOV, LJUPCO
Southern Trail, The (1982)
I Told You So (1984)
Happy New Year--1949 (1986)
Hi-Fi (1987)

KONT, PAUL
Brutality (Flight into the
Reeds) (1953)

KONTE, LAMINE
Dignity (1982)

KOO, JOSEPH
Drummer, The (1983)
Better Tomorrow, A (1986)
Better Tomorrow II, A (1987)
Mirage (1987)

KOOPMAN, MAARTEN
Tracks in the Snow (1985)

KOPP, FREDERICK
Creeping Terror, The (1974)

KOPPEL, ANDERS
John's Secret (1985)
Thumbscrew, The (1986)
Redtops Meets Tyrannos, The
(1988)

KOPPELMAN, MARTIN
Bear, The (1984)

KOPS, PIM
Looking for Eileen (1987)

KORENI, BELA
Our Johnny (1980)

KORINEK, MIROSLAV
Very Late Afternoon of a
Faun, The (1984)

KORNGOLD, GEORGE
Laurel & Hardy Laughtoons
(1979)

KOROKU, REJIRO
Godzilla (1985)

KORVEN, MARK
I've Heard the Mermaids
Singing (1987)

KORWIN, EDWARD
Paul Cadmus: Enfant Terrible
at 80 (1986)

KORZYNSKI, ANDRZEJ
Olympics 40 (1980)
Salad Days (1980)
Man of Iron (1981)
Possession (1981)
Fair Game (1984)
Silver Globe, The (1988)

KOSINAKI, RICHARD KOZ
Enemy Territory (1987)

KOSMA, JOSEPH
Rules of the Game (1939)
Devil's Envoys, The (1942)
Petit Soldat, Le (1947)
Wench, The (1949)
Hans the Sailor (1949)
Love Locked Out (1949)
Here Is the Beauty (1950)
Crossroads of Passion (1951)
Lovers of Verona (1951)
Grand Terrace, The (1951)
Bethsabee (1951)
Curious Adventures of Mr.
    Wonderbird, The (1952)
Paris Is Always Paris (1952)
Red Curtain, The (1952)
Children of Love, The (1953)
Paris Incident (1954)
Fugitives, The (1955)
People of No Importance
    (1956)
Along the Sidewalks (1956)
That Is the Dawn (1956)
Je Reviendrai a Kandara
    (1957)
Paris Does Strange Things
    (Elena and the Men) (1957)
Picnic on the Grass (1959)
Man Wants to Live! (1961)

KOSTIC, VOJISLAV
Who's That Singing Over
    There? (1980)
Berlin Kaput (1981)
Great Guy at Heart, A (1981)
Sunday Lunch (1982)
Train to Kraljevo, The (1982)
Tight Spot, A (1983)
My Temporary Father (1983)
Balkan Spy, The (1984)

Nothing But Words of Praise
    for the Deceased (1984)
Life Is Beautiful (1985)

KOSTIDAKIS, YANNIS
City Never Sleeps, The
    (1984)

KOSUGI, TAICHIRO
Cyborg 009--Underground
    Duel (1967)
Blood Vendetta (1971)
Swords of Death (1971)
Women Smell of Night (1971)

KOTONSKI, WLODZIMIERZ
Labyrinth (1962)

KOTTUKAPALLY, ISAAC THOMAS
Esthappan (1980)

KOUNADIS, ARGHYRIS
Girl in Black, The (1956)
Our Last Spring (1960)
Your Neighbor's Son (1981)
Noose, The (1987)

KOUROUPOS, GEORGE
Blood of the Statues, The
    (1982)

KOURY, REX
Gunsmoke (1955)

KOUYATE, SOTIGUI
Days of Torment (1985)

KOVAC, KORNELIJE
Dreams, Life, the Death of
    Filip Filipovic (1980)
Season of Peace in Paris
    (1981)
Living Like the Rest of Us
    (1982)
Hello, Taxi (1983)
Igman March, The (1983)
Time of Leopards, The (1985)
Volunteers (1986)
Blackbird (1988)

KOVAC, ROLAND
48 Hours to Acapulco (1968)

KOVACH, KORNELL
Montenegro (1981)

KOVACS, GYORGY
Vulture, The (1983)

KOWALSKI, OLIVIER
Pierre and Djemila (1987)

KOYAMA, SEIICHIRO
Fables from Hans Christian
Andersen (1969)

KOYAMA, TOMOHIRO
High School Outcasts (1971)

KOZ, JEFF
Last Horror Film, The (1984)
Mission Kill (1985)

KOZINA, MARIJAN
Peaceful Valley, The (1957)

KOZLOWSKI, LEOPOLD
Austeria (1983)

KRAEMER, NICHOLAS
Honor, Profit and Pleasure
(1985)

KRAFT, GENE
Master, The (1984)

KRAFT, ROBERT
Moving Day (1987)
Day by Day (1988)

KRAFT, WILLIAM
Chisholms, The (1980)
Bill (1981)
Fire and Ice (1983)

KRAJEWSKI, SEWERYN
Without Love (1980)

KRANZ, GEORGE
Cop and the Girl, The
(1985)
Magic Sticks (1987)

KRATOCHVILI, MARTIN
Dark Sun (1980)

KRAUS, VLADIMIR (KRAUS-
RAJTERIC)
Road a Year Long, The (1958)
Non-Scheduled Train, A
(1959)
War (Rat) (1960)
14 Days, The (1961)
Evening Bells (1986)

KRAUSE, BERNARD
Dark Circle (1982)
Wildrose (1984)

KRAUSE, ZYGMUNT
Smaller Sky (1981)

KRAUS-RAJTERIC, VLADIMIR
see KRAUS, VLADIMIR

KRAUSHAAR, RAOUL
Lassie (1954)
Back from the Dead (1957)
Bonanza (1959)
September Storm (1960)
Beachcomber, The (1961)
Children of Divorce (1980)

KRAUSS, ROLI
Mama Happy ...? (1984)

KREUDER, PETER
Burg Theater (1936)
Children of Fortune (1936)
Hokum (1936)
Wedding Dream, A (1936)
Confession (1937)
Feminine Wiles (1951)

"KREUNERS GROUP"
Congo Express (1986)

KRICKA, JAROSLAV
Merry Wives, The (1938)

KRISHNA, BALAMURALI
Madhvacharya (1987)

KRISHNAMURTHY, V.
Jagan Mohini (1978)

LAGE, KLAUS
  Zabou (1987)

LAI, FRANCIS
  Berlin Affair (1970)
  Beyond the Reef (1981)
  Ins and the Outs, The (1981)
  Madame Claude 2 (1981)
  Edith and Marcel (1983)
  Dog Day (1984)
  Ripoux, Les (1984)
  Here Comes Santa Claus
    (1985)
  Marie (1985)
  AIDS--A Danger for Love
    (1985)
  Man and a Woman: 20 Years
    Later, A (1986)
  Sins (1986)
  Association of Wrongdoers
    (1987)
  Attention, Bandits (1987)
  Dark Eyes (1987)
  Bernadette (1988)
  Blue Pyramids, The (1988)
  Itinerary of a Spoiled Child
    (1988)

LAI, MICHAEL
  Body Is Willing, The (1983)
  Happy Din Don (1986)
  Police Story (1986)

LAIRD, MARVIN
  Keep on Truckin' (1975)
  Lost Saucer, The (1975)
  Baxters, The (1979)
  Hamptons, The (1983)

LAIRD, WAYNE
  Death in the Family, A (1987)

LAJTHA, LÁSZLO
  Murder in the Cathedral
    (1952)

LAKONNY, REINHARD
  ... Difficult to Become
    Engaged (1983)

LALANNE, JEAN-FELIX
  Passage, The (1986)

LaLOGGIA, FRANK
  Fear No Evil (1981)
  Lady in White (1988)

LAM, TANG SIU
  Older Master Cute (1981)
  Head Hunter, The (1982)
  To Hell with the Devil (1982)
  Shaolin Drunkard (1983)

LAM, VIOLET
  Secret, The (1979)
  Father and Son (1981)
  Ah Ying (1983)
  Love Unto Waste (1987)

LAMB, ROBERT
  Dublin Suite, The (1986)

LAMBERT, JERRY
  Texas Chainsaw Massacre
    Part 2, The (1986)

LAMBERT, PAUL
  Bloodthirsty Fairy, The
    (1968)

LAMBERTH, ARNE
  Youth at Play (1957)

LAMBRO, PHILIP
  Crypt of the Living Dead
    (1973)

LAMMERS, KELLY
  Planet of the Dinosaurs
    (1980)

LANCTOT, FRANCOIS
  Homme a tout Faire, L' (1980)

LANDAU, MICHAEL
  Killing Cars (1986)

LANDAU, RUSS
  Senior Week (1988)

LANDEE, DONN
  Wild Life, The (1984)

LANDGREN, NILE
  Rat Winter (1988)

LANE, JAMES
   Murder Lust (1987)

LANG, HANS
   Eva Inherits Paradise (1951)
   Twin Maneuver (1956)
   Candidates for Marriage (1958)
   Vienna, City of My Dreams
     (1958)
   Youth Comes Only Twice
     (1958)

LANG, MICHAEL
   Suicide Club, The (1973)
   House Calls (1979)
   Hollywood Harry (1985)

LANGE, ARTHUR
   Love Under Fire (1937)
   This Is My Affair (1937)
   Western Gold (1937)
   Wife, Doctor and Nurse (1937)
   Undying Monster, The (1952)
   99 River St. (1953)

LANGE, JOHNNY
   Black Dragons (1941)
   Invisible Ghost, The (1941)
   Corpse Vanishes, The (1942)

LANGEVIN, PIERRE
   Choice of a People, The
     (1985)

LANGFORD, GORDON
   Egghead's Robot (1970)
   Troublesome Double, The
     (1971)

LANGHORNE, BRUCE
   Jimmy B. & Andre (1980)
   Night Warning (1980)
   Melvin and Howard (1980)
   Word of Honor (1981)
   Fourth Wise Man, The (1985)
   Smart Alec (1986)

LANGKILDE, HENRIK
   Ophelia Hits Town (1985)

LANGLOIS, JEROME
   Pale Face (1985)

LANOE, HENRI
   Roaring Forties, The (1982)

LANOIS, DANIEL
   Surrogate, The (1984)

LANZ, JUAN
   San Antonito (1986)

LANZARONE, BEN
   Out of the Blue (1979)
   Shirley (1979)
   Goodtime Girls (1980)

LAPICKI, ANDRZEJ
   World of Horror (1968)

LAPIDES, FRED
   Assault of the Killer Bimbos
     (1988)

LAPOUBLE, POCHO
   Gone to Seed (1984)
   Goodbye, Robert (1985)

LAR, ROBERTO
   Nights Without Moons or
     Suns (1984)

LARA, AUGUSTIN
   Devil and the Lady, The
     (1983)

LARA, CATHERINE
   Men Prefer Fat Girls (1981)

LAROCHELLE, DENIS
   Henri (1986)
   Gaspard and Son (1988)

LARSEN, KIM
   In the Middle of the Night
     (1984)

LARSON, GLEN A.
   Switch (1975)
   Nancy Drew Mysteries, The
     (1977)
   B.J. and the Bear (1978)
   Battles: The Murder That
     Wouldn't Die (1980)
   Galactica 1980 (1980)

LARSON, GREY
Tuck Everlasting (1981)

LARSSON, LARS-ERIK
Lights of the Night (1958)

LASA, XABIER
Segovia Escape, The (1981)

LA SALLE, JOHN
Hello, Larry (1979)

LA SALLE, RICHARD
Tank Battalion (1958)
Purple Hills, The (1961)
Mermaids of Tiburon, The
   (1962)
Room 222 (1969)
Aquasex (1970)
City Beneath the Sea (1971)
Run, Joe, Run (1974)
Adventures of the Queen
   (1975)
Swiss Family Robinson (1975)
Westwind, The (1975)
Big John, Little John (1976)
Flood (1976)
McDuff, the Talking Dog
   (1976)
Monster Squad, The (1976)
Fire! (1977)
New Adventures of Wonder
   Woman, The (1977)
Return of Captain Nemo, The
   (1978)
Brenda Starr, Reporter (1979)
Hanging by a Thread (1979)
Memory of Eva Ryker, The
   (1980)
When, Jenny, When? (1980)
Code Red (1981)
Cave-In! (1983)
Night the Bridge Fell Down,
   The (1983)

LA SANDRA, JOHN
Scalpels (1980)

LASKO, EDWARD
Immoral Mr. Teas, The
   (1960)

LASLO, SANDOR
Cafe Moscow (1936)

LASRY, TEDDY
Clowns of God, The (1986)

LASZLO, ALEXANDER
Renegade Satellite, The (1954)
Narcotics Story, The (1958)
Night of the Blood Beast
   (1958)
Atomic Submarine, The (1960)

LATTANZI, MICHAEL
Class of Nuke 'Em High (1986)

LAUBER, KEN
Things in Their Season (1974)
Hatfields and the McCoys, The
   (1975)
Journey from Darkness (1975)
Returning Home (1975)
Studs Lonigan (1979)
Where's Poppa? (1979)
Camp Grizzly (1980)
Mr. and Mrs. Dracula (1980)
Little Dragons, The (1980)
Kent State (1980)
Babies Having Babies (1986)

LAUBERT, ANNE
Coffin Affair, The (1980)

LAUMANN, HOLGER
Imprudent Lover, The (1982)

LAUREL, BOBBY
Rosary Murders, The (1987)

LAURIE, LINDA
Land of the Lost (1974)

LAURISIN, MIKLOS
Puszta Princess (1939)

LAUZON, ROBERT
Last Straw, The (1987)

LAVA, WILLIAM
Smiling Ghost, The (1941)
Mysterious Doctor, The (1943)

Jungle Captive (1945)
50 Years Before Your Eyes
    (1950)
Tobor the Great (1954)
Monster on the Campus (1958)
Horse With the Flying Tail,
    The (1961)
Sword of Ali Baba, The (1965)
Pink Blueprint, The (1967)
Pink Panther, The (1969)
O'Hara, United States
    Treasury: Operation Cobra
    (1971)
Road Runner Show, The
    (1971)
Sylvester and Tweety (1976)
Bugs Bunny's Third Movie:
    1001 Rabbit Tales (1982)

LAVAGNINO, FRANCESCO
Strange Appointment (1950)
Bachelor, The (1956)
Manfish (1956)
Rice Field, The (1956)
White Vertigo (1956)
Don't Trifle With Women (1957)
Women Times Three (1957)
Passionate Summer (1958)
Pezzo, Capopezzo e Capitano
    (1958)
Soledad (1958)
Calypso (1959)
Follies of Barbara, The (1959)
First Love (1959)
Gorgo (1960)
Night They Killed Rasputin,
    The (1960)
Ulysses Against the Sons of
    Hercules (1961)
Corsican Brothers, The
    (1961)
Gioia Vivere, Che (1961)
Grand Olympiade, The (1961)
Samson vs. the Pirates (1963)
Castle of the Living Dead,
    The (1964)
Hercules Against Rome (1964)
Hercules and the Tyrants of
    Babylon (1964)
Invincible Three, The (1964)
War Between the Planets,
    The (1965)

America, God's Country
    (1966)
Bitter Bread (1966)
Million Dollars for Seven
    Assassins, A (1966)
Red Roses for Angelique
    (1966)
Spies Love Flowers (1966)
Zorro the Rebel (1966)
Gungala, the Virgin of the
    Jungle (1967)
Something is Creeping in the
    Dark (1970)
Queens of Evil, The (1971)
Naked Magic (Shocking Can-
    nibals) (1974)

LAVANDIER, HERVE
Catwalk, The (1988)

LAVILLIERS, BERNARD
Snow (1981)
Rue Barbare (1984)

LAVIN, TOM
Out of the Blue (1980)

LAVISTA, RAUL
Midnight Phantom, The
    (1939)
Man Without a Face, The
    (1950)
Susana (1950)
Woman Without Love, A
    (1951)
Absentee, The (1952)
Right to Be Born, The (1952)
Return to Youth (1953)
Mr. Photographer (1953)
Witch, The (1955)
Hidden One, The (1956)
Lovers, The (1956)
Felicidad (1957)
Tizoc (1957)
Cucuracha, La (1959)
Happiness (1959)
Skeleton of Mrs. Morales,
    The (1959)
Sleepless Years (1959)
Up and Down (1959)
I, a Sinner (1960)
Impatient Heart, The (1960)
Macario (1960)

To Each His Life (1960)
Little Red Riding Hood and
the Monster (1960)
Cat, The (1961)
Invasion of the Zombies
(1961)
Simon of the Desert (1965)
She Wolf, The (1965)
Night of a Thousand Cats
(1974)

LAVSKY, RICHARD
Beginner's Luck (1986)

LAWRENCE, ALFRED
Flying Doctor, The (1936)

LAWRENCE, BRUNO
Pallet on the Floor (1984)

LAWRENCE, ELLIOTT
Search for Tomorrow (1951)
Edge of Night, The (1956)
Your Money or Your Wife
(1972)
Texas (1980)
Baker's Dozen (1982)
Cradle Will Fall, The (1983)

LAWRENCE, STEPHEN
Michele Lee Show, The (1974)
It Happened One Christmas
(1977)
Alice, Sweet Alice
(Communion) (1978)
Sooner or Later (1979)
Dorothy in the Land of Oz
(1981)
Trackdown: Finding the
Goodbar Killer (1983)
Mirrors (Marianne) (1984)
Red Riding Hood (1987)
Baby on Board (1988)
Meet the Munceys (1988)

LAWS, MAURY
Original TV Adventures of
King Kong, The (1966)

Tom of T.H.U.M.B. (1966)
Mad Monster Party, The
(1967)
Jackson Five, The (1971)
Last Dinosaur, The (1977)
Bermuda Depths, The (1978)
Bushido Blade, The (1978)
Ivory Ape, The (1980)
Leprechaun's Christmas Gold,
The (1981)
Wind in the Willows, The
(1985)

LAY, CHRIS
Outtakes (1987)

LAYTON, EDDIE
Love Is a Many-Splendored
Thing (1967)
Where the Heart Is (1969)

LAZAROIU, JEAN
Snapshot Around the Family
Table (1981)

LEAF, IMER
Miss Leslie's Dolls (1972)

LEAHY, RONNIE
Ascendency (1983)

LEANDER, MIKE
Privilege (1967)
Run a Crooked Mile (1969)

LEAO, FOTU
Paradise (1974)

LECAROS, ROBERTO
With Burning Patience (1983)

LECOEUR, JACQUES
Turn-On (1985)

LECOEUR, MAURICE
Erendira (1983)

LEDENEW, R.
Trumpet Solo (1986)

LEDUC, PIERRE
Few Days More, A (1981)

LEE, BILL
She's Gotta Have It (1986)
School Daze (1988)

LEE, DAVID
Kitchen, The (1961)

LEE, GERALD
Satan's Cheerleaders (1977)

LEE, JONG-GU
Man With Three Coffins, The
(1987)

LEE, LINDSAY
Front Line (1981)

LEE, S. C.
Papa, Can You Hear Me
Sing? (1984)

LEE, WILLIE
Dream On (1981)

LEENEN, ERNST
90 Minute Stop (1936)

LEFEBVRE, JEAN-PIERRE
To the Rhythm of My Heart
(1983)
"S" Day, The (1984)
Box of Sun, The (1988)

LEFEVRE, TOMAS
Conceived Desires (1982)

LEGRAND, MICHEL
Gold and Lead (1966)
Go-Between, The (1971)
Brian's Song (1971)
Adventures of Don Quixote,
The (1973)
It's Good to Be Alive (1974)
Mountain Men, The (1980)
Hunter, The (1980)
Atlantic City, U.S.A. (1980)
Hinotori (1980)
Falling in Love Again (1980)
Gift, The (1982)
What Makes David Run? (1982)
Best Friends (1982)
Slapstick (1982)

Woman Called Golda, A (1982)
Love in Germany, A (1983)
Never Say Never Again (1983)
Yentl (1983)
Secret Places (1984)
Words and Music (1984)
Jesse Owens Story, The (1984)
Hell Train (1984)
Palace (1985)
Departure, Return (1985)
Parking (1985)
Promises to Keep (1985)
Crossings (1986)
Casanova (1987)
Lonely Hearts Club (1987)
Spiral (1987)
Switching Channels (1988)
Three Seats for the 26th
(1988)

LEGRAND, RAYMOND
Three Sinners (1952)
Manon of the Spring (1953)
Public Enemy No. 1 (1954)

LEHMAN, LEW
Search and Rescue: The
Alpha Team (1977)

LEHTINEN, RAUNO
Niskavouri Saga, The (1985)

LEIMER, K.
Land of Look Behind (1982)

LEIPOLD, JOHN
Death Takes a Holiday (1934)

LEKAJ, KRIST
Proka (1986)

LEKAS, DEMETRIS
Electric Angel (1981)

LELANN, ERIC
Elsa! Elsa! (1985)
With All Hands (1986)

LEMA, RAY
Black Hanky Panky (1986)

Little Friend (1934)
Man with 100 Faces (1938)
Mad Men of Europe (1940)
Night Train (1940)
So Little Time (1953)

LEVY, SHUKI
Dawn of the Mummy (1981)
Inspector Gadget (1983)
Littles, The (1983)
Fatal Games (1984)
Get Along Gang, The (1984)
Going Bananas (1984)
Kidd Video (1984)
Wolf Rock TV (1984)
Escape from Grumble Gulch
(1984)
Here Come the Littles (1985)
Rainbow Brite and the Star
Stealer (1985)
Kissyfur (1985)
Bay Coven (1987)
Perfect Victims (1988)

LEWIN, FRANCIS
First Love (1982)

LEWIN, FRANK
Brookhaven Spectrum (1967)
Year Toward Tomorrow, A
(1967)
Jake's Way (1980)

LEWIS, HERSHELL GORDON
(SHELDON SEYMOUR)
Blood Feast (1963)
She-Devils on Wheels (1968)
Blood Bath (1971)

LEWIS, LAURIE
Evil Touch, The (1973)
On the Run (1982)

LEWIS, MICHAEL J.
Man Who Haunted Himself,
The (1970)
In Search of ... (1976)
Medusa Touch, The (1978)
Lion, the Witch, and the
Wardrobe, The (1979)
Sphinx (1981)

Unseen, The (1981)
Naked Face, The (1984)

LEWIS, MORGAN
Helen Keller in Her Own
Story (1954)

LEWIS, RICHARD WARREN
Rhoda (1974)

LEWIS, ROBERT
She-Devils on Wheels (1968)

LEWIS, W. MICHAEL
Secrets of the Bermuda
Triangle (1978)
Shogun Assassin (1980)
New Year's Evil (1981)
Ninja, The (1981)
Killing of America, The
(1982)
Enter the Ninja (1982)
Ballad of Gregorio Cortez,
The (1983)
Revenge of the Ninja (1983)
Hot Child in the City (1987)

LEWIS, WEBSTER
Hearse, The (1980)
My Tutor (1983)
Go Tell It on the Mountain
(1984)

LEXMANN, JURAJ
Bloody Lady (1981)

LEY, BRUCE
Confidential (1986)

LIANG, DAVID
Great Wall Is a Great Wall,
The (1986)

LIBACK, SVEN
Inner Space (1975)

LIBERATORI, FABIO
Soap and Water (1983)
Two Cops, The (1985)
Me and My Sister (1988)
Volpone (1988)

LIBONATI, DANA
  American Taboo (1984)

"LIBRA"
  Beyond the Door II (1979)

LICHTMANN, JAKOB
  In the Land of My Parents
    (1982)
  Melek Leaves (1985)

LICKS, AUGUSTO
  Green Years (1984)
  That Couple (1985)

LIEBAU, JO
  Golge (1980)

LIEBER, ED
  Anita--Dances of Vice (1987)

LIEBERMAN, ROBERT
  Warning: Medicine May Be
    Hazardous to Your Health
    (1988)

LIFSHITZ, MARCOS
  Macho That Barks Doesn't
    Bite II (1987)
  Poking Fun at the Border
    Patrol (1987)
  Race Never Loses--It Smells
    Like Gas, The (1987)
  Tonight Pancho Dines Out
    (1987)

LIGUORI, GAETANO
  Come Dire (1983)
  Okay, Okay (1983)

LINDAHL, THOMAS
  Ake and His World (1984)
  Princess of Babylonia, The
    (1986)
  Pirates of the Lake (1987)
  Emma's Shadow (1988)

LINDBERG, EDVIN
  South of the Highway (1937)

LINDEMAN, OSMO
  Mysterious Case of Rygseck
    Murders (1960)
  Red Dove, The (1961)

LINDERHOLM, GOESTA
  Rasmus Hits the Road (1982)

LINDH, BJOERN JASON
  Grass Widowers (1982)
  Man from Mallorca, The
    (1984)

LINDQUIST, FREDDY
  On the Threshold (1984)

LINDSAY, CREIGHTON
  Bad Night (1986)

LINDSAY, MARK
  Shogun Assassin (1980)
  Killing of America, The (1982)

LINDSEY, STEVE
  Behind Enemy Lines (1986)

LINDUP, DAVID
  Journey to the Unknown
    (1968)
  Spiral Staircase, The (1975)
  Rising Damp (1980)

LINE, LINDA
  Return to Peyton Place (1972)

LINK, PETER
  Great Niagara, The (1974)
  Nightmare (1974)

LINKE, PAUL
  Girl from the Chorus, A
    (1937)
  Secretly, Quietly and Softly
    (1953)

LINKOLA, JUKKA
  Snow Queen, The (1987)

LINN, MICHAEL (MIKE)
  Breakin' 2 Electric Boogaloo
    (1984)

Rappin' (1985)
American Ninja (1985)
Allan Quatermain and the
    Lost City of Gold (1987)
Evil Town (1987)
Survival Game (1987)

LINNET, ANNE
Inside Woman (1980)
Chronic Innocence (1985)
Street of My Childhood (1986)
Time Out (1988)

LINSEY, TONY
Souvenir (1988)

LIPSKER, SCOTT
Joy of Sex (1984)

LIPVOSEK, MARIJAN
Good Old Piano, The (1959)

LISBOA, NEI
Green Years (1984)

LISK, ALAN
Codename: Kyril (1988)

LISKA, A.
Inspiration (1949)

LISKA, ZDENEK
Lullaby (1948)
Treasure of Bird Island, The
    (1952)
Naughty Ball, The (1956)
Weapons of Destruction (1958)
Day of Reckoning, The (1960)
Where the Devil Cannot Go
    (1960)
White Dove, The (1960)
At the Terminus (1961)
High Princip (1961)
Baron Munchausen (1961)
Murder, Czech Style (1966)
Flat, The (1968)
Valley of Bees, The (1968)
Castle for a Young Hangman,
    A (1970)
Divine Emma (1980)
Medal, The (1980)

Death Made to Order
    (1981)

LITMANOWITSCH, ANDREAS
Noah and the Cowboy (1986)

LITTLE, RUSS
Too Outrageous! (1987)

LIU, ZHUENG
Young Teacher, The (1982)

LIVANELI, ZULFI (ZUIFU)
Guelibik (1984)
Blood (1986)
Iron Earth, Copper Sky
    (1987)

LJUPCO-KONSTANTINOV
Red Horse, The (1981)
Years of Crisis (1981)

LLOYD, MICHAEL
Sigmund and the Sea Monsters
    (1973)
Land of the Lost (1974)
Far-Out Space Nuts (1975)
Lost Saucer, The (1975)
Love's Dark Ride (1978)
Shipshape (1978)
Strangers in Our House (1978)
Me and Maxx (1980)
Grambling's White Tiger (1981)
Beach Girls, The (1982)
Tough Enough (1983)
Savage Streets (1984)
Tomboy (1985)
Staff of "Life," The (1985)
Body Slam (1987)
Garbage Pail Kids, The (1987)
Ultimate Stuntman: A Tribute
    to Dar Robinson, The
    (1987)

LLOYD, NORMAN
Moment in Love, A (1956)

LO, ISMAILA
Camp Thiaroye (1988)

LO, LOWELL
Infatuation (1985)

Passion (1986)
Autumn's Tale, An (1987)
Prison on Fire (1987)
Painted Faces (1988)
People's Hero (1988)

LOBACHEV, C. G.
Gypsies (1936)

LOBO, EDU
Pictures from the Unconscious
(1988)

LOCKHART, ROBERT
On the Black Hill (1988)

LOCKYER, MALCOLM
Strictly Confidential (1959)
Island of the Burning Doomed
(1967)
Face of Eve, The (1968)
Dr. Who (1973)

LO DUCA, JOE (JOSEPH)
Evil Dead, The (Book of the
Dead) (1980)
Thou Shalt Not Kill ...
Except (1987)

LOEFFLER, JOHNNY
Rush (1981)

LOFFREDO, MUZZI
False One, The (1986)

LOGARIDIS, STAVROUS
Woman Across the Way, The
(1983)

LOGGINS, KENNY
Between the Lines (1980)

LOGIADIS, MANOLIS
Children of Chronos (1985)

LOJEWSKI, HARRY
Young Doctor Kildare (1972)
Jigsaw John (1976)
Diner (1983)

LOLASCHWILI, ENRI
Robinsoniad: Oh, My English
Grandfather (1986)

LOMUTO, FRANCISCO
College Girls (1939)

LONGO, ACHILLE
Pact With the Devil (1949)

LOOSE, WILLIAM
Reflections (1967)
Tarzan and the Jungle Boy
(1968)
Night of the Living Dead
(1968)
Blacksnake (1973)
'Gator Bait (1973)
Last of the Wild (1974)
Between the Wars (1978)
Lucifer Complex, The (1978)
Mysterious Island of Beautiful
Women (1979)
Alien Encounters, The (1979)
Devil Times Five, The (1979)
Camp Wilderness (1980)
Man Who Saw Tomorrow, The
(1981)
E.T. & Friends--Magical Movie
Visitors (1982)
Mystery Mansion (1983)
Prime Times (1983)
Heroes and Sidekicks--Indiana
Jones and the Temple of
Doom (1984)
Four Americans in China
(1985)
In the Shadow of Vesuvius
(1987)
African Odyssey (1988)
Grotesque (1988)

LOPEZ, DANIEL
Treasure of the Amazon, The
(1985)

LOPEZ, FERNANDO M.
Cave of Ali Baba, The (1954)

LOPEZ, FRANCIS
Rita (1950)

Andalousie (1951)
Susanna and Me (1957)
It Happened on the 36
   Candles (1957)
Tabarin (1958)

LOPEZ SAES, JOSE MIGUEL
False Eyelashes (1982)

LORING, GLORIA
Jo's Cousins (1974)
Diff'rent Strokes (1978)
Facts of Life, The (1979)
Parkers, The (1981)

LOTHAR, MARK
White Hell of Pitz-Palu, The
   (1952)
Keepers of the Night
   (Night Watch) (1953)
Angelika (1954)
His Royal Highness (1954)
Sauerbruch (1954)
Devil in Silk, The (1956)
Faust (1960)

LOTKA, FRAN
Unconquered People (1950)

LOUBE, CARL
Cow Girl of St. Catherine
   (1955)

LOUBET, ROGER
Is There a Frenchman in the
   House? (1982)
Boodle, The (1985)

LOUIE, ALEXINA
Martha, Ruth and Edie
   (1988)

LOUIE, DIANE
Latino (1985)

LOUIE, ZINA
Gordon Pinsent and the Life
   and Times of Edwin Alonzo
   Boyd (1982)

LOUIGUY
Toa (1949)

Treasure of Cantenac, The
   (1950)
Poison, Le (1952)
Heroes Are Tired, The (1955)
Frou-Frou (1955)
Eye for an Eye, An (1957)

LOUIS, EDDY
Tabataba (1988)

LOUSSIER, JACQUES
Sky Above Heaven (1964)
Man Who Went Up in Smoke,
   The (1981)

LOVAS, ROBERT
Hunting Ground (1982)

LOVE, GEOFF
Bless This House (1977)

LOW, BEN
Kid Who Couldn't Miss, The
   (1983)
Keeping Track (1987)

LOWE, MUNDELL
Love on a Rooftop (1966)
Attack on Terror: The
   F.B.I. vs. the Ku Klux
   Klan (1975)
Deadly Game, The (1977)
Girl in the Empty Grave,
   The (1977)
Tarantulas: The Deadly
   Cargo (1977)
B.A.D. Cats (1980)
Cassie and Company (1982)

LOWRY, TONY
Not Wanted on the Voyage
   (1957)

LU-DING, HO
Crossroads (1937)

LUBAT, BERNARD
Juliette's Fade (1983)
Miss Mona (1987)

LUBIN, HARRY
One Step Beyond (1958)

LUBROCK, MARK
Nana (1977)

LUCAS, LEIGHTON
Portrait of Clare (1950)
Yangtse Incident (1957)
Desert Attack (Ice Cold in
Alex) (1958)
Serious Charge (1959)

LUCAS, TREVOR
Cassandra (1987)
Mullaway (1988)

LUDOVIC, VINCIO
Beyond Silence (1987)

LUDWIG, JOACHIM VAN
Julie Darling (1982)

LUI, TSUN-YUEN
Four Americans in China
(1985)

LUKIN, GABOR
Eskimo Woman Feels Cold
(1984)

LUMSDEN, JAMES D.
Self-Portrait in Brains
(1980)

LUN, YU
Emperor Lee (1968)
Father and Son (1981)

LUNDQUIST, TORBJORN
Love Mates (1968)

LUNDSTEN, RALPH
Inside Woman (1980)
Flight Level 450 (1980)

LUNN, MARTI
Instructor, The (1983)

LUNNY, DONAL
Eat the Peach (1986)
Return, The (1988)

LURIE, EVAN
Doomed Love (1984)
Little Devil (1988)

LURIE, JOHN
Permanent Vacation (1982)
Variety (1983)
Stranger Than Paradise
(1984)
City Lights (1985)
Down by Law (1986)
Monster Manor (1988)

LUSSIER, RENE
Last Glacier, The (1985)
Passiflora (1986)

LUSTIG, GORDON
Foley Square (1985)

LUTYENS, ELISABETH
World Without End (1954)
Malpas Mystery, The (1960)
Never Take Candy from a
Stranger (1960)
Dr. Terror's House of Hor-
rors (1964)
Psychopaths, The (1965)
Terrornauts, The (1966)

LYMAN, RICHARD
Josie (1983)

LYNNER, DOUG
Killers, The (1984)

LYUBENOV, RAICHO
Return to Earth (1987)

MAAS, DICK
Flodder (1986)
Amsterdamned (1988)

MABARAK, CARLOS JIMENEZ
Poison for Fairies (1986)

MACAULEY, TONY
Beast in the Cellar, The
(1971)
Percy's Progress (It's Not the
Size That Counts) (1979)

McBRIDE, ROBERT
   Farewell to Yesterday (1950)

McBROOM, AMANDA
   Eisenhower & Lutz (1988)

McCABE, JOHN
   Fear in the Night (1972)
   Come Back, Little Sheba
      (1977)

McCALL, TOM
   Jennie: Lady Randolph
      Churchill (1975)

McCALLUM, JON
   Surf Nazis Must Die (1987)

McCALLUM, PAUL
   Death Wish 4: The
      Crackdown (1987)

McCALLUM, VALENTINE
   Assassination (1987)
   Death Wish 4: The
      Crackdown (1987)

McCARTHY, DENNIS
   Enos (1980)
   Hoyt Axton Show, The (1981)
   Legends of the West: Truth
      and Tall Tales (1981)
   Private Benjamin (1981)
   Pray TV (1982)
   Rainbow Girl, The (1982)
   Cutter to Houston (1983)
   Goodnight, Beantown (1983)
   Gun Shy (1983)
   Mississippi, The (1983)
   Off the Wall (1983)
   Small and Frye (1983)
   Kid With the 200 I.Q., The
      (1983)
   V (1984)
   V: The Final Battle (1984)
   Playing with Fire (1985)
   On Our Way (1985)
   Houston: The Legend of
      Texas (1986)
   Houston Knights (1987)
   Star Trek--The Next

Generation (1987)
   Sword to Silence (1987)

McCARTNEY, DAVE
   Queen City Rocker (1987)

McCARTY, MICHAEL
   Dangerously Close (1986)

McCAULEY, JOHN
   Deadly Intruder (1984)

McCAULEY, MATTHEW
   In the Custody of Strangers
      (1982)
   Matter of Sex, A (1984)
   Undergrads, The (1985)
   Many Happy Returns (1986)

McCAULEY, TIM
   Love (1982)
   Screwballs (1983)
   Blue City Slammers (1988)

MACCHI, EGISTO
   Truth on the Savolta Affair,
      The (1980)
   Authorized Instructor (1980)
   Charlotte (1981)
   Beast, The (1982)
   Minuet (1982)
   Circle of Passions (1983)
   Stone in the Mouth, A (1983)
   Last Diva: Francesca Bertini,
      The (1983)
   November Moon (1985)
   Mussolini: The Decline and
      Fall of Il Duce (1985)
   Brothers (1985)
   Malady of Love, The (1986)
   Salome (1986)
   Diary of a Mad Old Man (1987)
   Havinck (1987)
   Mascara (1987)
   Woman Destroyed, A (1988)

MACCHI, LAMBERTO
   Carefree Giovanni (1986)
   He Looks Dead ... But He
      Just Fainted (1986)
   Whoever Is Here, Is Here

(1987)
Special Affections (1988)

McCLINTOCK, STEVE
Deadly Prey (1987)
Mankillers (1987)
Night Wars (1988)

McCOY, CHARLIE
Grady Nutt Show, The (1981)

McCRAW, SKEETS
Bombs Away (1985)

McCUBBERY, JOHN
Future Schlock (1984)

McCURDY, STEPHEN
Came a Hot Friday (1985)
Shaker Run (1985)
Leave All Fair (1985)
Bridge to Nowhere (1986)

MacDERMOT, GALT
Moon Over the Alley (1980)

MacDONALD, CATHERINE
Right Out of History--The
Making of Judy Chicago's
Dinner Party (1980)

McDONALD, COUNTRY JOE
Secret Agent, The (1984)

McDONALD, GARRY
Second Time Lucky (1984)
Robbery Under Arms (1985)
My Brother Tom (1986)
Playing Beatie Bow (1986)
Far Country, The (1987)
Flying Doctors, The (1987)

McDUFF, JEFF
Jarrett (1973)

MACERO, TEO
Face of Genius, The (1967)
Opus Op (1968)
Sergeant Matlovich vs. the
U.S. Air Force (1978)

Top Secret (1978)
Friday the 13th ... The
Orphan (1979)
Virus (1980)
Ted Kennedy Jr. Story, The
(1986)
Special Friendship, A (1987)
Bodywatching (1988)
Inside the Sexes (1988)

McEUEN, JOHN
Man Outside (1987)

McEVOY, MICHAEL
Vroom (1988)

McGINNIS, DAVID
Young and the Restless, The
(1973)

McGINNIS, DON
Fiend with the Electronic
Brain, The (1965)
Man with the Synthetic Brain,
The (1971)

McGLASHAN, DON
Other Halves (1984)

McGUFFIE, BILL
Challenge, The (1960)
Golden Rabbit, The (1962)
Dr. Who (1973)

MACHA, OTMAR
Jan Amos' Peregrination
(1984)

McHUGH, DAVID
Nobody's Perfekt (1981)
Moscow on the Hudson (1984)
Pumping Iron II: The Women
(1985)
One More Saturday Night
(1986)
Welcome Home, Bobby (1986)
Willy/Milly (1986)
Jocks (1987)
Mr. North (1988)
Mystic Pizza (1988)

McINTYRE, KEN
    Diggers (1986)

MACKAY, DAVID
    Number One (1984)

McKAY, HARPER
    Storefront Lawyers, The
        (1970)
    Men at Law (1971)
    Delphi Bureau, The (1972)
    Jigsaw (1972)
    Full House (1976)

MACKEBEN, THEO
    Love, Death and the Devil
        (1934)
    Student of Prague, The (1935)
    Intermezzo (1936)
    Lessons in Love (1937)
    City of Torment (1950)
    Miracles Still Happen (1952)

McKELVEY, FRANK
    Ozzie's Girls (1973)
    Boggy Creek II (1985)

McKENNIT, LOREENA
    Bayo (1985)
    To a Safer Place (1987)
    Heaven on Earth (1988)

MacKENZI, MALCOLM, JR.
    Train of Dreams (1987)

McKEOWN, TERENCE
    Strangers in a Strange Land:
        The Adventures of a
        Canadian Film Crew in
        China (1988)

MACKEY, PERCIVAL
    ·Accused (1936)
    This Man Is News (1939)

McKINLEY, PETER
    Save the Lady (1982)

McKUEN, ROD
    Borrowers, The (1973)
    Lisa, Bright and Dark (1973)

MACLAIN, GREG
    Allies (1983)

McLAUGHLAN, MURRAY
    Alligator Shoes (1981)

McLEOD, JENNY
    Silent One, The (1984)
    Neglected Miracle, The (1985)
    Haunting of Barney Palmer,
        The (1987)

McLEOD, JOHN
    Another Time, Another
        Place (1983)

McLEOD, MURRAY
    Evil Roy Slade (1972)
    Rolling Man (1972)
    Savages (1974)
    Dooley Brothers, The (1979)
    240-Robert (1979)
    Young Guy Christian (1979)
    Brett Maverick (1981)
    Long Summer of George Adams,
        The (1982)
    Paramedics (1988)

McLERNON, MICHAEL
    Cold in Colombia (1985)

McMAHON, GERARD
    Defiance (1980)

McMAHON, KEVIN
    Video Dead, The (1986)

MACMILLAN, ALLAN
    Silence of the North (1981)

McMILLIN, BOB
    King of Kensington (1977)

McNEELY, JOEL
    You Talking to Me? (1987)
    Davy Crockett: Rainbow in
        the Thunder (1988)
    Splash, Too (1988)

MACPHERSON, CAMERON
    Dawn to Dawn (1934)

McRITCHIE, GERIG
  Night Stalker (1974)
  International Animation
    Festival, The (1975)
  Code Red (1981)

McSHERRY, MARK
  Eating Your Heart Out (1985)
  In Between (1987)

McVAY, JAMES
  P.O.W.--American in Enemy
    Hands (1987)
  Top Flight (1987)
  Destined to Live (1988)

"MADRID JUDEO-SPANISH
  MUSICAL GROUP"
  Stilts, The (1984)

MAEDA, NORIO
  Star Wolf (1978)

MAGAINO, SHUN-ICHI
  To Love Again (1971)

MAGDIC, JOSIP
  Endeavor (1982)

MAGENTA, GUY
  Oh! Que Mambo (1959)

MAGNE, MICHEL
  Living Bread, The (1955)
  Devil and the Ten Command-
    ments, The (1962)
  Fantomas (1964)
  Shadow of Evil (1964)
  O.S.S. Mission for a Killer
    (1965)
  Exterminators, The (1965)
  Heart Trump in Tokyo for
    O.S.S. 117 (1966)
  S.A.S.--Terminate with
    Extreme Prejudice (1983)
  Informer, The (Indic, L')
    (1983)
  Surprise Party (1983)
  Emmanuelle 4 (1984)
  New Year's Eve at Bob's
    House (1985)

MAGNUS, NICK
  Bloody New Year (1987)

MAHADEVAN, K. V.
  Jewel of Shiva, The (1981)
  Thyagayya (1982)

MAHALINGAM, T. R.
  Mind of Clay, The (1986)

MAHANA, GEORGE
  Groovie Goolies, The (1971)
  My Favorite Martian (1973)
  Flash Gordon (1979)
  Sport Billy (1982)

MAHDI, SALAH
  Man of Ashes (1986)

MAHPATRA, SHANTANU
  Search, The (1981)

MAIBORODA, PLATON
  Years of Youth (1960)

MAIMONE, GERALD
  Insomniac on the Bridge,
    The (1985)

MAINARDI, DANIELE
  Deep Lakes (1986)

MAINAT, JOSEP M.
  Vicar of Olot, The (1981)

MAINOTTI, STEFANO
  Italian Postcards (1987)

MAIOLI, CLAUDIO
  Teresa (1987)

MAIOROVICI, H.
  Phalanstery, The (1981)

MAIZTEGUI, ISIDORO
  Emergency Ward (1952)
  Leap to Fame (1959)
  Sonatas (1959)

MAJEWSKI, HANS-MARTIN
  Men at Dangerous Age (1954)

Double Destiny (1955)
Golden Pestilence, The (1955)
Ingrid: Story of a Model
   (1955)
Master Over Life and Death
   (1955)
Second Life, The (1955)
Star of Africa (1957)
Fox of Paris, The (1958)
Catcher, The (1958)
And That on Monday Morning
   (1959)
Labyrinth (1959)
Boomerang (1960)
Darkness Fell on Gotenhafen
   (1960)
Division Brandenberg (1960)
Three Moves to Freedom
   (1960)
Marriage of Mr. Mississippi,
   The (1961)
Miracle of Malachias (1961)
Sacred Waters (1961)
Beyond the Darkness (1974)
Elixir of the Devil (1977)
Star Without a Sky (1981)
Society Limited (1982)

MAKEBA, MIRIAM
   Amok (1983)

MAKINO, YUKATA
   Temptress, The (1958)
   Dawn of Judo (1970)
   Secret Zone of Tokyo (1971)

MAKLAKIEWICZ, JAN
   Love or a Kingdom (1937)
   Pan Twardowski (1937)

MAKMUDOV, MIKHAIL
   Granny General (1986)

MAKSYMIUCK, JERZY
   World of Horror, The (1968)
   Birthday, The (1980)
   Boldyn (1981)
   Barbed Wire (1981)
   Pastorale Heroica (1983)
   Who Is That Man? (1985)
   Write and Fight (1985)

Memoirs of a Sinner, The
   (1986)

MAKULOLUWA, W. B.
   Before the Dawn (1982)

MALALLEMO, GABRIEL AND
   EDUARDO
   It's My Life (1986)

MALAPARTE, CURZIO
   Forbidden Christ (1951)
   Strange Deception (1953)

MALATESTA, LUIGI
   Scream of the Demon Lover,
   The (1970)

MALAVASI, CLAUDIO
   Picaros, The (1987)

MALAVASI, MAURO
   Fortunate Pilgrim, The (1988)

MALAVOI, GROUPE
   Street of the Black Shacks
   (1983)

MALECKI, MACIEJ
   Queen's Father, The (1980)

MALEK, AHMED
   Aziza (1980)
   One Way Ticket (1981)
   Roof, a Family, A (1982)

MALERAS, CARLOS
   Metamorphosis (1971)

MALJEAN, JEAN-FRANCOIS
   Black Orchestra, The (1985)

MALKEN, JACK
   Nesting, The (1981)

MALNECK, MATTY
   Witness for the Prosecution
   (1957)

MALONE, MICHAEL
   Dream House (1983)

MALONE, WIL
Raw Meat (1972)

MALONEY, PETER
Cold in Colombia (1985)

MALOVEC, JOSEF
Pictures of the Old World
(1988)

MALVICINO, NORACIO
Nut in Action, A (1983)

MAMANGAKIS, NICOS (NIKOS)
Arpa-Colla (1982)
Homeland (1984)
Loafing and Camouflage
(1984)
Bordello (1985)
Living Dangerously (1987)

MAMECIER, MECHE
Tokyo-Ga (1985)

MAMISSACHVILI, NODAR
Hey, Maestro! (1988)

MAMIYA, YOSHIO
Little Norse Prince (1969)
Expo '70 (1971)

MAMORSKY, MORRIS
With These Hands (1950)

MAN-YEE, LAM
Hong Kong, Hong Kong
(1983)
Love in a Fallen City (1984)

MANABE, RIICHIRO
Cruel Story of Youth (1960)
Vampire Doll, The (1970)
Godzilla vs. Hedorah (1971)
Lake of Dracula (1971)
Godzilla vs. the Smog
Monster (1972)
Godzilla vs. Megalon (1973)
Evil of Dracula (1975)
Possessed, The (1976)
Gate of Youth--Part II, The
(1978)

Inferno, The (1979)
Taro of the Dragons (1979)

MANCINA, MARK
Mankillers (1987)
Night Wars (1988)

MANCINI, HENRY
It Came from Outer Space
(1953)
Cade's County (1971)
Columbo (1971)
Curiosity Shop, The (1971)
Blue Knight, The (1975)
Invisible Man, The (1975)
What's Happening? (1976)
Moneychangers, The (1976)
Kingston: Confidential
(1977)
Sanford Arms (1977)
Family Upside Down, A (1978)
Best Place to Be, The (1979)
Co-Ed Fever (1979)
Shadow Box, The (1980)
Little Miss Marker (1980)
Change of Seasons, A (1980)
Back Roads (1981)
S.O.B. (1981)
Condorman (1981)
Mommie Dearest (1981)
Victor/Victoria (1982)
Newhart (1982)
Trail of the Pink Panther
(1982)
Second Thoughts (1983)
Curse of the Pink Panther
(1983)
Better Late Than Never
(1983)
Man Who Loved Women, The
(1983)
Thorn Birds, The (1983)
Harry & Son (1984)
Angela (1984)
That's Dancing! (1985)
Lifeforce (1985)
Santa Claus--the Movie
(1985)
Fine Mess, A (1986)
Great Mouse Detective, The
(1986)

That's Life! (1986)
Blind Date (1987)
Circus (1987)
Glass Menagerie, The (1987)
Justin Case (1988)
Sunset (1988)
Without a Clue (1988)

MANCINI, UMBERTO
These Children (1937)
Two Mothers, The (1940)

MANCO, BARIS
Number 14 (1986)

MANCUSI, GUIDO
Borderline (1988)

MANDEL, JOHNNY
Trackers, The (1971)
M*A*S*H (1972)
Call Holme (1972)
Turning Point of Jim Malloy,
The (1975)
Code Name: Hercules (1976)
Not Until Today (1979)
Too Close for Comfort (1980)
Baltimore Bullet, The (1980)
Caddyshack (1980)
Evita Peron (1981)
Deathtrap (1982)
Soup for One (1982)
Lookin' to Get Out (1982)
Verdict, The (1982)
Family Business, The (1983)
Letter to Three Wives, A
(1985)
Jack and Mike (1986)
Assault & Matrimony (1987)
Foxfire (1987)
LBJ: The Early Years (1987)
Great Escape II: The Untold
Story, The (1988)

MANDIS, NIMAL
Village in the Jungle (1981)

MANDOZZI, GRAZIANO
Metin (1982)
Innocence (1986)
Secret Life of Sergei
Eisenstein, The (1987)

MANFREDINI, HARRY
Danny (1979)
Friday the 13th (1980)
Children, The (1980)
Friday the 13th Part 2 (1981)
Swamp Thing (1982)
Friday the 13th--Part 3
(1982)
Returning, The (1983)
Zombie Island Massacre (1983)
Hills Have Eyes II, The (1983)
Friday the 13th--The Final
Chapter (1984)
Friday the 13th V: A New
Beginning (1985)
April Fool's Day (1985)
Friday the 13th: Part VI:
Jason Lives (1986)
House (1986)
House II: The Second Story
(1987)
Friday the 13th Part VII--
The New Blood (1988)

MANGESHKAR, HRIDAYANATH
Throne, The (1981)
Chakra (1981)

MANGIAGALLI, RICCARDO PICK
Rose of Bagdad, The (1949)

MANKEWITZ, LOTHAR
Concerto for the Right Hand
(1987)

MANN, BARRY
Days of Our Lives (1965)

MANN, LUDVIK
Between the Times (1985)

MANNE, SHELLEY
Like Father, Like Son (1961)
All That Glitters (1977)

MANNEN, LELIJKE
Failure, The (1986)

MANNINO, FRANCO
Bellissima (1952)

MANSFIELD, DAVID
  Heaven's Gate (1980)
  Year of the Dragon (1985)
  Club Paradise (1986)
  Into the Homeland (1987)
  Sicilian, The (1987)

MANSFIELD, KEITH
  Fist of Fear, Touch of
    Death (1980)

MANSON, EDDIE
  Weddings and Babies (1958)
  Crash (1978)
  Love Affair: The Eleanor
    and Lou Gehrig Story, A
    (1978)
  Woman Inside, The (1981)
  Tiger Town (1983)
  Eye on the Sparrow (1987)

MANSUYAN, TIGRAN
  Slap in the Face, A (1981)
  Tango of Our Childhood
    (1985)
  Lit Lantern, The (1986)
  Master, The (1986)

MANUEL, ROLAND
  Bandera, La (1935)
  Odd Mr. Victor (1938)
  Strangers in the House
    (1949)

MANY, CHRIS
  Heart (1987)

MANZANERO, ARMANDO
  On the Line (1984)
  Challenge to Life (1987)

MANZIE, JIM
  From a Whisper to a Scream
    (1987)

MAR-HAIM, YOSSI
  Flames in the Ashes (1986)

MARATTE, SARATH CHANDRA
  Salt (1988)

MARCEL, LEONARD
  Video Dead, The (1986)

MARCELLO, ALEXANDRO
  Island Wind, The (1988)

MARCHESE, PINO
  Cop's Honor (1985)
  Wolves Among Themselves,
    The (1986)

MARCHETTI, GIOVANNI
  Secret Diary of a Minor
    (1968)

MARCHI, VIRGINIO
  Lost in the Dark (1949)

MARCHITELLI, LELE
  Specters (1987)

MARCOEUR, ALBERT
  Two Lions in the Sun (1980)
  Sweet Inquest on Violence
    (1982)

MARCUS, TONI
  Summerspell (1983)

MARCZEWSKI, PIOTR
  Coup d'Etat (1980)
  If Your Heart Can Feel
    (1980)

MARES, KAROL
  Hordubal (1980)

MARGO, MITCH
  Fantastic World of D. C.
    Collins, The (1984)
  Goddess of Love, The (1988)

MARGOLIN, STUART
  Evil Roy Slade (1972)
  Rolling Man (1972)
  Long Summer of George
    Adams, The (1982)

MARGOSHES, STEVEN
  Date Rape (1988)

MARIANO, CESAR CAMARGO
    I Love You (1981)

MARIANO, CHARLY
    Put on Ice (1980)

MARIANO, DETTO
    Give Me Five (1980)
    Can-Cannes (1980)
    I Made a Splash (1981)
    Taming of the Scoundrel
        (1981)
    Ace (1981)
    Please Look After Amelia
        (1981)
    Street Corner Kids (1982)
    Really .... Incredible (1982)
    Toxic Love (1983)
    Tomorrow I'm Getting
        Married (1984)
    Exterminators of the Year
        3000, The (1984)
    Bi and the Ba, The (1986)
    Department Store (1986)
    Italian Fast Food (1986)
    Yuppies, Youngsters Who
        Succeed (1986)
    Grouch, The (1987)

MARIE, VINCENT
    Calm Night (1987)

MARIN, CARLOS TORRES
    All Life Long (1987)
    Black Side of Blackie, The
        (1987)
    Cocked Gun (1987)
    One Straight and Two With
        Salt (1987)
    Pleasure of Vengeance, The
        (1987)

MARINELLI, ANTHONY
    Rigged (1985)
    Nice Girls Don't Explode
        (1987)
    Pinocchio and the Emperor of
        the Night (1987)
    Young Guns (1988)

MARINI, GIOVANNA
    Cafe Express (1980)

Mystery of the Morca, The
    (1984)
Love Story (1986)

MARINO, LEO
    Beyond Passion (1986)

MARINUZZI, GINO, JR.
    Appointment for Murder
        (1954)
    South Wind (1960)
    Hercules and the Captive
        Women (1961)
    Venus Against the Son of
        Hercules (1962)
    Patriarchs of the Bible (1963)
    Matchless (1966)
    Operation "Three Yellow
        Cats" (1966)
    Peaceful Nights (1966)

MARIO, MASAO
    Bokuchen's Battlefield (1986)

MARION, JEAN
    Roi, Le (1950)
    Mousetrap, The (1950)
    Simple Case of Money, A
        (1952)
    Cadet-Rousselle (1954)
    One Bullet Is Enough (1955)

MARKOVIC, MILIVOJ
    Erogenous Zone (1981)

MARKOWITZ, RICHARD
    Operation Dames (1959)
    Wild Wild West, The (1965)
    Mission: Impossible (1966)
    Scalplock (1966)
    Summer Children, The (1967)
    Weekend of Terror (1970)
    Beg, Borrow ... or Steal
        (1973)
    Police Story (1973)
    Stranger, The (1973)
    Voyage of the Yes, The
        (1973)
    Girl on the Late, Late Show,
        The (1974)
    Hanged Man, The (1974)
    Panic on the 5:22 (1974)

Policewoman (1974)
Joe Forrester (1975)
Return of Joe Forrester, The (1975)
Brink's: The Great Robbery (1976)
Kiss Me, Kill Me (1976)
Mayday at 40,000 Feet (1976)
Most Wanted (1976)
Tales of the Unexpected (1977)
Washington: Behind Closed Doors (1977)
Doctors' Private Lives (1978)
Hunters of the Reef (1978)
Operation: Runaway (1978)
Standing Tall (1978)
Wild Wild West Revisited, The (1979)
Death Car on the Freeway (1979)
Mystique (1981)
Neighborhood, The (1982)
Law and Harry McGraw, The (1987)

MARKOWSKY, JAN
Astronauts, The (1959)

MARKS, ALAN
Anita--Dances of Vice (1987)
Zacharias (1987)

MARKS, FRANKLYN
Legend of the Boy and the Eagle, The (1968)

MARKS, WALTER
Father on Trial (1972)

MARKUSH, FRED
Plain Girl (1935)

MARLO, MARIO
World Safari II (1984)

MAROIS, REJEAN
Sweet Lies and Loving Oaths (1982)

MARQUEZ, GILBERTO
Cubagua (1988)
Treasure (1988)

MARQUEZ, JUAN
House for Swap (1985)
Tupac Amaru (1985)
Partner of God, The (1987)
Dueling Techniques (1988)
Krik? Krak! Tales of a Nightmare (1988)

MARSH, HUGH
Waterwalker (1984)

MARSHALL, JACK
Giant Gila Monster, The (1959)
Munsters, The (1964)
Something for a Lonely Man (1968)
Debbie Reynolds Show, The (1969)

MARSHALL, JOHN
Carry On Laughing (1980)

MARSHALL, JULIAN
Old Enough (1984)

MARSHALL, MAURICE
Hounds ... of Notre Dame, The (1980)
War Story, A (1982)

MARSHALL, PHIL
Prime Risk (1985)
Last of Philip Banter, The (1986)
Rolling Vengeance (1987)
Student Exchange (1987)
Full Moon in Blue Water (1988)
Illegally Yours (1988)

MART, ZDENEK
Radical Cut (1983)

MARTA, ISTVAN
Miklos Akli (1987)

MARTEL, FERNAND
   Last Straw, The (1987)

MARTEL, PIERRE
   Night on Bare Mountain, The
      (1962)

MARTELL, CYRIL
   Song of Paris (1952)

MARTELL, PHILIP
   Miss Pilgrim's Progress
      (1950)
   Spy Killer, The (1969)
   Foreign Exchange (1970)

MARTELLI, CARLO
   Witchcraft (1964)
   Prehistoric Women (1967)
   Serpent God, The (1970)

MARTHA, ISTVAN
   Lost Illusions (1983)
   Duck and Drake Adventure,
      A (1984)
   Annunciation (1984)
   Fond Farewell to the Prince,
      A (1987)

MARTIN, ADELA
   Swallow It, Dog (1981)

MARTIN, GEORGE
   Yellow Submarine, The (1968)
   Honky Tonk Freeway (1981)
   Give My Regards to Broad
      Street (1984)

MARTIN, HERB
   Dooley Brothers, The (1979)

MARTIN, PERRY
   Tattoo Connection, The
      (1980)

MARTIN, PETER
   Hope and Glory (1987)

MARTIN, RAY
   It's Great to Be Young (1956)
   Yield to the Night (1956)

MARTIN, SIMON MICHAEL
   Heartaches (1981)

MARTINEAU, JEAN-CLAUDE
   Krik? Krak! Tales of a
      Nightmare (1988)

MARTINEZ, ARTURO
   Difficult Days (1988)

MARTURET, EDUARDO
   Oriana (1985)

MARTYNEC, EUGENE
   Alligator Shoes (1981)

MARUYAMA
   Tradition in the World of
      Spirit, A (1982)

MARX, BILL
   Deathmaster, The (1971)
   Terror House (1972)
   Keeper of the Wild (1977)

MAS, JEAN-PIERRE
   Ma Cherie (1980)
   Passing Killer, A (1981)
   Coast of Love, The (1982)
   Laisse-Beton (1984)
   Flag (1988)

MAS, JOSEF
   Lead Soldiers (1984)

MASHUKOV, ALEXI
   Woman in Love with Mechanic
      Gavrilov, The (1982)

MASIK, JANOS
   Idiots May Apply (1986)
   Tandem (1986)
   Damn Real (1988)

MASON, BENEDICT
   Tom Machine, The (1981)
   Stranger Than Fiction (1985)

MASON, GLEN
   Go for a Take (1972)

MASON, IAN
Jenny Kissed Me (1985)
Cassandra (1987)

MASON, NICK
White of the Eye (1987)

MASSARA, NATALE
Kansas (1988)

MASSARA, PINO
Growing Up (1988)

MASSARI, JOHN
Killer Klowns from Outer
Space (1988)
Wizard of Speed and Time,
The (1988)

MASSENBURG, GEORGE
Certain Fury (1985)
Smooth Talk (1985)

MASSETTI, ENZO
Tomb of the Angels (1937)
Kiss of a Dead Woman (1949)
Lure of the Sila (1950)
Sicilian Uprising (1950)
Bullet for Stefano, A (1950)
Volcano (1950)
Musolino the Bandit (1951)
Last Meeting, The (1952)
Red Shirts (1952)
Eager to Love (1953)
Voice of Silence (1953)
Hercules and the Queen of
Lydia (1958)

MASSEY, CURT
Beverly Hillbillies, The
(1962)
Petticoat Junction (1963)

MASSO, ALEJANDRO
Evening Performance (1981)
Witching Hour, The (1985)
Rowing With the Wind (1988)

MASSON, ASKELL
Outlaw: The Saga of Gisli
(1982)

MASSON, DIEGO
Spirits of the Dead (1967)

MASUO, MOTOAKI
Making It (1982)

MATHIESON, MUIR
South Riding (1938)
Who Goes There? (1952)
After the Ball (1957)
Canadians, The (1961)
Mr. Horatio Knibbles (1971)

MATHISEN, LEO
Take It Easy (1986)

MATHISON, T.
Testament (1988)

MATLOVSKY, SAMUEL
Dangerous Days of Kiowa
Jones, The (1966)
Wings of Fire (1967)
Salty (1974)

MATSIEVSKI, IGOR
Left-Hander (1987)

MATSON, SASHA
Daddy's Boys (1988)
Shadows in the Storm (1988)

MATSUI, HACHIRO
My Friend Death (1960)

MATSUMURA, TEIZO
Long Darkness, The (1973)
Rise, Fair Sun (1974)
Assassination of Ryoma, The
(1975)
Preparations for the Festival
(1976)
Sea and Poison, The (1987)

MATSUTOYA, MASATAKA
Little Girl Who Conquered
Time, The (1983)

MATTES, WILLI
Fruit Without Love (1956)
Penalty Battalion 999 (1960)

MAZUREK, BOHDAN
    Epitaph for Barbara Radziwill,
        An (1983)

MAZZA, GIANNI
    Beach House, The (1980)
    Jealousy Tango (1981)

MEAD, ABIGAIL
    Full Metal Jacket (1987)

MECHELEN, CLOUS VAN
    Black Rider (1983)

MEDAGLIA, JULIO
    Seven Female Vampires,
        The (1986)
    Me, Myself and I (1987)

MEDEROS, RODOLFO
    Entire Life, The (1987)
    Hotel du Paradis (1987)
    Things Forgotten and Not
        (1988)

MEEGAN, PADDY
    Angel (1982)

MEEHAN, TONY
    Movement, Movement (1969)

MEHAMA, HANI
    Love Atop the Pyramids
        (1985)

MEID, LOTHAR
    Theo Against the Rest of
        the World (1980)
    Asphalt Night (1980)
    Heartbreakers, The (1983)
    Danni (1983)

MEISL, WILLI
    Champion of Pontresina
        (1934)
    Annette in Paradise (1936)
    Paloma, La (1936)
    Waltz for You, A (1936)
    Every Woman Has a Secret
        (1937)
    Family on Parade (1937)

MEJIA, MAURICIO
    Train of the Pioneers, The
        (1986)

MELACHRINO, GEORGE
    Things Happen at Night
        (1948)
    House of Darkness, The
        (1948)
    Now Barabbas Was a Robber
        (1949)
    Old Mother Riley (1952)
    Eight O'Clock Walk (1954)
    Gamma People, The (1955)
    Odongo (1956)

MELBOURNE, HIRINI
    Mauri (1988)

MELICHAR, ALOIS
    Private Life of Louix XIV,
        The (1936)
    Love's Awakening (1936)
    This Girl Irene (1936)
    For You Only (1938)
    Ulli und Marei (1949)
    Maria Theresia (1952)
    April 1, 2000 (1953)

MELL, GARY LEE
    Psycho Lover, The (1969)

MELLE, GIL
    My Sweet Charlie (1970)
    If Tomorrow Comes (1971)
    Night Gallery (1971)
    Psychiatrist, The (1971)
    Astronaut, The (1972)
    Judge and Jake Wyler, The
        (1972)
    Lieutenant Schuster's Wife
        (1972)
    That Certain Summer (1972)
    Victim, The (1972)
    Cold Night's Death, A (1973)
    Frankenstein: The True
        Story (1973)
    Partners in Crime (1973)
    President's Plane Is Missing,
        The (1973)
    Savage (1973)

Six Million Dollar Man, The
  (1973)
Tenafly (1973)
Trapped (1973)
Evel Knievel (1974)
Hitchhike! (1974)
Imposter, The (1974)
Killdozer (1974)
Last Angry Man, The (1974)
Night Stalker, The (1974)
Questor Tapes, The (1974)
Art of Crime, The (1975)
Crime Club, The (1975)
Cry for Help, A (1975)
Death Scream (1975)
Missing Are Deadly, The
  (1975)
Dynasty (1976)
Executive Suite (1976)
Perilous Voyage (1976)
Gold of the Amazon Women
  (1979)
Vacation in Hell, A (1979)
Borderline (1980)
Rape and Marriage: The
  Rideout Case (1980)
Attica (1980)
Curse of King Tut's Tomb,
  The (1980)
Blood Beach (1981)
Intruder Within, The (1981)
Last Chase, The (1981)
Traitor Within, The (1981)
World War III (1982)
Through Naked Eyes (1983)
Sweet Revenge (1984)
Best Kept Secrets (1984)
Flight #90: Disaster on the
  Potomac (1984)
Jealousy (1984)
Starcrossed (1985)
When Dreams Come True
  (1985)
Hot Target (1985)
Circle of Violence: A Family
  Drama (1986)
Deliberate Stranger, The
  (1986)
Killer in the Mirror (1986)
Still Watch (1987)

MELO, GUTO GRACA
  Kiss, The (1981)
  Boy from Rio, The (1982)
  Best Wishes (1988)

MELVOIN, MICHAEL (MIKE)
  Mongo's Back in Town (1971)
  Thicker Than Water (1973)
  Pete 'n' Tillie (1974)
  Last Survivors, The (1975)
  Aspen (1977)
  Lou Grant (1977)
  Magic Mongo (1977)
  King of the Mountain (1981)
  Return of the Rebels (1981)
  Yearbook: Class of '67
    (1985)
  Big Town, The (1987)
  Sharing Richard (1988)

MENDELSOHN, BRIAN
  China Run (1987)

MENDEZ, BETO
  Devil and the Lady, The
    (1983)

MENDEZ, GUILLERMO
  Spell II, The (1986)

MENDEZ, JAIME
  O Desterrado (1949)
  Ribatejo (1949)

MENDEZ, NACHO
  Dr. Tarr's Torture Dungeon
    (1976)
  Seven in the Viewfinder
    (1985)
  Don Mouse and Don Thief
    (1985)
  Night on the Town, A (1986)

MENDO, LUIS
  Closed Case (1985)
  Wolves' Moon (1988)

MENDOZA-NAVA, JAIME
  Grass Eater, The (1961)
  Legacy of Blood (1971)
  Garden of the Dead (1972)

MIKLIN, KARL-HEINZ
    Purgatory (1988)

MIKROUTSIKOS, THANOS
    Journey to the Capital (1984)

MILANES, PABLO
    Girlfriend for David, A
        (1985)

MILANO, TOM
    Breeders (1986)
    Necropolis (1987)

MILENA, LUCIO
    Teddy Boys (1961)

MILHAUD, DARIUS
    Inhumaine, L' (1923)
    Beloved Vagabond, The (1937)
    Life Begins Tomorrow (1952)
    Pictura (1952)

"MILLADOIRO"
    Half of the Sky (1986)

MILLER, BRUCE
    Outing, The (1987)

MILLER, FRANKIE
    Sense of Freedom, A (1981)
    Act of Vengeance (1986)

MILLER, MARCUS
    Siesta (1987)

MILLER, PETER
    Rainbow Serpent, The (1985)

MILLER, RANDY
    Bloodspell (1988)

MILLER, ROBERT WILEY
    Daughter of Dr. Jekyll,
        The (1957)

MILLO, MARIO
    Against the Wind (1979)
    Aussie Assault (1984)
    Lighthorsemen, The (1987)
    Always Afternoon (1988)

MILLS-COCKELL, JOHN
    Terror Train (1980)
    John Huston's Dublin (1985)

MILLUTIN, YURI
    In the Far East (1937)

MINAMI, KOSETSU
    Triton of the Seas (1979)
    Straits (1982)

MINARD, MICHAEL
    Mutilator, The (1984)
    Special Effects (1985)
    Return to Salem's Lot, A
        (1987)

MINDEL, DAVID
    Real Life (1984)

MING, JI
    Come Back Swallow (1981)

MING, TAM KAR
    Kill to Love (1981)

MING, WANG
    Intimate Friends: An Historic
        Legend (1982)
    Bao and His Son (1984)
    Corner Forsaken by Love,
        The (1986)
    Girl in Red, The (1986)

MING-TAO, LO
    Coldest Winter in Peking,
        The (1981)
    Battle for the Republic of
        China, The (1982)

MINGXIN, DU
    Savage Land, The (1981)

MINKOV, MARC
    Fire on East Train 34 (1984)
    Zina, Dear Zina (1988)

MINSKY, SUSAN
    Love in a Taxi (1980)

MINSUP, CHUNG
    Bell for Nirvana, A (1983)

MINUCCI, ULPIO
  Robert Scott and the Race
    for the South Pole (1968)

MIRALLES, RICARDO
  Almeria Case, The (1984)
  Spinach Face (1987)

MIRANDA, CARLOS
  Midsummer Night's Dream,
    A (1984)
  Pleasure of Killing, The
    (1988)

MISAKA, YO
  Detective Story (1982)

MISRA, BHUBANESWAR
  Event, An (1985)

MISRAKI, PAUL
  Moutonnet (1936)
  Cheri-Bibi (1938)
  Return to the Dawn (1938)
  I Was an Adventuress (1939)
  Battement de Coeur (Heart-
    beat) (1940)
  Duraton Family, The (1940)
  If Youth Only Knew (1947)
  All Roads Lead to Rome (1949)
  We Shall Go to Paris (1950)
  Prize, The (1952)
  Femmes de Paris (1954)
  Dames Get Along (1954)
  Ali Baba and the 40 Thieves
    (1954)
  French Touch, The (1954)
  Intermediate Landing in Paris
    (1955)
  Lost Dogs Without Collars
    (1955)
  Confidential File (1956)
  Attack of the Robots (1962)
  Bubble, The (1976)

"MISSING LINK, THE"
  Mistress of the Apes (1979)

MITCHELL, MARK
  Captive Rage (1988)

MITCHELL, RICHARD
  Born American (1986)

MITRA, RAJA
  Portrait of a Life (1988)

MITSOUKO, RITA
  Keep Up Your Right (1987)

MIYAGAWA, HIROSHI
  Arrevederci Yamato (1978)
  Grand Prix Hawk (1978)
  Space Cruiser Yamato--The
    New Voyage (1979)
  Be Forever Yamato (1980)
  Yamato 3 (1980)
  Space Cruiser Yamato--Final
    (1982)

MIYAGAWA, YASUSHI
  Rendezvous, The (1972)

MIYAGI, MARIKO
  Silk Tree Ballad, The (1974)
  Mariko-Mother (1977)

MIYAKE, HARUNA
  Abracadabra (1988)

MIYAUCHI, KUNIO
  Human Vapor, The (1964)
  Ultraman (1965)
  Godzilla's Revenge (1971)

MIZRAHI, SHLOMO
  Koko at 19 (1985)

MIZZY, VIC
  Addams Family, The (1964)
  Green Acres (1965)
  Reluctant Astronaut, The
    (1966)
  Captain Nice (1967)
  Deadly Hunt, The (1971)
  Very Missing Person, A
    (1972)
  Daddy's Girl (1973)
  New Temperatures Rising
    Show, The (1973)
  Hurricane (1974)

Terror on the 40th Floor
(1974)
Million Dollar Rip-Off, The
(1976)
Quincy (1976)
Delta House (1979)
Munster's Revenge, The
(1981)

MOCHIACH, ILAN (MOKHIAKH)
You've Been Had ... You
Turkey! (1980)
Hairdresser, The (1984)

MOCKRIDGE, CYRIL
Hot Spot (I Wake Up Scream-
ing) (1941)
Undying Monster, The (1942)
Where the Sidewalk Ends
(1950)
Peyton Place (1964)

MODAK, ANAND
22nd June, 1897 (1980)

MODUGNO, MARCELLO
All That Rhythm (1984)

MOECKEL, HANS
Golden Ox Inn (1958)
S.O.S. Glacier Pilot (1959)

MOFFAT, MARK
Bingo, Bridesmaids and
Braces (1988)

MOFFIATT, MARK
Fields of Fire (1987)
High Tide (1987)

MOHAUPT, RICHARD
Farewell to Yesterday (1950)

MOHRI, DURODO
For Kayako (1985)

MOICHANOV, K.
Great Is My Country (1959)

MOKHIAKH, ILAN see
MOCHIACH

MOLETTA, CARLOS
It's Nice to Meet You (1982)
Luz del Fuego (1982)

MOLINO, MARIO
Angels of 2000, The (1975)

MOLLEDA, JOSE see MUNOZ
MOLLEDA, JOSE

MOLLIN, FRED
Spring Fever (1983)
Loose Screws (1985)
My Father, My Rival (1985)
Incredible Ida Early, The
(1987)
Friday the 13th Part VII--
The New Blood (1988)
Friday the 13th: The
Series (1988)

MOLONEY, PADDY
Ballad of the Irish Horse
(1985)

MOLONEY, WILLIAM
Cavanaughs, The (1986)

MONAHAN, STEVE
I Married a Vampire (1986)

MONALDI, GIANFRANCO
Nobody Can Judge Me (1966)
Pardon (1966)

MONK, MEREDITH
Plainsong (1982)
Modern American Composers
I (1984)
Book of Days (1988)

MONKMAN, FRANCIS
Long Good Friday, The (1980)
Innocent, The (1985)

MONN-IVERSEN, EGIL
Captive of the Dragon (1985)
Rising Stock (1987)

MONTAGNINI, E.
Peddlin' in Society (1949)

MONTAGNINI, FELICE
  Emperor of Capri, The (1950)

MONTANARI, PIERO
  Zucchini Flowers (1988)

MONTE, TONY
  Madhouse Brigade, The
    (1978)

MONTENEGRO, HUGO
  I Dream of Jeannie (1965)
  Here Come the Brides (1968)
  Partridge Family, The (1970)
  Getting Together (1971)
  Say Goodbye, Maggie Cole
    (1972)

MONTES, MICHAEL
  Pumping Iron II: The Women
    (1985)
  Firehouse (1987)
  Hangmen (1987)

MONTES, OSVALDO
  Wasp, The (1986)
  Straight from the Heart
    (1988)

MONTGOMERY, BRUCE
  Eyewitness (1956)
  Carry On, Teacher (1959)
  Carry On, Constable (1960)
  Too Young to Love (1960)
  Carry On, Regardless (1961)

MONTILOR, OVIDI
  Hector (1984)

MONTSALVAGE, JAVIER
  Goya (1985)
  Dragon Rapide (1986)
  Lights and Shadows (1988)

MOODY, JAMES
  Navy Lark, The (1959)

MOOKERJI, ANUPAM
  Bhombal Sardar (1985)

MOON, GUY
  Creepozoids (1987)

MOONEY, HAL
  Longest Night, The (1972)
  Lady Luck (1973)
  My Darling Daughters'
    Anniversary (1973)
  Runaway! (1973)
  Tom Sawyer (1973)
  Case of Rape, A (1974)
  Chadwick Family, The (1974)
  Execution of Private Slovik,
    The (1974)
  Tribe, The (1974)
  Ellery Queen (1975)
  One of Our Own (1975)
  Sunshine (1975)
  City of Angels (1976)
  Operation Petticoat (1977)
  Nobody's Perfect (1980)

MOORE, ANTHONY
  Uliisees (1983)
  What Really Happened Between
    the Images? (1986)

MOORE, DOUGLAS
  Power and the Land (1940)

MOORE, DUDLEY
  Derek and Clive Get the
    Horn (1981)
  Six Weeks (1982)

MOORE, FRANK LEDLIE
  American Vision, The (1967)

MOORE, GENE
  Carnival of Souls (1962)

MORALES, MIGUEL
  We Must Undo the House
    (1987)

MORALES, ROLAND
  Reunion (1987)

MORALI, JACQUES
  Monique (1979)

MORAN, CHILO
  Carrasco's Escape (1987)

550 Composers and Their Films

MORAN, MIKE
Time Bandits (1981)
Missionary, The (1982)
Water (1985)
Taggart (1987)

MORANTE, MASSIMO
Unsane (1987)

MORAVEC, PAUL
Born Again: Life in a
Fundamentalist Baptist
Church (1987)

MORAWECK, LUCIEN
Massacre River (1949)

MORAZ, PATRICK
Lost Way, The (1980)
Stepfather, The (1986)

MORETTI, BRUNO
Big Deal on Madonna Street
--20 Years Later (1986)

MORGAN, DAVID
Distortions (1987)

MORGAN, HOWARD
Freedom Fighters (1988)

MORGAN, JOHN
Aftermath, The (1980)
Flicks (1987)

MORGAN, PAM
Finding Mary March (1988)

MORGAN, PATRICIA
Adventures of Faustus
Bidgood, The (1986)

MORGAN, PIERO
Guendalina (1957)
Ballerina and God, The
(1958)

MORI, KURODO
Antonio Gaudi (1985)

MORILLO, FERNANDO GARCIA
Fantasia ... 3 (1966)

Case of the Two Beauties,
The (1968)
Kiss Me, Monster (1968)

MORIOKA, KENICHIRO
Return of the Champ (1981)
This Is Noriko (1982)

MORLEY, ANGELA
New Adventures of Wonder
Woman, The (1977)
Friendships, Secrets and
Lies (1979)
McClain's Law (1981)
Madame X (1981)
Summer Girl (1983)

MORLEY, GLENN
Overnight (1986)

MORLIER, JEAN
Ladies' Turn (1982)
Marriage of the Century,
The (1985)

MORODER, GIORGIO
American Gigolo (1980)
Foxes (1980)
Cat People (1982)
Flashdance (1983)
Metropolis (1983)
Scarface (1983)
D.C. Cab (1983)
Neverending Story, The
(1984)
Electric Dreams (1984)
Over the Top (1987)
Mamba (1988)

MOROSS, JEROME
Grizzly! (1968)

MOROZOV, ALEXANDER
Ovation (1986)

MORRICONE, ENNIO
Martians Have Arrived, The
(1964)
Hawks and the Sparrows,
The (1965)
Agent 505 (1965)
Adultery, Italian Style (1966)

Adventurer, The (1966)
Dollar a Head, A (1966)
Long Days of Vengeance,
    The (1966)
Pistol for Ringo, A (1966)
Quien Sabe? (1966)
River of Dollars, A (1966)
Seven Wives for the McGregors
    (1966)
Wake Up and Kill (1966)
Woman and the General, The
    (1966)
You'll See Me Come Back
    (1966)
Harem (1968)
Man from Shiloh, The (1970)
Sicilian Clan, The (1970)
Devil in the Brain (1972)
What Have You Done With
    Solange? (1972)
Without Apparent Motive
    (1972)
Romantic Agony, The (1973)
Spasm (1974)
Magic Man, The (1976)
Moses--The Lawgiver (1976)
Windows (1980)
I As In Icarus (1980)
Todo Modo (1980)
Fun Is Beautiful (1980)
Good Thief, The (1980)
Island, The (1980)
Almost Human (1980)
Woman Banker, The (1980)
Men or Not Men (1980)
Cage aux Folles II, La
    (1980)
True Story of Camille, The
    (1981)
Man's Tragedy, A (1981)
Butterfly (1981)
So Fine (1981)
Disobedience (1981)
Professional, The (1981)
Rise Up, Spy (1982)
Marco Polo (1982)
Thing, The (1982)
White Dog (1982)
Scarlet and the Black, The
    (1983)
Treasure of the Four Crowns
    (1983)

Ruffian, The (1983)
Order of Death (1983)
Key, The (Chiave, La) (1983)
Outsider, The (1983)
Time to Die, A (1983)
Sahara (1983)
Thieves After Dark (1984)
Don't Kill God (1984)
Hundra (1984)
Once Upon a Time in
    America (1984)
Link, The (1985)
Red Sonja (1985)
Forester's Sons, The (1985)
Cage, The (1985)
Repenter, The (1985)
Cage Aux Folles III, La (1985)
C.A.T. Squad (1986)
Mission, The (1986)
Octopus--Pt. 2, The (1986)
Venetian Woman, The (1986)
Control (1987)
Gold-Rimmed Glasses, The
    (1987)
Moscow Farewell (1987)
Neighborhood (1987)
Rampage (1987)
Untouchables, The (1987)
C.A.T. Squad: Python Wolf
    (1988)
Frantic (1988)
New Paradise Cinema (1988)
Time of Destiny, A (1988)

MORRIS, JOHN
    ABC After School Special,
        The (1972)
    Adams Chronicles, The (1976)
    Scarlet Letter, The (1979)
    Dr. Franken (1980)
    Mating Season, The (1980)
    In God We Trust (1980)
    Elephant Man, The (1980)
    History of the World--Part I
        (1981)
    Splendor in the Grass (1981)
    Electric Grandmother, The
        (1982)
    Table for Five (1983)
    Yellowbeard (1983)
    To Be or Not To Be (1983)
    Firm, The (1983)

Ghost Dancing (1983)
Woman in Red, The (1984)
Johnny Dangerously (1984)
Doctor and the Devils, The
   (1985)
Clue (1985)
Fresno (1986)
Haunted Honeymoon (1986)
Dirty Dancing (1987)
Fig Tree, The (1987)
Ironweed (1987)
Little Match Girl, The (1987)
Spaceballs (1987)
Wash, The (1988)

MORRISON, VAN
Lamb (1985)

MORROS, BORIS
Land of Promise (1935)

MORSE, FUZZBEE
Ghoulies II (1988)

MORTAROTT, JOHN
Women of Russia (1981)

MORTIFIE, ANN
Surfacing (1981)

MORTON, ARTHUR
Riding on Air (1937)
Swingin' Along (1962)
Peyton Place (1964)
Waltons, The (1972)
Medical One (1975)
Medical Story (1975)
Swiss Family Robinson (1975)

MOSALINI, JUAN JOSE
Beto Nervio Against the
   Powers of the Shadows
   (1981)
Autograph, The (1984)

MOSELEY, JERRY
Blood Tide (1980)
Frightmare (1981)

MOSER, ROLAND
Interrupted Traces, The
   (1982)

MOTHERSBAUGH, MARK
Revenge of the Nerds II:
   Nerds in Paradise (1987)
Slaughterhouse Rock (1988)

"MOTORHEAD"
Eat the Rich (1987)

MOTTA, PEPE
In the Name of the Son
   (1987)

MOTTOLA, TONY
Running on Empty (1988)

MOTZING, WILLIAM
Prisoner: Cell Block H
   (1979)
Dead Easy (1982)
Return of Captain Invincible,
   The (1983)
Undercover (1984)
Stanley (1984)
One Night Stnad (1984)
Silver City (1984)
Cowra Breakout, The (1985)
Coca-Cola Kid, The (1985)
Room to Move (1987)
Shadows of the Peacock (1987)
Vietnam (1987)
Jack Simpson (1988)
Melba (1988)
Young Einstein (1988)

MOUCKA, JUROSLAV
Krabat (Sorcerer's Apprentice,
   The) (1982)

MOULAERT, PIERRE
Black Shadows (1949)

MOUNSEY, BOB
News Is the News, The (1983)

MOURA, PAULO
Partners of Adventure (1980)
Parahybe Woman (1983)
Good Bourgeois, The (1984)

MOURA, TAVINHO
Cabaret Mineiro (1980)
Loved One, The (1983)

Hinterland Nights
(1984)

MOZART, ODDSON W. A.
Beast, The (1986)

MUTUME, JAMES
Native Son (1986)

MUELLER, HANNS CHRISTIAN
Man Spricht Deutsch (1988)

MUELLER, MARIUS
Hard Asphalt (1986)
Pathfinder (1987)

MUELLER, ROLF-SANS
Veil of Blood (1978)

MUHLBRADT, HORST
Not Nothing Without You
(1985)
Burning Beds (1988)

MUIR, JAMES
Ghost Dance (1983)

MULDERS, MICHEL
Pointsman, The (1986)
Egg (1988)

MULDOWNEY, DOMINIC
Betrayal (1983)
Ploughman's Lunch, The
(1983)
Loose Connections (1983)
Laughterhouse (1984)
1984 (1984)
Insurance Man, The (1985)

MULE, GIUSEPPE
Jeanne Dore (1939)

MULIC, ZORAN
Stallion Didn't Like Him,
The (1988)

MULLE, RADZO
Captain Leshi (1960)

MULLENDORE, JOSEPH
Daniel Boone (1964)
Lancer (1968)

MULLER, VERONIQUE
Black Spider, The (1983)

MULLIGAN, JERRY
Help, My Snowman Is Burning
Down (1964)

MULLIGAN, KEVIN
One Woman or Two (1985)

MUNDI, COATI
Spike of Bensonhurst
(1988)

MUNKACSI, MURT
Koyaanisqatsi (1982)

MUNOZ, ANGEL
Gulf of Biscay (1985)
Be Unfaithful and Don't Be
Concerned With Whom
(1985)
Lulu by Night (1986)
Let Down Your Hair (1988)
Most Amusing Game, The
(1988)

MUNOZ, MANUEL
On the Line (1984)

MUNOZ-MOLLEDA, JOSE
Andalusian Nights (1938)
As Long as You Live (1955)

MUNRO, MURRAY
Private Investigations (1987)

MUNROW, DAVID
Six Wives of Henry VIII,
The (1971)

MUNSEN, JUDY
Bon Voyage, Charlie Brown

(And Don't Come Back)
(1980)
Street Music (1981)

MUNTANER, RAMON
Diamond Square (1982)

MURAI, KUNIHIKO
Rhyme of Vengeance, A
(1978)

MURAVLOV, ALEXEI
Vasily and Vasilisa (1982)

MURCIANO, PAUL
Living Dreams (1988)

MURILLO, ENRIC
Daniya, Garden of the Harem
(1988)

MURPHEY, MICHAEL MARTIN
Hard Country (1981)

MURPHY, MICHAEL
Bobby Jo and the Big Apple
Goodtime Band (1972)

MURPHY, ROBERT
Backroads (1981)
Judgment in Stone, A (1986)

MURPHY, WALTER
Savage Bees, The (1976)
Raw Force (1982)
Tricks of the Trade (1988)

MURRAY, LYN
Dragnet (1951)
Prowler, The (1951)
Daniel Boone (1964)
Time Tunnel, The (1966)
Escape to Mindanao (1968)
Now You See It, Now You
Don't (1968)
Smugglers, The (1968)
Don't Push, I'll Charge
When I'm Ready (1969)
Dragnet (1969)
Love, Hate, Love (1971)
Magic Carpet (1972)

MURRAY, SEAN
Scorpion, The (1986)

MURTAUGH, JOHN
Connection (1973)
Strike Force (1975)
African Queen, The (1977)

MUSCH, JAN
Taste of Water, The (1982)

MUSCHIETTI, ALFREDO E.
Favorites and Winners (1983)

MUSKETT, JENNIE
People of the Forest (1988)

MUSSER, JOHN
Some Kind of Wonderful (1987)

MUSTAMU, ZETH
And Never the Twain Shall
Meet (1985)

MUSUMURA, ROMANO
Woman of My Life, The (1986)
Malady of Love (1987)
Childhood of Art (1988)
Faceless (1988)

MUSY, JEAN
My Heart Is Upside Down
(1980)
Tanya's Island (1981)
Sideroads (1983)
Bird Watch, The (1983)
Gramps Is in the Resistance
(1983)
False Confidences, The
(1984)
Diary of a Madman, The
(1987)
Johnny Monroe (1987)

MUSZYNSKI, ROBERT
Charles Burchfield--Fifty
Years of His Art (1967)

MUTSU, HIROSHI
Wet Sand in August
(1975)

MYER, JOHN
Captain Kangaroo (1955)

MYERS, PETER
Stark (1985)
Death of an Angel (1985)
Dynasty II: The Colbys
(1985)
Crazy Dan (1986)
Stark: Mirror Image (1986)

MYERS, STANLEY
Divorce His/Divorce Hers
(1973)
House of Whipcord (1974)
Frightmare (1975)
Schizo (1976)
Comeback, The (1977)
Confessional, The (1977)
Summer of My German
Soldier, The (1978)
Day the Screaming Stopped,
The (1979)
Martian Chronicles, The
(1980)
Watcher in the Woods, The
(1980)
Next One, The (1981)
Gentleman Bandit, The (1981)
Absolution (1981)
Lady Chatterly's Lover
(1981)
Incubus, The (1982)
Beyond the Limit (1983)
Eureka (1983)
Blind Date (1984)
Success Is the Best Revenge
(1984)
Zany Adventures of Robin
Hood, The (1984)
Nancy Astor (1984)
Florence Nightingale (1985)
Chain, The (1985)
Insignificance (1985)
My Beautiful Laundrette
(1985)
Lightship, The (1985)
Dreamchild (1985)
Wild Horses (1985)
Castaway (1986)
New World (1986)

Second Victory, The (1986)
Strong Medicine (1986)
Pack of Lies (1987)
Prick Up Your Ears (1987)
Sammy and Rosie Get Laid
(1987)
Wind, The (1987)
Wish You Were Here (1987)
Zero Boys, The (1987)
Baja Oklahoma (1988)
Boost, The (1988)
Most Dangerous Man in the
World, The (1988)
Nature of the Beast, The
(1988)
Paperhouse (1988)
Stars and Bars (1988)
Taffin (1988)
Track 29 (1988)
Trading Hearts (1988)

MYGGEN, BENT
Smokey Bites the Dust (1981)

MYHRE, LARS MARTIN
Henry's Back Room (1982)

MYLONAS, COSTAS
Polk File on the Air (1988)

MYROW, FRED
In Search of America (1971)
Message to My Daughter
(1973)
Pray for the Wildcats (1974)
Secret Life of John Chapman,
The (1976)
On the Nickel (1980)
Journey to Spirit Island
(1988)
Phantasm II (1988)

"MYSTICS, LES"
Ablakon (1985)

NACHON, JEAN-CLAUDE
Secret Passage (1985)

NADER, HERMELINO
Lady from the Shanghai
Cinema, The (1988)

Chase (1973)
I Love a Mystery (1973)
Money to Burn (1973)
Six Million Dollar Man, The
  (1973)
Matt Helm (1975)

NELSON, STEVE
Cheers (1982)
Star of the Family (1982)
Webster (1983)
Last Resort (1986)

NELSSON, ANDERS
Tattoo Connection, The
  (1980)
Seven Years Itch (1987)

NEMEC, JAN
Codename: Wildgeese (1986)

NESCHLING, JOHN
Strangers--The Road to
  Liberty (1980)
Pixote, Survival of the
  Weakest (1981)
Lucio Flavio (1981)
Family Album (1981)
Kiss of the Spider Woman
  (1985)

NESMITH, MICHAEL
Timerider (1983)

NETO, TO
Lives (1984)

NEUBRAND, HEINZ
My Daughter Patricia (1959)

NEUBURG, ETHAN
Bum Rap (1988)

NEUFELD, DAN
Lemora, the Lady Dracula
  (1975)

NEUMANN, DREW
Scalps (1983)
Biohazard (1983)

NEUMANN, WOLFGANG
Nuclear Split (1987)

"NEUROTIC GROUP"
Peter in Wonderland (1988)

NEVES, OSCAR CASTRO
Blame It on Rio (1984)

NEWBORN, IRA
All Night Long (1981)
Police Squad (1982)
Sixteen Candles (1984)
Never Again (1984)
Into the Night (1985)
Weird Science (1985)
Ferris Bueller's Day Off
  (1986)
Wise Guys (1986)
Dragnet (1987)
Guilty of Innocence: The
  Lennel Geter Story (1987)
Planes, Trains and Auto-
  mobiles (1987)
Caddyshack II (1988)
Naked Gun, The (1988)

NEWKIRK, BILL
Sidney Shorr (1980)

NEWMAN, ALFRED
Wee Willie Winkie (1937)
Egyptian, The (1954)
Mark of Zorro, The (1974)

NEWMAN, CHARLES
Litterbugs (1943)

NEWMAN, DAVID
Critters (1986)
Vendetta (1986)
Brave Little Toaster, The
  (1987)
Kindred, The (1987)
Malone (1987)
My Demon Lover (1987)
Throw Mama from the Train
  (1987)

NEWMAN, EMIL
Woman on the Run (1950)

Guns, Girls and Gangsters
(1958)

NEWMAN, LIONEL
Death in Small Doses (1957)
Daniel Boone (1964)
Peyton Place (1964)
Boston Strangler, The (1968)
Land of the Giants (1968)
Bracken's World (1969)
Room 222 (1969)
Fireball Forward (1972)
M*A*S*H (1972)
When Michael Calls (1972)
Planet of the Apes (1974)
Swiss Family Robinson (1975)

NEWMAN, RANDY
Whatever Happened to Dobie
Gillis? (1977)
Ragtime (1981)
Natural, The (1984)
Huey Long (1985)

NEWMAN, THOMAS
Reckless (1984)
Revenge of the Nerds (1984)
Grandville, U.S.A. (1984)
Seduction of Gina, The
(1984)
Desperately Seeking Susan
(1985)
Girls Just Want to Have Fun
(1985)
Man With One Red Shoe, The
(1985)
Real Genius (1985)
Gung Ho (1986)
Jumpin' Jack Flash (1986)
Less Than Zero (1987)
Light of Day (1987)
Lost Boys, The (1987)
Great Outdoors, The (1988)

NEWTON, JON
Shadow Play (1986)

NICHOL, JIMMIE
Anti-Climax (1970)

NICHOLAS, JEREMY
Quartermain's Terms (1987)

NICHOLAS, MARK
Death Warmed Up (1984)

NICHOLS, LEO
Cruel Ones, The (1966)

NICHOLS, TED
Birdman (1967)
New Adventures of Huckle-
berry Finn, The (1968)
Perils of Penelope Pitstop,
The (1969)
Pebbles and Bamm Bamm
(1971)
Scooby-Doo/Dynomutt Hour,
The (1976)

NICK, EDMUND
Court Concert (1937)

NICOLAI, BRUNO
Apocalypse in Berlin (1966)
Cisco, El (1966)
Django Spara per Primo (1966)
Kiss Kiss ... Bang Bang
(1966)
Operation Lady Chaplin (1966)
Christ of the Ocean (1971)
Excite Me (1972)
Night of the Blood Monster
(1972)
Who Put Those Drops of
Blood on the Body of
Jennifer? (1972)
Tempter, The (1974)
All the Colors of Darkness
(1976)
Eyeball (1978)
Persian Lamb Coat, The
(1980)
Camminacammina (1983)
Buckeye and Blue (1988)

NICOLAU, DIMITRI
Panagoulis Lives (1980)

NICOLOSI, ROBERTO
Sixth Continent, The (1954)
Cote d'Azur (1959)
Esther and the King (1960)
Eye of the Labyrinth
(1971)

NIEDERBERGER, MAX
  Dance Music (1935)
  Love at Court (1936)

NIEHAUS, LENNIE
  Tightrope (1984)
  City Heat (1984)
  Pale Rider (1985)
  Sesame Street Presents:
    Follow That Bird (1985)
  Heartbreak Ridge (1986)
  Ratboy (1986)
  Emanon (1987)
  Bird (1988)
  Child Saver, The (1988)

NIELSEN, ELISABETH G.
  Suzanne and Leonard (1984)
  Pinky's Gang (1986)

NIEMAN, CZESLAW
  Charge (1981)
  Polonia Restituta (1981)

NIESSEN, CHARLEY
  My Niece Doesn't Do That
    (1960)

NIETO, JOSE
  Black Hand, The (1980)
  I'm in a Crisis! (1982)
  Odds and Evens (1982)
  Rogues (1983)
  Queen of Mate, The (1985)
  Extramurals (1985)
  Knight of the Dragon, The
    (1986)
  Captain James Cook (1987)
  El Lute--Forge On or Die
    (1987)
  Enchanted Forest, The (1987)
  Tomorrow I'll Be Free (1988)

"NIGHTWORK"
  Land of Cops and Robbers
    (1983)

NIGRA, SAMBUCA
  Malady of Death, The (1985)

NIKOLAIS, ALWIN
  Fusion (1968)

NIKOLIC, KORNELIJE
  Love, Love, But Don't Lose
    Your Head (1981)

NIKOLOV, VESSELIN
  All Is Love (1980)

NILSEN, LILLEBJORN
  Bluecher (1988)

NILSSON, HARRY
  Courtship of Eddie's Father,
    The (1969)
  Popeye (1980)

NILSSON, STEFAN
  Sally and Freedom (1981)
  Big Bang in Bender, The
    (1983)
  Inside Man, The (1984)
  Smuggler King, The (1985)
  False as Water (1985)
  Cat's Whiskers and Green
    Peas (1986)
  Jim & the Pirates (1987)
  Pelle the Conqueror (1987)
  Serpent's Way Up to the
    Naked Rock, The (1987)
  Age of the Wolf (1988)
  Sweetwater (1988)

"1984"
  Back-Jet Family, The (1985)

NISHI, GORO
  Rikisha Man, The (1943)

NISHIYAMA, HOBURU
  Living Skeleton, The (1968)

NITTELS, DEAD
  Gasping (1984)

NITZSCHE, JACK
  Cruising (1980)
  Cutter and Bone (Cutter's
    Way) (1981)
  Personal Best (1982)
  Cannery Row (1982)
  Officer and a Gentleman, An
    (1982)
  Without a Trace (1983)

Breathless (1983)
Windy City (1984)
Razor's Edge, The (1984)
Starman (1984)
Stripper (1985)
Jewel of the Nile, The (1985)
Nine-and-a-Half Weeks (1986)
Stand By Me (1986)
Streets of Gold (1986)
Whoopee Boys, The (1986)
Seventh Sign, The (1988)

NOCENZI, GIANNI
In the Lost City of Sarzana
(1980)
Very Old Man with Enormous
Wings, A (1988)

NOCK, MIKE
Strata (1983)

NOER, EMBIE C.
Dawn, The (1983)

NOGISTO, JAANUS
Ideal Landscape (1986)

NOLIN, MAGGIE
Night of the Zombies (Gamma
693) (1979)

NONO, LUIGI
Successful Man, A (1986)

NORDGREN, ERIK
Eva (1949)
She Only Danced One Summer
(Sommerlek) (1951)
Seventh Seal, The (1957)
Magician, The (1958)
Rainbow Dilemma, The (1958)
Wild Strawberries (1958)

NORDHEIM, ARNE
Witch Hunt, The (1981)
Skin (1986)

NORELL, TIM
One Way Ticket (1988)

NORGAARD, PER
Babette's Feast (1987)

NORMAN, LON
Sting of Death (1966)
I Eat Your Skin (1974)

NORMAN, MONTY
Dickens of London (1977)

NORTH, ALEX
Playhouse 90 (1956)
77 Sunset Strip (1959)
Man and the City, The (1971)
Rich Man, Poor Man, Book I
(1976)
Rich Man, Poor Man, Book II
(1976)
Word, The (1978)
Wise Blood (1979)
Carny (1980)
Dragonmaster (1981)
Sister, Sister (1982)
Under the Volcano (1984)
Prizzi's Honor (1985)
Private Conversations (1985)
Dead, The (1987)
Good Morning, Vietnam (1987)
John Huston and the Dubliners
(1987)
Penitent, The (1988)

NORTON, ED
Beyond Atlantis (1973)

NOVAK, JAN (JANOS)
Cybernetic Grandmother
(1962)
Jester's Tale, A (1964)
Philadelphia Attraction, The
(1985)
Cowboys (1986)
Whooping Cough (1987)

NOVAK, JERKO
Displaced Person (1982)

NOVEMBRE, TOM
Signed Heart (1985)
Follow My Gaze (1986)

NOVOTNY, PAUL
Blue Monkey (1987)
Dixie Lanes (1988)

NOYEN, ENGIN
Swallow Storm, The (1986)

NOZAWA, MATSUNOSUKE
Love Suicides at Sonezaki,
The (1982)

NUNEZ, JUAN CARLO
Wedding, The (1982)
House of Water (1984)

NUNEZ PALACIO, ALBERTO
Collapse (1987)

NUNNES, JUAN CARLOS
Wanted: Good Looking
Receptionist and Messenger
with His Own Motorcycle
(1982)

NUTI, GIOVANNI
Blame It on Paradise (1986)
Bewitched (1987)

NUTTER, MAYF
Deadly Stranger (1988)

NYBERGET, NISSA
Something Entirely Different
(1986)
Feldmann Case, The (1987)

NYKJAR, ELIT
Closing Time (1988)

NYMAN, MICHAEL
Draughtsman's Contract,
The (1982)
Nelly's Version (1983)
Cold Room, The (1984)
Zed and Two Noughts, A
(1985)
Drowning by Numbers (1988)
Man Who Mistook His Wife
for a Hat, The (1988)

NYRO, LAURA
Broken Rainbow (1985)

"O.K. CHARLIE"
Ostria (1984)

OBER, ARLON
Hospital Massacre (1980)
Galaxina (1981)
X-Ray (1981)
Eating Raoul (1982)
Happy Birthday (1982)
Crimewave (1985)
Bloody Birthday (1986)
In the Shadow of Kilimanjaro
(1986)

OBERMEYER, KLAUS
Fear Not, Jacob! (1981)

OBIEDO, RAY
Method, The (1987)

OBRADOVIC, DIMITRIJE-MIKAN
Like Grandfather, Like
Grandson (1983)

OCAL, TARIK
Wrestler, The (1985)
Handful of Paradise, A (1986)
Voice, The (1987)

OCAMPO, OSCAR CARDOZO
From the Abyss (1980)
Untamable Shrews, The
(1982)
Open Day and Night (1982)
There Will Be No More Sor-
rows Nor Oblivion (1983)
Deathstalker (1984)
Passengers of a Nightmare
(1984)
Eva Peron Mystery, The
(1988)
Stormquest (1988)

OCSKO, MICHAEL
Walls (1984)

ODA, YUICHIRO
Dirty Hero (1983)

ODDIE, BILL
Goodies, The (1976)

ODLAND, BRUCE
Land of Little Rain (1988)

O'DONOHUE, RORY
Fatty Finn (1980)

O'FARRELL, CHICO
New Voice, The (1973)
Guaguasi (1982)

O'FARRELL, MARC
It Can't Be Winter, We
Haven't Had Summer Yet
(1981)
Choice of a People, The
(1985)

OFIR, URI
Avanti Popolo (1986)

O'GALLEHUR, EAMONN
You Can't Fool an Irishman
(1950)

OGAWA, HIROYOSHI
Utamaro, Painter of Women
(1960)

OGAWA, NIROAKI
Manster, The (1959)

O'HEARN, PATRICK
Destroyer (1988)

OHKAWA, SHINNOSUKE
Ohan (1985)

OHMORI, SEITARO
Cobra (1975)

OHMURO, HITOSHI
My Voiceless Friends (1972)

OHNE, KATSUO
Yen Family (1988)

OHNO, YUJI
Inugamis, The (1977)
Space Cobra (1983)
Mighty Orbots, The (1984)

"OHPSST"
Berlin Chamissoplatz (1981)

OHTA, HERB
White House on the Beach,
The (1978)

OKADA, KAZUO
Tattered Banner, The (1975)
Things That Teachers Do
(1982)

OKADA, KYOKO
Village, The (1976)

OKADA, TORU
Lonely Hearts (1982)

OKAWA, SHINNOSUKE
Sasame Yuki (1983)

O'KENNEDY, JOHN
Stripped to Kill (1987)

OKI, MASAO
Story of a Pure Love, The
(1958)

OKUSAWA, HAJIME
From Three to Sex (1972)

OLAFSSON, EGILL
Twins, The (1982)

OLDFIELD, ALAN
Invisible Strangler (1976)
Forest, The (1981)
Deep Space (1988)

OLDFIELD, MIKE
Charlotte (1975)
Dogs (1976)
Space Movie, The (1980)
Milan '83 (1984)
Killing Fields, The (1984)

OLDFIELD, TERRY
Land of the Tiger (1985)
In Search of the Trojan War
(1986)
Australia's Twilight of the
Dreamtime (1988)

OLEA, ANTONIO PEREZ
Requiem for a Secret Agent

(1966)
Nightmare Hotel (1973)
Blood-Spattered Bride, The
(1974)
Royal Romp (1981)

OLIAS, LOTAR
Uncle from America (1953)
Loving Couples (1955)

OLIVER, CHRISTOPH
Tarot (1986)

OLIVER, STEPHEN
Love's Labor's Lost (1985)
After Pilkington (1986)
Lady Jane (1986)

OLIVIERO, JAMES
Impure Thoughts (1986)
Funland (1987)
Mace (1987)
Sleepaway Camp 2: Unhappy
Campers (1988)

OLMSTED, JEFFREY
Abuse (1983)
Buddies (1985)

OLSEN, OLLIE
With Time to Kill (1987)

OLSSON, MATS
Fear Has a Thousand Eyes
(1971)

OLVIS, WILLIAM
Nightingales (1988)

O'MARTIN, MICHAEL
Go Ask Alice (1973)
Leg Work (1987)

OMORI, SEITARO
Monster from a Prehistoric
Planet (1967)
Three Seconds to Zero Hour
(1969)
Oh, My Comrade! (1971)
Waterfront Blues (1971)
Weird Trip (1972)

Dancer and the Warrior, The
(1981)

O'NEILL, SHARON
Smash Palace (1981)

ONG, LANCE
Initiation, The (1982)

ONI, UGI
House of Terror (1976)
Lupin III (1978)

ONIONS, OLIVER
After the Fall of New York
(1985)

ONO, KATSUO
Pool Without Water, A (1982)
Dropout, The (1983)
Mosquito on the Tenth Floor
(1983)
Comic Magazine (1986)

ORBIT, WILLIAM
Youngblood (1986)
Hotshot (1987)

ORENSTEIN, LARRY
But Mother! (1979)

O'RIADA, SEAN
Echoes of a Distant Drum
(1988)

ORLANDI, NORA
Beckett Affair, The (1966)
Sheriff All in Gold, A (1966)

ORM, PETER & PAVEL
Round My Head in 40 Days
(1986)

ORNADEL, CYRIL
Brief Encounter (1974)
Flesh and Blood Show, The
(1974)
Edward the King (1980)

ORNELAS, NIVALDO
Dance of the Dolls (1987)

ORN-IEM, MONTRI
   They Call Him Hurricane
      (1980)

"ORPHANAGE, THE"
   Run, Simon, Run (1970)
   Bounty Man, The (1972)
   Can Ellen Be Saved? (1974)
   New Land, The (1974)
   They Only Come Out at
      Night (1975)

ORR, BUXTON
   Fiend Without a Face, The
      (1958)

ORTEGA, CHICO ROJO
   Tokyo-Ga (1985)

ORTEGA, FRANK
   Rosie: The Rosemary
      Clooney Story (1982)

ORTH, FRANK
   Mummy's Curse, The (1944)

ORTIZ, LUIS see PERICO
ORTIZ, LUIS

ORTOLANI, RIZ
   Ursus in the Valley of the
      Lions (1961)
   Horror Castle (1963)
   Castle of Terror (1964)
   Girl from Bersagliere, The
      (1966)
   I Don't Love War, I Love
      Love (1966)
   Operation Goldman (1966)
   Special Code (1966)
   Top Crack (1966)
   Girl Who Couldn't Say No,
      The (1969)
   Tigers in Lipstick (1971)
   Cannibal Holocaust (1979)
   Help Me Dream (1981)
   Ghost of Love (1981)
   Madhouse (1980)
   Valentina (1982)
   Revenge of the Dead (1982)
   1919 (1983)

School Outing, A (1983)
Giuseppe Fava: Sicilian Like
   Me (1984)
Proper Scandal, A (1984)
We Three (Noi Tre) (1984)
House on the Edge of the
   Park, The (1985)
Employees (1985)
Christopher Columbus (1985)
Graduation Party (1985)
Miranda (1985)
Christmas Present (1986)
Capriccio (1987)
Investigation, The (1987)
Last Moment (1987)
Rome, 2072 A.D.--The New
   Gladiators (1987)

OSBORN, JASON
   High Season (1987)

OSBORNE, LESLIE
   Howard's Way (1985)

OSBORNE, TONY
   Beware the Brethren (1972)

OSHRATH, KOBI
   Mute Love (1982)
   Kuni Lemel in Cairo (1983)

OSKAR, LEE
   My Road (1981)

OSSA, BERNARDO AND
   GABRIEL
   Pure Blood (1982)

OSTENDORF, JENS-PETER
   Due to an Act of God (1983)
   Yasemin (1988)

OSTERMANN, WILLI
   Dream of the Rhine (1935)

OSTMAN, ARNOLD
   Gosta Berling's Saga (1986)

O'SULLEABHEIN, MICHAEL
   It's Handy When People Don't
      Die (1981)

OSZAN, SARPER see OZHAN

OTANI, KAZUO
  Good Luck Love (1982)

OTSUKA, GULLIVER
  Blind Alley (1985)

OUEDRAOGO, GEORGES
  Zan Boko (1988)

OVCHINNIKOV, VYACHESLAV
  Boris Godunov (1986)

O'VERLIN, JOHN
  Planet of Dinosaurs (1980)

OVTSHINSKAIA, L.
  More Light! (1988)

OWEN, REG
  Very Important Person, A
    (1961)

OWENS, JAMES W.
  Freedom (1957)

OYA, KAZUO
  Vienna Story--Gemini Y and
    S (1983)

OZDEMIROGLU, ATILLA
  Frogs, The (1986)
  Her Name Is Vasfiye (1986)
  Motherland Hotel (1987)
  Mr. Muhsin (1988)
  Night Journey (1988)

OZHAN, SARPER
  Guard, The (1985)
  Water Also Burns (1987)
  Hunting Time (1988)

OZKAN, HALUK
  Last Man of Urfa, The (1987)

PA, TON
  Return to Eden (1983)

PACELLI, OSCAR
  When the Skin Burns (1966)

PACENCIA, PEDRO
  Lovers of the Lord of the
    Night, The (1984)

PACHAIYO, SARAVUTH
  Miss Keow (1980)

PACHECO, ADOLFO
  Accordionist's Wedding, The
    (1988)

PADILLA, JOSE
  El 113 (1936)

PADMANABHAN, A.
  Wandering Soul (1980)

PAES, JOAO
  Benilde, ou a Virgem Mae
    (1975)
  Love of Perdition (1980)
  Francisca (1981)

PAGAN, JOSE MANUEL
  Lola (1986)
  Anguish (1987)
  With Feathers (1988)

PAGANI, MAURO
  Midsummer Night's Dream, A
    (1983)
  Ladies and Gentlemen (1984)

PAGE, GENE
  Annie Flynn (1978)
  Friends (1978)
  Pryor's Place (1984)

PAGE, GLEN
  Who's On Call? (1979)

PAGE, JIMMY
  Death Wish II (1982)
  Death Wish 3 (1985)

PAGE, SCOTT
  Three Kinds of Heat (1987)

PAGEL, HAYES
  Phantom Planet, The (1961)

PAHANI, MAURO
  Sweet Absence (1986)

PAICH, MARTY
  Ironside (1967)
  Riddle at 24,000 (1974)

PAINE, AIME
  Geronima (1986)

PAIS, JOAO
  My Case (1986)

PAIVA, MANUEL
  Last Faust, The (1986)
  Suburban Angels (1987)

PAKSY, JOSEPH
  Gay Misery (1938)

PAL, VED
  Girl from India (1982)

PALACIO, ALBERTO see
  NUNEZ PALACIO, ALBERTO

PALERMO, CHRIS
  Momma the Detective (1981)

PALESTER, ROMAN
  Young Forest (1935)
  Last Stop, The (1949)

PALJATIC, GORAN
  Sugar Water (1984)

PALLUMBO, JOHN
  Adventure of the Action
    Hunter, The (1987)

PALMER, DAVID
  Royal Romance of Charles
    and Diana, The (1982)

PALMER, SHELDON LEIGH
  Xtro (1983)
  For All People, For All
    Time (1984)

PALMERS, BENGT
  Charter Trip, The (1980)

Business Is Booming (1985)
Package Tour II--Snowroller,
  The (1985)

PALOMBO, BERNARDO
  El Salvador: Another Vietnam
    (1981)
  Good Fight, The (1984)

PANCHENKO, VLADISLAV
  Miss Million (1988)

PANNACH, GERULF
  Fatherland (1986)

PAOLETTI, TONIO
  Masoch (1980)

PAOLI, GINO
  Woman in the Mirror, A
    (1984)

PAPADAKIS, GEORGE
  Roads of Love Are Night
    Roads, The (1981)
  On the Time of Hellenes
    (1981)
  Theofilos (1987)

PAPADEMETRIOU, DEMETRIS
  Homecoming Song (1983)
  Revenge (1983)
  Enchantress, The (1985)
  Trees We Were Hurting, The
    (1986)
  Potlatch (1987)
  In the Shadow of Fear (1988)

PAPADIAMANDIS, PIERRE
  Week's Vacation, A (1980)

PAPATHANASSIOU, VANGELIS
  (EVANGELOS) see VANGELIS

PAPIR, VICTOR
  Frozen Child, The (1937)
  Tommy (1937)

PAPP, ZOLTAN
  Peephole and the Key, The
    (1985)

PAUL, EDWARD
  Mahatma Gandhi--20th Century
    Prophet (1953)

PAULAVICUS, ALGIRDAS
  Gardener, The (1988)

PAVAO, RICARDO
  Land for Rose (1988)

PAVLICEK, MICHAEL
  Why (1988)

PAVLOSKY, CHARLES
  Ninja Turf (1986)

PAWLUSKIEWICZ, JAN KANTY
  Chance (1980)
  Moth, The (1980)
  Fever (1981)
  Lonely Woman, A (1981)
  Hero of the Year (1987)

PAXTON, GLEN
  American Image, The (1968)
  Wyeth Phenomenon, The
    (1968)
  You Are There (1971)
  Clone Master, The (1978)
  Two Worlds of Jennie Logan,
    The (1979)
  Charlie and the Great Balloon
    Race (1981)
  Dark Night of the Scarecrow
    (1981)
  Isabel's Choice (1981)
  Vital Signs (1986)

PAYNE, ADRIAN
  Fantasy Man (1984)

PAYNE, BILL
  Certain Fury (1985)
  Smooth Talk (1985)

PAYNE, HAROLD
  Joy of Sex (1984)

PEAK, KEVIN
  Windrider (1986)

PEAKE, DON
  Legend of Bigfoot, The
    (1975)
  Sister Terri (1978)
  Battered (1978)
  Beane's of Boston (1979)
  California Fever (1979)
  Flatbed Annie and Sweetiepie:
    Lady Truckers (1979)
  Makin' It (1979)
  Further Adventures of Wally
    Brown, The (1980)
  House Where Death Lives,
    The (1980)
  Prey, The (1980)
  Camp Wilderness (1980)
  I, Desire (1982)
  Knight Rider (1982)
  Code of Vengeance (1985)
  Dalton: Code of Vengeance
    II (1986)

PEARCE, DONALD
  Fast Friends (1979)

PEARL, HOWARD
  Angie (1979)
  New Kind of Family, A (1979)
  Blue Jeans (1980)
  Bosom Buddies (1980)
  Joanie Loves Chachi (1982)
  New Odd Couple, The (1982)
  One More Try (1982)
  Oh Madeline (1983)
  Brothers (1984)
  His and Hers (1984)
  Johanna (1985)
  Mary (1985)
  In the Lion's Den (1987)

PECHECO, JOHNNY
  Mondo New York (1988)

PECK, BILL
  Plainsong (1982)

PEDACE, ANTONIO
  After a Night of Love (1935)

PEDERSEN, GUNNAR MOELLER
  Next Stop Paradise (1980)

Beauty and the Beast, The
(1983)
Baby Doll (1988)

PEEK, KEVIN
Battletruck (1982)

PEGURI, GINO
Bloody Pit of Horror (1965)
For a Thousand Dollars a
Day (1966)
Nostalgia (1983)

PEIER, GIACOMO
After Darkness (1985)

PEJOVSKI, ILJA
Lead Brigade, The (1980)

PELLEGRINO, STEPHEN
Lightning Over Braddock:
A Rustbowl Fantasy (1988)

PELLETIER, JEAN-CLAUDE
Beyond Love and Evil (1970)

PENA, ANGEL (CUCCO)
Gran Fiesta, La (1987)

PENDERECKI, KRYZYSTOF
Hands Up! (1981)

PENDERGRASS, TEDDY
Choose Me (1984)

PENNELL, CHUCK
Trespasses (1987)

PEPPER, ANNA
Outer Touch (Spaced Out)
(1979)

PEPPER, JIM
Weave of Time, A (1987)

PERAK, RUDOLF
Stronger Than Paragraphs
(1936)
On Both Sides of the Rollbahn
(1953)
Till Five Minutes Past
Twelve (1953)

PERATHONER, SERGE
Paco the Infallible (1980)
Strictly Personal (1985)
Kangaroo Complex, The (1986)

PEREZ, GATO
Blonde at the Bar, The (1987)

PEREZ, GEORGE
Santo Attacks the Witches
(1964)

PEREZ, JAIME
Exorcism's Daughter (1974)

PEREZ HERRERA, JORGE
Criminal Life of Archibaldo
de la Cruz, The (1955)
Diabolical Axe, The (1964)

"PERFORMER'S BAND, THE"
Private Passions (1985)

PERICO ORTIZ, LUIS
Mondo New York (1988)

PERILSTEIN, MICHAEL
Deadly Spawn, The (1981)
Hollywood Chainsaw Hookers
(1988)

PERJANIK, MIKE
Norman Loves Rose (1982)
Bush Christmas (1983)
Warming Up (1984)
Home and Away (1988)

PERKINSON, COLERIDGE-TAYLOR
Love Is Not Enough (1978)
Woman Called Moses, A (1978)
Freedom Road (1979)
Talk to Me (1982)

PERKOV, BOJIDAR
Home for Gentle Souls, A
(1981)

PERRER, ROSITA
Teo the Redhead (1986)

PERRET, PIERRE
    Wolf-Cubs of Niquoluna, The
        (1980)

PERRONE, MARC
    Trace, The (1983)

PERRY, WILLIAM
    Life on the Mississippi (1980)

PERSHING, D'VAUGHN
    Bizarre (1979)

PERSSON, BO ANDERS
    Fox, The (1986)

PESKANOV, ALEXANDER
    He Knows You're Alone
        (1980)
    Killing Hour, The (1981)

PESKANOV, MARK
    He Knows You're Alone
        (1980)

PESKO, GYORGY
    Let Ye Inherit (1985)

PESKO, ZOLTAN
    Yerma (1985)

PETERDI, PETER
    To See the Light (1985)

PETERS, RANDOLPH
    Tramp at the Door (1986)

PETERSEN, LEIF SYLVESTER
    Circus Casablanca (1981)
    Have You Seen Alice? (1981)
    Felix (1982)
    Rocking Silver (1983)

PETERSON, JOHN
    Atrapados (1981)

PETIT, JEAN-CLAUDE
    Tusk (1980)
    Vive la Sociale! (1983)
    Bill, The (1984)
    Sadness and Beauty (1985)

Red Caviar (1985)
Billy Ze Kick (1985)
Slices of Life (1985)
As Long As There Are Women
    (1987)
F...ing Fernand (1987)
Savannah (1988)

PETITGAND, LOORIE
    Tokyo-Ga (1985)

PETITGIRARD, LAURENT
    Asphalt (1981)
    King of Jerks, The (1981)

PETKOV, BOZHIDAR
    Journey, The (1981)
    Measure for Measure (1981)
    Hotel Central (1983)
    Black Swans (1987)

PETROV, ANDREI
    Blue Bird, The (1976)
    Station for Two (1983)
    Ruthless Romance (1985)
    Forgotten Tune for the
        Flute, A (1988)

PETROV, VADIM
    Rabbit Case, The (1980)
    Escapes Home (1981)
    I Am Not Afraid Anymore
        (1985)

PETROVIC, BOSCO
    Crazy Leg (1965)

PETROVICS, ELEK
    Volley for a Black Buffalo
        (1985)

PETROVICS, EMIL
    Boys of Paul Street, The
        (1969)

PFEIFFER, JACK
    Vladimir Horowitz: The Last
        Romantic (1986)

PHELOUNG, BARRINGTON
    Friendship's Death (1987)

PHILIP, HANS-ERIK
Time of Wolves, A (1981)
Parallel Corpse, The (1982)
Flight of the Eagle, The
(1982)
Flight of the Raven (1984)
Stravinsky--a Life (1985)
Ophelia Hits Town (1985)
In the Shadow of the Raven
(1988)

PHILIPS, BARRE
Top Speed (1982)
Doc's Kingdom (1988)

PHILLIPS, ART (ARTHUR)
Lucky Star, The (1980)
Devil at Your Heels, The
(1982)
American Caesar (1985)
Killing 'Em Softly (1985)

PHILLIPS, FREDDIE
Frog Prince, The (1954)
Gallant Little Tailor, The
(1954)
Grasshopper and the Ant,
The (1954)
Hansel and Gretel (1954)
Jack and the Beanstalk
(1954)
Puss in Boots (1954)

PHILLIPS, SHAWN
Abuse (1983)

PHILLIPS, STU
Monkees, The (1966)
Curious Female, The (1969)
McCloud (1970)
Six Million Dollar Man, The
(1973)
Switch (1975)
Quincy (1976)
Benny and Barney, Las
Vegas Undercover (1977)
Hardy Boys Mysteries, The
(1977)
Nancy Drew Mysteries, The
(1977)
New Adventures of Wonder

Woman, The (1977)
What Really Happened to the
Class of '65? (1977)
Spiderman Strikes Back (1978)
Battlestar Galactica (1978)
Evening in Byzantium (1978)
Islander, The (1978)
B.J. and the Bear (1979)
Buck Rogers in the 25th
Century (1979)
Battles: The Murder That
Wouldn't Die (1980)
Eyes of Texas, The (1980)
Galactica 1980 (1980)
Waikiki (1980)
Conquest of the Earth (1980)
Midnight Lace (1980)
Fall Guy, The (1981)
Fitz and Bones (1981)
Rooster (1982)
Terror at Alcatraz (1982)
Chicago Story (1982)
How Do I Kill a Thief--Let
Me Count the Ways (1982)
Knight Rider (1982)
Automan (1983)
Masquerade (1983)

PHILLIPS, VAN
Big Money, The (1958)

PHYX, BILL
Devil's Ecstasy, The (1977)

PIAZZA, ANDREA
Caffe Italia (1985)

PIAZZI, GIUSEPPE
Dynamite Brothers, The
(1949)

PIAZZOLLA, ASTOR
So Feared a Hell (1980)
North Bridge (1981)
Come Back (1982)
Bella Donna (1983)
Tango Is History (1984)
Enrico IV (1984)
Between the Times (1985)

Tangos--Gardel's Exile (1985)
Madres: The Mothers of
    Plaza de Mayo, Las (1986)
South (1988)

PICARD, NICK
Scavengers (1988)

PICCIONI, PIERO
Adua and the Colleagues
    (1960)
Via Margutta (1960)
Viaccia, La (1961)
Matchless (1966)
Pardon Me, But Are You For
    or Against? (1966)
Precarious Bank Teller, The
    (1980)
Catherine and I (1981)
Three Brothers (1982)
Fighting Back (1982)
I Know That You Know That
    I Know (1982)
My Trip with Dad (1982)
Open Grave ... an Empty
    Coffin, An (1982)
Cabbie, The (1983)
Put 'Em All in Jail (1984)
Chronicle of a Death Foretold
    (1987)

PICKERING, BOB
Ellie (1984)

PIEMONTESE, RENATO
Altra Donna, L' (1981)

PIERANUNZI, ENRICO
Boy Like Many Others, A
    (1983)

PIERCE, DAVID
Flipside of Dominick Hyde,
    The (1980)

PIERETIS, PIERIS
Agitated Winds (1984)

PIERRE, ALAIN
End of the Journey, The
    (1981)
Wildschut (1985)

PIERRE, PIERRE
Still Point, The (1986)

PIERSANTI, FRANCO
Sweet Dreams (1981)
Strike at the Heart (1982)
Bianca (1984)
Yellow Hair and the Pecos
    Kid (1984)
Mamma Ebe (1985)
Ferrywoman, The (1986)
House Poised on the Edge, A
    (1986)
Taste of Corn, The (1986)
Three Sisters (1988)
Tottering Lives (1988)
Woman in the Moon (1988)

PIESTRUP, LARRY
King of the Road (1978)

PIGA, ALDO
Playgirls and the Vampire,
    The (1960)
Curse of the Blood Ghouls,
    The (1962)
Vampires and the Ballerina,
    The (1962)
Tarzan and the Leopard Man
    (1964)
Z-7 Operation Thunderbolt
    (1967)

PIGNATELLI, GABIO
Unsane (1987)

PIJI, ZHANG
Strange Friends (1983)
Blood Is Always Hot (1984)

PIKE, NICHOLAS
Graveyard Shift (1987)
Critters 2: The Main Course
    (1988)
Nightmare on Elm Street--
    Freddy's Nightmare: The
    Series, A (1988)

PILGER, PAUL
Cavanaughs, The (1986)

PILHOFER, HERB
  On the Edge (1985)

PILON, ROGER
  Hey Babe! (1984)

PIMENTEL, GUSTAVO
  Better Than Bread (1987)
  Female Cabbie, The (1987)
  Mofles' Escapades (1987)
  Muffler and the Mechanics
    (1987)
  Narcotics Police (1987)

PIMPERE, CLAUDE
  Follies of Elodie, The (1981)

PINA, ANGEL OLIVER
  Please, Don't Shoot the
    Cannon (1966)

PINDAR, MARC
  Lame Ducks (1982)

PING, ZHAO JI
  Buddha's Lock (1987)

PINTO, ARTURO KIKE
  Maruja in Hell (1983)

PIOVANI, NICOLA
  Perfume of the Woman in
    Black, The (1974)
  Flavia, Priestess of Violence
    (1975)
  Leap Into the Void (1980)
  Vacations in Val Trebbia (1980)
  Minestrone (1981)
  Fit to Be Untied (1981)
  Girl with the Red Hair, The
    (1981)
  Marquis of Grillo, The (1982)
  Enchanted Sail, The (1982)
  Night of the Falling Stars
    (Night of San Lorenzo)
    (1982)
  Eyes, the Mouth, The (1982)
  Trace, The (1983)
  Desire (1984)
  Chaos (1984)
  Scorpion, The (1984)

Bertoldo, Bertoldino and
    Cacasenno (1984)
  Secrets Secrets (1985)
  Two Lives of Mattia Pascal,
    The (1985)
  Mass Is Over, The (1985)
  Ginger and Fred (1985)
  Let's Hope It's a Girl (1986)
  Professor, The (1986)
  Bride Was Radiant, The
    (1987)
  Exploits of a Young Don
    Juan, The (1987)
  Federico Fellini's Interview
    (1987)
  Good Morning, Babylon (1987)
  Camels, The (1988)
  It'll Happen Tomorrow (1988)
  Life is Strange (1988)
  Manifesto (1988)
  Train of Lenin, The (1988)

PIPIN, RAMON
  Move Along, There's Nothing
    to See (1983)
  Favorite, The (Rock and
    Torah) (1983)

PIPPIN, DONALD
  Eat and Run (1986)

"PI-RATA"
  Neighbor, The (1987)

PIRAZZOLI, PINUCCIO
  Bingo Bongo (1983)

PIRONKOV, SIMEON
  Hole, The (Dupkata) (1967)
  Big Night Bathe, The (1981)
  Window, The (1981)
  Khan Asparukh (1981)
  681 A.D. The Glory of Khan
    (1984)

PISANO, FRANCO (BERTO)
  Spy Who Came from the Sea,
    The (1966)
  Superargo vs. Diabolicus
    (1966)
  Three Violent Nights
    (1966)

Dorellik (1967)
Pierino Against the World
(1981)

PISIEUR, SUSANNE
After Darkness (1985)

PITTS, CLAY
I Drink Your Blood (1971)

PIZZETTI, ILDEBRANDO
Scipio, the African (1937)
Mill on the Po, The (1949)

PLACENICIA, PEDRO see
PLASCENCIA, PEDRO

PLANA, SEBASTIAN
I Was Born in Buenos Aires
(1959)

PLASA, FRANZ
Crazy Boys (1987)

PLASCENCIA, PEDRO
Mexican, You Can Do It
(1986)
Terror and Black Lace (1986)
Mexican Double Entendre
(1987)

PLAZA, JULIAN
Sentimental (1981)

PLEES, JACK
Dusty's Trail (1973)

PLENIXIO, GIANFRANCO
Spaghetti House (1982)
And the Ship Sails On (1983)
One Rainy Night (1984)

PLESSAS, MIMIS
He Is Heading to the Glory
Again (1980)

PLOQUIN, RAOUL
Adieu, les Beaux Jours
(1934)

PLUNDER, NIGEL
Shark's Paradise (1986)

PODDANY, EUGENE
Tom and Jerry Show, The
(1966)
How the Grinch Stole Christmas (1966)

PODELL, ART
Black Room, The (1981)

PODOLAR, RICHARD A.
Bigfoot (1972)

POGGIS, ANDREAS
Youth of Athens (1949)

"POGUES, THE"
Straight to Hell (1987)

POHL, WERNER
Fair, The (1960)

POITEVIN, ROBBY
Battle of the Mods, The
(1966)
Technique of a Murder
(1966)

POKRASS, BROTHERS
If War Comes Tomorrow (1938)

POLEDOURIS, BASIL
Congratulations, It's a Boy
(1971)
Tintorera (1977)
Defiance (1980)
Blue Lagoon (1980)
Whale for the Killing, A
(1980)
Conan the Barbarian (1982)
Summer Lovers (1982)
Making the Grade (1984)
Conan the Destroyer (1984)
Red Dawn (1984)
Amazons (1984)
Protocol (1984)
Sheriff and the Astronaut,
The (1984)

Flesh and Blood (1985)
Iron Eagle (1986)
Amerika (1987)
Island Sons (1987)
No Man's Land (1987)
Robocop (1987)
Cherry 2000 (1988)
Intrigue (1988)
Spellbinder (1988)
Split Decisions (1988)

POLEN, DENNIS
Cavanaughs, The (1986)

POLGAR, TIBOR
New Squire, The (1936)
Bride of Tarocke (1937)
Sensation (1937)
Storm of the Plains (1937)
Deadly Spring (1940)
In Soldier's Uniform (1957)

POLIKER, YEHUDA
Because of That War (1988)

POLLECUTT, DAVE
Shaka Zulu (1986)

POLNAREFF, MICHEL
Vengeance of the Plumed
Serpent, The (1984)

POLONIAK, ZDENEK
Incomplete Eclipse (1983)

"POLYGRAM"
Without a Promised Land (1980)

PONS, MIGUEL
Vicious Circle (1980)

PONTY, JEAN-LUC
Witchcraft Through the
Ages (1969)

POOT, MARCEL
Evil Eye, The (1937)

POPA, TOMISTOCLE
Clowns, The (1985)

POPE, CAROL
Deadline (1979)
Track Two (1983)

POPESCU, CORNEL
Story of Love, The (1981)

POPOECK, AUGUST
Romance (1936)

"POPOL VUH"
Heart of Glass (1976)
Nosferatu, Phantom of the
Night (1979)
Fitzcarraldo (1982)
SL-1 (1983)
Slave Coast (1988)

POPOVICI, ILEANA
Revenge (1981)

POPP, MARIUS
Stand-Off, The (1981)

POPPER, WALTER
Seven Ravens, The (1953)

PORTAL, MICHEL
Red Shadow, The (1981)
Return of Martin Guerre, The
(1982)
Stray Bullets (1983)
Horseman of the Storm, The
(1984)
King of China, The (1984)
Voyage, The (1984)
Operation Judas (1985)
Max My Love (1986)
Brightness (1987)
Field of Honor (1987)
Sorceress (1987)
Bengali Night, The (1988)
History of Wind, The (1988)
No Harm Intended (1988)
Two More Minutes of Sunlight
(1988)
Women in Prison (1988)

PORTE, PIERRE
Blue Like Hell (1986)

PORTER, LEW
    Black Dragons (1941)
    Invisible Ghost, The (1941)
    Corpse Vanishes, The (1942)

PORTER, ROBIE
    Some Kind of Miracle (1979)

PORTMAN, RACHEL
    Privileged (1982)
    Reflections (1984)
    Four Days in July (1984)
    Sharma and Beyond (1986)
    Fearnot (1987)
    Storyteller, The (1987)
    Luck Child, The (1988)

PORTNOY, GARY
    Popcorn Kid (1987)

PORTOCALOGLOU, NICOS
    And Two Eggs from Turkey
        (1987)

POSEGGA, HANS
    Caspar David Friedrich (1987)

POST, MIKE
    Two on a Bench (1971)
    Gidget Gets Married (1972)
    Griff (1973)
    Needles and Pins (1973)
    Toma (1973)
    Locusts (1974)
    Morning After, The (1974)
    Rockford Files, The (1974)
    Texas Wheelers, The (1974)
    Bob Crane Show, The (1975)
    Invasion of Johnson County,
        The (1976)
    Richie Brockelman: Missing
        24 Hours (1976)
    Scott Free (1976)
    Black Sheep Squadron, The
        (1977)
    Charlie Cobb: Nice Night for
        a Hanging (1977)
    Off the Wall (1977)
    Doctor Scorpion (1978)
    Richie Brockelman: Private
        Eye (1978)

White Shadow, The (1978)
Big Shamus, Little Shamus
    (1979)
Captain America (1979)
Captain America II (1979)
Duke, The (1979)
416th, The (1979)
Night Rider, The (1979)
Operating Room (1979)
240-Robert (1979)
Stone (1979)
Tenspeed and Brownshoe
    (1980)
Scout's Honor (1980)
Hill Street Blues (1980)
Coach of the Year (1980)
Greatest American Hero, The
    (1981)
Palms Precinct (1982)
Quest, The (1982)
Tales of the Gold Monkey
    (1982)
Will, G. Gordon Liddy (1982)
A-Team, The (1983)
Adam (1983)
Bay City Blues (1983)
Big John (1983)
Hardcastle and McCormick
    (1983)
Riptide (1983)
Rousters, The (1983)
Running Brave (1983)
Four Eyes (1984)
Hadley's Rebellion (1984)
Hard Knox (1984)
No Man's Land (1984)
Return of Luther Gillie, The
    (1984)
River Rat, The (1984)
Welcome to Paradise (1984)
Heart of a Champion (1985)
Stingray (1985)
Adam: His Song Continues
    (1986)
L.A. Law (1986)
Last Precinct, The (1986)
Destination America (1987)
Hooperman (1987)
Sirens (1987)
Wiseguy (1987)

Murphy's Law (1988)
Sonny Spoon (1988)

POTAMIAMOS, GEORGE
Aphrousa (1971)

POTOTSKY, SERGEI
Guerrilla Brigade (1942)

POTTS, STEVE
Bengali Night, The (1988)

POULENC, FRANCIS
Trip to America, A (1952)

POULICACOS, DEMETRIS
Barbecue Them! (1981)

POULY, ROGER
Paris Seen By ... 20 Years
After (1984)

POUSHKOV, V.
Peasants (1935)

POUSSIQUE, H.
Rare Bird (1935)

POWDER, STEVE
Piranha II (Spawning, The)
(1981)

POWELL, ANDREW
Ladyhawke (1985)
Rocket Gibralter (1988)

POWELL, DAVE
Hot Resort (1985)

POWELL, MEL
Lonely Night, The (1954)

POWELL, REG
Far-Out Space Nuts (1975)

POYTEN, PAUL
Massive Retaliation (1984)

PRADO, PEREZ
Hell's Kitchen (1952)

PRASAD, BADRI
Double Cross (1938)

PREDIN, ZORAN
Cormorant (1986)

PREGADIO, ROBERTO
Eve, the Savage Venus (1968)
King of Kong Island (1968)

PREISNER, ZBIGNIEW
No End (1985)
Touching (1986)
Short Film About Killing, A
(1988)
Short Film About Love, A
(1988)

PRENDERGAST, ROY
Those Amazing Animals (1980)

PRENEN, PAUL
Four Hands (1987)

PRESSER, GABOR
Ham Actors (1981)
Afternoon Affair, An (1984)

PRESTON, DON
Being, The (1980)
Android (1982)
Blood Diner (1987)
Underachievers, The (1988)

PRESTON, JAN
Pictures (1981)
Among the Cinders (1984)
Trial Run (1984)
Illustrious Energy (1988)

PRETENDERS, THE
Heroin (1980)

PREUS, ANNE-GRETE
Black Crows (1983)
Sweet 17 (1985)

PREVIN, ANDRE
Sun Comes Up, The (1949)

PREVIN, CHARLES
Flying Hostess (1936)

Sinners in Paradise (1938)
Devil's Party, The (1938)
Son of Frankenstein (1939)

PREVIN, DORY
Third Girl from the Left
(1973)

PREVITALI, FERNANDO
Flesh Will Surrender (1950)

PREVITE, ROBERT
Chain Letters (1985)

PRIALE, FERNANDO
Death of a Tycoon (1981)

PRICE, ALAN
Britannia Hospital (1982)
Plague Dogs, The (1982)
Whales of August, The (1987)

PRICE, GEORGE S.
Guyana: Cult of the Damned
(1980)

PRICE, HENRY
Incredibly Strange Creatures
Who Stopped Living and
Became Mixed-Up Zombies,
The (1963)
Thrill Killers, The (1965)
Sinthia, the Devil's Doll
(1979)

PRICE, JIM
Heated Vengeance (1985)

PRIETO, ANTONIO
Vacations in Acapulco (1961)

PRIMATA, FRANK
Mausoleum (1981)

PRINCE, ROBERT (BOB)
Happiness is a Warm Clue
(1970)
Alias Smith and Jones (1971)
Columbo (1971)
Little Game, A (1971)
What's a Nice Girl Like
You...? (1971)

Cool Million (Mask of Mar-
cella) (1972)
Gargoyles (1972)
Circle of Fear (1973)
Scream, Pretty Peggy (1973)
Big Rose (1974)
Cry in the Wilderness, A
(1974)
Strange and Deadly Occur-
rence, The (1974)
Where Have All the People
Gone? (1974)
Blue Knight, The (1975)
Dead Don't Die, The (1975)
Desperate Miles, The (1975)
Fantastic Journey, The (1977)
New Adventures of Wonder
Woman, The (1977)
Snowbeat (1977)
Flying High (1978)
Gathering, Part II, The (1979)
Return of Charlie Chan, The
(1979)
Seduction of Miss Leona, The
(1980)
Violation of Sarah McDavid,
The (1981)

PRITIKIN, KAREN
What You Take for Granted
(1984)

PRIVSEK, JOZE
My Dad, the Socialist Kulak
(1988)

PRODROMIDES, JEAN
Spirits of the Dead (1967)
Danton (1982)

PROFES, ANTON
Shadows of the Past (1936)
Eternal Mask, The (1937)
Talking About Josephine
(1937)
Vagabonds (1949)
Grandstand for the General
Staff, A (1953)
Girl Days of a Queen (1955)
Seven Year's Bad Luck (1957)
Embezzled Heaven (1958)

PROFETA, LAURENTIU
  Bride on the Train, The
    (1981)

PROHASKA, MILJENKO
  Lion Tamer, The (1961)
  Kind-Hearted Ant, The (1965)
  High Voltage (1981)
  Cyclops (1982)

PROKOP, SKIP
  Dr. Frankenstein on Campus
    (1970)

PRONCET, VICTOR
  Celina's Cry (1975)
  Dear Friends (1980)
  Unpredictable Guy (1980)

PROST, GEORGES
  Risk of Living, The (1980)

PUCHAN, DAVE
  Witchfire (1985)

PUEYO, S.
  Strange Case of Dr. Faustus,
    The (1969)

PUGLIESE, OSVALDO
  Tango Is History (1984)

PULIDO, LUIS
  Accordionist's Wedding, The
    (1988)

PULLICINO, GERARD
  Burning Land (1984)

PUPNIK, IVAN
  Miss Stone (1959)

PUSCHNIG, WOLFGANG
  Skin of the Fool (1982)

PUSHKOV, V.
  City of Youth (1938)
  New Teacher, The (1941)
  Wings of Victory (1941)
  Big Family, A (1955)

PYARELAL, LAXMIKANT
  Nagin (1975)
  Festival (1984)

PYLKKANEN, TAUNO
  Joha (1957)

QGULLO, ALFONSO
  Sea Devils (1982)

QINGSHI, TANG
  Well, The (1988)

QIXIONG, CHEN
  Yamaha Fish Stall (1985)

QUARESMA, SIDONIO PAIS
  Mortu Nega (1988)

"QUEEN"
  Flash Gordon (1980)

QUESADA, PANCHI
  Invitation, The (1982)

QUIMING, LU
  Chilly Nights (1985)

QUINLAN, NOEL
  Aces Go Places III (1984)
  Maybe It's Love (1984)

QUINTANO, JOSE ANTONIO
  In the Name of God (1987)

QUINTERO, JOAQUIN
  Nail, The (1949)

QUINTERO, JUAN
  Duchess of Benameji, The
    (1950)
  Sister Unafraid (1954)

"QUINTESSENCE"
  Midnight (1982)

QUIPING, ZHAO
  Big Parade, The (1987)

RAAB, LEONID
  He Walked by Night (1948)

RABEN, PEER
  Ortlieb Women, The (1980)
  Portrait of a Female
    Drunkard (1980)
  German Spring (1980)
  Purity of Heart (1980)
  Berlin Alexanderplatz (1980)
  Mosch (1980)
  Lili Marleen (1981)
  Malou (1981)
  Moon's Only a Naked Ball,
    The (1981)
  Lola (1981)
  Veronika Voss (1982)
  Day of the Idiots (1982)
  Wizard of Babylon, The
    (1982)
  Querelle (1982)
  Nothing Left to Lose (1983)
  Woman Flambee, A (1983)
  Open Ends (1983)
  Swing, The (1983)
  Giarres (1984)
  Cheaters, The (1984)
  Image of Dorian Gray in the
    Yellow Press, The (1984)
  Air of Crime, The (1984)
  Flaming Hearts (1986)
  Inside Out (1986)
  Tommaso Blu (1986)
  Sins of the Fathers (1988)
  Venus Trap, The (1988)

RABENALT, PETER
  Escapade (1980)
  Bicycle, The (1982)
  Old Henry (1985)

RABENJA, DEL
  Falcon, The (1983)

RABINOWITZ, BARRY
  Love for Lydia (1979)
  Reilly, Ace of Spies (1984)

RABINOWTISCH, STUART
  Video Dead, The (1986)

RADEN, FRANKI
  Roro Mendut (1984)
  Narrow Bridge, The (1985)

Moon and Sun (1987)

RADETIC, ZORAN
  Live Broadcast (1982)

RADHAKISHMAN, M. G.
  Dead End, A (1980)

RADIC, DUSAN
  Don't Meddle With Fortune
    (1961)
  Salonka Terrorists, The
    (1961)
  Violence at the Square
    (1961)

RADWAN, STANISLAW
  In Broad Daylight (1981)

RAGLAND, ROBERT O.
  Mansion of the Doomed (1975)
  Glove, The (1978)
  High Ice (1979)
  Brain Waves (1982)
  Q, The Winged Serpent (1982)
  10 to Midnight (1983)
  Lovely But Deadly (1983)
  Time to Die, A (1983)
  Evils of the Night (1985)
  Supernaturals, The (1986)
  Assassination (1987)
  Nightstick (1987)
  Prettykill (1987)
  Deep Space (1988)
  Messenger of Death (1988)
  Moon in Scorpio (1988)

RAGUE, STEPHEN
  Some Kind of Wonderful (1987)

RAHBANY, ZIAD
  Return to Haifa (1982)
  What Happened Next Year
    (1986)

RAI, MICHAEL
  Armour of God, The (1986)

RAIM, WALTER
  Behind the Spaceman (1967)

RAJ, ZBIGNIEW
  Three Feet Above the
    Ground (1985)
  In an Old Manor House (1987)

RAJA, ILAYA
  Indian Summer (1987)

RAKSIN, DAVID
  Over-the-Hill Gang Rides
    Again, The (1970)
  Ghost of Flight 401, The
    (1978)
  Suicide's Wife, The (1979)
  Day After, The (1983)

RAMEAU, JEAN-PHILIPPE
  Lark, The (1988)

RAMES, REY
  Virgin People (1983)

RAMIN, RON
  Next Step Beyond, The
    (1978)
  Hart to Hart (1979)
  New Mike Hammer, The
    (1986)
  Diamond Trap, The (1988)
  Stranger on My Land (1988)

RAMIN, SID
  Nancy (1970)
  All My Children (1970)
  Miracle on 34th Street
    (1973)
  Pop! (1975)

RAMIREZ, ROSALIO
  Day With the Devil, A
    (1945)
  Satan's Five Warnings (1945)
  Heritage of the Crying Women,
    The (1946)
  Adventure in the Night
    (1947)

RAMLEE, R.
  Devouring Rock, The (1959)

RAMONE, PHIL
  Mind Snatchers, The (1972)
  Puppetman (1987)

RAMSEY, KENNARD
  Heavenly Kid, The (1985)
  Uncle Tom's Cabin (1987)
  Home Free (1988)

RAMSEY, WILLIS ALAN
  Second-Hand Hearts (1980)

RAMSING, ROY
  Before Stonewall (1984)

RAND, RICHARD
  Princess (1980)

RANDLES, ROBERT
  Beyond Reason (1977)

RANKI, GYORGY
  New Squire, The (1936)
  Bit of Immortality, A (1967)

RAO, GANPAT
  Kuruk Shetra (1946)

RAPEE, ERNO
  Dead March, The (1937)

RAPH, PIERE
  Requiem for a Vampire (1971)
  Night in the Cemetery, A
    (1973)
  Rose of Iron, The (1973)
  Demoniaques, Les (1974)

RAPHAVA, VIJAY
  10 Days in Calcutta (1984)

RAPOS, DUSAN
  Hurry, He's Coming! (1988)

RAPOSO, JOE
  Sesame Street (1969)
  We'll Get By (1975)
  Ivan the Terrible (1976)
  That Was the Week That Was
    (1976)

Visions (1976)
Three's Company (1977)
Joe and Valerie (1978)
Ropers, The (1979)
Dennis the Menace: Mayday
    for Mother (1981)
Foot in the Door (1983)
No Place Like Home (1985)
Kingdom Chums: Little
    David's Adventure, The
    (1986)

"RAREVIEW"
Sidekicks (1986)
Hot Pursuit (1987)

RASKIN, RUBY
Hidden World, The (1967)
That's Hollywood (1977)

RASMUSSEN, ERIC
Scalps (1983)
Biohazard (1983)

RASSI, ALI JIHAD
Women from South Lebanon
    (1986)

RATHAUS, KAROL
Loves of a Dictator (1935)
Queen of Spades (Pique Dame)
    (1937)

RATHBURN, ELDON
Champions Part 3--The Final
    Battle, The (1986)

RATZER, KARL
Head-Stand (1981)

RAUE, MATTHIAS
Come Along to Monte Carlo
    (1982)
River Trip with Hen (1984)
Chick for Cairo, A (1985)

RAVAN, KAMBIZ ROSHAN
Frosty Roads (1987)

RAVEL, WINSTON
Affair, The (1985)

RAVN, PERNILLE URZON
Glass Heart, The (1988)

RAWSTHORNE, ALAN
Pandora and the Flying
    Dutchman (1951)
Secret Flight (1951)

RAY, CYRIL
Everything Is Rhythm (1940)

RAY, DON B.
Hawaii Five-O (1968)

RAY, GREG
Ladies of the Lotus (1987)

RAY, SATYAJIT
Deliverance (1982)
Phatik and the Juggler (1983)
Home and the World, The
    (1984)

RAYNOR, EDDIE
Rikky and Pete (1988)

REA, CHRIS
Now or Never (1986)

REA, DANIELE
Specters (1987)

READE, PAUL
Great Expectations (1982)

RECCHION, TOM
Private Practices: The Story
    of a Sex Surrogate (1985)

RECHARDT, PEKKA
In the Year of the Ape (1983)

RECHT, COBY
Apple, The (1980)

RECHTER, YONI
Off the Air (1981)
Stigma (1982)
Nadia (1986)

"RED CLAY RAMBLERS, THE"
Far North (1988)

REDDING, OTIS
Kid, The (1986)

REDFORD, J. A. C.
James at 15 (1977)
Dooley Brothers, The (1979)
Brett Maverick (1981)
Honeyboy (1982)
King's Crossing (1982)
Long Summer of George
Adams, The (1982)
St. Elsewhere (1982)
Happy Endings (1983)
Bliss (1984)
Hawaiian Heat (1984)
Helen Keller--The Miracle
Continues (1984)
Going for the Gold: The
Bill Johnson Story (1985)
Key to Rebecca, The (1985)
Trip to Bountiful, A (1985)
Alex: The Life of a Child
(1986)
City, The (1986)
Cry from the Mountain (1986)
Easy Prey (1986)
Extremities (1986)
Independence (1987)
Long Journey Home, The
(1987)
Annie McGuire (1988)
Oliver and Company (1988)

REDSTONE, WILLY
Flying Doctor, The (1936)

REED, HENRY
John Wesley (1954)

REED, LES
Creepshow 2 (1987)

REESEN, EMIL
Wedding of Palo (1937)

REHM, ENGLEBERT
Westler (1986)

REICHEL, ACHIM
Va Banque (1986)

REICHERT, JAMES
All My Children (1970)

REILLY, TOMMY
Navy Lark, The (1959)

REIM, CHRISTIAN
Nedtur (1980)

REINHARDT, DJANGO
Swindle, The (1980)

REISER, CLUTCH
Brain Damage (1988)

REISER, NIKKI
So What? (1987)

REISER, RIO
Chinese Are Coming, The
(1987)

REISMAN, JOE
Cop and the Kid, The (1975)

REITMAN, IVAN
They Came from Within
(1976)
House by the Lake, The
(1977)
Rabid (1977)

REMAL, GARY
Dark Circle (1982)
Wildrose (1984)
Breakin' (1984)
Maria's Lovers (1984)
Missing--Have You Seen
This Person? (1985)

REMY, TONY
Passion of Remembrance, The
(1986)

RENAUD
Come to My Place, I'm Living
at My Girlfriend's (1981)

RENDISH, MICHAEL
    First Killing Frost, The (1987)

RENFROW, ROBERT
    Future-Kill (1985)

RENLIDEN, MIKAEL
    Seppan (1988)

RENNERT, ADI
    Joshua, Joshua (1988)

RENUCCI, SERGIO
    Surprise Party (1983)

RENZETTI, JOE (JOSEPH)
    Cotton Candy (1978)
    Diary of a Hitchhiker, The
        (1979)
    Elvis (1979)
    Exterminator, The (1980)
    Fatso (1980)
    Marathon (1980)
    Dead and Buried (1981)
    Under the Rainbow (1981)
    Through the Magic Pyramid
        (1981)
    Mysterious Two, The (1982)
    Wanted: Dead or Alive (1987)
    Child's Play (1988)
    Poltergeist III (1988)

REPETE, PETE
    Murder in the Dark (1986)
    Murder in Paradise (1988)

RESETAR, ROBERT J.
    White Phantom (1987)

RESS, GUNTER
    November Cats (1986)

RETTBERG, ROBERT
    Goofballs (1987)

REUTLINGER, HEINZ
    Flight Year, The (1982)

REVALLO, JOZEF
    Doom of the Berhof Lonely
        Farm, The (1984)
    Scalpel, Please (1985)

REVAUX, JACQUES
    Syringe, The (1984)

REVERBERI, GIANFRANCO
    Reincarnation of Isabel (1973)
    Not Quite Jerusalem (1985)

REVUELTAS, SYLVESTRE
    Wave, The (Redes) (1937)

REYES, EDDIE
    Chair, The (1988)

REYES, GIL
    Fire and Passion (1988)

REYES, JORGE
    Orozco Family, The (1982)

"RHEINGOLD"
    Trance (1982)

RHODES, BURT
    Good Neighbors (1980)

RIBAS, MIKE
    TV and the Hotel, The (1985)

RIBERO, TITO
    Muddy Waters (1953)
    Descent into Hell (1954)
    Sacred Call, The (1954)
    Gringalet (1959)

RICCI, LUIGI
    Song of the Butterfly (1939)

RICH, FREDERIC EFREM
    Walk in the Sun, A (1945)

"RICH LOOK"
    Happy Birthday, Gemini (1980)
    Refuge (1981)

RICHARDS, BOBBY
    Black Torment, The (1964)
    Doctors Wear Scarlet (1970)

RICHEPIN, TIARKO
    Stream, The (1938)

RICHMOND, KIM
  Kojak (1973)
  Harry O (1974)
  It Happened at Lake Wood
    Manor (1977)

RICHTER, ROLAND SUSO
  Kolp (1985)

RICKETS, DAVID
  Echo Park (1985)

RIDDLE, NELSON
  Hawk (1966)
  Emergency! (1972)
  Blue Knight, The (1973)
  Happy Anniversary and
    Goodbye (1974)
  Caribe (1975)
  Mobile One (1975)
  Mobile Two (1975)
  Promise Him Anything ...
    (1975)
  Runaway Barge, The (1975)
  City of Angels (1976)
  Executive Suite (1976)
  How to Break Up a Happy
    Divorce (1976)
  Seventh Avenue (1977)
  79 Park Avenue (1977)
  Project U.F.O. (1978)
  Runaways, The (1979)
  Guyana: Cult of the Damned
    (1980)
  Rough Cut (1980)
  Strike Force (1981)
  Harper Valley P.T.A. (1981)
  Mickey Spillane's Margin for
    Murder (1981)
  Help Wanted: Male (1982)
  Matt Houston (1982)
  Newhart (1982)

RIEDEL, GEORG
  Morianna--I the Body (1968)
  Rooster, The (1981)
  Children of Bullerby Village,
    The (1986)
  More About the Children of
    Bullerby Village (1987)
  Katinka (1988)

RIEHM, ROLF
  September Wheat (1980)
  Report from an Abandoned
    Planet (1985)

RIESENFELD, HUGO
  Wandering Jew, The (1935)
  Little Men (1935)

RIETHMUELLER, HEINRICH
  Parson of Kirchfeld, The
    (1955)

RIETI, VITTORIO
  Cuckoo Clock, The (1938)

RIGAUD, JEAN YVES
  Love and Death (1985)

RILEY, TERRY
  No Man's Land (1985)

RINALDO, SUSANA
  Tango Is History (1984)

RINCON, MIGUEL ANGEL
  Kapax: The Man from the
    Amazon (1987)

RINDER, LAURIN
  In Search of ... (1976)
  Secrets of the Bermuda
    Triangle (1978)
  New Year's Evil (1981)
  Enter the Ninja (1982)

RINNE, HANNO
  Microscope, The (1988)

RIOPELLE, JERRY
  Evil Roy Slade (1972)

RISSI, MARK M.
  Tragedy of the Afghan, The
    (1986)

RIST, GARY
  Soldier's Revenge (1986)

RITENOUR, LEE
  American Flyers (1985)
  Rock 'n' Roll Mom (1988)

RITZ, WALTER
    Thunder Warrior 2 (1987)

RIVARD, MICHEL
    Jacques and November (1985)
    Marie in the City (1988)

RIVAS, MIKE
    Little Devil from the Quarter
        (1983)

RIVERA, SCARLET
    Las Vegas Weekend (1986)

RIVRON, ROWLAND
    Leave to Remain (1988)

RIWANE, NASS EL
    Transes (1981)

RIZZATI, WALTER
    House Outside the Cemetery,
        The (1981)
    1990: The Bronx Warriors
        (1983)

RIZZONE, FIORENZO
    Sadness of Knowing, The
        (1985)

ROA
    10 Days in Calcutta (1984)

ROBBINS, RICHARD
    Jane Austen in Manhattan
        (1980)
    Quartet (1981)
    Heat and Dust (1983)
    Bostonians, The (1984)
    Room With a View, A (1986)
    Sweet Lorraine (1987)
    Perfect Murder, The (1988)

ROBELLAZ, JACQUES
    Campo Europa (1984)
    Poisons (1987)

ROBERGE, JIM
    Joey (1985)

ROBERT, MAX
    Rumpelstiltskin (1987)

ROBERTS, ANDY
    Loose Connections (1983)
    Reefer and the Model (1988)

ROBERTS, BRUCE
    Jinxed! (1982)
    Things Are Looking Up (1984)
    Best Times, The (1985)

ROBERTS, HOWARD
    Cindy (1978)

ROBERTS, JAMES
    Last Electric Knight, The
        (1986)

ROBERTS, JONATHAN
    I Was a Teenage Zombie
        (1987)

ROBERTS, KENYON (KEN)
    My Son, My Son (1980)
    Hot Water (1985)

ROBERTSON, B. A.
    Heavenly Pursuits (1986)

ROBERTSON, ERIC
    M-3: The Gemini Strain
        (Plague) (1979)
    Spasms (1981)
    If You Could See What I
        Hear (1982)
    Shocktrauma (1982)
    That's My Baby (1985)
    Home Is Where the Hart Is
        (1987)

ROBERTSON, HARRY see
    ROBINSON, HARRY

ROBERTSON, ROBBIE
    King of Comedy (1983)
    Color of Money, The (1986)

ROBIDOUX, MICHEL
    Day in a Taxi, A (1982)

ROBIN, TEDDY
    Saviour, The (1980)
    All the Wrong Clues (for the
        Right Solution) (1981)

Play Catch (1983)
Perfect Wife, The (1983)
Working Class (1985)
City on Fire (1987)

ROBINSON, EARL
Maybe I'll Come Home in the
Spring (1971)
Great Man's Whiskers, The
(1973)
Huckleberry Finn (1975)

ROBINSON, HARRY (HARRY
ROBERTSON)
Danny the Dragon (1966)
Blinker's Spy Spotter (1971)
Johnstown Monster, The
(1971)
Fright (1972)
Demons of the Mind (1973)
House in Nightmare Park
(1973)
Boy With Two Heads, The
(1974)
Flying Sorcerer, The (1975)
Legend of the Werewolf, The
(1975)
Glitterball, The (1977)
Hitch in Time, A (1978)
Sammy's Super T-Shirt (1978)
When Havoc Struck (1978)
Electric Eskimo, The (1979)
There Goes the Bride (1980)
Hawk the Slayer (1980)
Prisoners of the Lost Universe
(1983)
Breakout (1984)
Terry on the Fence (1985)

ROBINSON, PETE (J. PETER)
Radioactive Dreams (1986)
Wraith, The (1986)
Bates Motel, The (1987)
Believers, The (1987)
Gate, The (1987)
J. Edgar Hoover (1987)
Rags to Riches (1987)
Cocktail (1988)
Kiss, The (1988)
Return of the Living Dead
Part II (1988)

ROBINSON, PETER MANNING
Pin (1988)

ROBLES, NESTOR
Beast of the Yellow Night
(1970)
Taste of Hell, A (1973)

RODER, MILAN
Supernatural (1933)
Death Takes a Holiday (1934)

RODGERS, JOHNNY
Getting Over (1981)

RODGERS, NILE
Soup for One (1982)
Alphabet City (1984)
Coming to America (1988)
Crack in the Mirror (1988)
Earth Girls Are Easy (1988)

RODREGO, JOAQUIN
Sister Unafraid (1954)

RODRIGUES, PADRE LUIS
Pintore a Cidade, O (1956)

RODRIGUEZ, FRANCISCO
Naked Man, The (1987)

RODRIGUEZ, PAUL
It's the Girl in the Red
Truck, Charlie Brown
(1988)

RODRIGUEZ, SILVIO
Refugees from Dead Man's
Cave, The (1983)
Becoming Aware (1985)
Like Life Itself (1985)

RODRIGUEZ, SUSAN (SUZY)
Death Game, The (1986)
Slaughter in Matamoros (1986)
Lady Coyote II, The (1987)
Operation Marijuana (1987)

ROEHRIG, WOLFRAM
Foxhole in Cairo (1960)

ROEMHELD, HEINZ
    Black Cat, The (1934)
    Fabulous Joe (1946)

ROEWE, SCOTT
    Viper (1988)

ROGALL, VOLKER
    Werewolf of W., The (1988)

ROGER, ROGER
    It's the Paris Life (1954)

ROGERS, ERIC
    Meet Mr. Lucifer (1953)
    Doctor Dolittle (1970)
    Barkleys, The (1972)
    Bailey's Comets (1973)
    In the Devil's Garden (1974)
    Return to the Planet of the
      Apes (1975)
    What's New, Mr. Magoo?
      (1978)
    Spider-Woman (1979)

ROGERS, SHORTY
    Mod Squad (1968)
    Mr. Deeds Goes to Town
      (1969)
    Gidget Grows Up (1969)
    Breakout (1970)
    Fools (1970)
    Interns, The (1970)
    Partridge Family, The (1970)
    Paul Lynde Show, The (1972)
    Starsky and Hutch (1975)
    Viva Valdez (1976)
    Tabitha (1977)
    Fantasy Island (1978)
    Vega$ (1978)
    Return of the Mod Squad
      (1979)

ROGERS, SIMON
    Daddy (1987)

ROGGERS, KLAUS
    To Live and Die in
      Westallgau (1986)

ROLAND, BRUCE
    Badlands 2005 (1988)

ROMANELLI, ROLAND (ROMAN)
    Rascals (1980)
    AIDS--A Danger for Love
      (1985)
    Sandwich Years, The (1988)

ROMANIS, GEORGE
    Medical Center (1969)
    U.M.C. (Operation Heartbeat)
      (1969)
    Cannon (1971)
    Assignment: Munich (1972)
    Crime Club, The (1973)
    Barnaby Jones (1973)
    Hawkins (1973)
    Maneater (1973)
    Reunion (1973)
    Live Again, Die Again (1974)
    Movin' On (1974)
    Police Woman (1974)
    Bronk (1975)
    Family Nobody Wanted, The
      (1975)
    McNaughton's Daughter (1976)
    Shark Kill (1976)
    Cabot Connection, The (1977)
    Feather and Father Gang,
      The (1977)
    She's Dressed to Kill (1979)
    Beyond Westworld (1980)
    Hagen (1980)
    Joe Dancer: The Big Black
      Pill (1980)
    Reunion (1980)
    Of Mice and Men (1981)
    Big Black Pill, The (1981)
    Monkey Mission, The (1981)
    Kentucky Woman (1983)
    Murder 1, Dancer 0 (1983)
    Hell Town (1985)

ROMANO, WALTER
    Gangster from Brooklyn,
      The (1966)

ROME, HAROLD
    Wonderful Things (1958)

ROMERO, TONY
    Debbie Reynolds Show, The
      (1969)
    No Holds Barred (1980)

ROMITELLI, SANTE MARIA
Three Supermen in the Jungle
(1971)
Hatchet for a Honeymoon, A
(1974)

ROOD, JURRIEN
Orion Nebula (1987)

ROOSA, JIMMY
Man with the Synthetic Brain,
The (1971)

ROS, TARRAGO
Dogs of the Night (1986)

ROSATI, GIUSEPPE
Rapture (1949)

ROSE, BOB
Nightforce (1987)

ROSE, DAVID
Bonanza (1959)
Men into Space (1959)
Monroes, The (1966)
High Chaparral, The (1967)
Bracken's World (1969)
Brady Bunch, The (1969)
Along Came a Spider (1970)
Birdmen, The (1971)
Devil and Miss Sarah, The
(1971)
Dream for Christmas, A
(1973)
Little House on the Prairie
(1974)
Suddenly Love (1974)
Loneliest Runner, The (1976)
Ransom for Alice (1977)
Killing Stone (1978)
Suddenly, Love (1978)
W.E.B. (1978)
Father Murphy (1981)
Little House: Look Back to
Yesterday (1983)
Sam's Son (1984)
Little House: The Last
Farewell (1984)
Little House: Bless All the
Dear Children (1984)
Highway to Heaven (1984)

ROSE, EARL
Thin Ice (1981)

ROSE, JEREMY
Raw Meat (1972)

ROSEN, ANDREW
Living Dreams (1988)

ROSEN, MILTON
Death Race (1973)

ROSENBAUM, JOEL
Voyagers (1982)
Outing, The (1987)
Psycho Girls (1987)

ROSENBERG, MARIANNE
Wild Bunch (1983)

ROSENBERGER, RAIMUND
Roses for the Prosecutor
(1960)
Judge for the Young, The
(1960)
Testament of Dr. Mabuse,
The (1962)
Mad Executioners, The (1963)

ROSENBLUM, YAIR
Troupe, The (1977)

ROSENFELS, GERHARD
Our Short Life (1981)
Paths of Life (1982)

ROSENGREN, BERNT
Children from Blue Lake
Mountain, The (1980)

ROSENMAN, LEONARD
Savage Eye, The (1959)
Virginian, The (1962)
Dr. Leakey and the Dawn of
Man (1967)
Stranger on the Run (1967)
Shadow Over Elveron (1968)
Any Second Now (1969)
Marcus Welby, M.D. (1969)
Man from Shiloh, The (1970)
Banyon (1971)
In Broad Daylight (1971)

Primus (1971)
Vanished (1971)
Bravos, The (1972)
Cat Creature, The (1973)
Judge Dee and the Monestary
    Murders (1974)
Nakia (1974)
Phantom of Hollywood, The
    (1974)
First 36 Hours of Dr. Durant,
    The (1975)
Sky Heist (1975)
Gibbsville (1976)
Kingston: The Power Play
    (1976)
Holmes and Yoyo (1976)
Lanigan's Rabbi (1976)
Sybil (1976)
Possessed, The (1977)
Rafferty (1977)
Other Side of Hell, The
    (1978)
Friendly Fire (1979)
Nero Wolfe (1979)
Hide in Plain Sight (1980)
City in Fear (1980)
Jazz Singer, The (1980)
Joshua's World (1980)
Murder in Texas (1981)
Making Love (1982)
Wall, The (1982)
Cross Creek (1983)
Miss Lonelyhearts (1983)
Heart of the Stag (1984)
Celebrity (1984)
Return of Marcus Welby,
    M.D., The (1984)
First Steps (1985)
Sylvia (1985)
Star Trek VI: The Voyage
    Home (1986)
Promised a Miracle (1988)

ROSENTHAL, LAURENCE
House That Would Not Die,
    The (1970)
How Awful About Allan (1970)
Night Chase (1970)
Last Child, The (1971)

Sweet, Sweet Rachel (1971)
Rookies, The (1972)
Call to Danger (1973)
Devil's Daughter, The (1973)
Satan's School for Girls (1973)
Death Sentence (1974)
Log of the Black Pearl, The
    (1975)
Home of Our Own, A (1975)
Murder on Flight 502 (1975)
Death at Love House (1976)
21 Hours at Munich (1976)
Young Pioneers (1976)
State Fair (1976)
Young Pioneers' Christmas
    (1976)
Amazing Howard Hughes (1977)
Logan's Run (1977)
And I Alone Survived (1978)
Fantasy Island (1978)
Return to Fantasy Island (1978)
Orphan Train (1979)
Rage (1980)
Revenge of the Stepford
    Wives, The (1980)
Day Christ Died, The (1980)
FDR--The Last Year (1980)
Clash of the Titans (1981)
Patricia Neal Story, The
    (1981)
Letter, The (1982)
Who Will Love My Children?
    (1983)
Heart Like a Wheel (1983)
Easy Money (1983)
George Washington (1984)
License to Kill (1984)
Lost Honor of Kathryn Beck,
    The (1984)
Hearst-Davies Affair, The
    (1985)
Blackout (1985)
Mussolini: The Untold Story
    (1985)
Anastasia: The Mystery of
    Anna (1986)
On Wings of Eagles (1986)
Peter the Great (1986)
Proud Men (1987)
Bourne Identity, The (1988)
Freedom Fighter (1988)

In the Line of Duty: The
    F.B.I. Murders (1988)
My Father, My Son (1988)
Street of Dreams (1988)
To Heal a Nation (1988)

ROSIER, MARINE
Husbands, Wives, Lovers
    (1988)

ROSS, AL
Psychopath (1974)

ROSS, JOHN
Frankenstein General
    Hospital (1988)

ROSSELLINI, RENZO
Woman (1947)
Machine That Kills Bad
    People, The (1948)
Doctor Beware (1951)
Signori in Carrozza (1951)
Without a Flag (1951)
Europe '51 (1952)
Man from Cairo, The (1953)
Neapolitans in Milan (1953)
Journey to Italy (1954)
Fear (Angst) (1955)
Strangers (1955)
World's Most Beautiful Woman,
    The (1955)
General Della Rovere (1959)
Night in Rome, A (1960)
We the Living (1988)

ROSSI, ALDO
Magic World of Topo Gigio,
    The (1964)

ROSSI, LUCIANO
This and That (1984)

ROSSI, UGO
Below the Chinese Restaurant
    (1987)

ROSSINI, ROGERIO
Man Labeled to Die, A
    (1984)

ROSTAING, HUBERT
Shot Pattern (1982)
Night Patrol (1984)
Abel Gance and His Napoleon
    (1984)
Where Is Parsifal? (1984)
Rumble, The (1985)
Prunelle Blues (1986)

ROTA, NINO
Prelude to Madness (Kreutzer
    Sonata) (1947)
Flight into France (1949)
Hey, Boy! (1949)
Under the Sun of Rome (1949)
Children of Chance (1950)
My Widow and I (1950)
Street Urchin (1951)
Women and Bandits (1951)
Neapolitan Millionaire (1951)
Angels of the District (1952)
Filumena Marturano (1952)
Husband and Wife (1952)
Something Money Can't Buy
    (1952)
Easy Years, The (1953)
His Last 12 Hours (1953)
Seven of the Big Bear (1953)
Face That Launched a Thousand
    Ships, The (1954)
Great Hope, The (1954)
Public Enemy No. 1 (1954)
Friends for Life (1955)
City at Night (1957)
Doctor and the Healer, The
    (1958)
Ghosts in Rome (1960)
Spirits of the Dead (1967)
Big Deal on Madonna Street--
    20 Years Later (1986)
Federico Fellini's Interview
    (1987)

ROTERS, ERNST
Axe of Wandsbek, The (1951)
Little Mook (1954)
Love Hangs on the Gibbet
    (1961)

ROTH, C. P.
Beach House (1982)

ROTH, FRANK
  Kolp (1985)

ROTMO, HANS
  Poachers (1982)

ROTTA, BECO
  Gigio (1987)

ROTTER, PETER
  Code Name: Zebra (1987)

"ROUGH TRADE"
  Deadline (1979)

ROUSSEL, JEAN-ALAIN
  Obsessed (1988)

ROVEN, GLENN
  Wide Net, The (1987)

ROWAN, PETER
  Hoxsey: The Quack Who
    Cured Cancer (1987)

ROWLAND, BRUCE
  Man from Snowy River, The
    (1982)
  Now and Forever (1983)
  Phar Lap (1983)
  All the Rivers Run (1984)
  Anzacs (1985)
  Cool Change (1986)
  Anzacs: The War Down
    Under (1987)
  Bigfoot (1987)
  Bushfire Moon (1987)
  Christmas Visitor, The (1987)
  Running from the Guns
    (1987)
  Backstage (1988)
  Danger Down Under (1988)
  Return to Snowy River
    (Part II) (1988)

ROWLEY, NICK
  Quatermass Conclusion (1980)

ROY, KANU
  Housewarming, The (1980)

ROZENVAL, ALEXANDER
  Two Hundred a Month (1936)

ROZSA, MIKLOS
  Criss Cross (1949)
  Eye of the Needle (1981)
  Dead Men Don't Wear Plaid
    (1982)

RUBALCABA, GONZALO
  Letters from the Park (1988)

RUBBERT, RAINER
  Anita--Dances of Vice (1987)

RUBENSTEIN, KEITH
  Vice Squad (1982)

RUBENSTEIN, MARTIN
  Prime Time, The (1960)

RUBIN, AMPARO
  Once Again (1987)
  What Is Caesar's (1987)

RUBIN, AMY
  Conversations with Willard
    Van Dyke (1981)

RUBIN, LANCE
  Barnaby Jones (1973)
  Fantasy Island (1978)
  Knot's Landing (1979)
  Breaking Away (1980)
  Leo and Loree (1980)
  Motel Hell (1980)
  Happy Birthday to Me (1981)
  Modern Romance (1981)
  Hear No Evil (1982)
  Emerald Point (1983)
  Six Pack (1983)
  Incredible Hulk Returns,
    The (1988)

RUBINI, MICHEL
  Powers of Matthew Starr,
    The (1982)
  Hunger, The (1983)
  Hitchhiker, The (1983)
  13 Thirteenth Avenue (1983)

Abducted (1986)
Band of the Hand (1986)
Manhunter, The (1986)
Crossing the Mob (1988)
Too Good to Be True (1988)

RUBINSTEIN, ARTHUR B., JR.
Phoenix, The (1972)
Easter Promise, The (1975)
Addie and the King of Hearts (1976)
Maureen (1976)
Flying High (1978)
Shirley (1979)
Great American Traffic Jam, The (1980)
Portrait of a Rebel: Margaret Sanger (1980)
Gridlock (1980)
Aunt Mary (1980)
Great Mysteries of Hollywood, The (1981)
Bulba (1981)
On the Right Track (1981)
Rivkin: Bounty Hunter (1981)
Whose Life Is It, Anyway? (1981)
Incident at Crestridge (1981)
Phoenix, The (1981)
Sherlock Holmes (1981)
Not Just Another Affair (1982)
Skeezer (1982)
Fake Out (1982)
Bring 'em Back Alive (1982)
Blue Thunder (1983)
War Games (1983)
Deal of the Century (1983)
Sawyer and Finn (1983)
Scarecrow and Mrs. King (1983)
Parade, The (1984)
Sins of the Past (1984)
It Came Upon a Midnight Clear (1984)
Lost in America (1985)
Doubletake (1985)
Best of Times, The (1986)
Doing Life (1986)

Hyper Sapien: People from Another Star (1986)
Sledge Hammer (1986)
Wizard, The (1986)
Betty Ford Story, The (1987)
Love Among Thieves (1987)
Roses Are for the Rich (1987)
Stakeout (1987)
Defense Play (1988)
Indiscreet (1988)
Inherit the Wind (1988)
Internal Affairs (1988)
Nightmare at Bitter Creek (1988)
Once Upon a Texas Train (1988)
Where the Hell's That Gold? (1988)

RUBINSTEIN, DONALD
Knightriders (1981)

RUBINSTEIN, JOHN
All Together Now (1975)
Family (1976)
Stalk the Wild Child (1976)
Fitzpatricks, The (1977)
New Maverick, The (1978)
Sticking Together (1978)
Champions: A Love Story (1979)
Lazarus Syndrome, The (1979)
MacKenzies of Paradise Cove, The (1979)
Ordeal of Patty Hearst, The (1979)
Amber Waves (1980)
To Race the Wind (1980)
Johnny Belinda (1982)
Choices of the Heart (1983)
Dollmaker, The (1984)
Conspiracy of Love (1987)
China Beach (1988)

RUCKER, STEVE
Pray for Death (1985)
Armed Response (1986)
... And God Created Woman (1988)
Bulletproof (1988)

RUDICH, ARIK (ERICH)
  Drifting (Nagua) (1983)
  Bar 51 (1986)
  House Committee Rivalry
    (1986)
  Shattered Dreams--Picking
    Up the Pieces (1987)
  China Ranch (1988)

RUDNER, TONY
  Quest for Love (1988)

RUDNICKY, ANTHONY
  Cossacks in Exile (1939)

RUDZINSKI, ZBIGNIEW
  Looming Shadow, A (1985)

RUEGGEBERG, MICHAEL
  Signs and Wonders (1982)

RUETH, LUDWIG
  Wackere Schustermeister
    (1936)

RUGG, MATHIAS
  Temptation, The (1988)

RUGOLO, PETE
  Doctor Kildare (1961)
  Outsider, The (1967)
  How to Steal an Airplane
    (Only One Lay Left Before
    Tomorrow) (1968)
  Sound of Anger, The (1968)
  Lonely Profession, The (1969)
  Set This Town on Fire (1969)
  Whole World Is Watching,
    The (1969)
  Young Country, The (1970)
  Death of Me Yet, The (1971)
  Do You Take This Stranger?
    (1971)
  Sam Hill: Who Killed the
    Mysterious Mr. Foster?
    (1971)
  Rookies, The (1972)
  Drive Hard, Drive Fast
    (1973)
  Letters, The (1973)
  Letters from Three Lovers
    (1973)

Love Thy Neighbor (1973)
Toma (1973)
Touch of Grace, A (1973)
Death Cruise (1974)
Story of Pretty Boy Floyd,
  The (1974)
Blue Knight, The (1975)
Death Stalk (1975)
Invisible Man, The (1975)
Last Hours Before Morning
  (1975)
Family (1976)
Jigsaw John (1976)
Carter Country (1977)
Kingston: Confidential (1977)
San Pedro Beach Bums, The
  (1977)
Jordan Chance, The (1978)
Last Convertible, The (1979)
Miss Winslow and Son (1979)
Home Front (1980)
Son-In-Law, The (1980)
Chu Chu and the Philly Flash
  (1981)
Revenge of the Gray Gang,
  The (1981)
For Lovers Only (1982)
O'Malley (1983)

RUHLMANN, JEAN JACQUES
  We Were One Man (1980)

RUIZ, FEDERICO
  Drop the Curtain (1955)
  Ladron de Cadaveres (Grave
    Robbers) (1956)
  Manon (1986)
  Black Sheep, The (1987)

RUIZ, FRANCISCO
  To the Four Winds (1955)

RUIZ, JORGE LOPEZ
  There Are Some Guys Down-
    stairs (1985)

RUIZ DE LUNA, SALVADOR
  Footsteps (1957)
  War Starts in Cuba (1958)
  Lazarillo (1959)
  Molokai (1959)

RUIZ DEL POZO, ARTURO
   Gregorio (1985)

RUMJAHN, MAHMOOD
   Family Affair, A (1984)
   Happy New Year (1985)
   Happy Ghost II, The (1985)
   Red Guards in Hong Kong
      (1985)
   Isle of Fantasy (1986)

RUMSHINSKY, JOSEPH
   Shir Hashirim (1935)
   Two Sisters (1938)

RUNDGREN, TODD
   Cold Feet (1983)
   Crime Story (1986)
   Under Cover (1987)

RUNJIC, ZDENKO
   Servants from a Small Town
      (1982)

RUNO, SVEN
   Asa-Nisse in Military
      Uniform (1959)

RUNSWICK, DARRYL
   Golden Sands (1985)
   No Surrender (1985)

RUSCONI, JEAN-PIERRE
   Mesrine (1984)

RUSHEN, PATRICE
   Hollywood Shuffle (1987)

RUSHKIN, WALLACE
   Charles Burchfield--Fifty
      Years of His Art (1967)

RUSSEL, BELLA
   Campaign (1988)

RUSSELL, WILLY
   Mr. Love (1985)

RUSSO, GUS
   Basket Case (1982)
   Brain Damage (1988)

RUSSO, WILLIAM
   Everybody Rides the Carousel
      (1976)

RUSSOVICH, ADRIAN
   Gombrowicz (1988)

RUST, FRIEDRICH WILHELM
   Castle Vogeloed (1936)
   Incognito (1937)

RUSTICHELLI, CARLO
   Accusation (1951)
   Road to Hope (1951)
   Bandit of Tacca del Lupo
      (1952)
   Behind Closed Doors (1952)
   Counterfeiters, The (1953)
   Railroad Man, The (1956)
   Man of Straw (1958)
   Mine, The (1958)
   Day the Sky Exploded, The
      (1958)
   Dubrovsky (1959)
   Uomo Facile, Un (1959)
   You're On Your Own (1959)
   Antinea (1961)
   My Son the Hero (1961)
   Lost Atlantis (1961)
   Rogopag (1962)
   Samson vs. the Giant King
      (1963)
   What? (1963)
   Conquest of Mycene (1963)
   Hercules of the Desert (1964)
   Long Hair of Death, The
      (1964)
   Almost Perfect Crime, The
      (1966)
   Kill or Be Killed (1966)
   Seasons of Our Love, The
      (1966)
   Wood of Love (1981)
   Blade Master, The (1982)
   All My Friends 2 (1983)
   Heads or Tails (1983)
   Glassful of Snow, A (1984)
   Woman of Wonders (1985)
   Monster of Florence, The
      (1986)

Throne of Fire, The (1986)

RUSTICHELLI, PAOLO
Heads or Tails (1983)
Violent Breed, The (1983)
Glassful of Snow, A (1984)
Woman of Wonders (1985)

RUSTICHESI, GIACOME
Toto Wants a Home (1950)

RUTHERFORD, MICHAEL
Shout, The (1978)

RUTHERFORD, PARIS
Crucible of Terror (1971)

RUTSTEIN, SONIA
Igor and the Lunatics (1985)

RYBNIKOV, ALEXEJ
Love and Lies (1982)
Mother Maria (1983)
Quarantine (1983)
Seraphim Polubes and Other
Humans (1984)

RYBRANT, STIG
Firebrand, The (1952)

RYCHKOV, BORIS
Star Inspector (1980)

RYCHLIK, JAN
Angel's Coat, The (1948)
Creation of the World (1958)
Bomb Mania (1959)

RYDER, ANDRE
Windfall in Athens (1956)
Shadow of the Past (1959)

RYDER, MARK
Future Cop (1985)
Savage Island (1985)

RYDMAN, KARI
Milka (1981)
Pessi and Illusia
(1984)

RYSLINGE, HELLE
Knife in the Heart, The (1981)
Awry in the Wings (1983)

RYUZAKI, TAKAMICHI
So This Is Love (1975)

SAAD, JAMES
Cyclone (1987)

SAARIAHO, KAIJA
Grand Illusion, The (1986)

SABAN, HAIM
Inspector Gadget (1983)
Littles, The (1983)
Escape from Grumble Gulch
(1984)
Get Along Gang, The (1984)
Going Bananas (1984)
Kidd Video (1984)
Wolf Rock TV (1984)
Here Come the Littles (1985)
Rainbow Brite and the Star
Stealer (1985)
Kissyfur (1985)

SABAR, JEAN-PIERRE
Rat Race, The (1980)

SABU, PAUL
American Drive-In (1985)

SACAVOLA, FRANCO
Carmela (1949)

SACS, NORMAN
Starting Fresh (1979)

SADAO, BETSUMIA
Matango (1963)

SAEGUSA, SHIGEAKI
Catch, The (1986)
Luminous Woman (1987)

SAENZ, PANCHO
Lovers of the Lord of the
Night, The (1984)

SAES, JOSE MIGUEL see
   LOPEZ SAES, JOSE MIGUEL

SAFAN, CRAIG
   Getting Married (1978)
   Survival of Dana (1979)
   Fade to Black (1980)
   Hardcase (1981)
   Cheers (1982)
   TAG (1982)
   Counterattack: Crime in
     America (1982)
   Nightmares (1983)
   Best of Times, The (1983)
   Angel (1984)
   Last Starfighter, The (1984)
   Imposter, The (1984)
   Poor Richard (1984)
   Detective in the House (1985)
   Legend of Billie Jean, The
     (1985)
   Warning Sign (1985)
   Remo Williams: The Adven-
     ture Begins (1985)
   Courage (1986)
   Help Wanted: Kids (1986)
   I-Man (1986)
   My Town (1986)
   Samaritan: The Mitch Snyder
     Story (1986)
   Lady Beware (1987)
   Spies (1987)
   Stranger, The (1987)
   Timestalkers (1987)
   Almost Grown (1988)
   Nightmare on Elm Street 4:
     The Dream Master, A
     (1988)
   Stand and Deliver (1988)

SAG, ARIF
   Hazal (1980)

SAGILD, KIM
   Forever Friends (1987)

SAHIN, OZAN GARIP
   Wall, The (1983)

SAHL, MICHAEL
   Bloodsucking Freaks (1976)
   Far from Poland (1984)

SAID, SABIR
   Revenge of the Vampire (1957)
   White Onion, Red Onion (1958)

ST. JAMES, JON
   Cave Girl (1985)

ST. JONS, ALAN
   Las Vegas Weekend (1986)

ST. LOUP, FLORA
   Malambo (1984)
   Glass Heaven, The (1988)

SAINT-PIERRE, MARTIN
   Blood of the Flamboyant Tree
     (1981)
   Dust (1985)

SAINTE-MARIE, BUFFY
   Stripper (1985)

SAINZ, ALFONSO
   Aoom (1970)

SAINZ DE LA MAZA, EDUARDO
   Boat Without a Fisherman,
     The (1964)

SAISSE, PHILIPPE
   Crack in the Mirror (1988)

SAITO, ICHIRO
   Golden Demon, The (1954)
   Girl in the Mist, The (1955)
   Women in Prison (1957)
   Love of a Princess, The
     (1981)

SAITO, KOJUN
   I Live, But ... (1985)

SAITO, MITSHUHIKO
   Yasha (1985)

SAKAC, BRANIMIR
   Girl and the Oak, The (1955)
   Piccolo (1959)
   Dreamer, The (Sanjar) (1961)
   Tifusari (1963)
   Masque of the Red Death,
     The (1969)

SAKAMOTO, RYUICHI
  Merry Christmas, Mr.
    Lawrence (1983)
  Adventures of Chatran (1986)
  Last Emperor, The (1987)

SAKATA, KOICHI
  Return of the Filthy Seven,
    The (1969)
  Killer, The (1971)

SAKURAI, HIDEAKIRA
  Sword of Vengeance (1972)

SALA, OSKAR
  Strangler of Blackmoor Castle,
    The (1963)

SALAM, MALEK
  Tragedy of the Afghan, The
    (1986)

SALAMA, GAMAL
  Egyptian Story, An (1982)
  Black Tiger, The (1983)
  Smoke Should Not Fly, The
    (1984)
  Victim, The (1986)

SALES, GARY
  Madman (1982)

SALINA, FRANCO
  Five Men with a Vendetta
    (1966)
  Velvet Hand (1966)

SALISBURY, TOM
  Condor (1986)

SALMON, BARRY
  Silent Madness (1983)

SALO, RAINE
  Ursula (1987)

SALOMON, DORON
  Vulture, The (1981)

SALTER, HANS J.
  Son of Frankenstein (1939)

Virginian, The (1962)
  Return of the Gunfighter
    (1967)

SALTON, JOHN
  Living Dreams (1988)

SALTUK, RAHMI
  Germany, Bitter Land (1980)

SALVADOR, DOM
  Two Worlds of Angelita, The
    (1983)

SALVATGE, XAVIER MORT
  Diego Corrientes (1959)

SALVATI, ALAIN
  Masterblaster (1987)

SALVAY, BENNETT
  Feel the Heat (1983)
  Young Hearts (1984)
  Better Days (1986)
  Aloha Summer (1988)

SALVI, ALDO
  Fascist Jew, The (1980)
  Malamore (1982)

SALVIUCCI, GIOVANNA MARINI
  Secret Access (1988)

SALZEDO, LEONARD
  Blonde Bait (1956)
  Revenge of Frankenstein
    (1958)

SAMIOU, DOMNA
  Factory, The (1982)

SAMPLE, JOE
  Code Name: Foxfire (1985)

SAMUEL, NICOLAS
  King of Jerks, The (1981)

SAMUELSSON, LASSE
  Raskenstam (1983)

SANADA, TSUTOMU
  Wet Highway (1972)

SANCHES, D. D.
  Devilish Dolls, The (1975)

SANCHEZ, HECTOR
  Narc--Red Duel, The (1986)

SANDAUER, HEINZ
  Family Schimek (1957)
  Unexcused Hour, The (1958)

SANDBURG, HERBERT
  Of Love and Lust (1960)

SANDIN, HANS
  Jonny Roova (1985)
  Inuksuk (1988)

SANDLOFF, PETER
  We Cellar Children (1960)
  Invisible Dr. Mabuse, The
    (1961)
  Return of Dr. Mabuse, The
    (1961)

SANDOR, JENO
  Borrowed Chateau (1937)
  Mammy (1937)

SANDRELLI, SERGIO
  D'Annunzio (1987)

SANFELICE, LEOPOLDO
  Francesca (1987)

SANG-KEY, HAN
  Noblewoman, The (1985)

SANGSTER, JOHN
  Funky Phantom, The (1971)
  Around the World in 80 Days
    (1972)
  Fluteman (1982)
  Dot and the Koala (1985)

SANGSUWAN, PISATE
  Gunman (1983)

SANOJA, CHUCHITO
  Adios Miami (1983)

SANTANA, CARLOS
  Bamba, La (1987)

SANTERCOLE, GINO
  Distinguishing Marks:
    Handsome (1983)

SANTIESTEBAN, L.
  Minister's Wife, The (1981)

SANTISTEBEN, ALFONSO
  Necrophagus (1971)

SANTOLALLA, GUSTAVO
  She Dances Alone (1981)

SANTORIO, SILVANO
  Paris Seen By ... 20 Years
    After (1984)

SANTOS, CARLOS
  Jet Lag (1981)

SANTOS, TURIBIO
  Pagu Forever (1988)

SANVOISIN, MICHAEL
  Biddy (1983)

SAPAROFF, ANDREA
  Appointment with Fear (1985)

SARACENI, SERGIO G.
  We Have Never Been So
    Happy (1984)
  Night (1985)
  Fulaninha (1986)
  Gavea Girls (1987)

SARARA, TARAK
  Train, The (1986)

SARDE, PHILIPPE
  Woman Cop, The (1980)
  I Sent a Letter to My Love
    (1980)
  Guignolo, Le (1980)
  Bad Son, A (1980)
  Boy Soldier, The (1981)
  Is This Really Reasonable?
    (1981)
  Stepfather (1981)
  Wings of the Dove (1981)
  Choice of Weapons (1981)
  Birgitt Haas Must be Killed

(1981)
Tales of Ordinary Madness
(1981)
Coup de Torchon (1981)
Ghost Story (1981)
Quest for Fire (1981)
Hotel of the Americas (1982)
Thousand Billion Dollars, A
(1982)
Strange Affair, A (1982)
North Star, The (1982)
Shock, The (1982)
Captain's Honor, A (1982)
Will the High Salaried Workers
Please Raise Their Hands!!!
(1982)
Lovesick (1983)
I Married a Dead Man (1983)
Stella (1983)
Friend of Vincent, A (1983)
Attention, One Woman May Be
Hiding Another (Double
Husbands) (1983)
First Desires (1983)
Garcon! (1983)
Fort Saganne (1984)
Pirate, The (1984)
Happy Easter (1984)
Devil in the Flesh (1985)
It Only Happens to Me (1985)
Signed Charlotte (1985)
Next Summer (1985)
Cowboy, Le (1985)
Rendezvous (1985)
Joshua Then and Now (1985)
Outlaws (1985)
Temptation of Isabelle, The
(1985)
Harem (1985)
Man With the Silver Eyes,
The (1985)
Every Time We Say Goodbye
(1986)
Manhattan Project, The (1986)
My Brother-In-Law Has Killed
My Sister (1986)
Pirates (1986)
Private Classes (1986)
Prude, The (1986)
Scene of the Crime, The
(1986)

State of Grace (1986)
April Is a Deadly Month
(1987)
Comedy! (1987)
Intimate Enemies (1987)
Last Summer in Tangiers
(1987)
No Drowning Allowed (1987)
Two Crocodiles (1987)
Bears, The (1988)
Color of the Wind, The
(1988)
Few Days With Me, A (1988)
For the Sake of Peace (1988)
House of Jade (1988)
Innocents, The (1988)
Murdered House, The (1988)
Transvestite, The (1988)

SARDI, IDRIS
Mementos (1986)
Mother (1987)

SARMANTO, HEIKKI
Goodbye, Mr. President
(1987)

SARSOZA, CHUCHO
Cemetery of Terror (1985)

SARY, LASZLO
Absentee, The (1986)

SASSE, KARL-ERNST
Fiancee, The (1980)
Moritz Inside the Advertising
Pillar (1984)
Saxon Splendor and Prussian
Glory (1986)

SASSE, KARL-HEINZ
Sabine Wulff (1980)
Don Juan, Karl-Liebknecht-
Str. 78 (1982)

SASSOVER, NATHAN
Lewis and Clark (1981)
Partners in Crime (1984)

SASSU, PIETRO
Habris (1984)

SATANOWSKI, JERZY
  Woman in a Hat (1985)
  Baritone, The (1985)
  O-Bi, O-Ba--The End of
    Civilization (1985)
  Lake of Constance, The
    (1986)
  Axiliad (1987)
  Magnate, The (1987)
  Siegfried (1987)
  Suspended (1987)
  Upstairs, Downstairs (1988)

SATHAKOVIT, OKAWEE
  I'll Love You Tomorrow
    (1980)

SATHYAM
  Lady James Bond (1972)

SATO, JUN
  My Champion (1981)

SATO, MASAHIKO
  Belladonna (1973)

SATO, MASARU
  Half Human (1955)
  Man Called Demon, A (1957)
  Gigantis, the Fire Monster
    (1959)
  Hidden Fortress, The (1959)
  Three Rascals in the Hidden
    Forest (1959)
  Throne of Blood (1961)
  Lost World of Sinbad, The
    (1964)
  Godzilla vs. the Sea Monster
    (1968)
  Admiral Yamamoto (1969)
  Emperor and a General, The
    (1969)
  Kill! (1969)
  Son of Godzilla (1969)
  City of Beasts (1970)
  Scandalous Adventures of
    Buraikan, The (1970)
  Battle of Økinawa (1971)
  Where Spring Comes Late
    (1971)
  Wolves, The (1972)

  Eternal Cause (1973)
  Home from the Sea (1973)
  Twilight Years (1973)
  Long Journey into Love (1974)
  Men and War (1974)
  Godzilla vs. Mechagodzilla
    (1975)
  Alaska Story, The (1977)
  Yellow Handkerchief, The
    (1978)
  U.F.O. Blue Christmas (1979)
  Toward the Terror (1980)
  Distant Cry from Spring, A
    (1980)
  Nomugi Pass (1980)
  There Was a War When I Was
    a Child (1982)
  Southern Cross, The (1982)
  At This Late Date, the
    Charleston (1982)
  Willful Murder (1982)
  Irezumi--Spirit of Tattoo
    (1983)
  Teacher, The (1983)
  Forest of Little Bear (1987)
  Tokyo Bordello (1987)
  Dun-Huang (1988)

SATOH, MITSHIKO
  Creature Called Man, The
    (1970)
  Love Can Make a Rainbow
    (1982)

SAUGUET, HENRI
  Scandals of Clochemerle (1950)
  This Is the Half Century
    (1950)
  Julie de Carnellhan (1950)
  When the Child Appears
    (1956)

SAULSKY, IGOR
  Gift of Life, The (1985)

SAUNDERS, LOUIS
  Warrior and the Sorceress,
    The (Kain of Dark Planet)
    (1983)

SAUNDERS, ROBIN
Amazing Years of Cinema,
The (1981)

SAUTER, EDDIE
Night Gallery (1971)
Switch (1975)
Beggarman, Thief (1979)

SAUVAGE, CAMILLE
Orloff and the Invisible Man
(1970)

SAUVAGEAU, JEAN
What Number? (1985)
Equinox (1986)

SAVAGE, PAM
On the Line (1984)

SAVATCHO, BUAN
Per, Jom and Phen (1980)

SAVERY, FINN
We Are All Demons! (1969)

SAVIN, DRAGUTIN
H 8 (1958)
Eighth Door, The (1959)
Quiet Summer, A (1961)

SAVIN, IGOR
Aloa--The Whore's Feast
(1988)

SAVINA, CARLO
Moralist, The (1959)
Europe By Night (1959)
I Love, You Love (1961)
Son of Hercules in the Land
of Fire (1963)
Terror in the Crypt (1963)
Secret Agent Fireball (1965)
A-077--Challenge to the
Killers (1966)
Fury at Marrakeck (1966)
Goldsnake "Killer's Company"
(1966)
Joe Dynamite (1966)
Singapore Zero Hour (1966)
Malenka (1968)

Young, the Evil and the
Savage, The (1968)
Invincible Invisible Man,
The (1969)
Amants del Diablo, Les (1971)
Hypnos (1971)
Night of the Damned, The
(1971)
Lisa and the Devil (1972)
Hunters of the Golden Cobra
(1984)
Future Is Woman, The (1984)
Pizza Connection, The (1985)

SAVINO, DOMENICO
Vivere (1937)

SAVIO, TATO
Hot Potato (1980)

SAWTELL, PAUL
Three Came to Kill (1960)

SBORDONI, ALESSANDRO
Kids from the South Side,
The (1985)

SCANNAVINI, CLAUDIO
Rose of the Names, The
(1987)

SCARIM, NICK
Tighten Your Belts, Bite the
Bullet (1981)

SCHACKMAN, AL
Palmerstown, U.S.A. (1980)

SCHAFER, KARL-HEINZ
Imprint of Giants, The (1980)
Exterior Nights (1980)
Polar (1982)

SCHARF, STUART
Autumn Flight (1967)

SCHARF, WALTER
That Girl (1966)
Alaska (1967)
Gasp! (1977)
Real American Hero, A (1978)

When Every Day Was the
   Fourth of July (1978)
Blind Ambition (1979)
From Here to Eternity (1979)
Salvage I (1979)
Triangle Factory Fire Scandal,
   The (1979)
Killin' Cousin, The (1980)
From Here to Eternity (1980)
Moviola: Scarlett O'Hara War,
   The (1980)
Long Days of Summer, The
   (1980)
This Is Elvis (1981)
Midnight Offerings (1981)
Twilight Time (1983)

SCHELLENBERG, GLENN
   Urinal (1988)

SCHENKER, RUDOLF
   Test of Strength (1982)

SCHER, FRED
   Jenny (Jadzia) (1937)

SCHERBACHEV, VLADIMIR
   Men of the Sea (1938)
   Men of Music (1953)

SCHERPENZEEL, TON
   Spetters (1980)

SCHICKELE, PETER
   Big People--Little People
      (1968)

SCHIERBECK, PAUL
   Day of Wrath (1943)
   Ordet (Word, The) (1955)

SCHIFRIN, LALO
   See How They Run (1964)
   Doomsday Flight (1966)
   Mission: Impossible (1966)
   How I Spent My Summer
      Vacation (Deadly Roulette)
      (1967)
   Hidden World, The (1967)
   Mannix (1967)
   Medical Center (1969)

Young Lawyers, The (1969)
Aquarians, The (1970)
Mask of Sheba, The (1970)
Young Lawyers, The (1970)
Earth II (1971)
Escape (1971)
Hunter (1971)
Partners, The (1971)
Welcome Home, Johnny Bristol
   (1972)
Hunter (1973)
Night Games (1974)
Petrocelli (1974)
Planet of the Apes (1974)
Bronk (1975)
Delancey Street: The Crisis
   Within (1975)
Foster and Laurie (1975)
Guilty or Innocent: The
   Sam Sheppard Murder
   Case (1975)
Starsky and Hutch (1975)
Brenda Starr (1976)
Most Wanted (1976)
Good Against Evil (1977)
Nativity, The (1978)
President's Mistress, The
   (1978)
Cat from Outer Space, The
   (1978)
Institute for Revenge (1979)
Serial (1980)
Back to the Planet of the
   Apes (1980)
Treachery and Greed on the
   Planet of the Apes (1980)
When Time Ran Out (1980)
Nude Bomb, The (1980)
Brubaker (1980)
Big Brawl, The (1980)
Loophole (1981)
Caveman (1981)
Skin, The (1981)
Fridays of Eternity, The
   (1981)
Chicago Story (1981)
Buddy Buddy (1981)
Robbers of the Sacred
   Mountain (Falcon's Gold)
   (1982)
Seduction, The (1982)

Stranger Is Watching, A
  (1982)
Falcon's Gold (1982)
Fast-Walking (1982)
Class of 1984 (1982)
Victims (1982)
Amityville II: The Possession
  (1982)
Wait Until Dark (1982)
Sting II, The (1983)
Doctor Detroit (1983)
Starflight: The Plane That
  Couldn't Land (1983)
Osterman Weekend, The
  (1983)
Sudden Impact (1983)
Princess Daisy (1983)
Rita Hayworth: The Love
  Goddess (1983)
Tank (1984)
Spraggue (1984)
Glitter (1984)
Breakfast Club, The (1985)
Hollywood Wives (1985)
New Kids, The (1985)
Private Sessions (1985)
A.D. (1985)
Bad Medicine (1985)
Bridge Across Time (1985)
Beverly Hills Madam (1986)
Black Moon Rising (1986)
Kung Fu: The Movie (1986)
Ladies Club, The (1986)
Triple Cross (1986)
Fourth Protocol, The (1987)
Jake's M.O. (1987)
Out on a Limb (1987)
Berlin Blues (1988)
Dead Pool, The (1988)
Earth Star Voyager (1988)
Little Sweetheart (1988)
Mission: Impossible (1988)
Shakedown on the Sunset
  Strip (1988)
Silence at Bethany, The
  (1988)

SCHIRMANN, PETER
  Barricade, The (1982)
  Rendezvous Leipzig (1985)

SCHITZE, PAUL
  Tale of Ruby Rose, The
    (1987)

SCHLEMM, GUSTAV ADOLF
  That Was Our Rommel (1953)

SCHLICHTER, VICTOR
  Master of Horror (1960)

SCHLOSS, ZANDER
  Space Rage (1987)

SCHMALSTICH, CLEMENS
  Woman of No Importance, A
    (1936)

SCHMIDT, IRMIN
  In the Heart of the Hurricane
    (1980)
  Last Stop Freedom (1981)
  Born for Diesel (1982)
  Man on the Wall, The (1982)
  Flight to Berlin (1984)
  Gathering of Spirits, A (1985)

SCHMIDT, KENDALL
  Neon Maniacs (1986)

SCHMIDT, OLE
  Kaj Munk (1986)
  Wolf at the Door, The (1986)

SCHMIDT-GENTNER, WILLY
  His Daughter Is Peter (1936)
  Private Secretary Marie (1936)
  Episode (1937)
  Maskerade (1937)
  Concert in Tyrol (1938)
  Angel with the Trumpet, The
    (1950)
  Wonder Child (1951)
  Wonder Boy (1952)
  Carnival Story (1954)

SCHMITT, PETER
  Banks and Robbers (1983)
  Lock and Seal (1987)

SCHMITZ, BERNHARD
  Quite Far Away (1983)

SCHMOELLING, JOHANNES
Hunger Years (1980)

SCHNEE, BILL
Go Ask Alice (1973)

SCHNEIDER, FLORIAN
Rorret (1988)

SCHNEIDER, HELGE
Uliisees (1983)
Johnny Flash (1987)

SCHNEIDER, NORBERT
JUERGEN
Carnival (1985)

SCHNEIDER, RALPH
Boy Who Had Everything,
The (1985)

SCHNITKE, ALFRED
Falling Stars (1981)
Fairy Tale of Wanderings, A
(1984)
Pushkin Trilogy, A (1985)

SCHOENER, EBERHARD
Lena Rais (1980)
Fear of Falling (1984)
Two Faces of January (1986)
Wild Clown, The (1986)

SCHOLASTIQUE, DAVID
Return to Eden (1983)

SCHON, PETER
Honeybunch (1988)

SCHONBERG, CLAUDE-MICHEL
Red Caviar (1985)

SCHONE, GERHARD
Boy With the Big Black
Dog, The (1987)

SCHOOF, MANFRED
Madonna Man, The (1988)

SCHOONDERWALT, HERMAN
If You Know What I Mean
(1983)

SCHRADER, BARRY
Galaxy of Terror (1981)

SCHREIBMAN, PHILIP
Seeing Things (1983)

SCHREYER, LINDA
Mandy's Grandmother (1980)
New York Nights (1984)

SCHROEDER, FRIEDRICH
Mailman Mueller (1953)
Charley's Aunt (1956)
Italian Journey--Love Included
(1958)

SCHROEDER, KURT
Dreiklang (1938)
His Official Wife (1936)

SCHTOREV, MITKO
My Darling, My Darling
(1986)

"SCHTUNG"
Kingpin (1985)

SCHUDSON, HOD-DAVID
Ghosts That Still Walk (1978)
Deadly Games (1979)
Brothers (1980)
Characters (1980)
Girl, the Gold Watch, and
Everything, The (1980)
Attic, The (1981)

SCHULMANN, PATRICK
Zig Zag Story (1983)
Aldo and Junior (1984)
P.R.O.F.S. (1985)
Ears Between the Teeth
(1987)

SCHULTZ, GREG
Fran (1985)

SCHULTZE, KRISTIAN
Anna's Mother (1984)
Aetherrausch (1988)

SCHULTZE, NORBERT
Cavalry Captain Wronski (1955)

Like Once Lili Marlene (1956)
Rosemary (1958)
Isn't Mama Fabulous? (1959)
Swindler and the Lord, The
(1961)

SCHULZE, KLAUS
Barracuda (1978)
Next of Kin (1982)
Fear (Angst) (1984)
Northern Lights (1985)

SCHUMAN, MORT
All-Stars (1980)
Psy (1981)

SCHUMANN, WALTER
Dragnet (1951)

SCHURMANN, GERARD
(GERBRAND)
Long Arm, The (1956)
Man in the Sky (1957)
Decision Against Time (1957)
Headless Ghost, The (1959)
Horrors of the Black Museum
(1959)
Crime of Silence (1960)
Konga (1961)
Lost Continent, The (1968)
Claretta (1984)

SCHWAB, RICH
Capiteau (1984)

SCHWALLER, ROMAN
Kovacs (1984)

SCHWARTZ, ABE
Love and Sacrifice (1936)

SCHWARTZ, DANIEL
Population: One (1986)

SCHWARTZ, DON
Our Street (1971)

SCHWARTZ, JEAN
Jaws of the Wolf, The (1981)
"Terrorists" in Retirement
(1986)

SCHWARTZ, LEV
New Gulliver, The (1935)
Concentration Camp (1939)
On His Own (1939)
University of Life (1941)
Leda and the Elephant (1946)
Stone Flower, The (1946)
Leningrad Skies (1960)

SCHWARTZ, NAN
Devlin Connection, The (1982)
Under the Influence (1986)
Home (1987)
Place at the Table, A (1988)
She Was Marked for Murder
(1988)

SCHWARTZ, SHERWOOD
Gilligan's Island (1964)
It's About Time (1966)

SCHWARTZ, STEPHEN
Echoes (1980)

SCHWARZ, ISAAK (see also
SHWARZ, ISAAK)
Marriage of Convenience (1986)
To Marry the Captain (1986)
Trial on the Road (1986)
Wild Dove, The (1986)

SCHYMAN, GARRY
Penitentiary III (1987)

SCIAMMARELLA, RUDOLFO
Wiseguy (Avivato) (1949)

"THE SCORPIONS"
Dog, The (1984)

SCOTT, ANDREW
Business as Usual (1987)

SCOTT, CHARLES
Iron Warrior (1987)

SCOTT, DEREK
Crimes of Passion (1976)

SCOTT, GARY
Final Exam (1981)

Deadly Force (1983)
Roadhouse 66 (1984)
Bronx Zoo, The (1987)

SCOTT, JOHN
Doomwatch (1972)
Quinns, The (1977)
Return of the Saint, The
(1979)
Final Countdown, The (1980)
Hostage Tower, The (1980)
Horror Planet (1982)
Assassination Run, The (1983)
Yor, the Hunter from the
Future (1983)
Greystoke: The Legend of
Tarzan, Lord of the Apes
(1984)
Shooting Party, The (1984)
Wet Gold (1984)
Jacques Cousteau: The First
75 Years (1985)
Harem (1986)
King Kong Lives (1986)
Lord Mountbatten: The Last
Viceroy (1986)
Whistle Blower, The (1986)
Man on Fire (1987)
Deceivers, The (1988)
Shoot to Kill (1988)

SCOTT, NATHAN
Dragnet (1951)
Lassie (1954)
My Three Sons (1960)
Family Affair (1966)

SCOTT, PATRICK JOHN
Berserk! (1967)
Those Fantastic Flying Fools
(1967)
Craze (1974)
Symptons (1976)
Satan's Slave (1976)
Inseminoid (1981)

SCOTT, PHIL (PHILLIP)
Those Dear Departed (1987)
Top Kid (1987)

SCOTT, RANDY
Jekyll and Hyde Portfolio,
The (1971)

SCOTT, ROBERT
Vicious (1988)

SCOTT, TOM
Class of '63 (1973)
Firehouse (1973)
Girls of Huntington House,
The (1973)
Trouble Comes to Town (1973)
Nine Lives of Fritz the Cat
(1974)
Starsky and Hutch (1975)
Twin Detectives (1976)
Aspen (1977)
Outside Man, The (1977)
Comedy Company, The (1978)
Baretta (1978)
Little Vic (1978)
Man Called Sloane, A (1979)
Our Family Business (1981)
Unit 4 (1981)
Why Us? (1981)
Family Ties (1982)
Hanky Panky (1982)
Square Pegs (1982)
Making the Grade (1982)
Going Berserk (1983)
Hard to Hold (1984)
Hawaiian Heat (1984)
Sara (1985)
Fast Forward (1985)
Sure Thing, The (1985)
Just One of the Guys (1985)
Badge of the Assassin (1985)
Soul Man (1986)
Taking It Home (1986)
Not Quite Human (1987)
Absent-Minded Professor,
The (1988)
Father's Homecoming, A (1988)
Run Till You Fall (1988)

SCOTT, WILLIAM
Sakura Killers (1987)

SCOTTO, TED
Christina (1984)
Love Scenes (1986)

SCOTTO, VINCENT
  Cesar (1936)
  Cinderella (1937)
  Sarati the Terrible (1937)
  Heartbeat (1939)
  Kiss of Fire (1940)
  Man of the Hour (1940)
  French Way, The (1952)

SCREAM, BILLY
  Closed Mondays (1974)
  Mark Twain (1985)

SCULLION, MICHELLE
  Bad Taste (1988)

SCULTHORPE, PETER
  Burke & Wills (1985)

SEAGRAVE, KAY
  Census Taker, The (1984)

SEAMAN, CRAIG
  I Was a Teenage Zombie
    (1987)

SEAR, WALTER
  Dr. Butcher M.D. (1982)
  Game of Survival (1985)
  Blood Sisters (1987)
  Lurkers (1988)
  Prime Evil (1988)

SEARLE, HUMPHREY
  Passionate Strangers, The
    (1957)
  Abominable Snowman, The
    (1957)
  Antarctic Crossing (1958)

SEAZER, J. A.
  Fruits of Passion, The (1981)
  Kusameikyu (1984)
  Farewell to the Ark (1985)

SEBAN, ANDREJ
  Salty Sweets (1986)

SEBASTIAN
  Hodja from Pjort (1985)

SEBASTIAN, JOHN
  Welcome Back, Kotter (1975)
  That's Cat (1977)
  Act, The (1984)
  Jerk, Two, The (1984)
  Care Bears Movie, The (1985)

SEBESKY, DON
  F. Scott Fitzgerald and "The
    Last of the Belles" (1974)
  How to Pick Up Girls! (1978)
  Hollow Image (1979)
  Rosary Murders, The (1987)

SECHI, ANTONIO
  Desiring Giulia (1986)

SECUNDA, SHOLEM
  Tevya (1939)
  God, Man and Devil (1950)

SEELOS, ANBROOS
  Obscene (1981)

SEELY, JOHN
  Hideous Sun Demon, The
    (1959)
  Road Runner Show, The
    (1971)
  Sylvester and Tweety (1976)

SEEMANN, HORST
  Levin's Mill (1981)
  Hotel Plan and Its Guests
    (1982)
  Lady Doctors (1984)

SEFFER, PAUL
  Adventures of Faustus Bid-
    good, The (1986)

SEGAL, JERRY
  Die Laughing (1980)

SEGAL, MISHA
  Cassie and Company (1982)
  Facts of Life Goes to Paris,
    The (1982)
  Baby Makes Five (1983)
  Contract for Life: The

S.A.D.D. Story (1984)
Knights of the City (1984)
Last Dragon, The (1985)
Young Lady Chatterley II
 (1985)
Lethal (1986)
Enemy Among Us, An (1987)
Lena: My 100 Children
 (1987)
Once We Were Dreamers
 (1987)
Home Sweet Homeless (1988)
New Adventures of Pippi
 Longstocking, The (1988)

SEGALL, BERNARDO
Congolaise (1950)
City: Time of Decision,
 The (1968)
Night Slaves (1970)
Columbo (1971)
Nichols (1971)
Moon of the Wolf (1972)
Girl Most Likely to ..., The
 (1973)
Turnover Smith (1980)

SEGERSTROM, MIKAEL
Inuksuk (1988)

SEGNITZ, PAUL
Slipper Episode (1938)

SEGURA, GREGORY
 (GREGORIO GARCIA SEGURA)
Carmen of Grenada (1959)
Sweet Sound of Death, The
 (1965)
Witch Without a Broom, A
 (1966)
Transplant (1970)
Hurrah for Adventure (1970)
... and the Third Year, He
 Resuscitated (1980)
Black Venus (1983)

SEIBER, MATYAS
Short Vision, A (1956)

SEIBERT, BUDI
Wurlitzer (1985)

SEKACZ, ILONA
Farmers Arms (1983)
Imaginary Friends (1987)
Intimate Contact (1987)

SELCUK, TIMUR
Season in Hakkari, A (1983)
Yusuf from Kuyucak (1986)

SELIGMAN, LORI
Before Stonewall (1984)

SELINSKY, WLADIMIR
Goodbye Raggedy Ann (1971)
Something Evil (1972)
Miles to Go Before I Sleep
 (1975)
Family Reunion (1981)

SELL, JACK M.
Outtakes (1987)

SELLERS, MAXINE
Joshua and the Blob (1972)

SELMECZI, GYORGY
Priceless Day, A (1980)
Wasted Lives (1982)
Daniel Takes a Train (1983)
Heavenly Hosts (1983)
Passing Fancy (1984)
Flowers of Reverie (1985)
Little Bit of You ... A Little
 Bit of Me, A (1985)
Time (1986)
Deserters, The (1987)
Fall, The (1987)
Laura (1987)
Cry and Cry Again (1988)

SELTZER, DOV
Seven Magnificent Gladiators,
 The (1982)
Mr. Leon (1982)
Savage Weekend (1983)
Megilah '83 (1983)
Ambassador, The (1984)
Forced Witness (1984)
Assisi Underground, The
 (1985)
Hame'ahev (1986)

Bouba (1987)
Hanna's War (1988)
Place by the Sea, A (1988)

SENANTE, JUAN C.
Caution to the Wind (1980)

SENDREY, AL
Remous (1935)

SENESE, JAMES
No Thanks, Coffee Makes Me
Nervous (1982)

SENIA, JEAN-MARIE
Weak Man, The (1981)
Lawful Violence (1982)
Words to Say It (1983)
Louise the Rebel (1985)
Song-Filled Tomorrows (1985)
Red Kiss (1985)
Moods (1986)
Brute, The (1987)
Fuegos (1987)
Romance in Paris, A (1987)
Wedding in Galilee, A (1987)
My Friend the Traitor (1988)

SENIGALLIA, RICCARDO
Before the Future (1985)

SENZA, LEON
Angel Dust (1987)

SEONG-JO, CHUNG
Deep Blue Night (1985)

SERAFINE, FRANK
Nightfall (1988)

SERBAN, RADU
Green, Green Grass of Home,
The (1977)

SERIO, RENATO
Alone in the Dark (1982)
Target Eagle (1982)
Invisibles, The (1988)

SEROCKI, KAZIMIERZ
Eighth Day of the Week,
The (1958)

Knights of the Teutonic
Order (1960)

SEROKA, HENRI
Funeral Ceremony (1985)
Flight of the Spruce Goose
(1986)

SERRA, ERIC
Last Combat, The (1983)
Subway (1985)
Kamikaze (1986)
Big Blue, The (1988)

SERRA, LUIS MARIA
My Days with Veronica (1980)
Fears (1980)
On the Far Side of Adventure
(1980)
Moments (1981)
From Mysterious Buenos Aires
(1981)
Nobody's Wife (1982)
Enemies, The (1983)
Lost Republic, The (1983)
Sting Is Over, The (1983)
Camila (1984)
Trapped Women (1984)
Count to Ten (1985)
Enraged Toy, The (1985)
Children of the War, The
(1985)
Days in June (1985)
Insomniacs, The (1986)
Lost Republic II, The (1986)
Miss Mary (1986)
Sophia (1987)

SERRANO, EDUARDO
Adolescence of Cain (1959)

SERVAIN, PHILIPPE
Beasts, The (1984)
Angel Skin (1986)

SE-TCHUNG, TUAN
Magic of the Kite (1957)

SEUBERTH, ERNIE
Mueller's Bureau (1986)
Muckrakers, The (1987)

SEVETAN, STEPHEN
    Paper Chase, The (1978)
    Paper Chase: The Second
        Year (1983)

SEYER, LARRY
    French Quarter Undercover
        (1985)

SEYMOUR, SHELDON see
    LEWIS, HERSCHELL GORDON

SFETSAS, KYRIACOS
    Paraguelia (1980)
    Mark, The (1982)
    Stigma (1984)
    Night with Silena, The (1986)

SHABAZIAN, FAREIDOUN
    Stony Lion (1987)
    Suitors, The (1988)

SHAFER, KARL-HEINZ
    Tender Dracula (1975)

SHAINDLIN, JACK
    Death of a Dream (1950)
    This Is Your Army (1954)
    Lowell Thomas Remembers
        (1975)

SHAKESPEARE, JOAN
    Ghost Goes Gear, The (1966)
    Beast of Morocco (1966)

SHAKESPEARE, JOHN
    Beast of Morocco (1966)
    Ghost Goes Gear, The (1966)
    Girl from Starship Venus,
        The (1978)
    Killer's Moon (1978)

SHANKAR, RAVI
    Awara (1956)
    Kabuliwala (1957)
    Philosopher's Stone (1957)
    Jungle Saga, The (1958)
    Love of Amiradka (1961)
    Alice in Wonderland (1966)
    Primordium (1968)
    Gandhi (1982)
    Genesis (1986)

SHAPIRO, COLIN
    My Country, My Hat (1983)

SHAPIRO, DAVID
    Evil Laugh (1988)
    Hell Comes to Frogtown (1988)

SHAPIRO, LEE
    Violated (1986)

SHAPIRO, TED
    Bloodeaters (1980)

SHAPORIN, Y.
    Prisoners (1937)

SHARGO, BECKY
    Footloose (1984)

SHARPLES, ROBERT
    Cosmic Monsters, The (1958)
    Unseen Heroes (1958)
    Strange World of Planet X,
        The (1958)
    Rivals of Sherlock Holmes,
        The (1975)
    Search for Alexander the
        Great, The (1981)

SHARPLES, WINSTON
    Leprechaun's Gold (1949)

SHATZMAN, POLDI
    On a Narrow Bridge (1985)

SHAW, CAROL CONNORS
    Overboard (1978)

SHAW, FRANCIS
    Family Affair, A (1982)

SHAW, GEORGE NEWMAN
    Axe (Lisa, Lisa) (1983)

SHAW, IAN
    Preppies (1984)
    R.S.V.P. (1984)
    Sex Appeal (1986)
    Warrior Queen (1987)
    Wimps (1987)

SHAW, ROLAND
  Straight On Until Morning
    (1972)

SHAWN, ALLEN
  My Dinner with Andre (1981)

SHCHEDRIN, RODION
  Communist, The (1957)

SHEBALIN, V. Y.
  Gobsek (1937)

SHEFFER, JONATHAN
  Vietnam War Story (1988)

SHEFTER, BERT
  Fly, The (1948)
  Black Scorpion, The (1957)
  Big Show, The (1961)
  Voyage to the Bottom of the
    Sea (1961)
  Young Guns of Texas (1962)
  Harbor Lights (1963)

SHEFTER, JONATHAN
  On Valentine's Day (1986)
  Rise and Rise of Daniel
    Rocket, The (1986)
  Story of a Marriage, Part I:
    Courtship, The (1987)
  In a Shallow Grave (1988)

SHEHU, BASHIM
  Five-Legged Hare, The (1982)

SHELABIN, V. J.
  Broken Shoes (1934)

SHELBY, MALCOLM
  Castle of Fu Manchu, The
    (1968)

SHELDON, ERNIE
  Hard Traveling (1985)

SHELDON, MAURIE
  Golden Pennies (1985)

SHELLER, WILLIAM
  Return in Bond (1980)
  Singles (1982)

SHELOBINSKI, V.
  Hectic Days (1935)

SHENOUDA, HANEY
  Lawyer, The (1984)

SHEPHERD, BILL
  Idle of Parade (1959)

SHERER, PETER
  Dinosaur! (1985)

SHERMAN, BOBBY
  Day the Earth Moved, The
    (1974)

SHERMAN, GARRY
  Johnny, We Hardly Knew Ye
    (1977)
  Stubby Pringle's Christmas
    (1978)
  Kid from Nowhere, The (1982)
  Don't Touch (1985)
  Child's Cry (1986)
  Whatever It Takes (1986)

SHERMAN, MICHAEL
  California Girls (1981)

SHERRILL, BILLY
  Take This Job and Shove It
    (1981)

SHETH, RAGHUNATH
  Bonded Until Death (1985)

SHEVAI, AMMAR
  Dreams of Hind and Camelia
    (1988)

SHIBUYA, TAKESHI
  Song of the Sun (1975)

SHIK, LIM WON
  Wedding Day, The (1957)

SHILKRET, NATHANIEL
  Jungle Cavalcade (1941)

SHIMIZU, YASUAKI
  Superslob (1985)

SHING, STEPHEN
  Human Lanterns (1982)
  Pure and the Evil, The (1982)
  Fist Full of Talons, A (1983)
  Men from the Gutter (1983)
  Family Light Affair (1984)
  Pale Passion (1984)
  Let's Make Laugh II (1985)
  Twisted Passion (1985)
  Love With the Perfect
    Stranger (1986)

SHINOZAKI, MASATSUGU
  River of Fireflies (1987)

SHIOMURA, OSAMU
  Main Theme (1984)
  Deaths in Tokimeki (1986)

SHIRAKAWA, GENPACHIRO
  Jongara (1974)

SHIRE, DAVID
  McCloud (1970)
  McCloud: Who Killed Miss
    U.S.A.? (1970)
  Forgotten Man, The (1971)
  Getting Together (1971)
  Harpy (1971)
  Impatient Heart, The (1971)
  Marriage Year One (1971)
  Priest Killer, The (1971)
  Sarge (1971)
  See the Man Run (1971)
  Is There a Doctor in the
    House? (1971)
  Rex Harrison Presents Short
    Stories of Love (1972)
  Isn't It Shocking? (1973)
  Love Story (1973)
  Doctor Dan (1974)
  Godchild, The (1974)
  Healers, The (1974)
  Killer Bees (1974)
  Lucas Tanner (1974)
  Sidekicks (1974)
  Tell Me Where It Hurts
    (1974)

Tribe, The (1974)
Virginia Hill Story, The
  (1974)
Joe and Sons (1975)
Oregon Trail, The (1975)
Three for the Road (1975)
Winner Take All (1975)
Amelia Earhart (1976)
McNaughton's Daughter (1976)
Alice (1976)
Practice, The (1976)
Sirota's Court (1976)
This Better Be It (1976)
Tales of the Unexpected
  (1977)
Daddy, I Don't Like It Like
  This (1978)
Defection of Simas Kudirka,
  The (1978)
Flying High (1978)
Night the Lights Went Out
  in Georgia, The (1981)
Dark Room, The (1981)
Only When I Laugh (1981)
Home Room (1981)
Norma Rae (1981)
Paternity (1981)
World According to Garp,
  The (1982)
Max Dugan Returns (1983)
Oh, God! You Devil (1984)
2010 (1984)
Do You Remember Love?
  (1985)
Return to Oz (1985)
Man About Town (1986)
'night, Mother (1986)
Promise (1986)
Short Circuit (1986)
Time Flyer (1986)
Backfire (1987)
Convicted: A Mother's Story
  (1987)
Echoes in the Darkness
  (1987)
God Bless the Child (1988)
Jesse (1988)
Monkey Shines (1988)
Vice Versa (1988)

SIMON, CARLY
  Heartburn (1986)
  Working Girl (1988)

SIMON, ERNST
  ... And Saucy at That!
    (1960)
  Young Sinner, The (1960)

SIMON, P.
  Gibralter (1939)

SIMON, PAUL
  One Trick Pony (1980)

SIMON, TIM
  Key Tortuga (1981)
  Family Ties (1982)
  Desperate Intruder (1983)
  Kudzu (1983)

SIMON, YVES
  Cocktail Molotov (1980)

SIMON, ZOLTAN
  Dawn, The (1986)
  Season of Monsters (1987)

SIMONEC, TOM
  Survival Game (1987)

SIMONETTI, CLAUDIO
  Warriors of the Wasteland
    (1983)
  Conquest (1984)
  Demons (1985)
  Cut and Run (1986)
  Hands of Steel (1986)
  Unsane (1987)

SIMONS, MARTY
  And Then You Die (1987)

SIMONYAN, M.
  Flying Carpet, The (1956)
  Snow Queen, The (1966)

SIMOVIC, TOMISLAV
  Great Fear, The (1958)
  Doll, A (1961)
  Game, The (1962)

Far Away I Saw Mist and Mud
    (1964)
  Ceremony, The (1965)
  Meeting at the Fashion Show
    (1965)
  Wall, The (1965)
  Tamer of Wild Horses (1966)
  Seventh Continent, The
    (1967)
  Between the Glass and the
    Lip (1968)
  Opera Cordis (1968)
  Stain on His Conscience, A
    (1968)
  Twiddle Twaddle (1968)
  Scabies (1969)
  Man Who Had to Sing, The
    (1970)
  Portraits (1970)
  Visitors from the Galaxy
    (1981)

SIMPSON, DUDLEY
  Moonbase 3 (1973)
  Blake's Seven (1980)
  Goodbye, Mr. Chips (1987)

SIMPSON, MICHAEL
  Hot Rod (1979)

SIMPSON, VALERIE
  Change at 125th Street
    (1974)

SINGARA, ANTONIO
  Sorry I'm Late (1983)

SINGER, LOU
  Gigantor (1966)

SINGH, GUNA
  Bangalore Bhoota (1975)

SINGH, UTAM
  Kasturi (1978)

SINHA, TAPAN
  Return of Robin Hood, The
    (1988)

SINZADZE, S.
  Otar's Widow (1958)

SIRLI, VASILE
   Glissandro (1985)

SIRVINSKAS, YUOZAS
   Woman and Her Four Men, A
     (1984)
   Prodigal Son, The (1986)

SISSMAN, PHILIPPE
   Raisins de la Mort, Les
     (1978)

SIU-LAM, TANG
   Zu (Warriors from the Magic
     Mountain) (1983)

SJOEHOLM, LENNART
   Leave Me Not Alone (1980)

SKEEL, CHRISTIAN
   Forever Friends (1987)

SKENE, GORDON
   Cosmos (1974)

SKILES, MARLIN
   Maze, The (1953)
   Hypnotic Eye, The (1960)
   Beachcomber, The (1961)
   Space Monster (1965)

SKINNER, DAVE
   Indecent Obsession, An
     (1985)
   Great Bookie Robbery, The
     (1986)

SKINNER, FRANK
   Son of Frankenstein (1939)

SKIPPER, SVEND
   Kurt and Valde (1983)

SKJOLD, SVEN
   Girl from a Mountain Village
     (1949)
   One Summer of Happiness
     (1952)
   Bread of Love, The (1954)

SKORNIK, GUY
   Tusk (1980)

SKORSKY, NICOLAS
   Gentle France (1986)

SKOUEN, SYNNE
   Guardians, The (1980)

SKRZEK, JOZEF
   Hands Up! (1981)
   War of the Worlds--Next
     Century, The (1981)

SLADE, JULIAN
   Love in a Cold Climate (1982)

SLANE, ROD
   Revenge (1986)

SLANEY, IVOR
   Spaceways (1953)
   Bad Blonde (1953)
   Terror Street (1953)
   Unholy Four, The (1954)
   Sally's Irish Rogue (1958)
   Prey (1977)
   Death Ship (1980)

SLAVIN, GIL
   Jacques Mesrine (1984)

SLEDGE, FRANKLIN
   Alien Dead, The (1980)

SLEITH, JOHN
   Vicious (1988)

SLIDER, DAN
   Demonwarp (1988)
   Uninvited (1988)

SLIOMIS, THOMAS
   Birthday Town (1987)

SLITR, JIRI
   Competition (1968)

SLOVAK, JOZEF
   Hurry, He's Coming! (1988)

SMAILA, UMBERTO
   Pony Express Boy, The
     (1986)
   My First 40 Years (1987)

SMALL, GEORGE
  Last Rites (1980)
  Splitz (1984)

SMALL, MICHAEL
  Magic Ring, The (1968)
  Draw Me a Telephone (1968)
  Miss Right (1980)
  Those Lips Those Eyes
    (1980)
  Boy Who Drank Too Much,
    The (1980)
  Postman Always Rings Twice,
    The (1981)
  Continental Divide (1981)
  Rollover (1981)
  Lathe of Heaven (1981)
  Chiefs (1983)
  Star Chamber, The (1983)
  Firstborn (1984)
  Target (1985)
  Brighton Beach Memoirs
    (1986)
  Dream Lover (1986)
  Nobody's Child (1986)
  Black Widow (1987)
  Jaws IV--The Revenge (1987)
  Orphans (1987)
  1969 (1988)

SMALLEY, JACK
  That's Hollywood (1977)
  Tourist (1980)

SMEATON, BRUCE
  Circle of Iron (1979)
  Grendel Grendel Grendel
    (1981)
  Last of the Knucklemen, The
    (1981)
  Town Like Alice, A (1981)
  Barbarosa (1982)
  Monkey Grip (1982)
  Squizzy Taylor (1982)
  Winds of Jarrah, The (1983)
  1893-1915 (1983)
  Undercover (1984)
  Double Deal (1984)
  Iceman (1984)
  Street Hero (1984)
  Naked Country, The (1985)

  Eleni (1985)
  Departure (1986)
  Roxanne (1987)
  Alien Years, The (1988)
  Cry in the Dark, A (1988)

SMEDLEY, DICK
  Beach Girls, The (1977)

SMITH, ARTHUR
  Lady Grey (1980)

SMITH, CLAY
  Lady Grey (1980)
  Day of Judgment, A (1980)

SMITH, CLIVE
  Liquid Sky (1982)

SMITH, DANIEL
  Alter Ego (1986)

SMITH, ERIC
  Flashpoint Africa (1978)

SMITH, HALE
  Eva's Dreams (1982)

SMITH, LARRY K.
  Pink Motel (Motel) (1983)

SMITH, PHIL
  Separate Tables (1983)

SMITH, TERI
  All My Children (1970)

SMITH, TOM
  Hello, Larry (1979)

SMITH, VINCENT
  One Way Out (1987)

SNEDDON, GREG
  Dunera Boys, The (1985)

SNIJDERS, RONALD
  Desiree (1984)

SNOW, MARK
  Starsky and Hutch (1975)

Boy in the Plastic Bubble,
  The (1976)
Family (1976)
Gemini Man, The (1976)
Visions (1976)
San Pedro Beach Bums, The
  (1977)
Big Bob Johnson and His
  Fantastic Speed Circus
  (1978)
Vega$ (1978)
Next Step Beyond, The
  (1978)
Brothers and Sisters (1979)
Flatbush (1979)
Hart to Hart (1979)
Return of the Mod Squad
  (1979)
Casino (1980)
When the Whistle Blows (1980)
Angel City (1980)
Cagney and Lacy (1981)
Strike Force (1981)
240-Robert (1981)
I'd Rather Be Calm (1982)
Six of Us, The (1982)
T. J. Hooker (1982)
Games Mother Never Taught
  You (1982)
Paper Dolls (1982)
John Steinbeck's "The Winter
  of Our Discontent" (1983)
Malibu (1983)
Packin' It In (1983)
Two Kinds of Love (1983)
Family Tree, The (1983)
Lottery (1983)
Good Sport, A (1984)
Off Sides (1984)
Something About Amelia (1984)
Crazy Like a Fox (1984)
Double Trouble (1984)
Not My Kid (1985)
Challenge of a Lifetime
  (1985)
International Airport (1985)
Lady from Yesterday, The
  (1985)

Rockhopper (1985)
Hometown (1985)
I Dream of Jeannie: 15
  Years Later (1985)
Acceptable Risks (1986)
Blood and Orchids (1986)
Bridges to Cross (1986)
Girl Who Spelled Freedom,
  The (1986)
Jake Speed (1986)
News at Eleven (1986)
One Police Plaza (1986)
One Terrific Guy (1986)
Cracked Up (1987)
Down the Long Hills (1987)
Father Clements Story, The
  (1987)
Hobo's Christmas, A (1987)
Kids Like These (1987)
Murder Ordained (1987)
Pals (1987)
Saint, The (1987)
Still Crazy Like a Fox (1987)
Warm Hearts, Cold Feet (1987)
Aaron's Way (1988)
Alone in the Neon Jungle
  (1988)
Bluegrass (1988)
Disaster at Silo 7 (1988)
Ernest Saves Christmas
  (1988)
In Crowd, The (1988)
Ladykillers (1988)
Return of Ben Casey, The
  (1988)
Secret Life of Kathy
  McCormick, The (1988)
Vietnam War Story (1988)

SOCCIO, GINO
  Hey Babe! (1984)

SOCIALIZMA, OTROCI
  Fatal Telephone, The (1987)

SODEN, BILL
  Great Wallendas, The (1978)

SODRE, FAIMUNDO
  Born for Diesel (1982)

SOHL, RICHARD
  Her Name Is Lisa (1987)

SOLA, JOSE
  Magician of Dreams (1966)

SOLAAS, EYVIND
  Little Ida (1981)

SOLANO, RAFAEL
  One-Way Ticket, A (1988)

SOLAS, ORREGO
  Confession at Dawn (1954)

SOLER, TOTI
  Hector (1984)

SOLERA, ANTONIO
  You Alone (1984)

SOLOMON, ELLIOT
  Dirty Laundry (1987)

SOLOMON, MARIBETH
  Kelly (1981)
  Improper Channels (1981)
  Ticket to Heaven (1981)
  Threshold (1981)
  Hard Feelings (1982)
  Abortion: Stories from
      North and South (1985)
  Lost! (1986)
  Milk and Honey (1988)

SOLOMON, MICKEY
  Utilities (1983)

SOLOVERA, PATRICIO
  Accomplished Fact, An (1985)

SOMEYA, KINGO
  Nitakayama Nobore (1968)

SOMLO, TAMAS
  Light Physical Injuries
      (1984)

SOMMER, HANS
  Baby Doctor Engel (1937)
  Fair and Warmer (1937)

Man Who Was Sherlock
    Holmes, The (1937)
  First Legion, The (1951)

SOMMERLATTE, ULRICH
  School for Connubial Bliss
      (1954)

SONDHEIM, STEPHEN
  Reds (1981)

SONGPAO, PRACHIN
  Jula Treekul River (1980)
  Red Mansion, The (1980)
  Hello, Cane Stick (1982)

"SONIC YOUTH"
  Made in U.S.A. (1987)

SONIK-OMI
  Dr. X (1972)

SONNINEN, AHTI
  Unknown Soldier, The (1956)

SONSTEVOLD, GUNNAR
  Boys from the Streets (1950)

SONSTEVOLD, MAJ
  Venner (1960)

SOPER, HARN
  Massive Retaliation (1984)

SORGHINI, M.
  Naked Exorcism (1975)

SORIANO, RAMIRO
  Santa Esperanza (1980)

SORVALI, UPI
  Betrayal, The (1988)

SOUD, HASSAN ABU EL
  Shame, The (1983)

SOUKUP, ONDREI
  Big Money (1988)

"SOUND X"
  Tin Star Void (1988)

SOUTH, HARRY
  Sweeney, The (1976)

SOUTHERLAND, JOE
  Day It Came to Earth, The
    (1979)

SOUTHGATE, BILL
  Jack the Ripper (1974)

SOUTHWORTH, LINDA
  My Son, the Vampire (1952)

SPADAVEKPIA, A.
  Horseman, The (1951)

SPANDOUDAKIS, STAMATIS
  Angel (1982)
  Sudden Love (1984)
  Stone Years (1985)
  Such a Long Absence (1985)
  Absences (1987)
  Striker With the No. 9 (1988)

SPANOS, GEORGE
  Agitated Winds (1984)

SPANOUDAKIS, STAMATIS see
  SPANDOUDAKIS, STAMATIS

SPEAR, DAVID
  Delta House (1979)
  Fear No Evil (1981)
  Creature Wasn't Nice, The
    (1981)
  Exterminator 2 (1984)
  Ratings Game, The (1984)
  Mortuary Academy (1988)

SPEAR, ERIC
  Shadow Man (Street of
    Shadows) (1953)
  Undercover Agent (1953)
  Golden Link, The (1954)
  Immediate Disaster (1954)
  Too Hot to Handle (1960)
  Coronation Street (1972)

SPEDDING, FRANK
  Architecture of Frank Lloyd
    Wright, The (1985)

SPEISS, LEO
  Phantom (1922)

SPENCE, JOHNNIE
  Amazing Spiderman, The
    (1977)
  Spider-Man (1977)
  Chinese Web, The (1978)

SPENCER, FRANK
  Cloudburst (1952)

SPENCER, HERBERT
  Make Room for Daddy (1953)

SPICER, MICHAEL
  Backlash (1986)

SPIES, MARKUS
  Something Becomes Evident
    (1982)

SPILLIT, OBERWALLISER
  Hidden Dances (1983)

"SPLIFF"
  Baby (1984)

SPOERRI, BRUNO
  Brain Burning (1982)
  Teddy Baer (1983)
  Umbruch (1987)

SPOLIANSKY, MISCHA
  King Solomon's Mines (1932)
  My Song for You (1935)
  Ghost Goes West, The (1936)
  Man Who Could Work Miracles,
    The (1936)
  Midnight Episode (1951)

"SPOONER"
  Dreams Come True (1985)

SPOTTS, ROGER HAMILTON
  Tongue (1976)

SPRINGER, PHILIP
  Medical Center (1969)

SREBOTNIAK, ALOJZ
Operation (1960)
Ballad About a Trumpet and
a Cloud, A (1961)

SRINIVASAN, M. B.
Rat Trap, The (1982)
Lekha's Death--A Flashback
(1984)
Face to Face (1986)
Monolog (1988)

SRNKA, KIRI
Krakatit (1951)

STABULNEIKS, ULDIS
Other People's Passions (1986)

STACK, LENNY
Shell Game (1975)
Bowzer (1981)

STAEBLER, GERHARD
King Kong's Fist (1985)

STAFFLER, R.
Toro! (1956)

STAIGER, BODO
Jagger & Spaghetti--The
Supper Bluffers (1984)

STAIKOV, IVAN
King for a Day (1985)

STALLING, CARL
Road Runner Show, The
(1971)
Sylvester and Tweety (1976)
Uncensored Cartoons (1982)
Bugs Bunny's Third Movie:
1001 Rabbit Tales (1982)

STAMPONE, ATILIO
Official History, The (1985)
Tango Bar (1988)

STAMPONI, HECTOR
Guapo del 1900, Un (1960)

STANGIO, FRANK
BMX Bandits (1983)

"STANISLAS"
Holcroft Covenant, The (1985)

STANISLAV, JIRI
Border (1987)

STANLEY, JAMES LEE
Cathy (1987)

STANOWSKI, JERZY
Man Unnecessary (1981)

STANSHALL, VIVIAN
Sir Henry at Rawlinson End
(1980)

STAPLES, KEVIN
Track Two (1983)

STARK, KARL
His Double Life (1933)

STATMAN, ANDY
Kaddish (1984)

STEAD, COLIN
Fighting Back (1982)
BMX Bandits (1983)
Last Bastion, The (1984)
Melvin, Son of Alvin (1984)

STEELE, DAVID
Tin Men (1987)

STEFANOVSKI, VLATKO
Three's Happiness (1986)
Forgotten Ones, The (1988)

STEFFLER, PAUL
Finding Mary March (1988)

STEIMEL, ADOLF
Tromba, the Tiger Man (1952)

STEIN, CHRIS
Union City (1980)
Polyester (1981)
Wild Style (1983)

STEIN, HERMAN
It Came from Outer Space
(1953)

Daniel Boone
(1964)

STEIN, JULIAN
Flesh Eaters, The (1964)

STEIN, RONALD
Day the World Ended, The
(1956)
It Conquered the World
(1956)
Not of This Earth (1956)
Oklahoma Woman, The (1956)
Phantom from 10,000 Leagues,
The (1956)
She-Creature, The (1956)
Invasion of the Saucer Men
(1957)
Naked Paradise (1957)
Undead, The (1957)
Hot Dog Gang (1958)
She-Gods of Shark Reef
(1958)
Tank Commandos (1959)
Last Woman on Earth (1960)
Journey to the Seventh
Planet (1961)
Ghosts That Still Walk (1978)
Frankenstein's Great Aunt
Tillie (1985)

STEINER, FRED
Perry Mason (1957)
Colossus of New York, The
(1958)
Daniel Boone (1964)
Hogan's Heroes (1965)
Star Trek (1966)
Wake Me When the War Is
Over (1969)
Carter's Army (1970)
Wild Women (1970)
River of Gold (1971)
Family Flight (1972)
Hec Ramsey (1972)
Heatwave! (1974)
Golden Age of Television,
The (1981)
Blood Feud (1983)
Case of the Shooting Star,
The (1986)

Perry Mason: The Case of
the Sinister Spirit (1987)
Perry Mason: The Case of
the Avenging Ace (1988)
Perry Mason: The Case of
the Lady in the Lake
(1988)

STEINER, GEORGE
Golden Age of Comedy, The
(1958)

STEINER, ITZHAK
Noa at 17 (1982)

STEINER, JERRY
Black Water Gold (1970)

STEINER, MAX
Phantom of Crestwood, The
(1932)
She (1935)
Gridiron Flash (1935)
Beyond the Forest (1949)

STEINMAN, JIM
Small Circle of Friends, A
(1980)
Dead Ringer (1982)

STEINMAN, ROGER
Best of the West, The (1981)
Family Man (1988)

STEKOL, RICHARD
Between the Lines (1980)

STELIO, MICHEL
Young Girl and Hell, The
(1986)

STELLARI, GIAN
Colossus and the Headhunters
(1962)

STEPANENCO, MAJA
Mike Test (1980)

STEPHEN, WILLIAM
Fetish and Dreams (1985)

STEREV, MITKO
Almost a Love Story (1980)

STERN, JACK
Champagne for Breakfast
(1981)

STERN, PAUL
Hero (1982)

STERN, THEODORE
Worm Eaters, The (1977)

STEVENETT, DARYL
Killpoint (1984)

STEVENS, LEITH
Daniel Boone (1964)
Mission: Impossible (1966)
Silent Gun, The (1969)
Immortal, The (1970)
Young Lawyers, The (1970)
Assault on the Wayne (1971)

STEVENS, MORTON
Gilligan's Island (1964)
Wild Wild West, The (1965)
Cimarron Strip (1967)
Hawaii Five-O (1968)
Storefront Lawyers, The
(1970)
Death of Innocence, A (1971)
Face of Fear, The (1971)
13th Day: The Story of
Esther, The (1971)
Deadly Harvest (1972)
She Waits (1972)
Strangers in 7A, The (1972)
Visions ... (1972)
Coffee, Tea or Me? (1973)
Guess Who's Sleeping in My
Bed? (1973)
Horror at 37,000 Feet, The
(1973)
Poor Devil (1973)
Apple's Way (1974)
Disappearance of Flight 412,
The (1974)
Kodiak (1974)
Police Woman (1974)
Khan! (1975)

Matt Helm (1975)
Banjo Hackett (1976)
F. Scott Fitzgerald in Holly-
wood (1976)
Spencer's Pilots (1976)
Time Travelers (1976)
Andros Targets, The (1977)
Code Name: Diamond Head
(1977)
Mulligan's Stew (1977)
Peter Lundy and the Medicine
Hat Stallion (1977)
Strange Possession of Mrs.
Oliver, The (1977)
W.E.B. (1978)
Wheels (1978)
13th Day: The Story of
Esther, The (1979)
Backstairs at the White
House (1979)
Billion Dollar Threat, The
(1979)
Flame of Love, The (1979)
Mandrake (1979)
Undercover with the KKK
(1979)
Women in White (1979)
Detour to Terror (1980)
Fugitive Family (1980)
Lucy Moves to NBC (1980)
M Station: Hawaii (1980)
Skag (1980)
Music Mart, The (1980)
Code Red (1981)
Judgment Day (1981)
Masada (1981)
Million Dollar Face (1981)
Hardly Working (1981)
Manions of America, The
(1981)
Great White (1982)
Memories Never Die (1982)
Knight Rider (1982)
Automan (1983)
Cocaine and Blue Eyes (1983)
I Married Wyatt Earp (1983)
Savage: In the Orient (1983)
Smorgasbord (1983)
Slapstick of Another Kind
(1984)
Alice in Wonderland (1985)

Outrage (1986)
They Still Call Me Bruce
    (1987)
Ann Jillian Story, The (1988)

STEYER, CHRISTIAN
Sabine Kleist, 7 Years Old
    (1983)
Pigeon Jill (1984)

"STING"
Brimstone and Treacle (1982)

STINNRBOM, LEIF
Gosta Berling's Saga (1986)

STIVIN, JIRI
House of Glass (1982)
Like Poison (1986)
Tandem (1986)

STOCKDALE, GARY
Hard Ticket to Hawaii (1987)
Arizona Heat (1988)
Picasso Trigger (1988)

STOKES, MICHAEL
Frank's Place (1987)

STOKLOSA, JANUSZ
Blows (1981)

STOLL, GEORGIE
Serenade (1959)

STOLLAR, YAKOV
Little Nightingale, The
    (1936)

STOLZ, ROBERT
My Friend Who Can't Say No
    (1950)

STOLZENWALD, FRANZ
What Am I Without You?
    (1935)

STONE, CHARLES
Princess (1980)

STONE, CHRISTOPHER (CHRIS)
It Can't Happen to Me (1979)

Covergirl (1981)
Trouble With Grandpa, The
    (1981)
Juggler of Notre Dame, The
    (1982)
Leadfoot (1982)
Nadia (1984)
Bet, The (1985)
Sword of Heaven (1985)
Naked Cage, The (1986)
Down and Out with Donald
    Duck (1987)
Phantasm (1988)

STONE, GREGORY
Jungle Princess, The (1936)

STONE, LAURIE
Second Time Lucky (1984)
Robbery Under Arms (1985)
My Brother Tom (1986)
Playing Beatie Bow (1986)
Far Country, The (1987)
Flying Doctors, The (1987)

STONE, RICHARD
North Shore (1987)
Summer Heat (1987)
Elvis & Me (1988)
Hiroshima Maiden (1988)
Longarm (1988)
Pumpkinhead (1988)

STORA, JEAN-PIERRE
Aphrodite (1982)
Jean-Louis Barrault--A Man
    of the Theater (1984)

STOREY, MICHAEL
Another Country (1984)
Every Picture Tells a Story
    (1984)
Coming Up Roses (1986)
Hidden City (1987)
Perfect Spy, The (1988)

STORRS, DAVID
P.O.W. The Escape (1986)
Sunset Strip (1986)

STORY, LIZ
Miss ... or Myth? (1987)

STOTT, WALLY (WALTER)
Will Any Gentleman? (1953)
For Better for Worse (1954)
Heart of a Man, The (1959)
Captain Nemo and the Under-
water City (1969)

STOTTER, PATRICIA LEE
Unfinished Business ... (1987)

STRAHAN, DEREK
Leonora (1986)

STRANGIO, FRANK
Dusty (1983)
Glass Babies (1985)
Dead-End Drive-In (1986)
Coda (1987)
Contagion (1988)
Dreaming, The (1988)
Fever (1988)

STRASSBURGER, JORG
Bitter Harvest (1985)

STRAUS, OSCAR
Little Schemer, The (1933)

STRAVIAK, EDWARD
Memoirs (1985)

STREAPY, F. L.
Little Flower of Jesus (1939)

STREINIKOV, N.
Poet and Tsar (1938)

STREISAND, BARBRA
Nuts (1987)

STRINGER, ROBERT
St. Benny the Dip (1951)

STROUSE, CHARLES
Just Tell Me What You Want
(1980)

STRUMMER, JOE
Walker (1987)
Permanent Record (1988)

STRYI, WOLFGANG
Wurlitzer (1985)

STRZELECKI, HENRY
Malibu Express (1985)

STUART, JOHN
Allies (1983)

STUART, JONATHAN
Doom Asylum (1988)

STUCKEY, MICHAEL
Citadel, The (1983)

STUCKEY, WILLIAM
Messenger, The (1987)

STUDER, JIM
Open House (1987)

STUPEL, YURI
Flying Machine, The (1981)

STUPPNER, HUBERT
Voices of the Sylphides,
The (1980)

STUR, SVETOZAR
Assistant, The (1982)
Concrete Pastures (1983)
Dead Teach the Living, The
(1984)

STURGES, JEFF
Hellhole (1985)

SU, CONG
Last Emperor, The (1987)

SUAREZ, GERARDO
Knockout (1984)

SUBRAMANIAM, L.
Salaam Bombay (1988)

"SUBURBANO"
Their Golden Years (1980)

SUGARMAN, SPARKY
Cinderella 2000 (1977)

SUGITA, KAZUO
    African Bird, The (1976)

SUGIYAMA, KOICHI
    Cyborg 009 (1974)
    Battle of the Planets (1977)
    Space Runway Ideon: A
        Contact (1982)
    Space Runway Ideon: Be
        Invoked (1982)
    Sea Prince and the Fire
        Child, The (1982)

SUJATOVICH, LEO
    Crooks (1987)
    Feelings: Mirta from Liniers
        to Istanbul (1987)
    Year of the Rabbit, The
        (1987)

SUKMAN, HARRY
    Bonanza (1959)
    Doctor Kildare (1961)
    Daniel Boone (1964)
    High Chaparral, The (1967)
    Genesis II (1973)
    Cowboys, The (1974)
    Family Kovack, The (1974)
    Planet Earth (1974)
    Beyond the Bermuda Triangle
        (1975)
    Jeremiah of Jacob's Neck
        (1976)
    Enigma (1977)
    Someone Is Watching Me!
        (1978)
    Hunter's Moon (1979)
    Salem's Lot (1979)

SULLIVAN, PETER
    Duet for Four (1982)
    As Time Goes By (1987)
    Slate, Wyn & Me (1987)
    Warm Nights on a Slow
        Moving Train (1987)

SULLIVAN, TOM
    Love's Dark Ride (1978)

SUMERA, LEPO
    Nest in the Wind (1980)

Keep Smiling, Baby! (1986)
Games for School Children
    (1987)

SUMMERS, ANDY
    Down and Out in Beverly
        Hills (1985)
    End of the Line (1988)
    Out of Time (1988)

SUMMERS, BOB
    Life and Times of Grizzly
        Adams, The (1977)
    Wind (1978)
    Deerslayer, The (1978)
    Donner Pass: The Road to
        Survival (1978)
    Greatest Heroes of the Bible
        (1978)
    Beyond Death's Door (1979)
    Legend of Sleepy Hollow, The
        (1979)
    Adventures of Nellie Bly
        (1980)
    Guyana: Cult of the Damned
        (1980)
    In Search of Historic Jesus
        (1980)
    Adventures of Nellie Bly,
        The (1980)
    Nashville Grab (1981)
    Adventures of Huckleberry
        Finn, The (1981)
    Rare Breed, The (1981)
    Boogens, The (1982)
    One Dark Night (1982)
    Capture of Grizzly Adams,
        The (1982)
    Fall of the House of Usher,
        The (1982)
    Romance Theater (1982)
    Uncommon Valor (1983)
    Eliminators (1986)
    Body Count (1988)

SUMMERS, DAVID
    Suffer Mammon (1987)
    Let Down Your Hair (1988)

SUMNER, WILL
    Personals, The (1982)

SUNDFOR, PAUL
    Attack of the Killer Tomatoes,
        The (1979)

SUNSET EDITORIAL
    In Name Only (1969)

SUOLA, LIU
    Sacrifice of Youth (1986)

SURMAN, JOHN
    Black Hills (1985)
    Permeke (1985)

SUSSKIND, H. W.
    Crisis (1939)

SUST, JIRI
    Wasted Sunday, A (1969)
    Short Cut (1981)
    Milo Barus--The Strongest
        Man in the World (1983)
    Snowdrop Celebrations (1984)
    My Sweet Little Village (1986)

SUTHERLAND, KEN
    Savannah Smiles (1982)
    Dark Before Dawn (1988)

SUZUKI, KUNIHIKO
    Wildcat Rock (1970)

SUZUKI, MASAKATSU
    Kamikaze, the Adventurer
        (1982)

SUZUKI, SEIICHI (SAEKO)
    Imposter, The (1955)
    Hours of Wedlock, The (1987)

SVARC, ISAAK
    Life Guard, The (1980)

SVENDSEN, STEIN B.
    Foxtrot (1988)

SVENSSON, GUNNAR RAYNIR
    Land and Sons (1980)
    SOPOR (1981)
    Rooster, The (1981)
    P & B (1984)

SVIRIDOV, GEORGY
    Red Bells: I've Seen the
        Birth of the New World
        (1983)

SVIRIDOV, YURI
    Skanderbeg (1954)

SVOBODA, JIRI
    Night of the Emerald Moon,
        The (1985)

SVOBODA, KAREL
    Fairy Tale of Honzik and
        Marenka, The (1981)
    Sing, Cowboy, Sing (1982)

SWADOS, ELIZABETH
    Tales of the Unexpected
        (1979)
    Too Far to Go (1979)
    Ohms (1979)
    Four Friends (1981)
    Rate It X (1985)
    Seize the Day (1986)
    Family Sins (1987)

SWEETEN, CLAUDE
    Tembo (1952)

SYGIETYNSKI, TADEUSZ
    Adventure in Warsaw (1955)

SYLVAIN, JULES
    Ready for Action (1937)
    Under a False Flag (1937)
    Jungle of Chang (1951)
    Lend Me Your Wife (1959)

SYLVIANO, RENE
    Francis the First (1947)

SYMONS, RED
    Empty Beach, The (1985)
    I Own the Racecourse (1986)

"SYNERGY"
    Jupiter Menace, The (1981)

SYREWICZ, STANISLAS
    Mad Love (1985)

Fantasist, The (1986)
Lair of the White Worm, The
  (1988)

SZATHMARY, IRVING
Get Smart (1965)

SZIGMONDY, PAUL
Lady Seeks Room (1937)

SZLATINAY, SANDOR
Sweet Stepmother (1935)
Kind Stepmother (1936)
My Daughter Is Different
  (1938)
Ripening Wheat (1939)

SZOLLOSY, ANDRAS
Baptism (1968)
Grimaces (1980)
Potteries (1981)

SZORENYI, LEHEL
So Goes the Day (1968)

SZORENYI, LEVENTE
Sunday Parents (1980)
Mascot (1982)
Miklos Akli (1987)

SZOSTAK, ZDZISLAW
Aria for an Athlete (1980)
Inspection of the Scene of a
  Crime 1901 (1980)
Knight, The (1980)
Shilly-Shally (1981)
Consul, The (1982)
Epitaph for Barbara Radziwill,
  An (1983)
Mrs. Latter's Pension (1984)
Tribulations of Balthazar
  Kobera (1988)

TABRIZI, DAVOOD
Hostage--The Christine Maresch
  Story (1983)
Surfer, The (1987)
Australian Daze (1988)
Navigator, The (1988)

TABUCHI, ERIC
Other Night, The (1988)

TABUCHI, KRISTIAN
Hit and Run (1985)

TAGLIAFERRI, E.
Three-Cornered Hat, The
  (1936)

TAKADA, HIROSHI
Blood (1974)

TAKADA, SHIN
Lusty Transparent Man, The
  (1978)

TAKAHASHI, YUJI
Michiko (1981)

TAKEI, TETSUO
Bundam (1980)

TAKEMITSU, TORU
Woman of the Dunes (1964)
Illusion of Blood (1966)
Dodes ka-Den (1971)
Inn of Evil (1972)
Dear Summer Sister (1973)
Time Within Memory (1973)
Himiko (1975)
Kaseki (1976)
Under the Blossoming Cherry
  Trees (1976)
Melody in Gray (1978)
Empire of Passion (1978)
Tears on the Lion's Mane
  (1980)
Glowing Autumn (1981)
A. K. (1985)
Fire Festival (1985)
Ran (King Lear) (1985)
Fate of a Family (1985)
Antonio Gaudi (1985)
Gonza the Spearman (1986)
Onimaru (1988)

TAKEMURA, JIRO
Lullaby of the Good Earth
  (1977)

TAKEO, KIYOSHI
Bus (1987)

TALBERT, THOMAS
    Struck by Lightning (1979)

"TALKING HEADS"
    Same As It Ever Was (1983)

TAM, ALAN
    Other Side of a Gentleman,
        The (1984)

TAMAKI, HIROKI
    Young Man's Stronghold, A
        (1970)
    Beat '71 (1971)
    Step on the Gas! (1971)
    Lineup of Kanto Outlaws
        (1971)
    Wildcat Rock-Beat '71 (1975)
    Mysterious Big Tactics
        (1978)

TAMASSY, ZDENKO
    Clowns on the Wall (1968)
    Happy Birthday, Marilyn!
        (1981)
    Matushka (Viadukt) (1983)
    Be Tough, Victor! (1983)
    Witches' Sabbath (1984)
    Embryo (1986)
    Roofs at Dawn (1987)
    Farewell to You (1988)

TAMBORRELLI, ALDO
    Tornado (1983)

TAMINDZIC, BORO
    Unseen Wonder (1984)

TANABE, SHINICHI
    Hell Island (1977)

TANAKA, MICHI
    No More Easy Going (1980)
    Four Seasons of Natsuko,
        The (1981)
    Love Letter (1987)

TANDLER, ADOLPH
    Queen Kelly (1929)

"TANGERINE DREAM"
    Spasms (1981)

Thief (1981)
About Judges and Other
    Sympathizers (1982)
Soldier, The (1982)
Kamikaze (1982)
Risky Business (1983)
Wavelength (1983)
Keep, The (1983)
Firestarter (1984)
Flashpoint (1984)
Heartbreakers (1984)
Street Hawk (1985)
Vision Quest (1985)
Forbidden (1985)
Red Heat (1985)
Zoning (1986)
Deadly Care (1987)
Near Dark (1987)
Shy People (1987)
Three O'Clock High (1987)
Tonight's the Night (1987)
Dead Solid Perfect (1988)
Miracle Mile (1988)
Red Nights (1988)

TANIGAWA, KENSAKU
    Actress (1987)

TANIMURA, SHINJI
    Imperial Navy (Great Fleet,
        The) (1982)
    Father and Child (1983)

TANO, ANEIRO
    Like Father, Like Daughter
        (1987)

TANO, TONY
    Like Father, Like Daughter
        (1987)

TAORMINA, CAL
    Jungle Raiders (1986)

TAPSCOTT, HORACE
    Checking In (1981)

TARANU, CORNEL
    Return from Hell (1983)
    Maiden of the Woods
        (1987)

TARDIF, GRAHAM
Tail of the Tiger (1984)
Incident at Raven's Gate
(1988)

TARDY, PIERRE
Time Masters, The (1982)

TARENSKEEN, BOUDEWIJN
Bastille (1984)
Frontier (1984)
Stranger at Home (1985)
Looking for Eileen (1987)
Thirst (1988)

TARP, SVEND ERIK
Golden Mountains (1958)
Faith, Hope and Witchcraft
(1960)

TARTAGLIA, JOHN ANDREW
Powderkeg (1971)
Adventures of Nick Carter,
The (1972)
Texas Wheelers, The (1974)
Barbary Coast, The (1975)
Islander, The (1978)
Sword of Justice (1978)
Misadventures of Sheriff
Lobo, The (1979)
Lobo (1980)
Nightside (1980)
Grace Kelly (1983)

TATRO, DUANE
Invaders, The (1967)
Hawaii Five-O (1968)
House on Greenapple Road,
The (1970)
Cannon (1971)
Paper Man (1971)
M*A*S*H (1972)
Barnaby Jones (1973)
F.B.I. Story, The: The
F.B.I. Versus Alvin
Karpis, Public Enemy
Number One (1974)
Manhunter, The (1974)
Bert D'Angelo/Superstar
(1976)
Love Boat, The (1977)
Keefer (1978)

Runaways, The (1979)
Murder Ink (1983)

TATSIS, NICOS
What My Eyes Are Going to
See (1984)

TATTERSALL, RICHARD
Carry On Laughing (1980)

TAUBE, EVERT
Our Boy (1936)

TAUBMAN, PAUL
Edge of Night, The (1956)

TAUTU, CORNELIA
Enchanted Grove, The
(1982)

TAYLOR, FRANCIS
2020 Texas Gladiators (1982)

TAYLOR, JAMES MICHAEL
Red Desert Penitentiary
(1986)

TAYLOR, LARRY
Cliffwood Avenue Kids, The
(1977)

TAYLOR, RICHARD
Joe Macbeth (1955)
Escapement (1958)

TEDESCO, MARIO CASTELNUOVO
Strictly Dishonorable (opera
sequence) (1951)

TELSON, BOB
Out of Rosenheim (1987)

TEMIZ, OKAY
Horse, The (1982)

TEMPERA, VINCENZO
Dracula in the Provinces
(1975)
I Like Her (1985)

TEMPERTON, ROD
Running Scared (1986)

TENNEY, DENNIS MICHAEL
Witchboard (1987)
Night of the Demon (1988)

TERASHIMA, MAOCHIKO
Happy Birthday, Mama (1982)

TERR, MICHAEL
King Dinosaur (1955)

TEXIER, HENRI
Filthy Business, A (1981)

THATCHER, MIKE
Put on Ice (1980)

THEISS, RICHARD
Day the Earth Got Stones,
The (1980)

THEODORAKIS, MIKIS
Walls (Falak) (1968)
Story of Jacob and Joseph,
The (1974)
Man with the Red Carnation,
The (1980)
Clowns of God, The (1986)

THEOFANIDES, MENELOS
Girl from Korfu, The (1957)

THICKE, ALAN
Jo's Cousins (1974)
Diff'rent Strokes (1978)
Facts of Life, The (1979)
Joe's World (1979)
Parkers, The (1981)

THIELMANS, TOOTS
One Woman or Two (1985)
Little Prosecutor, The (1987)

THIRIET, MAURICE
Devil's Envoys, The (1942)
Wolves of the Malveneurs,
The (1942)
Pretty Little Beach, A (1949)
Portrait of an Assassin (1950)
Lucrece Borgia (1953)
Bernadette of Lourdes
(1960)

"THIRTEEN MOONS"
Summer Nights (1987)

"39 CLOCKS, THE"
Nightfall (Head Shot) (1982)

THOMAS, LIONEL
Dracula Sucks (1980)

THOMAS, PETER
Ingeborg (1960)
Escape to Berlin (1961)
Indian Scarf, The (1963)
Blood Demon, The (1967)
Females, The (1970)
Hand of Power (1971)
Mysteries of the Gods (1976)

THOMAS, WHITEY
Mark of the Witch (1970)
Nail Gun Massacre (1987)

THOMASS, EUGEN
Meat (1979)

THOME, JEAN
Invisible Terror, The (1963)

THOMPSON, ANDY
Legend of Wolf Lodge, The
(1987)

THOMPSON, RICHARD S.
Deadly Games (1979)

THOMPSON, STEPHEN
Citizen: The Political Life
of Allard K. Lowenstein
(1983)

THOMS, TONI
Boundary Fire (1936)
Those Three About Christine
(1936)

THOR, JAN-MIKI
Zombie Nightmare (1987)

THORARENSSON, LEIFUR
Frozen Leopard, The
(1986)

THORN, MIKE
  Memoirs of a Survivor (1981)

THORNE, KEN
  Bed Sitting Room, The (1968)
  Persuaders, The (1971)
  Zoo Gang, The (1975)
  Wolf Lake (1978)
  Arabian Adventure (1979)
  House Where Evil Dwells,
    The (1982)
  Hunchback of Notre Dame,
    The (1982)
  Superman III (1983)
  White Water Rebels (1983)
  Lassiter (1984)
  Finders Keepers (1984)
  Evil That Men Do, The
    (1984)
  Protector, The (1985)
  Lost in London (1985)
  Return of Sherlock Holmes,
    The (1987)
  Trouble with Spies, The (1987)

THORNHILL, RUSTY
  Return of Josey Wales, The
    (1986)

THORUP, JOERGEN
  Elvis Hansen--A Pillar of
    Society (1988)

THURBER, H. KINGSLEY
  Don't Go in the Woods
    (1980)

THURNER, FRANS
  Fairy of Happiness (1949)

TIEN, LI HSIAO
  On the Wrong Track (1983)

TIGHRENT, LAHLOU
  Mint Tea (1984)

TIKANMAKI, ANSSI
  Glan: Tale of the Frogs,
    The (1985)
  Love Movie, The (1985)

TILLAR, JACK
  Last of the Wild (1974)
  Between the Wars (1978)
  Mysterious Island of Beautiful
    Women, The (1979)
  Mystery Mansion (1983)
  Heroes and Sidekicks--Indiana
    Jones and the Temple of
    Doom (1984)
  Four Americans in China
    (1985)
  In the Shadow of Vesuvius
    (1987)
  African Odyssey (1988)

TILLAR, NORMAN
  True Life Stories (1981)

TILLEY, ALEXANDRA
  Life Classes (1987)

TILSEY, REG
  Invasion of the Body Stealers,
    The (1969)

TIMM, DOUG
  Terror in the Aisles (1984)
  Streetwalkin' (1985)
  Man Who Fell to Earth, The
    (1987)
  Nightflyers (1987)
  Winners Take All (1987)
  Dirty Dozen, The (1988)

TIMMLER, THOMAS
  Polish War Worker, The
    (1986)

TIMMS, COLIN
  Australian Dream (1987)

TIMOFEYEV, N.
  Professor Mamlock (1938)
  Great Beginning, The (1940)

TIMPELAN, HELMUT
  Reason Asleep (1984)

TIOMKIN, DIMITRI
  Mad Love (1935)
  Moscow Strikes Back (1942)

TIPPET, KEITH
    Supergrass, The (1985)

TIPTON, GEORGE ALICESON
    Courtship of Eddie's Father,
        The (1969)
    Home for the Holidays (1972)
    No Place to Run (1972)
    Affair, The (1973)
    Gun and the Pulpit, The
        (1974)
    Hit Lady (1974)
    Remember When (1974)
    Stranger Who Looks Like Me,
        The (1974)
    Barbary Coast, The (1975)
    Fay (1976)
    Griffin and Phoenix (1976)
    I Want to Keep My Baby
        (1976)
    Mr. T and Tina (1976)
    Love Boat, The (1977)
    Loves Me, Loves Me Not
        (1977)
    Mulligan's Stew (1977)
    Soap (1977)
    Julie Farr, M.D. (1978)
    Three on a Date (1978)
    With This Ring (1978)
    Benson (1979)
    Christmas Lilies of the Field
        (1979)
    Sweepstakes (1979)
    Gift, The (1979)
    Seizure: The Story of Kathy
        Morris (1980)
    I'm a Big Girl Now (1980)
    It's a Living (1980)
    Trouble in High Timber
        Country (1980)
    Yeagers, The (1980)
    In Trouble (1981)
    Making a Living (1981)
    Private Benjamin (1981)
    Night at O'Rear's (1981)
    It Takes Two (1982)
    Side by Side: The True
        Story of the Osmond
        Family (1982)
    Condo (1983)
    Demon Murder Case, The
        (1983)

Just Married (1985)
Gidget's Summer Reunion
    (1985)
Moscow Bureau (1986)
One Big Family (1986)
Tough Cookies (1986)
Empty Nest (1988)

TIPTON, JEFFREY
    National Lampoon's Two
        Reelers (1981)

TISO, WAGNER
    He, the Dolphin (1987)
    Kiss Me a Lot (1987)

TITUS, HIRAM
    Christmas Carol, A (1982)

TOCCHI, GIAN LUCA
    I Will Give a Million (1937)

TODD, B.
    Young and the Restless, The
        (1973)

TODOROVSKIJ, PETR
    Front Romance, A (1984)

TOGASHI, MASAHIKO
    Tales from the Magino Village
        (1987)

TOLEDO, PAQUITO
    Magic Samurai, The (1969)

TOLLAND, GERRY
    Plumber, The (1980)

TOMARO, ROBERT
    Slime City (1988)

TOMASI, HENRI
    Man from the Niger, The
        (1940)

TOMASSI, SERGE
    Faüburg Saint-Martin (1986)

TOMITA, ISAO
    Hunger Canal (1964)
    Black Lizard (1960)

Prophecies of Nostradamus
(1975)
Demon Pond (1980)

TOMMASI, AMEDEO
Thomas and ... the Bewitched
(1970)
Off Season (1980)

TOP, YAVUZ
Enemy, The (1980)

TOPOLSKY, KEN
Thunder Alley (1985)

TORAK, FRED
Horses in Winter (1988)

TOROSSI, STEFANO
Shiver of Skin, A (1966)

TORQUE, HENRY
Mammame (1986)

TORRANCE, TIM
Perfect Match, The (1987)

TORRES, CARLOS
That Mad Mad Hospital
(1986)
Kill or Die (1987)
Shameless ... But Honorable
(1987)

TORRES, JAIME
Debt, The (1988)

TOTARI, GEORGE
Gaza Ghetto: Portrait of a
Palestinian Family,
1948-84 (1985)

"TOTO"
Dune (1984)

TOUSSAINT, ALLEN
Maid for Pleasure (1974)

TOWERS, MICHAEL
Simon and Simon (1982)

TOWNS, COLIN
Full Circle (1977)
Slayground (1984)
Shadey (1985)
Bellman and True (1987)
Born of Fire (1987)
Fear, The (1988)
Vampire's Kiss (1988)

TOY, HOLY
X (1986)

TOYO, GEOFFREY
Rembrandt (1936)

TOZER, SCHAUN
Is That It? (1985)
Ballet Black (1986)
Further and Particular (1988)

TRAMPETTI, PATRIZIO
Love of My Heart (1982)

TRAMPLER, WALTER
Of Stars and Men (1961)

TRANTOW, HERBERT
Cold Heart (Heart of Stone)
(1950)
Girls Behind Bars (1950)
Punktchen und Anton (1954)
Love Laughs at All (1957)
Until Money Departs You
(1960)

TREDE, GERHERD
Strange Places (1973)
Wild Wild World of Animals,
The (1973)

TREMBLAY, DOMINIQUE
Alfred Laliberte, Sculptor
(1987)

TREPANIER, GUY
Great Land of Small, The
(1987)
Tadpole and the Whale (1988)

"TRIO"
Mother's Meat and Freud's
Flesh (1984)

TRIPATHI, S. N.
  Naag Champag (1976)

"TRITONZ, THE"
  Edge of Hell, The (1987)

TROIANO, DOMENIC
  Night Heat (1985)
  Hot Shots (1986)
  Gunfighters, The (1987)

TROJAN, VACLAW
  Emperor's Nightingale, The
    (1951)

TROOST, ERNEST
  Sweet Revenge (1987)
  Dead Heat (1988)
  Tiger Warsaw (1988)

TROVAJOLI, ARMANDO
  White Slave Trade, The
    (1952)
  Girls Marked Danger (1954)
  18-Year-Olds (1956)
  Hercules' Pills (1960)
  Pleasures of Saturday Night
    (1960)
  Atom Age Vampire (1960)
  Grand Olympiade, The (1961)
  Hercules Against the Haunted
    World (1961)
  Mole Men vs. the Son of
    Hercules (1961)
  Planets Against Us (1961)
  Giant of Metropolis, The
    (1962)
  Monk of Monza, The (1963)
  America, God's Country
    (1966)
  Devil in Love, The (1966)
  Dynamite in the Pentagon
    (1966)
  Fate, The (1966)
  Great Coup of the 7 Golden
    Men, The (1966)
  Maigret in Pigalle (1966)
  Operation San Gennaro (1966)
  Our Husbands (1966)
  Spies Love Flowers (1966)
  Story of a Night, The (1966)

Terrace, The (1980)
Passion of Love (1981)
Shut Up When You Speak!
  (1981)
Orderly, The (1982)
Night of Varennes, The
  (1982)
Life Is Wonderful (1982)
Grand Hotel Excelsior (1982)
Ballad of Mamlouk, The
  (1982)
Count Tacchia (1983)
Mystere (1983)
Frankenstein 90 (1984)
Macaroni (1985)
Island, An (1986)
Family, The (1987)
Miss Arizona (1988)

TRUMAN, TIM
  Coming of Age (1988)

TRUNZO, JOE
  One Down Two to Go (1982)

TRYTELL, WILLIAM
  Lily of Kilarney (1934)
  Is Your Honeymoon Really
    Necessary? (1953)

TRZASKOWSKI, ANDRZEJ
  Creeps (1981)
  Star Wormwood, The (1988)

TRZCINSKI, WOJCIECH
  Woman and a Woman, A
    (1980)
  Scream, The (Krzyk) (1983)

TSANG, JOHNNY
  Mission Thunderbolt (1983)

TSANG, STEPHEN
  Ninja Thunderbolt (1985)

TSANGUARIS, GIORGOS
  Wrong Timing (1984)
  Caravan Palace (1986)
  Children of the Swallow,
    The (1987)

TSCHEDIN, MICHAEL
  Camp Wilderness (1980)

TSCHERBATCHOV, VLADIMIR
  Thunderstorm (1934)
  Peter the First (1937)
  Conquest of Peter the Great,
    The (1939)

TSFASMAN, A.
  Variety Stars (1955)

TSIBOULKA, KIRIL
  Truck, The (1981)

TSUKERMAN, SLAVA
  Liquid Sky (1982)

TSUKIMISATO, TAICHI
  Castle Orgies (1972)
  Temptation of the Collora
    (1972)

TSUMIKI, SO
  Mako, the Bad Girl (1971)

TSUNO, MORITSUNE
  Door (1988)

TSUSHIMA, TOSHIAKI
  Magic Serpent, The (1966)
  Grand Duel in Magic (1967)
  Sex Comedy, Quick on the
    Trigger (1971)
  Tokyo Bad Girls (1971)
  Lone Assassin, A (1972)
  Nun at Casino (1972)
  Killing Blows (1975)
  Operation Summit (1975)
  War in Space, The (1978)
  Earthquake Islands (1979)

TSUTSUI, HIROSHI
  Voltus V (1979)
  Superelectromagnetic Robot
    "Combatler V" (1982)

TSUTSUMI, KYOHEI
  Blue Jeans Memory (1982)

TSVETKUV, IGOR
  Love by Request (1983)

TUCCI, GIORGIO
  Zombie (1980)

TUCHINDA, SAHAT
  Kun Pi (1975)

TUCKER, JOHN
  Bedroom Eyes (1984)

TUDO, FEDERIGO MARTINEZ
  Spy Spying (1966)

TUDOR, WILLIAM-JOHN
  Passing, The (1985)

TULLIO, JIM
  Pink Nights (1985)

TULLY, COLIN
  Gregory's Girl (1982)

TUNC, OMNO
  Aah, Belinda! (1987)

TUNCER, GULSEN
  Cloth Doll (1988)

TUNG, CHANG
  Red Army's Bridge, The
    (1964)

TUNICK, JONATHAN
  Flying High (1978)
  America 2100 (1979)
  Rendezvous Hotel (1979)
  Swan Song (1980)
  Blinded by the Light (1980)
  Comedy of Horrors (1981)
  Fort Apache, the Bronx
    (1981)
  Endless Love (1981)
  I Am the Cheese (1983)
  Brotherly Love (1985)
  B.R.A.T. Patrol, The (1986)
  You Ruined My Life (1987)
  Tattinger's (1988)

TUR-EL, ALONA
  Real Game, The (1980)

TURINA, JOAQUIN
  Sister Unafraid (1954)

TURNER, SIMON FISHER
Caravaggio (1986)

TURRIN, JOSEPH
New Life, A (1988)

TUSQUES, FRANCOIS
Vampire Women, The (1967)
Royal Vacation (1980)
Eyes of the Birds (1983)

"TUXIDEMOON"
Field of Honor, The (1983)

TWAIN, ART
Gossip (1979)

TWARDOWSKI, ROMUALD
Angel of Fire (1985)

TYCHO, TOMMY
Frenchman's Farm (1987)
Young Einstein (1988)

TYGEL, DAVID
Man With the Black Coat,
The (1986)
Color of Destiny, The (1987)
Leila Diniz (1987)

TYRELL, STEVE
Midnight Crossing (1988)

UDELL, PETER
It's a Dog's World (1967)

UGOLINELLI, REMO
Immacolata and Concetta:
The Other Jealousy (1980)

UHER, BRUNO
I and My Wife (1953)

UHL, ALFRED
This Is China (1937)

UIGH, MIHALY
Autumn Almanac (1984)

UKAN, GYORGY
Housewarming, The (1984)

ULFIG, WALTER
Green Is the Heath (1935)
Pappi (1936)

ULFIK, RICK
Street Trash (1987)

ULRICH, KEITH
From Pole to Equator (1987)

ULRYCH, PETR
Sonata for a Redhead (1983)
Courageous Blacksmith, The
(1984)

UMILIANI, PIERO
Red Lips (1960)
Omicron (1963)
00-2 Secret Agents (1964)
Samson and the Mighty Chal-
lenge (1964)
Operation Poker (1965)
Stroke of a Thousand Million
(1966)
How to Steal the Crown of
England (1966)
Agent 3S3, Massacre of the
Sun (1966)
Black One, The (1966)
Coup of a Thousand Milliards,
A (1966)
Duel Over the World (1966)
It's a Long and Difficult
Summer, But ... What a
Night, My Dears (1966)
Jerry Land, Spy Hunter
(1966)
Operation Goldseven (1966)
Password: Kill Agent Gordon
(1966)
Secret (1966)
Technique for a Massacre
(1966)
Testadirapa (1966)
Two Men of the Mafia Against
Al Capone (1966)
Two Sanculotti, The (1966)
Two Sons of Ringo, The
(1966)
Rififi in Amsterdam (1967)
Goldface, the Fantastic

Superman (1967)
Chinese and Miniskirts (1968)
Witchcraft '70 (1969)
I Hate Blondes (1981)

UMNHOYOSHI, SHIGARU
And Then (1986)

UNDERWOOD, IAN
Fugitive from the Empire
(1981)

UNENGE, DAG
Blood Tracks (1986)

UNO, SEIICHIRO
Jack and the Witch (1967)
Madcap Island (1967)
Fables from Hans Christian
Andersen (1968)
Ali-Baba and the Forty
Thieves (1971)

URAYAMA, HIDEHIKO
To Sleep So As to Dream
(1986)

URBAN, MAX
Phantom of the Convent
(1934)
Mystery of the Pallid Face,
The (1935)
Blessed Rose, The (1937)

URBANIAK, MICHAEL
Astonished (1988)

URBONT, JACQUES
Video Vixens (Black Socks)
(1972)
Supercops (1975)
Littlest Hobo, The (1980)

URCHS, MARKUS
Morning in Alabama (German
Lawyer, A) (1984)

URETTA, ALICE
Chamber of Fear (1968)
House of Evil (1968)
Snake People, The (1968)

Incredible Invasion, The
(1971)

URIBE, ALEJANDRO see
BLANCO URIBE, ALEJANDRO

URIBE, FERNANDO
Crystalstone (1988)

URMUZESCU, PAUL
Wasps' Nest, The (1988)

USAI, REMO
Sin in the Vestry (1975)

USUELLI, TEO
Patriarchs of the Bible (1963)
Operation Atlantis (1965)
Fischio al Naso, Il (1966)
Rete Piena di Sabbia, Una
(1966)
Seventh Floor, The (1966)
Seed of Man, The (1970)

UTTAL, JAI
West Is West (1988)

UYTTEBROECK, PAUL
Petzi (1968)

UZAKI, RYUDO
Station (1982)
Tattoo (1982)
Miracle of Joe Petrel, The
(1984)
Nuclear Gypsies, The (1985)

VACEK, MILES
Word of a Cat, The (1960)

VAITHILAXMAN
Seventh Man, The (1983)

VALAZQUEZ, LEONARDO
Man with the Mandolin, The
(1985)
Childstealers (1987)

VALCARCEL, JORGE
Deal, The (1983)

VALDEZ, DANIEL
Zoot Suit (1981)

VALDEZ, DOMINIC
Magic Typewriter, The (1970)

VALERO, JEAN-LOUIS
Pauline at the Seaside (1983)
Summer (1986)
Four Adventures of Reinette
and Mirabelle (1987)
My Girl Friend's Boy Friend
(1987)

VALERY, FRANCOIS
Joy (1983)
Summer in Hell, A (1984)
Chicks, The (1985)

VALKEAPAA, NILS-ASLAK
Pathfinder (1987)

VALLI, ANTONIO
Holy Nun, The (1949)

VALLI, CELSO
Blood Ties (1986)
Quite by Chance (1988)

VALPOLA, HEIKKI
Flame Top (1981)
Big Blonde (Iso Valee)
(1983)

VALTKAYA, CENGIZ
Luggage of the Gods (1983)

VAN BRUGGE, PAUL MICHAEL
Love Is a Fat Woman (1987)

VAN CAMPEN, BERINGTON
In Dangerous Company (1988)

VAN DER HORST, HERMAN
Ardent Love (1960)

VAN DER KOOIJ, FRED
Noise Kill, The (1985)

VAN DER WURFF, ERIK
Splitting Up (1981)
Ciske the Rat (1984)

VAN DONSELAAR, ROB
Month Later, A (1987)

VAN ECHEREN, WILLEM
Day at the Beach, A (1984)

VAN GELDER, CHARLOTTE
Karkalou (1984)

VAN HALEN, EDWARD
Wild Life, The (1984)

VAN HEMERT, RUUD
Mama Is Mad! (1986)
Honeybunch (1988)

VAN HET GROENEWOUD,
RAYMOND
Brussels by Night (1983)
Crazy Love (1987)

VAN MECHELEN, CLOUS
White Delusion, The (1984)

VAN NOORD, ADRIAAN
Love Odyssey (1987)

VAN OTTERLOO, ROGIER
Flax Field, The (1983)
Outsider in Amsterdam (1983)
Good Hope, The (1986)

VAN PARYS, GEORGES
Mother Love (1938)
Advocate d'Amour (1938)
Escadrille of Change (1938)
My Foster Sister (1938)
Abused Confidence (1938)
Cafe de Paris (1938)
Cocoanut (1939)
Circumstantial Evidence
(1939)
Histoires Extraordinaires
(1950)
Lady Paname (1950)
Mr. Peek-a-Boo (1951)
Two Pennies Worth of Violets
(1951)
Grand Melies, Le (1952)

Jupiter (1952)
Belle Otero, La (1954)
Mam'selle Nitouche (1954)
Meeting in Paris (1956)
Man in the Raincoat, The
   (1957)
Charming Boys (1958)
Frantic (Double Deception)
   (1960)
Millionairess, The (1960)
Mr. Topaze (1961)

VAN ROOYEN, LAURENS
   Castle of Lust (1968)
   Succubus (1968)
   Kiss Me, Monster (1975)
   Woman Like Eve, A (1980)
   Dear Boys (1980)
   Flight of Whimbrels, A
      (1982)
   Burning Love (1983)

VAN T'HOFT, JASPER
   Put on Ice (1980)

VAN TIEGHEM, DAVID
   Working Girls (1986)

VAN WARMERDAM, VINCENT
   Abel (1986)

VANDER, MAURICE
   Break-In (1983)

VANGELIS
   Mother, Dearly Beloved (1980)
   Defiant Delta (1980)
   Chariots of Fire (1981)
   Missing (1982)
   Pablo Picasso (1982)
   Blade Runner (1982)
   Antarctica (1984)
   Bounty, The (1984)
   Wild and Beautiful (1985)

VANNELLI, ROSS
   Born to Race (1988)

VANNIER, JEAN-CLAUDE
   Night Beast (1983)
   Clean Loving Never Stays
      That Way for Long (1985)

VANSTON, JEFFREY
   Pink Nights (1985)

VARGA, MARIAN
   Another Love (1986)

VARGAS, ANTONIO PINHO
   Hard Times (1988)

VARKONYI, MATYAS
   Right Man for a Delicate
      Job, The (1985)

VARMAN, AJIT
   Cry of the Wounded (1981)
   Blood of Brothers (1986)

VARS, HENRY
   Love Maneuvers (1936)
   Happy Days (1937)
   Neighbors (Apartment Above)
      (1939)

VARTKES, BARONIJAN
   On the Road to Katanga
      (1987)

VASANTHA, E.
   Raja Nartakiya Rahasya
      (1977)

VASILE, PAOLO
   Squeeze, The (1980)

VASILENKO, S. N.
   Golden Riaga (1935)

VASILENKO, V.
   Golden Lake (1936)

VASSEGHI, ISMAIL
   Prince and the Fawn, The
      (1982)

VASSEUR, DIDIER
   Cathy's Curse (1980)
   Dogface (1985)

VAUGHAN, CLIFFORD
   Raven, The (1935)

VEALE, JOHN
  No Road Back (1957)
  Postmark for Danger (1956)
  Invisible Creature, The
    (1960)

VEITCH, TREVOR
  Dreams (1984)

VELARDE, MIKE
  Horror of the Blood Monsters
    (Creatures of the Prehis-
    toric Planet) (1970)

VELAZCO, EMIL
  Stallion Canyon (1949)

VELAZQUEZ, LEONARDO
  Mystery (1983)
  Trip to Paradise (1987)

VELOSO, CAETANO
  India, Daughter of the Sun
    (1982)
  Dede Mamata (1988)

VELOSO, RUI
  Skinny Chico (1983)
  Story of the Good Scoundrels,
    The (1984)

VENDITTI, ANTONELLO
  He's Too Much (1986)

VENKATESH, G. K.
  Naa Ninna Bidenu (1978)

VERDUN, HENRI
  Southern Bar (1938)
  Woman Thief, The (1938)
  Missing from St.-Agil
    (1938)
  Deserter, The (1939)
  I Accuse (1939)
  Inn of Sin, The (1950)
  Monsignor (1950)
  Napoleon Bonaparte (1955)
  Tower of Nesle, The (1955)

VERES, SANDOR
  Treasured Earth (1951)

VERETTI, ANTONIO
  Siege of the Alcazar (1941)
  Heaven Over the Marshes
    (1949)
  Three Forbidden Stories
    (1952)
  Devotion (1953)

VERHEES, EVERT
  One Woman or Two (1985)

VERMAN, AJIT
  Half-Truth (1984)

VERMEERSCH, PETER
  Silent Ocean, The (1984)

VERMEULEN, MATTHIJS
  Last Voyage, The (1988)

VERRACHIA, ALBERT
  Deborah (1974)

VERTAZARYAN, MARTYN
  To Love a Long Life (1980)

VERWOHLT, FINN
  Suzanne and Leonard (1984)

VESALA, EDWARD
  Tomorrow (1986)

VESEGHI, A.
  Suitors, The (1988)

VESTERGAARD, YORGEN
  Tomorrow It Is Over (1988)

"VESZI"
  End of the Miracle, The (1984)

VEZINA, PHILIP
  Memoirs (1985)

VIANELLO, EDOUARDO
  Taste of Sea, A (1983)

VICARI, CLEM
  Redeemer ... Son of Satan,
    The (1978)
  Mother's Day (1980)

VICENTE, JULINHO
  Ghost from Bahia, The (1984)

VICTOR, PATRICK
  Return to Eden (1983)

VIDOVSZKY, LASZLO
  Narcissus and Psyche (1981)
  Red Countess, The (1985)
  Last Manuscript, The (1987)

VIERU, ANATOL
  Return of the Banished,
    The (1980)

VIG, TOMMY
  Terror Circus (1973)
  Forced Entry (Last Victim,
    The) (1975)
  Sweet Sixteen (1981)
  Fistful of Chopsticks, A
    (1982)
  Kid With the Broken Halo,
    The (1982)

VIGH, MIHALY
  Eskimo Woman Feels Cold
    (1984)
  Damnation (1988)

VIGNES, MARIO GOMEZ
  Flesh of Your Flesh (1984)

VIKLICKY, EMIL
  Landscape with Furniture
    (1988)

VILAR, STEPHANE
  Last Song (1986)

VILDANOV, RUMIL
  Mirages of Love (1988)

VILLAMIL, JORGE
  Ambassador from India,
    The (1988)

VILLASEKA, RODRIGO
  Images of an Everyday
    War (1986)

VINCELLI, ANDRE
  20th Century Chocolate Cake,
    A (1983)

VINCENT, DON
  Night God Screamed, The
    (1971)
  Run, Stranger, Run (1973)
  Switch (1975)

VINCENT, PAUL
  Sprinter, The (1984)

VINCENT, ROLAND
  Strangler, The (1972)
  C'est La Vie! (That's Life)
    (1980)
  At the Top of the Stairs
    (1983)
  Fine Weather, But Storms
    Due Towards Evening
    (1986)
  I Hate Actors (1986)
  Rosa-the-Rose, Public Woman
    (1986)
  Summer on a Soft Slope (1987)
  Encore (1988)

VINCZE, IMRE
  Bondage (1968)

VINICIUS, MARCUS
  Next Victim, The (1984)
  Time of the Star, The (1985)

VINNIK, YURI
  How Young We Were Then
    (1986)

VIRTZBERG, ILAN
  Smile of the Lamb, The
    (1986)
  Himmo, King of Jerusalem
    (1987)

VISVANATHAN, M. S.
  Water Water (1982)

VITALE, LITO
  Hole in the Wall, The (1982)
  Diapason (1986)

VITIER, JOSE MARIA
  Red Dust (1982)
  Heart on the Land, The
    (1985)
  Very Old Man with Enormous
    Wings, A (1988)

VITIER, SERGIO
  Maluala (1980)
  Capablanca (1986)
  Placido (1986)

VIVES, RAMON
  Back to the Door (1959)

VIZKI, MORT
  Forever Friends (1987)

VIZZIELLO, CARLOS
  Supernatural (1981)
  Everybody Is Good (1982)
  Sahara (1985)
  I Need a Moustache (1986)

VLAD, ROMAN
  Behind the Barriers (1949)
  Demon in Art, The (1950)
  Walls of Malapaga (1950)
  Last Days of Pompeii, The
    (1950)
  Midsummer Holiday (1950)
  Three Steps North (1951)
  Tragic Spell (1952)
  Pictura (1952)
  I Chose Love (1953)
  Women of Destiny (1953)
  Monsieur Ripois (1954)
  Pepote (1956)
  Devil's Commandment, The
    (1956)
  Vampires, The (1957)
  Dreams in a Drawer (1957)
  Paradise on Earth (1957)
  Challenge, The (1958)
  Caltiki, the Immortal
    Monster (1959)
  Mystery of Three Continents,
    The (1959)
  Hell in the City (1959)
  Where the Hot Wind Blows
    (1960)

Girl in the Window (1961)
Horrible Dr. Hitchcock, The
  (1962)
Hypnosis (1962)
Ghost, The (1963)

VOIGT, WOLFGANG
  Island on the Lake, The
    (1980)

VOLTZ, GERNOT
  Dorado--One Way (1984)

VOMVOLOS, COSTAS
  Doxobus (1987)

VON BUDAY, DENES see
  BUDAY, DENES

VON DALLWITZ, BURKHART
  Bachelor Girl (1987)

VON EICHWALD, HAKAN
  Woman in White (1949)
  Girls in Tails (1957)

VON FEILITZSCH, KARL
  Krammer, The (1959)

VON GROTHE, FRANZ
  Abduction (1936)

VON SLATINA, ALEXANDER
  Three Men in the Snow
    (1955)

VONWILLER, ADRIAN
  Black and Without Sugar
    (1986)

VOSS, BERNHARD
  Transit Dreams (1986)
  Stadtrand (1987)

VRANJESEVIC, BRANCA
  Picnic Among the Poplars
    (1981)

VRANJESEVIC BROTHERS
  (MLADEN AND PREDRAG)
  Just Once More (1983)

End of the War, The (1985)
Oktoberfest (1987)
Magpie's Strategy, The
(1987)

VRIENTEN, HENNY
Prey, The (1985)
In the Shadow of Victory
(1986)
Vanishing, The (1988)

VRONTOS, H. S.
Showdown (1982)

VUH, POPOL see "POPOL
VUH"

VUJICSIES, TIHAMER
Girl Who Danced into Life,
The (1964)

VUKAN, GYORGY
Balint Fabian Meets God
(1980)
Temporary Paradise (1981)
Day Before Yesterday, The
(1982)
Oh, Bloody Life! ... (1984)
Mr. Clock (1985)
Banana Skin Waltz (1987)
Dead Ball, The (1987)
Train to Holland (1987)
Hanussen (1988)

VYAS, GAURANG
Folk Tale, A (1981)

VYAS, SHANKAR RAO
Lav Kush (1951)
Ganga Malya (1953)

WADA, HIROSHI
I Go to Tokyo (1986)

WADSWORTH, DEREK
Space: 1999 (1975)
Day After Tomorrow, The
(1975)

WAGERINGEL, BERNHARD
Luther Is Dead (1984)

WAGNER, KAREL
Shoe Called Melichar, A
(1984)

WAGNER, OSKAR
Trip to the Moon, A (1959)

WAGNER, REINHARDT
Coverup (Crime, La) (1983)

WAGNER, ROGER
Outer Space Connection, The
(1975)

WAHEB, MOHAMMED ABDEL
What Will We Do on Sunday?
(1984)

WAHLBERG, ULF
About Love (1986)

WAITS, TOM
One from the Heart (1982)
Streetwise (1985)
Where To Go? (1988)

WAITZMAN, ADOLFO
Unknown Hour, The (1964)

WAKEMAN, RICK
Burning, The (1981)
She (1982)
G'Ole (1983)
Crimes of Passion (1984)
Creepshow 2 (1987)

WAKEMIYA, SADAI
Nitakayama Nobre (1968)

WAKS, NATHAN
Kangaroo (1986)
Twelfth Night (1986)

WALACINSKI, ADAM
Zamach (Partisan Prison)
(1959)
Plunderers of the Moon
(1962)

WAL-BERG
Katia (1938)

Affair Lafont, The (1939)
French Way, The (1952)

WALDEN, CHARLES
Mighty Gorga, The (1970)

WALDEN, STANLEY
Desperado City (1981)

WALDEN, W. G. SNUFFY
Wonder Years, The (1988)

WALDIMIR, SUNE
Youth of Today (1936)
Girl from the Dress Circle,
The (1949)
Girl from Jungfrusund (1950)

WALDMAN, JACK
Marriage, A (1983)

WALKER, BILL
Catcher, The (1972)
Bog (1978)

WALKER, DON
Freedom (1982)

WALKER, KENNETH
Alien Factor, The (1976)

WALKER, SHIRLEY
Tucker's Witch (1982)
Touched (1983)
Ghoulies (1985)
Dungeonmaster, The (1985)

WALKER, SIMON
Run, Rebecca, Run! (1982)
Wild Duck, The (1983)
Annie's Coming Out (1984)

WALLACE, OLIVER
Ben and Me (1953)

WALLACE, ROB
Child, The (Kill and Go
Hide) (1977)

WALLACK, JUNE
Larose, Pierrot et al Luce
(1983)

WALLER, BERT
These Dangerous Years (1957)

WALLIN, BENGT ANRE
Bat Winter (1988)

WALLIN, PETER
Visitor, The (1988)

WALSH, BOB (ROB)
My Therapist (1982)
Bugs Bunny's Third Movie:
1001 Rabbit Tales (1982)
Revenge of the Ninja (1983)
Dungeons and Dragons (1983)
My Little Pony (1986)

WALSH, JOE
Fast Times at Ridgemont
High (1982)

WALTER, GEORGE
Dangerous Secrets (1938)

WALTON, BRYN
Secret Rites (1971)

WANCHUM, SHI
Girl of Good Family, A (1986)
Two Virtuous Women (1988)

WANG, EDDIE
Convict Killer, The (1980)
Clan of the White Lotus
(1980)
Two Champions of Shaolin
(1980)
Rebel Intruders, The (1980)
Legend of the Fox (1980)
Lost Souls (1980)
Boxer from the Temple, The
(1980)
My Young Auntie (1981)

WANG, PATRICIO
Cannot Run Away (1988)

WANNBERG, KEN
Great American Beauty Con-
test, The (1973)
Amateur, The (1982)
Mother Lode (1982)

Losin' It (1983)
Of Unknown Origin (1983)
Blame It on Rio (1984)
Draw! (1984)
Miles to Go (1986)
Vanishing Act (1986)
Red River (1988)

WARD, JOSEPH
Lost Empires (1986)

WARMAN, CARLOS
Mariana, Mariana (1987)

WARNE, DEREK
Killer's Moon (1978)

WARR, TERRY
House That Vanished, The
(1974)

WARREN, MICHAEL
Dallas (1978)

WARREN, RICHARD LEWIS
Rhoda (1974)
Dallas (1978)
Remington Steele (1979)
Cover-Up (1984)
Carly's Web (1987)
Shell Game (1987)

WATANABE, CHUMEI
100 Monsters (1968)
Haunted Castle, The (1969)
Giant Iron Man 1-7--The
Ariel Battleship (1977)

WATANABE, HIROAKI
Alone With Ghosts (1964)

WATANABE, MICHIAKI
When the Skin Burns (1966)

WATANABE, SOICHIRO
Tower of the Lilies (1982)

WATANABE, TAKEO
Crimson Bat-Oichi: Wanted,
Dead or Alive (1970)
Live My Share, Mother (1971)

WATTS, TOMMY
Night We Got the Bird, The
(1961)

WAX, STEVE
Tough Enough (1983)

WAXMAN, FRANZ
Liliom (1934)
Bride of Frankenstein, The
(1935)
Love and Kisses--Veronica
(1936)
Brighton Strangler, The
(1945)
King of the Roaring Twenties
(1961)
Longest Hundred Miles, The
(1967)

WAYNE, HAYDEN
Tainted (1985)

WAYNE, JEFF
McVicar (1980)

WAYNE, PAUL
Love and Learn (1979)

WE, OU
Come Back Swallow (1981)

WEBB, JIMMY
Last Unicorn, The (1982)
E/R (1984)
Hanoi Hilton, The (1987)

WEBB, ROGER
Burke and Hare (1971)
Strange Report, The (1971)
Bedtime with Rosie (1974)
Miss Jones and Son (1977)
Godsend, The (1980)
Death of a Centerfold: The
Dorothy Stratten Story
(1981)
George and Mildred (1984)
Boy in Blue, The (1986)

WEBB, ROY
Clash by Night (1952)
River Changes, The (1956)

WEBB, SIMON
    Playing Away (1986)

WEBBER, HAMILTON
    Tall Timbers (1937)
    Let George Do It (1938)
    Mr. Chedworth Steps Out
        (1939)

WEBER, EBERHARD
    Red Stocking, The (1980)
    Strawberry Fields (1985)

WEBER, JOE
    Great Wallendas, The (1978)

WECHTER, JULIUS
    Midnight Madness (1980)

WECK, URSULA
    Zechmeister (1981)

WECKER, KONSTANTIN
    White Rose, The (1982)
    Peppermint Peace (1983)
    Gasping (1984)
    Voyager (1984)
    Martha Dubrinski (1985)

WEGENER, SIEGFRIED
    Blazing Sand (1960)

WEHLE, PETER
    Cuckoo's Egg, The (1959)

WEILL, LARRY & TOM
    Day My Kid Went Punk, The
        (1987)

WEINBERG, FRED
    Violins Came With the
        Americans, The (1987)

WEINBERG, MOISSEJ
    Donkey Skin (1985)

WEINER, JEAN
    Bandera, La (1935)
    Maria Chapdeleine (1935)
    Man of the Hour (1940)
    Appointment with Life (1949)

Living Corpse, The (1950)
No More Vacation for the
    Good Lord (1950)

WEINSTEIN, SHALOM
    Tel Aviv-Berlin (1987)

WEISS, JOSEPH
    Gideon's Trumpet (1980)
    My Husband Is Missing (1978)

WEISS, LARRY
    Me and Ducky (1979)

WELCH, ED
    Shillinbury Blowers, The
        (1980)
    Dangerous Davies--The Last
        Detective (1981)
    Out of the Darkness (1985)

WELCH, KEN AND MITZI
    Movers & Shakers (1985)

WELLER, PAUL
    Business as Usual (1987)

WELLINGTON, LARRY
    2,000 Maniacs (1964)
    How to Make a Doll (1967)
    Wizard of Gore, The (1971)

WELLMAN, MARITA M.
    No Dead Heroes (1987)

WELLS, DANNY
    Never Say Never (1979)

WELLS, JOSEPH
    My Husband Is Missing (1978)

WELLS, TOM
    Kallikaks, The (1977)
    WKRP in Cincinnati (1978)
    Semi-Tough (1980)
    Open All Night (1981)
    Cass Malloy (1982)
    Buffalo Bill (1983)
    Sitcom (1983)
    There Goes the Neighborhood
        (1983)

We Got It Made (1983)
Duck Factory, The (1984)

WEMBA, PAPA
Life Is Rosy (1987)

WENGLER, MARCEL
Stammheim (1986)

WENJING, GUO
Chess King (1988)

WENNELS, FRITZ
Lost Valley (1936)

WENZEL, HANS JURGEN
I Dreamed of My Elk (1987)

WERESKY, MARTY
Mystery Mansion (1983)

WERLE, LARS JOHAN
Hour of the Wolf (1968)

WERNER, FRED
Eight Is Enough (1977)
Fitzpatricks, The (1977)
MacKenzies of Paradise Cove,
The (1979)
Sweepstakes (1979)
Death of Ocean View Park,
The (1979)
Flo (1980)
Small Killing, A (1981)

WERNLE, CORNELIUS
Schilten (1980)
Nest Break (1980)

WERZLAUD, JOACHIM
Sun Searchers, The (1986)

WESS, RICHARD
I Dream of Jeannie (1965)

"WEST BLOCK"
Windy Places: Torn Apart
(1983)

WESTBROOK, MIKE
Caught on a Train (1980)

Caught in a Web: L'Impasse
(1987)

WESTHEIMER, PETER
Kadaicha (1988)
Out of the Body (1988)

WESTPHAL, LONZO
Boran--Time to Aim (1987)

WETHERWAX, MICHAEL
Sorority House Massacre
(1987)

WHEATLEY, DAVID
Herndon and Me (1983)
At Your Service (1984)
Women's Club, The (1987)

WHEATON, JACK W.
Penitentiary II (1982)

WHEELER, CHERYL
Mickey & Nora (1987)

WHEELER, HAROLD
Benny's Place (1982)
Gift of Amazing Grace, The
(1986)

WHELAN, BILL
At the Cinema Palace--Liam
O'Leary (1983)

WHIBLEY, BURNELL
Virgin Witch, The (1970)

WHITE, DANIEL J.
Wedding in Monaco, The
(1956)
Hand of a Dead Man (1963)
Diabolical Dr. Z, The (1965)
Dr. Mabuse (1971)
Bare-Breasted Countess,
The (1975)
Kiss and Kill (1968)
Carrousel Boreal (1959)

WHITE, JACK
Voyage of the Rock Aliens
(1988)

WHITE, RICK
  Paradise Motel (1985)

WHITELAW, REID
  Nocturne (1975)

WHITFIELD, TED
  Blame It on the Night (1984)

WHITLEY, LARRY
  Snowballing (1987)

WHITSETT, CARSON
  Wonder Woman (1973)
  Stuckey's Last Stand (1980)

WHITTAKER, DAVID
  Dominique (1978)
  Sword and the Sorcerer,
    The (1982)

WIDELITZ, STACY
  Stranded (1987)

WIENER, ELISABETH
  Cap Canaille (1983)

WIENER, JEAN
  Maria Chapdelaine (1935)
  Dr. Knock (1937)
  Lower Depths, The (1937)
  Slipper Episode (1938)
  Future Stars (1955)
  Garconne, La (1957)
  Stars Never Die (1957)
  Golem, Le (1966)
  From Somalia with Love (1984)

WILCZYNSKI, MAREK
  Planet "Tailor," The (1983)

WILEN, BARNEY
  Kiss and Kill (1968)

WILHELM, JOHN
  Axe (Lisa, Lisa) (1983)

WILHELM, ROLF ALEXANDER
  08/15 at Home (1956)
  Heritage of Bjoerndal (1960)
  Kreimhild's Revenge (1965)

Siegfried (1965)
From the Life of the Marion-
  ettes (1980)
Wonderful Years, The (1980)
Doktor Faustus (1982)
Odipussi (1988)

WILK, SCOTT
  City Girl, The (1984)
  Plain Clothes (1988)

WILKINS, DON
  Mission Hill (1982)
  First Killing Frost, The
    (1987)

WILKINS, GEORGE
  Black Market Baby (1977)

WILKINS, RICK
  Changeling, The (1980)

WILKINSON, ARTHUR
  Travellers Joy (1951)

WILKINSON, CHARLES
  My Kind of Town (1984)

WILKINSON, MARC
  Man and the Snake, The
    (1972)
  Return, The (1973)
  Quatermass Conclusion (1980)
  Fiendish Plot of Dr. Fu
    Manchu, The (1980)
  Kim (1984)
  Visitors (1987)

WILLEMETZ, BETTY
  Abel Gance and His
    Napoleon (1984)

WILLIAMS, CHARLES
  Terror House (1943)
  Romantic Age, The (1949)
  Flesh and Blood (1951)

WILLIAMS, EDWARD
  Unearthly Stranger, The
    (1963)

WILLIAMS, GRACE
  Blue Scar (1988)

WILLIAMS, GRAHAM
  Boy Soldier (1986)

WILLIAMS, JACK ERIC
  Nightmare (1981)

WILLIAMS, JEFF
  Sex Symbol, The (1974)

WILLIAMS, JOHN
  Gilligan's Island (1964)
  Heidi (1968)
  Land of the Giants (1968)
  Jane Eyre (1971)
  Screaming Woman, The
    (1972)
  Cowboys, The (1974)
  Empire Strikes Back, The
    (1980)
  Raiders of the Lost Ark (1981)
  Heartbeeps (1981)
  E.T., The Extra-
    Terrestrial (1982)
  Monsignor (1982)
  Return of the Jedi (1983)
  Superman III (1983)
  Indiana Jones and the Temple
    of Doom (1984)
  River, The (1984)
  Heroes and Sidekicks--
    Indiana Jones and the
    Temple of Doom (1984)
  Amazing Stories (1985)
  Space Camp (1986)
  Empire of the Sun (1987)
  Superman IV: The Quest
    for Peace (1987)
  Witches of Eastwick, The
    (1987)
  Accidental Tourist, The
    (1988)

WILLIAMS, PATRICK (PAT)
  Headmaster (1970)
  Mary Tyler Moore Show, The
    (1970)
  San Francisco International
    Airport (1970)

  Failing of Raymond, The (1971)
  Funny Face (1971)
  Incident in San Francisco
    (1971)
  Lock, Stock and Barrel
    (1971)
  Terror in the Sky (1971)
  Travis Logan, D.A. (1971)
  Bob Newhart Show, The
    (1972)
  Moonchild (1972)
  Hardcase (1972)
  Sandy Duncan Show, The
    (1972)
  Short Walk to Daylight (1972)
  Streets of San Francisco,
    The (1972)
  Hitched (1973)
  Magician, The (1973)
  Ordeal (1973)
  Time for Love, A (1973)
  Topper Returns (1973)
  Friends and Lovers (1974)
  Mrs. Sundance (1974)
  Murder or Mercy (1974)
  Hex (1975)
  Crossfire (1975)
  Doc (1975)
  Lives of Jenny Dolan, The
    (1975)
  Stowaway to the Moon (1975)
  Ace (1976)
  Bert D'Angelo/Superstar
    (1976)
  Don't Call Us (1976)
  Good Heavens (1976)
  Most Wanted (1976)
  Tony Randall Show, The
    (1976)
  Andros Targets, The (1977)
  Stonestreet: Who Killed the
    Centerfold Model? (1977)
  Chopped Liver Brothers, The
    (1977)
  Lou Grant (1977)
  Man With the Power, The
    (1977)
  Escapade (1978)
  Many Loves of Arthur, The
    (1978)
  Last Resort, The (1979)
  Man Called Sloane, A (1979)

Muppet Movie, The (1979)
Mother and Me, M.D. (1979)
Hero at Large (1980)
Wholly Moses! (1980)
Used Cars (1980)
It's My Turn (1980)
Princess and the Cabbie, The
    (1981)
Maggie (1981)
Stephanie (1981)
Miracle of Kathy Miller, The
    (1981)
Two of Us, The (1981)
Charlie Chan and the Curse
    of the Dragon Queen (1981)
Devlin Connection, The (1982)
Family in Blue (1982)
In Security (1982)
James Boys, The (1982)
Some Kind of Hero (1982)
Moonlight (1982)
Best Little Whorehouse in
    Texas, The (1982)
Tomorrow's Child (1982)
Toy, The (1982)
Girl's Life, A (1983)
Mr. Smith (1983)
Marvin and Tige (1983)
Fighter, The (1983)
Two of a Kind (1984)
Buddy System, The (1984)
Down Home (1984)
Empire (1984)
Swing Shift (1984)
All of Me (1984)
Best Defense (1984)
Suzanne Pleshette Is Maggie
    Briggs (1984)
Walter (1984)
Slugger's Wife, The (1985)
Seduced (1985)
Fathers and Sons (1985)
Faculty, The (1986)
Heart of the City (1986)
Just Between Friends (1986)
Oceans of Fire (1986)
Violets Are Blue (1986)
Barrington (1987)
Days and Nights of Molly
    Dodd, The (1987)
Mr. President (1987)
Reno and Yolanda (1987)

Double Standard (1988)
Eisenhower & Lutz (1988)
Fresh Horses (1988)
Maybe Baby (1988)

WILLIAMS, PAUL
    Boy in the Plastic Bubble,
        The (1976)
    McLean Stevenson Show,
        The (1976)
    Anna and the King (1978)
    Sparrow (1978)
    Another Day (1978)

WILLIAMSON, LAMBERT
    Don't Ever Leave Me (1949)
    Green Grow the Rushes
        (1951)
    Cosh Boy (1953)
    Forbidden Cargo (1954)

WILLIAMSON, MALCOLM
    Nothing But the Night (1975)

WILSON, ANDREW THOMAS
    Chain Reaction (1980)

WILSON, ART
    High Five (1982)

WILSON, DENNIS
    Fawlty Towers (1977)

WILSON, GERALD
    My Buddy (1979)

WILSON, MORTON
    Scarecrow, The (1982)

WILSON, PHILIP
    Clarence and Angel (1980)

WILSON, STANLEY
    Radar Patrol vs. Spy King
        (1949)
    King of the Rocket Men
        (1949)
    Invisible Monster, The (1950)
    Dragnet (1951)
    Radar Men of the Moon
        (1951)

Zombies of the Stratosphere
(1952)
Love Slaves of the Amazon
(1957)
Hanged Man, The (1964)
Name of the Game, The (1968)
Sunshine Patriot, The (1968)
Deadlock (1969)
Trial Run (1969)
Movie Murderer, The (1970)
Paris 7000 (1970)

WINANS, SAM
Enemy Territory (1987)
Party Line (1988)

WINDING, KASPAR
Flying Devils, The (1985)

WINDT, HERBERT
Fahrmann Maria (1935)
Sharpshooter Bruggler (1936)
Flight of the Tertia (1953)
Inferno (1959)

WING-FAI, LO (LAW)
Boat People (1982)
Women (1985)

WINWOOD, STEVE
They Call That an Accident
(1982)

WIREN, DAG
Only a Mother (1950)
Korkarlen (1959)

WIRTH, ROBERT
Silver Spoons (1982)

WIRTZBERG, ILAN
Beyond the Walls (1984)

WISNIAK, ALAIN
Joy (1983)
Public Woman, The (1984)
Black List (1984)
Year of the Medusa (1984)

WISSMANN, FRIEDBERT
Interrogation of the
Witness (1987)

WITKIN, BEATRICE
Wild Wild World of Animals,
The (1973)

WITTSTADT, HANS
Taxi to the Loo (1981)
Our Bodies Are Still Alive
(1981)
What Now, Little Man? (1982)

WITTWER, STEPHAN
Right Way, The (1983)
Flies in the Light (1986)

WOHL, STEFAN
Ghost Hunter, The (1975)

WOLFE, TOM
Ritual (1984)

WOLFF, ALBERT
Itto (1935)
Tender Enemy (1936)

WOLFF, FRANK
Blind Spot (1981)
It Is Cold in Brandenburg--
Kill Hitler (1981)
Martin Niemoeller (1985)

WOLFF, JONATHAN
Charmings, The (1987)

WOLFF, LARRY
Joshua and the Blob (1972)

WOLFSON, SETVEN
Summer (1984)

WOLGERS, TOM
Fairytale Country, The
(1988)

WOLINSKI, HAWK
Wildcats (1986)

WOLL, BJOERN
Rendezvous with Forgotten
Years (1957)

WOLMAN, AMMON
Hide 'n' Seek (1980)

WONG, JAMES
   Peking Opera Blues (1986)
   Chinese Ghost Story, A (1987)

WOOD, J.
   Young and the Restless, The
    (1973)

WOOD, JEFFREY
   Gunpowder (1987)
   Mind Killer (1987)

WOODHEAD, DAVID
   No Sad Songs (1985)

WOOLDRIDGE, JOHN
   Paper Gallows (1950)
   Blackmailed (1951)
   RX Murder (Family Doctor)
    (1958)

WOOLFENDEN, GUY
   Secrets (1984)

WORONTSCHAK, GEORGE
   Snow, the Movie (1984)

WORRALL, TOM
   Wild Women of Chastity
    Gulch, The (1982)
   Herbie, the Love Bug (1982)
   Tales of the Apple Dumpling
    Gang (1982)

WORTH, FRANK
   Bride of the Monster (1955)

WORTH, JODY TAYLOR
   Up the Academy (1980)

WORTH, PAUL
   King Midas Jr. (1942)
   Imagination (1943)

WORTH, STAN
   George of the Jungle (1967)
   Dudley Do-Right Show,
    The (1969)

WOUT, ERIK VAN'T
   Cool Lakes of Death, The
    (1982)

WOZNICKI, PAUL
   Fiend (1981)

WRIGHT, CLIVE
   South of Reno (1987)

WRIGHT, GARY
   Endangered Species (1982)

WRIGHT, GEOFFREY
   Ships With Wings (1942)
   Behind the Mask (1958)

WRIGHT, RAYBURN
   Christ Is Born (1967)

WRIGHT, ROBB
   Welcome to the Parade (1986)

WU, DAVID
   Heartbeat 1000 (1987)

WYATT, ROBERT
   Animals Film, The (1981)

WYKES, DENISE
   Front Line (1981)

WYKES, ROBERT
   Time of the West (1967)
   Monument to the Dream (1968)
   Quality and Promise (1968)

WYLE, GEORGE
   Living in Paradise (1981)
   Scamps (1982)

WYMAN, BILL
   Green Ice (1981)
   Digital Dreams (1983)

WYMAN, DAN
   Return, The (1980)
   Without Warning (1980)
   Hell Night (1981)

WYOMING-BENDER, PETE
   Wolf's Bride, The (1985)

XARHACOS, STAVROS
   Rebetico (1983)
   Sweet Country (1987)

XAVIER, LUIZ HENRIQUE
Happy Old Year (1988)

XIAOYUAN, ZHAO
Swan Song (1986)

XIASONG, QU (XIXIAN, QU)
Rickshaw Boy (1983)
Sacrifice of Youth (1986)
Big Parade, The (1987)
King of the Children (1988)

YAGI, MASAO
Drifting Avenger (1969)
Industrial Spy (1969)
Night Guy (1969)
Kamikaze Cop, A (1970)
Kamikaze Cop, The Poison
  Gas Affair (1971)
Duel at the Cape Shiretoko
  (1971)
Kamikaze Cop, Marihuana
  Syndicate (1971)
Kamikaze Cop, No Epitaph
  to Us (1971)
Legend of Dinosaurs and
  Monster Birds (1977)
Funny Note (1978)

YAMADA, KOSAKU
New Earth, The (1937)

YAMAGUCHI, TADASHI
Return of the Giant Monsters,
  The (1967)

"YAMAHA" see KAWAKAMI,
  GEN-ICHI

YAMAKAWA, SHIGERU
Forward, God's Army (1987)

YAMAMOTO, HOZAN
Samurai Reincarnation (1982)

YAMAMOTO, KIMINARI
Empire of Punks (1981)

YAMAMOTO, NAOZUMI
Computer Free-for-All (1969)
Gangster VIP (1969)
Return of the Filthy Seven

(1969)
Space Giants, The (1969)
Treasure Island (1971)
Tora-san, the Good Samaritan
  (1971)
Tora-san's Love Call (1972)
Tora-san's Dream Come True
  (1973)
Tora-san Loves an Artist
  (1974)
Three Old Women (1975)
Tora-san's Rise and Fall
  (1976)
Tora-san's Sunrise and Sunset
  (1977)
Mysterious Big Tactics (1978)
Tora-san Meets His Lordship
  (1978)
Tale of Africa, A (1981)
Imperial Japanese Empire,
  The (1982)
Tradition in the World of
  Spirit, A (1982)
Burmese Harp, The (1985)
Final Take: The Golden
  Days of the Movies (1986)

YAMANI, GARY
Liar's Dice (1980)

YAMASHITA, STOMU
Man Who Fell to Earth, The
  (1976)
Tempest (1982)

YAMASHITA, TAKEO
Ballad of Death (1971)
Boss with the Samurai Spirit,
  A (1971)
Gamblers in Okinawa (1971)
Lute of the Blind Monks of
  Satsuma, The (1985)

YAMASHITA, YOSUKE
Kidnapping Blues (1982)

YAMAUCHI, TADASHI
Sex Check, The (1969)
Hot Little Girl, The (1971)

YAMAZAKI, HAKO
Gate of Youth, The (1982)

YAN, GE
   Legend of Tianyun Mountain
      (1983)
   Hibiscus Town (1988)

YAN, WONG TSE
   Aililia (1975)

YAN-XI, LIU
   Our Aunt Tao (1983)

YANCHENKO, OLEG
   Go and See (1985)

YANG, EDWARD
   Summer at Grandpa's, A
      (1985)
   Taipei Story, The (1985)

YANNE, JEAN
   Quarter to Two Before Jesus
      Christ, A (1982)
   Liberty, Equality, Sauer-
      kraut (1985)

"YANNI"
   Heart of Midnight (1988)

YANNIDES, J.
   Girl Refugee, The (1938)

YANNOULATOS, GEORGE
   Trial of Junta, The (1981)

YARED, GABRIEL
   Everyone for Himself in Life
      (1980)
   Malevil (1981)
   Invitation to a Trip (1982)
   Little Wars (1982)
   Moon in the Gutter, The
      (1983)
   Sarah (1983)
   Shadow Dance (1983)
   Hannah K. (1983)
   Lucie Sur Seine (1983)
   Scarlet Fever (1984)
   Fire on Sight (1984)
   Nemo (Dream One) (1984)
   Telephone Always Rings
      Twice, The (1985)

Dangerous Moves (1985)
Adieu, Bonaparte (1985)
Scout Forever, A (1985)
Betty Blue (1986)
Certain Desire, A (1986)
Disorder (1986)
Red Zone (1986)
Beyond Therapy (1987)
Light Years (1987)
Testament of a Murdered
   Jewish Poet, The (1987)
Trouble Agent (1987)
Veiled Man, The (1987)
Camille Claudel (1988)
Clean and Sober (1988)
Night at the National
   Assembly, A (1988)
Seasons of Pleasure, The
   (1988)

YARMOLINSKY, BENJAMIN
   44 or Tales of the Night
      (1985)

YARROW, PETER
   Willmar 8, The (1981)

YATOVE, JEAN
   Jour de Fete (1949)
   Bonjour Paris (1953)

YAU, HERMAN
   Reunion (1987)

YEE, LAM MUN
   Family, The (1986)

"YELLO"
   Black Spider, The (1983)

YEN, K. S.
   Sable Cicada (1942)

YEN-SI, CHEN
   New Year's Sacrifice (1957)

YERMATOV, T.
   Sky of Our Childhood, The
      (1967)

YI, LIN MIN
   Pale Passion (1984)

YIANNIDE, COSTA
  Last Mission, The (1952)

YODA, NOBORU
  She Beasts' Warm Bodies
    (1972)

YOKOTA, TOSHIAKI
  Ghost Festival at Saint's
    Village (1979)
  Farewell, Beloved Land
    (1982)

YOKOUCHI, SHOJI
  Final Winner?, The (1969)

YOKOYAMA, SEIJI
  Space Fantasy Emeraldus
    (1978)
  Space Pirate Captain Harlock
    (1978)
  Tomb of Dracula (1980)
  Future War 198X (1982)

"YOLLO"
  Schmutz (1986)

YON-JOO, CHONG
  Eunuchs (1987)

YONG, HAN
  Stand-In, The (1987)

YOSHIDA, SATORU
  Gondola (1987)

YOSHIDA, TAKURO
  Journey into Solitude (1973)

YOUFU, XU
  On a River Without Navigation
    Marks (1984)
  Wild Mountains (1986)
  Old Well, The (1987)

YOUNG, BOB
  Hands of Cormac Joyce,
    The (1972)
  Lady, Stay Dead (1982)
  Dot and Santa Claus (1982)
  Dot and the Bunny (1983)
  Camel Boy, The (1984)

Brothers (1984)
Dot and the Koala (1985)

YOUNG, CHRIS (CHRISTOPHER)
  Pranks (1982)
  Def-Con 4 (1983)
  Oasis, The (1984)
  Power, The (1984)
  Avenging Angel (1985)
  Desert Warrior (1985)
  Nightmare on Elm Street,
    Part 2: Freddy's Revenge,
    A (1985)
  Barbarian Queen (1985)
  Getting Even (1986)
  Invaders from Mars (1986)
  Torment (1986)
  Trick or Treat (1986)
  American Harvest (1987)
  Flowers in the Attic (1987)
  Hellraiser (1987)
  Bat 21 (1988)
  Haunted Summer (1988)
  Hellbound: Hellraiser II
    (1988)
  Telephone, The (1988)

YOUNG, DANNY
  Ninja Mission, The (1984)

YOUNG, MARL
  Here's Lucy (1968)

YOUNG, NEIL
  Where the Buffalo Roam (1980)

YOUNG, PAUL M.
  Kamikaze Hearts (1986)

YOUNG, VICTOR
  Gun Crazy (Deadly Is the
    Female) (1949)

YOUNOUS, HAJ
  Nightmare (1985)

YU, CHAN YANG
  Black Magic II (1977)

YU, LO TA
  Cabaret Tears (1983)

YUAN, CHEN CHI
Last Night of Madam Chin,
The (1984)

YUAN, TSO HONG
Spring in Autumn (1982)

YUASSA, JOHJI (YUASA, JOJI)
Island of the Evil Spirit
(1981)
Funeral, The (1985)

YUN-CHU, CHONG
Wheel, The (1984)

YUTHAWORN, VIRAT
Teenaged Girl (1983)

ZABKA, STAN
Turn the Key Softly (1959)

ZACCARO, MARIO VALERIO
Asa Branca--A Brazilian
Dream (1988)

ZADEJA, CESK
Skanderbeg (1954)

ZADOR, EUGENE
Florian (1940)
Gallant Sons (1940)
More About Nostradamus
(1940)
Mortal Storm, The (1940)

ZAFRED, MARIO
Girls of San Frediano, The
(1955)
Young Husbands (1958)

ZAHARIAN, HAJG
Taulant Wants a Sister
(1985)

ZAHLER, GORDON
Night of the Ghouls (1959)
First Spaceship on Venus,
The (1959)
Shock Corridor (1963)
Navy vs. the Night Monsters,
The (1966)

Journey to the Center of the
Earth (1967)
Fantastic Voyage, The (1968)
Hardy Boys, The (1969)

ZAHLER, LEE
Galloping Ghost, The (1931)
Lightning Warrior, The (1931)
Vanishing Legion, The (1931)
Last of the Mohicans, The
(1932)
Fighting with Kit Carson
(1933)
Mystery Squadron (1933)
Three Musketeers, The
(1933)
Whispering Shadow, The
(1933)
Wolf Dog, The (1933)
Burn 'Em Up Barnes (1934)
Law of the Wild (1934)
Lost Jungle, The (1934)
Mystery Mountain (1934)
Adventures of Rex and Rinty,
The (1935)
Fighting Marines, The (1935)
Miracle Rider, The (1935)
Phantom Empire, The (1935)
Lost City, The (1935)
Green Archer, The (1941)
Iron Claw, The (1941)
Secret Code, The (1942)

ZAMBRINI, BRUNO
Fracchia vs. Dracula (1986)
Thief Academy (1986)

ZAMFIR, GHEORGHE
Ion, the Curse of Land
(1981)
Red Caviar (1985)

ZAMPA, RICCARDO
Little Fires (1985)

ZAMPINO, BILL
Joe Louis--For All Time
(1984)

ZANDENAT, RICARDO
Orloff and Tarakanova (1938)
Betrayal (1939)

ZANDRINI, BRUNO
Madly in Love (1982)

ZANESI, CHRISTIAN
Time Masters, The (1982)

ZARYCKI, ANDRZEJ
Provincial Actors (1980)
Battlefield (1985)

ZARZOSA, JESUS (CHUCHO)
Braggarts, The (1960)
Song to Remember, A (1960)
Beautiful and Beloved Mexico
(1961)
Other, The (1985)
From Neither Here Nor
There (1987)
Narcotics Terror (1987)

ZARZOSA, JONATHAN
Delinquent (1987)

ZARZOSA, JORGE
One More Saturday (1987)

ZAVALA, JOSE ANTONIO
Antonieta (1982)

ZAVOD, ALLAN
Big Hurt, The (1986)
Death of a Soldier (1986)
Marsupials: The Howling
III, The (1987)
Time Guardian, The (1987)
Sebastian and the Sparrow
(1988)

ZAYANI, GEORGE KAZA
Hunger (1986)

ZAZA, PAUL J.
Murder by Decree (1979)
Prom Night (1980)
Kidnapping of the President,
The (1980)
My Bloody Valentine (1981)
Gas (1981)
Being Different (1981)
Porky's (1981)
American Nightmare (1982)
Melanie (1982)

Modesty Blaise (1982)
Curtains (1983)
Sentimental Reasons (1984)
Isaac Littlefeathers (1984)
Turk 182 (1985)
Breaking All the Rules (1985)
Birds of Prey (1986)
Bullies (1986)
Frankenstein '88 (1986)
Pink Chiquitas, The (1986)
Blindside (1987)
From the Hip (1987)
Hello Mary Lou: Prom Night
II (1987)
High Stakes (1987)
Higher Education (1987)
Meatballs II (1987)
Brain, The (1988)

ZAZOU, HECTOR
Komba, God of the Pygmies
(1986)

ZECEVIC, KSENIJA
Days of Dreams (1980)
Distant Sky, The (1982)

ZELJENKA, ILJA
Miraculous Virgin (1967)
Genii (Devils) (1969)

ZELLER, WOLFGANG
Atlantide, L' (1932)
Wajan (1934)
Governor, The (1939)
Unholy Wish, The (1939)
Bedeviled Gold (1942)
Palace Scandal (1949)
Life Begins at 17 (1954)

ZELONY, JACK
Sunny Youth (1935)

ZEPEDA, ANTONIO
Ulama, The Game of Life and
Death (1987)

ZERVOS, NICOS
Barbecue Them! (1981)

ZESSES, NICK
Sugar Hill (1974)

ZGRAJA, ZYGMUNT
    Sinful Life of Franciszek
        Bula, The (1980)

ZGUR, DECO
    Apprenticeship of Snail the
        Inventor, The (1982)

ZHUBANOV, A.
    Amangeldy (1939)

ZHUBOVSKY, E.
    Bountiful Summer (1952)

ZHUN, HUANG
    Two Stage Sisters (1981)

ZHURBIN, ALEXANDER
    Letters from a Dead Man
        (1986)

ZIDAKIS, NICOS
    Mania (1985)

ZIEGLER, ERICH
    Kingdom for a Horse, A
        (1949)

ZIEGLER, PABLO
    Goodbye, Robert (1985)

ZIELINSKI, JUAN PABLO MUNOZ
    Bastard Brother of God,
        The (1986)

ZIEN, WANG
    Snuff Bottle (1988)

ZILLIG, WINFRIED
    Jonas (1957)

ZIMA, AL
    South Bronx Heroes (1983)

ZIMMER, HANS
    Success Is the Best Revenge
        (1984)
    Wild Horses (1985)
    Wind, The (1987)
    Zero Boys, The (1987)
    Burning Secret (1988)
    Fruit Machine, The (1988)

Nature of the Beast, The
    (1988)
Paperhouse (1988)
Prisoner of Rio (1988)
Rain Man (1988)
Taffin (1988)
World Apart, A (1988)

ZIMMERMAN, BOB
    An Bloem (1983)

ZIMMERMAN, UDO
    April Has 30 Days (1980)

ZINGARO, CARLOS
    Jester, The (1987)

ZINSMEISTER, HORST
    Finders Keepers (1984)

ZINZI, GIORGIO
    Assassin 77, Life or Death
        (1966)

ZITTERER, CARL
    Children Shouldn't Play With
        Dead Things (1972)
    Blood Orgy of the She Devils
        (1973)
    Death Dreams (Night Andy
        Came Home, The) (1974)
    Murder by Decree (1979)
    Prom Night (1980)
    Lovers' Exile, The (1981)
    Porky's (1981)
    Porky's II: The Next Day
        (1983)
    Christmas Story, A (1983)

ZIVKOVIC, BRANISLAV (BRANA)
    Redeemer, The (1977)
    Melody Haunts My Reverie,
        The (1981)
    Jaws of Life, The (1984)
    My Uncle's Legacy (1988)

ZOLLER, ATTILA
    Hansel and Gretel Get Lost
        in the Woods (1970)

ZORN, JOHN
  She Must Be Seeing Things
    (1987)

ZOROV, ALEXANDER
  Caravan to Russia (1959)

ZOURABICHVILL, NICOLAS
  Thieves (Voleurs) (1984)

ZUBIRIA, AMAIA
  Segovia Escape, The (1981)
  Arder and Yul (1988)

ZULUETA, IVAN
  Rapture (1980)

ZWART, JACQUES
  Out of Order (1984)
  Deadline (1987)
  Helsinki Napoli All Night
    Long (1988)

ZWETKOFF, PETER
  Bums, The (1984)
  Land of Fathers, Land of
    Sons (1988)

ZYKAN, OTTO M.
  Exit ... But No Panic (1980)

RECORDED MUSICAL SCORES: A DISCOGRAPHY

compiled by H. Stephen Wright

This discography lists domestic (U.S.) recordings of film music
on 33-1/3 rpm records or compact discs issued in the years 1980
through 1987. As in the previous volume in this series, Keeping
Score, it is arranged in four separate alphabetical sequences: "Recorded Musical Scores," "Recorded Musical Scores--Anthologies,"
"Recorded Musical Scores--Television," and "Recorded Musical Scores--
Television Anthologies."

The sections "Recorded Musical Scores" and "Recorded Musical
Scores--Television" contain entries for recordings of music devoted
entirely to individual productions, as well as excerpts or suites on
recorded anthologies lacking collective titles. Each entry gives
the film or program title, the producing studio or network (or country of origin in the case of non-U.S. productions), date of release
(or date of first broadcast in the case of television programs), and
the composer's name. Omissions indicate that the information is
unknown. Citations to recordings list the manufacturer's name and
the recording's serial number; compact discs are represented by
the abbreviation (CD). Underlined citations indicate that the entire
recording, or a substantial portion of it, is devoted to a single
score; a lack of underlining generally indicates a brief excerpt.

The sections "Recorded Musical Scores--Anthologies" and "Recorded Musical Scores--Television Anthologies" list recordings of
music from various films issued under a single collective title. Each
entry gives the album title, performers' names (if known), a list
of the films or programs represented on the recording, and the
manufacturer's name and recording serial number.

Recordings of film versions of stage muscials and anthologies
of classical music used in films are not included; reissues of pre-
1980 recordings are not included unless the identifying information
(label name and/or serial number) is different.

A phenomenon in film music recording which exploded into
prominence in the 1980s (and which is much in evidence in this
discography) is the soundtrack album consisting entirely of pop
or rock songs, usually of diffuse or uncertain authorship. Such

items can be identified herein by the phrase "various composers" in place of a single composer credit. The composer credits in this discography reflect what is found on the recording, not what is in the film's credits; thus a film with the "various composers" credit may have a traditional background score that is represented minimally, or not at all, on the soundtrack album.

Tape cassettes were issued for many of the items in this discography, though they are not cited; generally, the cassette version's serial number differs only in its prefix (for example, STV 81249 for a disc, CTV 81249 for a cassette). Despite their acceptance by consumers, cassettes are shunned by collectors of film music.

RECORDED MUSICAL SCORES

ABOUT LAST NIGHT ... (Tri-Star, 1986) various composers
EMI SV 17210

ABSOLUTE BEGINNERS (Britain, 1986) various composers
EMI SV 17182

ACCADE AL PENITENZIARIO (Italy, 1955) Nino Rota
Cerberus CST-0205

ADVENTURES OF DON JUAN (Warner Bros., 1948) Max Steiner
Tony Thomas Productions TT/MS-11 (private)

THE ADVENTURES OF ROBIN HOOD (Warner Bros., 1938) Erich
Wolfgang Korngold
Varese Sarabande 704.180; VCD 47202 (CD)

AFTER THE FOX (United Artists, 1966) Burt Bacharach
MCA 25132

AGAINST ALL ODDS (Columbia, 1984) Michel Colombier, Larry
Carlton
Atlantic 80152-1; 80152-2 (CD)

AGNES OF GOD (Columbia, 1985) Georges Delerue
Varese Sarabande STV 81257

AIRPLANE! (Paramount, 1980) Elmer Bernstein
Regency RY 9601

ALAMO BAY (Tri-Star, 1985) Ry Cooder
Slash 25311-1

THE ALCHEMIST (Empire, 1986) Richard Band
  Varese Sarabande STV 81262

ALEXANDER NEVSKY (Russia, 1938) Sergei Prokofiev
  Vox Cum Laude 3-VCL 9004X

ALIENS (Twentieth Century-Fox, 1986) James Horner
  Varese Sarabande STV 81283; VCD 47263 (CD)

ALL THAT JAZZ (Columbia/Twentieth Century-Fox, 1979) various
    composers
  Casablanca NBLP 7198

ALL THE RIGHT MOVES (Twentieth Century-Fox, 1983) various
    composers
  Casablanca 814 449-1 M-1

THE ALLNIGHTER (Universal, 1987) various composers
  Chameleon CHST 9601, CHPD 9601 (picture disc)

AN ALMOST PERFECT AFFAIR (Paramount, 1979) Georges Delerue
  Varese Sarabande STV 81132

ALTERED STATES (Warner Bros., 1980) John Corigliano
  RCA ABL 1-3983, AGL 1-5066

AMADEUS (Orion, 1984) Wolfgang Amadeus Mozart
  Fantasy WAM 1791, 1205; FCD 1791, 1205 (CD)

AMAZING GRACE AND CHUCK (Tri-Star, 1987) Elmer Bernstein
  Varese Sarabande STV 81312; VCD 47285 (CD)

AMERICAN ANTHEM (Columbia, 1986) various composers
  Atlantic 81661-1; 81661-2 (CD)

AMERICAN FLYERS (Warner Bros., 1985) Lee Ritenour, Greg
    Mathieson
  GRP A 2011

THE AMERICAN FRIEND (France/West Germany, 1977) Jurgen
    Knieper
  Enigma SJ 73286

THE AMERICAN GAME (World Northal, 1979) Jeffrey Kaufman
  Buddah BDS 5724

AMERICAN GIGOLO (Paramount, 1980) Giorgio Moroder
  Polydor PD-1-6259

AMERICAN POP (Columbia, 1981) various composers
  MCA 5201

AN AMERICAN TAIL (Universal, 1986) James Horner
  MCA 39096; MCAD 39096 (CD)

ANASTASIA (Twentieth Century-Fox, 1956) Alfred Newman
  Varese Sarabande STV 81125

ANATOMY OF A MURDER (Columbia, 1959) Duke Ellington
  Columbia Special Products JCS 8166
  Rykodisc RCD 10039 (CD)

ANDY WARHOL'S DRACULA (Bryanston, 1975) Claudio Gizzi
  Varese Sarabande STV 81156

ANDY WARHOL'S FRANKENSTEIN (Bryanston, 1974) Claudio Gizzi
  Varese Sarabande STV 81157

ANIMAL HOUSE see NATIONAL LAMPOON'S ANIMAL HOUSE

ANIMALYMPICS (Lisberger Studios, 1980) Graham Gouldman
  A&M SP-4810

ANY WHICH WAY YOU CAN (Warner Bros., 1980) various composers
  Warner Bros. HS 3499

APOLOGY (Peregrine Entertainment Ltd., 1986) Maurice Jarre
  Varese Sarabande STV 81284

APRIL FOOL'S DAY (Paramount, 1986) Charles Bernstein
  Varese Sarabande STV 81278

ARMED AND DANGEROUS (Columbia, 1986) various composers
  Manhattan SJ 53041

AROUND THE WORLD IN 80 DAYS (United Artists, 1956) Victor
    Young
  MCA 37086

ARTHUR (Orion/Warner Bros., 1981) Burt Bacharach
  Warner Bros. BSK-3582

L'ASSOLUTO NATURALE (Italy, 1972) Ennio Morricone
  Cerberus CEM-S 0112

ATLANTIC CITY (Paramount, 1981) Michel Legrand
  DRG SL 6104

ATLANTIS, THE LOST CONTINENT (Metro-Goldwyn-Mayer, 1961)
    Russell Garcia
  GNP Crescendo GNPS 8008; GNPD 8008 (CD)

THE ATOMIC CAFE (Archives Project, 1982) various composers
  Rounder 1034

THE AVIATOR (Metro-Goldwyn-Mayer/United Artists, 1985) Dominic
    Frontiere
    Varese Sarabande STV 81240

THE AWAKENING (Orion, 1980) Claude Bolling
    Entr'acte ERS 6520

BACHELOR PARTY (Twentieth Century-Fox, 1984) various composers
    International Record Syndicate SP 70047

BACK TO SCHOOL (Orion, 1986) various composers
    MCA 6175

BACK TO THE BEACH (Paramount, 1987) various composers
    Columbia SC 40892; CK 40892 (CD)

BACK TO THE FUTURE (Universal, 1985) various composers
    MCA 6144

BAD BOYS (Universal, 1983) various composers
    Capitol ST-12272

BAD GUYS (InterPictures, 1986) various composers
    Casablanca 826 610-1

LA BAMBA (Columbia, 1987) various composers
    Slash/Warner Bros. 25605-1; 25605-2 (CD)

BAND OF ANGELS (Warner Bros., 1957) Max Steiner
    Entr'acte ERM 6003
    Label "X" LXCD 3 (CD)

BAND OF THE HAND (Tri-Star, 1986) various composers
    MCA 6167

BARABBAS (Columbia, 1962) Mario Nascimbene
    Citadel CT 7034

BATTLE BEYOND THE STARS (New World, 1980) James Horner
    Rhino RNSP 300

BATTLE OF BRITAIN (Britain, 1969) Ron Goodwin, William Walton
    MCA 25008

THE BATTLE OF NERETVA (American International, 1969) Bernard
    Herrmann
    Southern Cross SCRS 5006; SCCD 5005 (CD)

BEACH PARTY (American International, 1963) various composers
    Rhino RNDF-204

THE BEASTMASTER (Metro-Goldwyn-Mayer/United Artists, 1982)
    Lee Holdridge
    Varese Sarabande STV 81174

BEAT STREET (Orion, 1984) various composers
    Atlantic 80154-1, 80158-1; 80154-2 (CD)

A BEAUTIFUL GIRL LIKE ME (France, 1972) Georges Delerue
    DRG SL 9519

THE BEDROOM WINDOW (De Laurentiis Entertainment Group, 1987)
    Michael Shrieve, Patrick Gleeson
    Varese Sarabande STV 81307

THE BELIEVERS (Orion, 1987) J. Peter Robinson
    Varese Sarabande STV 81328

BELIZAIRE THE CAJUN (Skouras Pictures, 1986) Michael Doucet,
    Howard Shore
    Arhoolie ARH 5038

BEN-HUR (Metro-Goldwyn-Mayer, 1959) Miklos Rozsa
    Varese Sarabande VC 81104; VCD 47268 (CD)

BERLIN ALEXANDERPLATZ (West Germany, 1983) Peer Raben
    Varese Sarabande STV 81217

BETTER OFF DEAD (Warner Bros., 1985) Rupert Hine
    A&M SP-5071

BEVERLY HILLS COP (Paramount, 1984) Harold Faltermeyer
    MCA 5547, 5553; MCAD 5553 (CD)

BEVERLY HILLS COP II (Paramount, 1987) various composers
    MCA 6207; MCAD 6207 (CD)

THE BIG CHILL (Columbia, 1983) various composers
    Motown 6062 ML, 6094 ML; 6062 MD (CD)

BIG JAKE (National General, 1971) Elmer Bernstein
    Varese Sarabande 704.350; VCD 47264

BIG TOWN (Columbia, 1987) various composers
    Atlantic 81769-1; 81769-2 (CD)

BIG TROUBLE IN LITTLE CHINA (Twentieth Century-Fox, 1986)
    John Carpenter, Alan Howarth
    Enigma SJ 73227; CDE 73227 (CD)

BILLION DOLLAR BRAIN (United Artists, 1968) Richard Rodney
    Bennett
    MCA 25091

BIRD OF PARADISE (RKO, 1932) Max Steiner
Medallion ML 305/6

BIRDY (Tri-Star, 1984) Peter Gabriel
Geffen GHS 24070

BIRTH OF A NATION (Epoch Producing Corp., 1915) Joseph Carl
Breil
Label "X" LXDR 701/2

BLACK BELLY OF THE TARANTULA (Italy, 1972) Ennio Morricone
Cerberus CEM-S 0116

THE BLACK CAULDRON (Buena Vista, 1985) Elmer Bernstein
Varese Sarabande STV 81253

THE BLACK STALLION (United Artists, 1979) Carmine Coppola
United Artists LOO 1040
Liberty LN-10279

THE BLACK STALLION RETURNS (Metro-Goldwyn-Mayer/United
Artists, 1983) Georges Delerue
Liberty LO-51144

BLADE RUNNER (Warner Bros., 1982) Vangelis
Full Moon 23748-1

BLAME IT ON RIO (Twentieth Century-Fox, 1984) Ken Wannberg
Varese Sarabande STV 81210

BLIND DATE (New Line, 1984) Stanley Myers, John Kongos
Varese Sarabande STV 81202

BLIND DATE (Tri-Star, 1987) Henry Mancini
Rhino 70705

BLOOD AND SAND (Twentieth Century-Fox, 1941) Vicente Gomez
Varese Sarabande STV 81117

BLOOD FEAST (Box Office Spectaculars, 1963) Herschell Gordon
Lewis
Rhino RNSP-305

BLOOD FOR DRACULA see ANDY WARHOL'S DRACULA

BLOOD SIMPLE (Circle Films, 1985) Carter Burwell
Varese Sarabande STV 81318; VCD 47284 (CD)

BLOODLINE see SIDNEY SHELDON'S BLOODLINE

BLOW-UP (Metro-Goldwyn-Mayer, 1966) Herbie Hancock
Verve UMF 1013

BLUE CITY (Paramount, 1986) Ry Cooder
   Warner Bros. 25386-1

THE BLUE LAGOON (Columbia, 1980) Basil Poledouris
   Marlin 2236

THE BLUE MAX (Twentieth Century-Fox, 1966) Jerry Goldsmith
   Varese Sarabande VCD 47238 (CD)

BLUE THUNDER (Columbia, 1983) Arthur B. Rubinstein, Jr.
   MCA 6122

BLUE VELVET (De Laurentiis Entertainment Group, 1986) Angelo
      Badalamenti
   Varese Sarabande STV 81292; VCD 47277 (CD)

BLUEBEARD (Italy, 1972) Ennio Morricone
   Cerberus CEM-S 0105

THE BOAT see DAS BOOT

BODY HEAT (Ladd Company/Warner Bros., 1981) John Barry
   Label "X" LXSE 1-002

BODY ROCK (New World, 1984) Sylvester Levay
   EMI SO 17140

BODY SLAM (Hemdale, 1987) various composers
   MCA 6197

BOLERO (France, 1982) Francis Lai, Michel Legrand
   Polydor PD-1-6353

BOLERO (Cannon, 1984) Peter Bernstein
   Varese Sarabande STV 81228

THE BOOGEY MAN (Jerry Gross, 1980) Tim Krog
   SST 101

DAS BOOT (West Germany, 1982) Klaus Doldinger
   Atlantic SD 19348

THE BORDER (Universal, 1982) Ry Cooder
   Backstreet BSR 6105

BORDER RADIO (Coyote Films, 1987) Dave Alvin
   Enigma SJ 73221; CDE 73221 (CD)

BOY ON A DOLPHIN (Twentieth Century-Fox, 1957) Hugo Friedhofer
   Varese Sarabande STV 81119

THE BOY WHO COULD FLY (Lorimar, 1986) Bruce Broughton
    Varese Sarabande STV 81299; VCD 47279 (CD)

BRAINSTORM (Metro-Goldwyn-Mayer/United Artists, 1983) James
    Horner
    Varese Sarabande STV 81197; VCD 47215 (CD)

THE BRAVE ONE (King Brothers, 1956) Victor Young
    AEI 3107

BREAKER MORANT (Australia, 1980) various composers
    First American FA 7783

THE BREAKFAST CLUB (Universal, 1985) Keith Forsey
    A&M SP-5045; CD-5045 (CD)

BREAKIN' (Metro-Goldwyn-Mayer/United Artists/Cannon, 1984)
    various composers
    Polydor 821 919-1; 821 919-2 (CD)

BREAKIN' 2: ELECTRIC BOOGALOO (Tri-Star, 1984) various
    composers
    Polydor 823 696-1; 823 696-2 (CD)

BREAKING GLASS (Paramount, 1980) Hazel O'Connor
    A&M SP-4820

THE BRIDE (Columbia, 1985) Maurice Jarre
    Varese Sarabande STV 81254

IL BRIGANTE (Italy, 1961) Nino Rota
    Cerberus CST 0204

BRIGHTON BEACH MEMOIRS (Universal, 1986) Michael Small
    MCA 6193

BRIMSTONE AND TREACLE (Britain, 1982) various composers
    A&M SP-4915, SP-3245

BRONCO BILLY (Warner Bros., 1980) various composers
    Electra 5E-512

THE BROTHER FROM ANOTHER PLANET (Cinecom International,
    1984) Mason Daring
    Daring DR 1007

BRUTE FORCE (Universal, 1947) Miklos Rozsa
    Tony Thomas Productions TT-MR-3 (private)

BURGLAR (Warner Bros., 1987) Sylvester Levay
    MCA 6201; MCAD 6201 (CD)

THE BURNING (Filmways/Orion, 1982) Rick Wakeman
  Varese Sarabande STV 81162

BUTCH CASSIDY AND THE SUNDANCE KID (Twentieth Century-
    Fox, 1969) Burt Bacharach
  A&M CD-3159 (CD)

BUTTERFLY (Analysis, 1982) Ennio Morricone
  Applause APLP 1017

CADDYSHACK (Orion, 1980) Kenny Loggins, Johnny Mandel
  Columbia JS 36737

LA CAGE AUX FOLLES (United Artists, 1979) Ennio Morricone
  Cerberus CEM-S 0102

LA CAGE AUX FOLLES II (United Artists, 1981) Ennio Morricone
  Cerberus CEM-S 0107

CAHILL, UNITED STATES MARSHALL (Warner Bros., 1973) Elmer
    Bernstein
  Varese Sarabande 704.350; VCD 47264

CAL (Ireland, 1984) Mark Knopfler
  Mercury 822 769-1; 822 769-2 (CD)

CALIFORNIA DREAMING (American International, 1979) Fred Karlin
  American International AILP 3001

CALIFORNIA SUITE (Columbia, 1978) Claude Bolling
  Columbia FM 36691
  RCA ARL 1-4148

CALIGULA (Penthouse Films, 1980) Paul Clemente, Toni Biggs
  Penthouse PR 101 CS

THE CANNIBALS (Italy, 1970) Ennio Morricone
  Cerberus CEM-S 0111

CAN'T STOP THE MUSIC (Associated Film Distribution, 1980)
    Jacques Morali
  Casablanca NBLP 7220

CAPTAIN KRONOS, VAMPIRE HUNTER (Britain, 1974) Laurie
    Johnson
  Starlog/Varese Sarabande SV-95002; VCD 47270 (CD)

THE CARDINAL (Columbia, 1963) Jerome Moross
  Entr'acte ERS 6518
  Preamble PRCD 1778 (CD)

CAREFUL, HE MIGHT HEAR YOU (Britain, 1984) Ray Cook
Varese Sarabande STV 81221

CARNY (United Artists, 1980) Alex North, Robbie Robertson
Warner Bros. HS 3455

CARRIE (United Artists, 1976) Pino Donaggio
Liberty LN-10276

CAST A GIANT SHADOW (United Artists, 1966) Elmer Bernstein
MCA 25093

CAT PEOPLE (Universal/RKO, 1982) Giorgio Moroder
Backstreet BSR 6107

CAT'S EYE (Metro-Goldwyn-Mayer/United Artists, 1985) Alan
    Silvestri
Varese Sarabande STV 81241

THE CENSUS TAKER (Seymour Borde, 1984) The Residents
Episode ED-21

CERTAIN FURY (New World, 1985) Bill Payne, Russ Kunkel
Varese Sarabande STV 81239

THE CHAIRMAN (Twentieth Century-Fox, 1969) Jerry Goldsmith
AEI 3110

CHAMPIONS (Britain, 1984) Carl Davis
Antilles ASTA 3

THE CHARGE OF THE LIGHT BRIGADE (Warner Bros., 1936) Max
    Steiner
Entr'acte ERM 6004
Label "X" LXCD 3 (CD)

CHARIOTS OF FIRE (Ladd Company/Warner Bros., 1981) Vangelis
Polydor PD-1-6335; 800 020-2 (CD)
Moss Music Group B-707

LE CHAT (France, 1978) Philippe Sarde
DRG SL 9512

CHE! (Twentieth Century-Fox, 1969) Lalo Schifrin
AEI 3111

CHEYENNE AUTUMN (Warner Bros., 1964) Alex North
Label "X" LXSE 1-003; LXCD 4 (CD)

CHILDREN OF A LESSER GOD (Paramount, 1986) Michael Convertino
GNP Crescendo GNPS-8007; GNPD-8007 (CD)

CHILDREN OF THE CORN (New World, 1984) Jonathan Elias
Varese Sarabande STV 81203

CHOICE OF ARMS (France, 1983) Philippe Sarde
DRG SL 9510

THE CHOSEN (American International, 1978) Ennio Morricone
Cerberus CEM-S 0103

CHRISTIANE F. (New World, 1982) David Bowie
RCA ABL 1-4239

CHRISTINE (Columbia, 1983) John Carpenter, Alan Howarth
Motown 6086 ML

CHRONOS (IMAX, 1985) Michael Stearns
Sonic Atmospheres 112; 312 (CD)

CHULAS FRONTERAS (Brazos Film, 1976) various composers
Arhoolie 3005

EL CID (Allied Artists, 1961) Miklos Rozsa
MCA 25005
Varese Sarabande VC 81104; VCD 47268 (CD)

THE CINCINNATI KID (Metro-Goldwyn-Mayer, 1966) Lalo Schifrin
MCA 25012

THE CITY (Civic Films, 1939) Aaron Copland
Argo ZRG 935

CITY HEAT (Warner Bros., 1984) Lennie Niehaus
Warner Bros. 25219-1

CLAN OF THE CAVE BEAR (Warner Bros., 1986) Alan Silvestri
Varese Sarabande STV 81274; VCD 47252 (CD)

CLASH OF THE TITANS (United Artists, 1981) Laurence Rosenthal
Columbia JS 37386

CLOSE ENCOUNTERS OF THE THIRD KIND (Columbia, 1977) John
Williams
RCA AGL 1-3650
Arista ARCD 8365 (CD)

CLUB PARADISE (Warner Bros., 1986) various composers
Columbia SC 40404

COAL MINER'S DAUGHTER (Universal, 1980) various composers
MCA 5107, 37226

COAST TO COAST (Paramount, 1980) various composers
Full Moon FM 3490

COBRA (Warner Bros., 1986) Sylvester Levay
Scotti Bros. SZ 40325; ZK 40325 (CD)

COCOON (Twentieth Century-Fox, 1985) James Horner
Polydor 827 041-1 Y-1; 827 041-2 (CD)

CODE OF SILENCE (Orion, 1985) David Frank
Easy Street ESA 9900

THE COLOR OF MONEY (Buena Vista, 1986) Robbie Robertson
MCA 6189; MCAD 6189 (CD)

THE COLOR PURPLE (Warner Bros., 1985) Quincy Jones
Qwest 25389-1, 25356-1; 25389-2 (CD)

THE COMANCHEROS (Twentieth Century-Fox, 1961) Elmer
    Bernstein
Varese Sarabande 704.280; VCD 47236 (CD)

COME NEXT SPRING (Republic, 1955) Max Steiner
Citadel CT 7019

THE COMEDIANS (Metro-Goldwyn-Mayer, 1967) Laurence Rosenthal
MCA 25002

THE COMPANY OF WOLVES (Britain, 1985) George Fenton
Varese Sarabande STV 81242

THE COMPETITION (Columbia, 1980) Lalo Schifrin
MCA 5185

CONAN THE BARBARIAN (Universal, 1982) Basil Poledouris
MCA 6108, 1566

CONAN THE DESTROYER (Universal, 1984) Basil Poledouris
MCA 6135

CONFIDENTIALLY YOURS (France, 1984) Georges Delerue
DRG SL 9519

THE COTTON CLUB (Orion, 1984) John Barry
Geffen GHS 24062; 24062-2 (CD)

COTTON COMES TO HARLEM (United Artists, 1970) Galt MacDermot
MCA 25133

COUNT THREE AND PRAY (Columbia, 1955) George Duning
Web ST-108

COUNTRY (Buena Vista, 1984) Charles Gross
Windham Hill WH 1039; WD 1039 (CD)

COUP DE TORCHON (France, 1981) Philippe Sarde
DRG SL 9511

THE COWBOYS (Warner Bros., 1972) John Williams
RC 31 (private)

CRAWLSPACE (Empire, 1986) Pino Donaggio
Varese Sarabande STV 81279

CREATURE FROM THE BLACK LAGOON (Universal, 1954) Hans J.
Salter
Tony Thomas Productions TT-HS-4 (private)

CREEPERS (Italy, 1985) various composers
Enigma SJ 73205

CREEPSHOW (Warner Bros., 1982) John Harrison
Varese Sarabande STV 81160

CRIMES OF THE HEART (De Laurentiis Entertainment Group, 1986)
Georges Delerue
Varese Sarabande STV 81298; VCD 47278 (CD)

CRITTERS (New Line Cinema, 1986) David Newman
Restless 72154-1

"CROCODILE" DUNDEE (Paramount, 1986) Peter Best
Varese Sarabande STV 81296; VCD 47283 (CD)

CROSSOVER DREAMS (Crossover Films, 1985) various composers
Elektra 60470-1

CROSSROADS (Columbia, 1986) Ry Cooder
Warner Bros. 25399-1

CRUISING (United Artists/Lorimar, 1980) Jack Nitzsche
Lorimar JC 36410

CRY FREEDOM (Universal, 1987) George Fenton, Jonas Gwangwa
MCA 6224; MCAD 6224 (CD)

CRY OF THE BANSHEE (American International, 1970) Les Baxter
Citadel CTV 7013

THE CZAR WANTS TO SLEEP (Russia, 1934) Sergei Prokofiev
Vox Cum Laude 3-VCL 9004X

D.C. CAB (Universal, 1983) Giorgio Moroder
MCA 6128

DANCE WITH A STRANGER (Britain, 1985) Richard Hartley
Varese Sarabande STV 81251

DANCERS (Cannon, 1987) Pino Donaggio
CBS SM 42565; MK 42565 (CD)

DANGEROUSLY CLOSE (Cannon, 1986) various composers
Enigma SJ 73204

DANTON (France, 1983) Jean Prodromides
DRG SL 9518

THE DARK CRYSTAL (Universal, 1982) Trevor Jones
Warner Bros. 23749-1

DARK EYES (Italy, 1987) Francis Lai
DRG SBL 12592; CDSBL 12592 (CD)

DARK STAR (Jack H. Harris, 1974) John Carpenter
Citadel CT 7022

DARK WATERS (United Artists, 1944) Miklos Roxsa
Tony Thomas Productions TT-MR-4 (private)

THE DAY AFTER HALLOWEEN (Group 1, 1980) Brian May
Citadel CT 7020

DAY FOR NIGHT (France, 1973) Georges Delerue
DRG SL 9519

DAY OF THE DEAD (United Film Distribution Company, 1985) John
    Harrison
Saturn SRLP 1701

THE DAY THE EARTH STOOD STILL (Twentieth Century-Fox,
    1951) Bernard Herrmann
Preamble PRCD 1777 (CD)

THE DAY TIME ENDED (Compass International, 1980) Richard Band
Varese Sarabande STV 81140

DEADLY FRIEND (Warner Bros., 1986) Charles Bernstein
Varese Sarabande STV 81291

THE DEADLY SPAWN (21st Century, 1983) Michael Perilstein
Deadly DS 6041

DEATH BEFORE DISHONOR (New World, 1987) Brian May
Varese Sarabande STV 81310

DEATH OF A SCOUNDREL (RKO, 1956) Max Steiner

Entr'acte ERM 6004
Label "X" LXCD 3 (CD)

DEATH WISH (Paramount, 1974) Herbie Hancock
Columbia PC 36825

DEATH WISH II (Filmways, 1982) Jimmy Page
Swan Song SS 8511

DEF-CON 4 (New World, 1985) Christopher Young
Cerberus CST-0212

THE DELTA FORCE (Cannon, 1986) Alan Silvestri
Enigma SJ 73201

DESPERATE TEENAGE LOVE DOLLS (1985) various composers
Enigma E 1140

DESPERATELY SEEKING SUSAN (Orion, 1985) Thomas Newman
Varese Sarabande STV 81320; VCD 47291 (CD)

DESTINATION MOON (Eagle Lion, 1950) Leith Stevens
Varese Sarabande STV 81130

THE DEVIL AT 4 O'CLOCK (Columbia, 1961) George Duning
Varese Sarabande STV 81136

DIAMONDS ARE FOREVER (United Artists, 1971) John Barry
Liberty LT-50301

DIRTY DANCING (Vestron, 1987) various composers
RCA 6408-1-R; 6408-2-R (CD)

DIRTY DINGUS MAGEE (Metro-Goldwyn-Mayer, 1971) Jeff Alexander
MCA 25095

THE DIRTY DOZEN (Metro-Goldwyn-Mayer, 1967) Frank de Vol
MCA 39064

DIRTY HARRY (Warner Bros., 1971) Lalo Schifrin
Viva 23990-1

DISORDERLIES (Warner Bros., 1987) various composers
Polydor 833 274-1; 833 274-2 (CD)

DIVA (France, 1982) Vladimir Cosma
DRG SL 9503
Rykodisc RCD 10010 (CD)

THE DIVINE NYMPH (Analysis, 1979) Cesare Bixio, Ennio Morricone
Cerberus CEM-S 0104

DOCTOR DETROIT (Universal, 1983) various composers
Backstreet BSR 6120

DR. NO (United Artists, 1963) Monty Norman
Liberty LT-50275

DR. STRANGELOVE (Columbia, 1964) Laurie Johnson
Starlog/Varese Sarabande SV-95002; VCD 47270 (CD)

DOCTOR ZHIVAGO (Metro-Goldwyn-Mayer, 1965) Maurice Jarre
MCA 39042; MCAD 39042 (CD)

DOGS IN SPACE (Australia, 1987) various composers
Atlantic 81789-1

DON'T MAKE WAVES (Metro-Goldwyn-Mayer, 1967) Vic Mizzy
MCA 25134

DOWN AND OUT IN BEVERLY HILLS (Touchstone, 1986) Andy
     Summers
MCA 6160; MCAD 6160, 31062 (CD)

DOWN TO THE SEA IN SHIPS (Twentieth Century-Fox, 1949) Alfred
     Newman
Preamble PRCD 1777 (CD)

DOWN TWISTED (Cannon, 1987) Berlin Game
Varese Sarabande STV 81305

DRAGNET (Universal, 1987) Ira Newborn
MCA 6210; MCAD 6210 (CD)

DRAGONSLAYER (Paramount, 1981) Alex North
Label "X" LXSE 2-001

THE DRAUGHTSMAN'S CONTRACT (Britain, 1983) Michael Nyman
DRG SL 9513

DREAMSCAPE (Twentieth Century-Fox, 1984) Maurice Jarre
Sonic Atmospheres 102; 302 (CD)

DRESSED TO KILL (Filmways, 1980) Pino Donaggio
Varese Sarabande STV 81148

DUDES (New Century-Vista, 1987) various composers
MCA 6212; MCAD 6212 (CD)

DUEL AT DIABLO (United Artists, 1966) Neal Hefti
MCA 1436

DUNE (Universal, 1984) Toto
Polydor 823 770-1; 823 770-2 (CD)

E.T., THE EXTRA-TERRESTRIAL (Universal, 1982) John Williams
  MCA 6109, 6113 (picture disc), 16014, 70000 (with narration);
    MCAD 37264 (CD)

THE EAGLE HAS LANDED (Columbia, 1977) Lalo Schifrin
  Label "X" LXCD 5 (CD)

EASY MONEY (Orion, 1983) Laurence Rosenthal, Billy Joel
  Columbia JS 38968

EATING RAOUL (Twentieth Century-Fox, 1982) Arlon Ober
  Varese Sarabande STV 81164

ECHO PARK (Atlantic, 1986) various composers
  A&M SP-5119

EDDIE AND THE CRUISERS (Embassy, 1983) John Cafferty
  Scotti Bros. BFZ 38929; ZK 38929 (CD)

EDITH AND MARCEL (France, 1984) Francis Lai
  Atlantic 80153-1

EDITH'S DIARY (West Germany, 1986) Jurgen Knieper
  Varese Sarabande STV 81255

EDUCATING RITA (Britain, 1983) David Hentschel
  Mercury MERL 23

EIGHT ON THE LAM (United Artists, 1967) George Romanis
  MCA 25096

84 CHARING CROSS ROAD (Columbia, 1987) George Fenton
  Varese Sarabande STV 81306

ELECTRIC DREAMS (Metro-Goldwyn-Mayer/United Artists, 1984)
    Giorgio Moroder
  Epic SE 39600

THE ELECTRIC HORSEMAN (Columbia/Universal, 1979) Dave Grusin
  Columbia JS 36327; CK 36327 (CD)

THE ELEPHANT MAN (Paramount, 1980) John Morris
  Pacific Arts PAC 8-143
  Twentieth Century T-1000

ELMER GANTRY (United Artists, 1960) Andre Previn
  MCA 39070

THE EMERALD FOREST (Twentieth Century-Fox, 1985) Junior
    Homrich, Brian Gascoigne
  Varese Sarabande STV 81244; VCD 47251 (CD)

THE EMPIRE STRIKES BACK (Twentieth Century-Fox, 1980) John
    Williams
    RSO RS-2-4201
    Chalfont SDG 313
    Varese Sarabande VCD 47204 (CD)
    Polydor 825 298-2 (CD)

THE ENCHANTED COTTAGE (RKO, 1945) Roy Webb
    Entr'acte ERM 6002

ENDLESS LOVE (Universal, 1981) Jonathan Tunick
    Mercury SRM 1-2001

ENEMY MINE (Twentieth Century-Fox, 1985) Maurice Jarre
    Varese Sarabande STV 81271; VCD 47249 (CD)

THE ENFORCER (Warner Bros., 1976) Jerry Fielding
    Viva 23990-1

ERASERHEAD (AFI/Libra, 1977) Peter Ivers
    International Record Syndicate SP 70027

UN EROE DE NOSTRI TEMPI (Italy, 1955) Nino Rota
    Cerberus CST-0205

ESCAPE FROM NEW YORK (Avco Embassy, 1981) John Carpenter,
    Alan Howarth
    Varese Sarabande STV 81134; VCD 47224 (CD)

THE ETERNAL SEA (Republic, 1955) Elmer Bernstein
    Citadel CT 7021

L'ETOILE DU NORD (France, 1982) Philippe Sarde
    DRG SL 9512

THE EUROPEANS (Levitt-Pickman, 1979) various composers
    Gramavision GR-1010

THE EVIL DEAD (New Line Cinema, 1983) Joseph LoDuca
    Varese Sarabande STV 81199

EVIL DEAD 2 (Rosebud Releasing, 1987) Joseph LoDuca
    Varese Sarabande STV 81313

EVIL UNDER THE SUN (Universal, 1982) Cole Porter
    RCA AYL 1-4309

EXCALIBUR (Orion/Warner Bros., 1981) Trevor Jones
    Warner Bros. WBS 49734

EXODUS (United Artists, 1960) Ernest Gold

RCA AYL 1-3872
MCA 39065

EXPLORERS (Paramount, 1985) Jerry Goldsmith
MCA 6148

EXTREME PREJUDICE (Tri-Star, 1987) Jerry Goldsmith
Intrada MAF 7001; 7001 (CD)

EYE OF THE NEEDLE (United Artists, 1981) Miklos Rozsa
Varese Sarabande STV 81133

F/X (Orion, 1986) Bill Conti
Varese Sarabande STV 81276

THE FALCON AND THE SNOWMAN (Orion, 1985) Pat Metheny, Lyle
    Mays
EMI SV 17150

THE FALL OF A NATION (National Films, 1916) Victor Herbert
Library of Congress OMP-103 (CD)

FAME (Cinema International, 1980) Michael Gore
RSO RX 1-3080; 800 034-2 (CD)

FANTASIA (Walt Disney Productions, 1940) various composers
Buena Vista 104; CD 001 (CD)

FAST FORWARD (Columbia, 1985) various composers
Qwest/Warner Bros. 25263-1

FAST TIMES AT RIDGEMONT HIGH (Universal, 1982) various
    composers
Full Moon/Asylum 60158-1

FATAL ATTRACTION (Paramount, 1987) Maurice Jarre
GNP Crescendo GNPS 8011; GNPD 8011 (CD)

FATAL BEAUTY (Metro-Goldwyn-Mayer, 1987) various composers
Atlantic 81809-1

FEAR NO EVIL (Avco Embassy, 1981) Frank LaLoggia, David Spear
Web ST-106

52 PICK-UP (Cannon, 1986) Gary Chang
Varese Sarabande STV 81300

THE FINAL CONFLICT (Twentieth Century-Fox, 1981) Jerry
    Goldsmith
Varese Sarabande STV 81272; VCD 47242 (CD)

THE FINAL COUNTDOWN (United Artists, 1980) John Scott
Casablanca NBLP 7232

FINAL EXAM (Bedford Entertainment Group, 1981) Gary Scott
AEI 3105

THE FINAL OPTION (Metro-Goldwyn-Mayer/United Artists, 1983) Roy
Budd
Varese Sarabande STV 81188

A FINE MESS (Columbia, 1986) various composers
Motown 6180 ML

FIRE AND ICE (Concorde Pictures, 1987) various composers
MCA 6206

FIRESTARTER (Universal, 1984) Tangerine Dream
MCA 6131

FIREWALKER (Cannon, 1986) Gary Chang
Varese Sarabande STV 81303

FIRST BLOOD (Orion, 1982) Jerry Goldsmith
Regency RY 9505

FIRST BLOOD PART II see RAMBO: FIRST BLOOD PART II

FIRST MEN IN THE MOON (Britain, 1964) Laurie Johnson
Starlog/Varese Sarabande SV-95002; VCD 47270 (CD)

FIRSTBORN (Paramount, 1984) Michael Small
EMI ST 17144

THE FISH THAT SAVED PITTSBURGH (United Artists, 1979) Thom
Bell
Lorimar SZ-36303

FITZCARRALDO (New World, 1982) Popol Vuh
Polydor PDH-1-6363

FITZWILLY (Metro-Goldwyn-Mayer, 1968) John Williams
MCA 25098

THE FLAMINGO KID (Twentieth Century-Fox/Edgewood, 1984)
various composers
Motown 6131 ML
Varese Sarabande STV 81232

FLASH GORDON (Universal, 1980) Queen
Elektra 5E-518

FLASHDANCE (Paramount, 1983) Giorgio Moroder
  Casablanca 811 492-1 M-1; 811 492-2 (CD)

FLASHPOINT (Tri-Star, 1984) Tangerine Dream
  EMI ST 17141

FLESH AND BLOOD (Orion, 1985) Basil Poledouris
  Varese Sarabande STV 81256

FLESH FOR FRANKENSTEIN see ANDY WARHOL'S FRANKENSTEIN

FLETCH (Universal, 1985) Harold Faltermeyer
  MCA 6142

THE FLY (Twentieth Century-Fox, 1986) Howard Shore
  Varese Sarabande STV 81289; VCD 47272 (CD)

THE FOG (Avco Embassy, 1980) John Carpenter
  Varese Sarabande STV 81191; VCD 47267 (CD)

FOLLOW THAT BIRD see SESAME STREET PRESENTS FOLLOW
    THAT BIRD

FOOL FOR LOVE (Cannon, 1985) Sandy Rogers
  MCA 6156

FOOTLOOSE (Paramount, 1984) various composers
  Columbia JS 39242, 9C9-39404 (picture disc); CK 39242 (CD)

FOR YOUR EYES ONLY (United Artists, 1981) Bill Conti
  Liberty L00-1109

FORBIDDEN WORLD (New World, 1982) Susan Justin
  Web ST-107

FORBIDDEN ZONE (Borack, 1980) Danny Elfman
  Varese Sarabande STV 81170

THE FORMULA (Metro-Goldwyn-Mayer/United Artists, 1980) Bill
    Conti
  Varese Sarabande STV 81153

THE FOUR MUSKETEERS (Twentieth Century-Fox, 1975) Lalo
    Schifrin
  Label "X" LXCD 5 (CD)

FOUR WIVES (Warner Bros., 1939) Max Steiner
  Entr'acte ERM 6004
  Label "X" LXCD 3 (CD)

THE FOURTH MAN (Netherlands, 1984) Loek Dikker
  Varese Sarabande STV 81222

THE FOURTH PROTOCOL (Britain, 1987) Lalo Schifrin
DRG SBL 12591

FOXES (United Artists, 1980) Giorgio Moroder
Casablanca NBLP 2-7206

FRANCES (Universal, 1982) John Barry
Southern Cross SCRS 1001

THE FRENCH LIEUTENANT'S WOMAN (United Artists, 1981) Carl
Davis
DRG SL 6106; CDRG 6106 (CD)

FRIDAY THE 13TH (Paramount, 1980) Harry Manfredini
Gramavision GR 1030

FRIDAY THE 13TH PART 2 (Paramount, 1981) Harry Manfredini
Gramavision GR 1030

FRIDAY THE 13TH PART 3 (Paramount, 1982) Harry Manfredini
Gramavision GR 1030

FRIENDLY PERSUASION (Allied Artists, 1956) Dimitri Tiomkin
Varese Sarabande STV 81165

FRIENDS (Paramount, 1971) Elton John
Pickwick SPC 3598

FRIGHT NIGHT (Columbia, 1985) various composers
Private I SZ 40087

FROM BEYOND (Empire, 1986) Richard Band
Enigma SJ 73240

FROM RUSSIA WITH LOVE (United Artists, 1964) John Barry
Liberty LT-55114

FROM THE HIP (De Laurentiis Entertainment Group, 1987) Paul
Zaza
Varese Sarabande STV 81309

FULL METAL JACKET (Warner Bros., 1987) Abigail Mead
Warner Bros. 25613-1; 25613-2 (CD)

FULL OF LIFE (Columbia, 1956) George Duning
Web ST-108

GABRIELA (Portugal, 1984) Antonio Carlos Jobim
RCA ABL 1-5186

GANDHI (Columbia, 1982) Ravi Shankar, George Fenton
RCA ABL 1-4557

GATOR (United Artists, 1976) Charles Bernstein
MCA 25014

THE GHOST AND MRS. MUIR (Twentieth Century-Fox, 1947)
Bernard Herrmann
Varese Sarabande 704.340; VCD 47254 (CD)

GHOST OF FRANKENSTEIN (Universal, 1942) Hans J. Salter
Tony Thomas Productions TT-HS-3 (private)

GHOST STORY (Universal, 1981) Philippe Sarde
MCA 5287, 27118

GHOSTBUSTERS (Columbia, 1984) various composers
Arista AL 8-8246, 6-8418; ARCD 8246 (CD)

GINGER AND FRED (Italy, 1986) Nicola Piovani
Varese Sarabande STV 81277

GIRLS JUST WANT TO HAVE FUN (New World, 1985) various
composers
Mercury 824 510-1; 824 510-2 (CD)

THE GLASS MENAGERIE (Cineplex Odeon, 1987) Henry Mancini
MCA 6222; MCAD 6222 (CD)

THE GLENN MILLER STORY (Universal, 1954) various composers
MCA 1624

GLORIA'S ROMANCE (George Kleine, 1916) Jerome Kern
Library of Congress OMP-103 (CD)

THE GO-BETWEEN (Columbia, 1971) Michel Legrand
Columbia M 35175

THE GODS MUST BE CRAZY (Botswana, 1984) John Boshoff
Varese Sarabande STV 81243

THE GOLDEN CHILD (Paramount, 1986) Michel Colombier, John
Barry
Capitol SJ 12544; CDP 46658 (CD)

GOLDEN EARRINGS (Paramount, 1947) Victor Young
Varese Sarabande STV 81117

THE GOLDEN SEAL (Samuel Goldwyn, 1984) John Barry, Dana
Kaproff
Compleat CSTR 6001

GOLDFINGER (United Artists, 1964) John Barry
Liberty LW-55117

GONE WITH THE WIND (Metro-Goldwyn-Mayer, 1939) Max Steiner
    Polygram PDM 1-7001
    MCA 39063; MCAD 39063 (CD)
    Polydor 817 116-2 (CD)

GOOD MORNING BABYLON (Italy/France, 1987) Nicola Piovani
    Varese Sarabande STV 81317

GOOD MORNING VIETNAM (Touchstone, 1987) various composers
    A&M SP-3913, CD-3913

THE GOOD, THE BAD AND THE UGLY (Italy, 1967) Ennio Morricone
    Liberty LN-10273

GOOD TO GO (Island Pictures, 1986) various composers
    Island 90509-1

GOODBYE, MR. CHIPS (Metro-Goldwyn-Mayer, 1969) Leslie Bricusse
    MCA 39066

THE GOONIES (Warner Bros., 1985) various composers
    Epic SE 40067, PS 40067; EK 40067 (CD)

GORKY PARK (Orion, 1983) James Horner
    Varese Sarabande STV 81206; VCD 47260 (CD)

GOSPEL (Aquarius, 1983) various composers
    Savoy SL 14753

GOSPEL ROAD (Twentieth Century-Fox, 1973) Johnny Cash
    Columbia KG 32253

GOTCHA! (Universal, 1985) various composers
    MCA 5596, 27112

GOTHIC (Britain, 1987) Thomas Dolby
    Virgin 90607-1

THE GRADUATE (Embassy, 1967) Paul Simon, Dave Grusin
    CBS CK 3180 (CD)

GRAND PRIX (Metro-Goldwyn-Mayer, 1966) Maurice Jarre
    MCA 25101

LA GRANDE BOURGEOISE (Italy, 1977) Ennio Morricone
    Cerberus CEM-S 0109

GREASE 2 (Paramount, 1982) Louis St. Louis
    RSO RS 1-3803

THE GREAT MUPPET CAPER (Universal/Associated Film

Distribution, 1981) Joe Raposo
Atlantic SD-16047

THE GREAT TRAIN ROBBERY (United Artists, 1978) Jerry Goldsmith
MCA 25102

THE GREATEST STORY EVER TOLD (United Artists, 1965) Alfred
Newman
MCA 39057

GREMLINS (Warner Bros., 1984) Jerry Goldsmith
Geffen GHSP 24044

THE GREY FOX (Britain, 1983) Michael Conway Baker
DRG SL 9515; CDSL 9515 (CD)

GREYSTOKE: THE LEGEND OF TARZAN (Britain, 1984) John Scott
Warner Bros. 25120-1

GUNS FOR SAN SEBASTIAN (Metro-Goldwyn-Mayer, 1968) Ennio
Morricone
MCA 25103

HAIL! HAIL! ROCK 'N' ROLL (Universal, 1987) Chuck Berry
MCA 6217; MCAD 6217 (CD)

HALLOWEEN (Falcon/Compass, 1978) John Carpenter
Varese Sarabande STV 81176; VCD 47230 (CD)

HALLOWEEN II (Universal, 1981) John Carpenter, Alan Howarth
Varese Sarabande STV 81152

HALLOWEEN III: SEASON OF THE WITCH (Universal, 1982) John
Carpenter, Alan Howarth
MCA 6115

HANG 'EM HIGH (United Artists, 1968) Dominic Frontiere
MCA 1435

HANNAH AND HER SISTERS (Orion, 1986) various composers
MCA 6190; MCAD 6190 (CD)

HANNIBAL BROOKS (United Artists, 1969) Francis Lai
MCA 25104

THE HAPPY ENDING (United Artists, 1970) Michel Legrand
MCA 25105

HARD COUNTRY (Associated Film Distribution, 1981) various
composers
Epic SE 37367

HARD TO HOLD (Universal, 1984) Tom Scott, Rick Springfield
    RCA ABL 1-4935; PCD 1-4935 (CD)

HARRY AND THE HENDERSONS (Universal, 1987) Bruce Broughton
    MCA 6208

HAWK THE SLAYER (Chips, 1980) Harry Robertson
    Chips CHLP-1

HEAD (Columbia, 1968) Ken Thorne
    Rhino RNLP 145

HEART BEAT (Orion, 1980) Jack Nitzsche
    Capitol S00-12029

HEARTS OF FIRE (Lorimar, 1987) various composers
    Columbia SC 40870; CK 40870 (CD)

HEAT AND DUST (Britain, 1983) Richard Robbins
    Varese Sarabande STV 81194

HEAVEN HELP US (Tri-Star, 1985) various composers
    EMI SV 17154

HEAVENLY BODIES (Metro-Goldwyn-Mayer/United Artists, 1985)
    various composers
    Private I SZ 39930

THE HEAVENLY KID (Orion, 1985) various composers
    Elektra 60425-1

HEAVEN'S GATE (United Artists, 1982) David Mansfield
    Liberty L00-1073

HEAVY METAL (Columbia, 1981) Elmer Bernstein
    Full Moon/Asylum 5E-547 (orchestral score), DP-90004 (rock
    music)

HEDDA (Britain, 1975) Laurie Johnson
    Starlog/Varese Sarabande SV-95002; VCD 47270 (CD)

HELLRAISER (New World, 1987) Christopher Young
    Cinedisc CDD 1001 (CD)

HEMINGWAY'S ADVENTURES OF A YOUNG MAN (Twentieth Century-
    Fox, 1962) Franz Waxman
    Entr'acte ERS 6516
    Label "X" LXRS 201; LXCD 1 (CD)

HENRY V (Britain, 1944) William Walton
    MCA 6187; MCAD 6187 (CD)

HERCULES (Cannon, 1983) Pino Donaggio
    Varese Sarabande STV 81187

HE'S MY GIRL (Scotti Bros., 1987) various composers
    Scotti Bros. SZ 40906

HIDING OUT (De Laurentiis Entertainment Group, 1987) various
        composers
    Virgin 90661-1; 90661-2 (CD)

HIGH ROAD TO CHINA (Warner Bros., 1983) John Barry
    Southern Cross SCAR 5003

HISTORY OF THE WORLD, PART I (Twentieth Century-Fox, 1981)
        John Morris
    Warner Bros. BSK-3579

THE HOLLYWOOD KNIGHTS (Columbia, 1980) various composers
    Casablanca NBLP 7218

HOLLYWOOD VICE SQUAD (Cinema Group, 1986) Chris Spedding
    Restless 72147-1

HOLOCAUST 2000 see THE CHOSEN

HOME MOVIES (United Artists Classics, 1980) Pino Donaggio
    Varese Sarabande STV 81139

HOME OF THE BRAVE (Cinecom, 1986) Laurie Anderson
    Warner Bros. 25400-1

THE HONEY POT (United Artists, 1967) John Addison
    MCA 25106

HONEYSUCKLE ROSE (Warner Bros., 1980) Willie Nelson
    Columbia S2 36752; CGK 36752 (CD)

HONKY TONK FREEWAY (Universal/Associated Film Distribution,
        1981) George Martin, Elmer Bernstein, Steve Dorff
    Capitol ST-12160

HONKYTONK MAN (Warner Bros., 1982) various composers
    Warner Bros./Viva 23739-1

HOOSIERS (Orion, 1986) Jerry Goldsmith
    Polydor 831 475-1 Y-1; 831 475-2 (CD)

HOPE AND GLORY (Columbia, 1987) Peter Martin
    Varese Sarabande STV 81329; VCD 47290 (CD)

HORROR EXPRESS (Britain, 1973) John Cacavas
    Citadel CT 7012

HORROR PLANET (Almi, 1982) John Scott
Citadel CT 7023

THE HOTEL NEW HAMPSHIRE (Orion, 1984) Jacques Offenbach
Capitol ST 12337

HOUSE (New World, 1986) Harry Manfredini
Varese Sarabande STV 81324; VCD 47295 (CD)

HOUSE II: THE SECOND STORY (New World, 1987) Harry Manfredini
Varese Sarabande STV 81324; VCD 47295 (CD)

HOW THE WEST WAS WON (Metro-Goldwyn-Mayer, 1962) Alfred
Newman
Lone Star LS-1983 (private)
MCA 39043

HOW TO BEAT THE HIGH COST OF LIVING (Filmways, 1980)
Patrick Williams
Columbia JS 36741

HOWARD THE DUCK (Universal, 1986) John Barry, Thomas Dolby
MCA 6173

THE HOWLING (Avco Embassy, 1981) Pino Donaggio
Varese Sarabande STV 81150

HUK (United Artists, 1956) Albert Glasser
Screen Archives 10.001 (private)

HUMANOIDS FROM THE DEEP (New World, 1980) James Horner
Cerberus CST-0203

HUNDRA (Italy, 1984) Ennio Morricone
Macola MRC 0903

THE HUNGER (Metro-Goldwyn-Mayer/United Artists, 1983) Michel
Rubini, Denny Jaeger
Varese Sarabande STV 81184; VCD 47261 (CD)

I WAS A TEENAGE ZOMBIE (Horizon Releasing, 1987) various
composers
Enigma SJ 73296

ICE STATION ZEBRA (Metro-Goldwyn-Mayer, 1968) Michel Legrand
MCA 25017

ICEMAN (Universal, 1984) Bruce Smeaton
Southern Cross SCRS 1006

THE IDOLMAKER (United Artists, 1980) Jeff Barry
A&M SP-4840

IF IT'S TUESDAY, THIS MUST BE BELGIUM (United Artists, 1969)
     Walter Scharf
     MCA 967

IN LOVE AND WAR (Twentieth Century-Fox, 1958) Hugo Friedhofer
     Preamble PRCD 1777 (CD)

IN THE MOOD (Lorimar, 1987) various composers
     Atlantic 81788-1; 81788-2 (CD)

INCHON (Cne Way Productions, 1981) Jerry Goldsmith
     Regency RI 8502

THE INCREDIBLE SHRINKING MAN (Universal, 1957) Hans J.
     Salter
     Tony Thomas Productions TT-HS-4 (private)

INDIANA JONES AND THE TEMPLE OF DOOM (Paramount, 1984)
     John Williams
     Polydor 821 592-1 Y-1; 821 592-2 (CD)

INNERSPACE (Warner Bros., 1987) Jerry Goldsmith
     Geffen GHS 24161; 24161-2 (CD)

INSEMINOID see HORROR PLANET

INSIDE MOVES (Associated Film Distribution, 1980) various
     composers
     Full Moon FMH-3506

INSPECTOR CLOUSEAU (United Artists, 1968) Ken Thorne
     MCA 25107

INTO THE NIGHT (Universal, 1985) Ira Newborn
     MCA 5561

INVADERS FROM MARS (Cannon, 1986) David Storrs (not used in
     the film)
     Enigma SJ 73226

INVASION U.S.A. (Cannon, 1985) Jay Chattaway
     Varese Sarabande STV 81263

INVESTIGATION OF A CITIZEN ABOVE SUSPICION (Italy, 1970)
     Ennio Morricone
     Cerberus CEM-S 0110

INVITATION AU VOYAGE (France, 1983) Gabriel Yared
     Varese Sarabande STV 81189

INVITATION TO THE DANCE (Metro-Goldwyn-Mayer, 1956) Jacques

Ibert, Andre Previn
MCA 25037

IRMA LA DOUCE (United Artists, 1963) Andre Previn
MCA 39068; MCAD 6178 (CD)

IRON EAGLE (Tri-Star, 1986) various composers
Capitol SV 12499

THE ISLAND (Universal, 1980) Ennio Morricone
Varese Sarabande STV 81147

ISLAND IN THE SKY (Warner Bros., 1953) Emil Newman, Hugo
Friedhofer
Varese Sarabande STV 81116

THE ISLAND OF DR. MOREAU (American International, 1977)
Laurence Rosenthal
Wells HG 4000 (private)

ISLANDS IN THE STREAM (Paramount, 1977) Jerry Goldsmith
Monogram JG-7711 (private)
Intrada RVF 6003; 6003 (CD)

IT LIVES AGAIN (Warner Bros., 1978) Bernard Herrmann, Laurie
Johnson
Starlog SR-1002

IT STARTED IN NAPLES (Paramount, 1960) Alessandro Cicognini
Varese Sarabande STV 81122

IT'S A MAD, MAD, MAD, MAD WORLD (United Artists, 1963) Ernest
Gold
MCA 39076

IT'S ALIVE 2 see IT LIVES AGAIN

IT'S MY TURN (Columbia, 1980) various composers
Motown M8-947 M1

IVAN THE TERRIBLE (Russia, 1947) Sergei Prokofiev
Vox Cum Laude 3-VCL 9004X

JAGGED EDGE (Columbia, 1985) John Barry
Varese Sarabande STV 81252

JAKE SPEED (New World, 1986) Mark Snow
Varese Sarabande STV 81285

JAMAA FANAKA'S PENITENTIARY III (Cannon, 1987) various
composers
RCA 6663-1-R8

JAMES CLAVELL'S TAI-PAN (De Laurentiis Entertainment Group,
      1986) Maurice Jarre
   Varese Sarabande STV 81293; VCD 47274 (CD)

JAWS 3-D (Universal, 1983) Alan Parker
   MCA 6124

THE JAZZ SINGER (Associated Film Distribution, 1980) Neil Diamond
   Capitol SWAV-12120

THE JEWEL OF THE NILE (Twentieth Century-Fox, 1985) various
      composers
   Arista JL 9-8406; ARCD 8406 (CD)

JO JO DANCER, YOUR LIFE IS CALLING (Columbia, 1986) various
      composers
   Warner Bros. 25444-1

JOHN PAUL JONES (Warner Bros., 1959) Max Steiner
   Varese Sarabande STV 81146

JOHNNY GUITAR (Republic, 1953) Victor Young
   Citadel CT 7026

JONATHAN LIVINGSTON SEAGULL (Paramount, 1973) Neil Diamond
   Columbia CK 32550 (CD)

JOSEPH ANDREWS (Paramount, 1977) John Addison
   Tony Thomas Productions TT-JA-2 (private)

JOURNEY INTO FEAR (Canada, 1976) Alex North
   Citadel CT 7014

JUDGMENT AT NUREMBERG (United Artists, 1961) Ernest Gold
   MCA 39055

JULIA (Twentieth Century-Fox, 1977) Georges Delerue
   DRG SL 9514

JULIUS CAESAR (Metro-Goldwyn-Mayer, 1953) Miklos Rozsa
   MCA 25022

JUMPIN' JACK FLASH (Twentieth Century-Fox, 1986) various
      composers
   Mercury 830 545-1

THE JUNGLE BOOK (Korda-United Artists, 1942) Miklos Rozsa
   Entr'acte ERM 6002
   Varese Sarabande VCD 47258 (CD)

THE JUPITER MENACE (Celebrity Releasing, 1981) Larry Fast
   Passport PB 6014

JUST BETWEEN FRIENDS (Orion, 1986) Patrick Williams
    Warner Bros. 25391-1

JUST ONE OF THE GUYS (Columbia, 1985) various composers
    Elektra 60426-1-E

JUST TELL ME YOU LOVE ME (1980) Dick Halligan
    MCA 3255

JUST THE WAY YOU ARE (Metro-Goldwyn-Mayer/United Artists,
    1984) Vladimir Cosma
    Varese Sarabande STV 81247

THE KARATE KID (Columbia, 1984) Bill Conti
    Casablanca 822 213-1

THE KARATE KID PART II (Columbia, 1986) various composers
    United Artists SW 40414

THE KENTUCKIAN (United Artists, 1955) Bernard Herrmann
    Preamble PRCD 1777 (CD)

KEYS OF THE KINGDOM (Twentieth Century-Fox, 1944) Alfred
    Newman
    Cine LP 1020 (private)

THE KILLERS (Universal, 1946) Miklos Rozsa
    Tony Thomas Productions TT-MR-4 (private)

THE KINDRED (F/M Entertainment, 1987) David Newman
    Varese Sarabande STV 81308

KING KONG (RKO, 1933) Max Steiner
    Southern Cross SCRS 5006; SCCD 901 (CD)

KING KONG LIVES (De Laurentiis Entertainment Group, 1986)
    John Scott
    MCA 6203

THE KING OF COMEDY (Twentieth Century-Fox, 1983) Robbie
    Robertson
    Warner Bros. 23765-1

KING OF KINGS (Metro-Goldwyn-Mayer, 1961) Miklos Rozsa
    MCA 39056
    Varese Sarabande VC 81104; VCD 47268 (CD)

KING SOLOMON'S MINES (Cannon, 1985) Jerry Goldsmith
    Restless 72106-1

KINGS ROW (Warner Bros., 1942) Erich Wolfgang Korngold

Chalfont SDG 305
Varese Sarabande VCD 47203 (CD)

KISS OF THE SPIDER WOMAN (Brazil, 1985) John Neschling, Wally
      Badarou
      Island 90475-1

KISSIN' COUSINS (Metro-Goldwyn-Mayer, 1963) various composers
      RCA AYL 1-4115

THE KNACK ... AND HOW TO GET IT (United Artists, 1964) John
      Barry
      MCA 25109

KNIGHTS OF THE CITY (New World, 1986) various composers
      Private I SZ 40317

KNIGHTS OF THE ROUND TABLE (Metro-Goldwyn-Mayer, 1953)
      Miklos Rozsa
      Varese Sarabande STV 81128; VCD 47269 (CD)

KOYAANISQATSI (New Cinema, 1983) Philip Glass
      Antilles ASTA 1, 90626-1; 90626-2 (CD)

KRAMER VS. KRAMER (Columbia, 1979) Henry Purcell, Antonio
      Vivaldi
      Columbia M 35873

KRULL (Columbia, 1983) James Horner
      Southern Cross SCRS 1004; SCCD 1004 (CD)

KRUSH GROOVE (Warner Bros., 1985) various composers
      Warner Bros. 25295-1

LABYRINTH (Tri-Star, 1986) Trevor Jones, David Bowie
      EMI SV 17206; CDP 46312 (CD)

LADY BEWARE (Scotti Bros., 1987) Craig Safan
      Scotti Bros. SZ 40971

LADYHAWKE (Warner Bros./Twentieth Century-Fox, 1985) Andrew
      Powell
      Atlantic 81248-1

LASSITER (Warner Bros., 1984) Ken Thorne
      Varese Sarabande STV 81208

THE LAST AMERICAN VIRGIN (Cannon, 1982) various composers
      Columbia JS 38279

THE LAST ANGRY MAN (Columbia, 1959) George Duning
      Web ST-108

THE LAST COMMAND (Republic, 1955) Max Steiner
Citadel CT 7019

THE LAST DRAGON (Tri-Star, 1985) various composers
Motown 6128 ML

THE LAST EMBRACE (United Artists, 1979) Miklos Rozsa
Varese Sarabande STV 81166

THE LAST EMPEROR (Columbia, 1987) David Byrne, Ryuichi Sakamoto
Virgin 90690-1; 90690-2 (CD)

THE LAST METRO (United Artists, 1981) Georges Delerue
DRG SL 9504, 9519

THE LAST RUN (Metro-Goldwyn-Mayer, 1971) Jerry Goldsmith
MCA 25116

THE LAST STARFIGHTER (Universal, 1984) Craig Safan
Southern Cross SCRS 1007; SCCD 1007 (CD)

LAWRENCE OF ARABIA (Columbia, 1962) Maurice Jarre
Arista ALB6-8380

LEGAL EAGLES (Universal, 1986) Elmer Bernstein
MCA 6172

LEGEND (Universal, 1986) Tangerine Dream
MCA 6165

LEGEND OF THE LONE RANGER (Universal, 1981) John Barry
MCA 5212

THE LEOPARD (Twentieth Century-Fox, 1963) Nino Rota
Varese Sarabande STV 81190

LESS THAN ZERO (Twentieth Century-Fox, 1987) various composers
Def Jam/Columbia SC 44042; CK 44042 (CD)

LETHAL WEAPON (Warner Bros., 1987) Michael Kamen, Eric Clapton
Warner Bros. 25561-1

LET'S GET HARRY (Tri-Star, 1986) Brad Fiedel
Varese Sarabande STV 81301

THE LETTER (Warner Bros., 1940) Max Steiner
Tony Thomas Productions TT-MS-12 (private)

LETTER TO BREZHNEV (Britain, 1986) various composers
MCA 6162

LIEUTENANT KIJE see THE CZAR WANTS TO SLEEP

LIFEFORCE (Tri-Star, 1985) Henry Mancini
Varese Sarabande STV 81249

LIGHT OF DAY (Tri-Star, 1987) various composers
Blackheart SZ 40654; ZK 40654 (CD)

LILI (Metro-Goldwyn-Mayer, 1953) Bronislau Kaper
MCA 1426

LILI MARLEEN (United Artists, 1981) Peer Raben
DRG SL 9506

LINK (Cannon, 1986) Jerry Goldsmith
Varese Sarabande STV 81294; VCD 47276 (CD)

LION OF THE DESERT (United Film Distribution, 1981) Maurice
    Jarre
Project 3 PR 5107

LIONHEART (Orion, 1987) Jerry Goldsmith
Varese Sarabande STV 81304, 81311; VCD 47282, 47288 (CD)

LIQUID SKY (Cinevista, 1983) Slava Tsukerman, Brenda I.
    Hutchinson, Clive Smith
Varese Sarabande STV 81181

THE LIQUIDATOR (Metro-Goldwyn-Mayer, 1966) Lalo Schifrin
MCA 25137

LISTEN, LET'S MAKE LOVE (Italy, 1968) Ennio Morricone
GSF 1003

THE LITTLE NUNS (Italy, 1965) Ennio Morricone
Cerberus CEM-S 0115

LITTLE SHOP OF HORRORS (American International, 1960) Fred
    Katz
Rhino RNSP-304

THE LIVING DAYLIGHTS (Metro-Goldwyn-Mayer/United Artists,
    1987) John Barry
Warner Bros. 25616-1; 25616-2 (CD)

THE LIVING WORD (unreleased, 1982) Edward David Zeliff
AEI 3112

LOCAL HERO (Warner Bros., 1983) Mark Knopfler
Warner Bros. 23827-1

LOLA (West Germany, 1982) Peer Raben
DRG SL 9508

LOLITA (Metro-Goldwyn-Mayer, 1962) Nelson Riddle, Bob Harris
MCA 39067

LONE WOLF McQUADE (Orion, 1983) Francesco DeMasi
Citadel CT 7024

THE LONELY GUY (Universal, 1984) Jerry Goldsmith
MCA 36010

THE LONELY LADY (Universal, 1983) Charles Calello
Allegiance AV 441

THE LONG RIDERS (United Artists, 1980) Ry Cooder
Warner Bros. HS 3448

LORCA AND THE OUTLAWS (Britain, 1985) Tony Banks
Atlantic 81680-1

THE LOST BOYS (Warner Bros., 1987) various composers
Atlantic 81767-1; 81767-2 (CD)

THE LOST HONOR OF KATHARINA BLUM (West Germany, 1975) Hans
Werner Henze
Varese Sarabande STV 81224

THE LOST WEEKEND (Paramount, 1945) Miklos Rozsa
Tony Thomas Productions TT-MR-2 (private)

LOUIE BLUIE (Corinth Films, 1985) various composers
Arhoolie 1095

LOUISIANE (Canada/France, 1984) Claude Bolling
CBS FM 39353

LOVE IS A FUNNY THING (France, 1970) Francis Lai
MCA 25111

LOVE SONGS (Canada/France, 1986) Michel Legrand
Varese Sarabande STV 81258

LOVING COUPLES (Twentieth Century-Fox, 1980) Fred Karlin
Motown M8-949 M1

LYDIA (Alexander Korda, 1941) Miklos Rozsa
Varese Sarabande STV 81166; VCD 47269 (CD)

MAD MAX (Australia, 1979) Brian May
Varese Sarabande STV 81144

MAD MAX 2 see THE ROAD WARRIOR

MAD MAX BEYOND THUNDERDOME (Australia, 1985) Maurice Jarre
Capitol SWAV 12429

MADE IN HEAVEN (Lorimar, 1987) various composers
Elektra 60729-1

MAGIC FIRE (Republic, 1954) Richard Wagner, Erich Wolfgang
Korngold
Varese Sarabande STV 81179

MAGNIFICENT OBSESSION (Universal, 1954) Frank Skinner
Varese Sarabande STV 81118

MAGNUM FORCE (Warner Bros., 1973) Lalo Schifrin
Viva 23990-1

MAKE HASTE TO LIVE (Republic, 1954) Elmer Bernstein
Citadel CT 7021

MAKING MR. RIGHT (Orion, 1987) Chaz Jankel
Varese Sarabande STV 81320; VCD 47291 (CD)

MAKING THE GRADE (Metro-Goldwyn-Mayer/United Artists/Cannon,
1984) Basil Poledouris
Varese Sarabande STV 81204

A MAN AND A WOMAN: 20 YEARS LATER (France, 1986) Francis
Lai
Finnadar 90562-1

THE MAN FROM SNOWY RIVER (Australia, 1983) Bruce Rowland
Varese Sarabande STV 81167; VCD 47217 (CD)

MAN OF A THOUSAND FACES (Universal, 1957) Frank Skinner
Varese Sarabande STV 81121

MAN ON FIRE (France/Italy, 1987) John Scott
Varese Sarabande STV 81343; VCD 47314 (CD)

THE MAN WITH BOGART'S FACE (Twentieth Century-Fox, 1980)
George Duning
Web ST-104

THE MAN WITH THE GOLDEN GUN (United Artists, 1974) John
Barry
Liberty LW-50358

MANHATTAN (United Artists, 1979) George Gershwin
CBS MK 36020 (CD)

THE MANHATTAN PROJECT (Twentieth Century-Fox, 1986) Philippe
    Sarde
    Varese Sarabande STV 81282

MANHUNTER (De Laurentiis Entertainment Group, 1986) various
    composers
    MCA 6182

MANIAC (Films Around the World, 1980) Jay Chattaway
    Varese Sarabande STV 81143

MARIE (Metro-Goldwyn-Mayer/United Artists, 1985) Francis Lai
    Varese Sarabande STV 81265

MARIE WARD (1986) Elmer Bernstein
    Varese Sarabande STV 81268

MARK DI SUVERO, SCULPTOR (Parrot Productions, 1977) Philip
    Glass
    Virgin VI 2085

MARVIN AND TIGE (Major Films, 1984) Patrick Williams
    Capitol ST 12307

MASK (Universal, 1985) various composers
    MCA 6140

MASTERS OF THE UNIVERSE (Cannon, 1987) Bill Conti
    Varese Sarabande STV 81333; VCD 47300 (CD)

MATEWAN (Cinecom, 1987) Mason Daring
    Daring DR 1011

MAURICE (Britain, 1987) Richard Robbins
    RCA 6618-1-RC; 6618-2-RC (CD)

MAXIMUM OVERDRIVE (De Laurentiis Entertainment Group, 1986)
    AC/DC
    Atlantic 81650-1; 81650-2 (CD)

McVICAR (Crown International, 1980) Roger Daltrey
    Polydor PD-1-6284

THE MEADOW (Italy, 1979) Ennio Morricone
    Cerberus CEM-S 0115

THE MEANING OF LIFE see MONTY PYTHON'S THE MEANING OF
    LIFE

LA MENACE (Canada/France, 1977) Gerry Mulligan
    DRG MRS 506

MERRY CHRISTMAS, MR. LAWRENCE (Britain/Japan, 1983) Ryuichiro
     Sakamoto
     MCA 6125

METROPOLIS (Germany, 1926) Giorgio Moroder
     Columbia JS 39526; CK 39526 (CD)

MIDNIGHT COWBOY (United Artists, 1969) John Barry
     Liberty LN-10290

MIDNIGHT EXPRESS (Columbia, 1978) Giorgio Moroder
     Casablanca 824 206-2 (CD)

A MIDSUMMER NIGHT'S SEX COMEDY (Warner Bros., 1982) Felix
     Mendelssohn-Bartholdy
     CBS SM 37789

MIKE'S MURDER (Ladd Co./Warner Bros., 1983) Joe Jackson
     A&M SP-4931

A MINOR MIRACLE (Entertainment Enterprises, 1983) Rick Patterson
     Varese Sarabande STV 81193

MISHIMA (Warner Bros., 1985) Philip Glass
     Nonesuch 79113-1; 79113-2 (CD)

THE MISSION (Warner Bros., 1986) Ennio Morricone
     Virgin 90567-1; 90567-2 (CD)

THE MISSOURI BREAKS (United Artists, 1976) John Williams
     MCA 25113

MISUNDERSTOOD (Metro-Goldwyn-Mayer/United Artists, 1984)
     Michael Hoppe, Carlos Frazetti
     Polydor 821 238-1

MODERN GIRLS (Atlantic, 1986) various composers
     Warner Bros., 25526-1

MOLIERE (France, 1980) Rene Clemencic
     Harmonia Mundi HM 1020

MON ONCLE D'AMERIQUE (France, 1981) Arie Dzierlatka
     DRG SL 9505

MONSIGNOR (Twentieth Century-Fox, 1982) John Williams
     Casablanca NBLPH 7277

MONTY PYTHON'S THE MEANING OF LIFE (Britain, 1983) Eric Idle,
     John du Prez
     MCA 6121

THE MOON IN THE GUTTER (France/Italy, 1983) Gabriel Yared
DRG SL 9516

MOONRAKER (United Artists, 1979) John Barry
Liberty L00-50971

MOSCOW ON THE HUDSON (Columbia, 1984) David McHugh
RCA ABL 1-5036

THE MOSQUITO COAST (Warner Bros., 1986) Maurice Jarre
Fantasy FSP 21005; FCD 21005 (CD)

MOVIE MOVIE (Warner Bros., 1978) Ralph Burns
Film Score FS 7914

THE MUPPETS TAKE MANHATTAN (Tri-Star, 1984) Ralph Burns,
    Jeff Moss
Warner Bros. 25114-1

MUSCLE BEACH PARTY (American International, 1964) various
    composers
Rhino RNDF-205

MUTANT (Film Ventures International, 1984) Richard Band
Varese Sarabande STV 81209

MUTINY ON THE BOUNTY (Metro-Goldwyn-Mayer, 1962) Bronislau
    Kaper
MCA 25007

MY DEMON LOVER (New Line Cinema, 1987) David Newman
Varese Sarabande STV 81322

THE NAKED CITY (Universal, 1948) Miklos Rozsa
Tony Thomas Productions TT-MR-3 (private)

NAPOLEON (France, 1927) Carmine Coppola
CBS FM 37230

NATIONAL LAMPOON'S ANIMAL HOUSE (Universal, 1978) various
    composers
MCA MCAD 31023 (CD)

NATIONAL LAMPOON'S VACATION (Warner Bros., 1983) Ralph
    Burns
Warner Bros. 23909-1

NATIVE SON (Cinecom, 1986) James Mtume
MCA 6198

THE NATURAL (Tri-Star, 1984) Randy Newman
Warner Bros. 25116-1

NEAR DARK (Near Dark Joint Ventures, 1987) Tangerine Dream
     Varese Sarabande STV 81345; VCD 47309 (CD)

NEVER ON SUNDAY (Greece, 1960) Manos Hadjidakis
     Liberty LN-10280

THE NEVERENDING STORY (West Germany, 1984) Klaus Doldinger,
     Giorgio Moroder
     EMI ST 17139

NEW ORLEANS (United Artists, 1947) various composers
     Giants of Jazz GOJ-1025

A NIGHT IN HEAVEN (Twentieth Century-Fox, 1983) Jan Hammer
     A&M SP-4966

NIGHT OF THE COMET (Atlantic, 1984) various composers
     Macola MRC 0900

NIGHT OF THE LIVING DEAD (Image Ten/Continental, 1968)
     various composers
     Varese Sarabande STV 81151

THE NIGHT OF THE SHOOTING STARS (Italy, 1982) Nicola Piovani
     Varese Sarabande STV 81175

NIGHT SHIFT (Warner Bros., 1982) Burt Bacharach
     Warner Bros. 23702-1

THE NIGHT THE LIGHTS WENT OUT IN GEORGIA (Avco Embassy,
     1981) David Shire
     Mirage WTG-16051

NIGHTHAWKS (Universal, 1981) Keith Emerson
     MCA BSR 5196

A NIGHTMARE ON ELM STREET (New Line Cinema, 1984) Charles
     Bernstein
     Varese Sarabande STV 81236; VCD 47255 (CD)

A NIGHTMARE ON ELM STREET, PART 2: FREDDY'S REVENGE
     (New Line Cinema, 1985) Christopher Young
     Varese Sarabande STV 81275; VCD 47255 (CD)

A NIGHTMARE ON ELM STREET 3: DREAM WARRIORS (New Line
     Cinema, 1987) Angelo Badalamenti
     Varese Sarabande STV 81314; VCD 47293 (CD)

NIJINSKY (Paramount, 1980) Various composers
     Columbia M 35861

9 1/2 WEEKS (Metro-Goldwyn-Mayer/United Artists, 1986) various

composers
Capitol SV 12470; CDP 46722 (CD)

9 TO 5 (Twentieth Century-Fox, 1980) Charles Fox, Dolly Parton
Twentieth Century T-627

1984 (Britain, 1985) Eurythmics
RCA ABL 1-5349

NO MERCY (Tri-Star, 1986) Alan Silvestri
TVT 3002

NO SAD SONGS FOR ME (Columbia, 1950) George Duning
Web ST-108

NO SMALL AFFAIR (Columbia, 1984) Rupert Holmes
Atlantic 80189-1

NO WAY OUT (Orion, 1987) Maurice Jarre
Varese Sarabande STV 81334; VCD 47301 (CD)

EL NORTE (1984) various composers
Antilles IVA 4

NORTH BY NORTHWEST (Metro-Goldwyn-Mayer, 1959) Bernard
Herrmann
Starlog/Varese Sarabande SV-95001
Varese Sarabande VCD 47205 (CD)

NORTH STAR see MARK DI SUVERO, SCULPTOR

NOTHING IN COMMON (Tri-Star, 1986) various composers
Arista AL 9-8438; ARCD 8438 (CD)

OCTOPUSSY (Britain, 1983) John Barry
A&M SP-4967

OF MICE AND MEN (United Artists, 1939) Aaron Copland
Argo ZRG 935

AN OFFICER AND A GENTLEMAN (Paramount, 1982) Jack Nitzsche
Island 90017-1

OLTRE LA PORTA (Italy, 1982) Pino Donaggio
Varese Sarabande STV 81213

ON GOLDEN POND (Universal, 1981) Dave Grusin
MCA 6106

ON THE WATERFRONT (Columbia, 1954) Leonard Bernstein
Deutsche Grammophon 2532 051

ONCE BITTEN (Samuel Goldwyn, 1985) various composers
   MCA 6154

ONCE UPON A TIME IN AMERICA (Warner Bros., 1984) Ennio
      Morricone
   Mercury 818 697-1; 822 334-2 (CD)

ONE FROM THE HEART (Columbia, 1982) Tom Waits
   Columbia FC 37703

1001 ARABIAN NIGHTS (Columbia, 1959) George Duning
   Varese Sarabande STV 81138

ONE-TRICK PONY (Warner Bros., 1980) Paul Simon
   Warner Bros. 3472-2 (CD)

THE OSTERMAN WEEKEND (Twentieth Century-Fox, 1983) Lalo
      Schifrin
   Varese Sarabande STV 81198

THE OTHER SIDE OF THE MOUNTAIN (Universal, 1975) Charles
      Fox
   MCA 1539

OUR TOWN (United Artists, 1940) Aaron Copland
   Argo ZRG 935

OUT OF AFRICA (Universal, 1985) John Barry
   MCA 6158; MCAD 6158 (CD)

OUT OF BOUNDS (Columbia, 1986) Stewart Copeland
   International Record Syndicate 6180

OUTLAND (Ladd Co./Warner Bros., 1981) Jerry Goldsmith
   Warner Bros. HS-3551

OVER THE TOP (Warner Bros., 1987) Giorgio Moroder
   Columbia SC 40655; CK 40655 (CD)

THE PARADINE CASE (Selznick, 1947) Franz Waxman
   Entr'acte ERM 6002

PARIS, TEXAS (Twentieth Century-Fox, 1984) Ry Cooder
   Warner Bros. 25270-1

A PASSAGE TC INDIA (Britain, 1984) Maurice Jarre
   Capitol SV 12389

PEGGY SUE GOT MARRIED (Tri-Star, 1986) John Barry
   Varese Sarabande STV 81295; VCD 47275 (CD)

PENITENTIARY III see JAMAA FANAKA'S PENITENTIARY III

PENNIES FROM HEAVEN (Metro-Goldwyn-Mayer, 1981) various
    composers
    Warner Bros. 2HW 3639

PERFECT (Columbia, 1985) various composers
    Arista AL 9-8278; ARCD 8278 (CD)

PETER RABBIT AND TALES OF BEATRIX POTTER (Metro-Goldwyn-
    Mayer, 1971) John Lanchbery
    Angel S 36789

PEYTON PLACE (Twentieth Century-Fox, 1957) Franz Waxman
    Entr'acte ERS 6515

PHANTOM OF THE PARADISE (Twentieth Century-Fox, 1974) Paul
    Williams, George Aliceson Tipton
    A&M SP-3176

PHAR LAP (Australia, 1984) Bruce Rowland
    Varese Sarabande STV 81230

THE PHILADELPHIA EXPERIMENT (New World, 1984) Ken Wannberg
    Rhino RNSP 306

THE PIRATE (France, 1984) Philippe Sarde
    Varese Sarabande STV 81227

PIRATES (Cannon, 1986) Philippe Sarde
    Varese Sarabande STV 81287; VCD 47265 (CD)

PLACES IN THE HEART (Tri-Star, 1984) various composers
    Varese Sarabande STV 81229

PLAN 9 FROM OUTER SPACE (Distributors Corp. of America, 1959)
    Gordon Zahler
    Hippo PLAN 9

PLANET OF THE APES (Twentieth Century-Fox, 1968) Jerry
    Goldsmith
    Project 3 PRD 5023 SD (CD)

PLATOON (Orion, 1986) various composers
    Atlantic 81742-1; 81742-2 (CD)

PLAYING FOR KEEPS (Universal, 1986) various composers
    Atlantic 81678-1

THE PLOW THAT BROKE THE PLAINS (Works Progress Administra-
    tion, 1936) Virgil Thomson

AEI ABM 3501
Angel CDC 7 47715 2 (CD)

POLICE ACADEMY 4: CITIZENS ON PATROL (Warner Bros., 1987)
     various composers
     Motown 6235 ML

POLTERGEIST (Metro-Goldwyn-Mayer/United Artists, 1982) Jerry
     Goldsmith
     MGM MG-1-5408

POLTERGEIST II: THE OTHER SIDE (Metro-Goldwyn-Mayer, 1986)
     Jerry Goldsmith
     Intrada RVF 6002; 6002 (CD)

POPEYE (Paramount, 1980) Harry Nilsson
     Boardwalk SW-36880

POPI (United Artists, 1969) Dominic Frontiere
     MCA 25044

PORKY'S REVENGE (Twentieth Century-Fox, 1985) various composers
     Columbia JS 39983

THE POWER (Film Ventures International, 1984) Christopher Young
     Cerberus CST-0211

PRANKS (New Image, 1982) Christopher Young
     Citadel CT 7031

PRETTY IN PINK (Paramount, 1986) various composers
     A&M SP-5113

PRIEST OF LOVE (Filmways, 1981) Joseph James
     That's Entertainment TER-1014
     SS 001 (private)

PRINCE OF DARKNESS (Universal, 1987) John Carpenter, Alan
     Howarth
     Varese Sarabande STV 81340; VCD 47310 (CD)

PRINCE OF THE CITY (Orion/Warner Bros., 1981) Paul Chihara
     Varese Sarabande STV 81137

THE PRINCESS BRIDE (Twentieth Century-Fox, 1987) Mark Knopfler
     Warner Bros. 25610-1; 25610-2 (CD)

PRISONER IN THE STREET (France, 1980) Third World
     Island ILPS-9616

PRIVATE LESSONS (Jensen Farley Pictures, 1981) various composers
     MCA 5275

PRIVATE SCHOOL (Universal, 1983) various composers
MCA 36005

PROVIDENCE (France, 1977) Miklos Rozsa
DRG SL 9502

PSYCHO II (Universal, 1983) Jerry Goldsmith
MCA 6119

PSYCHO III (Universal, 1986) Carter Burwell
MCA 6174

PUMPING IRON II: THE WOMEN (Cinecom, 1985) various composers
Island 90273-1

PURPLE RAIN (Warner Bros., 1984) Prince
Warner Bros. 25110-1

THE PURPLE ROSE OF CAIRO (Orion, 1985) Dick Hyman
MCA 6139

THE PURSUIT OF D. B. COOPER (Universal, 1981) James Horner
Polydor PD-1-6344

Q (UFD, 1982) Robert C. Ragland
Cerberus CST-0206

QUADROPHENIA (World Northal, 1979) The Who
Polydor PD-2-6235

QUANDO L'AMORE E SENSUALITA (Italy, 1973) Ennio Morricone
Cerberus CEM-S 0113

QUARTET (New World, 1981) Richard Robbins
Gramavision GR 1020

QUERELLE (West Germany, 1983) Peer Raben
DRG SL 9509

QUEST FOR FIRE (Twentieth Century-Fox, 1982) Philippe Sarde
RCA ABL 1-4274

QUICKSILVER (Columbia, 1986) Tony Banks
Atlantic 81631-1, 81680-1; 81631-2 (CD)

QUO VADIS (Metro-Goldwyn-Mayer, 1951) Miklos Rozsa
MCA 39075

RAD (Tri-Star, 1986) various composers
MCA/Curb 6166

RADIO DAYS (Orion, 1986) various composers
Novus 3017-1-N9; 3017-2-N (CD)

RAGTIME (Paramount, 1981) Randy Newman
Elektra 5E-565

RAIDERS OF THE LOST ARK (Paramount, 1981) John Williams
Columbia JS 37373, 37696 (with dialogue)
Polydor 821 583-1 Y-1; 821 583-2 (CD)

RAISING ARIZONA (Twentieth Century-Fox, 1987) Carter Burwell
Varese Sarabande STV 81318; VCD 47284 (CD)

RAMBO: FIRST BLOOD PART II (Tri-Star, 1985) Jerry Goldsmith
Varese Sarabande STV 81246; VCD 47234 (CD)

RAN (Japan, 1985) Toru Takemitsu
Fantasy FSP 21004

RAPPIN' (Cannon, 1985) various composers
Atlantic 81252-1

RASHOMON (Japan, 1950) Fumio Hayasaka
Varese Sarabande STV 81142; VCD 47271 (CD)

RAW DEAL (De Laurentiis Entertainment Group, 1986) Cinemascore
Varese Sarabande STV 81286

THE RAZOR'S EDGE (Columbia, 1984) Jack Nitzsche
Southern Cross SCRS 1009; SCCD 904 (CD)

THE RE-ANIMATOR (Empire, 1985) Richard Band
Varese Sarabande STV 81261

RED DAWN (Metro-Goldwyn-Mayer/United Artists, 1984) Basil
Poledouris
Intrada RVF 6001

THE RED PONY (Republic, 1949) Aaron Copland
Varese Sarabande STV 81259

RED SONJA (Metro-Goldwyn-Mayer/United Artists, 1985) Ennio
Morricone
Varese Sarabande STV 81248

REDS (Paramount, 1981) Stephen Sondheim, Dave Grusin
Columbia BJS 37690

REFORM SCHOOL GIRLS (New World, 1986) various composers
Rhino RNLP 70310

THE REINCARNATION OF PETER PROUD (American International,
    1975) Jery Goldsmith
    Monogram JG-7711 (private)

REPO MAN (Universal, 1984) various composers
    San Andreas SAR 39019

THE RETURN OF MARTIN GUERRE (France, 1983) Michel Portal
    DRG SL 9514

RETURN OF THE JEDI (Twentieth Century-Fox, 1983) John Williams
    RSO 811 767-1 Y-1; 811 767-2 (CD)
    RCA CRC 1-4748; RCD 1-4748 (CD)

RETURN OF THE LIVING DEAD (Orion, 1985) various composers
    Enigma 72004-1

RETURN OF THE SEVEN (United Artists, 1966) Elmer Bernstein
    Liberty LN-10281

RETURN TO OZ (Buena Vista, 1985) David Shire
    Sonic Atmospheres 113

RETURN TO WATERLOO (Britain, 1985) Ray Davies
    Arista AL 6-8386

REVENGE OF THE NERDS (Twentieth Century-Fox, 1984) various
    composers
    Scotti Bros. BFZ 39599

REVENGE OF THE NINJA (Metro-Goldwyn-Mayer/United Artists,
    1983) Rob Walsh
    Varese Sarabande STV 81195

REVENGE OF THE PINK PANTHER (United Artists, 1978) Henry
    Mancini
    Liberty LN-10277

RHINESTONE (Twentieth Century-Fox, 1984) Dolly Parton
    RCA ABL 1-5032; PCD 1-5032 (CD)

THE RIGHT STUFF (Warner Bros., 1983) Bill Conti
    Varese Sarabande 704.310; VCD 47250 (CD)

RIO GRANDE (Republic, 1950) Victor Young
    Varese Sarabande STV 81124

THE RIVER (Farm Security Administration, 1937) Virgil Thomson
    Angel CDC 7 47715 2 (CD)

THE RIVER (Universal, 1984) John Williams
    MCA 6138

THE RIVER RAT (Paramount, 1984) Mike Post
RCA CBL 1-5310

RIVER'S EDGE (Island Pictures, 1987) Jurgen Knieper
Metal Blade SJ 73242; CDE 73242 (CD) (rock music)
Enigma SJ 73286 (score)

THE ROAD WARRIOR (Australia, 1982) Brian May
Varese Sarabande STV 81155; VCD 47262 (CD)

ROADIE (United Artists, 1980) various composers
Warner Bros. 2HS 3441

ROBOCOP (Orion, 1987) Basil Poledouris
Varese Sarabande STV 81330; VCD 47298 (CD)

ROCK BABY, ROCK IT (Freebar, 1957) various composers
Rhino RNSP-309

ROCK, ROCK, ROCK (Vanguard Productions, 1956) various composers
Chess CH 9254

ROCKERS (New Yorker, 1980) various composers
Mango MLPS-9587

ROCKIN' THE BLUES (1955) various composers
U.G.H.A. 001

ROCKY (United Artists, 1976) Bill Conti
Liberty CDP 7 46081 2 (CD)

ROCKY II (United Artists, 1979) Bill Conti
Liberty CDP 46082 (CD)

ROCKY III (Metro-Goldwyn-Mayer/United Artists, 1982) Bill Conti
Liberty LO 51130; CDP 7 46561 2 (CD)

ROCKY IV (Metro-Goldwyn-Mayer/United Artists, 1985) various
composers
Scotti Bros. SZ 40203; ZK 40203 (CD)

ROLLER BOOGIE (United Artists, 1979) Bob Esty
Casablanca NBLP-2-7194

A ROOM WITH A VIEW (Britain, 1986) Richard Robbins
DRG SBL 12588; CDSBL 12588 (CD)

THE ROSE (Twentieth Century-Fox, 1979) various composers
Atlantic SD 16010; 16010-2 (CD)

ROUND MIDNIGHT (Warner Bros., 1986) Herbie Hancock
    CBS SC 40464; CK 40464 (CD)

ROXANNE (Columbia, 1987) Bruce Smeaton
    Cinedisc CDC 1000 (CD)

RUMBLE FISH (Universal, 1983) Stewart Copeland
    A&M SP-6-4983

RUNAWAY (Tri-Star, 1985) Jerry Goldsmith
    Varese Sarabande STV 81234; VCD 47221 (CD)

RUNAWAY TRAIN (Cannon, 1985) Trevor Jones
    Enigma SJ 73200

THE RUNNER STUMBLES (Twentieth Century-Fox, 1979) Ernest
        Gold
    EG 1001 (private)

RUNNING SCARED (Metro-Goldwyn-Mayer, 1986) various composers
    MCA 6169, 39321; MCAD 31053 (CD)

THE RUSSIANS ARE COMING, THE RUSSIANS ARE COMING
        (United Artists, 1966) Johnny Mandel
    MCA 1428

RUSTLER"S RHAPSODY (Paramount, 1985) Steve Dorff
    Warner Bros. 25284-1

RUTHLESS PEOPLE (Buena Vista, 1986) various composers
    Epic SE 40398; EK 40398 (CD)

RYAN'S DAUGHTER (Metro-Goldwyn-Mayer, 1970) Maurice Jarre
    MCA 25142

SAHARA (Metro-Goldwyn-Mayer/United Artists, 1984) Ennio
        Morricone
    Varese Sarabande STV 81211

ST. ELMO'S FIRE (Columbia, 1985) various composers
    Atlantic 81261-1

SALT AND PEPPER (United Artists, 1968) John Dankworth
    MCA 25035

SANDS OF IWO JIMA (Republic, 1949) Victor Young
    Citadel CT 7027

SANTA CLAUS: THE MOVIE (Tri-Star, 1985) Henry Mancini
    EMI SJ 17177

SATURDAY NIGHT FEVER (Paramount, 1977) various composers
RSO 800 068-2 (CD)

SAVAGE STREETS (Motion Picture Marketing, 1984) Michael Lloyd,
John D'Andrea
MCA 6134

SAY AMEN, SOMEBODY (United Artists, 1983) various composers
DRG SB2L 12584; CDSBXP 12584 (CD)

THE SCALPHUNTERS (United Artists, 1968) Elmer Bernstein
MCA 25042

SCARFACE (Universal, 1983) Giorgio Moroder
MCA 6126

SCREAM FOR HELP (Lorimar, 1984) John Paul Jones
Atlantic 80190-1

SCREAMERS (New World, 1981) Luciano Michelini
Web ST-101

THE SEARCHERS (Warner Bros., 1956) Max Steiner
Entr'acte ERM 6004
Label "X" LXCD 3 (CD)

SECRET ADMIRER (Orion, 1985) various composers
MCA 5611

THE SECRET LIFE OF PLANTS (Paramount, 1979) Stevie Wonder
Tamla T13 371 C2

THE SECRET OF MY SUCCESS (Universal, 1987) various composers
MCA 6205

THE SECRET OF NIMH (Metro-Goldwyn-Mayer/United Artists, 1982)
Jerry Goldsmith
Varese Sarabande STV 81169; VCD 47231 (CD)

THE SECRET OF SANTA VITTORIA (United Artists, 1969) Ernest
Gold
MCA 25034

SECRET PLACES (Britain, 1985) Michel Legrand
Shanachie 82005

SESAME STREET PRESENTS FOLLOW THAT BIRD (Warner Bros.,
1985) Van Dyke Parks, Lennie Niehaus
RCA CBL 1-5475

THE SEVEN SAMURAI (Japan, 1956) Fumio Hayasaka
Varese Sarabande STV 81142; VCD 47271 (CD)

THE 7TH VOYAGE OF SINBAD (Columbia, 1958) Bernard Herrmann
    Varese Sarabande STV 81135; VCD 47256 (CD)

THE SHAPE OF THE LAND (Japan, 1986) Philip Aaberg
    Windham Hill WH 1055; WD 1055 (CD)

SHARKEY'S MACHINE (Orion/Warner Bros., 1981) various composers
    Warner Bros. BSK-3653

SHEENA (Columbia, 1984) Richard Hartley
    Varese Sarabande STV 81225

SHE'S GOTTA HAVE IT (Island Pictures, 1986) Bill Lee
    Island 90528-1

THE SHINING (Warner Bros., 1980) various composers
    Warner Bros. HS 3449

SHOCK TREATMENT (Twentieth Century-Fox, 1981) Richard
    Hartley, Richard O'Brien
    Ode/Warner Bros. LLA-3615

THE SHOES OF THE FISHERMAN (Metro-Goldwyn-Mayer, 1968) Alex
    North
    MCA 25130

SHOGUN ASSASSIN (New World, 1980) W. Michael Lewis, Mark
    Lindsay
    Baby Cart 1001

THE SHOOTING PARTY (Britain, 1985) John Scott
    Varese Sarabande STV 81235

THE SHOOTIST (Paramount, 1976) Elmer Bernstein
    Varese Sarabande 704.350; VCD 47264 (CD)

THE SICILIAN (Twentieth Century-Fox, 1987) David Mansfield
    Virgin 90682-1; 90682-2 (CD)

SID & NANCY (Britain, 1986) various composers
    MCA 6181

SIDNEY SHELDON'S BLOODLINE (Paramount, 1979) Ennio Morricone
    Varese Sarabande STV 81131

SIESTA (Lorimar, 1987) Miles Davis, Marcus Miller
    Warner Bros. 25655-1; 25655-2 (CD)

SILKWOOD (Twentieth Century-Fox, 1983) Georges Delerue
    DRG 6107

SILVER BULLET see STEPHEN KING'S SILVER BULLET

SILVERADO (Columbia, 1985) Bruce Broughton
   Geffen GHS 24080

SISTERS (American International, 1973) Bernard Herrmann
   Southern Cross SCRS 5004; SCCD 903 (CD)

633 SQUADRON (United Artists, 1964) Ron Goodwin
   MCA 25043

SIX PACK (Twentieth Century-Fox, 1982) Charles Fox
   Allegiance AV 430

SIXTEEN CANDLES (Universal, 1984) Ira Newborn
   MCA 36012

SKATETOWN U.S.A. (Columbia, 1979) various composers
   Columbia JC 36292

SKY BANDITS (Britain, 1986) Alfie Kabiljo
   Varese Sarabande STV 81297

SLAM DANCE (Island Pictures, 1987) Mitchell Froom
   Island 90662-1

SLAPSTICK OF ANOTHER KIND (International Film Marketing,
      1984) Michel Legrand, Morton Stevens
   Varese Sarabande STV 81163

THE SLUGGER'S WIFE (Columbia, 1985) various composers
   MCA 5578

SMOKEY AND THE BANDIT 2 (Universal, 1980) various composers
   MCA 6101

SMOKEY AND THE BANDIT PART 3 (Universal, 1983) various
      composers
   MCA 36006

SNOW WHITE AND THE THREE STOOGES (Twentieth Century-Fox,
      1961) Harry Harris
   Columbia Special Products ACS 8450

SOLOMON AND SHEBA (United Artists, 1959) Mario Nascimbene
   MCA 1425

SOME KIND OF WONDERFUL (Paramount, 1987) various composers
   MCA 6200; MCAD 6200 (CD)

SOMETHING WILD (Orion, 1986) various composers
   MCA 6194; MCAD 6194 (CD)

SOMEWHERE IN TIME (Universal, 1980) John Barry
  MCA 5154; MCAD 5154 (CD)

SONG OF BERNADETTE (Twentieth Century-Fox, 1943) Alfred
    Newman
  Varese Sarabande STV 81116

SONGWRITER (Tri-Star, 1984) Kris Kristofferson, Willie Nelson
  Columbia FC 39531

SONNY AND JED (Italy, 1973) Ennio Morricone
  Cerberus CEM-S 0111

SOPHIE'S CHOICE (Universal, 1982) Marvin Hamlisch
  Southern Cross SCRS 1002; SCCD 902 (CD)

SOUL MAN (New World, 1986) various composers
  A&M SP-3903; CD-3903 (CD)

SOUP FOR ONE (Warner Bros., 1982) various composers
  Mirage WTG 19353

SOUTH SEAS ADVENTURE (Cinerama, 1958) Alex North
  Citadel CT 7014

SPACEBALLS (Metro-Goldwyn-Mayer/United Artists, 1987) John
    Morris
  Atlantic 81770-1; 81770-2 (CD)

SPACECAMP (Twentieth Century-Fox, 1986) John Williams
  RCA ABL 1-5856

SPIES LIKE US (Warner Bros., 1985) Elmer Bernstein
  Varese Sarabande STV 81270; VCD 47246 (CD)

SPRING BREAK (Columbia, 1983) Harry Manfredini
  Warner Bros. 23826-1

THE SPY WHO LOVED ME (United Artists, 1977) Marvin Hamlisch
  Liberty LO-50774

STAND BY ME (Columbia, 1986) various composers
  Atlantic 81677-1; 81677-2 (CD)

STAR TREK: THE MOTION PICTURE (Paramount, 1979) Jerry
    Goldsmith
  Columbia PS 36334; CK 36334 (CD)

STAR TREK II: THE WRATH OF KHAN (Paramount, 1982) James
    Horner
  Atlantic SD 19363

STAR TREK III: THE SEARCH FOR SPOCK (Paramount, 1984) James
      Horner
   Capitol SKBK 12360; CDP 46089 (CD)

STAR TREK IV: THE VOYAGE HOME (Paramount, 1986) Leonard
      Rosenman
   MCA 6195; MCAD 6195 (CD)

STAR WARS (Twentieth Century-Fox, 1977) John Williams
   RCA AGL 1-3650
   RSO 800 096-2 (CD)

STARMAN (Columbia, 1984) Jack Nitzsche
   Varese Sarabande STV 81233; VCD 47220 (CD)

STARSTRUCK (Cinecom International, 1982) Phil Judd
   OZ SP 4938

THE STATE OF THINGS (West Germany, 1982) Jurgen Knieper
   Enigma SJ 73286

STAVISKY (France/Italy, 1974) Stephen Sondheim
   RCA RCD 2-7128 (CD)

STAYING ALIVE (Paramount, 1983) various composers
   RSO 813 269-1 Y-1; 813 269-2 (CD)

STEPHEN KING'S SILVER BULLET (Paramount, 1985) Jay Chattaway
   Varese Sarabande STV 81264

STEVIE (Britain, 1978) Patrick Gowers
   Epic SE 37726

THE STING (Universal, 1973) Scott Joplin, Marvin Hamlisch
   MCA MCAD 1625, 31034 (CD)

THE STING II (Universal, 1983) Lalo Schifrin
   MCA 6116

A STOLEN LIFE (Warner Bros., 1946) Max Steiner
   Entr-acte ERM 6004
   Label "X" LXCD 3 (CD)

STOP MAKING SENSE (Cinecom International, 1984) Talking Heads
   Sire 25186-1; 25186-2 (CD)

THE STORY OF NAOMI UEMURA see THE SHAPE OF THE LAND

STRAIGHT TO HELL (Island Pictures, 1987) various composers
   Enigma SJE 73308; CDE 73308 (CD)

STRANGE BREW (Metro-Goldwyn-Mayer/United Artists, 1983) Charles
    Fox
    Mercury 814 104-1 M-1

THE STRANGE LOVE OF MARTHA IVERS (Paramount, 1946) Miklos
    Rozsa
    Medallion ML 314

STRANGER THAN PARADISE (Samuel Goldwyn, 1984) John Lurie
    Enigma SJ 73213; CDE 73213 (CD)

STREETS OF FIRE (Universal, 1984) Ry Cooder
    MCA 5492

STROKER ACE (Universal/Warner Bros., 1983) Al Capps
    MCA 36003

THE STUNT MAN (Twentieth Century-Fox, 1980) Dominic Frontiere
    Twentieth Century T-626

SUBURBIA (New Horizons, 1984) Alex Gibson
    Enigma E 1093

SUBWAY (France, 1985) Eric Serra
    Varese Sarabande STV 81269

SUDDEN IMPACT (Warner Bros., 1983) Lalo Schifrin
    Viva 23990-1

SUMMER AND SMOKE (Paramount, 1962) Elmer Bernstein
    Entr'acte ERS 6519

SUMMER LOVERS (Orion, 1982) Basil Poledouris
    Warner Bros. 23695-1

SUMMER SCHOOL (Paramount, 1987) various composers
    Chrysalis OV 41607; VK 41607 (CD)

THE SUN SHINES BRIGHT (Republic, 1953) Victor Young
    Citadel CT 7027

A SUNDAY IN THE COUNTRY (France, 1984) various composers
    Varese Sarabande STV 81227

SUNNYSIDE (American International, 1979) Alan Douglas, Harold
    Wheeler
    American International AILP 3002

SUNRISE AT CAMPOBELLO (Warner Bros., 1960) Franz Waxman
    Preamble PRCD 1777 (CD)

SUPERGIRL (Tri-Star, 1984) Jerry Goldsmith
   Varese Sarabande STV 81231; VCD 47218 (CD)

SUPERMAN II (Warner Bros., 1981) John Williams, Ken Thorne
   Warner Bros. HS-3505

SUPERMAN III (Warner Bros., 1983) Ken Thorne, Giorgio Moroder
   Warner Bros. 23879-1

SURRENDER (Warner Bros., 1987) Michel Colombier
   Varese Sarabande STV 81348; VCD 47312 (CD)

SWAMP THING (Embassy, 1982) Harry Manfredini
   Varese Sarabande STV 81154

THE SWAN (Metro-Goldwyn-Mayer, 1956) Bronislau Kaper
   MCA 25086

SWANN IN LOVE (France, 1984) Hans Werner Henze
   Varese Sarabande STV 81224

SWEET DREAMS (Tri-Star, 1985) various composers
   MCA 6149; MCAD 6149 (CD)

THE SWORD AND THE SORCERER (Group I, 1982) David Whittaker
   Varese Sarabande STV 81158

SYLVESTER (Columbia, 1985) various composers
   MCA 39026

TAI-PAN   see   JAMES CLAVELL'S TAI-PAN

TAKE THIS JOB AND SHOVE IT (Avco Embassy, 1981) Billy
      Sherrill
   Epic SE 37177

TAXI DRIVER (Columbia, 1976) Bernard Herrmann
   Arista ARCD 8179 (CD)

TEACHERS (Metro-Goldwyn-Mayer/United Artists, 1984) various
      composers
   Capitol SV 12371

TEEN WOLF (Atlantic, 1985) Miles Goodman
   Southern Cross SCRS 1010
   Metronome 829 092-2 (CD)

TEMPEST (Columbia, 1982) Stomu Yamashita
   Casablanca NBLP 7269

THE TEN COMMANDMENTS (Paramount, 1956) Elmer Bernstein
   MCA 2-4159

10 TO MIDNIGHT (Cannon, 1983) Robert O. Ragland
    Varese Sarabande STV 81172

TENDER MERCIES (Universal, 1983) various composers
    Liberty LO-51147

TEPEPA (1968) Ennio Morricone
    Cerberus CEM S-0106

THE TERMINATOR (Orion, 1984) Brad Fiedel
    Enigma 72000-1; 72000-2 (CD)

TERMS OF ENDEARMENT (Paramount, 1983) Michael Gore
    Capitol SV 12329; CDP 46076 (CD)

TERRORVISION (Empire, 1986) Richard Band
    Restless 72120-1

TESS (Columbia, 1980) Philippe Sarde
    MCA 5193

THE TEXAS CHAINSAW MASSACRE, PART 2 (Cannon, 1986) various
    composers
    International Record Syndicate 6184

THAT WAS THEN ... THIS IS NOW (Paramount, 1985) Keith Olsen,
    Bill Cuomo
    Easy Street ESA 9903

THEY CALL IT AN ACCIDENT (France, 1982) various composers
    Island ILPS 9757

THIEF (United Artists, 1981) Tangerine Dream
    Elektra 5E-521

THE THIEF OF BAGDAD (United Artists, 1940) Miklos Rozsa
    Varese Sarabande VCD 47258 (CD)

THIEF OF HEARTS (Paramount, 1984) Harold Faltermeyer
    Casablanca 822 942-1; 822 942-2 (CD)

THE THING (Universal, 1982) Ennio Morricone
    MCA 6111

THIS COULD BE THE NIGHT (Metro-Goldwyn-Mayer, 1957) George
    Stoll
    MCA 39085

THIS IS ELVIS (Warner Bros., 1981) various composers
    RCA CPL 2-4031

THIS IS SPINAL TAP (Embassy, 1984) Christopher Guest, Michael
    McKean, Harry Shearer, Rob Reiner
    Polydor 817 846-1

THREE AMIGOS (Orion, 1986) Elmer Bernstein, Randy Newman
    Warner Bros. 25558-1

THREE BITES OF THE APPLE (Metro-Goldwyn-Mayer, 1967) Eddy
    Manson
    MCA 25010

THREE FOR THE ROAD (New Century/Vista, 1987) Barry Goldberg
    Varese Sarabande STV 81319

THREE O'CLOCK HIGH (Universal, 1987) Tangerine Dream, Sylvester
    Levay
    Varese Sarabande STV 81339; VCD 47307 (CD)

THE THREE WORLDS OF GULLIVER (Columbia, 1959) Bernard
    Herrmann
    Citadel CT 7018

THUNDERBALL (United Artists, 1965) John Barry
    Liberty LT-55132

TIME AFTER TIME (Warner Bros., 1979) Miklos Rozsa
    Southern Cross SCCD 1014 (CD)

THE TIME MACHINE (Metro-Goldwyn-Mayer, 1960) Russell Garcia
    GNP Crescendo GNPS 8008; GNPD 8008 (CD)

TIME OUT OF MIND (Universal, 1947) Miklos Rozsa, Mario
    Castelnuovo-Tedesco
    Tony Thomas Productions TT-MR-4 (private)

A TIME TO DIE (Almi, 1983) Ennio Morricone
    Cerberus CEM-S 0119

A TIME TO SING (Metro-Goldwyn-Mayer, 1968) various composers
    MCA 1458

TIMES SQUARE (AFD, 1980) various composers
    RSO RS-2-4203

TO BE OR NOT TO BE (Twentieth Century-Fox, 1983) John Morris
    Antilles 8 ASTA 2

TO KILL A MOCKINGBIRD (Universal, 1962) Elmer Bernstein
    Citadel CT 7029

TO LIVE AND DIE IN L.A. (New Century, 1985) Wang Chung
    Geffen GHS 24081

TOGETHER? (Italy, 1979) Burt Bacharach
RCA ABL 1-3541

TOKYO FILE 212 (RKO, 1951) Albert Glasser
Screen Archives 10.002 (private)

TOM JONES (Britain, 1963) John Addison
MCA 39068; MCAD 6178 (CD)

TOOTSIE (Columbia, 1982) Dave Grusin
Warner Bros. 23781-1

TOP GUN (Paramount, 1986) various composers
Columbia SC 40323; CK 40323 (CD)

TOP SECRET (Paramount, 1984) Maurice Jarre
Varese Sarabande STV 81219 (orchestral score)
Passport PB 3603 (songs)

TOPKAPI (United Artists, 1964) Manos Hadjidakis
MCA 25118

TOUCH OF EVIL (Universal, 1960) Henry Mancini
Citadel CT 7016

TOUGH ENOUGH (Twentieth Century-Fox, 1983) Michael Lloyd, Steve
Wax
Liberty LT-51141

TOUGH GUYS DON'T DANCE (Cannon, 1987) Angelo Badalamenti
Varese Sarabande STV 81346

TRAIL OF THE PINK PANTHER (Metro-Goldwyn-Mayer/United
Artists, 1982) Henry Mancini
Liberty LT-51139

LE TRAIN (France, 1973) Philippe Sarde
DRG SL 9512

TRANSFORMERS: THE MOVIE (De Laurentiis Entertainment Group,
1986) Vince DiCola
Scotti Bros. SZ 40430

TRANSYLVANIA 6-5000 (New World, 1985) Lee Holdridge
Varese Sarabande STV 81267

TRE DONNE (Italy; n.d.) Ennio Morricone
Cerberus CEM-SP 0117

TRICK OR TREAT (De Laurentiis Entertainment Group, 1986)
Fastway
Columbia SC 40549; CK 40549 (CD)

TROLL (Marvin Films, 1986) Richard Band
  Restless 72119-1

TRON (Buena Vista, 1982) Wendy Carlos
  CBS SM 37782

TROUBLE IN MIND (Alive Films, 1985) Mark Isham
  Island 90501-1

TRUE CONFESSIONS (United Artists, 1981) Georges Delerue
  Varese Sarabande STV 81141

TRUE GRIT (Paramount, 1969) Elmer Bernstein
  Varese Sarabande 704.280; VCD 47236 (CD)

TRUE STORIES (Warner Bros., 1986) David Byrne
  Sire 1-25515 (score), 1-25512 (songs)

A TUESDAY IN NOVEMBER (U.S. Office of War Information, 1945)
    Virgil Thomson
  AEI ABM 3501

TUFF TURF (New World, 1985) Jonathan Elias
  Rhino RNSP-308

THE TWELVE CHAIRS (UMC, 1970) John Morris
  Varese Sarabande STV 81159

TWILIGHT ZONE--THE MOVIE (Warner Bros., 1983) Jerry Goldsmith
  Warner Bros. 23887-1

TWO FOR THE SEESAW (United Artists, 1962) Andre Previn
  MCA 25016

TWO OF A KIND (Twentieth Century-Fox, 1983) various composers
  MCA 6127

2000 MANIACS! (Box Office Spectaculars, 1964) Herschell Gordon
    Lewis
  Rhino RNSP-305

2001: A SPACE ODYSSEY (Metro-Goldwyn-Mayer, 1968) various
    composers
  Polydor 1665096-PSI
  MCA 39049; MCAD 39049 (CD)

2010 (Metro-Goldwyn-Mayer/United Artists, 1984) David Shire
  A&M SP-5038; CD-5038 (CD)

UCCIDETE IL VITELLO GRASSO E ARROSTITELO (Italy, 1969)
    Ennio Morricone
  Cerberus CEM-SP 0117

UMBRELLAS OF CHERBOURG (Allied Artists, 1964) Michel
    Legrand
    Columbia M 35175

THE UNDEFEATED (Twentieth Century-Fox, 1969) Hugo Montenegro
    Lone Star LS-1983 (private)

UNDER FIRE (Orion, 1983) Jerry Goldsmith
    Warner Bros. 23965-1

UNDER THE CHERRY MOON (Warner Bros., 1986) Prince
    Warner Bros. 25395-1

UNDERCOVER (Cannon, 1987) Todd Rundgren
    Enigma SJ 73276; CDE 73276 (CD)

UNTIL SEPTEMBER (Metro-Goldwyn-Mayer/United Artists, 1984)
    John Barry
    Varese Sarabande STV 81226

THE UNTOUCHABLES (Paramount, 1987) Ennio Morricone
    A&M SP-3909; CD-3909 (CD)

UP THE ACADEMY (Warner Bros., 1980) various composers
    Capitol S00 12091

UP THE CREEK (Orion, 1984) various composers
    Pasha SZ 39333

URBAN COWBOY (Paramount, 1980) various composers
    Asylum DP-90002
    Epic SE-36921

URGH! A MUSIC WAR (Lorimar, 1982) various composers
    A&M SP-6019

UTU (New Zealand, 1984) John Charles
    Southern Cross SCRS 1008

THE V.I.P.S (Metro-Goldwyn-Mayer, 1963) Miklos Rozsa
    MCA 25001

VACATION see NATIONAL LAMPOON'S VACATION

VALLEY GIRL (Atlantic, 1983) various composers
    Epic FE 38673
    Roadshow RS 101

VAMP (New World, 1986) Jonathan Elias
    Varese Sarabande STV 81288

VERONIKA VOSS (West Germany, 1982) Peer Raben
  DRG SL 9508

LA VEUVE COUDERC (France, 1971) Philippe Sarde
  DRG SL 9512

VICTOR/VICTORIA (Metro-Goldwyn-Mayer, 1982) Henry Mancini
  MGM/Polygram MG 1-5407

VIDEODROME (Universal, 1983) Howard Shore
  Varese Sarabande STV 81173

A VIEW TO A KILL (Britain, 1985) John Barry
  Capitol SJ 12413

VISION QUEST (Warner Bros., 1985) various composers
  Geffen GHS 24063; 24063-2 (CD)

VOYAGE OF THE DAMNED (Embassy, 1977) Lalo Schifrin
  Label "X" LXCD 5 (CD)

WAGNER (Britain, 1983) Richard Wagner
  London CS 7252

A WALK ON THE WILD SIDE (Columbia, 1962) Elmer Bernstein
  Citadel CT 7028

WALKABOUT (Britain, 1971) John Barry
  GSF 1005 (private)

WALKER (Universal, 1987) Joe Strummer
  Virgin 90686-1; 90686-2 (CD)

WAR OF THE WORLDS (Paramount, 1953) Leith Stevens
  Quasi PAL-1953 (private)

WARGAMES (Metro-Goldwyn-Mayer/United Artists, 1983) Arthur B.
     Rubinstein, Jr.
  Polydor 815 005-1 Y-1

WARNING SIGN (Twentieth Century-Fox, 1985) Craig Safan
  Southern Cross SCRS 1012

WAVELENGTH (New World, 1983) Tangerine Dream
  Varese Sarabande STV 81207; VCD 47223 (CD)

THE WAY WE WERE (Columbia, 1973) Marvin Hamlisch
  CBS CK 32801 (CD)

THE WAY WEST (United Artists, 1967) Bronislau Kaper
  MCA 25045

WE STILL KILL THE OLD WAY (Italy, 1968) Luis Enrique Bacalov
MCA 25039

WEIRD SCIENCE (Universal, 1985) various composers
MCA 6146

WELCOME TO L.A. (United Artists, 1976) Richard Baskin
MCA 25040

WESTWORLD (Metro-Goldwyn-Mayer, 1973) Fred Karlin
MCA 25004

WETHERBY (Britain, 1985) Nick Bicat
Varese Sarabande STV 81247

WHAT COMES AROUND (A.W.O. Associates, 1986) Al Delory
Capitol ST-12444

WHEN THE WIND BLOWS (Britain, 1987) Roger Waters
Virgin 90599-1

WHEN WORLDS COLLIDE (Paramount, 1951) Leith Stevens
Quasi PAL-1951 (private)

WHERE EAGLES DARE (Metro-Goldwyn-Mayer, 1969) Ron Goodwin
MCA 25082

WHERE THE BOYS ARE '84 (Tri-Star, 1984) Sylvester Levay
RCA ABL 1-5039

WHERE THE BUFFALO ROAM (Universal, 1980) Neil Young
Backstreet MCA 5126

WHERE THE RIVER RUNS BLACK (Metro-Goldwyn-Mayer, 1986)
James Horner
Varese Sarabande STV 81290; VCD 47273 (CD)

THE WHISPERERS (Britain, 1967) John Barry
MCA 25041

THE WHISTLE BLOWER (Britain, 1987) John Scott
Varese Sarabande STV 81315

WHITE NIGHTS (Columbia, 1985) various composers
Atlantic 81273-1

WHO'S THAT GIRL (Warner Bros., 1987) various composers
Sire 25611-1; 25611-2 (CD)

THE WICKED LADY (Metro-Goldwyn-Mayer/United Artists, 1983)
Tony Banks
Atlantic 80073-1

THE WILD BUNCH (Warner Bros., 1959) Jerry Fielding
    Varese Sarabande STV 81145

THE WILD LIFE (Universal, 1984) various composers
    MCA 5523, 27103

THE WILD ROVERS (Metro-Goldwyn-Mayer, 1971) Jerry Goldsmith
    MCA 25141

WILD STYLE (First Run Features, 1983) various composers
    Animal APE 6005

WILDCATS (Warner Bros., 1986) various composers
    Warner Bros. 25388-1

WINDWALKER (Pacific International Enterprises, 1982) Merrill Jenson
    Cerberus CST 0202

THE WITCHES OF EASTWICK (Warner Bros., 1987) John Williams
    Warner Bros. 25607-1; 25607-2 (CD)

WITHNAIL AND I (Britain, 1987) David Dundas, Rick Wentworth
    DRG SBL 12590; CDSBL 12590 (CD)

WITNESS (Paramount, 1985) Maurice Jarre
    Varese Sarabande STV 81237; VCD 47227 (CD)

THE WOMAN IN RED (Orion, 1984) Stevie Wonder, John Morris
    Motown 6108 ML; 6108 MD (CD)

THE WOMAN NEXT DOOR (France, 1981) Georges Delerue
    DRG SL 9507, 9519

THE WONDERFUL WORLD OF THE BROTHERS GRIMM (Metro-Goldwyn-
    Mayer, 1962) Leigh Harline, Bob Merrill
    MCA 39091

THE WRAITH (New Century Productions Ltd., 1986) various com-
    posers
    Scotti Bros. SZ 40429

XANADU (Universal, 1980) Barry DeVorzon, Jeff Lyne, John Farrar
    MCA 6100

THE YEAR OF LIVING DANGEROUSLY (Australia, 1983) Maurice
    Jarre
    Varese Sarabande STV 81182; VCD 47222 (CD)

YEAR OF THE DRAGON (Metro-Goldwyn-Mayer/United Artists, 1985)
    David Mansfield
    Varese Sarabande STV 81266

YENTL (Metro-Goldwyn-Mayer/United Artists, 1983) Michel Legrand
   Columbia JS 39152; CK 39152 (CD)

YES, GIORGIO (Metro-Goldwyn-Mayer/United Artists, 1982) Michael
      J. Lewis, John Williams
   London PDV 9001

YOL (Triumph Films, 1982) Sebastian Argol
   Warner Bros. 23816-1

YOR, THE HUNTER FROM THE FUTURE (Columbia, 1983) John
      Scott, Guido De Angelis, Maurizio De Angelis
   Southern Cross SCRS 1005

YOU ONLY LIVE TWICE (United Artists, 1967) John Barry
   Liberty LT-50289

YOUNG BILLY YOUNG (United Artists, 1969) Shelly Manne
   MCA 25031

THE YOUNG LIONS (Twentieth Century-Fox, 1958) Hugo Friedhofer
   Varese Sarabande STV 81115

YOUNG SHERLOCK HOLMES (Paramount, 1985) Bruce Broughton
   MCA 6159

THE YOUNG WARRIORS (Cannon, 1983) Rob Walsh
   Varese Sarabande STV 81186

YOUNGBLOOD (Metro-Goldwyn-Mayer/United Artists, 1986) various
      composers
   RCA ABL 1-7172; PCD 1-7172 (CD)

YOURS, MINE AND OURS (United Artists, 1968) Fred Karlin
   MCA 1434

ZAPPED! (Embassy, 1982) various composers
   Regency RY 38-152

ZIGGY STARDUST AND THE SPIDERS FROM MARS (Britain, 1983)
      David Bowie
   RCA CPL 2-4862

ZONE TROOPERS (Empire, 1986) Richard Band
   Varese Sarabande STV 81262

ZOOT SUIT (Universal, 1982) Daniel Valdez
   MCA 5267

ZULU DAWN (American Cinema, 1980) Elmer Bernstein
   Cerberus CST-0201

RECORDED MUSICAL SCORES--ANTHOLOGIES

AISLE SEAT: GREAT FILM MUSIC (John Williams Conducting the
        Boston Pops Orchestra)
    E.T. The Extra-Terrestrial
    Raiders of the Lost Ark
    Chariots of Fire
    Yes, Giorgio
    Gone with the Wind
    Friendly Persuasion
        and other themes
        Philips 6514 328; 411 037-2 (CD)

ANDRE KOSTALANETZ
    Cuba
    The Electric Horseman
    The Muppet Movie
    Star Trek: The Motion Picture
    The Secret Life of Plants
    Breaking Away
    The Main Event
    The Black Hole
    The Rose
    Yanks
        Columbia JC 36382

BIG CONCERTO MOVIE THEMES (Geoff Love and His Orchestra)
    Dangerous Moonlight [Warsaw Concerto]
    Spellbound
    Love Story [Cornish Rhapsody]
    While I Live [The Dream of Olwyn]
    The Way to the Stars
        and other themes
        Moss Music Group B-706

THE BIG GUNDOWN: JOHN ZORN PLAYS THE MUSIC OF ENNIO
        MORRICONE
    The Big Gundown
    Peur sur la Ville
    Once Upon a Time in America
    Milano Odea
    The Burglars
    Battle of Algiers
    Duck, You Sucker
    La Classe Operaia va in Paradiso
    Once Upon a Time in the West
        Nonesuch 79139-1; 79139-2 (CD)

BIG LOVE MOVIE THEMES (Geoff Love and His Orchestra)
    Gone With The Wind

Doctor Zhivago
A Summer Place
The Sandpiper
Romeo and Juliet
La Strada
Casablanca
The Umbrellas of Cherbourg
A Man and a Woman
Love Story
    and other themes
    Moss Music Group B-701

BRITISH MUSIC FOR FILM & TELEVISION (Marcus Dods conducting
    the City of Birmingham Symphony Orchestra)
A Bridge Too Far
Yanks
The Battle of Britain
An Ideal Husband
Christopher Columbus
Colditz (TV)
Watership Down
The Overlanders
Lady Caroline Lamb
Frenzy
Malta G.C.
    DRG MRS 703

BY REQUEST: THE BEST OF JOHN WILLIAMS AND THE BOSTON
    POPS
The Cowboys [on CD edition only]
Close Encounters of the Third Kind
Midway
Return of the Jedi
E.T. The Extra-Terrestrial
Superman
Raiders of the Lost Ark [on CD edition only]
The Empire Strikes Back
1941
Jaws
NBC Nightly News (TV)
Star Wars
    and other themes
    Philips 420 178-1; 420 178-2 (CD)

CAPTAIN FROM CASTILE: THE CLASSIC FILM SCORES OF
    ALFRED NEWMAN (Charles Gerhardt conducting the National
    Philharmonic Orchestra)
Captain from Castile
How to Marry a Millionaire
Wuthering Heights
The Robe

Airport
Down to the Sea in Ships
Anastasia
The Best of Everything
The Bravados
The Song of Bernadette
   RCA AGL 1-4367

CASABLANCA: CLASSIC FILM SCORES FOR HUMPHREY BOGART
   (Charles Gerhardt conducting the National Philharmonic
   Orchestra)
Casablanca
Passage to Marseille
Treasure of the Sierra Madre
The Big Sleep
The Caine Mutiny
To Have and Have Not
The Two Mrs. Carrolls
Sabrina
The Left Hand of God
Sahara
Virginia City
Key Largo
   RCA AGL 1-3782

CINEMAGIC (Dave Grusin with the London Symphony Orchestra)
On Golden Pond
Heaven Can Wait
Tootsie
The Heart is a Lonely Hunter
The Goonies
The Champ
Three Days of the Condor
Falling in Love
The Little Drummer Girl
   GRP GR-1037; GRD-1037 (CD)

CLASSIC FILM SCORES FOR BETTE DAVIS (Charles Gerhardt
   conducting the National Philharmonic Orchestra)
Now, Voyager
Dark Victory
A Stolen Life
The Private Lives of Elizabeth and Essex
Mr. Skeffington
In This Our Life
All Above Eve
Jezebel
Beyond the Forest
Juarez
The Letter
All This and Heaven Too
   RCA AGL 1-3706

CLOSE ENCOUNTERS OF THE THIRD KIND (Geoff Love and His
    Orchestra)
    Close Encounters of the Third Kind
    Logan's Run
    The Time Machine
    Blake's 7 (TV)
    The Omega Man
        and other themes
        Moss Music Group B-705

DIGITAL FIREWORKS (Robert Henderson conducting the Utah
    Symphony Orchestra)
    Mondo Cane
    Rocky
        and other themes
        Varese Sarabande VCDM 1000.80

DIGITAL PREMIERE RECORDINGS FROM THE FILMS OF LEE
    HOLDRIDGE (Charles Gerhardt conducting the London Symphony
    Orchestra)
    Wizards and Warriors (TV)
    Splash
    Jonathan Livingston Seagull
    The Great Whales (TV)
    East of Eden (TV)
    The Hemingway Play (TV)
    The Beastmaster
    Going Home
        Varese Sarabande 704.290; VCD 47244 (CD)

DIGITAL SPACE (Morton Gould conducting the London Symphony
    Orchestra)
    Windjammer
    Star Wars
    Airport
    The Red Pony
    Things to Come
    The Big Country
    That Hamilton Woman
    The Invaders [49th Parallel]
    Spitfire [The First of the Few]
        Varese Sarabande VCD 47229 (CD)

ENNIO MORRICONE'S GREATEST THEMES
    The Good, the Bad and the Ugly
    A Fistful of Dollars
    For a Few Dollars More
    The Master and Margherita
    Sixty Seconds to What
    Violent City
        Accord 193220 (CD)

THE FANTASTIC FILM MUSIC OF ALBERT GLASSER, VOL. 1
  The Cyclops
  The Amazing Colossal Man
  Beginning of the End
  The Boy and the Pirates
  The Buckskin Lady
  Big Town (TV)
  Top of the World
  Cisco Kid (TV)
    Starlog SR-1001

FILM CLASSICS
  Altered States
  Gandhi [on CD edition only]
  Return of the Jedi [on CD edition only]
    and classical music used in other films
    RCA XRL 1-4020; 6366-2-RC (CD)

FILM CLASSICS, TAKE 3
  Sophie's Choice
  The Sting II
  M*A*S*H
  Unfaithfully Yours
  La Traviata
  Gandhi
  Return of the Jedi
    RCA XRL 1-4867

FILM MUSIC (Mark Isham)
  Mrs. Soffel
  The Times of Harvey Milk
  Never Cry Wolf
    Windham Hill WH 1041; WD 1041 (CD)

FILM MUSIC OF ALFRED NEWMAN (Alfred Newman, conductor)
  Captain from Castile
  All About Eve
  Pinky
  Wuthering Heights
  A Royal Scandal
  Song of Bernadette
  The Razor's Edge
  How Green Was My Valley
  A Letter to Three Wives
    Citadel CT 7015

FILM MUSIC OF BRONISLAU KAPER (Bronislau Kaper, piano)
  Mutiny on the Bounty
  Lili
  The Glass Slipper
  Butterfield 8

Auntie Mame
The Chocolate Soldier
Invitation
The Brothers Karamazov
Green Dolphin Street
The Swan
Lord Jim
San Francisco
    Facet FCD 8101 (CD)

FILM MUSIC OF MAX STEINER
Santa Fe Trail
A Star is Born
Life with Father
Bird of Paradise
    Medallion ML 309

FILM MUSIC, VOLUME 1 (Ennio Morricone)
The Good, the Bad and the Ugly
Come Maddalena
The Sicilian Clan
Chi Mai
Investigation of a Citizen Above Suspicion
Moscow Farewell
Marcia in La
Lady Caliph
The Battle of Algiers
The Infernal Trio
Dedicace
For Love One Can Die
Sacco and Vanzetti
La Tragedia di un Uomo Ridicolo
On Earth as It Is in Heaven
    Virgin 90674-1; 90674-2 (CD)

THE FINAL FRONTIER (Roy Budd conducting the London Symphony
    Orchestra)
Star Trek (TV)
Star Trek: The Motion Picture
Star Trek II: The Wrath of Khan
Star Trek III: The Search for Spock
Star Wars
The Empire Strikes Back
Return of the Jedi
E.T. The Extra-Terrestrial
Sinbad and the Eye of the Tiger
Alien
The Final Conflict
Dr. Who (TV)
Raiders of the Lost Ark
Indiana Jones and the Temple of Doom

The Wild Geese
Supergirl
The Mark of Zorro
Superman
    Mobile Fidelity MFCD 2-831 (CD)

FOUR CLASSIC FILM SCORES
    Tomorrow Is Forever
    Treasure of the Sierra Madre
    Johnny Belinda
    The Fountainhead
       Tony Thomas Productions TT-MS-13/14 (private)

FRANCIS LAI PERFORMS HIS GREAT FILM MUSIC (Francis Lai,
    piano, with Christian Gaubert conducting the Royal Philhar-
    monic Orchestra)
    Un homme qui me plait
    Un homme et une femme
    Vivre pour vivre
    Cinq pour l'aventure
    Mayerling
    Toute une vie
    La bonne annee
    Love Story
       DRG MRS 508

FROM DR. NO TO OCTOPUSSY: JAMES BOND 21ST ANNIVERSARY
    (Nicky North Orchestra)
    Dr. No
    From Russia with Love
    Goldfinger
    Thunderball
    You Only Live Twice
    On Her Majesty's Secret Service
    Diamonds Are Forever
    Live and Let Die
    The Man with the Golden Gun
    The Spy who Loved Me
    Moonraker
    For Your Eyes Only
    Octopussy
       Bainbridge BT 6253

GREAT ACTION FILM THEMES/GREAT HORROR FILM THEMES
    The Domino Principle
    Black Sunday
    Silver Streak
    Voyage to the Bottom of the Sea
    The Manchurian Candidate
    Marathon Man
    The Betsy

The Shootist
Machine Gun Kelly
Nightmare Castle
Twins of Evil
The Tender Dracula
Night of the Living Dead
The Man Who Haunted Himself
Horror Castle
The Rip Van Winkle Caper [The Twilight Zone] (TV)
Night of the Blood Monster
Cat o'Nine Tails
    GSF 1002 (private)

GREAT FILM MUSIC (Stanley Black conducting the London Festival
    Orchestra; Bernard Herrmann conducting the National Phil-
    harmonic Orchestra)
The Battle of Britain
Henry V
Oliver Twist
The Invaders
Richard III
Escape Me Never
Things to Come
    London/Viva 411 837-1

GREAT FILM THEMES (Stanley Black conducting the London Festival
    Orchestra; Mantovani and His Orchestra; Ronnie Aldrich)
Limelight
Born Free
Moulin Rouge
Exodus
Casablanca
2001: A Space Odyssey
High Noon
Love Story
The Big Country
Gone With the Wind
Lawrence of Arabia
Around the World in Eighty Days
The Go-Between
The Godfather
Doctor Zhivago
    London MCPS 820 040-2 (CD)

THE GREAT MOVIE THEMES, VOL. 1
Missing
Raise the Titanic
The In-Laws
Big Wednesday
Hero at Large
Zelig

The Final Conflict
They Might Be Giants
The Devil and Max Devlin
Used Cars
Norma Rae
The Beast Within
Scavenger Hunt
The Lone Ranger and the Lost City of Gold
Chapter Two
    DLP 105 (private)

GREAT SCIENCE FICTION FILM MUSIC
Jack the Giant Killer
Kiss of the Vampire
Godzilla
Theater of Blood
Danger: Diabolik
Return of Dracula
The Omega Man
The Time Machine
The Green Slime
The First Men in the Moon
The Blob
Damnation Alley
The Mysterians
Dracula Has Risen from the Grave
War of the Worlds
Kronos
I Bury the Living
Mothra
The Incredible Shrinking Man
    GSF LP-1001 (private)

GREAT STAGE AND FILM SCORES (Wilford Holcombe conducting the
    London Philharmonic Orchestra)
Chariots of Fire
2001: A Space Odyssey
Elvira Madigan
Doctor Zhivago
   and other themes
    Moss Music Group B-707

GREATEST SCIENCE FICTION HITS (Neil Norman and His Cosmic
    Orchestra)
Moonraker
Alien
Star Trek (TV)
Battlestar Galactica (TV)
The Outer Limits (TV)
Close Encounters of the Third Kind
Superman

Star Wars
Space: 1999 (TV)
The Day the Earth Stood Still
Godzilla
2001: A Space Odyssey
One Step Beyond (TV)
The Black Hole
    and other themes
    GNP Crescendo GNPS 2128; GNPD 2128 (CD)

GREATEST SCIENCE FICTION HITS II (Neil Norman and His Cosmic
    Orchestra)
The Empire Strikes Back
Voyage to the Bottom of the Sea (TV)
Sinbad and the Eye of the Tiger
The Time Tunnel (TV)
The Twilight Zone (TV)
Star Trek: The Motion Picture
Buck Rogers in the 25th Century (TV)
Vampire Planet
Dr. Who (TV)
The Adventures of Superman (TV)
Dark Star
    and other themes
    GNP Crescendo GNPS 2133; GNPD 2133 (CD)

GREATEST SCIENCE FICTION HITS III (Neil Norman and His
    Cosmic Orchestra)
Land of the Giants (TV)
Space: 1999 (TV)
The Thing
The Angry Red Planet
Blade Runner
Lost in Space (TV)
Capricorn One
The Prisoner (TV)
Raiders of the Lost Ark
E.T. The Extra-Terrestrial
The Invaders (TV)
U.F.O. (TV)
Star Trek (TV)
Flash Gordon
War of the Worlds
Return of the Jedi
    and other themes
    GNP Crescendo GNPS 2163; GNPD 2163 (CD)

HANS SALTER'S FANTASY FILM MUSIC
The Golden Horde
The Black Shield of Falworth
The Prince Who Was a Thief
    Medallion ML 312

HOLLYWOOD: THE POST-WAR YEARS, 1946-1949
   A Double Life
   Time Out of Mind
   Bandit of Sherwood Forest
   Force of Evil
      AEI 3104

HOLLYWOOD'S GREATEST HITS, VOLUME 1 (Erich Kunzel conduct-
      ing the Cincinnati Pops Orchestra)
   Twentieth Century-Fox Fanfare
   Captain Blood
   Gone with the Wind
   Ben-Hur
   Exodus
   Doctor Zhivago
   Lawrence of Arabia
   Romeo and Juliet
   Goldfinger
   Love Story
   A Summer Place
   Jaws
   Summer of '42
   Rocky
   Terms of Endearment
   Out of Africa
   Chariots of Fire
      Telarc CD-80168 (CD)

IN THE PINK (James Galway, flute; Henry Mancini conducting the
      National Philharmonic Orchestra)
   The Pink Panther
   The Thorn Birds
   Breakfast at Tiffany's
   The Molly Maguires
   Victor/Victoria
   The Great Race
   Hatari
   Two for the Road
   Days of Wine and Roses
   Charade
      and other themes
      RCA CRC 1-5315; RCD 1-5315 (CD)

JAMES BOND: 13 ORIGINAL THEMES
   The James Bond Theme
   From Russia with Love
   Goldfinger
   Thunderball
   You Only Live Twice
   On Her Majesty's Secret Service
   Diamonds are Forever
   Live and Let Die

The Man with the Golden Gun
The Spy Who Loved Me
Moonraker
For Your Eyes Only
Octopussy
    Liberty LO 51138
    Capitol CDP 46079 (CD)

JARRE BY JARRE: THE FILM THEMES OF MAURICE JARRE
    (Maurice Jarre conducting the Royal Philharmonic Orchestra)
    Lawrence of Arabia
    Ryan's Daughter
    Doctor Zhivago
    A Passage to India
    Witness
    Is Paris Burning?
    The Damned
    Mad Max Beyond Thunderdome
    Villa Rides!
        CBS FM 42307; MK 42307 (CD)

JOHN WILLIAMS' SYMPHONIC SUITES (Frank Barber conducting the
    London Symphony Orchestra and the National Philharmonic
    Orchestra)
    E.T. The Extra-Terrestrial
    Star Wars
    Close Encounters of the Third Kind
        Angel RL-32109

MANCINI'S CLASSIC MOVIE SCORES (Henry Mancini and His
    Orchestra)
    The Pink Panther
    Charade
    Hatari!
    Breakfast at Tiffany's
        RCA 4938-2-RC (CD)

MAX STEINER ... MEMORIES
    Escapade in Japan
    Dr. Ehrlich's Magic Bullet
    A Dispatch from Reuters
    Arsenic and Old Lace
    Fighter Squadron
        Tony Thomas Productions TT-MS-17 (private)

MIKE POST
    The A-Team (TV)
    Riptide (TV)
    Footloose
    St. Elsewhere (TV)
    Against All Odds

Terms of Endearment
   and other themes
      RCA AFL 1-5183, 1-5415; PCD 1-5183 (CD)

MOVIE AND TV THEMES (Composed and conducted by Elmer
   Bernstein)
   The Rat Race
   Take Five (TV)
   Sudden Fear
   Anna Lucasta
   Saints and Sinners (TV)
   The Sweet Smell of Success
   The Man with the Golden Arm
   Walk on the Wild Side
      and other themes
      Mobile Fidelity MFCD 851 (CD)

MOVIE GREATS
   Jaws
   E.T. The Extra-Terrestrial
   Beverly Hills Cop
   Back to the Future
   Somewhere in Time
   Fletch
   The Sting
   Jesus Christ Superstar
   Love Story
   The River
   Out of Africa
      MCA 6183; MCAD 6183 (CD)

THE MOVIE THEME TEAM II (Ferrante and Teicher, dual pianos)
   The Seventh Dawn
   M*A*S*H
   Goldfinger
   The April Fools
   The Bible
   One-Eyed Jacks
   Funny Girl
   Judith
   The Lion in Winter
   You Only Live Twice
      Liberty LN 10210

MUSIC FOR MILDRED PIERCE AND OTHER MELODRAMATIC LADIES
   Mildred Pierce
   Without Honor
   Caged
   Breaking Point
   Four Daughters
      Tony Thomas Productions TT-MS-15 (private)

MUSIC FOR SHAKESPEAREAN FILMS (Sir Charles Groves conducting
    the Royal Liverpool Philharmonic Orchestra)
    Richard III
    Hamlet
    Henry V
       Angel DS 38088

MUSIC FROM ALFRED HITCHCOCK FILMS (Charles Ketcham conduct-
    ing the Utah Symphony Orchestra)
    Family Plot
    Strangers on a Train
    Suspicion
    Notorious
       Varese Sarabande 704.250; VCD 47225 (CD)

MUSIC FROM EPIC MOTION PICTURES
    Cimarron
    El Cid
    King of Kings
    Cleopatra
    War and Peace
       AEI 3114

MUSIC FROM FILMS FOR PIANO AND ORCHESTRA (Daniel Adni,
    piano; Bournemouth Symphony Orchestra; Kenneth Alwyn,
    conductor)
    Dangerous Moonlight [Warsaw Concerto]
    While I Live [The Dream of Olwen]
    Spellbound [Spellbound Concerto]
    Love Story [Cornish Rhapsody]
    Rhapsody in Blue
       Angel SZ 37757

MUSIC FROM GREAT AUSTRALIAN FILMS (William Motzing conduct-
    ing the Australian Broadcasting Commission Philharmonic
    Orchestra)
    Newsfront
    Gallipoli
    My Brilliant Career
    Tall Timbers
    Cathy's Child
    Eliza Fraser
    Breaker Morant
    The Chant of Jimmy Blacksmith
    The Picture Show Man
    Picnic at Hanging Rock
    The Mango Tree
    Dimboola
    Caddie
       DRG SBL 12582; CDSBL 12582 (CD)

MUSIC FROM THE GALAXIES (Ettore Stratta conducting the London
    Symphony Orchestra)
  Superman
  Moonraker
  Meteor
  Star Trek (TV)
  Star Wars
  Alien
  The Black Hole
  Battlestar Galactica (TV)
    Columbia IC 35876, FM 37266

THE MUSIC OF MIKLOS ROZSA (Elmer Bernstein conducting the
    Utah Symphony Orchestra)
  The World, the Flesh and the Devil
  Lydia
  Time Out of Mind
  Because of Him
  Spellbound
    Varese Sarabande 704.260; VCD 47226 (CD)

THE MUSIC OF REPUBLIC (James King, conductor)
  The Three Mesquiteers
  The Painted Stallion
  King of the Royal Mounted
  Daredevils of the Red Circle
  The Border Legion
  Down Mexico Way
    Varese Sarabande STV 81250

NEW RECORDINGS FROM THE FILMS OF FRANZ WAXMAN (Richard
    Mills conducting the Queensland Symphony Orchestra)
  The Horn Blows at Midnight
  Mister Roberts
  The Bride of Frankenstein
  Taras Bulba
  Botany Bay
  The Paradine Case
    Varese Sarabande 704.320

NINO ROTA: 14 MOVIE THEMES (Carlo Savina, conductor)
  The Godfather
  The Taming of the Shrew
  La Dolce Vita
  Rocco and his Brothers
  Napoli Milionaria
  Romeo and Juliet
  War and Peace
  The Leopard
  Amarcord
  La Strada

La Notti di Cabiria
Juliet of the Spirits
I Vitelloni
8 1/2
   Polydor 822 747-2

OUT OF THIS WORLD (John Williams conducting the Boston Pops
      Orchestra)
   2001: A Space Odyssey
   E.T. The Extra-Terrestrial
   Alien
   Star Trek (TV)
   Battlestar Galactica (TV)
   Star Trek: The Motion Picture
   Twilight Zone (TV)
   Return of the Jedi
      Philips 411 185-1; 411 185-2 (CD)

POPS AROUND THE WORLD (John Williams conducting the Boston
      Pops Orchestra)
   The Cowboys
      and other overtures
      Philips 6514 186; 400 071-2 (CD)

POPS IN SPACE (John Williams conducting the Boston Pops Orches-
      tra)
   Superman
   The Empire Strikes Back
   Star Wars
   Close Encounters of the Third Kind
      Philips 9500 921

POPS ON THE MARCH (John Williams conducting the Boston Pops
      Orchestra)
   Midway
   Captain from Castile
      and other marches
      Philips 6302 082

ROUND-UP (Erich Kunzel conducting the Cincinnati Pops Orchestra)
   The Magnificent Seven
   The Furies
   Bonanza (TV)
   Rawhide (TV)
   Wagon Train (TV)
   The Rifleman (TV)
   How the West Was Won
   Gunfight at the O.K. Corral
   High Noon
   The Big Country
   Silverado

and other themes
Telarc DG 10141; CD 80141 (CD)

THE SEA HAWK: THE CLASSIC FILM SCORES OF ERICH WOLFGANG
    KORNGOLD (Charles Gerhardt conducting the National Philhar-
    monic Orchestra)
The Sea Hawk
Juarez
Anthony Adverse
The Adventures of Robin Hood
Devotion
Deception
King's Row
Captain Blood
The Constant Nymph
Escape Me Never
Of Human Bondage
Between Two Worlds
    RCA AGL 1-3707

SECRET AGENT FILE
Octopussy
I Spy (TV)
The Rockford Files (TV)
The Prisoner (TV)
Reilly: Ace of Spies (TV)
The Man from U.N.C.L.E. (TV)
Casino Royale
The Ipcress File
Get Smart (TV)
Thunderball
Our Man Flint
Moonraker
The Spy Who Came In From the Cold
You Only Live Twice
Goldfinger
    and other themes
    GNP Crescendo GNPS 2166; GNPD 2166 (CD)

SOUNDTRACK MEMORIES
Close Encounters of the Third Kind
Lawrence of Arabia
Brian's Song (TV)
Cactus Flower
Taxi Driver
Foul Play
Ice Castles
Billy Jack
Head
Funny Lady
    Arista ABM 2005

SOUNDTRACKS, VOICES AND THEMES FROM GREAT MOVIES
      (Morris Stoloff, conductor)
   From Here to Eternity
   The Bridge on the River Kwai
      and other themes
      DRG MRS 509

STAR TRACKS (Erich Kunzel conducting the Cincinnati Pops
      Orchestra)
   Star Wars
   The Empire Strikes Back
   Return of the Jedi
   Superman
   Raiders of the Lost Ark
   Close Encounters of the Third Kind
   E.T. The Extra-Terrestrial
   Star Trek (TV)
      Telarc DG 10094

STAR TRACKS II (Erich Kunzel conducting the Cincinnati Pops
      Orchestra)
   Superman
   Back to the Future
   Star Trek: The Motion Picture
   Star Trek II: The Wrath of Khan
   Star Trek IV: The Voyage Home
   Spacecamp
   Cocoon
   Lifeforce
   Return of the Jedi
   The Right Stuff
      and other themes
      Telarc CD-80146 (CD)

THE STAR WARS TRILOGY (Varujan Kojian conducting the Utah
      Symphony Orchestra)
   Star Wars
   The Empire Strikes Back
   Return of the Jedi
      Varese Sarabande 704.210; VCD 47201 (CD)

THE STEINER TOUCH
   Jezebel
   Dark Victory
   My Reputation
   Marjorie Morningstar
      Tony Thomas Productions TT-MS-16 (private)

SUNSET BOULEVARD: THE CLASSIC FILM SCORES OF FRANZ
      WAXMAN (Charles Gerhardt conducting the National Philhar-
      monic Orchestra)

Sunset Boulevard
The Bride of Frankenstein
A Place in the Sun
Prince Valiant
Rebecca
The Philadelphia Story
Old Acquaintance
Taras Bulba
RCA AGL 1-3783; RCD 1-7017 (CD)

THERE'S SOMETHING GOING ON OUT THERE
2001: A Space Odyssey
Rosemary's Baby
A Clockwork Orange
Jaws
The Bride of Frankenstein
Star Wars
Close Encounters of the Third Kind
The Exorcist
Superman
Experiment in Terror
The Day the Earth Stood Still
Psycho
RCA OPL 1-0003

TIME WARP (Erich Kunzel conducting the Cincinnati Pops Orchestra)
2001: A Space Odyssey
Star Trek: The Motion Picture
Star Trek (TV)
Battlestar Galactica (TV)
Superman
Star Wars
Alien
Telarc DG-10106; CD-80106 (CD)

WESTERN SCORES OF HANS SALTER
Battle of Apache Pass
Walk the Proud Land
Man Without a Star
Bend of the River
The Spoilers
Day of the Bad Man
The Tall Stranger
The Oklahoman
Untamed Frontier
Four Guns to the Border
The Far Horizons
Medallion ML 313

RECORDED MUSICAL SCORES--TELEVISION

ANASTASIA: THE MYSTERY OF ANNA (NBC, 1986) Laurence
    Rosenthal
    Southern Cross SCRS 1015; SCCD 1015 (CD)

THE AVENGERS (Britain, 1961) Laurie Johnson
    Starlog/Varese Sarabande ASV-95003

BALLAD OF THE IRISH HORSE (PBS, 1984) Paddy Moloney
    Shanachie 79051

BRIDESHEAD REVISITED (Britain, 1981) Geoffrey Burgon
    Chrysalis CHR 1367

CHARLOTTE'S WEB (1972) Richard M. Sherman, Robert B. Sherman
    MCA 13302 (picture disc)

CHRISTOPHER COLUMBUS (CBS, 1985) Riz Ortolani
    Varese Sarabande STV 81245

THE COSBY SHOW (NBC, 1985) Stu Gardner
    Columbia FC 40270, 40704; CK 40270, 40704 (CD)

COSMOS (PBS, 1980) various composers
    RCA ABL 1-4003

COUSTEAU AMAZON (1984) John Scott
    Varese Sarabande STV 81220

DALLAS (CBS, 1970) John Parker, Jerrold Immel
    First American FA 7780

DARK SHADOWS (ABC, 1966) Robert Cobert
    Media MS 00001

DINOSAURS (Midwich Entertainment Productions) David Spear
    Cerberus CST 0213

DREAMS (CBS, 1984) various composers
    Columbia BFC 39886

EAST OF EDEN (ABC, 1981) Lee Holdridge
    Elektra 5E-520

EDWARD AND MRS. SIMPSON (Britain, 1980) Ron Grainer
    Stet DS 15019

EDWARD THE KING (Britain, 1979) various composers
    DRG DARC 2-1104

ENOLA GAY (NBC, 1980) Maurice Jarre
   Varese Sarabande STV 81149

AN EVENING WITH EDGAR ALLAN POE (American International,
      1970) Les Baxter
   Citadel CTV 7013

THE EWOK ADVENTURE (ABC, 1984) Peter Bernstein
   Varese Sarabande STV 81281

EWOKS: THE BATTLE FOR ENDOR (ABC, 1985) Peter Bernstein
   Varese Sarabande STV 81281

FAME (NBC/Syndicated, 1981) various composers
   RCA AFL 1-4259, 1-4525, 1-4842, 1-4961

THE FAR PAVILIONS (HBO, 1984) Carl Davis
   Chrysalis FV 41464

HERE COMES GARFIELD (CBS, 1982) Ed Bogas
   Epic FE 38136

HOLLYWOOD (Britain, 1979) Carl Davis
   Stet DS 15006

THE HONEYMOONERS (CBS, 1955) Jackie Gleason
   Murray Hill 000237

THE IRISH R.M. (1983) Nick Bicat
   Release RRL 8012

JESUS OF NAZARETH (NBC, 1977) Maurice Jarre
   RCA ABL 1-4284

JEWEL IN THE CROWN (Britain, 1984) George Fenton
   Chrysalis FV 41465

KENT STATE (NBC, 1981) Ken Lauber
   RCA ABL 1-3928

LIBERTY (NBC, 1986) William Goldstein
   Citadel CTD 8100

MARCO POLO (NBC, 1982) Ennio Morricone
   Arista AL 8304

MASADA (ABC, 1980) Jerry Goldsmith
   MCA 5168

MIAMI VICE (NBC, 1984) Jan Hammer
   MCA 6150, 6192; MCAD 6150, 6192 (CD)

MISTRAL'S DAUGHTER (CBS, 1984) Vladimir Cosma
   Carrere SZ 39902

MOONLIGHTING (ABC, 1985) various composers
   MCA 6214; MCAD 6214 (CD)

MOUNTBATTEN: THE LAST VICTORY (Britain, 1985) John Scott
   Varese Sarabande STV 81273

THE NEW AVENGERS (Britain, 1978) Laurie Johnson
   Starlog/Varese Sarabande ASV-95003

NICHOLAS NICKLEBY (Britain, 1983) Stephen Oliver
   DRG SBLC-12583

NORTH AND SOUTH (ABC, 1985) Bill Conti
   Varese Sarabande 704.310; VCD 47250 (CD)

OCEANQUEST (NBC, 1985) William Goldstein
   CBS FM 42226

ONE STEP BEYOND (ABC, 1959) Harry Lubin
   Varese Sarabande STV 81120

PETER THE GREAT (NBC, 1985) Laurence Rosenthal
   Southern Cross SCCD 1011 (CD)

THE PROFESSIONALS (Britain, 1980) Laurie Johnson
   Starlog/Varese Sarabande ASV-95003

RETURN TO EDEN (Australia, 1985) Brian May
   Varese Sarabande STV 81260

ROBIN OF SHERWOOD (1984) Clannad
   RCA AFL 1-5084

SAVING THE WILDLIFE (PBS, 1985) Chip Davis
   American Gramophone AG 2086

THE SCARLET AND THE BLACK (CBS, 1983) Ennio Morricone
   Cerberus CEM-S 0120

SHADES OF LOVE (made-for-home-video series) various composers
   Capitol ST 12571

SHAKA ZULU (PBS, 1987) Dave Pollecutt
   Cinedisc CDD 1002 (CD)

SHOGUN (NBC, 1980) Maurice Jarre
   RSO RX-1-3088

SILK ROAD (Japan, 1983) Kitaro
  Gramavision 18-7009-1, 18-7011-1, 18-7019-1; 18-7009-2, 18-7011-2,
    18-7019-2 (CD)

STAR TREK (NBC, 1966) Alexander Courage, Fred Steiner, George
    Duning, Gerald Fried, various other composers
  Label "X" LXDR 703, 704; LXCD 703, 704 (CD)
  GNP Crescendo GNPS 8006; GNPD 8006 (CD)
  Varese Sarabande 704.270, 704.300; VCD 47235, 47240 (CD)

A STREETCAR NAMED DESIRE (ABC, 1984) Marvin Hamlisch
  Allegiance AV 439

A TOWN LIKE ALICE (Britain, 1981) Bruce Smeaton
  Southern Cross SCCD 1013 (CD)

THE TWILIGHT ZONE (CBS, 1959) Marius Constant, Bernard
    Herrmann, Jerry Goldsmith, Fred Steiner, various other
    composers
  Varese Sarabande STV 81171, 81178, 81185, 81192, 81205; VCD
    47233, 47247 (CD)

THE UNCLE FLOYD SHOW (Syndicated, 1974) various composers
  Mercury 811 149-1

THE VELVETEEN RABBIT (1985) George Winston
  Dancing Cat DC 3007; CD 3007 (CD)

VICTORY AT SEA (NBC, 1952) Richard Rodgers
  RCA 6660-2-RC (CD)

THE WINDS OF WAR (ABC, 1983) Robert Cobert
  Varese Sarabande STV 81180

THE YEAR OF THE FRENCH (Ireland, 1983) Paddy Moloney
  Shanachie 79036

RECORDED MUSICAL SCORES--TV ANTHOLOGIES

BERNARD HERRMANN'S OUTER SPACE SUITE
  The Outer Space Suite (composed as "stock music" for the CBS
    music library)
  The Moat Farm Murders (radio music)
  The Hitchhiker (radio music)
    Cerberus CST-0208

BERNARD HERRMANN'S WESTERN SAGA
  Western Saga

The Desert Suite
The Indian Suite
(Suites composed as "stock music" for the CBS music library)
Cerberus CST 0207

BRITISH MUSIC FOR FILM & TELEVISON (Marcus Dods conducting
    the City of Birmingham Symphony Orchestra)
Colditz
    and other themes (for film contents see entry in "Recorded
    Musical Scores--Anthologies" section)
    DRG MRS 703

BY REQUEST: THE BEST OF JOHN WILLIAMS AND THE BOSTON
    POPS
NBC Nightly News
    and other themes (for film contents see entry in "Recorded
    Musical Scores--Anthologies" section)
    Philips 420 178-1; 420 178-2 (CD)

CARL DAVIS MUSIC FOR TELEVISION (Carl Davis conducting the
    Royal Philharmonic Orchestra)
The Snow Goose
Our Mutual Friend
Wuthering Heights
The Mayor of Casterbridge
Marie Curie
The Long Search
    DRG MRS 704

CLOSE ENCOUNTERS OF THE THIRD KIND (Geoff Love and His
    Orchestra)
Blake's 7
    and other themes (for film contents see entry in "Recorded
    Musical Scores--Anthologies" section)
    Moss Music Group B-705

DALLAS (Floyd Cramer, piano, with orchestra)
Dallas
Knots Landing
Laverne and Shirley
Incredible Hulk
The Young and the Restless
M*A*S*H
Taxi
The Waltons
All in the Family
    RCA AHL 1-3613, AYL 1-4066

DIGITAL PREMIERE RECORDINGS FROM THE FILMS OF LEE
    HOLDRIDGE (Charles Gerhardt conducting the London
    Symphony Orchestra)

Wizards and Warriors
The Great Whales
East of Eden
The Hemingway Play
    and other themes (for film contents see entry in "Recorded
    Musical Scores--Anthologies" section)
    Varese Sarabande 704.290; VCD 47244 (CD)

THE EXCITING TELEVISION MUSIC OF RON GRAINER
Tales of the Unexpected
Edward and Mrs. Simpson
Malice Aforethought
Dr. Who
Born and Bred
Rebecca
Paul Temple
    and other themes
    Stet DS 15018

THE FANTASTIC FILM MUSIC OF ALBERT GLASSER, VOL. 1
Big Town
Cisco Kid
    and other themes (for film contents see entry in "Recorded
    Musical Scores--Anthologies" section)
    Starlog SR-1001

FAVORITE TV THEMES (Sounds of the Screen Orchestra)
The A-Team
Dallas
M*A*S*H
Hill Street Blues
Taxi
Knight Rider
Star Trek
The Thorn Birds
The Rockford Files
Dynasty
Fame
    Bainbridge BT 6261; BCD 6261 (CD)

THE FINAL FRONTIER (Roy Budd conducting the London Symphony
    Orchestra)
Star Trek
Dr. Who
    and other themes (for film contents see entry in "Recorded
    Musical Scores--Anthologies" section)
    Mobile Fidelity MFCD 2-831 (CD)

GREAT ACTION FILM THEMES/GREAT HORROR FILM THEMES
The Rip Van Winkle Caper [The Twilight Zone]
    and other themes (for film contents see entry in "Recorded

Musical Scores--Anthologies" section)
GSF 1002 (private)

GREATEST SCIENCE FICTION HITS (Neil Norman and His Cosmic
      Orchestra)
   Star Trek
   Battlestar Galactica
   The Outer Limits
   Space: 1999
   One Step Beyond
      and other themes (for film contents see entry in "Recorded
      Musical Scores--Anthologies" section)
      GNP Crescendo GNPS 2128; GNPD 2128 (CD)

GREATEST SCIENCE FICTION HITS II (Neil Norman and His Cosmic
      Orchestra)
   Voyage to the Bottom of the Sea
   The Time Tunnel
   The Twilight Zone
   Buck Rogers in the 25th Century
   Dr. Who
   The Adventures of Superman
      and other themes (for film contents see entry in "Recorded
      Musical Scores--Anthologies" section)
      GNP Crescendo GNPS 2133; GNPD 2133 (CD)

GREATEST SCIENCE FICTION HITS III (Neil Norman and His Cosmic
      Orchestra)
   Land of the Giants
   Space: 1999
   Lost in Space
   The Prisoner
   The Invaders
   U.F.O.
   Star Trek
      and other themes (for film contents see entry in "Recorded
      Musical Scores--Anthologies" section)
      GNP Crescendo GNPS 2163; GNPD 2163 (CD)

MARK TWAIN CLASSICS (William Perry)
   The Adventures of Huckleberry Finn
   Pudd'nhead Wilson
   Life on the Mississippi
   Innocents Abroad
   The Private History of a Campaign that Failed
   The Mysterious Stranger
      Trobriand TRO 1001

MIKE POST
   The A-Team
   Riptide

St. Elsewhere
and other themes (for film contents see entry in "Recorded
Musical Scores--Anthologies" section)
RCA AFL 1-5183, 1-5415; PCD 1-5183 (CD)

MOVIE AND TV THEMES (Composed and conducted by Elmer Bern-
stein)
Take Five
Saints and Sinners
and other themes (for film contents see entry in "Recorded
Musical Scores--Anthologies" section)
Mobile Fidelity MFCD 851 (CD)

MUSIC FOR RADIO AND TELEVISION (Bernard Herrmann)
The Walt Whitman Suite (radio music)
Brave New World (radio music)
Collector's Item
The Landmark Theme
Cerberus CST-0210

MUSIC FROM THE GALAXIES (Ettore Stratta conducting the London
Symphony Orchestra)
Star Trek
Battlestar Galactica
and other themes (for film contents see entry in "Recorded
Musical Scores--Anthologies" section)
Columbia IC 35876, FM 37266

OUT OF THIS WORLD (John Williams conducting the Boston Pops
Orchestra)
Star Trek
Battlestar Galactica
Twilight Zone
and other themes (for film contents see entry in "Recorded
Musical Scores--Anthologies" section)
Philips 411 185-1; 411 185-2 (CD)

OUTER SPACE SUITE see BERNARD HERRMANN'S OUTER SPACE
SUITE

ROUND-UP (Erich Kunzel conducting the Cincinnati Pops Orchestra)
Bonanza
Rawhide
Wagon Train
The Rifleman
and other themes (for film contents see entry in "Recorded
Musical Scores--Anthologies" section)
Telarc DG 10141; CD 80141 (CD)

SECRET AGENT FILE
I Spy

The Rockford Files
The Prisoner
Reilly: Ace of Spies
The Man from U.N.C.L.E.
Get Smart
    and other themes (for film contents see entry in "Recorded
    Musical Scores--Anthologies" section)
    GNP Crescendo GNPS 2166; GNPD 2166 (CD)

SOUNDTRACK MEMORIES
    Brian's Song
    and other themes (for film contents see entry in "Recorded
    Musical Scores--Anthologies" section)
    Arista ABM 2005

STAR TRACKS (Erich Kunzel conducting the Cincinnati Pops
    Orchestra)
    Star Trek
    and other themes (for film contents see entry in "Recorded
    Musical Scores--Anthologies" section)
    Telarc DG 10094

STUCK ON T.V. (Warren Schatz with the Universal City Orchestra)
    The Munsters
    Magnum, P.I.
    Kojak
    Baretta
    Night Gallery
    Quincy
    The Six Million Dollar Man
    MCA 5380

TELEVISION THEME SONGS (Mike Post)
    Hill Street Blues
    The Greatest American Hero
    The White Shadow
    Magnum P.I.
    The Rockford Files
    Richie Brockelman, Private Eye
    Elektra E1-60028

TELEVISION'S GREATEST HITS
    Captain Kangaroo
    The Little Rascals
    The Flintstones
    The Woody Woodpecker Show
    Bugs Bunny
    Casper, the Friendly Ghost
    Felix the Cat
    Popeye
    Yogi Bear

Magilla Gorilla
Top Cat
The Jetsons
Fireball XL-5
Howdy Doody
The Beverly Hillbillies
Petticoat Junction
Green Acres
Mister Ed
The Munsters
The Addams Family
My Three Sons
The Donna Reed Show
Leave It To Beaver
Dennis the Menace
Dobie Gillis
The Patty Duke Show
The Dick Van Dyke Show
Gilligan's Island
McHale's Navy
I Dream of Jeannie
I Love Lucy
The Andy Griffith Show
Star Trek
Lost in Space
The Twilight Zone
Alfred Hitchcock Presents
Superman
Batman
Flipper
Combat
The Rifleman
Bonanza
Branded
F Troop
Rin Tin Tin
Daniel Boone
The Wild Wild West
The Lone Ranger
The Roy Rogers Show
Mission: Impossible
The Man from U.N.C.L.E.
Get Smart
Secret Agent
Dragnet
Perry Mason
Adam 12
The F.B.I.
Hawaii Five-O
77 Sunset Strip
Surfside 6

Ironside
Mannix
The Mod Squad
The Tonight Show
    TeeVee Toons TVT 1100; TVT 1100 CD (CD)

TELEVISION'S GREATEST HITS, VOLUME II
The Three Stooges
Merrie Melodies
Rocky and Bullwinkle
Huckleberry Hound
Mighty Mouse
Courageous Cat and Minute Mouse
Pink Panther
Road Runner
George of the Jungle
Jonny Quest
Spider-Man
Underdog
Looney Tunes
Peanuts
Mister Rogers' Neighborhood
The Odd Couple
The Courtship of Eddie's Father
Mary Tyler Moore
Gidget
That Girl
Bewitched
Love, American Style
The Honeymooners
I Married Joan
The Monkees
The Brady Bunch
The Partridge Family
My Mother the Car
Car 54, Where Are You?
It's About Time
My Favorite Martian
Jeopardy
Hogan's Heroes
Gomer Pyle, U.S.M.C.
Rat Patrol
Twelve O'Clock High
Time Tunnel
Voyage to the Bottom of the Sea
Sea Hunt
Daktari
Tarzan
The Adventures of Robin Hood
Rawhide
Bat Masterson

Maverick
Wagon Train
Have Gun Will Travel
The Virginian
The Rebel
Peter Gunn
Route 66
I Spy
The Avengers
The Saint
Hawaiian Eye
The Green Hornet
The Outer Limits
Dark Shadows
Ben Casey
Medical Center
NBC Mystery Movie
ABC's Wide World of Sports
The Jackie Gleason Show
Smothers Brothers Comedy Hour
Monty Python's Flying Circus
    TeeVee Toons TVT 1200; TVT 1200 CD (CD)

THEMES FROM MASTERPIECE THEATRE
  Volume I:
    Masterpiece Theatre Series Music
    The First Churchills
    Upstairs, Downstairs
    Poldark
    Country Matters
    Elizabeth R
    Lord Peter Wimsey
    Lillie
    Shoulder to Shoulder
    I, Claudius
    Love for Lydia
    The Duchess of Duke Street
    Disraeli
    Pride and Prejudice
  Volume II:
    The Citadel
    Pictures
    To Serve Them All My Days
    The Good Soldier
    The Irish R.M.
    The Jewel in the Crown
    The Flame Trees of Thika
    Edward and Mrs. Simpson
    The Tale of Beatrix Potter
    Flickers
    By the Sword Divided

On Approval
A Town Like Alice
Masterpiece Theatre Series Music
Sine Qua Non 5057-1, 5052-1 (volume II only)

TIME WARP (Erich Kunzel conducting the Cincinnati Pops Orchestra)
Star Trek
Battlestar Galactica
and other themes (for film contents see entry in "Recorded
Musical Scores--Anthologies" section)
Telarc DG-10106; CD-80106 (CD)

THE TV THEME SONG SING-ALONG ALBUM
I Love Lucy
Bonanza
The Beverly Hillbillies
Hogan's Heroes
The Andy Griffith Show
Star Trek
Rawhide
Leave It To Beaver
The Monkees
Green Acres
Petticoat Junction
Mission: Impossible
Perry Mason
Dobie Gillis
American Bandstand
Rhino RNLP-703

WESTERN SAGA see BERNARD HERRMANN'S WESTERN SAGA

APPENDIX: FILM MUSIC NECROLOGY

William Alwyn (1905-1985)
Daniele Amfitheatrof (1901-1983)
Richard D. Aurandt (1905-1984)
Georges Auric (1899-1983)
George Bruns (1914-1983)
Lucien Calliet (1893-1985)
Pete Carpenter (1915-1987)
Luchi de Jesus (1923-1984)
James Dietrich (1894-1984)
Carmen Dragon (1915-1984)
Franco Ferrara (?-1985)
Hugo Friedhofer (1902-1981)
Ron Grainer (1923-1981)
Walter Greene (1910-1983)
Johnny Guarnieri (1917-1985)
Kenyon Hopkins (1912-1983)
Gordon Jenkins (1911-1984)
Bronislau Kaper (1902-1983)
Anton Karas (1910-1985)
Bernhard Kaun (1900-1980)
Gail Kubik (1915-1984)
Michel Magne (1930-1984)

Shelly Manne (1920-1984)
Emil Newman (1911-1984)
Lionel Newman (1917-1989)
Nino Oliviero (1918-1980)
Edward Powell (1910-1984)
Nelson Riddle (1921-1985)
Heinz Roemheld (1902-1985)
Renzo Rossellini (1908-1982)
Rudolf Schramm (1903-1981)
Humphrey Searle (1916-1982)
Richard Shores (c1918-1985)
Paul Smith (1907-1985)
Mischa Spoliansky (1899-1985)
Ronald Stein (1930-1988)
George Stoll (1906-1985)
Peggy Stuart (Coolidge)
   (1914-1981)
Harry Sukman (1912-1984)
Alexandre Tansman (1896-1986)
Sir William Walton (1902-1983)
Roy Webb (1888-1982)
Jean Wiener (1896-1982)
Meredith Willson (1902-1984)

FILM TITLE INDEX

ABC After School Special, The
    (1972)
A. D. (1985)
A.E.S. Hudson Street (1978)
A for Andromeda (1962)
A. K. (1985)
A-Team, The (1983)
A-077--Challenge to the Killers
    (1966)
A-008 Operation Exterminate
    (1965)
Aah, Belinda! (1987)
Aan (Pride) (1952)
Aaron's Way (1988)
Abandon (Afzien) (1986)
Abandoned (1982)
Abbott and Costello Show, The
    (1952)
Abducted (1986)
Abduction, The (1936)
Abduction of Kari Swenson, The
    (1987)
Abduction of Saint Anne, The
    (1975)
Abdul the Damned (1936)
Abel (1986)
Abel Gance and His Napoleon
    (1984)
Ablakon (1985)
Abominable Dr. Phibes, The
    (1971)
Abominable Snowman, The
    (1957)
Abortion: Stories from North
    and South (1985)
About Judges and Other
    Sympathizers (1982)
About Last Night (1986)
About Love (1987)
Above the Law (1988)
Abracadabra (1988)
Absence of Malice (1981)
Absences (1987)
Absentee, The (1952)
Absentee, The (1986)
Absent-Minded Professor, The
    (1988)

Absolution (1981)
Abuse (1983)
Abused Confidence (1938)
Abyss, The (1988)
Acapulco (1961)
Acceptable Levels (1983)
Acceptable Risks (1986)
Accidental Family (1967)
Accidental Tourist, The (1988)
Accomplices (1988)
Accomplished Fact, An (1985)
According to Pontius Pilate (1988)
Accordionist's Wedding, The (1988)
Accusation (1951)
Accused (1936)
Accused, The (1988)
Ace (1976)
Ace (1981)
Ace Crawford, Private Eye (1983)
Ace of Aces (1982)
Aces Go Places (1982)
Aces Go Places III (1984)
Aces Up (1974)
Acorn People, The (1981)
Act, The (1984)
Act of Love (1981)
Act of Vengeance (1986)
Act of Violence (1979)
Act of Violence (1980)
Acting: Lee Strasberg and the
    Actors Studio (1981)
Action (1957)
Action (1980)
Action Jackson (1988)
Actress, The (1988)
Actress (Eiga Joyu)(1987)
Adam (1983)
Adam and Eve (1950)
Adam and Eve (1956)
Adam and Yves (1974)
Adam: His Song Continues (1986)
Adam Mackenzie Story, The (1963)
Adam-12 (1968)
Adam 2 (1969)
Adams Apple (1986)
Adams Chronicles, The (1976)
Adam's House (1983)

Adams of Eagle Lake (1975)
Adam's Rib (1973)
Addams Family, The (1964)
Addams Family, The (animated)
   (1973)
Addicted to His Love (1988)
Addie and the King of Hearts
   (1976)
Addressee Unknown (1983)
Adela (1985)
Adieu, Bonaparte (1985)
Adieu, les Beaux Jours (1934)
Adios Gringo (1968)
Adios Miami (1983)
Admiral Yamamoto (1969)
Adolescence of Cain (1959)
Adolescent Sugar of Love, The
   (Gazi El Banat) (1985)
Adua and the Colleagues (1960)
Adultery, Italian Style (1966)
Adventure at the Center of the
   Earth, The (1965)
Adventure at the Door (1961)
Adventure in the Night (1947)
Adventure in Warsaw (1955)
Adventure of Salvator Rosa, An
   (1940)
Adventure of the Action Hunters,
   The (1987)
Adventurer, The (1966)
Adventurer, The (1972)
Adventures in Babysitting (1987)
Adventures in Paradise (1959)
Adventures in Vienna (1952)
Adventures of Baron
   Munchaussen (1943)
Adventures of Buckaroo Banzai:
   Across the 8th Dimension, The
   (1984)
Adventures of Captain Fabian,
   The (1951)
Adventures of Champion, The
   (1955)
Adventures of Chatran, The (1986)
Adventures of Dr. Dolittle (1928)
Adventures of Don Quixote, The
   (1973)
Adventures of Enrique and Ana,
   The (1981)
Adventures of Faustus Bidgood,
   The (1986)
Adventures of Huckleberry Finn
   (1981)
Adventures of Jonny Quest, The
   (1964)
Adventures of Long John Silver,
   The (1956)

Adventures of Nellie Bly (1980)
Adventures of Nick Carter, The
   (1972)
Adventures of Ozzie and Harriet,
   The (1952)
Adventures of Pinocchio, The (1975)
Adventures of Pollyanna, The (1982)
Adventures of Rex and Rinty, The
   (1935)
Adventures of Rin-Tin-Tin, The
   (1954)
Adventures of Robin Hood, The
   (1955)
Adventures of Sherlock Holmes,
   The (1985)
Adventures of Sun Wu Kung (1958)
Adventures of Takla Makan (1965)
Adventures of the Queen (1975)
Adventures of Til Eulenspiegel
   (1957)
Adventuress, The (1951)
Advice to the Lovelorn (1981)
Aerodrome, The (1983)
Aeroport: Charter 2020 (1980)
Aetherrausch (1988)
Affair, The (1973)
Affair, The (Relasyon) (1985)
Affair at Akitsu (1962)
Affair in Port Said (1966)
Affair Lafont, The (1939)
Affairs of a Model (1952)
Affairs of a Rogue, The (1949)
Affairs of China Smith, The (1952)
Affairs of Maupassant (1938)
Afflicted, The (1988)
Affliction (Dahan) (1986)
Afraid to Dance (1988)
African, The (1983)
African Bird, The (1976)
African Holiday (1937)
African Odyssey (1988)
African Queen, The (1977)
After a Night of Love (1935)
After Darkness (1985)
After Hours (1985)
After Love (1983)
After Midnight (1982)
After Pilkington (1986)
After Rubicon (1987)
After the Ball (1957)
After the Fall of New York (1985)
After the Promise (1987)
Aftermath, The (1980)
Afternoon Affair, An (1984)
Again Forever (Dime Novel) (1985)
Against All Odds (1984)
Against the Wind (1979)

Agatha (1985)
Agatha Christie's "A Caribbean
  Mystery" (1983)
Agatha Christie's "Murder Is Easy"
  (1982)
Agatha Christie's "Sparkling
  Cyanide" (1983)
Age of Love, The (1954)
Age of the Earth, The (1980)
Age of the Wolf (1988)
Agee (1980)
Agency (1980)
Agent 505 (1965)
Agent on Ice (And Then You Die/
  Silent Partners) (1986)
Agent Sigma 3--Mission Goldwather
  (1968)
Agent 353, Massacre in the Sun
  (1966)
Agent Z-55: Desperate Mission
  (1966)
Agitated Winds (1984)
Agnes of God (1985)
Agony (1985)
Ah Ying (1983)
AIDS--A Danger for Love (1985)
Aililia (1975)
Air Heroes (1957)
Air of Crime, The (1984)
Air Strike (1955)
Airplane (1980)
Airplane II: The Sequel (1982)
Airship, The (1983)
Airwolf (1984)
Ake and His World (1984)
Akropolis Now (1984)
Al di La (1981)
Al Qadisiyya (1981)
Aladdin and the Wonderful Lamp
  (1969)
Aladdin Takes Off (Dringue,
  Castrito y la Lampara de
  Aladino) (1954)
Alamo Bay (1985)
Alamo: 13 Days to Glory, The
  (1987)
Alaska (1967)
Alaska (1971)
Alaska Story, The (1977)
Alaskans, The (1959)
Alberto Giacometti (short) (1967)
Alcatraz: The Whole Shocking
  Story (1980)
Alchemist, The (1986)
Alcove, The (1985)
Aldo and Junior (1984)
Aleksa Dundic (1958)

Alerte au Sud (1953)
Alex and the Doberman Gang (1980)
Alex: The Life of a Child (1986)
Alexander the Great (O
  Megalexandros) (1980)
Alexander the Little (1983)
Alexander: The Other Side of
  Dawn (1977)
Alexandre (1983)
Alexyz (1984)
Alf, Bill and Fred (short) (1964)
Alfred Laliberte, Sculptor (1987)
Ali Baba and the 40 Thieves (1954)
Ali Baba and the Forty Thieves
  (1971)
Alias John Preston (1955)
Alias Smith and Jones (1971)
Alias Will James (1988)
Alice (1976)
Alice in Wonderland (1966)
Alice in Wonderland (1985)
Alice, Sweet Alice (Communion)
  (1978)
Alice to Nowhere (1986)
Alien, The (De Plaats van de
  Vreemdeling) (1980)
Alien Contamination (1980)
Alien Dead, The (1980)
Alien Encounters, The (1979)
Alien Factor, The (1976)
Alien 2 (1982)
Alien Years, The (1988)
Aliens (1986)
Aliens Are Coming, The (1980)
Alif Laila (1953)
Alive and Kicking (1959)
All-American Pie (1980)
All at Sea (1957)
All Because of a Wedding Dress
  (1986)
All Creatures Great and Small
  (1975)
All Fired Up (Tout Feu, Tout
  Flamme) (1982)
All for Mary (1956)
All God's Children (1980)
All in the Family (1971)
All Is Love (1980)
All Life Long (1987)
All Men Are Apes (1965)
All Mixed Up (1985)
All My Children (1970)
All My Darling Daughters (1972)
All My Friends 2 (1983)
All-New Popeye Hour, The (1978)
All Night Long (1981)
All of Me (1984)

All-Out Game, The (1971)
All Quiet on the Western Front
   (1979)
All Right, My Friend (1983)
All Roads Lead to Rome (1949)
All-Stars (Tous Vedettes) (1980)
All That Glitters (1977)
All That Rhythm (1984)
All the Colors of Darkness (They're
   Coming to Get You) (1976)
All the Kind Strangers (1974)
... All the Marbles (1981)
All the Right Moves (1983)
All the Rivers Run (1984)
All the Way (1988)
All the Wrong Clues (for the
   Right Solution) (1981)
All the Wrong Spies (1983)
All Together Now (1975)
Alla en el Rancho Grande (1936)
Allan Quatermain and the Lost
   City of Gold (1987)
Allegement, L' (1983)
Allegro Non Troppo (short)
   (1962)
Alley Cat (1980)
Alley Cat, The (Matou, Le) (1985)
Alliance (Wedding Ring, The)
   (1970)
Allies (1983)
Alligator Shoes (1981)
Allnighter, The (1987)
All's Fair (1976)
Almacita de Desolata (1986)
Almafuerte (1950)
Almeria Case, The (1984)
Almonds and Raisins (1984)
Almost a Love Story (1980)
Almost Grown (1988)
Almost Heaven (1978)
Almost Human (Milano Odia) (1980)
Almost Partners (1987)
Almost Perfect Crime, The (1966)
Almost Transparent Blue (1980)
Almost You (1984)
Aloa--The Whore's Feast (1988)
Aloha Means Goodbye (1974)
Aloha Summer (1988)
Alone Among His Own (1985)
Alone at Last (1980)
Alone in the Dark (1982)
Alone in the Neon Jungle (1988)
Alone with Ghosts (1964)
Along Came a Spider (1970)
Along the Barbary Coast (1961)
Along the Sidewalks (1956)
Alpha Caper, The (Inside Job)
   (1973)

Alphabet City (1984)
Alpine Fire (1985)
Alraune (Daughter of Evil) (1928)
Alsino and the Condor (1983)
Alter Ego (Letters from a Doctor in
   Africa) (1986)
Altered States (1980)
Altitude 3,200 (1938)
Altra Donna, L' (1981)
Always Afternoon (1988)
Amada (1983)
Amagi Pass (1983)
Amanda Fallon (1972)
Amanda's (1983)
Amangeldy (1939)
Amants del Diablo, Les (1971)
Amateur, The (1982)
Amateur Night at the Dixie Bar and
   Grill (1979)
Amazing Chan and the Chan Clan,
   The (1972)
Amazing Grace and Chuck (1987)
Amazing Howard Hughes, The (1977)
Amazing Mr. Blunden, The (1972)
Amazing Monsieur Fabre, The (1952)
Amazing Spiderman, The (1977)
Amazing Stories (1985)
Amazing Three, The (1967)
Amazing Transparent Man, The
   (1960)
Amazing Years of Cinema, The
   (short) (1981)
Amazons (1984)
Amazons (1987)
Ambassador, The (IND) (1984)
Ambassador, The (YUG) (1984)
Ambassador from India, The (1988)
Amber Waves (1980)
Ambush at Devil's Gap (1966)
Ambush Murders, The (1982)
Ambushers, The (1967)
Amelia Earhart (1976)
Amerasia (1986)
America (1972)
America and Americans (1968)
America, God's Country (1966)
America 3000 (1986)
America 2100 (1979)
America, Unknown Land (1988)
American Anthem (1986)
American Caesar (1985)
American Christmas Carol, An
   (1979)
American Commandos (Hitman)
   (1986)
American Dream (1981)
American Dreamer (1984)
American Drive-In (1985)

Angels of Iron (1981)
Angels of the District (1952)
Angels of the Streets (1950)
Angels of 2000, The (1975)
Angelus Novus (1987)
Angie (1979)
Angkor-Cambodia Express (1981)
Angry Red Planet, The (1959)
Anguish (1987)
Aniki-Bobo (1942)
Animals Film, The (1981)
Anita--Dances of Vice (1987)
Ann in Blue (1974)
Ann Jillian Story, The (1988)
Anna (Une Mere, Une Fille) (1981)
Anna and Elizabeth (1936)
Anna and the King (1972)
Anna and the King (1978)
Anna's Mother (1984)
Anne Devlin (1984)
Anne of Avonlea (1987)
Anne Trister (1986)
Annette in Paradise (1936)
Annie Flynn (1978)
Annie McGuire (1988)
Annie Oakley (1954)
Annie Oakley (1985)
Annie's Coming Out (1984)
Annunciation (1984)
Another Chance (1988)
Another Country (1984)
Another Day (1978)
Another Life (1981)
Another Love (Ina Laska) (1986)
Another Man's Shoes (1984)
Another Time, Another Place
   (1983)
Another Woman's Child (1983)
Another World (1964)
Antarctic Crossing (1958)
Antarctica (1984)
Antarctica Project, The (1988)
Anti-Climax (1970)
Anti-Clock (1980)
Antinea (Atlantide, L') (1961)
Antique Dealer's Wife, The
   (1983)
Antonieta (1982)
Antonio di Padova (1949)
Antonio Gaudi (1985)
Anxiety (1954)
Any Body ... Any Way (1980)
Any Second Now (1969)
Anzacs (1985)
Anzacs: The War Down Under
   (1987)
Aoom (1970)

Apartment Zero (1988)
Ape, The (1940)
Aphrodite (1982)
Aphrousa (1971)
Apocalypse in Berlin (1966)
Apology (1986)
Appalling Days (Schoene Tage)
   (1982)
Appeal on the Cross (1957)
Appearances (1964)
Apple, The (short) (1962)
Apple, The (1980)
Apple of Our Eye, The (Eszterlanc)
   (1985)
Apple's Way (1974)
Appointment for Murder (1954)
Appointment in Liverpool (1988)
Appointment with a Killer (1975)
Appointment with Death (1988)
Appointment with Fear (1985)
Appointment with Life (1949)
Appointment with Venus (1951)
Apprentice to Murder (1988)
Apprenticeship of Snail the Inventor,
   The (1982)
April 1, 2000 (1954)
April Fool's Day (1985)
April Fool's Day (1986)
April Has 30 Days (1980)
April Is a Deadly Month (1987)
April Morning (1988)
Aquanauts, The (1960)
Aquarians, The (1970)
Aquasex (1970)
Arabian Adventure (1979)
Arch of Triumph (1985)
Archie (1976)
Archie Bunker's Place (1979)
Archie Comedy Hour, The (1970)
Archie's TV Funnies (1971)
Architecture of Frank Lloyd Wright,
   The (1985)
Arctic Sea Calls, The (1984)
Ardent Love (1960)
Arder and Yul (1988)
Are We Winning, Mommy? America
   and the Cold War (1986)
Are You in the House Alone? (1978)
Arena (1969)
Arhats in Fury (1985)
Aria for an Athlete (1980)
Arizona and Its Natural Resources
   (short) (1967)
Arizona Colt (1966)
Arizona Heat (1988)
Ark of the Sun God, The (1983)
Ark II (1976)

Armed and Dangerous (1986)
Armed Response (Jade Jungle)
  (1986)
Armour of God, The (1986)
Army Wives (1987)
Arnie (1970)
Arnold's Closet Review (1971)
Around the World in 80 Days
  (1972)
Around the World in Eighty Ways
  (1986)
Aroused (1968)
Arpa-Colla (1982)
Arrevederci Yamato (1978)
Arriving Tuesday (1986)
Arsenic and Old Lace (1949)
Arshin Mal Alan (1937)
Art of Crime, The (1975)
Art of Getting Along, The (1955)
Art of Love, The (1983)
Art Scene USA (short) (1967)
Arthur (1981)
Arthur & the Britons (1971)
Arthur the King (1985)
Arthur 2 on the Rocks (1988)
Artichoke (1982)
Article 519, Penal Code (1953)
Artist's Entrance (1938)
As Is (1986)
As Long as There Are Women
  (1987)
As Long as You Live (1955)
As the Sea Rages (1960)
As the World Turns (1956)
As Time Goes By (1987)
Asa Branca--A Brazilian Dream
  (1988)
Asaki Yumemishi (1975)
Asa-Nisse in Military Uniform
  (1959)
Ascendancy (1983)
Ash Wednesday (1958)
Ashes to the Wind (1942)
Asik Kerib (1988)
Ask Max (1986)
Aspen (1977)
Asphalt (1981)
Asphalt Cowboy, The (1980)
Asphalt Night (1980)
Assa (1988)
Assam Garden, The (1985)
Assassin (1986)
Assassin 77, Life or Death (1966)
Assassination (Attentat) (1980)
Assassination (1987)
Assassination of Ryoma, The
  (1975)

Assassination Run, The (1983)
Assassin's Quarry (1975)
Assault, The (1986)
Assault & Matrimony (1987)
Assault of the Killer Bimbos (1988)
Assault on Precinct 13 (1976)
Assault on the Wayne (1971)
Assignation, The (short) (1953)
Assignment Africa (1986)
Assignment Earth (1968)
Assignment: Munich (1972)
Assignment Outer Space (Space
  Men) (1960)
Assignment--Paris (1952)
Assignment: Vienna (1972)
Assisi Underground, The (1985)
Assistant, The (Pomocnik) (1982)
Association of Wrongdoers (1987)
Asterix and Cleopatra (1968)
Asterix in Britain (1986)
Asterix vs. Caesar (1985)
Astic (1956)
Astonished (1988)
Astounding She Monster (1950)
Astronaut, The (1972)
Astronauts, The (short) (1959)
Astronauts, The (1960)
Astro-Zombies, The (1969)
Asya (1982)
Asylum (1972)
Asylum of Satan (1974)
At Close Range (1986)
At Ease (1983)
At Green Cockatoos by Night (1958)
At Mother's Request (1987)
At the Cinema Palace--Liam O'Leary
  (1983)
At the Photographer's (short) (1959)
At the Terminus (1961)
At the Top of the Stairs (1983)
At This Late Date, the Charleston
  (1982)
At Your Own Request (1979)
At Your Service (1984)
Athalia (1984)
Atlanta Child Murders, The (1985)
Atlantic City, U.S.A. (1980)
Atlantide, L' (Lost Atlantis) (1932)
Atom Age Vampire (Seddok) (1960)
Atomic Power Today (short) (1967)
Atomic Station (1984)
Atomic Submarine, The (1960)
Ator (1983)
Atrapados (1981)
Attack of the Killer Tomatoes, The
  (1979)
Attack of the Mayan Mummy (1963)

Attack of the Monsters (1969)
Attack of the Puppet People, The
    (Six Inches Tall) (1958)
Attack of the Robots (Cards on
    the Table) (1962)
Attack on Terror: The F.B.I.
    vs. the Ku Klux Klan (1975)
Attempt at a Crime (1956)
Attention (1985)
Attention, Bandits (1987)
Attention, One Woman May Be
    Hiding Another (Double
    Husbands) (1983)
Attic, The (1981)
Attic: The Hiding of Anne
    Frank, The (1988)
Attica (1980)
Augh! Augh! (1980)
August (1988)
August Requiem, An (1982)
Aunt Alexandra (1980)
Aunt Mary (1980)
Aurelia (1987)
Aurora Encounter, The (1986)
Auschwitz Street (1980)
Aussie Assault (1984)
Austeria (1983)
Australia, Australia (1981)
Australian Daze (1988)
Australian Dream (1987)
Australia's Twilight of the Dream-
    time (1988)
Author! Author! (1982)
Authorized Instructor (1980)
Autobiography of Miss Jane
    Pittman, The (1974)
Autograph, The (1984)
Automan (1983)
Autumn Almanac (1984)
Autumn Born (1983)
Autumn Flight (short) (1967)
Autumn's Tale, An (1987)
Avanti Popolo (1986)
Ave Maria (1984)
Avengers, The (1966)
Avenging Angel (1985)
Avenging Force (1986)
Avia's Summer (1988)
Avocate d'Amour (1938)
Awakening, The (1980)
Awakening Land, The (1978)
Awakening of Candra, The (1983)
Awara (1956)
Awesome Lotus (1986)
Awry in the Wings (1983)
Axe (Lisa, Lisa) (1983)
Axe of Wandsbeck, The (1951)

Axe of Wandsbek, The (1982)
Axiliad (1987)
Azimat (1958)
Aziza (1980)
Azra (1988)
Azul (1988)
Azure Express (1938)

B.A.D. Cats (1980)
B. B. Beegle Show, The (1980)
B. J. and the Bear (1978)
B. J. and the Bear (1979)
BMX Bandits (1983)
B.R.A.T. Patrol, The (1986)
Babes in Bagdad (1952)
Babette's Feast (1987)
Babies Having Babies (1986)
Baby (1984)
Baby (1985)
Baby and the Battleship, The (1956)
Baby Boom (1987)
Baby Come Home (1980)
Baby Doctor Engel (1937)
Baby Doll (1988)
Baby Girl Scott (1987)
Baby, I'm Back (1978)
Baby M (1988)
Baby Makes Five (1983)
Baby on Board (1988)
Baby Sister (1983)
Baby the Rain Must Fall (1965)
Babylon (1980)
Bacchantes, The (1960)
Bach and Broccoli (1987)
Bachelor, The (1956)
Bachelor Girl (1987)
Bachelor of Hearts (1958)
Bachelor Party (1984)
Back from the Dead (1957)
Back Roads (1981)
Back to Nature (1936)
Back to School (1986)
Back to the Beach (1987)
Back to the Door (1959)
Back to the Future (1985)
Back to the Planet of the Apes
    (1980)
Back Together (1984)
Backfire (1987)
Back-Jet Family, The (1985)
Backlash (1986)
Backroads (1981)
Backstage (1988)
Backstairs at the White House
    (1979)
Bad Blonde (1953)

Barretts of Wimpole Street, The
   (1955)
Barricade, The (1982)
Barrington (1987)
Basic Training (Up the Pentagon)
   (1983)
Basket Case (1982)
Basket of Mexican Tales (1956)
Bastard, The (1983)
Bastard Brother of God, The
   (1986)
Bastard/Kent Family Chronicles,
   The (1978)
Bastille (1984)
Bat People, The (It Lives by
   Night) (1974)
Bat 21 (1988)
Batch '81 (1982)
Bates Motel, The (1987)
Batman (1966)
Baton Rouge (1985)
Baton Rouge (1988)
Battement de Coeur (Heartbeat)
   (1940)
Battered (1978)
Batteries Not Included (1987)
Battle, The (1936)
Battle at Bloody Beach (1961)
Battle at Poziralnik, The (1982)
Battle Beyond the Stars (1980)
Battle for the Republic of
   China, The (1982)
Battle of Okinawa (1971)
Battle of the Mods, The (1966)
Battle of the Planets (1977)
Battle of the Planets (1978)
Battle of the Rails (1946)
Battlefield (1985)
Battles of Chief Pontiac (1952)
Battles: The Murder That
   Wouldn't Die (1980)
Battlestar Galactica (1978)
Battletruck (1982)
Baxters, The (1979)
Bay Boy (1984)
Bay City Blues (1983)
Bay Coven (1987)
Bayo (1985)
Bayou (1957)
Be Dear to Me (1957)
Be Forever Yamato (1980)
Be Good unto Death (1936)
Be Tough, Victor! (1983)
Be Unfaithful and Don't Be
   Concerned With Whom (1985)
Beach Balls (1988)
Beach Girls, The (1977)

Beach Girls, The (1982)
Beach House, The (Casotto, Il)
   (1980)
Beach House (Down the Shore)
   (1982)
Beach Patrol (1979)
Beachcomber, The (1961)
Beaches (1988)
Beacon Hill (1975)
Beads of One Rosary, The (1980)
Beaks (Birds of Prey) (1987)
Beane's of Boston (1979)
Bear, The (1984)
Bear Island (1980)
Bear-Skinned Man (1987)
Bearcats! (1971)
Bearn (1983)
Bears, The (1988)
Beast, The (1982)
Beast, The (1986)
Beast, The (1988)
Beast in the Cellar, The (1971)
Beast Must Die, The (1974)
Beast of Morocco (1966)
Beast of Yucca Flats, The (1961)
Beast with a Million Eyes, The
   (1955)
Beast Within, The (1982)
Beastmaster, The (1982)
Beasts, The (1984)
Beasts Are on the Streets, The
   (1978)
Beat, The (1987)
Beat Generation--An American
   Dream, The (1987)
Beat '71 (1971)
Beauf, Le (1987)
Beautiful Adventure (1959)
Beautiful and Beloved Mexico (1961)
Beautiful Dreamer, The (1953)
Beautiful Galatea, The (1950)
Beautiful Stranger (1954)
Beauty and the Beast (1976)
Beauty and the Beast, The (1983)
Beauty and the Beast (1987)
Beauty and the Thieves (1952)
Beauty of Vice, The (1986)
Beaver Track, The (1985)
Because of That War (1988)
Beckett Affair, The (1966)
Becoming Aware (1985)
Bed, The (Lit, Le) (1983)
Bed of Grass (1957)
Bed Sitting Room, The (1968)
Bedeviled Gold (1942)
Bedroom Eyes (1984)
Bedroom Window, The (1986)

Bedrooms (1984)
Bedtime with Rosie (1974)
Bee-Hive, The (Colmena, La)
    (1982)
Bee Keeper, The (1986)
Beer (1985)
Bees, The (1979)
Beethoven Concerto (1937)
Beetlejuice (1988)
Before & After (1985)
Before Stonewall (1984)
Before Sundown (1956)
Before the Battle (1983)
Before the Dawn (A Rutana Pera)
    (1982)
Before the Future (1985)
Beg, Borrow ... or Steal (1973)
Beggarman, Thief (1979)
Beggars, The (1987)
Beginner's Luck (1986)
Beginning of a Story, The (1988)
Beginning or the End, The (1957)
Behind Closed Shutters (1952)
Behind Enemy Lines (1986)
Behind Locked Doors (1948)
Behind the Barriers (1949)
Behind the Facade (1939)
Behind the Mask (1958)
Behind the Screen (1981)
Behind the Show Window (1957)
Behind the Spaceman (short)
    (1967)
Being, The (Easter Sunday)
    (1980)
Being Different (1981)
Beirut: The Last Home Movie
    (1987)
Bela Lugosi Meets a Brooklyn
    Gorilla (1952)
Believe It or Not (Impossible
    Things) (1986)
Believers, The (1987)
Bell, Book and Candle (1978)
Bell Diamond (1987)
Bell for Nirvana, A (1983)
Bella Donna (1983)
Belladonna (1973)
Belle Otero, La (1954)
Belle Starr (1980)
Bellman and True (1987)
Bells (Murder by Phone)(1980)
Bells of Autumn (Autumn Chimes)
    (1980)
Belly of an Architect, The (1987)
Beloved Corrine (1957)
Beloved of the World (1949)
Beloved Vagabond, The (1937)

Below the Belt (1980)
Below the Chinese Restaurant (1987)
Belzaire the Cajun (1986)
Ben and Me (short) (1953)
Ben Casey (1961)
Bender (1979)
Beneath the World (1987)
Beneficiary, The (1980)
Bengali Night, The (1988)
Beni Walks by Himself (1985)
Benilde, ou a Virgem Mae (1975)
Benji the Hunted (1987)
Bennett Brothers, The (1987)
Benny and Barney, Las Vegas
    Undercover (1977)
Benny's Place (1982)
Benson (1979)
Benvenuta (1983)
Bergslagsfolk (1938)
Berlin Affair (1970)
Berlin Affair, The (1985)
Berlin Alexanderplatz (1980)
Berlin Blues (1988)
Berlin Chamissoplatz (1981)
Berlin Kaput (1981)
Berlin Love Story, A (1985)
Berlin Tunnel (1981)
Berliner Ballade (1949)
Bermuda Depths, The (1978)
Bermuda Triangle, The (1978)
Bernadette (1988)
Bernadette of Lourdes (1960)
Berrenger's (1985)
Berserk! (1967)
Berserker (1987)
Bert D'Angelo/Superstar (1976)
Bertoldo, Bertoldino and
    Cacasenno (1984)
Beryl Markham: A Shadow on the
    Sun (1988)
Best Defense (1984)
Best Father in the World, The
    (1941)
Best Friends (1982)
Best Kept Secrets (1984)
Best Legs in the Eighth Grade, The
    (1984)
Best Little Girl in the World, The
    (1981)
Best Little Whorehouse in Texas,
    The (1982)
Best Man, The (1986)
Best of the West, The (1981)
Best of Times, The (1983)
Best of Times, The (1986)
Best Place to Be, The (1979)
Best Seller (1987)

Best Times, The (1985)
Best Wishes (1988)
Bet, The (short) (1985)
Bethsabee (1951)
Beto Nervio Against the Powers
  of the Shadows (1981)
Betrayal (Taran Kova) (1939)
Betrayal (1974)
Betrayal (1978)
Betrayal (1983)
Betrayal, The (Petos) (1988)
Betrayed (1988)
Betrayed by Innocence (1986)
Better Days (1986)
Better Late Than Never (1979)
Better Late Than Never (1983)
Better Off Dead (1985)
Better Than Bread (1987)
Better Tomorrow, A (1986)
Better Tomorrow II, A (1987)
Betty Blue (1986)
Betty Ford Story, The (1987)
Betty Hutton Show, The (1959)
Betty White Show, The (1977)
Between Brothers (1982)
Between Friends (1983)
Between Midnight and Dawn
  (1950)
Between Parallel Mirrors (1981)
Between the Glass and the Lip
  (1968)
Between the Lines (1980)
Between the Nets (1967)
Between the Times (1985)
Between the Wars (1978)
Between Two Women (1986)
Beulah Land (1980)
Beverly Hillbillies, The (1962)
Beverly Hills Buntz (1987)
Beverly Hills Cop (1984)
Beverly Hills Cop II (1987)
Beverly Hills Madam (1986)
Beware the Brethren (1972)
Beware Spooks! (1939)
Bewitched (1964)
Bewitched (Stregati) (1987)
Bewitching Love of Madam Pai,
  The (1956)
Beyond Atlantis (Sea Creatures)
  (1973)
Beyond Death's Door (1979)
Beyond Evil (1980)
Beyond Love and Evil (1970)
Beyond Passion (1986)
Beyond Reason (Mati) (1977)
Beyond Reasonable Doubt (1980)
Beyond Silence (1987)

Beyond Sorrow, Beyond Pain (1984)
Beyond the Bermuda Triangle
  (1975)
Beyond the Darkness (Magdelena--
  Possessed by the Devil) (1974)
Beyond the Door (1982)
Beyond the Door II (Shock/
  Suspense) (1979)
Beyond the Forest (1949)
Beyond the Limit (1983)
Beyond the Reef (1981)
Beyond the Rising Moon (1988)
Beyond the River (1922)
Beyond the Time Barrier (1960)
Beyond the Walls (1984)
Beyond Therapy (1987)
Beyond Westworld (1980)
Beyond Witch Mountain (1983)
Bhombal Sardar (1985)
Bi and the Ba, The (1986)
Bianca (1984)
Bible ... in the Beginning, The
  (1966)
Bicycle, The (1982)
Bicycles Are for the Summer (1984)
Biddy (1983)
Big (1988)
Big Bad Mama II (1987)
Big Bang, The (1987)
Big Bang in Bender, The (1983)
Big Black Pill, The (1981)
Big Blonde (Iso Valee) (1983)
Big Blue, The (1988)
Big Bob Johnson and His Fantastic
  Speed Circus (1978)
Big Brawl, The (1980)
Big Brother, The (1982)
Big Business (1937)
Big Business (1988)
Big Carnival, The (1983)
Big Chamorro Circus, The (1955)
Big City Comedy (1980)
Big Daddy (1973)
Big Deal on Madonna Street--20
  Years Later (1986)
Big Easy, The (1982)
Big Easy, The (1986)
Big Eddie (1975)
Big Family, A (1955)
Big Game, The (1972)
Big Hawaii (1977)
Big Hurt, The (1986)
Big John (1983)
Big John, Little John (1976)
Big Joys, Small Sorrows (1986)
Big Meat Eater (1982)
Big Money, The (1958)

Big Money (1988)
Big Night Bathe, The (1981)
Big Parade, The (1987)
Big Pardon, The (Grand Pardon,
  Le) (1982)
Big People--Little People (short)
  (1968)
Big Picnic, The (1981)
Big Race, The (1987)
Big Red One, The (1980)
Big Ripoff, The (1975)
Big Road, The (1987)
Big Rose (1974)
Big Score, The (1983)
Big Shamus, Little Shamus (1979)
Big Shots (1985)
Big Shots (1987)
Big Show, The (1961)
Big Top Pee-Wee (1988)
Big Town (1950)
Big Town, The (1987)
Big Town Girl (1937)
Big Trouble (1986)
Big Trouble in Little China (1986)
Big Valley, The (1965)
Bigfoot (1972)
Bigfoot (1987)
Bigfoot--Man or Beast? (1975)
Bill (1981)
Bill, The (Addition, L') (1984)
Bill Cosby Show, The (1969)
Bill on His Own (1983)
Billboard (1987)
Billion Dollar Threat, The (1979)
Billionaire Boys Club (1987)
Billy (1979)
Billy: Portrait of a Street Kid
  (1977)
Billy Ze Kick (1985)
Biloxi Blues (1988)
Bimini Code (1985)
Bingo Bongo (1983)
Bingo, Bridesmaids and Braces
  (1988)
Biography (1962)
Biohazard (1983)
Bionic Woman, The (1976)
Biquefarre (1983)
Bird (1988)
Bird in the Hand Is Worth ..., A
  (1987)
Bird Watch, The (1983)
Birdman (1967)
Birdmen, The (1971)
Birds of Prey (1973)
Birds of Prey (1986)
Birds Will Fly (1985)

Birdy (1984)
Birgitt Haas Must Be Killed (1981)
Birthday, The (1980)
Birthday Present, The (1957)
Birthday Town (1987)
Biskitts, The (1983)
Bit of Immortality, A (1967)
Bit of Living, A (Croque la Vie)
  (1982)
Bit Part, The (1987)
Bite, The (1985)
Bitter Bread (1966)
Bitter Coffee (1986)
Bitter Harvest (1981)
Bitter Harvest (1985)
Bitter Truth, The (1986)
Bizarre (1979)
Black and Without Sugar (1986)
Black Angel (short) (1981)
Black Beauty (1978)
Black Box Affair, The (1966)
Black Caldron, The (1985)
Black Cat, The (1934)
Black Cat, The (1984)
Black Crows (1983)
Black Diamonds (1938)
Black Dragons (1941)
Black Ermine (1953)
Black Eye, A (1987)
Black Flag (1986)
Black Goddess (1983)
Black Gown for a Killer, A (1981)
Black Hand, The (1980)
Black Hanky Panky (1986)
Black Hen, The (1982)
Black Hills (1985)
Black List (1984)
Black Lizard (1969)
Black Magic II (1977)
Black Marble, The (1980)
Black Market Baby (1977)
Black Mirror (1981)
Black Monk, The (1988)
Black Moon Rising (1986)
Black Noon (1971)
Black One, The (1966)
Black Orchestra, The (1985)
Black Pearls (1958)
Black Pirate, The (1939)
Black Rider (1983)
Black Room, The (1981)
Black Saddle (1959)
Black Scorpion, The (1957)
Black Shadows (1949)
Black Sheep (1935)
Black Sheep, The (1987)
Black Sheep Squadron, The (1977)

Black Side of Blackie, The (1987)
Black Spider, The (1983)
Black Stallion Returns, The (1983)
Black Swans (1987)
Black Tanner (1986)
Black Tiger, The (1983)
Black Torment, The (1964)
Black Vampire, The (1981)
Black Venus (1983)
Black Water Gold (1970)
Black Widow (1954)
Black Widow (1987)
Blackbird (1988)
Blacke's Magic (1986)
Blackmailed (1951)
Blackout (1985)
Blackout (1986)
Blackout (1988)
Blacksnake (Slaves/Sweet Suzy)
   (1973)
Blackstar (1981)
Blade in the Body, The (1966)
Blade in the Dark, A (1983)
Blade Master, The (Ator the
   Invincible) (1982)
Blade Runner (1982)
Blake's Seven (1980)
Blame It on Paradise (1986)
Blame It on Rio (1984)
Blame It on the Night (1984)
Blancheville Monster, The (1963)
Blansky's Beauties (1977)
Blastfighter (1983)
Blazing Sand (1960)
Blazing Sun, The (Deng-Byod)
   (1985)
Bleak House (1985)
Bless This House (1977)
Blessed Rose, The (1937)
Blind Alley (Mienai) (1985)
Blind Ambition (1979)
Blind Chance (Przypadek) (1987)
Blind Date (1984)
Blind Date (1987)
Blind Endeavor (1986)
Blind Justice (1986)
Blind Spot (1981)
Blind Woman's Curse, The (1970)
Blinded by the Light (1980)
Blindside (1987)
Blinker's Spy Spotter (1971)
Bliss (1984)
Bliss (1985)
Bliss on Earth (1957)
Blob, The (1988)
Blonde at the Bar, The (1987)
Blonde Bait (1956)

Blondie (1957)
Blondie (1968)
Blondie Hits the Jackpot (1949)
Blood (1974)
Blood (Kan) (1986)
Blood and Honor: Young Under
   Hitler (1982)
Blood and Orchids (1986)
Blood Bath (Gore-Gore Girls, The)
   (1971)
Blood Beach (1981)
Blood Beast from Outer Space
   (Night Caller) (1965)
Blood Brothers (1983)
Blood Demon, The (1967)
Blood Diner (1987)
Blood Feast (1963)
Blood Feud (1983)
Blood Hook (1987)
Blood Is Always Hot (1984)
Blood of Brothers (Aghaat) (1986)
Blood of Others, The (1984)
Blood of the Flamboyant Tree (1981)
Blood of the Statues, The (1982)
Blood of the Vampires (Dugo No
   Vampires) (1970)
Blood Orgy of the She Devils
   (1973)
Blood Relations (1977)
Blood Rose (1971)
Blood Simple (1984)
Blood Sisters (Slash) (1987)
Blood-Spattered Bride, The (1974)
Blood Sport (1973)
Blood Sport (1986)
Blood Tide (Red Tide, The) (1980)
Blood Ties (1986)
Blood Tracks (1986)
Blood Vendetta (1971)
Blood Waters of Dr. Z, The (1972)
Blood Wedding (1981)
Bloodeaters (1980)
Bloodline--A Modern Tale (1981)
Bloodspell (1988)
Bloodsport (1988)
Bloodsucking Freaks (Incredible
   Torture Show, The) (1976)
Bloodthirsty Fairy, The (short)
   (1968)
Bloody Birthday (1986)
Bloody Brood, The (1959)
Bloody Lady (1981)
Bloody New Year (1987)
Bloody Pit of Horror (1965)
Bloody Weed (1987)
Blow Out (1981)
Blows (Ciosy) (1981)

Blue and the Gray, The (1982)
Blue Bird, The (1976)
Blue City (1986)
Blue City Slammers (1988)
Blue DeVille (1986)
Blue Heaven (1985)
Blue Iguana, The (1988)
Blue Jeans (1980)
Blue Jeans Memory (1982)
Blue Knight, The (1973)
Blue Knight, The (1975)
Blue Lagoon (1980)
Blue Lamp, The (1950)
Blue Light, The (1966)
Blue Like Hell (1986)
Blue Mammy, The (1986)
Blue Money (1985)
Blue Monkey (1987)
Blue Mountains, The (1985)
Blue Movies (1988)
Blue Paradise (Adam and Eve)
   (1982)
Blue Pyramids, The (Paradise
   Calling) (1988)
Blue Scar (1988)
Blue Skies (1988)
Blue Skies Again (1983)
Blue Sunshine (1977)
Blue Thunder (1983)
Blue Thunder (1984)
Blue Velvet (1986)
Blue Window (1987)
Bluebeard (1984)
Blueberry Hill (1988)
Bluecher (1988)
Bluegrass (1988)
Blues for Lovers (1966)
Bluffing It (1987)
Boat, The (Boot Ist Voll, Das/
   Full House) (1981)
Boat People (1982)
Boat Without a Fisherman, The
   (1964)
Boatman, The (1984)
Bob & Carol & Ted & Alice (1973)
Bob Crane Show, The (1975)
Bob Newhart Show, The (1972)
Bobby Jo and the Big Apple
   Goodtime Band (1972)
Bobby Parker and Company
   (1974)
Boccaccio (Love Tales of
   Boccaccio) (1936)
Bodily Restraint (1988)
Body Beat (Dance Academy) (1988)
Body Count (1988)
Body Double (1984)

Body Heat (1981)
Body Is Willing, The (1983)
Body of Evidence (1988)
Body Slam (1987)
Bodywatching (1988)
Bog (1978)
Bogart (1967)
Boggy Creek II (1985)
Bogie (1980)
Bokuchan's Battlefield (1986)
Boldyn (1981)
Bolero (1983)
Bolero (1984)
Bolivar, Tropical Symphony (1982)
Bom, the Soldier (1949)
Bomb Mania (1959)
Bomb Was Stolen, A (1962)
Bombs Away (1985)
Bon Plaisir, Le (1984)
Bon Soir, Paris, Bonjour L'Amour
   (1957)
Bon Voyage, Charlie Brown (And
   Don't Come Back) (1980)
Bona (1981)
Bonanza (1959)
Bonanza: The Next Generation
   (1988)
Bonchi (1981)
Bondage (Kotolek) (1968)
Bonded Until Death (Damul) (1985)
Bonjour Monsieur Lewis (1982)
Bonjour Paris (1953)
Boodle, The (Pactole, Le) (1985)
Boogens, The (1982)
Boogeyman (1980)
Boogeyman II (1983)
Book of Days (1988)
Boomerang (1960)
Boone (1983)
Boost, The (1988)
Boran--Time to Aim (1987)
Bordello (1985)
Border, The (1981)
Border, The (1982)
Border (1987)
Border Pals (1981)
Border Town (1963)
Borderline (1980)
Borderline (1988)
Borgia Stick, The (1967)
Boris Godunov (1986)
Born Again (1984)
Born Again: Life in a Fundamental-
   ist Baptist Church (1987)
Born American (1986)
Born Beautiful (1982)
Born for Diesel (1982)

Born Free (1974)
Born in East L.A. (1987)
Born Innocent (1974)
Born of Fire (1987)
Born Reckless (1937)
Born to Be Sold (1981)
Born to Race (1988)
Borrowed Chateau (1937)
Borrowers, The (1973)
Borrowing Trouble (1937)
Bosom Buddies (1980)
Boss' Wife, The (1986)
Boss with the Samurai Spirit, A
    (1971)
Boston Blackie (1951)
Boston Strangler, The (1968)
Boston Terrier, The (1962)
Bostonians, The (1984)
Bottoms Up (1960)
Bouba (1987)
Boulevard of Broken Dreams
    (1988)
Boundaries of the Heart (1988)
Boundary Fire (1936)
Bounder, The (1984)
Bountiful Summer (1952)
Bounty, The (1984)
Bounty Killer, The (1966)
Bounty Man, The (1972)
Bourbon Street Beat (1959)
Bourgeois Gentilhomme, Le
    (Would-Be Gentleman, The)
    (1982)
Bourne Identity, The (1988)
Bowzer (1981)
Box of Sun, The (1988)
Boxer from the Temple, The
    (1980)
Boxoffice (1982)
Boy (1940)
Boy and a Girl, A (1984)
Boy and the Bridge, The (1959)
Boy Detectives, The (1956)
Boy from Ebalus, The (1984)
Boy from Rio, The (1982)
Boy in Blue, The (1986)
Boy in the Plastic Bubble, The
    (1976)
Boy Like Many Others, A (1983)
Boy Soldier, The (1981)
Boy Soldier (1986)
Boy Who Could Fly, The (1986)
Boy Who Disappeared, The (1984)
Boy Who Drank Too Much, The
    (1980)
Boy Who Had Everything, The
    (1985)

Boy With the Big Black Dog, The
    (1987)
Boy With Two Heads, The (1974)
Boys from the Streets (1950)
Boys in Blue, The (1984)
Boys of Paul Street, The (1969)
Bracken's World (1969)
Braddock: Missing in Action III
    (1988)
Brady Brides, The (1981)
Brady Bunch, The (1969)
Brady Girls Get Married, The (1981)
Brady Kids, The (1972)
Brady's Escape (1984)
Braggarts, The (1960)
Brain, The (Vengeance) (1962)
Brain, The (1969)
Brain, The (1988)
Brain Burning (Hirnbrennen) (1982)
Brain Damage (1988)
Brain Eaters, The (1958)
Brain from Planet Arous, The (1958)
Brain Leeches, The (1978)
Brainiac, The (Baron of Terror) (1960)
Brainstorm (1983)
Brain Waves (1982)
Branagan and Mapes (1983)
Brand Marks (1982)
Brand New Day (1987)
Brand New Life, A (1973)
Branded (1965)
Brass Bottle, The (1964)
Brave Little Toaster, The (1987)
Brave New World (1980)
Brave Seaman (1936)
Bravestarr (1988)
Bravos, The (1972)
Brazil (1985)
Brazil Year 2000 (1970)
Bread, Love and Fantasy (1954)
Bread, Love and Jealousy (1955)
Bread of Love, The (1954)
Break Away (Przed Odlotem) (1980)
Break-In (Effraction) (1983)
Break of Dawn (1988)
Breakdown (1981)
Breaker Morant (1980)
Breakfast Club, The (1985)
Breakfast in Paris (1982)
Breakfast with Les & Bess (1985)
Breakin' (1984)
Breakin' 2 Electric Boogaloo (1984)
Breaking (Shovrim) (1985)
Breaking All the Rules (1985)
Breaking Away (1980)
Breaking Loose (1988)
Breaking Point (1963)

Breaking Silence (1985)
Breaking the Silence: The
    Generation After the Holocaust
    (1984)
Breaking Up (1978)
Breaking Up Is Hard to Do (1979)
Breakout (1970)
Breakout (1984)
Breath of Air, A (DIH) (1983)
Breathless (Ademloos) (1982)
Breathless (1983)
Breed Apart, A (1984)
Breeders (1986)
Brenda Starr (1976)
Brenda Starr, Reporter (1979)
Brett Maverick (1981)
Brewster's Millions (1985)
Brian's Song (1971)
Bricklayers Day, Part II (1986)
Bride, The (1985)
Bride for a Night (1952)
Bride from Hades, The (1968)
Bride of Boogedy (1987)
Bride of Frankenstein, The
    (1935)
Bride of Tarocke (1937)
Bride of the Monster (1955)
Bride on the Train, The (1981)
Bride Was Radiant, The (1987)
Brides of Fu Manchu (1966)
Brideshead Revisited (1981)
Bridge Across Time (1985)
Bridge to Nowhere (1986)
Bridger (1976)
Bridges to Cross (1986)
Bridget Loves Bernie (1972)
Brief Encounter (1974)
Brief Encounters (1967)
Brief Rapture (1952)
Bright Lights, Big City (1988)
Brightness (Yeelen) (1987)
Brighton Beach Memoirs (1986)
Brighton Strangler, The (1945)
Brilliant Benjamin Boggs (1966)
Brimstone and Treacle (1982)
Bring 'em Back Alive (1982)
Bring Me the Head of Dobie
    Gillis (1988)
Bringing Up Buddy (1960)
Brink's: The Great Robbery
    (1976)
Britannia Hospital (1982)
Broadcast News (1987)
Broadside (1964)
Broadway (1955)
Broadway Boys (1984)
Broadway Danny Rose (1984)

Brock's Last Case (1973)
Broken Angel (1988)
Broken April (1987)
Broken Arrow (1956)
Broken Arrow 29 (1986)
Broken English (1981)
Broken-Hearted Love Story, A
    (1983)
Broken Hearts and Noses (see
    Crimewave)
Broken Images (1986)
Broken Melody (1938)
Broken Mirrors (1984)
Broken Promise (1980)
Broken Rainbow (1985)
Broken Shoes (1934)
Broken Sky (1982)
Broken Victory (1988)
Broken Vows (1987)
Bronco (1958)
Bronco, El (1986)
Bronco Billy (1980)
Bronk (1975)
Bronx Zoo, The (1987)
Brood, The (1979)
Brookhaven Spectrum (short)
    (1967)
Brother from Another Planet, The
    (1984)
Brotherhood of the Bell, The
    (1970)
Brotherly Love (1985)
Brothers, The (1956)
Brothers (1980)
Brothers (1982)
Brothers (1984)
Brothers (Fratelli) (1985)
Brothers and Sisters (1979)
Brothers and Sisters (1980)
Brothers-in-Law (1957)
Brownout (1969)
Brubaker (1980)
Bruja, La (Witch, The) (1955)
Brussels by Night (1983)
Brutality (Flight into the Reeds)
    (1953)
Brute, The (1987)
Bubble, The (1966)
Bubble, The (1976)
Buccaneers, The (1956)
Buck Rogers in the 25th Century
    (1979)
Buckeye and Blue (1988)
Buckskin (1958)
Bud and Lou (1978)
Budapest Candy Store (1936)
Buddha's Lock (1987)

Buddies (1983)
Buddies (1985)
Buddy Buddy (1981)
Buddy System, The (1984)
Buffalo Bill (1983)
Buffalo Bill, Jr. (1955)
Buffalo Soldiers, The (1979)
Buford and the Ghost (1971)
Bugaloos, The (1970)
Bugs Bunny's Third Movie: 1001
    Rabbit Tales (1982)
Build a House, Plant a Tree
    (1980)
Bulba (1981)
Bull Durham (1988)
Bulldog Breed, The (1960)
Bulldogs and Cherries (1984)
Bullet for Stefano, A (1950)
Bullet Train Blast (1975)
Bulletproof (1988)
Bullies (1986)
Bullseye (1987)
Bullshot (1983)
Bullwinkle Show, The (1964)
Bum Rap (1988)
Bumpers (1977)
Bums, The (Strawanzer) (1984)
Bunco (1977)
Bunker, The (1981)
Bureau, The (1976)
Burg Theater (1936)
Burglar (1987)
Buried Alive (1980)
Burke and Hare (1971)
Burke & Wills (1985)
Burke's Law (1963)
Burlesque (1955)
Burmese Harp, The (1985)
Burn 'Em Up Barnes (1934)
Burnin' Love (1987)
Burning, The (1981)
Burning an Illusion (1982)
Burning Angel (1984)
Burning Beds (1988)
Burning Bush (1987)
Burning Court, The (1961)
Burning Flowers (1985)
Burning Land (1984)
Burning Love (1983)
Burning of a Thousand Suns,
    The (1965)
Burning of the Imperial Palace,
    The (1983)
Burning Secret (1988)
Burst of Lead (1986)
Bus (1987)
Bus Driver, The (1982)

Bus Stop (1961)
Bush Christmas (1983)
Bush Doctor (1982)
Bushfire Moon (1987)
Bushido Blade, The (1978)
Business as Usual (1987)
Business Is Booming (1985)
Busted Up (1986)
Buster (1988)
Buster Keaton: A Hard Act to
    Follow (1987)
Busters, The (1978)
Buster's World (1984)
Bustin' Loose (1981)
Busting Loose (1977)
Bu-Su (1988)
But I Don't Want to Get Married!
    (1970)
But Mother! (1979)
Butch Cassidy and the Sundance
    Kids (1973)
Butterflies (1982)
Butterflies and Flowers (1986)
Butterfly (1981)
Buy and Cell (1988)
Buying Time (1988)
By Design (1981)
By the Sword Divided (1988)
Bye Bye Brazil (1980)

C.A.T. Squad (1986)
C.A.T. Squad: Python Wolf (1988)
C.B. Bears, The (1977)
C.H.U.D. (1984)
C.O.D. (Snap) (1981)
C.P.O. Sharkey (1976)
Cabaret Mineiro (1980)
Cabaret Tears (Send in the Clowns)
    (1983)
Cabbie, The (1983)
Cable Car Murder, The (1971)
Caboblanco (1981)
Cabot Connection, The (1977)
Cache, The (Battant, Le) (1983)
Caddyshack (1980)
Caddyshack II (1988)
Cade's County (1971)
Cadet-Rousselle (1954)
Cafe de Paris (1938)
Cafe Express (1980)
Cafe Moscow (1936)
Cafe Odeon (1959)
Caffe Italia (1985)
Caftan of Love (1988)
Cage, The (1985)
Cage aux Folles II, La (1980)

Cage aux Folles III, La (1985)
Cage Without a Key (1975)
Caged Fury (1984)
Caged Women (1984)
Cain (1987)
Cain and Abel (1982)
Cain's Hundred (1961)
Cal (1984)
Calacan (1986)
Calamari Union (1985)
Calamity Jane (1984)
Caldi Amori di una Minorenne, I
   (1969)
Caldron of Blood (1967)
Calendar Girl Murders, The
   (1984)
California Fever (1979)
California Girls (1981)
California Gold Rush (1981)
California Kid, The (1974)
California Summer (1985)
Caliph Stork (short) (1954)
Call Holme (1972)
Call Me (1988)
Call Me Genius (Rebel, The)
   (1961)
Call Me Mister (1987)
Call of the Wild, The (1976)
Call to Danger (1973)
Call to Glory (Air Force) (1984)
Callahan (1982)
Caller, The (1987)
Callie & Son (1981)
Calling Paul Temple (1948)
Calling the Shots (1988)
Calm Night (Nuit Docile) (1987)
Calmos (Femmes Fatales) (1977)
Caltiki, the Immortal Monster
   (1959)
Calucci's Department (1973)
Calypso (1959)
Camarena Taken Hostage (1986)
Came a Hot Friday (1985)
Camel Boy, The (1984)
Camels, The (1988)
Camila (1984)
Camille (1984)
Camille Claudel (1988)
Camminacammina (1983)
Camomille (1988)
Camorra (1986)
Camp Grizzly (1980)
Camp Runamuck (1965)
Camp Thiaroye (1988)
Camp Wilderness (1980)
Campaign (1988)
Campo Europa (1984)

Campus Man (1987)
Can Ellen Be Saved? (1974)
Can She Bake a Cherry Pie (1983)
Can You Feel Me Dancing? (1986)
Can You Hear the Laughter?: The
   Story of Freddie Prinze (1979)
Canadians, The (1961)
Canaguaro (1981)
Canaris (1955)
Canary Cage, The (1985)
Can-Cannes (1980)
Candidates for Marriage (1958)
Cannery Row (1982)
Cannibal Holocaust (1979)
Cannibals in the Streets (1980)
Cannon (1971)
Cannonball Run II (1984)
Cannot Run Away (1988)
Canon (short) (1964)
Can't Buy Me Love (1987)
Canterville Ghost, The (1974)
Canterville Ghost, The (1986)
Cap Canaille (1983)
Capablanca (1986)
Cape Canaveral Monster, The (1960)
Capitol (1982)
Capriccio (Letters from Capri)
   (1987)
Captain America (1979)
Captain America II (1979)
Captain and His Hero, The (1955)
Captain Caveman and the Teen
   Angels (1980)
Captain Gallant of the Foreign
   Legion (1955)
Captain Grant's Children (1939)
Captain James Cook (1987)
Captain Kangaroo (1955)
Captain Khorshid (1988)
Captain Leshi (1960)
Captain Midnight (1954)
Captain Nemo and the Underwater
   City (1969)
Captain Nice (1967)
Captain Scarlet and the Mysterons
   (1967)
Captain Sinbad (1963)
Captains and the Kings (1976)
Captains Courageous (1977)
Captain's Honor, A (1982)
Captive (1986)
Captive Hearts (1987)
Captive of the Dragon (1985)
Captive Rage (1988)
Capture of Grizzly Adams, The
   (1982)
Capture That Capsule! (1961)

Car 54, Where Are You? (1961)
Car Wash (1979)
Cara Williams Show, The (1964)
Caravaggio (1986)
Caravan Palace (1986)
Caravan to Russia (1959)
Carbon Copy (1981)
Care Bears Movie, The (1985)
Care Bears Movie II: A New
    Generation (1986)
Career Woman (1936)
Carefree Giovanni (1986)
Careful, He Might Hear You (1983)
Caribe (1975)
Caribe (1988)
Carl Gustav, the Gang and the
    Parking Lot Bandits (1982)
Carlton, Your Doorman (1980)
Carly's Web (1987)
Carmela (1949)
Carmen (1983)
Carmen of Granada (1959)
Carnage (Antefatto) (1971)
Carnation Killer, The (1973)
Carne: The Man Behind the
    Camera (1985)
Carnet de Bal, Un (1937)
Carnival (1985)
Carnival (Fasnacht) (1985)
Carnival Night (1957)
Carnival of Souls (1962)
Carnival Story (1954)
Carny (1980)
Carol (1967)
Carol for Another Christmas, A
    (1964)
Caro's Escape--Kill the Fugitive
    (1987)
Carpenter, The (1988)
Carpet Change (Knock on the
    Wrong Door) (1984)
Carpetbaggers, The (1964)
Carpool (1983)
Carrasco's Escape (1987)
Carrefour (1938)
Carrousel Boreal (1959)
Carry Me Back (1982)
Carry On, Constable (1960)
Carry On Laughing (1980)
Carry On Regardless (1961)
Carry On, Teacher (1959)
Carter Country (1977)
Carter's Army (1970)
Cary Grant: A Celebration (1988)
Casablanca (1983)
Casanova (1981)
Casanova (1987)

Case Against Paul Ryker, The
    (1963)
Case Is Closed, The (Kharij) (1983)
Case of Irresponsibility, A (1984)
Case of Poisons, The (1955)
Case of Rape, A (1974)
Case of the Murdered Madam, The
    (1987)
Case of the Scandalous Scoundrel,
    The (1987)
Case of the Shooting Star, The
    (1986)
Case of the Two Beauties, The
    (1968)
Casino (1980)
Casino de Paris (1957)
Caspar David Friedrich (1987)
Casper and the Angels (1979)
Cass Malloy (1982)
Cassandra (1987)
Cassette Love (1981)
Cassie and Company (1982)
Castaway (1986)
Castaways on Gilligan's Island, The
    (1979)
Castillo de las Bofetadas, El (1945)
Castle, The (Linna) (1986)
Castle for a Young Hangman, A
    (1970)
Castle in Flanders (1936)
Castle Is Swinging, The (1959)
Castle of Fu Manchu, The (Assign-
    ment Istanbul) (1968)
Castle of Lust (1968)
Castle of Sand, The (1975)
Castle of Terror (Danse Macabre)
    (1964)
Castle of the Living Dead, The
    (1964)
Castle of the Monsters (1957)
Castle Orgies (1972)
Castle Rock (1981)
Castle Vogeloed (1936)
Castles in the Air (1952)
Casual Sex? (1988)
Cat, The (1961)
Cat, The (1988)
Cat City (Macskafogo) (1987)
Cat Creature, The (1973)
Cat from Outer Space, The (1978)
Cat on a Hot Tin Roof (1976)
Cat on a Hot Tin Roof (1984)
Cat People (1982)
Cat Women of the Moon (1953)
Catacombs (1988)
Catalan Cuckold (Salut I Forca al
    Canut) (1980)

Charlie Bravo (1980)
Charlie Brown and Snoopy Show,
    The (1983)
Charlie Chan and the Curse of the
    Dragon Queen (1981)
Charlie Chan at Monte Carlo (1937)
Charlie Chan at the Circus (1936)
Charlie Chan at the Olympics (1937)
Charlie Chan at the Opera (1936)
Charlie Chan at the Race Track
    (1936)
Charlie Chan at Treasure Island
    (1939)
Charlie Chan in Shanghai (1935)
Charlie Chan on Broadway (1937)
Charlie Chan's Secret (1935)
Charlie Cobb: Nice Night for a
    Hanging (1977)
Charlie Dingo (1987)
Charlie Wooster--Outlaw (1963)
Charlie's Angels (1976)
Charlotte (1975)
Charlotte (1981)
Charmer, The (Joli Coeur, Le)
    (1984)
Charming Boys (1958)
Charmings, The (1987)
Charmurti (1978)
Charter Trip, The (1980)
Chase (1973)
Chase (1985)
Chase That Man (1972)
Chasing Rainbows (1988)
Cheap Detective, The (1980)
Cheap Shots (1988)
Cheaper to Keep Her (1980)
Cheaters, The (Tricheurs, Les)
    (1984)
Chechechela--A Girl of the Barrio
    (1987)
Check Is in the Mail, The (1986)
Checker Player, The (1939)
Checkers (1937)
Checking In (1981)
Checkmate (1960)
Cheech and Chong's Next Movie
    (1980)
Cheech & Chong's Nice Dreams
    (1981)
Cheech & Chong's The Corsican
    Brothers (1984)
Cheerleader Camp (1988)
Cheerleaders, The (1976)
Cheers (1982)
Chekhov in My Life (1985)
Cheri-Bibi (1938)
Cherokee Trail, The (1981)

Cherry Blossoms in the Air--The
    Suicide Raiders--Oh, Buddies!
    (1970)
Cherry 2000 (1988)
Chess King (1988)
Chevalier de la Nuit (1954)
Chewingum (1984)
Cheyenne (1956)
Chicago Story (1981)
Chicago Story (1982)
Chicago Teddy Bears, The (1971)
Chicano Connection, The (1986)
Chicherin (1986)
Chick for Cairo, A (1985)
Chicks, The (Nanas, Les) (1985)
Chico and the Man (1974)
Chidambaram (1986)
Chief Zabu (1988)
Chiefs (1983)
Chieftain, The (1984)
Child, The (Kill and Go Hide)
    (1977)
Child Bride of Short Creek (1981)
Child God, The (1986)
Child in the House (1956)
Child of Divorce (1980)
Child of Glass (1978)
Child Saver, The (1988)
Child Stealer, The (1979)
Child Woman, The (1980)
Childhood Garden, A (1984)
Childhood of Art (1988)
Childhood of Maxim Gorky, The
    (1938)
Children, The (1980)
Children, The (1985)
Children from Blue Lake Mountain,
    The (1980)
Children from No. 67, The (1980)
Children in the Crossfire (1984)
Children, Mother and a General
    (1955)
Children Must Laugh (1938)
Children Nobody Wanted, The
    (1981)
Children of a Lesser God (1986)
Children of An Lac, The (1980)
Children of Babylon (1980)
Children of Bullerby Village, The
    (1986)
Children of Chance (1950)
Children of Chronos (1985)
Children of Divorce (1980)
Children of Fortune (1936)
Children of God's Earth (1983)
Children of Love, The (1953)
Children of Pride (1984)

Children of the Cold War (1986)
Children of the Corn (1984)
Children of the Night (1985)
Children of the Snow Country
  (1975)
Children of the Steps (1984)
Children of the Swallow, The
  (1987)
Children of the War, The (1985)
Children of the Wind (1980)
Children of Times Square (1986)
Children Shouldn't Play With
  Dead Things (1972)
Children's Dream (short) (1960)
Children's Island (1981)
Child's Cry (1986)
Child's Play (1957)
Child's Play (1988)
Childstealers (1987)
Chile, I Do Not Call Your Name
  in Vain (1984)
Chiller (1985)
Chilly Nights (Han Ye) (1985)
Chiltern Hundreds, The (see
  Amazing Mr. Beecham--1949)
Chimimoryo (1972)
China Beach (1988)
China Girl (1987)
China Ranch (1988)
China Rose (1983)
China Run (1987)
China: The Roots of Madness
  (1967)
China Venture (1953)
Chinese and Mini-Skirts, The
  (1968)
Chinese Are Coming, The (1987)
Chinese Boxes (1984)
Chinese Ghost Story, A (1987)
Chinese Web, The (1978)
Chinese White (1988)
Chip on the Shoulder (1960)
Chipmunk Reunion, A (1985)
Chips Are Down, The (1947)
Chisholms, The (1979)
Chisholms, The (1980)
Chocolate (1988)
Choice, The (Yam Daabo) (1987)
Choice of a People, The (1985)
Choice of Weapons (1981)
Choices (1986)
Choices of the Heart (1983)
Choke Canyon (1986)
Choose Me (1984)
Chopped Liver Brothers, The
  (1977)

Chopper (1986)
Chopper One (1974)
Chopping Mall (Kilbots) (1986)
Chosen, The (1981)
Chousans! (1988)
Christ in Bronze (1959)
Christ Is Born (1967)
Christ of the Ocean (1971)
Christina (1984)
Christine (1983)
Christmas Carol, A (1982)
Christmas Carol, A (1984)
Christmas Comes to Willow Creek
  (1987)
Christmas Eve (1982)
Christmas for Boomer, A (1979)
Christmas Lilies of the Field (1979)
Christmas Memory, A (1966)
Christmas Miracle in Caufield, U.S.A.
  (1977)
Christmas Present (1985)
Christmas Present (1986)
Christmas Snow (1986)
Christmas Star, The (1986)
Christmas Story, A (1983)
Christmas That Almost Wasn't, The
  (1965)
Christmas to Remember, A (1978)
Christmas Vacation (1984)
Christmas Visitor, The (1987)
Christmas Wife, The (1988)
Christmas Without Snow, A (1979)
Christopher Columbus (1985)
Christopher Crumpet (short) (1953)
Christopher Crumpet's Playmate
  (short) (1955)
Chromophobia (short) (1965)
Chronic Innocence (1985)
Chronicle of a Death Foretold (1987)
Chronopolis (1982)
Chu Chu and the Philly Flash (1981)
Churchill and the Generals (1979)
Ciao Nemico (Bridge Between, The)
  (1982)
Ciascuno il Suo, A (1966)
Ciboulette (1933)
Cimarron Strip (1967)
Cinderella (1937)
Cinderella '80 (1984)
Cinderella 2000 (1977)
Cindy (1978)
Circle of Children, A (1977)
Circle of Danger (1951)
Circle of Fear (1973)
Circle of Iron (1979)
Circle of Passions (1983)
Circle of Two (1980)

Circle of Violence: A Family Drama
   (1986)
Circumstantial Evidence (1939)
Circus (short) (1954)
Circus (1987)
Circus Casablanca (1981)
Circus Maximus (1981)
Cisco, El (1966)
Cisco Kid, The (1950)
Ciske the Rat (1984)
Citadel, The (1983)
Citadel, The (1988)
Citadel of Silence (1937)
Citizen: The Political Life of
   Allard K. Lowenstein (1983)
City, The (1971)
City, The (1977)
City, The (1986)
City and the Dogs, The (1985)
City at Night (1957)
City Beneath the Sea, The
   (1971)
City Birds (1981)
City Girl (1937)
City Girl, The (1984)
City Heat (1984)
City Hero (1985)
City in Fear (1980)
City Limits (1985)
City Never Sleeps, The (1984)
City of Angels (1976)
City of Beasts (1970)
City of Pirates (1985)
City of the Walking Dead (Night-
   mare City) (1980)
City of Torment (1950)
City of Women (1980)
City of Youth (1938)
City on Fire (1987)
City Park (1951)
City Rats (1987)
City That Never Sleeps, The
   (1953)
City: Time of Decision, The
   (short) (1968)
Claire and Darkness (1982)
Clan of the Cave Bear, The
   (1986)
Clan of the White Lotus (1980)
Clan: Tale of the Frogs, The
   (1985)
Clandestine Destinies (1988)
Clara and the Swell Guys (1981)
Clara's Heart (1988)
Clarence and Angel (1980)
Claretta (1984)
Claretta and Ben (1974)

Clash by Night (1952)
Clash of the Titans (1981)
Class (1983)
Class Murmurs (1982)
Class of 1984 (1982)
Class of Nuke 'Em High (1986)
Class of '63 (1973)
Class Whispers (see Class Murmurs)
Classified Love (1986)
Classroom No. 205 (1975)
Claws (1977)
Clean and Sober (1988)
Clean Loving Never Stays That
   Way for Long (1985)
Clean Machine, The (1988)
Clear and Present Danger, A (1970)
Clerk and the Coat, The (1955)
Cliff Dwellers, The (1966)
Cliffhangers (1979)
Cliffwood Avenue Kids, The (1977)
Climb, The (1987)
Climb an Angry Mountain (1972)
Clinic on 18th Street (1974)
Clinton and Nadine (Blood Money)
   (1988)
Cloak and Dagger (1984)
Clockwise (1986)
Clone Master, The (1978)
Clones, The (1972)
Close Behind the Door (1984)
Close Ties (1983)
Close to Home (1986)
Closed Case (1985)
Closed Mondays (short) (1974)
Closing Ranks (1987)
Closing Time (1988)
Cloth Doll (1988)
Cloud Dancer (1980)
Cloud Dancing (1987)
Cloudburst (1952)
Clowns, The (1985)
Clowns of God, The (1986)
Clowns on the Wall (1968)
Club, The (1980)
Club Med (1986)
Club Paradise (1986)
Clue (1985)
Clue Club, The (1976)
Clue: Movies, Murder and Mystery
   (1986)
Coach! (1987)
Coach of the Year (1980)
Coal Miner's Daughter (1980)
Coast of Love, The (1982)
Coast to Coast (1980)
Cobalt Blue (1985)
Cobra (1975)

Cobra (1986)
Cobra Girl (1962)
Coca-Cola Kid, The (1985)
Cocaine and Blue Eyes (1983)
Cocaine: One Man's Seduction
  (1983)
Cocked Gun (1987)
Cocktail (1988)
Cocktail Molotov (1980)
Cocktales (1978)
Cocoanut (1939)
Cocoon (1985)
Cocoon: The Return (1988)
Coda (1987)
Code Name: Diamond Head (1977)
Code Name: Emerald (1985)
Code Name: Foxfire (1985)
Code Name: Heraclitus (1967)
Code Name: Hercules (1976)
Code Name: The Russian (1988)
Code Name: Zebra (1987)
Code of Silence (1985)
Code of Vengeance (1985)
Code R (1977)
Code Red (1981)
Codename: Kyril (1988)
Codename: Wildgeese (1986)
Co-Ed Fever (1979)
Co-Fathers, The (1983)
Coffee, Tea or Me? (1973)
Coffin Affair, The (1980)
Cohen and Tate (1988)
Cold Feet (1983)
Cold Heart (Heart of Stone) (1950)
Cold in Colombia (1985)
Cold March (1988)
Cold Night's Death, A (1973)
Cold River (1982)
Cold Room, The (1984)
Cold Steel (1987)
Coldest Winter in Peking, The
  (1981)
Collapse (1987)
Collar and the Bracelet, The
  (1987)
College Girl, The (1938)
College Girls (Girls Who Study)
  (1939)
Colonel Bogey (1947)
Colonel March of Scotland Yard
  (1957)
Color Him Dead (1974)
Color of Destiny, The (1987)
Color of Money, The (1986)
Color of the Wind, The (1988)
Color Purple, The (1985)
Colorado C.I. (1978)

Colors (1988)
Colossal (1971)
Colossus (1963)
Colossus and the Headhunters
  (1962)
Colossus of New York, The (1958)
Colt .45 (1957)
Columbo (1971)
Comando de Asesinos (1966)
Combat (1962)
Combat High (1986)
Combat Shock (1986)
Come Along to Monte Carlo (1982)
Come Back (Volver) (1982)
Come Back, Little Sheba (1977)
Come Back Swallow (1981)
Come Dire (1983)
Come In, Jupiter (short) (1955)
Come Out, Come Out, Wherever You
  Are (1974)
Come to My Place, I'm Living at My
  Girlfriend's (1981)
Comeback, The (Day the Screaming
  Stopped, The) (1977)
Comeback (1982)
Comeback (1983)
Comeback Kid, The (1980)
Comeback Trail, The (1970)
Comedy! (1987)
Comedy Company, The (1978)
Comedy of Horrors (1981)
Comedy Shop, The (1978)
Comfort and Joy (1984)
Comic Magazine (1986)
Coming of Age (1988)
Coming Out of the Ice (1982)
Coming to America (1988)
Coming Up Roses (1986)
Commanding Sea, The (1981)
Commando (1985)
Commissar (1967)
Committed (1984)
Communications Primer, A (short)
  (1956)
Communist, The (1957)
Companions in Nightmare (1968)
Company of Wolves, The (1984)
Competition (1968)
Compromise, The (1988)
Compromising Positions (1985)
Computer Free-for-All (1969)
Computer Glossary, A (short) (1967)
Computerside (1982)
Comrade President Center-Forward
  (1960)
Comrades (1986)
Conan the Barbarian (1982)

Conan the Destroyer (1984)
Conceived Desires (1982)
Concentration Camp (1939)
Concert at the End of Summer
  (1980)
Concert in Tyrol (1938)
Concerto for the Right Hand
  (1987)
Concrete Beat (1984)
Concrete Cowboys (1979)
Concrete Cowboys (1981)
Concrete Jungle, The (1982)
Concrete Pastures (1983)
Condo (1983)
Condominium (1980)
Condor (1986)
Condorman (1981)
Confession (1937)
Confession at Dawn (1954)
Confession Under Four Eyes
  (1954)
Confessional, The (1977)
Confessions of a Married Man
  (1983)
Confidential (1986)
Confidential File (1956)
Conflict (1956)
Conflict of Wings (1954)
Confusion (Yessa Mossa) (1953)
Con-fusion (1980)
Congo Express (1986)
Congolaise (1950)
Congratulations, It's a Boy!
  (1971)
Connection (1973)
Conquest (1984)
Conquest of Albania, The (1983)
Conquest of Mycene (1963)
Conquest of Peter the Great, The
  (1939)
Conquest of the Earth (1980)
Conquest of the Moon (1960)
Conspiracy of Love (1987)
Conspiracy of Terror (1975)
Constance (1984)
Consul, The (Daimler-Benz
  Limuzvna) (1982)
Consuming Passions (1988)
Contagion (1988)
Contender, The (1980)
Continental Divide (1981)
Contraband (1940)
Contraband Aces (1986)
Contract (Kontrakt) (1980)
Contract for Life: The S.A.D.D.
  Story (1984)
Contract Mother (Sibaji) (1987)

Contract on Cherry Street (1977)
Contract with Death (1985)
Contrary Warriors (1985)
Control (1987)
Conversations with Willard Van
  Dyke (1981)
Convict Killer, The (1980)
Convicted: A Mother's Story (1987)
Convoy (1965)
Cook & Peary: The Race to the
  Pole (1983)
Cool Change (1986)
Cool Lakes of Death, The (1982)
Cool Million (Mask of Marcella)
  (1972)
Coolangatta Gold, The (1984)
Cop (1988)
Cop and the Girl, The (1985)
Cop and the Kid, The (1975)
Copacabana, Mon Amour (1975)
Cops and Robbers (1952)
Cops and Robin (1978)
Cop's Honor (1985)
Coral Jungle, The (1976)
Cordelia (1980)
Corey: For the People (1977)
Cormorant (1986)
Corn Is Green, The (1979)
Corner Bar, The (1972)
Corner Forsaken by Love, The
  (1986)
Coronation Street (1972)
Coronet Blue (1967)
Corpse Grinders, The (1972)
Corpse Vanishes, The (1942)
Corruption (1987)
Corsican Brothers, The (1961)
Corsican Brothers, The (1985)
Cosh Boy (1953)
Cosmic Monsters, The (Strange
  World of Planet X, The) (1958)
Cosmos (1974)
Cossacks in Exile (1939)
Cote d'Azur (1959)
Cotton Candy (1978)
Cotton Club, The (1984)
Couch Trip, The (1988)
Count Dracula (1978)
Count of Monte Cristo, The (1975)
Count Tacchia (1983)
Count to Ten (1985)
Count Your Blessings (1987)
Countdown (1986)
Counterattack: Crime in America
  (1982)
Counterblast (1948)
Counterfeit Commandos (see

Cutter and Bone (1981)
Cutter to Houston (1983)
Cutter's Trail (1970)
Cybernetic Grandmother (short) (1962)
Cyborg 009 (1974)
Cyborg 009--Underground Duel (1967)
Cyborg 2087 (1966)
Cyclone (1987)
Cyclone Tracy (1986)
Cyclops (1982)

D.A., The (1971)
D.A.: Conspiracy to Kill, The (1971)
D.A.: Murder One, The (1969)
D.A.R.Y.L. (1985)
D.A.'s Man, The (1959)
D.C. Cab (1983)
D.C. Cop (1986)
D-Day (1962)
Da (1988)
Da Capo (1985)
Dadah Is Death (1988)
Daddy (1987)
Daddy Dearest (1984)
Daddy, I Don't Like It Like This (1978)
Daddy's Boys (1988)
Daddy's Girl (1973)
Dads (1986)
Dain Curse, The (1978)
Dakota (1988)
Dakotas, The (1963)
Daktari! (1966)
Dallas (1978)
Dallas Cowboys Cheerleaders, The (1979)
Dallas: The Early Years (1986)
Dalton: Code of Vengeance II (1986)
Dalton Gang, The (1949)
Dames Get Along (1954)
Damien: The Leper Priest (1980)
Damn Real (1988)
Damnation (1988)
Damsel of Bard (Destino, Il) (1938)
Dan August (1970)
Dan Raven (1960)
Dance Music (1935)
Dance Music (1984)
Dance of the Dolls (1987)
Dance With a Stranger (1985)
Dancer and the Warrior, The (1981)

Dancer and the Worker, The (1936)
Dancers (1987)
Dances Sacred and Profane (1985)
Dancing Daze (1986)
Dancing in the Rain (1961)
Dancing on Water (1986)
Dandin (1988)
Danger (1950)
Danger Down Under (1988)
Danger in Paradise (1977)
Danger Man (1961)
Danger Within (1959)
Danger Zone, The (1987)
Dangerous Characters (1987)
Dangerous Company (1982)
Dangerous Davies--The Last Detective (1981)
Dangerous Days of Kiowa Jones, The (1966)
Dangerous Exile (1957)
Dangerous Game (1988)
Dangerous Guests (1950)
Dangerous Liaisons (1988)
Dangerous Life, A (1988)
Dangerous Moves (1985)
Dangerous Orphans (1986)
Dangerous Secrets (1938)
Dangerously Close (1986)
Dangerously Yours (1937)
Daniel & the Towers (1987)
Daniel Boone (1964)
Daniel Takes a Train (1983)
Daniya, Garden of the Harem (1988)
Danni (1983)
D'Annunzio (1987)
Danny (1979)
Danny and the Mermaid (1978)
Danny the Dragon (1966)
Dan's Motel (1982)
Dante (1960)
Danton (1982)
Danube Waltzes (1984)
Darinda (1977)
Dark August (1975)
Dark Before Dawn (1988)
Dark Circle (1982)
Dark Crystal, The (1982)
Dark End of the Street, The (1981)
Dark Enemy (1984)
Dark Eyes (1938)
Dark Eyes (Oci Ciornie) (1987)
Dark Lullabies (1985)
Dark Mansions (1986)
Dark Mirror (1984)
Dark Night (1986)
Dark Night of the Scarecrow (1981)
Dark Room, The (1981)

Dark Room, The (1982)
Dark Secret of Harvest Home, The
  (1978)
Dark Shadows (1966)
Dark Side of Innocence, The
  (1976)
Dark Side of Midnight, The (1988)
Dark Star, The (1955)
Dark Star (1974)
Dark Sun (Temne Slunce) (1980)
Dark Victory (1976)
Darker Side of Terror, The (1979)
Darkness (Tamas) (1988)
Darkness Fell on Gotenhafen (1960)
Darkside, The (1987)
Darlings! (1984)
Darwaza (1978)
Dastardly and Muttley and Their
  Flying Machines (1969)
Date by the Danube (1937)
Date Rape (1988)
Date With an Angel (1987)
Daughter of Dr. Jekyll, The
  (1957)
Daughter of the Mind (1969)
Daughter of the Sands (1952)
Daughters of Fire (1978)
Daughters of Joshua Cabe, The
  (1972)
Daughters of Joshua McCabe
  Return, The (1975)
Dauphins, The (1960)
David (1988)
David Cassidy--Man Undercover
  (1978)
David Copperfield (1970)
Davy Crockett (1954)
Davy Crockett: Rainbow in the
  Thunder (1988)
Dawn, The (1983)
Dawn, The (1986)
Dawn of Judo (1970)
Dawn of the Mummy (1981)
Dawn: Portrait of a Teenage
  Runaway (1976)
Dawn to Dawn (1934)
Dawning, The (1988)
Day After, The (1983)
Day After Halloween, The
  (Snapshot/One More Minute)
  (1981)
Day After Tomorrow, The (1975)
Day at the Beach, A (1984)
Day Before Yesterday, The
  (Tegnapelott) (1982)
Day by Day (Grands Engants,
  Les) (1981)

Day by Day (1988)
Day Christ Died, The (1980)
Day for Thanks on Waltons Mountain,
  A (1982)
Day in a Taxi, A (1982)
Day in Moscow, A (1957)
Day It Came to Earth, The (1979)
Day Longer Than the Night, The
  (1984)
Day My Kid Went Punk, The (1987)
Day of Fear (1957)
Day of Judgment, A (1980)
Day of Reckoning (short) (1960)
Day of the Dead (1957)
Day of the Dead (1985)
Day of the Idiots (1982)
Day of the Owl (1968)
Day of the Panther (1988)
Day of the Triffids, The (1982)
Day of the Vistula, The (1980)
Day of Wrath (1943)
Day of Wrath (1986)
Day Pedro Infante Died, The (1984)
Day the Bubble Burst, The (1982)
Day the Earth Got Stoned, The
  (1980)
Day the Earth Moved, The (1974)
Day the Loving Stopped, The
  (1981)
Day the Screaming Stopped, The
  (Comeback, The) (1979)
Day the Sky Exploded, The (1958)
Day the Women Got Even, The
  (1981)
Day the World Ended, The (1956)
Day They Came to Arrest the Book,
  The (1987)
Day Time Ended, The (1980)
Day to Day (1987)
Day with the Devil, A (1945)
Daybreak in Udi (short) (1950)
Days and Nights of Molly Dodd,
  The (1987)
Days in June (1985)
Days of Dreams (1980)
Days of Hell (1986)
Days of Love (1954)
Days of Our Lives (1965)
Days of Torment (1985)
Days to Remember (1987)
Dead, The (1987)
Dead and Buried (1981)
Dead Ball, The (1987)
Dead Don't Die, The (1975)
Dead Easy (1982)
Dead End, A (Peruvaziambalan)
  (1980)

Dead-End Drive-In (1986)
Dead End Kids (1986)
Dead End Street (1982)
Dead Heat (1988)
Dead Man on the Run (1975)
Dead Man Walking (1988)
Dead Man's Folly (1986)
Dead March, The (1937)
Dead Men Don't Wear Plaid (1982)
Dead Men Tell No Tales (1971)
Dead of Night (1977)
Dead of Winter (1987)
Dead or Alive (Elve Vagy Halva)
   (1980)
Dead or Alive (1988)
Dead Pool, The (1988)
Dead Ringer (1982)
Dead Ringers (1988)
Dead Solid Perfect (1988)
Dead Teach the Living, The
   (1984)
Dead Wrong (1983)
Dead Zone, The (1983)
Deadhead Miles (1972)
Deadliest Season, The (1977)
Deadline (1987)
Deadline (1988)
Deadline (Anatomy of a Horror)
   (1979)
Deadlock (1969)
Deadly Addiction (1988)
Deadly Blessing (1981)
Deadly Business, A (1986)
Deadly Care (1987)
Deadly Circuit (1983)
Deadly Dream, The (1971)
Deadly Dreams (1988)
Deadly Force (1983)
Deadly Friend (1986)
Deadly Game, The (1977)
Deadly Game (Jaeger, Die) (1982)
Deadly Games (1979)
Deadly Harvest (1972)
Deadly Hunt, The (1971)
Deadly Illusion (Love You to
   Death) (1987)
Deadly Impact (1983)
Deadly Intent (1988)
Deadly Intentions (1985)
Deadly Intruder (1984)
Deadly Lessons (1983)
Deadly Odor, The (1970)
Deadly Passion (1985)
Deadly Prey (1987)
Deadly Spawn, The (1981)
Deadly Spring (1940)
Deadly Stranger (1988)

Deadly Tower, The (1975)
Deadly Triangle, The (1977)
Deadman's Curve (1978)
Deaf in the City, The (1987)
Deal, The (1983)
Deal of the Century (1983)
Dear America (1987)
Dear Augustin, The (1960)
Dear Boys (Lieve Jongens) (1980)
Dear Cardholder (1987)
Dear Dead Delilah (1972)
Dear Detective (1979)
Dear Family (1957)
Dear Friends (1980)
Dear Gorbachev (1988)
Dear Karl (Lieber Karl) (1984)
Dear Mr. Prohack (1949)
Dear Mr. Wonderful (1982)
Dear Summer Sister (1973)
Dear Teacher (1981)
Death Among Friends (1975)
Death at Love House (1976)
Death Be Not Proud (1975)
Death Before Dishonor (1987)
Death by Hanging (1968)
Death by Invitation (1971)
Death by Witchcraft (1957)
Death Car on the Freeway (1979)
Death Cruise (1974)
Death Curse of Tartu, The (1966)
Death Dream (Night Andy Came
   Home, The) (1974)
Death Game, The (1986)
Death Hunt (1981)
Death in California, A (1985)
Death in Canaan, A (1978)
Death in Deep Water (1975)
Death in Love (1950)
Death in Small Doses (1957)
Death in Small Doses (1973)
Death in the Family, A (1987)
Death in the Vatican (1982)
Death Made to Order (1981)
Death March (Morte Cammina con
   Loro, La) (1966)
Death Moon (1978)
Death of a Beautiful Dream (1987)
Death of a Centerfold: The
   Dorothy Stratten Story (1981)
Death of a Dream (1950)
Death of a Friend (1959)
Death of a Patriot (1985)
Death of a Soldier (1986)
Death of a Tycoon (1981)
Death of an Angel (1985)
Death of Innocence, A (1971)
Death of Mario Ricci, The (1983)

Devil's Messenger (1962)
Devil's Mistress, The (1966)
Devil's Mountain, The (1976)
Devil's Nightmare, The (1971)
Devil's Paradise (1987)
Devil's Party, The (1938)
Devil's Triangle, The (1973)
Devil's Wanton, The (Fangelse) (1948)
Devil's Web, The (1974)
Devlin (1974)
Devlin Connection, The (1982)
Devonsville Terror, The (1982)
Devotee to the God (1955)
Devotion (1953)
Devouring Rock, The (1959)
Devude Gelichad (1976)
Diabolic Pact, The (1968)
Diabolica (1977)
Diabolical Axe, The (1964)
Diabolical Dr. Z, The (1965)
Diabolique (1955)
Diagnosis: Danger (1963)
Dial a Deadly Number (1975)
Dial Hotline (1970)
Dial M for Murder (1981)
Diamond City (1949)
Diamond Square (1982)
Diamond Trap, The (1988)
Diamond Wizard, The (1954)
Diana (1973)
Diapason (1986)
Diary (Naplo) (1984)
Diary for My Lovers (1987)
Diary of a Hitchhiker, The (1979)
Diary of a Mad Old Man (1987)
Diary of a Madman, The (1987)
Diary of a Perfect Murder, The (1986)
Diary of Anne Frank, The (1980)
Diary of Sueko, The (1960)
Dick and the Duchess (1957)
Dick Smart 2/007 (1966)
Dick Tracy Show, The (1961)
Dick Tracy vs. Crime Incorporated (1941)
Dick Van Dyke Show, The (1961)
Dickens of London (1977)
Did Your Hear About Josh and Kelly? (1980)
Didi and His Double (1984)
Didi and the Revenge of the Disinherited (1985)
Die Hard (1988)
Die Laughing (1980)
Die, Sister, Die! (1978)

Diego Corrientes (1959)
Different Affair, A (1987)
Difficult Days (1988)
... Difficult to Become Engaged (1983)
Diff'rent Strokes (1978)
Dig (short) (1972)
Diggers (1986)
Digital Dreams (1983)
Dignity (Jom) (1982)
Dim Sum: A Little Bit of Heart (1985)
Dimension 5 (1966)
Dina and Django (1981)
Diner (1983)
Dinner Is Served (1936)
Dinosaur! (1985)
Dion Brothers, The (1974)
Dionysus (short) (1963)
Direct-Line Heir, The (1982)
Dirt Bike Kid, The (1986)
Dirt Cheap (1986)
Dirtwater Dynasty, The (1988)
Dirty Dancing (1987)
Dirty Dealings Between Friends (1988)
Dirty Dozen, The (1983)
Dirty Dozen: Next Mission, The (1985)
Dirty Dozen: The Fatal Mission, The (1988)
Dirty Hero (Yogoreta Eiya) (1983)
Dirty Laundry (1987)
Dirty Rotten Scoundrels (1988)
Dirty Sally (1974)
Dirty Story (1985)
Dirty Story of the West, A (1968)
Dirty Tricks (1981)
Disappearance of Aimee, The (1976)
Disappearance of Flight 412, The (1974)
Disappearance of Harry, The (1983)
Disaster at Silo 7 (1988)
Disaster on the Coastliner (1980)
Disbanded, The (1955)
Disciple of Satan (1970)
Disciples, The (1985)
Disciples of Hippocrates (1981)
Disco of Love, The (1980)
Disconnected (1986)
Discotheque, The (1984)
Disembodied, The (1967)
Dishonor (1952)
Dishonored (1950)
Disintegrating Ray, or the Adventures of Quique and Arthur the Robot, The (1965)

Dollar a Head, A (1966)
Dollar Between the Teeth, A (1966)
Dollmaker, The (1984)
Dolly In (Travelling Avant) (1987)
Dolores (1949)
Domani non Siamo piu Qui (1966)
Domestic Life (1984)
Domina--The Burden of Lust (1985)
Dominic's Dream (1974)
Dominick and Eugene (1988)
Dominique (Dominique Is Dead) (1977)
Domino (1982)
Don Juan, Karl-Liebknecht-Str. 78 (1982)
Don Mouse and Don Thief (1985)
Don Quintin, the Bitter (1935)
Don Quixote (1984)
Don Rickles Show, The (1972)
Donkey Skin (1985)
Donna Donna! (1988)
Donner Pass: The Road to Survival (1978)
Donovan's Brain (1953)
Don't Answer the Phone (1980)
Don't Be Afraid of the Dark (1973)
Don't Be Offended, Beatrice (1953)
Don't Call Me Charlie (1962)
Don't Call Us (1976)
Don't Ever Leave Me (1949)
Don't Give a Damn (1987)
Don't Go in the House (1980)
Don't Go into the Woods (1980)
Don't Go to Sleep (1982)
Don't Kill God (1984)
Don't Look Back (1981)
Don't Look in the Basement (1973)
Don't Meddle with Fortune (1961)
Don't Open Till Christmas (1984)
Don't Panic, Chaps! (1959)
Don't Panic, Please! (1983)
Don't Press the Button (1987)
Don't Push, I'll Charge When I'm Ready (1969)
Don't Touch (1985)
Don't Trifle With Women (1957)
Dooley Brothers, The (1979)
Doom Asylum (1988)
Doom of the Berhof Lonely Farm, The (1984)
Doomed Love (1984)
Doomsday Chronicles, The (1979)
Doomsday Flight (1966)
Doomwatch (1972)

Door (1988)
Door in the Wall (short) (1957)
Door on Heaven, A (1988)
Door on the Left as You Leave the Elevator, The (1988)
Door Remains Open, The (1959)
Door with No Name, The (1951)
Doorway to Danger (1952)
Dorado--One Way (1984)
Dorellik (1967)
Doris Day Show, The (1968)
Dormire (1985)
Dorotej (1981)
Dorothy (1979)
Dorothy in the Land of Oz (1981)
Dot and Santa Claus (1982)
Dot and the Bunny (1983)
Dot and the Koala (1985)
Dot and the Whale (1986)
Double, The (Kagemusha) (1980)
Double Agent (1987)
Double-Barrelled Detective Story (1965)
Double Cross (1938)
Double Dare (1985)
Double Deal (1984)
Double Decker (1984)
Double Destiny (1955)
Double Feature (Sesion Continua) (1984)
Double Indemnity (1973)
Double Kill (1975)
Double Life of Henry Phyfe, The (1966)
Double Negative (1980)
Double Standard (1988)
Double Start to Act, The (1985)
Double Switch (1986)
Double Talk (1986)
Double Trouble (1982)
Double Trouble (1984)
Doubletake (1985)
Dougal and the Blue Cat (Pollux and the Blue Cat) (1972)
Down and Out in Beverly Hills (1985)
Down and Out with Donald Duck (1987)
Down by Law (1986)
Down Home (1984)
Down the Long Hills (1987)
Down to Earth (1947)
Down with the Germans (1985)
Downtown (1986)
Doxobus (1987)
Dracos (1956)
Dracula (1974)

Dylan Thomas' A Child's Christmas
    in Wales (1987)
Dynamite Brothers, The (1949)
Dynamite in the Pentagon (1966)
Dynasty (1976)
Dynasty II: The Colbys (1985)
Dyurado (1966)

E/R (1984)
E. T. & Friends--Magical Movie
    Visitors (1982)
E. T., the Extra-Terrestrial
    (1982)
Eager to Love (1953)
Eames Lounge Chair (short) (1956)
Early Frost, An (1985)
Early Snowfall in Munich (1984)
Ears Between the Teeth (1987)
Earth Girls Are Easy (1988)
Earth Star Voyager (1988)
Earth II (1971)
Earth vs. the Spider (Spider,
    The) (1958)
Earthling (1981)
Earthlings, The (1984)
Earthquake Islands (1979)
East of Eden (1981)
East Side/West Side (1963)
Easter Promise, The (1975)
Easy Money (Plata Dulce) (1982)
Easy Money (1983)
Easy Prey (1986)
Easy Street (1986)
Easy Times Are Over, The (1984)
Easy Years, The (1953)
Eat and Run (1986)
Eat the Peach (1986)
Eat the Rich (1987)
Eaten Alive (Death Trap) (1976)
Eating Raoul (1982)
Eating Your Heart Out (1985)
Ebony, Ivory and Jade (1979)
Ebony Tower, The (1987)
Ecce Homo (1937)
Echo of Theresa, An (1973)
Echo Park (1985)
Echoes (1980)
Echoes in the Darkness (1987)
Echoes of a Distant Drum (1988)
Eclipse (Grhana) (1980)
Ed Wynn Show, The (1958)
Eddie and Herbert (1977)
Eddie and the Cruisers (1983)
Eddie Capra Mysteries, The (1978)
Eddie Macon's Run (1983)
Eden Miseria (1988)

Edge of Darkness (1985)
Edge of Hell, The (Rock 'n' Roll
    Nightmare) (1987)
Edge of Night, The (1956)
Edith and Marcel (1983)
Edith's Diary (1983)
Edo Porn (1982)
Educating Father (1936)
Educating Rita (1983)
Edward and Mrs. Simpson (1980)
Edward the King (1980)
Egan (1973)
Egg (Ei) (1988)
Egghead's Robot (1970)
Egon Schiele--Excess and Punish-
    ment (1981)
Egyptian, The (1954)
Egyptian Story, An (1982)
Eight Is Enough (1977)
Eight Is Enough: A Family Reunion
    (1987)
Eight Kilos of Happiness (1980)
Eight Men Out (1988)
8 Million Ways to Die (1986)
Eight O'Clock Walk (1954)
18 Again (1988)
1893-1915 (1983)
18-Year-Olds (1956)
Eighth Day of the Week, The (1958)
Eighth Door, The (1959)
84 Charing Cross Road (1987)
87th Precinct (1961)
Eijanaika (1982)
Eischied (1979)
Eisenhower & Lutz (1988)
El Lute--Forge On or Die (1987)
El Salvador: Another Vietnam
    (1981)
Eleanor and Franklin (1976)
Eleanor and Franklin: The White
    House Years (1977)
Eleanor, First Lady of the World
    (1982)
Electra Woman and Dyna Girl (1976)
Electric Angel (1981)
Electric Blue (1988)
Electric Dreams (1984)
Electric Eskimo, The (1979)
Electric Grandmother, The (short)
    (1982)
Eleftherios Venizelos 1919-1927
    (1980)
Elegie (Agit) (1981)
Element of Crime, The (1984)
Eleni (1985)
Elephant Got Lost, An (1986)
Elephant Man, The (1980)

Elephant Story (1980)
Elevator, The (1974)
Elevator to the Gallows (1958)
Eleventh Hour, The (1962)
11th Victim, The (1979)
Elfego Baca (1958)
Elge, Queen of Snakes (1965)
Eliminators (1986)
Elisabeth McQueeney Story, The (1959)
Elixir of the Devil, The (1977)
Elizabeth of Ladymead (1949)
Ellery Queen (1975)
Ellery Queen (Too Many Suspects) (1975)
Ellery Queen: Don't Look Behind You (1971)
Ellie (1984)
Ellis Island (1984)
Elsa! Elsa! (1985)
Elvira, Mistress of the Dark (1988)
Elvis (1979)
Elvis & Me (1988)
Elvis and the Beauty Queen (1981)
Elvis Hansen--A Pillar of Society (1988)
Emanon (1987)
Embalmer, The (1965)
Embezzled Heaven (1958)
Embryo (1986)
Emerald Point (1983)
Emergency! (1972)
Emergency! (1979)
Emergency (1985)
Emergency Room (1983)
Emilio Varela's Band (1987)
Emmanuelle and the Last Cannibals (Trap Them and Kill Them) (1977)
Emmanuelle 4 (1984)
Emmanuelle 5 (1987)
Emmanuelle 6 (1988)
Emma's Shadow (1988)
Emoh Ruo (1985)
Emperor and a General, The (1969)
Emperor Caligula: The Untold Story, The (1986)
Emperor Lee (1968)
Emperor of California (1936)
Emperor of Capri, The (1950)
Emperor's Nightingale, The (1951)
Empire (1962)
Empire (1984)
Empire (1985)
Empire of Passion (1978)

Empire of Punks (Gaki Teikoku) (1981)
Empire of the Sun (1987)
Empire Strikes Back, The (1980)
Employees (Impiegati) (1985)
Empty Beach, The (1985)
Empty Nest (1988)
Empty Star, The (1960)
Enchanted Dollars, The (1986)
Enchanted Forest, The (1987)
Enchanted Grove, The (1982)
Enchanted Sail, The (1982)
Enchanting Shadow (1960)
Enchantress, The (1985)
Encore (1980)
Encore (Once More) (1988)
Encounter of the Spooky Kind (1981)
End of August at the Hotel Ozone, The (1965)
End of Innocence (1960)
End of Milton Levi, The (1981)
End of the Day (1939)
End of the Journey, The (1981)
End of the Line (1988)
End of the Miracle, The (1984)
End of the Road, The (1954)
End of the Trail (1967)
End of the War, The (Kraj Rata) (1985)
End of the World, The (1930)
End of the World (1977)
End of the World Man, The (1985)
Endangered Species (1982)
Endeavor (1982)
Endgame (1986)
Endless Dream (1986)
Endless Love (1981)
Enemies, The (1983)
Enemy, The (Dusman) (1980)
Enemy Among Us, An (1987)
Enemy Mine (1985)
Enemy Territory (1987)
Englishman Abroad, An (1983)
Enigma (1977)
Enjo (1959)
Enola Gay (1980)
Enos (1980)
Enraged Toy, The (1985)
Enrico IV (Henry IV) (1984)
Ensign O'Toole (1962)
Enter the Devil (1971)
Enter the Ninja (1982)
Entertainer, The (1976)
Entire Life, The (1987)
Entity, The (1982)
Epilog (1984)

Episode (1937)
Epitaph for Barbara Radziwill, An (1983)
Equalizer 2000 (1987)
Equator (1983)
Equinox (1967)
Equinox (1986)
Equipage, L' (1938)
Er Woo Dong (Entertainer, The) (1985)
Erendira (1983)
Eric (1975)
Ernest Goes to Camp (1987)
Ernest Saves Christmas (1988)
Ernie Kovacs: Between the Laughter (1984)
Erogenous Zone (1981)
Erotica (1981)
Erotomania Daimyo, The (1975)
Errant Lives (1984)
Escadrille of Change (1938)
Escapade (1978)
Escapade (1980)
Escape (1950)
Escape (1971)
Escape (1973)
Escape (1980)
Escape, The (Firar) (1985)
Escape Artist, The (1982)
Escape from Brogen County (1977)
Escape from Grumble Gulch (1984)
Escape from Iran: The Canadian Caper (1980)
Escape from New York (1981)
Escape from Sobibor (1987)
Escape from the Bronx (1985)
Escape from Women's Prison (1978)
Escape to Berlin (1961)
Escape to Mindanao (1968)
Escapement (1958)
Escapes Home (1981)
Escarlotta (1969)
Eskimo Woman Feels Cold (1984)
Espionage in Tangiers (1965)
Espy (1975)
Essence, The (Susman) (1987)
Esthappan (1980)
Esther and the King (1960)
Ete and Ali (1985)
Eternal Cause (1973)
Eternal Evil (1988)
Eternal Feelings, The (1984)
Eternal Fire (1985)
Eternal Mask, The (1937)
Eternal Return, The (1943)
Eternal Street (1938)

Ethel Is an Elephant (1980)
Eugenio (1980)
Eulalia (1987)
Eunice (1974)
Eunuchs (1987)
Eureka (1983)
Europe by Night (1959)
Europe '51 (1952)
Eva (1949)
Eva: Guerrillera (1987)
Eva Inherits Paradise (1951)
Eva Peron Mystery, The (1988)
Evangeline (1929)
Eva's Dreams (1982)
Eve Arden Show, The (1957)
Eve, the Savage Venus (1968)
Eve Wants to Sleep (1958)
Evel Knievel (1974)
Evening Bells (1986)
Evening Dress (1986)
Evening in Byzantium (1978)
Evening Performance (1981)
Evening with Edgar Allan Poe, An (1970)
Event, An (1985)
Everlasting Secret Family, The (1988)
Every Day Has Its Secret (1958)
Every Man Needs One (1972)
Every Picture Tells a Story (1984)
Every Sparrow Must Fall (1964)
Every Stray Dog and Kid (1981)
Every Time We Say Goodbye (1986)
Every Woman Has a Secret (1937)
Everybody Is Good (1982)
Everybody Rides the Carousel (1976)
Everybody's All-American (1988)
Everybody's Woman (1936)
Everyone for Himself in Life (1980)
Everything for the Woman (1936)
Everything Happens to Me (1961)
Everything Is Rhythm (1940)
Everything's Archie (1973)
Everything's Relative (1987)
Evil Dead, The (Book of the Dead) (1980)
Evil Eye, The (1937)
Evil Eye, The (Maldiccio) (1975)
Evil Laugh (1988)
Evil of Dracula (1975)
Evil Roy Slade (1972)
Evil Spawn (Alive by Night/Deadly Sting) (1987)
Evil Speak (1981)
Evil That Men Do, The (1984)
Evil Touch, The (1973)
Evil Town (1987)
Evils of the Night (1985)

Evita Peron (1981)
Evita--Who Wants to Hear May
   Hear (1984)
Ewoks: The Battle for Endor
   (1985)
Excalibur (1981)
Exception to the Rule (1937)
Excite Me (1972)
Execution of Private Slovik, The
   (1974)
Execution of Raymond Graham,
   The (1985)
Executioner's Song, The (1982)
Executive Suite (1976)
Exile Express (1939)
Exit ... But No Panic (1980)
Exo-Man (1977)
Exorcism (1974)
Exorcism's Daughter (1974)
Exorcist--Italian Style, The (1975)
Exploits of a Young Don Juan,
   The (1987)
Explorers (1985)
Explosion Happens at Five O'Clock,
   The (1985)
Expo '70 (1971)
Exposed (1983)
Exquisite Corpses (1988)
Exterior Night (1980)
Exterminator, The (1980)
Exterminator 2 (1984)
Exterminators, The (1965)
Exterminators of the Year 3000,
   The (1984)
Extra Day, The (1956)
Extramurals (1985)
Extreme Prejudice (1987)
Extremities (1986)
Eye for an Eye, An (1957)
Eye for an Eye, An (1981)
Eye of the Labyrinth, The
   (Blood) (1971)
Eye of the Needle (1981)
Eye on the Sparrow (1987)
Eye to Eye (1985)
Eyeball (1978)
Eyes Behind the Stars (1978)
Eyes Have It, The (1974)
Eyes of a Stranger (1981)
Eyes of Fire (1984)
Eyes of Texas, The (1980)
Eyes of the Birds (1983)
Eyes, the Mouth, The (1982)
Eyes Without a Face (Horror
   Chamber of Dr. Faustus/
   Shadowman) (1963)
Eyewitness (1956)

Eyewitness (1983)

F.B.I., The (1965)
F.B.I. Code 98 (1962)
F.B.I. Story: The F.B.I. Versus
   Alvin Karpis, Public Enemy Num-
   ber One (1974)
FDR--The Last Year (1980)
F...ing Fernand (1987)
FM--Frequency Murder (1988)
F. Scott Fitzgerald and "The Last
   of the Belles" (1974)
F. Scott Fitzgerald in Hollywood
   (1976)
F Troop (1965)
F/X (1986)
Fabian (1980)
Fable of the Beautiful Pigeon Fan-
   cier, The (1988)
Fables from Hans Christian Ander-
   sen (1968)
Fables from Hans Christian Ander-
   sen (1969)
Fabulous Funnies, The (1978)
Fabulous Joe (1946)
Face of Darkness, The (1976)
Face of Eve, The (1968)
Face of Fear, The (1971)
Face of Genius, The (1967)
Face of Rage, The (1983)
Face of Terror (1962)
Face of the Screaming Werewolf,
   The (House of Terror) (1959)
Face That Launched a Thousand
   Ships, The (1954)
Face to Face (1985)
Face to the Sun (1980)
Faceless (Night Predators) (1988)
Faces in the Dark (1960)
Factory, The (1982)
Factory B (1959)
Facts of Life, The (1979)
Facts of Life Down Under, The
   (1987)
Facts of Life Goes to Paris, The
   (1982)
Faculty, The (1986)
Fade to Black (1980)
Faerie Tale Theater (1982)
Fahrmann Maria (1935)
Failing of Raymond, The (1971)
Failure, The (1986)
Fair, The (1960)
Fair and Warmer (1937)
Fair at Dharamtalia, The (1987)
Fair Exchange (1962)

Fair Game (Freiwild) (1984)
Fair Game (1986)
Fairy of Happiness (1949)
Fairy Tale of Honzik and
   Marenka, The (1981)
Fairy Tale of Wanderings, A
   (1984)
Fairy Tales (1979)
Fairytale Country, The (1988)
Faith, Hope and Witchcraft
   (1960)
Faithful River, The (1987)
Fake Five (1987)
Fake-Out (1982)
Falasha: Exile of the Black Jews
   (1983)
Falcon, The (Banovic Strahinja)
   (1981)
Falcon, The (1983)
Falcon and the Snowman, The
   (1985)
Falcon Crest (1981)
Falcon's Gold (1982)
Fall, The (1987)
Fall and Rise of Reginald Perrin,
   The (1978)
Fall Guy, The (1981)
Fall Guy, The (1985)
Fall of Italy (1981)
Fall of the House of Usher, The
   (1982)
Fallen Angel (1981)
Falling in Love (1984)
Falling in Love Again (1980)
Falling Stars (Zvezdopad) (1981)
Falsch (1987)
False as Water (1985)
False Confidences, The (1984)
False Eyelashes (1982)
False One, The (1986)
False Passport, The (1959)
False Word, The (1987)
Fame (1980)
Fame and the Devil (1950)
Fame Is the Name of the Game
   (1966)
Family (1976)
Family, The (1986)
Family, The (1987)
Family Affair (1966)
Family Affair, A (1982)
Family Affair, A (1984)
Family Again, A (1988)
Family Album (1981)
Family Bonus (1938)
Family Business (1983)
Family Council (1986)

Family, Fine, Thanks, The (1980)
Family Flight (1972)
Family Holvak, The (1975)
Family in Blue (1982)
Family Kovack, The (1974)
Family Light Affair (1984)
Family Man, The (1979)
Family Man (1988)
Family Nobody Wanted, The (1975)
Family on Parade (1937)
Family Planning (short) (1968)
Family Relations (Rodnia) (1983)
Family Reunion (1981)
Family Rico, The (1972)
Family Rock (1982)
Family Schimek (1957)
Family Secrets (1984)
Family Sins (1987)
Family Ties (1982)
Family Tree, The (1983)
Family Upside Down, A (1978)
Family Viewing (1987)
Famous Adventures of Mr. Magoo,
   The (1964)
Fan, The (1981)
Fanatics, The (1960)
Fandango (1985)
Fando and Lys (Tar Babies) (1968)
Fang Face (1978)
Fanny and Alexander (1982)
Fanny by Gaslight (1982)
Fantabulous Inc. (1967)
Fantasia ... 3 (1966)
Fantasies (1982)
Fantasist, The (1986)
Fantasize (1984)
Fantastic Ballad (1968)
Fantastic Four, The (1967)
Fantastic Journey, The (1977)
Fantastic Voyage, The (1968)
Fantastic World of D. C. Collins,
   The (1984)
Fantastica (1980)
Fantasy Island (1977)
Fantasy Island (1978)
Fantasy Man (1984)
Fantomas (1964)
Fantomas vs. Fantomas (1947)
Fantozzi Against the World (1980)
Fantozzi Takes It on the Chin
   Again (1984)
Far Away I Saw Mist and Mud
   (1964)
Far Country, The (1987)
Far East (1982)
Far from Moscow (1951)
Far from Poland (1984)

Feminist and the Fuzz, The (1971)
Femme de l'Hotel, La (1984)
Femmes (1983)
Femmes de Paris (1954)
Ferat Vampire (1983)
Fer-de-Lance (1974)
Ferdinanda, La (1982)
Fernand (1980)
Ferocious (1984)
Ferris Bueller's Day Off (1986)
Ferrywoman, The (1986)
Fertility God, The (1978)
Fess Parker Show, The (1974)
Festival (Utsav) (1984)
Festival of Fire (Holi) (1985)
Fetish and Dreams (1985)
Fetters (1986)
Fever (Goraczka) (1981)
Fever (1988)
Fever Pitch (1985)
Few Days in Weasel Creek, A
  (1981)
Few Days More, A (1981)
Few Days With Me, A (1988)
ffolkes (1980)
Fiancee, The (Verlobte, Die)
  (1980)
Fiancee Who Came in From the
  Cold, The (1983)
Fictive Marriage (1988)
Field Agent, The (1987)
Field of Honor, The (1983)
Field of Honor (1987)
Fields of Fire (1987)
Fiend (1981)
Fiend with the Electronic Brain,
  The (Psycho a Go-Go) (1965)
Fiend Without a Face, The (1958)
Fiendish Plot of Dr. Fu Manchu,
  The (1980)
Fifi la Plume (1964)
15 Pounds in 7 Days (1986)
Fifth Missile, The (1986)
5th Movement, The (1981)
Fifth of July, The (1982)
50 Years Before Your Eyes (1950)
50 Years of Action! (1986)
52 Pick-Up (1986)
Fig Tree, The (1987)
Fight for Life, The (1940)
Fight for the Red Cow, The
  (1987)
Fighter, The (1983)
Fighting Back (1982)
Fighting Choice (1986)
Fighting Cuban Against the
  Demons, The (1972)

Fighting for Two (1982)
Fighting Marines, The (1935)
Fighting Nightingales, The (1978)
Fighting Stallion, The (1950)
Fighting with Kit Carson (1933)
File It Under Fear (1973)
Film Without a Name, The (1950)
Filthy Business, A (1981)
Filthy Rich (1982)
Final Arrangement, The (1988)
Final Assignment (1980)
Final Call (1984)
Final Conflict--Damien III, The
  (1981)
Final Countdown, The (1980)
Final Cut (1980)
Final Exam (1981)
Final Executioner, The (1983)
Final Jeopardy (1985)
Final Justice (1985)
Final Mission (1986)
Final Take: The Golden Days of
  the Movies (1986)
Final Terror, The (1981)
Final Season (1988)
Final Winner?, The (1969)
Finals (1983)
Find a Way, Comrade (1981)
Finder of Lost Loves (1984)
Finders Keepers (1984)
Finding Mary March (1988)
Fine Mess, A (1986)
Fine Weather, but Storms Due
  Towards Evening (1986)
Fire! (1977)
Fire and Ice (1983)
Fire and Ice (1987)
Fire and Passion (1988)
Fire Festival (Himatsuri) (1985)
Fire from the Mountain (1987)
Fire in the Night (1986)
Fire in the Sky, A (1978)
Fire on East Train 34 (1984)
Fire on Sight (Tir a Vue) (1984)
Fire Test (Agni Pariksha) (1951)
Fire With Fire (1986)
Fireball Forward (1972)
Fireball on the Highway (1975)
Firebrand, The (Eldfageln) (1952)
Firefighter (1986)
Firefox (1982)
Firehouse (1973)
Firehouse (1974)
Firehouse (1987)
Firestarter (1984)
Firewalker (1986)
Fireworks (1954)

Firm, The (1983)
Firm Forever, A (1984)
First Affair (1983)
First Among Equals (1987)
First & Ten (1984)
First Baby, The (1936)
First Blood (1982)
First Contact (1984)
First Deadly Sin, The (1980)
First Desires (1983)
First Family (1980)
First Front, The (1949)
First Hundred Years, The (1962)
First Legion, The (1951)
First Killing Frost, The (1987)
First Love (1959)
First Love (Ahava Rishona) (1982)
First Olympics--Athens, The (1984)
First Son (1985)
First Spaceship on Venus, The
   (1959)
First Steps (1985)
First 36 Hours of Dr. Durant,
   The (1975)
First Time, The (Goldmine) (1980)
First Time, The (1982)
First Time, Second Time (1980)
First Voyage (1980)
First You Cry (1978)
Firstborn (1984)
Fischio al Naso, Il (1966)
Fish (1977)
Fish Called Wanda, A (1988)
Fisherman's Wharf (1981)
Fist Full of Talons, A (1983)
Fist of Fear, Touch of Death
   (1980)
Fistful of Chopsticks, A (1982)
Fists in the Dark (1987)
Fit for a King (1982)
Fit to Be Untied (Matti da
   Slegare) (1981)
Fitz and Bones (1981)
Fitzcarraldo (1982)
Fitzpatricks, The (1977)
Five and the Skin (1982)
Five Corners (1987)
Five Days--Five Nights (1961)
Five Days One Summer (1982)
Five Desperate Women (1971)
$5.20 an Hour Dream, The (1980)
Five Fingers (1959)
Five Forks (Cinco Tenedores)
   (1980)
Five-Forty (1939)
500-Pound Jerk, The (1973)
Five-Legged Hare, The (1982)

Five Men with a Vendetta (1966)
Five Minutes of Paradise (1959)
Five Nerds Take Las Vegas (1987)
Five-O-One (1984)
Five of Me, The (1981)
5% Risk (1980)
Flag (Flagrante Delicto) (1988)
Flag, Class A, Grade 4, The (1977)
Flambards, The (1980)
Flame in the Streets (1961)
Flame Is Love, The (1979)
Flame Top (Tulipaa) (1981)
Flame Trees of Thika, The (1982)
Flames in the Ashes (1986)
Flaming Hearts (1986)
Flamingo Road (1980)
Flash Gordon (1953)
Flash Gordon (1979)
Flash Gordon (1980)
Flash Gordon--The Greatest Adven-
   ture of All (1983)
Flash of Green, A (1984)
Flashdance (1983)
Flashpoint (1984)
Flashpoint Africa (1978)
Flat, The (Byt) (1968)
Flatbed Annie and Sweetiepie:
   Lady Truckers (1979)
Flatbush (1979)
Flatbush/Avenue J (1976)
Flatfoots (1982)
Flavia, Priestess of Violence (1975)
Flax Field, The (1983)
Flesh and Blood (1951)
Flesh and Blood (1979)
Flesh & Blood (1985)
Flesh and Blood Show, The (1974)
Flesh and the Fiends (1960)
Flesh Eaters, The (1964)
Flesh Is Weak, The (1957)
Flesh of Your Flesh (1984)
Flesh Will Surrender (1950)
Fleshburn (1984)
Fletch (1985)
Flicks (Hollyweird/Loose Joints)
   (1987)
Fliers, The (1965)
Flies in the Light (1986)
Flight (1960)
Flight into France (1949)
Flight Level 450 (1980)
Flight #90: Disaster on the Potomac
   (1984)
Flight of the Eagle, The (1982)
Flight of the Navigator (1986)
Flight of the Raven (1984)
Flight of the Sphinx, The (1984)

Flight of the Spruce Goose (1986)
Flight of the Tertia (1953)
Flight of Whimbrels, A (1982)
Flight to Berlin (1984)
Flight to Holocaust (1977)
Flight 222 (1986)
Flight Year, The (Flugjahr, Das)
  (1982)
Flintstones Comedy Hours, The
  (1972)
Flipper (1964)
Flipside of Dominick Hyde, The
  (1980)
Flirt (1983)
Flo (1980)
Flodder (1986)
Flood (1976)
Flor de Mayo (1959)
Florence Nightingale (1985)
Florian (1940)
Florida Straits (1986)
Flourishing Times (1980)
Flower in the Raining Night, A
  (1983)
Flowers in the Attic (1987)
Flowers of Reverie (1985)
Floyd Gibbons, Reporter (1962)
Fluteman (1982)
Fly, The (1958)
Fly, The (1986)
Fly Away Home (1981)
Flyer, The (1987)
Flying (1986)
Flying Carpet, The (1956)
Flying Devils, The (1985)
Flying Doctor, The (1936)
Flying Doctors, The (1987)
Flying Dutchman, The (1957)
Flying High (1978)
Flying High (1978)
Flying Hostess (1936)
Flying Machine, The (Letaloto)
  (1981)
Flying Sorcerer, The (1975)
Flying Without Wings (1977)
Foes (1977)
Fog, The (1980)
Fog Island (1945)
Foggy Landscapes (1984)
Foley Square (1985)
Folk Tale, A (1981)
Folks and Robbers of Cardamom
  City (1988)
Follies of Barbara, The (1959)
Follies of Elodie, The (1981)
Follow a Star (1959)
Follow My Gaze (1986)

Follow That Horse (1960)
Follow the Sun (1961)
Fond Farewell to the Prince, A
  (1987)
Fond Memories (Beaux Souvenirs,
  Les) (1982)
Fontamara (1980)
Fonz and the Happy Days Gang
  (1980)
Fool for Love (1985)
Foolin' Around (1980)
Foolish Virgin (1938)
Foolish Years of the Twist, The
  (1983)
Fools (1970)
Fools, Females and Fun (1974)
Fools on the Hill, The (1986)
Foot in the Door (1983)
Footloose (1984)
Footrot Flats (1986)
Footsteps (1957)
Footsteps (1972)
For a Few Dollars Less (1966)
For a Few Dollars More (1966)
For a Thousand Dollars a Day
  (1966)
For a Young Lady and Her Male
  Companions (1984)
For All People, For All Time (1984)
For Better for Worse (1954)
For Better or Worse (1959)
For Freedom and Love (1938)
For Kayako (1985)
For Keeps (1987)
For Ladies Only (1981)
For Love and Honor (1983)
For Love ... For Magic ... (1966)
For Lovers Only (1982)
For Queen and Country (1988)
For the Love of It (1980)
For the People (1965)
For the Sake of Peace (1988)
For the Taste of Killing (1966)
For Them That Trespass (1949)
For Those I Loved (1983)
For 200 Grand, You Get Nothing
  Now (1982)
For You Only (1938)
For Your Eyes Only (1981)
For Your Heart Only (1985)
Forbidden (1985)
Forbidden Affair (1971)
Forbidden Cargo (1954)
Forbidden Christ (1951)
Forbidden Desert (1957)
Forbidden Fruit, The (1971)
Forbidden Jungle (1949)

Francis the First (1947)
Francisca (1981)
Francois Reichenbach's Japan
  (1983)
"Frank" and I (Liberated Lady)
  (1984)
Frankenstein (1931)
Frankenstein (1973)
Frankenstein Conquers the World
  (1966)
Frankenstein '88 (Vindicator, The)
  (1986)
Frankenstein 90 (1984)
Frankenstein General Hospital
  (1988)
Frankenstein: The True Story
  (1973)
Frankenstein, the Vampire and Co.
  (1962)
Frankenstein's Bloody Terror (1971)
Frankenstein's Daughter (1958)
Frankenstein's Great Aunt Tillie
  (1985)
Frank's Place (1987)
Frantic (Double Deception) (1960)
Frantic (1988)
Franza (1986)
Fraternity Vacation (1985)
Freaks (1932)
Fred and Barney Meet the Thing
  (1979)
Free Country (1978)
Freebie and the Bean (1981)
Freedom (1957)
Freedom (1982)
Freedom Fighter (1988)
Freedom Fighters (Mercenary
  Fighters) (1988)
Freedom Radio (1941)
Freedom Road (1979)
Freeway (1988)
French Atlantic Affair, The
  (1979)
French Lieutenant's Boys, The
  (1984)
French Quarter Undercover (1985)
French Touch, The (1954)
French Way, The (1952)
French Without Dressing (1965)
Frenchman's Farm (1987)
Fresh Horses (1988)
Fresno (1986)
Friday Is Not the Weekend (1981)
Friday the 13th (1980)
Friday the 13th Part 2 (1981)
Friday the 13th--Part 3 (1982)
Friday the 13th [IV]--The Final

Chapter (1984)
Friday the 13th V: A New Begin-
  ning (1985)
Friday the 13th, Part VI: Jason
  Lives (1986)
Friday the 13th Part VII--The New
  Blood (1988)
Friday the 13th ... The Orphan
  (Don't Open the Door) (1979)
Friday the 13th: The Series (1988)
Fridays of Eternity, The (1981)
Friend of a Jolly Devil, The (1987)
Friend of Vincent, A (1983)
Friend or Foe (1982)
Friendly Expression, Please (1936)
Friendly Fire (1979)
Friendly Persuasion (1975)
Friends (1978)
Friends (1979)
Friends (1988)
Friends and Enemies (1987)
Friends and Lovers (1974)
Friends for Life (1955)
Friends of Eddie Coyle, The (1973)
Friendship's Death (1987)
Friendships, Secrets and Lies
  (1979)
Fright (1972)
Fright Night (1985)
Fright Night Part 2 (1988)
Frightened Ghosts (1951)
Frightmare (1975)
Frightmare (Horror Star, The (1981)
Fringe Dwellers, The (1986)
Frisson des Vampires (Sex and the
  Vampire) (1970)
Frog Dreaming (1985)
Frog Prince, The (short) (1954)
Frogs, The (1986)
From a Bird's Eye View (1971)
From a Far Country--Pope John
  Paul II (1981)
From a Whisper to a Scream (1987)
From Beyond (1986)
From Here to Eternity (1979)
From Here to Eternity (1980)
From Hollywood to Deadwood (1988)
From Mysterious Buenos Aires (1981)
From Neither Here Nor There (1987)
From Normandie to Berlin: A War
  Remembered (1985)
From Pole to Equator (1987)
From Somalia with Love (1984)
From the Abyss (Desde el Abismo)
  (1980)
From the Hills to the Valley (1939)
From the Hip (1987)

From the Life of the Marionettes
(1980)
From Three to Sex (1972)
Front Line (1981)
Front Page Story (1954)
Front Romance, A (1984)
Frontier (De Grens) (1984)
Frontier (1986)
Frontier Circus (1961)
Frosty Paradise (1988)
Frosty Roads (1987)
Frou-Frou (1955)
Frozen Child, The (1937)
Frozen Heart, The (1980)
Frozen Leopard, The (1986)
Fruit Machine, The (1988)
Fruit Without Love (1956)
Fruits of Passion, The (1981)
Fuegos (1987)
Fugitive, The (1963)
Fugitive Family (1980)
Fugitive from the Empire (1981)
Fugitives, The (1955)
Fugitives, The (1986)
Fukusuke (Top Heavy Frog,
The) (1957)
Fulaninha (1986)
Full Circle (1977)
Full House (1976)
Full House (1983)
Futt Metal Jacket (1987)
Full Moon (Pelnia) (1980)
Full Moon (1988)
Full Moon High (1986)
Full Moon in Blue Water (1988)
Full Treatment, The (1961)
Fun (Boarding House) (1983)
Fun and Games (1980)
Fun Is Beautiful (Sacco Bello,
Un) (1980)
Funeral, The (1985)
Funeral Ceremony (1985)
Funeral Home (1982)
Funeral Racket, The (1981)
Funhouse (1981)
Funky Phantom, The (1971)
Funland (1987)
Funny Face (Sandy Duncan Show,
The) (1971)
Funny Farm, The (1983)
Funny Farm (1986)
Funny Farm (1988)
Funny Money (1983)
Funny Note (1978)
Funny World of Fred and Bunni,
The (1978)
Further Adventures of Wally

Brown, The (1980)
Further and Particular (1988)
Further Perils of Laurel & Hardy,
The (1967)
Further Up the Creek (1958)
Fury at Marrakeck (1966)
Fusion (short) (1968)
Future Cop (1976)
Future Cop (1977)
Future Cop (1985)
Future Interior, The (1984)
Future Is Woman, The (1984)
Future-Kill (1985)
Future of Emily, The (1984)
Future Schlock (1984)
Future Stars (1955)
Future War 198X (1982)
Fuzz Brothers, The (1973)

G.I. Executioner, The (Wit's End/
Dragon Lady) (1971)
G.I.'s (1980)
Gabe and Walker (1981)
Gabriela (1983)
Gabrielle (1950)
Gaby--A True Story (1987)
Gadfly, The (1956)
Gag Kings, The (1985)
Gaiety Girls (1938)
Galactic Gigolo (1988)
Galactica 1980 (1980)
Galaxina (1981)
Galaxy Express 999 (1982)
Galaxy Goofups, The (1978)
Galaxy of Terror (1981)
Gallant Little Tailor, The (short)
(1954)
Gallant Sons (1940)
Galloping Ghost, The (1931)
Galloping Major, The (1951)
Gambler, The (1980)
Gambler (1988)
Gambler III, The Legend Continues,
The (1987)
Gamblers in Okinawa (1971)
Game, The (short) (1962)
Game of Survival (Tenement) (1985)
Gamera vs. Jiger (1970)
Gamera vs. Viras (1969)
Gamera vs. Zigra (1971)
Games for School Children (1987)
Games Mother Never Taught You
(1982)
Games of Angels (1964)
Games of Artifice (1987)
Gamma People, The (1955)

Gandhi (1982)
Gang Leader (1961)
Ganga Avtaran (1935)
Ganga Malya (1953)
Ganga Maya (1984)
Gangster Chronicles, The (1981)
Gangster from Brooklyn, The
   (1966)
Gangster VIP (1969)
Gapi (1982)
Garbage Pail Kids, The (1987)
Garbagemen (1986)
Garbo Talks (1984)
Garcon! (1983)
Garconne, La (1957)
Garden of the Dead (Tomb of the
   Undead) (1972)
Gardener, The (1982)
Gardener, The (Sadovnik) (1988)
Gardens of Stone (1987)
Garfield Goes Hollywood (short)
   (1987)
Gargoyles (1972)
Garrison's Gorillas (1967)
Gary Cooper, Who Art in Heaven
   (1981)
Gas (1981)
Gasp! (1977)
Gaspard and Son (1988)
Gasping (Atemnot) (1984)
Gate, The (1987)
Gate of Youth, The (1982)
Gate of Youth--Part II, The (1978)
Gates of Flesh, The (1988)
Gates of Hell, The (1980)
Gathering, The (1977)
Gathering of Old Men, A (1987)
Gathering of Spirits, A (1985)
Gathering, Part II, The (1979)
'Gator Bait (1973)
Gaucho (1954)
Gaucho War, The (1942)
Gauguin the Savage (1980)
Gavea Girls (1987)
Gavilan (1982)
Gay Misery (1938)
Gaza Ghetto: Portrait of a
   Palestinian Family, 1948-84
   (1985)
Gazija (1981)
Geek (1987)
Geierwally (1988)
Gemini Affair--A Diary, The
   (1973)
Gemini Man (1976)
Gemini Man, The (1976)
General Delle Rovere (1959)

General Document on Chile (1986)
General Electric Theater, The (1953)
General Electric Theater (1958)
General Hospital (1963)
Generals Without Buttons (1938)
Generation (1985)
Generation Apart, A (1984)
Genesis (1986)
Genesis II (1973)
Genie, The (1953)
Genii (Devils) (1969)
Genocide (1982)
Gentle Ben (1967)
Gentle France (1986)
Gentle Julia (1936)
Gentleman, The (1986)
Gentleman Bandit, The (1981)
Gentlemen (1988)
George and Mildred (1984)
George Burns Comedy Week (1985)
George McKenna Story, The (1986)
George of the Jungle (1967)
George Stevens: A Filmmaker's
   Journey (1984)
George Washington (1984)
George Washington: The Forging
   of a Nation (1986)
Georgia (1988)
Georgia Peaches, The (1980)
Gerald McBoing Boing (1956)
Gerald McBoing Boing on the Planet
   Moo (short) (1955)
German Destiny (1936)
German Dreams (1986)
German Revolution, A (1982)
German Sisters, The (1981)
German Spring (1980)
Germany, Bitter Land (1980)
Germany, Pale Mother (1980)
Geronima (1986)
Gervaise (1956)
Get Along Gang, The (1984)
Get Christie Love! (1974)
Get Crazy (1983)
Get Outta Town (1960)
Get Smart (1965)
Getting Even (1981)
Getting Even (Hostage: Dallas)
   (1986)
Getting It On (1983)
Getting Married (1978)
Getting Over (1981)
Getting Physical (1984)
Getting There (1980)
Getting Together (1971)
Ghost, The (1963)
Ghost and Mrs. Muir, The (1968)

Ghost Busters, The (1975)
Ghost Chasers (1951)
Ghost Dance (1983)
Ghost Dancing (1983)
Ghost Festival at Saint's Village
  (1979)
Ghost Fever (1987)
Ghost from Bahia, The (1984)
Ghost Goes Gear, The (1966)
Ghost Goes West, The (1936)
Ghost Goes Wild, The (1947)
Ghost Hunter, The (1975)
Ghost in the Garden, A (1985)
Ghost in the Noonday Sun (1973)
Ghost Jesters, The (1964)
Ghost of a Chance (1980)
Ghost of a Chance (1987)
Ghost of Flight 401, The (1978)
Ghost of Love (1981)
Ghost Story (1972)
Ghost Story (1973)
Ghost Story (1981)
Ghost Town (1988)
Ghost Valley, The (1987)
Ghostbusters (1984)
Ghosts in Rome (1960)
Ghosts of Berkeley Square, The
  (1947)
Ghosts of Buxley Hall, The (1980)
Ghosts of Cape Horn (1980)
Ghosts of the Civil Dead (1988)
Ghosts That Still Walk (1978)
Ghoul, The (1933)
Ghoulies (1985)
Ghoulies II (1988)
Giant from the Unknown (1958)
Giant Gila Monster, The (1959)
Giant Iron Man 1-7--The Ariel
  Battleship (1977)
Giant of Metropolis, The (1962)
Giarres (City of Wolves) (1984)
Gibbsville (1976)
Gibralter (1939)
Gideon's Trumpet (1980)
Gidget (1965)
Gidget Gets Married (1972)
Gidget Grows Up (1969)
Gidget Makes the Wrong
  Connection (1973)
Gidget's Summer Reunion (1985)
Gift, The (1979)
Gift, The (Cadean, Le) (1982)
Gift Horse, The (1952)
Gift of Amazing Grace, The (1986)
Gift of Life, The (1982)
Gift of Life, The (1985)
Gift of Love, The (1978)

Gift of Love: A Christmas Story,
  The (1983)
Gift of Oscar, The (short) (1965)
Gift of the Fox, The (1971)
Gigantis, the Fire Monster (1959)
Gigantor (short) (1966)
Gigio (1987)
Gilligan's Island (1964)
Gilligan's Planet (1982)
Gilsodom (1986)
Gimmie a Break (1981)
Gimmie an "F" (1984)
Ginger and Fred (1985)
Ginger Meggs (1982)
Gioia Vivere, Che (1961)
Girdhar Gopal Ki Mira (1949)
Girl, The (1987)
Girl and the Oak, The (1955)
Girl Called Hatter Fox, The (1977)
Girl Cops--Counterattack of the
  Three Sisters (1988)
Girl Days of a Queen (1955)
Girl Friends, The (1955)
Girl from a Mountain Village (1949)
Girl from Bersagliere, The (1966)
Girl from India (1982)
Girl from Jungfrusund (1950)
Girl from Korfu, The (1957)
Girl from Mani, The (1986)
Girl from Millelire Street, The
  (1980)
Girl from Starship Venus, The (Diary
  of a Space Virgin) (1978)
Girl from the Chorus, A (1937)
Girl from the Dress Circle, The
  (1949)
Girl from the Salt Fields, The (1957)
Girl from U.N.C.L.E., The (1966)
Girl from Valladolid (1958)
Girl in a Swing, The (1988)
Girl in Black, The (1956)
Girl in Red, The (1986)
Girl in the Empty Grave, The
  (1977)
Girl in the Window (1961)
Girl Most Likely to ..., The (1973)
Girl Named Sooner, A (1975)
Girl of Good Family, A (1986)
Girl on the Late, Late Show, The
  (1974)
Girl on the Run (1958)
Girl Refugee, The (1938)
Girl, the Gold Watch, and Every-
  thing, The (1980)
Girl, the Gold Watch & Dynamite,
  The (1981)
Girl Thief, The (1938)

Girl Who Came Gift-Wrapped, The (1974)

Girl Who Couldn't Say No, The (1969)

Girl Who Danced into Life, The (1964)

Girl Who Spelled Freedom, The (1986)

Girl with a Sea Shell (1981)

Girl with Something Extra, The (1973)

Girl with the Golden Panties, The (1980)

Girl with the Horse, The (1982)

Girl with the Red Hair, The (1981)

Girlfriend, The (1988)

Girlfriend for David, A (1985)

Girls (Banoth) (1985)

Girls at Sea (1958)

Girls Behind Bars (1950)

Girls' Dormitory (1936)

Girls in Tails (1957)

Girls in the Office, The (1979)

Girls Just Want to Have Fun (1985)

Girl's Life, A (1983)

Girls Marked Danger (1954)

Girls of Huntington House, The (1973)

Girls of San Frediano, The (1955)

Girls of the White Orchid (1983)

Girls School Screamers (1986)

Girl's Tear, A (1981)

Giro City (1982)

Giuseppe Fava: Sicilian Like Me (1984)

Give a Dog a Bone (1966)

Give Me Five (Qua la Mano) (1980)

Give My Regards to Broad Street (1984)

Give Us This Day (Christ in Concrete) (1949)

Gladiator, The (1986)

Gladiator School (1988)

Glass Babies (1985)

Glass Heart, The (1988)

Glass Heaven, The (1988)

Glass Menagerie, The (1973)

Glass Menagerie, The (1987)

Glassful of Snow, A (1984)

Gleisdreick (1937)

Glembays, The (1988)

Glissandro (1985)

Glitter (1984)

Glitterball, The (1977)

Glitz (1988)

Global Assembly Line, The (1986)

Gloria (1980)

Gloria (1982)

Gloria Comes Home (1982)

Glorious Times in the Spessart (1967)

Glory Days (1988)

Glory of Faith (1938)

Glove, The (1978)

Gloves (1986)

Glowing Autumn (1981)

Glynis (1963)

Go and See (1985)

Go Ask Alice (1973)

Go-Between, The (1971)

Go for a Take (1972)

Go Tell It on the Mountain (1984)

Go Toward the Light (1988)

Go--U.S.A. (1975)

Go West, Young Girl (1978)

Goat, The (Chevre, La) (1982)

Gobsek (1937)

God Bless the Child (1988)

God Bless the Children (1970)

God, Man and Devil (1950)

God Told Me To (Demon) (1976)

Godchild, The (1974)

Goddess of Love, The (1988)

God's Gift (see Wend Kuuni)

Godsend, The (1980)

Godson, The (1986)

Godzilla (1985)

Godzilla, King of the Monsters (1956)

Godzilla Power Hour, The (1978)

Godzilla vs. Gigan (1972)

Godzilla vs. Hedorah (1971)

Godzilla vs. Mechagodzilla (1975)

Godzilla vs. Megalon (1973)

Godzilla vs. the Sea Monster (Ebirah) (1968)

Godzilla vs. the Smog Monster (1972)

Godzilla's Revenge (1971)

Goin' All the Way (1982)

Going Ape! (1981)

Going Bananas (1984)

Going Berserk (1983)

Going for the Gold: The Bill Johnson Story (1985)

Going My Way (1962)

Going Places (1973)

Going Sane (1986)

Going to the Chapel (1988)

Going Undercover (1988)

Goke, Body Snatcher from Hell (1969)

Gokul (Shepherd) (1947)

Gold (Or, L') (1934)

Gold and Lead (1966)

Gossip Columnist, The (1980)
Gosta Berling's Saga (1986)
Gotamah the Buddha (1956)
Gotcha (1985)
Gothic (1986)
Governor, The (1939)
Governor and J.J., The (1969)
Goya (1985)
Grace Kelly (1983)
Graduation Day (1981)
Graduation Party (1985)
Grady (1975)
Grady Nutt Show, The (1981)
Grambling's White Tiger (1981)
Gramps Is in the Resistance (1983)
Gran Fiesta, La (1987)
Grand Ceremonial, The (1968)
Grand Duel in Magic (1967)
Grand Hotel Excelsior (1982)
Grand Illusion, The (1986)
Grand Jete (short) (1968)
Grand Jury (1960)
Grand Melies, Le (1952)
Grand Olympiade, The (1961)
Grand Prix Hawk (1978)
Grand Terrace, The (1951)
Grandfather Automobile, The
   (1957)
Grandpa Goes to Washington (1978)
Grandpa Max (1975)
Granny General (1986)
Grandstand for the General Staff,
   A (1953)
Grandview, U.S.A. (1984)
Grass Eater, The (1961)
Grass Is Always Greener Over
   the Septic Tank, The (1978)
Grass Is Singing, The (1981)
Grass Recruits (1981)
Grass Widowers (1982)
Grasshopper and the Ant, The
   (short) (1954)
Grasshopper and the Ant, The
   (short) (1955)
Grave of the Vampire (1975)
Graveyard Shift (1987)
Great Adventure, The (1963)
Great Alligator, The (1981)
Great American Beauty Contest,
   The (1973)
Great American Traffic Jam, The
   (1980)
Great American Tragedy, A
   (1972)
Great Beginning, The (1940)
Great Bookie Robbery, The
   (1986)

Great Cash Giveaway Getaway, The
   (1980)
Great Citizen, The (1939)
Great Coup of the 7 Golden Men,
   The (1966)
Great Day, The (1957)
Great Day (1977)
Great Day (1983)
Great Escape II: The Untold Story,
   The (1988)
Great Expectations (1974)
Great Expectations (1982)
Great Fear, The (short) (1958)
Great Gildersleeve, The (1954)
Great Grape Ape Show, The (1977)
Great Guy at Heart, A (1981)
Great Hope, The (1954)
Great Hospital Mystery, The (1937)
Great Ice Rip-Off, The (1974)
Great Is My Country (Wide Is My
   Country (1959)
Great John Ericsson, The (1938)
Great Land of Small, The (1987)
Great Man's Whiskers, The (1973)
Great Mouse Detective, The (1986)
Great Mysteries of Hollywood, The
   (1981)
Great Niagara, The (1974)
Great Outdoors, The (1988)
Great Wall Is a Great Wall, The
   (1986)
Great Wallendas, The (1978)
Great White (1982)
Greater Promise, The (1936)
Greatest American Hero, The (1981)
Greatest Gift, The (1974)
Greatest Heroes of the Bible (1978)
Greatest Show on Earth, The (1963)
Greatest Thing That Almost Hap-
   pened, The (1977)
Greece on the March (1941)
Green Acres (1965)
Green Archer, The (1941)
Green Emperor, The (1939)
Green Eyes (1976)
Green Fields (1937)
Green, Green Grass of Home, The
   (1977)
Green, Green Grass of Home (1982)
Green Grow the Rushes (1951)
Green Hornet, The (1966)
Green Ice (1981)
Green Is the Heath (1935)
Green Mansions (1959)
Green Mare, The (1959)
Green Shadow, The (1955)
Green Years (1984)

Greenhouse (1985)
Gregorio (1985)
Gregory's Girl (1982)
Gremlins (1984)
Grendel Grendel Grendel (1981)
Grey Fox, The (1982)
Greystoke: The Legend of
   Tarzan, Lord of the Apes
   (1984)
Gridiron Flash (1935)
Gridlock (1980)
Grievous Bodily Harm (1988)
Griff (1973)
Griffin and Phoenix (1976)
Grilling, The (Garde a Vue)
   (1981)
Grimaces (1980)
Grindl (1963)
Gringalet (1959)
Gringo (1985)
Gritta of the Rat Castle (1986)
Grizzlies, The (1987)
Grizzly! (1968)
Grog (1982)
Groovie Goolies, The (1971)
Gros Bill, Le (1949)
Grotesque (1988)
Grouch, The (1987)
Ground Zero (1987)
Groundstar Conspiracy, The
   (1972)
Growing Pains (Acne '80) (1980)
Growing Pains (1984)
Growing Up (De Grande) (1988)
Grown Up Today (1986)
Gruenstein's Clever Move (1985)
Grunt! The Wrestling Movie
   (1985)
Guaguasi (1982)
Guapo del 1900, Un (1960)
Guard, The (Bekci) (1985)
Guardian Angel (1987)
Guardian of the Atom (short)
   (1968)
Guardians, The (Formynderne)
   (1980)
Guardianus of the Fog (1988)
Guelibik (1984)
Guendalina (1957)
Guepiot, Le (1981)
Guerrilla Brigade (1942)
Guerrilla from the North (1983)
Guess Who's Sleeping in My Bed?
   (1973)
Guestward Ho! (1960)
Guide for the Married Woman, A
   (1978)
Guiding Light, The (1952)

Guignolo, Le (1980)
Guilt Is My Shadow (1950)
Guilty Conscience (1985)
Guilty Melody (1936)
Guilty of Innocence: The Lennel
   Geter Story (1987)
Guilty or Innocent: The Sam
   Sheppard Murder Case (1975)
Guilty or Not Guilty (1966)
Gulag (1985)
Gulf of Biscay (1985)
Gulliver's Travels (1983)
Gulliver's Travels Beyond the
   Moon (1965)
Gumby Special, The (1957)
Gun and the Pulpit, The (1974)
Gun Crazy (Deadly Is the Female)
   (1949)
Gun in the House, A (1981)
Gun Shy (1983)
Gundam (1980)
Gunfighters, The (1987)
Gung Ho (1986)
Gungala, the Virgin of the Jungle
   (1967)
Gunman (Meu-Peun) (1983)
Gunpowder (1987)
Guns, Girls and Gangsters (1958)
Guns of Will Sonnett, The (1967)
Gunsmoke (1955)
Guru, The (1969)
Gus Brown and Midnight Brewster
   (1985)
Guy de Maupassant (1982)
Guyana: Cult of the Damned
   (1980)
Guyana Tragedy: The Story of
   Jim Jones (1980)
Gwen, or the Book of Sand (1985)
Gwendoline (1984)
Gymkata (1985)
Gypsies (1936)
Gypsy, The (1986)

H 8 (1958)
Ha-Ha (1987)
Habris (Ybris) (1984)
Hadley's Rebellion (1984)
Hagen (1980)
Hairdresser, The (1984)
Haiti Express (1983)
Haitian Corner (1988)
Half Brothers (1988)
Half Human (1955)
Half Moon Street (1986)
Half 'n' Half (1988)

Half of Life, A (1985)
Half of Love (1985)
Half of the Sky (1986)
Half-Truth (Ardh Satya) (1984)
Hall of Kings (1968)
Halloween II (1981)
Halloween III: Season of the
   Witch (1982)
Halloween 4: The Return of
   Michael Myers (1988)
Halls of Ivy, The (1954)
Ham Actors (Ripacsok) (1981)
Hambone and Hillie (1984)
Hamburger Hill (1987)
Hamburger--The Motion Picture
   (1986)
Hame'ahev (1986)
Hamlet (1970)
Hammerhead Jones (1987)
Hammett (1982)
Hamptons, The (1983)
Hamsin (1982)
Hand, The (1981)
Hand of a Dead Man (1963)
Hand of Power (1971)
Handful of Dust, A (1988)
Handful of Paradise, A (1986)
Hands of Cormac Joyce, The
   (1972)
Hands of Orlac (1960)
Hands of Steel (After the Fall of
   New York (1986)
Hands of the Ripper (1971)
Hands Up! (Rece Do Gory) (1981)
Handwritten (short) (1959)
Hangar 18 (1980)
Hanged Man, The (1964)
Hanged Man, The (1974)
Hanging by a Thread (1979)
Hanging In (1979)
Hangman (short) (1964)
Hangman's Noose (1941)
Hangmen (1987)
Hank (1965)
Hanky Panky (1982)
Hannah K. (1983)
Hanna's War (1988)
Hanoi Hilton, The (1987)
Hans, Life Before Death (1983)
Hans the Sailor (1949)
Hansel and Gretel (short) (1954)
Hansel and Gretel Get Lost in
   the Woods (1970)
Hanussen (1988)
Happeners, The (1967)
Happily Ever After (1978)
Happiness (1959)

Happiness Is a Three-Legged Dog
   (short) (1967)
Happiness Is a Warm Clue (1970)
Happiness of Three Women, The
   (1954)
Happiness Strikes Again (1986)
Happy (1983)
Happy Alcoholic, The (1984)
Happy Anniversary and Goodbye
   (1974)
Happy Birthday, Gemini (1980)
Happy Birthday (Creeps/Bloody
   Birthday) (1982)
Happy Birthday, Mama (1982)
Happy Birthday, Marilyn! (1981)
Happy Birthday to Me (1981)
Happy Days (1937)
Happy Days (1970)
Happy Days (1974)
Happy Din Don (1986)
Happy Easter (1984)
Happy End (short) (1958)
Happy End (1988)
Happy Endings (1983)
Happy Ghost II, The (1985)
Happy Homecoming, Comrade (1986)
Happy Hour (1987)
Happy New Year (1985)
Happy New Year (1987)
Happy New Year--1949 (1986)
Happy Old Year (1988)
Happy Valley, The (1986)
Harbor Command (1957)
Harbor Lights (1963)
Hard Asphalt (1986)
Hard Choices (1984)
Hard Country (1981)
Hard Feelings (1982)
Hard Game (1986)
Hard Knocks (1981)
Hard Knox (1984)
Hard Ticket to Hawaii (1987)
Hard Times (1988)
Hard to Hold (1984)
Hard Traveling (1985)
Hardbodies 2 (1986)
Hardcase (1972)
Hardcase (1981)
Hardcastle and McCormick (1983)
Hardesty House (1986)
Hardhat and Legs (1980)
Hardly Working (1981)
Hardy Boys, The (1969)
Hardy Boys Mysteries, The (1977)
Harem (1968)
Harem (1985)

Heartbeat (1939)
Heartbeat (1988)
Heartbeat 100 (1987)
Heartbeeps (1981)
Heartbreak Hotel (1988)
Heartbreak Ridge (1986)
Heartbreak Yakuza, The (1987)
Heartbreakers, The (1983)
Heartbreakers (1984)
Heartburn (1986)
Heartland (1980)
Hearts and Guts (1982)
Hearts of Fire (1987)
Heat (1987)
Heat and Dust (1983)
Heat and Sunlight (1987)
Heat Line, The (1988)
Heated Vengeance (1985)
Heathcliff and Dingbat Show, The
  (1980)
Heatwave! (1974)
Heatwave (1981)
Heaven (1987)
Heaven and Hell (1988)
Heaven Can Wait (1961)
Heaven Earth Man (1984)
Heaven Help Us (1985)
Heaven on Earth (1981)
Heaven on Earth (1979)
Heaven on Earth (1988)
Heaven over the Marshes (1949)
Heaven Without Love (1959)
Heavenly Hosts (1983)
Heavenly Kid, The (1985)
Heavenly Pursuits (1986)
Heaven's Gate (1980)
Heavy Metal (1981)
Hec Ramsey (1972)
Hecate (1982)
Heck's Angels (1976)
Hectic Days (1935)
Hector (1984)
Hector (1988)
Heels Go to Hell (1956)
Heidi (1968)
Heidi's Song (1982)
Heinrich Heine Revue (1980)
Heinrich Penthesilea von Kleist
  (1983)
Heiress, The (1961)
Heist, The (1972)
Held for Questioning (1983)
Helen and Fernanda (1970)
Helen Keller in Her Own Story
  (Unconquered, The) (1954)
Helen Keller--The Miracle
  Continues (1984)

Hell Comes to Frogtown (1988)
Hell in the City (1959)
Hell Island (1977)
Hell Night (1981)
Hell on Earth (1934)
Hell Riders (1983)
Hell Squad (1983)
Hell Town (1985)
Hell Train (1984)
Hellbound: Hellraiser II (1988)
Hellfire (1986)
Hellhole (1985)
Hellinger's Law (1980)
Hellish Love (1949)
Hello Again (1987)
Hello, Cane Stick (1982)
Hello, Larry (1979)
Hello Mary Lou: Prom Night II
  (1987)
Hello, Taxi (1983)
Hellraiser (1987)
Hell's Kitchen (1952)
Hell's Kitchen (Kiez) (1983)
Help! I'm an Heir! (1937)
Help! It's the Hair Bear Bunch
  (1971)
Help Me Dream (1981)
Help, My Snowman Is Burning Down
  (short) (1964)
Help Wanted: Kids (1986)
Help Wanted: Male (1982)
Helsinki Napoli All Night Long (1988)
Helter Skelter (1976)
Helter-Skelter (1984)
Hemingway (1988)
Hen With the Wrong Chick, The
  (short) (1965)
Henderson Monster, The (1980)
Hennesey (1959)
Henri (1986)
Henry's Back Room (1982)
Her Life as a Man (1984)
Her Melody (1942)
Her Name Is Lisa (1987)
Her Name Is Vasfiye (1986)
Her Panelled Door (1951)
Her Secret Life (1987)
Herbie Goes Bananas (1980)
Herbie, the Love Bug (1982)
Hercule (1938)
Hercules (1983)
Hercules Against Rome (1964)
Hercules Against the Haunted World
  (1961)
Hercules Against the Moon Men
  (1964)
Hercules Against the Sun (1964)

His Daughter Is Peter (1936)
His Double Life (1933)
His Excellency (1952)
His Hand Slipped (1952)
His Last 12 Hours (1953)
His Master's Eye (Oeil du Maitre,
  L') (1980)
His Official Wife (1936)
His Royal Highness (1954)
Histories Extraordinaries (1950)
History (1986)
History of the World--Part 1
  (1981)
History of Wind, A (1988)
Hit, The (1984)
Hit and Run (1982)
Hit and Run (1985)
Hit Lady (1974)
Hitch in Time, A (1978)
Hitched (1973)
Hitcher, The (1986)
Hitchhike! (1974)
Hitchhiker, The (1983)
Hitlerjunge Quex (1934)
Hizzoner (1979)
Hoax (1936)
Hobo's Christmas, A (1987)
Hobson's Choice (1983)
Hockey Fever (1983)
Hodja from Pjort (1985)
Hogan's Heroes (1965)
Hokum (1936)
Holcroft Covenant, The (1985)
Hold the Dream (1986)
Hold-Up (1985)
Hole, The (Dupkata) (1967)
Hole in the Wall, The (1982)
Holes in the Soup (1988)
Holiday Australia (1987)
Holidays in the Snow (1966)
Hollow Image (1979)
Hollow Triumph (Scar, The)
  (1948)
Holloway's Daughters (1966)
Holly and the Ivy, The (1954)
Hollywood (1980)
Hollywood and the Stars (1961)
Hollywood Chainsaw Hookers
  (1988)
Hollywood Cop (1988)
Hollywood Harry (1985)
Hollywood High Part II (1981)
Hollywood Hot Tubs (1984)
Hollywood Shuffle (1987)
Hollywood: The Golden Years
  (1961)
Hollywood Vice Squad (1986)

Hollywood Wives (1985)
Holmes and Yoyo (1976)
Holocaust (1978)
Holy Heritage (1957)
Holy Innocents, The (1984)
Holy Island, The (1959)
Holy Nun, The (1949)
Holy Robe of the Shaolin Temple,
  The (1985)
Holy Terror, The (1937)
Home (1987)
Home and Away (1988)
Home and the World, The (Ghare
  Baire) (1984)
Home at Hong Kong (1983)
Home Country, USA (1968)
Home for Gentle Souls, A (1981)
Home for the Holidays (1972)
Home Free (1988)
Home Free All (1983)
Home from the Sea (1973)
Home Front, The (1980)
Home in My Heart (1971)
Home Is Where the Hart Is (1987)
Home of Our Own, A (1975)
Home Remedy (Xero) (1987)
Home Room (1981)
Home Sweet Homeless (1988)
Home to Stay (1978)
Homeboy (1988)
Homecoming, The (1971)
Homecoming (1984)
Homecoming Song (1983)
Homeland (1984)
Homeland Fever (Shigaon Shel
  Moledeth) (1980)
Hometown (1985)
Homeward Bound (1980)
Homework (Growing Pains) (1979)
Homme a tout Faire, L' (1980)
Homo Sapiens (short) (1959)
Hondo (1967)
Honest, Decent and True (1985)
Honestly, Celeste! (1954)
Honey West (1965)
Honeyboy (1982)
Honeybunch (1988)
Honeymoon (1983)
Honeymoon (1985)
Honeymoon Suite (1972)
Honeymoon with a Stranger (1969)
Hong Kong (1960)
Hong Kong Graffiti (1985)
Hong Kong, Hong Kong (1983)
Hong Kong Phooey (1974)
Hong Kong Playboys (1983)
Honky Tonk (1974)

Honky Tonk Freeway (1981)
Honkytonk Man (1982)
Honor, Profit and Pleasure (1985)
Honor Thy Father (1973)
Hookers on Davie Street (1984)
Hooperman (1987)
Hooray Brazil (1982)
Hoosiers (1986)
Hoover vs. the Kennedys: The Second Civil War (1987)
Hope and Glory (1987)
Hoppla, Now Comes Eddie (1959)
Hopscotch (1980)
Hopscotch (Pisingana) (1985)
Horatio I.P.I. (1983)
Hordubal (1980)
Horizon, The (1984)
Horoscope of the Hesselbach Family (1956)
Horrible Dr. Hitchcock, The (1962)
Horror at 37,000 Feet, The (1973)
Horror Castle (Virgin of Nuremberg) (1963)
Horror Hospital (1975)
Horror Hotel (1963)
Horror of Dracula (1958)
Horror of Party Beach (1963)
Horror of the Blood Monsters (Creatures of the Prehistoric Planet) (1970)
Horror of the Zombies (1976)
Horror on Snape Island (1971)
Horror Planet (Inseminoid) (1982)
Horror Vacui (1984)
Horrors of the Black Museum (1959)
Horse, The (1982)
Horse Boy, The (1957)
Horse of Pride (1980)
Horse With the Flying Tail, The (1961)
Horseman, The (1951)
Horseman Riding By, A (1982)
Horsemen of the Storm, The (1984)
Horses in Winter (1988)
Horse's Mouth, The (Oracle, The) (1953)
Hospital Massacre (1980)
Hostage (1988)
Hostage Flight (1985)
Hostage Heart, The (1977)
Hostage--The Christine Maresch Story (1983)
Hostage Tower, The (1980)

Hot and Deadly (Retrievers, The) (1981)
Hot Blood (1936)
Hot Child in the City (1987)
Hot Dog Gang (1958)
Hot Dog--The Movie (1984)
Hot Dreams (Free Love) (1974)
Hot L Baltimore (1975)
Hot Little Girl, The (1971)
Hot Men Observed (1984)
Hot Moves (1984)
Hot Paint (1988)
Hot Potato (Patata Bollente, La) (1980)
Hot Pursuit (1984)
Hot Pursuit (1987)
Hot Resort (1985)
Hot Rod (1979)
Hot Shots (1986)
Hot Spot (I Wake Up Screaming) (1941)
Hot Summer in Kabul, A (1983)
Hot Target (1985)
Hot to Trot (1988)
Hot Touch (1982)
Hot W.A.C.S. (1981)
Hot Water (1937)
Hot Water (1985)
Hot Wheels (1969)
Hotel (1983)
Hotel Adlon (1955)
Hotel Central (1983)
Hotel Colonial (1987)
Hotel de Paree (1959)
Hotel du Nord (1939)
Hotel du Paradis (1987)
Hotel Kikelet (1937)
Hotel New York (1984)
Hotel of the Americas (1982)
Hotel Polan and Its Guests (1982)
Hotel Sahara (1951)
Hotel St. Pauli (1988)
Hotline (1982)
Hotshot (1987)
Houndcats, The (1972)
Hounds ... of Notre Dame, The (1980)
Hour of the Assassin (License to Kill) (1987)
Hour of the Wolf (1968)
Hours of Wedlock, The (1987)
House, The (1983)
House (1986)
House Across the Bay, The (1940)
House Arrest (1982)
House by the Lake, The (1977)
House by the Railway Tracks, The (1988)

House by the River, The (1950)
House by the Sea, The (1980)
House Calls (1979)
House Committee Rivalry (1986)
House for Swap (1985)
House for Two, A (1988)
House in Nightmare Park (1973)
House in the Park (1983)
House of Bamboo (1955)
House of Dark Shadows, The
   (1970)
House of Darkness, The (1948)
House of Death (Pee-Mak) (1981)
House of Evil (1968)
House of Fright (1961)
House of Games (1987)
House of Glass (1982)
House of Gloom (1986)
House of Greed (1934)
House of Jade (1988)
House of Life (1953)
House of Science (short) (1962)
House of Secrets (1956)
House of Terror (1976)
House of the Long Shadows (1983)
House of the Maltese (1938)
House of the Sleeping Virgins,
   The (1969)
House of the Yellow Carpet (1983)
House of Water, The (1984)
House of Whipcord (1974)
House on Bare Mountain, The
   (1962)
House on Carroll Street, The
   (1988)
House on Fire (1987)
House on Garibaldi Street, The
   (1979)
House on Greenapple Road, The
   (1970)
House on Sorority Row, The
   (1983)
House on the Edge of the Park,
   The (1985)
House on the Moon, The (1963)
House on the River, The (1986)
House Outside the Cemetery,
   The (1981)
House Poised on the Edge, A
   (1986)
House That Screamed, The (1970)
House That Vanished, The (1974)
House That Wouldn't Die, The
   (1970)
House II: The Second Story
   (1987)
House Where Death Lives, The

(Delusion) (1980)
House Where Evil Dwells, The
   (1982)
Houseboat No. 70 (1982)
Housekeeping (1987)
Housemaid, Highly Presentable,
   Seeks Job (1951)
Housewarming, The (Grihapravesh)
   (1980)
Housewarming, The (1984)
Houston Knights (1987)
Houston: The Legend of Texas
   (1986)
Houston, We've Got a Problem
   (1974)
How Awful About Allan (1970)
How Chileans   Love (1984)
How Do I Kill a Thief--Let Me
   Count the Ways (1982)
How I Spent My Summer Vacation
   (Deadly Roulette) (1967)
How the Grinch Stole Christmas
   (short) (1966)
How the West Was Won (1977)
How to Break Up a Happy Divorce
   (1976)
How to Furnish a Flat (short)
   (1960)
How to Make a Doll (1967)
How to Make a Monster (1958)
How to Pick Up Girls! (1978)
How to Steal an Airplane (Only
   One Day Left Before Tomorrow)
   (1968)
How to Steal the Crown of England
   (Argoman Superdiabolico) (1966)
How We Stole the Atomic Bomb
   (1967)
How Young We Were Then (1986)
Howard the Duck (1986)
Howard's Way (1985)
Howdy Doody (1947)
Howling, The (1981)
Howling IV ... The Original Night-
   mare (1988)
Howling in the Woods, A (1971)
Howling II ... Your Sister Is a
   Werewolf, The (1984)
Hoxsey: The Quack Who Cured
   Cancer (1987)
Hoyt Axton Show, The (1981)
Huckleberry Finn (1975)
Huey Long (1985)
Human Cargo (1936)
Human Experiments (1980)
Human Feelings (1978)
Human Jungle, The (1964)

Human Lanterns (1982)
Human Monster, The (Dark Eyes of London) (1939)
Human Target (1971)
Human Vapor, The (1964)
Humanoids of the Deep (1980)
Humongous (1982)
Hunchback of Notre Dame, The (1978)
Hunchback of Notre Dame, The (1982)
Hundra (1984)
Hunger, The (1983)
Hunger (1986)
Hunger Canal (1964)
Hunger Years (1980)
Hungry Wives (1972)
Hunk (1987)
Hunted (1952)
Hunted Lady, The (1977)
Hunter, The (1952)
Hunter (1971)
Hunter (1973)
Hunter (1977)
Hunter, The (1980)
Hunter of Fall (1936)
Hunter of the Heart (1984)
Hunters Are for Killing (1970)
Hunter's Blood (1987)
Hunter's Moon (1979)
Hunters of the Golden Cobra (1984)
Hunters of the Reef (1978)
Hunting Ground (1982)
Hunting Time (1988)
Hurrah for Adventure (1970)
Hurricane (1974)
Hurry, He's Coming! (1988)
Husband and Wife (1952)
Husbands, Wives and Lovers (1978)
Husbands, Wives, Lovers (1988)
Hussy (1980)
Hussy, The (Effrontee, L') (1985)
Hustle (1975)
Hustler of Muscle Beach, The (1980)
Hustlers (1984)
Hustling (1975)
Husty (1984)
Hyena of London, The (1964)
Hyper Sapien: People from Another Star (1986)
Hypnos (1971)
Hypnosis (1962)
Hypnotic Eye, The (1960)

I, a Sinner (1960)
I Accuse (1939)
I Am a Fugitive from a Chain Gang (1932)
I Am Longing for You (1936)
I Am Maria (1980)
I Am Not Afraid Anymore (1985)
I Am the Cheese (1983)
I Am the Greatest: The Adventures of Muhammad Ali (1977)
I and My Wife (1953)
I and You (1954)
I As in Icarus (1980)
I Chose Love (1953)
I, Claudius (1979)
I Confess (1981)
I Cover Times Square (1950)
I, Desire (1982)
I Dismember Mama (Poor Albert and Little Annie) (1972)
I Do (1983)
I Do 'em In (1987)
I Don't Love War, I Love Love (1966)
I Don't Want to Be Grown-Up (1984)
I Dream of Jeannie (1965)
I Dream of Jeannie: 15 Years Later (1985)
I Dreamed of My Elk (1987)
I Drink Your Blood (1971)
I Eat Your Skin (1974)
I Gave at the Office (1984)
I Go to Tokyo (1986)
I Had Three Wives (1985)
I Hate Actors (1986)
I Hate Blondes (1981)
I Hear the Whistle (1971)
I Heard the Owl Call My Name (1973)
I Know That You Know That I Know (1982)
I Know Why the Caged Bird Sings (1979)
I Like Her (1985)
I Like Mike (Surprise Party) (1961)
I Live, But ... (1985)
I Love a Mystery (1973)
I Love Dollars (1986)
I Love N.Y. (1987)
I Love You (Eu te Amo) (1981)
I Love You (Je Vous Aime) (1981)
I Love You (1987)
I Love You, Goodbye (1974)
I Love, You Love (1961)
I Love You Only (1936)

I Made a Splash (1981)
I-Man (1986)
I Married a Dead Man (1983)
I Married a Spy (1938)
I Married a Vampire (1986)
I Married Dora (1987)
I Married Wyatt Earp (1983)
I, Monster (1972)
I Need a Moustache (1986)
I Only Arsked (1958)
I Ought to Be in Pictures (1982)
I Own the Racecourse (1986)
I Passed for White (1960)
I Remember Mama (1949)
I Saw What You Did (1988)
I Sent a Letter to My Love
  (Chere Inconnue) (1980)
I Shall Always Stand Guard
  (1984)
I Spy (1956)
I Spy (1965)
I Take These Men (1983)
I, the Executioner (1987)
I, the Jury (1982)
I Told You So (1984)
I Want to Keep My Baby (1976)
I Want to Live (1982)
I Want to Live! (1983)
I Want to Live with Joy (1938)
I Was a Mail Order Bride (1982)
I Was a Prisoner in Siberia
  (1952)
I Was a Teenage Zombie (1987)
I Was an Adventuress (1939)
I Was Born in Buenos Aires
  (1959)
I Was Caught in the Night (1986)
I Will Fight No More Forever
  (1975)
I Will Give a Million (1937)
Ice Birds (Isfugle) (1983)
Ice Palace, The (1988)
Ice Pirates, The (1984)
Icebreaker (1988)
Iceman (1984)
Ichabod and Me (1961)
I'd Rather Be Calm (1982)
Idea, The (short) (1934)
Ideal Husband, An (1937)
Ideal Landscape (1986)
Ideal Woman, The (1959)
Ideal Woman Sought (1952)
Idiots May Apply (1986)
Idle on Parade (1959)
Idol (1985)
If All the Women in the World
  (Operation Paradise) (1966)

If I Had Seven Daughters (1955)
If I Love You, Am I Trapped For-
  ever? (1974)
If I Were for Real (1983)
If It's a Man, Hang Up (1975)
If Looks Could Kill (1987)
If the Sun Never Returned (1987)
If Things Were Different (1980)
If Tomorrow Comes (1971)
If Tomorrow Comes (1986)
If Versailles Were Told to Me (see
  Royal Affair in Versailles--1954)
If War Comes Tomorrow (1938)
If You Could See What I Hear
  (1982)
If You Know What I Mean (1983)
If Youth Only Knew (1947)
If Your Heart Can Feel (1980)
Igman March, The (1983)
Igor and the Lunatics (1985)
Iguana (1988)
Ike (1979)
Ikiru (1957)
I'll Be Home for Christmas (1988)
I'll Carry You on My Hands (1959)
I'll Get You (1953)
I'll Love You Tomorrow (1980)
I'll Never Forget What's Her Name
  (1976)
I'll Take Manhattan (1987)
Illegally Yours (1988)
Illusion (1980)
Illusion of Blood (1966)
Illusionist, The (1983)
Illusions (1983)
Illusive Summer of '68, The (1984)
Illustrious Energy (1988)
I'm a Big Girl Now (1980)
I'm All Right Jack (1959)
I'm Blushing (1981)
I'm Dancing as Fast as I Can (1982)
I'm Dickens ... He's Fenster (1962)
I'm Getting a Yacht (1981)
I'm Going to Be Famous (1983)
I'm Gonna Git You Sucka (1988)
I'm in a Crisis! (1982)
I'm Not Living With You Anymore
  (1983)
I'm Photogenic (1980)
I'm the Girl He Wants to Kill (1974)
I'm the Law (1953)
Image of Dorian Gray in the Yellow
  Press, The (1984)
Imagemaker, The (1986)
Images of an Everyday War (1986)
Images of Indians (1980)
Imaginary Friends (1987)

Imagination (short) (1943)
Immacolata and Concetta: The
    Other Jealousy (1980)
Immediate Disaster (1954)
Immigrants, The (1978)
Immoral Mr. Teas, The (1960)
Immortal, The (1969)
Immortal Garrison, The (1957)
Immortelle, L' (1962)
Impatient Heart, The (1960)
Impatient Heart, The (1971)
Imperative (1982)
Imperial Japanese Empire, The
    (1982)
Imperial Navy (Great Fleet, The)
    (1982)
Impossible on Saturday (1964)
Impossible Spy, The (1987)
Imposter, The (1955)
Imposter, The (1974)
Imposter, The (1984)
Imprint of Giants, The (1980)
Improper Channels (1981)
Imprudent Lover, The (1982)
Impulse (1984)
Impure Thoughts (1986)
In a Glass Cage (1986)
In a Shallow Grave (1988)
In an Old Manor House (1987)
In Between (1987)
In Blood and Sand (1988)
In Broad Daylight (1971)
In Broad Daylight (1981)
In Crowd, The (1988)
In Dangerous Company (1988)
In God We Trust (1980)
In Heaven All Hell Is Breaking
    Loose (1985)
In Her Own Time (1985)
In Just the Wink of an Eye
    (1982)
In Love and War (1987)
In Love, But Doubly (1960)
In Love With an Older Woman
    (1982)
In My Life (Honningmane) (1980)
In 'n' Out (Gringo Mojado) (1986)
In Name Only (1969)
In Olden Days (1952)
In Retirement (1987)
In Search of ... (1976)
In Search of America (1971)
In Search of Famine (1981)
In Search of Historic Jesus (1980)
In Search of the Trojan War (1986)
In Security (1982)
In Self Defense (1987)

In September (1982)
In Soldier's Uniform (1957)
In Tandem (1974)
In the Beginning (1978)
In the Custody of Strangers (1982)
In the Dead of Night (1969)
In the Devil's Garden (1974)
In the Far East (1937)
In the Glitter Palace (1977)
In the Heart of the Hurricane
    (1980)
In the Heat of the Night (1988)
In the King of Prussia (1982)
In the Land of My Parents (1982)
In the Last Resort (1987)
In the Line of Duty: The F.B.I.
    Murders (1988)
In the Lion's Den (1987)
In the Lost City of Sarzana (1980)
In the Matter of Karen Ann Quinlan
    (1977)
In the Middle of the Night (1984)
In the Mood (Woo Woo Kid, The)
    (1987)
In the Name of God (1987)
In the Name of the Law (1986)
In the Name of the People (1987)
In the Name of the Son (1987)
In the Nick (1960)
In the Pope's Eye (1981)
In the Shadow of Fear (1988)
In the Shadow of Kilimanjaro (1986)
In the Shadow of the Raven (1988)
In the Shadow of the Wind (1987)
In the Shadow of Vesuvius (1987)
In the Shadow of Victory (1986)
In the Shite City (1983)
In the Year of the Ape (1983)
In This House of Brede (1975)
In Trouble (1981)
Inch High, Private Eye (1973)
Inchon (1981)
Incident at Crestridge (1981)
Incident at Raven's Gate (1988)
Incident in San Francisco (1971)
Incident of the Half-Meter, The
    (1983)
Incident on a Dark Street (1973)
Incinerator, The (1984)
Incognito (1937)
Incomplete Eclipse (1983)
Incredible Hulk, The (1978)
Incredible Hulk Returns, The
    (1988)
Incredible Ida Early, The (1987)
Incredible Invasion, The (1971)
Incredible Journey of Dr. Meg

Israel (short) (1960)
Issa's Valley (1983)
Issue de Secours (1988)
Istanbul Express (1968)
Istvan Bors (1939)
It All Depends on Girls (1980)
It Came from Outer Space (1953)
It Came Upon a Midnight Clear
    (1984)
It Can't Happen to Me (1979)
It Can't Be Winter, We Haven't
    Had Summer Yet (1981)
It Conquered the World (1956)
It Couldn't Happen to a Nicer
    Guy (1974)
It Goes Better with Raspberry
    Juice (1960)
It Happened at Lake Wood Manor
    (1977)
It Happened Here (1966)
It Happened on the 36 Candles
    (1957)
It Happened One Christmas (1977)
It Happens in Spain (1958)
It Is Cold in Brandenburg--Kill
    Hitler (1981)
It Only Happens to Me (1985)
It Takes a Thief (1963)
It Takes Two (1982)
It Takes Two (1988)
It Was Not in Vain (1957)
Italian Fast Food (1986)
Italian Journey--Love Included
    (1958)
Italian Night (1987)
Italian Postcards (1987)
Italians, The (1985)
Itinerary of a Spoiled Child (1988)
It'll Happen Tomorrow (1988)
It's a Dog's World (1967)
It's a Great Life (1954)
It's a Living (1980)
It's a Long and Difficult Summer,
    But ... What a Night, My
    Dears (1966)
It's a Man's World (1962)
It's a World Full of Children
    (1980)
It's About Time (1966)
It's Alive III: Island of the Alive
    (1987)
It's Always Jan (1955)
It's Gary Shandling's Show (1986)
It's Good to Be Alive (1974)
It's Great to Be Young (1956)
It's Handy When People Don't
    Die (1981)

It's My Life (Noa Noa 2, El) (1986)
It's My Turn (1980)
It's Nice to Meet You (Muito
    Prazer) (1982)
It's Not Easy (1983)
It's Not Me, It's Him (1980)
It's the Girl in the Red Truck,
    Charlie Brown (1988)
It's the Paris Life (1954)
Itto (1935)
Ivan the Terrible (1976)
Ivanhoe (1957)
Ivanhoe (1982)
I've Heard the Mermaids Singing
    (1987)
I've Lost My Husband (1937)
I've Made a Love Match (1938)
I've Never Stolen in My Life (1939)
Ivory Ape, The (1980)

J. Edgar Hoover (1987)
JFK Years--A Political Trajectory,
    The (1980)
J. O. E. and the Colonel (1985)
Jabberjaw (1976)
Jack (1978)
Jack and Mike (1986)
Jack and the Beanstalk (short)
    (1954)
Jack and the Witch (1967)
Jack of Spades (1984)
Jack Simpson (1988)
Jack the Ripper (1959)
Jack the Ripper (1974)
Jack the Ripper (1988)
Jackals (1986)
Jack's Back (1988)
Jackson Five, The (1971)
Jacob Behind the Blue Door (1988)
Jacobo Timerman: Prisoner Without
    a Name, Cell Without a Number
    (1983)
Jacqueline Bouvier Kennedy (1981)
Jacqueline Susann's Valley of the
    Dolls 1981 (1981)
Jacques and November (1985)
Jacques Costeau: The First 75
    Years (1985)
Jacques Mesrine (1984)
Jade Love (1985)
Jade Mask, The (1945)
Jadu Tona (1977)
Jagan Mohini (1978)
Jagged Edge (1985)
Jagger & Spaghetti--The Supper
    Bluffers (1984)

Jumping for Joy (1956)
Jungle, The (1952)
Jungle Captive (1945)
Jungle Cavalcade (1941)
Jungle Girl (1941)
Jungle Jim (1955)
Jungle of Chang (1951)
Jungle Princess, The (1936)
Jungle Raiders (1986)
Jungle Saga, The (1958)
Jungle Warriors (1983)
Junior Miss (1957)
Jupiter (1952)
Jupiter Menace, The (1981)
Just a Big, Simple Girl (1949)
Just a Game (1983)
Just a Little Inconvenience (1977)
Just an Old Sweet Song (1976)
Just Ask for Diamond (1988)
Just Before Dawn (1981)
Just Between Friends (1986)
Just Forget It (1988)
Just Friends (1979)
Just in Time (1988)
Just Married (1985)
Just Me and You (1978)
Just My Luck (1957)
Just Once More (1983)
Just One of the Guys (1985)
Just Our Luck (1983)
Just Tell Me What You Want (1980)
Just the Way You Are (1984)
Just Whistle a Little (1981)
Justin Case (1988)
Juvi (1987)

K. u. K. (1984)
Kabuliwala (1957)
Kadaicha (1988)
Kaddish (1984)
Kadoyng (1972)
Kaidan Botan Doro (1968)
Kaiser and One Night (1985)
Kaj Munk (1986)
Kalamazoo (1988)
Kaleidoscope (Challchitra) (1981)
Kaliyugaya (1982)
Kallikaks, The (1977)
Kamikaze (1982)
Kamikaze (1986)
Kamikaze Cop, A (1970)
Kamikaze Cop, Marihuana Syndicate (1971)
Kamikaze Cop, No Epitaph to Us (1971)
Kamikaze Cop, The Poison Gas Affair (1971)

Kamikaze Hearts (1986)
Kamikaze, the Adventurer (1982)
Kamilla and the Thief (1988)
Kaminsky (1985)
Kandyland (1988)
Kane and Abel (1985)
Kangaroo (1986)
Kangaroo Complex, The (1986)
Kangaroos in the Kitchen (1982)
Kanikosen (1957)
Kansas (1988)
Kansas City Massacre, The (1975)
Kapax: The Man from the Amazon (1987)
Karamoja (1954)
Karate Kid, The (1984)
Karate Kid Part II, The (1986)
Karate Lady in Danger (1975)
Karen (1964)
Karen (1975)
Kargus (1981)
Karkalou (1984)
Karla's Marriages (1981)
Karma (1988)
Karnal (1984)
Karsh: The Searching Eye (1986)
Kaseki (1976)
Kasturi (1978)
Kate and Allie (1984)
Kate Bliss and the Ticker Tape Kid (1978)
Kate Loves a Mystery (1979)
Kate McShane (1975)
Katia (1938)
Katie: Portrait of a Centerfold (1978)
Katinka (1988)
Katrina (1949)
Katzensteg, Der (1938)
Kaz (1978)
Keefer (1978)
Keegans, The (1976)
Keep, The (1983)
Keep On Truckin' (1975)
Keep Smiling, Baby! (1986)
Keep Up Your Right (1987)
Keeper of the Wild (1977)
Keepers of the Night (Night Watch) (1953)
Keeping Track (1987)
Keeping Up with the Joneses (1984)
Kellers Hof--Portrait of a German Farmer (1982)
Kelley (1981)
Kelly's Kids (1974)
Kemira: Diary of a Strike (1984)
Kennedy (1983)

Kenny Rogers as the Gambler--
   The Adventure Continues (1983)
Kent State (1980)
Kentucky Jones (1964)
Kentucky Woman (1983)
Kermesse Heroique, La (1935)
Key, The (Chiave, La) (1983)
Key Exchange (1985)
Key to Rebecca, The (1985)
Key Tortuga (1981)
Key West (1973)
Khan! (1975)
Khan Asparukh (1981)
Khandar (1984)
Kickapoo Juice (short) (1945)
Kid, The (Mome, Le) (1986)
Kid Brother, The (1987)
Kid from Left Field, The (1979)
Kid from Nowhere, The (1982)
Kid Power (1972)
Kid Who Couldn't Miss, The
   (1983)
Kid Who Wouldn't Quit/The Brad
   Silverman Story, The (1987)
Kid with the Broken Halo, The
   (1982)
Kid with the 200 I.Q., The
   (1983)
Kidd Video (1984)
Kidnapped (1987)
Kidnapping, The (1982)
Kidnapping, The (Rapt, Le)
   (1984)
Kidnapping Blues (1982)
Kidnapping of the President, The
   (1980)
Kids from C.A.P.E.R., The
   (1976)
Kids from the South Side, The
   (1985)
Kids Like These (1987)
Kifaru (1970)
Kill! (1969)
Kill and Kill Again (1981)
Kill Johnny Ringo (1966)
Kill Me If You Can (1977)
Kill or Be Killed (1966)
Kill or Die (1987)
Kill Squad (1982)
Kill the Referee (1984)
Kill the Shogun (1981)
Kill to Love (1981)
Kill Zone (1985)
Killdozer (1974)
Killer, The (1971)
Killer, The (1983)
Killer Bees (1974)

Killer by Night (1972)
Killer in Every Corner, A (1974)
Killer in the Family, A (1983)
Killer in the Mirror (1986)
Killer Instinct (1988)
Killer Klowns from Outer Space
   (1988)
Killer on Board (1977)
Killer Party (1986)
Killer Shrews, The (1959)
Killer Who Wouldn't Die, The (1976)
Killer With Two Faces, The (1974)
Killer Workout (Aerobicide) (1987)
Killers, The (Kilas, O Mau da Fita)
   (1980)
Killers, The (1984)
Killers Are Challenged (1965)
Killer's Moon (1978)
Killers of Kilimanjaro (1960)
Killin' Cousin, The (1980)
Killing Affair, A (1977)
Killing Affair, A (1988)
Killing Auntie (1985)
Killing at Hell's Gate (1981)
Killing Blows (1975)
Killing Cars (1986)
Killing 'em Softly (1985)
Killing Fields, The (1984)
Killing Game, The (1975)
Killing Hour, The (Clairvoyant,
   The) (1981)
Killing Machine, The (1986)
Killing of America, The (1982)
Killing of Angel Street, The (1981)
Killing of Randy Webster, The
   (1980)
Killing Stone (1978)
Killing Time, The (1987)
Killpoint (1984)
Kim (1984)
Kimiko (1937)
Kincaid (1963)
Kind-Hearted Ant, The (short)
   (1965)
Kind of English, A (1986)
Kind Stepmother (1936)
Kindred, The (1987)
King (1978)
King and His Fool, The (1981)
King and His Movie, A (1986)
King and the Mockingbird, The
   (1979)
King August the Strong (1937)
King Blank (1983)
King Crab (1980)
King David (1985)
King Dinosaur (1955)

Krabat (Sorcerer's Apprentice, The)
 (1982)
Krakatit (1951)
Krammer, The (1959)
Kreimhild's Revenge (re-issue)
 (1965)
Kreutzer Sonata (1938)
Kreutzer Sonata, The (1987)
Krik? Krak! Tales of a Night-
 mare (1988)
Krull (1983)
Kudzu (1983)
Kuei-Mei, A Woman (1986)
Kukan (1941)
Kukla, Fran and Ollie (1948)
Kukurantumi--The Road to Accra
 (1983)
Kulicka (1963)
Kun Pi (1975)
Kung Fu (1972)
Kung-Fu (1980)
Kung Fu Master! (1988)
Kung Fu: The Movie (1986)
Kung Fu: The Next Generation
 (1987)
Kuni Lemel in Cairo (1983)
Kuroneko (1969)
Kurt and Valde (1983)
Kuruk Shetra (1946)
Kusameikyu (1984)

L.A. Law (1986)
LBJ: The Early Years (1987)
Labyrinth (1959)
Labyrinth (short) (1962)
Labyrinth (1986)
Lac aux Dames (1934)
Lace (1984)
Lace II (1985)
Lacy and the Mississippi Queen
 (1978)
Ladies and Gentlemen (1984)
Ladies Choice (1981)
Ladies Club, The (1986)
Ladies in Blue (1980)
Ladies' Man (1980)
Ladies of the Lotus (1987)
Ladies' Turn (American Quarter
 Hour, The) (1982)
Ladron de Cadaveres (Grave
 Robbers) (1956)
Lady and Death, The (1946)
Lady Beware (1987)
Lady Blue (1985)
Lady Called Andres, A (1970)
Lady Chatterley's Lover (1981)

Lady Coyote II, The (1987)
Lady Doctors (Arztinnen) (1984)
Lady Escapes, The (1937)
Lady Frankenstein (1971)
Lady from the Shanghai Cinema, The
 (1988)
Lady from Yesterday, The (1985)
Lady Grey (1980)
Lady in a Cage (1964)
Lady in White (1988)
Lady James Bond (1972)
Lady Jane (1986)
Lady Killer (1937)
Lady Killer (1973)
Lady Luck (1973)
Lady Mobster (1988)
Lady of the House (1978)
Lady Paname (1950)
Lady Seeks Room (1937)
Lady, Stay Dead (1982)
Lady With a Lamp (1951)
Ladyhawke (1985)
Ladykillers (1988)
Lair of the White Worm, The (1988)
Laisse-Beton (1984)
Lake of Constance, The (1986)
Lake of Dracula (1971)
Lamb (1985)
Lambert Is Threatened (1949)
Lame Devil, The (1970)
Lame Ducks (1982)
Lame Go Christmas, The (1988)
Lamentations (Dung-Aw) (1981)
Lancer (1968)
Land, The (1942)
Land and Sons (1980)
Land Before Time, The (1988)
Land for Rose (1988)
Land in Two (1985)
Land of Cops and Robbers (1983)
Land of Doom (1984)
Land of Fathers, Land of Sons
 (1988)
Land of Fire All Night Long (1981)
Land of Hope (1976)
Land of Look Behind (1982)
Land of Little Rain (1988)
Land of Love, The (Pendin Heng
 Kuam Rak) (1980)
Land of Miracles (1984)
Land of No Return, The (1981)
Land of Promise (1935)
Land of the Brave (1987)
Land of the Giants (1968)
Land of the Lost (1974)
Land of the Minotaur (1977)
Land of the Tiger (1985)

Last Summer in Tangiers (1987)
Last Survivors, The (1975)
Last Tango, The (1986)
Last Temptation of Christ, The
  (1988)
Last Tenant, The (1978)
Last Unicorn, The (1982)
Last Voyage, The (1988)
Last War, The (1961)
Last Warning, The (1928)
Last Winter, The (1983)
Last Wishes (1983)
Last Witness, The (1961)
Last Woman on Earth (1960)
Late Great Planet Earth, The
  (1978)
Late Matthew Pascal, The (1937)
Late Summer Blues (1987)
Latent Image (1988)
Lathe of Heaven (1981)
Latino (1985)
Latitude 55° (1982)
Latitude Zero (1970)
Laughing at Trouble (1937)
Laughter in Paradise (1951)
Laughterhouse (1984)
Laura (1968)
Laura (1987)
Laura (From Heaven to Hell)
  (1987)
Laura Lansing Slept Here (1988)
Laura: Shadows of Summer (1980)
Laurel & Hardy Laughtoons (1979)
Lav Kush (1951)
Lavender Hill Mob, The (1951)
Laverne and Shirley (1976)
Laverne and Shirley in the Army
  (1981)
Laverne and Shirley with the Fonz
  (1982)
Law and Harry McGraw, The
  (1987)
Law and Mr. Jones, The (1960)
Law and Order (1976)
Law of the Land (1976)
Law of the Outlaw (1971)
Law of the Plainsman, The (1959)
Law of the Wild (1934)
Lawful Violence (1982)
Lawman (1958)
Lawyer, The (1984)
Lazarillo (Ragamuffin of Tormes)
  (1959)
Lazarus Syndrome, The (1979)
Lead Brigade, The (1980)
Lead Soldiers (1984)
Leadfoot (1982)

Leading Edge, The (1987)
League of Gentlemen (1960)
Leap from the Bridge, The (1980)
Leap into the Void (Salto nel Vuoto)
  (1980)
Leap of Faith (1988)
Leap to Fame (1959)
Leave All Fair (1985)
Leave 'Em Laughing (1981)
Leave It to Beaver (1957)
Leave Me Not Alone (1980)
Leave to Remain (1988)
Leave Yesterday Behind (1978)
Leaves Are Wide, The (1981)
Lecture on Man, A (short) (1962)
Led by the Nose (1984)
Leda and the Elephant (short)
  (1946)
Left-Hander (Levsha) (1987)
Left Without Leaving an Address
  (1982)
Leg Work (1987)
Legacy of Blood (1971)
Legacy of the Brave (1987)
Legal Eagles (1986)
Legend (1985)
Legend of Bigfoot, The (1975)
Legend of Bigfoot, The (1976)
Legend of Billie Jean, The (1985)
Legend of Custer, The (1967)
Legend of Dinosaurs and Monster
  Birds (1977)
Legend of Hillbilly John, The (1971)
Legend of Jesse James, The (1965)
Legend of Julian Makabayan, The
  (1980)
Legend of Lizzie Borden, The (1975)
Legend of Plumeria--Heaven's Kiss,
  The (1983)
Legend of Sleepy Hollow, The (1958)
Legend of Sleepy Hollow, The (1979)
Legend of Sleepy Hollow, The (1986)
Legend of Suram Fortress, The
  (1985)
Legend of the Boy and the Eagle,
  The (1968)
Legend of the Drum, The (1982)
Legend of the Fox (1980)
Legend of the Glass Mountain, The
  (Glass Mountain, The) (1949)
Legend of the Golden Gun (1979)
Legend of the Lone Ranger, The
  (1981)
Legend of the Mermaid (1984)
Legend of the 7 Golden Vampires,
  The (7 Brothers Meet Dracula,
  The) (1979)

Legend of the Skylark, The (short) (1967)
Legend of the Spider Forest, The (1974)
Legend of the Werewolf, The (1975)
Legend of the White Serpent, The (White Madam's Strange Love) (1956)
Legend of the Wolf Woman (Werewolf Woman) (1976)
Legend of Tianyun Mountain (1983)
Legend of Valentino, The (1975)
Legend of Walks Far Woman, The (1982)
Legend of Wolf Lodge, The (1987)
Legends of Anika (1956)
Legends of the West: Truth and Tall Tales (1981)
Legs (1978)
Legs (1983)
Legions of Honor (1938)
Leif (1987)
Leila Diniz (1987)
Lekha's Death--A Flashback (1984)
Lemon Sky (1987)
Lemora, the Lady Dracula (Child's Tale of the Supernatural, A) (1975)
Lena (1981)
Lena: My 100 Children (1987)
Lena Rais (1980)
Lend Me Your Wife (1959)
Lenin in 1918 (1939)
Lenin in October (1938)
Lenin in Paris (1981)
Leningrad Skies (1960)
Leo and Liz in Beverly Hills (1986)
Leo and Loree (1980)
Leonard Part 6 (1987)
Leonora (1986)
Leopard, The (1984)
Leopard Men of Africa (1940)
Leprechaun's Christmas Gold, The (1981)
Leprechaun's Gold (short) (1949)
Les Patterson Saves the World (1987)
Less Than Zero (1987)
Lesson of a Dead Language (1980)
Lessons in Love (1937)
Let Down Your Hair (1988)
Let George Do It (1938)
Let It Be Sunday (1983)
Let Them Kill Me Once and For All (1986)

Let Ye Inherit (1985)
Lethal (KGB--The Secret War) (1986)
Lethal Pursuit (1988)
Lethal Weapon (1987)
Let's Get Harry (1987)
Let's Get Married (1960)
Let's Go On (1982)
Let's Hope It's a Girl (1986)
Let's Make Laugh II (1985)
Let's Switch (1975)
Letter, The (1982)
Letter to Brezhnev (1985)
Letter to Loretta, A (1953)
Letter to Three Wives, A (1985)
Letters, The (1973)
Letters from a Dead Man (1986)
Letters from Frank (1979)
Letters from the Park (1988)
Letters from Three Lovers (1973)
Letters to an Unknown Lover (1985)
Letting Go (1985)
Levin's Mill (1981)
Levy and Goliath (1987)
Lewis and Clark (1981)
Lianna (1983)
Liar's Dice (1980)
Liberace (1988)
Liberace: Behind the Music (1988)
Liberators, The (1987)
Liberty at Night (1984)
Liberty Belle (1983)
Liberty, Equality, Sauerkraut (1985)
License to Drive (1988)
License to Kill (1984)
Licensed to Love and Kill (1979)
Lie of Nina Petrovna, The (1937)
Lie of the Land, The (1985)
Lies (1983)
Lieutenant Schuster's Wife (1972)
Life and Adventures of Santa Claus, The (1985)
Life and Assassination of the Kingfish, The (1977)
Life and Blood of the Polish (1983)
Life and Loves of a She-Devil, The (1986)
Life and Times of Eddie Roberts, The (L.A.T.E.R.) (1980)
Life and Times of Grizzly Adams, The (1977)
Life Around Us (1959)
Life Begins at 17 (1954)
Life Begins Tomorrow (1952)
Life Classes (1987)
Life Goes On (1981)

Life Guard, The (1980)
Life in Emergency Ward 10 (1959)
Life in the Balance (short) (1967)
Life in Wittstock (1985)
Life in Your Hands (1959)
Life Is a Circus (1960)
Life Is a Dream (1987)
Life Is a Long Quiet River (1988)
Life Is a Novel (1983)
Life Is Beautiful (1985)
Life Is Rosy (1987)
Life Is Strange (1988)
Life Is Wonderful (1982)
Life, Love, Tears (1985)
Life of Chikuzan, Tsugaru
  Shamisen Player, The (1978)
Life of Don Bosco, The (1936)
Life of Riley, The (1949)
Life of Riley, The (1953)
Life of the Party: The Story of
  Beatrice (1982)
Life of the Summer People, The
  (1981)
Life on the Hegns Farm (1939)
Life on the Mississippi (1980)
Life With Alkis (1988)
Life with Father (1953)
Lifeforce (1985)
Light Blast (1985)
Light Cavalry (1936)
Light of Day (1987)
Light Physical Injuries (1984)
Light Up the Sky (1960)
Light Years, The (Annees
  Lumiere, Les) (1981)
Light Years (Gandahar) (1987)
Lighted Lantern, The (1987)
Lighthorsemen, The (1987)
Lighthouse, The (1958)
Lightning Over Braddock: A
  Rustbowl Fantasy (1988)
Lightning Over Water (Nick's
  Movie) (1980)
Lightning Warrior, The (1931)
Lights and Shadows (1988)
Lights of the Night (1958)
Lights Out (1949)
Lightship, The (1985)
Like a Stranger (1981)
Like Father, Like Daughter (1987)
Like Father, Like Son (1961)
Like Father, Like Son (1987)
Like Grandfather, Like Grandson
  (1983)
Like Life Itself (1985)
Like Mom, Like Me (1978)
Like Normal People (1979)

Like Once Lili Marlene (1956)
Like Poison (Jako Jed) (1986)
Li'l Abner (1971)
Lili Marleen (1981)
Liliom (1930)
Liliom (1934)
Lill, My Darling Witch (1972)
Lily (1986)
Lily in Love (1985)
Lily of Kilarney (Bride of the Lake)
  (1934)
Lime Street (1985)
Limpan (1983)
Linda (1973)
Lindbergh Kidnapping Case, The
  (1976)
Line, The (1987)
Line One (1988)
Line-Up, The (1954)
Lineup, The (1958)
Lineup of Kanto Outlaws (1971)
Link, The (1985)
Link (1986)
Lion of Africa, The (1987)
Lion of Flanders, The (1984)
Lion of the Desert (1981)
Lion Tamer, The (short) (1961)
Lion, the Witch and the Wardrobe,
  The (1979)
Lionheart (1987)
Lion's Den, The (1988)
Liquid Sky (1982)
Lisa and the Devil (1972)
Lisa, Bright and Dark (1973)
Lisi and the General (1986)
Listen to the City (1984)
Listen to the Sound of the Wind
  (1982)
Listen to Your Heart (1983)
Lit Lantern, The (1986)
Litan (1982)
Little Ball, The (short) (1963)
Little Bit of You ... A Little Bit
  of Me, A (1985)
Little Black Sambo Hunts the Tiger
  (short) (1957)
Little Brother, The (1983)
Little Bull, The (1985)
Little Bunch, The (1983)
Little Darlings (1980)
Little Devil (1988)
Little Devil from the Quarter (1983)
Little Dragons, The (1980)
Little Drummer Girl, The (1984)
Little Fires (1985)
Little Flower of Jesus (1939)
Little Friend (1934)

Little Game, A (1971)
Little Girl Lost (1988)
Little Girl Who Conquered Time, The (1983)
Little Girl Who Lives Down the Lane, The (1977)
Little Gloria ... Happy at Last (1982)
Little House: Bless All the Dear Children (1984)
Little House: Look Back to Yesterday (1983)
Little House on the Prairie, The (1974)
Little House: The Last Farewell (1984)
Little Ida (1981)
Little Jerk (P'tit Con) (1984)
Little Joseph (1982)
Little Kidnappers, The (Kidnappers, The) (1954)
Little Klas in the Trunk (1984)
Little Ladies of the Night (1977)
Little Lord Fauntleroy (1980)
Little Love of My Life (1952)
Little Lulu (1978)
Little Match Girl, The (1987)
Little Men (1935)
Little Miss Marker (1980)
Little Miss Nobody (1936)
Little Mo (1978)
Little Mook (1954)
Little Mother (1935)
Little Nightingale, The (1936)
Little Nikita (1988)
Little Norse Prince (1969)
Little One (1959)
Little People, The (1972)
Little People (1982)
Little Prince and the Eight-Headed Dragon, The (1963)
Little Prosecutor, The (1987)
Little Rascals, The (1982)
Little Red Riding Hood and Her Friends (1959)
Little Red Riding Hood and the Monster (1960)
Little Schemer, The (1933)
Little Sex, A (1982)
Little Shop of Horrors, The (1961)
Little Shop of Horrors, The (1986)
Little Shots (1983)
Little Siren, The (1980)
Little Sister, The (1985)
Little Sister, The (1986)
Little Spies (1986)

Little Sweetheart (1988)
Little Town Will Go to Sleep, The (1954)
Little Train Robbery, The (1984)
Little Vic (1978)
Little Virgil and Frogeater Orla (1980)
Little Wars (1982)
Little Women (1971)
Little Women (1978)
Littles, The (1983)
Littlest Hobo, The (1964)
Littlest Hobo, The (1980)
Live Again, Die Again (1974)
Live and Learn (1971)
Live Broadcast (1982)
Live My Share, Mother (1971)
Live Today; Die Tomorrow! (1971)
Lives (Vidas/Survivors) (1984)
Lives of Jenny Dolan, The (1975)
Living Bread, The (1955)
Living Corpse, The (1940)
Living Dangerously (1987)
Living Daylights, The (1987)
Living Dreams (1988)
Living Head, The (1959)
Living in Paradise (1981)
Living Legends (Amagleba) (1988)
Living Like the Rest of Us (1982)
Living Off Love (1985)
Living Planet, The (1985)
Living Skeleton, The (1968)
Living Together (1975)
Liza (1978)
Lloyd Bridges Show, The (1962)
Lloyd Bridges Water World (1972)
Loafing and Camouflage (1984)
Lobo (1980)
Local Hero (1983)
Lock and Seal (1987)
Lock 17 (1986)
Lock, Stock and Barrel (1971)
Locusts (1974)
Lodz Ghetto (1988)
Log of the Black Pearl, The (1975)
Logan's Run (1977)
Lois Gibbs and the Love Canal (1982)
Lokis (1970)
Lola (1981)
Lola (1986)
Lon, the Curse of Land (1981)
London and Davis in New York (1984)
Lone Assassin, A (1972)
Lone Ranger, The (1949)
Lone Runner, The (1988)

Lot of Bills to Pay, A (1981)
Lots of Luck (1985)
Lotsa Luck (1973)
Lottery (1983)
Lou Grant (1977)
Lou, Pat and Joe D. (1988)
Louis Armstrong--Chicago Style
  (1976)
Louis L'Amour's "The Shadow
  Riders" (1982)
Louise the Rebel (1985)
Louisiana (1984)
Lounge Chair, The (1988)
Love (Kaerleken) (1980)
Love (1982)
Love Affair: The Eleanor and
  Lou Gehrig Story, A (1978)
Love, American Style (1969)
Love Among the Ruins (1975)
Love Among Thieves (1987)
Love and Chatter (1958)
Love and Death (1971)
Love and Death (1985)
Love and Kisses--Veronica (1936)
Love and Learn (1979)
Love and Lies (1982)
Love and Marriage (1959)
Love & Money (1982)
Love and Sacrifice (1936)
Love and the Happy Days (1972)
Love Around the Corner (1986)
Love at Court (1936)
Love at Every Fair, A (1961)
Love at First Sight (1980)
Love Atop the Pyramids (1985)
Love Betrayed (1974)
Love Between the Raindrops (1980)
Love Boat, The (1976)
Love Boat, The (1977)
Love Boat II, The (1977)
Love Butcher, The (1975)
Love by Request (1983)
Love Can Make a Rainbow (1982)
Love Child (1982)
Love Circles (1985)
Love, Death and the Devil (1934)
Love for Eternity (1971)
Love for Lydia (1979)
Love for Rent (1979)
Love Forgives (1981)
Love Hangs on the Gibbet (1961)
Love, Hate, Love (1971)
Love in a Cold Climate (1982)
Love in a Fallen City (1984)
Love in a Minefield (1987)
Love in a Taxi (1980)
Love in Bagdad (1986)

Love in Germany, A (1983)
Love in Pawn (1953)
Love Is a Fat Woman (1987)
Love Is a Many-Splendored Thing
  (1967)
Love Is Forever (1983)
Love Is Never Silent (1985)
Love Is Not an Argument (1984)
Love Is Not Enough (1978)
Love Is Strange (1988)
Love Is Where the Trouble Begins
  (1984)
Love Laughs at All (1957)
Love Letter (Koibumi) (1986)
Love Letter (1987)
Love Lives On (1985)
Love Locked Out (1949)
Love, Love, But Don't Lose Your
  Head (1981)
Love Maneuvers (1936)
Love Mates (1968)
Love, Mother (1987)
Love Movie, The (1985)
Love, Natalie (1980)
Love Odyssey (1987)
Love of a Princess, The (1981)
Love of Anuradka (1961)
Love of Life (1951)
Love of My Heart (Core Mio) (1982)
Love of Perdition (1980)
Love on a Budget (1938)
Love on a Rooftop (1966)
Love on the Run (1985)
Love or a Kingdom (1937)
Love Scenes (1986)
Love, Sex and Marriage (1983)
Love, Sidney (1981)
Love Slaves of the Amazon (1957)
Love Stopped the Runaway Train
  (1974)
Love Story (1973)
Love Story (Storia d'Amore) (1986)
Love Strange Love (1985)
Love Streams (1984)
Love Suicides at Sonezaki, The
  (1982)
Love Tapes, The (1980)
Love That Bob (1955)
Love Thy Neighbor (1973)
Love Thy Neighbor (1984)
Love Till First Blood (1986)
Love Till Second Blood (1988)
Love Under Fire (1937)
Love Unto Death (1984)
Love Unto Waste (1987)
Love War, The (1970)
Love With a Perfect Stranger (1986)

Lovebirds, The (1979)
Loved One, The (1983)
Lovelock (1987)
Lovely But Deadly (1983)
Lover, The (Asheke, Al) (1986)
Lovers, The (1956)
Lovers and Other Strangers (1983)
Lovers' Exile, The (1981)
Lovers of the Lord of the Night,
   The (1984)
Lovers of Verona (1951)
Loves and Poisons (1950)
Love's Awakening (1936)
Love's Dark Ride (1978)
Love's Labor's Lost (1985)
Loves Me, Loves Me Not (1977)
Loves of a Dictator (1935)
Loves of Angelica, The (1966)
Loves of Salammbo, The (1963)
Love's Savage Fury (1979)
Lovesick (1983)
Lovey: A Circle of Children,
   Part II (1978)
Loving (1983)
Loving Couples (1955)
Loving Couples (1980)
Loving Walter (1986)
Low Blow (1986)
Low Midnight (1960)
Low Visibility (1984)
Lowell Thomas Remembers (1975)
Lower Depths, The (1937)
Loyalty of Love (1937)
Luana, Daughter of the Virgin
   Forest (1968)
Luc ou la Part des Choses (1982)
Lucan (1977)
Lucas (1986)
Lucas Tanner (1974)
Lucie Sur Seine (1983)
Lucifer Complex, The (1978)
Lucifer Rising (1981)
Lucio Flavio (1981)
Luck Child, The (short) (1988)
Lucky Galoshes (1958)
Lucky Ravi (1987)
Lucky Star, The (1980)
Lucrece Borgia (1953)
Lucy Arnaz Show, The (1985)
Lucy Moves to NBC (1980)
Lucy Show, The (1962)
Luggage of the Gods (1983)
Lullaby (1948)
Lullaby of the Good Earth (1977)
Lulu by Night (1986)
Luminous Woman (1987)
Lunar Rainbow (1984)

Lunch Wagon (1981)
Lupin III (1978)
Lure of the Sila (Wolf of the Sila)
   (1950)
Lurkers (1988)
Lust for Freedom (1987)
Lust in the Dust (1984)
Lusty Transparent Man, The (1978)
Lute of the Blind Monks of Satsuma,
   The (1985)
Luther Is Dead (1984)
Lux Video Theater (1950)
Luxury Liner (1963)
Luz del Fuego (1982)
Lynx (Rys) (1981)

M (1951)
M.A.D.D.: Mothers Against Drunk
   Drivers (1983)
M*A*S*H (1972)
M Squad (1957)
M Station: Hawaii (1980)
M-E: The Gemini Strain (Plague)
   (1979)
Ma and Pa (1974)
Ma Cherie (1980)
Mabel and Max (1987)
Mac and Me (1988)
Macahans, The (1976)
Macario (1960)
Macaroni (1985)
MacArthur's Children (1985)
Macbeth (1960)
Macbeth (1971)
McClain's Law (1981)
McCloud (1970)
McCloud: Who Killed Miss U.S.A.?
   (1970)
McCoy (1975)
McDuff, the Talking Dog (1976)
Mace (1987)
McGruder & Loud (1985)
McGuffin, The (1985)
MacGyver (1985)
McHale's Navy (1962)
Machine Gun Kelly (1958)
Machine That Kills Bad People, The
   (1948)
Macho That Barks Doesn't Bite II
   (1987)
Maciste and the Queen of Samar
   (1964)
Maciste, Gladiator of Sparta (1964)
McKeever and the Colonel (1962)
Mackenzie (1982)
MacKenzies of Paradise Cove, The

(1979)
McLaren's Riders (1977)
McLean Stevenson Show, The
    (1976)
McMillan (1976)
McMillan and Wife (1971)
McNaughton's Daughter (1976)
Macross--Super Time Fortress
    (1983)
Macu, the Policeman's Wife (1987)
Macunaima (1972)
McVicar (1980)
Mad About Men (1954)
Mad About You (1988)
Mad Bull (1977)
Mad Doctor of Blood Island
    (1969)
Mad Dog (Wsciekly) (1980)
Mad Executioners, The (1963)
Mad Love (1935)
Mad Love (Amour Braque, L')
    (1985)
Mad Max Beyond Thunderdome
    (1985)
Mad Max 2 (1981)
Mad Men of Europe (1940)
Mad Monster Party, The (1967)
Mad Woman, The (1952)
Madame Claude 2 (Intimate
    Moments) (1981)
Madame Sin (1972)
Madame Sousatzka (1988)
Madame X (1981)
Madcap Island (Kyokkori Hyotan
    Jima) (1967)
Made in Argentina (1987)
Made in Heaven (1952)
Made in Heaven (1987)
Made in U.S.A. (1987)
Mademoiselle Docteur (1937)
Madhouse (Scared to Death/I Will
    Scare You to Death/There Was
    Once a Child) (1980)
Madhouse (1982)
Madhouse Brigade, The (1978)
Madhvacharya (1987)
Madigan (1972)
Madly in Love (Innamorato Pazzo)
    (1982)
Madman (1982)
Madman at War (1985)
Madness My Love (1986)
Madonna, Che Silenzio c'e
    Stasera (Wow, How Quiet It
    Is Tonight) (1982)
Madonna Man, The (1988)
Madonna, Where Are You? (1936)

Madres: The Mothers of Plaza de
    Mayo, Las (1986)
Madrid (1987)
Mae West (1982)
Mafia Princess (1986)
Magdalena Viraga (1987)
Maggie (1981)
Maggie (1986)
Magic Boy, The (1959)
Magic Carpet (1972)
Magic Fountain, The (1961)
Magic Guitar, The (1968)
Magic Is Alive, My Friends (1985)
Magic Man, The (1976)
Magic Moments (1984)
Magic Mongo (1977)
Magic Mountain (1936)
Magic Mountain, The (1982)
Magic of the Kite (short) (1957)
Magic Ring, The (short) (1968)
Magic Samurai, The (1969)
Magic Serpent, The (1966)
Magic Snowman, The (1987)
Magic Sticks (1987)
Magic Strings (short) (1955)
Magic Sword, The (1949)
Magic Toyshop, The (1986)
Magic Typewriter, The (short)
    (1970)
Magic World of Topo Gigio, The
    (1964)
Magician, The (1958)
Magician, The (1973)
Magician and the Police Commis-
    sioner, The (1985)
Magician of Dreams (1966)
Magilla Gorilla Show, The (1964)
Magnate, The (1987)
Magnificence in Trust (1967)
Magnificent Magnet of Santa Mesa,
    The (1977)
Magnificent Seven, The (1960)
Magnificent Warriors (1987)
Magnum, P.I. (1980)
Magpie's Strategy, The (1987)
Mahatma Gandhi--20th Century
    Prophet (1953)
Maid for Pleasure (1974)
Maid in America (1982)
Maid to Order (1987)
Maiden of the Woods (1987)
Maiden Voyage (1988)
Maidstone (1971)
Maigret in Pigalle (1966)
Mailman Mueller (1953)
Main Theme (1984)
Maine-Ocean Express (1986)

Majdhar (1984)
Majin Strikes Again (1967)
Majin, the Hideous Idol (1966)
Major and the Steers, The (1956)
Make a Note of This Face (1986)
Make Me an Offer (1980)
Make Room for Daddy (1953)
Make Room for Daddy (1967)
Make Room for Granddaddy (1970)
Make-Up (Kesho) (1985)
Makin' It (1979)
Making a Living (1981)
Making It (Ningyo Girai) (1982)
Making Love (1982)
Making Mr. Right (1987)
Making of a Model, The (1983)
Making of the President, The
   (1963)
Making the Grade (1982)
Making the Grade (1984)
Mako, the Bad Girl (1971)
Malady of Death, The (1985)
Malady of Love, The (1986)
Malady of Love (1987)
Malambo (1942)
Malambo (1984)
Malamore (1982)
Malayunta (1986)
Male and Female (1985)
Malenka (1968)
Malevil (1981)
Malibu (1983)
Malibu Express (1985)
Malibu Run (1961)
Malice in Wonderland (1985)
Mallory: Circumstantial Evidence
   (1976)
Malone (1987)
Malou (1981)
Malpas Mystery, The (1960)
Malauala (1980)
Mama Dracula (1980)
Mama Happy ...? (1984)
Mama Is Mad! (1986)
Mama's Family (1983)
Mamba (Fair Game) (1988)
Mambru Went to War (1986)
Mamele (1939)
Mamma (1982)
Mamma Ebe (1985)
Mammame (1986)
Mammy (1937)
Mam'selle Nitouche (1954)
Mamula Camp (1959)
Man About Town (1986)
Man and a Woman: 20 Years
   Later, A (1986)

Man and the City, The (1971)
Man and the Monster, The (1959)
Man and the Snake, The (1972)
Man Called Demon, A (1957)
Man Called Intrepid, A (1979)
Man Called Sloane, A (1979)
Man Eaters (1988)
Man for All Seasons, A (1988)
Man from Atlantis, The (1977)
Man from Boulevard des Capucines,
   The (1988)
Man from Cairo, The (1953)
Man from Denver, The (1959)
Man from Galveston, The (1963)
Man from Independence, The (1962)
Man from Interpol, The (1960)
Man from Mallorca, The (1984)
Man from Moscow, The (1985)
Man from Nowhere, The (1976)
Man from S.E.X., The (1978)
Man from Shiloh, The (1970)
Man from Snowy River, The (1982)
Man from the Niger, The (1940)
Man from UNCLE, The (1964)
Man in a Cocked Hat, The (Carlton-
   Browne of the F.O.) (1959)
Man in a Suitcase (1968)
Man in Love, A (1987)
Man in the Iron Mask, The (1977)
Man in the Middle (1964)
Man in the Middle (1972)
Man in the Moon, The (1986)
Man in the Raincoat, The (1957)
Man in the Santa Claus Suit, The
   (1979)
Man in the Sky (1957)
Man in the Top Hat, The (1983)
Man Is a Social Being (short) (1960)
Man Labeled to Die, A (1984)
Man Looking Southeast (1986)
Man of Africa (1956)
Man of Aran (1934)
Man of Ashes (1986)
Man of Conflict (1953)
Man of Fashion (1980)
Man of Iron (1981)
Man of Music (1953)
Man of My Measure, A (1983)
Man of Straw (1958)
Man of the Foreign Debt, The
   (1987)
Man of the Hour (1940)
Man of the Moment (1955)
Man of the World (1962)
Man on a False Flight (1971)
Man on Fire (1987)
Man on the Move (1972)

Many Happy Returns (1964)
Many Happy Returns (1986)
Many Loves of Arthur, The (1978)
Many Passed By (1956)
Marathon (1980)
Marathon Runners, The (1982)
Marauders (1987)
Maravillas (1981)
Marciano (1979)
Marco Polo (1982)
Marcus-Nelson Murders, The (1973)
Marcus Welby, M.D. (1969)
Marcus Welby, M.D.--A Holiday
    Affair (1988)
Margie (1961)
Marguerite Drei (1939)
Marguerite of the Night (1955)
Maria (1986)
Maria Chapdeleine (1935)
Maria Chapdelaine (1983)
Maria de mi Corazon (1984)
Maria the Servant (1936)
Maria Theresia (1952)
Mariah (1987)
Marian Rose White (1982)
Mariana, Mariana (1987)
Maria's Lovers (1984)
Marie (1979)
Marie (1985)
Marie Curie (1979)
Marie in the City (1988)
Marie Ward (1985)
Marija Valewska (1936)
Mariko-Mother (1977)
Marilyn: The Untold Story (1980)
Marine Boy (1966)
Mario (1984)
Mark, The (Stigma, To) (1982)
Mark, I Love You (1980)
Mark of Death, The (1961)
Mark of the Beast (1981)
Mark of the Witch (1970)
Mark of Zorro, The (1974)
Mark Twain (1985)
Market of the Humble (1986)
Markham (1959)
Marlo and the Magic Movie Machine
    (1977)
Marmalade Revolution, The (1980)
Marquis of Grillo, The (1982)
Marriage, A (1983)
Marriage Is Alive and Well (1980)
Marriage of Convenience (1986)
Marriage of Mr. Mississippi, The
    (1961)
Marriage of the Century, The
    (1985)

Marriage Year One (1971)
Married for the First Time (1980)
Married Man, A (1984)
Married: The First Year (1979)
Married to the Mob (1988)
Marshal of Gunfight Pass, The
    (1950)
Marsupials: The Howling III, The
    (1987)
Martha Dubronski (1985)
Martha, Ruth and Edie (1988)
Marthe Richard (1937)
Martian Chronicles, The (1980)
Martians Have Arrived, The (1964)
Martin in the Clouds (1961)
Martin Niemoeller (1985)
Martin's Day (1985)
Maruja in Hell (1983)
Marva Collins Story, The (1981)
Marvin and Tige (1983)
Mary (1985)
Mary and Joseph: A Story of Faith
    (1979)
Mary Hartman, Mary Hartman (1976)
Mary Jane Harper Cried Last Night
    (1977)
Mary Tyler Moore Show, The (1970)
Mary White (1977)
Masada (1981)
Mascara (1987)
Maschenka (1987)
Mascot (Kabala) (1982)
Masculine Mystique, The (1984)
Mask, The (1988)
Mask of Marcella, The (1972)
Mask of Sheba, The (1970)
Masked Marvel, The (1943)
Maskerade (1937)
Masks (1987)
Masoch (1980)
Masque of the Red Death, The
    (short) (1969)
Masquerade (1983)
Masquerade (1988)
Mass Appeal (1984)
Mass Is Over, The (1985)
Mass Miracle (1981)
Massacre River (1949)
Massarati and the Brain (1982)
Massey Sahib (1986)
Massive Retaliation (1984)
Master, The (1984)
Master, The (1986)
Master of Ballantrae, The (1984)
Master of Boyana, The (1981)
Master of Horror (1960)
Master of the Game (1984)

Master over Life and Death (1955)
Masterblaster (1987)
Masters of the Universe (1987)
Mata Hari (1985)
Matador (1986)
Matagi (Old Bear Hunter, The)
   (1982)
Matango (Attack of the Mushroom
   People) (1963)
Matchless (1966)
Maternity (1935)
Matewan (1987)
Mathematical Peep Show (short)
   (1961)
Mating Season, The (1980)
Matlock (1986)
Matt Helm (1975)
Matt Houston (1982)
Matt Lincoln (1970)
Matter of Dignity, A (1960)
Matter of Heart (1986)
Matter of Life and Death, A
   (1987)
Matter of Sex, A (1984)
Matter of Wife and Death, A
   (1975)
Matushka (Viadukt) (1983)
Maureen (1976)
Mauri (1988)
Mausoleum (1981)
Maverick (1957)
Max (1983)
Max Dugan Returns (1983)
Max Headroom (1987)
Max My Love (1986)
Maxie (1985)
Maximum Overdrive (1986)
Maximum Security (1985)
Maxwell Street Blues (1981)
May We Borrow Your Husband?
   (1986)
Maya (1949)
Maya (1967)
Maya Manushya (1976)
Maybe Baby (1988)
Maybe I'll Come Home in the
   Spring (1971)
Maybe It's Love (1984)
Mayberry R.F.D. (1968)
Mayday at 40,000 Feet (1976)
Mayflower: The Pilgrim's
   Adventure (1979)
Mayhem (Scream, Baby, Scream)
   (1969)
Mayor of the Town (1954)
Maytime in Mayfair (1949)
Maze, The (1953)

Me and Ducky (1979)
Me and Maxx (1980)
Me and Mrs. C (1986)
Me and Mom (1985)
Me and My Sister (1988)
Me and the Chimp (1972)
Me, Light and Darkness (1983)
Me, Myself and I (Eu) (1987)
Me Want You (1985)
Mean Season, The (1985)
Means and Ends (1987)
Meantime (1983)
Meantime, It's Already Noon (1988)
Measure for Measure (1981)
Meat (1979)
Meatballs II (1984)
Meatballs II (1987)
Med Kaerlig Hilsen (Love Me,
   Darling) (1971)
Medal, The (1980)
Medic (1954)
Medical Center (1969)
Medical One (1975)
Medical Story (1975)
Mediterranean, The (1983)
Medium (Deja Vu) (1985)
Medusa Touch, The (1978)
Medusa vs. the Son of Hercules
   (1962)
Meet Corliss Archer (1951)
Meet Mr. Kringle (1957)
Meet Mr. Lucifer (1953)
Meet the Munceys (1988)
Meeting at the Fashion Show (1965)
Meeting in Paris (1956)
Megaforce (1982)
Megilah '83 (1983)
Melanie (1982)
Melba (1988)
Melek Leaves (1985)
Melo (1986)
Melody Haunts My Reverie, The
   (1981)
Melody in Gray (1978)
Melody of Hate (1975)
Melody of Love (1954)
Melvin and Howard (1980)
Melvin Purvis--G-Man (1974)
Melvin, Son of Alvin (1984)
Melzer (1983)
Member for Chelsea, The (1981)
Memed My Hawk (1984)
Mementos (1986)
Memoirs (1985)
Memoirs of a Sinner, The (1986)
Memoirs of a Survivor (1981)
Memorial Day (1983)

Memories Never Die (1982)
Memories of Fear (1981)
Memories of Me (1988)
Memories of You (Love Story)
   (1988)
Men (Manner) (1985)
Men and War (1974)
Men and Wolves (1957)
Men at Dangerous Age (1954)
Men at Law (1971)
Men from Shiloh, The (1970)
Men from the Gutter (1983)
Men into Space (1959)
Men of Action Meet Women of
   Dracula (1969)
Men of the Dragon (1974)
Men of the Sea (1938)
Men on Wings (1935)
Men or Not Men (1980)
Men Prefer Fat Girls (1981)
Men's Club, The (1986)
Merchant of Slaves (1949)
Merchant of Venice, The (1953)
Mercy or Murder? (1987)
Mermaids of Tiburon, The (1962)
Merry Christmas, Mr. Lawrence
   (1983)
Merry Marriage, The (1984)
Merry Wives, The (1938)
Mesmerized (1986)
Mesrine (1984)
Message to My Daughter (1973)
Messalina, Messalina (1977)
Messenger, The (1937)
Messenger, The (1987)
Messenger Boy (Kurier) (1987)
Messenger of Death (1988)
Metalstorm: The Destruction of
   Jared-Syn (1983)
Metamorphosis (1971)
Meteor and Shadow (1985)
Method, The (1987)
Metin (1982)
Metropolis (reissue) (1926)
Metropolis (reissue) (1983)
Metropolitan Avenue (1985)
Mexican, The (1957)
Mexican Double-Entendre (1987)
Mexican, You Can Do It (1986)
Mexico in Flames (1982)
Mga Hagibis (1970)
Miami Vice (1984)
Michael Shayne, Private Detective
   (1960)
Michel Strogoff (1957)
Michele Lee Show, The (1974)
Michiko (1981)

Mickey (1964)
Mickey & Nora (short) (1987)
Mickey Mouse Club, The (1955)
Mickey Spillane's Margin for Murder
   (1981)
Mickey Spillane's Mike Hammer:
   More Than Murder (1983)
Mickey Spillane's Mike Hammer:
   Murder Me, Murder You (1983)
Micki & Maude (1984)
Microscope, The (1988)
Microwave Massacre (1978)
Midas Touch, The (Eldorado) (1988)
Midas Valley (1985)
Middle Age Crazy (1980)
Midnight (1982)
Midnight Caller (1988)
Midnight Crossing (1988)
Midnight Episode (1951)
Midnight Happenings (1938)
Midnight Hour, The (1985)
Midnight Lace (1980)
Midnight Madness (1980)
Midnight Movie Massacre (1988)
Midnight Offerings (1981)
Midnight Phantom, The (1939)
Midnight Rehearsal (1983)
Midnight Run (1988)
Midnight Spares (1983)
Midnight Taxi (1937)
Midnight Tradition (1939)
Midsummer Holiday (1950)
Midsummer Night's Dream, A (1983)
Midsummer Night's Dream, A (1984)
Mighty Gorga, The (1970)
Mighty Hercules, The (1960)
Mighty Mouse Playhouse, The
   (1955)
Mighty Orbots, The (1984)
Mignon Has Gone (1988)
Migrants, The (1974)
Migrating Birds (1987)
Migration of Sparrows (1980)
Mike Test (1980)
Mike's Murder (1984)
Miklos Akli (1987)
Milagro Beanfield War, The (1988)
Milan '83 (1984)
Miles from Home (1988)
Miles to Go (1986)
Miles to Go Before I Sleep (1975)
Milionario and Ze Rico in the High-
   way (1980)
Milizia Territoriale (1936)
Milk and Honey (1988)
Milk Train (1988)
Milka (1981)

Mill, The (1987)
Mill of the Stone Women (1960)
Mill on the Po, The (1949)
Millennial Bee, The (1983)
Million Dollar Duck, The (1971)
Million Dollar Face, The (1981)
Million Dollar Infield (1982)
Million Dollar Mystery (1987)
Million Dollar Rip-Off, The (1976)
Million Dollars for Seven Assassins,
   A (1966)
Millionaire, The (1955)
Millionaire, The (1978)
Millionairess, The (1960)
Mills of Power (Part 1) (1988)
Milo Barus--The Strongest Man
   in the World (1983)
Milpitas Monster, The (1976)
Milton the Monster Cartoon Show,
   The (1965)
Mimi (1935)
Mind Killer (1987)
Mind of Clay, The (1986)
Mind of Mr. Soames, The (1969)
Mind Over Murder (1979)
Mind Snatchers, The (1972)
Mine, The (1958)
Minestrone (1981)
Mini-Skirt Gambler, A (1970)
Minister's Friend, The (1939)
Minister's Wife, The (1981)
Minstrel Man (1977)
Mint Tea (1984)
Minuet (1982)
Miracle, The (1987)
Miracle in Milan (1951)
Miracle in Soho (1957)
Miracle Mile (1988)
Miracle of Joe Petrel, The (1984)
Miracle of Kathy Miller, The
   (1981)
Miracle of Malachias (1961)
Miracle of the Heart: The Boys
   Town Story (1986)
Miracle on Ice (1981)
Miracle on 34th Street (1973)
Miracle Rider, The (1935)
Miracle Worker, The (1979)
Miracles (1987)
Miraculous Virgin (Panna
   Zazranica) (1967)
Mirage, The (Maya Miriga) (1984)
Mirage (1987)
Mirages of Love (1988)
Miranda (1985)
Mirele Efros (1939)
Mirror, The (1984)

Mirror Crack'd, The (1980)
Mirror, Mirror (1979)
Mirror of Deception, The (1975)
Mirrors (Marianne) (1984)
Mirza Nowrouz's Shoes (1986)
Misadventures of Sheriff Lobo, The
   (1979)
Mischief (Frevel) (1984)
Mischief (1985)
Mischief Makers, The (1960)
Miser, The (L'Avare) (1980)
Miser, The (1988)
Miserables, Les (1934)
Miserables, Les (1978)
Mishima (1985)
Miss All-American Beauty (1982)
Miss April (1959)
Miss Arizona (1988)
Miss Cuple (1959)
Miss Jones and Son (1977)
Miss Keow (Keow) (1980)
Miss Leslie's Dolls (1972)
Miss Lonelyhearts (1983)
Miss Mary (1986)
Miss Million (1988)
Miss Mona (1987)
Miss ... or Myth? (1987)
Miss Pilgrim's Progress (1950)
Miss Right (1980)
Miss Stone (1959)
Miss Winslow and Son (1979)
Missile to the Moon (1958)
Missing (1982)
Missing Are Deadly, The (1975)
Missing from St.-Agil (1938)
Missing--Have You Seen This
   Person? (1985)
Missing in Action (1984)
Missing in Action 2--The Beginning
   (1985)
Missing Link, The (1980)
Mission, The (1986)
Mission Hill (1982)
Mission: Impossible (1966)
Mission: Impossible (1988)
Mission Kill (1985)
Mission Magic (1973)
Mission of No Return (1984)
Mission Thunderbolt (1983)
Missionary, The (1982)
Mississippi, The (1983)
Mississippi Burning (1988)
Mistakes Will Happen (1938)
Mr. Adams and Eve (1957)
Mr. & Mrs. & Mr. (1980)
Mr. and Mrs. Bo Jo Jones (1971)
Mr. and Mrs. Cop (1974)

Mr. and Mrs. Dracula (1980)
Mr. and Mrs. Ryan (1986)
Mr. Boogedy (1986)
Mr. Broadway (1964)
Mr. Chedworth Steps Out (1939)
Mr. Clock (What Time Is It, Mr.
    Clock?) (1985)
Mr. Deeds Goes to Town (1969)
Mr. Denning Drives North (1952)
Mr. District Attorney (1951)
Mr. Ed (1960)
Mr. Fabre's Mill (1986)
Mr. Garlund (1960)
Mr. Horatio Knibbles (1971)
Mr. Horn (1979)
Mr. Inside/Mr. Outside (1973)
Mister Jericho (1970)
Mr. Leon (1982)
Mr. Love (1985)
Mr. Lucky (1959)
Mr. Magoo (1963)
Mr. Merlin (1981)
Mr. Mom (1983)
Mr. Mom (1984)
Mr. Muhsin (1988)
Mr. Nice Guy (1987)
Mr. North (1988)
Mr. Patman (1980)
Mr. Peek-a-Boo (1951)
Mr. Peepers (1952)
Mr. Photographer (1953)
Mr. President (1987)
Mr. Roberts (1965)
Mr. Rogers' Neighborhood (1970)
Mr. Slotter's Jubilee (1979)
Mr. Smith (1983)
Mr. Success (1984)
Mr. Sunshine (1986)
Mr. T and Tina (1976)
Mr. Terrific (1967)
Mr. Topaze (1961)
Mr. Vampire (1986)
Mr. Walkie Talkie (1952)
Mr. Wrong (1985)
Mistral's Daughter (1984)
Mistress, The (1959)
Mistress (1987)
Mrs. Columbo (1979)
Mrs. Delafield Wants to Marry
    (1986)
Mrs. G Goes to College (1961)
Mrs. Latter's Pension (1984)
Mistress of Paradise (1981)
Mistress of the Apes (1979)
Mrs. R.'s Daughter (1979)
Mrs. Soffel (1984)
Mrs. Sundance (1974)

Mrs. Warren's Profession (1960)
Misunderstanding (1984)
Misunderstood (1984)
Mitchell and Woods (1981)
Mix-Up (Meli-Melo) (1986)
Mixed Blood (1984)
Moa (1987)
Mob War (1984)
Mobile One (1975)
Mobile Two (1975)
Mod Squad (1968)
Mode in France (1985)
Model Behavior (1984)
Modern American Composers I (1984)
Modern Day Houdini (1983)
Modern Girls (1937)
Modern Girls (1986)
Modern Problems (1981)
Modern Romance (1981)
Moderns, The (1988)
Modesty Blaise (1982)
Mofles' Escapades (1987)
Moju (Blind Beast, The) (1969)
Mole Men vs. the Son of Hercules
    (1961)
Moll Flanders (1975)
Molokai (1959)
Moloka'i Solo (1988)
Molotov Cocktail (see Cocktail
    Molotov)
Mom, the Wolfman and Me (1980)
Moment, The (1980)
Moment in Love, A (short) (1956)
Moment of Adventure, The (1983)
Moments (1981)
Moments of Play (1986)
Momma the Detective (1981)
Mommie Dearest (1981)
Momo (1987)
Mona Lisa (1986)
Mona McCluskey (1965)
Monchhichis (1983)
Monday, a Parody (1985)
Mondo New York (1988)
Money on the Side (1982)
Money Pit, The (1986)
Money to Burn (1973)
Moneychangers, The (1976)
Mongo's Back in Town (1971)
Monique (Flashing Lights/New York
    After Dark) (1979)
Monk, The (1969)
Monk of Monza, The (1963)
Monkees, The (1966)
Monkey Grip (1982)
Monkey Mia (1985)
Monkey Mission, The (1981)

Monkey Shines (1988)
Monkey's Paw, The (1948)
Monolith Monsters, The (1957)
Monolog (1988)
Monroes, The (1966)
Monsieur de Pourceaugnac (1985)
Monsieur Ripois (1954)
Monsignor (1950)
Monsignor (1982)
Monsignor Quixote (1987)
Monster Club, The (1981)
Monster Dog (1986)
Monster from a Prehistoric Planet (Gappa) (1967)
Monster from Green Hell, The (1957)
Monster from the Ocean Floor, The (1954)
Monster in the Closet (1986)
Monster Island (1981)
Monster Manor (1988)
Monster of Florence, The (1986)
Monster of Highgate Ponds, The (1966)
Monster of the Island, The (1973)
Monster on the Campus (1958)
Monster Shark (Red Ocean) (1986)
Monster Squad, The (1976)
Monster Squad, The (1987)
Monster Zero (1970)
Monstrosity (1964)
Monte Napoleone (1987)
Montecarlo Gran Casino (1988)
Montecarlo, Montecarlo (1987)
Montefuscos, The (1975)
Montenegro (Pigs and Pearls) (1981)
Month in the Country, A (1987)
Month Later, A (1987)
Monty Nash (1971)
Monty Python and the Holy Grail (1975)
Monty Python's Flying Circus (1974)
Monument to the Dream (1968)
Moods (Etats d'Ame) (1986)
Moon and Sun (1987)
Moon in Scorpio (1988)
Moon in the Gutter, The (1983)
Moon of the Wolf (1972)
Moon Over Parador (1988)
Moon Over the Alley (1980)
Moonbase 3 (1973)
Moonchild (1972)
Moonfleet (1955)
Moonlight (1982)
Moonlighting (1985)

Moon's Only a Naked Ball, The (1981)
Moonshine Bowling (1983)
Moonstruck (1987)
Moonwalker (1988)
Moral (1983)
Moralist, The (1959)
Morality (1936)
More About Nostradamus (short) (1940)
More About the Children of Bullerby Village (1987)
More Light! (1988)
More Than Broken Glass: Memories of Kristallnacht (1988)
More Than Friends (1978)
More Things Change, The (1985)
More Wild, Wild West (1980)
Morgan Stewart's Coming Home (1987)
Morianna--I the Body (1968)
Moritz Inside the Advertising Pillar (1984)
Mork and Mindy (1978)
Mork and Mindy (animated) (1982)
Morning After, The (1974)
Morning After, The (1986)
Morning in Alabama (German Lawyer, A) (1984)
Morning Man, The (1987)
Morning Mist (1984)
Morning Patrol (1987)
Moro Affair, The (1986)
Morons from Outer Space (1985)
Mortal Storm, The (1940)
Mortu Nega (1988)
Mortuary (1981)
Mortuary Academy (1988)
Mosch (1980)
Moscow Bureau (1986)
Moscow Farewell (1987)
Moscow Laughs (1935)
Moscow on the Hudson (1984)
Moscow Strikes Back (1942)
Moses--The Lawgiver (1975)
Mosquito Coast, The (1986)
Mosquito on the Tenth Floor (1983)
Moss-Covered Asphalt (1983)
Most Amusing Game, The (1988)
Most Dangerous Man in the World, The (1988)
Most Deadly Game, The (Zig Zag) (1970)
Most Wanted (1976)
Motel (1984)
Motel Hell (1980)
Moth, The (Cma) (1980)

Mother (Ibunda) (1987)
Mother and Daughter: The Loving
     War (1980)
Mother and Me, M.D. (1979)
Mother Courage and Her Children
     (1961)
Mother, Dearly Beloved (1980)
Mother Lode (1982)
Mother Love (1938)
Mother Maria (1983)
Mother of Kings, The (1987)
Mother Song (1938)
Mother Teresa (1985)
Motherland (1960)
Motherland Hotel (1987)
Mother's Day (1980)
Mother's Day on Waltons Mountain
     (1982)
Mothers-in-Law, The (1967)
Mother's Meat and Freud's Flesh
     (1984)
Motor Mouse (1970)
Mt. Hakkoda (1978)
Mountain Calls, The (1938)
Mountain Men, The (1980)
Mountains of the Moon (1987)
Mountaintop Motel Massacre (1986)
Mouse Factory, The (1972)
Mousetrap, The (1950)
Mousey (1973)
Moutonnet (1936)
Move Along, There's Nothing to
     See (1983)
Movement, Movement (1969)
Movers & Shakers (1985)
Movie Murderer, The (1970)
Movin' On (1972)
Movin' On (1974)
Moving (1988)
Moving (see "On the Move")
Moving Day (1987)
Moving Targets (Zielscheiben)
     (1985)
Moving Violations (1985)
Moviola: The Scarlett O'Hara
     War (1980)
Moviola: The Silent Lovers
     (1980)
Moviola: This Year's Blonde
     (1980)
Ms. 45 (1981)
Muckrakers, The (1987)
Muddy Waters (1953)
Mueller's Bureau (1986)
Muffler and the Mechanics (1987)
Muggable Mary: Street Cop
     (1982)

Mulatto, The (1950)
Mulberry Tree, The (Pong) (1986)
Mullaway (1988)
Mulligan's Stew (1977)
Mummy, The (1932)
Mummy's Curse, The (1944)
Munsters, The (1964)
Munster's Revenge, The (1981)
Muppet Family Christmas, A (1987)
Muppet Movie, The (1979)
Muppets Take Manhattan, The (1984)
Murder at the Mardi Gras (1978)
Murder at the Nation's Senate (1984)
Murder at the World Series (1977)
Murder by Decree (1979)
Murder by Natural Causes (1979)
Murder Can Hurt You (1980)
Murder, Czech Style (1966)
Murder in Coweta County (1983)
Murder in Ecstasy (1984)
Murder in Music City (1979)
Murder in Paradise (1988)
Murder in Peyton Place (1977)
Murder in Texas (1981)
Murder in the Blue Room (1944)
Murder in the Central Committee
     (1982)
Murder in the Dark (1986)
Murder Ink (1983)
Murder Is a One-Act Play (1974)
Murder Lust (1987)
Murder Motel (1975)
Murder of Mary Phagan, The (1988)
Murder on Flight 502 (1975)
Murder on the Midnight Express
     (1975)
Murder Once Removed (1971)
Murder One (1988)
Murder 1, Dancer 0 (1983)
Murder or Mercy (1974)
Murder Ordained (1987)
Murder, She Wrote (1984)
Murder Will Out (1952)
Murdered House, The (1988)
Murders in the Rue Morgue (1986)
Murdock's Gang (1973)
Murphy Brown (1988)
Murphy's Law (1986)
Murphy's Law (1988)
Murphy's Romance (1985)
Murrow (1986)
Museum of Horror, The (1963)
Music Mart, The (1980)
Music of Covind (short) (1947)
Music School (1956)
Musical Story, A (1941)
Musolino the Bandit (1951)

My World Dies Screaming (1958)
My Young Auntie (1981)
Mystere (1983)
Mysteries from Beyond Earth
  (1975)
Mysteries from Beyond the
  Triangle (1977)
Mysteries of Black Magic, The
  (1957)
Mysteries of Paris (1937)
Mysteries of the Gods (1976)
Mysterious Big Tactics (1978)
Mysterious Case of Rygseck
  Murders (1960)
Mysterious Castle in the Car-
  pathians (1981)
Mysterious Doctor, The (1943)
Mysterious Island of Beautiful
  Women, The (1979)
Mysterious Two, The (1982)
Mysterious Uncle Silas (1947)
Mystery (1983)
Mystery Mansion (1983)
Mystery Mountain (1934)
Mystery of Bellavista, The (1986)
Mystery of Life, The (1973)
Mystery of Picasso (Picasso)
  (1956)
Mystery of the Morca, The (1984)
Mystery of the Pallid Face, The
  (1935)
Mystery of the Wax Museum, The
  (1933)
Mystery of Three Continents, The
  (1959)
Mystery Squadron (1933)
Mystic Pizza (1988)
Mystic Warrior, The (1984)
Mystique (1981)

N.Y.P.D. (1967)
Naa Ninna Bidenu (1978)
Naag Champag (1976)
Nacha Regules (1950)
Nadia (1984)
Nadia (1986)
Nadine (1987)
Nagin (1976)
Nail, The (1949)
Nail Gun Massacre (1987)
Naked Cage, The (1986)
Naked City (1958)
Naked Country, The (1985)
Naked Evil (1966)
Naked Exorcism (1975)
Naked Face, The (1984)

Naked Gun, The (1988)
Naked Love (1981)
Naked Magic (Shocking Cannibals)
  (1974)
Naked Man, The (1987)
Naked Paradise (1957)
Naked Sun, The (1959)
Naked Truth, The (1957)
Naked Vengeance (1986)
Nakia (1974)
Name for Evil, A (1970)
Name of the Game, The (1968)
Name of the Rose, The (1986)
Nameless Band, A (1981)
Nana (1977)
Nana (1985)
Nancy (1970)
Nancy Astor (1984)
Nancy Drew Mysteries, The (1977)
Nanny and the Professor (1970)
Nanou (1986)
Naples of Former Days (1938)
Naples That Never Dies (1939)
Naples Under the Kiss of Fire
  (1938)
Napoleon (re-issue) (1981)
Napoleon and Josephine: A Love
  Story (1987)
Napoleon Bonaparte (reissue) (1955)
Narc--Red Duel, The (1986)
Narcissus (1956)
Narcissus and Psyche (1981)
Narcotics Police (1987)
Narcotics Story, The (1958)
Narcotics Terror (1987)
Narrow Bridge, The (1985)
Nashville Grab (1981)
Nashville 99 (1977)
National Gallery of Art, The (1968)
National Lampoon's Class Reunion
  (1982)
National Lampoon's European Vaca-
  tion (1985)
National Lampoon's Two Reelers
  (1981)
National Lampoon's Vacation (1983)
National Snoop, The (1983)
National Velvet (1960)
Native Pony (1954)
Native Son (1951)
Native Son (1986)
Nativity, The (1978)
Natural, The (1984)
Natural Look, The (1977)
Nature of the Beast, The (1988)
Nature's Revenge (1984)
Naughty Ball, The (short) (1956)

Naughty Boys (1984)
Navigator, The (1988)
Navy Lark, The (1959)
Navy vs. the Night Monsters,
  The (1966)
Navy Wife (1935)
Nazi Hunter: The Beate Klarsfeld
  Story (1986)
Neapolitan Millionaire (1951)
Neapolitans in Milan (1953)
Near Dark (1987)
Necessary Parties (1988)
Necrophagus (1971)
Necropolis (1970)
Necropolis (1987)
Nedtur (If Music Be the Food of
  Love) (1980)
Needles and Pins (1973)
Neglected Miracle, The (1985)
Negresco (1968)
Neighbor, The (1987)
Neighborhood, The (1982)
Neighborhood (1987)
Neighborhood--Oh, Those Hot
  Mexicans, The (1986)
Neighbors (Apartment Above)
  (1939)
Neighbors (1981)
Neighbours (1985)
Neither Chana Nor Juana (1985)
Nelly's Version (1983)
Nemesio (1986)
Nemo (Dream One) (1984)
Nenita Unit (1954)
Neon Ceiling, The (1971)
Neon Maniacs (1986)
Nero Wolfe (1979)
Nero Wolfe (1981)
Nest, The (1988)
Nest Break (1980)
Nest in the Wind (1980)
Nesting, The (1981)
Nestor Burma, Detective of Shock
  (1982)
Net, The (1953)
Neutron Against the Death Robots
  (1961)
Neutron and the Black Mask
  (1961)
Nevada Smith (1975)
Never Again (1984)
Never Cry Wolf (1983)
Never Say Die (1988)
Never Say Never (1979)
Never Say Never Again (1983)
Never Take Candy from a
  Stranger (1960)

Neverending Story, The (1984)
New Adventures of Batman, The
  (1977)
New Adventures of Gilligan, The
  (1974)
New Adventures of Huckleberry
  Finn, The (1968)
New Adventures of Perry Mason,
  The (1973)
New Adventures of Pinocchio, The
  (1961)
New Adventures of Pippi Longstock-
  ing, The (1988)
New Adventures of Superman, The
  (animated) (1966)
New Adventures of Wonder Woman,
  The (1977)
New Andy Griffith Show, The
  (1972)
New Archie/Sabrina Hour, The
  (1977)
New Avengers, The (1978)
New Breed, The (1961)
New Daughters of Joshua Cabe,
  The (1976)
New Delhi Times (1986)
New Dick Van Dyke Show, The
  (1971)
New Earth, The (1937)
New Fred and Barney Show, The
  (1979)
New Gulliver, The (1935)
New Healers, The (1972)
New Horizons (1939)
New Invisible Man, The (1957)
New Kids, The (1985)
New Kind of Family, A (1979)
New Land, The (1974)
New Life, A (1988)
New Maverick, The (1978)
New Mike Hammer, The (1986)
New Morning of Billy the Kid, The
  (1986)
New Odd Couple, The (1982)
New Operation Petticoat, The (1978)
New, Original Wonder Woman, The
  (1975)
New Paradise Cinema (1988)
New People, The (1969)
New Phil Silvers Show, The (1969)
New Schmoo, The (1979)
New Squire, The (1936)
New Super Friends Hour, The
  (1977)
New Teacher, The (1941)
New Temperatures Rising Show,
  The (1973)

New Three Stooges, The (1966)
New Voice, The (1973)
New World (1986)
New Year's Eve at Bob's House (1985)
New Year's Evil (1981)
New Year's Sacrifice (1957)
New York Nights (1984)
New York Ripper (1982)
Newhart (1982)
Newman's Drug Store (1976)
News at Eleven (1986)
News Is the News, The (1983)
Next of Kin (1982)
Next of Kin (1986)
Next One, The (1981)
Next Step Beyond, The (1978)
Next Stop Paradise (1980)
Next Summer (1985)
Next Victim, The (1975)
Next Victim, The (1984)
Next Year If All Goes Well (1981)
Nice Girls Don't Explode (1987)
Nichols (1971)
Nichols and Dymes (1981)
Nick and the Dobermans (1980)
Nickel Mountain (1985)
Nickel Ride, The (1974)
Nicky's World (1974)
Niel Lynne (1985)
Niemann's Time--A German "Heimatfilm" (1985)
Night (1985)
Night After Death (1983)
Night and Its Price, The (1984)
Night Angels (1987)
Night at the National Assembly, A (1988)
Night Beast (Bete Noir, La) (1983)
Night Butterflies (1971)
Night Caller (1985)
Night Chase (1970)
Night Court (1984)
Night Cries (1978)
Night Editor (1946)
Night Friend (1988)
Night Gallery (1969)
Night Gallery (1971)
Night Games (1974)
Night Games (1980)
Night God Screamed, The (1971)
Night Guy (1969)
Night Hair Child (1971)
Night Heat (1985)
Night in Heaven, A (1983)

Night in Hell, A (1958)
Night in Rome, A (1960)
Night in the Cemetery, A (1973)
Night in the Life of Jimmy Valentine, A (1988)
Night Journey (1988)
Night Magic (1985)
'night, Mother (1986)
Night of a Thousand Cats (1974)
Night of Courage (1987)
Night of Destiny (1982)
Night of Terror (1972)
Night of the Blood Beast (1958)
Night of the Blood Monster (Throne of Fire) (1972)
Night of the Bloody Apes, The (Horror and Sex) (1968)
Night of the Creeps (1986)
Night of the Damned, The (1971)
Night of the Demon (1988)
Night of the Emerald Moon, The (1985)
Night of the Falling Stars (Night of San Lorenzo) (1982)
Night of the Ghouls (1959)
Night of the Juggler (1980)
Night of the Living Dead (1968)
Night of the Marten, The (1988)
Night of the Mayas (1939)
Night of the Pencils, The (1986)
Night of the Seagulls (1977)
Night of the Witches (1970)
Night of the Wolves (1982)
Night of the Zombies (Gamma 693) (1979)
Night of the Zombies (Hell of the Living Dead/Apocalipsis Canibal) (1980)
Night of Varennes, The (1982)
Night on the Town, A (1986)
Night Partners (1983)
Night Patrol (Ronde de Nuit) (1984)
Night Prowl (1958)
Night Rider, The (1979)
Night River (1981)
Night School (Terror Eyes) (1981)
Night Shadows (Mutant) (1984)
Night Shift (1982)
Night Slaves (1970)
Night Soldier (1984)
Night Stalker, The (1972)
Night Stalker, The (1974)
Night Stalker, The (1985)
Night Strangler, The (1973)
Night Terror (1977)
Night That Panicked America, The (1975)

Night the Bridge Fell Down, The
  (1983)
Night the Lights Went Out in
  Georgia, The (1981)
Night They Arrested Fatima, The
  (1984)
Night They Killed Rasputin, The
  (1960)
Night They Saved Christmas, The
  (1984)
Night They Took Miss Beautiful,
  The (1977)
Night Train (1940)
Night Train to Kathmandu, The
  (1988)
Night Voyage (1987)
Night Warning (Thrilled to Death/
  Momma's Boy/Butcher, Baker,
  Nightmare Maker) (1980)
Night Wars (1988)
Night We Dropped a Clanger, The
  (1959)
Night We Got the Bird, The
  (1961)
Night with Hortense, The (1988)
Night with Silena, The (1986)
Night with the Emperor, A (1937)
Night Without Stars (1951)
Night Zoo (1987)
Nightfall (Head Shot) (1982)
Nightfall (1988)
Nightflyers (1987)
Nightforce (1987)
Nighthawks (1981)
Nightingales, The (1979)
Nightingales (1988)
Nightmare (1974)
Nightmare (1981)
Nightmare (1985)
Nightmare at Bitter Creek (1988)
Nightmare at Shadow Woods
  (1987)
Nightmare Hotel (1973)
Nightmare in Badham County
  (1976)
Nightmare in Chicago (1964)
Nightmare on Elm Street, A
  (1984)
Nightmare on Elm Street, Part 2:
  Freddy's Revenge, A (1985)
Nightmare on Elm Street 3: Dream
  Warriors, A (1987)
Nightmare on Elm Street 4: The
  Dream Master, A (1988)
Nightmare on Elm Street--
  Freddy's Nightmare: The
  Series, A (1988)

Nightmare Weekend (1986)
Nightmares (1983)
Nights at O'Rear's (1981)
Nights in White Satin (1987)
Nights Without Moons or Suns
  (1984)
Nightside (1980)
Nightsongs (1984)
Nightstick (1987)
Nine-and-a-Half Weeks (1986)
9 Deaths of the Ninja (1985)
Nine Lives of a Cat, The (1970)
Nine Lives of Fritz the Cat (1974)
Nine to Five (1980)
Nine to Five (1982)
Nine Ways to Approach Helsinki
  (1982)
1918--A Man and His Conscience
  (1957)
1984 (1984)
1919 (1983)
1919 (1984)
1990: The Bronx Warriors (1983)
1969 (1988)
Ninety Days (1985)
90 Minute Stop (1936)
99 River Street (1953)
Ninja, The (1981)
Ninja Mission, The (1984)
Ninja Thunderbolt (1985)
Ninja Turf (L.A. Streetfighters)
  (1986)
Ninth Circle, The (1961)
Ninth Heart, The (1980)
Niskavouri Saga, The (1985)
Nitakayama Nobore (1968)
Nitwits (1987)
No Clues (1983)
No Dead Heroes (1987)
No Drowning Allowed (1987)
No End (1985)
No Funny Business (1934)
No Harm Intended (1988)
No Harvest But a Thorn (1985)
No Holds Barred (1980)
No, Honestly (1975)
No Man's Land (1984)
No Man's Land (1985)
No Man's Land (1987)
No Mercy (1986)
No More Easy Going (1980)
No More Vacation for the Good
  Lord (1950)
No One Twice (1984)
No Other Love (1979)
No Place for Jennifer (1950)
No Place Like Home (1985)

No Place to Hide (1981)
No Place to Run (1972)
No Retreat No Surrender (1986)
No Road Back (1957)
No Sad Songs (1985)
No Small Affair (1984)
No Soap, Radio (1982)
No Surrender (1985)
No Terrace-House for Robin Hood
  (1981)
No Thanks, Coffee Makes Me
  Nervous (1982)
No Time for Sergeants (1964)
No Time for Tears (1957)
No Time to Die (1958)
No Time to Die (1986)
No Way Out (1987)
Noa at 17 (1982)
Noah and the Cowboy (1986)
Noah's Ark (1956)
Noah's Ark Principle, The (1984)
Noble House (1988)
Noblewoman, The (1985)
Nobody Can Judge Me (1966)
Nobody's Boy (1970)
Nobody's Child (1986)
Nobody's Fool (1986)
Nobody's Perfect (1980)
Nobody's Perfekt (1981)
Nobody's Wife (Senora de Nadie)
  (1982)
Nobody's Women (1984)
Nocturna (1978)
Nocturna (1979)
Nocturnal Voyage, The (1986)
Noise Kill, The (Schalltot) (1985)
Noistottus (1987)
Nomads (1985)
Nomugi Pass (1980)
Non-Scheduled Train, A (1959)
Noose, The (1987)
Norah O'Neale (1934)
Norliss Tapes, The (1973)
Norma Rae (1981)
Norman Loves Rose (1982)
Norman Rockwell's "Breaking Home
  Ties" (1987)
North & South, Book II (1986)
North Beach and Rawhide (1985)
North Bridge (Pont du Nord, Le)
  (1981)
North Shore (1987)
North Star, The (1982)
Northern Lights (Havlandet) (1985)
Nosferatu (1922)
Nosferatu in Venice (1988)
Nostalgia (1983)

Not Everything Is True (1986)
Not for Hire (1959)
Not Guilty (1974)
Not in Front of the Children (1982)
Not in Front of the Kids (1984)
Not Just Another Affair (1982)
Not My Kid (1985)
Not Nothing Without You (1985)
Not of This Earth (1956)
Not Quite Human (1987)
Not Quite Jerusalem (1985)
Not Since Casanova (1988)
Not Tonight, Henry (1961)
Not Until Today (1979)
Not Wanted on the Voyage (1957)
Not With You, Not Without You
  (1985)
Notes for an African Orestes (1979)
Nothing But the Night (1975)
Nothing But Words of Praise for
  the Deceased (1984)
Nothing in Common (1986)
Nothing in Common (1987)
Nothing Left to Do But Cry (1985)
Nothing Left to Lose (1983)
Nothing to Lose (Time, Gentlemen,
  Please) (1953)
Nothing Underneath (1985)
Notorious Nobodies (1985)
November Cats (1986)
November Moon (1985)
Now and Forever (1956)
Now and Forever (1983)
Now Barabbas Was a Robber (1949)
Now I Know (1988)
Now or Never (1986)
Now You See It, Now You Don't
  (1968)
Nowhere to Hide (1977)
Nowhere to Hide (1987)
Nowhere to Run (1978)
Nuclear Gypsies, The (1985)
Nuclear Split (1987)
Nucleus Zero (1984)
Nude Bomb, The (1980)
Nuit des Traquees, La (1980)
Number 14 (1986)
Number 96 (1980)
Number One (1984)
Number 111 (1938)
Number One With a Bullet (1987)
Nun at Casino (1972)
Nurse (1980)
Nursemaid Mine (1987)
Nut House, The (1964)
Nut in Action, A (1983)
Nutcracker (1982)

Pale Passion (1984)
Pale Rider (1985)
Pallet on the Floor (1984)
Pallisers, The (1977)
Palmerstown, U.S.A. (1980)
Palms Precinct (1982)
Paloma, La (1936)
Pals (1987)
Pan Twardowski (1937)
Panache (1976)
Panagoulis Lives (1980)
Pancho (1967)
Pancho Barnes (1988)
Pancho Villa Returns (1950)
Panda and the Magic Serpent
    (1958)
Pandemonium (1982)
Pandemonium (Thursday the
    12th) (1982)
Pandemonium (1988)
Pandora and the Flying Dutch-
    man (1951)
Panic! (1957)
Panic in Echo Park (1977)
Panic on the 5:22 (1974)
Pankow '95 (1984)
Panther Squad (1986)
Paolo and Francesca (1953)
Papa, Can You Hear Me Sing?
    (1984)
Paper Bird (1984)
Paper Bridge, The (1987)
Paper Chase, The (1978)
Paper Chase: The Second Year,
    The (1983)
Paper Dolls (1982)
Paper Gallows (1950)
Paper Gramophone, The (1988)
Paper Heart (1982)
Paper Man (1971)
Paperhouse (1988)
Pappi (1936)
Parade, The (1984)
Parade of the Planets (1985)
Paradise (1974)
Paradise (1982)
Paradise (1986)
Paradise (1988)
Paradise and Fire Oven (Heaven
    and Hell) (1959)
Paradise Camp (1986)
Paradise Connection, The (1979)
Paradise for All (1982)
Paradise Motel (1985)
Paradise on Earth (1957)
Paradise View (1985)
Paraguelia (1980)

Parahyba Woman (1983)
Parallel Corpse, The (1982)
Parallel Divergences (1983)
Parallels (1980)
Paramedics (1988)
Parasite (1982)
Pardon (1966)
Pardon Me, But Are You For or
    Against? (1966)
Parent Trap II, The (1987)
Parents Terribles, Les (1949)
Parfait Amour (1985)
Paris (1979)
Paris Commune (1937)
Paris Incident (1954)
Paris Is Always Paris (1952)
Paris Midnight (1986)
Paris Seen By ... 20 Years After
    (sequence) (1984)
Paris 7000 (1970)
Paris, Texas (1984)
Park Place (1981)
Parkers, The (1981)
Parking (1985)
Parodontosis Now (1984)
Parole (1982)
Parson of Kirchfeld, The (1955)
Partisan Stories (1960)
Partner of God, The (1987)
Partners, The (1971)
Partners (1982)
Partners in Crime (1973)
Partners in Crime (1984)
Partners of Adventure (1980)
Partridge Family, The (1970)
Partridge Family: 2200 A.D., The
    (1974)
Party, The (1981)
Party Camp (1987)
Party Line (1988)
Party II, The (1982)
Pascali's Island (1988)
Pasi Spre Luna (1963)
Paso Doble (1983)
Paso Doble for Three (1986)
Pass the Ammo (1988)
Passage, The (1986)
Passage to India, A (1984)
Passengers of a Nightmare (1984)
Passengers of the Garden, The
    (1982)
Passerby of the San Souci Cafe,
    The (1982)
Passiflora (1986)
Passing, The (1985)
Passing Fancy (1984)
Passing Killer, A (1981)

Passing Strangers (1976)
Passing the Course (1987)
Passion (1986)
Passion Flower (1986)
Passion of Beatrice, The (1987)
Passion of Love (1981)
Passion of Remembrance, The
   (1986)
Passionate People (1983)
Passionate Strangers, The (1957)
Passionate Summer (1958)
Passport to Shame (1958)
Passport to Treason (1956)
Password: Kill Agent Gordon
   (1966)
Past Caring (1985)
Past, Present, Future (Trikal)
   (1986)
Pastorale Heroica (1983)
Patakin (1985)
Paternity (1981)
Pathetic Fallacy (Ajantrik) (1988)
Pathfinder (1987)
Paths of Life (Lebenslaeufe)
   (1982)
Patience (Ayoub) (1984)
Patriarchs of the Bible (1963)
Patricia Neal Story, The (1981)
Patrick Stone (1965)
Patriot, The (1938)
Patriot, The (1986)
Patti Rocks (1987)
Patty Duke Show, The (1963)
Patty Hearst (1988)
Pauk (short) (1969)
Paul Bernard--Psychiatrist (1972)
Paul Cadmus: Enfant Terrible at
   80 (1986)
Paul Chevrolet and the Ultimate
   Hallucination (1985)
Paul Lynde Show, The (1972)
Paulette (1986)
Pauline at the Seaside (1983)
Paul's Awakening (1985)
Pavlova (1984)
Peaceful Days (1984)
Peaceful Nights (1966)
Peaceful Valley, The (1957)
Peanut Butter Solution, The
   (1985)
Peanuts (1965)
Pearl (1978)
Pearl Harbor (1967)
Pearl of the Caribbean, The (1981)
Pearls of the Crown (1937)
Peasants (1935)
Pebbles and Bamm Bamm (1971)

Peck's Bad Girl (1959)
Peddler (Matlosa) (1981)
Peddlin' in Society (1949)
Pedro and the Captain (1984)
Peephole and the Key, The (1985)
Peeping Tom (Face of Fear) (1960)
Pee-Wee's Big Adventure (1985)
Peggy Sue Got Married (1986)
Peking Central (1986)
Peking Opera Blues (1986)
Pelle the Conqueror (1987)
Penalty Battalion 999 (1960)
Penitent, The (1988)
Penitentiary II (1982)
Penitentiary III (1987)
Penmarric (1982)
People, The (1972)
People of No Importance (1956)
People of the Forest (1988)
People vs. Jean Harris (1981)
People's Choice, The (1955)
People's Hero (1988)
Pepito and the Monster (1957)
Pepo (1935)
Pepote (1956)
Peppermint Peace (1983)
Per, Jom and Phen (1980)
Percy's Progress (It's Not the Size
   That Counts) (1979)
Perennial Weed, The (1976)
Perfect (1985)
Perfect Gentlemen (1978)
Perfect Marriage, A (Beau Mariage,
   Le) (1982)
Perfect Match, A (1980)
Perfect Match, The (1987)
Perfect Murder, The (1988)
Perfect People (1988)
Perfect Spy, The (1988)
Perfect Strangers (Blind Alley)
   (1983)
Perfect Victims (1988)
Perfect Wife, The (1983)
Perfectionist, The (1985)
Perfume of the Woman in Black,
   The (1974)
Perilous Voyage (1976)
Perils of Penelope Pitstop, The
   (1969)
Permanent Record (1988)
Permanent Vacation (1982)
Permeke (1985)
Perri (1957)
Perry Mason (1957)
Perry Mason Returns (1985)
Perry Mason: The Case of the
   Avenging Ace (1988)

Perry Mason: The Case of the
Lady in the Lake (1988)
Perry Mason: The Case of the
Lost Love (1987)
Perry Mason: The Case of the
Notorious Nun (1986)
Perry Mason: The Case of the
Sinister Spirit (1987)
Persian Lamb Coat, The (1980)
Personal Best (1982)
Personal Foul (1987)
Personals, The (1982)
Persuaders, The (1971)
Perverse Tales (1980)
Pessi and Illusia (1984)
Pest, The (Tete a Claques) (1982)
Pesti-Mese (1937)
Pestonjee (1988)
Pete and Gladys (1960)
Pete Kelly's Blues (1959)
Pete 'n' Tillie (1974)
Pete Roleum and His Cousins
(short) (1939)
Peter (1935)
Peter and Paul (1981)
Peter Gunn (1958)
Peter in Wonderland (1988)
Peter Loves Mary (1960)
Peter Lundy and the Medicine Hat
Stallion (1977)
Peter No-Tail (1982)
Peter No-Tail in America (1985)
Peter Potamus Show, The (1964)
Peter the First (1937)
Peter the Great (1986)
Peter von Scholten (1987)
Peter Voss, Hero of the Day
(1960)
Petit Soldat, Le (short) (1947)
Petrija's Wreath (1980)
Petrocelli (1974)
Petrol, Petrol (1981)
Petrov Affair, The (1987)
Petticoat Junction (1963)
Petzi (short) (1968)
Peyton Place (1964)
Peyton Place: The Next Genera-
tion (1985)
Pezzo, Capopezzo e Capitano
(1958)
Phalanstery, The (1981)
Phantasm II (1988)
Phantom (1922)
Phantom, The (Widziadlo) (1984)
Phantom Chariot, The (1940)
Phantom Empire, The (1935)
Phantom from 10,000 Leagues, The

(1956)
Phantom of Crestwood, The (1932)
Phantom of Hollywood, The (1974)
Phantom of the Convent (1934)
Phantom of the Opera (1983)
Phantom of the Operetta, The (1960)
Phantom of the Red House, The
(1954)
Phantom Planet, The (1961)
Phar Lap (1983)
Pharaoh's Court (1985)
Phatik and the Huggler (1983)
Phil and Mikhy (1980)
Phil Silvers Show, The (1955)
Philadelphia Attraction, The
(Uramisten) (1985)
Philip Marlowe, Private Eye (1983)
Philosopher's Stone (1957)
Phobia (1980)
Phobia (1988)
Phoenix, The (1972)
Phoenix (1978)
Phoenix, The (1981)
Photograph, The (1986)
Photographing Patricia (1984)
Phyllis (1975)
Piano for Mrs. Cimino, A (1982)
Pianoforte (1984)
Picaros, The (1987)
Picasso Trigger (1988)
Piccadilly Third Stop (1960)
Piccolo (short) (1959)
Picking Up the Pieces (1985)
Pickles Make Me Cry (1988)
Pickup (1951)
Pick-Up Artist, The (1987)
Pick-Up Summer (1981)
Picnic Among the Poplars (1981)
Picnic on the Grass (1959)
Pico, El (Needle, The) (1983)
Picone Sent Me (1984)
Picture Hunters, The (1986)
Picture Mommy Dead (1966)
Picture of Dorian Gray, The (1973)
Pictures (1981)
Pictures from the Unconscious
(1988)
Pictures of the Old World (1988)
Piece of Blue Sky, A (1961)
Piece of the Royal Pie, A (1986)
Pieces (1981)
Pied Piper of Hamelin, The (Krysar)
(1986)
Pierino Against the World (1981)
Pierre and Djemila (1987)
Pigeon, The (1969)
Pigeon Feathers (1988)

Pigeon Jill (1984)
Pigs, The (Daddy's Deadly
  Darling) (1972)
Pigs (1984)
Pigs and Battleships (1961)
Pilgrimage to Japanese Baths
  (1971)
Pimp, The (Zegen) (1987)
Pimpernel Svensson (1953)
Pin (1988)
Pinchcliffe Grand Prix (1981)
Pine Canyon Is Burning (1977)
Pine Lake Lodge (1961)
Ping Pong (1986)
Pink Blueprint, The (short)
  (1967)
Pink Chiquitas, The (1986)
Pink Motel (Motel) (1983)
Pink Nights (1985)
Pink Panther, The (1969)
Pinky's Gang (1986)
Pinocchio and the Emperor of the
  Night (1987)
Pinot, Just a Cop (1984)
Pintore a Cidade, O (1956)
Pioneer Spirit (1969)
Pioneer Woman (1973)
Pioneers, The (1960)
Pioneers, The (1980)
Piper's Pets (1979)
Piranha II (Spawning, The)
  (1981)
Piranha 2 (1982)
Pirate, The (1984)
Pirates, The (1983)
Pirates (1986)
Pirates of the Lake (1987)
Pistol for Ringo, A (1966)
Pistols 'n' Petticoats (1966)
Pit, The (1980)
Pitiless Colt of the Gringo, The
  (1966)
Pixote, Survival of the Weakest
  (1981)
Pizza Connection, The (1985)
Place at the Coast, The (1987)
Place at the Table, A (1988)
Place by the Sea, A (1988)
Place in the Sun, The (1988)
Place to Call Home, A (1987)
Place to Die, A (1974)
Places in the Heart (1984)
Placido (1986)
Plague Dogs, The (1982)
Plagues (1988)
Plain Clothes (1988)
Plain Girl (1935)

Plainlands (1988)
Plains of Heaven, The (1982)
Plainsong (1982)
Plan of His 19 Years, The (Jukyu-
  Sai no Chizu) (1980)
Planes, Trains & Automobiles (1987)
Planet Earth (1974)
Planet of Dinosaurs (1980)
Planet of the Apes (1974)
Planet "Tailor," The (1983)
Planetary Robot Vanguard: Ace
  Naval Battle in Space (1978)
Planets Against Us (1961)
Plasticman Comedy/Adventure Show,
  The (1979)
Platoon (1986)
Platoon Leader (1988)
Play ... Boy (1987)
Play Catch (1983)
Play Dead (1986)
Play It Cool (1970)
Play on the Tenne, The (1937)
Playgirls and the Vampire, The
  (1960)
Playhouse 90 (theme) (1956)
Playing Away (1986)
Playing Beatie Bow (1986)
Playing for Time (1980)
Playing with Fire (1985)
Playmates (1972)
Please Don't Eat the Daisies (1965)
Please, Don't Shoot the Cannon
  (1966)
Please Look After Amelia (1981)
Please Stand By (1978)
Pleasure Cove (1979)
Pleasure Garden, The (short)
  (1952)
Pleasure of Killing, The (1988)
Pleasure Palace (1980)
Pleasure of Vengeance, The (1987)
Pleasures (1986)
Pleasures of Saturday Night (1960)
Ploughman's Lunch, The (1983)
Plum Juice (1981)
Plumber, The (1980)
Plumber, The (1987)
Plumbum, or a Dangerous Game
  (1987)
Plunderers of the Moon (1962)
Plutonium Incident, The (1980)
Poachers (Krypskyttere) (1982)
Poet and Tsar (1938)
Point 905 (1960)
Pointsman, The (1986)
Poison, Le (1952)
Poison for Fairies (1986)

Poisons (1987)
Poker Alice (1987)
Poker Face (1986)
Poking Fun at the Border Patrol
  (1987)
Polar (1982)
Police (1985)
Police Academy (1984)
Police Academy 2: Their First
  Assignment (1985)
Police Academy 3: Back in
  Training (1986)
Police Academy 4: Citizens on
  Patrol (1987)
Police Academy 5: Assignment
  Miami Beach (1988)
Police Mondaine (1937)
Police Squad! (1982)
Police Story (1973)
Police Story (1986)
Police Story: The Freeway
  Killings (1987)
Police Surgeon (1972)
Police Woman (1974)
Policewoman Centerfold (1983)
Polish War Worker, The (1986)
Polk File on the Air (1988)
Polonia Restituta (1981)
Poltergeist (1982)
Poltergeist II (1986)
Poltergeist III (1988)
Polyester (1981)
Pomegranate Girl (1940)
Ponirah Terpidana (1984)
Pony Express (1960)
Pony Express Boy, The (1986)
Pool Without Water, A (1982)
Poor Albert and Little Annie
  (1972)
Poor Devil (1973)
Poor Little Rich Girl, The
  Barbara Hutton Story (1987)
Poor Man's Orange (1987)
Poor Richard (1984)
Pop! (1975)
Popcorn Kid (1987)
Pope John Paul II (1984)
Pope of Greenwich Village, The
  (1984)
Popeye (1980)
Popeye Doyle (1986)
Popi (1976)
Poppy Is Also a Flower, The
  (1966)
Population: One (1986)
Porky's (1981)
Porky's Revenge (1985)

Porky's II: The Next Day (1983)
Port Sinister (Beast of Paradise
  Isle) (1952)
Portia Faces Life (1954)
Portrait of a Female Drunkard
  (1980)
Portrait of a Life (1988)
Portrait of a Rebel: Margaret
  Sanger (1980)
Portrait of a Showgirl (1982)
Portrait of a Woman, Nude (Nudo di
  Donna) (1981)
Portrait of an Assassin (1950)
Portrait of an Escort (1980)
Portrait of Clare (1950)
Portrait of the Soviet Union (1988)
Portraits (short) (1970)
Possessed, The (Witch Yoba, The)
  (1976)
Possessed, The (1977)
Possessed, The (1988)
Possession (1973)
Possession (1981)
Possession (1985)
Post No Bills! (short) (1967)
Postcard from a Journey (1985)
Postman Always Rings Twice, The
  (1981)
Postmark for Danger (1956)
Post-Mortem (Moyna Tadanta)
  (1981)
Potlatch (1987)
Potteries (1981)
Pottsville (1980)
Poulet au Vinaigre (1985)
Pouvoir Intime (1986)
Powaqqatsi (1988)
Powderkeg (1971)
Power (1980)
Power, The (1984)
Power (1986)
Power and the Glory, The (1961)
Power and the Land (1940)
Power of Evil, The (1985)
Power of Men Is the Patience of
  Women, The (1980)
Power Within, The (1979)
Powerhouse (1982)
Powers of Matthew Starr, The
  (1982)
Powwow Highway (1988)
PPPerformer, The (1986)
Practice, The (1976)
Practice of Love, The (1985)
Prague (1985)
Pranks (1982)
Pray for Death (1985)

Pray for the Wildcats (1974)
Pray TV (1982)
Prayer for the Dying, A (1987)
Praying Mantis (1982)
Precarious Bank Teller, The
  (1980)
Precipice, The (1958)
Predator (1987)
Prehistoric Women (1967)
Prelude to Madness (Kreutzer
  Sonata) (1947)
Premiere (1937)
Preparations for the Festival
  (1976)
Preppies (1984)
Prescription: Murder (1968)
President's Mistress, The (1978)
President's Plan Is Missing, The
  (1973)
Presidio, The (1988)
Pretenders, The (1981)
Pretty in Pink (1986)
Pretty Little Beach, A (1949)
Pretty Smart (1987)
Prettykill (1987)
Prey (1977)
Prey, The (1980)
Prey, The (1985)
Price of Love, The (1984)
Price of Survival, The (1980)
Priceless Day, A (Ajandek ez a
  Nap) (1980)
Prick Up Your Ears (1987)
Prickly Pears (Fico d'India)
  (1980)
Pride and Prejudice (1980)
Pride of Jesse Hallam, The (1981)
Pride of the Family (1953)
Priest Killer, The (1971)
Priest of Love (1981)
Primal Fear (1980)
Primary English Class, The
  (1977)
Prime Evil (1988)
Prime of Miss Jean Brodie, The
  (1979)
Prime Risk (1985)
Prime Suspect (1982)
Prime Time, The (1960)
Prime Times (1983)
Primordium (short) (1968)
Primus (1971)
Prince and the Fawn, The (1982)
Prince Charming (1984)
Prince Jack (1984)
Prince of Bel Air (1986)
Prince of Central Park, The (1977)

Prince of Darkness (1987)
Prince of Homburg, The (1981)
Prince of the City (1981)
Princes, The (1983)
Princess (1980)
Princess Academy, The (1987)
Princess and the Cabbie, The (1981)
Princess Bride, The (1987)
Princess Daisy (1983)
Princess Mermaid (1975)
Princess of Babylonia, The (1986)
Princess Sen, The (1954)
Princess Tarakanova (1938)
Principal, The (1987)
Prison, The (1949)
Prison (1988)
Prison on Fire (1987)
Prison Ship (Star Slammer) (1987)
Prisoner, The (1968)
Prisoner: Cell Block H (1979)
Prisoner of Corbal (1939)
Prisoner of Love (1954)
Prisoner of Rio (1988)
Prisoner of the Cannibal God (1978)
Prisoner 1.040 (1959)
Prisoners (1937)
Prisoners of the Lost Universe
  (1983)
Private Battle, A (1980)
Private Benjamin (1980)
Private Benjamin (1981)
Private Classes (1986)
Private Conversations (1985)
Private Eye (1987)
Private Eyes, The (1980)
Private Function, A (1984)
Private Investigation (1987)
Private Investigations (1987)
Private Life, A (1983)
Private Life of Louis XIV, The
  (1936)
Private Matter, A (1966)
Private Passions (Clair) (1985)
Private Practices: The Story of a
  Sex Surrogate (1985)
Private Secretary (1953)
Private Secretary Marie (1936)
Private Sessions (1985)
Private Show (1985)
Privates on Parade (1982)
Privilege (1967)
Privileged (1982)
Prize of Peril, The (1983)
Prizzi's Honor (1985)
Probe (1972)
Probe (1988)
Procureau Hallers, Le (1930)

Rappel Immediat (1939)
Rappin' (1985)
Rapture (1949)
Rapture (Arrebato) (1980)
Rapture at Two-Forty (1965)
Rare Bird (1935)
Rare Breed, A (1981)
Rascals (Turlupins, Les) (1980)
Rascals and Robbers--The Secret
    Adventures of Tom Sawyer and
    Huck Finn (1982)
Raskenstam (1983)
Rasmus Hits the Road (1982)
Rat Patrol, The (1966)
Rat Race, The (Je Vais
    Craquer!) (1980)
Rat Trap, The (1982)
Rat Winter (1988)
Ratboy (1986)
Rate It X (1985)
Ratings Game, The (1984)
Rats, The (1955)
Rattlerat, The (1987)
Ravagers (1979)
Raven, The (1935)
Raw Force (1982)
Raw Meat (1972)
Rawhide (1959)
Razorback (1984)
Razor's Edge, The (1984)
Reaching Out (1983)
Ready for Action (1937)
Ready for the People (1964)
Ready or Not (1974)
Real American Hero, A (1978)
Real Game, The (1980)
Real Genius (1985)
Real Life (1984)
Real McCoys, The (1957)
Really ... Incredible (1982)
Realm of Fortune, The (1986)
Re-Animator (1985)
Rearview Mirror (1984)
Reason Asleep (1984)
Reason Nobody Hardly Ever
    Seen a Fat Outlaw in the Old
    West Is as Follows:, The
    (1967)
Rebel (1985)
Rebel Intruders, The (1980)
Rebel Love (1986)
Rebellion of the Ghosts (1946)
Rebelote (1984)
Rebels, The (1979)
Rebetico (1983)
Reborn (1981)
Recess (short) (1969)

Reckless (1984)
Record, The (1985)
Recruits (1986)
Red (1976)
Red Alert (1977)
Red Ants (Passkey to Paradise)
    (1987)
Red Army's Bridge, The (1964)
Red Badge of Courage, The (1974)
Red Bells: I've Seen the Birth of
    the New World (1983)
Red Blossoms (1961)
Red Boogie (1983)
Red Caviar (1985)
Red Countess, The (1985)
Red Curtain, The (1952)
Red Dawn (1984)
Red Desert Penitentiary (1986)
Red Dock (1988)
Red Dove, The (1961)
Red Dragon, The (1945)
Red Dust (Polvo Rojo) (1982)
Red Flag: The Ultimate Game
    (1981)
Red Guards in Hong Kong (1985)
Red Heat (1985)
Red Heat (1988)
Red Horse, The (1981)
Red Inn, The (1951)
Red Kiss (1985)
Red Light District (1956)
Red-Light Sting, The (1984)
Red Lips (1960)
Red Mansion, The (1980)
Red Nights (1988)
Red Pony, The (1973)
Red Rain (1950)
Red Riding Hood (1987)
Red River (1988)
Red Roses for Angelique (1966)
Red Shadow, The (1981)
Red Shirt, The (1987)
Red Shirts (1952)
Red Sonja (1985)
Red Sorghum (1988)
Red Spider, The (1988)
Red Stocking, The (1980)
Red Village, The (1935)
Red Zone (1986)
Redd Foxx Show, The (1986)
Redeemer ... Son of Satan, The
    (1978)
Redigo (1963)
Redondela (1987)
Reds (1981)
Redtops Meet Tyrannos, The
    (1988)

Reefer and the Model (1988)
Reference (1985)
Reflections (short) (1967)
Reflections (1984)
Reflections of Murder (1974)
Reform School Girls (1986)
Refuge (1981)
Refugees from Dead Man's Cave,
  The (1983)
Regina (1987)
Regular Fellow, A (1936)
Rehearsal for Murder (1982)
Reilly, Ace of Spies (1984)
Reincarnation of Isabel (Ghastly
  Orgies of Count Dracula) (1973)
Rejuvenator, The (1988)
Relative Merits (1987)
Relatives (1985)
Relentless (1977)
Reluctant Astronaut, The (1966)
Reluctant Heroes, The (1971)
Rembrandt (1936)
Remedy (1984)
Remember When (1974)
Remembering Marilyn (1988)
Remembrance (1988)
Remembrance of Love (1982)
Remington Steele (1979)
Remo Williams: The Adventure
  Begins (1985)
Remote Control (1988)
Remounting the Champs-Elysee
  (1938)
Remous (1935)
Rendezvous (1952)
Rendezvous, The (1972)
Rendezvous (1985)
Rendezvous Hotel (1979)
Rendez-vous in Melbourne (1957)
Rendezvous Leipzig (1985)
Rendezvous with Forgotten Years
  (1957)
Renegade Satellite, The (1954)
Renegades, The (1982)
Renfrew of the Royal Mounted
  (1937)
Reno and Yolanda (1987)
Rent-A-Cop (1988)
Rentadick (1972)
Repeat Dive (1982)
Repenter, The (1985)
Report from an Abandoned Planet
  (1985)
Report on Pollution at the Women's
  Kingdom (1988)
Reporter, The (1964)
Reporter X (1986)

Reptile, The (1966)
Requiem for a Secret Agent (1966)
Requiem for a Spanish Peasant (1985)
Requiem for a Vampire (1971)
Rescue, The (1988)
Rescue 8 (1958)
Rescue from Gilligan's Island (1978)
Research in Mark Brandenburg
  (1983)
Resting Place (1986)
Restless Gun, The (1957)
Restless Natives (1985)
Resurrection (1980)
Rete Piena di Sabbia, Una (1966)
Retouche (1986)
Retribution (1987)
Return, The (1973)
Return, The (1980)
Return (1985)
Return, The (1988)
Return Engagement (1978)
Return Engagement (1983)
Return from Hell (1983)
Return in Bond (1980)
Return of a Citizen (1986)
Return of Ben Casey, The (1988)
Return of Captain Invincible, The
  (1983)
Return of Captain Nemo, The (1978)
Return of Charlie Chan, The (1979)
Return of Desperado, The (1988)
Return of Dr. Mabuse, The (1961)
Return of Dr. X, The (1939)
Return of Frank Cannon, The (1980)
Revenge of Frankenstein (1958)
Return of Hickey, The (1988)
Return of Joe Forrester, The (1975)
Return of Josey Wales, The (1986)
Return of Luther Gillis, The (1984)
Return of Marcus Welby, M.D., The
  (1984)
Return of Martin Guerre, The (1982)
Return of Mickey Spillane's Mike
  Hammer, The (1986)
Return of Robin Hood, The (1988)
Return of Sherlock Holmes, The
  (1987)
Return of the Banished, The (1980)
Return of the Beverly Hillbillies,
  The (1981)
Return of the Champ (1981)
Return of the Filthy Seven, The
  (1969)
Return of the Giant Majin, The
  (1967)
Return of the Giant Monsters, The
  (Gammera vs. Gaos) (1967)

Riding on Air (1937)
Rififi in Amsterdam (1967)
Rifleman, The (1958)
Rigged (1985)
Right at the Bottom (1986)
Right Bank, Left Bank (1984)
Right Hand Man, The (1987)
Right Man, The (1960)
Right Man for a Delicate Job,
   The (1985)
Right of Way (1983)
Right Out of History--The Making
   of Judy Chicago's Dinner Party
   (1980)
Right Stuff, The (1983)
Right to Be Born, The (1952)
Right to Die, The (1987)
Right to Kill? (1985)
Right Way, The (1983)
Riker (1981)
Rikisha Man, The (1943)
Rikky and Pete (1988)
Riko Na Oyome-San (1959)
Ring, The (1988)
Ring Around the Clock (1953)
Ring of Passion (1978)
Ringo and Gringo Against All
   (1966)
Ringo: The Face of Revenge
   (1966)
Rio Zone Norte (1958)
Ripcord (1961)
Ripening Wheat (1939)
Ripoux, Les (1984)
Riptide (1983)
Rise and Rise of Daniel Rocket,
   The (1986)
Rise and Shine (1981)
Rise, Fair Sun (1974)
Rise Up, Spy (1982)
Rising Damp (1980)
Rising from the Surface (1981)
Rising Stock (1987)
Risk of Living, The (1980)
Risky Business (1983)
Rita (1950)
Rita Hayworth: The Love
   Goddess (1983)
Rita la Zanzara (1966)
Rita Moreno Show, The (1978)
Rita, Sue and Bob Too (1987)
Ritual (1984)
Ritual of Evil (1970)
Rivalry, The (1975)
Rivals of Sherlock Holmes, The
   (1975)
River, The (1984)

River Changes, The (1956)
River of Dollars, A (1966)
River of Fireflies (1987)
River of Gold (1971)
River of Mystery (1971)
River Rat, The (1984)
River Trip with Hen (1984)
Riverbed, The (1986)
Riverboat (1959)
River's Edge (1986)
Rivkin: Bounty Hunter (1981)
Road, The (Droga) (1981)
Road, The (Yol) (1982)
Road a Year Long, The (1958)
Road Games (1981)
Road Home, The (1988)
Road of Life, The (1956)
Road Runner Show, The (1971)
Road South, The (1988)
Road to Hope (1951)
Road West, The (1966)
Roadhouse 66 (1984)
Roadie (1980)
Roads of Love Are Night Roads,
   The (1981)
Roanoak (1986)
Roar (1981)
Roarin' Fifties, The (1983)
Roaring Forties, The (1982)
Roaring Twenties, The (1960)
Robbers of the Sacred Mountain
   (Falcon's Gold) (1982)
Robbery Under Arms (1985)
Robert Frost (1988)
Robert Herridge Theater, The
   (1960)
Robert Kennedy and His Times
   (1985)
Robert Scott and the Race for the
   South Pole (1968)
Robin Hood and the Sorcerer (1984)
Robin's Nest (1977)
Robinson Crusoe (1974)
Robinsoniad: Or, My English
   Grandfather (1986)
Robocop (1987)
Robot Monster (1953)
Robot vs. the Aztec Mummy, The
   (1959)
Rocinante (1986)
Rock and a Hard Place, A (1981)
Rock & Rule (1983)
Rock Disconcert (1982)
Rock 'n' Roll Mom (1988)
Rock Rainbow, The (1978)
Rockabye (1986)
Rocket Robin Hood (1967)

Rocket Gibralter (1988)
Rocket to Nowhere (1962)
Rockets Galore (1958)
Rockford Files, The (1974)
Rockhopper (1985)
Rockin' Road Trip (Summertime
  Blues) (1986)
Rocking Silver (1983)
Rocktober Blood (1984)
Rocky and His Friends (1959)
Rocky III (1982)
Rocky IV (1985)
Rodeo Girl (1980)
Roger and Harry: The Mitera
  Target (1977)
Roger Doesn't Live Here Anymore
  (1982)
Roger Rabbit & the Secrets of
  Toontown (1988)
Rogopag (1962)
Rogue of the North (1988)
Rogues, The (1964)
Rogues (Truhanes) (1983)
Roi, Le (1950)
Rojo, El (1966)
Roll, Freddy, Roll! (1974)
Roll of Thunder, Hear My Cry
  (1978)
Roll Out! (1973)
Roller Blade (1986)
Rollergirls, The (1978)
Rolling Man (1972)
Rolling Vengeance (1987)
Rollover (1981)
Roman Holidays, The (1972)
Roman Tales (1956)
Romance (1936)
Romance (1986)
Romance and Riches (Amazing
  Adventure, The) (1937)
Romance in Budapest (1934)
Romance in Paris, A (1987)
Romance of Betty Boop, The
  (1985)
Romance of Ida (1934)
Romance Theater (1982)
Romance with Amelie (1982)
Romancing the Stone (1984)
Romaneto (1981)
Romantic Age, The (1949)
Romantic Agony, The (Vaarwel)
  (1973)
Romantic Comedy (1983)
Romantic Story (1983)
Romantic Story (1986)
Rome, 2072 A.D.--The New
  Gladiators (1987)

Rona Jaffe's "Mazes and Monsters"
  (1982)
Ronya--The Robber's Daughter
  (1984)
Roof, a Family, A (1982)
Roofs at Dawn (1987)
Rookies, The (1972)
Room, The (1987)
Room at the Top (1959)
Room for One More (1962)
Room in Town, A (1982)
Room 666 (1982)
Room to Move (1987)
Room 222 (1969)
Room Upstairs, The (1987)
Room with a View, A (1986)
Roommates (1982)
Roommates (1984)
Rooster, The (Tuppen) (1981)
Rooster (1982)
Roots (1977)
Roots: The Gift (1988)
Roots: The Next Generation (1979)
Ropers, The (1979)
Roro Mendut (1984)
Rorret (1988)
Rosa (1982)
Rosa Luxemburg (1986)
Rosa-the-Rose, Public Woman (1986)
Rosary Murders, The (1987)
Rose of Bagdad, The (1949)
Rose of Iron, The (1973)
Rose of the Border (1987)
Rose of the Names, The (1987)
Rose of the Winds, The (1983)
Rosenthal and Jones (1975)
Roses Are for the Rich (1987)
Roses for the Prosecutor (1960)
Rosetti and Ryan (1977)
Rosi and the Big City (1981)
Rosie: The Rosemary Clooney
  Story (1982)
Rosso (1985)
Rothschild (1938)
Rotten Fate! (Sale Destin!) (1987)
Rough and the Smooth, The (1959)
Rough Cut (1980)
Roughnecks (1980)
'Round Midnight (1986)
Round My Head in 40 Days (1986)
Rounders, The (1966)
Rousters, The (1983)
Route 66 (1960)
Rowing With the Wind (1988)
Roxanne (1987)
Roxie (1987)
Royal Romance of Charles and

Sally's Irish Rogue (1958)
Salome (1986)
Salonka Terrorists, The (1961)
Salt (Uppu) (1988)
Salt of the Earth (1954)
Salt on the Skin (1985)
Salty (1974)
Salty Sweets (1986)
Salvador (1986)
Salvage I (1979)
Sam (Alone) (1959)
Sam (1978)
Sam Benedict (1962)
Sam Hill (1961)
Sam Hill: Who Killed the
    Mysterious Mr. Foster? (1971)
Samaritan: The Mitch Snyder
    Story (1986)
Same As It Ever Was (1983)
Sammy and Rosie Get Laid (1987)
Sammy's Super T-Shirt (1978)
Sampson (1961)
Sam's Son (1984)
Samson and Delilah (1984)
Samson and the Mighty Challenge
    (1964)
Samson in King Solomon's Mines
    (1964)
Samson vs. the Giant King (1963)
Samson vs. the Pirates (1963)
Samuel Lount (1985)
Samurai (1979)
Samurai Reincarnation (1982)
San Antonito (1986)
San Francisco International Air-
    port (1970)
San Pedro Beach Bums, The
    (1977)
Sanctuary of Fear (1979)
Sand (1986)
Sand Castles (1972)
Sandakan No. 8 (1975)
Sandokan the Great (1965)
Sands of the Desert (1960)
Sandwich Years, The (1988)
Sandy Duncan Show, The (1972)
Sanford (1980)
Sanford and Son (1972)
Sanford Arms (1977)
Sanford Meisner--The Theater's
    Best Kept Secret (1985)
Sanka (1973)
Santa Barbara (1984)
Santa Claus (1959)
Santa Claus Conquers the
    Martians (1964)

Santa Claus Is a Louse (1982)
Santa Claus--the Movie (1985)
Santa Esperanza (1980)
Santo and the Daughter of Franken-
    stein (1972)
Santo Attacks the Witches (1964)
Santo Vs. the Black Magic (1972)
Santo vs. the Blue Demon in
    Atlantis (1968)
Sara (1976)
Sara (1985)
Sarah (The Seventh Match) (1982)
Sarah (1983)
Sarah T.--Portrait of a Teenage
    Alcoholic (1975)
Sarati the Terrible (1937)
Sarge: The Badge or the Cross
    (1971)
Sarraounia (1986)
Sasame Yuki (1983)
Satan of All Horrors (1972)
Satanik (1968)
Satan's Cheerleaders (1977)
Satan's Empire (Beginning, The)
    (1986)
Satan's Five Warnings (1945)
Satan's Mistress (1980)
Satan's School for Girls (1973)
Satan's Slave (1976)
Satan's Triangle (1975)
Satellite in the Sky (1956)
Satin Spider, The (1985)
Satisfaction (1988)
Saturday Night and Sunday
    Morning (1960)
Saturday Night at the Palace (1987)
Saturday the 14th (1981)
Saturday's Children (1962)
Saturday's Hero (1951)
Saturn 3 (1980)
Sauerbruch (1954)
Savage (1973)
Savage Bees, The (1976)
Savage Breed (Razza Selvaggia)
    (1980)
Savage Creatures in Heat (1987)
Savage Curse, The (1974)
Savage Eye, The (1959)
Savage Harvest (1981)
Savage: In the Orient (1983)
Savage Island (1985)
Savage Land, The (Yuan Ye)
    (1981)
Savage Streets (1984)
Savage Sunday (1962)
Savage Weekend (1983)

Savage Women (1984)
Savages (1974)
Savamala (1982)
Savannah (Ballade, La) (1988)
Savannah Smiles (1982)
Save the Lady (1982)
Saviour, The (1980)
Savoy Lancers (1938)
Sawdust (short) (1987)
Sawyer and Finn (1983)
Saxon Splendor and Prussian
    Glory (1986)
Say Goodbye, Maggie Cole (1972)
Scabies (short) (1969)
Scalpel, Please (1985)
Scalpels (1980)
Scalplock (1966)
Scalps (1983)
Scamp, The (1957)
Scamps (1982)
Scandal (Shuban) (1950)
Scandal, The (1966)
Scandalous (1984)
Scandalous Adventures of
    Buraikan, The (1970)
Scandalous Gilda (1985)
Scandals of Glochemerle (1950)
Scanners (1981)
Scarecrow, The (1982)
Scarecrow and Mrs. King (1983)
Scared Silly (1982)
Scared Stiff (1987)
Scared Straight: Another Story
    (1980)
Scared to Death (1946)
Scared to Death (1980)
Scarface (1983)
Scarlet and the Black, The
    (1983)
Scarlet Fever (1984)
Scarlet Letter, The (1979)
Scarlet Pimpernel, The (1982)
Scavengers (1988)
Scenario (1985)
Scene of the Crime, The (1984)
Scene of the Crime, The (1986)
Scent of Death (1987)
Scent of Quince, The (1982)
Schilten (1980)
Schinderhannes, Der (1959)
Schizo (1976)
Schizoid (1980)
Schlagerparade (Hit Parade)
    (1954)
School Daze (1988)
School for Connubial Bliss
    (1954)

School for Scoundrels (1960)
School for Vagabonds (1955)
School for Vandals (1986)
School Outing, A (1983)
School Spirit (1985)
Schoolmaster, The (1981)
Schumtz (1986)
Scipio, the African (1937)
Scooby-Doo and Scrappy-Doo (1979)
Scooby-Doo/Dynomutt Hour, The
    (1976)
Scooby-Doo, Where Are You? (1969)
Scoop (1982)
Scorpio Letters, The (1967)
Scorpion, The (1984)
Scorpion (Summons, The) (1986)
Scotland Yard (1957)
Scott Free (1976)
Scoundrels, The (Cannales, Los)
    (1969)
Scout Forever, A (1985)
Scout's Honor (1980)
Scream (Outing, The (1981)
Scream, The (Krzyk) (1983)
Scream for Help (1984)
Scream from Nowhere, A (Hidden
    Beast, The) (1977)
Scream of the Demon Lover, The
    (1970)
Scream of the Wolf (1974)
Scream, Pretty Peggy (1973)
Screamer (1974)
Screamers (1982)
Screaming Skull, The (1958)
Screaming Woman, The (1972)
Screamplay (1985)
Screen Test (1985)
Screwball Academy (1987)
Screwballs (1983)
Scrooged (1988)
Scrubbers (1982)
Scruples (1980)
Sea and Poison, The (1987)
Sea Devils (1982)
Sea Fury (1958)
Sea Gypsies, The (1961)
Sea of Roses (1980)
Sea of Sand (1958)
Sea Prince and the Fire Child, The
    (1982)
Sea Serpent, The (1984)
Sea Shall Not Have Them, The
    (1954)
Sea Wolves, The (1980)
Seal, The (1981)
Sealab 2020 (1972)
Sealed With a Kiss (1981)

Seeing Things (1983)
Seekers, The (1979)
Seems Like Old Times (1980)
Segovia Escape, The (1981)
Seize the Day (1986)
Seizure: The Story of Kathy
  Morris (1980)
Self-Portrait in Brains (1980)
Semi-Tough (1980)
Semmelweis (1940)
Semmelweis (1980)
Send a Gorilla (1988)
Sender, The (1982)
Senior Trip! (1981)
Senior Week (1988)
Senior Year (1974)
Senorita de Travelez, La (1936)
Sensation (1937)
Sensations (1988)
Sense of Freedom, A (1981)
Sensi (Evil Senses) (1986)
Sensitive, Passionate Man, A
  (1977)
Sentimental (1981)
Sentimental Reasons (1984)
Separate Tables (1983)
Seppan (1988)
September Gun (1983)
September Storm (1960)
September Wheat (1980)
Sequa, La (1985)
Seraphim Polubes and Other
  Humans (1984)
Serenade (1959)
Serge (1960)
Sergeant Matlovich vs. the U.S.
  Air Force (1978)
Sergeant Ryker (1963)
Sgt. T. K. Yu (1979)
Serial (1980)
Serie Noir (1955)
Serious Charge (1959)
Serpent and the Rainbow, The
  (1988)
Serpent God, The (1970)
Serpent's Poison (Hadi Jed)
  (1982)
Serpent's Way Up to the Naked
  Rock, The (1987)
Serpico (1976)
Serpico: The Deadly Game (1976)
Servants from a Small Town (1982)
Sesame Street (1969)
Sesame Street Presents: Follow
  That Bird (1985)
Sessions (1983)
Set in Berlin (1987)

Set This Town on Fire (Profane
  Comedy, The) (1969)
Seven Brothers (1980)
Seven Dials Mystery, The (1981)
Seven Female Vampires, The (1986)
Seven Golden Women Against Two
  07s (1966)
Seven Hours to Judgment (1988)
Seven in Darkness (1969)
Seven in the Viewfinder (1985)
Seven Journeys (1951)
Seven Little Foys, The (1964)
Seven Lively Arts, The (1957)
Seven Magnificent Gladiators, The
  (1982)
Seven of the Big Bear (1953)
Seven Ravens, The (1953)
Seven Thunders (1957)
Seven Waves Away (1957)
Seven Wives for the McGregors
  (1966)
Seven Women for Satan (Count Zaroff)
  (1974)
Seven Year's Bad Luck (1957)
Seven Years Itch (1987)
Seventh Avenue (1977)
Seventh Continent, The (1967)
Seventh Floor, The (1966)
Seventh Man, The (1983)
Seventh Satellite, The (1968)
Seventh Seal, The (1957)
Seventh Sign, The (1988)
Seventh Target, The (1985)
79 Park Avenue (1977)
77 Sunset Strip (1959)
77 Sunset Strip (1958)
Severance (1988)
Severed Arm, The (1973)
Sex and the Married Woman (1977)
Sex and the Single Parent (1979)
Sex and the Vampire (Vampire
  Thrills/Frisson des Vampires,
  Les) (1970)
Sex Appeal (1986)
Sex Check, The (1969)
Sex Comedy, Quick on the Trigger
  (1971)
Sex Express (1975)
Sex Machine, The (1976)
Sex Mission (Seksmisja) (1984)
Sex Symbol, The (1974)
Sexorcists, The (1974)
Sexpot (1988)
Shadey (1985)
Shadow Box, The (1980)
Shadow Chasers, The (1985)
Shadow Dance (1983)

Shadow Dancing (1988)
Shadow in the Streets, A (1975)
Shadow Line (1980)
Shadow Man (Street of Shadows) (1953)
Shadow of Chikara, The (1977)
Shadow of Deception (1971)
Shadow of Evil (1964)
Shadow of the Past (1950)
Shadow of the Past (1959)
Shadow of Sam Penny, The (1983)
Shadow of the Earth (1983)
Shadow on the Land (1968)
Shadow Over Elveron (1968)
Shadow Play (1986)
Shadow Within, The (1970)
Shadows Are Getting Longer, The (1961)
Shadows in the Storm (1988)
Shadows of the Future (1985)
Shadows of the Past (1936)
Shadows of the Peacock (1987)
Shadows of the West (1949)
Shaft (1973)
Shaka Zulu (Part 1) (1986)
Shakedown (1988)
Shakedown on the Sunset Strip (1988)
Shaker Run (1985)
Shallow Grave (1988)
Shame, The (El-aar) (1983)
Shameful Secrets of Hastings Corners, The (1970)
Shameless ... But Honorable (1987)
Shamrock Hill (1949)
Shane (1966)
Shanghai Surprise (1986)
Shannon (1961)
Shannon (1981)
Shanty Town (1936)
Shaolin Drunkard (1983)
Shaping Up (1984)
Sharing Richard (1988)
Shark Kill (1976)
Shark Woman, The (1941)
Shark's Paradise (1986)
Sharma and Beyond (1986)
Sharon: Portrait of a Mistress (1977)
Sharpshooter, The (1958)
Sharpshooter Bruggler (1936)
Shattered Dreams--Picking Up the Pieces (1987)
Shattered Innocence (1988)
Shattered Spirits (1986)
Shattered Vows (1984)

Shaved Heads (1987)
Shazam! (1974)
Shazzam! (1967)
She (1935)
She (1982)
She Beasts' Warm Bodies (1972)
She Creature, The (1956)
She Cried "Murder!" (1973)
She Dances Alone (1981)
She Demons (1958)
She-Devils on Wheels (1968)
She Didn't Say "No" (1958)
She Freak (1966)
She-Gods of Shark Reef (1958)
She Had to Eat (1937)
She Must Be Seeing Things (1987)
She Waits (1972)
She Was Marked for Murder (1988)
She-Wasps' Challenge (1972)
She Wolf, The (Horrors of the Black Forest) (1965)
She-Wolf of the Devil's Moon, The (Devil's Bed, The) (1978)
Sheena (1984)
She'll Be Wearing Pink Pajamas (1985)
Shell Game (1975)
Shell Game (1987)
Shelley (1987)
Sheriff, The (1971)
Sheriff All in Gold, A (1966)
Sheriff and the Astronaut, The (1984)
Sheriff and the Satellite Kid, The (1979)
Sheriff of Fractured Jaw, The (1959)
Sheriff's Strange Son, The (1986)
Sherlock Holmes (1954)
Sherlock Holmes (1981)
Sherlock Holmes in New York (1976)
She's Dressed to Kill (1979)
She's Gotta Have It (1986)
She's Having a Baby (1988)
She's in the Army Now (1981)
Shillingbury Blowers, The (1980)
Shilly-Shally (Wahadelko) (1981)
Shining Season, A (1979)
Ships with Wings (1942)
Shipshape (1978)
Shipwreck of Liguria, The (1985)
Shir Hashirim (1935)
Shiralee, The (1957)
Shiralee, The (1988)
Shirley (1979)
Shirley Temple's Storybook (1958)
Shirley's World (1971)

Silver Globe, The (1988)
Silver Spoons (1982)
Silver Star, The (1955)
Silverado (1985)
Simon (1980)
Simon and Simon (1982)
Simon Lash (1960)
Simon of the Desert (1965)
Simple Case of Money, A (1952)
Sin in the Vestry (1975)
Sin of Innocence (1986)
Sinful Life of Franciszek Bula,
   The (1980)
Sing, Cowboy, Sing (1982)
Singapore, Singapore (1969)
Singapore Zero Hour (1966)
Singin' in the Corn (1946)
Single Life, The (1980)
Singles (Ma Femme s'Appelle
   Reviens) (1982)
Singoalla (1950)
Sinners in Paradise (1938)
Sins (1986)
Sins of Dorian Gray, The (1983)
Sins of the Father (1985)
Sins of the Fathers (1988)
Sins of the Past (1984)
Sinthia, the Devil's Doll (1979)
Sir Henry at Rawlinson End
   (1980)
Sirens (1987)
Siren's Song, The (Canto de la
   Sirena, El) (also, Song of the
   Siren) (1948)
Sirota's Court (1976)
Sister Maria (1937)
Sister, Sister (1982)
Sister, Sister (1987)
Sister Terri (1978)
Sister Unafraid (Path to the
   Kingdom) (1954)
Sisters of Nishijin (1952)
Sitcom (1983)
Six Against the Rock (1987)
Six Days in June (1985)
681 A.D. the Glory of Khan
   (1984)
Six Million Dollar Man, The
   (1973)
Six O'Clock Follies, The (1980)
Six of Us, The (1982)
Six Pack (1982)
Six Pack (1983)
6 Rms Riv Vu (1974)
Six Weeks (1982)
Six Wives of Henry VIII, The
   (1971)

Sixteen Candles (1984)
16 Days of Glory (1986)
Sixth Continent, The (1954)
Sixth Day, The (1986)
Sixth Gear (Sesta Brzina) (1981)
Sixth Sense, The (1972)
Sixth Sense, The (1986)
'68 (1987)
Sixty Years of Seduction (1981)
Sizzle (1981)
Skag (1980)
Skanderbeg (1954)
Skanor-Falsterbo (1939)
Skatebirds, The (1977)
Skeezer (1982)
Skeleton of Mrs. Morales, The
   (1959)
Ski Chase, The (1938)
Ski Lift to Death (1978)
Ski Troop Attack (1960)
Skies of Haruo, The (1978)
Skin, The (1981)
Skin (Hud) (1986)
Skin Deep (1987)
Skin of the Fool (Narrohut) (1982)
Skinny Chico (1983)
Skipper, The (Abba Ganuv) (1987)
Sky Above Heaven (1964)
Sky Bandits (1986)
Sky Commando (1953)
Sky Heist (1975)
Sky Is Red, The (1952)
Sky King (1951)
Sky of Our Childhood, The (1967)
Sky on Location, The (1983)
Sky Over Berlin, The (Wings of
   Desire) (1987)
Sky Pirates (1986)
Skyhawks, The (1969)
Skyhigh (1985)
Sky's No Limit, The (1984)
Skyward (1980)
Skyway to Death (1974)
Slam Dance (1987)
Slammer Girls (Big Slammer, The)
   (1985)
Slap in the Face, A (1981)
Slapstick (1982)
Slapstick of Another Kind (1984)
Slate, Wyn & Me (1987)
Slattery's People (1964)
Slaughter in Matamoros (1986)
Slaughter in San Francisco (1973)
Slaughterhouse (1988)
Slaughterhouse Rock (1988)
Slave Coast (Cobra Verde) (1988)
Slave Girls from Beyond Infinity

(1987)

Slave Merchant (see Merchant of Slaves)

Slave of Paradise, The (1968)

Slayer, The (1981)

Slayground (1984)

Sledge Hammer (1986)

Sleep Well, My Love (1987)

Sleepaway Camp (1983)

Sleepaway Camp 2: Unhappy Campers (1988)

Sleeping Tiger, The (1954)

Sleepless Years (1959)

Sleeps Six (1984)

Sleepwalk (1986)

Sleepwalker (1975)

Sleight of Hand (Jogo de Mao) (1983)

Slices of Life (1985)

Slime City (1988)

Slime People, The (1963)

Slipper Episode (1938)

Sloane (1984)

Slugger's Wife, The (1985)

Slumber Party Massacre, The (1982)

Slumber Party Massacre II (1987)

Small and Frye (1983)

Small Circle of Friends, A (1980)

Small Killing, A (1981)

Smaller Sky (1981)

Smart Alec (1986)

Smash Hit, A (Trhak) (1981)

Smash Palace (1981)

Smash-Up on Interstate 5 (1976)

Smile, Jenny, You're Dead (1974)

Smile of the Lamb, The (1986)

Smiley's People (1982)

Smiling Gentleman, The (1937)

Smiling Ghost, The (1941)

Smith Family, The (1971)

Smithereens (1982)

Smoke Should Not Fly, The (1984)

Smokey and the Bandit II (1980)

Smokey and the Bandit--Part 3 (1983)

Smokey Bites the Dust (1981)

Smokey the Bear Show, The (1969)

Smoky Mountain Christmas, A (1986)

Smooth Talk (1985)

Smorgasbord (1983)

Smuggler King, The (1985)

Smugglers, The (1968)

Smurfs, The (1981)

Smurfs and the Magic Flute, The

(1983)

Snails, The (1965)

Snake People, The (Isle of the Dead) (1968)

Snakes: Eden's Deadly Charmers (1988)

Snapshot Around the Family Table (1981)

Snatched (1973)

Sniffing Around (1985)

Sniper, The (1952)

Sniper, The (1980)

Sno-Line (Texas Sno-Line) (1984)

Snoop Sisters, The (1972)

Snoop Sisters, The (1974)

Snorks (1984)

Snow (Miege) (1981)

Snow Country Elegy (1971)

Snow Fairy, The (Yuki) (1982)

Snow Ghost, The (1968)

Snow Queen, The (1966)

Snow Queen, The (1987)

Snow, the Movie (1984)

Snowballing (1987)

Snowbeast (1977)

Snowdrop Celebrations (1984)

Snowman, The (1985)

Snuff Buttle (1988)

So Feared a Hell (1980)

So Fine (1981)

So Goes the Day (1968)

So Little Time (1953)

So Long, Stooge (Tchao Pantin) (1983)

So Many Dreams (1987)

So This Is Hollywood (1955)

So This Is Love (1975)

So What? (Eijanaika) (1981)

So What? (1987)

Soap (1977)

Soap and Water (1983)

Society Limited (Feine Gesellschaft, Beschraenkte Haftung) (1982)

Softly ... Softly (1985)

Solarbabies (1986)

Soldier, The (1982)

Soldier in Love (1967)

Soldier's Revenge (1986)

Soldier's Story, A (1984)

Soldier's Tale, A (1988)

Soldiers--365 Till Dawn (1987)

Sole Survivor (1970)

Soledad (1958)

Solitary Man, The (1979)

Solitary Man Attacks, The (1968)

Solo Sailor, The (1988)

Solo Sunny (1980)

Some Kind of Hero (1982)
Some Kind of Miracle (1979)
Some Kind of Wonderful (1987)
Somebody's Stolen the Thigh of
  Jupiter (1980)
Someday, Somewhere (1976)
Someone at the Top of the Stairs
  (1973)
Someone Behind the Door (1971)
Someone I Touched (1975)
Someone Is Watching Me! (1978)
Someone to Watch Over Me (1987)
Somerset (1970)
Something About Amelia (1984)
Something About Love (1988)
Something Becomes Evident (1982)
Something Entirely Different
  (1986)
Something Evil (1972)
Something for a Lonely Man (1968)
Something for Joey (1977)
Something in Between (1983)
Something in Common (1986)
Something Is Creeping in the Dark
  (1970)
Something Is Out There (1988)
Something Like That (No Yonamono)
  (1982)
Something Money Can't Buy (1952)
Something Out of Nothing (1980)
Something So Right (1982)
Something Wicked This Way Comes
  (1983)
Something Wild (1986)
Somewhere in Berlin (1949)
Somewhere in Time (1980)
Sommarlek (She Only Danced One
  Summer) (1951)
Son-in-Law, The (1980)
Son of D'Artagnan (1950)
Son of Godzilla (1969)
Son of Hercules in the Land of
  Fire (1963)
Son of Samson (1960)
Son of the Pusta (1937)
Son Rise: A Miracle of Love
  (1979)
Sonata for a Redhead (1983)
Sonatas (1959)
Song-Filled Tomorrows (1985)
Song for Europe, The (1985)
Song of Paris (1952)
Song of the Butterfly (1939)
Song of the Demon (1976)
Song of the Streets (1939)
Song of the Sun (1975)
Song to Remember, A (1960)

Songwriter (1984)
Sonny Spoon (1988)
Sons and Daughters (1974)
Sooner or Later (1979)
Sophia! (1968)
Sophia (1987)
Sophia Loren in Rome (1964)
Sophia Loren: Her Own Story
  (1980)
Sophie's Choice (1982)
Sophisticated Gents, The (1981)
Sorceress (1987)
Sorority House Massacre (1987)
Sorry I'm Late (1983)
Sorry to Have Imposed (1980)
Soul (1987)
Soul Is Greater Than the World,
  The (1985)
Soul Man (1986)
Soul to Devils, A (Chimimorya)
  (1971)
Sound of Anger, The (1968)
Sound of Horror, The (1964)
Soup for One (1982)
Soursweet (1988)
Sous-Doues, Les (Less Gifted, The)
  (1980)
South (Sur) (1988)
South Bronx Heroes (Runaways/
  Revenge of the Innocents) (1983)
South of Reno (1987)
South of the Highway (1937)
South Riding (1938)
South Wind (1960)
Southern Bar (1938)
Southern Comfort (1981)
Southern Cross, The (1982)
Southern Roses (1936)
Southern Trail, The (1982)
Souvenir (1988)
Souvenirs, Souvenirs (1984)
Space (1985)
Space Academy (1977)
Space Cobra (1983)
Space Cruiser Yamato (1982)
Sapce Cruiser Yamato--Final (1982)
Space Cruiser Yamato--The New
  Voyage (1979)
Space Fantasy Emeraldus (1978)
Space Firebird 2772 (Hi No Tori-
  2772) (1982)
Space Ghost (1966)
Space Giants (1969)
Space Kidettes (1966)
Space Monster (1965)
Space Movie, The (1980)
Space 1999 (1975)

Stories of the Century (1956)
Storm, The (Jhor) (1980)
Storm (1985)
Storm Fear (1956)
Storm of the Plains (1937)
Storm over Asia (1938)
Stormbound (1952)
Stormin' Home (1985)
Stormquest (1988)
Storms in May (1938)
Stormy Crossing (1958)
Stormy Monday (1988)
Story of --, The (1962)
Story of a Goldfish, The (short)
  (1959)
Story of a Good Guy, The (1980)
Story of a Marriage, Part I:
  Courtship, The (1987)
Story of a Night, The (1966)
Story of a Pure Love, The (1958)
Story of a Trickster, The (1936)
Story of an Encounter (1983)
Story of an Unknown Man (1980)
Story of David, A (1960)
Story of Fausta, The (1988)
Story of Hollywood--Part 1, The
  (1988)
Story of Jacob and Joseph, The
  (1974)
Story of Louis Pasteur, The (1935)
Story of Love, The (1981)
Story of Piera (1983)
Story of Pretty Boy Floyd, The
  (1974)
Story of the Good Scoundrels,
  The (1984)
Storyteller, The (1977)
Storyteller, The (1987)
Stowaway (1936)
Stowaway to the Moon (1975)
Straight from the Heart (1988)
Straight on Until Morning (1972)
Straight to Hell (1987)
Straits (Kaikyo) (1982)
Stranded (1976)
Stranded (1986)
Stranded (1987)
Strange Affair, A (1982)
Strange and Deadly Occurrence,
  The (1974)
Strange Appointment (1950)
Strange Bargain (1949)
Strange Brew (1983)
Strange Case of Dr. Faustus, The
  (1969)
Strange Case of Dr. Jekyll and Mr.
  Hyde, The (1967)

Strange Case of Dr. Jekyll and Mr.
  Hyde, The (1987)
Strange Deception (1953)
Strange Fascination (1952)
Strange Friends (1983)
Strange Fruits (Eisenhans) (1983)
Strange Gods, The (1958)
Strange Guest, A (1936)
Strange Guests (1959)
Strange Holiday (1942)
Strange Homecoming (1974)
Strange Invaders (1983)
Strange Love (1984)
Strange Mr. Gregory, The (1946)
Strange New World (1975)
Strange Passion, A (1984)
Strange Places (Other People, Other
  Places (1973)
Strange Possession of Mrs. Oliver,
  The (1977)
Strange Report, The (1971)
Strange Vengeance of Rosalie, The
  (1972)
Strange Voices (1987)
Strange World of Planet X, The
  (1958)
Stranger, The (1954)
Stranger, The (1973)
Stranger, The (1987)
Stranger at Home (1985)
Stranger in Our House (1978)
Stranger Is Watching, A (1982)
Stranger on My Land (1988)
Stranger on the Run (1967)
Stranger Than Fiction (1985)
Stranger Than Paradise (1984)
Stranger Waits, A (1987)
Stranger Who Looks Like Me, The
  (1974)
Stranger Within, The (1974)
Strangers (1955)
Strangers in a Strange Land: The
  Adventures of a Canadian Film
  Crew in China (1988)
Strangers in Paradise (1983)
Strangers in 7A, The (1972)
Strangers in the House (1949)
Stranger's Kiss (1983)
Strangers--The Road to Liberty
  (1980)
Strangers: The Story of a Mother
  and Daughter (1979)
Strangler, The (1972)
Strangler of Blackmoor Castle, The
  (1963)
Strangler vs. Strangler (1984)
Strata (1983)

(1982)
Tales of the Gold Monkey (1982)
Tales of the Unexpected (1977)
Tales of the Unexpected (1979)
Tales of Tomorrow (1951)
Tales of Wells Fargo, The (1957)
Talk Radio (1988)
Talk to Me (1982)
Talking About Josephine (1937)
Talking Walls (1982)
Tall Man, The (1960)
Tall Timbers (1937)
Talmae and Pomdari (1987)
Talpa (1957)
Tame re Champo ne Ame Kel (1978)
Tamer of Wild Horses (short)
  (1966)
Taming of the Scoundrel
  (Bisbetico Domato, Il) (1981)
Tammy (1965)
Tammy Grimes Show, The (1966)
Tandem (1986)
Tandem (1987)
Tanga-Tika (1953)
Tango Bar (1988)
Tango in the Belly (1985)
Tango Is History (1984)
Tango of Our Childhood (1985)
Tango: Our Dance (1988)
Tangos--Gardel's Exile (1985)
Tank (1984)
Tank Battalion (1958)
Tank Commandos (1959)
Tanya (1942)
Tanya's Island (1981)
Tapeheads (1988)
Taps (1981)
Tarantulas: The Deadly Cargo
  (1977)
Tarao Bannai (1978)
Target (1985)
Target Eagle (Playing with Death)
  (1982)
Target ... Earth (1980)
Target for Killing, A (1966)
Target: Harry (1980)
Target Risk (1975)
Target: The Corrupters (1961)
Taro of the Dragons (1979)
Tarot (1986)
Tarzan and the Leopard Man (1964)
Tarzan (1966)
Tarzan and King Kong (1965)
Tarzan and Lone Ranger Adventure
  Hour, The (1980)
Tarzan and the Jungle Boy (1968)
Tarzan and the Super Seven (1978)

Tarzan and the Valley of Gold
  (1965)
Tarzan: Lord of the Jungle (1976)
Tarzan the Ape Man (1959)
Tarzan, the Ape Man (1981)
Tarzan's Three Challenges (1963)
Tasio (1984)
Taste of Corn, The (1986)
Taste of Evil, A (1971)
Taste of Hell, A (1973)
Taste of Sea, A (1983)
Taste of Sin, A (1983)
Taste of Water, The (1982)
Tattered Banner, The (1975)
Tattered Web, A (1971)
Tattinger's (1988)
Tattoo (1981)
Tattoo (1982)
Tattoo Connection, The (1980)
Taulant Wants a Sister (1985)
Taxi (1978)
Taxi Boy (1986)
Taxi Driver Baenz (1957)
Taxi to Cairo (1987)
Taxi to the Loo (1981)
Taxing Woman, A (1987)
Taxing Woman II, A (1988)
Tea in the Harem of Archimedes
  (1985)
Teacher, The (Sensei) (1983)
Teachers Only (1982)
Teacher's Pet (1973)
Tears Are Flowing (1983)
Tears in Florence (1985)
Tears in the Rain (1988)
Tears on the Lion's Mane (1980)
Technique for a Massacre (1966)
Technique of a Murder (1966)
Technopolice 21-C (1982)
Ted Kennedy Jr. Story, The (1986)
Ted Knight Show, The (1978)
Teddy Baer (1983)
Teddy Bear (Mis) (1981)
Teddy Boys (Potota, La) (1961)
Teen Wolf (1985)
Teen Wolf Too (1987)
Teenage Casanova (1958)
Teenage Caveman (1958)
Teenage Monster (1958)
Teenaged Girl (1983)
Tel Aviv-Berlin (1987)
Telephone, The (1988)
Telephone Always Rings Twice, The
  (1985)
Telephone Bar, The (1980)
Tell Me a Riddle (1980)
Telethon (1977)

Thanksgiving Promise, The (1986)
Thanksgiving Visitor, The (1968)
That Certain Summer (1972)
That Championship Season (1982)
That Couple (1985)
That Damned Meat (1985)
That Darned Kid (1956)
That Girl (1966)
That House in the Outskirts (1980)
That I May Live (1937)
That Is the Dawn (1956)
That Mad Mad Hospital (1986)
That Secret Sunday (1986)
That Thing on ABC (1978)
That Was Our Rommel (1953)
That Was the Year That Was (1976)
That Woman Opposite (1957)
That Wonderful Guy (1950)
That's Cat (1977)
That's Dancing! (1985)
That's Hollywood (1977)
That's Life! (1986)
That's My Baby (1985)
That's My Line (1980)
That's My Mama (1974)
That's TV (1982)
That's Why (1981)
Theater of Shimmering Heat (1982)
Theatre of Mr. and Mrs. Kabal, The (1967)
Theft of the Mummies of Gunjuato (1972)
Their Golden Years (1980)
Then Came Bronson (1969)
Then Nothing Was the Same Anymore (1987)
Theo Against the Rest of the World (1980)
Theofilos (1987)
There Are Some Guys Downstairs (1985)
There Goes the Bride (1980)
There Goes the Neighborhood (1983)
There Is Another Sun (1951)
There Must Be a Pony (1986)
There Was a Village (1987)
There Was a War When I Was a Child (1982)
There Was No Sun (1984)
There Were Nine Bachelors (1939)
There Were Times, Dear (1985)
There Will Be No More Sorrows Nor Oblivion (1983)
There's Always Room (1973)

There's But One Love (1937)
Therese Raquin (1981)
These Are the Days (1974)
These Children (1937)
These Children Survive Me (1983)
These Dangerous Years (1957)
They Call Him Hurricane (Jao Payu) (1980)
They Call It Murder (1969)
They Call That an Accident (1982)
They Came from Within (Shivers/ Parasite Murders, The) (1976)
They Died in the Middle of the River (1987)
They Don't Wear Black Ties (1981)
They Live (1988)
They Only Come Out at Night (1975)
They Still Call Me Bruce (1987)
They Wanted Peace (1940)
They Were Nobody (1982)
They're Playing With Fire (1984)
Thicker Than Water (1973)
Thief (1971)
Thief (1981)
Thief Academy (1986)
Thief in the Bedroom, The (1960)
Thief of Bagdad, The (1979)
Thief of Hearts (1984)
Thieves (Voleurs) (1984)
Thieves After Dark (1984)
Thin Blue Line, The (1988)
Thin Ice (1981)
Thin Man, The (1957)
Thing, The (1982)
Thing of Beauty, A (1967)
Things Are Looking Up (1984)
Things Change (1988)
Things Forgotten and Not (1988)
Things Happen at Night (1948)
Things in Their Season (1974)
Things That Teachers Do (1982)
Think! (View from the People Wall, The) (short) (1963)
Think Fast, Mr. Moto (1937)
Thinkin' Big (1988)
Third Commandment, The (1959)
Third Dragon, The (1986)
Third Girl from the Left (1973)
Third Key, The (1983)
Third Sex, The (1957)
Third Time Lucky (1948)
Thirst (Dorst) (1988)
13 at Dinner (1985)
13 Girls Smile at the Sky (1938)
13 Queens Boulevard (1979)
13 Thirteenth Avenue (1983)

Thirteenth Bride of the Prince,
   The (1987)
13th Day: The Story of Esther,
   The (1971)
'38 (1986)
Thirty Million Rush, The (1987)
32nd of December, The (1988)
Thirty Seconds of Love (1937)
36 Chowringhee Lane (1982)
This Age Without Pity (1980)
This and That (1984)
This Better Be It (1976)
This England (1941)
This Girl for Hire (1983)
This Girl Irene (1936)
This House Possessed (1981)
This Is America, Charlie Brown
   (1988)
This Is China (1937)
This Is Elvis (1981)
This Is Kate Bennett ... (1982)
This Is My Affair (1937)
This Is Noriko (1982)
This Is Not Our Destination (1987)
This Is the Half Century (1950)
This Is Your Army (1954)
This Love of Mine (1988)
This Man Is News (1939)
This Man Stands Alone (1979)
This Was the West That Was (1974)
This Woman Is Mine (1935)
Thomas and Senior on the Track of
   Barend the Brute (1986)
Thomas and ... the Bewitched
   (1970)
Thompson's Last Run (1986)
Thorn Birds, The (1983)
Thorn in the Flesh (1981)
Thorn Under the Fingernail, A
   (1988)
Thornwell (1981)
Thorvald and Linda (1982)
Those Amazing Animals (1980)
Those Dear Departed (1987)
Those Fantastic Flying Fools
   (Rocket to the Moon/Blast-Off)
   (1967)
Those Lips Those Eyes (1980)
Those Three About Christine (1936)
Thou Shalt Not Commit Adultery
   (1978)
Thou Shalt Not Kill (1982)
Thou Shalt Not Kill ... Except
   (1987)
Thousand and One Daisies, A
   (1986)
Thousand Billion Dollars, A (1982)

Thousand Eyes (1983)
Thousand Little Kisses, A (1981)
Thrashin' (1986)
Threat, The (1987)
Three Amigos (1986)
Three Argentines in Paris (1938)
Three Brothers (1981)
Three Came to Kill (1960)
Three Coins in the Fountain (1970)
Three-Cornered Hat, The (1936)
Three Crowns of the Sailor, The
   (1983)
Three Eyes (1982)
Three Feet Above the Ground (1985)
Three Fifteen (1986)
Three for Tahiti (1970)
Three for the Road (1975)
Three for the Road (1987)
Three Forbidden Stories (1952)
Three Girls Named Anna (1960)
Three Golden Men (1966)
Three Hundred Miles for Stephanie
   (1981)
Three Kinds of Heat (1987)
Three Kings, The (1987)
Three Men and a Baby (1987)
Three Men in the Snow (1955)
Three Men to Destroy (1980)
Three Minus Me (1988)
Three Moves to Freedom (1960)
Three Musketeers, The (1933)
Three O'Clock High (1987)
Three Old Women (1975)
Three on a Date (1978)
Three Quarters of a Sun (1959)
Three Rascals in the Hidden Forest
   (1959)
Three Robonic Stooges, The (1978)
Three Romeos and a Juliet (1961)
Three Sailors and a Blonde (1937)
Three Seats for the 26th (1988)
Three Seconds to Zero Hour (1969)
Three Sinners (1952)
Three Sisters (Fear and Love) (1988)
Three Sorts of Slovene Madness
   (1984)
Three Sovereigns for Sarah (1985)
Three Steps North (1951)
Three Supermen in the Jungle
   (1971)
330 Independence S.W. (1962)
3,000 Mile Chase, The (1977)
Three Times Daley (1976)
Three to Get Ready (1988)
Three Treasures, The (1960)
Three Violent Nights (1966)
Three Wishes of Billy Grier (1984)

Three Wives of David Wheeler,
  The (1979)
Three's a Crowd (1969)
Three's Company (1977)
Three's Happiness (1986)
Threshold (1981)
Thrill Killers, The (1965)
Thrill Seekers (1973)
Thriller (1960)
Thriller (1973)
Thrillkill (1984)
Throb (1986)
Throne, The (1981)
Throne of Blood (1961)
Throne of Fire, The (1986)
Through Naked Eyes (1983)
Through the Magic Pyramid (1981)
Throw Momma from the Train
  (1987)
Thumbscrew, The (1986)
Thundarr the Barbarian (1980)
Thunder (1977)
Thunder Alley (1985)
Thunder Run (1986)
Thunder Warrior (1986)
Thunder Warrior 2 (1987)
Thunderbirds (1968)
Thunderbirds to the Rescue (1980)
Thundercrack! (1975)
Thunderstorm (1934)
Thursday's Child (1983)
Thursday's Game (1971)
Thus Ends the Night (1950)
Thus Spake Bellavista (1984)
Thyagayya (1982)
Ticket to Heaven (1981)
Tickets Please (1988)
Tifusari (short) (1963)
Tiger Bay (1959)
Tiger of Eschnapur, The (1959)
Tiger von Eschnapur (1938)
Tiger! Tiger! (1969)
Tiger Town (1983)
Tiger Walks, A (1964)
Tiger Warsaw (1988)
Tigers in Lipstick (1979)
Tiger's Tale, A (1987)
Tight Spot, A (Tesna Koza)
  (1983)
Tighten Your Belts, Bite the
  Bullet (1981)
Tightrope (1959)
Tightrope (1984)
Till Five Minutes Past Twelve
  (1953)
Tim Conway Show, The (1970)
Time (Ido Van) (1986)

Time After Time (1985)
Time and Tide (1981)
Time Bandits (1981)
Time Bomb (1953)
Time Bomb (1984)
Time Destroyed: Letters from a
  War, 1939-40 (1985)
Time Express (1979)
Time Flyer (1986)
Time for Love, A (1973)
Time for Miracles, A (1980)
Time for Revenge (1981)
Time Guardian, The (1987)
Time Lock (1957)
Time Machine, The (1978)
Time Masters, The (1982)
Time of Desire (1957)
Time of Destiny, A (1988)
Time of Leopards, The (1985)
Time of Massacre (1966)
Time of the Star, The (1985)
Time of the West (short) (1967)
Time of Violence (1988)
Time of Wolves, A (Ulvetid) (1981)
Time Out (1988)
Time Out for Romance (1937)
Time Slip (1981)
Time Stops (1986)
Time That Remains, The (1986)
Time to Be Happy (1982)
Time to Die, A (1983)
Time to Die, A (1985)
Time to Live, A (1985)
Time to Live and a Time to Die, A
  (1986)
Time to Triumph, A (1986)
Time Travelers (1976)
Time Tunnel, The (1966)
Time Walker (1982)
Time Within Memory (1973)
Timerider (1983)
Times of Harvey Milk, The (1984)
Timestalkers (1987)
Timing (1985)
Timmy and Lassie (1957)
Tin Man (1983)
Tin Men (1987)
Tin Star Void (1988)
Tinker, Tailor, Soldier, Spy (1980)
Tintorera (1977)
Tiznao (1984)
Tizoc (1957)
To a Safer Place (1987)
To All My Friends on Shore (1972)
To Be a Man (1967)
To Be or Not to Be (1983)
To Catch a Cop (1984)

To Catch a King (1984)
To Church and Work You Go (1986)
To Die a Little (1981)
To Each His Life (1960)
To Find My Son (1980)
To Heal a Nation (1988)
To Hell with the Devil (1982)
To Hurt and to Heal (1987)
To Kill a Cop (1978)
To Kill a Priest (1988)
To Kill a Stranger (1982)
To Live a Long Life (1980)
To Live and Die in L.A. (1985)
To Live and Die in Westallgau (1986)
To Love Again (1971)
To Love the Damned (1980)
To Marry the Captain (1986)
To Our Late Unlamented Husband (1988)
To Race the Wind (1980)
To Rome With Love (1969)
To See the Light (Eszmejes) (1985)
To Sleep So As to Dream (1986)
To the Devil, a Daughter (1976)
To the Four Winds (1955)
To the Last Drop (1980)
To the Manor Born (1982)
To the Rhythm of My Heart (1983)
Toa (1949)
Tobor the Great (1954)
Toby McTeague (1986)
Today Is for the Championship (1980)
Today's F.B.I. (1981)
Todo Modo (1980)
Together (1956)
Together (Juntos) (1987)
Together We Stand (1986)
Tokay Rhapsody (1938)
Tokyo Bad Girls (1971)
Tokyo Blackout (1987)
Tokyo Bordello (1987)
Tokyo-Ga (1985)
Tokyo Pop (1988)
Tolerance (1987)
Tom and Jerry Show, The (1966)
Tom and Joann (1978)
Tom, Dick and Mary (1964)
Tom Horn (1980)
Tom Machine, The (1981)
Tom of T.H.U.M.B. (1966)
Tom Sawyer (1973)
Tom Swift and Linda Craig Mystery Hour, The (1983)
Tom Terrific (1957)

Toma (1973)
Tomb, The (1985)
Tomb of Dracula (1980)
Tomb of Lygeia, The (1964)
Tomb of the Angels (1937)
Tomboy (1985)
Tombs of the Blind Dead (1973)
Tommaso Blu (1986)
Tommy (1937)
Tommy the Toreador (1960)
Tomorrow (1986)
Tomorrow I'll Be Free (Lute II, El) (1988)
Tomorrow I'm Getting Married (1984)
Tomorrow It Is Over (1988)
Tomorrow We Dance (1982)
Tomorrow's Child (1982)
Tongue (1976)
Tonight for Sure (1961)
Tonight Pancho Dines Out (Bachelor Party) (1987)
Tonight's the Night (1987)
Toni's Boys (1980)
Tony Draws a Horse (1951)
Tony Randall Show, The (1976)
Too Close for Comfort (1980)
Too Far to Go (1979)
Too Good to Be True (1983)
Too Good to Be True (1988)
Too Hot to Handle (1960)
Too Many Crooks (1959)
Too Much (1987)
Too Much Kissing (Qui Trop Embrasse) (1986)
Too Outrageous! (1987)
Too Scared to Scream (Doorman, The) (1982)
Too Young the Hero (1988)
Too Young to Love (1960)
Tooth for a Tooth, A (On the Tracks of the Killers) (1985)
Tootsie (1982)
Top Crack (1966)
Top Flight (1987)
Top Gun (1986)
Top Kid (1987)
Top of the Hill (1980)
Top Secret (1978)
Top Secret (1984)
Top Speed (Toute Allure, A) (1982)
Topos (1985)
Topper (1953)
Topper (1979)
Topper Returns (1973)
Tora! Tora! Tora! (1970)
Tora-san Loves an Artist (1974)
Tora-san Meets His Lordship (1978)

Tora-san, the Good Samaritan
    (1971)
Tora-san's Dream Come True
    (1973)
Tora-san's Love Call (1972)
Tora-san's Rise and Fall (1976)
Tora-san's Sunrise and Sunset
    (1977)
Torchlight (1984)
Torment (1986)
Tormento (1953)
Torn Allegiance (1984)
Torn Between Two Lovers (1979)
Tornado (1983)
Toro! (1956)
Torpedo Planes (1985)
Torso (1974)
Toto Wants a Home (1950)
Tottering Lives (House on a Limb,
    A) (1988)
Touch and Go (1986)
Touch of Blue, A (1988)
Touch of Grace, A (1973)
Touch of Spice, A (1987)
Touched (1983)
Touched by Love (1980)
Touching (1986)
Tough Cookies (1986)
Tough Enough (1983)
Tough Guys (1986)
Tough Guys Don't Dance (1987)
Toughest Man in the World, The
    (1984)
Toughlove (1985)
Tour of Duty (1987)
Tourist (1980)
Toward Magic Island (1982)
Toward the Terror (1980)
Towards the Year 2000 (1977)
Tower of Nesle, The (1955)
Tower of Terror (1941)
Tower of the Lilies (1982)
Town Bully, The (1988)
Town Is Full of Secrets, The
    (1955)
Town Like Alice, A (1981)
Town Mayor, The (1984)
Town Tale (Pueblerina) (1949)
Toxic Avenger, The (1985)
Toxic Love (1983)
Toxic Time Bomb (1984)
Toy, The (1982)
Toy Soldiers (1984)
Trace, The (1983)
Track 29 (1988)
Track Two (1983)
Trackdown (1957)

Trackdown: Finding the Goodbar
    Killer (1983)
Tracker, The (1988)
Trackers, The (1971)
Tracks in the Snow (Pervola) (1985)
Trading Hearts (1988)
Trading Places (1983)
Tradition in the World of Spirit, A
    (1982)
Tradition of Terror: Frankenstein,
    A (1982)
Tragedy of the Afghan, The (1986)
Tragic Earthquake in Mexico (1987)
Tragic Spell (1952)
Trail, The (1983)
Trail of the Pink Panther (1982)
Train, The (Kettar, Al) (1986)
Train for Hollywood (1987)
Train for the Stars, A (1987)
Train Goes East, The (1949)
Train of Dreams (1987)
Train of Lenin, The (1988)
Train of the Pioneers, The (1986)
Train to Holland (1987)
Train to Kraljevo, The (1982)
Traitor Within, The (1981)
Traitors (1957)
Traitors, The (1983)
Tramp at the Door (1986)
Trance (1982)
Transformers, The (1986)
Transes (1981)
Transit (1980)
Transit Dreams (1986)
Transplant (1970)
Transplant (1979)
Transportation USA (short) (1967)
Transvestite, The (1988)
Transylvania 6-5000 (1985)
Trapeze (1934)
Trapp Family, The (1956)
Trapp Family in America, The
    (1958)
Trapped (1973)
Trapped Beneath the Sea (1974)
Trapped Women (Atrapadas) (1984)
Trapper John, M.D. (1979)
Trauma (1984)
Trauma Center (1983)
Travellers Joy (1951)
Travelling Man (1987)
Travels with Charley (1968)
Travis Logan, D.A. (1971)
Travis McGee (1983)
Traxx (1988)
Treachery and Greed on the Planet
    of the Apes (1980)

Treasure (1988)
Treasure Island (1971)
Treasure of Bird Island, The (short) (1952)
Treasure of Cantenac, The (1950)
Treasure of San Teresa (1959)
Treasure of the Amazon, The (1985)
Treasure of the Four Crowns (1983)
Treasure of the Moon Goddess (1987)
Treasured Earth (1951)
Tree Grows in Brooklyn, A (1974)
Tree Under the Sea, The (1985)
Trees We Were Hurting, The (1986)
Treichville Story (1987)
Trenchcoat (1983)
Trespasses (1983)
Trespasses (1987)
Trial of Chaplain Jensen, The (1975)
Trial of Junta, The (1981)
Trial of Lee Harvey Oswald, The (1977)
Trial on the Road (1986)
Trial Run (1969)
Trial Run (1984)
Trials of O'Brien, The (1965)
Trials of Oscar Wilde, The (1960)
Triangle Factory Fire Scandal, The (1979)
Tribe, The (1974)
Tribe, The (Smala, La) (1984)
Tribes (Soldier Who Declared Peace, The) (1970)
Tribulations of Balthazar Kobera (1988)
Trick or Treat (1986)
Tricks of the Trade (1988)
Trilogy of Terror (1975)
Trip Across Paris, The (1956)
Trip to America, A (1952)
Trip to Bountiful, A (1985)
Trip to Paradise (1987)
Trip to the Moon, A (1959)
Trip to the Sea, A (1988)
Triple Cross (1986)
Triton of the Seas (1979)
Triumph of the Just (1987)
Triumphs of a Man Called Horse, The (1984)
Trokadero (1981)
Troll (1986)
Trollenberg Terror, The (Crawling Eye, The) (1958)

Trollkins (1981)
Tromba, the Tiger Man (1952)
Tron (1982)
Troopship (1938)
Trouble Agent (1987)
Trouble Comes to Town (1973)
Trouble in High Timber Country (1980)
Trouble in Mind (1985)
Trouble with Dick, The (1987)
Trouble with Grandpa, The (1981)
Trouble With Spies, The (1987)
Trouble with 2-B, The (1972)
Troubled Heart (1938)
Troublesome Double, The (1971)
Troupe, The (Halahaka) (1977)
Trout, The (1982)
Truck, The (1981)
True and Accurate Report, A (1987)
True as a Turtle (1957)
True Colors (1987)
True Confessions (1981)
True Grit (1978)
True Life Stories (1981)
True Story of Camille, The (1981)
Truman Capote's The Glass House (1972)
Trumpet Solo (1986)
Truth on the Savolta Affair, The (1980)
Truxa (1937)
Try and Get Me (Sound of Fury, The) (1951)
Tub Studs (1985)
Tuck Everlasting (1981)
Tucker: The Man and His Dream (1988)
Tucker's Witch (1982)
Tudawali (1988)
Tuesday Wednesday (1987)
Tuff Turf (1984)
Tug of Love (Etincelle, L') (1984)
Tulips (1981)
Tunnel, The (1988)
Tunnel Under the World, The (1968)
Tupac Amaru (1985)
Turk 182 (1985)
Turkey Shoot (1983)
Turn of the Screw (1974)
Turn of the Screw, The (1985)
Turnabout (1979)
Turncoat, The (1985)
Turning Point of Jim Malloy, The (1975)
Turn-On (Declic, Le) (1985)
Turn the Key Softly (1959)
Turnover Smith (1980)

Up from the Depths (1979)
Up in the World (1957)
Up Line (1987)
Up Pompeii (1971)
Up the Academy (1980)
Up the Chastity Belt (1971)
Up the Creek (1958)
Up the Creek (1984)
Up to a Certain Point (1984)
Uphill All the Way (1984)
Ups & Downs (1983)
Upstairs, Downstairs (1974)
Upstairs, Downstairs (1988)
Uptown Saturday Night (1979)
Urban Cowboy (1980)
Urge to Kill, The (1987)
Urinal (1988)
Ursula (1987)
Ursus in the Valley of the Lions
    (1961)
Us Real Men (1987)
Used Cars (1980)
Used Cars (1984)
Users, The (1978)
Utamaro, Painter of Women (1960)
Utilities (1983)
Utopia (1983)
Utu (1983)

V (1983)
V (1984)
V--The Final Battle (1984)
Va Banque (1986)
Va Banque II (1985)
Vacation in America (1984)
Vacation in Hell, A (1979)
Vacation with a Gangster (1952)
Vacations in Acapulco (1961)
Vacations in Val Trebbia (1980)
Vagabond (1985)
Vagabond Hero (1966)
Vagabonds (1949)
Vagrants (Fariaho) (1984)
Valentina (1982)
Valentine for Maria, A (short)
    (1965)
Valentine Magic on Love Island
    (1980)
Valentine's Day (1964)
Valerie (1986)
Valet Girls (1987)
Valhalla (1986)
Valiant Years, The (1960)
Valley Forge (1976)
Valley of Bees, The (1968)
Valley of the Dinosaurs (1974)

Valley of the Dolls 1981 (see
    Jacqueline Susann's Valley of
    the Dolls 1981)
Valley of the Zombies (1946)
Vamp (1986)
Vamping (1984)
Vampire (1979)
Vampire at Midnight (1988)
Vampire Doll, The (1970)
Vampire Dracula Comes to Kobe:
    Evil Makes Women Beautiful
    (1979)
Vampire Hookers, The (1978)
Vampire Women, The (1967)
Vampires, The (1957)
Vampires (Abadon) (1988)
Vampires and the Ballerina, The
    (1962)
Vampire's Kiss (1988)
Vampyres (1975)
Van Dyke Show, The (1988)
Van Gogh (short) (1949)
Vandedevatha (1976)
Vanished (1971)
Vanishing, The (1988)
Vanishing Act (1986)
Vanishing Legion, The (1931)
Varan, the Unbelievable (1962)
Vargas Inn (1959)
Variety (1983)
Variety Stars (1955)
Variola Vera (1982)
Vasectomy: A Delicate Matter
    (1986)
Vasily and Vasilisa (1982)
Vassa (1983)
Vault of Horror, The (Tales from
    the Crypt II) (1972)
Vaya con Dios Gringo (1966)
Vayanadan Thampan (1978)
Vega$ (1978)
Veil, The (1958)
Veil of Blood (Devil's Plaything,
    The (1978)
Veiled Man, The (1987)
Velvet (1984)
Velvet Hand (1966)
Velvet Hands (1980)
Velvet Vampire, The (1971)
Vendetta (1986)
Venetian Black (Damned in Venice)
    (1978)
Venetian Woman, The (1986)
Vengeance Is Mine (1980)
Vengeance of the Plumed Serpent,
    The (1984)
Vengeance: The Story of Tony

Voice of the Heart, The (1937)
Voices (1973)
Voices of the Sylphides, The
   (1980)
Volcano (1950)
Volga Boatman, The (1938)
Volga Volga (1941)
Volley for a Black Buffalo (1985)
Volpone (Big Fox, The) (1988)
Voltus V (1979)
Volume One (1949)
Volunteers (1985)
Volunteers (1986)
Voodoo Woman (1957)
Voyage, The (1984)
Voyage Beyond (1988)
Voyage of the Brigantine Yankee
   (1966)
Voyage of the Canoe "Che-Che-
   Meni," The (1977)
Voyage of the Rock Aliens (1988)
Voyage of the Yes, The (1973)
Voyage to Cythera (1984)
Voyage to Nowhere (1986)
Voyage to the Bottom of the Sea
   (1961)
Voyage to the Bottom of the Sea
   (1964)
Voyager (1984)
Voyagers (1982)
Vroom (1988)
Vulcan, Son of Jupiter (1962)
Vulture, The (1981)
Vulture, The (1983)
Vultures, The (1984)

W.E.B. (1978)
WKRP in Cincinnati (1978)
Wackere Schustermeister (1936)
Wackiest Ship in the Army, The
   (1965)
Wacko (1983)
Wacky Races, The (1968)
Wagner (1983)
Wagon Train (1957)
Waikiki (1980)
Wait for Me a Long Time (1983)
Wait for Me in Heaven (1988)
Wait Till Your Father Gets Home
   (1972)
Wait Till Your Mother Gets Home!
   (1983)
Wait Until Dark (1982)
Waiting for Daddy (1980)
Waiting for Darkness (1986)
Waiting for the Pallbearers (1987)

Wajan (Son of a Witch) (1934)
Wake Me When the War Is Over
   (1969)
Wake Up and Kill (1966)
Walk in the Sun, A (1945)
Walk Like a Man (1987)
Walk on the Moon, A (1987)
Walker (1987)
Walking After Midnight (1988)
Walking Dead, The (1936)
Walking Tall (1981)
Walking the Edge (1985)
Walking Through the Fire (1979)
Wall, The (1965)
Wall, The (1982)
Wall, The (Mur, La) (1983)
Wall Driller, The (Falfuro) (1986)
Wall Street (1987)
Wallenberg: A Hero's Story (1985)
Walls (Falak) (1968)
Walls (1984)
Walls of Malapaga (1950)
Wally Gator (1962)
Walter (1984)
Walter and Carlo: Up at Dad's Hat
   (1985)
Waltons, The (1972)
Waltz Across Texas (1983)
Waltz for You, A (1936)
Wanderers, The (1974)
Wandering Jew, The (1935)
Wandering Soul (Ashwathama) (1980)
Wanted: Dead or Alive (1958)
Wanted: Dead or Alive (1987)
Wanted: Good Looking Receptionist
   and Messenger with His Own
   Motorcycle (1982)
Wanted: Loving Father and Mother
   (1988)
Wanted: The Sundance Woman
   (1976)
War (Rat) (1960)
War (1988)
War & Remembrance (1988)
War Between the Planets, The
   (1965)
War Between the Tates, The (1977)
War Games (1983)
War Gods of the Deep (1965)
War in Space (1977)
War in Space, The (1978)
War in the Air (short) (1956)
War of Children, A (1972)
War of the Colossal Beast, The
   (1958)
War of the Gargantuas (1970)
War of the Giants (1966)

War of the Insects (Genocide)
(1968)
War of the Monsters (1966)
War of the Wizards (Phoenix, The)
(1978)
War of the Worlds--Next Century,
The (1981)
War Starts in Cuba (1958)
War Story, A (1982)
Warlock Moon (1974)
Warm Hearts, Cold Feet (1987)
Warm Nights on a Slow Moving
Train (1987)
Warming Up (1984)
Warning: Medicine May Be
Hazardous to Your Health
(1988)
Warning Sign (1985)
Warrior and the Sorceress, The
(Kain of Dark Planet) (1983)
Warrior of the Lost World (1983)
Warrior Queen (1987)
Warriors of the Apocalypse (1987)
Warriors of the Wasteland (1983)
Wars, The (1983)
Was It He? Yes! Yes! (1952)
Wash, The (1988)
Washington Affair, The (1977)
Washington: Behind Closed
Doors (1977)
Washington Mistress (1982)
Wasp, The (1986)
Wasp Woman, The (1960)
Wasps' Nest, The (1988)
Wasted Lives (1982)
Wasted Sunday, A (1969)
Wasteland (1982)
Watch Out for Love (1955)
Watcher in the Woods, The (1980)
Watchers (1988)
Water (1985)
Water Also Burns (1987)
Water and Man (short) (1985)
Water Babies, The (1978)
Water in the Ground (1934)
Water Spider, The (1971)
Water Water (Thaneer Thaneer)
(1982)
Waterfront (1954)
Waterfront Blues (1971)
Waterwalker (1984)
Wave, The (Redes) (1937)
Wave of Lust (1975)
Wavelength (1983)
Waverly Wonders, The (1978)
Waves (Golven) (1982)
Waxwork (1988)

Way Back Home (1981)
Way It Is or Eurydice in the Avenues,
The (1985)
Way of the Lotus, The (1987)
Way Out, Way In (1970)
Way Upstream (1987)
Ways of Love Are Strange (1937)
Ways of the Lord Are Finite, The
(1987)
We Are All Demons! (1969)
We Are from Kronstadt (1936)
We Are the Children (1987)
We Are the Guinea Pigs (1981)
We Cellar Children (1960)
We Got It Made (1983)
We Have Never Been So Happy
(1984)
We Must Undo the House (1987)
We of the Never Never (1982)
We Shall Go to Paris (1950)
We Shall See (1964)
We the Living (1988)
We Think the World of You (1988)
We Three (Noi Tre) (1984)
We Were One Man (1980)
We Were Seven Sisters (1938)
We Won't Commit Hara-Kiri (1981)
Weak Man, The (1981)
Weapons Man (1963)
Weapons of Destruction (1958)
Weapons of Gordon Parks, The
(short) (1968)
Weapons of Vengeance (1963)
Weather in the Streets, The (1983)
Weave of Time, A (1987)
Webster (1983)
Wedding, The (Boda, La) (1982)
Wedding Day, The (1957)
Wedding Dream, A (1936)
Wedding in Galilee, A (1987)
Wedding in Monaco, The (1956)
Wedding of Palo (1937)
Wedding on Waltons Mountain, A
(1982)
Weddings and Babies (1958)
Wednesday Night Out (1972)
Wee Willie Winkie (1937)
Weeds (1987)
Weekend at Dunkirk (1966)
Weekend Nun, The (1972)
Weekend Pass (1984)
Weekend of Terror (1970)
Weekend War (1988)
Weekend Warriors (1986)
Week's Vacation, A (Une Semaine
de Vacances) (1980)
Weird Science (1985)

Who's That Singing Over There?
   (1980)
Who's Watching the Kids? (1978)
Whose Life Is It Anyway? (1981)
Why (Proc) (1988)
Why Albert Pinto Is Angry (1981)
Why Didn't They Ask Evans?
   (1981)
Why Me? (1984)
Why on Earth? (1988)
Why Us? (1981)
Why Would I Lie? (1980)
Wichita Town (1959)
Wicked Lady, The (1983)
Wicker Man, The (1974)
Wide Net, The (1987)
Wide Open Faces (1938)
Widow (1976)
Widow Montiel, The (1980)
Wife, The (Savithri) (1980)
Wife, Doctor and Nurse (1937)
Wife for My Son, A (1983)
Wife of an Important Man (1987)
Wild and Beautiful (1985)
Wild and the Free, The (1980)
Wild and Woolly (1937)
Wild and Wooly (1978)
Wild Beasts (1982)
Wild Bunch (1983)
Wild Clown, The (1986)
Wild Daisy, The (1982)
Wild Dove, The (1986)
Wild Duck, The (1983)
Wild Flowers (1982)
Wild Geese II (1985)
Wild Horses (1983)
Wild Horses (1985)
Wild Kingdom (1963)
Wild Life, The (1984)
Wild Mountains (1986)
Wild 90 (1968)
Wild Pair, The (1987)
Wild Pony, The (1987)
Wild Side, The (Suburbia) (1983)
Wild Strawberries (1958)
Wild Style (1983)
Wild Swans, The (1978)
Wild Thing (1987)
Wild Things (1988)
Wild Times (1980)
Wild Weed (1949)
Wild Wild West, The (1965)
Wild Wild West Revisited, The (1979)
Wild Wild World of Animals, The
   (1973)
Wild Wind, The (1986)
Wild Women (1970)

Wild Women of Chastity Gulch, The
   (1982)
Wildcat Rock (1970)
Wildcat Rock-Beat '71 (1975)
Wildcats (1986)
Wildfire (1988)
Wildrose (1984)
Wilds of Ten Thousand Islands,
   The (1978)
Wildschut (1985)
Wildside (1985)
Wilhelm Tell (1961)
Will Any Gentleman? (1953)
Will, G. Gordon Liddy (1982)
Will the High Salaried Workers
   Please Raise Their Hands!!!
   (1982)
Will the Real Jerry Lewis Please Sit
   Down? (1970)
Will There Really Be a Morning?
   (1983)
Will to Conquer (1971)
Willa (1979)
Willful Murder (1982)
Willie and Phil (1980)
Willing and Abel (1987)
Willmar 8, The (1981)
Willow (1988)
Willow B: Women in Prison (1980)
Willy/Milly (1986)
Wilma (1977)
Wimps (1987)
Winchester '73 (1967)
Wind (1978)
Wind, The (1987)
Wind in the Willows, The (1985)
Windfall in Athens (1956)
Windmills of the Gods (1988)
Window, The (Prozoretsut) (1981)
Window on Main Street (1961)
Windows (1980)
Windrider (1986)
Winds of Change (Metamorphosis)
   (1978)
Winds of Jarrah, The (1983)
Winds of Kitty Hawk, The (1978)
Winds of War, The (1983)
Windshade (1986)
Windsong (short) (1958)
Windwalker (1980)
Windy City (1984)
Windy Places: Torn Apart (1983)
Winged Serpent, The (1982)
Winged World, The (1968)
Wings of Fire (1967)
Wings of the Dove (1981)
Wings of Victory (1941)

Woman from the Provinces, The
    (1985)
Woman Hater, The (1972)
Woman He Loved, The (1988)
Woman in a Fur Coat, The (1958)
Woman in a Hat (1985)
Woman in Love with Mechanic
    Gabrilov, The (1982)
Woman in Red, The (1984)
Woman in the Mirror, A (1984)
Woman in the Moon (1988)
Woman in White (1949)
Woman Inside, The (1981)
Woman Like Eve, A (1980)
Woman Next Door, The (1981)
Woman of Evil (1949)
Woman of My Life, The (1986)
Woman of No Importance, A (1936)
Woman of Substance, A (1984)
Woman of the Dunes (1964)
Woman of the Year (1976)
Woman of Wonders (1985)
Woman on the Run (1950)
Woman Thief, The (1938)
Woman to Woman (1987)
Woman Wise (1937)
Woman Without Camelias, The
    (1953)
Woman Without Love, A (1951)
Woman's Day (1987)
Wombling Free (1977)
Women (1985)
Women and Bandits (1951)
Women from South Lebanon (1986)
Women in Chains (1972)
Women in Prison (1957)
Women in Prison (1987)
Women in Prison (1988)
Women in White (1979)
Women of Destiny (1953)
Women of Niskavuori (1938)
Women of Russia (1981)
Women of San Quentin (1983)
Women of Valor (1986)
Women of the Frontier (1987)
Women on the Verge of a Nervous
    Breakdown (1988)
Women Smell of Night (1971)
Women Three Times (1957)
Women Who Care (short) (1968)
Women's Affair, A (1988)
Women's Club, The (1987)
Women's Love (1981)
Women's Prison (1938)
Women's Prison Massacre (1985)
Women's Room, The (1980)
Wonder Boy (1952)

Wonder Child (1951)
Wonder Girl (1973)
Wonder Woman (1973)
Wonder Woman (1974)
Wonder Woman (1976)
Wonder Years, The (1988)
Wonderbug (1976)
Wonderful Things (1958)
Wonderful Times (1951)
Wonderful World of Philip Malley,
    The (1981)
Wonderful Years, The (1980)
Wood of Love (1981)
Word, The (1978)
Word of a Cat, The (short) (1960)
Word of Honor (1981)
Words and Music (1984)
Words to Say It (1983)
Work (Avodah) (1936)
Worker's Life, A (1987)
Working Class (1985)
Working Girl (1988)
Working Girls (1986)
Working Stiffs (1979)
World According to Garp, The (1982)
World Apart, A (1988)
World at War, The (1973)
World Beyond, The (1978)
World Gone Wild (1988)
World of Darkness, The (1977)
World of Horror (1968)
World Safari II (1984)
World, The Flesh and the Devil,
    The (1960)
World War I (1964)
World War III (1982)
World Without End (1954)
Worlds Apart (see "Don't Ask Me If
    I Love"--1979)
World's Greatest Superheroes, The
    (1978)
World's Most Beautiful Woman, The
    (1955)
Worm Eaters, The (1977)
Would You Believe It (1981)
Wraith, The (1986)
Wrestler, The (Pehlivan) (1985)
Write and Fight (Pismak) (1985)
Wrong Guys, The (1988)
Wrong Is Right (1982)
Wrong Timing (1984)
Wrong World (1985)
Wurlitzer (1985)
Wyeth Phenomenon, The (short)
    (1968)